Biographical and Historical Memoirs of Mississippi

VOL. II
PART II

Biographical and Historical Memoirs  of Mississippi

VOL. II

EMBRACING AN

AUTHENTIC AND COMPREHENSIVE ACCOUNT OF THE CHIEF EVENTS IN
THE HISTORY OF THE STATE, AND A RECORD OF THE
LIVES OF MANY OF THE MOST WORTHY AND
ILLUSTRIOUS FAMILIES AND INDIVIDUALS

VOL. II PART II

ILLUSTRATED

Gretna 1999

Manufactured in the United States of America
Published by Pelican Publishing Company, Inc.
1000 Burmaster Street, Gretna, Louisiana 70053

Table of Contents.

CHAPTER XVI.
Sketches of individual life, P.. 547

CHAPTER XVII.
Memoirs of a few families, Q.. 632

CHAPTER XVIII.
Other prominent persons, R.. 634

CHAPTER XIX.
Selected memorials, S.. 717

CHAPTER XX.
Conspicuous residents of the state, T... 876

CHAPTER XXI.
A few special notices, U.. 937

CHAPTER XXII.
A glance at individual records, V.. 941

CHAPTER XXIII.
Brief notices of prominent persons, W.. 962

CHAPTER XXIV.
Concluding individual and family notices, Y... 1083

ERRATA...1091

SUPPLEMENTARY INDEX FOR VOLUME I...1093

POPULATION OF 1880–1890...1094

INDEX..1111

ILLUSTRATIONS.

	PAGE.
Stephen Thrasher	555
Agricultural college	571
Robert H. Peel	587
L. T. Baskett	619
J. A. Payne	651
John P. Richardson	667
H. L. Taylor	683
W. W. Moore	699
Helena, Battle of	715
Raymond, Battle of	715
Brice's Cross Roads, Battle of	715
E. T. Clark	731
J. J. White	763
Fred Beall	779
R. F. Beck	811
J. H. Jamison	827
Corinth, Battle of	843
C. Williams	859
B. F. Ward	891
M. G. Davis	907
Thomas W. East	923
T. D. Isom	939
John Clark	955
E. F. Lowe	971
Blind asylum, Jackson	987

Chapter XVI.

SKETCHES OF INDIVIDUAL LIFE, P.

THE following is a brief sketch of the life of the Hon. J. R. Pace, of Conehatta, Miss., one of Newton county's most enterprising citizens. He was born in Copiah county, Miss., January 2, 1832. His parents removed to Yazoo county in 1833, and in 1835 to Newton county, where he grew to manhood. He is the eldest of a family of twelve children, and was educated in the common schools. When it came time to select an occupation whereby he might gain an honorable livelihood he chose that of agriculture. In 1852 he was married to Miss M. J. Mathews, a daughter of William Mathews, and born in Perry county, Miss., in 1830. This union has been blessed by the birth of ten children, only six of whom are still living: Julia A., wife of James Anderson, Jr.; Matilda J. (deceased); Martha S., wife of R. A. Hattaway; T. B. (living), James N. (deceased), A. J. (living), Sarah E. (deceased); Mary C., wife of H. C. Bufkin, G. W. (living), and Hattie E. (deceased). Mr. Pace responded to the call for men to go to the defense of the country, and enlisted in the Thirty-ninth Mississippi as a private under Captain McElroy, company D. He participated in the battles of Corinth, Port Hudson, and was wounded at Atlanta, Ga., on August 10, 1864; he was confined in the hospital for some time, and when he was able to go about again he returned to his home, and resumed the more peaceful occupation of farming. The people of Newton county have testified to the confidence which they have in Mr. Pace by retaining him as a member of the board of supervisors for twelve years. He was further honored by being elected to the state legislature in the fall of 1887, and served in this capacity until 1890. He has also filled the office of county school commissioner of Newton county. He belongs to the Masonic order, and is also a member of the Farmers' Grange. In the autumn of 1886 he embarked in the mercantile trade at Conehatta, and does a business of $8,000 a year in connection with his farming. He has one thousand acres of land, two hundred of which he has reduced to a high state of cultivation. The family are members of the Baptist church, and are zealous workers in the cause which they have espoused.

R. B. Pace, one of the most extensive and prosperous farmers of Conehatta, Newton county, Miss., is a native of this county, born in 1839. His father, T. J. Pace, was born in the state of Alabama in 1810, and the mother, Jerusha Ann Tuchtone Pace, was a native of Copiah county, Miss., born in 1811. There were twelve children in the family, of whom R. B. is the fifth. The parents were married in 1833 in Copiah county, and the father engaged in farming, in which he continued until his death. He passed out of this life in October, 1864. He and his wife were useful members of the Baptist church, and all religious and educational enterprises found ready sympathy and support in them. R. B. Pace began life upon his own responsibility in 1862. In that same year he abandoned his private interests and went into the service of his country. He enlisted in the Thirteenth Mississippi regiment as a private under Captain Carleton, and saw one year of active duty. He participated in the battle of Ball's Bluff, and in June, 1863, he was honorably discharged at Richmond, Va. He then returned to his home and resumed his agricultural pursuits. He was married September 30, 1862, to Miss Elizabeth Horalson, daughter of William and Carmelia Horalson, who was born in Georgia in 1843. To them were born eleven children, ten of whom are living: Edith F., wife of M. M. McCuden; Exah V., wife of R. A. Sprened; Phebe E., wife of J. L. Frazier; Onia L., wife of O. A. Eddy; Lawrence J., Laura J., William J., Bruce M., Orent B., and Kirthla M. Mr. Pace engaged in the mercantile trade, and in 1876, 1877 and 1878 he handled $20,000 worth of goods annually. He then moved the store to his plantation, about four miles northwest of town, but soon after returned to the old stand. This was in 1884, and he continued there seven years. On account of a failure of his health he abandoned merchandising and retired to his farm in April, 1891. He owns about four thousand acres of land and has five hundred under cultivation; it is one of the best improved farms in the community. Mr. Pace's family are members of the Baptist church, in which society their zeal finds ready expression.

H. G. Paden, M. D., was born in Fayette county, Tenn., August 25, 1844, the youngest in a family of five children belonging to Alexander and Sarah (McCauley) Paden. The father was a native of Greenville district and the mother of Chester district, S. C. They grew up, were married in the Palmetto state and removed thence to Tennessee, where Mr. Paden bought land in Fayette county and settled there, engaging in planting. After four years' residence there he removed to Tishomingo county and located at old Castle Garden, now known as Burnt Mills, where he built a grist and sawmill, which he ran in connection with his planting enterprise. He was one of the earliest and in many respects one of the most influential citizens of the county. He did not aspire to any official position in the management of its concerns, but was content to be known as an honorable man of affairs, a kind and benevolent neighbor and a high-minded, Christian gentleman. Before the war he had accumulated considerable property in the way of land and slaves. He and his wife were members of the Presbyterian church, and died in this county, Mr. Paden in 1870 in the sixty-fifth year of his age, while Mrs. Paden passed away in 1873. Only four of the family are now living. These are: William D., who lives in Cameron, Tex.; David R., Mary J., wife of John H. Aughey, living in the Indian territory, and the subject of this sketch. The latter began life for himself and for his country at the early age of sixteen years, enlisting in 1862 in a company of the Thirty-second Mississippi infantry, under the command of Col. M. P. Lowrey, which was included in the department of the army of the Tennessee. He was in the battles of Chickamauga, Chattanooga, Missionary ridge, Lookout mountain, Kenesaw mountain, Atlanta, Franklin, Bentonville and numerous engagements of minor importance. At the battle of Franklin, Tenn., every member of his company was killed except two, and he was one of the two survivors, the other being a man named Dean. Although he was in some of the most hotly contested battles of the war, he was never wounded nor taken prisoner. At the end of the struggle he was paroled after the surrender, the company being disbanded at Greensboro, N. C. Returning to Tishomingo county, he engaged in farming and took up the study of medicine in the office of Dr. John Gordon at Rienzi, Miss., in the year 1868, with whom he remained for four years, meanwhile in the winter of 1869-70 taking a course of lectures at Louisville Medical college, Louisville, Ky. In 1872 he located on the old homestead at Burnt Mills, where he has since been engaged very successfully in the practice of his profession, carrying on planting in connection therewith. He is the owner of two hundred and forty acres of land, fifty acres of which are in a good state of cultivation, and are as productive as any in this part of the state. The Doctor was married in 1873 to Eusebia Thompson, a daughter of John Thompson and Eusebia (Hodges) Thompson. Her father was a native of Alabama and her mother of Tennessee. Mr. and Mrs. Paden have had four children to consecrate their union—three sons and one daughter: Ward, Sallie, Charles and John. The eldest is attending the Iuka Normal institute. The Paden family are extensively known throughout this part of the state, having been first among the pioneers and always among the leading citizens of Tishomingo county. The Doctor has a lucrative practice, the reputation of being a physician of skill and learning, and is regarded as an honorable practitioner, second to none in this part of the state. Although his interest in the public welfare is deep and abiding, he has never consented to accept any official position nor any of the numerous offices thrust upon him. His contributions to religious and educational as well as to charitable and beneficial interests generally have been frequent and generous. He and his estimable wife are members of the Methodist Episcopal church, and their home is ever open with the true Southern hospitality.

G. R. Page, planter, Clarksdale, Miss., was originally from Mississippi, his birth occurring in Tallahatchie county in 1854, and was the youngest of seven children born to George H. and Rebecca (Crawley) Page, the former a native of Virginia, and the latter of North Carolina. The father came to Mississippi when a young man, settled and married in Tallahatchie county, and followed the occupation of a planter. He came to Coahoma county in 1854, and his death occurred there four years later. He was a prominent citizen of the county, and was a descendant of an old and honored Virginia family. The mother died in 1874. They had two sons in the Confederate army: Robert (killed at Atlanta in 1864), and James (who died at Camp Douglas prison, Illinois, in April, 1865); two daughters died in infancy; Thomas W. (died in this county in 1882) and Albert B. (died the same year in Los Angeles, Cal., whither he had gone for his health). G. R. Page received a thorough education in the University of Mississippi, graduated in the class of 1878, and then practiced law at Friar's Point until 1882. After the death of his brother he moved to the homestead plantation, adjoining Clarksdale, consisting of six hundred acres, with five hundred acres under cultivation, and there he has since remained. He is thoroughgoing and progressive in his ideas, and has his land well improved and equipped. Politically he is a worker for the democratic party. In 1884 he was elected secretary of the board of levee commissioners for the Yazoo (Miss.) delta, with W. L. Hemingway as treasurer. In 1889 the offices of treasurer and secretary were combined, and Mr. Page was elected to fill both offices. He is treasurer of the Yazoo Delta Investment company, and is a director in the same. He is also a director and stockholder of the Clarksdale Brick and Manufacturing company, and has been identified with and a promoter of all enterprises of a public nature. He is tall, has dark hair and eyes, and is a shrewd, careful business man. Aside from his planting interest he is the owner of a number of lots in Clarksdale. March 12, 1891, Mr. Page was married to Miss Annie L. Murphy, a daughter of the late C. M. Murphy, of Durant, Miss., and they now reside at their beautiful home, Myrtle Hall, just outside the city limits of Clarksdale.

L. Page, planter, is a Mississippian by birth, born October 13, 1851, the youngest of thirteen children born to Maj. Warren A. and Mrs. (Reed) Page, the former of whom was born in Nashville, Tenn., in 1808, and in his early manhood came to Mississippi, settling in De Soto county in 1851. After remaining there five years he moved to Calhoun county and there followed the occupation of planting until his death in 1870. His wife was also a native of Tennessee and came of a family of planters. L. Page received his initiatory training in the common schools, after which he entered Leddin's Commercial school of Memphis, Tenn., from which he graduated in 1874. After leaving school he went to northern Mississippi, where he spent six years, at the end of which time he went to Texas, remaining in the Lone Star state two years. He next spent some time in Concordia parish, La., and during the six years that he remained in that state he was engaged in planting. The six subsequent years were spent in Mississippi, near Natchez, but in 1887 he left that place and came to Warren county, and in partnership with Mr. Pipes, of Natchez, he purchased the Ursena plantation, in Davis' bend. This plantation contains about two thousand acres, nine hundred of which are under cultivation, and is especially well adapted to the raising of stock, being well watered, etc. This entire tract was at one time heavily covered with timber, but a considerable portion of it has been cleared and other parts of it have gone back to Bermuda grass, which is very nutritious and affords the best of pasture. The old bed of the river is gradually filling up and adding to his acreage, and this too is growing up in grass. He is already raising an excellent grade of beef cattle and is expecting to engage in this enterprise very extensively in the near future. He has taken no interest in politics, being content to devote his time to his planting interests, at which he is making money. He is unmarried.

Junius G. Parham, the owner and proprietor of Parham hotel at Rolling Fork, also a planter of Sharkey county, Miss., was born in New Orleans in 1833 to Dr. John G. and Eliza (Moss) Parham, the former of whom was born at Hickford, Greene county, Va., in 1800. He was reared to a knowledge of farm life, and after obtaining a common-school education he began the study of medicine, graduating from a medical institution of Philadelphia, Penn. When in his early manhood he came to Vicksburg, Miss., where he was first married to a Miss Merritt, by whom he became the father of several children, among whom were: Prof. John, who was the superintendent of public instruction at New Orleans prior to the war, and died at Bessemer, Ala., a few years ago; Eugene, who is now at New Orleans, and Victoria, wife of a Mr. De Mallory, a prominent attorney of Hickford, Va. Mr. Parham's second marriage was to Miss Moss, by whom he became the father of the following children: James, who died when young; Henry; Rosy, wife of Solomon Frank, of Erath county, Tex.; Junius G.; Edinas P. (deceased), and Lucinda, wife of Willard Chamberlain, of Erath county, Tex. Dr. Parham was a leading medical practitioner of Vicksburg for many years, and in that city he was also an extensive dealer in real estate. His residence was at Parham hill, two miles east of Vicksburg, until 1849, when he removed to New Orleans, where he hired out his negroes for levee work. In 1860 he removed to Amite City, near which place he died on the 25th of July, 1862, after a long and well-spent life. Although he received but little schooling in his youth, he was ambitious and persevering, and throughout his life was a hard student, applying himself to his studies to such purpose that he became a man of profound learning, a highly successful physician and a leading politician. He was at one time the choice of the whig party as a candidate for congress, this being while he was a resident of Vicksburg, but he was defeated. He was afterward offered a nomination for the position of mayor of New Orleans, but declined. He was a prominent Mason, and was also a leading member of the Felicita Road Methodist church at New Orleans. His father was James Parham. Mrs. Parham, the mother of Junius G. Parham, was born in Vicksburg in 1827, and died in Amite City in April, 1889, having been the wife of Hon. Martin Haney, a member of the lower house of the Louisiana legislature. She was the daughter of Col. H. A. Moss, a native of Vermont, who left home at the age of thirteen years and came to Vicksburg, Miss., where he grew to manhood and was married to Miss Eliza Vick, a daughter of Gen. William Vick, a brother of the founder of Vicksburg (see sketch of N. J. Vick). Colonel Moss was a merchant and planter, and very well to do. He spent some years in Tennessee and Texas, and was a colonel in the Mexican war, his death occurring in New Orleans in 1859. Junius Parham was educated in Amite City, La., and at the age of sixteen years began for himself as a planter near Amite City, but in 1875 came to Anguilla, Miss., and took charge of Colonel Vick's Anguilla plantation. In 1877 he was married to Alice, daughter of Eli Stevens, who was a planter of Warren county, where he passed from life, having previously been a planter of Claiborne county. His wife died when their daughter, Mrs. Parham, was two years old. The latter has borne her husband one son and three daughters; the former, a bright little boy, was drowned in Huntonia landing, Sunflower river, near their home, in the high water of 1882. In 1883 Mr. Parham purchased a fine plantation of five hundred and eighty-six acres near Anguilla, about three hundred acres of which are under cultivation, producing from one hundred and ten to two hundred bales of cotton per year. He also owns a residence and four lots in Anguilla, and a hotel and store building in Rolling Fork, which he has the satisfaction of knowing has been acquired by his own efforts. From 1885 until 1889 he was a merchant of Anguilla, but since October, 1890, he has resided in Rolling Fork, where he is the proprietor of Parham hotel, which is an admirably kept hostelry, and commands a paying patronage. Mr. Parham has always been active in public affairs, and no effort has been spared on his part for the general advancement of the community. In 1879 he was the candidate of the fusionists for sheriff of Sharkey county, but was defeated by a small majority. In 1887 he was the choice of the democratic party for county treasurer, but was opposed by an independent candidate who obtained the support of the republicans and defeated Mr. Parham by thirty-five votes. In 1890 he was census enumerator for districts one and two in Sharkey county, and was at one time the democratic congressional committeeman for Sharkey county. He is a prominent member of the Knights of Honor of Rolling Fork, and he and his wife are consistent workers in and active members of the Methodist church.

Dr. John T. Parker is an active medical practitioner of Chickasaw county, Miss., located at Buena Vista. He is a son of Eleazer and Mary Parker, of South Carolina, and grandson of Isaac and Susan (Gibson) Parker, Isaac being a native of Virginia and a planter by occupation. His father was born in Wales, and in the sixteenth century came to America and located in Virginia, where he became an extensive stockdealer and very wealthy. Eleazer and Mary Parker became the parents of the following children: John T., Mary H. (Surrat), Naomi J. (Davis), Isaac L. (deceased), Meek C., Emeline (McLuncy), Joseph E. (deceased), and Elizabeth (Surrat), deceased. Dr. John T. Parker was educated in the South Carolina Military academy, and afterward fitted himself for his profession in the Jefferson Medical college, of Philadelphia, Penn., and the South Carolina Medical college, graduating from the last named institution in 1861. He first located at Fort Mill, S. C., but became a resident of Chickasaw county, Miss., in 1871, locating at Buena Vista, becoming a member of the Buena Vista and Houston Medical association, and its first president. He became secretary of the same in 1875, and the following year its vice president. He was also a member of the Mississippi State Medical association, and during the year of 1878 was its vice president. He entered the Confederate army as first lieutenant and was promoted to the captaincy of his company, in which capacity he served until the war closed. He was in all the skirmishing and fights on the coast of South Carolina; the engagements around Richmond, Petersburg; was under Stonewall Jackson in Maryland, and was at Appomattox Courthouse at the time of Lee's surrender. In December, 1866, he was married to Miss Louisa, a daughter of Minor Sadler, Esq., of York, S. C., but in 1876 he was called upon to mourn her death, she leaving him with three children: Pearl, Victor S. and Louis S. His second marriage, in 1881, was to Mrs. Annetta Conner Hill, who died in 1883, leaving him with one child to care for, John William. Dr. Parker is a member of the Masonic order at Buena Vista. He is a member of the Presbyterian church, and in 1886-7 was county superintendent of public schools of Chickasaw county. He has been one of the trustees and directors of Buena Vista college ever since that institution was established, and has otherwise interested himself in the public affairs of this section, being the present mayor of the town. As a physician he is well known, for he is skilled and experienced, and his patronage is large and lucrative.

John T. Parker, merchant, Graysport, Miss., a member of the well-known mercantile firm of Parker Bros., is a general trader, and in connection is actively engaged in planting. His father, William Parker, was a native of Anson county, N. C., where he was married in 1839 to Miss Isabella F. Harris, also a native of that county. After marriage the parents came to Lowndes county, Miss., remained there for three years and then removed to Carroll county, where they continued to reside until 1857. Mr. Parker was a very successful planter and a man of excellent business ability, although he had but a limited education. He accumulated a large fortune by his industry and economy. He died in 1875, and his wife in 1884. He was a member of the Baptist and she a member of the Methodist church. The paternal grandfather, James Parker, was a native of America, but of Scotch-Irish descent. He was a planter and died in North Carolina. Daniel Harris, the maternal grandfather, was a native of America and followed the occupation of a planter and miller. He was very wealthy, owning a distillery and gold mine, and passed his last days in the Old North state. John T. Parker is the eldest of the following children, born to the above mentioned union: Young A. was a merchant in Yalobusha county, was educated in Mississippi and died in 1867 (he was in company D, Forty-eighth Mississippi infantry and served with the Virginia army in a brave and faithful manner. He was severely wounded near Petersburg); William J. is in business in Graysport with John T. (he was married to Miss Lula F., daughter of Dr. L. M. Mays, who has been a prominent physician of Graysport since 1870); Henry W., and Ada (wife of L. F. Provine, who is a merchant of Coffeeville). John T. Parker was born in Tishomingo county in 1839, educated principally in Carroll county, and at the age of eighteen years he began as clerk at Graysport for B. F. Johnson and has resided here ever since, except during the war. In 1861 he joined company E, Fifteenth Mississippi infantry, and the first battle in which he participated was Fishing creek, Ky. On January 19, 1862, he was captured and imprisoned at Camp Chase, Ohio, where he remained until the 26th of April, when he was taken to Johnson island. He remained there until May and was then returned to Camp Chase, where he continued until September, 1862, when he was exchanged at Vicksburg. After this, on account of ill health, he went home and there remained until after the fall of Vicksburg, when he joined the Forty-eighth Mississippi, company E, and operated in the Virginia army until the close of the war, or just before, when he returned home on account of an old wound. In February, 1866, he engaged in merchandising at Graysport, the firm being Badeheimer & Parker; continued until 1876, and from that time until 1880 Mr. Parker was not in business. At the last mentioned date he engaged in business alone, and six years later the present firm was established. He and his brother do an annual business of over $40,000 and are live, energetic men. Mr. Parker is well and favorably known all over the county and is an excellent financier. He is progressive and liberal in his support of all public enterprises of a laudable nature. He is also the owner of two thousand acres of land in different tracts, and is well respected for his many qualities as a business man, citizen and member of society. In 1866 he married Miss Martha A. Clark, a native of what is now Grenada county, and the daughter of Zenas A. and Ann Clark, natives of Tennessee and Virginia respectively. Mr. and Mrs. Clark removed to Grenada county, Miss., at a very early date and there the father passed the life of a planter and was also a real-estate speculator. His death occurred in 1865 and his wife's in 1863. To Mr. and Mrs. Parker were born four interesting children. Mrs. Parker died in 1884. She was a worthy member of the Presbyterian church. Mr. Parker's second marriage occurred in 1884, to Miss Laura Clark, sister of his first wife, who has borne him one child, a son. Mr. Parker is one of the oldest settlers of Graysport and one of its best citizens. He was a member of the Masonic fraternity, Graysport lodge (now defunct) No. 289, and was secretary of the lodge for a number of years. This lodge was chartered a few years after the war and was in operation for ten or twelve years. Mr. Parker is also a prominent member of the Presbyterian church.

Among the prosperous planters of Yazoo county is Robert A. Parker, Craigs, Yazoo county, Miss., who has resided here since 1874. He was born in Holmes county, Miss., in 1848, and is a son of Peter A. Parker, who was one of the earliest settlers of the state, and one of the largest and most successful planters. He died in 1890, at the age of eighty years; he was a citizen of Holmes county at the time of his death, and had been a resident fifty years. Robert A. passed his schooldays in Holmes county and at Oxford university, from which institution he was graduated in 1870. During the last few months of the war he was in the service of the state, where he proved himself capable and efficient. In 1871 he entered the ranks of the schoolteacher, and for four years at Ebenezer, Holmes county, Miss., he was devoted to the schoolroom. In 1878 he purchased the plantation on which he lives in Yazoo county, to which he had removed four years previously. He cultivates six hundred acres of land, the principal crops being corn and cotton; of the latter he produces three hundred bales annually. He takes an active interest in the politics of the county and now holds the office of magistrate. All movements of a benevolent and philanthropic character have found in Mr. Parker a ready and sympathetic supporter, and much of the improvement and advancement of his community are due to his efforts. He is an ardent admirer of the Spring creek valley, and considers it one of the most salubrious and delightful spots in which to dwell.

Col. Elisha A. Parrish, a planter of Yalobusha county, was born in Williamson county, Tenn., 1824. He was the son of Matthew F. and Priscilla E. (North) Parrish, natives of Virginia. The former was born in May, 1789, the latter September 20, 1792. They moved with their parents to Williamson county, Tenn., where they were married June 10, 1812, and where Mr. Parrish died May 30, 1830. In 1837 the family came to Yalobusha county, but about 1845 Mrs. Parrish returned to Williamson county, where she died in 1846. She was a daughter of Elisha North, a native of Virginia but an early settler of Williamson county, Tenn., at a time when the county was little more than a vast canebrake, becoming a well-known settler and dying prior to 1837. He was of English descent. His wife was Rhoda Reese, who died when our subject was a small boy. Colonel Parrish's grandfather, Joel Parrish, was of French descent, but was born in Virginia, and was another of the pioneers of Williamson county, Tenn., where he became a planter of considerable prominence and died at a comparatively early date. His wife was Susannah Maury, a native of Virginia, who survived him but a few years. Eight children were born to them. Colonel Parrish is the sixth in order of their birth. The eldest and the youngest two are buried in Tennessee and the rest removed to this county, and all except Colonel Parrish are dead. Our subject was educated principally in Williamson county, Tenn., but he has supplemented his common-school education with a large amount of general information acquired by practical contact with the world. He began for himself as a planter at about the age of twenty. He was first married in 1853 to Catherine Jones, a native of Alabama, where her father died during her girlhood, she coming with her mother to Panola county. She died in 1860, having been for a long time a member of the Baptist church. In 1867 he married Mary Susan, daughter of John N. and Sarah Ann Herron; the former was born in Williamson county February 23, 1815, and the latter was born in Greene county, Ala., April 13, 1814, both coming with their parents to Mississippi, where they were married November 6, 1838, when they removed to Tallahatchie county, where they were engaged in planting until 1853. Then they removed to Coffeeville because of its superior educational advantages, keeping a hotel there until 1860. In the year last mentioned they removed to a farm eight miles northeast of Oakland, where Mr. Herron died in June, 1863. His wife was so unfortunate as to lose her eyesight soon after, and she died March 14, 1881. Both were members of the Cumberland Presbyterian church, though she had formerly been of the Old School Presbyterian faith. She was a daughter of Alexander Shaw, who was born in Ireland about 1774 and was orphaned when a little boy. He stole his passage to America and located at Charleston, S. C., where he learned the cabinetmaker's trade and married a Miss Harden. Thence he removed to Greene county, Ala., and about 1834 he came to Yalobusha county. Afterward he moved to Lafayette county and thence to De Soto county, where he died a wealthy planter in 1860. He was three times married. His first wife, Mrs. Herron's mother, died in Lafayette county. Mrs. Parrish's father was once treasurer of Yalobusha county and was in other respects a prominent man. His father was Andrew Herron, a native of North Carolina, and was among the pioneers of Williamson county, Tenn. He removed, in 1834, to Lafayette county, Miss., where he died. He was of Irish descent and was a planter during most of his life. His wife, who was Mary Ann McAllister, died at Seguin, Tex., about 1858. Mrs. Parrish was born in Lafayette county November 10, 1841, and has borne her husband five children, three of whom are living: Epper S. (who received her education at Oxford and McMinnville, Tenn., and later was a student at the Clara Conway, Memphis, Tenn.), Robert, Isam and John Herron. Since 1852 Colonel Parrish has resided on his present plantation, three miles northeast of Oakland, which consists of two thousand seven hundred acres of well-improved and highly productive land. This fine property he has acquired by his own efforts, for he is one of the self-made men of this county. During the war he was a member of the sixty days' regiment attached to Alcorn's brigade. He ranked as second lieutenant and saw considerable service in Tennessee and Kentucky. At the expiration of his term of enlistment his regiment was disbanded at Columbus, Ky. He found himself in such poor health that he did little military service afterward, though he was for a short time afterward in a militia organization. He has for many years been a member of Oakland lodge No. 82, A. F. & A. M. He and his wife are devout and consistent members of the Cumberland Presbyterian church, with which his sons are also connected. Colonel Parrish is a man above reproach, widely known and respected. He is one of the few residents of the county who serve as a connecting link of Yalobusha county of the present and Yalobusha county of the pioneer days. He is energetic, enterprising and public-

spirited, a man devoted to his home and home interests. Justly proud of his family he spares no pains to make their home pleasant, and affords his children the best educational facilities obtainable.

David W. E. Parsons, planter, Canton, Miss., the youngest of three children born to D. C. M. and Dorcas L. (Harold) Parsons, owes his nativity to Missouri, his birth occurring in Pike county on the 20th of November, 1845. He was reared and educated in Mississippi, finished his schooling at Central academy, Madison county, and later started out as a planter, which occupation he has continued to follow up to the present time. He is now the owner of one thousand acres of land, six hundred acres of which are under plow. In 1862 he enlisted with Harvey's scouts and was with the same for about eighteen months. He was then transferred to Wirt Adams' regiment, cavalry, and remained with this until the close of the war. He was not in any of the regular engagements, but as he belonged to a scouting party he of course did a great deal of fighting that is not mentioned in history. Mr. Parsons is one of the county's most practical and enterprising citizens. He contributes liberally of his means to all public enterprises of a laudable nature, and has the respect of all. He was first married in 1867 to Miss Mattie Southerland, a native of Mississippi, and the daughter of John A. and Eliza Southerland, natives also of that state. Mr. and Mrs. Parsons' union was blessed by the birth of two children: Cora D. and Annie E. Mr. Parsons was married, the second time, in 1874, to Miss Mary Dinkins, who was born in Mississippi, and whose parents, James A. and Margaret Dinkins, were natives of North Carolina and Mississippi, respectively. The second marriage resulted in the birth of seven children: Mollie M., Mary, John R., Lillie, D. C. M., Maggie and James. Mr. Parsons' parents were natives respectively of Virginia and Kentucky. The father was a prominent character in Missouri, and was sent to the state legislature from Pike county of that state in 1842. At the time of his death, which occurred in 1845, he was a candidate for congress, but died before the election. He was in the Black Hawk war and was among the pioneers of Missouri.

Frank Parsons, farmer and miller, resides five miles north of Brookhaven. He was born in Virginia in 1844, a son of Isaac and Sarah (Pugh) Parsons, both of whom were born and married in that state. His father was a farmer, mechanic and merchant, a son of Robert Parsons and his wife, who was a Miss Wilbourne, whose parents were both born in Virginia. Sarah Pugh, the mother of our subject, was a daughter of Robert and Pollie (Thomas) Pugh. Both of them were also natives of the Old Dominion. On his father's side Mr. Pugh is of English descent, and on his mother's side of Welsh descent. He removed to Kentucky with his parents when quite a young man, where his mother died. After about four years' residence in that state they removed to Ohio, where the father died. Frank Parsons is the fifth in a family of twelve children, seven of whom lived to maturity, and four of whom are yet living. The family originally consisted of six boys and six girls, and of this round dozen five died in infancy. The names of the remaining seven are: Robert R., who lives in Jones county, Miss., and has three children; Mollie, who is deceased, and left two children; Stephen, who is in South America; Rhoda (deceased), and for whom one child mourns; Frank, our subject; Virginia (deceased), and John W., who lives in Copiah county, where he is a prominent planter, and has four children. Mr. Parsons received a good English education in the common schools of Virginia. He removed from Ohio to Tennessee, and from there, in 1872, to Mississippi. He was married in Holmes county in 1874, to Miss Cornelia Gage, a daughter of M. and Patience W. (Sandress) Gage. Her father was a native of Mississippi, and her mother of Alabama, she herself claiming Mississippi as the state of her nativity. Mrs. Parsons is the eighth in a family of twelve children. Of these Mary, now a widow, has one child; Matthew was assassinated in Holmes county; Jerry was killed in battle at fateful Gettysburg; George died young; Robert lives in Holmes county; Georgia (deceased) left two children; Louie lives in Holmes county; Anna E., wife of Judge Evans, lives at Enterprise with her family of two children; Cornelia, the wife of our subject; Charles, who lives with his two children at Brookhaven; Ada, now Mrs. Dabbs, of Clarke county, and Virgie G., who lives in Clarke county with her widowed sister Mary. Mr. and Mrs. Parsons have six children: Hazlett, who is living with the father and mother, as are also Frank, Anna B. and Sexton; two are dead: Virgie Lou and an unnamed infant. Mr. Parsons enlisted in the Union army June 12, 1862, in Seredo, Va., in company G, of the Fifth Virginia infantry, under the command of Colonel Ziegler. He served in the northern Virginia campaign, and was discharged on account of ill health in 1863. He was in the battle of Cross Keys, and in all of General Rosecrans' campaigns until his discharge. After the war he engaged in photography and chemistry, filling for a time the position of chemist in an oil refinery in Mason county, Ky. During four years, while a resident of Tennessee, he was engaged in the manufacture of lumber. He removed to Mississippi, and worked for a time as a millwright. He purchased the place upon which he resides in 1875, and here he has established a planing-mill and general wood-working and machine shop, in which he carries on a large business. He is the owner of one of the most excellent vineyards in the state, and manufactures wine on a large scale. He is a stanch republican, and cast his first presidential vote for Abraham Lincoln. He is a Master Mason, and a liberal and reliable supporter of religious and educational interests, and of all measures tending to the public good, while his wife is a member of the Presbyterian church.

Charles W. Partee, merchant and planter, Belen, Miss., who inherits French blood from the paternal and English from the maternal side of the house, was originally from Tennessee, where his birth occurred on the 22d of March, 1845. His parents, Squire Boone and Martha A. (Douglass) Partee, were natives of North Carolina and Tennessee, respectively. The parents emigrated to Mississippi about 1848, located in Panola county, and there the father engaged in planting, which pursuit he followed successfully until his death in 1862. He was an honored citizen and held many positions of trust in his county. He was married twice, his first wife being a Miss Edwards, who bore him three children. Charles W. Partee, the fifth of seven children born to the second union, came to Mississippi with his parents when but three years of age, and was reared and educated in this state. He and a brother served through the Civil war. He enlisted as a volunteer in 1861 in company H, Twelfth Mississippi regiment, Sardis blues, a company organized at Sardis, and was in the second battle of Manassas, Seven Pines, and several battles in Mississippi. He surrendered at Gainesville, Ala., at the close of the war, and returned home, where he resumed his planting interests. This occupation he has continued since, and in connection is also engaged in merchandising. He is the owner of about two thousand four hundred acres of land, and has about six hundred acres under cultivation, all of which he has cleared in the last six years. He has a good business house, and carries a stock of general merchandise valued at about $3,500. He erected his residence in Belen in 1888. He was married in 1871 to Miss Lizzie Jackson, a native of Mississippi, and the daughter of James and Mary I. (Askew) Jackson, natives of the Bayou state. This union was blessed by the birth of the following children: Pattie Belle, Birdie, Charlie W., Carrie May, Nina Fontaine. Mrs. Partee died on the 10th of January, 1891, and in her death the town of Belen, as well as her family, sustained an irreparable loss. She was not only the life of her home, but of the little town, and her name was a synonym for goodness. She was a devoted Christian, and spent much of her time in caring for the sick, and helping those in want and distress. Mr. Partee is a quiet, unassuming gentleman, and is one of the representative and substantial citizens of the county. He held the office of treasurer for some time, and discharged the duties incumbent upon this office in a very satisfactory manner.

Dr. I. P. Partin, of the firm of Thompson, Hyer & Partin, physicians and surgeons, of Meridian, Miss., was born in Lauderdale county, Miss., in the year 1852, a son of Charles P. Partin, who is also a practicing physician in Newton county, Miss., where he resides. Before the war he was postmaster in charge of an office in Lauderdale county, Miss., and major of the Thirty-sixth Mississippi Confederate regiment. He has three sons, of whom our subject was the second in order of birth, and is the one who has followed in the line of his father's footsteps professionally. Dr. I. P. Partin received his literary education in the counties of Lauderdale and Newton, and at an early age began to study medicine. He graduated at the medical college of Alabama, at Mobile, in the year 1886, and in 1887 formed a partnership with Dr. M. J. Thompson, which relationship he has since continued. He is a general practitioner and is highly esteemed as such. He is a member of the State Medical association and of the Lauderdale county Medical association, and was vice president of the latter association in the year 1890. He is a member of the Masonic fraternity, belongs to the Knights of Pythias, the Knights of the Golden Rule, and the Knights of Honor. He was married in 1872 to Miss Martha J. Warren, a native of Lauderdale county, Miss. Of the children born to this union, three are living: Walter C., Charles E., and William F. One son, Albert S. is deceased. The Doctor and his family are members of the Methodist Episcopal church. The family take high rank in the county, and the Doctor himself is esteemed and respected throughout the community.

W. N. Pass is not only one of the prosperous merchants and successful planters of Grenada, Grenada county, Miss., but is vice president of the Merchants' bank and the Grenada Compress company, and is one of the directors of the Grenada Ice factory. He was born in Grenada, Miss., on the 28th of March, 1836, and is a son of John B. and Elizabeth (Ewing) Pass, natives of Georgia and Alabama, and born in 1802 and 1812, respectively. Mr. and Mrs. Pass came to Mississippi in 1832, and settled in what is now Grenada, where Mr. Pass is credited with erecting the first brick building. He was also one of the first merchants. Sometime afterward he moved to the country near Grenada and engaged in planting, and there resided until his death, in April, 1865. Previous to the war he was the owner of large tracts of land and many slaves, but lost all during the struggle. He was a member of Masonic lodge No. 31, of Grenada, and was one of the county's leading citizens. He was familiarly known as Major Pass. Mrs. Pass followed her husband to the grave in the fall of the same year. They were Baptists in belief and liberal supporters but not members of any church. To them were born eight children, three sons and three daughters yet living. W. N. Pass, the third in order of birth of the above mentioned family, was reared in what is now Grenada county, and owns the property on which he was born. He quite recently erected a large brick building, two stories in hight, and with a number of large rooms and many offices. He served during the war in Colonel Stanford's battery as a private, and operated in Tennessee, Kentucky and Alabama, participating in all the battles of his brigade. He was paroled in Alabama at the close of the war, and returned to Mississippi, where he was engaged in merchandising in Providence for some time. In 1867 he went to Duck Hill, and from there to Grenada in 1868, where he has since resided. He is a self-made man, and what he has won in the way of this world's goods is wholly due to his own good fighting qualities. He is one of the class of men singled out by nature to show what a man can do when he sets his mind upon accomplishing a certain object. Since residing in Grenada he has been busily employed in merchandising, carries a general stock, and does an annual business of from $75,000 to $140,000. He is also quite extensively engaged in planting, owning large tracts of land, besides valuable property in Memphis, Tenn., and New Orleans, La. He owns five brick buildings in Grenada with other property in town and county valued at $65,000. He is one of the sharpest, shrewdest business men, and one of the oldest merchants of the place. He was married in 1881 to Miss Mollie Ragsdale, who was reared and educated in Grenada, and who is the daughter of George W. and Elizabeth (Berry) Ragsdale, natives of Mississippi. Mr. and Mrs. Pass' marriage has been blessed by the birth of two children— a son and daughter: Louis and Alma. Mrs. Pass is a member of the Episcopal church. Mr. Pass affiliates with the democratic party in politics, and socially is a member of the I. O. O. F. lodge, No. 6.

Dr. Benjamin F. Passmore, merchant and planter, Passonia, Madison county, Miss. Dr. Passmore's parents, Ellis Pusey Passmore and Hester A. Saunders, were born in Pennsylvania and Mississippi, respectively, and the fruits of their union were five children, of whom Benjamin F. was the youngest and is the only one living, the rest having died before maturity without issue. The father was a very prominent character in his day and represented Franklin county, Miss., in the state legislature in 1830. He was a very prominent physician also. His death occurred in 1839. His father, Ellis Passmore, Sr., was of English descent, and was a native of the Keystone state, and a member of the society of Friends. The maternal grandparents, Hugh Saunders and Nepsy Campbell, were natives of Wales and Scotland, respectively. Benjamin F. Passmore was born in Madison county, Miss., on the 13th of April, 1838, and was educated in the private schools of the same until seventeen years of age. He then entered the Mississippi college, at Clinton, remained there from 1854 until 1857, and would have graduated in 1858, but left school. In 1858 and 1859 he attended the Jefferson Medical college, Philadelphia, Penn., and in the last-named year and 1860 he attended the medical department of the University of Louisiana, graduating from the same in that year. Immediately afterward he began the practice of medicine in Madison county, Miss., where he has remained ever since and has a lucrative and extensive practice. He is quite a prominent character in the politics of Madison county, but has never held office. He is county lecturer for the Alliance of Madison county and is also a member of the state executive committee of the same. In 1890 he was president of the Board of Alliance exchange. Besides his profession, Dr. Passmore is engaged in merchandising and planting, and is the owner of three thousand acres of land, one thousand five hundred acres under cultivation. He is considered one of the most successful planters of the county and is a safe and reliable business man. He has been a frequent contributor to the press on public topics, is one of the most prominent men of the Farmers' Alliance in the state, and has written some very able articles in opposition to the sub-treasury scheme promulgated by the National Alliance, over which the Alliance in Mississippi is now divided. He is strongly democratic in his political views. He is always ready and willing to give aid and countenance to all worthy enterprises for the public weal. His farm is in a fine state of cultivation and everything about the place indicates to the beholder that the owner is a progressive and thoroughgoing man. He began life for himself at the age of thirteen years with a small capital and had accumulated quite a fortune before the war. During that stirring period he lost a great portion of it, and in 1882 he had to begin anew, having made all of his property since that time. He was assistant surgeon and was in hospital service during the late war. Dr. Passmore was married March 13, 1863, to Miss Eleanor Jane Richey, a native of Clinton, Hinds county,

Miss., and the daughter of James Richey and Eliza Nichol, natives of Ireland. To Dr. and Mrs. Passmore have been born in Mississippi two children: Ellis L. Passmore, who married on January 15, 1890, Miss Ella Russell; and Leila G. Passmore, who was married January 4, 1884, to W. B. Cordts and has two sons: Leroy Passmore Cordts and Walter Richey Cordts.

P. W. Patterson was born in Franklin county, Ala., November 2, 1845. He was the third child in a family of ten children of W. C. and Sarah (Scoggins) Patterson, both of whom were natives of Ohio, and removed with their parents when small children to Alabama. Mr. Patterson's paternal grandfather was one of the pioneers of Alabama, and his parents grew up and were married in Franklin county of that state, and removed to Tishomingo county in 1867, locating near Bay Springs, where his father bought land and engaged in planting, which, although he is a minister of the Missionary Baptist church, and does considerable evangelical work in Tishomingo and adjoining counties, he has made his principal occupation through life. Mr. Patterson's mother died in 1881 at her home near Bay Springs, having been long a member of the Baptist church, and lived an exemplary Christian life. Rev. Mr. Patterson has never aspired to any official position, but has always been content to live the simple life of a tiller of the soil, and devote his talents and energies to the salvation of souls. Of the ten children of Mr. and Mrs. Patterson, seven are now living, and three of them are residents of Iuka. The Patterson family is well known throughout the county, and its representatives are regarded as good citizens, and are held in high respect by the public at large. Our subject began planting on his own account near Bay Springs at the age of twenty-one. In 1863 he enlisted in company E, of the Fifth Alabama cavalry, under Colonel Warren, and in General Forrest's command. He was in the engagement at Sulphur Trestle, Athens, Decatur, Selma, Dixie and Harrisburg, and in numerous others of more or less importance, serving until the close of the war, without being wounded or taken prisoner. He was paroled at Danville, Ala., May 19, 1865, and he returned to Marion county of that state. In 1867 he removed to Mississippi, where he has since made his home. In 1869 he married Miss Mary Ann Shackelford, daughter of Capt. W. A. H. Shackelford, of Tishomingo county. Down to the year 1888 Mr. Patterson planted with considerable success, in the meantime holding the office of magistrate for two years. In that year he was elected chancery clerk of Tishomingo county, and he is the present incumbent of that office. He has devoted himself closely to its duties, and is regarded as one of the most obliging and efficient officials in the county. He is the owner of half a block and considerable residence property in Iuka, and of four acres of land in the suburbs of that town. He takes a great interest in the progress of Iuka, and has always contributed his full share toward the advancement of its general interests. He and his wife are honored members of the best social circles, and Mrs. Patterson is a communicant of the Primitive Baptist church.

James V. Patton is one of the prominent and successful business men of Senatobia and may well feel proud of his career as a self-made man. Born April 2, 1850, in that part of Tate county which was then De Soto county, he was well educated in Mississippi and Tennessee and in 1874 began life as a teacher. Preferring the more active career to be found in a mercantile life, he became salesman and bookkeeper for Echols & Echols, with whom he remained five years, beginning with a small salary, which was gradually increased according to the value of his services. At the end of that time he was offered a better position with Gabbert & Co., and with this firm he remained until 1886, when he entered upon an independent business for himself under the firm name of J. V. Patton & Co. At the close of the first year J. F. Carlock became partner and the firm has since been Carlock &

Patton. They do an extensive business amounting to $35,000 annually, carrying a complete line of general merchandise. Mr. Patton has a pleasant home in Senatobia, which is enlivened by the presence of his wife and six bright children. In 1877 he married Miss Mary L. McFadden, who was also a native of Mississippi. Her parents, William D. and Eliza A. (Neely) McFadden were South Carolinians. The six children born to Mr. and Mrs. Patton are, Anna L., William L., Agnes E., James V., Mary W. and a little son who is yet unnamed. The parents of Mr. Patton, William E. and Agnes A. (Carr) Patton, born November 27, 1817, and May 30, 1821, respectively, were both natives of South Carolina, James V. being the sixth of their ten children. William E. Patton removed to Tennessee at an early age and was educated in that state, being there married in 1840 to Miss Carr, a daughter of William and Esther (Boyd) Carr, who were from the Palmetto state. In 1848 Mississippi became his home, since which time he has led the quiet life of a planter on his fine estate of four hundred acres in Tate county. All but one of his children lived to bless his old age. He and his family are members of the Presbyterian church, in which both he and his son, James V., are elders. The latter is a wideawake and enterprising man, and has always taken great interest in public affairs, being complimented by his fellow-citizens by election to office, having been secretary and treasurer of Senatobia four years and a member of its city council. Secret societies claim some of his attention, he being a member of the Knights of Honor and Knights and Ladies of Honor. He enjoys the confidence of his neighbors as a safe business man who has won his present high position by honorable methods as a Christian gentleman.

J. W. Patton is one of the prominent planters of Itawamba county, Miss. He was born in this state July 15, 1843. He is the son of G. W. and Catherine (Reed) Patton. He was reared to farm life, and received a practical education in the common schools of his neighborhood. In 1872 he married Miss Susan C. Martin, a native of Alabama, and a daughter of R. Martin and Teressa (Robinson) Martin, both natives of that state, and members of two of its most prominent families. To Mr. and Mrs. Patton have been born nine children, of whom the six here named are living: Charles M., Ellac, James L., John L., Levona and Edgar. In 1861 Mr. Patton enlisted in Capt. B. Tucker's company H, of the Twenty-eighth Mississippi cavalry, formed at Aberdeen. The principal engagements in which he participated were those at the siege of Vicksburg, the affairs at Carson's Landing and at Thompson's station. At Carter's Mills, Tenn., he was captured by the Federals and carried to City Point, Va., as a prisoner. After his exchange he was sent to the hospital at Chattanooga, where he remained for four months. At the expiration of that time he again entered active service and was sent to Clinton, Miss., and took part in the battle of Harrisburg. He was paroled in 1865, and, returning home to his native county, engaged in farming. The war left him in an impoverished condition, and he may be said to have practically began life at its close. He is now the owner of about eleven hundred acres of land, which he has acquired by his own unaided efforts, and ranks among the leading planters of this county. Politically he is a democrat, and his interest in the state and national affairs of importance is exceeded only by his interest in his county and town affairs. He is a Master Mason and a good citizen, stands high in the public estimation, being liberal in his contribution to churches, schools and all other objects having a view to the general advancement and development of his county and state.

William Hinkle Patton is a prominent merchant of Shubuta, Clarke county, Miss. He was born September 7, 1847, near Jacinto, in old Tishomingo county, the eldest son of a family of five children born to James J. and Sarah A. (Hinkle) Patton, three of whom are yet living. His father was born in Tennessee August 23, 1822, and gave his life for the Confederate cause in 1862, dying at his home in Clarke county of typhoid pneumonia contracted in camp at Columbus, Miss. He was a member of company E, of the Thirty-seventh Mississippi regiment, ranking as orderly sergeant. Mr. and Mrs. Patton were married in Chickasaw county. Their children were: William H.; Mary J. G., now Mrs. Martin, and living at Rome, Ga.; James L., of Micanopy, Fla.; Margaret D., who died at Mobile, Ala., when sixteen years of age; Luellah R., who died at the age of six in Shubuta, Clarke county. The mother of our subject was born in the northern part of the state in 1826. She was a daughter of Jacob Hinkle, and died at Shubuta in 1870. The family settled in Clarke county in 1859, and Mr. Patton engaged in planting. He was an enterprising man who exhibited much public spirit. Both he and his wife were members of the Presbyterian church, but there being no Presbyterian church near them after their settlement here, they connected themselves with the Methodist church. Previous to the war he had been an old-line whig, was opposed to secession, but after the die was cast he joined his fortunes with his fellow-citizens for better or for worse. At the death of our subject's father the burden of the family's support, and the education of his brother and sisters fell principally on his shoulders, which interfered materially with his obtaining an education. Such schooling as he had, however, he received in the country schools of Texas, Louisiana and Mississippi, except one session at Mansfield, La., near where his family were living at the time. From 1850 to 1856 they lived in Texas, moving thence to De Soto parish, La., where they lived until 1859, when they returned to this state. Mr. Patton's early life was spent on a farm, and when he was but fourteen years old he was orphaned by the loss of his father. Not being very strong he came to Shubuta and found employment suited to his strength, as a clerk in the postoffice and drug store for Dr. D. M. Dunlap. There he remained for two years. Mrs. Dunlap was exceedingly kind to him, and her advice and counsel were heeded by him. Mr. M. P. Collins, who was station agent at Shubuta at that time, was very ready to render him any assistance in his power or to advise him on perplexing questions. In 1863 he learned telegraphy, and for a year before the close of the war he had charge of the office at Shubuta, where he could be with the family. He remained there while the line was in the hands of the Federal government and some three months afterward, when he resigned. His name appears in the history of the military telegraph during the Civil war in the United States, by William R. Plum, LL. B. At the close of the war the Adams Express company established its lines in the South, and, through the influence of his friends, he was made agent at Shubuta while only seventeen years of age without bond, which position he held six years, when, owing to the ill health of his wife, he resigned. At the close of the war he took what was left after supporting his mother's family from his salary as telegraph operator and express agent and engaged in a small mercantile business, but in about a year his store was destroyed by fire with no insurance, entailing upon him an almost total loss. Later, in connection with his office as express agent, he kept books and clerked in a store. In 1870 he married Miss Drucilla, daughter of Rev. T. B. and A. C. Heslep, of Shubuta, and formed a copartnership with his father-in-law, under the firm name of Heslep & Patton. Two years later Mr. Heslep died and Mr. Patton continued the business in his own name, in which he has engaged successfully till the present time. Mrs. Patton was an artist of exquisite finish, a favorite pupil of the celebrated Miss Julia A. Spear, of Judson institute, Marion, Ala., where she graduated. She was also a devoted Christian, and died in March, 1872, leaving one child, Thomas H., who is now living at Shubuta. In 1873 Mr. Patton married Miss Kate Heslep, a sister of his first wife, who died in February, 1883, at Micanopy, Fla., where she had gone in the hope of regaining her health, leaving three children: Early N., Annie

L. and Willie J. She was a fine musician, having taken a special course in music at the Judson institute, after her literary graduation. She was an earnest devotee to all church work and zealous in dispensing deserved charity.

Mr. Patton was married the third time, December 26, 1883, to Mrs. Regina C. Joiner, formerly Miss Spann. She was educated at Columbus, Miss.; was the mother of three sons by her first marriage: Charles S., a merchant of Pheba, Miss.; Samuel W., of Shubuta, and Robert E., who died in 1889, at Shubuta. She is a very active worker in all church work, and a leader in all the missionary and aid societies connected with the church. Since the organization of the Woman's Christian Temperance Union in Mississippi, she has been president of the local union, and state superintendent of temperance literature. Mr. Patton has been successful as a business man, and now does a trade of about $60,000 annually, carrying a very large stock, and he is very popular with the planters around about. He owns an orange grove in Marion county, Fla., and several hundred acres of land in this county, besides a fine water-power sawmill, cottongin and gristmill. He is interested in all things that pertain to the advancement of the community, and has been a member of the city council of Shubuta since 1876, except during one term of two years, and then he was not a candidate. He has also served as treasurer of the corporation. About 1875 he joined a temperance organization, known as the Murphy's, and since that time he has been an active worker in the temperance cause. Whenever a petition was before the city council for license, he took an active part in circulating remonstrances, and if the license was granted, he saw to it that the law was complied with. In 1884 he was a leader in circulating a petition to the legislature that secured statutory prohibition for Clarke county, and since the passage of the local option law for the entire state he has canvassed the county twice in the interest of prohibition, and the county has gone for prohibition with overwhelming majorities at both local option elections. He has also assisted in this work in adjoining counties; has attended all the state prohibition conventions, both nonpartisan and third party; has been a member of the state prohibition executive committee ever since the organization, and secretary of the party prohibitionists; and he is one of the vice presidents of the National Temperance society and Publication House of New York city. In 1883 three saloon keepers waylaid and attempted to assassinate him for no other reason than that he had circulated a counter petition against one of them, and contested his petition before the city council when he failed to secure his license. He has long taken an interest in education, and has served for years as a trustee of the Shubuta Male and Female academy, and of the free school, and is now serving the county as school commissioner. He and his family are members of the Baptist church. Soon after he joined the church, in 1872, he was chosen assistant superintendent of the Sunday-school, and he was later made superintendent, which position he still holds. Some ten years ago he was ordained deacon, and is now clerk and treasurer of the church. He is nearly always chosen delegate to the Mississippi Baptist State convention, in their annual meetings, having served as one of the vice presidents of the convention. He has served several terms of three years each as trustee of Mississippi college at Clinton, Miss., and as trustee in several other institutions of learning. He is also a zealous Sunday-school worker, and is one of the vice presidents of the state Sunday-school convention and district organizer, and has been selected as delegate to the National Sunday-school convention. Mr. Patton has never offered himself for any office except alderman, although he has been solicited to represent the county in the legislature. He sometimes attends the county mass meetings and state democratic conventions. In state issues he votes the democratic ticket; but he always scratches every nominee he knows to be openly immoral, or who drinks intoxicating liquors, or treats others to obtain their votes, or any one who is not in favor of the suppression of the liquor traffic. For the last eight years he has voted the national prohibition ticket, and was one of ten who met in Jackson, Miss., to put out an electoral ticket for Fisk and Brooks for president and vice president of the United States on the prohibition party ticket. He has also been a leader in introducing the Woman's Christian Temperance Union into the state of Mississippi, and has been one of their "standbys" since its organization in the state, having attended all of its conventions except one. He was secretary of Wayne lodge No. 102, A. F. & A. M., when it surrendered its charter, and he is also a Royal Arch Mason. He is dictator of the Knights of Honor at Shubuta, and has held the office of state treasurer of the I. O. G. T., and has been a delegate to the grand lodge of that order. Mr. Patton is a graduate of Clarke's school of embalming, and is a funeral director and embalmer in Shubuta, and is serving his second term as president of the Mississippi Funeral Directors' association. Mr. Patton has one of the nicest homes in east Mississippi, and is very happy in the society of his family. His store building is one of the neatest and best arranged on the line of the Mobile & Ohio railroad, and it was built after his own design. He has owned two turpentine distilleries, but at the writing of this sketch is not engaged in this enterprise.

Hon. Robert C. Patty was born in Winston county, Miss., July 9, 1846, and died December 31, 1890. He was the second son in a family of eleven children, born to John W. and Adaline (Hickman) Patty, who settled in Winston county early in the forties. Joshua Hickman, the maternal grandfather, was a son of William and Lettice (Cole) Hickman, the first mentioned of whom was born in 1732, the latter in 1740. He married Susannah, daughter of William and Mary (Goff) Ellis, all of whom were from Virginia. The Patty family was of English origin. John W. Patty was a merchant at Louisville, Winston county. While there Robert C. Patty obtained the rudiments of an education. He was a studious youth, with the faculty of rapid acquisition of knowledge, and with a memory so retentive that he was said to have never forgotten anything he read. He entered on his business career at Durant, Miss., and removed from there to Grand Junction, Tenn., where he filled for a brief time a position in the employ of a railway company, which he left to undertake the duties of a similar position at Jackson. At the beginning of the war he enlisted in Colonel Muldrow's regiment of Mississippi troops, and was made orderly sergeant of his company. In one of the battles in Georgia he received a slight wound. In 1868 he engaged in merchandising at Macon, Miss., but closing out his interests there, he soon went to New Orleans, where he was employed for one year in a railway office. November 18, 1869, he married Miss Ella, daughter of Dr. W. G. and Anna (Brotherton) Campbell, of Memphis, Tenn. Returning to Macon he was soon elected chancery clerk, an office which he held with credit for sixteen years. He was a member of the last constitutional convention of Mississippi, and was made chairman of the most important committee in that body, that on elections and franchise, and it was the arduous work of this position that precipitated his death. He was generous to a fault, giving freely of his means to all worthy objects and all helpful public enterprises. The Presbyterian church building in Macon, an elegant structure, was built almost entirely at his expense. He was a ruling elder in the church, and superintendent of its Sunday-school. Not long before his death he erected an elegant residence, one of the finest in the state. After his death the *New Mississippian* contained the following eulogium: "The honored chairman of the state democratic executive committee, the beloved president of the Mississippi Farmers' Alliance, the late worthy grand master of the Masons, the late president of the Sunday-school convention, the efficient chancery clerk of Noxubee county, the vigilant state commissioner, the gallant Knight of Pythias, the loyal citizen and model, exemplary gentleman is dead, and Mississippi mourns. Although life's sun with him had not reached its zenith, and its shadows were still falling to the west, he had been generously crowned with public honors, and had obtained a position in popular confidence and esteem of enviable character, almost impossible of replacement. Of almost every organization that sought the material advancement of the state, the purification of public service, the elevation of individual morals, or the judicious distribution of charity, he was a member, and membership with him was not a mere nominal connection, but in every instance it meant the assumption and discharge of the major part of the work. To business sagacity and quick perception he added untiring industry; to industry a peculiarly analytical mind and rare executive ability; while humility, patience, decision of character and affability of manner were blended in him in specially happy proportions. With no chart save that of justice, with no compass save that of charity, life's course with him was always toward the harbor of duty. If honorable preferment and high official trust and station were his, they came, not as the result of self-seeking, but in recognition of his wondrous capabilities, and as the reward of virtuous merit. That his death was precipitated by his three weeks' incessant labors as chairman of the franchise committee of the constitutional convention there can be no question. Peace hath its sacrifices as well as its victories, no less renowned than war. As his life had been spent in the public service for the advancement of the public good, so was it closed in death upon the bier of public duty. His nature was sweet as summer to his fellow-men, and in his death a personal loss has been sustained by every citizen of Mississippi. Over the new-made grave of Macon the flowers, planted by tender hands, will bloom in perpetual fragrance, fit emblems of the bowers of beauty that will blow for his bliss as the Master welcomes to the sunlit shores of Paradise the brave, bright soul of Robert C. Patty." As a husband and father, he was kind and indulgent; as a neighbor, courteous and obliging; as a friend, constant and true; as a citizen, upright and patriotic; as a public officer, scrupulously honest and conscientious, and as a Christian gentleman, his daily walk and conversation were such as to commend him to good men and women everywhere as worthy of their confidence and esteem.

Among the younger members of the Mississippi bar who are admirably adapted to honorably prosecute this most exalted of professions is Alexander G. Paxton, attorney at law of Indianola, Miss., who may truly be said to be one of nature's noblemen, for he possesses that ease and grace of manner which can only be acquired by those of broad intellect who are sufficiently learned and sufficiently familiar with the world's ways to discern man's own littleness, and to recognize that all are equal before man's as before God's tribunal. He was born in Washington county, Miss., January 16, 1858, and was given a thorough and practical education in the Washington and Lee university of Virginia. After finishing the literary course he entered the law department, from which he graduated in 1880, soon after which he returned to his home in Arcola, where he opened an office and began practicing, also following the occupation of a planter. He has made a study and a specialty of land litigation from the first, and has given the principal part of his time and attention to this department of his practice, and has carried some very important and extensive cases to a successful termination. He is at the head of this practice in this part of the state and ranks second to none in his knowledge and management of delta tax titles. He has also been quite an extensive dealer in land and is now the owner of about eight hundred acres in Sunflower county, besides a good plantation in Washington county. He is an admirable type of the cultured and keen Southerner, and his logical and financial ability, his high sense of propriety and justice and his profound knowledge of the law have made his name a familiar one in legal circles throughout the state. He has been a resident of Indianola since 1888, soon after which the present law partnership of Chapman & Paxton was formed. This firm has a complete set of abstracts, and the extensive practice which they now command is but a natural result of their individual and confederate action. They have a large clientage, their judgment is regarded as conscientious and safe, and in speech they are logical, concise and to the point. Mr. Paxton was married in Warren county, Miss., on the 12th of December, 1882, Miss Mary H. Noland, a daughter of H. P. Noland, becoming his wife. She was born, reared and educated in Warren county and died in the month of February, 1890. She was a lady of very superior mental endowments, and in the domestic circle was a model wife and mother, being passionately devoted to her family, whose happiness and comfort was her chief aim and object in life. Her death was deeply lamented, not only by her immediate and sorrowing family, but by all who knew and loved her in life. She left three bright little daughters: Annie Aldridge, Jennie Ruth and Mary Noland. The Paxtons were among the first families of Virginia and in the Old Dominion A. J. Paxton, the father of the subject of this sketch, was born. He obtained a very superior education at Washington college, and in his native state fitted himself for the practice of law. In 1837, when a young man, he came to Mississippi and for several years practiced his profession at Vicksburg, after which he removed to Jackson, continuing his practice there. In 1854 he located on a plantation in Washington county, and for several years past has been retired from the active practice of his profession. He is quite a distinguished character of Washington county, and has always taken an active interest in all questions pertaining to political affairs or to the advancement and building up of his state and county, being a member of the last constitutional convention. He was married at Jackson, Miss., to Miss Hannah M. Beazley, a native of that city.

Col. A. J. Paxton has long been a resident of this section of the state, but was born in Rockbridge county, Va., on the 18th of March, 1816, being the third of seven children born to Elisha and Margaret (McNutt) Paxton, both of whom were Virginians, the former being a farmer by occupation and a son of William Paxton, a native of Pennsylvania, but a farmer and resident of Virginia. The Paxtons are of Scotch-Irish descent. The wife of Elisha Paxton was a daughter of Alexander McNutt, a native of England, and once governor of Nova Scotia, who reared a large family of children. Col. A. J. Paxton was reared in his native state and received his education in what is now known as Washington and Lee university, and in the Virginia university, where he studied law. He began the practice of that profession in Jackson, Miss., in 1838, but in 1850 came to Arcola, cutting his own road as he came, and engaged in planting, being now the owner of two thousand acres of as fine land as there is in this section of the country. Of this valuable plantation he has one thousand four hundred acres under cultivation, on which, in 1888, he erected a handsome and commodious residence. He was married in 1847 to Miss Hannah M. Beazley, a native of Tennessee and a daughter of Samuel P. and Susanna (Smith) Beazley, both of whom were Virginians. To Mr. and Mrs. Paxton, the following children have been born: Lucy, who is the wife of Frank Aldridge, a merchant and planter, resides with her parents; Andrew J., is married to Lena Wilmot, and is engaged in planting near his father; Alexander G., was married to a Miss Noland (now deceased) and is practicing law at Indianola; Hannah M., is the wife of A. J. Aldridge and lives at Arcola; Cornelia, is the wife of Porter C. Chapman, a lawyer of Indianola; Elisha and Samuel, who are at school at Sewanee, Tenn. Mr. Paxton enlisted in the Confederate army in the year 1864, being in the quartermaster's department at Lynchburg, Va. He was a member of the constitutional convention held in Jackson in 1890, and in his political views has always been a democrat. He is one of the oldest settlers in the delta, and has since taken an active interest in county affairs although he is not a politician. Being a nephew of ex-Governor McNutt, he was very intimate with him, resided in his family, and was his law partner for many years. In his younger days he had every opportunity of indulging his love of hunting, and being an excellent shot, many a bear has fallen a victim to his skill with the rifle. Although he is now seventy-five years of age he carries himself perfectly erect, and wears his hair and beard, which are almost white, quite long. He is neat and precise in his dress, is courteous and kindly in his manners, and is a very intelligent and entertaining conversationalist. He has long been a member of the Methodist Episcopal church, and for his many worthy traits of character is honored and respected by all.

W. G. Paxton, a member of the firm of A. M. Paxton & Co., is a foundry machinist and manufacturing agent at Vicksburg, in which city he was born in 1838, being the eldest of eight children born to Alexander M. and Mary (Ellis) Paxton, both of whom were members of old Virginia families, the paternal ancestors having been residents of that state for many generations. Alexander M. Paxton was educated in the University of Virginia, after which he studied law and came to Vicksburg, Miss., to practice his profession, this being about the year 1830. In 1853 he purchased an established foundry and machine shop and conducted it with success until his death in 1886. He was a promoter of humane and benevolent institutions of the city, was active in educational matters, and was president of the city board of trustees of the public schools of Vicksburg, and was a member of the board of trustees of the Agricultural and Mechanical college at Starkville, Miss. He was of distinguished and dignified appearance, was over six feet tall, and weighed about two hundred and forty pounds. He was an active member of the Masonic fraternity. W. G. Paxton was educated in the Military institute at Lexington, Va., from which he graduated in 1860. In March, 1861, he became a member of a regiment of state troops that went to Florida, but in November of the same year he was transferred to Wirt Adams' regiment of cavalry at Bowling Green, Ky., and was appointed adjutant. He was in the battle of Shiloh, and was there placed in command of one hundred men, was assigned to Morgan's regiment, and started for Kentucky. He was captured at Lebanon, Tenn., and was confined in Nashville, Camp Chase, and on Johnson's island, being exchanged at Vicksburg, September 1, 1862. He afterward served as captain of an artillery brigade, provost-marshal, major of Miller's regiment of cavalry, and took part in the Georgia campaign, terminating in the fall of Atlanta, and was paroled at Jackson early in July, 1865. He at once embarked in business with his father, and has since devoted his attention to the foundry business. He was made secretary of the Vicksburg Hotel company at its organization and has otherwise interested himself in the business affairs of the city. He is a member of Vicksburg lodge No. 26 of the A. F. & A. M., and in this organization has been a member of Royal Arch chapter No. 3, and Magnolia commandery No. 2. He has presided over these branches, and in 1878 was grand commander of the Knights Templar and grand master of Masons in 1889. He is president of the Howard Associate society of the Red Cross. In 1867 he was married to Miss Lucy Gibbs, a native of Grenada, Miss., daughter of E. F. Gibbs, a merchant of Vicksburg, who died in 1855. To Mr. Paxton's union eight children were born, seven of whom are living: Janie, widow of W. M. Klein; Mary Lou; Alexander, who died in infancy; Lucy, W. G., Jr., Henry C., Edward G. and Shelby. The family are members of the Methodist Episcopal church, and in this church Mr. Paxton has been superintendent and teacher in the Sunday-school. He is a member of the board of managers of the Young Men's Christian association. Charles B. Paxton, brother and partner of W. G. Paxton, was born in 1846, and was educated in the University of Virginia. Upon arriving at suitable years he engaged in business with his father, but since the latter's death has been associated with his brother. He is a wideawake and enterprising young business man and is doing well financially. He is a member of the following secret and social societies: The K. of H., the K. of P., the A. L. of H., the A. O. U. W., the Order of Elks, Vicksburg lodge No. 95, and the Nogales Social club.

George H. Payne, one of the most prominent citizens and most successful planters in Tallahatchie county, was born in this county in 1857, a son of Dr. George W. and Florida (Simmons) Payne. His father was born in Virginia, his mother in Georgia. Dr. Payne was reared in his native state, and came with three brothers to Mississippi, afterward reading medicine and graduating from the Medical college at Louisville, Ky. He married in Tallahatchie county, and passed the remainder of his life there, ranking among the leading physicians and planters. He practiced his profession with marked success until his death in 1878. He fell a victim to yellow fever, and fifteen of his relatives, including two of his brothers, died also. These brothers were Joseph H. Payne, M. D., a prominent physician of Garner station, and William, a planter. His other brother, who came to Mississippi, died before the war. Dr. Payne was energetic, industrious, and in all the relations of life strictly honorable. He was a successful business man, and acquired a good home and considerable property. He was identified with the Masonic fraternity, having long been a member of the George Washington lodge No. 157, A. F. & A. M. His widow still resides on the old homestead. Before her marriage to Dr. Payne she had been married to Dr. Foster H. Thompson, who died in Tallahatchie county. Her father, Stern Simmons, was a native of Georgia who came at an early date to Mississippi, where he died before the war. He was twice married, his first wife, Mrs. Payne's mother, having died in Georgia. George H. Payne is the third of four children—two sons and two daughters. Of these, Robert died while young; Virginia is the wife of Henry C. Montgomery, of Le Flore county; our subject is the next in order of birth; Florida S. is the wife of Dr. J. R. Crow, of Charleston. Mrs. Payne had four children by her first husband, Dr. Thompson: Joseph, a planter of Tallahatchie county; John and Graham, both deceased, and Nannie, wife of Bolivar Bowen. Mr. Payne received his education at Charleston and at Garner station, and was reared to the life of a practical farmer on the farm where he was born and has always lived and will probably live the balance of his life. This old homestead consists of five hundred and sixty acres of land, about two hundred acres of it being cleared. It is considered one of the best improved farms in the county, and has good buildings and fences and other evidences of prosperity. In 1885 Mr. Payne married Willie Blanche Herron, whose father came from Tennessee and was for some years a merchant at Charleston, where he died. His widow married R. Denman, and died in 1887. Mrs. Payne was born in Charleston, and was educated at Oxford Female college. She has borne her husband two sons and one daughter. Mr. Payne is a member of George Washington lodge No. 157, A. F. & A. M., at Charleston. He is also a member of A. Macon Leigh lodge, Knights of Honor, No. 3233, of the same place. Mr. Payne is a man who stands high in every way among his fellow-men. He is a progressive, wideawake farmer and a practical one as well. He is looked upon with confidence and trust, and is an earnest, useful citizen.

The commercial circle of Hernando, De Soto county, Miss., has no more conspicuous figure than Jordan A. Payne, whose career will be briefly outlined in the following space. He is the fifth of a family of nine children, and was born September 1, 1842, to Jordan and Nettie (Joyner) Payne. His father removed from Tennessee to De Soto county in 1833 and engaged in planting. He was reasonably successful in his occupation, and was recognized as a man of sterling worth by all who knew him. He was a son of William and Sarah (Burrus) Payne, natives of North Carolina. The mother of our subject was a daughter of Isaac and C. (Davis) Joyner, of North Carolina. They were all agricultural people and free from political ambitions. Jordan A. passed his boyhood and youth in De Soto county, attending the private schools of the neighborhood. When the late war came he was not slow to take up arms in defense of his country. He enlisted in 1861 in company K, Ninth Mississippi regiment, and served until he was honorably discharged. He then went to Virginia and attached himself to company C, Forty-second Mississippi, remaining with this regiment until the battle of Gettysburg, when he was taken prisoner; he was sent to Fort Delaware and held there as a prisoner of war until June 18, 1865. After his release he returned to his home and went to work with a will to replace what the ravages of war had swept from the country. He now owns upward of two thousand acres of land, which he is cultivating in cotton, corn and grasses. He owns a half interest in the business of Payne & Bell, which firm is one of the most reliable in the state, doing a business of $60,000 to $80,000 annually, and carrying a stock of $7,000 to $10,000; the house of business is owned by the firm and is one of the best built in the place. Mr. Payne was united in marriage in 1873 to Miss Mary Banks, of De Soto county, a daughter of Lemuel and Louisa (Tate) Banks, natives of Georgia. She died in 1874, leaving no children. Mr. Payne was married a second time in 1880 to Miss Sallie Bowdre, a Mississippian, and a daughter of Maj. A. R. and Lucy (Meriwether) Bowdre, of Georgia. Five children are the result of this marriage: Albert Bowdre, Lelia, Ava P., Clifford and Henry Grady. Mr. and Mrs. Payne are members of the Baptist church and he is a Knight of Honor. He is a man of unquestioned probity of character and enjoys the esteem of all who know him.

L. C. Payne, a successful planter of Lee county, was born in Tennessee in 1839, and is a son of James and Elizabeth Payne, natives of Kentucky. James Payne was the son of Lawrence and Mary Payne. The subject of this notice received a fair English education, and at the age of sixteen years started out in life on his own responsibility. He was married November 7, 1860, to Miss Martha J. Moore, a native of Alabama, born May 20, 1845, and a daughter of John A. and Jane K. Moore, natives of North Carolina. The father was born November 24, 1807, and the mother was born November 7, 1814. They were both worthy members of the Cumberland Presbyterian church. They reared a family of nine children, eight of whom lived to maturity: Thomas F., deceased; William J , deceased; Sarah E., deceased; Robert G., who married Sarah Brombley; Jane K., wife of John English; Abraham, deceased; Lelia, deceased; and Martha J., the wife of Mr. Payne. Mr. and Mrs. Payne have reared a family of eleven children, nine of whom still survive: Reuben F., married Belle Morgan; Willard J. married Emma Knowles; Amy E., wife of Samuel Scribner; Elizabeth J., wife of T. Monaghan; Ada A., wife of Nathaniel Coggins; Abraham A.; Jesse T.; Leo N.; Martha A.; John A., born January 4, 1865, died June 19, 1887; and Albert W., born June 29, 1877, and died October 7, 1881. Mr. Payne is the third in a family of five children. In 1861 he enlisted under Capt. John M. Simonton, and throughout the remainder of the war saw a great deal of active service. He was taken ill the first year of his enlistment, and came home, remaining six months; he reënlisted under Captain Ashcraft, in the Forty-first Mississippi regiment, and participated in some of the most noted engagements of 1862. He was sent back to Mississippi and transferred to the First Mississippi regiment, participating in the engagement at Port Hudson, where he was captured; he was paroled, returned to his home, and after six months went to Atlanta, and thence to

Tennessee, and after the surrender came back home again. He has since been devoted to planting, and owns a farm of six hundred acres, all of which is well improved and under good cultivation. Politically he affiliates with the democratic party. He is a member of the Methodist Episcopal church, and contributes liberally to its support.

J. H. Peace was born in Coahoma county, Miss., July 22, 1861, the only child born to Dr. James A. and Elvira T. (Badget) Peace, the former of whom was born in North Carolina. He came to Coahoma county, Miss., in 1842, and here began the practice of medicine, having graduated from the Louisville Medical college. He became eminent as a medical practitioner, and also became prominent in the political affairs of this section, and served with distinction in the Mississippi legislature for one term. He was well known and highly honored throughout the county, and although very successful in the practice of medicine he gave this up in 1880, and from that time until his death, in 1890, he devoted his whole time to his large planting interests. J. H. Peace was reared on the plantation on which he is now residing, and acquired his education in the University of Mississippi at Oxford. For eight years prior to his father's death he acted as manager for him on the home plantation, in which capacity he was successful and showed good business tactics. By inheritance he has become the owner of a very fine plantation of four thousand five hundred acres, and has twelve hundred acres under cultivation. He erected his handsome residence in 1889 at a cost of $2,500, and has in other ways improved and increased the value of his property. He is extremely enterprising, is much averse to continually keeping in one rut, but shows much forethought and prudence in his ventures, and has never yet had occasion to regret the adoption of new and improved methods in conducting his affairs. His home is the abode of peace and plenty, and has about it an air of refinement and taste which does not belie the character of the inmates. In 1890 he was married to Miss Rose B. Strickland, a native of Mississippi and a daughter of Jacob and Frances (Bobo) Strickland, the former a native of Mississippi, and the latter of South Carolina. Mrs. Peace is a member of the Methodist Episcopal church, and Mr. Peace is a Mason and a democrat. He is a cultivated and polished gentleman, and he and his wife move in the highest social circles.

Robert N. Pearce was born in Sumter county, Ga., in 1833, and is the elder of two children of Edmond and Amanda F. (Belcher) Pearce, who were also natives of Georgia. The parents emigrated to Yazoo county in 1841 and settled near Benton. The father died in 1844 and the mother lived until 1863. Both children lived to maturity. Mary E. married George H. Shell and bore him two children. She died in 1862. Mr. Pearce passed his youth in his native county, receiving but a limited education. This was due to the death of his father, as he was then thrown upon his own resources. He went to work on a farm and followed this vocation until he was twenty-two years of age. In February, 1862, he entered the Confederate service, enlisting in company I, Third Mississippi volunteer infantry, Colonel Dyer, of Benton, commanding. He was in the engagements at Peachtree creek, Jonesboro, Atlanta, Bentonville and smaller battles and skirmishes. He was promoted to the office of first lieutenant. and at the time of the surrender was at Greensboro, N. C. On July 20, 1864, at Peachtree creek, he was wounded, though not seriously, in the back of the neck. After the battle of Franklin, Tenn., he was the only commissioned officer present belonging to his company, and the command naturally devolved upon him. He later commanded two other companies, whose officers were killed, until the surrender. Mr. Pearce was married in 1857 to Miss Frances E. White, a daughter of Nathan and Rebecca (Hannon) White. The following year he settled on the plantation where he now lives. It then consisted of seven hundred and twenty acres, but he has made additions to the original until it now covers not less than one thousand eight hundred acres. He has improved the place with fencing, good substantial buildings and a comfortable, convenient residence. His principal crops are cotton and corn, and he has made the beginning of great improvements in the breed of his livestock. He now has some of the finest Jersey and Holstein cattle, with which the place in time will be fully stocked. The politics of the county have always been of interest to Mr. Pearce, and for four years he has been a member of the board of supervisors. He belongs to the P. B. Tutt lodge No. ——, A. F. & A. M., of which he he has been junior warden. He is also a member of the Knights of Honor, and is the lecturer of the Farmers' Alliance. Mr. and Mrs. Pearce are worthy members of the Rocky Springs Missionary Baptist church. They are the parents of six children: Cora R., deceased; Mamie, wife of S. W. Johnson; Josie S., wife of W. F. Heard, of Sunflower county; Edmond B.; Robert N.; and Mercy E., a student at Clinton, Miss. Mr. Pearce has ever been keenly alive to the needs of the community in which he lives, and has been generous in giving of his means to aid in its growth and development. He is a man of great popularity, and is the present candidate for sheriff of Yazoo county.

> "They shunned not labor when 'twas due,
> They wrought with right good will;
> And for the homes they won for them,
> Their children bless them still."

The first of the Pearcefield family to locate in the state of Mississippi was James B. Pearcefield, the father of the subject of this sketch, who left his native state to locate here when a young man, he being one of the earliest pioneers of Jefferson county. He was born on blue grass soil, as was his father before him, his family being among the very first of the pioneer settlers of Kentucky. After his removal to Mississippi, J. B. Pearcefield was married here to Miss Isabella Montgomery, daughter of John B. Montgomery, who was one of the first settlers of this region from the Palmetto state. After the celebration of his nuptials Mr. Pearcefield settled on a plantation, and in following this calling his efforts were attended with good results and he became well to do. After having passed a useful life he died in 1854, his wife surviving him several years, dying in 1878. The father of the latter located on the farm on which his grandson, P. M. Pearcefield, is now living, but at that early day the land was in a very primitive condition, heavily covered with timber and canebrake, which furnished homes for innumerable wild animals, many of which fell victims to Mr. Montgomery's trusty rifle. On this plantation he reared his family and resided until his death. P. M. Pearcefield and a sister, Mrs. James Lowe, of Harriston, Miss., are the only children born to their parents. The former was born in the county in which he is at present residing, on September 22, 1844, and obtained his education in a private school in this county. Upon the opening of the late war in 1861 he joined the Jefferson artillery, in Capt. Put Darden's battery, and served with him until the close of the war, being gunner of his battery. He was blown up by the explosion of an ammunition chest in one engagement, but aside from being quite badly burned he was uninjured. At the close of the war he was paroled with his company at Meridian, Miss., and returned to his home to take up the occupation of farming once more, the details of which calling he had learned of his father, and this has since received his attention. He has been fortunate in his enterprises, and is now the owner of his grandfather Montgomery's old homestead, which is a good, and under Mr. Pearcefield's watchful care, an admirably cultivated one. He was married in Franklin county, Miss., May 29, 1867, to Mrs. Amelia J. Herring, daughter of J. Monroe Brown, a native of Franklin county, but now a resident of McNair. Mrs. Pearcefield was born in Jefferson county, but was educated at Port Gibson, Claiborne county, Miss., leaving school an intelligent and accomplished young lady.

AGRICULTURAL COLLEGE BUILDINGS, STARKVILLE.

She was first married in Franklin county to Mr. Herring, who died while in prison at Camp Morton, Ind., while serving in the Confederate army. To her first marriage three children were born: D. M. Herring, who is a railroad agent and resides at McNair; Jennie, wife of S. L. Davis, a railroad contractor of Seneca, Kas., and Ida, an accomplished young lady. Mr. Pearcefield carries on all his operations according to the most advanced and progressive ideas, and he has long since gained the reputation of being among the very foremost agriculturists of this portion of the county. He early became acquainted with the duties of farm labor, and this fact, in connection with the industry, perseverance and energy which he has ever manifested, has done much toward bringing about his present good fortune. He owns about twelve hundred acres of excellent land, about three hundred acres of which are open and devoted to the raising of the usual Southern products. He has been interested in local politics, and has served as a delegate to a number of county and congressional conventions. He is a Master Mason, and he and his accomplished and amiable wife, who is a member of the Methodist Episcopal church, have many warm friends and are favorites with all who know them.

A. V. Pearcifield, planter, Benoit, Miss., is a native Kentuckian, born in 1822, and his parents, Henry and Lovey (Pearce) Pearcifield, were natives also of the Blue Grass state. The paternal grandfather was a native of the famous Emerald isle. He left his native land to come to the United States and settled in the Old Dominion at an early date. The maternal grandfather, Robert Pearce, was a native of Virginia, but at an early date emigrated to Kentucky, where he followed planting until his death in 1832. A. V. Pearcifield was reared and educated in his native state, but in 1839 came to Mississippi, settling first in Jefferson, then Adams, and finally in 1856 in Bolivar county, on Egypt ridge. In 1866 he settled on his present place, on Egypt ridge, four miles from Benoit, and is now the owner of one thousand two hundred and forty acres in different tracts, with seven hundred acres under cultivation. In 1854 he was married to Miss Narcissa Noble, of Natchez, and the fruits of this union were two children: Margaret (deceased) and Emma. Mrs. Pearcifield died in 1860. After settling upon his present property Mr. Pearcifield entered actively upon the work of clearing and improving, and his career since that time has been marked by industry and strict attention to his calling. His plantation is beautifully improved, and everything about the place shows the energy and good management for which he has ever been noted. In the management of this fine plantation he does not lose sight of the stock industry and raises some fine animals, being the owner at the present time of a fine stallion. Mr. Pearcifield is above the average hight, rather inclined to be portly, marked features and hair turning toward the silver tint. He is strong, hearty and robust. During the war he was placed in charge of the wagons at the salt mines (or works) in Alabama by the Confederate government.

William L. Pearman. Bolivar county, Miss., has become well known for its prosperous planters, and this reputation has been acquired by the energy and enterprise of such planters as William L. Pearman, whose labors to acquire a competency have been earnest, persistent and continuous. He was born in the Palmetto state, March 1, 1845, being the fourth in a family of nine children born to Benjamin and Drucilla (McGregor) Pearman, their entire lives being spent in South Carolina, where Mr. Pearman was engaged in planting and died on his old homestead in 1880, having reached a ripe old age. His father was Weldon C. Pearman and his mother's maiden name was Shirley, the ancestors of both having come from England and settled near Petersburg, Va., in the welfare of which section they interested themselves, becoming substantial and honored residents of the Old Dominion. The maternal grandfather was William McGregor and the maternal grandmother's name was Dean, natives of Scotland

and Wales, respectively. In the town of Anderson, S. C., William L. Pearman was reared, his education being received in a private school, and although his advantages were not of the best, he made fair progress in his studies, and up to the age of sixteen years, when the war opened, he was as far advanced as any youth of his age. Although but a boy, he immediately enlisted in the Confederate army, becoming a member of company E, Twentieth South Carolina regiment, under L. M. Keith, and until the war closed was one of the tried and true soldiers of the Confederacy. He was in the siege of Charleston, Cold Harbor, besides nearly all the engagements in Virginia, and although severely wounded in the head at Berryville, his good constitution and determination stood him in good stead and it was not long before he was again ready for duty. At the time of Lee's surrender he was at Charlotte, N. C., soon after which he returned to his home and in 1866 came to Mississippi, and became overseer for Dr. Mart Ellis, in Tippah county, but continued with him for only one year. At the end of that time he made a short visit to his old home in South Carolina, but soon returned to Mississippi and took an interest in a drug store, at Baldwin, but this venture not proving a success, he went to Texas, after spending a short time in Bolivar county. Six months later he returned to Mississippi and was here married, in 1874, to Miss Viola Reeves, a native of this state and a daughter of Sylvester K. and Elizabeth (Bird) Reeves, native Mississippians, and by her he became the father of eight children: William M., Eveline (deceased), Margaret, Roberta, Minnie, Arthur C., Pearl and Reuben, the living ones still making their home under the parental roof. Mr. Pearman began life very poor in purse, but has succeeded in accumulating one thousand four hundred acres of land, and by his own efforts has cleared and improved six hundred acres. In 1885 he erected a neat and pretty residence at a cost of $2,500, and is the owner of about $5,000 worth of real estate in Cleveland. He is one of the oldest settlers of this part of Bolivar county, having come here when there were only three men within a radius of fifteen or twenty miles, his nearest postoffice (Concordia) being thirty miles distant. His land was heavily covered with timber and canebrake, but he now has a valuable and highly productive plantation, a state of affairs that has been brought about by his own efforts. He has never engaged in speculation to any extent, but has made what he now has by the sweat of his brow, and throughout his quiet, uneventful life has continued to pursue the even tenor of his way, and has never meddled with affairs that did not concern him. He and his wife and two children are active members of the Methodist Episcopal church, and socially he belongs to the Knights of Honor. Mr. Pearman is very highly esteemed by all who know him, and by his numerous friends was elected to the constitutional convention at Jackson, but was beaten out of his seat through fraud. He has a very comfortable and pleasant residence, and he and his wife have a very interesting and intelligent family of children.

"Lo! I declare I deem him blest
Whose foot, here pausing, findeth rest."

Charles A. Pearson (deceased) in times now past, had been closely identified with the welfare and material and social happiness of this region, and here the greater number of his days of usefulness were spent. Even in his youth he possessed an intellect of no ordinary ability, and the power and originality of his genius was felt by all with whom he came in contact in after years. His birth occurred in Fredericksburg, Va., in 1805, he being the only son of a family of ten children born to his parents, three members only of whom are living at the present time: Mary, Margaretta and Martha. He was a direct descendant of the old Quaker stock of William Penn, and possessed in an eminent degree the love of truth and simple tastes of his time-honored ancestor. He was educated in the schools of Fredericksburg and throughout his long and useful career he was a stanch friend of education and believed in the universal education of the masses. He was especially devoted to scientific researches, astronomy and mathematics being his special delight, and from the study of these branches he derived much profit and pleasure. He was very kind, affectionate and charitable in disposition, was filled with the milk of human kindness for all, but being chary of having his "right hand know what his left hand doeth," many of his charities remained unknown. He was at all times very public-spirited, for he loved his country better than life, and did everything in his power to advance her interests and promote her progress and development. The most of his business life was spent as a cotton merchant, the old and well-known firm of Pearson & Hume being established in Grand Gulf, Miss., the same year as his arrival here, and as a man of business he possessed far more than ordinary ability. The business of this large firm extended from the Pearl river in Lawrence County, Miss., to Liverpool, England, and in point of commercial credit and for business capacity it was known in every city of any importance in the Union. He began life at the bottom of the ladder, for previous to his removal to Port Gibson he was a salesman on a salary. After being in Mississippi for some time, he traveled throughout the Southwest, and by trade purchased some six thousand acres of land in Texas, a large portion of which is still in possession of his family. At the opening of the Civil war, Mr. Pearson had accumulated a comfortable fortune, but in his love for the South he became conspicuous as a devoted Confederate, and in 1862 his elegant home was laid in ashes and he was in numerous other ways plundered of his property. At the bombardment of Grand Gulf, he stood by the side of Col. Wade, aiding the Confederate commander by his knowledge of the topography of the country, until the latter fell dead at his feet. While on a trip to England he was present at the coronation of Queen Victoria. He was married March 26, 1846, to Miss Clara Warren, a native of Oswestry, Shropshire, England, her birth occurring in that town, which is one of the oldest in England, January, 11, 1826, the name of her home being Brynmorda. Mrs. Pearson received excellent advantages in her youth, a principal portion of her education being received in France, one of her teachers being Madame Collyer, who kept a French school for English girls. Mrs. Pearson's sisters were also educated there. Her union with Mr. Pearson resulted in the birth of eleven children—seven sons and four daughters—of whom there are nine living: George B., who is a successful pharmacist of Fredericksburg, Va.; Charles W., who is head bookkeeper, cashier and correspondent in the celebrated clothing house of Schwab & Co., of St. Louis, Mo.; William J. who is a cotton planter and a member of the board of supervisors at Grand Gulf, Miss.; Alfred M., a successful telegrapher of the state of Washington.; Isaac C. is a resident of Vicksburg, Miss., and is manager of the telephone exchange; Lawrence is a commercial traveler for Schwab & Co., in the state of Arkansas; Clara P. is the widow of Thomas M. Harwood, who was engaged in the municipal affairs of Claiborne county (Mrs. Harwood is an accomplished lady, having been a teacher of Grand Gulf previous to her marriage, and is very skillful with her needle, having been awarded first mention for point lace at the World's fair at New Orleans in 1885); Eleanor resides at home; Mary G. is the wife of Sprig Harwood, a relative of the Harwoods of Boston, and resides in Los Angeles, Cal.; Harriet died in infancy, and Henry, who was the sixth of the family, died of yellow fever at Grand Gulf at the age of twenty-one years, and would in all probability have been a machinist of note had his life been spared. Mr. Pearson was a man who always held a high place in the estimation of his fellow-citizens and lived, as he died, an earnest member of the Episcopal church. He had frequent premonitions that his death would be sudden, and was several times, within a few years, prostrated with heart disease, which at last caused his death Sunday, January, 11, 1878, the funeral services being conducted by Rev. Mr. Cary, who read the services of the Episcopal church at the grave. The pallbearers were: Messrs. William Brown, Sr., J. L. Foote, John Burnet, J. L. Kennard, Joseph A. Gage, Charles Shreve, W. T. Morris, J. S. Mason, of Port Gibson, and Charles Johnson, Sr., A. A. Nichols, Henry Simonson and J. P. Taylor, of Grand Gulf. So ended the life of one of Mississippi's most illustrious sons. He was a great lover of horses all his life, and at the time of his death he left valuable real estate in Mississippi, Louisiana and Texas amounting to about four thousand acres.

Dr. William E. Pearson, a well-known practitioner of Scooba, Kemper county, Miss., resides three and a half miles east of Scooba. He was born in Greene county, Ala., in 1836, and is a son of John and Margaret (Forbes) Pearson. His father was born in South Carolina about the year 1785; he was descended from one of two brothers who came to America, and were brigadier-generals in the War of the Revolution. The parents were married in North Carolina and removed to Alabama, where the father died shortly after the birth of our subject in 1836; he was a large planter and owned a large estate. The mother was born in North Carolina in 1816 and died in 1856; she was a member of the Christian church and the father belonged to the Baptist church. William E. was their only child. He spent his early life in Alabama in Greene and Sumter counties. He received his literary education near Nashville, Tenn., at Franklin college, his medical education at Charleston, S. C., and New Orleans, and began the practice of medicine in 1859, having located at Gainesville, Ala. In 1860 he removed to his present home, where he has since resided. In 1862 he enlisted in the Confederate army and was attached to the First Tennessee Regiment as assistant surgeon. He never missed a march or battle from the time of his enlistment until the surrender. He was at Gettysburg and in the seven days' fight around Richmond. He was taken prisoner and afterward paroled. In 1861 the Doctor was united in marriage to Miss C. F. Harwood, of Gainesville, Ala., a daughter of Samuel and Elizabeth (Ellison) Harwood, natives of Virginia. Mrs. Pearson was born in Virginia in 1835. Four children were born of this union: John F. and William E., Jr., are at home; William and Edward died in childhood. Dr. Pearson is identified with the democratic party. He is a member of the Masonic order, belonging both to the Blue lodge and chapter. He is a member of the Knights of Honor, lodge No. 2534. He has given some attention to farming, in addition to his professional duties. He owns sixteen hundred acres of land, which have been improved under his direction. He has been very successful in his medical practice and has a large patronage. He is a man of kind and generous impulses, and is ready always to aid the needy and to be of service to the general public in any way that is presented. He is a member of the Presbyterian church, while his wife belongs to the Methodist Episcopal church.

Dr. John B. Pease, the oldest practicing physician of Bolivar county, and a popular druggist at Gunnison, is the son of John B. and Elizabeth (Dibrell) Pease, his birth occurring in Nashville, Tenn., while his parents were there on a visit. The father was born in Utica, N. Y., and there grew to manhood, and received an excellent education. He came to Mississippi about 1834 or 1835, located in Yazoo county, and secured a large tract of land upon which Yazoo City is now built. In 1837 or 1838 he married Miss Dibrell, a native of Tennessee, and afterward made his home on his estate in Yazoo City. He not only became a very extensive planter, but was also a successful merchant at Manchester, now Yazoo City. Although active in politics and very pronounced in his views in regard to competent officials, he was no officeseeker himself. The Pease family trace their origin to Otho I, emperor of Germany 961-983. This emperor knighted an officer of his army named Pease and granted him a coat of arms with the motto: "Sic itur ad astra, optime de patra meruit." In 1637 Robert Pease came to America, settled near Enfield, Conn., and entered the site of Martha's Vineyard from the crown of England. His descendants may be found in every state and territory in the Union, also the provinces of Canada, and every political office from governor down has been filled by some one bearing the family name. This name is also to be found upon the army rolls of every state, in the Civil war, both North and South, and frequent instances occurred where officers of that name opposed each other in battle. On the mother's side the Dibrells descended from French Huguenots. Grandfather Edwin Dibrell, was in the treasury department under President Polk, and was a prominent citizen of Nashville, Tenn. The mother's cousin, Gen. George Dibrell, was a member of congress from Tennessee for many years, and was a brigadier-general in the Civil war. He was covering the retreat of President Davis when the latter was captured. Dr. John B. Pease, to whom has descended the family name, was reared in Yazoo county, Miss., and was left fatherless when but two years of age. He received his literary and medical education in the University of Virginia, and in 1860 entered the medical department of the University of Louisiana, from which he graduated the following year. He then began practicing at Yazoo City, remained there until 1862, when he enlisted in the sixty days' troops as private. At the expiration of that time he was appointed assistant surgeon in the reserve corps, and in reorganizing the medical staff of the corps under General Forrest he was made surgeon, filling that position until the close of hostilities. In 1865 he came to Bolivar county, located at Holmes lake, and there engaged in planting until 1869, when he moved to Concordia, where he practiced his profession. There he resided until 1891, and in connection with his practice was also engaged in planting. In 1890 he erected a drug store at Gunnison, and in the following year erected a residence into which he moved soon after. Dr. Pease was married in 1862 to Miss Emma C. Evens, a native of Claiborne county, Miss., and daughter of James Evens. Six children have been the fruits of this union, one of whom is deceased: Loudie D., married Dr. Jones and died in 1891; John B., Jr.; George Evens, Herbert W., Minrette and Standifer W. The family hold membership in the Methodist Episcopal church. Mr. Pease is a member of the Masonic fraternity, and is a master of Concordia lodge No. 347; is past grand dictator of the state in the Knights of Honor, and is past chancellor of the Knights of Pythias. He was the organizer of the Knights of Pythias lodge No. 67, of Gunnison. He was quite active in politics formerly. Mr. Pease has a store well stocked with fancy goods and toilet articles as well as a full line of drugs, and by his pleasant social manner and gentlemanly conduct has already built up a good trade. His eldest son, who graduated from the Medical college at Little Rock, is associated with his father in practice.

A. C. Peatross, of the firm of Peatross, Cameron & Co., extensive coal merchants, of Vicksburg, Miss., was born in Virginia in 1861, the eighth in a family of ten children born to Samuel D. and Angelina (Seay) Peatross, the parents being also Virginians, the father a successful planter by occupation. He died in 1866. A. C. Peatross was educated in Virginia, and followed clerking and working on a farm in his native state until 1870, when he came to Mississippi, and for some time clerked in the city of Jackson. He became a resident of Vicksburg in 1878, and after clerking in various establishments until 1889, he became a member of the present firm, which is a very prosperous one, and of which he is one of the active and enterprising members. He was married to Mrs. (Mattingly) Teay, a daughter of A. D. Mattingly, and to their union a family of six children have been born: Charles E., Lee, Mary Ann, Kate G., Edith and Regina. By her former husband Mrs. Peatross became the mother of two children: Austin and Joe. She is a member of the Catholic church, and is a worthy and useful member of society. Socially, Mr. Peatross is a member of the A. L. of H. and the K. of P. fraternities.

G. F. Peek, M. D., of Rose Hill, Miss., was a native of Autauga county, Ala., and was born August 12, 1836. He is a son of George and Sarah E. (Saxon) Peek. The father was a native of Virginia, and the mother of South Carolina. They were married in Lawrence county, of the latter named state, and shortly afterward settled in Autauga county, Ala., removing thence to Coosa county, Ala., where they resided until their deaths. They were the parents of seven children, named: Nancy E., Charlotte E., Sophia E., George F., James S., Benjamin F. and William R. Dr. Peek was educated at the Central institute, of Coosa county, and in 1856 began reading medicine with Dr. Thomas Edwards, of that county. In the winter of 1857-8 he attended the Reform Medical college, of Macon, Ga., after which he returned home, and in 1859 came from there to Jasper county, Miss., locating about five miles southeast of Garlandville, where he began the practice of his profession. In the winter of 1859-60 he took his second term of lectures at the Reform Medical college at Macon, from which institute he was graduated in the spring of 1860. Returning to Jasper county, he resumed his medical practice there. In August, 1861, he enlisted in the Tolson's guards, of which he was elected first lieutenant, then at the organization of the regiment was elected major, and with that rank served with credit until the reorganization of the regiment in 1862, when he returned home, and organized a cavalry company, which was attached to the Fifty-sixth Alabama cavalry, and soon afterward transferred to the Twelfth Mississippi cavalry, in which organization he was captain until the close of the war. Taking up his residence again in Jasper county, he again hung out his shingle as a medical practitioner. He has been one of the most successful physicians of the county since that time, having built up a large and extensive practice and gained the confidence of the public to an unusual degree. February 28, 1866, he was married to Miss Saphronia A., the daughter of James and Mildred (Risher) McCormick, who has borne him eight children, as follows: Ocie R., William E., Edwin F., Luna Pearl, Luta R., Lura C., Saphronia A., and an infant, who died before being named. March 24, 1884, Mrs. Peek died, regretted by all who knew her, leaving a name among her neighbors as a consistent Christian woman, an affectionate wife and a model mother. Dr. Peek is a member of the Masonic order and of the Methodist Episcopal Church South. He is the owner of twenty-two hundred acres of land, of which three hundred acres are under cultivation. He is a successful and helpful citizen, well liked in the community, and influential in all his relations.

Dr. R. H. Peel, a prominent physician of north Mississippi, now practicing his profession at Holly Springs, is the second child and eldest son of Volney and Charlotte Royston Peel. Volney Peel, the father of Dr. R. H. Peel, was the eldest son of Hunter Peel, and was born in Bedford county, Va., whence the family moved to north Alabama, and there settled near Huntsville in the early history of that state. There he studied civil engineering and practical surveying, and was employed as draughtsman in the land office at Florence, Ala. During this time he married Charlotte Royston, the daughter of an old Virginia gentleman, a soldier under Washington during the Revolution. His parents dying, Volney Peel lived for a short time near Courtland, Lawrence county, Ala., where Robert H. Peel was born, September 30, 1832. Receiving an appointment from the government to survey the territory, embracing all north Mississippi, then occupied by the Chickasaw and Choctaw Indians, he left his young wife and child with her parents, who had moved to Hardeman county, Tenn., and at once hastened to the scene of his labors, which required two years of hardship, toil and exposure in an unexplored wilderness, inhabited only by Indians. Having completed his work to the entire satisfaction of the government, he bought a large tract of land in Marshall county, and hastily building some rude cabins, he moved his family to a pioneer home in 1834, the first white man to settle in the county. The Indians being removed by the government, a white population began to pour into the country with astonishing rapidity. Wealthy planters owning hundreds of slaves purchased the lands and opened large cotton plantations, and such was the great fertility of the virgin soil that agriculture flourished, and then began what has been called the flush times of Mississippi. Being two years of age at the time his father emigrated to Mississippi, Robert Peel grew to manhood on a cotton plantation, receiving his education principally from the common schools of the county. At the age of fifteen he entered St. Thomas Hall, of Holly Springs, with the eminent Dr. Hawks as principal, with the view of taking a thorough collegiate course of study. Among his classmates were our distinguished senator, Gen. Ed Walthall, Gen. J. R. Chalmers, Col. J. A. Autry and others who have distinguished themselves in the profession of law and in political and military life. His father dying the same year he entered college, he was called, at the age of fifteen years, to assume the grave responsibility of watching over an invalid mother and six young brothers, besides engineering a large farming interest, employing over one hundred slaves. As his mother's waning days showed the sands of life were almost run, she requested a solemnization of his marriage with Miss Virginia M. Matthews, which event was deferred on account of the critical condition of his mother's health. In October, 1852, he was united in marriage with Miss Virginia M. Matthews, third child and daughter of Dr. B. D. Matthews, who had moved to Marshall county, Miss., in 1835, a successful practitioner and speculator in the early history of the county. In his wife he found an able counselor; possessing great force of character and rare personal endowments, she presided a sacred priestess about the altar of home, dispensing the blessing of domestic love, assuming and faithfully performing the duties of mother to an orphaned household. Two daughters were the fruits of this marriage, both of whom died in infancy, and after three years of unalloyed happiness, his wife was called to join her angels in the skies. Placing his brothers at school, his two elder brothers, Albert and Addison, at the Military school of Kentucky, he turned his back upon his beautiful and palatial home and sought a balm for a wounded spirit in the study of medicine, spending several years in New Orleans, where he received a diploma from the School of Medicine, Louisiana. Returning to his home, then densely populated by wealth and influence, he devoted himself to the practice of his chosen profession and to his farming interest. The representative of a time-honored family and from his own individual worth, he soon ranked among the first practitioners of his age. At the breaking out of the late war he raised a company of his friends and neighbors and went to Richmond, Va., with the Nineteenth Mississippi regiment, commanded by Colonel Matt, killed at Williamsburg, and Lieut.-Col. L. Q. C. Lamar, the distinguished senator from the state and now one of the supreme judges of the United States. Arriving at Richmond, Dr. R. H. Peel was tendered the position of assistant surgeon of the Nineteenth Mississippi regiment, which he declined, but soon after accepted a position as surgeon of the Nineteenth regiment, and also a commission as surgeon of Gen. C. M. Wilcox's brigade, and at once began operating upon the wounded Federal soldiers at the old stone house on the first battlefield of Manassas. And here we would state that, with that philanthropy of which his life has been such a beautiful expression, he so won upon the hearts of a rough soldiery in his efforts to soothe and encourage them amid the painful operations of the knife, they exclaimed, "My God! why are we fighting such men?" After the state troops were brigaded, the Nineteenth Mississippi regiment was placed in a brigade commanded by General Posey, who was killed at Bristow station, and subsequently by Gen. W.

S. Featherstone, who was transferred to the department of Mississippi, after which it was commanded by Gen. Nat Harris, of Vicksburg, until the surrender. In February, 1865, Dr. Peel was transferred, by his own request, to the department of Mississippi. Returning home on a short furlough, to look after the interest of his younger brothers, he was married to Miss Alice Maud Matthews, a younger sister of his former wife, and repaired at once to his new field of duty at Lee hospital, near Lauderdale springs, in Mississippi, where he remained on duty until the surrender of the Southern army. Three of Dr. Peel's younger brothers followed his fortunes in the army of Virginia, two of whom were killed—Thomas in the seven days' fight around Richmond, and Albert, the adjutant of the Nineteenth Mississippi regiment, was killed at Spottsylvania Courthouse, falling within three feet of the oak tree, twenty-two inches in diameter, which was cut down with rifle balls at the "bloody angle," as it is called in history, where General Grant had massed seven lines of battle, to force his way through General Lee's lines at this place. The stump of this tree is now in the museum at Washington city. Another brother, Addison Peel, was captured at Spottsylvania, and remained in prison at Fort Delaware until the surrender. Volney Peel, the youngest brother, then a mere boy, was wounded while with General Forrest's command at Franklin, Tenn., but recovered soon. He was married to Miss Holt, of Virginia parentage, who died several years ago, leaving to her husband's care a daughter and three sons, who now reside sixteen miles south of Holly Springs, upon a fine farm with five hundred acres under cultivation. Andrew Peel, the third brother, removed to Texas in 1858, in quest of a more salubrious climate. He located a large stock farm and owned a large land estate at his death, which occurred some years ago, leaving a wife and five children to inherit his wealth. Returning home when our banner had been furled o'er dead hopes and wasted lives, the three brothers met upon the spot they once called home, now a deserted, desolate spot. Fire, as well as the sword, had done its work, and naught remained to tell of the beauty and grandeur of old Hickory park, save its walls, which were built of brick, the first in Marshall county, and which stood defiantly frowning at the midnight torch and marauding mob of an invading army. Near by, fanned by the evening zephyr, garlanded by trailing vines and lovely flowers, shaded by the willow's bending boughs, where the song-bird trilled a mournful requiem, slept the parents from whom they inherited a spirit which knew no defeat, and, gathering up the ashes whose fires had long burnt out, they went forth to battle with an untried future. The hand which had wielded the sword, handled the rifle and skillfully guided the amputating knife soon learned to hold the plow and guide the faithful mule, and with a fixed determination to rebuild their ruined fortunes. For years Dr. Peel has devoted his time to his profession and a large farming interest, and is now living in Holly Springs, with a large and lucrative practice, and at the age of fifty-eight is as active, vigorous and usefully employed as in years gone by, when the impulse of life's dawning manhood quickened into action the energy which has crowned the nobility of his life with its own green laurels. Residing in the northern part of our town, in a grand old residence surrounded by majestic oaks, and a beautiful lawn terraced by lovely flowers, where his wife and accomplished daughter and only child, Mary G. Peel, preside, dispensing the hospitality which not only entertains, but invites all to its welcome shades, a benefactor and friend, lives Dr. Peel, a noble Christian gentleman whom all delight to honor.

George H. Peets, M. D., one of Wilkinson county's worthy planters and a leading physician, is located near Buffalo river, fourteen miles northwest of Woodville. The Doctor is very well known and has a large circle of friends and an extensive practice, and by reason of his superior skill, long years of practice and excellent judgment receives and merits the confidence of the community. He is a native of Louisiana, and was born near Laurel Hill, on the West Feliciana railroad, and was the eldest of a family of three—one son and two daughters, the latter two dying in infancy and named Mary Eliza and Maria L. They were the children of Lee Peter and Cassandra (Davis) Peets, natives of Louisiana and Tennessee respectively. The mother was born near Greeneville, Tenn., and was brought to Louisiana when a child by her parents. Samuel Davis, her father, was born in Richmond, Va., and came down the river to Fort Adams, and later, going to Louisiana, settled near Tunica, where he reared a large family. He was a leading member of the Methodist Episcopal church, and built a church in the same vicinity that still stands as a monument to his religious character and his honored memory. He was very active in church work, and at his death had accumulated a handsome competency for himself and family, valued at about $70,000. He was very industrious, a hard worker and an honest man. He is said to have shortened his days by unceasing activity and unflagging hard work, but his name of high integrity is the common heritage of the county and state. The mother of George H. was his eldest child, and was reared in Louisiana, where she married. Her brother, Richard Davis, is living in Holmes county, Miss. Mrs. Peets died in 1844, at the age of thirty-six years, an earnest member of the Methodist Episcopal church, in which she was very active. Mr. Peets, the father, and his brother George W. were left orphans at a very early age. The father settled on the property where Baton Rouge is now located, and later, when deprived of his rights here, had in view the education of his younger brother George in the law for the purpose of fitting and posting themselves in securing their rights in that city. George read law in Minden, La., under Judge Murray, a famous lawyer of that district, and was admitted to the bar of Louisiana at the age of twenty-two years, and held the office of circuit judge for several years. He also served in the legislature, and was very popular in political circles. He died in the thirty-seventh year of his age, a single man. His whole object in life was to repay his brother for the pains taken in securing his education and in supporting him until his education was finished. He had attended Centenary college for several years, and was splendidly educated and possessed naturally the highest talents. He was of unusually good address, of a commanding appearance—six feet one inch in hight, weighed one hundred and eighty pounds, had dark hair, light brown eyes, and was a fluent and finished debater. The father in early life began planting on a very small scale, but by energy and economy gradually gathered together enough to comfortably sustain and educate his family. He was an honored citizen, greatly loved and respected by all. He died in 1854, at the age of forty years. George H. Peets was reared in the first location in which his parents settled, attended the public schools and later the Mississippi college, at Clinton, a Baptist school. He then attended Shelby college, Kentucky, and finally went to Philadelphia, at the age of twenty years. He remained in that city and took up the study of medicine under Charles Pendleton Tutt, of Virginia, and graduated from the Medical college of Philadelphia in March, 1860. He returned to Mississippi and commenced the practice of the profession. When the war broke out he entered company E, of the Twenty-first Mississippi regiment, as second lieutenant, and was promoted to assistant surgeon, and later to surgeon of the Twenty-first Mississippi regiment in the army of northern Virginia, and served thus until the surrender of Appomattox. He participated in the following engagements under General Magruder: Dam No. 2, in Virginia; at Savage Station (after which he entered the medical corps); the second battle of Fredericksburg, in which he took active part, and was in the trenches and fired nine shots. He was at that time assistant surgeon. After the war he returned to the home place, where he practiced medicine for some years. He then married and commenced planting on his present place. He was married to Josephine Crow, daughter of Levi Crow, of Mississippi. Mrs. Peets was born and reared on the present place, where she died two years after her marriage, leaving no children. Mr. Peets was again married to the sister of his first wife, Eliza, who died, leaving six children, all of whom are yet living and all are at school: Richard Davis, Levi Crow, George H., Josephine (a very bright student of fifteen years, who took the full course of French at Whitworth college, Mississippi; she is now at McGehee college, at Woodville), Mary E. and Lee Percy. Richard and George are at the Centenary college, one in the junior and one in the sophomore class. Richard attended Vanderbilt university, Nashville, Tenn. Dr. Peets was married, the third time, to Anna Brown, a native of this county, the daughter of Thomas Brown, a Methodist Episcopal minister and school superintendent of this county, which latter office he has held for a number of years. He is a man of fine education and refinement. His wife, Mary Smith, was a native of New York, educated in Buffalo at Miss Willard's school. She was the niece of Fitz Smith, of New York city. Miss Anna Brown was very highly educated at home by her esteemed mother, taking a full classical course, and is a very highly accomplished and a most estimable lady. She was at the time of her marriage to Dr. Peets the principal of the McGehee college, and one of the ablest and most highly esteemed instructors. To this union were born three children: Anna Cupples, Kate Lee and Grandville Hunter. Dr. and Mrs. Peets are active members of the Methodist Episcopal church, as are four of their oldest children. Dr. Peets has held the office of church steward and Sunday-school superintendent. He is a member of the A. F. & A. M., of Woodville. He was elected to the state legislature in 1883, and is a member of the board of trustees of the Agricultural and Mechanical college and a trustee of Centenary and McGehee colleges, and is one of the county's most prominent and respected planters. He has nearly four thousand five hundred acres, with about one thousand acres under cultivation. He owns eight miles frontage on the Buffalo river.

W. C. Pegram, a well-known and prominent attorney at Vicksburg, Miss., a native of the city, son of Tilford and Margaret (McLemore) Pegram, is a graduate of the law department of the University of Louisville, Ky. In 1878 was a member of the lower house of the Mississippi legislature. As a criminal lawyer he ranks deservedly high, being regarded one of the best in the state. In 1890 he married Harriet Willis Barnes. On her mother's side she is descended from the Montgomerys. The Barnes and Montgomery families are among the earliest settlers of the state. A number of them have been quite prominent in the state's history.

The Pepper family, of which R. B. Pepper, Deasonville, Miss., is a member, is one of the largest and most influential in the county of Yazoo, and is worthy of mention in this record of the leading families of Mississippi. Zedekiah Pepper was born in South Carolina, January 13, 1800, and at the age of eighteen years removed to Tennessee, and thence to Lawrence county, Miss., where he married Sarah Bull. In 1835 he came to Yazoo county, where he was a large and prosperous planter before the war. He owned two thousand two hundred and fifty acres of land, the most of which was in a high state of cultivation. He died in 1886, at the age of eighty-six years. His wife died in 1882. They reared a family of twelve children, all of whom settled in Yazoo county. At the time of the father's death he had a direct succession of more than one hundred descendants: Elisha married Miss Rachel West and reared a family of five sons; Lovy married S. Z. Dixion, and to them were born twelve children; E. B. married Miss Elizabeth Kuhn, and they had two children; Zedekiah, Jr., married Miss Matilda Beall, and they had eight children born to them; William J. married Miss Cornelia Mathews, and they had one child, who died in 1859; S. J. lived to be about fifty years of age and was unmarried; Sarah married F. M. Beall, and died some years ago, they had two children; A. G. married Miss Amanda Stubblefield, and they had seven children; J. J. married Miss Rachel Penny, and they have eight children; J. H. married Miss Betty Penny, and to them were born ten children; Mary, the fourth child, died in infancy; R. B., the subject of this notice, was born in Yazoo county in 1839, and is the eleventh of the twelve children of Zedekiah and Sarah (Bull) Pepper. Mr. Pepper was married to Miss Agnes Handley, and eight children have been born to them. With six of his brothers, Mr. Pepper saw three years' service in the Civil war. He was with A. G. in the engagement at Port Hudson; J. H. was in the engagement at Vicksburg, and J. J. fought gallantly at Blakely. E., Z., Jr., and S. J. were on light duty. The two others were then deceased.

Col. W. A. Percy was born in Huntsville, Ala., though he lived in Washington county, Miss., from his boyhood to the time of his death. His father was a native of Adams county, in this state, where his grandfather, Captain Percy, of the British naval service, settled in the early days of the Natchez province. Graduating at Princeton college, Colonel Percy came home to the plantation owned by his brothers and himself on Deer creek. He resumed his studies in the law school of the University of Virginia, where he took so high place in his class that his teacher, Professor Minor, predicted for him the station in the front rank of his profession which he afterward achieved. He married Miss Armstrong, daughter of General Armstrong, a distinguished soldier of the regular army. Before beginning active practice the war came on, and though an uncompromising opponent of secession, he raised and led to the camps the first company that left his county. He subsequently, after having been elected colonel of his regiment, was transferred to the staff of General Bowen, on which he served during the siege of Vicksburg. He was next assigned to duty with Gen. A. S. Long, chief of artillery of the Second corps, army of northern Virginia. The war over, Colonel Percy returned to his plantation home, soon moving to Greenville, however, and engaging in the active practice of law. He at once received a large business, which continued to grow as long as he lived. Absorbed as he was in the management of his law business, the dire needs of the state at this, the reconstruction period, drew him much into political affairs. This divergence did not accord with his tastes, but was an imperative duty—as much so as the response to the call to arms in time of war. His home, the Yazoo delta, was the very core of the black belt, where the carpetbaggers flourished and grew fattest. It was the central point in the succeeding struggle for the building up of stable white supremacy—at times threatening the peace of the state and the institution of home government. Through all of the years from 1870 to 1888 Colonel Percy was the acknowledged leader and guide of the delta counties in the trials and perplexing emergencies growing out of what is known as the race question. He was one of the famous committee of seven which in June, 1875, issued a call for the reorganization of the state democracy preliminary to the profound struggle which resulted in the overthrow of base and alien rule. He was elected to the legislature in that year and to that of two years later, by which he was chosen speaker. This was his only official experience, except as delegate from the state at large to the national democratic convention of 1880, and from the district in 1884. During the period stated Colonel Percy was the champion and acknowledged authority of the levee interests, the problem of overflow protection only a degree less important than that of home rule. These questions, the political redemption, the levee protection, and the full development of the Yazoo delta, embraced the duties on which his life work was centered. The following of Colonel Percy, the Gray Eagle of the Delta, as his friends and admirers were wont to call him, is taken from the history of Mississippi by Messrs. McCaudle and Lowry: "He possessed the highest of nature's gifts—personal magnetism—by which were drawn to him men of all classes, creeds and conditions. At the time of his untimely death he had taken such place in the minds of Mississippians that it was only a question of time when he would have been called to high official station. How great would have been his services upon a broader field of action there are no means of judging, for he was equal to every opportunity presented, to all obstacles encountered." This outline of his life may serve to awaken memories of him in the thousands of those who knew and loved him, but it presents but a shade of what Colonel Percy was to the people of the Yazoo delta, among whom his lot was cast, or of that wonderful influence which he exerted, apparently unconsciously to himself, over all who came in contact with him, by which he seemed to bind chance acquaintances as well as friends to him with hooks of steel; of how he was looked up to, implicitly leaned upon and confided in. He filled the measure of statesmanship. Animated by genius for justice and truth, possessing courage of convictions in and above all things, with a true heart, broad sympathies and a wise brain, he was, where he lived, first in popular affection and admiration, above envy and beyond rivalry. "Great thoughts, great feelings, came to him like instincts unawares."

Le Roy Percy, a member of the legal firm of Yerger & Percy, Greenville, Miss., is a native of Mississippi, his birth having occurred in Washington county, on the 9th of November, 1861. He attended the University of the South at Sewanee, Tenn., and graduated from that institution in 1879, after which he read law in his father's office. He subsequently entered the University of Virginia (where his father and two brothers had graduated) and finished his course there in 1881, being examined on his twenty-first birthday. Since then he has been practicing at Greenville, and though young in years is a fluent and ready speaker, and is well fitted for the profession he has chosen. He was married on the 9th of December, 1883, to Miss Camille E. Bourges, a native of Louisiana, and to them has been born one child, William A. Mrs. Percy is a member of the Catholic church. Mr. Percy is active in politics and has been chairman of the county executive committee. He was in partnership with his father and Mr. Yerger until the former's death, and since then the firm has continued as Yerger & Percy. Mr. Percy was the second of five children born to Col. William Alexander and Nannie E. (Armstrong) Percy, the father a native of Alabama and the mother of Tennessee. The children were named as follows: Fannie (died in 1882), Le Roy, W. A. (a lawyer of Memphis), Walker (a lawyer in Birmingham), and Lady (wife of Charles McKinney, of Knoxville, Tenn.). When quite a lad the father came with an elder brother to Washington county, Miss., opened a tract of land, and passed his youthful days in that state and in Alabama. He attended Princeton college, New Jersey, also the University of Virginia, and there took a course in law, graduating about 1854 or 1855. He afterward returned to Washington county, Miss., and there made his permanent home. He was married about 1856 or 1857 to Miss Nannie Armstrong, of Tennessee, who is still living. In 1861 he entered the Confederate army, and with the rank of captain took the first company from Washington county. He served until the close of the war. During the siege of Vicksburg he was on the staff of General Bowen, and later he was in the army of Virginia, surrendering at the close as colonel. In 1875 he was a member of the executive committee and soon after was elected to the state legislature from Washington county. He was reëlected the next term and was afterward made speaker of the house. From this time on he could have been elected to almost any office, but declined to have his name placed in nomination. It may be said of his character that he was upright and honorable in all his dealings, and had hosts of friends whose confidence and esteem was his highest eulogium. He died on the 19th of January, 1888, a worthy member of the Episcopal church. A poem, "The Sunstruck Eagle," was written by Eleanor Percy Lee in the year 1843, and was dedicated to the memory of Col. W. A. Percy by her daughter on account of the strange coincidence of his being called "The Gray Eagle of the South":

THE SUNSTRUCK EAGLE.

I saw an eagle sweep the sky,
The God-like seeking his place on high;
With a strong and wild and rapid wing,
A dark, and yet a dazzling thing,
And his arching neck, his bristling crest,
And the dark plumes quivering upon his breast,
And his eye bent up to each beam of light,
Like a bright sword flash'd, with a sword in flight.

I saw him rise o'er the forest trees;
I saw his pinions ride the breeze;
Beyond the clouds I watched him tower
On his path of pride, his flight of power;
I watched him wheeling stern and lone,
Where the keenest ray of the sun was thrown,
Soaring, circling, bathed in light —
Such was that desert eagle's flight.

Suddenly, then, to my straining eye,
I saw the strong wing slack on high,
Failing, falling to earth once more,
The dark breast covered with foam and gore,
The dark eyes' glory dim with pain,
Sick to death with a sunstruck brain;
Reeling down from that hight divine,
Eagle of heaven, such fall was thine.

Even so we see the sons of light
Up to the day-beam steer their flight,
And the wing of genius cleaves the sky,
As the clouds rush on when the wind is high;
Then comes the hour of sudden dread:
Then is the blasting sunlight shed,
And the gifted fall in their agony,
Sunstruck eagle, to die like thee.

The Hon. Charles H. Perkins, of Yazoo City, was born in Benton, Yazoo county, Miss., February 24, 1850, and is the twelfth of a family of fourteen children. His parents, R. S. G. and Judith N. (Hurst) Perkins, were natives of Virginia and Mississippi respectively. The father was prominently identified with the earlier political history of the county. He was district attorney for four years, and for some time held the office of probate judge. For four years he represented the people of his county in the state legislature, exerting a marked influence in that body, and giving entire satisfaction to his constituency. He was graduated in law at the age of eighteen years, when he was admitted to the bar by a special act of the legislature. He vigorously prosecuted all his duties as a public servant, and as a citizen he was never found wanting. He died at the age of fifty-seven years, in 1862. His wife survived until 1887, when she passed away at the age of seventy-five years. He was of Scotch lineage, and Mrs. Perkins was a relative of Gen. Robert E. Lee. Charles H. was reared in Yazoo county, and was educated in the common schools. His opportunities were very limited, so that it was mainly through his own exertions he was fitted for the path in life which he chose for himself. He has been dependent upon his own resources since he was a lad of fourteen years. After the war he engaged in farming, which he continued ten years. In 1874 he took up the study of law, reading in the evening after the day's work was done. He worked along in this way until 1878, when he was admitted to the bar, and has been engaged in professional duties since that time. In 1887 he was elected to the legislature, and filled the same chair in that honorable body which his father had occupied forty years before him. He is truly "a chip of the old block," and is destined to make his mark high above the point ordinarily attained. In connection with his professional work he finds time to attend to a considerable amount of planting, and is an excellent manager. He is a member of the Methodist Episcopal church, and belongs to the I. O. O. F. fraternity. He is a man of a great deal of individuality and determination, and it is probably due to these two traits that he has won the position he so ably fills.

Ebenezer M. Perkins, Booneville, Miss., who owns a large and well-improved farm seven miles southwest of Booneville, and who is one of the enterprising farmers of the county, was originally from the Old North state, born in 1813. His parents, Samuel and Elizabeth (Marsh) Perkins, were natives also of that state, but the father moved his family to Giles county, Tenn., and became one of the most extensive planters in that county. His children, six in number, were named as follows: Hugh (deceased), John (deceased), William (deceased), Ebenezer, Solomon (deceased), and Lucinda (resides in Tennessee). The mother of these children was a consistent member of the Baptist church and received her final summons in Tennessee. The father was afterward married to Mrs. Anna Dill, who bore him eight children: Amanda, Hardiman, Catherine (deceased), Joe, Simeon, Samuel, Eliza and Anna. The father died in 1850 and his body is interred in Hardin county, Tenn. Ebenezer M. Perkins received a common-school education in Tennessee, commenced farming for himself when young, and in 1858 moved to Mississippi, settling on a farm in Prentiss county. Previous to this, while a resident of Tennessee, he met and married Miss Elizabeth Usserry, a native of Tennessee, born in 1823, and the daughter of William and Jane (Marsh) Usserry, both natives of North Carolina. Mrs. Perkins was one of the following children: Eli, Lucinda, Ellen, Sallie, Jane, Thomas, Eliza, Patrick and Elizabeth. To Mr. and Mrs. Perkins were born six children: Patrick, married Miss Annie Miller (deceased) and subsequently married Mrs. Caddie Johnson, who at that time had two children; Samuel and Baxter, with their mother in Prentiss county; Amanda, widow of Benjamin Donalson, resides at Corinth with her three children: Anna, Dora and John; Thomas, married Mrs. Mary Wallace, who at that time had one child, William (they now reside in Palestine, Tex.); Mollie, wife of William Duke, resides in Coryell county, Tex., and is the mother of five children: Emma, Basil, Samuel, Marsh and Etna; Callie (deceased) was the wife of Thomas Braden and left two children: Callie and Paul; and Sallie, wife of James Miller, resides in Booneville and is the mother of six children: Terry, Lizzie, Albert, Katie, Lushion and Estma. Mr. Perkins' first wife died in 1882 and is buried at Booneville. She was an excellent woman and a devout Christian. Mr. Perkins was married the second time to Miss Fannie Lucus, daughter of Willis and Louisa (Smith) Lucus. Mr. and Mrs. Lucus have two children: Pearl and Allice. Mr. Perkins is a democrat in politics. He is a liberal contributor to churches, schools and all public enterprises and he and Mrs. Perkins are members of the Christian church.

Elisha O. Perkins is a highly esteemed planter of Coffeeville, Yalobusha county, and it is fitting that the following space should be given to a brief outline of his career. He was born in Pickens county, Ala., in 1826, and is a son of Robert and Elizabeth C. (Hooper)

Perkins, natives of Virginia and Georgia, respectively. The father died in 1874, in his eightieth year; the mother died in 1889, aged eighty-one years. They removed to Mississippi in 1849, and settled on the place where our subject now resides; the father purchased the land and devoted all his energies to its improvement and development until the time of his death. He served as a soldier in the War of 1812. He was a member of the Masonic lodge at Tuscaloosa, Ala., and in his death the community lost a valued citizen. His wife was a member of the Baptist church and was an earnest Christian. The family consisted of ten children: Elisha O., the subject of this notice; Mrs. Sarah A. Vann; Elizabeth V., who is a widow now living in Texas; James H., deceased; Watson R., deceased; Nicholas C., deceased; William H., deceased; Daniel P., deceased; Marion A., and Julia F., the wife of W. D. York. Mr. Perkins did not forsake the parental roof until he was twenty-nine years of age, when he engaged in farming near the home place. He was married in 1855 to Edith A. Murphree, who was born in Yalobusha county in 1835, a daughter of Solomon Murphree; the father was a native of Tennessee, and was married in Alabama to Frances Brown, of Tuscaloosa, Ala. In 1834 they removed to Mississippi and in 1860 the parents and eight of the children removed to Texas; the father died in 1864, aged fifty-four years; the mother died in 1865, aged forty years. Mr. and Mrs. Perkins are the parents of ten children, six of whom are still living: Mrs. Julia A. Hyde lives near the home place, and has a family of five children; Elisha O. lives in Texas (he is married and has two children); William H. lives in Texas and is unmarried; Fannie E. lives at home; Ranson D., a resident of Texas, is unmarried; James H. is at home; Sallie, the youngest, died at home; Robert S. died at the age of fourteen years; Lena died at the age of five years, and the other child died in infancy.

When there was a call for men to go to the defense of their country, Mr. Perkins left his home and family and went to the front; he enlisted in the First Mississippi cavalry and served from February, 1863, until the close of the war; he was promoted to the office of sergeant and participated in many battles and skirmishes. Before the war, from 1845 to 1860, he was engaged in boating on the Yalobusha, Tallahatchie and Tombigbee rivers and their tributaries. It was while in the business of boating that he acquired the title of captain. He is a member of the Masonic lodge, No. 297, at New Hope Church, and of the chapter No. 101, Royal Arch Masons, at Coffeeville, Miss. Politically he affiliates with the democratic party. He is the owner of a fine tract of eight hundred acres of land, three hundred of which he has brought to a good state of cultivation; he has devoted his time and attention to the different branches of farming, and has met with marked success. Mrs. Perkins is a member of the Baptist church.

Among the pioneers who went from the older states in the first quarter of the century, to build up new commonwealths along the Mississippi, was the subject of this sketch, Jesse Perkins. He was of English descent, his mother, Agnes Clopton, a lineal descendant of the Cloptons of Clopton Hall, near Stratford-on-Avon. Tradition says that Charlotte Clopton, a daughter of the family, who lived in the days of Shakespeare, returned to consciousness after having been consigned to the ancestral tomb, and upon this incident England's great bard founded his story of Romeo and Juliet. Colonel Perkins emigrated from Virginia in 1821, and traveling on horseback through the country between that state and the Mississippi river, finally settling at Natchez and engaged in mercantile pursuits. There he became the friend of S. S. Prentiss, Hiram G. Runnels, General Quitman, William L. Sharkey, Colonel McClung, and nearly all those great lights who made brilliant the early years of Mississippi's history. At that epoch the code duello was recognized by all gentlemen as the proper resort for the settlement of personal difficulties, and in common with many prominent men of his time, he became engaged in several affairs of honor; on one occasion he appeared on the field as the second of Governor Runnels. He knew well the celebrated James Bowie, who liked him so much he made him a present of one of the first specimens of his famous weapon known to this day as the bowie-knife. Colonel Perkins never indulged in political aspirations, and though often tendered positions of honor and responsibility, could never be induced to accept office. He concerned himself with the practical affairs of life, and amassed a large fortune. As a business man he did his full share in the great work of building up his state and making her prosperous and great. He was truly a representative man of the old South, of that regime when men made duty their guiding star and honor their best monitor.

William P. Perkins (deceased) was one of the early pioneers of Mississippi, and emigrated from Kentucky to Williamson county, of the former state, as early as 1820. From there he went to Madison county, thence in 1840 to Bolivar county, and settled on the Mound plantation, on the Mississippi river. This was a wilderness at that time, covered with canebrakes, but he went vigorously to work and soon had cleared two thousand acres, and made many improvements. He was married in that county, about 1820, to Miss Jane Stewart, daughter of Charles Stewart, who was of Scotch descent, and who settled in Wilkinson county about 1810, where he became one of the most extensive planters. To Mr. and Mrs. Perkins were born a large family, seven of whom were living at the time of his death, in 1850: Ann, Jane, Noland, Charles, William, Daniel and James. Mrs. Perkins survived her husband ten years, her death occurring on the old home place. They are interred in the family burial lot on the summit of one of three Indian mounds on this place, which suggested the name for the plantation, and also gave name to the locality. A postoffice was established at an early day, and still retains the name of Mound Landing. Mr. Perkins was educated at one of the colleges at Nashville, and was a man of strong character and excellent judgment. He was of medium hight, complexion dark and ruddy, and his eyes were blue. He and wife were members of the Methodist church. Jane, the only surviving child, resides on the old homestead and is a refined, well-educated and intelligent lady. She was first married in 1853 or 1854 to S. B. Curry, a native of South Carolina, who died in 1861 and is buried on the Mound. In personal appearance he was tall and a decided blonde. In 1865 Mrs. Curry married Col. M. H. Moore, a native of Kentucky, and a lawyer by profession, and they afterward moved to Missouri. The Colonel was in the Confederate army with General Price, and served as commissary, for, his eyesight being very poor, he did not hold the rank of colonel long. Returning to Mississippi in 1865, he was there married to Mrs. Curry. He was an energetic, public-spirited citizen, and although he did not practice law, he often advised the negroes for their good. His death occurred in Texas in 1878. He was a member of the Presbyterian church, and his widow holds membership in that church at the present time. The Colonel was tall and portly in appearance, fair complexion, with blue eyes and dark hair. When the railroad was built a station was located on Mrs. Moore's plantation, and she sold a number of lots. Soon several stores and dwellings were erected, and Moore's became quite a busy place. It is in a rich and populous country, and its future prospects for growth and prosperity are very good indeed. The Mound plantation now consists of about one thousand acres of the most productive cotton land in the Yazoo delta; about six hundred acres under a high state of cultivation, and consequently kept in the best of order by the mistress. She has a pleasant residence on the banks of Williams' bayou, well-shaded by large trees, and her home is well furnished, the walls being hung with family portraits. It is a beautiful place of residence, and a strong, new levee has just been completed

along the river front, which gives all promise of future protection from the Mississippi river floods.

William W. Perkins, merchant and planter, Batesville, Miss., was born in Yalobusha county, Miss., on the 4th of March, 1838, and was the third of ten children born to John W. and Louisa A. (Melugin) Perkins, natives of Hickman county, Tenn. The father came to Yalobusha county, Miss., in 1836, when it was chiefly populated with Indians, and was engaged most of his life in agricultural pursuits. He was a good, intelligent citizen, and one who took little interest in political matters, though a stanch Douglas democrat. He was opposed to the secession until Mississippi seceded, and then, as a son of his mother state, he stood by her. Though not in the war himself on account of age, he gave the Confederacy a noble gift in four of his sons, all gallant soldiers, and one laid down his life as a sacrifice for the Southern cause. Mr. Perkins died in 1877, at the age of sixty-eight years, and his wife, now surviving him, is enjoying good health at the age of seventy-eight years. The paternal grandfather, Wright Perkins, was of direct Scotch descent, his father being a native of that country and coming to the United States with a brother. The maternal grandfather, Melugin, married a Miss Gee, who was of Irish lineage. Our subject's early ancestors here were Revolutionary soldiers, and Melugin was shot through the throat by an Indian while crossing a stream in a boat. The arrow penetrated between the jugular vein and the windpipe, and he saved his life by stuffing the wound with tow, which stopped the flow of blood until medical aid could be had. William W. Perkins remained in Yalobusha county until sixteen years of age, attending the district schools, and from that time until the present he has been a resident of Panola county. He remained with his father until the war cloud broke over the nation and then, in March, 1861, he enlisted in Panola guards and left for Pensacola, Fla., where he remained until January. From there his company went to Cumberland Gap and participated in the skirmishing there. At the reorganization he attached himself to company B, Yates' battery, with which he remained as lieutenant of his company until the close, participating in the battles of Corinth, Chickasaw bayou, and siege of Vicksburg. From there he went to parole camp at Enterprise, Miss., and was afterward in recruiting camp at Mobile, Ala. In 1864 he joined the army of Tennessee at Good Hope Church, and was in the retreat through Georgia. In Quarles' brigade, on the 28th of July of that year, in a hard fight his command was nearly all killed. He was in almost constant engagements from the time he enlisted until the close of the war, and his career was marked with bravery and faithfulness. He surrendered at Greensboro, N. C., on the 26th of April, 1865, and then returned home, bringing surviving members of his company and others with him. He came all the way on foot, reached home footsore and sick and found himself and the entire family destitute and his father's property a wreck. He and his brothers went to work and in a measure restored the home to its wonted prosperous condition. In the winter of 1866 Mr. Perkins came to Batesville with one Confederate suit of clothes and a silver half dollar which his brother, while dying at Vicksburg, had given him. On coming to Batesville Mr. Perkins became clerk in a general store, remained there until 1868, and then he and his present partner, M. B. Jones, purchased the stock and began merchandising with a joint capital of $2,400, $710 of which was Mr. Perkins'. Since then they have conducted a successful business, carry a stock of general merchandise valued at $6,000, and do an annual business of about $45,000. The firm also owns about six thousand acres of land, with one-half under cultivation, and in this they are equally interested. They also own their place of business, a large gin factory in Batesville and manufacture ginstands, feeders, etc. This is one of the best enterprises of the county and is a credit to it. Mr. Perkins was married in 1870 to Miss

Mary J. Jones, a native of Mississippi and a daughter of Peter B. and Emiline (Polk) Jones, the mother a relative of James K. Polk. Mr. and Mrs. Perkins are the parents of six children: Howard J., Florence N., Louis M., Clifford P., Fred P. and Gladys. Mr. and Mrs. Perkins are members of the Methodist church, as are all the children with the exception of the two youngest. The eldest child is at Oxford university and Florence is attending school at Columbus, Miss. Mr. Perkins is a most worthy Christian gentleman and stands high in the esteem of all. He is scrupulously honest and upright in every way and is a very entertaining conversationalist. He is a member of the Knights of Honor and the American Legion of Honor.

J. C. Perry, circuit clerk and deputy chancery clerk of Grenada county, also a member of the well-known firm of Kimbrough & Perry, general merchants, is the eldest of six children—four sons and two daughters—born to Col. Oliver H. and Elizabeth (Williamson) Perry, the father a native of the Palmetto state, and the mother of what is now Grenada county, Miss. The children were named in the order of their births as follows: J. C., Oliver H., Charles E., Mary L., widow of W. P. Williamson; Belle, wife of John Thompson, of Stockdale; and Robert E. When quite young Col. Oliver H. Perry came with his parents to Grenada county, Miss., was married in this state, and there spent the closing scenes of his life, his death occurring in 1868. His wife had died a year previous. Both were members of the Presbyterian church. The father was a prominent and wealthy farmer, owning at one time two thousand acres of land. He was a man of learning, and was colonel of the militia, serving a short time in the late war. He was at one time a member of the board of police of Yalobusha county. He was active in politics, and was a man of considerable influence, doing considerable public business in a private way, such as the writing of deeds, etc. He was a member of the Masonic fraternity. His father, Zaddock Perry, was a native of South Carolina, where he spent all his early life, but came to Yalobusha (now Grenada) county about fifty years ago (1842), and settled six or seven miles east of Grenada, where he improved a good farm. There his death occurred about 1849. He was of the same family as Commodore Oliver H. Perry. His wife also died in this county. The maternal grandfather, Maj. Jack Williamson, was a native of South Carolina, and came to Grenada county about 1835 or 1836, being one of the very earliest settlers in that section. He assisted in opening the road east of Grenada, and the county then was almost a vast wilderness. He was a prominent planter, trader and river man, boating on the Yalobusha river. He was also engaged in merchandising to some extent. He was major of militia, and was a man well and favorably known over the county. J. C. Perry was born in Grenada in 1851, and comes of honored and representative families on both sides of the house. He secured a fair education in the public schools of his native town, and in 1868, when seventeen years of age, he engaged in planting, continuing this for a number of years. He then spent two years in Canton as assistant secretary of an insurance company there, after which he returned to Grenada and resumed planting until 1880. After this he engaged in merchandising at Gray's Port, remained there for six years, or until 1887, when he was elected circuit clerk of Grenada county, and later deputy chancery clerk. For two years he has been a member of the firm of Kimbrough & Perry, and they do an annual business of about $30,000; he is the owner of four hundred acres of land. He is a member of the Grenada lodge, I. O. O. F., No. 6, and of the encampment, being secretary for two years of the former. In 1873 he wedded Miss Nannie, daughter of Benjamin F. and Mary (Sledge) Johnson, a native of Grenada. The parents died in Grenada in 1868 and 1867, respectively, and both were members of the Baptist church. Mr. Johnson is a well-to-do planter, and was probably a native of

Virginia as was also his wife. To Mr. and Mrs. Perry have been born two sons and two daughters. Both are members of the Baptist church.

T. H. Pettit is a native of Warren county, Miss., born January 29, 1855, a son of Absolom Pettit, a native of West Virginia, born in 1798. He came to Mississippi about 1818, and in the county of Jefferson was employed as overseer on the plantation of James Turpin for two years, at the end of which time he came to Warren county and followed the same calling for Judge Covington, whose daughter he married soon after. He then moved onto a plantation, which he entered as government land, and where he remained up to the day of his death in 1883. After the death of his first wife he married Miss Rollins, of Mississippi, and took for his third wife Miss Rachel F. Knight, who was born in Ohio, their marriage taking place in 1834. His first and second unions resulted in the birth of three children, but to his last union fifteen children were born. Absolom Pettit was a minister of the Methodist Episcopal church, was a close student, and wrote some pamphlets on religious subjects that were considered very fine. He was very liberal in his views, so much so that he was at one time tried by his church for the free utterance of his views, but was acquitted. The early education of T. H. Pettit was somewhat limited, but up to the age of eleven years he was under the instruction of a private tutor. The two subsequent years were spent in Magruder college, of Baton Rouge, at the end of which time he returned home and started upon the career of a planter, in connection with which he has done a general merchandise business since 1886, and has built up a trade that amounts to $15,000 annually. His plantation consists of eight hundred and fifty acres, two hundred of which are under cultivation, three hundred and fifty acres being covered with fine oak timber. He has always been an excellent manager, and keeps his place in excellent repair, everything about the plantation indicating that a man of discretion, energy and ability is at the helm. He at one time was elected to the position of justice of the peace, but on account of his extensive business he refused to qualify. In 1876 he was married to Miss Sophia Whitaker, of Warren county, a daughter of William Whitaker. Mrs. Pettit died in 1878 of yellow fever, and in 1879 Mr. Pettit took for his second wife Miss Ella Stanford, a daughter of A. D. Stanford, of Warren county, and by her is the father of six living children: Gertrude, Fannie, Doctor, Dixon, Lizzie, Ella, and one that died in infancy. The family are members of the Methodist Episcopal church.

The following space will be devoted to a brief sketch of Col. Thomas F. Pettus, one of Newton county's most prominent citizens. He was born in Lauderdale county, Ala., in August, 1828. His father, Winston P. Pettus, was born in Charlotte county, Va., in 1806, and was a son of Horatio Pettus, a native of Lunenburg county, Va., born April 15, 1775. His father, John Pettus, was born in Lunenburg county, Va., April 22, 1736. The family is descended from English stock. John Pettus married Miss Susanna Winston, who comes of a noted family. The children of John Pettus and his wife were: Thomas P. Pettus, born April 7, 1759; Amos Pettus, born August 17, 1761; John P. Pettus, born August 17, 1765; Sarah Pettus, born October 7, 1767; Susanah Pettus, born April 20, 1769; Overton Pettus, born August 16, 1770; Mary Pettus, born December 7, 1772; Horatio Pettus, born April 15, 1775; William Pettus, born June 9, 1777; Elizabeth Pettus, born November 11, 1781. The descendants of these ten children are in almost every Southern state, especially Alabama, Tennessee, Texas and Mississippi. Horatio Pettus married Mary, daughter of Philip Poindexter, of Virginia. Winston P. Pettus married Miss Mary D., daughter of Amos Williams, who came to the frontier with Daniel Boone. The subject of this notice was born of this marriage. He remained in Alabama during his youth and early manhood; he served as doorkeeper and sergeant-at-arms of the Alabama senate during the session of 1851-2.

He was elected colonel of the Eleventh regiment, Alabama militia, in 1853. He was a stanch adherent to the principles of the whig party during its existence and was elected by that body. He removed to the city of Jackson, in 1859, and soon after came to Morton, Scott county, Miss., where he resided fourteen years, with the exception of a short period during the war. He raised the first company that was mustered in Scott county. In 1861 he went to Lynchburg, Va., and served a few months in West Virginia (General Lee commanding), but on account of illness he came home and did no active service until 1863–4; he then served voluntarily in the commissary department for about one year; at the end of that time he returned to his home and engaged in mercantile business with James R. Stevens, under the firm name of Pettus & Stevens. In 1871 he sold out at Morton and formed a partnership with his brother in the same town. It was not until 1873 that he came to Newton, taking charge of the business of Richardson & Co., of which he was a member. He managed this until 1881 and then sold out his interest to Mr. Richardson. In 1884 and 1885 he bought cotton, and in September, 1886, he was appointed by President Cleveland to the consulate at Ningpo, China. He served in this capacity until June, 1890, when he was succeeded by a republican from Massachusetts. He was a delegate to the national convention at Chicago in 1884, and has always been actively interested in the movements of his party. He has also been a delegate to many of the state conventions. Colonel Pettus is a worthy member of the Methodist Episcopal church and belongs to the A. F. & A. M. and Knights of Pythias and Knights of Honor. His first wife was Annie M., daughter of Stephen Cowley, of Virginia; five children were born of this marriage. Mrs. Pettus died in January, 1888, in China. The Colonel was married a second time, to Mrs. Elizabeth Hart, a sister of his first wife.

G. M. Petty is a planter and liveryman of Woodville, Miss., but was born at Centerville in 1852, the eldest of eleven children born to Sylvanus and Malinda J. (Fly) Petty, who were born in Kentucky and Sharon, Miss., respectively, the latter being the daughter of Rev. A. T. M. Fly, one of the first Methodist Episcopal ministers of the section, who died at Natchez in 1855, of yellow fever, at which time he was in charge of a church at that place, and was doing a noble and successful work. The paternal grandfather, James Petty, was a Virginian, who removed to Kentucky with the pioneers of that state, settling in the central portion thereof. There he followed planting, and reared a large family. He died about 1835. Sylvanus Petty spent his early days on blue grass soil, receiving but a limited education, but at the age of about twenty years, or in 1844, he removed to Wilkinson county, Miss., where he and an older brother, who had preceded him, began the life of planters, a calling he continued to follow there until 1849, when he, like so many of the young, as well as the old, men of that day was taken with the gold fever, and started for California, where he followed gold mining for one year. In 1850 he returned to Mississippi and bought a plantation near Centerville, on which he has since resided. He was married in 1851, and of the children born to himself and wife the following are now living: George M.; Annie M., wife of Charles Anderson, of Centerville; Louisa M., wife of E. E. Riggs, now residing at Monroe, La.; Hattie Fly, wife of James Petty, of Abbeville, La.; Sallie E., wife of Henry Chevis, of Louisiana; Fredonia, wife of R. C. Way, at Centerville; Martha W., wife of A. W. Riggs, of Centerville; James Marshall, and John Henry. Sylvanus and Nellie died in infancy. The parents of these children still reside on the old home place; are earnest members of the Methodist Episcopal church, the father having been a steward in that church at Centerville for many years. G. M. Petty was reared and educated in the town of his birth, and was married at the age of twenty-one to Miss Emma E., daughter of Lieutenant Hanford

Lanehart, of this county. He began life as a planter, and followed that occupation exclusively until 1884, when he moved to Woodville and opened a livery stable, where he also deals in stock. He erected his own establishment, which is a good and substantial one, and has also one at Centerville, both of which are well conducted and equipped with vehicles of all kinds and excellent horses. He owns a pleasant and comfortable home in Woodville, besides still owning his plantation, which comprises about four hundred and fifty acres of land, of which about one hundred acres are under cultivation, a tract of forty acres near Woodville, which has been recently purchased, and two residences in Centerville. Mr. Petty and his wife are members of the Methodist Episcopal church, and he is a very agreeable and social gentleman, although very unassuming. He is a wideawake and progressive man of business, and has become possessed of a comfortable competency.

Dr. Alonzo J. Phelps is retired from the active life of a medical practitioner, and is devoting his attention to planting, being the owner of Nitta Yuma plantation, at Nitta Yuma, Miss. He was born in Pike county, Ohio, in the year 1835, a son of Dr. Orlando J. and Nancy (Watkins) Phelps, the former of whom was born in Meigs county, Ohio, and the latter in Greenbrier county, Va. (now West Virginia). They were married in Virginia, but afterward took up their residence in Pike county, Ohio, where they resided for many years. Dr. Phelps, Sr., was a man of fine mental endowments and his thorough knowledge of his profession won him a large practice, which he commanded up to the time of his demise. He graduated from a medical college of his native state in his early manhood, and throughout his well-spent life he showed himself to be a man of noble attributes, and a medical practitioner of more than ordinary ability. He and his wife were members of the Presbyterian church, and he was a member of the A. F. & A. M. His paternal grandfather, James E. Phelps, was born in Hartford, Conn., and shortly before the birth of Dr. Orlando J., he removed to Meigs county, Ohio, where he spent the rest of his life on his farm near Pomeroy. He was an associate judge of his district, and his home was the favorite resort of the members of the bar at that early day. The first of the Phelps family to come to America were three brothers, who became residents of America about the year 1630. The maternal grandfather, Francis Watkins, was born in Enniskillen, Ireland. He and two brothers came to America prior to the Revolutionary war, and the two latter were killed at the battle of Cowpens. Mr. Watkins first located in Greenbrier county, Va. (now West Virginia), of which he was one of the very earliest settlers. He afterward moved to Mason county, where he died, having at one time been high sheriff of his district. Dr. Alonzo J. Phelps, the subject of this sketch, is the eldest of seven children, and he and a brother, Judge William G. Phelps, a prominent attorney of Greenville, Miss., are the only members of the family now living. He received a fine classical education in the University of Ohio, after which he studied medicine with his father, and in 1852 graduated from the Starling Medical college at Columbus, Ohio, taking a diploma two years later from the New York Medical college. He then practiced his profession in partnership with his father until the opening of the war of the states, when he was made surgeon of the Thirty-third Ohio volunteers, and soon afterward was ordered before the regular medical army board for examination, and was commissioned as staff surgeon or surgeon of volunteers. He was then made medical director of the fourth division of the army commanded by General Wood, which position he held until the army was divided into corps, and was then made successively medical director of the Twenty-first and Fourth army corps, and when General Grant was placed in command in Virginia, Dr. Phelps was ordered to the army of the Potomac, and was made general director and inspector and placed in charge of the general field hospitals, in the forward movement of that army, which position he retained until about October, 1864, when he was relieved of field duty, at his own request, having been constantly in front field duty from the beginning of the war. He was then ordered to Columbus, Ohio, and was placed on light duty, superintending the examination of recruits, where he spent the winter of 1864-5, at the end of which time he was ordered to Louisville, Ky., and was made medical director of the department of Kentucky, on the staff of Maj.-Gen. John M. Palmer, now Senator Palmer, with the rank and pay of colonel. While there he met Miss Mary Vick, a native of Vicksburg, Miss., whom he married on October 18, 1865. Afterward, resigning his position in the army, January 4, 1866, he practiced his profession in Louisville for some time, but as his attention became too much engrossed in other interests and planting in Mississippi, where his wife owned the fine Nitta Yuma estate, to permit of his giving proper attention to his practice, he retired from the profession, and since that time has made his home alternately at Louisville, Ky., and at Nitta Yuma, Miss. The Nitta Yuma plantation, lying on Deer creek, is one of the finest in the South. The Louisville, New Orleans & Texas railroad passes through it, and near his residence is located the station and postoffice of Nitta Yuma, taking its name from the plantation. The public spirit and enterprise of Dr. Phelps were manifested recently by his appropriating a town site for Nitta Yuma. The site of this place is one unexcelled in beauty by any other along the Louisville, New Orleans & Texas railroad, between Memphis and New Orleans. Although it has been a principal station, with considerable improvements since the building of this road, and has done a very large business, the ground has been held from public purchase until the spring of 1891, when, in consideration of the rapid increase of the surrounding population and the demand for facilities adequate to meet the growth of business, the Doctor determined to open a town site to the public for purchase. Deer creek, on the southern boundary, courses to the left, with a constant running stream between sloping banks rising twenty-five feet above the bottom of the channel, and is spanned by a roadbridge two hundred and fifty feet long, besides a railroad bridge. The Mississippi Valley road, from Memphis to New Orleans, runs north and south along the eastern border, with ample yard facilities and a fine passenger and freight depot and conveniences of telegraph and express. The soil is sandy and the drainage complete. There is no section in the bottom safer from overflow. It is distant twenty miles from the Mississippi river, on the Deer creek ridge, where it has never been overflowed. Its healthfulness is remarkable, and unexcelled by the upland districts of the state. A broad, open country surrounds it, unmarred by slashes or stagnant pools. Lots are donated for church and school purposes by the proprietor, and the community is assured against the presence of saloons by terms of sale, so that families can here find a place where they will have all the conditions of peaceful rest and orderly society, and opportunities for education and religious privileges. Dr. Phelps and his wife have four children, named: Nannie W., Henry Vick, Mary P. and Ellen B. His family are Episcopalians, and he is a member of the A. F. & A. M. In politics the Doctor was nurtured a whig, but he has never engaged in political strife. By the unanimous wish of his district he became a member of the Mississippi Levee board, and is now serving his second term of four years. As a business man he possesses much practical ability and foresight. His wife is a daughter and only surviving child of Col. Henry W. Vick, a native of South Carolina, and a son of Maj. Burwell Vick, who came to this state at an early day and was one of the original settlers and founders of Vicksburg, Miss., from whom the town derived its name. Col. Henry Vick was married to Miss Sarah Pearce, of Louisville, Ky., in 1861. Miss Pearce was a member of one of the oldest families of Kentucky. Her grandfather, Maj. Gen. Jonathan Clarke, served as such with great distinction in the Revolutionary war, and his brother, Gen.

George Rogers Clarke, of whom it has been said by Senators Sherman and Daniels and other senators on the floor of the senate of the United States, that to him more than to any one else is our country indebted for the conquest and redemption of the territory of the great Northwest. His military possession of it at the close of the Revolution was the controlling fact that compelled Great Britain to yield anything west or north of the Ohio river, and south of the lakes, in final settlement of the war. Another younger brother, William Clarke, was the Rocky mountain explorer, and led the first expedition beyond the Mississippi, known as the Lewis and Clarke expedition.

W. G. Phelps, lawyer, Greenville, Miss., the second of seven children born to Orlando John and Nancy (Watkins) Phelps, was originally from the state of Ohio. His birth occurred in 1837. All of his brothers and sisters have died except Dr. A. J. Phelps, who resides in Sharkey county, Miss. His father was also a native of the state of Ohio, and resided there all his life, and the greater part of the time in Pike county. He was a physician by profession. The paternal grandfather, James E. Phelps, was originally from Connecticut, but in the year 1802 emigrated with his family to Meigs county, Ohio. He followed the occupation of a farmer. The mother of W. G. Phelps died in 1874. She was a native of Virginia. Her father, Francis Watkins, came from Ireland, and settled in the western part of the Old Dominion, at Charleston, now West Virginia. Her mother, Nancy Watkins, was the daughter of Colonel Donnelly, who owned a fort on the frontier of Virginia in the time of Daniel Boone. W. G. Phelps was educated in Ohio, began the study of law in 1858, attended Harvard law school in 1859, and was admitted to the bar in 1860 in Columbus, Ohio. In 1865 he came to Washington county, Miss., and engaged in planting, and in 1874 began the practice of law in Greenville. In 1878 he was appointed chancellor of the fourth judicial district of the state, held that office nearly nine years, and then resigned to resume his practice. His marriage to Miss Virginia Thompson, of Louisville, Ky., who belonged to one of the oldest families in Kentucky whose ancestors served with great distinction in the Revolutionary war, was consummated in January, 1879. He is a member of the Masonic fraternity and the Knights of Pythias. Judge Phelps owns a plantation in Sunflower county, Miss., and has considerable city property. He is an able lawyer and one of the county's best citizens.

Hon. Eli Phillips, ex-probate judge of Itawamba county, was born in Moore county, N. C., in 1825. He is a son of John and Mary (Dowd) Phillips, natives of North Carolina, but of Scotch-Irish descent. His father, a son of Mark Phillips, was born in 1793, and was a planter, and served his country in the War of 1812 as a soldier. The father and mother of our subject were members of the Baptist church. The former died in 1855, and the latter in 1886. Judge Phillips began at an early age to assist his father in his work on the plantation, and received a good, practical education. He took up life's battle for himself as overseer of a large plantation. Later he was a clerk in an establishment devoted solely to general merchandise. He removed to this state in 1844, and settled in the southwest part of the county, and there he married Miss Irene Collins, in 1853. She was a daughter of John and Mary (Wortham) Collins, and was born in Maury county, Tenn., in 1835. She has borne her husband seven children, named as follows: Mary I., now Mrs. A. C. Betts; Travis, Laura, Martha and Dickinson all died when young; Sula, wife of M. C. Betts, died in 1889, and Sumter is now living in Washington, D. C. In the period before the war Judge Phillips was an old-line whig in his political ideas, and with might and main he opposed the secession of Mississippi from the Union, but since the war, believing that the best interests of the white population of the South were dependent to a great extent upon the democratic party for their perpetuation, he affiliated with that body. He has held numerous offices by election and appointment. He was postmaster at Fulton for sixteen years, and, upon making a final settlement to the government, owed only the small sum of $2.02. His first county office was that of probate clerk, which he held for five terms. He was later elected probate judge and served as such a year and a half. He was appointed United States commissioner for this district, and served with credit to himself and with satisfaction to all concerned. In 1870-71 he represented Itawamba county in the state legislature. He has lived in this state for forty-seven years, and has been a resident of Fulton for thirty-two years. He is one of the old, reliable and honored residents of Itawamba county, to all of whose varied interests he has always lent his advocacy and practical aid. He has been for many years a Royal Arch Mason, and has been long identified with the Baptist church.

Among the many successful practitioners of the healing art in Holmes county, Miss., deserving special mention, is Dr. George C. Phillips, Lexington, Miss., who was born in Uniontown, Ala., October 4, 1835. His father, Hon. F. W. Phillips, was born in Dallas county, Ala., in 1809, and received his literary education in that state. He then graduated at Transylvania Medical college, Kentucky, and also at New York Medical college. He was married, in his native state, to Miss Martha Shearer, daughter of Gen. Gilbert Shearer, of Alabama. The Doctor practiced in Alabama a number of years, and in 1842 moved to Mississippi, settling in the northern part of Holmes county, where he was among the pioneer physicians, practicing for a number of years. He took an active part in political matters, served several terms in the legislature, was delegate to the secession convention from Holmes county, and a member of the constitutional convention after the war. He abandoned his practice in 1860, and lived retired until his death, in 1879. His wife died in 1872. He was an old line whig and voted against secession, but after the stand was made he was a strong Confederate, standing with his state. He wrote numerous articles for the press, both before and after the war, contributed to the local papers, and was considered authority of whig ideas in the county before the war. He was well known all over the state, was a great humorist and a good speaker. His family consisted of three children, two of whom died in early youth. The remaining member, Dr. George C. Phillips, received his literary education in the University of Mississippi, graduating in the class of 1857, and after studying medicine with his father took a course of lectures at the New Orleans School of Medicine, from which he graduated in the spring of 1860. On May 29, of the same year, he was married to Miss A. R. Chew, a native of Wilkinson county, Miss., but who was reared in Carroll county of that state, receiving her education at Black Hawk, in the latter county. She was the daughter of Dr. W. S. Chew, of Carroll county, Miss. After his marriage Dr. Phillips practiced his profession and managed his father's plantation until 1861, when he enlisted in the Confederate army, Black Hawk rifles, which company was formed on the county line between Holmes and Carroll counties. He entered as a private, and soon afterward joined the Twenty-second Mississippi infantry, called the First Mississippi war regiment. He was soon promoted to assistant surgeon, and in 1862 to surgeon, which position he held until the close of the war. In 1863 he was made brigade-surgeon under General Featherston, and was present in all the battles of his regiment with the exception of one, Bentonville, Va. During the latter part of the war the Doctor kept a complete record of the regiment, but gave it to Colonel Claiborne to use in his history of Mississippi. He surrendered at Greensboro, N. C., with Gen. Joseph Johnston. He was in the battles of Shiloh, Corinth, first siege of Vicksburg, Fort Pemberton, Jackson, Georgia campaign, Hood's campaign in Tennessee, and was in the fights of Nashville and Franklin. After the war Dr. Phillips resumed the practice of his profession at home, and in 1878 moved to Lexington, where he continued practicing until July,

1888. He then located at Greenville, practiced there until 1890, and in March of that year returned to Lexington. He is now in partnership with Dr. G. W. Farr. He has a large practice, and is one of the leading practitioners of the county. He is a member of the State Medical association, and was county health officer for a number of years. He takes a prominent part in local politics, and was chairman of the executive committee for a number of years. Mrs. Phillips died in 1878, leaving three children—a daughter and two sons: Dr. F. M., licensed by the state board of health to practice; Walter C., and Lu Gay, wife of J. P. Phillips, of Birmingham, Ala., and bookkeeper for a large mercantile house. Dr. Phillips was married again, at Lexington, May 4, 1880, to Miss L. H. Dyer, daughter of Judge James Dyer, one of the prominent old settlers. One child, a daughter, Cornelia Dyer, has been born to this union. Socially the Doctor is a Royal Arch Mason, a member of the grand lodge of Mississippi, and has served a number of times as past master and high priest. He is also a member of the Knights of Pythias and the Knights of Honor. In religion the Doctor is an Episcopalian, and Mrs. Phillips is a Presbyterian.

H. W. Phillips is a rising young merchant and planter of the Silver creek valley, and is entitled to mention in this record of Mississippi's stanch, reliable citizens. He was born in Orangeburgh county, S. C., and is a son of W. F. and A. E. (Reaheimer) Phillips, natives of South Carolina. He passed his schooldays in the county of his birth, and when he grew to man's estate he started out to face the world, and to make his own fortune. His first venture was as commercial traveler for a large leather house in the East. In 1880 he decided to locate in the South, and the wisdom of this decision has been clearly demonstrated by the success with which his efforts have been rewarded. As he had but little capital to invest, he first acted as agent for one of the large plantations until he could lay up some capital to invest. He was economical in his habits and finally purchased two hundred acres of land lying in the delta of the Yazoo, which is so rapidly rising in value; the cotton raised in this section invariably commands the highest price in the market. Mr. Phillips is also doing a flourishing business in mercantile lines; he has two stores in the Yazoo delta, carries stocks valued at $5,000 and does an annual business of $30,000. He is a man of indefatigable energy, push and pluck, and has made all obstacles yield to his forceful touch. Such traits must make themselves felt in the new South.

Seldon F. Phillips has lived a useful and well-spent life, and being possessed of those advanced ideas and progressive principles regarding agricultural life necessary to a successful following of that calling he is now in independent circumstances. He is a Virginian, his birth occurring in Hanover county in 1849, being the second of eight children born to William and Caroline (Eacho) Phillips, they being also born in the Old Dominion, the former's birth occurring in 1822. He enlisted in company I, Fifteenth Virginia regiment of the Confederate States army in 1862 and served as a private until the close of the war, taking part in the battles of Cold Harbor, Watts Farm and Fair Oaks. He was called from life in his native state in 1883. His wife, who was a daughter of John A. Eacho, was born in 1824. The subject of this sketch was reared in Hanover county, but received his education in Lexington. While attending school at this place his studies were interrupted by the war, but, notwithstanding this fact, he is one of the most intelligent gentlemen of the county. He began life for himself in 1870 as a planter in Washington county, Miss., and has continued to follow this calling up to the present time, being now the owner of a one-half interest in one thousand six hundred and forty acres of land valued at $5 per acre, and is working one thousand three hundred acres of leased land. He also has a one-half interest in the very prosperous business of C. E. Livingston, at Livingston, Miss., their stock of goods being valued at about $20,000. He was married in 1873 to Miss Sally I. Hogan, a native of Mississippi, and a daughter of William Hogan, a planter of this state, and by her has two children: George Fall and Jennie Hogan, who are attending school in Cleveland, Tenn., and Hiwassee, Tenn., respectively. Mr. Phillips has always been a democrat in his political views, and he and his wife are members of the Methodist Episcopal church. His paternal grandfather, William Phillips, was a Virginian, in which state he followed the life of a planter. He served throughout the War of 1812, and passed from life in 1860. His wife, formerly a Miss Wicker, was also born in the Old Dominion. The maternal grandfather of Mr. Phillips was John A. Eacho, his wife being a Miss Dudley, of Virginia. To William and Caroline (Eacho) Phillips the following children were born: Deborah Carter is the wife of James Southall, a planter, of Virginia; Lafayette Fariss is also a planter of that state; Caroline Hall was married to a Mr. French, of Baltimore, Md., in which city he was a merchant, but she is now a widow and resides in Richmond, Va.; William is a bookkeeper of Baltimore; Mercy Carter is the wife of a Mr. Elliott, a mechanic of Richmond, Va., and Seldon F. The latter is now worth about $10,000, all which has been acquired by his own good management and industry, for he began life for himself with no means. He is a thorough and practical business man, and has had every need of being such, for his father, being left penniless at the close of the war, could give him no pecuniary aid. He, however, inherited an abundant supply of grit and believed that honest labor would not go unrewarded, and has lived to see his belief fulfilled. He was manager of a plantation for quite a while, but afterward leased some land, and has been reasonably successful. He weighs about one hundred and eighty pounds, and in complexion is a brunette. His wife was the adopted daughter of Col. G. R. Fall. She is a well-educated and refined lady, an admirable housekeeper and a most faithful wife.

Among the popular hotel men of the Mississippi valley may be mentioned Vincent Piazzo, who is the kindly and courteous landlord of the Piazzo hotel, of Vicksburg, of which he is sole proprietor and manager. He was born in Italy in 1842, and at the age of sixteen years immigrated to America, for he decided that in the land of the free opportunities were offered young men that were not given them in any country of Europe. He attended school in his native land, and also after coming to the United States, for he discovered that a knowledge of the English language was very necessary for success in any business here, and in the country of his adoption he immediately began qualifying himself for useful citizenship. He first learned the trade of wood carving, and after following it for some years in New York city, he in 1865 came to Mississippi, and for seven years thereafter was engaged in merchandising at Crystal Springs, Miss. In 1872 he came to Vicksburg, and until 1879 was engaged in the saddlery and harness business with N. and Joseph Piazzo, but in the latter part of the same year, relinquishing that, he embarked in the hotel business in a small way, in the management of which he gave such general satisfaction that his hostelry soon became known as one of the leading establishments of the kind in this section of the state. The trade which had been built up by Mr. Piazzo by 1889 was so extensive that more room was necessary to do justice to his business, and during that year he erected a handsome brick building, consisting of one hundred and eight rooms, the structure being five stories in hight. It is fitted up with all modern improvements, such as elevators, fire escapes, etc., is elegantly and tastefully furnished throughout, has a comfortable reading and writingroom, also handsome offices, and last, but not least, his tables are supplied with the best the market affords, well and carefully prepared. The diningroom is cool and commodious, and his guests are well served by a finely drilled corps of servants. A cordial and ready welcome is extended to all by the genial host, whether they are guests of the hotel or not, and traveling men find his hotel especially satisfactory and homelike. This hotel, under its present efficient management, is one of the most desirable places from Memphis to New Orleans, for Mr. Piazzo caters to the taste of the public, and gives all to understand that it is his pleasure so to do. He is accounted one of the most progressive men of Vicksburg, for few, if any, have done more toward building up and helping to sustain the reputation of the place as a thriving and progressive city than he. He is always to be found among the leaders in charitable and public enterprises, but does not confine his charities entirely to Vicksburg, as the poor of other cities can testify. He has never sought any office at the hands of his fellow-citizens, and his time is fully occupied with his hotel and other interests. He was married in 1877 to Miss Katie Botto, a native of Vicksburg, but of Italian and Irish parentage. Mr. and Mrs. Piazzo are the parents of the following children: Effizia, Mary, Louise, Katie and Vincent, Jr. The entire family are members of the Catholic church, of Vicksburg. Mr. Piazzo is a son of A. Piazzo, who was a wine manufacturer and merchant of his native land, in connection with which he carried on the grocery business, although he made a specialty of handling fine wine. He died about 1854, leaving the following children fatherless: John P., who resides in his native land; Nathaniel, who is engaged in the saddlery and carriage business in Vicksburg; Joseph, a farmer at Crystal Springs, Miss.; Frank and Louis, grocers of this city, and Mary, who is in Italy, and the subject of this sketch.

M. Pickett, Redmondville, has for many years been identified with the history of Yazoo county, and the following space will be devoted to a brief sketch of his personal career. He was born in Sicily Island, La., November 29, 1812, and is the youngest in a family of nine children. His parents, William and Mary (King) Pickett, were natives of South Carolina. The family is descended from English ancestors, who emigrated to America and settled in Virginia. The father came with his family to Mississippi in 1807, making the journey by a flatboat down the Tennessee and Mississippi rivers to Franklin county; there he and his wife spent the remainder of their days with the exception of a few years passed in Sicily Island, La. Mr. Pickett received his early education in the primitive log schoolhouse with a dirt floor and slab seats. At the age of fourteen years he was sent to Franklin, Tenn., and afterward to Danville, Ky., and finished his education at the University of Virginia. He then took up agriculture in Franklin county, Miss., which he continued until 1839. On Christmas eve of that year he arrived on the plantation which he has made his home since that time; it then covered nine hundred acres, the greater portion of which he opened to cultivation; he added to the first purchase until he owned at one time seven thousand acres. At the beginning of the Civil war he owned one hundred and ninety-six slaves, and livestock enough to carry on his farm. He raised meat and provisions for two hundred and twenty-five people, and milked as many as sixty-four cows. The plantation was one of the best improved in the county, and was carried on in the most systematic and approved manner. Eight hundred and thirty bales of cotton were produced annually, and fifteen thousand bushels of corn. Owing to ill health, Mr. Pickett was unable to enter the Confederate service. He now owns about twenty-five hundred acres of land. He was married at Jackson, Miss., in 1844, to Miss Jane E. Clark, a daughter of Gen. William and Louisa (Lanier) Clark. Mrs. Pickett was born in Pitt county, N. C. Two sons were born of this union, both of whom died in infancy. Mrs. Pickett was taken from this life in December, 1879. Ten years later, in the month of December, Mr. Pickett was again united in marriage to Miss Harriet Amanda Rucker, a daughter of Col. John W. Rucker, of Tennessee. He has always taken an active interest in the politics of his county. He is a member of the Christian church, while his wife belongs to the Baptist church. They are both people of unusual attainments, and of refined, cultivated tastes. Mr. Pickett is a widely traveled man, having visited almost every portion of the United States. He has witnessed the development of the South from the destruction of the war to its present advanced position, and takes a just pride in the courage of the Southern spirit.

Dr. James Pipes, a planter of Natchez, and a descendant of one of the pioneer families of Adams county, where his birth occurred on Sandy creek in 1835, is a son of Lewis and Mary (Holmes) Pipes, both born in Adams county, the father in 1800 and the mother in 1801. The parents were married in 1821, settled in the woods on Sandy creek, and opened a large farm on which they lived until 1858, when they removed near Natchez on St. Catherine's creek on Oak Ridge plantation, where his death occurred in 1869. His wife died in 1882. She was a member of the Methodist church for many years. Mr. Pipes was a self-made man, started with nothing, and became very wealthy although like others he lost heavily during the war. At one time he owned several valuable plantations, viz.: The home plantation, Franklin, Pinelog, Smithland, Anchorage and Pine Ridge, the latter his birthplace. He raised on an average fifteen hundred bales of cotton per year for a few years prior to the war, and was a man of industry and economy. At one time he was a member of the board of supervisors. Of his father, John L. Pipes, it is not known whether he was a native of Adams county or not, but at least he was one of the pioneers. He lived and died on Pine Ridge plantation, and was also a prominent planter. He was of Scotch-Irish origin. He reared a family of three sons and three daughters: David, Levi, John L., Jane, Mary and Eliza, all now deceased. Grandfather John Holmes was also an early settler here, if he was not born in this county. He married a Miss Ford, and was a wealthy and prosperous planter. He was the father of ten sons and seven daughters, of whom our subject's mother was the last to die. Dr. James Pipes was the ninth of twelve children—six sons and six daughters—and he and his youngest brother, Lewis, are the only ones now living. Three brothers were in the army: Hon. Charley was first in the Jefferson Davis legion, in the Virginia army, afterward lieutenant of artillery in Sander's battery in Mississippi, etc. He became a wealthy planter, a successful lawyer of Vidalia, and served about four years as sheriff and taxcollector of Concordia parish, holding that office at his death. He was at one time a member of the Mississippi legislature, and was a popular and successful official. He was educated at Oakland college and at the University of Virginia. Lewis, who is now a well-to-do planter of Natchez, was educated at Centenary college and at the University of Virginia. During the war he served in Breckinridge's guards in the Tennessee army. Dr. James Pipes was also educated at Centenary college and the University of Virginia, and in 1858 graduated from the medical department of the University of Tennessee, but never devoted much of his time to his profession, preferring the life of a planter instead. He resided on his plantation and operated it extensively and very successfully until recently, when he removed to Natchez on account of the ill health of his wife, who is an invalid. He owns a fine plantation consisting of one thousand seven hundred and forty acres in Warren county, and a residence in Natchez, principally the result of his own good management. He is a member of the Knights of Honor, Bluff City lodge No. 1145, and both he and wife are members of the Episcopal church. He was married in 1869 to Miss Mary Wright, a native of Washington, Miss., born in 1839, and educated in that city. They have no children. Mrs. Pipe's parents were natives of Adams county, where they spent all their days. Mr. Wright was a successful planter of Washington, and died in 1841. His wife died in July, 1889. She was a daughter of Dr. Daniel Rawlings, who, after marriage, came from Maryland to Adams county at a very early period.

He was a man of more than ordinary intelligence, was a frequent contributor to various journals, and was a prominent physician and planter. He was quite well off. In June, 1861, Dr. Pipes joined the Adams troop as sergeant, and served all through the war in the Virginia army, fighting first at first Bull Run, then Chancellorsville, Antietam, Gettysburg, seven days' fight around Richmond, and many others in Virginia. Just before Lee's surrender he was sent with Gen. Wade Hampton into North Carolina, and fought at Bentonville. He was with his regiment at every roll call, and was slightly wounded at Brandy station. He surrendered with General Johnston, and then returned home.

John C. Pitchford, planter and merchant, Shoccoe, Miss., was born in Warren county, N. C., on the 26th of January, 1834, and was the eldest of fourteen children born to the union of Thomas J. and Matilda H. (Cheek) Pitchford, natives of the Old North state also. The father was quite a noted physician in his native state, and was also a prominent politician, serving as state senator for a number of years before the war. He died in 1883, and the mother in 1881. The paternal grandparents of our subject, Matthew and Elizabeth Pitchford, were natives of North Carolina, as were also his maternal grandparents, Robert T. and Mary A. Cheek. The Pitchford family is of Scotch-Irish origin. John C. Pitchford was educated in the private schools of North Carolina principally, attending school at Warrenton until seventeen years of age, and then entered the Baptist college at Wake Forest, where he graduated in 1855, taking first honors. He subsequently taught school, and continued this until 1861, when he began planting, and this has been his occupation since. He is the owner of one thousand two hundred acres of land, with four hundred acres under the plow, and in connection he is also engaged in merchandising, carrying a stock of goods valued at $600. Mr. Pitchford has made all his property by his own exertions, and is honored and respected by all who are intimately acquainted with him. Miss Harriet E. Day, who became his wife in 1861, was born in North Carolina, and was the daughter of W. H. and Mary B. Day, natives also of that state. The ten children born to Mr. and Mrs. Pitchford are named in the order of their births as follows: Robert L., Sterling, Lucy M., John C., Thomas J., William D., Annie L., Landon C. and Marshall N. Mr. Pitchford's sympathies were with the South during the Civil war, and in 1862 he enlisted in the Madison artillery, with which he remained until cessation of hostilities. He was in the following battles: Mine Run, Bristoe Station, Wilderness, Spottsylvania, Hanover Junction, Cold Harbor, Appomattox Courthouse, and all the battles around Petersburg. He was dangerously wounded at the battle of Cold harbor, being struck three times in ten minutes, and was disabled for three months. In politics he is a democrat. He holds the offices of justice of the peace and postmaster, is public-spirited, and is a liberal contributor to all laudable enterprises such as schools, churches, etc. He has been unusually successful, and what he has accumulated in the way of this world's goods is the result of his own unaided efforts.

George Planchet, Bay St. Louis, Miss., was born at the Logis de Romefort, department de la Charente, France, May 28, 1840, and is a son of George Planchet, who did a large agricultural business. He was educated in his native land, at the college of La Rochefoucauld. In 1859 he went to Angouleme city, and clerked there in a drygoods store until about the middle of the year 1860, and then went to Paris, where he also clerked in the same line of business until 1862. During this time he became familiar with the different lines of goods handled in the business, and went out as a traveling salesman. He was thus employed until 1870. During that year he entered the corps of the Mobilises, in the French army, and went through the Franco-Prussian war, ending his service in March, 1871. In October of the same year he sailed for America, landing at New Orleans

December 24, 1871. He secured a situation in a drygoods store, which he held until May, 1872. In July of that year he came to Bay St. Louis, and established himself in the drygoods business. His long years of experience in the employ of other men and in his own business have been of incalculable use to him. He is a complete master of the details of the trade, and by close attention and industry he has accumulated a competency. He is treasurer of the St. Joseph society, of the Catholic Knights of America, branch 486, and of the People's Building and Loan association of Bay St. Louis, and in all these positions he displays that excellent judgment and wise management that have characterized his private dealings. Mr. Planchet was married to Miss Louise Chiona, and they have had born to them four children. Besides his commercial interests he owns a considerable amount of property, and is in very comfortable circumstances.

Poitevent & Favre. One of the most gratifying examples of business expansion presented by the history of Hancock county, Miss., is that of the corporation known as the Poitevent & Favre Lumber company of Pearlington, Miss. It was established on a small scale in 1866, by the above mentioned gentlemen, and owing to their excellent business qualification it has become the largest plant of the South. They do a business of immense proportions, the annual product of their establishment amounting to forty million feet; their lumber being principally of pine, cypress and mahogany. They own nine forty-to-fifty-ton schooners, six large schooners and brigs, which ply between Mexico, Buenos Ayres, and other foreign ports; also one light-draught stern-wheel boat, running from Jackson, Miss., to New Orleans, employed in carrying cotton, and four tugboats of ten to seventy-five tons each. Their mill premises are equipped with an elaborate outfit of every description of machinery adapted to the requirements of their business, including a large amount of valuable special machinery; the mill is kept constantly running to its full capacity, and gives employment to about one hundred and fifty workmen, one hundred of whom are employed on their schooners and brigs, and the rest as lumbermen and in the sawmill. Their mill is a two-story structure, 300x82 feet; has brick floors, corrugated galvanized iron siding, slate roof; boiler shed, 65x75 feet, with slate roof; twelve steel boilers, forty-two inches in diameter and thirty feet long, and four flues. The mill proper cost $150,000, not including their finely equipped planing-mill, dry houses, wharves, etc. They own about ninety-five thousand acres of good timber land in Hancock county, Miss., and St. Tammany parish, La., which keeps their mill constantly supplied with the finest timber. They were the originators of the East Louisiana railroad, which they still own, but it is run under another corporation. Thirty additional miles of railroad were built to tap the Northeast railroad, and their road is now out of debt and paying a large profit. It was built with money made from the sawmill and vessels owned by Poitevent & Favre, who have never had occasion to regret the investment of their money for this purpose. Their trains run immediately from their mill to the city of New Orleans, there being also a daily train from Covington to that place. They keep in constant use eleven coaches, two baggage cars, four fast freight cars, eight ordinary freight cars, sixteen long cars of forty thousand pounds' capacity, three passenger and two freight engines, all of which are equipped with power brakes. These cars were built in New Orleans and are models in their way, four of the passenger cars being especially handsome. This road is one of the finest in the South, is largely patronized and has proven a very paying enterprise. In addition to this they are the proprietors of three good retail stores, two being at Pearlington, and one on the line of their railroad at Florenville. John Poitevent, the senior member of the firm, was born in Mississippi in 1840 to William J. and Mary A. (Russ) Poitevent, natives of North Carolina, the father being a descendant of the French

Huguenots. The paternal grandfather, John Poitevent, and the maternal grandfather, Samuel Ross, were both natives of the Old North state. William J. Poitevent came to Mississippi in 1835, and located in Hancock county, on the Pearl river. He was a steamboat and sawmill man, and died in his adopted county in 1890, his wife being also deceased. Of a family of eight children born to them, seven are now living—four sons and three daughters: June, John, Adolph, Samuel, Mrs. Nicholson, Mrs. McAvoy, of St. Tammany parish, La., and Mrs. Lola Carter, wife of the clerk of the court of Panola county, Miss. Mr. Poitevent was reared in the county of his birth, and was partially educated in New Orleans. In 1862 he enlisted in the Commodore Holland navy, and served until New Orleans was taken by Butler, when he was sent to Norfolk, Va., thence to Mobile, Ala., at which place he remained one year. He then entered the trans-Mississippi department under Gen. Dick Taylor, remaining with him until the close of the war. He was acting master in the navy, and was wounded at Fort Derusa by a gunshot, receiving several flesh wounds. After the close of hostilities he engaged in sawmilling, with the above mentioned results. He has had long experience in this business, and being a gentleman of superior executive ability the business has flourished under his skillful and experienced supervision. He takes a deep and abiding interest in everything that concerns the welfare of Hancock county, and it may be justly said that no enterprise in this section has added more to its importance as a manufacturing center than has the Poitevent & Favre Lumber company. He was married in 1866 to Miss Toomer, by whom he has two children, Mary and William. His second union was celebrated in 1877, Miss Mary Hansbrough becoming his wife, and the mother of his six children: Emily, John, Eads, June, Callie and Helouise. Mr. Poitevent is a member of the Knights of Honor.

G. W. Pollock is engaged in the sawmilling business, but also devotes much attention to planting, his home plantation being situated about four miles southeast of Brandon, Miss. He was born in the state in which he is now residing, on the 7th of August, 1861, and in Kemper county he was reared and educated, being an attendant of the public schools. He became familiar with the details of planting and milling while growing up, for his father followed these callings, and like the majority of sons, he followed in his father's footsteps. His plantation was admirably tilled, devoted to the raising of cotton and corn principally, and on this he has erected a fine sawmill, which brings him in a handsome sum annually, for the work which he does is strictly first class. He is pleasant, courteous, yet unassuming in manners, and being full of energy, pluck and perseverance, his future is bright with promise. He was married in 1889 to Miss Florence Robinson, a native of Mississippi. His father, L. B. Pollock, is a Mississippian by birth, born about 1836, and still devotes his attention to planting and milling. He is a member of the A. F. & A. M., the Farmers' Alliance, and is a public-spirited and whole-souled gentleman. In 1860 he was married to Miss Josephine Hall, by whom he became the father of ten children—seven sons and three daughters. He and his wife are residents of Kemper county.

W. A. Pollock, banker at Greenville, Washington county, Miss., was born in Jefferson county, Va., in 1845. He was the eldest in a family of three children born to Addison G. and Martha E. (Graham) Pollock, both of whom were natives also of the Old Dominion. W. A. Pollock was educated at Oxford, Ohio, and at the age of twenty years, or in 1866, he engaged in business at Vicksburg as a cotton factor, continuing there for four years. In 1869 he came to Greenville, was engaged with the Levee board for one year, and during that time organized the first bank of the place. After a year or two he sold out, and in 1876 was the main mover in organizing the Bank of Greenville, of which he has been president ever since. In

1886 he organized the Greenville Compress and Warehouse company, and is president of this also. In 1877 he erected his fine residence in Greenville, and this not only exceeds any in the town, but is one of the finest buildings in the state. It has all the modern improvements, and is a model of beauty, comfort and convenience. Mr. Pollock is most extensively engaged in planting, and is the owner of Lake Vista plantation, consisting of twenty-five hundred acres, with thirteen hundred acres under cultivation, and one of the best improved on the delta. He also owns Auburn plantation, in Washington county, consisting of five hundred acres, with three hundred and fifty acres improved; and Geneva plantation of fifteen hundred acres, with one-half under cultivation. He has made many and vast improvements on all. Mr. Pollock was married in 1870 to Miss Olive H. Bowen, a native of the Buckeye state, and a representative of a prominent family of that state. To this union have been born two children: Olive and Elise. Mr. and Mrs. Pollock are members of the Episcopal church. Mr. Pollock has been most active in promoting the welfare of Washington county, and since his residence here has been the moving spirit in almost every commercial enterprise. He has made a large fortune here, and contributes bounteously to all enterprises of a public nature. No man in the delta is held in higher estimation than Mr. Pollock, who is ever engaged in some good work for the people, and whose open-heartedness and generosity are fully appreciated by all. He is most pleasant and courteous in his manners, and has a host of warm friends.

Seth P. Pool is a well-to-do planter of Clay county, Miss., and has been a resident of the state since 1837. He was born in North Carolina December 26, 1818, to Philip and Anna (Winfrey) Pool of North Carolina, in which state they were born, reared, educated and married. Of fourteen children born to them only two are now living: Seth P. and Carrie A., wife of Mr. Beaver, a well-to-do and prosperous planter of Person county, N. C. Seth P. Pool is a strictly self-made man, for when he started out in life for himself it was at about the age of fifteen years, prior to which his educational advantages had not been of the best, and he never went to school more than six months all told. After coming to Mississippi he began working at the carpenter's trade but later turned his attention principally to planting and is now the most extensive landholder in the county, the principal part of his land lying near West Point. He also owns the Central hotel, three first-class storehouses and a dwellinghouse in West Point. The wealth that he has so honorably gained is not selfishly hoarded, but is used generously in the support of worthy causes, and although he early learned to know the value of a dollar he does not count the cost when a friend is to be aided or in the purchase of anything that may add to the comfort and happiness of himself and wife. On the 14th of April, 1842, he was married to Miss Martha J. Hullomon, in what was then Lowndes, but is now Clay county, but their union has not been blessed by the birth of any children. Out of the kindness of their hearts they gave a home to Alice Hulsey, an orphan, and she is now the wife of Lemuel Crump. Mr. Pool and his wife are members of the Presbyterian church, and he has held the office of supervisor of the county six years, first while it was Lowndes county, and was the first supervisor after it was organized as Clay county. He made a faithful and capable official, and in every relation of life has discharged his duties in a manner becoming an upright Christian gentleman.

John and Jacob Pope removed to Marion county, Miss., about the year 1812. All the older members of the family have passed away, but there is a large and prominent connection scattered throughout the Southern states. John Pope married Elizabeth Regan, and they had born to them seven children: Harriet became Mrs. Bridges, and was afterward married to John Erwin; Nancy S. married Felix Ford, he died and she married Samuel G. Foxworth;

Henry P. and Augustus L.; William H. started to California in 1849 and died before he had reached the end of his journey; Delilah married Hugh Ervin; Sophronia married Benjamin Williams. Henry P. Pope, son of John Pope, removed to Hinds county, Miss., where he made a fortune planting; later on he went to Bossier parish, La., and afterward to Texas, where he died in 1862, leaving a family of four children.

Jacob Pope married Sarah Lee and they reared a family of eight children: James, Benjamin, Sampson, Jacob, Richard, Mary A., who married a Mr. Morgan, and after his death was united in marriage to Judge Ebenezer Ford; Clarissa, wife of Benjamin B. Barnes, and Sarah, who married Solomon Ford, and after his death was married a second time, to Watson Ford. Sampson Pope, son of Jacob Pope, married Esther Barnes. They became the parents of sixteen children, thirteen of whom grew to maturity: William, Mary, Jacob, Dickerson, Joseph, Harris, Sarah, Henry, James, Amanda, Allen, Willis, Salonia, Cordelia, Albert, and one who died in infancy.

Port Gibson Female college. This admirable institution of learning was established on the 3d of April, 1844, at which time a meeting of the board of trustees agreed that Mr. and Mrs. Harvie should open the school on Monday the 15th, both for boarding and day pupils. It is later recorded that the articles of agreement of the association were entered into September 11, 1843, and were signed by J. H. Maury, Benjamin G. Humphreys, Elias Bridgers, Joseph Devenport, John S. Chambliss, Peter C. Chambliss, D. G. Humphreys, D. S. Humphreys, E. S. Jefferies, N. Jefferies, Samuel Cobun, H. T. Ellett and G. N. Humphreys. The college was founded in 1844, and in 1854 was incorporated, and in 1869 was deeded to the Mississippi annual conference of the Methodist Episcopal Church South. The main building was completed and opened for pupils in 1844, and the annex has been built since the war. The present board of trustees are as follows: Hon. G. W. Humphreys, J. H. Gordon, John Burnett, Hon. E. S. Drake, G. J. Bahin, Hon. J. Millsaps, Henry Key, H. G. Millsaps, Rev. J. A. B. Jones, Rev. B. F. Jones, Hon. J. McMartin and Rev. J. A. Ellis. The present president is Miss M. E. Compton, and the students number ninety. The curriculum embraces the following departments: The primary and preparatory, in which the common branches are taught; the collegiate, which is divided into the schools of mathematics, natural science, moral science, history and the languages, and the musical department, in which special attention is paid to voice culture. The terms of the institution are within the reach of all, and, as the best of instructors are employed, the establishment is liberally patronized. The buildings can not be surpassed for convenience of arrangement. The rooms and halls are well ventilated, and the grounds, being extensive and well shaded, are well adapted to the health, comfort and improvement of the pupils.

Mrs. Celestia A. Porter, a resident of Coahoma county, Miss., and a lady of marked business ability, was originally from Cobb county, Ga., her birth occurring in that state on the 22d of November, 1824. She was the eldest of three children born to the union of Thomas R. and Eliza (Legg) Johnson, both natives of Georgia. The father was a soldier in the Mexican war, was also a participant in the Florida war, and received his final summons about that time. The mother moved to Mississippi in 1862 and died here in 1888. The maternal grandparents were Nathaniel and Lucy (Hampton) Legg, and the grandmother was a sister of Gen. Wade Hampton, the noted politician of Georgia. Mrs. Porter was reared in Georgia, Alabama and Mississippi, and received her education in the private schools of those states, having moderately good educational advantages. She came to Mississippi in 1848, and was here married on Feburary 18, 1851, to Mr. Edward D. Porter, a native of Ohio who came to Mississippi in 1837. Mr. Porter was in the Civil war, and held the rank of captain of his company until cessation of hostilities. He figured very prominently in all the fighting in Mississippi, and was an intrepid officer and a valiant soldier. His death occurred in 1871. Mrs. Porter is the owner of three hundred acres of land, and has one hundred and seventy-five acres under cultivation. She is a lady of more than ordinary business ability, and displays excellent judgment and discretion in the management of her fine farm, gathering from seventy-five to one hundred bales of cotton from the same, annually. The farm, which is situated on the Sunflower river, five miles south of Clarksdale, is in a good state of cultivation, and everything indicates industry and prosperity. Mrs. Porter is a member of the Methodist church and is a devout Christian.

J. C. Porter, of Lauderdale Station, Miss., was born on the 15th of October, 1815, in Union district, South Carolina, being the fourth of a family of seven children born to Elisha P. and Hollie (Cooper) Porter, both of whom were born in South Carolina, the descendants of Revolutionary parents. They grew up and were married in the state of their birth, residing there for about thirty years, finally emigrating to Mississippi early in the forties, settling at Houston, in Chickasaw county. They purchased land near that town, and the father followed planting throughout the remainder of his days, becoming quite well to do. He was the owner of many slaves as well as a large amount of real estate, and became well and favorably known throughout his adopted county. He was an excellent citizen and neighbor, and he and his wife were worthy Christians. They died at their home in Chickasaw county in 1873 and 1865 respectively. Only two of their family are now living, Captain J. C., and Mary S., wife of Isaac Paulk, of Chickasaw county. Capt. J. C. Porter began planting for himself at the age of twenty-one years, but after some time removed from his native state to Alabama, and was married in Sumter county of that state in 1839 to Miss Nancy G. Lavender, by whom he became the father of fourteen children—six sons and eight daughters, eight of whom are living: Elmira J., wife of W. B. Clark; Elizabeth, wife of T. P. Porter, deceased; Eugenie, wife of Robert Taylor; Ellen B., widow of Dr. J. R. Webb; Hollie, wife of Robert Hunter; Alice, wife of D. L. Barr; Lemuel, a farmer and miller of Kemper county; and Isaac D., a merchant of Lauderdale. Captain Porter removed from Alabama to Mississippi in 1846, and took up his abode in Chickasaw county, where he was engaged in planting for six years, after which he returned to Alabama and there remained for seven years. At the end of this time he returned to Mississippi, and after spending some time in Kemper county, he came to the place where he is now living, at Lauderdale Station, in 1865. He successfully carried on merchandising at this point for twenty years, and succeeded in securing a large patronage throughout the country, doing an annual business of $30,000 to $60,000. He retired from the active duties of life in 1886, owing to defective eyesight, and has since lived in retirement. He has been a member of the board of county supervisors, was justice of the peace of Lauderdale county for a number of years, and for four years was mayor of Lauderdale Station. His wife died at her home in this county, in 1884, a consistent member of the Christian church, but Captain Porter has been a member of the Protestant Methodist church for many years, and has for the past forty years been a member of the A. F. & A. M. He is the owner of six thousand acres of land in Kemper county, seven hundred acres in Sumter county, Ala., one hundred acres in Lauderdale county, and a handsome residence and business property in Lauderdale; also five tenement houses. The Captain has been very energetic and enterprising, and has proven himself a man of shrewd business tactics, and sound and practical views. He is well known throughout the county, is the soul of honor in the conduct of his business, and has numerous warm friends. His property has been earned by hard and persistent endeavor, but he has been very liberal in the use of his means, and worthy enterprises find in him a hearty supporter. The Porters are noted for their generosity, warm-heartedness and upright principles, and being among the prominent citizens of Lauderdale county they have always moved in the highest social circles.

Dr. James G. Pou, a physician and merchant of Courtland, Miss., who, by his own ability, has become prominent in his different callings, owes his nativity to Panola county, Miss., born January 24, 1849. His father, Henry P. Pou, was a native of the Palmetto state, was married there to Miss G. M. Chapman, also a native of that state, and subsequently, or in 1846, immigrated to Panola county, where he was engaged in tilling the soil. He was a soldier in the Creek Indian war, and for a few months also served in the Civil war. He is now seventy-six years of age and is still engaged in his life's calling. Of the eight children born to his marriage, Dr. James G. was the fifth in order of birth. The latter was educated in the public schools of Panola county, and the war coming on at a time when he should have been in school, prevented his getting more than an ordinary English education. However, by close application to the duties of life, he has gleaned a great deal of valuable knowledge since. He graduated in medicine from Tulane university, New Orleans, La., in 1871, and immediately entered upon the practice of his profession in the place of his birth and boyhood, where he has continued successfully since. He is a clever and scientific practitioner, and is known all over the county. In 1880 he established a drug business in Courtland, and conducted the same under the firm name of J. G. Pou until 1890, when J. M. Fowler purchased one half interest in the business, and it is now conducted under the firm title of J. G. Pou & Co. They do a good business and are thoroughgoing, enterprising men. Dr. Pou was married in 1873 to Miss Mary E. Nelms, a native of Mississippi, and a daughter of Samuel H. and Mary (Caldwell) Nelms, natives of Alabama and Tennessee, respectively. Four children have been born to Dr. and Mrs. Pou: Mary Blanche, James Virgil, Arrah Viola and Theodora Alice, all at home. Dr. Pou started out to fight life's battles for himself, with limited means, and, by his success as a practitioner and his excellent business ability, has become the owner of five hundred acres of land, one hundred acres of which are under cultivation, his place of business and his fine home being in Courtland. He is a man of few words and is very attentive to business and his profession.

Absalom C. Powell, planter and dealer in livestock, Mount Carmel, Miss., is a well-known resident of Covington county. He was born in Darlington district, S. C., in 1811, the third of a family of seven children, named as follows: Sallie, who married David Dalrymple; Mary, wife of Kindred Griffith; Absalom C.; Martha; Margaret; Kate, wife of Benjamin Diggs, and John. The parents, James and Melissa (Stewart) Powell, were natives of Darlington district, S. C. The father was born in 1780, and was a son of John Powell, a native of North Carolina, and a soldier of the Revolutionary war. He was born in 1752, and died in 1834. He was a planter by occupation. James Powell was a soldier in the War of 1812. The subject of this sketch removed to Covington county in 1835, and settled within one mile of the plantation which he occupies. He was married in 1840 to Miss Angeline Lott, and of this union there have been born ten children, seven of whom are still living: Robert, Nancy, (wife of Benjamin Eastland), John, Katie (wife of Alexander Leonard), Thomas (deceased), William, Joseph, Melissa (deceased), Morgan and Howard (deceased). Mr. Powell had two sons in the Civil war, but both lived through the conflict. He belongs to no church, nor to any secret societies. He is a man of the highest character and a loyal citizen. Before the war he had thirty-three slaves, and like many of the Southern people lost heavily by the war. He has placed his land under cultivation, and it is well stocked with good grades of animals.

The name of Isaac T. Powell is synonymous in Prentiss county with successful agriculture, for he has been one of its successful planters for many years. He was born in Hardeman county, Tenn., in 1839, and is the son of William and Sarah (Ingram) Powell, the father a native of South Carolina, born in 1800, and the mother of the same state, born in 1812. William Powell was reared to farm life, and after receiving the usual schooling of his day, started out to make his own way in life. He was married in his native state to Miss Ingram, who is a descendant of one of the prominent families of South Carolina, and soon after moved to Tennessee, where their children were born and reared. The children were named in the order of their birth as follows: John R., who died before the war; Nancy, Mrs. Sanders, also died before the war; Needham J., in Texas; Alice, Mrs. Holmes, is now deceased; Amanda, Mrs. Crawford, now deceased; Louisa, Mrs. Brint, now deceased; William was taken prisoner during the war confined at Alton, Ill., and there died; he left three children: Richard H. resides near the old homestead in Tennessee; Isaac T., our subject; Mary, Mrs. Moore, died in Arkansas, and James was killed at the battle of Cross Roads, Lee county, Miss. The parents died in Hardeman county, Tenn., near Cranesville, in 1863, nearly at the same time, not a day between their deaths. The father was an honest, industrious citizen, was an old-line whig in politics, and was justice of the peace for a number of years. He and wife reared all their children. The paternal grandfather of our subject served in the War of 1812. Isaac T. Powell grew to manhood in Hardeman county, Tenn., secured good educational advantages, and at the age of twenty-one years enlisted in the Middleton legions, and was attached to the Ninth Tennessee infantry, commanded by Gen. Douglas. Mr. Powell enlisted as a private, and later was promoted to the rank of orderly sergeant. He participated in the battle of Corinth, and was all through the county where he now lives. He was at Coldwater, Shiloh and the fight around Jackson, Tenn. He was never wounded or taken prisoner, and was paroled at Corinth, Miss., in 1865. After the war he followed the occupation of his father, farming, and this has continued to be his chosen industry since. He was married, in 1865, to Miss Mattie Donaldson, daughter of John B. and Sarah (Fulghur) Donaldson, natives of Tennessee. Mr. and Mrs. Donaldson moved to Mississippi before the war, and both are now deceased, the mother dying before and the father after that eventful period. They had one son, Ben F., in the Confederate army. To Mr. and Mrs. Powell were born four interesting children, three of whom are living: Anna L., Sarah (died in 1883), Henry and John. The children are all at home. Mr. Powell is quite an extensive farmer, and has about twelve thousand acres of what is called the black land. He has of this about one hundred and fourteen acres under cultivation. He and Mrs. Powell hold membership in the Baptist church. He is a Master Mason, a member of Booneville lodge No. 305, and is also a member of the Knights of Honor. He is an active member of the democratic party. He is a selfmade man, having accumulated all his property by his own energy and enterprise, and has been a resident of this county since the war.

Capt. John Powell, a prominent commission merchant of New Orleans, and president of the Merchants' bank, also the Grenada Compress and Oil company at Grenada, where he has his residence, was born in Nottoway county, Va., in 1825, and is the son of Thomas W. and Martha Anderson (Leigh) Powell, natives of Nottoway and Amelia counties, Va., respectively. The parents were married in the latter county, and there Mr. Powell died in 1830, at the age of forty-five, being clerk of the county at the time. He also engaged in merchandising and was a prominent and successful business man. Mrs. Powell moved to northern Alabama in 1831, and five years later to Mississippi. Her death occurred in Yalobusha county in 1865, at the age of seventy-two years. She was the daughter of Rev. Zachery Leigh, a native of the Old Dominion, a planter, and a Baptist minister of considerable prominence. He was captain of a cavalry company under General Washington during the Revolutionary war. To Mr. and Mrs. Powell were born eight children—three sons and five daughters—only two besides our subject now living—two sisters who reside in Yalobusha county. One brother, Thomas, served in the Confederate army, cavalry, and died in Grenada, of yellow fever, in 1878. He was a planter by occupation. Another brother, Dr. William, was a prominent physician, and died in Grenada county in 1890. Capt. John Powell was educated at Grenada and in the languages at Preston, Miss. When twenty years of age he began for himself as a clerk in Troy, then Yalobusha county, and in 1855 the mercantile firm of Conley & Powell was formed at Grenada. Two years later they were burned out, and after this Mr. Powell served for about two years as station agent for the Mississippi Central railroad company. In 1860 he was elected to fill an unexpired term as sheriff of Yalobusha county, and was reëlected at the next general election, serving about two and a half years in all, but when the war broke out he joined company H, Fifteenth Mississippi infantry, and operated in east Tennessee. He was in the battles of Rock Castle, Fishing Creek, etc., and after about six months came home to collect the taxes of his county, that being a part of his official duties as sheriff. Early in 1862 he organized a company (H), which he commanded, and joined the Forty-second Mississippi infantry. He served in the Virginia army and fought at Cold Harbor, Hagerstown, and many other places. In June, 1864, he was severely wounded in the thigh at Drewrey's Bluff, was disabled from further service, and from this wound he has never fully recovered. He spent some time in the hospital in Richmond and then came home. When he had sufficiently recovered he was employed as a traveling agent for different commission houses of New Orleans for five years, and in 1875 he founded the cotton commission house of Chaffe, Hamilton & Powell, of New Orleans, which was afterward Chaffe & Powell, and now Chaffe, Powell & West, one of the best known commission houses of the city. To this Captain Powell devotes most of his time, and his presence is required in New Orleans. In 1865 he was made treasurer of the Mississippi Central Railroad company, but at the end of about sixteen months was compelled to resign on account of his disability and wound. He placed himself in the hands of the celebrated surgeons, Drs. Warren Strong and Thomas G. Richardson, of New Orleans, and after a severe operation, in which they removed a portion of the thigh bone, he found much relief. Captain Powell has extensive planting interests in the Yazoo delta, and one plantation in Tallahatchie county furnishes employment for about one hundred negroes. The Captain started in life a poor boy, and lost what property he had accumulated prior to the war, being obliged, like many others, to start anew. For many years he has been a member of the Grenada lodge, A. F. & A. M., No. 31. Although quiet and unpretentious, Captain Powell is one of Grenada county's most esteemed and worthy citizens. He is connected with its most worthy enterprises, both financially and officially, and possesses, in more than ordinary degree, the natural attributes essential to a successful public as well as private career. He is a thoroughgoing and live business man, and is practically a selfmade man in a business point of view. In 1875 he was married to Miss Winnie, daughter of Dr. Willis M. and Sarah (Wilson) Lea, and a native of Mississippi. Her parents were born near Leesburg, N. C., and Danville, Va., respectively, and came to Marshall county, Miss., at a rather early date. The father was a successful physician and planter for many years, and died about 1880. He was a member of the secession convention, and had three sons killed in the Confederate army. Mrs. Lea is still living, and is seventy-eight years of age. Captain and Mrs. Powell are worthy members of the Baptist church, which he joined many years ago.

John M. Powell is one of the most successful planters of Coahoma county and one whose honesty has never been questioned. His beautiful home is a model of neatness, taste and comfort, and indicates the refined taste and culture of both Mr. Powell and his wife. Mr. Powell was born in the county in which he is now residing, February 16, 1854, being the youngest of five children born to John M. and Cordelia (Penrice) Powell, the former born in the Old North state and the latter in Tennessee. Mr. Powell came to Mississippi in 1850 and located on the plantation on which his son, John M., is now residing, and engaged in planting, in which he was very prosperous. He was one of the first contractors on the Mississippi levee, being in partnership with Jacob Thompson, who was secretary under James Buchanan. Mr. Powell was one of the most prominent men in the delta, but died in New York in 1875. His parents were Ransom and Myra (Rolen) Powell, natives of North Carolina, where they were wealthy planters. The great-grandparents were Thomas R. and Myra (Lewis) Powell, also of North Carolina. The maternal grandparents, Frank and Elizabeth (Smith) Penrice, as well, and the maternal great-grandparents, John and Amy (Herod) Smith, were North Carolinians. The Penrice family originally came from Wales and settled in Tennessee. John M. Powell was principally reared in Ohio, but received his education in Oxford, Miss., Ohio and Illinois. Upon leaving school he returned to his home in Mississippi and began merchandising and planting, the latter calling being conducted on the plantation which then belonged to his father and of which he is now the owner. He started in life with $1,000, and by a free use of brain and brawn he has made the remainder of his property by his own efforts, being now the owner of one thousand eight hundred and fifty acres of land, of which seven hundred and fifty acres are under cultivation, the most of which he has brought to its present excellent state of fertility by his own efforts. He has greatly improved his property in the way of building, and in 1890 erected his handsome residence. Everything about his place indicates that a man of thrift, energy and enterprising views has the management of affairs. He is very thorough in everything that he undertakes, takes great pride in beautifying and adorning his home, is kind and considerate in his family, and is ever thoughtful of the comfort and happiness of his mother, who makes her home with him. He was first married in 1876, to Miss Ella Smith, a native of this state and a daughter of Jesse and Lucinda (Carr) Smith, natives of Kentucky. In 1885 his wife was called from earth, leaving one child: Lou S., who is now attending school at Helena, Ark. In 1890 he took for his second wife Mrs. Minnie C. Thomas, a native of Helena, Ark., and daughter of Alexander and Mary (Estell) Clemens, the former of whom was born in Arkansas and the latter in Louisiana. To Mrs. Powell's first union a daughter, Julia Estell, was born, who is attending school in her mother's native town. Mr. Powell is a member of the Presbyterian church, while his wife and mother are Episcopalians, the latter being now in her seventy-fourth year. Mr. Powell has a sister living who is the wife of Rev. D. B. Ramsey, of Louisville, Ky. He is well educated, a good business man and, socially, is a member of the K. of P. He is deeply religious, honorable, philanthropic and public-spirited, and, as a business man, has not his superior in this section of the country. Although he is a lineal descendant of George Washington's and Gen. Dick Lewis' families, he does not boast of his ancestry, being sufficiently democratic to believe that "worth makes the man," no matter who the father may have been. His career has been such that the standard of morality among young men has become much higher in the community in which he resides, and in numerous ways he has helped to make Coahoma county a most desirable place in which to live. He is of commanding presence, tall and slender, with fair hair and complexion and handsome and intelligent gray eyes. He is very neat in dress, is very courteous and hospitable, and takes great delight in entertaining his friends. His wife ably seconds him in every worthy movement, is devoted to her family, and does all in her power to make their home a cheerful and happy one. She is quite a talented artist, and the walls of their parlors are hung with the results of her brush.

Joseph F. Powell was born in Northampton county, N. C., February 14, 1836, and is the seventh of a family of thirteen children. His father, George W. Powell, was born in Virginia in the year 1800, and spent the early part of his life there. He was a minister of the Methodist Episcopal church. In the year 1825 he removed to North Carolina, where he resided until 1840. Then he came to Mississippi, locating in Warren county. There he engaged in agricultural pursuits, which he followed until his death, in 1866. He was a man of industrious habits and accumulated considerable property. He was of Irish origin. His wife, whose maiden name was Mary Ramsey, was a native of North Carolina. Joseph F. was reared within the borders of Warren county, Miss., but his educational advantages were extremely meager. His school days did not cover a single year, but, fortunately, experience is a wise teacher, albeit a severe one, and to-day he has few equals in practical business knowledge. When about twenty-two years of age he was appointed deputy sheriff of Warren county, discharging the duties of this office for two years. He then clerked in the postoffice at Vicksburg, and was afterward in the offices of the Vicksburg & Meridian railroad at Vicksburg. He was afterward employed by the railroad company as station agent at Bolton and other points along the line. In 1866 he became a resident of Yazoo City, and for a period of thirteen years he clerked for F. Barkdale. In the meantime he made some good investments, from which he realized a handsome profit. In 1877 he embarked in the general mercantile trade and has conducted a large and growing business. He is the originator of the first cotton warehouse company that was organized in Yazoo City, of which he is the efficient president. He is a director and heavy stockholder in the Bank of Yazoo City. He is a charter member of the Lintonia Land company, which is one of the most worthy business enterprises. He is treasurer of the Yazoo Valley Telephone company, of which he is also a stockholder. He is also one of the largest stockholders of the Yazoo Commercial company and was the first president of the organization. From this brief review it will be seen that there are few business corporations to which he has not lent a helping hand, either by investment or personal supervision. He is thoroughgoing, energetic, courteous and kind of manner, and a man whom it is the pleasure of the stranger in a strange land to meet. Mr. Powell was united in marriage in 1861 to Miss Mary Redding, a native of Yazoo City, and a daughter of James Redding of South Carolina. One child was born of this marriage, John F., who is in business with his father. Mrs. Powell is a member of the Methodist Episcopal church, and her husband, while not a member of the society, is a liberal contributor to its support.

William H. Powell, who stands at the head of the legal profession in Madison county, Miss., is a native of that county, born on the 16th of November, 1856, and is the fifth of six children born to J. R. and Frances A. (Smith) Powell, natives of the Old Dominion. The father emigrated to North Carolina at an early day, thence to Mississippi in 1850 and settled in Madison county, where he has since lived as a cotton-factor and planter, meeting with fair success. He was president of the board of supervisors of Madison county for many years, and although not a politician he is an ardent democrat. He and wife are both living, he at the age of seventy-two and she at the age of sixty-eight years. William H. Powell was reared in his native county, received his education at Oxford and graduated before eighteen years of age. He had read law at home, was admitted to the bar, and before he was nineteen years of age had commenced practicing. He is a warm and hearty advocate and supporter of democracy, and although he is not an office-seeker, few men stand higher in the estimation of the people than he. Although frequently urged to run for the office of representative, senator and other positions of honor and trust, he has always respectfully declined. His life is devoted wholly to his business and his family. He has a large and successful practice in the supreme and Federal courts as well as the lower courts, and stands at the head of the bar. Believing that his clients should have his time, he is ready to prosecute their claims to the extent of his ability. In fact he is a man of business and one who believes that whatever is worth doing at all is worth doing well. He has occupied the same office since practicing and has built up his now large practice in the place of his birth, thus forcibly illustrating the confidence that the people have in him. He is an excellent business man, is the owner of three thousand five hundred acres of land and has a fine residence in Canton. He is a stockholder in the Mississippi state bank and of the Canton Cotton Compress and Warehouse company. Mr. Powell was married in 1881 to Miss Sallie Cage, a native of Canton, Miss., and the daughter of Dr. A. H. Cage, who was born in Kentucky. Her father was an able physician and died during the yellow-fever epidemic of 1878. Mr. Powell has three living children by this union: Amanda, Robert and Louise. Mr. and Mrs. Powell are members of the Baptist church and he is a Knight of Pythias.

There are few citizens of Mississippi more generally or more favorably known than Col. J. L. Power, of Jackson, of which city he has been a resident since April, 1855. Colonel Power was born in Ireland in 1834, and has a lively recollection of the great agitation of 1848, and remembers having seen Daniel O'Connell, William Smith O'Brien, Thomas Francis Meagher, John Mitchell, and other prominent leaders, as they moved among and addressed the people. His father died when subject was about six years of age, and his mother, remarrying, came to the United States, leaving him to the care of relatives who were barely able to provide for themselves. For ten years of his young life his experience was an exceptionally hard one, and it is often a matter of surprise to him, as well as of gratitude, that he survived the trying ordeals of his early years. When he was not quite sixteen years of age he resolved to come to America. He traveled on foot a long distance to the city of Waterford, thence by steamer to Liverpool, where he embarked on a sailing vessel, and after a six weeks' voyage, narrowly escaping shipwreck, he arrived in New York in December, 1850. He was thinly clad and had only a few dimes in his pocket, but he was cared for, as he always has been, by a kind Providence, and the next day he was placed on a Hudson river steamer for Albany. Arriving there, he expected to work his way to Lockport, in the western part of the state, where his mother lived, but the canal was frozen and navigation closed for the winter. He then went to the railway station, found the conductor and told him his story, who told him to get aboard, and who permitted him to ride as far as Batavia. There was no railroad to Lockport in those days, and when he alighted from the train a heavy snow was falling, and his heart sank within him. Cold and hungry, without money, and seemingly without friends, the prospect seemed gloomy indeed; but a kind-hearted gentleman took in the situation and he was again provided for, and after being nourished and wrapped in buffalo robes, he was taken to Lockport in a splendid sleigh. After the subject of this sketch had resided in Lockport for a short time, he became identified with the Presbyterian Sabbath-school and church. Through the influence of his teacher he obtained employment in the office of the Lockport *Journal*, where he soon became proficient in all departments of the printing business. It so happened that a family from New Orleans were visiting Lockport in the summer of 1854, and they talked so much about Dixie and the sunny South, he resolved to go with them when they returned, and so on the 31st of August, 1854, he started for the Crescent city. Yellow fever was prevailing there and in other cities of the South, and after passing Vicksburg he was prostrated with the fever, but passed the crisis of the disease before the steamer reached New Orleans, and soon convalesced. He found steady and profitable employment, and though much attached to the Crescent city, he accepted an invitation to go to Jackson, Miss., in April, 1855, where he has since resided and has been for many years one of its most active, progressive and useful citizens. He was married in December, 1857, to Miss Jane Wilkinson, and they have raised quite a large family. When the war came on Mr. Power was engaged in the publishing business in Jackson, but on the organization of Wither's regiment of light artillery he enlisted as a private in company A. He was appointed orderly sergeant, and soon after became adjutant of the regiment. He was in the siege of Vicksburg. In 1864 he was commissioned superintendent of army records, under a joint act of congress and the states, with the rank of colonel, and hence the title by which he has since been known. He was thus engaged at Richmond when the city fell, on April 2, 1865.

On his return to Mississippi he was, for many months, without employment, but when Provisional Governor Sharkey called a convention to adopt a constitution that should conform to the changed condition of affairs, Mr. Power was offered for secretary, and was elected over three formidable competitors. His earnings from this he pooled with equal sums by two others in starting a newspaper called the Mississippi *Standard*, which was merged with the *Clarion* in 1866. It was the official journal of the state, and so continued until the beginning of the reconstruction period, when a military order transferred the printing to an office deemed loyal by the party in power. His associate for many years was Hon. Ethel Barksdale. In 1875 the firm of Power & Barksdale was elected state printer, and reëlected for five biennial terms. After the election of Mr. Barksdale to congress, the *Clarion* was merged with the *State Ledger*, in January, 1888, and Colonel Power is the business manager. But he has also the pen of a ready writer, and employs it as inclination and time admit. Colonel Power is one of the best known secretaries in the state. He was clerk of the house of representatives in 1867, secretary of the constitutional convention of 1865, reported the proceedings of the secession convention of 1861 and of the constitutional convention of 1890, and has been secretary of many of the political state conventions that have been held at the capitol. But it is as grand secretary of Masons that he is most widely known, and his name is familiar to the craft throughout the Union. He was elected to that office in 1869, and is now serving his twenty-third year. He is also secretary of the three other Masonic grand bodies. He is a past grand master of Odd Fellows, and was grand treasurer of that order for several years, and has received many special testimonials of his efficiency. He is also an active member of the Knights of Honor and Knights of Pythias; is a ruling elder in the Presbyterian church, and for twenty years was superintendent of its Sabbath-school. Colonel Power's greatest work, and the one of which he is especially proud, is in connection with the great yellow fever scourge of 1878. He received and judiciously disbursed to more than thirty stricken communities nearly $100,000, being vested by the contributors with unlimited discretion as to its use. He visited many of the afflicted towns, during and after the epidemic, and distributed relief to all, regardless of race, creed or fraternity. His work was examined and warmly commended by the grand lodge. Colonel Power's rough experience in his early youth implanted in him a disposition to help the orphan and the friendless, and hence it is that the Protestant Orphan asylum at Natchez has found in him a friend indeed. The lady managers have placed in its parlor a large portrait of him, from which is suspended a beautiful card, "The Lord will provide;" and that he has been an instrument in the Lord's hands in providing food and raiment for the fatherless is ample compensation for all that he has done in that direction. Immediately after the epidemic of 1878, and occasionally since, Colonel Power's name has been mentioned in connection with the office of governor, but he has always been too busy to give the matter a serious thought, and he has been satisfied in the consciousness that there were others more willing to seek and more able to fill that high station.

Capt. Homer C. Powers, banker, Starkville, Miss. Captain Powers' grandfather, Jacob Powers, was a native of Pennsylvania and one of the pioneers of Mahoning valley, in Ohio, where he opened up a large farm in the wilderness. He became one of its wealthy and well-known citizens, was also an extensive stocktrader, and gave each of his seven children a good start in life after educating them. He was in the War of 1812. His wife was a Virginia lady. Both died in the Buckeye state. One of their sons, John W. Powers, father of subject, was born in Beaver county, Penn., in 1812, and at a very early day removed with his parents to Ohio, where he was married to Miss Miranda Gee, a native probably of New York state. Her father, Rev. Nicholas Gee and his wife were natives of the state of New York, and were also pioneers of the Mahoning valley, Ohio, where the father became an extensive landowner. He was for many years a prominent Methodist minister and of great service to the church. Besides rearing thirteen children of his own to become well-to-do and prosperous citizens, Mr. Gee reared two adopted children, both of whom he gave good educational advantages. He lived to be about ninety-five years of age, and was a very useful man. After his marriage to Miss Gee, Mr. Powers settled in Mahoning valley and became one of the largest landowners and stockdealers in the country. He was well educated, was a man of great industry and good judgment. He excelled as a business man and was a noted financier. He reared seven children, all of whom were well educated. Capt. Homer C. Powers, the fourth in order of birth of this family, all of whom are living with the exception of one son who was killed while railroading in the West, was born in Youngstown, Ohio, in 1842, and there received his early education. At the breaking out of the war he was a pupil of the lamented President Garfield, and during the vacation of 1861 he joined the one hundred-day troops, and spent a few weeks in Kentucky. After that, he being a minor, his services were not needed and he returned home. His father, while being in favor of the war, said the war could be put down without enlisting minors (the North having so many resources), and he was not allowed to enter the service further, but instead, in the fall of 1861, he entered the Michigan university at Ann Arbor, from which he graduated in 1865. During his first year in college he was a roommate of a cousin, R. C. Powers, who afterward became a colonel in the Federal army. After the war the latter removed to Noxubee county, Miss., became one of the wealthiest planters, and was lieutenant-governor with Governor Alcorn. Upon the election of Governor Alcorn to the United States senate Colonel Powers became governor of the state. He afterward returned North, and is now a resident of Arizona. After completing his education Captain Powers' father started him in the merchandising business in the oil regions of Pennsylvania, and after a very successful career of about nine months he lost all by fire. On September 20, 1866, he was married in Cleveland, Ohio, to Miss Matilda, daughter of J. S. and Matilda (Kimbal) Tilden, natives of New York state but early settlers of Cleveland, Ohio, where Mr. Tilden was a prominent merchant and large landowner and where he still lives. Mrs. Tilden died in 1873. Mrs. Powers was born in Cleveland, Ohio, and is a consistent member of the Presbyterian church. To Mr. and Mrs. Powers were born four children, two now living. Immediately after the war Captain Powers came to Oktibbeha county, Miss., where his father had purchased a large cotton plantation in 1865, and resided on the same for five years, since which time he has resided in Starkville, although he still carries on his planting interests quite extensively. He pays the third largest tax in the county, and most of his property is the result of his own industry. During the constitutional convention of 1867 he was made reading clerk, and while holding that position a vacancy occurred in the sheriff's office of Oktibbeha county, and in January of the following year he was appointed to that office, serving ten years in succession, being elected once after the democrats came into power. He afterward served one year as deputy revenue collector of this district, and was a delegate to the national republican convention in Chicago in 1884, that nominated James G. Blaine. Captain Powers has shown his appreciation of secret organizations by becoming a member of the Masonic fraternity, Albert lodge No. 89, the I. O. O. F., Ridgely lodge No. 23, the Knights of Honor, Starkville lodge No. 783, and of the Knights of Pythias. In 1877 Captain Powers established the Starkville bank, which he controlled until 1887, when it was made a national bank, of which he has since been president, L. D. McDowell, vice president, and E. L. Terry, cashier. The capital stock is $60,000; it has declared an annual dividend of ten per cent. and now has a surplus of $6,500.

A gratifying example of what can be accomplished by determination and energy is demonstrated in the career of L. C. Prather, merchant, Baldwyn, Miss., who started out to fight life's battles with limited means, and who is to-day one of the leading business men and substantial citizens of the county. He is a native of the Palmetto state, and was the eldest of eight children, five of whom are living, born to the union of John T. and Harriet (Ramage) Prather. The paternal grandfather followed planting and smithing for a livelihood, and died while in his prime. John T. Prather was born in Maryland in 1815, but was reared in Laurens district, S. C., where he resided until 1846, when he and family moved to Mississippi, settling near Satillo, then in Itawamba (now Lee) county, where they resided until 1852. They then moved to Tippah county, located in the southeast corner, and there purchased land, which they cultivated until 1884. At that date they moved to Saltillo, Miss., where the father carried on merchandising until 1890, since which time he has retired from active pursuits. He is a stanch democrat, and while a resident of Tippah county held the office of justice of the peace for some time. He has been a cripple all his life, is a man of good judgment, and is well posted on all the leading topics of the day. He is a member of the Christian church, and his wife, who was born in 1825, and is also living, holds membership in the same. The four children, besides our subject, now living, are named as follows: Mrs. Nannie T. Hardin, resides in Tippah county, Miss.; Mrs. Ophelia Wesson, of Saltillo, Miss.; Mrs. Caroline Chisholm, of Blue Springs, Miss., and Mrs. Harriet McElroy, residing at Graham, Union county, Miss. L. C. Prather's early life was spent in Tippah county, and there he received a good practical education in the common schools. In 1867 he commenced business for himself at Baldwyn with the firm of J. D. Bills & Co., which was subsequently changed to Bills & Prather. In 1878 Mr. Prather bought out his partner, and has since been engaged in the business alone. His annual sales amount to $35,000, and he handles about six hundred bales of cotton every year. Aside from this he is also interested in farming to a considerable extent in this vicinity, and has made a success of this as he has with all other enterprises undertaken. Hosts of patrons and friends throughout this and adjoining counties will bear voluntary testimony to his honesty and uprightness, both in business and social affairs. His marriage to Miss America Allen, daughter of David Allen, a prominent citizen of the county, resulted in the birth of five sons: Walter, Brooks, Forest, LeRoy and Claude. In politics he is identified with the democratic party. He is an A. F. & A. M., and is a member of the Christian church, having been clerk in the same ever since its organization.

Francis B. Pratt, lawyer, Canton, Miss. Originally from Worcester, Mass., Mr. Pratt's birth occurred on April 19, 1841, and he was the eldest of eight children born to Ezra K. and Abigail D. (Brigham) Pratt, natives, also, of that state. The father was an agriculturist and spent his life in his native state. He was a son of Otis and Lidia (Mason) Pratt, natives of Connecticut, his father also being engaged in farming. The Pratts are of English, and the Brighams of Irish ancestry. Francis B. Pratt was reared and received a common-school education in Massachusetts. Until seventeen years of age he worked in the cottonmill, and then went to California, where he worked in the mines and cooked for a hotel. He subsequently ran a blacksmith shop and a hotel. After remaining in California for six years he succeeded in accumulating a few thousand dollars, after which he returned to Massachusetts. He resided in that state for a few years, and then, in 1866, came to Madison county, Miss., where he followed planting for five years. Then, not finding it as profitable as he wished, he abandoned it, read law, was admitted to the bar in 1870, and has practiced his profession continuously ever since. He is very successful, and is noted for his pertinacity, industry and strict fidelity to the interests of his clients. He was justice of the peace for some time, president of the board of supervisors from 1870 to 1875, was district attorney for some time, and from 1876 to 1880 he was state senator. He held the position of postmaster of Canton under President Garfield for four years, and is the present postmaster at Canton. He owns the building he occupies as his office and the postoffice. Though a republican in his political views, Mr. Pratt has won the friendship and respect of the people of Madison county, and no man is more interested in its welfare than is he. The offices given him have been filled with credit to himself and to the entire satisfaction of his constituents.

James Rhea Preston, of Jackson, Miss., the present superintendent of public instruction for that state, was born in Washington county, Va., January 22, 1853, being a son of Col. James T. and Fannie (Rhea) Preston. About the seventeenth century the Prestons removed from England, the country of their birth, to Ireland, from which they came to America. The paternal grandfather, who bore the name of John, was a resident of Walnut Grove, Va. Col. James T. Preston served in the Confederate army in the army of Virginia. His wife was of Scotch ancestry, and was born in Blountville, Tenn. They were the parents of six children: John, James R., Walter E., Robert F., Fannie R. and Francis M., all of whom are living, with the exception of Fannie and Walter. The father was a lawyer by profession, but was also engaged in tilling the soil. John, his son, is at present superintendent of the State Lunatic asylum at Terrell, Tex. The early life of James Rhea Preston was spent at home, where he received his preliminary education under private teachers. At the age of sixteen he entered Georgetown university, and after remaining in that institution for two years he entered Emory and Henry college, Virginia, to finish his course of studies, and from that institution was graduated in 1873, and in 1875 received the degree of A. M. Soon after leaving college he became a teacher and followed this occupation one year each in Tennessee and Indiana. In 1875 he removed to Mississippi and located at Okolona, where he taught school for three years, and during his leisure moments studied law, being admitted to the bar at the above-mentioned place. In 1878 he removed to Center Point, Noxubee county, Miss., at which place he conducted the high school for three years, and resigning, was elected superintendent of public schools at Water Valley. He held this position for four years and a half, at the end of which period he received the nomination at the democratic state convention and was elected state superintendent of public schools November, 1885. At Water Valley he established a fine system of schools, which attracted the attention of the public and led to his promotion. He was reëlected state superintendent in 1889, and by the provisions of the new constitution his term is extended two years. Mr. Preston has made education his study, and has introduced several very important reforms into the school system of Mississippi, among which may be mentioned the following, which were adopted and passed by the legislature at his suggestion: one providing for uniform examinations to test the scholarship of applicants so that they could be paid according to their qualifications, the county superintendent being required to fix the salary of each teacher, with due regard not only to his scholarship but his experience, ability and the scholastic population of his district. Another reform was providing a system of districts to limit the number of schools and to make each large enough to justify the employment of a competent teacher. A third provision was one requiring the superintendent to inspect the work of teachers, also to arrange and manage the institutes for the advancement of teachers in the best methods of instruction and discipline. Another important reform was one requiring continuous sessions so that the school fund might not be frittered away, and also that all schools of a term should be in session at the same time, that the work of supervision might be systematic and effective. A salary system based upon the average attendance had been in vogue, which was a fruitful source of unjust discriminations and of many frauds. This was abolished, and the salaries of the teachers of the different grades were fixed between a maximum and minimum limit. Mr. Preston is a very popular official, and is doing a great work toward the advancement of education in Mississippi. He is a man of good stature, well-proportioned, and in personal appearance attractive. He has dark hair and beard, and dark, expressive eyes. In politics Mr. Preston has always been a stanch democrat, and in 1875 assisted in redeeming the state from radical misrule. Under his administration the public schools of the state have rapidly improved. Graded-school systems have been established in more than twenty-five towns, and the impulse for advancement has penetrated every country district.

Armead Price was born in Mississippi in September, 1840, the second in a family of eight children born to Washington and Frances (Harris) Price, a history of whom is given elsewhere in this work. Armead Price was educated principally in Oxford, Miss., but after the death of his father, and when only a small boy, he went to North Carolina and made his home with an uncle, after which he attended Chapel Hill college in that state and an educational institution of Lebanon, Tenn. After attaining manhood he returned to Oxford, and took up the study of law in the University of Oxford, and would have graduated in 1861, had not the war come up. He dropped his books when the first alarm sounded, enlisted in the Confederate service and was sent to Pensacola, Fla., where he remained twelve months. At the end of this time he returned to Oxford, but soon after joined the Eleventh Mississippi infantry, and was sent directly to the front, being in the seven days' fight in front of Richmond, being also in the engagements of Gettysburg and Sharpsburg. In the last engagement he was wounded, being shot through the leg below the knee, and after remaining in the hospital a few days he was removed to a private residence, where he was cared for until he was able to return to his home in Oxford. Upon recovering he returned to his command in Virginia, with which he remained until the surrender of General Lee, when he was taken to Fort Delaware, where he was kept for some time, not reaching his home until October, 1865. The University of Oxford being about broken up, he did not again resume his legal studies, but engaged in farming, and in November, 1865 was married to Miss Sallie G. Slate, a daughter of Peterson James and Henrietta (Delbridge) Slate. She and her parents were born in Virginia, Mr. and Mrs. Slate being also married there. When Mrs. Price, who was their eldest child, was one year old, they removed to Lafayette county, Miss., in 1844, and here afterward became the parents of eight more children. The Slates were of English descent, the paternal grandfather of Mrs. Price having come to America from England. During the Revolutionary war, he acted as courier for General Washington, and was among the very earliest settlers of Virginia. They are a long-lived race and the grandfather Slate lived to be ninety years of age. The marriage of Mr. Price resulted in the birth of seven children: Manfred (deceased), Nellie, Manfred, Walter (deceased), Prentiss, Fannie and Blanche. Mr. Price, by hard work and good management, became the owner of thirteen hundred acres of land, six hundred of which are under cultivation, and was perfectly contented to pursue the even tenor of his way without aspiring to any office. He was very domestic in his tastes and much preferred a quite life with his family to the honors of public life. He was refined in his tastes and was regarded by all as a high-minded gentleman. He was an earnest member of the Methodist Episcopal church, and was very generous in the use of his means, contributing liberally to schools, churches, etc. His death, which occurred January 20, 1880, was deeply regretted by his numerous friends, and Lafayette county lost one of her most worthy citizens and successful planters. Mrs. Price and five children survive him, and since the death of her husband she has been quite successful in the management of her business affairs, and has given her children good educational advantages. Prentiss took a commercial course in Ledden Commercial college of Memphis, Tenn., and has been employed by the Merchants' Bank of Grenada, Miss., for about one year. His health then began to fail him and he quit the bank and is now in the Indian territory, in charge of a trader's post. Manfred took a course in the Jackson (Miss.) Commercial college, one daughter is attending school at Oxford, and another is in the Grenada Collegiate institute. Mrs. Price and family are members of the Methodist Episcopal church, and move in the highest social circles. They have one of the loveliest homes in Lafayette county, and their residence is surrounded by grand old oak trees and beautiful and ornamental evergreens.

Among the most progressive and prosperous residents of Oxford, Lafayette county, Miss., is Mr. Bem Price, cashier of the Bank of Oxford. He was born in this county, March 8, 1850, and is the fifth of a family of nine children. The parents, Washington and Frances Bushord (Harris) Price, were natives of the state of North Carolina. The paternal grandfather, Thomas Price, settled in Wake county, N. C., about one hundred years ago, where he married Rebecca Robertson. To this union there were born three sons and two daughters, and the lands upon which he settled have been occupied continuously by his descendants up to the present time. Washington Price, the eldest, born October 17, 1803, removed from North Carolina to west Tennessee, near Jackson, where he married Frances B. Harris, in February, 1837, and soon thereafter removed to the southeast portion of Lafayette county, Miss., where he became an extensive and successful planter. In addition to his agricultural pursuits he carried on other important interests. He erected a number of the business buildings in Oxford and with Maj. Paul B. Barringer, built the University hotel, which became the most popular in the place, and continued until burned by the Federal troops, in 1862, with all the rest of the business property of the town. He was also prominent in securing the subscription to the Mississippi Central railroad. He was a man of strong and vigorous mind, active, enterprising and energetic. Having been educated at Chapel Hill, N. C., his tastes and fondness for books were afterward evinced in the collection of a library, regarded at one time the finest in the county. In politics he was a whig of the strongest persuasion. While actively engaged in the duties and responsibilities of citizenship that promised more than ordinary success, he was cut off in his prime, in the year 1855; his wife died in 1856. They were both honored members of the Old School Presbyterian church. There were born to this union nine children: Huldrick, Armead, Grosswald, Ethboll, Relbue, Bem, Anna, Manford and an infant daughter who died unnamed. Grosswald and Manford also died in early childhood. Bem Price was thus left an orphan at the early age of five years. After the death of his parents, he, with the remaining four brothers and one sister, was taken to Wake county, N. C., where he lived with an uncle for nearly ten years, receiving his education from a private tutor. In 1865, with three brothers and a sister (one brother having died while at Hillsboro, N. C., attending school), he returned to Lafayette county and went to live in the old home. He was occupied on the farm until he reached his majority, attending two sessions of school in the meantime. In 1871 he embarked in the mercantile trade in partnership with Paul B. Barringer and Thomas L. Harris, under the firm name of Harris, Price & Barringer, in Oxford, Miss., which business continued until the latter part of 1875, when it was dissolved by consent of all partners. Then with Charles Roberts he organized the Southern bank, at Oxford, with a paid-up capital of $50,000, he being elected cashier. The Southern bank was in successful operation for two years, when its affairs were wound up by mutual consent, and the building erected by them for their use was sold to and is now occupied by the Bank of Oxford. Mr. Price was then engaged in operating with his private funds until 1880. In June of that year he was elected cashier of the Bank of Oxford and treasurer of the University of Mississippi, and in 1886, secretary of the board of trustees of the university, which positions he still holds. He now owns one thousand acres of his father's old plantation and other valuable real estate in the county and town. He was one of the promoters and organizers of a number of banking institutions in the state, all of which are in successful operation, and is now a large stockholder and director in them. It will quickly be recognized that he is a man of much more than ordinary business talent, and that he has made the most of his opportunities, preserving in all of his dealings a character of highest honor. Mr. Price was united in marriage in November, 1876, to Mary Delle Bowles, a native of this state and county, and a daughter of James R. Bowles. Mr. Bowles was born in Virginia, his father being a pioneer from that state to this. Mr. and Mrs. Price are members of the Old School Presbyterian church.

Angus M. Price, a prominent planter and miller, residing and doing business two miles southwest of Shubuta, in Wayne county, Miss., was born near Frost Bridge, in that county, in 1854. He is the youngest of ten children born to and reared by Allen and Effie (McDonald) Price. His father, who was a son of David Price, was born in South Carolina in 1815, and became a planter and removed to Wayne county in 1836, locating at Frost Bridge, where he has come to be a large landholder and a prominent citizen. Mr. Price's mother was a native of South Carolina and became the wife of Mr. Price in 1835. Soon after, they immigrated to Mississippi, where they were among the pioneers. Of their union were born the following children: William, who served during the late war and died soon after in Clarke county; Malcolm, also a soldier in the Confederate service, who died during the war; Quillie, who died in infancy; George, who died in the Confederate service at Columbus, Miss.; Catherine E., now Mrs. Dr. Evans, of Clarke county; John, who is a planter of Wayne county; Maggie, now Mrs. Howard and residing in Wayne county; Joseph, of Clarke county, who is the inventor and patentee on a mill-dress; Anna, who married Mr. William Price, and who died soon after, and Angus M., the subject of our sketch. His parents were members of the Methodist Episcopal church and his father was identified with the Masonic order. He has been one of the most successful planters in this part of the country. He is a democrat in politics and in the highest degree public-spirited, and is interested in every movement pertaining to the good of the community and state. His mother died in Clarke county in 1870. Angus M. Price was reared and educated in Clarke county. He began life for himself in 1875 as a farmer, in which he was engaged exclusively until 1889. In that year he embarked in the mill business and is the owner of a sawmill, cottongin and gristmill, located on Eucutta creek, which affords good water power. This establishment has a capacity to turn out five thousand feet of lumber a day, twelve bales of cotton per day, and one hundred and fifty bushels of meal a day. He also has a plantation of one hundred and eighty acres of land, his home farm consisting of about fifty acres. He was married in 1876 to Miss Lizzie Seales, the daughter of Benjamin Seales, of Lowndes county, who was born in 1861 and who died August 8, 1891, having borne him six children: Allen, Benjamin, Minnie, Mary, Henry and Alma, all of whom are living. Mrs. Price was a member of the Methodist Episcopal church, of which Mr. Price is also a member. Mr. Price, who has through life been a democrat, takes a deep interest in all national questions of importance. He has always been a liberal contributor toward the establishment of schools and churches, and has been prompt and generous in his aid to all worthy objects. He is entitled to a certain amount of pride in the fact that he has been architect of his own fortune.

Dr. Daniel T. Price, one of the successful physicians of the county, is also engaged in farming and fruit-growing and is prominently identified with the growth and prosperity of Prentiss county. He is a native Mississippian, born in Tishomingo (now Prentiss) county, within three miles of Booneville, on the 23d of November, 1839, and is the son of Richard and Sarah (Eppes) Price, natives of Knox county, Tenn., where they were reared and married. The parents came to Mississippi in 1838, settled three miles northwest of what is now Booneville at a time when the country was very sparsely settled, and the father purchased wild land, paying $8 per acre for it. Other families came there the same year, among them being Thomas Eppes, brother of Mrs. Price, who had also been a resident of Knox county, Tenn. Mr. Price continued to reside on his farm for about five years and then sold out, moving to a place south of Booneville, where he purchased land, now near the limits of Booneville, and there resided until his death in 1889, at the age of eighty-five years. He was a quiet, unobtrusive man and was universally respected. He was an old line whig in politics, later a democrat, and his first democratic vote was for James Buchanan. He was a man well posted on all the current topics of the day, a constant reader and at the time of his death could see to read, by aid of glasses, as well as in middle life. He was a member of the Methodist church. He was colonel of the militia of east Tennessee, and during the war enlisted for sixty days to assist General Alcorn in his campaign at Bowling Green, Ky., as a high private. He had two or three brothers in the early Indian wars. One brother, Daniel Price, was killed in Florida. He was captain of a company and had his head cut off and stuck up on a stake by the Indians. Mr. Price was the youngest of twelve children born to Edward and Sarah (Webb) Price, both natives of the Palmetto state. Edward Price and wife moved from South Carolina to Tennessee with an oxcart at an early day, settled in Knox county and there the father engaged in planting. He died in Knox county many years ago, but the mother lived to be eighty-four years old and died when the subject of this sketch was a boy. Richard Price's wife died in 1854, at the age of forty years. She was a member of the Methodist church. Their family consisted of twelve children, two sons and one daughter dying in childhood. The others were: Mrs. Judith Bracking, on the old home place; Mrs. Martha Patterson, near Aberdeen; Daniel T., subject; Mrs. Amanda Gresham,

wife of W. G. C. Gresham; William E., farmer of Prentiss county; John T., undertaker and dealer in furniture, of Booneville; Oscar, a successful merchant of Tyler, Tex.; James J., at Hillsboro, Tex., engaged in merchandising, and Mrs. Sarah E. Burns, wife of the present county treasurer. Dr. D. T. Price supplemented a common-school education by attending the academy at Rienzi. He commenced the study of medicine at the latter place in the fall of 1860 under Dr. J. M. Taylor, a leading physician of the place and now one of the most prominent in the state, and attended lectures at Richmond, Va., in 1864 and 1865. With the exception of the time he took lectures he served as hospital steward of the Twenty-sixth Mississippi regiment during the war. He attended lectures at Richmond, Va., by special permission from the secretary of war. He graduated from Jefferson Medical college in 1866 and came to Booneville, where he commenced practicing his profession. There he has continued since and is one of the leading physicians of the county. He is the present health officer of the county and stands in the front ranks of the medical fraternity. He was married to Miss Victoria McCrory, a native of Marshall county, Tenn., and the daughter of Robert and Nancy (Williams) McCrory, who came with their family to Mississippi in 1848. To Dr. Price and wife were born five children, four now living: Claude B., John W., R. C. and Robert G. The one deceased died unnamed. Claude B. is acting midshipman on the United States ship Baltimore, with headquarters at Washington, D. C. He was a graduate of the United States naval academy, at Annapolis, from the engineering division of the class of 1890, standing second in his class. During the four years he was in that institution he stood twenty-third in his class the first year, nineteenth the second year, twelfth the third year and second the last year in the engineering division of the class. The graduating class, according to a recent act of congress, is divided into the line and engineering divisions in order that each cadet in the last year's course may receive special instruction to better qualify him for his particular work or line of service. Mr. Price chose the engineering division and graduated in that division as above. He is now in his twenty-third year. John W. completed the course for the junior year at the Mississippi Agricultural and Mechanical college, and is now studying medicine with his father. He is past the junior year at the Agricultural and Mechanical college of Mississippi and will later attend the University of Virginia. The other children are at home. Dr. Price and family enjoy a very pleasant home adjoining Booneville, where he is engaged in fruit-growing in connection with his practice. He is a member of the state horticultural society, in which he takes a deep interest. Politically he is a democrat.

In the commercial circles of Yalobusha county, Miss., no name stands higher than that of George W. Price, proprietor of the Blue Front store of Water Valley, Miss. He was born in Pontotoc county, Miss., July 9, 1842, and is a son of John and Nancy (Ragland) Price, natives of Georgia. His father was born February 4, 1808, and his mother in March, 1810; they were married in Jasper county, Ga., February 9, 1831, and removed to Mississippi, settling in Pontotoc county. To them were born six children—two sons and four daughters. The father died April 2, 1872, honored and respected by all who knew him. His father, John Price, Sr., a descendant of the Prices of Virginia, was a very successful planter, and for many years a magistrate. After the death of his first wife, in 1845, he was married to Miss Tabitha Thomas, of Georgia, who died in 1876. The father and mother of Mr. Price were members of the Primitive Baptist church, of which Mr. Price's father was also a member. The eldest and first child of Mr. Price's father's family, born December 11, 1831, was named Julia Ann. She married Robert C. Hellum, and died October 19, 1855, leaving three children: John W., William Lewis and Mary Ellen Hellum, and her husband, who married again, died in 1863 while in service in the late war. The second, a daughter also, named Martha Jane, married Wilson or "Dock" Hellum, a brother of Robert C. Hellum. She was born September 22, 1833, and died May 4, 1860, leaving five children: Nancy, George W., Julia Ann, John T. and Robert Wilson Hellum; her husband, who was a member of company K, of the Seventeenth Mississippi regiment, died in the army at Richmond, Va., in 1864. The third daughter, Susan Caroline, was born August 6, 1835, and married Samuel T. Crimm, who was also a member of company K, of the Seventeenth Mississippi regiment, and died during the war (1862) at Richmond, Va.; she had three children by Mr. Crimm: Mary Ann, Rachel and Samuel T. She afterward married John F. Stewart, by whom she had five children. The family settled near Sherman, Grayson county, Tex., in 1878. The fourth daughter, Mary Morgan, was born September 28, 1837, and married Henry Lynch in 1858, and he died near Atlanta, Ga., in 1864, a member of company E, of the First Mississippi cavalry. She had by him two children: Madora Tobitha and Mary V. Lynch. By her second husband, Hardy McGlaune, she had three children named Francis, Helen and George Washington McGlaune. She and her husband removed to near Temple, Bell county, Tex., in 1878, where she died May 21, 1883. Dr. John Ragland Price, the fifth child and eldest son, was born September 16, 1839, and was educated at Sparta academy in Calhoun county, Miss. He was third lieutenant of company E, of the First Mississippi cavalry, and was wounded in the knee at Abbeville, Miss., and is a cripple for life. He married Miss Maggie Duncan, a daughter of Dr. M. I. Duncan, of Sarepta. He is a high Mason, and was county treasurer of Calhoun county, Miss., in 1869 and 1870. After the war he sold goods at Pittsboro and at Banner. Later he took up the practice of medicine, and has devoted himself to it during the past eighteen years, and is regarded as one of the leading practitioners of the county. He has had nine children, two of whom are dead. The eldest two, William Duncan and John Washington, are twins, and were born November 30, 1864; the second is a daughter, named Minnie; the others are named James, Eddie, Dale, Lou, Claude and Ruby. Dr. Price is the purchasing agent for the Alliance at Banner, Miss. One of his two sons, John Washington Price, is a candidate for county treasurer of Calhoun county. George Washington, the youngest of the family, was born July 9, 1842. To return to the gentleman whose history follows: He passed his early youth in the county of his birth, and received his education in the common schools, and in the academy at Sarepta, Calhoun county, Miss. In 1861, when there was a call for men to go to the defense of their country, he abandoned his private interests, and enlisted in company K, of the Seventeenth Mississippi volunteer infantry, of Barksdale's brigade, for one year; he was soon made third sergeant; at the battle of Bull Run he acted as orderly sergeant, and at the battle of Yorktown he was made third lieutenant. He was soon promoted to be second lieutenant, and was finally made captain, but never received his commission on account of losing his right leg below the knee at Fredericksburg. He was wounded at the same time in the left foot, and was slightly wounded also at the battle of Bull Run. He was afterward in many important engagements, and was again slightly wounded in the right thigh at the battle of Antietam, and in the battle of Fredericksburg. Of the twenty-eight men who were at the pontoon crossing below the market house, twenty-three were killed or wounded, he being one of the twenty-three, and receiving such serious wounds in the right leg and left foot that amputation was necessary, and, although the captaincy had been conferred upon him, he was unfit for the duties of the office. He had an artificial limb made, and was able to take part later in several cavalry scouts, serving until the close of the war. The art of making artificial limbs has been brought to such perfection that Mr. Price has been enabled to supply the missing limb with such success that he suffers little inconvenience. While he was in a crippled condition at Harrisburg, he captured two prisoners and two horses by himself.

After the close of the war he returned to Pontotoc county, but shortly went to Memphis, Tenn., where he engaged in the livestock business. After a time he came back to Pontotoc county and embarked in the mercantile trade, and in 1866 formed a partnership with H. J. Ragland, his uncle, at Banner, Calhoun county, Miss. This relationship was ended by the death of Mr. Ragland in 1870. Mr. Price continued the business alone till 1873, at which time he came to Water Valley and formed a partnership with H. W. Rogers and A. Collum, the firm being known as Collum, Price & Rogers. Mr. Price retired and entered into business relations with Capt. W. A. Herring. Four years later the firm of G. W. Price & Co. was established, and did a large and successful business until the yellow-fever epidemic in 1878 swept over the South. After this a partnership was formed by Mr. Price with H. E. Wagner, who died. Four years later Capt. Z. D. Jinnings became a member of the firm, and Mr. Price finally sold his interest in the business to Z. D. Jinnings & Son. He then retired to his farm and followed agriculture for a time and merchandising at Belen, Quitman county, Miss. for two years. He then rented his land and returned to Water Valley, and in February, 1890, established his present business. He carries a fine, fresh stock of general merchandise, and does a thriving business. Mr. Price was united in marriage to Frances Oregon Freeman, a daughter of Simeon Freeman, who was born in Jasper county, Ga., in 1808, and came to Mississippi in the early history of the state, and there reared a family of thirteen children. Mrs. Price grew up in Pontotoc county, and received her education at the academy of Sarepta, Calhoun county, Miss. She became the mother of five children: Guy Hartwell (aged sixteen years), Mary Ida (aged nine years), Frances C. (aged four years), Edgar E. (second child, who died at the age of fourteen years), and Elnora C. (first child, who died when but five months old). Mrs. Frances O. Price is a member of the Knights and Ladies of Honor. Mr. Price is a member of the A. O. U. W., of the Knights of Honor, and of the Knights and Ladies of Honor. In his political opinions he adheres to the principles of the democratic party. He is now the nominee for county treasurer. Mrs. Price is an earnest member of the Presbyterian church. The family is one of the leading ones of the county, and its members have the respect and esteem of the entire community.

Dr. J. J. Price is one of the prominent druggists of Clarksdale, and by his social and pleasing manners has built up a good trade and won a host of warm friends. He is the third of five children born to John J. and Sarah R. (Hunter) Price, his birth occurring in Alabama in 1844. The parents were natives of South Carolina, in which state their nuptials were celebrated, and in 1837 or 1838 they removed to Alabama, where the father was engaged in tilling the soil until his death in 1850. He was an officer of the county militia. The mother's death occurred in 1888. Both were members in good standing in the Methodist Episcopal church. J. J. Price attained his growth and received a good practical education in Alabama. In 1861 he came to Mississippi, settled at Enterprise, Clarke county, and early in 1862 entered the Confederate Military hospital at Enterprise as assistant druggist. There he remained until December, 1862, when he enlisted in Company B, Thirty-seventh Mississippi regiment infantry, and was in many of the most prominent engagements, from the battle of Resaca to Atlanta. For a time he was in the medical department, then in the ranks, and was with General Hood in his campaign in Tennessee, taking part in all those battles—Franklin, Spring Hill, etc. He was at Greensboro, N. C., at the time of the surrender. After this he went to Enterprise, followed farming until the fall, and then engaged in clerking, which he continued until 1872. He went from there to Augusta, Ark., and three years later embarked in business for himself as a merchant under the firm name of Price & Wise. In 1875 he sold out and came to Clarksdale to take charge of the mercantile business of John Clark. Remaining with Mr. Clark until December, 1879, he then started his present drug business at Clarksdale. He erected a neat cottage residence a few years ago, and in 1889 erected his fine business building and another brick store on Front street; he also owns a tract of timber land. Mr. Price was married in Hinds county, Miss., in 1870, to Miss Bettie McRae, a native of that county, and the daughter of William McRae. Her mother's maiden name was Wells, and she was a descendant of an old and very prominent family. Mrs. Price is also related to Governor McRae. To Mr. and Mrs. Price have been born five children, two daughters living and three sons deceased. Those living are Maud and Blanche. Mr. Price was one of the organizers of the Clarksdale Bank and Trust company, and has been a member of the city council since the incorporation of Clarksdale, with the exception of one year. He is one of the promoters of all public enterprises in Clarksdale, Coahoma county. He is a member of the Knights of Honor and the Knights of Pythias orders. In addition to the complete stock of drugs that he carries, Mr. Price has toilet articles, paints, oils, glass, school books, and stationery.

Melville C. Priddy, planter, owes his nativity to the state of Tennessee, his birth having occurred in Shelby county, October 10, 1838. He was the third of eight children born to his parents, John H. and Mariah A. (Priddy) Priddy, native Virginians. The father removed from his native state to Tennessee about 1830, and was a contractor and builder and a very fine architect of Shelby county for many years. In 1870 he removed to Memphis, where he is now residing at the age of seventy-seven years. He was left a widower in 1870, and four years later he married a Mrs. Smith of Memphis. The Priddys are of Scotch-Irish ancestry and were among the oldest and most prominent families of Virginia. The paternal grandfather, William Priddy, and the grandmother, whose maiden name was Crenshaw, were also natives of the Old Dominion. Melville C. Priddy was brought up in Memphis, but was educated in Macon, Tenn. At the age of thirteen years he became a salesman in a country store, where he remained three years, after which he went to Memphis and kept books for John C. Lonsdale for three years, subsequently becoming clerk on a steamboat plying on the Mississippi. He retained this position until the breaking out of the war when he, from New Orleans, enlisted in company H, Miles' Louisiana legion, and was at once made orderly sergeant. Soon after this he was promoted to sergeant major of his command and in the siege of Port Hudson received a slight wound. Being cut off from his command after the surrender of this place he joined Morton's Tennessee battery of Forrest's artillery and served until the war closed, participating in all the engagements of his company. He surrendered at Gainesville, Ala., in May, 1865, and returned to Memphis, where he remained two years, after which he came to Coahoma county and began merchandising. Seven years later he went to Friar's Point and for four years held the office of chancery and circuit court clerk of the county, after which he entered the employ of the Mobile & Northwestern railroad company as bookkeeper and cashier, in which position he remained three years. He then filled a responsible and remunerative position in Helena, Ark., for six years, and in 1887 came to his present plantation, which contains two thousand three hundred and eighty-two acres, of which six hundred and fifty are under cultivation. All this property he has made through his own exertions, and although his early labors were severe he surmounted the many difficulties that strewed his pathway and in the various employments in which he has been engaged he has acquitted himself creditably. He is genial, hospitable, and possesses a kind heart, and his intercourse with those around him has been very harmonious and cordial. He was married in 1870 to Miss Emma Stothart, a native of Tennessee, but her death occurred three years later. In 1876 Mr. Priddy took for his second wife Miss Blanche Miles, of Mississippi, a daughter of William P. and Musidora (Alcorn) Miles, the mother being a 'sister of ex-Governor Alcorn. To Mr. and Mrs. Priddy one child has been born, Miles, who is attending school at Clarksdale, Miss. Mr. Priddy is a member of the Methodist Episcopal church, is a Mason and a member of the American Legion of Honor. His wife is a member of the Presbyterian church.

Capt. John T. Priestly, planter, Canton, Miss. Captain Priestly's father, James Priestly, was born in Tennessee, and came to Mississippi in 1832, locating among the first settlers of Canton, the county seat of Madison county. He was quite a prominent physician, and ministered to the physical wants of his fellow-men in that county until his death, in 1855, of yellow fever. He married Miss Susan Nelson, also a native of Tennessee, and her death occurred in 1890. His parents, John T. and Hannah Priestly, were natives of Tennessee, and the maternal grandfather, Bevily Nelson, was also born in that state. Of the seven children born to James and Susan Priestly, Capt. John T. was the third in order of birth. He was born in Madison county, Miss., April 3, 1840, and was educated in the Canton high school until 1857, when he took a commercial course in Gundrey's Commercial college, Cincinnati, Ohio, graduating the same year. He has figured quite prominently in the politics of the county, was sheriff from 1875 to 1881, and was an efficient officer. He is considered one of the leading citizens of Madison county. During the early portion of his life he followed merchandising, but failing health compelled him to retire to the farm, where he has resided since 1872. He is a planter, and, jointly with his wife, owns nineteen hundred acres of land, with nine hundred and fifty under cultivation. He also has some buildings in Canton valued at $3,000. Mr. Priestly was married, in 1868, to Miss Stella Shackleford, a native of Mississippi, and the daughter of Judge Thomas and Sarah T. (Moon) Shackleford, natives, respectively, of Mississippi and Tennessee. This union resulted in the birth of three children: Thomas S., Pauline and Sadie. During the Civil war, or in 1861, Mr. Priestly enlisted in company I, Tenth Mississippi regiment infantry, a volunteer company known as the Madison rifles, and served in the same until 1862, when the company was disbanded, the time of enlistment having expired. He then went to Virginia with Gen. S. D. French, and was with him until after the fall of Vicksburg. After this he joined a company known as Harvey's scouts, with which he remained until the war closed. He was in all of General Sherman's raids, and being with a scouting party was in many dangerous places. He was shot through the left lung while in the mountains of Georgia, and was disabled for duty for a short time. He was in active service at the time of the surrender. Mr. Priestly and family are members of the Episcopal church, and he has shown his appreciation of secret organizations by becoming a member of the Masonic fraternity, Knights of Honor and Knights of Pythias. He has ever been identified with the best interests of the county, and is held in high regard by his friends and neighbors.

Francis M. Prince, the present sheriff of Kemper county, has for many years been prominently connected with the history of this section of country, and is deserving of a place in the record of Mississippi's loyal citizens. He was born at Jones' Bluff, Sumter county, Ala., September 25, 1835, and is a son of Richard and Susan R. (Jackson) Prince. The father was born in Virginia in 1804, and was a son of John Prince; he removed with his father from Virginia to South Carolina at an early day, and there received his education in the common schools. In his youth he determined to follow husbandry, and removed to Alabama, locating in Sumter county, where he became a prosperous planter. He was married in Barbour county, Ala., but resided in Sumter county until his death, which occurred in 1845. He was a member of the Baptist church, and a stanch adherent to the principles of the democratic party. He was a soldier in some of the Indian wars, and was once justice of the peace. The mother of our subject was born in Alabama in 1812, and was a daughter of Randie Jackson; her family were from Georgia, but removed to Barbour county, Ala., at an early day. Richard Prince and wife were the parents of children named: Martha, Sophronia, Francis M., John R., William, Enos, Mary and Jefferson. The mother died in 1880. She belonged to the Baptist church. Francis M. grew to man's estate in his native county, and then removed with his mother and the rest of the family to Noxubee county, Miss., where they settled on a farm. Just before the war he was married to Miss Sarah E. Coleman, a daughter of James Coleman, and a native of Sumter county, Ala., born in 1837. Her father was a native of Georgia, and her mother was born in Alabama; both died in Mississippi. Mr. and Mrs. Prince have reared a family of three children: Maud, Ina and Ella. Maud married H. F. Weever, and Ella is the wife of J. J. Chetham. Mr. Prince enlisted, in 1861, in company C, Third Mississippi volunteer infantry, and took part in many of the fiercest of battles; among them, Shiloh, Missionary Ridge, Chickamauga, Perryville, Murfreesboro and Franklin, but he was never taken prisoner. On coming home he engaged in agriculture, and in 1865 he removed to Kemper county, harvesting his first crop in 1866. He and his wife are both members of the Christian church. Politically he is a democrat. In 1878 he was elected justice of the peace, and again in 1889, the people of the county further showed the confidence which they repose in Mr. Prince by electing him sheriff of Kemper county. He has been a brave and most efficient official, and has been true to his convictions under all circumstances. He is a member of Summerville lodge No. 133, A. F. & A. M., and also belongs to the chapter. He is a member of the Farmers' Alliance. He has met with marked success in all his business undertakings, and especially in his farming; he owns about eleven hundred acres of land, and in view of the fact that he has accumulated his property solely through his own efforts, too much can not be said in praise of his excellent judgment and wise management.

One of the wealthiest planters of the state is Capt. W. Berry Prince, Carrollton, Miss. He was born in Jefferson county, Miss., September 26, 1826, and is a son of the Hon. W. Berry Prince. The father was a native Mississippian, and a well-known planter of Washington county. He was a member of the legislature at the time of his death, which occurred about the year 1830. Captain Prince passed his boyhood and youth in Washington county; he attended school at Alton, Ill., and at Frankfort, Ky.; he finished his college course at Oakland college, Mississippi, graduating in the class of 1849. In June, 1850, he was united in marriage to Miss Eliza K. Terry, a daughter of the Hon. William Terry, of Jefferson county. Mr. Terry afterward became a resident of Carroll county, and was one of the most successful planters within her borders, accumulating a large estate. Mrs. Prince was born near Rodney, Jefferson county, Miss., and is one of a family of three daughters: Mrs. William Helm is now deceased; Mrs. Sarah T., wife of Evan Jeffries, of Claiborne county, and Mrs. Prince. The mother of Captain Prince, after the death of her husband, was married a second time; her second union was with Mr. John A. Miller, of Greenville, Miss. He was a large planter, and left a fine estate. Mrs. Miller had four daughters by her second marriage. Captain Prince is the only son. Soon after his marriage he located in Carroll county, on Pine Bluff plantation. Before the war he was the second largest planter in the state of Mississippi, but in 1862 he abandoned his private interests, and enlisted in the Confederate army.

He was made captain of a company, and served as a scout and home guard. At the close of the first year he was compelled to resign on account of failing health; after a short rest at home he took a number of his slaves and went to the Alabama Salt works, and manufactured salt for the Confederate army, remaining there until the close of the war. After the final surrender he returned to his home in Carroll county, and again took up the pursuits of peace. He has devoted his time and attention exclusively to planting, and has been eminently successful. At this time he is one of the most extensive planters in the state, owning two plantations in Carroll county, one in Le Flore, and another in Washington county. Captain and Mrs. Prince have had born to them two children: Robert Prince, and a daughter, Shelby, a young lady greatly beloved for her many fine traits of character. Captain Prince and family reside on the plantation adjoining the town of Carrollton; this place is well improved, having a large, two-story dwelling, and many modern conveniences. Mrs. Prince is a lady of amiable disposition, and has won many warm friends.

William B. Prince, grandfather of Robert Prince, planter, Greenville, Miss., was one of the first settlers of Washington county, Miss., locating on Lake Washington, and was among the best known of the pioneers of that county. He acquired a good property, held numerous positions of trust and honor, and died at Clinton while on his way to the legislature at Jackson, to represent his people in that body. He was a man of sterling qualities, and had the respect of all. His son, William B. (father of subject of this sketch), is a resident of Carroll county, Miss., where he is well known and highly esteemed, and was a gallant officer in the Confederate army during the Civil war. He was married to Miss Eliza K. Terry, a native of Mississippi and daughter of Maj. William Terry, a man well and favorably known in central Mississippi. Robert Prince, who was born to the above mentioned union, owes his nativity to Claiborne county, Miss., born March 26, 1851, and was reared on his father's plantation. He attended preparatory school at Dinwiddie Station, Va., and afterward entered Washington and Lee university, Virginia, where he remained two years. He subsequently attended the Western Military academy of Henry county, Ky., at that time presided over by Gen. Kirby Smith, where he completed the course. He then returned to Washington county, Miss., and has since been engaged in planting. He has always favored all enterprises of a laudable nature, is liberal and whole-souled, and a man who has a host of warm friends. He devotes his time and energy to his plantation, and is now the owner of twenty-two hundred acres of land, with twelve hundred under cultivation. He has farmed extensively and successfully and is one of the leading men of Washington county. He now resides in Greenville, whither he lately moved in order to educate his children.

Hon. R. N. Provine is a native-born resident of Calhoun county, Miss., his birth occurring within a few rods of where he now lives, in 1840. His parents, Samuel and Elizabeth (Creekmore) Provine, were married and settled the above place in 1839. There the father resided until his death in 1846. He was born in Tennessee in 1808, and was the son of John Provine, a native of South Carolina, who moved from his native state to Tennessee, and was one of the founders of the Cumberland Presbyterian church. The latter died in the last named state at the age of seventy years, an honored and esteemed citizen. His family consisted of five children—four sons and one daughter—all of whom lived to be grown, but all now deceased with the exception of the youngest son, who is now living in Tennessee. The latter is a retired minister in the Cumberland Presbyterian church, and is one of its most noble and earnest workers. The father of our subject was the eldest member of this family and was reared in Tennessee. He came to Mississippi in about 1836, settled below Grenada, and there sold goods until coming to the above place at Cole's Creek. His marriage to Miss Creekmore occurred after coming to this state. Mrs. Provine's father, Dr. Creekmore, was a native of North Carolina, but moved from that state to Tennesse and thence to Mississippi, where he was among the early settlers. The country was then in a wild and unbroken state, Indians were plentiful, and Dr. Creekmore, although often warned to leave the country, continued to reside there and practiced his profession until age prevented. He was a man universally respected, and was ever ready to extend a helping hand to all in distress. He was a liberal supporter of the church, and was in favor of all Christian denominations. He was strongly opposed to secret organizations, and was a man of more than ordinary intelligence. He was a soldier in the War of 1812, and for his services his second wife now draws a pension. He died in 1868, at the age of seventy-seven years, and was one of the county's best men. To his first marriage were born ten children—five sons and five daughters—two of his sons being killed in the war, James M., at Seven Pines, and Leonidas at a battle in Virginia. His daughter Elizabeth (Mrs. Provine), is also deceased. She was born in Tennessee in 1823, and died in the year 1866. She was a member of the Baptist church, and one of the most active and earnest workers in the same. Her father was married the second time to Miss McKelvy, of Mississippi, who is yet living on the old home place, settled by him in 1835. She is in her seventy-second year, is highly respected, and is a worthy member of the Baptist church. The remainder of the children by the Doctor's first marriage are: Hiram C., William R., H. C. (resides in Texas), Mrs. Nancy E. Martin (resides near the home place), Mrs. Sarah G. Simpson (near by), Mrs. Mary F. Bryant (resides at Grenada), Millinium (wife of Dr. West of Grenada), and Robert (who died at the home place after the war). After his marriage Mr. Provine resided on the home place, and carried on farming until his death, as above stated, in 1846. He was a member of the Baptist church. At his death he left a wife and four children, of whom R. N. is the eldest. John W. enlisted in the Forty-eighth Mississippi regiment in the army of north Virginia, and was killed at the battle of Spottsylvania, Va., on the 12th of May, 1864. Foster is a merchant of Coffeeville, Miss. (see sketch), and Nancy J. (wife of I. C. Stoole) resides in Banner, Calhoun county. The mother continued to reside on the home place until 1857, when she was married to Mr. T. A. Mitchell, who located in Pittsboro, Miss., where they resided until the war, after which they returned to the home place in Calhoun county, and there she died soon after. Mr. Mitchell died in 1888. R. N. Provine passed his youthful days on the home place, and as he was but a boy six years old when his father died, a great prospective responsibility rested on his shoulders, he being the eldest child. He was married at the age of twenty years to Mrs. Nancy Goyen, a native of Alabama, in Pickens county, born 1840. She was left an orphan at an early age, was reared by her brothers and sisters, and received her education in the common schools. To Mr. and Mrs. Provine have been born nine children—eight sons and one daughter: J. Finley was educated at Oxford university, Miss., and the Nashville university, and is now engaged in merchandising at Coffeeville, Miss; John W. is now in Germany, taking a special course in chemistry (in 1888 and 1889 he was assistant professor of chemistry at Oxford, Miss., where he was educated and where he was appointed to the position. He always stood at the head of his classes, and is an unusually bright young man); Robert F. also attended the University of Oxford, and is also well educated (he is now engaged in merchandising at Big Creek, Miss.); Charles graduated at Oxford in 1890, was well advanced in his classes, and is now taking law courses in Austin, Tex.; George H. is in the junior class at Oxford; James M. is now in the sophomore year in the same institution; Edgar, in the preparatory department; Oscar T. is at home taking lessons under his brother, preparatory for the university; and Lizzie May, attending Lancaster Female college at Oxford. Mr. and Mrs. Provine are rearing an orphan, Emma McMahan; though not taking their name she is treated in all respects as one of their own children. They have taken great pains to educate their family, and before sending their children away to school Mr. Provine erected a school building, employed a teacher, and had school ten months every year. This school he kept up until 1890, making it free to all the poor of his neighborhood. He has been very successful as a planter and merchant, and assists liberally in all public enterprises for the good of the county. During the late war he enlisted in company F, Twenty-ninth Mississippi regiment volunteer infantry, and served from 1862 until the close of the war. He was in the battles of Murfreesboro and Chickamauga, and was slightly wounded at the battle of Lookout Mountain, where he was captured. He was sent to Johnson's island, and there remained until the surrender. He was in command of a company all the time of his service, and held the commission of first lieutenant. When not in command of his company he was in command of some other, taking charge of a company of sharpshooters at one time. When peace was declared he left Johnson's island, returned to the home place, and met his wife and child, whom he had not seen since August, 1862. In speaking of it, Mr. Provine says, "That day was the happiest day of my life." After the war Mr. Provine had very little left, but eighty acres of land, and on this he laid the foundation of his present fortune. He is now the owner of four thousand five hundred acres of choice land, and has about fourteen hundred acres under cultivation, lying along Yalobusha river. This he has well stocked, and under a fine state of cultivation. In 1868 he had one store at Cole's Creek, and an interest in one at Coffeeville, Miss. He is now one of the leading merchants of the county. Mrs. Provine and all her children are members of the Baptist church, and liberal supporters of the same. In politics Mr. Provine is a democrat, and represented Calhoun county, Miss., in the legislature in 1882 and 1883.

L. F. Provine is the senior member of the firm of Provine Bros. & Co., Coffeeville Miss., and occupies a conspicuous position in the business circles of Yalobusha county, where he was born in 1844. He is a son of Samuel F. and Elizabeth (Creekmore) Provine, natives of Tennessee. The father was born in 1808, and was the son of John Provine, a native of Kentucky, who was a son of John Provine, a native of North Carolina. His father was also named John, and he emigrated from Ireland to America, although he was descended from a family of French Huguenots. The grandfather was a minister in the Cumberland Presbyterian church. He was married in Tennessee to Nancy Calhoun, whose family had been early settlers in that state. To them were born five children—four sons and one daughter. The father of our subject was the eldest child. He was reared near Lebanon, Tenn., and received his education in the common schools. He remained under the paternal roof until he was twenty-five years of age, and then came to Natchez, Miss. In 1837 he came to Yalobusha county, and invested in lands. He was engaged in farming, and also dealt in real estate to a large extent, owning lands in Chickasaw and Calhoun counties. He was a stanch whig, and member of the Baptist church. His death occurred in 1846, in December. His wife was born in 1823, and was a daughter of Robert W. Creekmore, an early settler of this county. He was born in Virginia in 1795, and was a soldier in the War of 1812. He came to Tennessee from Virginia, and was there married to Nancy McGowen, of Virginia. They settled in Tallahatchie county, Miss., and in 1835 they came to Yalobusha county, where they passed the remainder of their days. Mrs. Creekmore died in 1856. To them were born ten children, all of whom lived to be grown. Mrs. Provine died in 1866. She was married a second time to Thomas A. Mitchell, of Mississippi, but no children were born of this union. The result of the first marriage was four children, all of whom lived to maturity: Robert N., a partner of the firm of Provine Bros. & Co., is a large planter in Calhoun county, and a prominent citizen; John W., was killed in the battle of the Wilderness, Virginia, leaving a wife and two daughters; Nancy J., is the wife of I. C. Steele, and resides in Calhoun county; L. F., passed his youth in Calhoun and Yalobusha counties, and obtained his education in the common schools. In 1861, when there was a call for men to go to the defense of the country, he forsook all his private interests, and enlisted in company C, Blythe's battalion, which was afterward known as Blythe's regiment. The most important engagements in which he participated were Shiloh, Murfreesboro, and Missionary Ridge. He was flagbearer after the battle of Shiloh, and was in many skirmishes around Corinth. He was paroled in North Carolina, and then returned to Pittsboro, Calhoun county, where he engaged in the more peaceful pursuits of mercantile life. One year later he came to Coffeeville, remaining there until 1872. He then went back to Calhoun county, resuming the same business, and in 1878 he came to Coffeeville again. The firm is one of the most substantial in the state, and does an annual business of $70,000. They pay cash for everything they buy, but never refuse credit to good men. Mr. Provine was married to Miss Ada P. Barker, a daughter of William and Isabella (Harris) Barker, natives of North Carolina. They came to Mississippi about the year 1840, and there reared a family of six children, of whom Mrs. Provine is the youngest. Mr. and Mrs. Provine are the parents of ten children: Kate, Broxton B., Finley, Pearl, Sallie M., Alline, Robert F. and Frank P. The other two died in infancy. The parents are members of the Cumberland Presbyterian church, and are zealous, active workers. Mr. Provine is a member of the Knights of Honor. Politically he affiliates with the democratic party. He is a typical Mississippi gentleman, has excellent business qualifications, and is in every way worthy of the high regard in which he is held.

James W. Prowell belongs to that sturdy, honest and independent class, the planters of Mississippi. His plantation comprises four thousand four hundred acres, is very fertile, and is so carefully tilled that it yields a large annual income. Mr. Prowell was born in Richland county, S. C., April 5, 1817, a son of David R. and Rachel (Morris) Prowell, both of whom were born in the Palmetto state, and were of French descent. James W. Prowell and his brother William resided in the state of their birth until the spring of 1832, when they came to Lowndes county, Miss., settling on a tract of land of which about two acres had been cleared by the Indians, the Choctaws. The following spring the father, David R. Prowell, removed to Lowndes county, Miss , with his family and preëmpted one hundred and sixty acres of land at $1.25 per acre, which is now in possession of his son, James W. The grandfather was a soldier in the Revolutionary war, and died in the state of South Carolina. The father resided in his adopted state for only two years, and on a visit to his brother in Tennessee was taken with cholera, and died in 1835. He was a soldier in the War of 1812; his wife then received a land warrant, which is still in the possession of her son, James W. His widow survived until 1872, when she was called from earth. James W. Prowell was educated in the schools of Plymouth, and afterward finished his knowledge of books in La Grange college, Alabama. In 1842 he was married to Miss Catherine, daughter of Joseph and Louisa Caldwell, natives of Virginia. His wife died in 1851, having borne him five children: Virginia, William, Eliza, Joseph and John. J. Mr. Prowell's second marriage took place in 1855, Miss Mary Madry becoming his wife. They have three children: Edward, Mary and James. Mr. Prowell is a member of the A. F. & A. M., of which order he has been a member for forty years, is a democrat politically, and is the oldest settler of the county.

It was but natural, perhaps, when starting out in life for himself, that James T. Pryor, of Slate Spring, Miss., should select planting as his chosen occupation for life, for his father, Samuel O., and both his paternal and maternal grandfathers followed that calling all their lives. The father was born in Tennessee in 1811, and when but a boy went with his parents to Tuscaloosa county, Ala., where he grew to manhood. There he met and married Miss Unity Fox, a native of Tennessee, born in 1810, and who also removed to Alabama with her parents when young. After marriage, or in 1836, they came to Choctaw, now Webster county, and settled in the woods on Lindsey's creek, where they improved a good farm and there passed the remainder of their days, the mother dying in 1855 and the father in 1859. Both were members of the Missionary Baptist church for many years. The grandfather, Joseph Pryor, was probably born in Kentucky, but was married in Tennessee, and at an early day went to Tuscaloosa county, Ala., where his death occurred. He was of Scotch-Irish descent. Grandfather Henry Fox also removed from Tennessee to Tuscaloosa county, Ala., and in 1835 came to Choctaw county, now Webster county, where he also received his final summons. He was one of the very first settlers of this vicinity. James T. Pryor is the sixth of seven sons and seven daughters, all of whom are living but two. Four of the sons served in the Confederate army, viz.: James T. (subject); Joseph, enlisted in the Fifteenth Mississippi infantry, was captured at Fishing creek, and was in prison at Fort Delaware for about eight months (after this he was captured again at Atlanta, Ga., and was in prison until the close); Jacob D., served in company K, Fifteenth Mississippi infantry, until the fall of Vicksburg, after which he was in the Third Mississippi of Forrest's cavalry until the close (he was a member of the board of supervisors two years, and then, from 1866 to 1890 he was sheriff of Webster county); John was in General Forrest's cavalry for two years. James T. Pryor was born in Tuscaloosa county, Ala., in 1836, but was reared on a farm in the wilds of Choctaw county. He received a limited common-school education and when eighteen years of age began for himself as a farmer. He was married in 1857 to Miss Mary J., daughter of Alex. B. and Isabell H. McKee, who came from Alabama to what is now Webster county, Miss., in 1839, and there passed the remainder of their days, the father dying in 1859 and the mother after the war. Both were members of the Missionary Baptist church. He was a wealthy planter and was justice of the peace for many years. Mrs. Pryor was born in Choctaw, now Webster county, Miss., and by her marriage became the mother of eight children, six now living: Belle, wife of J. B. Spencer, a merchant of Slate Springs; James, a merchant of Grenada; Alonzo, farmer and merchant with his father; Cora, wife of Prof. W. J. Taylor, a teacher of Winona; Minnie and Samuel Tilden. Mr. Pryor lived on the old farm until the father's death, and then settled on Sabougla creek, where he remained until 1870. He then removed to Slate Spring, and has resided alternately there and on his farm ever since. He owns six hundred acres with three hundred acres cleared, and has improved it all since 1873, at which time he settled in the woods. All this he has accomplished by his own exertions. Since 1871 he has also been engaged in merchandising at Slate Spring, Grenada and Duck Hill respectively, the present firm being Spencer & Pryor. They do an annual business of about $6,000. In 1861 Mr. Pryor joined company G, Forty-second Mississippi infantry, and served in the army of Virginia until the close. He was on provost duty at Richmond for a long time, and the first general engagement was at Gettysburg. After this he was in the battle of Falling Water, Wilderness, Spottsylvania, and around Richmond and Petersburg. After this he obtained a furlough and came home. He was captured soon after the battle of Gettysburg, but was soon after released. He was also wounded in the first day's fight at Gettysburg, and after the war he returned to his family. He filled the office of justice of the peace for a number of years, and has been junior and senior warden of the Masonic fraternity, Slate Spring lodge. He and wife and family are members of the Missionary Baptist church. Mr. Pryor is one of the most energetic, thoroughgoing planters of Webster county, is strictly honest and is well and favorably known. He is giving his children good advantages for an education.

James Pryor, of the firm of James Pryor & Co., dealers in dry goods, groceries, millinery, etc., at Grenada, although young in years is one of the wideawake, thoroughgoing business men of the town. He was born in Calhoun county, Miss., in 1862, and is a son of James T. and Mary J. (McKee) Pryor, natives respectively of Alabama and Mississippi. When young the elder Pryor came with his parents to Mississippi, and after growing up was married in Choctaw county, where he resided until 1890. He then removed to Winona and is now retired from the active duties of life. He is one of the prominent farmers and has also been engaged in merchandising for many years. He lost a handsome property during the war and was obliged to start anew. He was all through the war in the Virginia army, and served in a creditable manner as a private. After the war he began at the bottom of the ladder, but has been very successful and is probably worth $50,000. He is the owner of about six hundred acres, producing about one hundred and fifty bales of cotton per year, and has everything convenient and comfortable about his place. He has been a member of the Masonic fraternity for a good many years. His father, Samuel O. Pryor, came from the Old Dominion to Mississippi many years ago, was a planter, and died before our subject was born. Mr. and Mrs. Pryor have been prominent Baptists for many years. Their family consisted of eight children, six now living, named in the order of their births as follows: Belle (wife of J. B. Spencer of Slate Spring, Miss.), James, Alonzo, Cora (wife of William J. Taylor, of Winona), Minnie and Tilden. James attended the public schools until sixteen years of age and then began business for himself at Slate Spring, where he continued for four years. After this he was at Duck Hill for two years, and in 1886 he came to Grenada, where he was engaged in business for the same length of time. He was subsequently bookkeeper for E. Cahn & Co. for some time, and on the 1st of January, 1891, the firm of James Pryor & Co. was established. Honest in his dealings and representations Mr. Pryor merits the esteem with which he is regarded. He is sole proprietor of the Grenada Saddlery company, which does an annual business of about $5,000. He is a stockholder in the Grenada bank and of the Building and Loan association. He was married in 1882 to Miss Jimmie McCord, a native of Calhoun county, Miss., and the daughter of James and Angie McCord, natives of Calhoun county also. Mr. McCord was killed in the early part of the war, while in service at Water Valley. His father, T. K. McCord, was a native Scotchman, who came to Mississippi at an early day and died in Greenwood, Miss. To Mr. and Mrs. Pryor have been born four children. Mrs. Pryor's maternal grandfather, William Cook, who was of Irish descent, at an early day settled in Calhoun county, where he still resides. He is about eighty-two years of age and is a wealthy planter. Mr. Pryor is a member of Grenada lodge, Independent Order of Odd Fellows, No. 6, and he and wife hold membership in the Baptist church.

James C. Purnell, president of the Citizens' bank at Winona, is a native born resident of Carroll, now Montgomery county, Miss., and was born March 17, 1847. He is the son of M. T. and Eunice E. W. (Read) Purnell, natives of the Old North state. His father was born in 1801, and his mother in 1809. M. T. Purnell was a man of fair business education, who carried on a merchandise business in connection with extensive planting. He moved West at an early day, and first located in west Tennessee, removing in 1839 to Carroll county, Miss. Mrs. Purnell died December 15, 1848. Her husband did not long survive her, dying August

26, 1849. He left a goodly estate in land and negro slaves to his five surviving children. The war swept away most of this property before the subject of this sketch had reached his majority. The five children were: M. T. Purnell, Jr., who died December 3, 1862, leaving no children; M. A. Purnell, who died September, 1866, leaving two boys: W. A. Purnell and M. A. Purnell; Elizabeth Helen, who married Capt. E. E. Foltz, a sketch of whom appears in this work; Eliza R., who is the wife of Capt. B. W. Sturdivant, of Tallahatchie county, and James C. Purnell, the youngest, the subject of this sketch. The three latter are the only survivors of the family at this date. Left an orphan at an early age, James C. Purnell grew to manhood in his native county, and received a fair education at Salem and Oxford, N. C. After completing his studies, and at the close of the war, he returned to Carroll county, and engaged in planting near Vaiden. May 24, 1870, he was married to Miss Jennie B. Hawkins, daughter of Maj. Frank Hawkins, a sketch of whom appears in this history. She was born and reared in Carroll county, but was educated at Jackson and Memphis, Tenn. In 1871 Mr. Purnell moved to Winona, and entered merchandise, in partnership with Joe C. Kittrell, the firm being Kittrell & Purnell, doing a successful business for three years. Mr. Purnell then formed a partnership with his brother-in-law, Frank Hawkins, Jr., under the firm name of Purnell & Hawkins. They carried on business successfully from 1874 till 1888, when they were burned out. They carried a large stock of general merchandise, and did a large furnishing business. After being burned out, the firm formed a private banking company, and engaged in banking. In September, 1890, a stock company was formed, and the Citizens' bank organized, when Mr. J. C. Purnell was made president; T. H. Somerville, vice president, and Frank Hawkins, Jr., cashier. Mr. J. C. Purnell is one of the enterprising business men of Winona, and is connected with a number of public enterprises. He was a town alderman for some years, president of the board of trade, and also of the Winona Land and Improvement company. He was the originator and first president of the Winona Warehouse company. Success has crowned all his various enterprises. Mr. and Mrs. Purnell have had eight children: Frank M., Mary H., Jennie H., James C., Jr., Anna E., Eunice Read, Rhesa H. and Eunice Elizabeth. Eunice Read died in August, 1884. Mr. Purnell is a member of the Episcopal church, of which he is junior warden, and also past master in the Masonic fraternity.

CHAPTER XVII.

MEMOIRS OF A FEW FAMILIES, Q.

D H. Quin, M. D., McComb City, Pike county, Miss. Peter Quin, Sr., grandfather of the subject of this sketch, came to Mississippi from Spartanville, S. C., in 1808, and settled on Tangipahoe. In 1812 he laid out the town of Holmesville, Pike county, Miss., as it now stands. He acted as governor of Mississippi territory for a short time. He was made a member of the convention that framed the first constitution of Mississippi. He had four sons, Daniel, Richard, Henry and Peter, and one daughter, Nancy. Dr. D. H. Quin is a descendant of his second son, Richard Quinn, who was a farmer by occupation. During his long life he was almost always connected with public duties. The Doctor was born February 16, 1821. At the age of fifteen he went to Kenyon college, Ohio, and finished his literary education there, and thence to Philadelphia, and finished his medical education in the Pennsylvania university. He was a physician in the hospital for two years, and graduated in the session of 1845 and 1846. He was married in 1848 to Mary F. Bickham. By this marriage were born two sons and two daughters; James and Oliver being the sons. O. B. Quin is now a physician and practitioner in McComb City, Miss. After the death of his first wife, the Doctor, in 1860, was married to Nannie Elezay, who died a short while after without issue. In the fall of 1864 he was married to Anna Beattie Long. They have two sons, Hillary and Richard. Hillary, the eldest, is a graduate of Mississippi university, Oxford, and now a professor at Fayette, Miss. Richard is yet young and unmatured.

Judge H. Murray Quin is among the pioneer families of Pike county, and among the more prominent in all its history this family has always taken superior rank. Col. Peter Quin, his father, who came to Pike county about 1813 and settled near where the town of Holmesville now is, was a native of South Carolina, having been born in York district of that state in 1787. He was reared and educated there and married Martha Moore, a native of North Carolina, and born and reared in Rutherford county. She was born in 1794. Soon after his marriage Mr. Quin emigrated to Mississippi, locating in the territory now embraced in the county of Pike. He assisted in the organization of the county and gave land at Holmesville upon which was erected the first county building, and at the first county election he was elected to represent the county in the legislature. He served also as a delegate from Pike county to the constitutional convention. Through all his active life he was one of the most prominent and useful citizens of the county. He died in 1839, his widow surviving him till 1864. Of the children of these worthy pioneers, Judge H. M. Quin is probably the best known. Mrs. S. A. Nicholson, widow of Dr. George Nicholson, is his eldest daughter; L. J. Quin, of McComb City, is also well known; he was sheriff of the county several years; Mrs. Louisa Bosworth, another daughter, is now dead; Dr. Irvin M. Quin, formerly of Brandon, was state senator from Rankin and Scott counties for eight years, and died at Arcola, in Sunflower county, in 1887, and was a prominent man in his day; Mrs. C. M. Leland, widow of Dr. L. C. Leland, late of Panola, resides at Holmesville; Col. Peter C. Quin, deceased, was state senator, representing Pike and Lawrence counties for four years; Capt. Josephus R. Quin, a prosperous merchant in Summit, was killed at the battle of Harrisburg, Ky., in 1864; DeWitt C. Quin, the youngest son, represented Pike county in the legislature, and died while a member of that body; Mrs. C. M. Wallace, another daughter, who became the wife of Dr. Jesse Wallace, died in New York. Judge Quin's younger days were passed upon his father's plantation, and it was in the common schools of his neighborhood that his education was begun; later he was a student for one year at Oakland college, afterward reading law at Holmesville, and being admitted to the bar in 1840, though he did not engage in the practice of his profession for several years thereafter, being in that year elected treasurer of Pike county, and serving in that capacity for four years. He was next elected, in 1845, to the office of circuit clerk; later, in 1846, he was elected to the office of clerk of the probate court and continued in that position as clerk of both circuit and probate courts for ten years, until his election as probate judge, in which office he served for eight years. After his retirement from office he continued his practice of law until 1871, when he became mayor of the town of Summit, since which time he has lived retired from active labor, devoting his attention to planting with much success. He first had as a partner in his law practice Judge Hurst, late judge of the supreme court, but later he became connected with Col. T. R. Stockdale, present member of congress, and later Judge H. Cassidy, Sr., also became a partner in said law firm. Excepting when the incumbent of some office, he was in the active practice of his profession from 1842 to 1871, a period of nearly thirty years. Prior to the war he became the owner of considerable property, including quite a number of slaves, but, in common with the rest of his friends and business associates of the South, he lost heavily as a consequence of the struggle. During the last twelve years he has served as justice of the peace, and he was one of the supervisors of the State Lunatic asylum, appointed by Governor Humphreys, serving in that capacity for six years. He was married September 1, 1842, to Miss Delilah Bearden, a daughter of Jeremiah Bearden, late of Pike county. Mrs. Quin, who was a native of this county, died in 1866, having left her husband five children: Dr. L. M. Quin, of Holmesville; Emma E., wife of L. W. Connerly, of Baton Rouge, La.; Wallace W., a farmer near Summit; George M. (now dead), and Lulu, who married Charles H. Rowan, and living at Point Pleasant, La. In May, 1867, Judge Quin married Miss Nannie Sumrall (his second wife), a daughter of Henry Sumrall, of Copiah county, by whom he had two children: Henry N., a bright young man of nineteen, who graduated from Jackson Commercial college in 1890, and is now a bookkeeper at Poplarville, Miss., and Ina M., who has recently graduated at Edward McGehee's college at Woodville. Judge Quin has been a Mason since 1848, and has been a Royal Arch Mason since 1855; is a member of the Holmesville lodge, A F. & A. M., is a member of the consistory of the Scottish Rites Masons, having taken eighteen degrees, and for the past thirty years has been a member of the Methodist Episcopal Church South. As a politician, he was a leader of the old whig party in his county, and after the late war he allied himself with the democratic party. He has occupied public positions in his county for fifty years and discharged his duties in all with such consummate ability as to gain unusual esteem and the confidence of his constituents.

Chapter XVIII.

OTHER PROMINENT PERSONS, R.

J C. Radgesky, merchant, Gunnison, Miss., a live, energetic business man, is a native of Europe, and when but a child four years of age came with his parents to the United States. They landed at New Bedford, Mass., in 1859. His father, Joseph Radgesky, upon coming to this country, first located in Mississippi, was one of the first settlers of Greenville, and was, it is believed, the third merchant at that place; and the fire in Greenville in 1875 or 1876 burned him out. He died there of yellow fever during the epidemic of 1878. In 1870 J. C. Radgesky embarked in business for himself at Concordia of this state, was very successful, and in 1872 and 1873 went to South Bend, Ark., where he opened a branch store on the Arkansas river in partnership with Clay Rice, then sheriff of Lincoln county, who died in 1873, when Mr. Radgesky returned to Concordia. Recognizing the advantages of Gunnison he located there in 1890, soon after the establishment of the station, and was the second to start business enterprises there. It is worthy of note that the business element of Gunnison is made up mostly of merchants and citizens of Concordia. There Mr. Ragdesky has invested in considerable property and has erected seven buildings, which he rents, and is completing a number more. In the winter of 1890 and 1891 he erected the first building at the station of Round Lake and now has a business interest there. He is also expecting to build on property in Rosedale. He has been rather active in politics and served as alderman of Concordia for three terms, filling that position in a creditable and satisfactory manner.

The ancestors of Samuel E. Ragland, planter, Delay, Miss., were originally from Wales, his grandfather having emigrated from that country to the United States with his parents when but an infant. His father, Pettis Ragland, was born in Hanover county, Va., about 1768 and followed tilling the soil and teaching school during his lifetime. He was a popular man and was ever ready with his time and means to assist in all enterprises pertaining to the welfare of his county. He was married to Miss Martha Carter, a native of North Carolina and a woman of marked intelligence and refinement. She was the daughter of Phillip Carter, who was an honorable and upright citizen and who served during the Revolutionary war. Samuel E. Ragland, who has Virginia blood in his veins, was born in Halifax county of that state on July 6, 1811, and was the eldest of seven children born to Pettis and Martha (Carter) Ragland. He had limited educational advantages during youth, but by observation and contact with the world he has become a well-informed man. At the age of seventeen, he began fighting life's battles for himself and located in Monroe county, W. Va., where he remained until 1832, when he located at Lynchburg. While a resident of that town he was engaged in the stage business, which he followed until 1835. While thus employed, he was elected to convey President Jackson's famous message of the nullification of South Carolina. This he accomplished successfully, making the distance of eighty miles in one night's ride. While a resident of Lynchburg he was united in marriage to Miss Elizabeth K. Hobson, and in 1836 they moved to Lafayette county, Miss. There Mr. Ragland was employed as manager and overseer on some of the most extensive plantations in the county, and in every instance his success was almost phenomenal, being commented on far and near. Besides this, he conducted a plantation of his own. When the war broke out he had charge of the big plantation of the Price heirs on the Yocona river in Lafayette county. There was his power and ability as an overseer and manager brought into full play. Not a single slave escaped that was in his charge, and he made a note of all the property carried away by the Union troops, the heirs being thereby enabled to collect damages from the government for the amount lost. By his efforts the county records were saved, as he had them boxed, and with two of his own teams hauled them home, a distance of fourteen miles, where he concealed and saved them. His wife died in 1866 leaving a family of five children, three of whom are still living. In 1870 he married Mrs. Elizabeth M. Hobson, who bore him one son, S. E. Ragland, Jr. Mr. Ragland is extensively engaged in farming, owns about three thousand acres of land and raises a good grade of horses, cattle, hogs and sheep. Although eighty years of age he is still active and energetic. He is of medium size and has a pair of keen black eyes. He is a man noted far and near for his bravery and nerve, and when he once undertook a task he kept steadily at it until it was accomplished.

In reviewing the lives of men, their abilities and attainments, we observe a marked difference in ages at which success is reached. To some it comes in early life, to others, not until the decline of life, and to some it is denied altogether. So that it is with pleasure we record the history of a man to whom many of the good things of the world have come within his first three-score years. William A. Ragsdale was born in Grenada, Miss., February 24, 1860, and is a son of George W. Ragsdale, who was born in Pickensville, Ala., about the year 1821. William Ragsdale, the father of George W., was also a native of Alabama, of Scottish ancestry. George W. grew to manhood in his native state, and received his education there. He came to Mississippi in 1841, and located at Grenada, where he became interested in a flouringmill; he continued in this business until after the late Civil war, and is now the owner of several large sawmills, being one of the heaviest lumber dealers in the state. His residence is at Macomb, Miss. William A. Ragsdale is one of a family of six children—four sons and two daughters. He spent his youth in his native town, attending the common schools, where he acquired a fair education. After leaving school he went to Mobile, Ala., where he entered the machine shops, and thoroughly mastered the machinist's trade. For several years he followed this business, and then went on the road as traveling salesman for an Eastern manufacturing company located at Chambersburg, Penn. He remained in the employ of this firm for three years, his territory being Mississippi. In 1890 he resigned this position, and established himself in business at Greenwood, Le Flore county, Miss.; he erected a large brick store, and placed a most complete stock of hardware on sale there. His early training in the machine shops and his later experience in handling these goods have fitted him for the work he has taken up, so that we anticipate for him a more than ordinarily prosperous future. He has also built and fully equipped an extensive foundry and machine shop, where any work in the line of casting and machine repairs can be done in the best style. Greenwood is greatly indebted to Mr. Ragsdale for this, one of the leading enterprises.

Although he began life without means, he has accumulated a handsome property, and has come to be recognized as one of the most substantial business men of the community. He was married in Grenada, Miss., November 18, 1882, to Miss Mary Wright, daughter of F. S. Wright, of Grenada. Mrs. Ragsdale was born, reared, and educated in Grenada. Two children have been born of this marriage: Emma, died at the age of four years in 1888; Mary, aged three years, survives. The parents are worthy members of the Methodist Episcopal church. Mr. Ragsdale is an active leader in the Knights of Pythias lodge.

Wilber Fisk Rainey is a prominent and influential planter of Coahoma county, Miss., but was born near Atlanta, Ga., March 12, 1848, being the eighth of eleven children born to Isom S. and Mary E. (Bell) Rainey, natives of North Carolina and Georgia, respectively. Isom S. Rainey came to Mississippi in 1848 and located in Monroe county, where he engaged in planting and merchandising, being very wealthy at the breaking out of the war. He took a prominent part in the political affairs of his section, and served two terms in the state legislature, acquitting himself with great credit. He died in 1872, his widow surviving him until 1882. The maternal grandfather, General Bell, was an eminent and distinguished politician and lawyer. Wilber Fisk Rainey was reared to manhood in Clay county, Miss., and received his literary education in the high school of West Point. After leaving school he sold goods in a mercantile establishment for seven years, at the end of which time he began planting and merchandising on his own account, and has continued in this business very successfully ever since. He began life for himself with $285 and by his own exertions has accumulated property, including one thousand acres of land, about four hundred acres of which he opened and improved himself; he also is a stockholder in the oil mills at Friar's Point. He is one of the most substantial of citizens, for he is public-spirited and enterprising. He is a true and steadfast friend, and has won the respect and esteem of all who know him; he takes great interest in church work, and is especially interested in the moral training of the young of the community. He is affable and agreeable in manners, and is very charitably inclined toward all his fellow creatures. As a planter he is systematic and thorough, and everything about his buildings and grounds shows neatness and order at once commendable and worthy of emulation. He is courteous and accommodating, and cheerfully and willingly extends the right hand of fellowship to those less fortunate than himself, and sends no one hungry from his door. He was married December 5, 1872, to Miss Mollie C. Brady, a native of this state, and a daughter of John and Mary Brady, native Tennesseeans, her father being a Confederate soldier during the Rebellion, dying in the service. Mr. Rainey and his wife are members of the Methodist Episcopal church, and he is a member of the American Legion of Honor, and the K. of P. He has held a number of offices of trust in this county, and in every instance proved a faithful and competent official. Of his brothers, William E., Thomas E., Preston, S. K. and A. Rainey were all members of the Confederate army, the first named dying during the service in Virginia. Preston was wounded at the battle of Corinth, but survived it.

Thomas J. Ramsey, a well-known planter of Copiah county, was a native or Jasper county, Ga., where he was born in 1819. He is the son of Noah and Elizabeth Ramsey, both natives of Georgia, his father having been born in 1764, and his mother in 1784, both of whom lived to be eighty-six years old, and both died in the same house in Copiah county. In his youth Mr. Noah Ramsey served his apprenticeship at the saddler's trade, at which he worked during his earlier days. In 1822 he moved to Lawrence county, Miss., where he located on a farm, which he cultivated, also working at his trade. He was the son of William Ramsey, one of the noble heroes who fought in the Revolutionary war under General Hancock. He married Elizabeth Deering, the daughter of William and Elizabeth Deering, of Georgia. Thomas J. Ramsey came to Mississippi with his parents at about the age of three years, and lived with them in Lawrence county until 1838, and then they moved to Copiah county, locating on the farm upon which he now lives. He was married in 1850 to Rebecca Womack, of Copiah county, a daughter of Jacob and Hezekiah Womack. To them have been born eighteen children—nine girls and nine boys—named as follows, fifteen of whom are yet living: Louzenberg B.; Melville; Emma; Silas; Anslum; J. Leonidas; Adela, deceased; Mattie; Joan; John W.; Cora, deceased; Jasper, deceased; Elizabeth; Lula; Simeon D.; Belle; Thomas; Rebecca. In 1847 he entered the Mexican war, enlisting in company B, First battalion of the Mississippi rifles, and served during the war. He was one of those veterans of that war who entered the Confederate army in the war of secession. In 1861 he enlisted in company B, of the Sixth Mississippi regiment, commanded by Colonel Thornton, of which he was first lieutenant, serving continuously until 1865. On account of the illness of his captain, he took command of the company a great portion of the time. Among the several engagements in which he took part were those of Harrisburg and Shiloh. Mr. Ramsey has been a member of the Masonic order since 1851, when he united with the Quitman lodge. In after years he became a Royal Arch Mason at Hazlehurst. He served four years as a member of the board of supervisors of this county. He and his wife are both worthy members of the Baptist church. Mr. Ramsey is a successful planter, and has property which is considered amongst the finest in this part of the state. His record as a business man and citizen is such that he commands the respect of the best people of this and surrounding counties.

L. Randall, one of the most prosperous and influential business men of Moss Point, Jackson county, was born in New England, in the town of Richmond, N. H., April 17, 1810. He was reared on a farm, attending school two or three months of the year, and spending the remainder of his time in the duties that usually fall to the lot of the boys on a farm. At the age of seventeen years he went to Boston, Mass., and was employed there in a hotel two or three years. Early in the thirties he removed to New Orleans, making the trip on a schooner. He secured a situation in a cookery house which he filled three years. In 1835, to escape the yellow fever, he came from New Orleans to West Pascagoula, Miss., and stopped at the McCrea house, which was then owned by Governor McCrea, and was a very popular hotel. Later, he went to Mobile, Ala., and was clerk in the Mansion house, of which Charles Cullom, a man widely known throughout the South, was proprietor. In the year 1840, Mr. Randall's friends, in the spirit of a joke, brought out his name as a candidate for the legislature against a prominent opponent. Greatly to the surprise of every one, he was elected by a large majority. He now declares that he knew nothing, and should have been on the farm, but he served through the session with much credit to himself. In 1847 he was elected sheriff of Jackson county, and held the office six years. These two offices are the only public positions he has held, or for which his name was ever offered. He was a member of the senatorial convention when Jefferson Davis made his first political speech. Mr. Randall was for some time a manufacturer of shingles at Scranton, Miss., and he has been in the mercantile and milling and steamboating business for many years. He is one of the old residents of Jackson county, and has witnessed many changes in the people and their surroundings. He has met with many ups and downs in his career, but with a buoyancy and courage characteristic of him he has risen to the top, and has made a success of every undertaking to which he has given his attention. He was married in 1842 to Miss I. M. Delmas, of Pascagoula, by whom he has had ten children.

William F. Randolph was born in Virginia, December 7, 1832. His father, Robert Lee Randolph, was a native of Fauquier county, Va., and his grandfather, Robert Randolph, was a captain of cavalry in the Revolutionary war, and was captured by the celebrated Colonel Tarleton, and sent to England as a prisoner of war. This family are related to John Randolph of Roanoke. They are also related to the celebrated Lee family of Virginia, our Robert Lee Randolph being a first cousin of Gen. Robert E. Lee. The history of these two distinguished families is, in a sense, the history of this great country. Mr. Randolph's mother was Mary Magill, a daughter of Col. Charles Magill, who was an aid to Gen. George Washington and General Gates. He was wounded at Cowpens, when the colonial army was so badly defeated. The Magills were among the best known people of the Old Dominion. Our subject's parents always resided in Virginia, on the old home plantation—Eastern View—which was in the family many years, and is now owned by Alfred M. Randolph, a brother of William F., and bishop of Virginia in the Episcopal church. Robert Lee Randolph and wife had four sons and one daughter. They were: William F., Alfred M., Beverly R., Buckner N. and Mary M., wife of Edward C. Turner, of Fauquier county, Va. All these children are residents of Virginia except William F., and are people of prominence and respectability. Buckner M. served with distinction in the Confederate army during the late war. William F. was reared upon the old plantation in Virginia. His education up to the time he was eighteen was acquired under private teachers at home, but was very thorough and practical. A short time after reaching his eighteenth year the gold fever was at its hight in California, and our young Randolph gained his father's consent and made the trip to that Eldorado via Panama. He mined there with varying success for five years, and in 1855 returned to his old home in Virginia. The next year he came to Mississippi and located on Deer creek, in Washington county. He brought with him thirty or forty negroes, given to him by his father, and from the time he came to the state to the breaking out of the war he was a prosperous and prominent planter. On learning of the secession of Virginia he returned to his native state, joined the Sixteenth Virginia cavalry, as a private, and served four years, until after the Valley campaign against General Banks, and after that he was captain of a company he had recruited, and which was placed with General Ewell as a body guard. He served with him until at the second battle of Manassas General Ewell was severely wounded, when the company was sent to Gen. T. J. Jackson, celebrated in history as Stonewall Jackson, to serve in like capacity. Sixteen men under the command of Captain Randolph constituted the guard on the night on which he received the wound that, with pneumonia, was the cause of his death. The loss of this gallant soldier was the dire result of a mistake incident to a panic among some raw North Carolina troops belonging to Lane's brigade. Of the sixteen men who were the escort only Captain Randolph escaped, every one of them having been killed or mortally wounded, and he escaped only by spurring his horse right through the column, amid a galling fire. Captain Randolph saw much hardship and much active service, and was a gallant and intrepid officer. One of the tenderest chords of his nature is touched when he speaks of and recalls the death of his beloved commander. A short time after the battle of Gettysburg, Penn., he was captured, and held a prisoner of war at Johnson's island until the close of the war. When he returned to Mississippi he found his slaves gone and his plantation devastated. He was united in marriage with Miss Nannie B. Carter, a native of Mississippi, and a daughter of Alfred G. Carter, one of the early settlers of Washington county, Miss., and a descendant of an old and respected Virginian family. By this union he has four children: Eleanor C., Alfred G., Hebe G. and Nannie B. Mr. Randolph's plantation consists of six thousand acres of land, two thousand acres of which are under a high state of cultivation. He has devoted his time to planting since he came to Mississippi with such success that he ranks among the well-to-do planters of this part of the state. He is a public-spirited, liberal-minded citizen, and has at heart the development and advancement of all of the best interests of this county and state.

W. T. Raney was born in Choctaw county, Ala., in 1862, but since 1883 has been a resident of Lauderdale county, Miss., where he has been engaged in farming on his own account since 1884. After a short experience in merchandising, he found that planting was much more congenial to his tastes, and accordingly gave up the former calling to obtain his living from the soil. In 1883 he made a purchase of land, which, by constant addition, now amounts to four hundred and sixty acres, all of which is exceptionally fertile land, well and carefully tilled. This land is located nine miles southeast of Meridian, and is devoted principally to the raising of cotton and corn. He has a large amount of timber land, on which is some of the finest longleaf pine in the state, and in addition to planting he is also engaged in lumbering. He has an interest in a sawmill plant, valued at $1,500, which turns off five thousand feet of pine lumber per day. Although the early educational advantages of Mr. Raney were poor, and the obstacles which beset his pathway many, yet he has surmounted all difficulties, soon paid off the debt which he owed upon starting out in life for himself, and is now well to do, and highly esteemed by all who know him. Although he is still young in years he has already manifested business ability of a high order, and bids fair to become one of the wealthiest citizens of the county. He is a member of the Farmers' Alliance. In December, 1887, he was married to Miss Maggie Brewster, by whom he has three children: Daniel, Hiram and Ethel. W. T. Raney is a son of Daniel H. Raney, who was born in Georgia about 1816, and was afterward united in marriage to Miss Matilda Carlisle.

William M. Rankin (deceased) was identified with the early history of Marion county, Miss., having removed there from South Carolina in 1818. He was born in Virginia, October 14, 1792. When he came to Mississippi he engaged in keelboating, which he carried on successfully for many years. He was married in the year 1820, to Martha, daughter of John Warren, and a native of Georgia. The result of this union was the birth of eleven children, ten of whom grew to maturity: Eliza L. (deceased) was born February 23, 1821; William J. (deceased) was born November 20, 1822; Mary J. (deceased) was born January 9, 1825; Martha R. (deceased) was born September 6, 1826; John W. (deceased) was born April 16, 1828; George W. was born March 31, 1830; H. Emily was born April 29, 1832; Elizabeth A. was born January 13, 1834; Louisa (deceased) was born November 6, 1835; Thomas J. (deceased) was born August 24, 1837, and S. Ed was born October 5, 1839. William J. Rankin married Miss Linian Harvey, and they had born to them four children, three of whom lived to maturity: Sarah E., William and Eliza. John W. married Miss Mary J. Fenn, and to them were born five children: J. Warren. Martha E., Floyd (wife of John Baylis), T. Jesse and Frank F. George W. married Miss Annie Fenn, and they reared five children: Harriet, Mary, Emily, Carrie and George M. Thomas J. had one son, G. Henry, a merchant at Spring College, Marion county. S. Ed married Miss Mary A. Ford, and unto them was born one son, S. Jesse. When the war between the North and South was begun in 1861, all the sons of William Rankin enlisted in the Seventh Mississippi regiment, and served faithfully and gallantly in the cause they had espoused. Jesse died at Brookhaven in 1861, and William J. was assassinated at his home before the conflict was ended. The Rankin family occupy a leading position in the social and political circles of Marion county. All the offices within the gift of the people have been bestowed upon some member of the family, who in turn have shown a great aptitude and ability for the discharge of public business. S. Ed Rankin occupies a dwelling whose walls, if they could speak, would unfold many pages of history. The house was probably erected as early as 1812, and was the first to be built on the Pearl river in Marion county. General Jackson occupied the house for a time during the War of 1812, and a stockade was erected about it. General Davidson, of the Federal army, with his division of cavalry, passed a night and a day there during the winter of 1864. In the same house was held a convention before the state of Mississippi was established, to fix the line of division between Mississippi and Alabama.

Among the wealthy plantation owners of Jasper county, Miss., is S. S. Ratcliffe, of Garlandville. He was born in Perry county, Miss., in the year 1821, and remained there during his early childhood. In 1826 he moved to Mobile with his parents, and there received a common-school education and attended Penney's college. His parents were born, reared and married in South Carolina, and removed to Mississippi in 1819. They had born to them seven children, of whom S. S. Ratcliffe was the second. The father was a farmer by occupation, but in the period of 1830-5 was engaged extensively in milling at Mobile. He sold his mills in 1835, and was most of the time until 1839 engaged in merchandising. In the year last mentioned he removed from Mobile to Jasper county, Miss., where he was a successful planter until 1856, when he again became a merchant at Enterprise, Clarke county, and carried on a profitable business until his death, which occurred in November, 1863. His wife survived until August, 1887. Both were worthy members of and liberal contributors to the Methodist Episcopal church. The subject of this notice spent a portion of his youth in Jasper county. He was united in marriage, in the year 1851, to Miss M. E. Boulton, a daughter of A. A. Boulton, a farmer of Jasper county, Miss. Of this union were born nine children. Mr. Ratcliffe engaged in farming near Garlandville, Miss., and followed this occupation until the breaking out of the late war. In 1863 he enlisted in Captain Porter's company, and was in the siege of Vicksburg, where he was wounded. He served through the conflict, and after peace was declared he returned to his business, which he has continued ever since. He owns fourteen hundred acres of choice land, six hundred acres of which are cleared and under excellent cultivation. He has given the closest attention to the pursuit of husbandry, and has followed it both as an art and science. Among his neighbors he is esteemed very highly, and as a citizen he would be an ornament to any community. He is a member of the Masonic fraternity.

John S. Ratliff, the pioneer of Verona, Miss., was born in Lincoln county, Ga., in 1806, a son of William and Mary Ratliff. He moved from Lincoln, Ga., to Monroe county, Ga., and there, in 1826, married Miss Grace Durham, a daughter of Matthew and Fannie Durham. He removed to Noxubee county, Miss., in 1833, and lived there about eighteen years. In December, 1850, he located at Verona, where he bought land of Newton Davis, and was a pioneer settler. Among the other early settlers here may be mentioned the Davises (Newton and Marion), Richard D. Scales and John Armstrong. The first store was opened here in 1850 by John O'Carrell, and that was the nucleus about which grew up the present town, its development from that time having been very rapid. Mr. Ratcliff engaged in merchandising, and also carried on planting to a considerable extent. Before the war he had at one time forty-two negroes, twenty-seven of whom were men. To Mr. and Mrs. Ratliff were born eight children: Fannie D., now Mrs. Armstrong; Lucy, now Mrs. Stovall; Mary, now Mrs. Ledbetter; Elizabeth A., now Mrs. Wear; Josephine, now Mrs. Caruth; Camilla, who became Mrs. Brown, and died in 1890; Georgia C., now Mrs. Anthony, and James William, who is a resident of Texas. They are members of the Baptist church, and Mr. Ratliff is a democrat in politics. It was in 1850 that this pioneer began to clear land at Verona, Miss. The Baptist church was organized there about 1852 with eight members. Its first house of worship was a log structure. The present more sightly building was erected in 1862, and the membership is now seventy. Not only in church advancement, but in every respect has Mr. Ratliff witnessed great changes since coming here. When he came the country was practically a wilderness, almost untouched by the hand of progress. What memories of the past a comparison of the site of Verona forty years ago with the busy town of to-day must bring to him—memories marked by successive steps in the work of civilization! All honor to the pioneer! Long may he be spared to enjoy the fruits of his toil, and to tell of the days before the railroad and the telegraph, the days of hardship and inconvenience, but of pleasures and sports unknown to the Mississippian of the present generation. It is such whose names most fittingly adorn the pages of local history.

Capt. William Ratliff was born in Madison county, Miss., in 1832, a son of John Ratliff, a native of Tennessee. The latter removed to Alabama early in life, where he married Miss Catherine Denson, after which he resided for one year in Rankin county, Miss. At the end of this time he moved to Madison county, where he operated a plantation and kept hotel on the old Natchez road. In 1835 he moved to Rankin county, and during the year 1849 he died. He accumulated considerable wealth, sufficient to give his children a good start in life, and also saw that they received fair educations. William Ratliff received his initiatory training in the common schools, and finished his education at St. Mary's college of Bardstown, Ky. Upon finishing his collegiate course he devoted his attention to the management of his plantation until the opening of the war. On the great issue that gave rise to the war, Mr. Ratliff stood with a great number of the best men of his section in favor of secession, for which his first vote was cast. Early in 1861 he enlisted as a private in company A, Eighteenth Mississippi regiment, and was assigned to duty in General Lee's army. In the winter of 1862 he was elected first lieutenant of the company, and was afterward promoted to captain. His career as a soldier was marked by intrepidity and courage, and he was highly respected and esteemed by his superior officers, as well as those beneath him in rank. At the time of the surrender he was in charge of a brigade, and he refused to surrender until his little remaining squad was literally overpowered, even then refusing to surrender his sword to a Federal lieutenant who demanded it, telling him that he would not surrender to an officer beneath him in rank. After the war he conducted a mercantile establishment for a short time at Forest, Miss., and in 1866 opened a similar business in Brandon, which he managed with remarkable success until he was burned out in 1868, from which he suffered a complete loss of everything invested in the business. After this unfortunate circumstance Captain Ratliff again took charge of his plantation, to which he has since given his chief attention. He has prospered, and is now the possessor of about eighteen hundred acres of land, well improved and stocked. In addition to this he also owns a store, and does a business that is constantly on the increase. For many years he has taken an active interest in local and state affairs, and in 1880 he was elected a member of the state senate, serving one term. While a member of that body he was recognized as an able, conscientious and incorruptible member, and did admirable service for his section. He has recently been solicited by many friends throughout Rankin county to allow his name to be used as a candidate for the senate for the ensuing term, and should he be elected he will be ranked among the leading members of that body. He has been married twice, his first wife being Miss Margaret Lucy, who died one year after their marriage, in 1860. In 1868 he was wedded to Miss Jennie Cavit, of Hinds county, by whom he has three sons and seven daughters.

Rev. William P. Ratliff is a Mississippian but was born in Leake county, on the 9th of February, 1847, his father, Z. L. Ratliff, being a native of Alabama. The latter took up his abode in Mississippi about 1828, and until he attained manhood he was a resident of Madison county. When a young man he became one of the early settlers of Leake county, and was married to Miss Sarah L. Adams, a member of a well known pioneer family of Attala county. Her father was a prominent member of the Methodist church, in which he was for many years a class leader. Z. L. Ratliff farmed up to 1856 in Leake county, at the end of which time he located and now resides in Attala county. He has been very successful as a planter, and is now in good circumstances. He is one of the stewards of the Methodist Episcopal church, is a member of the A. F. & A. M., and is a public-spirited and law abiding citizen. He served in the Confederate army for a short time under Colonel George. Rev. William P. Ratliff is the eldest of his five sons and five daughters, all of whom are living and all of whom are heads of families, with the exception of three. Mr. Ratliff attained manhood in Attala county, and received his primary education in the common schools. The war came up and he joined the Confederate forces in 1863, first going into the service as a substitute for his father, but afterward joining on his own account. He became a member of Colonel Lay's regiment, Adams' brigade, and did service in Louisiana until the close of the war. After its close he returned home and engaged in planting in Attala county, and on the 22d of October, 1868, he was united in marriage to Miss Cornelia B. Mitchell, a daughter of Albert Mitchell, a member of one of the old families of the county. Mr. Ratliff was left destitute at the close of the war and had to once more commence the battle of life for himself. Being a good manager and full of pluck he fought the battle of life bravely and successfully, and although his first purchase was small and on time, he succeeded in paying off the debt and soon after purchased more land. He now has three good plantations, comprising one thousand one hundred acres of land, and is one of the thriftiest planters of the county. One of the plantations is located near Ethel and on this place about eleven acres are devoted to strawberries, at the raising of which Mr. Ratliff has had remarkable success. In 1866 he joined the Methodist church and in 1878 was licensed to preach, since which time he has been a local preacher and is one of the prominent and leading members of the church in Kosciusko. He is a member of the A. F. & A. M., and in his political views is a democrat. He has held several local political positions in the county, and in 1875 was elected county assessor and made two assessments of the county. Mr. and Mrs. Ratliff are the parents of the following children: Anna L., Mary Belle, Sudie, John B., Zach M., Katie E., Florence C., Albert W., Pinkney and Grady. Mr. Ratliff purchased some excellent residence property in Kosciusko in 1890, and moved with his family to town in September of that year, for the purpose of giving his children the advantages of the town schools. He is, himself, mostly self-educated since coming to years of maturity. He has a well-selected library, and keeps well posted on the current topics of the day. He is progressive, enterprising and successful as a business man, and is a superior manager and a shrewd financier. He is very kindly and social in his manners, and is a man whom to know is to honor.

Capt. William C. Raum is one of the leading citizens of Vicksburg, Miss., but was born in Charleston, Jefferson county, Va., in 1829, being the second child born to the union of William C. Raum and Elizabeth Moody, both of whom were born in the Keystone state, the father being reared and educated in Cannonsburg. He studied medicine at Baltimore, graduating from a fine medical institution of that city, and his first practice was done in Gettysburg. After a time he moved to Charleston, Va., where he made his home until his death, being one of the leading medical practitioners of this town. His ancestors were of

German descent and were early settlers of what is now Shippensburg, Penn., his grandfather having been born in that town. The Moody family are of Irish lineage and became residents of Pennsylvania during colonial times, the grandfather, Rev. John Moody, being born at Shippensburg on the 4th of July, 1776. Dr. William C. Raum died in 1863, but his widow survived him until 1888, when she died at her old home in Virginia. They were earnest members of the Presbyterian church, in which the father had been an elder. Capt. William C. Raum received his education in Charleston academy and began life as a clerk in Virginia. In 1848 he came to Vicksburg, Miss., and after working as clerk for some time engaged in the dry goods business for himself, but at the end of two years turned his attention to auctioneering and the real estate business, which callings he continued to follow until the opening of the war. Although opposed to secession, when Mississippi withdrew from the Union he remained true to what he considered her interests, and in 1861 raised a company for the Confederate army and entered the service as a first lieutenant. In about one month he was chosen captain of the company and participated in the engagements at Shiloh, Perryville, Murfreesboro, Nashville, Franklin, and all the battles of the Georgia campaign. He was paroled at Greensboro, N. C., after which he returned to Vicksburg, and for two years followed the calling of a planter, being compelled to commence anew the battle of life, as nearly all his property had been swept away during the war. After giving up planting, he followed the calling of a clerk for a short time, and then secured an interest in a steamboat and became captain of the Era, No. 8, which plied on the Sunflower and Yazoo rivers. He continued as a steamboat captain for about seven years, then devoted one year to the auction and furniture business. In 1878 he was made deputy United States revenue collector for his district, and filled this position to the satisfaction of all concerned until 1881, when he was appointed United States marshal for the southern district of Mississippi by President Arthur, and held the office for four years. In the month of April, 1890, he took charge of a trader ship in the Indian territory, but one year later, in the month of May, he entered the postoffice of Vicksburg as assistant postmaster, the duties of which position he is still discharging. He was married in 1852 to Miss Ann Gwinn, a native of Virginia, who came to Vicksburg in youth, dying in Mississippi in 1865. The Captain's second marriage took place in 1866, to Miss Augusta Henshaw, a daughter of Major Henshaw, of Louisiana, and resulted in the birth of five children, who are living: William C., who is chief clerk of the Singer Sewing Machine company of Mississippi and Louisiana; Emma, wife of Dr. Sherard, Vicksburg; Elizabeth, Jennie and John. The family are regular attendants at church, and although Captain Raum is not a member of any religious organization he gives liberally of his means in their support. In appearance he is of medium stature, rather portly, has gray hair and mustache, and possesses agreeable and courteous manners. Raumville is a beautiful suburb in the southern part of Vicksburg, consisting, originally, of about twenty-seven acres, on which many handsome residences have been built. It is proving very popular as a residence section, for it overlooks the river, and the view, as far as the eye can reach, abounds in beautiful scenery. It was laid out and named by Captain Raum, who now owns some fifteen of its dwellings. His own residence, which is in this suburb, is a very handsome one, and is surrounded by fine old forest trees.

Maj. John Rawle, who is a leading business man of the city of Natchez, Miss., was born at Point Plaquemine, La., August 21, 1837, being the youngest son of the late Judge Edward Rawle and Appolina S. C. Saul, daughter of Joseph Saul, of New Orleans. Judge Edward Rawle was born in Germantown, a suburb of Philadelphia, September 22, 1797, but was married in the city of New Orleans on April 19, 1827, his wife dying on February 27, 1844. The

Judge departed this life at New Orleans November 4, 1880. He was a graduate of the University of Pennsylvania on January 15, 1815, having been one of the founders of the Philomathean society of that institution in 1813. January 2, 1823, he was admitted to the Philadelphia bar and afterward became a member of the Washington Benevolent society of Philadelphia, and on February 22, 1823, he delivered the annual address on Washington, before that body. In 1824 he moved to New Orleans, at which place he became the founder of the public-school system, and was a member of the first school board of the second municipality, acting as its president for many years. He was one of the founders, and a life member of the Second Municipal Public School Lyceum and Library society of that city, and in 1839 was chosen attorney for the second municipality, in which office he served for several years. In 1856 he was elected a fellow of the New Orleans Academy of Science, and for many years he was a prominent member of the Keystone association of New Orleans, and for a portion of that time acted as its president. Prior to this he was appointed associate judge of the city court and upon his retirement from the bench he resumed the practice of law, which he continued until advancing years forced him to retire from active life. He was a man of high aspirations, of noble character, and his brilliant intellect was strengthened and enriched by the highest culture. His mind was well poised and analytical and the most difficult subjects were handled by him with ease. As a lawyer he was one of the most brilliant of his time and as an orator his style was pleasing, convincing and forcible, and impressed one at once with his depth of mind and breadth of views. His father was the distinguished jurist, William Rawle of Philadelphia, one of the honored and trusted friends of George Washington. He held the office of United States district attorney in Pennsylvania during that eventful era known as the whisky rebellion of that state, and in the prosecution resulting therefrom he acquitted himself with great distinction and ability. The crowning act of his life was his commentary upon the Federal constitution, written in 1787, in which he displayed remarkable judgment and a high order of statesmanship. So admirably were the objects of this work devised and so skillfully were they matured, that it became a standard text-book in many or all of the colleges of the United States at that time, and up to about 1860 was used in the military academy at West Point. A life-size medallion of himself now adorns Medallion hall in the beautiful municipal buildings of his native city, Philadelphia. This distinguished family is of English descent. An ancestor of the American branch came to this country with, and was secretary for, William Penn. In 1724 one Francis Rawle, wrote a work on political economy entitled Ways and Means for the Inhabitants of Delaware to Become Rich. This book was the first that was ever printed by Benjamin Franklin. A reprint, for private distribution, was made in 1878, by William Brooke Rawle of Philadelphia, a copy of which, with the following letter, is full of interest, historically.

PHILADELPHIA, March 23, 1878.

MY DEAR UNCLE: I have had reprinted a few copies of a small book, or pamphlet, as we should call it in these days, written by our ancestor, Francis Rawle, who came over with his father in 1686, from Plymouth, Devonshire, to settle here. I send you a copy of it by book post. The only copy of the original was lost for some years, and has but recently been found. I have fulfilled a vow, that in case the book should ever turn up, I would thus save it from oblivion. The book is interesting for several reasons. Franklin told your father at Passy, in 1782, that this was the first book he ever printed with his own hand. It is supposed to have been the first book on political economy which issued from the press of this, if not of any American colony. When we consider that at the time it was written, 1724, there were few books and no libraries in this country, I think the work shows its author to have been a man of considerable information and education. Yours very sincerely,

WILLIAM BROOKE RAWLE.

HON. EDWARD RAWLE.

The following extract from the life of Benjamin Franklin, by Jared Sparks, refers to the preceding:

"One day at his dinner table at Passy, France, surrounded by men of rank and fashion, a young gentleman was present who had just arrived from Philadelphia. He showed a marked kindness to the young stranger, conversed with him about friends he had left at home, and then said: 'I have been under obligations to your family; when I set up business in Philadelphia, being in debt for my printing materials, and wanting employment, the first job I had was a pamphlet written by your grandfather. It gave me encouragement, and was the beginning of my success.'" This young stranger was the Hon. William Rawle, grandfather of the immediate subject of this sketch. Maj. John Rawle was educated in New Orleans, and in 1853 began life as a mercantile clerk, but the coming clash of arms caused him to cast aside personal considerations to enlist as a private soldier, April, 1861, in the Louisiana guards, Drew's battalion, and he was promoted through the various grades until in June, 1863, he was made major, and was appointed chief of artillery in General Forrest's army. He was in many battles, and at all times was found in the performance of his duty, but providentially escaped without a wound. After the war was over he returned to New Orleans and embarked in the cotton commission business, but came to Natchez, Miss., in 1867 and began planting. In 1877 he founded his present business, that of an insurance and real estate agent, and as he is unerring in his estimate of values, his judgment is sought and relied upon by capitalists, who consider him one of the most cautious as well as enterprising and successful followers of the business. He is regarded as authority upon such matters throughout this section, and deals in all classes of property, from residence sites in towns to plantations in this and adjoining states. In his insurance branch he represents the best companies in the United States, and does a general business in life, fire, marine and tornado insurance. He is a practical business man in every sense of the word, possessed of untiring energy, and is one of the leading men of Natchez. By leniency, fair dealing and honest integrity he has won many warm friends. He was married in 1867 to Miss Elizabeth H. Stanton (see sketch of Stanton family), and to them seven children have been born: Juliet (wife of L. R. Martin), Bessie (wife of W. C. Martin), Ethel, Hulda, John, Jr., Georgie (deceased), and Cecil. Major Rawle and his family are members of the Episcopal church, and of this church he has been senior warden for many years. He is a member of the A. F. & A. M., the K. of H., the K. of P., the A. L. of H., and the I. O. O. F. He is president of the M., A. & G. railroad, and secretary of the Mississippi Valley railroad. He has never been in politics, but he has been active in agitating railroad projects and other public enterprises for Natchez, and several of them may yet be developed for the future prosperity of this city. The Major's home is the mansion erected by his wife's father in 1857, and is one of the most beautiful and stately of Southern homes which were erected in ante-bellum days. It is furnished throughout in almost royal magnificence, and here he and his wife dispense hospitality with true Southern generosity to the numerous friends who delight to gather beneath their roof-tree.

Dr. Robert W. Rea, a prominent physician and surgeon of Wesson, Miss., was born at Old Gallatin, the old county seat, in 1844, a son of George and Sarah (Simpson) Rea. His father was born in Clarion county, Penn., in 1808, and the mother in Feliciana parish, La., in 1813. The former received a moderate education in his native state, and there also acquired a knowledge of the tailor's trade. After leaving Pennsylvania, he worked as a journeyman tailor in New Orleans and Louisville, and in other places, finally locating at Gallatin about 1833. There he was married the following year, and lived during the balance of his life, gaining a reputation as an honest, upright and progressive citizen. He abandoned his trade, however, before the war, and engaged in planting, with such success that he accumulated considerable property. Previous to the war, he served his county as a member of the board of supervisors, as school commissioner, and in other official positions. Not long after the war he was appointed sheriff of the county, in which capacity he served for a short time. Though he was not identified with any church, he was a strictly moral man. He was a member of the A. F. & A. M. and I. O. O. F. He was a great reader, which rendered him conversant with general history and the Scriptures, and he was noted as being a fine conversationalist, and the fact that he was one of the pioneers of the county, made his reminiscences peculiarly interesting for the residents of this part of the state. He was one of seventeen children born to Joshua and Sarah Rea, who were born and passed their lives in Pennsylvania, though his father was of Scotch origin. Mrs. Rea is still living, and is possibly the oldest inhabitant of the county. She is the daughter of Samuel Simpson, who is thought to have been born in Kentucky, and gone from there to Louisiana, where his wife died while Mrs. Rea was an infant, and where he married again and remained, Mrs. Rea being brought by her aunt, Mary Cairns, while yet an infant, to Gallatin when central Mississippi was an almost unbroken wilderness and inhabited chiefly by wild animals and Indians. Mrs. Rea is the mother of twelve children, six of them yet living: Captain William, now circuit clerk of Copiah county (he was captain of company G, of the Twelfth Mississippi regiment, and served with the army of Virginia); George, deceased (he was first lieutenant of company G, of the Thirty-sixth Mississippi regiment, and died at Mobile, from the effects of a wound received at Nashville); Thomas, now at Port Gibson, was with company B, of the Twelfth Mississippi regiment during the entire war period; Dr. Robert W., our subject; Sarah E., wife of Capt. A. L. Ard; Anna, wife of Albert Carter; Ellen, who is unmarried. Dr. Robert received his primary education in the public schools. It was not until after the war that he was enabled to take advantage of better educational opportunities. In 1862 he joined company G, of the Thirty-sixth Mississippi regiment, and fought at Farmington, Iuka, Corinth, Cold Water, and in the siege at Vicksburg; he was also with General Johnston's army at Resaca, Ga., and fought in the Atlanta campaign, and back under Hood to Franklin and Nashville, and on their retiring to Mobile, where he was detailed, and was located at Columbus, Miss., at the time of the surrender. During a portion of this time he held the rank of first sergeant. He was quite severely wounded at Corinth.

Returning home, he taught school and read medicine with Dr. William Shan, of Gallatin; graduated from the Louisiana university of New Orleans in 1869. After practicing for a few months at Gallatin, he located at Wesson, where he has since resided, and built up a large and still growing practice, having come to be recognized as one of the leading physicians of the county, as well as one of its most prominent citizens. He is the owner of about seventeen hundred acres of good timbered and tillable land, all of which he has acquired by his own efforts. He is a member of the A. F. & A. M., and he and his family are members of and attendants upon the services of the Presbyterian church. He was married in 1874 to Rilla E., a daughter of Capt. William and Mary (Calloway) Oliver. Mrs. Rea was born in Georgia and educated at Staunton, Va. She has borne her husband eight children, five of whom are living. She is a woman of fine intellect and attractive social qualities, and is respected and admired by a large circle of friends. Her mother died in 1883. Her father, Captain Oliver, was born in Georgia in 1828, was reared there, and there was married at the age of nineteen. About this time he removed to Louisiana and engaged in merchandising, which he followed with marked success until the war, when he entered the Confederate service, serving in the quartermaster's department of the Western army, with a rank as captain, with great distinction until the close of the war. After the war he located at Trenton, La., and again engaged in trade as a general merchant. A short time afterward he became a partner of John T. Hardy, a prominent and wealthy commission merchant of New Orleans, who was also owner of the Mississippi mills at Wesson, Miss. In 1870 the Captain purchased an interest in these mills, which then constituted only a small factory compared with the dimensions of the present concern. The following year the original mills were burned, but they were at once rebuilt on a much larger scale. Since his connection with the mills the Captain has devoted his entire attention to their management, and it is due in no small degree to his extraordinary business capacity that they have become one of the most complete and extensive cotton and woolen factories in the South. The Captain is a born financier, and possesses an indomitable will and energy combined with the best natural abilities. These qualities, backed up by his long business experience, have naturally made the Captain a man of wealth. He has gained a wide reputation as being one of the foremost business men and financiers of the South. When Dr. Rea resumed the battle of life after the war, he found himself so broken in fortune as to be practically destitute, but his devotion to his profession and business interests has been so great that he has attained not only the highest professional standing but ranks among the prominent business men of this section.

John J. Reaves, planter, Bently, has been a resident of Calhoun county, Miss., for the past forty years, and his principal occupation during that time has been farming. He has attended to his adopted calling with such energy and thoroughness that successful results have been reaped, and he is at the present time possessed of a large tract of land, and has over two hundred acres under cultivation. His grandparents, Stephen and Sarah (Flowers) Reaves, were natives of Georgia, and the grandfather was accidentally killed while spiling posts in a water gap in that state. He was a democrat in politics, and he and wife were members of the Baptist church. She lived to be quite aged. Both were very highly respected, and were the owners of considerable property. Of their nine children all lived to be grown, and one is now living, Mrs. Sarah Huckelby, who resides in the Lone Star state. The father of John J. Reaves, William Reaves, was the fourth in order of birth of this family. He was born in Virginia in 1805, but was reared in Georgia, where in 1827 he was married to Miss Sarah Lakey, also a native of the Old Dominion, born in 1810. There they resided until 1852, when they emigrated to Mississippi, settled near Bentley, and there made their home until 1887. The father was a very successful planter in early days, and owned a considerable amount of property, but in a later period his fortunes were less bright. He was in the Indian war in Florida in 1836. In politics he affiliated with the democratic party. He was a consistent member of the Primitive Baptist church, as is also his widow, who now resides with her youngest son near the old home place. Their family consisted of nine children, three, besides John J., now living: William, resides in Webster county, Miss.; Josiah Thomas, also in Webster county; and Susan, wife of C. G. Bently. Those deceased were: Mrs. Sarah McDowell, died in Webster county, leaving four children; Mrs. Mary J. Rigell, died at Bentley, Miss.; Mrs. Amanda Tabb, died in Webster county, leaving one child; and Benjamin, died in Alabama from the effects of a wound received during the war. The others died when small. John J. Reaves was born in Georgia in 1833, but attained his growth in Mississippi, whither he had moved with his parents. At the breaking out of hostilities he enlisted in company B, Thirty-first Mississippi regiment, infantry, and served until the close of war. He was wounded in the ankle and foot near Dalton, and was captured at Baker's creek in the first attack of Vicksburg, Miss.; taken to Indianapolis, Ind., and thence to Fort Delaware,

Md., where he was exchanged four months later. He afterward returned to his regiment in Alabama, and at the time of the surrender was in the hospital. From that time to the present he has never been free from pain in his ankle from the wound. Returning to Mississippi after the war he resumed agricultural pursuits, and in 1866 he was wedded to Mrs. T. J. Few, nee Tobitha Bently, widow of Jasper Few, who died during the war. By Mr. Few she had two children, William C. Few, and Susan, who died when ten years of age. To Mr. and Mrs. Reaves have been born two children, Samuel D., died near Denver, Colo., in December, 1889, at the age of twenty-two years, and J. Charles, who died at his home in 1887, when seventeen years of age. William C. Few is the only child now living of either marriage. He was reared by Mr. and Mrs. Reaves, and resides with them at the present time. He was married to Miss Connie Douglas, a native of Bently, and the daughter of T. J. Douglas, who is now deceased, but who was sheriff of Calhoun county for some time. Mrs. Douglas resides on the home place in Bently, and has seven living children. One, Dr. Thomas O., is a successful physician of Bently. In politics Mr. Reaves is a democrat. He was a member of the board of supervisors of Calhoun county, Miss., in 1885 and 1886, and he and Mrs. Reaves are members of the Methodist Episcopal church. He is a member of the Masonic fraternity, Atlanta lodge, of Chickasaw county, Miss.

Dr. Joseph Redhead, one of the early settlers of Wilkinson county, and a prominent physician and planter, was a native of England, and was born October 14, 1812, in Northumberland county, and was the eldest of a family of three daughters and two sons born to John and Anna Redhead, natives of England. When Dr. Joseph was seven years of age they came to the United States and settled in Cincinnati, Ohio, where the father engaged in an iron foundry. The parents remained in that city until their respective deaths at advanced years. Dr. Joseph started out for himself at the age of sixteen years, and coming South clerked for a time in Alabama. He carefully saved his earnings, and returned to Cincinnati, where he read medicine under one of Cincinnati's most prominent physicians, and later graduated with distinction from the Cincinnati Medical college. He then went to Springfield, Ill., where he practiced successfully for a time, during which period he became very well acquainted and was upon intimate terms with Abraham Lincoln, who took up his residence there in 1837. From Springfield the Doctor went to Peoria, where he remained several years practicing his profession. He finally started down the Illinois river on a flatboat, his sole possession being a horse, saddle and saddle-bag. Landing at Natchez in 1834 he rode to Woodville, and from there to Rose Hill, Amite county, where he practiced his profession, remaining with Mr. Eli Cappell for three or four years. He then came to Wilkinson county and settled at Montrose plantation, which had been the stand of several other physicians. This stand for doctors was the site of the Jackson academy, incorporated in 1814 and named in honor of General Jackson. It flourished for a number of years and was the resort of many of the leading physicians of this county. After the college went down it was known only as the stand for physicians. The Doctor soon after settling at Montrose married, March 25, 1847, the lady of his choice in Amite county. She was Mary, the daughter of Agrippa and Margaret Gayden. The Gaydens were early settlers from South Carolina. Mrs. Redhead was born March 17, 1830, and was from a family of three daughters and three sons, all of whom are deceased but Ivison G. Gayden, who served in the Mexican war. He now lives in East Feliciana parish, La., engaged in planting. George and Frank settled in Bolivar county, Miss. Frank was a soldier in the late war and was the first prisoner exchanged between the North and the South. He was captured in Missouri and exchanged the same day. He held a captain's commission and died several years after the war. George died in 1861. Minerva died in girlhood, and Mary became the wife of Mr. Redhead. Elvira married A. G. Cage, of Terre Bonne parish, La., a prominent sugar planter. She died in 1863, leaving six small children. Mary, mother of John A., was educated in Liberty, Amite county, and died April 21, 1851. She was a member of the Presbyterian church. She was a good woman and a dutiful wife and mother. By this union were born two children, Mary H. and John A. Mary H. first married Dr. Hamilton, and upon his death a Mr. Morrill, and lives in Newburyport, Mass. John A. lives on the home place. Dr. Redhead was actively engaged in the practice of medicine until about the close of the war. He was a public-spirited man, but would not accept an office, and was a Jacksonian democrat. After the war he devoted his time and attention to his plantation. While being a man of social temperament, fond of life and its enjoyments, he was withal a philosopher, and always looked at life with practical though charitable eyes. He traveled a great deal, spending his summers in the cool resorts of the North. He was a natural mechanical genius—could make anything—and at one time made an artificial leg for General Brandon, and a hand for Albert Cage, the latter being so perfect that he could use the hand to write with. He died September 7, 1881, with congestion of the bowels. He came in possession of a large estate through his wife, and was among the county's most respected and well-to-do citizens. He was a member of the A. F. & A. M. and the I. O. O. F., in which he took very active part until late in life. His son, John A., was born October 28, 1849, on the place where he now resides, and was educated at Albert Lyon's high school, in Pike county, Miss., and by private tutors at home, and by his own exertions. He was married in 1878 to Miss Julia Norwood, of East Feliciana parish, La. She was the daughter of Judge Norwood, a very prominent man of Louisiana. Mrs. Redhead was educated in Clinton, La., and is a very highly respected and very estimable lady. To this union were born three children: Joseph, John and Ella. John A. served two terms as a member of the board of supervisors of this county, and was elected in 1878 to the legislature. He is devoted to his family, and is one of the most successful and progressive planters in the county. He has about one thousand eight hundred acres well under cultivation, and is a member of the A. F. & A. M. and K. of H. He has a beautiful residence located near the site of the old Jackson academy, on an elevation of ground and surrounded with handsome shade trees.

D. M. Redmond, of Osyka, Pike county, Miss., was born in this county, near where he now resides, December 6, 1825. Jesse Redmond, his father, was born in Barnwell district, S. C., April 4, 1791, came to Mississippi when a young man in 1812 and settled in the territory now embraced in Pike county. February 7, 1825, he married here a Miss Elizabeth Carter, also a native of Barnwell district, S. C. After his marriage he located where the town of Osyka has since grown up, becoming a well-known planter. He served in the War of 1812 as a soldier under General Jackson, and received a pension from the government until his death in 1876, which, after his death, was paid to his widow until she died, which occurred June 10, 1888. D. M. Redmond is the eldest of a family of ten, of whom four sons and one daughter died young. He was reared in this county and received such an education as was afforded by the public schools. May 25, 1855, he was married at New Orleans to Miss Bridget Joyce, a native of Ireland, but who was reared in the state just mentioned. Soon after his marriage Mr. Redmond located where he now lives in Osyka, having previously purchased part of the old homestead of his father, adjoining the village. Although he has never operated on a very extensive scale, he has been a very successful planter and acquired a competency, owning at this time, besides his plantation, considerable residence property in Osyka. His political affiliations are with the democratic party. He has held many local positions of trust and honor, being at this time mayor of Osyka and a justice of the peace. He is highly esteemed for his integrity and sterling qualities. He has three children grown to manhood and womanhood, and occupying honorable positions in society. They are: Florilla, a young lady of superior education and fine abilities, who occupies the position of telegraph operator at Osyka; James M., a well-educated young man of good business capacity, who is the station agent at Aquila, Sunflower county, Miss., and Mary E., wife of P. E. Triche. Mr. Redmond is a member and holds the office of treasurer of the Baptist church of Osyka. During his long life Mr. Redmond has been faithful to every trust reposed in him, and in every relation of life to which he has been called he has done his whole duty with an honesty of purpose which has been his distinguishing characteristic, and now in his old age he is loved and venerated by his family and wide circle of friends, and is highly esteemed by the entire community. Among his most interesting reminiscences are those of his services in the Confederate army during the late war. In 1862 he enlisted as a private in company F, of the Fourteenth Mississippi cavalry. He was soon promoted to be orderly sergeant, and as such served till he received his discharge at the close of the war. He participated in a number of important engagements and was captured at Liberty while on detached duty as courier for Colonel Dillon, and was held a prisoner of war at Liberty, Baton Rouge and New Orleans, but the most of the time at Ship island, where he was kept in close confinement until the end of the war came. During his military life Mr. Redmond often found himself in the thick of some of the hardest fought battles of the war, with missiles of war flying fast and furious on all sides of him, but he escaped, almost miraculously as it were, without even a bullet hole in his clothes.

W. B. Redus, Shannon, Lee county, Miss. The Rev. J. W. Redus was born in Marion county, Ala., November 15, 1820. At the age of thirteen years he united with the Methodist Episcopal Church South, and in 1856 was licensed as a minister. He preached throughout northern Mississippi, and in 1863 enlisted in the Confederate service under Captain Welterall. He passed through all the experiences of warfare, being taken prisoner in the battle of Egypt; he was held twenty-two days, and then released. He was a son of William Redus. The father was born in Tennessee in 1796, and the mother in South Carolina in 1799. Her maiden name was Brown. John W. Redus was united in marriage November 20, 1845, to Miss Emily Saunders. She was a daughter of John F. and Catherine Gilberth. Their union was blessed by the birth of four children: Mrs. Catherine Cunningham, widow of William Cunningham; Laura, wife of C. A. Henly; R. C., a lawyer of Birmingham, Ala.; and W. B., the subject of this sketch. He was born in what was then a portion of Pontotoc county, now Lee county, Miss., March 31, 1850. The war, with all its disasters, deprived him of a collegiate education, but he made the most of the opportunities that were afforded him in the ungraded schools of the country. When he left school he was employed as a clerk by W. M. Cunningham for a period of nine years. He acted in the same capacity for F. G. Thomas for four years. In September, 1878, he embarked in business for himself at Shannon, and has met with more than ordinary success. His long years of experience in the service of older merchants have been invaluable to him. He carries a stock of $10,000, and does a large business. In 1872, November 27, Mr. Redus was married to Miss Sallie J. Wright, a daughter of Judge N. C. and J. K. Wright, natives of Tennessee. She was born April 22, 1854. Her father was a soldier in the late war, and is a Mason of high degree. He is a strong advocate of prohibition, and is a member of the Farmers' Alliance and of the Knights of Labor. He is now a resident of Shannon, and has a wide circle of friends. At the age of twenty-one years he united with the Cumberland Presbyterian church, and has been an elder

J A Payne

of the church ever since. Politically he affiliates with the democratic party. His wife's maiden name was Jennie McDaniels. She is now deceased. They had born to them six children: Mattie, wife of John Lasetter; James T.; Annie E. (deceased) was the wife of Silas Nelson; Mary E., wife of John S. Henley; Fannie (deceased) was the wife of G. A. Henley, and Sallie J., the wife of Mr. Redus. Mr. and Mrs. Redus are the parents of five children: Lena D., James N., J. Frank, Minnie Gertrude, and Fannie, the fourth-born, deceased. Mr. Redus is a zealous supporter of democratic principles, having cast his first presidential vote for Samuel J. Tilden. For thirteen years he was express agent at Shannon, and discharged the duties of this position with much promptitude. He and his wife are members of the Cumberland Presbyterian church, and he has been an elder since they united with the society in 1864. He has been a citizen desirous of aiding in the growth and development of the county, and has contributed both by giving his means and influence to all enterprises of public benefit. He has traveled over the United States, usually on business, but has seen nothing to compare with the sunny South.

Maj. Thomas Reed, a citizen of Mississippi, who was esteemed as a man of high integrity and ability, and a lawyer of reliability and talent, was born on April 11, 1817, in Butler county, Penn. His father, Thomas Reed, was a native of the same state, and his mother, Mary Patterson, was from the state of Virginia. When only three years of age Major Reed's parents removed to Warren county, Miss., and in the neighborhood in that county known as Warrenton, about ten miles distant from the city of Vicksburg, which was then but a small village, Major Reed spent several of his happy boyhood years. He often referred to his childhood days in that vicinity as a pleasant remembrance. As early as 1828 he came with his mother's family to Natchez, and here and in the adjoining county of Jefferson he spent the remaining long and useful years of his life. When but a small boy his father died of yellow fever in Alvaredo, Mexico, whither he had gone on a business venture, leaving the widowed mother with very little means to support herself and several children. Still, she was a woman of persevering ability and energy, and above all a devoted Christian. By industrious effort, aided by the children themselves, she raised three of her children (the others having died while quite young) to honored manhood and womanhood, a comfort to her until her death, which occurred in the city of Natchez on November 18, 1863. Major Reed's education was, by reason of his mother's circumstances, limited to that obtained in ordinary day schools, and a short attendance upon Jefferson college, a high school for boys situated in the historic town of Washington, about six miles from Natchez. But he loved books, and soon learned to be a student. His reading was extensive and thorough, and he became a man whose mind was well stored with varied knowledge and useful information. His great attachment for books was shown by the large library of publications of the best grade which he accumulated. During his long life he made many addresses before schools and literary societies, and was always in thorough sympathy with the educational interests and efforts in the state of his residence. Acting often in the capacity of trustee, or as a member of the visiting committee to these institutions of learning, he also gave liberally of his means toward the support of the various colleges and schools. Major Reed was not only well known as a speaker and a lecturer, but was also known as a writer. Often did he give aid and encouragement to a worthy cause by well-written and strong communications to the state press, and to the journal that was the official organ of the church to which he belonged. In 1876, by appointment and request, he prepared a Centennial history of Jefferson county, where he then resided, which was published with many favorable comments. While growing up he clerked in stores and learned the mercantile business, and before he was of legal age, with his brother James, who was only two years his senior, though well matured for his age, he engaged in general merchandising on quite a large scale. But neither he nor his brother seemed suited to this kind of life, and their career as merchants was soon ended by an adverse turn in their business affairs, causing the failure of the firm of J. P. & T. Reed. After this they both studied law, but James P. Reed returned in a few years to his favorite work as a pharmacist, and Thomas Reed, having held the office of clerk of the criminal court for several years, entered upon the active practice of law, which profession he followed for nearly a half century, and until his death. These brothers, who had been so intimately associated with each other during their boyhood and early manhood, seemed now, by the vicissitudes of life, to be separated. For while quite a young man James P. Reed, moved by a spirit of adventure which always seemed strong within him, and a desire to champion the weak but deserving side of every struggle, went to Texas and fought with the noble men of that state for their independence. He was a brave and daring man. Having served also in the capacity of scout and special interpreter for Gen. John A. Quitman during the war with Mexico, and though advanced in years and enfeebled by former hard service, he enlisted in the Confederate army, and with the boys who wore the gray battled for the lost cause. The remaining years of his life were spent in the city of San Antonio, Tex., and in that place he died in July, 1887, after some years of suffering, caused by wounds and injuries received during his career as a soldier, leaving a wife and three sons, who still live to cherish the memory of a true man and kind father.

Major Reed studied law with the well-known firm of Quitman & McMurran. General John A. Quitman, of that firm, was his warm personal friend. After practicing some years in Natchez he moved to Jefferson county in 1852, and there residing on his plantation two miles from the town of Fayette, he for about thirty years successfully followed his profession. He then removed to Natchez, the home of his early days, and in this picturesque city of the bluffs he spent the remainder of his long and useful life in his chosen profession. He was widely known as a lawyer whose character was above reproach, who would not stoop to any trick or dishonorable act, and his clients had great confidence in him. A brother lawyer, in referring to him, said, that he was an honorable, kind-hearted, courteous gentleman, who amid all the dusty purlieus of the law had kept the whiteness of his soul; that his strict integrity amidst all of the temptations of his profession was an eloquent and convincing evidence of a singularly pure and virtuous heart. He was a patriotic politician; he loved his country, and was always willing to do what he could for its welfare and prosperity. He was prominent in conventions, and made many political speeches, being generally a leader, but he was not an officeseeker; he did not follow politics for gain. The good of his native land was uppermost in his heart. He was for a long number of years a whig, afterward and during the remainder of his life a democrat. He volunteered for service during the Mexican war. His friend, General Quitman, appointed him major on his staff, but before he saw service the war had ended. However, the title of major followed him ever after. At the time of the Civil war, he opposed secession, but when his beloved Mississippi withdrew from the Union he felt it his first duty to fight for his own state, and he at once enlisted, and served as an officer of the Jefferson artillery until after the battle of Shiloh, when his health having entirely failed he returned to his home, and as soon as he sufficiently recovered he began duties as a civil officer of the Confederate government. He was glad when the unfortunate struggle was over, and was an active and faithful worker in the effort to restore to proper order and prosperity the affairs of the state. Major Reed was a faithful and consistent Christian, being from the time of his youth a member of the Methodist Episcopal church. He followed closely the footsteps of his Divine Master. His heart seemed to overflow with love for his fellow-man. He was long engaged in the Sunday-school cause, being for about thirty-five years a superintendent. Through every portion of the state he was known as a Christian worker. He with soldier-like firmness championed the religion of Jesus, and at last gave his pure soul to his Captain, Christ, under whose banner he had served so long. Major Reed was twice married; in 1847 he married Lavinia West, the daughter of Charles West, who was a descendant of Cato West, a provincial governor of Mississippi. This lady a few years after her marriage died, leaving two children, Kate, who died when about fourteen years of age, and Charles W., who now resides in the city of Natchez. In October, 1852, he married Miss Mary J. Forman, the daughter of Stephen S. Forman and Keziah Howell. This marriage took place at the very historic residence on Springfield plantation in Jefferson county, which was then and for a long number of years owned by the late William Holmes, one of the honored citizens of the state, who was a dear and fatherly friend of Mrs. Reed. This residence is a substantial brick structure, erected over one hundred years since by Thomas Green, one of the pioneer leaders of the state, and a relative of both the West and Forman families. It was on this place that Gen. Andrew Jackson was married, and near it that Aaron Burr was captured. Both the West and Forman families were among the oldest and most prominent in the state; the two families being closely connected and related. To Major Reed and his second wife five children were born: Mary, who married Jacob Guice, and died some years since; Janie, who died in infancy, and Susan Holmes, Richard Forman and Thomas James, all of whom now reside with their mother in Natchez, Miss. The tender devotion and loving care shown by Mrs. Reed to her husband during the closing years of his life is a blessed memory now to their children and friends. In truth, the kindness of heart and unselfishness of service to all with whom she is associated, have drawn to Mrs. Reed many loving friends. While Major Reed was early separated from his brother, as has been stated, still during the long years of his life he has been closely associated with his sister, Mrs. Susan R. Guice, who was the wife of the late Stephen L. Guice, an able lawyer and good man. She is a woman of many excellent traits of character, having a clear and strong intellect, a tender, loving heart, and with all being a consecrated Christian, it is a privilege to be with her, and she is held in high esteem by a large circle of friends. Mrs. Guice survives her brother and now resides with her daughter, Mrs. F. A. Dicks, in the city of Natchez.

After having lived seventy-four years of active usefulness, on August 4, 1891, in the city of Natchez, where he had so long resided, Major Reed passed from his earthly dwelling-place to his eternal home in heaven. During his last sickness he was tenderly cared for by his family and many friends. The great esteem for him by the people was shown at his funeral, when every class of persons was largely represented, besides the attendance in a body of the Masonic fraternity, the Independent Order of Odd Fellows and the Confederate veterans. He had been for nearly half a century a member of the I. O. O. F., and was the oldest living past grand master of the order.

He also took an active interest in the two other associations named. He was a good man, a patriotic citizen, a consecrated Christian. His life was an honor to his state, and the beneficial influence therefrom will be felt for long years to come. The following is a portion of a notice of Major Reed's life, published a day or two after his demise in an influential Southern newspaper: "Major Reed has from early manhood taken a great interest in politics. Though he was never an officeseeker he always took a prominent part in the councils of the democratic party. During the Mexican war he was appointed to the rank of major on General Quitman's staff, but the war closed before he saw any active service. He served in the late Civil war in aid of the Confederate cause. He was, at the time of his death, the oldest living past grand master of the Independent Order of Odd Fellows in the state. For more than forty years he had been a prominent member of this order. From early boyhood he was a member of the Methodist church, and he lived a sincere and faithful Christian life. One who knew him well said to the writer this morning that he made it a rule never to allow anything to stand in the way of church duties. He said further that he had never seen him absent from Sunday-school in the Jefferson Street church until he was taken sick two weeks ago. Major Reed leaves a devoted widow and a family of three sons and one daughter, all grown, to mourn his death. To them and his numerous relatives and friends we tender our sympathy. The funeral proceeds from the Jefferson Street Methodist church at five o'clock this evening. The Mississippi lodge of the Independent Order of Odd Fellows will attend in a body."

W. S. Reed, Free Run, was born in Yazoo county, Miss., in 1847, and is the son of J. H. and Elizabeth L. (Hurst) Reed. The father was born in Adams county, Miss., and is a son of the Hon. Thomas B. Reed, United States senator, of Adams county, who settled in Mississippi about the year 1816. Senator Reed died in 1829. The mother of our subject was a daughter of Thomas Hurst, a pioneer of Adams county. J. H. Reed was educated in Kentucky at Center college, and settled in Yazoo county in 1837. He opened up and improved a large plantation near Benton, where he was an influential and honored citizen. He died in 1874, but his wife still survives. They reared a family of four children, two of whom are deceased. Ella E., wife of J. W. Waterer, and Betty, wife of W. E. Philipps, are not living; Mary C., wife of Dr. J. E. McGehee, and W. S. are the other members of the family. The maternal grandfather was a native of Virginia, from which state he removed to Mississippi in the year 1806. Mr. Reed spent his boyhood and youth in Yazoo county, where he received his education. In 1864 he entered the Confederate service, enlisting in company K, Woods' Mississippi cavalry. He was at Gainesville, Ala., at the time of the surrender in 1865. After the close of the war he engaged in farming. In 1860 the family had settled on the place which he now occupies. It now covers an area of four hundred and forty acres, two hundred being under cultivation. Mr. Reed was wedded in 1869 to Miss Florence Hurst, a daughter of Chatham and Ann (Gaskins) Hurst, who were from Virginia. Six children have been born of this union: I. Shelby, John H., Chatham, William and Pearl (twins), and Dudley. Mrs. Reed and the eldest son are members of the Methodist Episcopal church. Mr. Reed belongs to the Knights of Honor, and is reporter of his lodge. He has always discharged his duties of citizenship faithfully, and is a man who has the entire respect of the community.

Among the representative, thoroughgoing and efficient officials of Prentiss county, Miss., there is probably no one more deserving of mention than Hon. W. H. Rees, chancery clerk, Booneville, Miss., for his residence within this state has extended through his entire life, his birth occurring in Tishomingo county (now Prentiss), near Rienzi, in 1847. He is a son of John and Elizabeth (Whitaker) Rees, and grandson of John Rees, a native of Virginia, who was one of the early settlers of Lincoln county, Tenn. The Whitaker family were originally from Kentucky. Grandfather Whitaker was a wealthy planter and a very active member of the Baptist church, taking great interest in all religious matters and building churches where he lived. The parents of W. H. Rees were natives of Lincoln county, Tenn., and came to Mississippi about 1834 or 1836, settling in Tishomingo county, where the father became one of the most prosperous and successful planters of the county, a model farmer in every respect. He died in 1859 at the age of fifty-eight years. He was a democrat in politics, was never an officeseeker, but took a very active part in political matters, and was influential in the politics of the county for some time. He was a member of the Methodist church, and socially was a member of the Masonic fraternity. Previous to his death his wife had received her final summons. They were the parents of nine children, five of whom are yet living: Mrs. Anna Bynum (of Rienzi), Mrs. Mary Bynum (of the same place), R. A. (resides in Lincoln county, Tenn.), Hardy W. (makes his home in Prentiss county) and W. H. Those deceased died young, with the exception of the eldest son, Jordon L., who was killed in the storm that swept over the county in 1875. W. H. Rees was the sixth in order of birth of the above mentioned children. He espoused the cause of the Confederacy, and at the breaking out of hostilities between the two sections he enlisted in company A, Thirty-second Mississippi regiment infantry, and served until the 8th of October, 1862, when he was wounded at the battle of Perryville, losing his left arm from the shoulder from the explosion of a shell. He was the first one of his company injured, and was captured by the Union soldiers. He was confined at Louisville but a short time, and was then exchanged at Vicksburg in December of the same year. After this he served in the quartermaster's department at Montgomery, Ala., until the close of the war, being paroled at Columbus, Miss., in May, 1865. Returning home he entered school at Oxford in 1868, and graduated from the law department of that institution, in a class of twenty, in 1869. He subsequently located at Booneville, Miss., and practiced his profession until finally ill health drove him to his farm. When he returned to his profession he was elected a member of the legislature for Alcorn and Prentiss counties as a floater, serving two terms, and in 1883 he was elected chancery clerk, and re-elected in 1887 without opposition. In politics he is active for the interests of the democratic party, and the very efficient manner in which he has discharged the duties of the different official positions he has held and is holding, testifies to the wisdom of the people's choice. The confidence they have in him is intelligently placed, for they have known him from boyhood and have had every opportunity to judge of his character and qualifications. He was married in Hinds county, Miss., to Miss Mary Farris, a native of Tishomingo county, and the daughter of A. J. Farris, who is a near relative of the Sivleys of Hinds county. Mrs. Rees was educated at Jacinto, and in a select school near Iuka, Miss., taught by Mrs. Brame. Mr. and Mrs. Rees are the parents of these children: John Jordon, Louise, William H., Jr., Mary Annie, Hamilton Sivley and Jefferson Davis Boone. Mr. Rees is a Knight of Honor, and he and wife are members of the Methodist church. Mr. Rees' house, with most of its contents, was burned in 1891. They had a beautiful and pleasant home.

Jesse J. Reeves, of Summit, was born in Pike county, Miss., November 14, 1820. He is the eldest of nine children born to John and Martha (Price) Reeves, both natives of South Carolina. John Reeves came to Mississippi in 1811, when the place was a territory inhabited by the Indians and wild beasts. He engaged in planting, which he continued until his death, which occurred in 1861. He was well known as one of the pioneers of the state. Jesse Reeves' paternal grandparents were Lazarus and Elizabeth Reeves, natives of Virginia. His grandfather settled on a farm about one-half mile from the present residence of Mr. Reeves. His maternal grandparents were William and Elizabeth Price, natives of South Carolina. Our subject was reared and educated in Mississippi, attending the private schools near his home. He is now a planter and owns four hundred and forty acres of land, about two hundred and fifty acres of which are under cultivation. In 1848 he was married to Miss Olive McCollough, a native of Mississippi and a daughter of William

McCollough. To them have been born twelve children: Mary A., Sarah J. (now deceased), James R. G., Tabitha, William H. C., Vashti P., Jasper M., Hannah E., John E., Martha A., Reuben W. (also deceased) and Dolly. Mr. Reeves and his family are members of the Baptist church. Mr. Reeves did not start out in life for himself until the age of twenty-eight years, and when he did begin for himself he had no means, but by close application and careful management has succeeded in collecting enough of this world's goods to live very comfortably the rest of his life. He is descended from one of the oldest families in the state, who were of English-Irish origin. Mr. Reeves is a Mason and a member of the Farmers' Alliance. He is deeply interested in all enterprises tending to the public good, and is a liberal contributor to the same.

William S. Regan (deceased). Among the earliest settlers who came to Marion county, Miss., and endured the privations and hardships incident to pioneer life, was John Regan, a native of North Carolina. He was married and reared a family of five children: Stephen A., Joe, William S., Nancy P., and Mary A. Stephen A. Regan married Elizabeth Applewhite, and they had thirteen children born to them, ten of whom grew to maturity: Ralph, Sarah A., John A., Mary J., William S., Nancy P., Rebecca E., Joe R., Melissa, and Thomas G. William S. Regan married Catherine Pittman, and they had a large family of children: Robinson, Rufus, Henry P., Elizabeth, John, Sarah, William P., Stephen A., Willis, and Nancy P. William S. Regan, son of Stephen A. Regan, was born April 27, 1832, and in 1851 he was married to Sarah A. Loe, by whom he had five children: Elizabeth, James K., Corinne, Abigail, and Caroline. The mother of these children died in 1863, and the father was married a second time, being united to Mrs. Susan Luter, widow of John Luter, and daughter of Daniel Scarborough. Eight children were born of this marriage: Mary J., Joseph, Willy, Nettie, Thomas G., Stephen A., Laura, and William H. Mr. Regan was an excellent business man and accumulated a considerable amount of property. At the time of his death he owned a large tract of land six miles south of Columbia. He was an honored member of the Methodist Episcopal church, and being possessed of many sterling traits of character, he had won an enviable position in the community in which he had resided so many years.

Judge H. P. Reid (deceased), was born April 28, 1839, at Greensboro, Ala., and was a descendant of an old and much honored family. He was left an orphan at an early age and was adopted by an uncle, Harrison P. Maxwell, who was one of the leading farmers of Tippah county. The Christian name of the uncle was given to young Reid. About the year 1854 or 1855 he was apprenticed in the Ripley *Advertiser* office, and before the war, and when still quite young, he worked on the *Bulletin* and other Memphis papers. When war was declared between the states he promptly entered the Confederate army and served with credit and ability throughout the entire struggle. He afterward entered the political field, served in the legislature and in party conventions, and was the means of accomplishing a great deal of good for the democratic party and the state of Mississippi. He was very conservative, and by his course set a good example in the community by which he was honored as a public servant and esteemed as a citizen. Judge Reid removed to Friar's Point before the war, and returning to that point after that eventful period he was almost without means. He started the *Coahomian* and conducted that paper for several years. During that time he studied law and was admitted to the bar in his county, afterward practicing in the courts of his own and adjoining counties and in the supreme court of the state at Jackson until the time of his death on the 3d of March, 1884, when but forty-five years of age. He was a self-made man in every sense of the word. He was married in 1869 to Miss Mary S.

Robinson, who now resides in Friar's Point, and to this union were born the following children: James Baxter, Alexander Morton, Frank Rochester, Harry Patton, Louie Wortham (died at the age of six months) and Samuel Warren (who also died in early boyhood). The Judge received his final summons at his home, from the exposure suffered on his trip to Jackson, Miss., to defeat a county site removal bill before the legislature. At his death he left a widow and five sons, one child having preceded him. He was the nephew of Dr. Bryan, a Presbyterian minister of Memphis, but he and his wife were members of the Methodist Episcopal Church South. He was tall and well formed, with dark brown hair, fair complexion and blue eyes.

Joseph Reid has for many years been noted for honorable, upright dealing, and his record is a clean and worthy one. The first of his family of whom he had any definite knowledge was his grandfather, Joseph Reid, who was of Scotch descent but a Virginian by birth. During the Revolutionary war, with three brothers, he served in that struggle against the British, holding the rank of lieutenant. He became a well-to-do planter of South Carolina, in which state he, for some time, filled the position of magistrate. He was also married in that state to Miss Isabella Baskin, of Irish descent, but a native of the Palmetto state. He died about 1830, and his widow in 1845, both being members of the Presbyterian church at the time of their deaths. Their son, Thomas B. Reid, the father of the subject of this sketch, was reared in Pickens district, S. C., his boyhood being spent on a farm. He was one of a family of three sons and six daughters, being the eldest son and the second of the family in order of birth. He received a common-school education, and throughout his entire life followed the calling of a planter, to which occupation he had been reared by his father. In 1823 he was married to Miss Sarah Nicholson, a native of Pickens district, S. C., and a daughter of William and Martha (Richardson) Nicholson, her father having been a planter in good circumstances, and died about 1820, being survived by his widow a number of years. In 1834 Thomas B. Reid removed with his family to Sumter county, Ala., where he remained one year, then came to Mississippi, reaching Chickasaw county December 25, 1835. He immediately purchased a section of land, and the succeeding year purchased a half section, and by the time of his death had accumulated a good and valuable property. He was in the war with the Seminole Indians, and was ensign in Captain Kelly's company. He died in 1858, his wife's death occurring in 1843, the latter being an earnest member of the Presbyterian church. They became the parents of eleven children, eight sons and three daughters: Joseph, William R., president of the topographical and engineering corps of Argentine Confederation, South America; Isabella (deceased), Thomas B., who was killed in Virginia during the Civil war; Samuel, who resides with the subject of this sketch; Lemuel N., who resides in Houston; Evan R., who was killed during the war at the battle of Seven Pines; Martha, widow of John G. Brooks, of Opelousas, La.; Sarah (deceased), Warren D., who resides with the subject of this sketch, and George, who was killed in the battle of Gaines' Mill, Va. The boyhood days of Joseph Reid were spent in his native state and Chickasaw county, Miss., and up to the age of seventeen years attended the common country schools five or six months throughout the year. At the age of twenty-one he began life for himself as an overseer on his father's plantation, continuing until the latter's death, when he purchased a portion of the old home place, afterward adding an addition to his share. He is now the owner of four hundred acres of fertile and well-tilled land. He was captain of militia prior to the war, and in 1862 was elected a member of the board of police, in which capacity he served until 1868 or 1869. From 1870 to 1872 he was a member of the board of supervisors, and in the discharge of all his official duties he was intelligent, faithful and active. He is a member of the Presbyterian church, and is unmarried. His brother, Warren D. Reid, was a sergeant in company H, Eleventh Mississippi, and while with the army of Virginia was wounded in a skirmish, from the effects of which he lost the use of his left arm. He was elected to the position of circuit clerk in 1886, the duties of which he faithfully discharged for two years. In December, 1865, he was married to Miss Jane McJunkin, a native of South Carolina, by whom he became the father of eight children, seven of whom are living: L. B., a teacher in Palestine, Tex.; Bessie C., Joseph B., James M., Minnie, Samuel E. and Warren D. Lemuel N. Reid, another brother of Joseph Reid, was in the same company as his brother, Warren D., during the war, and while in the battle of Gettysburg received two severe wounds in the thigh. After remaining at home on furlough for some time he soon recovered from the effects of his wounds, and endeavored to rejoin his command, but owing to communication being cut off he was unable to do so, and joined a cavalry company, with which he served in the winter of 1864-5. He was married to Miss Anna Moffett, a native of Houston, Miss., and a daughter of William Moffett, by whom he became the father of four children: William J., Harriet, Sarah and Thomas B. Samuel Reid, another brother, was also in company H, Eleventh Mississippi, and was captured at the battle of Gettysburg and taken to Fort Delaware, whence he escaped with a companion, and made his way to the Confederate lines. He went to the Black Hills during the gold fever, where he remained ten years. He is now the postmaster of Ridge, Miss. He is unmarried.

D. Reinach, merchant and planter, Riverton, Miss. The firm of Frank & Reinach, at Riverton, Bolivar county, Miss., carry a stock of goods valued at $20,000, and do an annual business of about $100,000. They are live, energetic business men, and in their dealings and representations, merit the esteem with which they are regarded. In 1884 they erected their large store building, one of the largest in the county, and their stock of assorted merchandise is of a character to suit the locality. Mr. Reinach was born in Bavaria in 1842, and his parents, Samuel and Mena (Arent) Reinach, were natives of that country also. There they passed their entire lives, the father dying in 1859 and the mother in 1875 or 1876. D. Reinach was educated in Bavaria and in 1860 came to the United States, residing for a short time in New York, after which he went to Cincinnati, O., and from there to Chicot county, Ark., where he clerked in a store at Grand Lake for nearly two years. He then came to Bolivar county, Miss., followed the same occupation for a short time, and then entered the Confederate service, Company H, First Mississippi cavalry, called Bolivar troops, and served in this company under Captain Montgomery during the entire war. He speaks in the highest praise of his late Captain, and quotes him as being one of the bravest and most fearless soldiers. Mr. Reinach embarked in business at Carson's, this county, in 1865, and there remained until 1869, when he came to his present locality, then called Pride's Point, but since changed to Riverton. He is a self-made man in every sense of the word, and although he could hardly speak the English language when coming here, he has, by his industry, good management and strict attention to business, become one of the most prosperous men in the county. The business grows under his supervision and is annually increasing. He also has a large plantation interest, about four thousand acres, and has two thousand acres of this under cultivation, it being thoroughly improved with gins, good buildings, etc. He has been postmaster at Riverton for a long time and was county treasurer for four years. Although formerly quite active in politics, he gives very little attention to the political issues of the day at the present time. He is a member of the Masonic order. He has a fine residence at Riverton and one of the largest orchards in the county.

The following is a brief sketch in memory of Isaiah P. Rembert, one of the most prominent pioneers or landmarks of early Mississippi. He was born in 1826, a son of John and Sarah Rembert, natives of South Carolina, who moved to Louisiana and from there came to Mississippi in 1820. He was one of nine chlidren: George, Judith, Nancy, Andrew, Amelia, Frank, Isaiah, Melissa and Sarah, all of whom are citizens of their native state and deserving of a remembrance in the memorial pages being dedicated to the subject of this sketch, who chose for his career, in his early manhood, a farmer's life. He was reared amidst the surroundings of a pioneer life. In 1850 he married Sarah Holliday, born in Copiah county in 1830, a daughter of John Johnson and Mary (Mangum) Ainsworth Holliday, the latter a daughter of James and Elizabeth Ainsworth. The former was a native of Georgia, the latter of Christian county, Ky., and they emigrated to this state in 1820, and here lived until death summoned them. They will be remembered as having been good citizens and useful workers in the Master's cause. At the opening of the war Mr. Rembert was a prosperous and contented man, whose large accumulations were due to his diligence and good management; but, like all true Southern men, he answered his country's call, leaving his happy home and large, splendid plantation of eleven hundred acres to the supervision of his wife and her mother, the latter, though, preferring her own home, living with her daughter, her Christian virtues, benevolence and experience rendering her capable of giving advice, such as none could fear to follow. Early in the war Mr. Rembert enlisted in Captain King's company as lieutenant, in which office he served faithfully, but, owing to his corpulency, he was considered unfit for active duty, and was transferred to the commissary department, in which he served until the close of the war. After the war he again engaged in planting, combining with his farm occupation the raising of hogs and horses. His widow resides on the old homestead. She has no children. Mr. Rembert was a member of the Hazlehurst lodge A. F. & A. M. In religious faith he worshiped with the Methodists. His wife is a member of the Methodist Episcopal Church South. The Remberts are of French descent, the first of the family having come to America and settled in South Carolina, before the war of the Revolution, in which they faithfully served their foster country. Mr. Rembert died April 8, 1884, after a protracted illness. His widow is a lady noted for her gentle, refined ways, and the modesty which is characteristic of her.

Isham B. Rembert, D. D. S., was born in Copiah county, Miss., July 14, 1859, the youngest of six children born to Frank M. and Sarah E. (Patrick) Rembert, natives of Mississippi, the former being born and reared in Copiah county, where he obtained such education as could be had in the common schools. He was reared on a farm and trained to hard work, but in later years he turned his attention to merchandising, in which he became very successful, accumulating valuable property. He is now residing in Hazelhurst. His father, John Rembert, was a native of South Carolina but emigrated to Mississippi in early life and was one of the first settlers of Copiah county. Isham B. Rembert received a good English education in his native county and in 1881 graduated in dental surgery from the Indiana Dental college at Indianapolis, Ind., immediately after which he located at Fayette, Jefferson county, where he practiced one year. At the end of this time he became a practitioner of Natchez, but in 1883 came to Jackson, where he has since remained. He has been exceptionally successful in the practice of his profession and now controls a large and lucrative patronage, which he well deserves, for he is careful and painstaking in his work and keeps fully abreast of the times in his profession. He is first vice president of the Mississippi State Dental association and is a rising young dentist, sure to make his mark in the world. He is gentlemanly and courteous in his intercourse with his fellows, and is a worthy member of one of the oldest and best known families of the state. In 1888 he was married to Miss

Alma Eyrich, a native of Mississippi, and daughter of George C. and Virginia Eyrich, but in 1889 was called upon to mourn her untimely demise. He is a member of the Episcopal church.

Ed. J. Rew, planter, Sageville, Lauderdale county, Miss., is a son of Southey Rew, who was born in Currituck county, N. C., about 1780, and was in the second war with Great Britain. His father, Southey Rew, was a patriot of the Revolution and figured in that struggle with distinguished credit. Southey married Mrs. Fannie Rew, of Craven county, N. C., about 1805, and died in December, 1836. Their son, Ed. J. Rew, was born on the banks of the river Neuse, Craven county, N. C., on March 31, 1815. He moved to Alabama in 1837, settled in the cane brake region, and remained there for fifteen years. He came to Lauderdale county, Miss., in 1852, settled in the southern portion, seven miles from Meridian and ten miles from Enterprise, Clarke county, where the weight of his energy and enterprise has been felt in church and state. He served as justice of the peace in his early manhood and sustained himself in that capacity, as only one appeal from his decision was ever made. He was married in 1839 to Miss Eliza J. Hooks, daughter of Charles Hooks, and granddaughter of Hon. Charles Hooks, of North Carolina, but afterward a citizen of Montgomery county, Ala. Mrs. Rew was educated at the Presbyterian institute at Tuscaloosa Ala. She is related to the celebrated Whitfield and Haywood families of North Carolina. Mr. Rew followed the trade of a mechanic in Alabama and was forward in developing the resources of the country in its pioneer days, He acquired a competency at his trade, but later engaged in agricultural pursuits, and was quite successful in this occupation. In 1860 he was appointed to canvass the county in favor of Bell and Everett. In this canvass he met the supporters of the opposing candidates, and stood boldly for what he conceived to be right. At the breaking out of the Civil war, Mr. Rew was successfully operating an extensive farm, tannery, mills, etc. One of Mr. Rew's exploits during the war is worthy of mention: When General Johnston was maneuvering to keep General Grant from Vicksburg, Major Young, quartermaster, stood in great need of mules. He therefore dispatched over twenty men to different sections to secure the needed supply; Mr. Rew was among the number. Of the three hundred and fifty mules secured, three hundred and thirty were due to the energy and enterprise of Mr. Rew, who was materially aided by Hon. Frank Lyon, Alfred Hatch, Captain Curry, quartermaster, and many others of Marengo county, Ala. The first named was a fine lawyer, the next a vast planter, and the others are first-class men in their professions. Toward the close of the war Mr. Rew was in the service of the state and Confederate departments. His position as a disunionist rendered him a conspicuous object for the wrath of Sherman's men, and accordingly his entire premises, dwelling house excepted, were burned and sacked. Among the losses he felt most bitterly were some of his most valuable agricultural records, etc. But for his Masonic allegiance and a sign accordingly from his wife, Mr. Rew would not have been left a single article. After the war he re-commenced farming and milling, and followed this with success. In 1872 Mr. Rew says the per-capita circulation was $52 and times flush, and accordingly, in the light of succeeding events, he attributes the recent stringency to the contraction of the currency. Mr. Rew has had an eventful history as the foregoing sketch discloses, but one laden with honor to himself and conformity to truth and sound principle, as reason enabled him to see, disdaining at all times a compromise with his convictions of right. Mr. Rew is the father of the following children: Fannie, Hattie B., Edward, Henrietta, Bettie, Charles H., George, and Comb; six are now living. The first Grange of Lauderdale county was organized in Mr. Rew's parlor by Major Wall, of Jackson, and Colonel Dennet, of New

Orleans. Mr. Rew has been long identified with the mechanical and agricultural interests of the county, such as fairs, organizations, etc., and is an uncompromising Alliance and sub-treasury man. He corresponds with the agricultural department and also with Northwest scientists. Mr. Rew is scientifically inclined, and has a splendid collection of marl, mineral and fossils. Mr. Rew is a Methodist in his religion and has been from childhood, and is identified with the church's best interests. His daughter, Miss Mary Fannie Rew, is the promoter of an enterprise, already chartered, for the education of orphan children, and she now has in care two widows and five children. Mr. Rew, by keeping abreast of the times, has been foremost in labors for the Agricultural and Mechanical college, takes great interest in all educational matters, and is prominently identified with other colleges, and in the development of a port of entry at Gulf Port, with its railroad contingencies. Mr. Rew is now in his seventy-sixth year, in robust health of body and mind, and as much interested in the public weal as ever.

Col. Reuben O. Reynolds (deceased) was born in Morgan county, Ga., and died at his home in Aberdeen, Miss., on the morning of Sunday, September 4, 1887. When he was yet a child, his father, Dr. Reynolds, removed with his family to Monroe county, Miss., and made his home a few miles north of Aberdeen. It was here at a school hard by that young Reynolds began his education. He fitted to enter La Grange college in Alabama, whither he went, but did not remain long before proceeding to the University of Georgia, where he graduated, receiving the degree of bachelor of arts. In 1855 he received the degree of bachelor of laws, from the University of Virginia, and returning to Aberdeen he soon wedded Miss Mollie English, who died shortly after. In 1856 he entered upon the practice of law in Aberdeen, and from the start gave promise of the high rank which he afterward attained. During 1856-7 he was associated in his practice with William G. Henderson, afterward chancellor of the Sea Coast district of this state; but in 1858 entered into partnership with Hon. Lock E. Houston, and until just prior to his death, when Judge Houston accepted a place on the circuit bench, the partnership continued unbroken, and at its dissolution was perhaps the oldest law firm in Mississippi. In 1861 Reuben O. Reynolds was among the first in his section to seek the Confederate service. He went to the field as first lieutenant of his company, the Van Dorn reserves, and by promotion successfully won the stars of captain, major and lieutenant colonel of the Eleventh Mississippi regiment. Colonel Reynolds was every inch a soldier, accomplished, gallant and chivalrous. He was twice wounded in battle: once in the leg at Sharpsburg, and later, near the close of the war, at the last engagement of Petersburg, and an empty sleeve ever remained as a reminder of the last wound. Early in 1865 he married Miss Sally B. Young, daughter of the late Col. George H. Young of Waverly, and their union was blessed by six children, who with his devoted wife survive him. In 1866 he was chosen reporter of the supreme court of Mississippi, then designated as the high court of errors and appeals, a position which he filled faithfully and efficiently. In the political revolution of his state, in 1875, Colonel Reynolds was elected to represent his district in the state senate and was a member of that body until his death, three successive terms, during which he was thrice elected president pro tem. of the senate. It was here that his high abilities and great usefulness began to attract general attention in the state. Few men were as ready and effective in debate; fewer still had his great capacity for mental labor, and his eager industry as a legislator, and no man in his time, of like capacity and influence, had fewer selfish purposes to hinder his pursuit of public duty. A co-worker with him through years in the senate, asserts that amid the vast legislative work he was identified with, no man can point to a single act he ever engineered for his own aggrandizement, or point to a private ax he ground for his own benefit. He was free from demagogical display and ostentatious service of the people, although always on the alert to oppose a fraud upon the state or to defeat the personal aim of a crooked bill. Through those twelve years of senatorial life, while he largely influenced the choice of governors, judges and United States senators, no man can justly charge him with pipe laying to achieve any of these fine positions for himself, although his influence was so potent that it required, perhaps, only self assertion and political barter to have brought any of these places within his grasp. As a lawyer, Colonel Reynolds ranked among the ablest and most efficient in the state. He pursued his profession with pride; was devoted to the elevation of its standards and kept abreast with its progress and reforms. He was a member of the American Bar association and one of the founders and chief promoters of the Bar association of Mississippi. His practice in the courts, both state and Federal, was for many years large and lucrative, and his great ability made it easy for him, unconsciously, to lead associates in the conduct of cases. He seemed to be a tireless mental laborer. He was equally effective before court and jury, equally efficient in criminal and civil practice. He was adroit and ingenious as a pleader, painstaking and elaborate in the preparation of his cases; skilled, spirited and earnest in presenting his client's side to the jury, and his mental agility surprised his adversary and delivered him from mishaps. In his legal arguments before the courts he was ever clear and concise, seeking to show the golden thread of principle which ran through all and did all unite. He did not seek rhetorical finish or oratorical phrasemaking, but spoke with directness and force. His fine clarion voice and knightly bearing, however, often thrilled the hearers with the tremor of genuine eloquence. No client ever had truer or more devoted counsel. He fought with dash and fire every inch of his rights. While quick of temper and impulsive of nature, in heated controversy, he never lost self-control, and was ever courteous, considerate and genial, and one of the pleasantest of legal adversaries. In private life, as citizen, friend, husband, father, it would be difficult to find a better example. He was a genuine patriot, and loved his country, his state and his town. While the state has experienced a great loss in his withdrawal from the legislative halls, Aberdeen has sustained a loss that for years will not be reparable, and which she sadly mourns. Mr. Reynolds was active in all her public enterprises, and gave without stint of purse, time or talent, to everything tending to secure her advancement or prosperity. He was frank, affable and sincere, independent in thought and action; free in the expression of his opinion, courageous, quick to resent and repel an insult and injury, but equally free and prompt to forgive. His nature was sympathetic and noble. He was clean of heart and hand, and his uprightness and integrity were unassailable. His religious convictions were clear and simple, and though he lived without cant or pretense to great piety, he ever struggled to imitate the example and obey the teachings of Jesus of Nazareth, and died a member of the Presbyterian church of his town, to which he had given much of his time and substance. The eminent juror, the honored legislator, the beloved husband and father, had been called to a higher sphere, and the sorrow of a great loss rests upon the state. There was little in his character to condemn, much to admire, and more to imitate and cherish. In the sanctity of the tomb he sleeps beneath the quiet of the stars in the land his genius defended.

Dr. John Henry Rhodes needs no introduction to the inhabitants of Hinds county, Miss., for in his professional capacity, as well as socially, he is well and favorably known, his skill and talent as a physician and his kindly and courtly manners in social circles winning him many warm friends. He was born in Rankin county, Miss., August 7, 1859, the third of four children born to Samuel D. and Jane (Ormand) Rhodes, natives of Mississippi and Alabama, respectively, the former's birth occurring in Rankin county in 1837. He was reared in the county of his birth and has been engaged in various industrial pursuits, and at present is engaged in farming. He has been sheriff of his county, is a member of the board of supervisors, and served through the Civil war with the Thirty-ninth Mississippi regiment. He was captured at Port Hudson and was imprisoned for twelve months. His parents, Henry and Katie (Crook) Rhodes, were native South Carolinians and were among the first settlers of Rankin county, where they were engaged in planting. Dr. John Henry Rhodes was reared in the county of his birth and was educated in the University of Mississippi, at Oxford, where his record as a student was very creditable and promising. He was editor of the university magazine while in college, and under his management it was a bright and newsy sheet. He afterward entered and graduated from the Louisville Medical college, and was valedictorian, completing his course in 1882, after which he immediately began practicing in Learned, Hinds county, Miss., where he has since remained, doing a large and constantly increasing practice. He has been chief health officer of the county for some time, and although a young man, has gained and sustained a reputation as a physician which many far older practitioners might well envy. He is not only a fine physician, but is a good business man as well, and is the owner of about eight hundred acres of land, and an excellent and well-appointed drug store in Learned. His life thus far has been crowned with success, and his future is bright with promise. He was married in 1887 to Miss Ella Sivley, a native of Mississippi and a daughter of William R. and Josephine (Stokes) Sively, both of whom were born in the state of Mississippi, and to this union one child has been born—John Sively. Mrs. Rhodes is a member of the Methodist Episcopal church, and the Doctor is a member of the A. F. & A. M. He is prepossessing in personal appearance and possesses many excellent traits of character. His fine intellect and thorough knowledge of his profession place him among the leading members of the medical fraternity, and he is a member of the Mississippi State Medical association.

Dr. Arthur H. Rice, physician and planter, Oktoc, Oktibbeha county, Miss., was born in Talladega, Ala., August 21, 1852, and comes of prominent and distinguished families on both sides of the house. His parents, John W. and Augusta (Hopkins) Rice, were natives, respectively, of South Carolina and Alabama, the father born in Chester district in 1815. The latter was educated at the University of Columbia, was a lawyer by profession, and when still a young man and after serving one term in the legislature, removed with his parents to Alabama. There he followed agricultural pursuits until the breaking out of the Mexican war, when he raised one of three companies in Alabama and soon was commissioned captain of Company I, Thirteenth United States infantry, and commanded this one year. Then on account of his father's death he resigned his commission to look after his father's estate, which was partly in Alabama and partly in Mississippi. His share of the property was in Mississippi, and he removed to Oktibbeha county and there followed the occupation of a planter. He was elected on the democratic ticket to represent Oktibbeha and Chickasaw counties in the state senate, holding that position at the time of his death, in 1857. He was first cousin of Governor and Senator Albert G. Brown, of Mississippi, first cousin of Judge William H. Foote, of Macon, and double first cousin of Samuel F. Rice, chief justice of Alabama. Mr. Rice was married in 1851 to Miss Augusta Hopkins, a native of Huntsville, Ala, born in 1831, and reared in Mobile. She was the daughter of Arthur F. Hopkins, who, although a whig, was elected justice of the Supreme court of Alabama by a democratic legislature and was made chief justice by his associates. Judge Hopkins was one of three commissioners sent by Alabama to Virginia to induce that state to secede from the Union. He was several times whig candidate for the United States senate and several times elector at large. He was also president of the Mobile & Ohio Railroad company. To John W. Rice's marriage were born two children—Arthur H. (subject) and Nannie H., wife of J. Simpson Walker, a civil engineer, now of Birmingham, and a son of Judge Richard W. Walker, of Alabama. Mrs. John W. Rice is still living, and makes her home first with one of her children and then with the other. She is a member of the Presbyterian church. John W. Rice's parents, John Sanders and Nancy Herndon Rice, were natives of Virginia and North Carolina, respectively, and the father was a public-spirited, enterprising citizen, who accumulated a considerable property. Dr. Arthur H. Rice was reared in Mobile, Ala., but spent a portion of each summer on the plantation in Oktibbeha county. He was educated in the private and public schools of Mobile, and when fourteen years of age went to Europe, spending three years in the schools of France and two years in the schools of Germany. Upon returning to the United States he began the study of medicine in Mobile Medical college, graduated in the class of 1873, and in the fall of that year went to New York, after practicing that summer in the county, and in the spring of 1874 graduated at the College of Physicians and Surgeons, taking an ad eundem degree. He subsequently spent six months in hospital service in the Orthopœdic Dispensary and Presbyterian hospital, and then went to St. Louis, Mo., where he practiced one year and was assistant to the clinic for women and children at the Sisters' hospital. In the winter of 1875, on account of failing health, he returned to this county and engaged in planting, in connection with his practice, until 1885, when he went to Mobile, practicing there during that and the following year. While in Mobile he served as visiting physician to the city hospital for one year, and then returned to Oktibbeha county, where he has since resided engaged in practicing medicine, planting and stockraising. He is the owner of one thousand seven hundred and sixty acres and has about eight hundred acres under the plow. He raises principally corn and cotton, and his stockraising is confined to trotting and pacing horses and Jersey cattle. In 1879 Dr. Rice was married to Fannie M. Smith, a native of Charlestown, Mass., and the daughter of Joseph H. and Harriet (McGarland) Smith, the father of Vermont and the mother of Massachusetts. Mr. Smith came to Mobile when a young man, engaged as clerk and was in the Confederate service. After the war he embarked in the railroad business; was at one time division superintendent of the Mexican Central railroad, and was afterward in charge of the railroad hotel system of the Southern Pacific. He is a first cousin of Senator Justin Morrill, of Vermont. To Dr. and Mrs. Rice have been born five interesting children: Augusta, Arthur, Frances, Nannie and Joseph. The subject has just been nominated by the democratic primaries for representative of Oktibbeha county in the state legislature.

E. P. Richards was born in Columbus, Miss., and save for a few years, has been a resident of the city from that time. He was at the University of Virginia at the inception of the war and returning home joined company A, Blythe's battalion Mississippi troops. He was with his command continually and participated in the battles of Belmont, Shiloh, Munfordville, Murfreesboro, Chickamauga, Missionary ridge and the battles of the Georgia campaign until he was wounded at Atlanta in the engagement of July 22, 1864, and saw no more active service. He entered the sheriff's office as deputy in 1880, and filled these duties until his election as chancery clerk in November, 1883, which office he has held continuously since.

Col. W. C. Richards, president of the First National bank of Columbus, Miss., was born to David C. and Elizabeth S. (Parrish) Richards in the year 1828, in Shelby county, Ala. His parents moved to Columbus, Lowndes county, in the year 1833, where he was reared and educated. He enlisted in the Confederate service March 27, 1861, going out as second lieutenant in Capt. W. B. Wade's company, the Southrons. In June, 1862, he was appointed major commanding the Ninth Mississippi battalion of sharpshooters, and was mustered out of the service as colonel of the Ninth Mississippi regiment, at Greensboro, N. C., upon the surrender of Gen. Joseph E. Johnston to General Sherman. He took part in almost all the battles in which the army of Tennessee was engaged and was twice severely wounded. After the surrender he returned to Columbus, took an active part in public affairs and became interested in most of the business enterprises of this prosperous little city. In 1870 he was united in marriage to Miss Sarah F. Evans, of Columbus, Miss., by whom he has had four children: William, Frank, Anna and John.

Edmund Richardson. There is, in the intensified energy of the business man, fighting the every day battle of life, but little to attract the attention of the idle observer or reader in search of a sensational chapter; but to the mind fully awake to the reality and meaning of human existence there are noble and immortal lessons in the life of the man who, without other means than a clear head, a strong arm and a true heart, conquers adversity, and who, toiling on through the workaday years of a long and arduous career, closes the evening of his life with an honorable competence and a good name; and it is to those who appreciate the value and would emulate the excellence of such lives that these pages are addressed. The history of the great commonwealths of the South contain many characters whose elements compose the great worth and excellence of American liberty and progression. The South has furnished its full quota of the men who have conserved and enriched the grand principles of our noblest of governments, men who have furnished practical illustrations of the value to society of the cardinal virtues of business life. The history of a country is best shown in the lives of the men who aid in making it great, and the record of the people of a state is the only true basis upon which to form judgment of the right of that state to the fullest enjoyment of the broad privileges accorded by the constitution that governs the whole. So true is this that the writers of human achievements stop to portray individual character before attempting to philosophize on civilization. The history of individuals, and not of events, has been the fundamental and the most popular theme from the beginning of the world, and the custom of recording their life accomplishments has descended, hoary with antique and solemn associations, to the present day. Men who live in the eye of the public, as incumbents of office conferred by the suffrage of the people, attain places in history by the force of circumstances, as well as by personal worth and the faithful employment of great abilities for the good of the nation. Men in business life can rise into prominence, and become objects of high consideration in public estimation, only by the development of the noblest attributes of manhood in enterprises that largely affect the well being of communities. The accidents of birth and fortune, and the adventitious aids of chance and circumstance, can do little to give these men position in history whose resources are within the limits of their brains and hands. The record of the life of Colonel Richardson finds easy and graceful place in history, not alone of his state, but in the records of the great commercial centers of America. It stands out preeminent, among the truly great men of his time, as a noble character whose force, whose sterling integrity, whose fortitude amid deep discouragements, whose good sense in the government of complicated affairs, whose control of agencies and circumstances, and whose marked success in establishing large industries and bringing to completion great schemes of trade and profit, have contributed more than any other to the development of the vast resources of two great commonwealths. In person he was of commanding presence; over six feet in hight he was stout in proportion, and in his younger days must have been a type of manly strength and physical perfection. The fine steel engraving of Colonel Richardson which faces this sketch was made expressly for this history, and is an excellent likeness. He may be justly termed a representative Southern man. He was by far the largest planter of cotton in the world, having for many years over twenty-three thousand acres of land under cultivation. To the practical planter, familiar with the difficulties of cotton planting, these figures speak volumes; no one else can appreciate the executive ability requisite to conduct successfully such immense planting operations.

In other fields of enterprise Colonel Richardson was equally prominent; the largest manufacturer of cotton in the South, he was also owner of extensive oilmills at Vicksburg, Miss., and was head of the firm of Richardson & May, New Orleans, the largest cotton commission house in the United States. Of his minor enterprises, such as his insurance business and his many stores in various places, there is not space here to speak in detail. As a capitalist he took first rank in the South. His great wealth, aggregating several millions, was accumulated in legitimate industry, and has never been used to crush feeble competitors. Communities have been made richer and thousands happier by his enterprise; in his mills alone, at Wesson, two thousand operatives and laborers find employment; nearly all of them have been drawn from the country in the vicinity of the mills, and by a liberal system of recompense and encouragement have been transformed into well-dressed, happy, self-supporting workers. With his careful attention to his own interests, Colonel Richardson combined much public spirit. His purchase of the Vicksburg, Shreveport & Pacific railroad required the expenditure of a large sum, kept the control of the road at home, and insured its completion. From its recent sale he derived a large profit. It is indicative of the nature and aspirations of the man and of the largeness of his operations, that while in the notes written out for a sketch of his life he enumerates with some pride the industrial honors conferred upon him, he omits all mention of his almost single-handed purchase of this railroad. But in the biography of any prominent and successful man, the most interesting part after all is that which tells the story of his early life. His later career is known to many; it is, so to speak, public property; but the early influences that determined his course in life, first set his feet in the path of success, and shaped his career are generally less known, although of most importance because the lesson they teach can be applied by others for their own benefit. Colonel Richardson was born in Caswell county, N. C., six miles from Danville, Va., then only a village, on June 28, 1818. His father, James Richardson, was a country merchant and planter, and died in 1826, leaving a widow and seven children. When about ten years of age Edmund Richardson was sent to what was then called an oldfield school. Even the limited opportunity for getting an education afforded him was diminished by the necessity he was under in assisting the field hands on his mother's farm on Saturdays, when other children of his age were either studying or enjoying their weekly holiday. That his efforts to secure an education did not cease with these four years of primitive schooling, and that he must afterward have studied diligently in his brief hours of respite from hard work, is shown by letters written by him, which are clear, precise, well worded, and such as any well-educated man might write. When the boy was fourteen years old his mother obtained for him a situation in a store in Danville, at $30 a year and board. That mother must have been a woman of great force of character and energy; so anxious was she that her boy should be able to save his salary that she had his clothes spun and woven at home, besides furnishing him with scanty pocket money for candy and other boyish necessaries of existence, and for an occasional visit to some passing circus. "And how much," he asks "do you suppose I saved out of that salary of $30 a year?" "Why, just $30."

Eng^d by H.B. Hall's Sons, NewYork.

In 1833, at the age of fifteen, he went to Brandon, Miss., where he took a position in a store at $40 per year. He held this position for two years and then continued for a working interest in the firm, and afterward at the settlement of his mother's estate, in 1840, the executor having turned over to young Edmund $2,800 in money and a few negroes, he added this money to his savings and bought out the firm and continued the business in his own name, establishing other mercantile houses in Canton and Jackson, Miss. From the day he obtained his situation in Brandon he was an ambitious student and was soon well up with the young men of his time and competent to keep the books and do the financiering for the firm. Nearly all the men who have risen to distinction in any walk of life have always been eager to make known their obligation to a mother's influence; to these Colonel Richardson is no exception; in concluding his own account of his career he said: "I owe my great success to early lessons in economy received from my mother, and to the assistance of my partners in business." He is careful to give full credit to the latter, saying in another place: "I have been very fortunate in partners." In 1847, while in New York buying goods, he met Margaret E. Patton, of Huntsville, Ala., a sister of ex-Governor Robert Patton of that state, who was visiting in New York, and in May, 1848, he married her. From the hour of the solemn ceremony to the end of his life, Colonel Richardson's marriage was of the most satisfactory and happy nature. It was a union of two affectionate hearts, with kindred impulses, sympathy and lofty ambitions, encouraged by high moral purpose; it was characterized throughout by the most gentle consideration and loving kindness, each to the other and both alike. It was a life-long honeymoon, that scattered sunshine over the lives of many and made their cares lighter and lives brighter by coming in touch with its warmth and gentleness. For more than a third of a century this sacred union continued, the advancing years adding to the honor and peace of the preceding ones. The tie was interrupted only by death. On January 11, 1886, Colonel Richardson was stricken with apoplexy and died in a few minutes. Mrs. Richardson was completely broken by her sad loss and on December 9th of the following year she followed her beloved husband to that mysterious realm of which we know only the brightness of a beautiful promise. From their marriage there were seven children, two of whom died: James S., William P., John P., Charles P. and Susie P., now the wife of William W. Gordon, of New Orleans, being the survivors of the family, James S. the eldest son being at the present time the head of the estates; interesting and instructive histories of whom will be found in the following pages. In 1850 Colonel Richardson went into business at Jackson with his brother and John W. Robinson as partners, and opened branch stores at Brandon, Canton, Morton and Newton. In 1852 he entered the cotton commission business in New Orleans, retaining his plantatation and country store interests until 1860, when he sold them. When the war broke out Colonel Richardson's house, Thornhill & Co., in New Orleans, suspended business, having acceptances out to the amount of $500,000; its assets amounted to between eight and nine hundred thousand dollars, but of course, most of these were lost. He had besides, some individual liabilities, and was working five plantations, most of them on the Mississippi river. The negroes on these were set free and the teams, stock and outfits, mostly lost or destroyed. The close of the war found Colonel Richardson seriously embarrassed financially and with his plantations in a dilapidated condition. As he himself said: "I would gladly have given up all I had to be free from debt;" but he felt that it was useless to remain inactive and nurse vain regrets. In the fall of 1865 he attempted to reorganize his places for planting, and with five hundred bales of cotton saved from the general wreck, reopened his commission house in New Orleans. He sold his plantations for good prices in cash, and his cotton enabled him to control his acceptances by paying half cash and extending the balance for twelve months. He then controlled the paper of his customers and went earnestly to work, collecting from some, compromising with others, settling in some way with all whose paper he held. In twelve months he was out of debt, and soon had capital in his business.

The traveling which Colonel Richardson did in these and the next succeeding years was marvelous; his activity was ceaseless; wherever his presence could be of service to his interests or those of his firm he managed to be. The whole reëstablishing of his fortune was an exhibition of energy and masterful appliance of the means at command, such as had scarcely ever before been witnessed, even under similar exceptional circumstances. Impossibilities were Colonel Richardson's opportunities, and what to most men would seem insurmountable obstacles Colonel Richardson leveled to his own convenience and order by the exercise of a courage, the remarkability of which was equaled only by its unswerving purpose. At the breaking out of the war Colonel Richardson owned eight hundred slaves and many large plantations, a possession so great as to sound like a romance. For four years during the war this vast business was entirely suspended. After the dissolution of his partnership with Mr. Thornhill in 1867, on account of the ill health of that gentleman, Colonel Richardson began to look around for a partner; he did not know Mr. A. H. May personally, but had heard of his great business qualities, and he started out to find him. He went to New Orleans and met Mr. May in front of No. 40 Perdido, and introduced himself; after a very few minutes' talk the firm of Richardson & May was formed; they stepped inside the office, 40 Perdido, and asked for a sheet of paper, and the articles of copartnership were written and signed, and Colonel Richardson hurried to catch his train, he having agreed to do the country work while Mr. May was to conduct the office. As he left Mr. May he said, "rent that office," which was done, and they have remained in the same office ever since. The Mississippi state penitentiary was, directly after the war, a great burden on the state; there were many prisoners and no money. Colonel Richardson made a proposition to the military governor to lease the penitentiary from the State for three years for $18,000 per annum, and in 1868 he became the lessee, and inaugurated the system of making cotton with convict labor. In 1871 the civil governor induced him to keep it another year. In order to employ all the prisoners he purchased many fine cotton plantations and leased many others. During the war the levees protecting the alluvial land of Mississippi from overflow were broken, washed away and caved into the river. There was no hope of reclaiming those valuable lands except by protection from overflow. Southern securities were not then wanted by capitalists. Colonel Richardson made a proposition to build these levees and take bonds for the work. The proposition was accepted, the levees built, and those magnificent lands reclaimed. He held these bonds until they were of good value, and it was always a source of pride to him to see the levee bonds, which had been such a drug, so eagerly sought after. A few years before his death the fifth district levee board of Mississippi decided to issue $200,000 of bonds. Colonel Richardson was wired to; he was then in New York. His reply was prompt that he would take the whole issue at par, and he took them. In 1873 Colonel Richardson had a talk with an Eastern gentleman well posted in cotton spinning of the world, and especially that of the East. Colonel Richardson argued that the place for the cotton mills of this country was near the cotton fields. The Eastern man argued that that was an impossibility, as the quality of the white labor in the South was not intelligent enough, and such a thing would not be possible in the South. Colonel Richardson decided to make the experiment, and built the Mississippi mills at Wesson, Miss. There is no foreign labor in the mills except Mr. John Hopkinson—Englishman—the superintendent, who has been with the mills since they were started, and to whom the great success of these mills is partly attributable. William Oliver, who was secretary and treasurer from the first, was a man of wonderful sagacity and energy. Mr. Oliver died in June of this year. Colonel Richardson was president of the World's Exposition in 1883. In 1879 the Northern Louisiana & Shreveport railroad was ordered foreclosed to pay the first bondholders, amounting to $1,250,000, and other cash liabilities amounting to about $400,000. Terms of sale, $60,000 cash to be deposited. Colonel Richardson bought the road, paid off the $400,000 cash, and assured the payments of the bonds. He ran the road for nine months, and sold the same to the Erlanger syndicate. This was a big job, the road in the worst possible condition, ties all rotted and rails worn and bent, and the roadbed in a dreadful state, requiring a great outlay of money to put it in shape so that it could be used.

Colonel Richardson was in partnership with Gen. N. B. Forrest in planting cotton on Prest island, near Memphis, from 1872 to General Forrest's death. He was also in partnership with Gen. Wade Hampton in planting cotton in Washington county, Miss. In addition to his many other engagements he was partner in Commendum, in the well known big grocery house of Goodrich & Raily, from 1869 to 1872. There are many remarkable instances upon record of the marked philanthropic character of Colonel Richardson; records that establish his great humanity to man and sympathy to those in distress. These records are living examples of Colonel Richardson's grateful remembrance of the friends of his early life and struggles, and of his great generosity to those who served him. Through all the many incidents placed before the eye of the writer, as indeed Colonel Richardson's whole life has proven, there is the ennobling presence of that high, moral purpose and unswerving allegiance to truth, so characteristic in the lives of truly great men. There is not space in this history to enumerate half of his kind acts to his fellowmen, or to set forth the footprints of his wonderful progress. Therefore a few of the incidents only can be related. When Colonel Richardson was on his way from North Carolina to Clinton, Miss., his horse died just before he reached there. He looked about to find someone from whom he could obtain a horse, and found a Mr. Hobson, who was a North Carolinian, and he cheerfully loaned him a horse to finish his journey. Mr. Hobson died shortly before Colonel Richardson's death, and one of the last acts of Colonel Richardson's life was to erect a monument over Mr. Hobson's grave, in remembrance of his kind act to him when he was a strange boy in a strange land. Among the bridal presents at the wedding of Colonel Richardson there were three valuable slaves: Dick Richardson, Martha Douglass and Sallie Rother. Dick was the trusty coachman until he was too old to do service, and was then given a monthly allowance until his death. During the war the family was in the Federal lines, and Dick was the messenger between his master and his family, making regular trips and carrying much money and valuables back and forth. He could have had his freedom any time, but he preferred to serve his master, for whom his devotion was worship. Sallie was the cook from 1848 to 1870. Martha Rother was the black mammy, who raised all the children. These three negroes were with the family in and out of the Federal lines many times during the war, never desiring to change their happy condition; they remained in the service of the family until their death.

James S. Richardson. It is the knowledge of the circumstances that tend to the formation of character, or the conditions which influence and direct the happiness of life, that constitute the advantage gained by the world from the publication of the lives of individuals; and the only objection which can possibly be raised against the time-honored custom of recording the lives of men while they live is that truth, in the hands of less painstaking biographers, is apt to be buried in panegyric. Under such circumstances there is an appearance of reason for the objection, and yet there are so many others against the objection that the balance is all on the side of truth and the usefulness and eminent propriety of memoirs. That we speak favorably of the subjects admitted in this history ought not to be considered a fault, as if we had nothing favorable to say of them they would not be admitted at all. It is not the design of history or the practice of historians or biographers to lavish praise indiscriminately, but rather to gather facts and state them fairly in a graceful manner; and such facts, published during the life of the subject, can with more certainty be relied on than such as may be gathered from his friends after death, when the maxim de mortuis nil nisi bonum, is most generally strictly observed. A virtuous life demands our reverence; public and private worth, our admiration; long and practical usefulness, our gratitude. It is the living presence of those elements that robs the task of the biographer of its melancholy and leaves it an agreeable duty to be performed for the instruction and guidance of the footsteps of those who follow after. Honor and fame are the legitimate reward of virtue and talent. Like wealth they may sometimes be unworthily bestowed and sometimes unworthily worn; but when yielded to merit or won by industry they adorn the wearer like a graceful robe, imparting dignity and commanding respect. Through the operation of the printing press and the careful writer they become the property of the present and the future, and appear as trophies to be won and worn by those who successfully contend against indolence and vice; and it is of rare occurrence in the history of any country that superior mental attainments, in alliance with moral worth, judiciously directed and actively employed, have failed in their attainment. An additional attestation of this universal truth will be found in this memoir.

Mr. J. S. Richardson, in many respects, is one of the most remarkable men in our history. He was born in Huntsville, Ala., on the 22d day of February, 1849, and is the eldest child of the late Col. Edmund Richardson, who was the founder of the great cotton firm of Richardson & May, as well as the greatest cotton planter in the world. His mother was Margaret Elizabeth Patton, a sister of ex-Governor Patton, of Alabama. Mr. J. S. Richardson's early education was obtained in the common schools at Brandon, Miss., where his father lived before the war, and at Huntsville, Ala., where he also spent part of his boyhood with his grandmother. During the war he had no opportunities for school. In 1863, when quite a boy, he was sent by his father into the Federal army to look after property belonging to his mother. He was arrested as a spy by General Granger and held a prisoner eight months at Huntsville, Ala., during which time he contracted the measles and had a relapse and came near dying. During General Granger's absence his adjutant took pity on the sick boy and released him and had him passed through the lines at Whitesburg. Being weak, without money or friends, and where no mail communications could reach his family, he had to walk nearly a hundred miles, when he borrowed an old mule and proceeded to where his father was refuging. Immediately after the war he was sent to Wilson's preparatory school in Alamance county, N. C., and he remained there a year, then entered the Virginia Military institute at Lexington, and having a taste for business, he was anxious to embark for himself. He left the military institute after the second year and went to Memphis, Tenn., and bought the interest of E. E. Clark, in the large cotton firm of Clark, Ely & Co., the firm then continuing under the name of Ely, Harney & Richardson.

In 1876 he bought his partners out and continued the business under the name of Richardson & Co. The yellow fever of 1879 forced him to move his office from Memphis to St. Louis. While there he determined to close up the cotton business in Memphis. He bought an interest in the well-known large grocery business of C. M. & G. M. Flanagan, the firm then becoming Flanagan & Richardson. This business was continued under that name for three years. The business of his father was increasing so fast that he needed help. Mr. Richardson sold his interest to his partners in 1881 and went South to assist his father, who was a firm believer in the gradual enhancement of values of good cotton lands, and Mr. James S. Richardson commenced in 1875 to follow out his father's idea—bought some cotton plantations and has continued ever since to enlarge his planting interest. When Colonel Richardson died, in 1886, he left no will, and the brothers and sisters of Mr. Richardson immediately issued powers of attorney and Mr. Richardson was put in the entire charge of the large estate of his father, which amounted to many millions. In the meantime Mr. Richardson's mother died, and afterward, when everything was in snug shape and ready for division, a meeting of all the heirs was called and the entire estate was divided pleasantly and to the entire satisfaction of all concerned, Mr. Richardson having caused large additions to his father's accumulations. The planting property of Mr. Richardson, inherited in addition to what he previously owned, makes him the largest cotton planter in the world, he having in all forty thousand acres of the fine alluvial cotton land, of which twenty thousand acres are in cultivation this year. The cotton firm of Richardson & May continues, and the Richardsons still own their father's stock in the Refuge Cotton oilmill at Wesson, which institution is now working over two thousand operatives. Probably one of the most remarkable incidents in Mr. Richardson's life was in 1871, during the yellow fever epidemic, while on a steamboat going up to his father's plantation he was taken sick with this fever. The crew and passengers became panicstricken with fright, and in the rain and wintry weather of November he was put ashore. The only house near was an old dilapidated one without chimneys, floor, doors or windows. He was placed in this house until friends came to his rescue, and in a short time, with the use of cloths, the openings were closed and a clapboard floor put in and straw and mud chimneys hurriedly built. The physician pronounced his recovery impossible, but his strong constitution pulled him through. One of the great attests of public faith and honor in the social organization of New Orleans, than which there is not a finer code in its usefulness and worthiness in the world, the annual election of the king of the carnival is the most distinguished. The selection of this personage is made solely upon personal popularity and worthiness; and it calls for an exhibition of great dignity, broad and liberal hospitality, and a distinguished personal appearance. There are no set rules for the ethics of the king upon this day, simply a prepared programme of his grand disembarkation from the steamer that has conveyed the royal host and party up the Mississippi river to the city, and the reception by the municipal authorities, and their escort of the king and his party to the city hall, where the keys of the city are turned over to Rex; the interpretation of the proper address of a king, his royal manner and dignity, before the eyes of a hundred thousand people is an ordeal of no common nature. More particularly is this true when the character is assumed by one of such pronounced American spirit as Mr. Richardson. In 1891 Mr. Richardson was elected to this distinguished social honor, and it is a matter of record, that while being full-charged with the spirit of democracy and liberty, Mr. Richardson possesses the high attainments requisite to the assumption of kingly favor and dignity. In personal appearance Mr. Richardson is six feet high and weighs about two hundred and thirty pounds. He has a compact figure and quick, decisive movement. His eyes are nearly as black as his father's and have the same searching, yet kindly, sympathetic, expression. He is the soul of considerate kindness, and is accessible to rich and poor alike. Among his happiest accomplishments is the one, which is truly a family trait, of placing strangers entirely at their ease,

At his lovely home, on St. Charles avenue, or in his city offices, Mr. Richardson can always be seen, and he will interrupt his busiest hour and give audience to friend and stranger alike. His liberality is a matter of note, and causes him no small degree of trouble. To all deserving public enterprises, he subscribes liberally; and while his private donations to those is distress are not known to the public, they are many, and are of the highest possible consideration, from the very fact of their silence. Of course, Mr. Richardson does not give to every supplicant, for if he did, he would be kept busy at that and nothing else. An instance of his appreciation of a good thing, and his quick wit, is related in the following incident of a begging letter of recent date: The pastor of some obscure church wrote Mr. Richardson a long letter, extolling his great charities and said, "I know you do not belong to our persuasion, but I know you will give liberally to this project—which is to build a church. You see, sir, we have a world of land, but no church, and we are anxious to raise the money to build one,"—and asked for an immediate reply. It was sent, and was as terse and crisp as any of the replies made by men of note, and deserves to be recorded here. It consisted of three words, "Sell some land." Mr. Richardson has never used his great wealth to oppress anyone or anything. His delight is to see every one prosperous and happy, and he will stop his royal four-in-hand on the roadside and talk to some lowly old darkey, who seems to bear life's burdens poorly, and with a few kind, cheering words, and a consistent amount of money, he will brighten and lighten the man's journey and forget all about it the next moment. To those who serve him he is ever just and kind, and for extra service, he always returns extra reward. Mr. Richardson has no political ambition whatever. He would decline a place in the United States senate for one-half the time with his friends and the people. His servants all love and respect him, and are as faithful to his interests as was Diana to her master. Mr. Richardson has traveled the world over, has driven through France and England, and is an ardent admirer and a friend of the horse, of which he keeps twelve in his city stables for pleasure driving. Very few men emulate the example of their fathers. Mr. J. S. Richardson is one of the few. When death came into his household, he assumed all the authority that was necessary. His acts were fully ratified by every member of the family, and what he has done for the great estate of Col. Edmund Richardson has been remarkable in the highest degree. His integrity is unquestioned, and his good name above reproach.

John P. Richardson, Wesson, Miss. It is a particular felicity of American institutions that they throw no impediment in the way of merit other than the competition of rival abilities. Into this career it may enter without encountering the repulses of artificial rank or royalty. As the father of an American family divides his favor and his fortune alike among his children, so the constitution of our greatest of republics gives the same impulse to all her sons, and receives in turn a larger contribution of their talents and services. The more conspicuous a man is rendered by his talents, energy, decision of character and unswerving principles, the more will he become the favorite of some, and the object of envy and reproach to others. In no country in the world are men's principles tried at the bar of public opinion as in America; nothing can alter this custom, this unwritten law, or change the result; nor is it desirable that it should be otherwise, unless, indeed, the bitterness and coarse invective of the indolent, the mentally shiftless, the morally indifferent, who oppose the advance above them of their opposites, should tend to moderate the custom or lessen its effect. Nothing is more becoming to a country, or affords better proof of the excellent spirit of its people, than to find the reward of popular praise, and popular honors bestowed upon those whose labors have been guided by a wise philanthropy, and whose objects have been largely the welfare and betterment of mankind.

There are many, no doubt, who have overcome greater embarrassments, who have had harder battles to fight, than the subject of this sketch, but there are few who have grasped the opportunities presented by the gods, and grasped them more firmly or to a better purpose, or who have made better use of the fruits of the possession than the typical American and Southern gentleman, of whom it is our pleasant task here to relate.

John P. Richardson was born at Brandon, Miss., May, 4, 1854, and is the second eldest son of Col. Edmund Richardson, whose brief biography appears in this history. The history of his boyhood is that of most boys who are blessed with wealthy and indulgent, but painstaking parents. He was educated at a private school at Jackson, Miss., until the age of fourteen, when he entered the Bellview high school for one year, and the following year entered a regular academic course of two years at the Virginia Military institute, at Lexington, Va., and finished his scholastic career with a term at the noted Kenmire high school, at Amherst Courthouse, Va. During all this time he was an earnest and conscientious student, and stored his brain with the knowledge which has so admirably captioned his business and social career. After his return home from school he accepted a position as assistant superintendent of the Mississippi mills, later removing to New Orleans, where he managed an agency for the mills. In 1879 he established a wholesale dry goods business at New Orleans, which business was successfully conducted under the firm name of Richardson & Cary, Mr. Richardson remaining a partner or sole owner until 1889, when the present firm of Richardson, Williams & Co. was organized. In 1886, after the death of his father, he was elected president of the Mississippi mills, and at once assumed the duties of this responsible position. He is a thorough, practical and methodical business man, and the organization of which he is the head has profited largely under his judicious management. Aside from his interests in this line, he is extensively engaged in planting and is the owner of eighteen thousand acres in the delta region of the state, all of which are under cultivation and require eight supply stores. On February 4, 1879, he was married to Miss Ella Oliver, a daughter of the late Capt. William Oliver, of Wesson. Four children have blessed this union, of whom one son and one daughter survive. An examination of the magnificent steel engraved portrait which faces this sketch will convey to the reader a true impression of the kindly elements that compose the character of Mr. Richardson. He is full six feet in hight, and has been abundantly favored by nature. Mr. Richardson weighs about two hundred pounds, and to the casual observer presents the appearance of being a finished student of some school of athletics. He is quick in his movement, without seeming to be in haste, and while in no way influenced by nervousness, he possesses an active, decisive temperament, that brooks no delay in the promulgation of his plans. He possesses his full share of the family courtliness and ethical consideration for those around him. He is, in a word, a broad-gauged gentleman, incapable of small or mean action. A bit of industrial history worthy of mention here, which serves to illustrate, not only the characteristics outlined in the preceding paragraph as belonging to the subject of this sketch, but to the father and all the sons alike, is this: In England, or in fact in the great weaving centers of the New England states of America, a manager or a proprietor of a cotton or woolen manufactory, would no more think of permitting another manufacturer of a similar line of goods to enter his factory, than he would of permitting a stranger to enter upon the secrets of his domestic affairs. In fact, in England, the visitor is obliged to take an oath that he is in no way, directly or indirectly, connected with any similar business that is directly or indirectly connected with or influenced by said mill or industry in England or elsewhere, before he can get a peep into the workings of the mill. The Richardsons are a remarkable opposite to that rigid and narrow understanding. Mr. James S. Richardson once almost dumbfounded a noted English cotton and woolen manufacturer who visited them at Wesson, by proposing to show him all the workings of their great mills. "What?" gasped the Englishmen, "you propose to permit me to enter your mills?" "Certainly," responded Mr. Richardson, and he forthwith proceeded to escort the rival manufacturer through each and every department, permitting him to examine at his leisure all of the original and improved methods, and to help himself to as much information as possible; saying, in the meantime: "What you see in mechanism for the protection of weave and advanced finish of fabrics is nearly a century in advance of English methods; but it is only the rudiments of American genius and our own original device; and when Europe creates its equal, we will proceed to step out another century in advance." The son of the Englishman, who was also present, was so impressed with the truth of what Mr. Richardson said, and with what he had seen, that he decided to remain in the United States; and he has done so, taking up his residence in the South, and devoting his time to re-learning the art of cotton and woolen spinning. What is probably a more remarkable evidence of their just confidence in the great strength and advantage of the Mississippi mills, came under the observation of the writer only a few days since: A gentleman from Carrollton, Miss., and the president of a new, necessarily competitive, cotton mill at that place, was visiting Wesson, and in company with the writer was shown through the vast labyrinth of machinery, and had the different workings described by the genial president, Mr. John P. Richardson, himself. These incidents may seem very unimportant to the casual observer, but to the mind fully informed as to the modus operandi of large manufacturing establishments even in America, they speak volumes in behalf of the advanced liberality and kindness of this noted family, and of the worthy example they set, even to those of superior years and pretentions.

The Mississippi mills, Wesson, Miss., a great industry, affording employment through which thousands of the citizens of a state are made brighter, happier and better, certainly lose identity as a mere place of mechanics, a work shop, and assume the advanced position of a leading factor in the organized methods of the social, moral and physical advancement of that state, and become as much a part of the deserving history of the state in which it is conducted as possibly can be ascribed to political organization or the organization of any great scheme for the betterment of mankind, for it is the inspiration of the latter and conserves the former. Particularly is this true where great industries bear so remarkable a likeness to the character, humanity and liberality of the master minds that worked so hard to make it great. There is no industry in the South, nor in the North, nor anywhere in the United States, that is blessed with so much of the broad-gauged humanity of its organizers, that is enriched with so complete a record of justice, equity and fellowship as that of the great institution of which it is our pleasure here to record. Within its massive walls during the busy work-a-day hours assigned to man, through which to discharge his obligations to the laws of creation, and earn his daily bread, there is a sufficient number of souls to populate a goodly sized city. Happy and contented, free from labor organization, free from trade's-union dictation, this honest little army of workers have for nearly a quarter of a century received their liberal pay without the cessation of a day. Regularly each morning, in response to the morning whistle of the mills, two thousand happy, bright faced healthy men and women flock from their pretty homes and enter the great white walls; within all is order, cleanliness and industry; the picture of cheerfulness observed upon the faces of the employes, while outside of the workrooms, is not in any degree lessened when they are at work; on the contrary it is enriched by the satisfaction they all have in knowing the importance of their work, for each and every individual in the great works has been educated by a system of liberal reward and kindness to feel that the success, the reputation of the mills, is in part dependent upon the character and faithfulness of his or her individual effort. They therefore take great pride in all they do. Such institutions as this cease to be a common place of toil. It is a vast school of labor, a college of instruction in the sacred precepts of American liberty and independence. The mind that for so many years directed them in their work, protected them in their rights, sympathized and aided them in their troubles, and who is now quietly sleeping the sleep of the just in the little churchyard at Wesson, never spoke of them as one of our men, or one of our factory hands, but as my people, my girls, my boys. He knew every one of the people by name, knew their condition in life, and this knowledge he used always to their betterment and satisfaction.

Personally, Col. Edmund Richardson was little known at the mills, but the beneficence of his spirit was ever present, and the people knew him almost as well as though his life had been spent among them. In every kindness, every evidence of thoughtful regard for their welfare which was made known to them, the people could trace the master mind of Colonel Richardson, and the kindly, executive hand of his able partner, Captain Oliver. It was impossible then even to look forward to the time, when, according to the course of human events, the grave must close upon the labors of these two men, without a feeling of profound sadness, for such men are the ornaments of every and any age. They arise only at distant intervals, to enlighten and elevate the human race. Death came. Like a flash of deadly lightning it grasped the towering mind, the strong physique of Colonel Richardson, when he has scarcely even approached the evening of his time, and leveled it to common earth. A wave of intense sorrow spread itself like a cold pall over the great commonwealth, and at the mills the two thousand operatives went about their work in a hushed and saddened manner. Great changes were anticipated by those who knew nothing of the delicate finish of the set principles of the great organization. But the great wheels turned just the same, the thousands of spindles flew just as fast. The man was dead, but his works still lived. Almost before the solemn cypress had been removed from the heads of those who mourned the death of Colonel Richardson, Captain Oliver was stricken down, and died. Again great changes were predicted. New and untried hands were to grasp the helm, and much fear was felt that there were breakers ahead for the interruption of the happy course of mill life; again were the outsiders disappointed, for it is ever a disappointment to those who predict all sorts of evil for mankind to learn the falsity and foolishness of their own minds. The son of his father came to the front, and assumed the chief executive. A meeting of the heirs and stockholders of the mill was held and John P. Richardson was elected president. Some changes were made, but they were only the changes suggested by a younger mind that perhaps was in closer touch with the world. The changes were only the abrogation of a few of the customs that had grown old and unnecessary by use. Like machinery and men, customs must grow old and as they can not be advanced to the improvement of a new age without rebuilding, they must be discarded. Hence the changes made by the sons of Edmund Richardson were for the greater happiness of their many people. And looking upon them to-day with a judgment sobered by time it is seen that they were just such alterations as would have been made by the father himself could he have lived to note their application to the needs of the time.

These mills are located at Wesson, Miss., about one hundred and thirty-five miles north of New Orleans and forty-five miles south of Jackson, on the Illinois Central railroad. A few years ago this was but a pine forest, worth at most $1 per acre, and now there stands here one of the most substantial towns anywhere along this line of railroad. Wesson, to-day, has a population of about four thousand, and a valuation of property of over one and one-half million of dollars. The Mississippi mills alone pay taxes this year on nearly $1,000,000 worth of property, and they have a large investment exempt from taxation for ten years, which will bring their property alone to nearly $1,500,000 dollars. It might be interesting to those who do not know anything about this large enterprise to know some of the particulars concerning it, and we here give a synopsis of the size and number of mills and their products. There are three mills, all of brick, as follows: No. 1, three stories, 50x350 feet; No. 2, four stories, 50x212 feet; No. 3 (new building), five stories, 50x240 feet, two towers, six stories high, twenty feet square, with five thousand gallon water tanks and automatic sprinklers throughout. The tower between No. 1 and No. 2 is eight stories, with a twenty thousand-gallon water tank, leading throughout every part of the works to automatic sprinklers, effectually obviating the danger of destruction by fire. A fourth building is 40x100 feet, two stories high, besides which the loom shed just erected is one story and basement, 175x340 feet.

In these buildings there are twenty-five thousand cotton spindles, twenty-six complete sets of woolen machinery and eight hundred looms, the latter to be increased to about twelve hundred in the near future. Besides the above mentioned there is an abundance of machinery used for dyeing, finishing, etc. It requires four engines with a combined force of one thousand horse power to furnish the necessary motive power. In connection with the above buildings, the mills have a large cotton warehouse, capacity 10,000 bales of cotton, which is about their requirements annually. In the basement of the loom shed they have a storage capacity of two million pounds of wool, and it will require almost this much after this year to supply their wants. The system of waterworks of these mills is excellent. They have a one hundred and fifteen thousand gallon cistern, connected with fire pumps and a six-inch water main and hydrants at convenient points for attaching hose, which form an efficient system of water works, driven by two Worthington pumps capable of forcing water over the highest building. The supply is taken from a spring creek, one and one-quarter miles distant and is inexhaustible.

One of the reasons for the success of these mills, is the great variety of their products. There is hardly any article in staple goods, made of cotton and wool, but what they can supply. The following is a list of their productions: Cassimeres, jeans, doeskins, tweeds, linseys, flannels, wool knitting yarn, cotton knitting yarn, cotton rope, cotton warp yarn, cottonades, flannelettes, gingham plaids, cheviots, checks, plaids, stripes, hickory, brown sheeting, shirting, drilling, eight-ounce osnaburgs, ticking for feathers and mattresses, sewing thread, sewing twine for bags and awnings, wrapping twine, honey comb towels, awning, balmoral skirts, etc. Samples and prices of all goods will be cheerfully furnished on application. Very soon they will be running knitting machinery which will turn out hose and underwear of a superior quality. These goods have a reputation for excellence that is not surpassed by the product of any mills in the world, and the trade for them is drawn from almost every state and territory in the union. These mills now employ about a thousand hands, but will have almost double that number when all the new machinery is started up. The present monthly pay roll is from $18,000 to $20,000, which will be almost doubled when the increase of hands is required. These employes are for the most part taken right from the surrounding country and adjoing counties. One of the blessings of this great enterprise is its benevolence in supplying employment for women and children that would be almost helpless without some work of this kind. The people are happy and contented, and everything moves along harmoniously. In order that any who may have a desire to immigrate this way, may see what inducements are offered, we attach hereto an article from the board of immigration, which offers inducements to home builders to come to the vicinity, well worth considering.

In a letter to Mr. A. E. Randle, of Washington, D. C., dated Aderdeen, Miss., October 5, 1890, the Hon. S. A. Jonas, United States Senator, speaking of the cotton industry of the South, said:—

"I do not doubt but that you are familiar with the plant and operations of most of our Mississippi factories, yet the following items may be interesting: The Mississippi mills, at Wesson, manufacture in woolen goods a more extensive assortment than any other factory in this country, and probably in the world. This is due to climatic advantages, suitable water for bleaching, etc., and the excellence of our native wools; while in cotton fabrics their range is very extensive, and in addition to cloths and threads, includes a vast line of cordage. The making of the peculiar twine used for fishing purposes on the North Pacific and Alaska coasts, has long been an extensive branch of their trade. The buildings of this factory cover about six acres of ground, are from three to five stories high. The factory proper includes three mills, huge brick affairs of most approved model. No. 1, three stories, 50x350 feet; No. 2, four stories, 50x212 feet; No. 3, completed last year, five stories, 50x240 feet, surmounted by two towers six stories high, with water tanks of 5,000 gallons capacity. There is another tower eight stories high, containing a 20,000 gallon tank, from which pipes and automatic sprinklers convey water for extinguishment of fires to all parts of the buildings. A fourth building is 40x1,000 feet and two stories high, and there is also a one story loom shed, 175x340 feet. To people living beyond our borders, and even to most of our own people, these figures are astounding.

"In these buildings are thirty thousand cotton spindles, thirty complete sets of woolen machinery and eight hundred looms; the latter to be increased to one thousand two hundred within the next few weeks. In addition to this plant is a complete outfit of the most approved machinery and appliances for dyeing, finishing, packing, etc., and the motive power is supplied by great engines aggregating over one thousand horse-power for actual service. These mills also have storage warehouses for six thousand bales of cotton, and wool rooms with capacity for over two million pounds. This amount of material is, I think, about the quantity of staples required annually by these mills. The cisterns have a capacity of one hundred and fifteen thousand gallons, supplied by pipes from a creek over a mile from the mills. In addition to other plants, they are now putting in knitting machinery, and will enter the market this season with hose and underwear made from our wonderful Lake wool. The number of hands employed now is two thousand, and I have good authority for saying that the force will be increased as soon as all of this new machinery is in place. A large proportion of the hands are women and children, and all, except the foreman and machinists, are from the surrounding country. You and I well remember when this mill site was a pine forest, hardly worth fifty cents an acre, and now it is a bustling factory town of about four thousand people, and the mill, though enjoying exemption for a term of ten years upon its new building and plant, still pays taxes on nearly a million dollars worth of property, and probably yields dividends of from thirty to forty per cent.

"I cite this mill particularly to show you the results of judicious management in that line in Mississippi, for it may be said that almost every dollar that is in this factory came out of it and was earned by it, with Mississippi owners, managers, employes, staples, water and fuel, they use wood; and every bit of machinery not controlled by patent outside is supplied by state builders. These mills and those at Natchez, Enterprise, Wanita, and elsewhere in the state are crowded with orders, and always pushed to full capacity of plant. When out at Cheyenne, Wyo., in 1888, I was surprised and gratified to find Governor Moonlight of that territory, Register Wilson, the secretary of state, the surveyor-general, and many other prominent officials, clothed in goods from the Wesson mills, and in 1882 both of the Mississippi and Georgia senators were clothed in beautiful suits of cloth made by the Wanita mills, of our state. But I tire you. I will only add that Mississippi offers greater advantages and facilities to the cotton and woolen manufacturers than any other state in the Union, and I am anxious to see you at once utilize this grand Carrollton property. Remember, that under the operation of the long and short haul of the inter-state commerce law, we enjoy a vast advantage over eastern mills in the trade with the trans-Mississippi country, China, Japan and the islands of the South seas in the all-controlling matter of freights to western seaboard."

Robert E. Williams, Wesson, Miss., although but a short time a resident of Mississippi, Mr. Williams has made himself decidedly popular with those around him, and as secretary and treasurer of the Mississippi mills, a position to which he was appointed in August, 1891, his career will be noted with no common interest. Mr. Williams was born at Port Royal, Va., June 11, 1846. His father was Dr. G. A. Williams, and his mother was Miss M. R. Blackmore, both native Virginians. At the age of fourteen he removed with his parents to Missouri, and his earlier efforts in life were those of assisting his father on the farm. Later in life he removed to St. Louis, Mo. where he engaged in commercial pursuits until his appointment to his present position. Mr. Williams has no organic connection with any church, but is a believer in divinity and christian organization. He is unmarried, and like most bachelors, contented with his lot. Personally, Mr. Williams is of a decidedly retiring disposition and of as equally pronounced modesty. He is of medium hight and good build and robust constitution. He has an open, frank face that wins confidence at once and a manner of speech that bids the stranger welcome. He is a brother of Mr. Williams of the large wholesale dry goods firm of Richardson, Williams & Co. of New Orleans. Mr. Williams' whole life since he arrived at early manhood has been devoted to clerical labors in which he is an expert. He was one of the organizers of the Office Men's club of St. Louis, a club of more than usual note.

In reviewing the names of the men in Newton county, who have made a career for themselves worthy of record, that of W. B. Richardson is found among the most prominent. He is a native of Caswell county, N. C., but was taken during his infancy by his parents to Christian county, Ky. There he passed an uneventful youth until the breaking out of the Civil war. He at once enlisted under Capt. Tom Woodward, of Christian county; the company went at once to Clarksville, Tenn., to be sworn into the service; thence, to Camp Boone, and afterward was the first company to enter Bowling Green, Ky., attended by eight other companies. Mr. Richardson's war record was rather phenomenal; he went through the entire conflict without receiving a single wound. Upon the declaration of peace he went back to his old home in Kentucky, remaining there until the fall of 1866; at that time he came to Brandon, Rankin county, Miss., and entered the employ of Stephens, Willis & Co., in whose service he continued three years. In 1869 he embarked in the mercantile trade at Newton on his own responsibility. The experience he gained while with this successful firm was the foundation of his own fortune. While at Newton, a period of three years, he did an extensive business of $250,000 under the firm name of Richardson & Co. He also established a business at Jackson, Miss., still retaining control of the business at Newton. In 1880 he returned to Newton, bought out his partner, and is now doing a business of

$150,000 annually; he handles more cotton than any firm between Vicksburg and Meridian, in the state of Mississippi. Mr. Richardson was united in marriage to Miss Elizabeth, a daughter of Col. Thomas E. Helm, of Jackson, Miss. She died in 1886, and he was married a second time to Miss Mattie Brown, daughter of A. J. Brown. Two sons have been born of this union: W. B., Jr., and James. Believing most earnestly in the bonds of friendship fostered in fraternities, Mr. Richardson is connected with the Knights of Pythias and the Knights of Honor. His wife is a consistent member of the Methodist Episcopal church. The father of W. B. Richardson was James Richardson, who was one of a family of four sons and four daughters.

Prof. S. R. Ricketts, A. M., one of the professors of Whitworth college, was born at Vicksburg, Miss., in 1843. He is the son of Rev. R. B. and Martha (Cosby) Ricketts, natives respectively of Kentucky and Georgia. His father was born in 1794, and was a son of Abraham Ricketts, of Maryland, and who was of Scotch and Welsh decent. The professor's great-grandfather was the original settler of the family in this country, and located at New Castle, Del., among the pioneers at that point. His son, Abraham, followed farming, and removed from Delaware to Marysville, Ky., where he became a well-to-do planter, and where he reared a large family of sons and daughters, of whom Rev. R. B. Ricketts was the youngest. The latter grew to maturity in Kentucky, and was there educated. Removing to Jefferson county, Miss., in 1833, he settled near Fayette, where he engaged in planting, in which he continued with considerable success. In 1839 he joined the Mississippi annual conference of the Methodist Episcopal church. In 1843 he removed to Louisiana and engaged in sugar planting, remaining there until 1860, when he took up his residence in Iberville parish, where he engaged in cotton planting until the war. After the war he removed to Baton Rouge, where he was made steward of the deaf and dumb asylum, which position he held until 1868, when he purchased a plantation near Summit, Pike county, Miss., from whence he removed in 1873 to Brookhaven, where he died in 1879. Although not all of his life engaged in preaching, he was ever an active worker for the church, devoting heart and soul to all of its varied interests. In politics he was a whig, and upon those questions which the division between the North and South turned, he espoused the Union cause. His wife was born in 1809, and was a daughter of James Cosby, a native of Georgia. Her mother, who was Miss Margaret (McCall) Cosby, was also a native of the same state and a first cousin of the wife of Judge Edward McGehee, of Wilkinson county. (See sketch of Judge McGehee.) The mother of our subject was one of a family of five children, four of whom were daughters, she being the youngest in order of birth. She was reared in Wilkinson county, Miss., where she had removed with her parents in her childhood. The other members of the family were: Eliza, who married Mr. Williams, and after living in Wilkinson county for a number of years removed to Hinds county, thence to California in 1869, dying there quite recently; Harriet married James Fuqua, and lived in Wilkinson county a great portion of her life, removing to Clinton, Miss., and thence to Baton Rouge, where she died; Louisa, who married Robert Germany, and lived and died in Centerville, Miss. (See sketch of Charles Germany). Martha, the mother of Prof. Ricketts, died in Summit in 1873, having been for many years an earnest and devoted worker in the Methodist church; Scott lived in Wilkinson county and died there in middle life. The father of Prof. Ricketts was first married to Miss Shaw, of Jefferson county, Miss., by whom he had two sons who removed with him to Baton Rouge and died while at college. His mother was first married to Mr. Chrissman, of Woodville. To Mr. and Mrs. Ricketts were born three sons and three daughters, of whom two sons and two daughters are yet living. Barron C. died in the army; Mary L. is now Mrs. Woodside, of Baton Rouge, La.; Patti died in her thirteenth year; Henry P. is the city editor of the Memphis *Scimitar*; Lucy is a teacher in the public schools of Memphis, Tenn.

Prof. Ricketts was reared near Baton Rouge and principally at the collegiate institutions of that time. Later he attended Centenary college, at Jackson, La. After receiving his degree at the last named college, he taught school for a short time in the collegiate institute, until 1862, when he joined the Second Louisiana cavalry, and a few months later he was tranferred to the Signal corps at Port Hudson. He was captured at the time of Bank's first movement at Port Hudson, and was a prisoner for a time at New Orleans. After his release on parole, he went to camp at Enterprise, Miss., being exchanged only after a year of inactivity. He reported to General Forrest, at Columbus, Miss., and was sent on signal duty to a point near Grand Gulf, where he remained until the close of the war, when he was paroled at Jackson, Miss. Removing with his family to Jackson, La., he taught for a short time in the collegiate institute, until he was appointed to a position in the United States revenue office at Baton Rouge, which he filled until February, 1867, when he removed to Port Gibson, and became a teacher in the collegiate academy, remaining there until 1873. During the last year of his connection with the institute he held the position of principal. He then became connected with Whitworth college, in which he has found a field of labor since, having taught the advanced classes in all of the departments, but having for the most part filled the chair of professor of mathematics. For years he was Dr. Johnson's chief assistant. His career as a teacher has been one of almost unexampled success, and his connection with this institution has brought to it much well deserved credit and prosperity. He married Miss Bertha Burnley, a graduate of Whitworth college, and a daughter of Col. Edwin and Maria Burnley, of Copiah county, Miss. Her father was a native of Virginia, who came to Mississippi in 1830, locating in Copiah county, and becoming a well-to-do planter. He was a very popular and influential man, having at one time held the office of secretary of state in Virginia. Her mother was a native of New Jersey, and came to Port Gibson as a teacher in 1843. She taught there and elsewhere in Mississippi. She is yet living, making her home with Professor Ricketts and his wife. She became the mother of three sons and one daughter, named: Robert, Edwin, John and Bertha. Professor Ricketts was first married to Miss Katy Bessy, the daughter of Judge T. T. Bessy, and who died in 1873. Mr. and Mrs. Ricketts are members of the Methodist Church South, and among its most liberal supporters. Prof. Ricketts is a member of the order of Knights of Honor.

Gen. Benjamin S. Ricks, Yazoo City, is entitled to a space in this record of the leading men of Mississippi, both on account of personal worth and the position he occupies in the business circles of Yazoo county. He is a son of Benjamin Sherrod and Frances (Winter) Ricks, natives of North Carolina and Virginia, respectively. His father was born in 1882, and was reared in Halifax county, N. C. He was graduated at Chapel Hill college, in 1823, and was also a graduate in medicine; he did not, however, enter into the practice of the profession, but in early life devoted himself to planting in Mississippi, to which state he had removed in 1830. In 1840 he went into the commission business in New Orleans in partnership with John Carroll, which he continued until 1862, though in the meantime he was associated with other men. He was a most excellent business man, and acquired a large fortune before the war. He was not an aspirant to political honors, and would never accept public office. Politically he was an old line whig, and a true and loyal friend of the sunny South. The maternal grandfather of our subject was Major Winter, a native of Virginia. The Ricks family is of Welsh extraction, and the Winters family is of English stock. The grandmother Winter was a daughter of Bailey Washington, who was a first cousin to Gen. George Washington. General Ricks was born in Madison county, Miss., May 24, 1843. He was educated at the Bingham school and Princeton university. The war coming on before he had finished his course, he left his books to go to battle. He enlisted in company C, Twenty-eighth Mississippi cavalry, and was promoted to first lieutenant and adjutant of his regiment. In 1880 he was made major general of the state militia by Governor Lowry. He served through the entire war with W. H. Jackson's division of cavalry in Frank Armstrong's brigade. He was in the battles of Atlanta and Adairsville, and in the latter engagement was wounded. After his recovery he was in many hard-fought battles in Tennessee. He was in Gainesville, Ala., at the time of the surrender. After his return from the war, he began planting in Yazoo county, where he has lived a retired, quiet life on his plantation, Belle Prairie. In 1882 he removed to Yazoo City, where he had built a handsome home. In 1873 he was married in Geneva, Switzerland, to Miss Fanny Jones, of Charlotte, N. C., a daughter of Edmond P. Jones, also a native of North Carolina. General Ricks has been a member of the levee board since 1884, and has done efficient service. He is one of the largest planters of the Yazoo delta, raising about three thousand bales of cotton annually. He owns not less than eighteen thousand acres of land, six thousand acres being under cultivation. He is interested in the Cotton Compress & Warehouse company, and other important enterprises of his city. Although not a member of any church, he has ever maintained a high moral standing, and as a citizen, business man and neighbor, he has few equals and no superiors.

William W. Rife, planter, Bolivar, Miss., is a Mississippian by birth and bringing up, and his parents, William and Martha J. (Collins) Rife were natives of that state also. The father was a pioneer of Washington county, Miss., and settled near the present site of Greenville before that town was founded. He was a farmer by pursuit and died in that county in 1843 or 1844, respected and honored by all. The mother received her final summons in 1853. William W. Rife was born near Greenville, Washington county, Miss., in 1835, and was liberally educated in Centenary college, Jackson, La. He came to Bolivar county in 1869, and as he had been trained to the duties of the plantation from early boyhood he very naturally chose that as his life's occupation. He now has about five hundred acres adjoining the village of Bolivar and has three hundred and fifty acres under a fine state of cultivation. This was formerly the home of General Vick, of Vicksburg, but it was a wilderness at the time Mr. Rife purchased it. He has it well improved and stocked and everything about the place indicates to the beholder that a thorough hand is at the helm. He is also the owner of a good steam cottongin with improved machinery, etc.

Thomas Rigby (deceased) who was for many years a resident of Vicksburg, was born in Manchester, England, in 1802, a son of George and Martha Ellen (Houson) Rigby, the former of whom was a minister of the Methodist church and came to America about 1820, locating in Missouri, where he preached the gospel and resided until his death, his wife also passing from life in that state. Thomas Rigby was educated in England and came to America with his parents, locating with them in Missouri, in which state his boyhood days were spent in tilling his father's farm, and in attending the public schools. After attaining a suitable age he taught school, but at about the time he attained his majority he determined to seek fresh fields and came to Vicksburg, Miss., which place was then known as Walnut Hills. Here he followed the calling of a builder and contractor for two years, at the end of which time he purchased a grocery store, which he successfully conducted for several years. During this time he also purchased some land from time to time, and in this manner soon became one of the largest landholders of the county. In the fifties, with several others, he purchased the railroad from Vicksburg to Jackson, and these gentlemen with their own private means completed the road to Meridian. After serving for many years as vice president of the road, Mr. Rigby became its president, continuing such until it was purchased by a syndicate, when he retired in 1882 at the age of eighty years. Prior to the Civil war he was very wealthy, but during the struggle between those two great factions he lost $500,000. In 1846 he erected the home on Grove street, where his widow now resides. He was married to Mrs. Mary Ann Stovall, nee Jewell, a native of Maine and a daughter of Joseph Jewell, who died in the North. Her first husband, Mr. Stovall, died in 1842, leaving one child, another child being born after his death. Mr. Rigby's marriage took place in 1845 and resulted in the birth of two sons and two daughters: Thomas M. died in infancy, George Henry died at the age of three and a half years, Mary Ellen became the wife of R. F. Beck, Thomasina became the wife of M. Wolsey, and resides at Selma, Ala. During the last six years of Mr. Rigby's life he was an invalid and died March 30, 1889, at the age of eighty-seven years, having been an earnest member of the Methodist church for many years, of which church Mrs. Rigby has been a member for fifty years. He had long been a well-known citizen of Vicksburg, and not one of its residents stood higher in the estimation of the public or lived a truer Christian life. He was about five feet ten inches in hight, with blue eyes and fair hair, and his face was always smoothly shaven. In disposition he was amiable and was kind to and considerate of the wants of his family. He was a self-made man, quite an extensive traveler, and almost from the foundation of the town he was identified with its progress and development. Mr. Rigby was a very old and very high Free Mason, and was buried with every Masonic honor. His widow survives him at the present writing (1891), a true type of noble womanhood.

Among the residents of Franklin county, Miss., the name of Dr. Reuben J. Right is a familiar one, for during the twenty-nine years that he has practiced his profession in this section he has become eminent as a medical practitioner, and is also highly respected and esteemed as a citizen and neighbor. He was born in this county in 1884 to Kendle and Louisa (Millsaps) Right, the former of whom was born in the state of Georgia in 1807, and about 1814 removed with his parents to Adams county, Miss., settling on a woodland plantation east of Washington. After residing here only a short time they became residents of Franklin county, taking up their abode on what is now known as Right's camp ground, on the Homochitto river. On this property the paternal grandfather died when the subject of this sketch was a small boy, being survived only one year by his widow. Kendle Right inherited German blood of his father, and many of the sterling business principles and characteristics of the German people, among which may be mentioned honesty, industry and frugality. He was married in Copiah county, but the first years of his married life were spent in this county, after which he moved to Copiah county, his death occurring there in 1857. He was a moderately successful planter, and had long been an earnest and worthy member of the Methodist Episcopal Church South. His widow died on the 13th of November, 1890, having attained to the advanced age of eighty-one years. She was also a Methodist in religious belief. Her father, William Millsaps, came from Alabama to Copiah county when this region was almost a wilderness, engaged in planting here, and soon became well known, for his intelligence and enterprise placed him among the leading men of this section. Dr. Reuben J. Right was one of twelve children born to his parents, five of whom lived to years of maturity: Elijah, who is residing on the old home place in Copiah county; Uriah W., deceased, was a prisoner at Camp Chase, Ohio, and died there, being captured on Hood's

raid through Nashville; the subject of this sketch is next in order of birth; Sarah E., wife of George W. Mock, of Kansas, and Margaret J., widow of Frank Sessions. The Doctor was given the advantages of the common schools of Copiah county, and in 1858 began pursuing the study of medicine, for which he had a natural inclination, and under the able instruction of Dr. Hugh McLaurin he made rapid progress in his studies. While preparing himself for the practice of medicine he was also engaged in teaching school for about four years, and in 1860-1 he attended the University of Louisiana, and since 1862 has practiced his profession with success, his first experience being in Adams county, where he was married, in March, 1861, to Miss Sarah E., daughter of Benjamin F. and Sarah Tate, who came to this state from Virginia, the latter dying in 1859, on the plantation of Robert Tate, the former in 1872 in Franklin county, at the residence of the Rights. Mrs. Tate was formerly a Miss Stephens, a relative of Alexander H. Stephens. Mrs. Right was born in Washington, Adams county, Miss., and after having lived an earnest Christian life died in 1874, leaving, besides her husband, a family of four children to mourn her death: Lula, wife of Ralph L. Weibin; Robert J.; Alice and Margaret J. Since 1867 the Doctor has been a resident of Franklin county, and has owned and operates Magnolia Grove plantation, which is situated about three miles southwest of Roxie and contains sixteen hundred acres, of which three hundred acres are under cultivation. Besides this he has five hundred and forty acres on Homochitto river, and the most of his property has been acquired by his own efforts. Since 1891 he has resided in Roxie. His second marriage was consummated in 1876, Miss Sarah E. Black becoming his wife. She was born in Pike county, and died in 1887, a member of the Methodist church. She bore the Doctor seven children, two of whom are living: Cecil and Stacy Ellen. The Doctor is a member of S. B. Stampley lodge No. 222 of the A. F. & A. M., at Roxie, in which order he has attained to the council degree. He is a man who ranks high in his profession, possesses excellent business qualifications, and is progressive and public-spirited in his views. He has been one of the substantial citizens of Franklin county, and would give prestige to any community in which he might choose to make his home.

F. L. Riley, Sr., a merchant of Hebron, Lawrence county, Miss., was born in this state in 1835, a son of E. M. and Mary (Shows) Riley. His father was a native of Georgia and a prominent planter, and his mother a native of Mississippi. F. L. Riley, Sr., is the sixth son and tenth child in a family of thirteen children, named as follows: John S., Elizabeth, Nancy, Ellender, James C., William, Mary, George W., Andrew J., Franklin L. (the subject of this sketch), Edward M., Sophronia A., and Missouri J. Mr. Riley received his education in this county, and afterward taught school for five years, until 1861, when he enlisted in company B, of the Sixteenth Mississippi regiment, under Captain Funtches. Being among the first volunteers he was sent to Virginia, and placed under the command of Stonewall Jackson. He took part in all the battles fought during Jackson's campaign in the Shenandoah valley, and in the seven days' fight around Richmond. He was in the engagements at second Bull run and Antietam. In the latter he was wounded and sent to Lynchburg, Va., where he remained a short time, until sent home on a furlough. He was at home about two months, and during that time married Miss Balsorah I. Weathersby. He rejoined his regiment at Fredericksburg in time to participate in the battle at that place, afterward taking part in the battles of Chancellorsville, Gettysburg, Spottsylvania, and all the other principal engagements in the Virginia campaign. A few days before the general surrender he was captured in Fort Gregg, in front of Petersburg, and taken to Point Lookout, where, after being kept a prisoner about three months, he was paroled July 1, 1865, and returned home. First he turned his attention to planting, and then, in 1871, he opened a store at

Hebron, Lawrence county, Miss., and has since done a successful business as a general merchant. To Mr. and Mrs. Riley have been born a large family, eight of whom are now living: Mollie E., Franklin L., Jefferson D., Balsorah, John B., James D., Ellen, and May. Those deceased are: Edward D., Robert E., and Maud E. Mollie is now the wife of Dr. J. R. Berry, and resides at Hebron. Mr. Riley is a democrat, and cast his first presidential vote for James Buchanan. He is a Master Mason, and he and his wife are members of the Baptist church. Besides a large and well-stocked store at Hebron, he owns about one thousand acres of land, a good proportion of which is in a high state of cultivation. Mr. Riley is an able business man and a very popular citizen. He gives his support to everything having a tendency to benefit the public.

F. L. Riley, Jr., son of F. L. Riley, Sr., was born in Simpson and reared in Lawrence county. After receiving a preparatory education in the common schools, he entered Mississippi college in 1884, where he received the degree of A. B. in 1889, taking first honors in a class of nine. He received the degree of A. M. in June, 1891. While in college he was editor-in-chief of the Mississippi College *Magazine*, and first lieutenant of the Mississippi College Invincibles. During the four and one half years of his college life he never received a demerit or a reproof from any member of the faculty of that institution. Immediately after graduation he was employed as principal of Hebron high school, and since that time has successfully conducted the affairs of that institution. He was married to Miss Fannie Leigh in July, 1891. She was born in Cleburne, Texas, but when quite young, owing to the death of her parents, made her home with her aunt, Mrs. M. L. Powell, in Grenada, Miss. She graduated at the Central Female institute in 1886. After graduating she taught in this institution two sessions. For the last two sessions she has been teaching music in the Hebron high school. Mr. Riley is a democrat, being a member of the democratic executive committee of Lawrence county. He is a very talented and promising young man, with a bright future before him, if his life be spared.

In reviewing the pioneer history of Carroll county, the name of Benjamin Roach is found as early as 1835, in which year he located near Carrollton; the town then consisted of a few houses, as it had but recently been laid out, and the time since it had been made the county-seat had not long passed. Mr. Roach made his home with Col. John L. Irwin, for three years, and one year of that time he was tutor to the Colonel's children. He next came to Carrollton and started a tannery, and did a large business for six years; in connection with this he carried on the manufacture of boots, shoes and saddles, attracting a fine patronage in this line of trade. Disposing of his manufacturing interests, he went to the country and engaged in farming, but in 1852, he returned to town and re-embarked in the mercantile trade, to which he has since devoted his time and energies. Mr. Roach is a native of Davidson county, N. C., born October 30, 1812; he was reared and educated in the county of his birth. John Roach, his father, was also a native of North Carolina; he was a man of good abilities, and had an unusually fine education for the time in which he lived; he was a surveyor by profession. The Roach family are descendants from English ancestors. John Roach married Margaret Miller, a native of North Carolina, and of German lineage. Benjamin Roach, their son, was married in Carroll county, Miss., September 6, 1838, to Nancy Ann Goodson, who was born in Hinds county, Miss., and is a daughter of James and Elizabeth Goodson. She died March 26, 1885, mourned by all who had known her. She was the mother of four sons and four daughters: Elizabeth, the wife of Joseph H. Lawrence, of Hinds county, Miss.; Margaret, wife of D. Mayes, of Oxford, Miss.; Ellen, wife of Dr. T. H. Matthews, of Carrollton, Miss.; Nannie, wife of M. Russell, of

Canton, Miss.; the sons were Thomas J., who was a soldier in the Confederate army, and was killed at the battle of Gettysburg; B. F., a merchant of Carrollton; James L., deceased leaving a wife and four children; and Charles B., who died at the age of seventeen years. Mr. Roach is a member of the Baptist church, and has been clerk of the same church for fifty years, his accomplishments in the way of penmanship well fitting him for that office. He also belongs to the Masonic fraternity, and is a royal and select Master Mason; he has served as secretary of his lodge for thirty years.

Dr. Joseph C. Robert, a physician of Centerville, Miss., is a native of Beaufort district, S. C., and is the second child and eldest son born to the marriage of William H. Robert and Georgia W. Clark, the former of whom was a native of the same district and the latter of Columbia, S. C. William H. Robert was born July 15, 1821. He was the son of James Jehu and Phœbe (McKenzie) Robert, natives of South Carolina and of Savannah, Ga., respectively. James Jehu Robert (who was familiarly known as Deacon Jehu), was the son of John and Elizabeth (Dixon) Robert; John Robert was the son of Jacques and Sarah (Jaudon) Robert, both of whom were natives of South Carolina; Jacques Robert was the son of Pierre and Judith (Videaunt) Robert; Pierre was the son of Rev. Pierre Robert (who was born near Basel, Switzerland), and Jean (Bayer) Robert (also a native of Switzerland). The father of Rev. Pierre Robert was Daniel Robert, of Saint Imier, Switzerland, whose paternal ancestors were from Wales. His wife was a Huguenot lady whose Christian name (Marie) only is known. Daniel Robert was born about the year 1625. One of his sons, Pierre Robert (mentioned above), was a minister. He was born in 1655, and being exiled by the revocation of the edict of Nantes, he came with other Huguenots to South Carolina in 1685 and settled near the Santee river. Of his presence there, Ramsey, the historian of South Carolina, makes prominent mention. He was pastor of the church at Santee from 1685 to 1715. He is mentioned by the Presbyterian historian, Rev. Dr. Howe, as a Waldensian pastor of Piedmont. The French colony on the Santee is thus described by Lawson, who visited them from England in 1700. He says: "They lived as comfortably as any planters in these Southward parts of America." He commended them for their temperance, industry and brotherly affection. "They are all of the same opinion of the Church of Geneva, there being no difference among them respecting the punctilios of their Christian faith. There is a happy and delightful concord in all other matters throughout the whole neighborhood, as kindred, everyone making it his business to share in the misfortunes and rejoice in the advance of the others of the community." Rev. Pierre Robert died in 1715, leaving three children: Pierre, Jean and Elias. Pierre, the eldest son, was born at Basel, Switzerland, in 1680, and came with his parents to South Carolina in 1685, and married Judith Videaunt in 1706. He died in March, 1731, leaving four children: Captain Pierre, Jacques, Madeline and Elizabeth (who married Elias Jaudon, a prominent man in the public affairs of the South Carolina colony). Jacques Robert, the second son, was born April, 1711, was married to Sarah Jaudon in 1735, and died in 1774. He left seven children: James, Peter, Elizabeth, John, Elias, Sarah and Judith. John Robert, the fourth child, was born in July, 1742, married, April 19, 1770, Elizabeth Dixon, a granddaughter of Landgrave Smith, and died February 24, 1826, leaving nine children: Mary H., Elizabeth Ann, John H., Thomas S., William H., James Jehu, Benjamin N., Sarah D. and Lucia. James Jehu, the sixth child, was born in November, 1781, and in 1802 he married Charlotte Lawton, by whom he had seven children: Thirza, Benjamin J., Joseph T., Eliza J., Alexander L., Sarah H. and Benjamin J.; and by his second marriage (in 1817 to Phœbe McKenzie) he had twelve children: Lawrence J., William H., Milton G., Adaline E., Juliana E., Charlotte H., Alexander J., Francis W., Richard F., J. Story, Benjamin F. and Edward A. The father of these children was a man of wealth and education, was highly religious and well respected. He was famous for his hospitality and generous disposition, and was prominent in everything he undertook. He was deacon of the Baptist church in Robertville, S. C., for thirty years. Of his nineteen children, thirteen lived to be grown, and at his death, in 1852, twelve were yet living.

The first wife was descended from Landgrave Thomas Smith, of England. She was born in 1788, and died in 1817. Her husband, James Jehu Robert, was descended from the same Thomas Smith on his mother's side. The second wife was born in 1797, and died in 1854. She was a woman of sterling Christian character, and was the granddaughter of Dr. George Mosse, deacon of the Baptist church at Savannah, Ga. William H., the second child of the second marriage, was born July 15, 1821, near Robertville, S. C., where he was reared. He was educated at South Carolina university. He started in business as a planter, and was married in 1840, becoming a Baptist minister about 1844, at his native town. He moved to Georgia in 1851, where he was pastor of the first Baptist church of

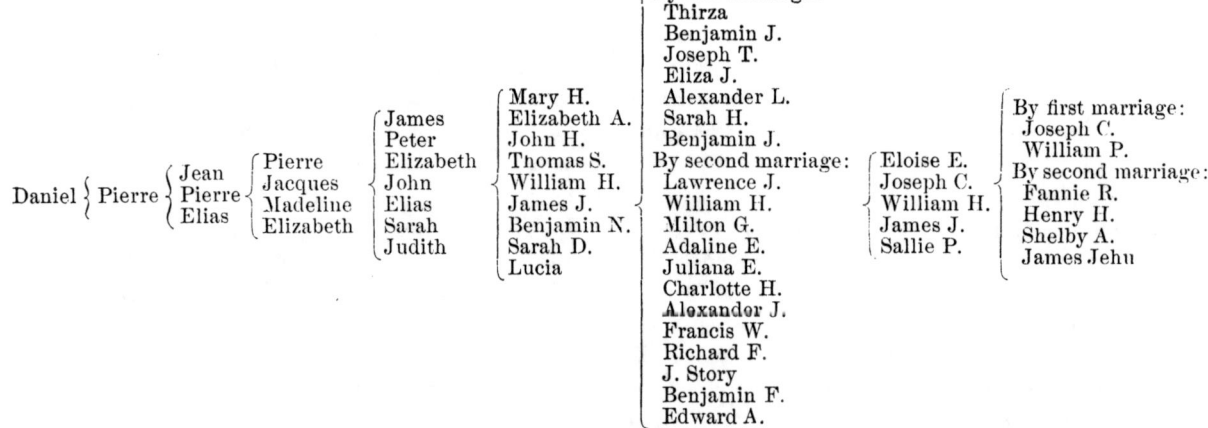

Atlanta, from 1852 to 1854. He filled the chair of mathematics at Cherokee Baptist college at Cassville, Ga., for two years, and was pastor of the Baptist church at Marietta, Ga., for two years. He was president of the Southern Female college at La Grange, Ga., for several years, and during the latter part of the war was appointed missionary to the Confederate troops. After the war he went to Little Rock, Ark., where he became pastor of the First Baptist church. He has been recently living in Denison, Tex., and was there engaged in ministerial work. Georgia W. Clark, his first wife, was born in Columbia, S. C., December 22, 1822, and died in 1870. She was the daughter of John W. and Mary (Roach) Clark, of Columbia, S. C. She was finely educated, and was a model Christian mother. To her marriage were born eight children, five of whom lived to be grown, and four of them are yet living: Eloise E., married Rev. Charner T. Scaife, of South Carolina, and died in 1872; Joseph C., the subject of this sketch; William H., who is now a druggist of Denison, Tex.; James Jehu, a prominent physician of Hillsboro, Tex., and Sallie P., who married J. W. Whitaker, of Wilkinson county, Miss. The father of these children was married the second time to Mrs. Power, nee Miss Lea, of Alabama, a lady of marked intelligence and piety, a sister-in-law of Gen. Sam Houston, of Texas. She died January 24, 1891. Dr.

Robert, the subject of this sketch, was born in 1844; was reared in Georgia, and was educated at the Cherokee Baptist college and at the Georgia Military institute. In 1862 he became a member of company E, Fourth regiment, Georgia infantry, and was afterward commissioned a lieutenant in the Confederate provisional army. At the close of the war he studied medicine, and graduated at the Nashville Medical college, Nashville, Tenn., in 1868. He then went to Arkansas where he practiced his profession for five years; then moved to Wilkinson county, Miss. (1873), locating in Centerville in 1874, where he has since resided and practiced his profession. He was married in March, 1870, to Miss Rebecca Whitaker of this county, who was born in 1849, and died in 1877, leaving a family of two children: Joseph C., now in the senior class of the Agricultural and Mechanical college of Mississippi, and William Pierre, of the United States Naval academy at Annapolis. The Doctor's second marriage was in January, 1879, to Fannie Harris, daughter of H. J. Harris, a prominent Methodist minister of this state. She was born in 1842 in Mississippi, and has borne her husband four children: Fannie R., Henry H., Shelby A. and James Jehu. Mrs. Robert is a member of the Methodist church, and Dr. Robert is a member and deacon of the Baptist church of Centerville.

In the midst of the failures and disasters of life it is a real pleasure to review the career of a man whose efforts have finally been crowned with success. Charles Roberts is an American by adoption, having been born in Plymouth, England, November 24, 1831. He was educated in the land of his birth, and did not emigrate to the United States until 1852. He spent six years in the East and the state of Ohio, and in 1858 he came to Mississippi, making a permanent settlement in Oxford. Since that time he has taken rank among the most progressive citizens of the town. At the outbreak of the Civil war he abandoned his business and entered the Confederate service. He was in Stanford's battery for two years, and participated in many a hard-fought battle. Among the most important are: Perryville, Murfreesboro and Chickamauga. He was offered at the end of two years a position in the quartermaster's department, and served as acting brigade quartermaster until the close of the war. He then returned to Oxford and was the first to resume business there. He erected a business building on the ruins of the former town, the business portion of which had been destroyed by the Federal soldiers. He soon won a very large patronage, and for many years past has been one of the leading merchants of the county. He has always taken an active interest in the young men in his employ, impressing on them that capacity and integrity was all the capital a young man required to insure success in life. He has three dry goods stores in the state, located at Oxford, Durant and Gunnison. These enterprises are in a flourishing condition, and the managing partners are all young men, selected on his theory that capacity and integrity are equivalent to capital. From 1878 to 1883 he was out of business in Oxford, and during that time was in New Orleans engaged in the cotton trade in the firm of Varden, Hawkins & Roberts. In 1875 he was one of the organizers of the Southern bank of Oxford. He is now president of the Merchants' and Farmers' bank of Oxford, and is vice president of the Bank of Yazoo City. He has assisted in the organization of many of the banks of Mississippi, and is a stockholder in seven different banking institutions. In 1854 Mr. Roberts was married, but this union was of short duration as his wife soon afterward died. He was married a second time to Miss Maggie McKee of Yazoo county, and this wife died in 1890, leaving four children. The Roberts home is one of the finest and most complete in the state. It is artistically furnished, surrounded by well-kept grounds, which are shaded by majestic water-oaks. Among other blessings, Mr. Roberts has always enjoyed the best of health, and is now in the prime of a vigorous, well-ordered manhood. He is a selfmade man in every sense of that term, having come to America without any means except that capital with which he had been endowed by nature. In the war he lost all that he had accumulated previously, and like so many other sons of the South, had to begin the struggle of life over again. He now pays taxes on thirty-seven thousand acres of land. Mr. Roberts has been a member of the Presbyterian church for the past twenty-five years.

In the list of the business establishments of Jackson, Miss., the insurance agency of Wharton & Roberts occupies a prominent position. H. C. Roberts, the junior member of the firm, was born near Edwards, Hinds county, Miss., in 1860, the youngest of three children born to Isaac and Martha (Todd) Roberts, the mother being the daughter of John Read, who was one of the earliest settlers of the county, and died at the age of eighty-four years. Isaac Roberts was a Mississippian by birth and spent the greater part of his life in Hinds county, in the progress and prosperity of which he was deeply interested. He was the owner of quite extensive plantation interests near Edwards, and prior to the Civil war was one of the largest planters in his section. In his latter years he was an invalid and died in July, 1874, at the age of eighty-four years, an earnest member of the Methodist Episcopal church. The maternal grandfather became the father of quite a large family, four of his sons serving in the Confederate army, Maj. Charles Read being a naval officer of considerable note. After the war he ran a vessel from New Orleans to Central America, his home being in the former place, where he held government offices. He died in 1890. John Read, another son, is now a Presbyterian minister in the Indian nation. William Read is a physician of Bryant, and another son, Joe, is a druggist of the same place. H. C. Roberts was educated in the University of Mississippi, but left school in 1881 and engaged in the mercantile business at Raymond with a brother, the firm name being J. W. Roberts & Co., which still continues to do the largest business of that place, a full supply of general merchandise and plantation supplies being kept constantly on hand. The stock which they carry amounts to about $15,000, and their annual sales equal $75,000 at least. In October, 1890, Mr. Roberts opened an insurance agency in Jackson, where they do fire, marine, life and accident insurance. The proprietors of this firm are business men of experience and sound judgment, and under their guidance the business has attained its present excellent proportions. Mr. Roberts owns a plantation of one thousand acres near Raymond, of which four hundred acres are in a fine state of cultivation. Mr. Roberts is a member of the A. F. & A. M., and as a business man, possesses ability of a high order. On April 26, 1888, he was married to Miss Corabel Wharton, a daughter of F. A. R. Wharton, an early settler of Mississippi, and to their union, one little daughter has been born: Corabel.

Although young in years, Perry B. Roberts, stockman, Calhoun, is one of the prosperous men of Madison county, Miss., and is engaged in the stock business at the present time. He was born in Iowa on the second of April, 1866, and was the second of three children born to Isaac P. and Margaret (Marr) Roberts, the father a native of New York state and the mother of Pennsylvania. The former was professor of agriculture in the Iowa State Agricultural college and has held several other important positions which he filled in a very creditable manner. Since 1873 he has been professor of agriculture in the Cornell university, Ithaca, N. Y., and is one of the prominent men of that state. His father was Edmond Roberts. The maternal grandparents, James and Mary Marr, were natives of Indiana. Perry B. Roberts was reared in York state and educated in Ithaca high school until seventeen years of age. He then entered the Cornell university in 1883, graduated from that institution four years later, and then came to Mississippi, where he has since been engaged in the stock business. He has three thousand acres of pasture and twenty-two hundred cattle, ranging all the way from calves to four year old steers. He does not raise, but buys and sells. He pastures about one thousand or twelve hundred through the summer and then fattens four or five hundred during the winter for market. He raises his own feed of various kinds suitable for fattening purposes, and thereby dispenses with the expense of buying his feed. He also handles sheep but not extensively, having about six hundred head last year. He has a trade all over the state, selling to butchers in different parts of the same, and he also ships to Chicago, New York and New Orleans. It pays better, however, to ship to points in the state and he makes that a specialty. He is a thoroughgoing, energetic young man and is justly deserving of success. He has a fine education and takes a great deal of interest in all modern literature.

Capt. Stokeley E. Roberts, of Fulton, Itawamba county, Miss., has a war record of which any man might well feel proud. In 1862 he enlisted at Columbus, Miss., in the Second Mississippi cavalry under Colonel Gordon, and was elected captain of one of the companies composing that regiment. He did gallant service in the battle of Harrisburg, and in various other engagements and skirmishes in northern Mississippi and Alabama, and was paroled at Decatur, Ala., in the spring of 1865. He was born January 23, 1825, a son of John and Sarah (Multins) Roberts, both of whom are natives of Georgia. He was educated in the common schools of Itawamba county. In 1847 he married Elizabeth R. Spearman, a native of Mississippi and a daughter of Elijah and Sydney Spearman, both natives of Tennessee. To Mr. and Mrs. Roberts have been born thirteen children, eight of whom lived to maturity: Sarah E., Mary M., Ophelia A., Ada E., Ida, Zerah, Rubuster, Cleo; and Lafayette, J. E., Ella, Elijah A. and another unnamed, all deceased. Mr. Roberts is a democrat politically, and is a member of the Farmers' Alliance. He served as deputy marshal for four years. He and his wife and all his children are members of the Methodist Episcopal church. He lives on a beautiful plantation, surrounded by all the comforts and most of the luxuries of life, and also owns a valuable farm of six hundred acres in Texas. As a citizen he stands deservedly high, having contributed his full share toward the development and improvement of the county, and takes a deep interest in all political questions, local, state and national.

Charles Henry Robertson, Hernando, Miss., has lived in De Soto county since he was a child three years of age. He was born in Hardeman county, Tenn., December 19, 1839, and is the youngest of a family of eight children. His parents, Gen. J. C. N. and Margaret (Reagan) Robertson, were natives of Washington county, Tenn. The father was born in 1792, and was well and favorably known throughout Tennessee. He was brigadier-general of the state militia, and for fifteen years was sheriff of Hardeman county. He was a member of the constitutional convention of the state, and was afterward a member of the state senate. He removed to Mississippi in 1842, and settled in De Soto county, three miles from Hernando, and engaged in planting. There he passed the remainder of his days, his death occurring in 1880. He was a soldier in the war of 1812, holding an official position. He was grand master of the Masonic lodge of Tennessee for a number of years. His wife survived him, and is still living, at the age of ninety-five years. She was born in 1795. The paternal grandparents were George and Susan (Nelson) Robertson, both of whom lived to be very old. They were of Scotch extraction. The maternal grandparents were John and Martha (Black) Reagan, the former being a native of Ireland, and the latter of North Carolina. The Blacks were originally from England. Charles Henry Robertson was sent to the public schools of his own county, and was also a student at La Grange, Tenn. Soon after leaving school, in 1860, he was united in marriage to Miss Emma L. Caffey, who was born in Hernando, Miss., a daughter of Thomas Y. and Louisa (Hanks) Caffey. (See sketch of T. Y. Caffey.) Five children were born to Mr. and Mrs. Robertson: Thomas Caffey, Charles Reagan, Emma L., John W. and Annie Bell. After his marriage Mr. Robertson embarked in the mercantile trade, and has followed the business continuously ever since. When there was a call for men to go to the country's aid he enlisted in 1862, in company I, Twenty-ninth Mississippi volunteer infantry, and served as sergeant-major for two years. He was in the battles of Stone river and Chickamauga, and at Lookout mountain he was taken prisoner. He was sent to Rock Island, where he was held until the surrender. After his release he returned to his home, and set about rebuilding his shattered fortunes. He has been successful in this effort, as he is now the owner of twenty-five hundred acres of land, two thousand of which are under cultivation. He also owns a half interest in the business of Robertson & Goodman, who handle $50,000 annually, and carry a stock valued at $10,000; they own their store building, which is worth $5,000. The people of De Soto county attested their confidence in Mr. Robertson by calling him to fill the office of treasurer, which he did for six years in a very satisfactory manner. He is a member of the Knights of Honor and of the I. O. O. F. fraternity. His wife is a consistent member of the Methodist Episcopal church. Mr. Robertson takes a just pride in his career, and is well worthy of the high esteem in which he is held by the people of his county. He gives freely of his means for the benefit of the public, and no more loyal citizen can be found.

G. M. Robertson was born in Huntsville, Ala., in 1842. During the Civil war he served in the Confederate army under Bragg, Forrest and Wheeler, was captured at Franklin, and imprisoned at Camp Chase, Ohio. He came to Noxubee county, Miss., in 1866, and in 1870 was wedded to Miss Ophelia Herron. They have five children: G. J., John M., William M., S. Lyttleton and Mary. Mr. Robertson was engaged in the mercantile business for fifteen years, and at the same time farmed very successfully—owning at present about thirteen hundred acres of choice land. He makes a specialty of growing lespedeza striata and melitotus alba. His sales from these two varieties of seeds, with the hay, aggregated $10,000 in the past five years. He contemplates the propagation of other grasses suited to the Southern climate. His hay and seed interests are very extensive, and his correspondence extends throughout the entire country south of, and including New York, Pennsylvania and California. Mr. Robertson also pays some attention to stockraising on his Oak Lawn seed and stock farm, located at Deer Brook, eleven miles northeast of Macon, and six miles east of Brookville. He is a thoroughgoing, progressive business man. Socially he is genial and pleasant, and is highly esteemed by the citizens of his county.

Dr. S. D. Robertson, physician and surgeon, Dover, Yazoo county, Miss., was born in Fairfield, S. C., in 1837, and is the second of a family of ten children. His parents are B. H. and A. M. (Dixon) Robertson, natives of South Carolina, where they still reside. The father is a farmer by occupation. He was a soldier in the Black Hawk, Mexican and Civil wars, and three of his sons served in the last named conflict. Seven of the ten children lived to maturity: Sarah, wife of Capt. Thomas Perry, of South Carolina; S. D.; Barnes, who fell at the charge of Drury's Bluff; Dixon, a planter of Fairfield, S. C.; Lee, a merchant of the same state, and two daughters who are living in South Carolina. Dr. Robertson was educated in the military school of Columbia, S. C., and came to Mississippi in October, 1857. Having chosen the profession of medicine for his life work, he entered the University of Pennsylvania, from which famous institution he was graduated in 1861. In May of the same year he entered the Confederate service, enlisting in company I, Eighteenth Mississippi volunteer infantry as first lieutenant. He was assigned to the army of Northern Virginia, and upon the reorganization of his regiment in 1862 he was elected captain of his company. He was wounded at Gettysburg, Penn., by a musket shot, after which he was on post duty for several months. He served through the entire war, and at the close of the struggle he returned to Mississippi, and located at Dover, Yazoo county, being among the earliest settlers there after the war. He entered on the practice of his profession, in which he has been very successful. With the exception of a short residence in Texas, he has been in Yazoo county since the war. He has a comfortable home, and is surrounded with peace and plenty. He was married in Hinds county, Miss., to Miss Sallie Garrett, a daughter of John and Mary Garrett. Five children were born to them and two lived, Annie and Mabel; the others died in infancy. Mrs. Robertson died in 1877, and in 1879 the Doctor was married a second time, being united to Miss Fanny Wilson, a daughter of S. J. and Caroline Wilson. They are the parents of three children: Wilson S., J. D. and Barnes. Dr. Robertson is a member of the Masonic order, belonging both to the blue lodge and chapter; he also belongs to the Knights of Pythias and the Knights of Honor. Mrs. Robertson is a member of the Baptist church, in which she is a zealous worker. The Doctor is a stanch supporter of all home interests, and an ardent believer in both the developed and the undeveloped resources of Yazoo county.

W. T. Robertson, of Forest, Miss., was born in Georgia in 1836. His father, W. H. Robertson, was a native of Virginia, born in 1807. His mother, Elizabeth Hardman, was born in 1809. They had nine children, of whom our subject was the fourth in order of birth. The marriage occurred in Georgia in 1828. There Mr. Robertson engaged in planting, and lived there until his removal to Scott county, Miss., in 1845, where he followed the same occupation with considerable success. Mr. and Mrs. Robertson were members of the Methodist Episcopal church. The latter died in 1854, and the former in 1862. W. T. Robertson grew to manhood in Scott county, Miss., receiving a common-school education. He was married in 1860 to Miss Lou Moore, daughter of Lod Moore, and a native of Scott county. They have had born to them four children, all of whom are living: W. T. Robertson, Jr., was educated at Harperville, Miss., graduating in 1880; Anna B. graduated from the same place in the class of 1885; while Pattie was educated at French Camp. Misses Anna and Pattie are successful schoolteachers, and the son, W. T. Robertson, Jr., is a bookkeeper at Greenville, Miss. Mr. Robertson has about five hundred acres of land, about two-fifths of which are under cultivation. He and his wife are members of the Methodist church. He is identified with the Masonic fraternity and with the Knights of Honor, being a member of the lodges at Morton and at Forest respectively. In 1861 Mr. Robertson enlisted in the Thirty-ninth Mississippi regiment, commanded by Col. W. B. Shelby. He fought at Port Hudson, Chickamauga, Murfreesboro, Atlanta, Kenesaw mountain, Columbia and Franklin. He was once slightly wounded, but served until the close of the war, returning home from Ship island in 1865. Mr. Robertson is a liberal friend of schools, churches, and all public institutions, and takes a great deal of interest in all matters pertaining to the good of the community.

Dr. J. R. Robinet, of Learned, Miss., was born in Yazoo county of this state in 1836, only child of J. R. and Winifred (Clark) Robinet, the father a native of the same state as himself. His ancestors came to the United States with the Count de Rochambeau during the Revolutionary war. Dr. J. R. Robinet received good educational advantages in his youth, and up to the age of twelve years was educated by a private teacher, at which time he was sent to a military school near Raymond, then to the Mississippi college at Clinton, from which he graduated in 1855 with the degree of A. M. He then entered upon the study of medicine in the office of Dr. M. D. Brown, and in 1856 went to Albany, N. Y., entering a medical college of that place, where he remained ten months, at the end of which time he went to New York city and took a course of lectures in the Bellevue Medical college. His next move was to Philadelphia, Penn., in which city he graduated from the Jefferson Medical college in May, 1858, after which he returned to his home and for one year was a practitioner at Richmond. Then on account of poor health he returned to the hill country and located at Bennett's Wells, where he practiced during the year 1859. Since then his practice has been confined to the country adjacent to his home. In addition to his profession he conducts a large planting interest which he commenced in 1865. He purchased the Ephraim Wells place in 1870, containing five hundred and eighty-eight acres of land, three hundred of which are under cultivation and one hundred acres heavily covered with valuable timber—oak, gum, poplar, etc. At the opening of the war the Doctor enlisted in the Charleston rifles, and was soon promoted to the medical department and assigned to the Second Arkansas regiment, then in the department of Tennessee. He took part in the Atlanta campaign and Bragg's invasion, during which time he was in Gen. Pat Cleburne's division. In 1859 he was married to a Miss Bush, a native of Mississippi, by whom he became the father of ten children, the following of whom are living: John Bush; Anna B., wife of Dr. Nelson, of Copiah county; Martin, Marshall, Frederick E. and J. R. Dr. Robinet has taken great interest in educational matters, is a member of the Farmers' Alliance, and he and his wife are members of the Presbyterian church.

Col. Jephthah Robins has for many years been a most conspicuous and influential member of the bar of Mississippi, and is worthy of mention in this record of the men who have been important factors in the development and cultivation of the resources of the state. He is a native of Pickens district, S. C., born in 1814, and is a son of Albert and Susan (Norton) Robins, natives of South Carolina and Virginia respectively. Albert Robins was a son of Michael Robins, a native of North Carolina, and a farmer by occupation. When Albert was a mere lad his father removed to Greenville Courthouse, S. C. The father was one of a family of eight sons and four daughters. He and all his brothers were soldiers in the Revolutionary war. He lived to the allotted age of man, three score and ten years. He reared a family of four sons and four daughters, all of whom lived to be grown. Albert was next to the youngest child, and was reared in South Carolina, where he resided until 1841. He then came to Fulton, Miss., where he lived at the time of his death, in 1849; he was seventy-eight years of age. His wife died two years later at about the same age. She was a consistent member of the Baptist church. To them were born three children: Levi died in South Carolina; Mrs. Arminda Copeland died in Fulton, Miss.; the Colonel was the second-born. He passed his youth in South Carolina, and received his education in the common schools. When he had reached his twentieth year he went to Moulton, Ala., where he clerked in a dry goods store for one year. Thence he went to Fulton, Miss., in 1836, and there he was employed as a clerk for some time. He then engaged in the mercantile trade on his own account, and while in this business he was elected treasurer of the county of Itawamba. After discharging the duties of this office for one term he was elected probate clerk for two years. He was then made clerk of the chancery court, the district comprising Itawamba, Monroe, Chickasaw and Tishomingo counties. He held this office eight years, and during that time he read law, and was admitted to the bar at Aberdeen, Judge Rogers presiding. He practiced his profession at Fulton until 1852, when he came to Lee county, and located at Guntown. For several years he devoted himself industriously to the law, but of late years he has paid more attention to agriculture, and has turned his practice over to his son, John Quitman Robins, a partner of the Hon. John M. Allen. Colonel Robins was attorney for the

Mobile & Ohio railroad, which position brought him many duties, and he still attends to all legal matters pertaining to the road. He is a man well read in all points of law and every class of literature. He is a man of rare judgment, quick insight and keen observation. He has won a wide reputation, and his ability is recognized in all legal circles throughout the South. He was married to Eliza D. Allen, a sister of the Hon. J. M. Allen, a native of Virginia. (See sketch of John M. Allen.) Nine children were born to this union, one of whom is deceased: Mrs. Belle Gore, Mrs. Mollie Allen, John Q., Jephthah (deceased), William, James, Edwin, Annie, and Harrison Lamar. The younger children are now attending some of the best educational institutions of the South, and all have had superior advantages in that line. Colonel Robins served on detached duty during the late Civil war, and was on intimate terms with Jefferson Davis, McNutt, Foote, Prentiss and Poindexter. He was a member of the Independent Order of Odd Fellows at Aberdeen, but the lodge is no longer in existence. He and his wife are members of the Methodist Episcopal church. The Colonel is a selfmade man, and is fully deserving of the honors that have been conferred upon him, and entirely worthy of the high regard in which he is held in the state.

Robinson & Brother, merchants, Friar's Point, Miss. These gentlemen are the proprietors of one of the largest, if not the largest, establishments in Friar's Point and have a patronage established that indicates appreciation of their reliable goods and fair dealing methods. They carry a full and well selected stock of dry goods, boots and shoes, hats and caps, groceries, hardware and a general line of plantation supplies. They do an annual business approximating $50,000. The members of the firm, Frank D. and James D. Robinson, are young men, natives of the town and are thoroughgoing and enterprising. Frank D. Robinson, senior member of the firm, was born in Friar's Point, Coahoma county, Miss., in 1854, and was the third in a family of eight children born to James D. and Catherine E. (Morton) Robinson. The father was one of the first settlers and merchants of Friar's Point and is spoken of as a good man and a law-abiding citizen. In 1861 he moved to Memphis, embarked in business as a cottonfactor and died there in 1868. The family then returned to Friar's Point, where the mother resides at the present time. Frank D. was educated in the common schools, took a legal course at Oxford, and graduated from that institution in 1878, standing fourth in a class of thirty-six. He at once began practicing with Messrs. Reid & Wynn, under the firm name of Reid, Wynn & Robinson, which continued until fall of 1879. Having previously graduated in bookkeeping in 1872, he gave up law and accepted a lucrative position at the desk, where he remained until 1882, when he and his brother formed the above-mentioned firm. In 1891 he was married to Miss Emma E. Slack, daughter of Dr. J. J. Slack, of Friar's Point. Mr. Robinson assisted in organizing the bank of Friar's Point, in which he is a stockholder, and is also a stockholder in the Friar's Point Building and Loan association, besides being a promoter of other corporations at Friar's Point. He held the position of postmaster at that place for over eight years, giving eminent satisfaction. Though not a member of any church he is a Christian in its broadest sense, and his wish is to see all sects united in one faith, one purpose and one eternal hope in working out the greatest good to all mankind. Mr. Robinson is a member of the Knights of Honor. In personal appearance he is a little under rather than above the medium size, and has brown hair and gray eyes; is quick and active in his movements and shows the thorough business man in word and action. He is now at the head of one of the most substantial firms in Mississippi. James D. Robinson, the junior member of the firm, was born in January, 1860, and educated in Friar's Point, his native place. For some time he filled the position of clerk in the drugstore of Dr. J. A. Cooper; and afterward held the position of assistant bookkeeper in the large furnishing house of J. W. Crowley & Co. In 1886 he was married to Miss Mattie L. Fisher, a native of Alabama, whose people were old settlers of Coahoma county. To them have been born two children: James and Milton. Mr. Robinson was one of the organizers of the bank at Friar's Point and is a director in the same. He and brother both own town property and a lot next to the bank building, on which they expect to erect a three-story brick block in the near future. Mr. Robinson is a member of the Knights of Pythias and he and his wife are both members of the Methodist Episcopal Church South. In personal appearance he is a blonde, of medium size and active in his movements; also a shrewd buyer and good salesman.

John L. Robinson is a native-born resident of Madison county, Miss., his birth having occurred on December 9, 1852, and comes of one of the prominent families of the state. He is the eldest of the children born to John and Sarah (Lowe) Robinson, natives of Mississippi. The father was an extensive planter in Madison county, and was one of its leading citizens. He died in 1879. The mother died in 1859. The paternal grandparents, John and Nancy (Collins) Robinson, were natives of Georgia and Mississippi, respectively, and the maternal grandparents, John and Sarah (Gatlin) Lowe, were natives of Mississippi. Our subject, John L. Robinson, is now residing on the old homestead. He was reared there, attended the public schools of the county until seventeen years of age, and then entered the Summerville institute, Noxubee county, Miss., where he remained for two years. Since that time he has followed planting, and of the two thousand five hundred acres in his plantation, one thousand five hundred acres are under cultivation. Miss Annie S. Hinton, who became his wife in 1878, is a native of Mississippi and the daughter of Eugene H. and Annie (Jones) Hinton, natives of the Old North state. Five children have been born to this union: Annie M., Helen B., Sarah, John and Pauline. Mr. and Mrs. Robinson are members of the Episcopal church. Mr. Robinson is also a member of the Knights of Pythias. He is democratic in his political views. All worthy movements receive his hearty support and he is a liberal contributor to the same. He is pleasant and agreeable in his intercourse with all and has many warm friends.

John W. Robinson, (deceased,) who was for many years one of the foremost business men of the state of Mississippi, was born in Chenango county, N. Y., and began life as a clerk in a country store in his native county. After continuing this occupation for some time he determined to seek his fortune in the South, and prior to attaining his majority he located in Jackson, where he continued his labors as a clerk for some time. He afterward engaged in business for himself in partnership with William Richardson, a brother of Ned Richardson, who in later years became the cotton king of Mississippi, and although he started out with limited means to begin with, he possessed correct business principles, and even then gave promise of becoming a shrewd and successful financier. Prior to the Civil war he became a citizen of Jackson, and here he opened a mercantile establishment in connection with a Mr. Windley, which they successfully conducted until the opening of the war. After Lee's surrender and the war-worn soldiers had returned home, the business of Robinson & Stevens was established and became one of the most extensive and prosperous wholesale and retail establishments in the city. He was one of the incorporators of the Mississippi cotton mill at Wesson, which is now one of the largest in the South; owned the Edwards house, one of the finest and best conducted hotels in Jackson; built the Jackson street railway, which he managed until his death, and also erected the Robinson operahouse of Jackson, besides many fine business houses of the city. After being prominently identified with the business life of Jackson for many years, Mr. Robinson was called from life in April, 1881, after which the mercantile firm in Jackson was dissolved. He was an exceptionally able financier, was a man of great force of character and profound intelligence, and his leading characteristics were a kindly and generous disposition, extreme frankness, honesty of purpose and indomitable will and energy. From a very small beginning he built up a business of magnificent proportions, and at his death he left a large fortune to his widow and children. He was keenly alive to the sufferings and misfortunes of others, and was never appealed to in vain for consolation or succor, for his early struggles to gain a foothold on the ladder of success made his heart warm for those less fortunate than himself. He was in every respect a model American citizen, and his career is eminently worthy of being emulated by the youth of the present day. He was married to Miss Mary J. Bradford, a native of Huntsville, Ala., and to their union six children were born, five of whom are now living: Mattie L.; Annie M., wife of R. L. Saunders (see sketch); John W.; Mary J., wife of C. M. Williamson (see sketch); Joseph F.; and a child that died in infancy. Mr. Robinson was a member of and an earnest worker in the Episcopal church, in which he had long been a vestryman, and socially he was a member of the A. F. & A. M. He was prepossessing in personal appearance, was above medium stature and had black hair, and clear, intelligent gray eyes. John W. Robinson, his eldest son, was born in the city of Jackson, in 1862, and in his birthplace he received a thorough and practical education. In 1890 he opened a wholesale and retail grocery house in Jackson, in connection with H. C. Roberts, of Raymond, Miss., and they are now doing an excellent annual business, which testifies to the correct business principles which they practice and to the reliability and variety of the goods they carry. Their place of business is situated on Pearl street, and was formerly occupied by Mr. Robinson's father. Mr. Robinson possesses in a marked degree the business attributes of his distinguished father, and these combined with a careful consideration for the needs of the public, have made his establishment a recognized synonym for all that is popular, progressive and honest. Mr. Robinson is the owner of a large amount of city and plantation property, one plantation being in Hinds county, and another in Madison county, there being seven hundred and eighty acres in each with one thousand two hundred acres under cultivation. All this land is fertile and that portion which is under cultivation is finely improved. In January, 1891, he was married to Miss Ida, the beautiful, accomplished and amiable daughter of Doctor Mitchell, and granddaughter of ex-Governor McWillie, of Mississippi. Mr. and Mrs. Robinson are worthy members of the Episcopal church. Joseph F. Robinson, a brother of John W., is a partner and the efficient treasurer of the Friedman-Shelton Clothing company, of Jackson, and was born on the 28th of January, 1869, the youngest son born to John W. and Mary J. (Bradford) Robinson, but was educated at Sewanee, Tenn., where he acquired a thorough and useful education. In 1886 he became correspondent for the First National bank of Jackson, the duties of which position he ably discharged for four years. On the 2d of March, 1891, he was one of the organizers of the Friedman-Shelton Clothing company, of Jackson, which has a capital stock of $20,000, and was immediately elected its treasurer. Their stock of goods, which is valued at $45,000, comprises a large line of ready-made clothing of all grades, including the finest imported goods and the best domestic fabrics. This establishment is fitted up with every convenience and auxiliary adapted to its successful prosecution, and as great care is taken in the selection of the stock, a large trade is enjoyed. Joseph F. Robinson owns some valuable business and residence property in Jackson, besides four fine plantations in Hinds, Yazoo and Rankin counties. Mr. Robinson is the youngest merchant of Jackson, and has adopted a business career from choice. Both he and his brother are destined to follow in their father's footsteps, and are agreeable and satisfactory gentlemen to meet.

Lee B. Robinson is a rising and successful young banker residing at Gloster, Miss., and as a business man has displayed a more than average amount of shrewdness, tact and ability. In all ages of the world's industry, perseverance and energy, where intelligently applied, have achieved the desired result, and Mr. Robinson is a striking example of what can be accomplished when the spirit of determination is exercised in connection with the everyday affairs of life. His enterprises have resulted most satisfactorily, and he is now wealthy. He was born near Liberty, July 4, 1850, to Col. John G. and Thirza (Jenkins) Robinson, a short history of whom is given in the sketch of Van W. Robinson, that appears below. The paternal grandfather, Moses Robinson, was of Scotch descent, was from one of the Carolinas, but during the early history of this section became one of its pioneer settlers. When only three years of age Lee B. Robinson was left motherless, and two years later his father also died. In his boyhood he was deprived of any great amount of schooling, but, like his brother, he possessed a naturally active mind, and managed to pick up here and there a considerable amount of valuable information. At the age of eighteen years he began clerking for G. H. Barney & Co., one of the leading firms of business men of Liberty, and here he was grounded most thoroughly in the practical and useful part of the business, and laid a solid foundation for future success. After remaining with this firm for about five years he engaged in the mercantile business for himself, but in a very humble way, and notwithstanding the fact that he had no money of his own, and that his capital was borrowed, he soon acquired a fair trade, for while with Barney & Co., he had, by his genial, accommodating and friendly manners, acquired many friends who gave him their patronage in his hour of need. By methodical business habits and superior management his business grew rapidly, and in connection with this he also dealt in cotton, and of late years has handled as high as two thousand bales annually. The annual sales of his mercantile establishment soon amounted to $200,000, but this establishment he sold out in December, 1889, with the view to taking a respite from his labors. In the summer of 1890 he decided to engage in the banking business at Gloster, and at that place he erected a suitable building, formed a stock company with G. H. Barney as president, L. B. Robinson, cashier, and E. S. Atkinson, assistant cashier. This bank was opened for business the first of September with very flattering prospects, and each month the business increased very rapidly and beyond the expectations of all. He was married in Liberty, November 21, 1873, to Miss Helen Barney, daughter of G. H. Barney, a pioneer, and one of the most successful business men of the county, and to them seven children have been born: Bertha, Emerson, Helen, Ary, Clara, Lee B., Jr. and Julio B. Mrs. Robinson was reared and educated in Liberty, and she and her husband are members of the Presbyterian church. Mr. Robinson belongs to the Masonic fraternity, in which he has attained to the council, and in this lodge has held official position. Mr. Robinson inherits many of the worthy traits of his Scotch ancestors, and is careful, prudent and economical, but not in the least penurious, and those who know him best recognize in him a good friend. He has a beautiful and pleasant home in Gloster, and here he and his intelligent and amiable wife dispense hospitality to their numerous friends.

Van W. Robinson is the leading officer of the law in Amite county, Miss., and in the discharge of his duties has proved himself courageous, conscientious and faithful. He was first elected to the office in November, 1883, and so noticeable was his devotion to the preservation of law and order, that he has been chosen to the position at each succeeding election, and his fidelity and ability have made a lasting impression on this sphere of public duty. As he was born in this county, near Liberty, on April 21, 1848, and has made his home here all his life, he is naturally interested in the progress and development of this section, and in his official capacity has done not a little to raise the standard of morality of the masses. His father, Col. John G. Robinson, was also born here, his birth occurring in the year 1812, and here he attained manhood and married, his wife, also of this county, being Miss Thirza Jenkins, a daughter of James Jenkins. Mr. Robinson was a practical farmer, and besides giving attention to the calling of an agriculturist found time to act in the capacity of a magistrate, as well as in other local positions of honor, and for some time was colonel of militia. He died in 1855, his wife having passed from life in 1852, and thus three young children were left to fight the battle of life for themselves without a father or mother's guidance. Their names are: Lee B., whose sketch appears herein; Ary, wife of Dr. J. R. Sample, a physician and druggist of Summit, Miss., and Van W. The latter spent his youth on a plantation, and, owing to the free and active life he led, became a healthy and vigorous young man, so that at the early age of sixteen years he was better fitted than the average to enlist in the service of the Confederacy. He became a member of the Tenth Mississippi cavalry, and served until Lee's surrender, when he was paroled at Gainesville, Ala. His company served as scouts, and was in a number of engagements and skirmishes. After the war he returned to his home in Mississippi, and for two years thereafter he attended school near Liberty, and during this time, as he was studious and naturally apt, made rapid progress in his studies. In 1869 he went to Texas, and after farming in that state for two years returned to Liberty, and went into a store with his brother, following the calling of a clerk for several years. He was united in marriage to Miss Emma Ratcliffe, a daughter of Peter Ratcliffe, a former sheriff of Amite county and one of the old and highly respected residents of the county. To Mr. and Mrs. Robinson five children have been born: John Worth, Ernest, Junius, Van and Myrtis. Mr. Robinson is a member of the Masonic fraternity, the K. of H. and the K. of P. He is one of the most social, hospitable and generous of men, as the numerous friends he has gathered around him can testify.

William W. Robinson, one of the successful business men of Ripley, was born in Madison county, Tenn., in 1835, and is the son of Hugh B. Robinson, who was also a native of Tennessee, born in Maury county. The elder Robinson left his native state and removed to Tippah county, Miss., in 1839, remaining there until his death in 1851. He was a man who took a deep interest in the welfare of his county, was tax assessor and sheriff, and was a leader of the democratic party there. He followed planting with considerable success up to the last years of his life. His father, James Robinson, was probably a native of North Carolina, whose parents immigrated direct from the Emerald isle. William W. Robinson was but four years of age when his parents located in Tippah county. He grew to maturity and was liberally educated in the schools of that county. While growing up he was afflicted with white swelling, and this has made him a cripple for life. When but fifteen years of age he was thrown on his own resources, and he has since been fortunate in the different occupations he has pursued. He has followed planting, merchandising and is now senior proprietor of the *Southern Sentinel*, of Ripley, which paper has an extensive circulation. Mr. Robinson is a representative citizen and has been connected with every office in the county. His method of conducting the duties assigned him was never questioned and never has he betrayed a trust confided to him. He was married in 1862, to Miss Armissa L. Wigington, a native of the Palmetto state, and they have four living daughters, of whom the eldest married L. Pink Smith, of Greenville, Miss. The others are at home. Mr. Robinson is a member of the Cumberland Presbyterian church, while his wife and two daughters hold membership in the Baptist church. He is a worthy member of the A. F. & A. M. and K. of H. organizations, and is a genial, pleasant gentleman, but one who makes little or no display. He is public-spirited and his name is associated with every enterprise for the advancement of the interests of his county. He owns a beautiful residence in Ripley, and is also an extensive land-owner.

Willie W. Robinson, of the wholesale and retail grocery firm of W. W. Robinson & Co., at West Point, Miss., was born in the town in which he is now residing April 21, 1866; a son of Capt. William Woodard and Margaret (Kilgore) Robinson, the former of whom was born in Pickens county, Ala., April 12, 1837, and reared on a farm, receiving a moderate education. He came to Mississippi when young, and in early life was engaged in merchandising when the town of West Point sprang into existence, and he was one of the first to embark in merchandising in that place. He continued with success until the war opened, when he organized a company with which he served under the Confederate flag until the war closed, doing good service in the cause he espoused. After the close of hostilities he resumed merchandising, which he continued with his usual success until his death, December 3, 1881, aged forty-four years. He was one of West Point's foremost citizens, active in everything for the town's advancement. It was said that his memory was so wonderful that he could call nearly every one for fifty miles around by their given names. He was a member of the A. F. & A. M., the K. of H. and the Methodist church, and his death was not only a loss to his family but to the public as well. He was one of a large family of children born to Alexander Robinson, the latter of whom was a planter and died in Clay county since the close of the war. The mother of the subject of this sketch was born in Chickasaw county, August 22, 1840, and died August 10, 1872. She was a daughter of Dr. Benjamin and Mary Dudley Kilgore. Her father, a native of South Carolina, at an early day came to Mississippi, settling near where West Point now is, where he practiced medicine and was engaged in planting for many years, dying at about the close of the war.* His acquaintance extended over a large territory, for he was well liked in his professional capacity as well as socially, and had been a resident of the county for many years. Willie W. Robinson, whose name heads this sketch, was the second of three children. Sidney, the eldest of the three, was educated in the schools of West Point and in the State university, and Minnie, who was educated in West Point also, is now engaged in teaching in the public schools of the place. Willie W. was educated in the state university at Oxford. He then clerked until 1887, at which time he established himself in the mercantile business at West Point, and for three years successfully conducted his affairs alone. In 1890 the firm of W. W. Robinson & Co. was established, and they are now doing a business of $50,000 annually, theirs being the leading grocery house in West Point. Mr. Robinson commenced business with a small capital, but was energetic, and the excellent business methods and practical ideas that he inherited from his father led to his prosperity. He is a genial, whole-souled gentleman, and is a member of the Methodist church. He is unmarried.

It will be seen from a perusal of this sketch of the life of M. T. Roby that his educational advantages in youth were quite meager, and, although perhaps deficient in general learning, his vigorous mind has so grasped and embraced the opportunities presented, that he is accounted one of the most intelligent and learned men of Attala county. He was from the very first taught everything connected with planting, and this has thus far been his life work. He was born in Georgia in 1828, and after becoming sufficiently qualified, taught for some time in the common schools. In 1853 he came to Mississippi, and soon after settled on the plantation on which he is now residing. He had been married in 1850 to Miss Mary

---

*See sketch of R. D. Kilgore, Clay county.

Eng'd by H.B. Hall's Sons, New York.

W. W. Moore,

Jane Boswell, of Georgia, and their union has resulted in the birth of the following children: Williamson B., who was born in 1852; D. C., born in 1854. M. L., born in 1856; J. E., born in 1859; E. Q. C., born in 1860; two daughters, Aurie S. and Virginia H., were born in 1864; Minnie L., born in 1870; Lilian, born in 1872; Edna E., born in 1874. The son, D. C., is a successful merchant of Durant, Miss. In May, 1861, Mr. Roby enlisted in company A, Fifteenth Mississippi regiment, and in May, 1862, was transferred to the Third Mississippi cavalry regiment, company B, commanded by Capt. T. M. Griffin. While in service he was in the following engagements: Fort Pillow, the three days' fight at Old Harrisburg, Miss., where he had two teeth shot out, and in the several battles during the siege of Atlanta, Ga. The last engagement in which he took part was at Eutaw, Ala. Upon his return home he resumed planting, and is now the owner of one thousand eight hundred and forty acres of land, the principal crop being cotton and corn. The success which has attended his efforts is well merited, for the property he has acquired is the result of honest industry and perseverance. He has been a member of the Masonic fraternity since 1857, and is now a member of the chapter. He is a courteous, agreeable and accommodating gentleman, well versed on all the current topics of the day, and is decidedly public spirited. He has a very handsome and comfortable residence about six miles from Sallis, and is well situated to enjoy the reward of his industry. His father, W. B. Roby, was born in Maryland in 1808, but his first work as a tiller of the soil was done in Wilkes county, Ga. From this place he removed to Putnam county, where he was married to Miss Elizabeth E. Sherman in 1826, their union resulting in the birth of four children: M. T., Aurie E., Henry W. and James R. W. B. Roby was quite an active politician, and filled the position of sheriff of Jasper county, Ga., a number of times. His father was a native of Maryland, and was there married to Miss Anna Roby. James Sherman, the maternal grandfather of the subject of this sketch, was a Georgian, and in the state of his birth also passed from life.

Dr. John U. Rochester, Friar's Point, the oldest practicing physician in Coahoma county and one of the few who connect the remote past, the pioneer period of Coahoma county with the present, was originally from Mercer county, Ky., where his birth occurred on February 8, 1818, and is a representative of a prominent English family. The paternal grandfather, John Rochester, was a native of Virginia and came to Kentucky at an early day. He was a farmer and merchant and a very active man in that day and time. He was a warm friend of Gen. Jackson, and although he was not in the war of 1812 (on account of his size, weighing over three hundred pounds) he contributed liberally to the cause and was a stanch believer in General Jackson. He died of cholera in 1833. The maternal grandfather, John Warren, was also a native of the old Dominion but came to Kentucky at an early period, and there followed the occupation of a farmer and merchant. He was quite active politically and was the private secretary of Governor Shelby, the first governor of Kentucky. His death occurred about 1822. Dr. John U. Rochester was the third in a family of four children born to William and Letitia E. (Warren) Rochester, both natives of the Bluegrass state. The father was a successful agriculturist and he received his final summons in 1824. Dr. Rochester was reared in Kentucky, attended college at Danville in that state and then clerked for an uncle for some time. In 1840 he began the study of medicine in the office of a physician at Danville, and later entered Transylvania college, where he received his medical education. He located at Friar's Point in 1846 and has practiced his profession here or in this county since. In 1848 he was married to Miss Margaret H. Saunders, a native of Tennessee, who was reared in this state, and whose father, George N. Saunders was an early pioneer. To Dr. and Mrs. Rochester were born four children, three deceased: Letitia E.

(died at the age of four years), two died in infancy, and Mariah Louise (wife of M. B. Collins a planter residing near Jonestown in Coahoma county). Mrs. Rochester is a member of the Methodist Episcpoal church. The Doctor is a member of the Masonic fraternity. In his personal appearance the Doctor is tall and venerable looking, walks erect, and were it not for his gray hair and long white beard he would pass for a much younger man. He is well educated, is a fluent and pleasing conversationalist and is one of the most highly esteemed citizens of Coahoma county. Hs was formerly engaged in planting but recently sold his interests.

As a tiller of the soil Capt. Lloyd W. Rogan is doing well, for although his plantation is not as large as a great many, yet the soil is very fertile, and as it is admirably tilled it yields a larger annual income than many more extensive places. In connection with looking after his plantation, which comprises eighty acres, he is also agent for the Port Gibson oil works, from which he derives a fair income. He was born in Vicksburg, Miss., in 1846, to William and Frances A. (Buley) Rogan, who were born, reared and married in Maryland, removing about 1833 to Vicksburg, Miss., at which time the place was a mere village. After the death of Mrs. Rogan, which occurred there in 1854, Mr. Rogan married again, his second wife being Mrs. Barnes, and for a third wife he took a Mrs. Smith, and spent the last of his life in Hinds county, dying in 1868. He was a merchant of Vicksburg, a planter of Hinds county, and in the former occupation acquired a large fortune, but was unsuccessful in the latter calling. He was quite a prominent member of the I. O. O. F., Warren lodge, of Vicksburg, and was an earnest member of the Methodist church. His father, Charles Rogan, was in all probability born in Ireland, but died in Maryland. He had two sons and a daughter that came to Vicksburg, the other sons and the daughter dying in that city. Capt. Lloyd W. Rogan is the fifth of nine children born to his father's first marriage, and is the only one of the family now living. Three elder brothers were in the Confederate army: James W. being a colonel in Rogan's regiment of Arkansas infantry, serving throughout the war and dying at Somerville, Tenn., in 1874, being a merchant of Memphis, Tenn., at the time of his death. He was a graduate of Sheron college, Mississippi, at which time it was one of the finest educational institutions of the South. Thomas G. was a private in the Eighteenth Mississippi infantry, and after being discharged from the service in 1861 on account of ill health, he died on his way home. Charles was a member of the Appeal battery of Memphis, and was killed in the siege of Vicksburg. Capt. Lloyd W. Rogan was educated in Hinds county, and upon the opening of the late war, although only fifteen years of age, he, with youthful enthusiasm, enlisted in the Confederate service, becoming a member of Gov. A. G. Brown's company, of the Eighteenth Mississippi infantry, Longstreet's corps of the army of Virginia, and fought at Leesburg, Savage Station, Sharpsburg and many others. In the summer of 1863 he was discharged, but soon after joined Wirt Adams' cavalry, and operated in Mississippi and Alabama until the close of the war, taking part in many severe engagements. After surrendering at Gainesville, he returned home, and until 1868 was successfully engaged in planting in Hinds county, when he came to Rolling Fork, and for some years was agent for different plantations. He was married, in 1873, to Miss Mattie, daughter of Bailey and Catherine A. Chaney, natives of Louisiana and Mississippi respectively. They were married in Wilkinson county, and died near Rolling Fork in 1874, the former having been a planter by occupation. Mrs. Rogan was born in this county, and of the nine children she has borne Mr. Rogan, six are living. Mr. Rogan was a justice of the peace for eight years, and socially is a member of Auburn lodge No 166 of the A. F. & A. M. of Hinds county. Mr. Rogan comes of a fine family, but throughout life has depended entirely upon his own merits, and has the respect and esteem of all who know him.

Simeon Rogers, the father of J. H. Rogers, of Pachuta, Clarke county, Miss., was born in South Carolina. He was married to Miss Margaret E. Hardee, of Mississippi, in August, 1858. Upon coming to Mississippi he settled in Clarke county, near the present town of Pachuta, and spent his life in agricultural pursuits, dying in 1871. His wife died in 1884. J. H. Rogers, the eldest son of Simeon and Margaret E. (Hardee) Rogers, was born August 18, 1859, near Pachuta, and began farming on his own account at the age of sixteen years. By his grandfather's death, which occurred at this time, he found himself at the head of the family affairs. Mr. Rogers attended the common schools and may be said to have had only ordinary advantages, educationally speaking. In 1882 he married Miss Sarah Gordon, a resident of the western part of Clarke county, Miss., a daughter of Sampson Gordon, one of the best citizens of this county. Mr. Rogers has four children: S. Rufus, Alma, Vane and Sheley. Mr. Rogers' brother, Rev. P. S. Rogers, is a graduate of Mississippi college. At the time of his marriage Mr. Rogers owned no landed interest. He now owns five hundred and sixty acres of the average land of the county, level and well watered, and produces corn, cotton, peas, potatoes, etc. He has begun fertilizing recently. His yield of cotton is twelve bales (one-half a bale per acre), of corn eighteen bushels per acre. He has much fine longleaf pine and does a turpentine business amounting to $800 annually, supplying Pachuta distillery. He also gins cotton by horsepower. He is a member of the Alliance and treasurer of the County Alliance, and he and his wife are members of the Missionary Baptist church and, though quite young, he has held the office of church clerk for eight years. Mr. Rogers is a friend to education and is identified with every movement tending to the upbuilding of the country on this line.

Timothy Rogers has been a life-long citizen of Covington county, Miss., having been born there in October, 1828. All these years he has lived within six miles of the scene of his birth. His father, Meshach Rogers, emigrated from South Carolina in 1822, and lived on the plantation where he first settled, until his death which occurred in 1875. He was an industrious, energetic man, a lover of law and order, and a citizen whom every one respected. He was an active member of the Missionary Baptist church for half a century. He was born in Pendleton district, S. C., about the year 1790, and was a son of Shadrach Rogers, a native of North Carolina, and a soldier in the war of the Revolution, who was noted for his bravery and courage, and high sense of honor. He removed to Covington county in 1822. His family consisted of eight children, named as follows: Timothy; Ailsey, wife of William West; Redock; Israel; Nisa, wife of Mr. Thames; Shadrach; Meshach; Elizabeth, wife of Matthew Thames. Meshach Rogers, the father of our subject, married Lucy Brunson, and they had born to them ten children: Sarah, wife of James M. Speed; Elizabeth, wife of Charles Carter; Caroline, wife of Jackson Edmundson (who at the time of her marriage to him was the widow of Benjamin Duckworth); Shadrach (deceased); Josiah; Timothy; Norval; Martha, deceased, wife of James West; Benjamin, and William. Six of the above are still living, and all of them reared families. Timothy Rogers was married in 1849 to Sarah E. Duckworth, and they had four children: Frances, who married Ransom Welch; Martha E., wife of J. S. Thompson; Mary A., wife of J. N. Welch; Nancy E., wife of J. M. Welch. The mother died in 1863, and Mr. Rogers was married a second time in 1866, to Miss Rebecca Duckworth. One child was born of this union, but died in infancy. In 1862 Mr. Rogers enlisted in the Confederate service, and participated in the siege of Vicksburg, went through the Georgia campaign, and was in the battle of Altoona. At the close of the war he returned to his home, and has since devoted his time and energies to agriculture. He owns seventeen hundred acres of excellent land which is well stocked. He is a member of the Baptist church at Leaf river, and has been a deacon since 1865. He is noted for his honesty and integrity, and is highly respected for his many sterling traits of character.

W. A. Rogers, planter, was born in Greenboro, Ala., in November, 1830, the eldest in a family of nine children, born to Alexander and Sally (Jolly) Rogers, the former of whom was born in Virginia, and the latter in Alabama. Alexander Rogers became a resident of the latter state when a young man, was married there, and there reared his family on a plantation. He died in 1853, but his widow still survives him, being a resident of Sumter county, Ala. W. A. Rogers began life for himself at the age of twenty years as a school teacher, a calling he followed for several years. In 1857 he was married to Miss Sallie Moore, a daughter of Nelson Moore, of Lauderdale county, Miss., and by her became the father of three sons and three daughters. His wife died in 1872, and he took for his second wife Miss Eliza Moore, a sister of his former wife, their marriage being celebrated in 1873. To them, also, have been born six children, five sons and one daughter. In 1862 Mr. Rogers enlisted in the Confederate army, becoming a member of company C, of the Second Mississippi cavalry, and being elected first lieutenant of the company, served in that capacity until the latter part of 1862, when he was promoted to the position of captain, and was in the battles of Dallas, Georgia, and in all the hard fighting around Atlanta. In one engagement he was shot through the thigh. He was captured at Oxford, Miss., and although he was to be imprisoned at Alton, Ill., he managed to make his escape from the boat just as they pulled into Alton, and returned to his command, with which he served until the close of the war. He was with General Forrest in all his raids, and after surrendering and being paroled at Gainesville, Ala., he returned to his home with the consciousness of having performed his duties with faithfulness and ability. After the war he resumed teaching, but after a few months began speculating in land, in which he met with remarkable success. He is now the owner of about five hundred acres of land, of which about one hundred and fifty acres are improved and under cultivation. The Captain has made planting and stock-dealing his chief business for several years, and now has some fine racehorses, which are his chief diverson, and in which he has been quite successful. He has spent large sums of money in educating his children, for he has given them the advantage of the best schools in the country, and has considered his money well spent. Eight of his children are living at the present time, and all of the older ones are especially well educated. Although Captain Rogers is not a member of any religious organization, he has always contributed liberally of his means in their support and, in fact, is generous toward all laudable enterprises. He is a member of the A. F. & A. M. and the K. of H., and is a wideawake, enterprising and public-spirited gentleman.

The medical fraternity of Bay St. Louis was reinforced in 1888 by the accession of Dr. W. B. Rohmer, a native of East Feliciana parish, La., born October 16, 1841. His father, Dr. F. J. B. Rohmer, was born in Alsace, France, and emigrated to America at the age of eighteen years. He was graduated in the first class of the University of Louisiana, taking his degree from the medical department. He located in East Feliciana parish, La., where he practiced his profession many years. He afterward moved to Baton Rouge, La., where he enjoyed an extensive practice. For some time he was surgeon-general of the state of Louisiana, and he also served as surgeon in the Confederate army, having charge of a laboratory at Mobile, Ala., where he exclusively manufactured chemicals and medicines for the Confederate government. He removed to Mobile, Ala., on account of its school facilities, and was appointed physician to Spring Hill college, a position which he held for a long number of years, until forced to resign on account of advanced age and declining health. He is now retired from active work. Dr. Rohmer was born in 1812, and married Alena Bell, of East Feliciana. To them were born six children, of whom Dr. W. B. Rohmer is the eldest son. He received his literary education at Spring Hill college, but in 1861, when there was a call for volunteers to go out in defense of the South, he abandoned his studies and went into the battlefield. He enlisted in the Mobile Cadets, which was the first company that left Mobile for service. He was in General Lee's army. After the surrender he entered Tulane university, resuming his studies as a resident student of the charity hospital, having been admitted into that institution, an unsurpassed school of clinical medicine, through the influence of Dr. Warren Stone, the world-renowned surgeon and noble-hearted man, with whom Dr. Rohmer was in the greatest bonds of friendship. He was graduated from this college in 1866 and began his professional work in Mobile, Ala. He was there but a short time when he was appointed assistant surgeon of a government hospital, a position he filled one year. At the end of that time he returned to Mobile, and practiced there and in that vicinity until 1888. As before stated, he came to Bay St. Louis in that year, and has been successfully engaged in professional duties. He is a physician to St. Stanislaus college and St. Joseph Female academy, and has won a large practice outside of these institutions. He is ambitious to keep up with the times in all medical discoveries, and is well posted on the various leading questions under discussion by the members of the profession. Dr. Rohmer was married in 1864 to Miss Octavia Duval, and they have six children.

Emanuel Rose is one of the substantial German-American citizens of Washington county, Miss., and since coming to America he has indentified himself with every interest of his county, and his inherited characteristics of honesty, industry and thrift have been put to good use. His parents, Simon and Caroline (Rose) Rose, were also native Germans, and his father was a successful grain speculator and died in his native land in 1875, the mother having passed from life in 1844. Emanuel Rose came to this country in 1852 and began dealing in horses and cattle, a calling he followed for a few years, after which he began merchandising and has continued in that capacity ever since. He was educated in the common schools of Germany and in 1864 began business for himself, but prior to this, in 1861, he enlisted in the Twenty-seventh Louisiana infantry and was in the battle and siege of Vicksburg, in which engagement he was also wounded. In 1863 he received an honorable discharge and returned home. He was married in 1887 to Mrs. Caroline Kaufman, a native of Louisiana, and a daughter of Jacob Sartovins, a native German. She was reared in Louisiana, and educated in Memphis, Tenn., and by her first husband became the mother of six children: Cora, Ike, Alfred, Mozart, Sophia and Birdie. By Mr. Rose she has no family. Since his Twenty-second year Mr. Rose has been making his own way in the world, and all of the property of which he is now the owner he has earned by the sweat of his brow and by his own good management. He is one of the pioneers of Leland, and almost ever since the town was organized he has been a member of the city council. He has a considerable amount of land in the county, some real estate in Leland and carries a stock of general merchandise valued at $18,000. Mr. Rose possesses excellent business qualifications, is a kind and considerate husband and is considered by all to be one of the substantial, progressive and enterprising residents of the county. He was a warm supporter of the Confederate cause, and until disabled fought bravely under the stars and bars. As he has resided in the South since coming to this country he has made her interests his own, and can at all times be relied upon to support any enterprise tending to her advantage.

Marx Rosenbaum, De Kalb, Kemper county, Miss., was born in Germany in 1813 and died at Meridian, Miss., in 1883. He was married in his native land to Caroline Heyman and soon after bade farewell to the scenes of his childhood and sailed away to the new world to seek the fortune which is always the portion of the industrious and temperate. He landed in New York and left his wife there while he came to the South. He was first employed as a traveling salesman and thus had an excellent opportunity to judge of the true merits of the country. He finally settled in Sumter county, Ala., and started a store at Patton Hill. In 1845 or 1847 he removed to Kemper county, and in 1852 he established a general mercantile trade in De Kalb; this he conducted until 1878, when he went to Meridian, where he passed the remainder of his days. In addition to his other possessions he owned a large tract of land in Kemper county, which was cultivated under his supervision. When the Civil war broke out he was too old to enter the service, but for a short time was in the state service. In his political opinions he occupied an independent position and after the war was identified with the republican party. He reared a family of ten children: Nannie died at the age of thirteen years; J. was killed in the battle of Gettysburg; Aaron was killed in Georgia during the war; Abraham is a dealer in real estate and resides at Meridian; Charles; Henry is in the general mercantile business at Scooba; William has a general store at De Kalb; Lewis and Joseph, twins, are planters in Kemper county; Isaac died in infancy. The mother of these children died in 1876, in De Kalb, Miss.

Charles Rosenbaum was born in Kemper county, Miss., and was educated at Summerville institute and in his native county. When a young man he entered his father's store, where he clerked until 1871. In that year he was appointed deputy sheriff and for five years held the position, W. W. Chisholm being sheriff. Since leaving the office he has been engaged in general speculations. He is a heavy real estate dealer and owns four thousand acres of land. He also has some commercial interests which are valuable. Politically he affiliates with the republican party. He is unmarried.

George W. Ross, a prominent merchant and planter of Calhoun county, Miss., owes his nativity to Monroe county, of that state, his birth occurring July 1, 1839, and is a son of John Leland and Mary Thompson (Boyd) Ross, natives of South Carolina. The parents were married in Monroe county, Miss., and there the father died October 11, 1850, at the age of forty years. They were members of the Primitive Baptist church, and in politics he adhered to the whig party. The mother was born on July 4, 1818, and was the daughter of Samuel Boyd, who was originally from South Carolina, Mr. Boyd moved to Monroe county, Miss., in 1826, and there resided until his death in 1850. He was the father of a large family of children. After the death of her first husband Mrs. Ross was united in marriage to his brother, Cyrus L. Ross, April 12, 1856, who died on May 20, 1890. To the first union were born six children, two besides our subject yet living: Frances Malinda (widow of Gilbert Garner), and Mary E. (wife of Thomas Garner). Those deceased are Lydia Caroline (who married James Sikes and both died, leaving one child), William L. (killed at the Peach Tree creek fight during the war) and Newton F. (took the measles at Bowling Green, Ky., and died while on the way home). To the second union were born these children: John C. (residing in Monroe counry), Sarah C. (also a resident of Monroe county and the widow of Samuel Gregory), Margaret E. (wife of J. J. Sealey) and Ebby (wife of John Cain). The paternal grandfather, John Ross, was born in Spartanburg, S. C., and with his son, John Leland Ross, moved to Monroe county, Miss., in 1837, taking a large number of slaves with him. He began clearing a farm, a small portion of which had been opened by the Indians, and the following year he brought his family from South Carolina. He made his home in Monroe county until his death in 1880 at the age of ninety-three years. He had been hale and hearty all his life until a few years before his death. He was a soldier in some of the early Indian wars. As long as he continued farming he was very successful, but later in life he embarked in the milling business and lost considerable property. At the time of his death he was living with his fourth wife. His son, John Leland Ross, was born to his first marriage with a Miss Furguson and was one of the following children: Nancy C. (single and resides in Mississippi), George (resides in Monroe county, where his death occurred), Eliza (married John Miller and is now deceased), Miles F. (died near Water Valley), Frank (resides in Texas) and Cyrus L. (who married the mother of our subject, and thus became his stepfather, died in Monroe county). The father of these children took for his second wife a Miss Ross, who bore him two children: William F. (died of measles during the war) and Francis M. (who also died during the war). Mr. Ross' third wife was a Miss Fowler, and after her death he married a Mrs. Angland, who was formerly a Miss Wells. She was born in Lowndes county, Miss., and is still living. By her first husband she had four children—two sons and two daughters: Almeta (married a Mr. Johnson and resides in Monroe county, Miss.), the other daughter married a Mr. Webb and is now deceased; Thaddeus A. and William H. (both reside in Tippah county, Miss.). George W. Ross began for himself as a farmer in Monroe county, Miss., in 1858, and in 1860 he moved to Calhoun county of this state. In 1861 he entered the Confederate army, served in the Magnolia guard corps and later in company K, Seventeenth Mississippi regiment, participating in all the engagements in which his regiment took part. He was captured at Knoxville, Tenn., and was carried to Rock Island, Ill., where he was confined for eighteen months and twenty days, or until the close of the war. At the time of his capture he was holding the rank of sergeant. Returning to Monroe county after the war he continued to reside there until September, 1865, when he moved to Calhoun county of that state, and there he has since made his home. His principal occupation has been farming, but in 1872 he began merchandising in Banner, and has continued this in connection with planting up to the present time. He held the position of postmaster from 1873 to 1877, and is the present mayor of Banner, which office he has held since 1886. He was appointed by the governor and then elected at the general election of 1889. Mr. Ross was married on March 4, 1866, to Mrs. Sarah C. Brown, nee Tedford, a native of Mississippi, born and reared in Monroe county. She came to Calhoun county in 1854, and was first married to L. W. Brown, of Mississippi, by whom she had one son, William J. (who died in Arkansas on May 1, 1889). To Mr. and Mrs. Ross have been born the following children: Mary C. (wife of J. H. Gors, of Banner, Miss.), Ulor B. (married and resides in Banner), Dennis V. (at home), Eleanor H. (resides in Belle county, Tex.), George Hicks (at home), Tapy (at home), Eva (at home) and three children that died in infancy. Mrs. Ross is a member of the Primitive Baptist church. Mr. Ross is a member of Banner lodge No. 329, A. F. & A. M., and in his political views is strictly democratic. He comes of a prominent family and is one of the substantial men of the county.

Benjamin Row, a distinguished planter of Wilkinson county, residing near Fort Adams, was born in West Feliciana parish, La., and was educated at the Brandon academy, in this county, with the Brandons, Pettibones and others. He is the son of Jacob Row and Sarah Gustavus, natives of Mississippi and Tennessee, respectively. Jacob was born in 1784 in Natchez, and was the third child born to John and Margaret Row, natives of Germany, born near Strassburg, the principal town of Alsace, on the Rhine. They came to America and settled in the Natchez district, where they resided for some years. To them were born five children: John, George, Jacob, Mary and William, all of whom lived to be grown and married. Three of the sons reared families, and Mary, the daughter, had one son who also passed away at the time of her death. She first married a Mr. Thompson, by whom the son was born, and after his death she married James Tanner. William married and settled in Louisiana, where he lived until his death. John died, leaving a large family in Louisiana. George also died in Louisiana, leaving a fine family. Jacob settled in West Feliciana parish, La., where he resided until his death in 1845, at the age of sixty-one years and nine months, and during life was an active, successful and extensive planter. He lived a quiet, unostentatious life, and died in comparatively early years full of honors with the highest respect of his neighbors. He was eminently a self made man, having educated himself, and built up his own career of usefulness and honor. His father, John Row, died about 1791, while the family were on the way to Louisiana, and lies buried at Clarksville, Miss. The mother of Benjamin died in 1868; she was born about 1786. To the parents of Benjamin were born ten sons: John G., George S., Micajah, William, who died an infant; Jacob A., Lewis, Henry, Francis, who died an infant; Vincent and Benjamin. John G. died in 1863 and left two sons. George died in 1850 but left no family. Micajah died in 1883, leaving four sons and two daughters. Three of his sons served gallantly in the Confederate army. Dr. Lewis Row, his eldest son, is deceased, but the others are yet living. Jacob died in 1872 leaving a family of ten children. Lewis died single in 1840. Henry died at twenty-one years of age. Vincent died in 1886 leaving eight children. He moved to Wilkinson county in 1849, where he resided and reared his family. Benjamin Row, the subject, just after the death of his father, was called home to take care of the property, and since that time has been engaged in planting. He settled on the present home place in 1853, where he has since lived. He continues to cultivate his land in Louisiana and in this county. During the war he was detailed by the secretary of the Confederate cabinet, under Majors Ewell and Mathews, to carry the mail across the Mississippi river from Fort Adams. While thus serving the South he had at one time $20,000,000 of Southern money in his house that belonged to the Confederate government, the same having been brought to this place from Richmond, Va. It was delivered to parties waiting on the river opposite who took it on to Alexandria, La., and sent from there to Kirby Smith, at Shreveport, to be used to pay the military expenses of the trans-Mississippi department. Since the war Mr. Row has devoted his time to his home. He has been an invalid since 1860, takes no active part in politics, but is well informed on public affairs. He was married in 1851 to Miss Eliza E. McNulty, a native of this county, the daughter of John and Evelyn (Orr) McNulty, natives of Mississippi and Pennsylvania, respectively. Her father came to Mississippi when a young man and engaged in merchandising in Fort Adams, where he was married to Miss Orr, who was born and reared in this county, her parents having been among the first settlers here. The grandfather of Evelyn Orr was Ruffin DeLoach, of French-Huguenot descent, who came to South Carolina at an early day. Mrs. Row died in 1855, leaving two little daughters, Ella Evelyn and Sarah Eliza, the latter now the wife of Darling Babersa, a prominent merchant of Fort Adams. Benjamin was again married in January, 1859, to Miss Sarah George, of Rapides parish, La. She was the daughter of Richard George, a native of Tennessee, who came to Louisiana early, and was married to Mrs. Lewis, nee Jones. William Jones, the father of the latter, was one of this county's very early settlers and prominent men. He married Miss Ogden, of this county, and moved to Louisiana. The Ogdens were also very early settlers and were very wealthy. To Benjamin and his second wife were born five children: Herbert, the eldest, died in 1864; Toly, married J. M. Lessley, a son of Dr. Lessley; Benjamin, died in 1868; Stella is yet single, living at home, and Bennie, Jr. The elder daughter was educated at Summit Lee college, and the younger, at home, by private tutors. Bennie is attending Jefferson college.

Hon. Elias Alford Rowan, M. D., a prominent physician and business man of Wesson, Miss., a son of Samuel and Jeanette (Alford) Rowan, natives of North Carolina, was born near Crystal Springs, December 31, 1837. His parents came to Mississippi in 1833, and located in the woods near the present site of Crystal Springs, where Mrs. Rowan died about 1883, aged seventy-five years, and where her husband (who will be eighty-six September 1, 1891), is still living. During the greater part of his life his occupation was that of an architect and builder, and his success is connected with the growth and development of this part of the country. He became known during his active career as an honest, industrious and thoroughly reliable man, and is held in high esteem and veneration by his present generation of friends, as possibly the only remaining pioneer whose fortunes have been identified with the history and progress of the county for sixty years. His family was of French descent. James Alford, the maternal grandfather of Mr. Rowan, was born in North Carolina, and was of Scotch and Irish descent, and came to Mississippi with Mr. Rowan, was a planter here, and here ended his days. The Doctor is the third of four sons and five daughters, of whom two sons and four daughters are living. He was reared on his father's farm, but received quite a liberal education. After reading medicine with Mr. J. M. K. Alford he attended lectures at the University of Louisiana (now Tulane university) in the session of 1860-1. In May, 1861, he enlisted in the Twelfth Mississippi infantry, but was soon taken sick and had to retire from the service. It was not long, however, before he recovered health and joined company G of the Sixth Mississippi infantry, and was made first lieutenant at the reorganization of the army; was detailed but served as assistant surgeon about two years, when he was promoted to the captaincy of his company. He was in engagements at Baker's creek, Port Gibson, and other points in the Georgia campaign; came back under Hood to Franklin, was in the Franklin battle and fights in front of Nashville, where he was captured in 1864, and kept a prisoner on Johnson's island, in Ohio, where he suffered much until released in June, 1865. Returning home, he resumed his medical studies and graduated from Tulane university in 1866, and went into the practice of his chosen profession, locating on Pearl river, in Lawrence county. Here he remained for three years and then removed to Wesson, in his native county. He has aided largely here in building up the town for twenty-one years, financially, morally and religiously, where he still resides, and where he has built up a large practice and become a leading physician, and is a member of the Mississippi Medical association, and also of the American Medical association. He is a working member of the Baptist church in Wesson, and always on hand to assist his pastor and brethren in church labors. He has been superintendent of the Sunday-school of that church for fifteen consecutive years, and largely to his efforts and influence with the children is due to the fact that it is the largest Sunday-school in the state, numbering at present over four hundred pupils and teachers. Three years ago he aided in organizing the inter-denominational Sunday-school convention in the county, and has been its president for three terms, declining at its last meeting a reëlection, wishing a president chosen from some one of the other denominations. He is a member of J. M. Wesson lodge, A. F. & A. M.; of the Harmony lodge No. 1851 of the Knights of Honor; of the Knights and Ladies of Honor; the I. O. O. F., and of the I. O. G. T. In the Odd Fellows he has served as noble grand, he has served as chief templar of the Good Templar's lodge of Wesson, and is at present grand chief templar of the State lodge.

In March, 1880, Dr. Rowan wrote and published in the county newspaper a strong article against intemperance, attacking the legalized liquor traffic prevailing at that time, when retail and pint saloons were common throughout the state. Many of his best friends thought that his attack on the saloons was an unwise step, but with a determination that nothing in the way of policy or the risk of personal popularity could shake his determination and will to succeed, he pressed the subject on the attention of the people, and three years later, in the legislature of 1884, of which he was a member, secured the passage of a prohibition enactment on petition for his county, and two years later he was one of the leading members who carried through the local option act, permitting each county to decide by vote upon the question of license within its own limits. In the contest in Copiah county, in the matter of prohibition, the personal liberty party made a determined fight, and there were no available means spared to carry their point, but Rowan and the friends who rallied to his side in the contest had the gratification of counting a majority of twelve hundred and seventy-eight votes in their favor. Nor has he abated in his zeal in behalf of prohibition, but hand to hand with its leading advocates in the state he is laboring and hoping for the time when the blot of licensed iniquity shall be removed from Mississippi. Politically his motto might be, Independent in all things, neutral in nothing. A consistent and uncompromising democrat, through his whole political record he holds that democracy as well as democrats should be consistent and uncompromising, and in the late trouble brought on by the irresponsible and unauthorized action of a convention which was not appointed with any view to political control or even advice in reading out of the democratic party the element that was affiliated with the Farmers' Alliance, he promptly took sides with the laborers and producers in pressing their just demands, and largely by an active and persistent canvass made, if not a victory, a very honorable drawn battle in this first skirmish between organized capital and rapidly organizing labor. He was married in December, 1867, to Miss Mary Augusta Mobley, of Lawrence county, who died in May, 1869. In December, 1874, he married Julia L., daughter of Isham and Martha B. Lamb, natives of Tennessee, who removed to Copiah county, where Mr. Lamb became a well-to-do lumberman, and died some years since. Mrs. Rowan was born in Tennessee, the second of seven children. She is connected with the Methodist Episcopal church. Dr. Rowan was elected to the state legislature in 1875, leading in the overthrow of radical and carpetbag rule in his county, and represented his county during the memorable sessions of the legislature in 1876 and 1877, acting as chairman of the committee on benevolent institutions, and aiding in the impeachment of Governor Ames and others. He was reëlected in 1883, and again in 1885. Financially, politically, socially and professionally he has been largely successful. As an evidence of his unabated popularity and the undiminished confidence felt in him by the people may be cited the fact of his election by a very large majority, at the late primary, as chairman of the democratic executive committee of Copiah county for the ensuing four years, over his opponent, Hon. W. C. Wilkinson, one of the ablest, truest and most effectively zealous democrats of the state. Dr. Rowan is a medium-sized man, strongly built. An excellent constitution, unimpaired by excesses, enables him to perform an immense amount of work. There are few men, possibly none, in Copiah county, whose influence equals his, or who devotes more time to the public interests than he. Taking the lead in all measures for the upbuilding of the people financially, morally and religiously, he is well and favorably known, not only through his own and adjoining counties, where he has spoken and served in leading campaigns for prohibition, etc., but throughout the state at large, and this reputation he richly deserves.

James H. Rowan, planter, Natchez, Miss. Daniel Rowan, grandfather of James H., was a native of the Emerald isle but when a young man came to America, settled in Tennessee, and was there married to Miss Sarah Basley. Mr. Rowan was high sheriff of

Dickson county, Tenn., for a number of years and was a man of no little influence and power. His death occurred in that state, and in 1798 his widow and seven children: Beal, Thomas, Lani, Mary, Jane J., James J. and Lion, moved to Mississippi. They settled in the wilderness about fourteen miles east of Natchez and on the farm they called Rowandale, where James H. Rowan now resides. There Mrs. Rowan died when the latter was but a little boy. James J. Rowan, her son and the father of James H., was born in Davidson county, Tenn., was reared on a farm in Adams county, Miss., and received a very meager education in the common schools, never attending more than three months altogether. Being naturally bright and quick witted, he became a man of rare business ability, and at an early age engaged in merchandising at Natchez. He soon became one of the foremost merchants and cotton buyers of the place, handling as many as thirty thousand bales of cotton annually. He was still engaged in business in that city when he married Mrs. Elizabeth (Handy) Leatherburg, a native of Sailsbury, Md., and the widow of Dr. Leatherburg who died in that state. She afterward came to Natchez. Mr. Rowan served as clerk of the county, and also filled the position of treasurer for a number of years. After a successful business career of many years, or in 1836, Mr. Rowan returned to the old homestead, where his death occurred in 1856. He was a prominent Mason and a member of the Methodist church. He was respected and esteemed by all. His wife, who was a member of the Episcopal church, was called to her final home in 1842. Her father, Dr. Handy, died in Maryland and but little is known of the family. Mrs. Rowan was an amiable, generous, noble woman, was very popular and a leader in society and in all works of charity or benevolence. By her union to Mr. Rowan she became the mother of two children: Alfred W., who graduated from Cambridge, Mass., became a well-to-do planter and his death occurred in 1872. The other and younger son, James. H. Rowan, was educated at home under a private tutor. In 1850 he was married to Miss Helen M. Merrick, a native of Natchez and the daughter of Phineas P. Merrick, who was born in Wilbraham, Mass., on the 7th of September, 1796. Mr. Merrick's wife, Hannah M., a native of Elizabethtown, N. J., born on the 15th of November, 1802, he married in St. George's church, New York city, on the 11th of August, 1822. They at once came to Natchez, and there for several years Mr. Merrick was engaged in merchandising, which he continued with success until his death on the 13th of May, 1833. He was vestryman in the Trinity church. He had been city clerk, and at the time of his death was prominently connected with the Agricultural bank of Natchez. He was a prominent Mason and a man of considerable wealth. His widow afterward married Judge William A. Stone, and died on the 14th of June, 1841. Samuel Merrick, the grandfather of Mrs. Rowan, was also a native of the Bay state, where he spent all his life. His father, James Merrick, was a son of Noah Merrick, who, it is supposed, came over in the Mayflower. Mrs. Rowan is one of five children, only she and a brother, Charles F., are now living. She was educated in New York city. To Mr. and Mrs. Rowan were born five children: Charles H., of Tensas parish, La., Mary E., wife of A. P. Miller, of Mew Mexico; Helen M., wife of William L. Foster; Lelah P., who died in 1873; and James B., who died December 29, 1885, from the effects of an accidental discharge of a gun while he was engaged in Christmas festivities. He was at that time a student of Jefferson college and a very promising young man. Mr. Rowan has spent nearly his entire life on the old homestead of his grandmother, and is now the owner of about seventeen hundred acres. He is trustee of Jefferson college, and since 1878 has been a member of the board of supervisors. He is a man of unblemished character, and his word is as good as his bond. He is one of the few men of his age who were born in Adams county and still resides there. Mrs. Rowan and daughter, Mrs. Foster, are members in good standing in the Presbyterian church.

E. Rubel, merchant, Corinth, Miss., is numbered among the prominent citizens of Alcorn county and is a member of the prominent mercantile firm of Abe Rubel & Co. He came originally from that grand old country, Germany, which seems somehow to instill into her sons the traits of character that make them successful, prosperous and popular wherever fate leads their footsteps. He was born in Bavaria on the 20th of June, 1837, to the union of Jacob and Veronica (Frauenthal) Rubel, both of whom were natives also of Germany, in which country they passed their entire days. E. Rubel was the ninth in order of birth of twelve children, nine of whom are living, but only our subject now in America. The latter emigrated to this country in 1854, peddled a short time in Philadelphia and country in Pennsylvania, and then attended boarding-school nine months in Bucks county of that state. He subsequently accepted a situation as clerk in a dry-goods business at Lexington, Va., and remained there two years, and returned to Philadelphia in April, 1858, remained there until May, and then accepted a clerkship with M. Simon & Co., Memphis, Tenn., where he continued until the fall of that year, when M. Simon opened a store at Corinth, Miss., in copartnership with James Dobbins, of that town, and Mr. Rubel came from Memphis to represent M. Simon in the business at Corinth. They started with a stock of general merchandise valued at about $3,500 under the firm name of Simon & Dobbins. About two months later the firm dissolved and was made Simon & Rubel, under which title the business was carried on by E. Rubel until the spring of 1862. Mr. Rubel, who was enthusiastic in the cause of the South, after the outbreak of the war collected funds for the purpose of making a uniform for the first company that had left Corinth for the seat of war at Pensacola, Fla., under command of Captain Kilpatrick and First Lieutenant F. E. Whitfield, Jr. Mr. Rubel purchased the goods and trimmings and had the uniforms made at Corinth, and forwarded the same to the company at Pensacola, Fla. After the battle of Shiloh he was requested to give up their storehouse for the use of the Confederate government and army, in consideration of which the government gave him transportation for himself and goods to Memphis, Tenn., and he left Corinth with his goods for Memphis on a train loaded with wounded soldiers from the battlegrounds of Shiloh and Pittsburg Landing. After arriving in Memphis he and Mr. Simon disposed of their goods, and Mr. Rubel started to Europe to visit his parents, of whom he had heard nothing during the war. Returning in the fall of 1863 he went again to Memphis, and engaged in merchandising and buying cotton, and immediately after the war started business again in Corinth, Miss., the firm known as E. Rubel & Co., L. Sekeles being the company. This continued until 1876, when Mr. Rubel's nephew, Abe Rubel, who prior to this clerked for the firm, was admitted into the business, and the firm title was changed to Rubel, Sekeles & Co. This continued until the spring of 1882, when E. Rubel sold his interest to the other members of the firm, and started in the cloak manufacturing business in Philadelphia, Penn. Later he gave this up, and, in connection with Abe Rubel, bought out Mr. Sekeles in 1889, the firm name being changed to Abe Rubel & Co. Abe Rubel has been connected with the firm since 1866. E. Rubel selected as his companion in life Miss Pauline Hochstadter, of Philadelphia, Penn., but a native of Fayette, Jefferson county, Miss., and their nuptials were celebrated in 1869 at Philadelphia. They became the parents of nine children, seven of whom are living: Florence, Carrie, Jacob, Jennie, Milton, Rose and Alfred. Florence and Carrie are graduates of the Philadelphia (Penn.) Normal High school; the eldest of the sons, Jacob, is attending the Philadelphia Manual Training school, and the younger members of the family are in school in Philadelphia, where E. Rubel has resided since his marriage. In his business career at Corinth the firm commenced on a small scale, but it has prospered, and has now one of the largest wholesale and retail enterprises in the state. They have a very handsome business building, erected by Rubel & Sekeles in 1873-4, and superintended and built by Mr. E. Rubel in person. He made his own brick, arranged everything, and the building, which is four stories in hight with a seventy-five foot front, cost over $40,000, and is not only an ornament to the city, but an honor to Mr. Rubel. They have a fine basement under all and carry a stock of goods valued at about $100,000. Their custom extends to Alabama, Tennessee and Mississippi. E. Rubel resides in Philadelphia, as above stated, but Abe Rubel resides in Corinth, and is a live, energetic business man. The latter was married to Miss Rachel Hirsh, of Memphis, Tenn., and is the father of seven children: Simon, Jacob, Charlotte, Lee, Milton, Carrie and Frank.

Atlas F. Rush, De Kalb, Miss., who for sixteen years has been chancery clerk of Kemper county, Miss., is entitled to the following space in this record of the leading men of the state. He was born in Kemper county, within six miles of De Kalb, in 1842, and is a son of William C. and Elizabeth (Crawford) Rush. His father was born in North Carolina in 1814, and removed to Kemper county in 1834, bringing his wife whom he had married in his native state. He was a planter and speculator, and was very successful. He was a member of the Methodist Episcopal church, and belonged to the Center Ridge lodge, A. F. & A. M. He was a man of wide and deep sympathies, whom the woes of the people touched, and it was to him the poor and needy were apt to turn for succor, knowing always that they would recieve aid. He died in 1873. His wife was born in North Carolina; she was a daughter of Mastin Crawford, and a woman of rare force of character. She belonged to the Methodist Episcopal church. Her death occurred in 1883. They reared a family of ten children: Thomas, Mastin, John, Charlotte, Julia, Mary, Atlas F., James, William and Mattie. Thomas, Mastin, Mary and James are deceased. Atlas F. was reared in the county of his birth, and received his education in the common schools. In 1861, at the age of eighteen years, he enlisted in company I, Twenty-fourth Mississippi volunteer infantry, and went out to aid the Confederate cause. He saw some active service, participating in the battles of Perryville, Murfreesboro, Chickamauga and Lookout Mountain; he was captured in the last named engagement, was sent to Johnson's island, where he was held twenty-two months, being paroled at the end of that period. He enlisted as a private, and was promoted to a lieutenancy before his capture. When the war was ended he returned to his home, and embarked in the mercantle trade in the town of De Kalb. He has a plantation of one thousand acres within two miles of De Kalb, which he has brought to a high state of cultivation. Politically he is identified with the democrat party. For the past sixteen years he has been clerk of the chancery court, and has discharged the business of that office with skill and fidelity that has won him a wide reputation. He is a member of the Masonic order, and also belongs to the Farmers' Alliance. Mr. Rush was united in marriage December 19, 1865, to Miss Cornelia Holton, a daughter of Col. John B. and Katie (McAlister) Holton, natives of North Carolina. Mrs. Rush was born in North Carolina in 1842, and is an only child. Ten children have been born to our subject and his wife: Inda H. is the wife of R. M. Hight, of Greenwood, Miss.; Anna married Dr. M. M. Warren, of Macon, Noxubee county, Miss.; Holton C.; Frank C. (deceased in 1888); Hugh B.; Kittie; Attie F.; Cornelia; and two who died in infancy. The parents are worthy members of the Baptist church.

Charles E. Rushing, the subject of this sketch, was born in Meltonville, Anson county, N. C., July 27, 1819. Leaving home at the early age of fifteen years to make his way in the world, he rode across the states on horseback to Mobile, Ala., accepting employment there as clerk in a wholesale shoe store. He married there in February, 1842, Miss Bridget C.

Collin. He remained in Mobile about two years after this, when his health failing he came to Marion, Lauderdale county, Miss., being one of the early settlers of the county. He there started in mercantile business, and how well he succeeded was attested by the fortune he was the possessor of when the war began, being the owner of many slaves, the largest land owner in the county, and interested in three mercantile houses. He was opposed to secession, but when the inevitable came he did his duty as a man and citizen. He held the office of tax assessor during the war. The only office that he ever held previous to this was county treasurer, which office he held for fifteen consecutive years. After the war he was elected and served as a member of the constitutional convention to frame a constitution for the state under the reconstruction act. He then set about to gather another fortune, one having been lost by the vicissitudes of war. He started a new mercantile business at Columbus, Ky., and continued in that until February, 1866, when he was elected vice president of the Mobile & Ohio railroad, in which capacity he served until May, 1874. He then returned to Marion, Miss., where he spent the remainder of his days in peace and quiet on his farm, dying December 30, 1881. His was a busy life. Many have cause to remember him for his charities, for he was a friend to the orphan. He was blessed with several children—four sons and two daughters—his two oldest sons being victims of the war. His oldest living son, H. P. Rushing, married Miss Anna J. Cole, of Meridian, Miss., in February, 1873, and settled at Toplin, Miss., on a farm, where he now resides, and does business as farmer and merchant. He owns one of the finest herds of Jersey cattle in the state, and has a dairy with all the latest improvements, run by steam. He has also a system of private water works to supply his house and cattle with water. J. C. Rushing, the other living son resides in Meridian, Miss., and is in the railroad business. The two daughters reside at the old homestead at Marion. The following is another account of Charles E. Rushing.

One of the useful citizens of Mississippi for many years and during his lifetime very prominent in public affairs was Charles E. Rushing (deceased). He was born in the Old North state in 1819 and after reaching manhood removed to Mobile, Ala., where he resided two years and was married to Miss Bridget Collin, a native of County Kildare, Ireland, where she was born in 1817. After their marriage they removed to Mississippi, settling at Old Marion, Lauderdale county, in 1844, where Mr. Rushing engaged in merchandising. After a few years he also established a good store at Marion station, on the then new Mobile & Ohio railroad, and at both these places he did a prosperous business until the opening of the Civil war. He filled the position of county treasurer ably and efficiently for some time and was otherwise interested in the political affairs of his section. When the war opened he was elected tax assessor of Lauderdale county, but was afterward in the commissary department and was instrumental in relieving the wants of those who were deprived of help and means by the devastations of war. When hostilities ceased he was completely bankrupt, much of his valuable property being destroyed by General Sherman's army. He was an extensive planter also in connection with his other enterprise, but after the war was over he embarked in the commission business in Columbus, Ky., and had been and was a director of the Mobile & Ohio railroad, and in 1866 was elected vice president of that road, which position he ably filled for nine years. After a well spent life he died at Old Marion, Miss., in 1881, his widow surviving him until 1889. Miss Clara L. Rushing, their daughter, resides with her sister, Mrs. M. E. Robinson, on the old homestead. These ladies are engaged successfully in conducting the plantation, Mrs. Robinson being chief of the domestic interests while Miss Rushing superintends the plantation. They have two thousand acres of good land, the cultivated portion of which yields from forty to fifty bales of cotton yearly. Their house is located seven miles east of Meridian, is pleasantly situated and makes them a comfortable and cozy home. These ladies are proving themselves good business women and are intelligent, wideawake and self-reliant. Mrs. Robinson has two sons: Clarence E. and Collin R. The Rushing family are Catholics. Charles E. Rushing was one of the incorporators and was afterward president of the Peoples' bank, Meridian, Miss.

Elijah Russell is a native of the state of South Carolina, born in the year 1817. He is a son of James D. and Susana (Gayden) Russell, also natives of South Carolina, of Irish descent. The family removed from South Carolina to Georgia where they remained two years, and in 1829 they came to Mississippi, and settled in Warren county, where the father died in 1834 and the mother died in Yazoo county in 1853. They were the parents of eleven children all of whom grew to maturity excepting two, and all of whom have passed away excepting two. Elijah Russell spent his early boyhood days in his native state. In 1843 he came to Yazoo county, and engaged in mercantile pursuits at Benton; he followed this busines a few years and then was employed in overseeing and farming for some time. He has resided on his present farm about ten years; it consists of three hundred acres of land, a portion of which is devoted to the raising of live-stock another to fruit, and the balance to general farming purposes; he has a fine herd numbering thirty head of graded Jersey breed, and six hundred bearing peach-trees, besides a great many apple, pear and quince trees. Mr. Russell was united in marriage January 16, 1845, to Miss Martha A. Erwin, a daughter of Abner and —— (Howard) Erwin. By this union eleven children were born, five of whom are still living: Mary, wife of John Birdwell of Louisiana; Abner, a farmer of Yazoo county; Reuben G., who resides in Indian territory; Howard, a resident of Washington county, and DeFrance, a resident of the same county. Mr. Russell lost the mother of these children in 1870. Three years later he was married to Mrs. Lucy (Hearn) Foster, a daughter of John and Mary (Montgomery) Hearn, natives of South Carolina. Four children have been born of this marriage: Ina, who died at the age of five years; Sera, Gaydon and Irene. The mother is a member of the Rock Springs Baptist church, and Mr. Russell belongs to the Methodist Episcopal church of Benton. He is also a member of the Masonic order. He is a man of public spirit, and has contributed both of his means and personal influence largely to the growth and advancement of Yazoo county.

Mrs. Laura V. Russell is the widow of W. H. Russell, who was born in Warren county, Miss., in 1828, a son of Arnold and Elizabeth (Grover) Russell, natives of Tennessee. Col. Arnold Russell came to this state while it was yet a territory, and entered quite a large body of land on the Yazoo river. A considerable portion of this property he afterward sold, but a large portion of what he reserved is now the property of Mrs. Laura V. Russell. Colonel Russell and his brother, James, were in the war of 1812, at which time the former was only nineteen years of age. James B. attained the rank of captain, and both afterward served with distinction in various Indian wars. W. H. Russell was educated in the schools of Nashville, Tenn., and was one of the finest educated men in Mississippi. Although he preferred the life of a planter to any other calling, many professions were opened to him, for his father was wealthy and generous, and would gladly have given his son every advantage. During the Rebellion W. H. Russell enlisted in the Confederate service, but owing to delicate health he was unable to stand the hardship and privations of army life, and shortly after he joined he was honorably discharged. He was the owner of quite a number of slaves but, of course, during the war lost them all, and after the cessation of hostilities found himself in a destitute condition. Not heeding the dark outlook he set energetically to work and possessing shrewd and practical views his efforts were well repaid, and at the time of his death was the owner of the old Russell estate consisting of about three thousand acres, and an estate of his own, the entire amount of land under cultivation on the two places amounting to eight hundred acres. In 1855 Mr. Russell was married to Miss Laura V. Jackson, and their union resulted in the birth of ten children, all of whom survive: Annie D., wife of C. F. Cassey, M. D., of Satartia, Miss.; Laura J., W. H. and Lauretta, twins; Seymour, Arnold, Mellen, Lee, Ruth and Ruby, twins. Mr. Russell was a Knight Templar in the A. F. and A. M. of Vicksburg, was very popular and well known throughout the county, and was highly honored and respected by his neighbors. Personally, and in every private relation and duty of life, he was liberal, generous and high minded, was the life of social intercourse, and the soul of true honor and unbounded greatness of heart. Mrs. Russell's parents, Stephen M. and Ann Dunn (Hill) Jackson, were natives of Virginia, being members of leading families of that state. Mrs. Jackson was a member of Dr. Dunn's family of Memphis, Tenn., who was quite a prominent citizen of this city. The maternal grandfather of Mr. Jackson was Littleberry Mason of Virgina. John Y. Mason, Sr., was his uncle, and John Y. Mason, Jr., of Confederate fame was his cousin. It was he who was with Slidell on recruiting service for the Confederacy in Canada, and was there captured. Mr. Jackson died in 1839, while just in the prime of life, and Mrs. Jackson, after remaining a widow eighteen years, married Dr. Seymour Halsey, of Vicksburg, who was one of the leading surgeons of Mississippi. He served in this capacity in the war with Mexico, throughout which war he was with Jefferson Davis. He was a member of the Halsey family of New Jersey, and when a young man came South, and first located at Baton Rouge, although the greater part of his life was spent in Vicksburg. He was very widely known, and a man whom to know was to honor. He died in 1851, and his widow in 1885, at the age of seventy-seven years. She bore Dr. Halsey no children, but her union with Mr. Jackson, who was born in 1800, resulted in the birth of four children, two of whom are living: Mrs. Laura V. Russell and Dr. D. D. Jackson, of Greenville.

Samuel D. Russell, planter and merchant at Missionary, Jasper county, Miss., was born near Decatur, Newton county, Miss., in 1854, one of the six children of Alexander and Elizabeth W. (Wilson) Russell (born, McDowell). Alexander Russell was born in Anson county, N. C., in 1816, and left home when but a youth to seek his fortune in the West, but located in Newton county, Miss., early in its history, and, while a resident there was engaged in planting, and in operating a small tannery on his place. In 1869 he became a merchant at Decatur, and as such proved a success, establishing a few years later a branch store at Newton, his partner in this enterprise being M. J. L. Hoye, his son-in-law. Mr. Russell was a man of remarkable business ability and great energy. Our subject, Samuel D. Russell, was reared in Newton county, where he received his primary education in the common schools, and later was a student at the college at Clinton for a year. He married Miss Bettie M. Longmire, daughter of Dr. G. E. Longmire, a native of Alabama. To Mr. and Mrs. Russell have been born three children: G. Longmire, R. Alexander and Samuel D., Jr. Mr. Russell located where he now lives in February, 1884, and is the owner of twenty-one hundred acres of land all in one body, besides about fifteen hundred acres in other tracts. In connection with his planting operations he has a general store, which is well stocked with such merchandise as is in demand in the country round about. He also has an interest in the store of Walton, Gallaspy & Russell, at Hickory, Miss. He is a thoroughgoing young man with the best business principles, and has made a success of each one of the several enterprises in which he has been engaged—his home store and the one at Hickory, each having a large trade, and his planting operations being as extensive as those of any other planter in his vicinity.

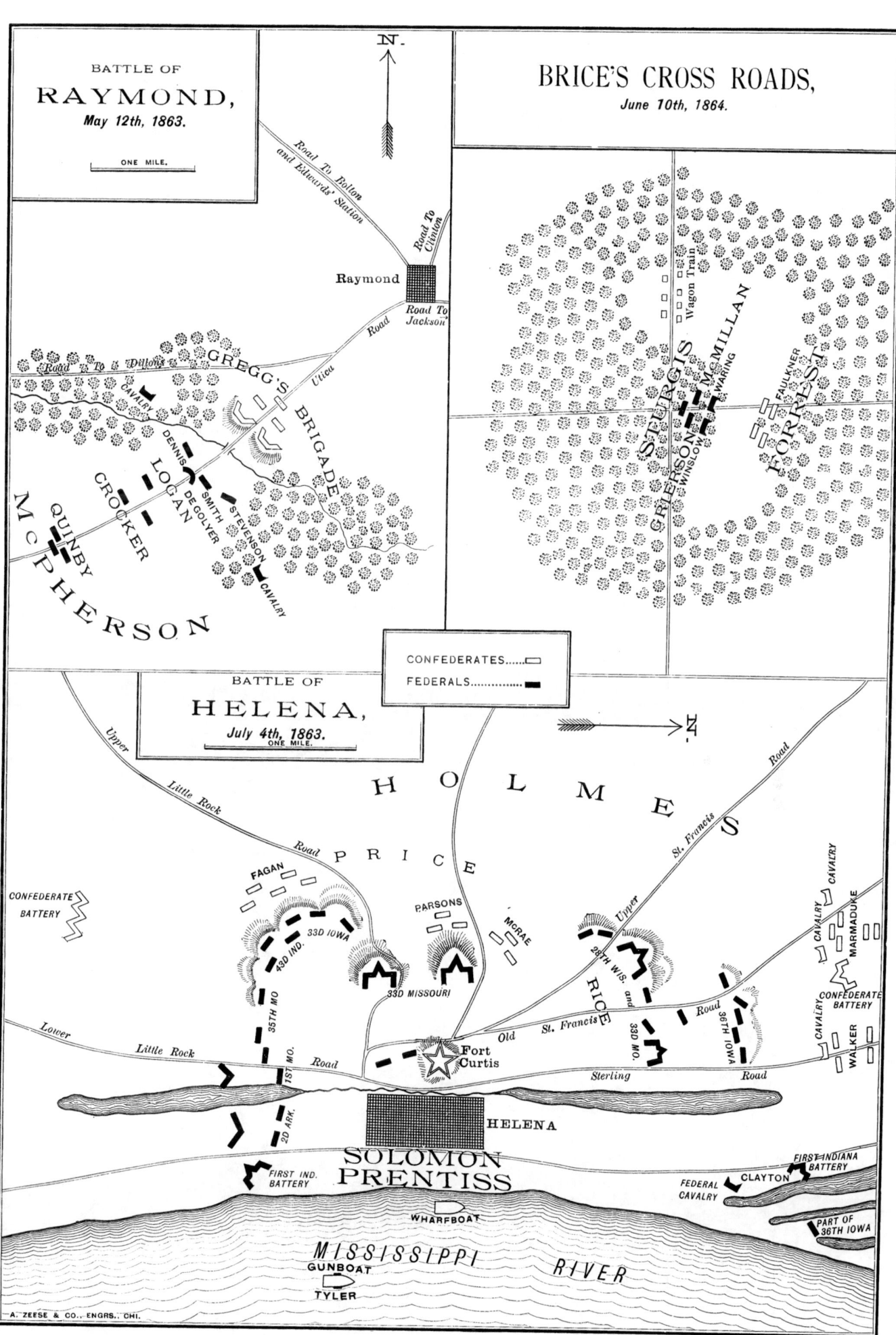

James M. Rutherford, sheriff, Ripley, Miss., was chosen to occupy his present responsible position by his party in October, 1881, and is now discharging the duties of that office in a manner highly creditable to himself and to the satisfaction of the community at large. This introduction is hardly necessary, for the people of Tippah county are not only perfectly familiar with Mr. Rutherford as a trustworthy official but honor and respect him as a man. He was born in Union county, Ga., in 1834 and was the second in a family of eleven children born to Thomas and Margaret A. (Lemmonds) Rutherford, natives of the old North State. The parents were reared in that state, and after their marriage, or in 1832, they moved to Georgia where they made their home until 1848. From there they moved to Tippah county, Miss., and there their family grew to maturity. The father was a mechanic, but in connection also carried on farming and was quite successful in both pursuits. He died on the 4th of February, 1891, at the age of eighty-seven years. James M. Rutherford was reared in Tippah county as above stated, and when the war broke out he was filled with an enthusiastic desire to assist the Confederacy. In April, 1862, he enlisted with three other brothers and with them served until the close. These brothers are all living at the present time. Another brother joined the cavalry and lived until 1890. After the final surrender, Mr. Rutherford returned to Tippah county with the consciousness of having served his cause faithfully and well. Previous to the war, in December, 1857, he selected Miss Harriet Reed as his companion in life, and their marriage has been blessed by the birth of four children, all of whom are now married and the heads of families. Mr. Rutherford followed planting until 1881, when he was elected to his present position. He now resides in Ripley and rents his farm. Although he makes no outward display, Mr. Rutherford attends strictly to the duties of his office in a manner highly trustworthy.

Dr. Charles Ryan, Elma, Miss., who is one of the successful physicians of Prentiss county, is a self-made man in every sense of that much abused term, and what he has accumulated in the way of this world's goods is the result of industry, perseverance and indomitable will power. His early life was one of hardship and privations, and, although in his subsequent career for many years he had a hard struggle to keep above water, he finally triumphed, and is to-day one of the substantial and much esteemed citizens of the county. He was born in Tuscaloosa county, Ala., on the 29th of January, 1820, and was the youngest of three children born to Charles and Sarah (Spaulding) Ryan, the father a native of one of the Carolinas, and the mother of Alabama. The parents were married in Alabama and there resided until the death of the father in 1820, the same year in which the Doctor was born. The mother was afterward married to Dorn Patton, who proved a hard taskmaster. This union resulted in the birth of eight children, one son and seven daughters. The mother died in Texas in 1868. Dr. Ryan, who was placed under his stepfathers care when a little child, did not fare very well at his hands, in fact, had a very hard time of it, and when about eight years of age had his left arm paralyzed by a limb from a tree striking it. This he has had to carry through life. When about ten years of age he was driven from home by his stepfather and started out to struggle for existence for himself. He engaged first as mail carrier from Waynesboro to Shelbyville, Tenn., receiving for his services the munificent sum of $5 per month. He followed this for eleven months, during which time his wages were increased to $15 per month, and after giving up his Tennessee contract he went to Alabama, where he succeeded in getting a position as mail carrier from Jasper to Blount Springs. There he remained for one year, receiving for his services $8 per month, and then went to Tishomingo county, Miss., where he took the contract for carrying the mail from Jacinto, Miss., to Tuscumbia, Ala., and rode that route. He retained that position for one year at $8 per month, and after that he began working in the office of the chancery clerk in Tishomingo county, Thomas Pate, assisting him in writing for three months. However, as he received nothing for his services except his board and clothes, he gave this up, and as he had studied hard when he had opportunity, he had sufficient education to teach a school of children. While thus employed he studied medicine, and at the end of six months, his school term ending, he went back to Alabama where he spent what money he had earned for books, and being the owner of a small pony, gave that to the professor of Spring Hill academy for ten months tuition in his school. He attended the fall term of 1844, and by that time, having obtained a fair literary education, he returned to Tishomingo county, Miss., in 1844, and engaged a five months school. This he taught, and in the following year was elected county assessor, when in his twenty-fifth year, serving one term in that capacity. In 1847 he was married to Miss Elizabeth Martin, who bore him nine children, three sons and six daughters: Sarah F. (wife of George T. Goddard), Kizzie A. (wife of A. J. Wilson), Elizabeth A. (wife of A. C. Stevens), Arthur M., Mary J. (wife of James E. Shackleford), Maggie C. (wife of W. C. Weems), Charles A., Melverdie R. (wife of Stephen W. Millican) and William P. Dr. Ryan is the owner of three hundred and forty-five acres of land in Prentiss county, and has one hundred acres of this under cultivation. As before stated, while teaching school he studied medicine, and decided to make that his profession, applying himself faithfully to this study for years. In 1853 he commenced practicing in Itawamba and Prentiss counties, and continued practicing until 1859, when he entered Memphis Medical college, graduating from that institution in 1860. He subsequently located at Bay Springs, Tishomingo county, remained there one year, and then moved to the farm where he now lives, three miles east of Elma. He was there during the war and had an extensive practice, being exempt from service on account of his crippled arm. He was about the only physician left in the county and had frequently to ride thirty miles to see a patient. The Doctor is still practicing, but in connection is also engaged in the drug business, having a store on his farm. He carries a stock of goods valued at about $1,000, drugs and general merchandise. Dr. Ryan's religious belief is as follows: He believes, "That the Holy Scriptures of the Old and New Testaments contain a revelation of the character of God, and of the duty, interest, and final destination of mankind; that there is one God, whose nature is Love, revealed in one Lord Jesus Christ, by one Holy Spirit of Grace, who will finally restore the whole family of mankind to holiness and happiness; that holiness and true happiness are inseparably connected, and that believers ought to be careful to maintain order, and practice good works, for these things are good and profitable unto men." He has been a member of the Masonic fraternity since 1866. He is well and favorably known all over the county. He was deputy sheriff of Itawamba county for about two years, and was an able and efficient officer. He has been a resident of Mississippi since 1835, and has ever been a liberal contributor to schools, churches, etc.

CHAPTER XIX.

SELECTED MEMORIALS, S.

A LEADING merchant and planter of Coahoma county, Miss., is William R. Sadler, who was born in Franklin county, Ala., December 24, 1843, being the sixth in a family of thirteen children born to Joseph M. and Maria E. (Owen) Sadler, the former a native of North Carolina and the latter of Tennessee. In the year 1846 they came to Mississippi, locating in Chickasaw county, where the father spent the remainder of his life as a progressive planter and a worthy and public-spirited citizen. At the opening of the late war he was strongly opposed to secession, but when the ordinance of secession was passed, he remained loyal to his state, and bent all his energies to the establishment of the Confederacy. He was one of the pioneers of the state, and here was called from life in 1882, at the age of seventy-six years. The paternal ancestors of William R. Sadler were from Germany, and settled in Pennsylvania upon coming to this country, where they became substantial, industrious and prosperous citizens. William R. has been a resident of Mississippi from the time he was three years of age, and in the schools of Chickasaw county he received his education. While fitting himself for college the war broke out, and as a loyal Southerner he joined the Confederate forces, becoming a member of company C, Thirteenth Mississippi cavalry, and served until the long struggle ended. He was one of the first to join his company, and was in every engagement in which it participated, but was never wounded, and during his protracted service he never received a furlough. He was at Iuka, Corinth, Franklin, and in the Georgia campaign. He was as brave and faithful a soldier as ever shouldered a musket, and although the cause was lost, he was conscious of having performed every duty faithfully and well. He began his business career after the war closed as a merchant and cotton speculator, in both of which he was very successful. In addition to these he has carried on planting successfully, and has become the owner of two thousand acres of land, seven hundred of which are in a good state of cultivation. The most of this he has opened and improved at great expense. He is a stockholder in the Friar's Point oilmill, and is part owner of the drug establishment of Sadler & Jones, in Jonestown. Like so many of the prosperous business men of the present day, he is essentially self-made, and by persistent and continous effort he has acquired his present property. He has been a member of the board of supervisors of Coahoma county for two terms, and was one of the first to settle in what is now Jonestown, being one of its most reputable and public-spirited citizens. He lives a quiet and happy life, with no aspirations for political honors, and is a very social and pleasant gentleman to meet, being by no means void of that hospitality characteristic of the Southern people.

J. G. Sallis, M. D., is a talented and skillful physician, who is well known throughout the state of Mississippi. He was born in Tuscaloosa county, Ala., October 28, 1825, and traces his ancestry back three generations to John Sallis, who was of English birth and came to America during its early history. His son, John S. Sallis, was born in Augusta, Ga., and became the father of John Sallis, the father of the subject of this sketch. John Sallis was born in Warren county, Ga., but the marriage of his parents was consummated in Augusta, in a fort, during Revolutionary times, their removal to Warren county taking place soon afterward. They became the parents of seven sons and seven daughters that grew to mature years. John Sallis, father of J. G. Sallis, M. D., was married in Warren county to Miss Mary Edmondson, a native of Warren county, and moved with his family to Tuscaloosa county, Ala., where he made his home for a few years. In 1849 he removed to Mississippi and settled in Attala county, where he died in 1866, at the age of seventy-six years. He had been a successful planter throughout life, and had accumulated a comfortable fortune. Dr. J. G. Sallis is one of a family of seven sons and three daughters, all of whom grew to mature years and became heads of families. Four brothers and one sister are the survivors. The youthful days of the Doctor were spent in Alabama, and there he was educated. In 1849 he came to Mississippi and began the study of medicine in Attala county, taking his first course of lectures in New Orleans in 1851, from which he graduated in the class of 1853 from Tulane university. He immediately returned to Attala county, and here has been one of the foremost medical practitioners ever since. He has had a very large and lucrative practice for forty years, and is, in addition to attending to his professional duties, one of the most extensive planters in the county, and has eleven hundred acres in one body, six hundred of which is open land in excellent farming condition. Upon the building of the Aberdeen branch of the Illinois Central railroad, a station was located on the Doctor's plantation, and was named Sallis, after him. He was married in 1852 to Miss M. A. Fleming, a daughter of John L. Fleming, of Madison county, Miss. Mrs. Sallis was born in Columbia, S. C., but reared in Madison county, Miss, and has borne the Doctor five children: William B., who is engaged in merchandising at Sallis; D. Fleming is attending medical lectures in Baltimore, Md.; Hattie M. is the wife of R. S. Clark, of Starkville, Miss., and Mary E. is the wife of Oscar Boyett, of Sallis. One son, Robert, died in 1872, at the age of eleven years. The Doctor and his wife are members of the Baptist church, and are worthy Christians and estimable citizens. Although the Doctor is approaching his three-score years and ten, his mind is as clear as ever and he is still active, physically. He has been active in all good works, but has been specially interested in church matters and for the past twenty-three years has been a deacon, and Sunday-school superintendent for twenty-three years.

A. D. Sample, farmer, Richland, Miss. Mr. Sample's father, Isaac Sample, was one of the pioneer settlers of Mississippi, leaving his native state, South Carolina, to come to the wilds of Mississippi in 1836. He located on a farm near old Franklin, and was married in 1840 to Mrs. Mary H. Barbour, who bore him four sons: John (died in infancy), J. H., A. D. and D. C. Mr. Sample was much attached to his family, was a kind and loving father, and a devoted husband. His death occurred in 1851. He was a member in good standing in the Masonic fraternity. His third son, A. D. Sample, is a native Mississippian, born in Holmes county in 1846, and there grew to manhood. He secured his early education in the Richland private schools, and in 1866 selected his companion in life in the person of Miss Ann Maria Ambrose, a native of Mississippi also. This union has been blessed by the birth of nine children. Previous to his marriage and when but sixteen years of age he enlisted in the Confederate army, as a private, in Harvey's scouts and their principal fields of operation were in Georgia, Alabama, Tennessee and Mississippi. He was captured at Selma, Ala., but escaped before the prison was reached. Returning home after cessation of hostilities, he resumed farming, has continued that vocation up to the present, and is the owner of one thousand and fifty acres of excellent land and of this six hundred acres are in a fine state of cultivation. This farm is located two miles west of Richland, Holmes county, and there the mother of our subject died in 1879. Mr. Sample takes great pride in his children and is rearing them to be honest, intelligent men and women.

Charles Sanger, builder and contractor, of Bay St. Louis, Hancock county, Miss., is a native of Germany, born in Wiesbaden in 1853. He is a son of George and Elizabeth Sanger, also natives of the Fatherland. Mr. Sanger was a stonecutter by trade. His death occurred in 1863, but his wife still survives. They reared a family of four children: Charles, Helena, Theresa and Frederick. Charles Sanger is the only member of this family who came to America. He remained in his native land until he was fourteen years of age, receiving a good education. In 1867 he sailed for the United States, and landed in New Orleans, where he had an uncle, Henry Sanger, a prominent builder and contractor of that city. The uncle died in 1870. Charles learned his trade from his uncle, and followed the business in New Orleans until 1873, when he came to Bay St. Louis, Miss. Here he has since resided. In 1871 he made a trip to the coast, being a contractor for the icehouses at Pass Christian and Biloxi. Since his residence at Bay St. Louis he has erected a great many buildings, and has taken some heavy contracts. He is a thorough master of the business, and his success is due to the excellent training he had under his uncle. He is now dealing exclusively in ice, and the most important part of this business is the sinking of artesian wells. He has sunk several, all of which have proven of best quality. Mr. Sanger was married in 1878 to Miss Lucy Jebenes, and one daughter has been born of the union, Augusta. They are members of the Roman Catholic church. Mr. Sanger is one of the most enterprising citizens of Bay St. Louis, and the superior character of all his work has won for him a first place in the business circles, not only of Hancock county, but also in the state of Mississippi.

George F. Sanders, Bright, De Soto county, Miss., was born in Wilkes county, Ga., May 4, 1835, and is the eldest of a family of five children. His parents, Marion and Lucy (Murphy) Sanders, were also natives of Georgia. The father was a planter by occupation. George F. was reared to farm life and received his education in the private schools of the neighborhood. At the age of nineteen years he started out in life for himself, with no capital excepting that with which nature had endowed him. She had been more generous with him, however, than she has been with some of her children, so he was well equipped for the struggle that must come to every earnest and ambitious young man. By diligence and wise management he has become the owner of six hundred and fifty acres of fine farm land, two hundred and fifty of which are under cultivation. He has a large, convenient residence, and all the surroundings are indicative of prosperity. Mr. Sanders was married in 1883 to Mrs. Sallie (Lauderdale) McNeese, a native of Mississippi, and a daughter of Abner D. Lauderdale, a full history of whom will be found on another page of this volume. This union resulted in the birth of four children: Marion A., Frank, both of whom are deceased; Lizzie W. and Millie. Our subject was a soldier in the late war, enlisting in the Thirty-seventh Georgia regiment, volunteer infantry. He took part in many battles, the most important being Resaca, Lost Mountain, Peachtree Creek and Murfreesboro. Although he served until the war was ended, he was neither wounded nor promoted. He has always been a liberal supporter of all public enterprises, and has been one of the most forceful factors in the development of his county. He has been successful in his business, but it has been through the exercise of good judgment and energetic effort. He is kind, courteous and hospitable, and is greatly respected by the entire community.

John W. Sanders, M. D. In reviewing the early history of Carroll county, the name of Sanders is conspicuous among the pioneers as far back as the thirties. It was in that decade that William Sanders, grandfather of our subject, emigrated to Carroll county and embarked in the mercantile trade. He was a native of Tennessee, where his ancestors were pioneers. Dr. John Sanders, the father of John W., was born in Carroll county in 1834. He was a man of more than ordinary attainments, being well educated both from a literary and professional standpoint. He was married in this county to Miss Sallie Young, a daughter of Thomas Young and a sister of Mrs. Senator George, of this county. Dr. Sanders, Sr., died in 1867, and Mrs. Sanders was married a second time to Judge Cothran, a former circuit judge of this judicial district, who died while in office. He was a very prominent man in political life, and was a Mason of high order. Mrs. Cothran survives him and is a hale, well-preserved old lady. Dr. John W. Sanders was born in Carroll county, Miss., July 5, 1859, and is one of a family of two sons. His brother, Dr. M. S. Sanders, of Terrell, Tex., is also a practicing physician. Our subject passed his youth in the county of his birth, and received a fair education in Clinton, Miss. He was in the junior class when he dropped his literary studies and took up medicine. His uncle, Dr. J. A. Sanders, was his preceptor for the first year. He took his first course of lectures at Louisville, Ky., in 1878-9, and was graduated in the class of 1880. He then located in his native town and has since been actively engaged in the practice of his profession. He is a young man, full of energy, and ambitious not only to succeed, but to succeed well. He devotes his time and thought to his work, and has won a large and loyal patronage. In 1890 he bought a stock of drugs and druggists' notions, and is doing a large business in that line. The Doctor was united in marriage, December 26, 1881, to Miss Della Davis, a daughter of George Davis, deceased. Three children have been born to these parents: Sadie, Kittie and Malcolm. Dr. Sanders is a member of the State Medical society, and keeps well abreast of the times in all medical discoveries and professional improvements. The Doctor's wife and mother are both members of the Baptist church.

R. L. Saunders. Jackson, Miss., has long been recognized as an important center of distribution for staple and fancy groceries of all kinds, and this business was among the earliest of all the mercantile branches to be established in the city. Many of the grocery houses of Jackson, both at wholesale and retail, are of old establishment and employ large capital and the best resources and facilities for carrying on a large business. The only wholesale grocery house of Jackson is the Jackson Grocery company, of which R. L. Saunders is president, which business was established in March, 1889, the stock of goods being valued at $20,000. This important and representative house has steadily carried on business since its establishment, and its history has been one of continuous growth, and the rapid expansion of its patronage is the surest evidence of Mr. Saunders' ability, popularity and correct system of conducting business. Mr. Saunders is a native Mississippian, born in 1848, the youngest of three children born to J. C. and Susan (Hudson) Saunders, both of whom were born in Tennessee. The father removed to Mississippi and here died soon after the birth of his son, R. L. Saunders. The latter was reared and educated in Jackson; began the battle of life for himself as a clerk, and in 1863 enlisted in the Twentieth Confederate cavalry, which operated in Louisiana, Mississippi and Alabama, and surrendered at Gainesville in the latter state. Upon his return to Jackson he followed clerking until 1878, when he became a partner in the business, the firm taking the name of Robinson, Stevens & Co., of which he was an active member until March, 1889. At that time Mr. Saunders organized the Jackson Grocery company and has since been its efficient president. Mr. Saunders is also vice president of the Jackson bank; president of the Jackson Fertilizer company; president of the Light, Heat and Water Works company; is treasurer of the Mississippi Compress and Warehouse company; was an organizer and is now a director of the First National bank; in 1881 became a director of the Mississippi mills at Wesson, Miss., and is a trustee of the Deaf and Dumb institute. As a business man his record has been a very successful one, and by his own efforts he has succeeded in accumulating a handsome competency. He was married in 1878 to Miss Annie M. Robinson, a native of Mississippi and a daughter of John W. Robinson, who was born in New York and came to Mississippi at an early day, becoming one of the foremost merchants of this section. To Mr. and Mrs. Saunders the following children have been born: Mattie, Annie (who died at the age of four years), Robert L., Frank (a daughter), John W., Marion P. and Mary J. The family worship in the Episcopal church, in which Mr. Saunders is an active worker. He is president of the board of trustees of the church property of the state, and is treasurer and vestryman of the church in Jackson. In 1890 he was appointed by President Harrison one of the commissioners of the World's Fair.

Phineas M. Savery, attorney at law, real estate and general insurance agent, is the senior member of the firm of P. M. & F. M. Savery, one of the most successful insurance agencies in the state. He is a native of New England, born in Massachusetts, July 30, 1830, a son of Dr. Phineas and Nancy (Messinger) Savery, natives of the same state. The said Dr. Phineas Savery was a leading physician of Attleboro, Mass., and a son of Phineas Savery who was born April 8, 1757, and married Hannah Swift in 1796. Samuel Savery, born August 18, 1718, was the father of the first Phineas Savery. They were of French descent. The father of our subject died in Massachusetts, and the mother died when he was an infant. He was reared and educated in his native state, receiving a practical business training. At the age of sixteen years he went to New York city, and thence to Mexico. In 1851 he returned to the United States, and settled in Clay county, Mo. He was employed as a clerk until 1853, when he was married to Miss Amanda G., the eldest daughter of Henry F. Mitchell, a native of Maryland, and a leading attorney of the state of Missouri. Soon after marriage Mr. Savery took up the study of law, and was admitted to the bar in 1858. When the war broke out between the North and the South, he joined the state troops, in which service he attained the rank of colonel, as provost-marshal-general of the state. In 1862 he entered the service of the Confederate States as captain of cavalry; was for a short time a major, as provost-marshal-general of army of the West and trans-Mississippi department, then resumed his place as captain of the Western rangers, a company of Missourians who went into service in May, 1861, and remained until the final surrender. After the fall of Vicksburg this company was consolidated with the Second Missouri cavalry, and was known as company C, of that regiment. In 1865 Mr. Savery resided in Memphis engaged as clerk and special collector. In 1866 he moved to Baldwyn, Miss., and went into business as commercial representative in Mississippi of University Publishing company of New York for a short time, then commenced the practice of law. In 1868 he entered into the life insurance business and in 1870 that of fire, since which time he has made insurance a specialty and confined his law practice to collection of claims. He moved to Tupelo in 1888, and still resides there, representing eighteen of the leading insurance companies of the United States. Mr. Savery takes great interest in societies and fraternities. As a Mason he has filled the highest office in each of the several grand bodies of Ancient York Masonry in Mississippi and is a member of Royal Solomon lodge at Jerusalem. He belongs to the Independent Order of Odd Fellows, Knights of Pythias, Knights of Honor, Knights of Golden Rule, etc., in each of which orders he has been highly honored. Mr. and Mrs. Savery are the parents of three children now living: Charles V., Finnie M. and Mary A. F. F. M. Savery is a partner in his father's business of insurance and real estate. One son, James M., died at the age of twenty-three years. Politically Mr. Savery and sons adhere to the principles of the democratic party. He and his wife and daughter are members of the Christian church or Church of the Disciples.

Capt. W. H. Scales, merchant of Macon, Miss. As a man of business Mr. Scales' reputation has been an enviable one, and every step of his financial and commercial career has been illustrated with acts of liberality and kindness. He was born in Williamson county, Tenn., in February, 1840, to Dr. N. F. and M. A. (Webb) Scales, natives of the Old North state, who emigrated with their parents to Tennessee when the country was in a wild and unsettled condition. The paternal grandfather, John Scales, became a well-known citizen of Williamson county, where he followed the life of a planter until his death. Dr. N. F. Scales graduated from the Louisville Medical college and for some time practiced his profession in Tennessee but in 1845 removed to Lowndes county, Miss., and located at Prairie Hill, where, in addition to practicing medicine, he carried on planting and merchandising successfully. He subsequently removed to Crawford, Miss., where he died in 1884, his wife's death occurring at the same place many years earlier, or in 1868. He was a man who commanded respect and esteem from all who knew him, and professionally was one of the foremost practitioners of the county. He and his wife became the parents of thirteen children, eight of whom are living: Mrs. E. Hosford, of Jackson, Tenn.; William H., of Macon; Thomas S., of Mobile, Ala.; Walter W. and Mrs. C. E. Gay, of Starkville; Samuel S., of Crawford; Noah, of Macon; and Charles M., of Macon. After the death of the mother of these children the father took for his second wife Mrs. Brooks, by whom he became the father of three children: Ella, Mattie L. and Ewell. Three sons served in the Confederate army during the war: W. H., Dr. T. S. and W. W. Capt. William H. Scales was reared in Lowndes county, Miss., and received his education in private schools. He was reared to a mercantile life at Crawford, but upon the bursting of the war cloud in 1861, he at once became a member of company C, First Arkansas infantry, under Fagan, enlisting from Camden, Ark., to which place he had gone in 1860 and opened a mercantile establishment. He entered the service as a lieutenant, but after the battle of Shiloh he was promoted to a captaincy. He was at the battles of Manassas, Perryville, Murfreesboro, Chickamauga and was also in all of the Georgia campaign, under Gen. J. E. Johnston, the battles of Spring Hill and Franklin, Tenn., and Bentonville, N. C. He was slightly wounded at Murfreesboro, and Franklin. After the surrender he returned to Mississippi, and began merchandising at Crawford, removing to West Point in 1872, and in 1878 to Mobile, Ala. In this city he was a successful cotton factor until 1888, when he became a resident of Macon, Miss., where he has since made his home, with the exception of two seasons, which were spent at West Point in purchasing cotton. He is interested in a large mercantile establishment in Macon, established by his brother Noah, and owing to the honorable business methods they have always practiced and to their desire to please their patrons, they have built up a paying trade. He is also largely interested in planting, and in connection with his brother is cultivating about twelve hundred acres of their own lands in Noxubee county. Captain Scales was married, in 1861, to Miss Sallie Flowers, of Arkansas, by whom he has four children: William

F., Lucius M., Anna E. and Mamie F. He and his wife are members of the Methodist Episcopal church, and with this church he has been prominently identified for many years. To show the extent of his mercantile operations, it is but necessary to state that he is a member of the firm of W. W. Scales & Co., of Starkville, Miss., and of S. S. Scales & Co., of Crawford, Miss., besides his business at Macon.

Thomas M. Scanlan, Newton, Miss. Edward Scanlan, deceased, was born in Cecil county, Md., about the year 1816. When he was four years of age his parents removed to Philadelphia, Penn., where he lived until the age of sixteen. He then went to Port Gibson, Miss., and in the year 1835 he located at the town of Union, the site of which was at that time in the northern part of Newton county; he embarked in mercantile pursuits, and continued there and in Decatur for ten or twelve years. He then removed to a point within a few miles of the present site of Newton, where he engaged in planting. He was a devout Roman Catholic, and politically he was identified with the Whig party. He took an active interest in all public questions, but would not accept a public office. He married Miss Sarah, daughter of Wellington Blalack, one of the pioneer settlers of Newton county. Of this union nine children were born, five of whom are still living. Edward Scanlan's father, Dr. James Scanlan, was a native of Maryland and a well-known planter and physician of Cecil county. He was largely interested in real estate in Pittsburgh, Penn., and Charlottesville, Va., and was a successful dealer. Thomas M. Scanlan, the subject of this notice, is the son of Edward and Sarah (Blalack) Scanlan. He was born in Newton county, Miss., in 1845, and grew to maturity in the county of his birth. He was reared to the occupation of a farmer, and attended the common schools of that day. Although they had not then reached their present advanced state, he acquired a practical knowledge which fitted him for all the duties which have fallen to his lot. At the tender age of sixteen years he entered upon the arduous labors of a soldier's life, enlisting in the Thirteenth Mississippi volunteer infantry, and served from 1861 until the battle of Gettysburg; in that engagement he was wounded and captured. He was afterward paroled, and returned to his home. After the war he resumed his mercantile interests, and has since been connected with that line of business. He has a general store at Newton, and does an extensive business. He is a member of the Knights of Pythias, and also of the Knights of Honor, belonging to the lodges at Newton. He is an active member of the Presbyterian church, giving a liberal and hearty support to all its efforts in the cause of the Master. Mr. Scanlan was united in marriage, in 1872, to Miss Bettie Murphy, of Macon, Miss. This union has been blessed by the birth of eight children, seven of whom are still living.

Hon. Isaac W. Scarborough is an able attorney of Kosciusko, Miss. He was born near Tarboro, Edgecombe county, N. C., April 17, 1816, his father, John R. Scarborough, being a native of the same state and county, and his grandfather, a native of Wales. The latter immigrated to the states at an early day, and settled in North Carolina, afterward serving with distinction in the Revolutionary war, holding the rank of major. He and a brother, William S., who settled in New York, are said to be the ancestors of all of that name in the United States. John R. was reared to manhood in North Carolina, and was married there to Miss Nancy M. Watkins, a native of Nash county, N. C., and in 1832 moved with his family to Alabama, where he made his home for several years. In 1838 he moved to Mississippi, and settled in Attala county, locating on the Big Black river, where he opened a large plantation, and resided until his death, January 30, 1846. His widow survived him until October, 1847, when she was called from life. Isaac W. Scarborough spent his youth in his native state and Alabama, receiving a fair education in Greene county of the latter state. After becoming sufficiently qualified, he began teaching school in Alabama, but in February, 1839, came to Mississippi, and for three years was engaged in merchandising, near the present town of Durant. In 1844 he removed to Kosciusko, which was then a village of about two hundred people, and here sold goods for several years. In November, 1847, he was elected to the position of probate clerk, in which capacity he served by re-election for over eleven years, and during this time showed an aptitude for the position which the citizens of the county were not slow to recognize. In 1862 his numerous friends elected him to the position of probate judge, and he served until removed by order of the government, in 1868. Prior to this, Mr. Scarborough had been a close student of law, and in 1869 he was admitted to the bar, and until a short time since when he retired he practiced his profession with great success. Of late years he has been devoting his attention to planting, and has now a good plantation near the town, which, when he settled here, was covered with a heavy growth of timber. He married in Attala county, in 1848, Miss Lucy J. Harrison, a daughter of John E. Harrison, a pioneer of this state, from Virginia. Mrs. Scarborough was born and reared in Orange county, Va., and has borne her husband twelve children: Otis W., an attorney of Arkansas; Othello C., a physician of that state; Fenton G., wife of J. W. Fletcher, a druggist of Batesville, Ark.; Isaac W., Jr., a dentist of Nashville, Tenn., and Lucy Lee, a young lady at home. Six children died in infancy, and Sule Sims died April 22, 1884, at the age of twenty-one years. Judge Scarborough and his family are members of the Methodist Episcopal church, in which he is steward and trustee, having held these positions since joining the church in 1855. He attends all district conferences as a delegate, and is very active in church work. In 1847 he became a member of the A. F. & A. M., and is now a Knight Templar, serving as master and high priest. He has been a delegate to all the grand lodges of the state since 1849, and has always been a very enthusiastic Mason. He has always been an exemplary citizen, and is highly honored by his neighbors and friends as one of the finest and most useful citizens of the county.

John W. Scarborough, M. D., is an eminent, skillful and experienced physician and surgeon of Kosciusko, Miss., and although he has resided in Attala county, Miss., since 1838, he was born in Edgecombe county of the Old North state in March, 1821. He is a son of John R. and Nancy M. (Watkins) Scarborough, for a sketch of whom see biography of Hon. Isaac W. Scarborough. Dr. John W. Scarborough attained manhood in Attala county, and with his father followed the calling of a planter. He was given the advantages of the schools of Carroll and Attala counties, and was also instructed by private tutors. He began the study of medicine with Dr. Bates, and took his first course of lectures at New Orleans in 1843-4, after which he practiced in Attala county, and again attended lectures during the winter of 1844-5, finishing the course in the spring of the latter year. After practicing until 1848 he entered the St. Louis Medical college, from which he graduated in the class of 1849, and has since been an active and highly successful medical practitioner of Kosciusko, and is the oldest resident physician of the place. He has served in the capacity of county physician, and as he has devoted the greater part of his life to healing the sick, and has met with the best of success, he has received a portion of his reward in this world, for he has the confidence, respect and love of his fellowmen, and the consciousness that he has driven sorrow and despair from many homes by his skill and talent as a physician. He has been married three times, first in Attala county in 1842 to Mrs. McCarter, who died a few weeks after their marriage. He next married Miss Martha E. Hanson, who died in 1873, and his third union was consummated in Kosciusko, his wife being Mrs. (Campbell) Nash, a sister of Judge Nash. The Doctor is a member of the

Methodist Episcopal church, but his wife is a Presbyterian. He belongs to the A. F. & A. M., in which he has attained to the chapter.

Emile Schaefer, Yazoo City, Miss., was born in Hanover, Germany, February 24, 1839, and is a son of Philip and Hannah (Benham) Schaefer. When he was a child his parents emigrated to America, and located in Biloxi, Harrison county, Miss. The father was educated in Germany, and received that thorough mental training for which the German nation is justly noted. All his life he has been engaged in mercantile pursuits, and has been fairly successful. He is still a resident of Biloxi, where he is an honored and respected citizen. Emile was reared in this place, and received his education there and in the city of New Orleans. When he was fourteen years of age he accepted a position as office boy in New Orleans, and was soon promoted with an increase of salary. In 1858 he went into business with his father, the partnership continuing until the war. He then enlisted in company A, Third Mississippi volunteer infantry, and served through the entire conflict. After peace was declared he came to Yazoo City, where he became an active member of commercial circles. He embarked in the dry goods trade, and by the exercise of excellent judgment he rapidly accumulated a comfortable fortune. In 1883 he disposed of these interests, and began planting, in which he has met with equal success. In 1886 he invested in the Yazoo Oil works, being elected treasurer of the corporation; these duties he has discharged faithfully and efficiently ever since. He owns about fifteen hundred acres of land in the Yazoo delta, and makes about two hundred and fifty bales of cotton annually. Politically he affiliates with the democratic party, of which he is one of the leaders in Yazoo county. He was a member of the city council for several terms, and was chairman of the democratic county committee; he served on the board of supervisors for two terms, and in all these positions he has proven himself worthy of the confidence reposed in him. He is a Mason of high standing, and has been Master of his lodge for years. He belongs to the I. O. O. F., and has filled some of its most important offices, among them those of grand high priest and deputy grand master of the grand lodge of Mississippi, I. O. O. F., as well as K. of H. In social, political and commercial circles he has been honored with positions of trust. Mr. Schaefer was married in 1860 to Caroline Weinschenk, a native of Louisiana, and a daughter of Solomon Weinschenk, who was born in Germany. She died in 1873, leaving five children: Valerie, Stella, Florence, Elvine and Cuthbert; three are married and live in Vicksburg and Hazlehurst, Miss. In 1877 Mr. Schaefer was married again to Julia Marx, who was born in Germany. This union resulted in the birth of four children: Marx, Hilda, Adeline and Solomon.

Chancellor Charles Scott was born in Knoxville, Tenn., on November 12, 1811. He was a descendant of a Virginia family noted for its production of many distinguished soldiers and eminent statesmen. He first began the practice of law in Nashville, Tenn., where he married and soon afterward removed to Jackson, Miss., and there pursued his profession in copartnership with George S. Yerger, who had married his sister. This firm was eminently successful, and enjoyed distinguished reputation; and the ability and stanch integrity of Charles Scott, together with his high sense of honor and amiability of character, commended him so highly to the people, that in a few years he was elected to the office of chancellor of Mississippi, and long presided over the superior court of chancery with great ability, and with the universal commendation of both bar and people. It was he who first rendered the decree in the great case of Johnson vs. the state of Mississippi, establishing the liability of the state for the payment of the bonds of the Union bank, that case having been first instituted in the chancery court; and notwithstanding that the popular sensibilities were adverse to the result, the ability, purity and sincere integrity which characterized his decision caused it to be generally received as a satisfactory emanation of conscientious duty. It was affirmed by the high court of errors and appeals. In 1859 Chancellor Scott removed to Memphis, Tenn., where he conceived a broader and more prolific field was presented to the practice of his profession, which he there entered upon with the opening prospects of a brilliant career, but so soon as the clouds of the war began to gather along the horizon he returned, in 1861, to Jackson, Miss., determined to cast his lot with his adopted state in the impending struggle. He had been a devoted friend of the Union, but when Mississippi seceded he promptly yielded to the demands of duty, and his heart and hand became warmly enlisted in her cause. He lived, however, but a short time after his return to Jackson, where he died, and was buried by his beloved brethren of the Masonic fraternity. Chancellor Scott was a most devoted Mason, and as such had a national reputation. He was for many years master of Silas Brown lodge, in Jackson, and afterward was grand master of the grand lodge of Mississippi. Chancellor Scott was not only an ardent, thorough student of the law, but he was also a ripe classical scholar, and was familiar with the standard poets and writers of modern times, particularly surpassing most of his contemporaries in his knowledge of that greatest of all modern poets, Shakespeare. His researches had even extended farther, and much of his time was devoted to sacred writers, while his knowledge of the Bible was thorough and extensive. His studies in this direction had convinced him of all the truths of religion, and he was an exemplary Christian. This sentiment pervaded his whole nature, and quickened a tender conscientiousness and amiability, which not only rendered him an ornament to society, but especially fitted him for the high office of chancellor. He was a man of noble candor and knightly courtesy, gentle and affable in his manners, devoted to his friends, unwearied in the performance of duty, and unswerving in fidelity to his high trust. A bright Mason, he cherished the virtue of charity; a cultivated lawyer, he loved the principles of justice; an able and upright judge, he promulgated the purest doctrines of equity, and a good man, his heart flowed in sympathy and generosity toward his fellowmen. Many of his comrades and friends are still living in Mississippi, and cherish his memory with sincere affection.

E. M. Scott, general manager of the Rosedale Grocery and Commission company, is a native of Jackson, Miss., born in 1842, and a son of Hon. Charles Scott (see sketch). He was educated in his native state and the University of Nashville, leaving the latter institution to enter the Confederate army in the spring of 1861. He enlisted in company K, Eighteenth Mississippi regiment, and was in the battles of Manassas, Ball's Bluff and Richmond. He was subsequently promoted and ordered to the western army as aid-de-camp to Gen. David W. Adams' Louisiana brigade, army of Tennessee. He was in the battles of Perryville, Murfreesboro, Chickamauga, and later in northern Alabama, where he participated in the New Hope Church battle and the Selma engagement. At the time of the surrender he was at Jackson, Miss., and after this he went to Vicksburg, where he clerked in the Prentiss hotel for fifteen months. He then went to Jackson, and was in Hotel Edwards for three years. In 1874 he embarked in merchandising, continuing at this in Jackson until 1887, when he came to Rosedale and carried on the same business until January 1, 1891, when he became manager for the Rosedale Grocery and Commission company, a large mercantile corporation of that town, of which his brother, Charles Scott, is president. The value of the stock is $30,000 and the store is one of the largest in the delta, if not in the county. Mr. Scott has been twice married, first, in 1867, to Miss Josephine Julienne, of Jackson, Miss., and daughter of Louis Julienne, an old resident of the latter place. Mrs. Scott died in 1874, leaving three children: Julienne, Charles and Edward M., Jr. Mr. Scott's second marriage was to Miss Eula Buckner, of this state, by whom he became the father of five children: Laura, Lizzie, Frank, Ida and Malcomb. Mr. and Mrs. Scott are members of the Catholic church. Mr. Scott predicts a prosperous future for Rosedale. He has chosen this city as his permanent home, and in 1890 erected one of the finest residences here.

George Y. Scott, sheriff of Bolivar county, Miss., is a painstaking, capable and zealous official, and is well qualified for the position, not only on account of his sound judgment but for his self-command and coolness in personal danger. He was born in Jackson, Miss., in 1845, the second of seven children born to Charles and Elizabeth M. (Bullus) Scott, for a sketch of whom see sketch of Hon. Charles Scott. In his native city George Y. was reared, but also spent a considerable portion of his youth in Memphis, Tenn., and received his education in the Nashville military college, which institution he left to enter the Confederate army at the early age of sixteen years. He served for two years as a private in company K, Wirt Adams' cavalry regiment, and was in the bloody battles of Shiloh, Bear Creek and Jackson, besides numerous sharp minor engagements and skirmishes. When Colonel Adams was made brigadier-general, Mr. Scott was promoted to first lieutenant and served throughout the remainder of the war as his aid-de-camp, and was afterward with Johnston and Hood until the close of the war, and at the time of General Lee's surrender he was at Gainesville, Ala. Mr. Scott immediately returned to Jackson, Miss., but soon after located in Vicksburg, as a clerk in the postoffice, where he remained for two years. At the end of this time he determined to try a different line of work, and with this end in view moved to Washington county, Miss., and engaged in planting on Deer creek. In 1870 he began the study of law in the office of Nugent & Yerger, at Greenville, and was admitted to the bar at Memphis, Tenn., and began the practice of his profession in Bolivar county, where he located in 1871. Two years later he formed a partnership with his brother Charles, with whom he remained associated until 1881. Two years later he was elected sheriff and tax collector of Bolivar county, and so ably in every way did he discharge the duties of this position that he was re-elected to the position in 1885-7 and 1889, which fact speaks volumes as to his popularity. He is interested in all measures of reform, and every movement for the improvement of the county or for the benefit of mankind finds in him a hearty and willing supporter. In 1873 Miss Lettie M. Baldwin of this county became his wife, and their union has resulted in the birth of a daughter, Annie B. Mrs. Scott is a daughter of George C. Baldwin, of Natchez, he, as well as his wife, being an early resident of Mississippi, his wife being a sister of Gov. Charles Clarke of this state. Mrs. Scott is an intelligent and amiable lady, is a kind and devoted wife and mother, and is an earnest member of the Methodist Episcopal church. Mr. Scott is a member of the A. F. & A. M., the Knights of Pythias and the Knights of Honor. In 1872, in connection with his brother Charles, he built the first land office and was the first lawyer of Rosedale, and the reputation he has gained as an attorney has been acquired largely through his own individual efforts, and at the expense of diligent study and hard practical experience. He erected him a pleasant and comfortable residence in 1886, an excellent two-story brick store in 1888, and in 1890 a two-story frame store building. He is one of the stockholders in the Bank of Rosedale and also of the Rosedale Grocery and Commission company. Mr. Scott is of a very practical turn of mind, and his career from an humble beginning in life to the present position which he occupies has been one of honor and reflects great credit upon him. In 1891 Mr. Scott received the democratic nomination for state senator from Bolivar county. The nomination being equivalent to election, it is reasonable to suppose that he will serve his county for the next four years as senator.

Hon. Charles Scott, lawyer and planter, Rosedale, Miss., is a native of the Bayou state, born in Jackson in 1847, and is the son of Hon. Charles Scott, who was chancellor of the state for many years (see sketch). Mr. Scott attended school until fourteen years of age and then, though under age, entered the Confederate army, in which he served gallantly until the close of the war. He was in the Washington cavalry, under Capt. W. E. Hunt, and participated in the battles of Franklin, Nashville, Jackson, Miss., and was at Gainesville, Ala., with General Johnston's army at the time of the surrender. He subsequently resided at Vicksburg, Miss., for one year, after which he came to Washington county of that state, located at Deer Creek, and there, in connection with planting, he read law. In 1868 he was admitted to the bar and on the 3d of June of the following year he came to Bolivar county, with whose interests he has been closely identified since. He first located at Beulah, but when the county seat was removed to Rosedale he became a resident of that city. Mr. Scott is not only a most eminent lawyer, but is one of the South's greatest planters and land owners. He has fourteen thousand acres in this county, the best in the delta, and has four thousand acres under cultivation. He owns vast tracts in different localities, embracing all kinds and qualities, both wild and improved, timber and grazing, and is the owner of Rosedale, Triumph, and other plantations, on which he has made many improvements. In 1885 he opened a store, organized a stock company, Rosedale Grocery and Commission company, with a paid-up capital of $30,000, and is president of this. He also held the position of president of the levee board of commissioners for two years, and as this board had the disposition of over $250,000 per annum, the position of president was naturally an important and responsible one. Mr. Scott is now president of the Mississippi Central Valley Railroad company, which is just now opening the road from Rosedale to Grenada, and he is chief stockholder in the hotel at the former place. On the organization of the Bank of Rosedale at that place, in 1889, he was made president. This bank has a paid up capital of $50,000 and a surplus of $10,000. No man has done more to advance the interests of this town and county than Mr. Scott, who is essentially a modern man, full of energy, enterprise and push, who by his own individual efforts has gained the proud position he now occupies. He ranks among the ablest and most distinguished jurists in the state, practicing in all the Federal and state courts, having carried to a successful issue many noted, important and complicated cases, and is very popular with both bench and bar. His practice is very extensive and is largely confined to important litigations involving large interests. He is the attorney for the Louisville, New Orleans & Texas railway company in Bolivar county. On the 26th of April, 1890, a convention of citizens from Arkansas, Illinois, Kansas, Kentucky, Louisiana, Mississippi and Tennessee, was convened at Vicksburg, Miss., for the purpose of considering the question of the improvement of the navigation of the Mississippi river and to endorse the levee system for protection from inundation. This convention formed itself into a permanent inter-state Mississippi River Improvement and Levee association, auxiliary to the Western Waterways association, and Mr. Scott, of Rosedale, was elected chairman of the association. On the 10th of March, 1870, Mr. Scott was married to Miss Malvina Yerger, daughter of Alexander Yerger (deceased), who was of Washington county, and by this union has four children: Alexander Y. (student at the University of the South), Lizzie, Malvina and Charlie.

Prominent among the eminent and very successful attorneys of Friar's Point stands the name of D. A. Scott, who was born in Jackson, Miss., in the year 1852, and whose father, Chancellor Charles Scott, was an esteemed and respected citizen of Jackson, Miss. (see sketch). D. A. Scott was liberally educated at Bay St. Louis and at other places in Mississippi, studied law in the office of his brother, Charles, at Rosedale, and was admitted to the bar at that place in 1872. Later he came to Friar's Point, and has been engaged in the active practice of his profession since. He is the attorney for the Louisville, New Orleans & Texas railroad, and the Western Union Telegraph company for Coahoma county. In 1890 Mr. Scott was the main organizer of the Bank of Friar's Point, and is president of the same at the present time. This bank has a paid-up capital of $50,000 and a fair surplus. He is also one of the organizers of the Friar's Point Oilmill, and holds the position of vice president of the same. He assisted in organizing the Friar's Point Box and Woodwork factory, of which he is treasurer, and he is president of the Friar's Point Land, Loan and Improvement company, an organization for town development and improvement, which is doing good work for Friar's Point. Mr. Scott takes an active and leading part in politics, is an active worker for the democratic party, but is not an officeseeker. His marriage occurred in 1874 to Miss Maria Lou Yerger, a native of Washington county, Miss., and the daughter of Col. Alexander Yerger, a prominent legal practitioner. The result of this union was the birth of five children: Nettie M., Charline, Elizabeth B., Daniel A., Jr., and Anna Louise. The family are members of the Episcopal church. At the present time Mr. Scott is engaged in erecting a large residence at a cost of about $8,000, and when finished it will be one of the finest in the county. He is also the owner of about five thousand acres of wild land. Mr. Scott's practice is very large, one of the largest in the state, and although he started with limited means he wields a remarkable influence, and to-day a review of his career demonstrates him to be an individual much above the ordinary. He is a leading spirit in all enterprises that have for their object the good of the county. In fact, he is among the foremost in every commendable enterprise. In personal appearance Mr. Scott bears a strong resemblance to a brother in Bolivar county, being rather slender and with dark hair and eyes, and his pleasing social qualities and courteous manners make him a pleasant companion and friend. He is a member of the Masonic and Knights of Pythias societies.

Frank M. Scott, planter, Rosedale, Miss., son of Chancellor Charles Scott and Elizabeth (Bullus) Scott (see sketch), was originally from Tennessee, his birth occurring in Memphis in 1859. He was educated in the University of Virginia and from 1878 until 1881 he was engaged as clerk in the office of his brother, Charles Scott, of Rosedale. During the fall of the last named year he entered the law department of the Oxford university, at Oxford, Miss., graduated from that institution in the summer of 1882, and at once entered upon the practice of his profession at Rosedale in partnership with Walter Sillers. In 1886 he was united in marriage to Miss Pearl Kirk, daughter of John C. Kirk, who located in Madison county, Miss., at an early date and who moved to Bolivar county in 1841. He located opposite the mouth of White river, on a large tract of land, made many improvements, and soon cleared two thousand acres. In character he was generous and wholesouled and straightforward to a marked degree. He died in 1887, when seventy-five years of age, leaving a widow and four children—two sons and two daughters: John M. (planter near Gunnison, Miss.), Pearl K., Albert L. and Anita (attending school at Columbia, Tenn.). Mrs. Kirk recently completed one of the handsomest residences in Rosedale. Mr. Scott owns two plantations, embracing eight hundred and fifty acres, with four hundred and sixty acres cleared, and this, with Mrs. Kirk's plantation, which he rents, he is engaged in cultivating—about one thousand acres in all. He and Mrs. Scott are members of the Episcopal church. Mr. Scott was left an orphan at an early age, and during his youth was cared for and later educated by his brother Charles. Since then he has most successfully carved his way in life and although he might easily have risen in the legal profession, he preferred to follow the ever-promising pursuit of planting, which occupation now occupies his attention wholly. A family likeness runs through the Scott family, and our subject not only resembles his brothers but also the fine picture of Chancellor Scott, seen in the office of Charles Scott. Mr. Scott is about the average hight, well-knit frame, dark hair and brown eyes, an intellectual forehead, and is distinguished looking. His personal appearance is greatly enhanced by a generous hospitality, courteous and amiable disposition.

N. B. Scott, lawyer, Rosedale, Miss., the third of five children born to William Parker and Fanny May (Bibb) Scott, owes his nativity to Yazoo county, Miss., his birth occurring on the 14th day of July, 1861. He is a nephew of Chancellor Charles Scott (see sketch), and his paternal grandparents were Edward and Sallie (Corde) Scott. On his mother's side Mr. Scott is a descendant of Stephen and Jennie (Eaton) Haynes, who prior to the Revolutionary war settled in Halifax county, N. C. They were wealthy and influential people. One of their daughters, Jennie Eaton Haynes, married Clement Wood about the close of the Revolution, and their daughter, Fanny Mayes Wood, married David Mason Dancy. One of the latter's daughters, Martha Haynes Dancy, graduated at Warrenton Female academy, North Carolina, and won the gold medal for scholarship in November, 1821. She moved with her parents to Mooresville, Limestone county, Ala., in 1821, where she married Dr. Joseph Wyatt Bibb, a native of Virginia and a very successful physician. Dr. Joseph Wyatt Bibb was a brother of William Wyatt Bibb, who was born in Virginia and removed to Georgia, where he was successively a member of the two branches of the legislature of Georgia and was a member of congress from 1807 till 1813, when he was chosen to the United States senate and retained his seat there till 1816. He removed to Alabama, then a territory, and was governor from 1817 to 1819, when it was admitted as a state and he was elected as its first executive. He died in July, 1820, and Thomas Bibb (another brother of Dr. Joseph Wyatt Bibb), who was then president of the Alabama senate, by virtue of his office became governor. He continued in office until 1821. Dr. Joseph Wyatt Bibb and wife were the grandparents of N. B. Scott. Their only daughter (Fanny May Bibb, mother of N. B. Scott), was born on the 6th day of October, 1827, at Mooresville, Limestone county, Ala. She married Rev. William Parker Scott, a native of Tennessee, and brother of Chancellor Charles Scott. Rev. William Parker Scott was an Episcopalian priest, and was ordained August 14, 1853. He lived in Yazoo county, Miss., at the time of his death, on November 9, 1865. He was educated at Knoxville, Tenn., and was rector of the church in Yazoo City, Miss., at the time of his death. His wife died April 14, 1868. N. B. Scott, the subject of this sketch, was educated in Alabama, studied law in the office of his cousin, Charles Scott, in Rosedale, Miss., and was admitted to the bar April 3, 1886. He married Miss Elizabeth Thomas, a native of Bolivar county, Miss., and daughter of Oscar D. Thomas and Mary (Yerger) Thomas. Mrs. Scott is a worthy member of the Episcopal church. Mr. Scott is practicing law in Rosedale, Miss.

Fourteen years devoted to the service of humanity sums up in a line the career, thus far, of Dr. S. A. Scruggs, who is one of the most successful and best known physicians of this section. The people of Lauderdale, as well as the surrounding counties, are familiar with his name, for twelve years of his professional career have been spent among them. He was born in Livingston, Sumter county, Ala., the sixth of nine children born to Josiah L. and Temperance (Arrington) Scruggs, the former of whom was born in Buckingham county, Va., and the latter in North Carolina. They both grew to maturity and attained their majority before coming to Alabama, where they married and spent the remainder of their lives. Josiah L. Scruggs was for many years in the drug business at Livingston, Ala. He died in

March, 1891, his wife having passed from life in 1875, both being worthy members of the Methodist Episcopal Church South. Dr. S. A. Scruggs was reared in Sumter county, Ala., and received a practical and thorough education in the common schools. He attended lectures at New Orleans during the winters of 1875, 1876 and 1877, and graduated in March of the latter year. He entered upon his practice in Natchitoches parish, La., but a few months later returned to his old home in Sumter county, Ala., where he remained until 1879, since which time he has been a resident of Lauderdale, Miss. Here his name has become a household world, for he has entered nearly every home in the town in his professional capacity, and where he has once been called, has been called again in case of need. Although his practice has always been a lucrative one, he conducts, in connection with it, a well-appointed drug store, which, under his able management, is proving a profitable source of revenue. He owns residence and business property in the town, and promises in time to win a handsome competency from his profession. Socially he belongs to the A. F. & A. M. and the K. of H., and while he is not a member of any church his wife is an esteemed member of the Episcopal church. He was married in Livingston, Ala., in 1882 to Miss Swassie Smith, a daughter of John T. Smith, and their union has resulted in the birth of three children: Ella Smith, Erma and Samuel A.

Wallace B. Scurr, Torrance, Miss., is one of the leading planters and stockgrowers of Yalobusha county. He was born in this county in 1840, and is a son of John L. and Lydia (Bray) Scurr. The parents were born in North Carolina, the father in 1806, and the mother in 1808; they were reared and married in their native state, and in 1837 they came to Mississippi, settling in the same place where our subject now resides. The father died there in 1867; he was an earnest worker in the Methodist Episcopal church, of which he was a steward for a number of years. In his political opinions he sided with the Whig party, and clung to the Union until his own state seceded, when he went out with it. The mother died in 1877; she was a member of the same church, where she did active and zealous service in the cause of her Master. She had born to her six children—four sons and two daughters—all of whom but one lived to maturity: Elizabeth died at the age of twelve years; Susan married Cornelius Moore, but is now deceased; Benjamin died in 1861 (he was a member of the Fifteenth Mississippi volunteer infantry, company G); Thomas died of wounds received in the war, July 27, 1864 (he was also a member of the Fifteenth Mississippi regiment); John W. is a resident of Sunflower county (he was a member of the Fifteenth Mississippi, and was wounded while in the service); Wallace B. is the fifth child; he was reared on the place where he now resides, and sleeps in the same room in which he was born. He passed his youth in the ordinary fashion of planters' sons, attending the common schools of the neighborhood; he also attended Bascom's college, a Methodist institution at Trenton, Tenn. In 1866 he started out in life upon his own responsibility, locating at Hillside Place on Holmes creek. He devoted his time to the cultivation of his farm until 1873, when he returned to the home place. He was married in 1863, to Miss Lydia M. Cook, who was born in Hinds county, Miss., in 1842, a daughter of McKinney L. Cook. Her father was a native of North Carolina, and removed to Mississippi in 1836 or 1837. Her mother's maiden name was Jeanette Scott Winters, and she was born in South Carolina; to her nine children were born: Mrs. W. D. Smith, Mrs. Z. Wordlaw, Mrs. W. T. Ratliff and William A.; those deceased are, David T., J. W., McKinney L., Alice. Mrs. Scurr was born in Hinds county, and to her were born nine children: Wallace B., Jr., John L., Edmond D., Winter S., Thomas, McWillie, and Esme; Jennie M. and Benjamin died in their childhood. Mr. Scurr entered the Fifteenth Mississippi volunteer infantry, company G, in 1861, and served until the surrender, excepting the time he was disabled. He was taken prisoner February 21, 1862, and was held seven weeks. He was in the hospital during this time, and was again captured in Mississippi; but was soon released, however, on account of his wounds. He was at the bombardment of Vicksburg, and during the latter part of the war served in the commissary department, his headquarters being at Grenada. While not taking an active part in politics, he does not fail of his duty to exercise the right of suffrage, voting with the democratic party. He is a member of the board of supervisors from district No. 4, and takes an active interest in the public schools, and is a liberal supporter of all movements having for their object the upbuilding of the community. He is the owner of one thousand and forty acres of land, as fine as can be found within the borders of the county, and is a man of deep integrity of character, and has the profound respect of all who know him.

Col. Roderick Seal, Mississippi City, Miss., is one of the oldest residents along the gulf. He was born in Richmond county, N. C., December 31, 1817, and is a son of Jacob and Catherine (Nicholson) Seal, also natives of North Carolina. The father was a planter, and removed to Mississippi at an early day. He first settled in Greene county, and came thence to Hancock county, where he passed the remainder of his days. He was ninety years old at the time of his death, and was in full possession of all his mental faculties; he could see to read without the use of glasses, and was quite active. He was a colonel of the state militia for many years, and served in the War of 1812. He reared a family of three sons and five daughters, five of whom survive: Roderick, Mrs. Boardman, Christian, Mrs. Patsey Boardman and Capt. D. B. Colonel Seal left home when he was eighteen years of age, and went to Bay St. Louis. In 1838 he was appointed deputy clerk of Hancock county, and during the time that he held this position he devoted all his leisure time to the study of law. In November, 1839, he was elected county clerk of Hancock county, and held that office continously eight years. In the meantime he engaged in the practice of law. The profession was not crowded at that day, and there was a wide field for his labors. He was elected to the legislature in 1850, and served one term. He had settled in Biloxi, Miss., and remained there until 1857. In that year he went to Pass Christian, Miss. In 1861 he was again elected a member of the legislature, and held the office until after the war was ended. In 1866 he was elected a member of the state senate, and was made president of the body. He was re-elected senator and discharged his duties to the entire satisfaction of his constituency. When the war ended, Colonel Seal found himself without a dollar, as all his means had been invested in slaves. He went to Mississippi City, and there resumed his legal practice. In 1888 he was again elected to the senate of the state, but resigned on account of ill health. He has held many offices in the gift of the people, and has always shown a fidelity and courage in caring for the interests of the people of his county that have won for him the highest regard of all classes of citizens. He is considered at the head of his profession, and there are few men on the coast better posted in all matters pertaining to the law. He owns a large amount of real estate along the coast, and large flocks of sheep and herds of cattle that are kept on Chandelier island. This is an island in the gulf, twenty-eight miles from Mississippi City, about forty miles long and two and a half miles wide; it has no timber, except myrtle wood, and is considered a very fine range. The Colonel is now somewhat advanced in years, but has an excellent memory, is quick in decision, and keen in judgment. He has been three times married. His first wife bore him four children, two of whom are living: Florian C., sheriff of Harrison county and Marshall.

Capt. D. B. Seal, attorney at law, Bay St. Louis, Miss., was born in Hancock county, Miss., February 24, 1836, and is a son of Jacob Seal. The father was born in Marion district, S. C., February 5, 1793, and was reared in his native state. He married Catherine Nicholson, who was of Scotch ancestry. She could speak the Gaelic language with great fluency. The paternal grandfather, Charles Seal, was a soldier in the Revolutionary war. He died in South Carolina. Jacob Seal served in the War of 1812, and was a colonel of the Mississippi state militia. He emigrated to Mississippi in 1823, and located in Hancock county, where he followed planting for a number of years. He died in Hancock county in 1883, at the age of eighty-nine years. He was one of the earliest settlers of the county, and while he was identified with the pioneer history of the county, he never sought public office. He had four sons and six daughters, four of whom are living: Roderick, a resident of Mississippi City; Mrs. Christian Seal and Mrs. Martha Boardman, and Capt. D. B., the subject of this notice. He is the youngest living member of the family. He was brought up on a plantation, and had just begun to think of starting out in life to make a place for himself when the war broke out, and the battlefield became the scene of action, instead of the busy marts of the city or the halls of justice. He enlisted in the Confederate cause and raised a company known as Hancock rebels. He went out as captain, and during the siege of Vicksburg he commanded the Thirty-eighth Mississippi regiment. Soon afterward he resigned, returning to his home. In 1865 he removed to Bay St. Louis. In 1861 he was elected a member of the legislature, and was re-elected in 1863; he served the full terms, getting a furlough for this purpose. In 1861 he was admitted to the bar, having studied law under Col. J. B. Deason, of Gainesville, Miss. After coming to the bay he began his professional work in earnest, and has since devoted himself to it most assiduously. He is the oldest lawyer in the bay, and has won a warm place in the hearts of the people, whom he has aided in many ways. In 1887 he was again elected to the legislature, and was re-elected in 1889. In 1867 he was elected a member of the constitutional convention, but this body never assembled. He was elected district attorney in 1872, and again in 1875. He was also city attorney for some time. He has held every office for which he has asked, and can truthfully say that he has received more votes than any opponent he has ever had. This is, indeed, a unique record in the political world. He has ever done credit to his constituency, and has acquitted himself, in the various positions he has held, with distinction. Captain Seal was united in marriage in 1867 to Miss Ivan Newman, of New Orleans, a native of Cincinnati, Ohio. Mrs. Seal is a devoted member of the Roman Catholic church.

Elbert B. Seale is a member of the prosperous mercantile firm of Seale & Byrd, of Roxie, Miss., the members of which, by their excellent management, business ability and efficiency, have built up an extensive patronage, and have done not a little to advance the reputation the county enjoys as a commercial center. Mr. Seale was born in Greene county, Ala., in 1827 (March 11), being the fourth of nine children born to Wright and Nancy (Cane) Seale, who were born in Georgia October 4, 1796, and February 13, 1804, respectively. They both came with their parents to what is now Amite county, Miss., in 1807, and were here married in 1821, removing three years later to Greene county, Ala., where they resided until 1832. At this date they returned to Amite county, and here Mrs. Seale was called from life in 1842. A year later Mr. Seale was married to Catherine Whittington, and in 1844 took up his abode in Franklin county, settling two miles south of the present town of Roxie, where he was called from earth in December, 1865. He had been a member of the Baptist church since 1826, and was a successful and practical farmer and a man of sound views, notwithstanding the fact that he received a limited education in early life. Thomas Seale, his father, was born in Georgia on the 7th of July, 1759, and was married five times. He was a private soldier during the Revolutionary war, was a planter by occupation, and died in Greene county, Ala., November 12, 1825. He was the father of fourteen children. The maternal grandfather, John Cane, was a Georgian, born June 24, 1751. In 1807 he brought his family to Amite county and improved a good place on Amite river. He died there about 1847. Elbert B. Seale is one of six surviving members of his father's family. Elijah W. is a planter of Morehouse parish, La., and was a soldier in the Confederate army during the war; Pascal H. was also in the Confederate army, and is a planter of Franklin county; Sarah J. is the wife of Charles F. Gates; Amanda is the wife of John Chambers, and William T., who was a private in the Confederate army and afterward served as a member of the board of supervisors of Franklin county, are the other members. Elbert B. was sent to the district schools near his home when his services were not needed on the home farm, and at the age of eighteen years he began farming for himself. In 1845 he was married to Miss Lizetta, daughter of Aaron and Lucretia Van Normand, natives of Canada, their marriage taking place on Long Island. They were early settlers of Amite county, the father dying here in 1862 and the mother in 1851, the former being a blacksmith by trade. Mrs. Seale was born in Liberty, Amite county, June 24, 1830, and died, having borne four children, of whom are living: Thomas G., and Nancy E., wife of Millard F. Byrd. His second union took place on the 23d of November, 1881, Mrs. Elizabeth Buffkin, a daughter of James Carlisle, becoming his wife. Mr. Carlisle died in Lawrence county, this state, in 1844, having come thither from Georgia. He was a soldier in the War of 1812, was with Jackson at New Orleans, was an earnest member of the Baptist church, and was an honest and upright citizen. His wife, formerly Miss Mary Bishop, was born in the state of Georgia, dying in Lawrence county in 1840, also a member of the Baptist church. Mrs. Seale was born in that county in 1830, and in 1850 was married there to Solomon Buffkin, who was born in Copiah county and died in Franklin county in December, 1877, she having borne him two daughters. When first married Mr. Seale resided for eight years in Liberty and kept a hotel. He then came to Franklin county and engaged in farming and merchandising six miles east of Roxie, where he continued until 1877, at which time he moved to the town, where he has since conducted a general mercantile establishment. In connection with this he owns and conducts five hundred and seventy-five acres of land, which is in three tracts, which is excellent and valuable property. He is the present mayor of the town, was formerly a member of the A. F. & A. M., and for thirty years has been a member of the Baptist church, his wife having been a member of the same for about forty years. Mr. Seale is quiet and unassuming in manner, but takes a deep interest in matters pertaining to the general welfare of the county. He has never aspired to office, his greatest aim being the advancement of the cause of Christianity.

S. Seaman, Handsboro, who has lived the greater portion of his life in Harrison county, Miss., was born in Jackson county, Miss., in 1831, and is a son of William C. and Catherine (Sheffield) Seaman. The father was a native of Staten Island, N. Y., and emigrated to Mississippi at an early day, locating in Jackson county. He subsequently removed to Harrison county, and was elected clerk of the circuit and chancery courts. He died near Biloxi, Miss. The mother of our subject was a native of South Carolina. They reared a large family of children, S. Seaman being the seventh born. He passed his youth in Harrison county, and was educated in the common schools. During the war he was detailed to work in the railroad shops. He had just opened business in partnership with J. T. Liddle, but this was necessarily suspended until the close of the war. He then resumed his plans, and carried them out successfully. When he had accumulated a comfortable fortune he retired from active business, and is now enjoying the fruits of his early years of industry and self-denial. He was married in 1865 to Miss Susan A. Baxter, a native of South Carolina. Four children were born to them: Emma A., W. S. Lily, May and Percy P. Mr. Seaman is a member of the Masonic fraternity. He is a man of excellent judgment, and superior business qualifications. He has been a loyal citizen, and has been an ardent supporter of home industries. Mrs. Seaman is a worthy member of the Baptist church.

Talbot H. Selby, one the most enterprising citizens of Newton county, Miss., was born in what is now Choctaw county, Ala., where he lived until he had reached man's estate. He then came to Lauderdale county, Miss., where he resided until 1860, a period of about one year; he then located in Newton county, where he has continuously resided excepting the time spent in the service of his country. He enlisted in company B, Second Mississippi cavalry, in May, 1862, and did valiant service; he was detailed to assist at regimental headquarters, and acted in this capacity until the close of the conflict. His associate in this work was Frank C. Armstrong. When the war was ended he came home, and secured a situation as bookkeeper with Watts & Nimocks, in whose employ he remained until the spring of 1869. He made a trip to New Orleans at this time, but did not stay any length of time; he came back to Newton and was employed by Richardson & Co., as bookkeeper; he is an expert accountant, and possesses the entire confidence of his employers. Mr. Selby was united in marriage in 1862 to Miss Kate, a daughter of Thomas H. Massey, of Fayetteville, N. C., and a most estimable woman. She has had born to her seven children, only four of whom survive: Robert is a minister in the Methodist Episcopal church, and is a member of the Mississippi conference (he is now located at Flora, Miss.), Eunice, Kate and Henry. Seth E. Selby, the father of our subject, was a native of North Carolina, where he lived until he was twenty years of age; he then removed to Alabama and was there married. About the 1856 he came to Mississippi, and in 1872 located in Newton. He died in October, 1887, but his widow still survives. He was a most exemplary man, a worthy member of the Methodist Episcopal church with which he united in early life, and a thoroughly respected citizen. Talbot H. Selby is connected with the Masonic order, the Knights of Pythias, and the Knights of Honor, belonging to the lodges at Newton. He is an untiring worker in the Methodist Episcopal Church South, of which he is a member.

A number of years passed in sincere and earnest endeavor to thoroughly discharge every duty incumbent upon the different official positions he has filled, and his success in the legal profession have served to place Hon. B. A. P. Selman, attorney, Booneville, Miss., among the leading and most influential men of the county. He was born in Itawamba county, Miss., in 1849, and of the eight children born to his parents, Dr. Thomas and Mrs. (Allen) Selman, he was the eldest in order of birth. His paternal grandparents, Benjamin and Sallie Selman, were natives of Tennessee and Virginia respectively. They moved from Tennessee to Texas in 1841, were among the pioneer settlers, and he was very prominent in politics, being a member of the legislature for some time. The maternal grandparents, Matthew and Rebecca (Drummond) Allen, were prominent citizens of Benton (now Calhoun) county, Ala., and he was an active politician, representing that county in the legislature for some time. Both died in Alabama, the grandmother in 1857, and the grandfather in 1866. Dr. Thomas Selman was a native of Franklin county, Tenn., born in 1819, and was reared to the arduous duties of the farm. He studied medicine and in 1842 moved to Itawamba county, Miss., where he practiced his profession seven years. In 1847 he was married in Jacksonville, Ala. to Miss Allen, a native of the Palmetto state, although reared in Alabama, and after his marriage the Doctor moved to Fulton, Itawamba county, Miss., where he resided for some time. From there he moved to Pontotoc county of that state, practiced medicine there for thirty years, and then settled in Baylor county, Tex., where he resides at tne present time. To his marriage were born the following children: B. A. P., A. K. (who died at the age of twenty-one years), Mattie A. (married H. S. Hunter and died at the age of thirty-five years, leaving a family): Mary E. (now Mrs. W. H. Elkins, resides in Texas); Cora (married Louis Deprew and died in 1889); Louella (died at the age of ten years); Alma (married Mr. Jones and her death occurred in 1888); and Ada (married S. Suttlemeyer and is now a resident of Baylor county, Tex.) The mother of these children died at her residence, five miles west of Guntown, Miss., in 1866. The father followed his profession all his life and in connection also carried on farming. He was one of the first treasurers of Itawamba county, and is honored and respected wherever known. He is a Master Mason and a member of the Missionary Baptist church, in which his wife also held membership. He is public-spirited and is active in all laudable enterprises. Hon. B. A. P. Selman divided his time in early life in assisting on his father's farm and in attending the common schools, where he received a good practical education. He then studied law with General Finley, of Tupelo, and in 1870, at the age of twenty-one years, he commenced practicing at Guntown. He came to Booneville in 1872 and has been a resident of that town ever since. He was married in 1879 to Mrs. Fannie E. Chamber, a native of Ripley, born in 1850, and the daughter of J. B. and Mary L. (Hindman) Ellis, both natives of Tennessee, the father born in 1819 and the mother in Knoxville, in 1823. She was a sister of General Thomas Hindman, who was killed at Helena, Ark., in 1867. Her father was Col. Thomas Hindman. Her parents moved to Ripley, Miss., about 1840 and the father practiced medicine up to the time of his death, at Booneville, in 1878. He was married about 1847. To our subject and wife were born two living children: Lucile (who died at the age of two years); Louis and Mabel. Mr. Selman is a Knight Templar in the Masonic fraternity and he is a member of the Knights of Honor organization. He is a prominent politician, represented Prentiss county in the legislature in 1882, 1884, 1886, was chairman of the committee in 1882, and was a member of the judiciary committee in 1884 and 1886. He takes part in and gives his hearty support to all enterprises worthy of notice. He has been engaged in gardening for the last four years and has been quite successful in a business way. He was mayor of Guntown for many years.

John H. Semmes is one of the foremost planters of Lauderdale county, where he owns a good and fertile plantation of four hundred acres, of which three hundred acres are under cultivation, which he devotes to the raising of vegetables and garden supplies for the city of Meridian. Corn and cotton are also raised to a considerable extent, and besides being exceptionally thorough and practical, he is also very energetic and enterprising. He was born in the county in which he now lives in January, 1850, the fourth of ten children born to Maj. Francis C., and Mary E. (Hubert) Semmes, the father a native of Maryland and the mother of Georgia. Francis C. Semmes was taken by his parents from his native state to Georgia, at which time he was but a lad, and there he grew to manhood, was educated and married. After spending some time in that state after the celebration of his nuptials he, in 1845, came to Lauderdale county, Miss., where he purchased land and engaged in planting, making this his chief occupation for the remainder of his days. He was a member of the Mississippi legislature at the time the ordinance of secession was passed, and voted for that measure. When the war opened he entered the Confederate service, and as he was in ill health and not able to perform active duty, he was placed in the quartermaster's department and during his service was stationed at Meridian, Miss. After the war he resumed his planting operations on the land now owned by the subject of this sketch, where he owned one thousand acres of land, having prior to the war been the owner of about sixty slaves. He was of a very hospitable and kindly disposition, and during the war his doors were thrown open to the sick and wounded soldiers, there often being as many as fifteen or twenty in his home. He was beloved and highly respected by all and at the time of his death, in November, 1867, he was a consistent member of the Catholic church. His widow, who died in November of the following year at her home near Meridian, Miss., was a member of the Methodist Episcopal church. When eighteen years of age John H. Semmes began to make his own way in life as a planter, and at the time of his marriage, in 1873, was in good circumstances. Miss Mary Scanlan became his wife, she being the daughter of Edwin Scanlan, of Newton county, Miss. To them three sons and six daughters have been born: Sarah, Jane, Katie, Joseph, John, Mary, Ella, William (deceased) and Celia. Mrs. Semmes has been an invalid since 1887, being partially paralyzed. Both Mr. and Mrs. Semmes are members of the Catholic church. Mr. Semmes has never aspired to any political position in his life, but has attended strictly to his business and now has a fair share of this world's goods. He is liberal in the use of his means.

Charles E. Sessions, the eldest of nine children born to Richard R. and Mary (Gibson) Sessions, owes his nativity to Chicot county, Ark., where his birth occurred on the 25th of March, 1854. He passed his youthful days in that state, and secured a thorough education in the Military university at Nashville, Tenn. When it became necessary for him to select some calling in life he very naturally, perhaps, chose the one to which he had been reared, and which he has continued to follow up to the present time. He started out to fight life's battle for himself when twenty years of age, and as his means were limited all he has made is the result of his own industry and good management. He is the owner of two thousand acres of land, thirteen hundred acres under cultivation, and he also owns stock in several enterprises in Friar's Point. Mr. Sessions chose Miss Mamie Hutchins as his companion in life, and their nuptials were celebrated on the 12th of April, 1878. She was born in Adams county, Miss., and is the daughter of John O. and Aubin Hutchins, natives of Mississippi and Virginia respectively. The result of this union has been the birth of four interesting children, all living: Richard M., Charles E., Aubin A. and Sidney D. In his political preference Mr. Sessions is a democrat of the first water. He is a member of the Knights of Honor and the Knights of Pythias. Although a young man Mr. Sessions is regarded as one of the representative citizens of the county, and is a thoroughgoing, enterprising young man. As far as his means will allow he has contributed to all worthy enterprises, and especially those pertaining to the good of the country. He is most social and pleasant in his intercourse with all, and has a host of warm friends. He is of medium hight, rather slender, and has a fair complexion. His parents were natives of Mississippi and Missouri, respectively, and were representatives of old and honored families. The father was an extensive planter and followed that industry until 1874, since which time he has retired from the active duties of life. He now lives alternately in Mississippi and Illinois. He has three sons residing in Friar's Point, all promising young men, one being postmaster at that place and the others prominent citizens. The maternal grandparents of Charles E. Sessions were John W. and Martha L. Gibson, natives of Scotland and Louisiana, respectively. The paternal parents were Richard Sessions and Nancy Cordell, of Sampson county, N. C.

Maj. J. F. Sessions, the gentleman whose name heads this sketch, is chairman of the Mississippi railroad commission and ex-officio chairman of the board of control of the Mississippi penitentiary. He was elected by the legislature in March, 1886, re-elected in 1888 and again in 1890. The late constitutional convention of Mississippi having changed the term from two to four years and made the office elective by the people, Major Sessions was again nominated by the democratic state convention on the 15th of July, 1891, for the term ending December 31, 1895, and will no doubt be again elected by the people in November, 1891. Major Sessions is a native of Franklin county, Miss., where he was born in 1838. His father was Jesse Sessions, who came from North Carolina to Mississippi about the beginning of the present century and was a successful planter. He died on his plantation near the present village of Knoxville, Franklin county, Miss., on the Louisville, New Orleans & Texas railroad, in 1842. He was preceded by his elder brother, Joseph Sessions, in the removal from North Carolina to Mississippi. This brother (together with several others who followed later) located in Adams county and was a successful planter, engaging somewhat in public affairs. He was a member of the constitutional convention which convened in the town of Washington, near Natchez, in 1817, and which formed the constitution under which the Mississippi territory was admitted into the Union as a state the same year. The grandfather of the subject of this sketch was Richard Sessions, who lived and died in Sampson county, N. C. His grandmother was Esther Boone, who was a daughter of Joseph Boone and a niece of Daniel Boone, who became famous as a frontiersman in Kentucky. His mother was Edney Kell, a native of Franklin county, where she died in 1847. Major Sessions was married in 1861 to Miss Eliza S. Dunckley, of Wilkinson county. They have two children—a son and daughter. The former is a medical student at Tulane university in New Orleans, and the daughter, Ada, is the wife of J. J. Proby, Esq., an attorney of Natchez, Miss. Major Sessions was a captain in the Seventh Mississippi regiment during the Civil war, until after the Kentucky campaign of General Bragg, when, on account of failing health, he resigned. After recovery he organized a cavalry company, which formed a part of the regiment commanded by Colonel Powers. In an engagement near Clinton, Miss., Captain Sessions, in July, 1864, lost an arm, after which he was promoted to be major of the regiment and served with it until the surrender, except during a few months while he was in command of the post at Woodville. After the surrender he began the practice of the law in Meadville, having graduated in 1860 at the law school of the University of Mississippi; he also graduated from Centenary college, Louisiana, in 1859. He was elected to the legislature from Franklin county in 1869 and re-elected in 1871, serving these two terms as one of a corporal's guard of democrats who withstood successfully many iniquitous schemes of the negroes and their carpetbag allies, during the dark days of reconstruction in Mississippi. He afterward served a fragmentary term in the state senate, representing the district composed of the counties of Lincoln, Lawrence and Pike, he having removed in 1873 to Lincoln county, locating at Brookhaven, and continuing in the practice of law until his election as railroad commissioner in 1886.

Among the steady and substantial old citizens of Jackson, Miss., Mr. E. von Seutter deserves a place in the front ranks. Though he himself remarked, "I am neither a politician nor a financier," yet we find him one of those happy and superior combinations of education, information, talent, æsthetic tastes, integrity, and push which stamp him as a citizen of unusual worth, notwithstanding his modesty and retiring habits. The youngest son of an aristocratic family in Germany, Mr. von Seutter, when twenty-one years of age, landed in New Orleans in 1848, to visit and see the far West. Soon disenchanted and homesick he accepted an urgent invitation from an old schoolfriend, Mr. Max Kuner, of the subsequent firm of Downing, Moody & Kuner, of Vicksburg, Miss., to join him in the jewelry business. Mr. von Seutter, with mechanical and artistic talents, enhanced by a careful education, including drawing and geometry, soon mastered the watchmaker's and jeweler's trade and taught himself engraving. In a few years, or in 1851, he established himself in business in Raymond. There he toiled and saved, and finally bought out a daguerrean artist, and added that financial lever to his business, and in two years, with plenty of money (hard and honorable earnings of toil), he went back to Austria to his family and "the girl he left behind him." He was married in grand style and brought his young bride, whose maiden name was Julia Hoch, to the home he had prepared for her in Mississippi, to be his life companion and the light of his home. The old inhabitants of Raymond speak in the highest terms of Mr. and Mrs. von Seutter, where they had made their home and prospered in business and children, until the Civil war swept away everything they had possessed. Undaunted, after the war Mr. von Seutter gradually paid his Northern creditors, and having moved to Jackson, Miss., slowly but surely ascended again in business. The following article is taken from the *Clarion-Ledger*, and only does Mr. von Seutter justice: "Seutter always succeeded in everything he has undertaken, and has guarded his honor all through as sacred, and as a thing of priceless value. His record has been an exemplary one, such as any man might be proud of. He is known thus in all portions of the land, and where he is best known, is where he is most admired. Without capital, speculation, or lucky windfall, step by step only, Mr. Seutter weathered the destructive war, epidemics, fires, bank failures, and hard times. It was slow work, slow but sure work, as Mr. Seutter with less covetousness than pride and integrity, ever discarded 'cheap goods' that yield large profits. But now he reaps the benefit of his honorable dealing and toil these forty years, by the most flattering appreciation and patronage of the public. So much for Mr. Seutter the jeweler."

There is nothing which more impresses the visitor to town or city with its refinement, prosperity or happiness, than elegant suburban dwellings clad in flowers and verdure, and in that respect Mr. von Seutter's Ivy cottage, the artist's home on North State street, presents a perfect little Eden, with its wealth of flowers and trees, its vines and waving banana trees and exotics, with its fresh, green lawn, its clean walks and general artistic and picturesque arrangement, all of which is the result of his active mind and hands. Here the genial Mr. von Seutter may be found, untiring in attending to and enjoying his home, after his indefatigable labors in his prosperous jewelry business. He is a business man of sterling qualities, ever ready to contribute to all worthy enterprises, and is an honor and ornament to the city of Jackson. His union with Miss Hoch, in 1853, resulted in the birth of seven children, three of whom are living: Armin, a photographer of Jackson; Edward Raymond, who is in the jewelry business and the optician of Meridian, is married to Miss Nettie Major, of Kentucky, and has two children; and Carl, who married Miss Mary Holbrook, a native of Mississippi, is associated in business with his father in Jackson. The family are members of the Episcopal church, and Mr. von Seutter is a member of the I. O. O. F. and K. of H. fraternities. His stock of goods, which is of the best quality, amounts to about $20,000, with which he does an annual business of about $18,000. He possesses decided literary tastes, and has written an autobiographical narrative of himself entitled "The Immigrant," published and copied by several papers, and some poetry of decided merit, of which the following is an example:

WOODLAND VOWS.

Woodland vows, meant for eternities,
 Though born and borne oft on the moment's wing,
In joy and hope carved on the silent trees,
 Ephemeral die with the departing spring.

This we are told, and often so it goes,
  But sometimes love and truth will keep
What these carved monograms propose,
  Though time and bark grew o'er the mark once deep.

'Tis one and thirty years—'tis long ago—
  I carved by stealth, with fear and mystery,
With beating heart and love's delicious throe,
  Our names united in the linden tree.

And when the summer waned, confessed my love:
  Ah, such a glory over woods and lea!
For, looking to the monogram above,
  We kissed our first kiss 'neath the linden tree.

Spring bloomed again—and with impetuous will
  To build a home for love beyond the sea,
I parted from my love—and pale and still
  We wept and vowed beneath the linden tree.

Five years beyond the stormy ocean's foam,
  I toiled 'neath Mississippi's tropic heat—
I carved a name, I built a cottage home,
  Returning, laid them at my darling's feet.

The church bells rang melodious on the air:
  "Mine! Mine!" they sang in happy glee;
And thus united with my bride so fair,
  Was heaven on earth beneath the linden tree.

We bade farewell the home the tree stands nigh—
  "Where thou goest, e'en beyond the ocean's flood,
There I will go; where thou diest, I will die;
  Thy people mine; thy God shall be my God!"

Thus spoke my love, and kept thro' grief and joy—
  Though sorrow, sickness, loss and death would bow
Her spirit oft—her troth without alloy,
  And I—I hope—have kept my woodland vow.

And thus life's battle we together fought;
  And on our silver wedding roamed to see
Once more our childhood's homes, and sought
  Our dear old monument, the linden tree.

Entwined in love, as thirty years ago,
  With joyous hearts, from toil and sorrow free,
As flew in crowds the sparrows to and fro,
  We stood once more beneath the linden tree.

There was no mark of letters—not a trace;
  The TREE had changed in size and every bough.
I pressed upon my heart her hand and face:
  "HERE, darling, HERE, read thou my woodland vow!"

Mr. Von Seutter also wrote a series of interesting letters on the World's exposition in Paris in 1878, and his continental travels in that year, which were published in the *Clarion*, of Jackson, Miss.

Hon. E. R. Seward, of the firm of Seward Bros., general merchants at Ackerman, Choctaw county, Miss., was born in Carroll county of that state in 1849, and is a son of

Richard A. and Sarah A. (Doyle) Seward, the father born in Virginia in 1808 and the mother a native of Alabama. When a boy, the elder Seward went to Tennessee with his parents, thence to Alabama and later to Mississippi. He was married in Pickens county, Alabama, but was a resident of Carroll county, Miss., at the time. He lived there until about 1852, when he removed to Choctaw county and settled near French Camp, afterward at La Grange, where he engaged in merchandising under the name of Seward, Boyd & Co. After the county seat was removed to Chester he located in that city and continued merchandising, the firm being Seward & Son. This was continued until shortly prior to Mr. Seward's death in 1887, when he retired. Mr. Seward was a good business man and a true Christian. He accumulated quite a fortune, and was one of the prominent men of the county. He was for some time circuit clerk of Carroll county, and although he had but an ordinary English education he possessed superior natural abilities. He was at one time a prominent stockholder in a cotton factory at Bankston. He was a member of the Masonic fraternity, D. Mitchell lodge, French Camp, now defunct. His father, Zachariah Seward, was a Virginian, but at an early day removed to Tennessee, thence to Alabama, from there to Carroll county, Miss., and afterward to Florida, where he and wife both died prior to the war. He was a planter by occupation, and was a soldier in the War of 1812. He reared a family of six sons and four daughters. His father was an Englishman. Grandfather Joseph Doyle, was probably a native of Alabama, but removed to Mississippi about 1840, settling near Winona, where his death occurred. He was also a planter. His wife died in Alabama, The mother of our subject was a member of the Christian church and died in 1858. After her death Mr. Seward married again and had one son, F. D., by the last union. The six children born to his first union were named in the order of their births as follows: Elizabeth V. (wife of R. J. Irving, of Texas), James A. (a planter of Texas, was all through the war, Confederate army, and was captured at Vicksburg and Mobile), Miss L. M. (a milliner at Ackerman), Hon. E. R. (subject), Emma (wife of M. M. Ridgeway, a planter of Choctaw county), and M. F. (a member of the firm of Seward Bros.). The fourth child in order of birth, Hon. E. R. Seward, passed his boyhood and youth on a farm, received his education at French Camp, and then taught school a short time. In 1872 he was elected chancery clerk of Choctaw county, and discharged the duties of that office in a very efficient manner until 1880, when he was elected to the legislature, serving one term and being on the committee on enrolled bills and on the committee on corporations. In the meantime, from 1880 to 1883, he was engaged in the practice of law, having prepared himself while clerking. He was married in 1873 to Miss L. M. Robinson, a native of Choctaw county, and the daughter of Samuel and R. E. Robinson, natives of Chester district, S. C., but who came to Choctaw county about 1853, and there passed their last days, the father dying in 1859, and the mother in 1875. Both were members of the Baptist church, and he was a planter by occupation. To Mr. and Mrs. Seward have been born three living children. Both are members of the Baptist church. Mr. Seward is one of the energetic business men of Ackerman. Shrewd and far seeing, strictly honest and upright, his high character, both in private and business life, places his methods above criticism and secures for him the patronage of a large portion of Choctaw county's citizens. He is a gentleman of experience, judgment and energy, has an extensive acquaintance, and is everywhere popular. The firm of Seward Bros. was established at Ackerman in 1884, and they do an annual business of about $30,000. This firm also has a store at McCool, in Attala county, under the name of F. D. Seward & Co., and does an annual business of about $25,000. Mr. Seward was made a Mason, in 1873, of La Grange lodge No. 363, but now of Snowsville lodge, at

Ackerman, No. 119, of which he was master two years. He is protector of Ackerman lodge, Knights and Ladies of Honor, No. 1290, and is past dictator of Ackerman lodge, Knights of Honor. No man stands higher in Choctaw county in the estimation of the people than Mr. Seward.

Hon. John F. Sexton, of Copiah county, was born in Rankin county, Miss., in 1844. He was the son of John C. and Mary E. Sexton, mention of whom as well as other members of the family will be found elsewhere in these pages. At about the age of twenty-two, Mr. Sexton began life for himself as a planter, in which interest he has been connected to the present time. His plantation is one of the largest and best improved in this part of the county, and he was so thoroughgoing an agriculturist that it may be said his was one of the most productive. In 1867 he was married to Elizabeth Hays, the daughter of Isaiah and Elizabeth Hays, of Copiah county, who has borne him four children: Willie F., Ollie, Eddie and Mary E., all of whom are members of their parents' household. Mr. Sexton is a member of numerous societies and secret orders, among which may be mentioned the Farmers' Alliance, of Copiah county, the Industrial Union, Knights of Honor, and Knights of Pythias, of Crystal Springs. He and his wife are members of the Methodist Episcopal church, worshiping with the congregation which meets at Crystal Springs. Four years before Mr. Sexton can be said to have begun life for himself in business, he made a departure which, except in the South, where such occasions were common enough among the youths at the outbreak of the Civil war, would have been, in view of his tender years, worthy of more than passing comment. In December, 1861, when he was seventeen years old, he enlisted in the Withers artillery regiment of Mississippi, where he served until the close of the war, participating in a number of hard fights. He was in the siege at Port Hudson, in Johnston's army in Georgia, and in Hood's army in Georgia and Tennessee. He was taken a prisoner by the Federals at Spanish Fort and kept a captive for sixty days. Although he was never wounded sufficiently to disable him, he received on several occasions slight wounds which, instead of breaking his spirit, stimulated him to fight the harder. In political life Mr. Sexton has been preferred beyond many of his more ambitious fellow-citizens. In 1888 he was elected to represent his county in the legislature, and has served during two consecutive terms. During the term of 1888-9 he was chairman of the committee on manufacturing, and also served on the committees of agriculture and temperance. During that session he introduced an assessment bill, out of which grew the present assessment law, Mr. Madison also introducing a similar bill that had an influence in the same direction. In the session of 1890-91 he served on the committee of education and on the committee of investigation of the state treasurer's and auditor's offices, a labor which proved of great value to the state. As a member of this committee he helped draw up the bill which, as a law, compelled the government to appoint a committee of three each year to count the cash and to investigate the books of the state treasurer. Previous to his election to the legislature he served as a member of the board of supervisors, and as one of the county school commissioners. Mr. Sexton is a tall, well-built man with sandy hair. He is of good address, genial, whole-souled, friendly and helpful. He commands the highest respect of all who know him, not only on account of his political life, but also because of his fine family connections, and he is widely known throughout the state. Olivar P. Sexton, a planter of Copiah county, was the son of John C. and Mary E. Sexton and a brother of Hon. John F. Sexton. He was born in Copiah county in 1849, and was known as a life-long planter who was very successful. In 1873 he married Mary E. Coor, daughter of Rufus and Mary Coor, the son of D. K. Coor, whose sketch appears in these pages. Mr. and Mrs. Sexton have had seven children, all of whom are living at home with their parents: Ada, Walter, Eula, Cora, Frank, Mary K. and Nora L. Mr. Sexton is a member of the Knights of Honor lodge at Crystal Springs, and he is a worthy member of society and a highly respected citizen.

Dr. Frank M. Sexton, a brother of the Hon. James S. Sexton (see sketch) is one of the prominent physicians and surgeons of Hazlehurst, Copiah county, Miss. He was born in this county, July 12, 1852, the third of five sons born to his parents, all of whom have taken a prominent part in the county of their birth. After receiving a liberal literary education, he entered the Tulane university, at New Orleans, La., from which he graduated in medicine in 1876, and has since practiced his profession with marked success among the people with whom he was reared. He was postmaster at Hazlehurst during Cleveland's administration. He is an active worker for the cause of education, and is a member of the board of control and a trustee of Hazlehurst's public schools, toward the upbuilding of which he has done as much as any other citizen. He is ranked as one of the most successful planters in the county, and is the owner of a large, well-cultivated plantation. In 1876 he married Sallie, a daughter of Joseph and Lovisa Price. Her father was born in Copiah county; her mother in Covington county, Miss. Mrs. Sexton was born in Copiah county, and has four children. Dr. Sexton is a Knight of Honor and a member of Hazlehurst lodge of that order. He is a genial, whole-souled gentleman, well known throughout this section of the country, and his standing is deservedly high professionally, commercially, socially and otherwise. He has a charming family, and his wife takes equal rank with himself, while she is greatly beloved by a large circle of friends and acquaintances for her many estimable qualities of heart and mind.

Hon. James S. Sexton, a prominent lawyer of Hazlehurst, was born in Copiah county in 1854. John Curtis Sexton, the father of James S., Frank M., and their brothers, was the son of William Sexton, who was born in Ireland and moved to America in childhood. He married a Miss Ewen, who died during the childhood of John Curtis Sexton. The latter was born March 4, 1801, in Tennessee. At the age of twenty-eight he removed from Tennessee to Rankin county, Miss., where he was married, August 30, 1840, to Mary Elizabeth Perry, the daughter of William and Jane Perry. Both of her parents were born in Ireland, from which place they removed with their parents in early childhood. Coming in the same vessel, their families settled, one in Newbury district and the other in Fairfield district, of South Carolina. Jane Perry's maiden name was Jane Seymour, one of whose brothers, John Seymour, is still living in Rankin county, Miss., and is over ninety years of age. After their marriage, John Curtis and Mary Sexton lived in Rankin county until 1849, when they moved to Copiah county and settled on a place then known as the John Wilson place, four miles southeast of Crystal Springs, on the old Jackson road. This property still remains in the family. John Sexton remained on this place, engaged in farming, until 1860, when he removed to Crystal Springs. Here he died, December 31, 1861. He was an old line whig, and was devoted to that party. He was a Royal Arch Mason, and a member of the Methodist church. There were nine children born of this marriage, five of whom are still living: John F., born June 6, 1844; Oliver P., born March 5, 1849; Frank M., born July 12, 1852; James S., born November 2, 1854, and Martin L., born October 11, 1857. Mrs. Sexton (now Mrs. Mullins) still lives, and is devoted to her family, of which she may well feel proud. She has spared no efforts to insure their welfare, and now she is being rewarded by their devotion and gratitude to her. Hon. John F. Sexton is a prominent planter of Copiah county, and a member of the legislature. He also served in company A, Bradford's battery, during the war. Oliver P. Sexton is a planter on the old home farm. Dr. Frank M. is a prominent physician of

Hazlehurst, and graduated at the Tulane university at New Orleans. James S. Sexton was the fourth in order of birth of the sons. Dr. Martin Luther Sexton is a prominent physician of Wesson, and graduated in a class of forty with the first honors, at the Tulane university, and has been recently elected a member of the faculty of that institution. He is one of the most prominent physicians of the state, and was once the president of the state association. He received his literary education at Oxford, Miss. James S. Sexton was reared principally to farm life by a widowed mother, who struggled successfully against adversity to afford her children a good education, and to impress upon their minds the advantage of becoming useful men. He received his early education at a country school, and was for three years a student at the State university. He then taught school for a few years, after which he read law with Judge T. E. Cooper, now one of the supreme judges of Mississippi, and was admitted to the bar in 1881. He immediately formed a partnership with R. R. Willing, which existed for about one year. For some years after its expiration he was alone in the practice of his profession, until a few years ago he became associated with R. H. Thompson, of Brookhaven, who has been associated with him ever since. Mr. Sexton has never sought office, but he was elected to represent the state at large at the recent constitutional convention, and was the youngest member of that body from the state at large. He is a member of the Knights of Honor. In 1875 he married Mary E., the daughter of William Wilson. She was born in Copiah county, and died in 1888, having been for a long time a member of the Methodist church. She left two children. In 1889 Mr. Sexton was married to Lillian W., the daughter of Dr. J. P. Wise. She has borne Mr. Sexton one child. She and her husband are both members of the Methodist Episcopal church. Mr. Sexton is a well-to-do man, and has a good income from his large practice. He is in the true sense of the term a self-made man, and is regarded as one of the best lawyers in this section. In person, he is of medium stature and noble bearing. His manners are genial and affable, and he enjoys the highest esteem of all who know him.

Luther Martin Sexton, M. D., ranks among the foremost physicians of the state of Mississippi, for his efforts in behalf of suffering humanity have been attended by results eminently satisfactory. He comes of Scotch-Irish stock, and inherits the traits of character, the industry, economy and integrity, common to those sturdy people. His father, John Sexton, was a relative of James A. Sexton, the present postmaster of Chicago, and Prof. S. S. Sexton, M. D., of New York, an eminent specialist and author of the elaborate and valuable treatise on the diseases and treatment of the eye, ear and throat. His father was also related to Sexton at present a member of the English parliament from Ireland and a prominent leader of the liberal party. His mother, Mary Elizabeth (Perry) Sexton, was of Irish descent, belonging to one of the first families in Mississippi. Dr. Luther Martin Sexton is a Mississippian by birth, his birth occurring at Crystal Springs, Copiah county, October 7, 1857. In the public schools of his native town he laid the foundations of a liberal education, and at the age of nineteen years he entered the University of Mississippi at Oxford, where he remained for two sessions, applying himself to his books with such diligence that he was awarded a gold medal for superiority in elocution and original address. He afterward became a teacher in the public schools of his native county, and in this vocation and in agriculture he sought means with which to continue his education. Having decided to enter into a profession, and having two brothers, both of whom had acquired considerable prominence in their respective professions of law and medicine, he was undecided as to which to choose for his life work, but the preference was finally almost given to law, as he had at college demonstrated his ability as an orator and public speaker.

As small objects sometimes turn the current of a stream, so unforeseen circumstances ofttimes exert a powerful influence upon the whole after lives of men, and never was this more ably illustrated than in the case of Dr. Sexton, for in 1878, while in the city of New Orleans, he happened one day to see a surgical operation performed in the hospital by Prof. T. G. Richardson, and the wonderful skill displayed in the alleviation of human suffering so won his admiration, that from that time forward he became an enthusiast upon the subject of the study and practice of medicine and surgery, and his eminent success as a physician and surgeon has demonstrated the wisdom of his choice. He immediately became a student in the medical department of the University of Louisiana (now known as Tulane university), where, with characteristic energy, he devoted himself to his studies. The following spring he applied for, and became one of the successful competitors for the position of resident student for the Charity hospital of New Orleans, and for the two years following served as interne at that institution. In 1881 he graduated with the first honors of his class, and became the proud possessor of the first gold medal ever conferred by the hospital upon a student for general proficiency in medicine and surgery. One of the most pleasant incidents of his college life, and a fitting testimonial of the high esteem in which he was held by his classmates, was when he was unanimously chosen by them as valedictorian. Appreciating the high honor thus conferred upon him, he delivered upon the occasion of their graduation an address that attracted much attention in medical circles and was widely published by the medical journals of the Southern states. In 1879 boats passing up the Mississippi river had conveyed to Memphis the dreaded yellow fever, by which this prosperous city and the surrounding country were almost completely depopulated, so fatal was the terrible scourge that swept over the country. The government was awakened to the necessity of quarantine stations on the river, and immediately following his graduation Dr. Luther Sexton was appointed government inspector of the national board of health, and was stationed on a government boat at Vicksburg, where it was his duty to inspect all boats passing up the river. In this position he continued until cold weather rendered further vigilance unnecessary. In 1882, at the strong solicitation of his friends, he located at Wesson, Miss., where he has since resided, and where he has risen to the topmost round of the ladder of success. He became a member of the Mississippi State Medical association, and in 1884 was chosen as its president. In the year last mentioned he was elected a member of the board of health for the seventh congressional district, and medical examiner for license to practice medicine in Mississippi. In 1890 he delivered an address before the St. Louis Medical society, and those present had the pleasure of listening to a master production of a master mind. The same year he was offered a professorship in the Marion Sims Medical college of St. Louis, the chair of genito-urinary surgery being tendered him, but interests at home prevented his acceptance. In 1891 he was elected lecturer and clinical instructor in surgery in Tulane university at New Orleans, his alma mater, thus becoming a member of the faculty of that institution. In 1881 he was united in marriage to Miss Katherine Ella Hartwell, of Wesson, in which city they reside, enjoying the respect and esteem of their fellow-citizens. Although the Doctor is but thirty-four years of age, he has, by frugality and industry, amassed a small fortune, and has the pleasure of knowing that his efforts in the pursuit of his profession have been eminently successful to a greater degree than those of any other physician of his age in the state, and it may be safely said in the South. He is, withal, an honored citizen, courteous and affable in his manner, of pleasing address and an interesting speaker. His success in life is but an illustration of what may be achieved by energy and determination.

Richard J. Shackelford is the third of a family of eight children born to James L. and Elvira (Payne) Shackelford, natives of South Carolina and Georgia respectively. The father removed to Mississippi in 1854, and died there in 1891. He was a son of William and Mariah Shackelford, who were of Irish lineage. The maternal grandparents were David and Martha Payne. Richard J. first saw the light of day August 3, 1841, in Franklin county, Ga. He spent his youth in Georgia and Mississippi, acquiring his education in the private schools. For his vocation in life he chose that of agriculture, and he now has one hundred and seventy acres of land under excellent cultivation. He owns six hundred and forty acres, and the whole will in time be cultivated. Mr. Shackelford has been twice married. In 1866 he was united to Miss Fannie Saunders, of Mississippi; of this marriage twelve children were born: Mary J., James J., Albert L., Francis T., Jesse M., Sallie A., Arthur L., Myrtie I., Ella V., Martha, John and Fanny. In 1885 he was married, a second time, to Martha Hordage, of Georgia. Our subject was a soldier in the late Civil war, being a member of the Fifth Mississippi volunteer infantry, company K. He was in the battles of Missionary ridge and Franklin, and served from 1861 to the end of the conflict. He adheres to the principles of the democratic party. He held the office of justice of the peace of Leake county for one term. He has not been behind in his support of all laudable movements having for their object the advancement of the community. He and his wife are active members of the Primitive Baptist church, and greatly respected by all who know them.

Col. Thaddeus H. Shackelford has been engaged in planting nearly all his life, for to this calling he was brought up by his father, Henry L. Shackelford, who was also a worthy tiller of the soil, in which calling his efforts were attended by success. The latter was a Virginian by birth, born in 1790, and upon reaching manhood was married to Miss Sarah Jane McGowan, of South Carolina, who bore him the following children: John; Thaddeus; Charles; Mary (Shannon); Martha J. (Tucker), widow of General W. F. Tucker; Jane, (Hodges), and Augusta (Evans). Mr. Shackelford was very finely educated, and as a planter became wealthy, thus enabling him to give his children excellent education and a good start in life. He served as a soldier in the Seminole war in Florida. Thaddeus H. Shackelford was partially educated by a private tutor at home, but received his literary education in Aberdeen, Miss., and in Parson Gladney's private school in Monroe county, Miss. He made the most of his opportunities, and upon finishing was exceptionally well informed, and was well calculated to battle successfully with the world. He came to Lowndes county, Miss., in 1831, after which he located in Oktibbeha county, and finally, in 1842, settled down to planting in Chickasaw county. He was married in 1852 to Miss Virginia E. Townsend, a daughter of Col. Thomas Townsend, of Lowndes county, Miss., and to them were born two children: Thomas T. (deceased) and William A., a planter of this county. After the death of the mother of the children, Mr. Shackelford took for his second wife Miss Virginia P. Tapley, their nuptials being celebrated in 1883, and to them two children have been born: Mary P. who died January 3, 1891, and Henry L. Mr. Shackelford has been a consistent and respected member of the Masonic order from his earliest manhood. He is also an earnest and faithful member of the Baptist church. At the opening of the Civil war, in 1861, he became captain of company E, Fifty-fourth Alabama regiment, Confederate States army, which was made up of men from different states, and in this capacity served one year, when he was promoted to the rank of major. He also filled this position one year, was then made lieutenant-colonel, in which capacity he served until the war closed. He took an active part in the engagements at Island No. 10 (at which place he was captured and exchanged at the end of five months), Vicksburg, Baker's Creek, Jackson, Resaca, Mobile and the Georgia campaign, in all of which he made an excellent record as a gallant soldier and for distinguished bravery. He started in life as a merchant at Okolona, Miss., in which place he built the second house in 1846. After remaining thus engaged for six years, he gave up merchandising and moved to his farm, where he has lived ever since.

Abram Keller Shaifer (deceased) was so closely and intimately identified with Claiborne county, Miss., and his name was so familiar to all its inhabitants that it is only just to dwell upon what he has done, and the influence his career has had upon others, not as empty words of praise, but the plain statement of a plain truth. He was born in Frederick, Md., in 1778 his parents being of Swiss origin, and in the city of Philadelphia, Penn., he learned the trade of a hatter, but afterward followed merchandising in Tennessee, a calling he pursued with good success. He was an old line whig in politics, and although not an active politician he at all times tried to exercise his right of franchise for men of principle and honor. His determination, enterprise and intelligence were soon recognized and he became a leader in Claiborne county, the residents of which showed their appreciation of his many excellent qualities by electing him to the office of sheriff, a position he filled in an admirable manner for four terms of two years each, after which he refused to be a candidate for re-election. He made a beau-ideal public officer, for he was prompt in the discharge of his duty, fearless in his support of truth and right, and honorable in every particular. He held high rank in the Masonic lodge of Nashville, Tenn., and was a charter member of Washington lodge at Port Gibson. Personally and in every private relation and duty of life too much can not be said in his praise, for he was generous, high-minded and possessed the instinct and training of a true gentleman. His life was illustrated with kind and charitable deeds, and as the wealth and education which he possessed were self-acquired he may with truth be said to have been a selfmade man. As a father he was kind and indulgent, and as a friend was true and tried. He died in 1861, at the advanced age of eighty-three years, and his remains now repose in the Port Gibson cemetery. He selected Miss Elizabeth Hannah Humphreys as his wife, she being a native of Claiborne county, Miss., and to them a family of eight children were born: Sallie Ann, who died at the age of seventeen years; Henry Faulk, married and residing in Vicksburg, Miss.; George Wilson Humphreys; S. P. (deceased); Esther Downing, who died at the age of thirteen years; Elizabeth K. is the wife of John Burnett, a merchant of Port Gibson; Margaret Smith, who died at the age of thirty years, was the wife of John C. Johnson, a planter of Copiah county; and Abraham Keller, who was named for his worthy progenitor. The latter is at the present time living on the old homestead four miles west of Port Gibson, on which place the battle of Port Gibson was fought May 3, 1863. Mr. Shaifer is well and favorably known by the citizens of Claiborne county, for he was born here on the 3d of May, 1833, and has resided here all his life, being one of its most reliable citizens. He was given the advantage of the country schools and the schools of Grand Gulf, and although he was mischievous and wideawake he managed to acquire a better education than the average boy. When a stripling he entered a mercantile establishment, where he remained six years, after which he began giving his attention to planting, and is now the owner of a fine plantation of four hundred acres, which he conducts in an admirable and skillful manner, everything about his home showing that a man of thrift, determination and energy is at the helm. He has been married twice, his first consort being Miss Elizabeth Chamberlain Giranet, a native of Claiborne county, Miss., their union taking place in the month of June, 1857, and resulting in the birth of four children: Benjamin Humphreys, a planter of the county; Abram Keller, who died at the age of eighteen years; George Giranet, who died young, and Edwin Thomas, also deceased. Mr. Shaifer lost his worthy wife in June,

1864, and her remains now repose in the cemetery of Port Gibson. On the 23d of November, 1865, Mr. Shaifer's second marriage was celebrated, his second wife being Miss Amanda C. Guice, whose birth occurred in Tensas parish, La., and resulted in the birth of a son, Percy Leon, who is a prosperous planter of the county and is married to Miss Lizzie Wheeler. Mr. Shaifer's love for his country caused him to enlist in the Confederate army in January, 1862, becoming a member of company K, First Mississippi light artillery, of which Capt. George Abby was commanding officer. Mr. Shaifer was mostly on garrison duty, which called him to Vicksburg, Port Hudson, Mobile, first siege of Vicksburg in 1862, and others. During the forty-nine days' siege of Port Hudson, Mr. Shaifer, with his command, suffered terribly for food, and for a long time was compelled to subsist on rats and mule carcasses. He tells many interesting anecdotes of the war, which are strictly authentic and would fill a large volume. The manner in which he and his brother comrades bore the untold hardships and privations of war proved that they were fighting for a principle and that their lives were nothing when compared with what they considered justice and right. At this siege Mr. Shaifer was paroled and was ordered to Selma, Ala., thence to Mobile, thence to Blakely and Spanish forts, his capture by the Union troops taking place at Fort Blakely. He was conveyed to Montrose, from there to Ship island on Mississippi sound, where he was kept three weeks, and was then taken to Vicksburg, then to Big Black bridge, where three thousand Confederates were paroled. Mr. Shaifer then returned home and began raising cotton, and although the war had caused many changes in Southern life, and reliable help was hard to obtain, yet he continued to prosper, and up to the present date has raised some cotton each year, although for the past fifteen years horticulture has received the greater part of his attention. He is an unswerving democrat, is warm in his support of his party, as a friend is true and stanch, and in his pleasant home he dispenses hospitality in an exceedingly liberal manner, and is well known for his polished and kindly manners. The house in which he resides was pierced by many bullets during the battle of Port Gibson, and a part of a shell and a whole shell passed through the roof. A musket ball crashed through the side of the house, piercing a frame which held the picture of Mr. Shaifer's mother. He and his wife are members of the Methodist Episcopal church, and socially he belongs to the Knights of Pythias, the Knights of Honor and the Knights and Ladies of Honor, all of Port Gibson. His brother, George Wilson Humphreys Shaifer, who makes his home with him on the old plantation, was educated in Oakland college. He was born on the 22d of January, 1822, and until the Civil war opened, with all its horrors, privations and sorrows, followed the life of a planter. Being an enthusiastic Southerner in heart, he heartily espoused her cause, and in the month of September, 1863, became a member of company K, Twelfth Mississippi volunteers, and was assigned to the army of northern Virginia, under Colonel Harris, and was in the thickest of the fight in the following bloody combats: Wilderness, Spottsylvania, where he was wounded in the left hand and right arm, being incapacitated for about sixty days, then took part in the engagements at Yellow Tavern, Petersburg, and Fort Gregg, which was the last engagement fought under General Lee, and was for the purpose of keeping back General Grant so that Lee could get back, gain his supplies and make good his escape, but as the supplies were not at hand the attempt was unsuccessful. Mr. Shaifer surrendered at Fort Gregg, April 3, 1865, and as soon as guards could be formed, was sent to City Point, thence to Lookout Point prison, and on the 1st of July was taken to Washington. From there he went to Baltimore, thence by rail to Cairo and down the Mississippi river to his home. He was married to Miss Charlotte L. Clarke, a native of Claiborne county, by whom he became the father of two children, one of whom is deceased.

The other, Mary, is the wife of L. C. Fisher, a merchant of Cayuga, Miss. Prior to the war Mr. Shaifer was a whig in his political views, but since that time he has been a stanch democrat. He was deputy sheriff of Claiborne county for four years, and was the first marshal of Port Gibson, being assiduous in his devotion to the duties of both offices. He was a volunteer in the Mexican war under command of Col. Jefferson Davis. He is a Master Mason and is a devout member of the St. James Episcopal church of Port Gibson. Both he and his brother Abram have inherited many of their father's worthy qualities, and have been prominently identified with the interests of this section from boyhood.

Hon. Garvin D. Shands, who was born in Spartanburg district, S. C., December 5, 1844, was the eldest child born to Dr. Anthony C. and his wife, Frances J. (Ferguson) Shands, both of whom were natives of South Carolina. Dr. Shands studied medicine in Augusta, Ga., and in 1842 took his degree at the age of twenty-six years, and at once entered upon his practice. In 1868 he removed to Mississippi, after which he retired from the practice of his profession to some extent, spending the remainder of his days in Tate county, two miles from Senatobia. By good management and perseverance he acquired a large practice before the war, but of course lost heavily during that period. He died in 1876. His father was a teacher, and a local minister of the Methodist church in South Carolina. As a family they were adherents of the Methodist church. They took but little interest in politics, not being desirous of distinction in that line. The maternal grandparents of the subject of this sketch were Miles and Mary (Beasley) Ferguson, who were also natives of the Palmetto state. They belonged to the old-time gentlefolk. Garvin Shands passed his early life at the family home, and was educated at Wofford college, South Carolina. Having a taste for law, he chose that for his profession, and took his degree at the University of Kentucky in 1870. At the outbreak of the war he responded to the call of duty, and entered the Confederate army, enlisting in Maj. Edward Manigault's battalion of South Carolina infantry, and at the end of one year in company C Sixth South Carolina cavalry, serving under Col. Hugh K. Aiken. These commands remained at and about Charleston, guarding that port until May, 1864, when the Sixth regiment was transferred to Gen. Wade Hampton's command, all further operations being conducted in Virginia. Mr. Shands participated in all the battles occurring in that state from May, 1864, to January, 1865. At the surrender he was at Hillsboro, N. C., with Johnston's army. In 1867 he removed to Panola county, Miss., where he engaged in teaching, and read law for two years; then, in 1869, went to Tate county, and from there to the law school of the University of Kentucky, graduating, as above mentioned, in 1870. Soon after this he opened an office in Senatobia, where he has built up an extensive practice. In political life he has won honor and distinction, having been a member of the state legislature from 1876 to 1880, and was lieutenant-governor of Mississippi from 1882 to 1890. In 1870 Mr. Shands was married to Miss Mary E. Roseborough, who was a native of Mississippi, her parents, W. D. and E. A. (Williamson) Roseborough, being natives of South Carolina. Mr. and Mrs. Shands have been blessed with five children. Hubert A., the eldest, graduated from the University of Mississippi at the early age of eighteen with high honor, and was immediately tendered the position of fellow in English literature. He is a brilliant young man, and fills the position with great ability. Mabel, the second child, aged seventeen, is in her graduating year at Whitworth college, Brookhaven, Miss., where she has developed great musical talent. The other children, Audley W., thirteen years old; Harley, aged eleven; and Cecil, aged eight, are attending school in Senatobia. Following out the family traditions: Mr. and Mrs. Shands and their two eldest children are members of the Methodist Episcopal church, and Mr. Shands has three times been a delegate to its general conference—at the sessions held in Nashville in 1882; in Richmond, Va., in 1886, and in St. Louis in 1890. He is an active member of the Knights of Honor. He has a large circle of friends who hold him in high regard, and in all his dealings is open and frank, fond and proud of his bright family, and justly proud of his honorable public record.

Dr. J. R. Sharman, Meridian, Lauderdale county, Miss. This well-known and popular physician and surgeon was born in Jasper county, Miss., April 4, 1851. His father, Dr. E. L. Sharman, is a native of Georgia who came to Mississippi about 1821, and located in Jasper county, where he was numbered among the pioneer settlers, Paulding having been at that time regarded as a place of much importance and of greater promise. He was a graduate of the University of Louisville, Louisville, Ky., and practiced at Paulding for thirty-five or forty years. As a matter of special interest it may be stated that he attended Sim Adams, the editor of the *Eastern Clarion*, in his last illness. He is now living retired from his active professional duties at Shubuta, Miss., in Clarke county, having acquired a competency. He had six sons and seven daughters, of whom two sons and one daughter survive. These are Dr. J. R. Sharman, James Sharman, now a student at the University of Oxford, and Mrs. A. R. Johnson, of Birmingham, Ala. Dr. J. R. Sharman obtained his literary education in the private schools of his native county. He began to study medicine in 1874, and was graduated from the Louisville Medical college in 1876, though he took a post-graduate course at the Polyclinic, New York city, N. Y., and two others at the University of Louisiana in New Orleans, La. He began his professional practice at Shubuta, Miss., and there lived until 1883, when he removed to Meridian, Miss., where he has met with much success. He is a member of both the county and state medical associations, and is regarded as an able and trustworthy physician. He was married in 1882 to Miss Mary Trueheart, a native of Mississippi, who was educated at Mobile, Ala. They are the parents of three children: Fannie, Kate and Nellie. The Doctor is a member of the Knights of Honor, and of the Methodist Episcopal church, while Mrs. Sharman is a member of the Protestant Episcopal church. The Doctor is the owner of considerable real estate and quite a number of buildings in Meridian, Miss. Among his other property there may be mentioned the new and elegant Planters' hotel, at the corner of Sixth street and Twenty-fifth avenue, a three-story brick structure, modern in style and well appointed in every respect. Dr. J. R. Sharman is a progressive, enterprising citizen, having at heart the advancement of the material interests of his town and county, and ranking high socially and professionally.

J. M. Sharp, merchant, Friar's Point, Miss., whose success in life is mainly due to his industry and good management, coupled with a pleasant, genial disposition, was born in Coahoma county, Miss., in 1863, and is the fifth of eight children, the result of the union of W. E. and Sarah (Rasor) Sharp. The parents were natives of South Carolina, and both were representatives of old and honored families. They emigrated to Mississippi about 1862, and the father followed the occupation of a planter until his death in 1875. The mother is still living and makes her home with her son, J. M. Sharp. The latter was left fatherless at the age of twelve years and the support of the family fell upon his shoulders principally. He worked and saved for the family, spending nearly all of his boyhood days thus employed, and as a consequence received but limited educational advantages. He remained on the farm until 1882 and then engaged as salesman at Friar's Point. In the fall of 1888 Mr. Sharp started in business for himself at the last mentioned place, and although he was in debt at that time, he has been very successful in his enterprises and is now considerered one of the most prominent business men of Friar's Point. He bought his store, 40x75 feet, one of the largest in town, and carries a full line of groceries, hardware, tinware, crockery, drugs, stationery, feed stuff, etc. His stock is valued at $2,500 and he does an annual business of $35,000. His marriage to Miss Minnie Johnson, of Memphis, occurred in 1889 and to this union one child, Robert L., has been born. Mr. Sharp has also bought a neat, comfortable residence at Friar's Point. He is a member of the Knights of Pythias.

John T. Sharp, planter and merchant, Sharpsburg, Miss., the third in order of birth of a family of eleven children, born to the marriage of Edward and Nancy (Kennedy) Sharp, owes his nativity to Abbeville district, S. C., his birth occurring in 1836. The parents were natives of the Palmetto state also, and were of English and Welsh descent, respectively. The Sharps were pioneers of South Carolina and one of the oldest and most respected families in that state. The grandmother of our subject was born, lived and died in the same house. She was one hundred and seven years of age at the time of her death. The great-grandfather was killed in the Revolutionary war. Edward and Nancy (Kennedy) Sharp removed from South Carolina to near Rome, Ga., in 1848, and there passed the remainder of their days, the father dying in 1884 at the age of eighty-four years, and the mother in February, 1886, at the age of seventy-four years. Most of the children born to this worthy couple died early in life, but five are now living: John T., C. A., Mrs. S. A. Barker, V. A. and J. C., a farmer on the old homestead in Georgia. All but John T. reside on or near the old homestead in Georgia. The last named remained in Georgia until twenty years of age, and there learned the carpenter's trade. In 1856 he came to Mississippi and the same year went from there to New Orleans with only about $40 in money. Four years later, at the beginning of the war, he was worth $75,000 in chattels and money, having been a large contractor in railroad works. He took large contracts in the New Orleans & Jackson railroad, Vicksburg & Meridian railroad and the Mississippi Central railroad. In 1862 he connected himself with the engineer corps of the army of Tennessee, which position he held until the surrender, at which time he was near Augusta, Ga. After this he was obliged to engage with the Federal government a few months to enable him to get home. He built a large bridge across the Chatthoochee river at that time. In September, 1865, he took a contract to reopen the Mississippi Central road from Holly Springs to Jackson, Tenn., and in the course of a few years was again worth $35,000 or $40,000. In 1868 he formed a partnership with E. Richardson and engaged in levee building, having erected forty miles of the levee in Washington and Bolivar counties. In 1875 he settled on his present farm, consisting of three thousand acres, and aside from this he is the owner of about two thousand seven hundred acres in Yazoo county. He did a big business in Vaughan station, in Yazoo county, for a number of years. In 1875 he also began merchandising at this place (Sharpsburg) and this business he still carries on. He now has under cultivation about two thousand five hundred acres, raises six hundred bales of cotton annually and besides raises all his own corn and forage. He is an active democrat in politics and frequently attends political conventions. Mr. Sharp was married in March, 1861, to Miss Susan Ewing, daughter of Jesse and Martha (Johnston) Ewing, both natives of Tennessee and early settlers of Mississippi. To Mr. and Mrs. Sharp were born two children: Lillie E., who died at the age of sixteen years with the yellow fever, and Thomas E., who is a partner with his father. Mrs. Sharp died in 1869, and in 1874 Mr. Sharp was married to Miss Ida V. Ewing, sister of his former wife. By this union were born four children: John T., Jr.; Edward, died at the age of five years; Leslie May and Ida Lee. Mr. and Mrs. Sharp are members of the Methodist church of South Chapel. Mr. Sharp has been a very successful farmer, and although several times his fortune has slipped from him, yet with indefatigable energy he has always been equal to the occasion. He is respected as one of the best and most useful citizens of the county.

Dr. J. W. Sharp, physician, Wall Hill, Miss. Wall Hill and vicinity have a number of physicians, among whom prominently stands Dr. J. W. Sharp, a native of Morgan county, Ala. He was born on the 14th day of March, 1839, and his parents, John and Rebecca (Gillespie) Sharp, were both natives of Virginia. The paternal grandparents, Thomas and Elizabeth (Hodge) Sharp, were born in America; but the maternal grandfather, Robert Gillespie, was a native of the Emerald isle, the maternal grandmother, Gillespie (Cathey), having been born in North Carolina. Dr. Sharp's parents removed from Alabama to Marshall county, Miss., in 1843, bought land two years later near Wall Hill, and there engaged in farming, that being the father's life occupation. He was justice of the peace in the county for a number of years, was one of the pioneers of the county, and was well and favorably known all over it. He and wife were worthy members of the Methodist Church South. The mother died in 1860, and the father in 1879. Dr. J. W. Sharp, the eighth of a family of twelve children, eight of whom are now living, began for himself by enlisting in the Confederate army at the age of twenty-one, Nineteenth Mississippi infantry, under Colonel Mott. He was in General Lee's army, and consequently in all the hard fighting throughout Virginia. He was wounded twice; first at Petersburg, where he received a bad wound in the right hand, and at the same place he was shot in the thigh. He was assistant surgeon of his regiment, and was in the hospital at Danville, Va., at the time of the surrender. After the war he returned to his home in Marshall county, finished his medical education that he had begun before the war, having attended one course of lectures prior to that eventful period in the New Orleans School of Medicine. He was examined by the army board of physicians, and found qualified for the position to which he was appointed in the army. He graduated in 1866 from the New Orleans School of Medicine, and began the practice of his profession the same year at Wall Hill, where he has continued ever since. He has practiced in this place for twenty-five years, and is well known all over the county as a high-minded citizen and a successful physician. In his youthful days he studied under Drs. Alexander and Mabry, and ranks now as one among the leading physicians of Marshall county. He is now in partnership with Dr. Mims, who is also a successful physician of the county. In 1868 he was married to Miss Mary E. Moring, daughter of J. S. Moring and Lucy (Dunn) Moring, and their union has been blessed by the birth of two sons and three daughters: Henrietta W., J. Sidney, Robert W., Minnie and Carrie. Henrietta is a graduate of the Grenada Collegiate institute at Grenada, Miss., and J. Sidney is now taking a literary course at the University of Mississippi, at Oxford. Dr. Sharp has been a member of the Masonic fraternity for thirty years, and was worshipful master for two years of Albert Pike lodge No. 385. He and Mrs. Sharp are members of the Methodist Episcopal Church South. He is also a member of the Tri-State Medical association of Mississippi, Tennessee and Arkansas.

Thompson A. Shaw is one of the prosperous general merchants of Jefferson county, Miss., and by his superior managment and rare business ability and efficiency he has done not a little to advance the reputation the county enjoys as a commercial center. He needs no special introduction to the people of Jefferson county, for he was born here on the 30th of December, 1851, has always resided here and has taken a deep interest in the progress and development of this section. His great-grandfather was born in Ireland and became one of the early settlers of South Carolina, and in that state, T. B. Shaw, his son, was brought up, but in the early part of the present century became a resident of Jefferson county, Miss. Here his son, William Shaw, was born in 1818, his education being obtained in Oxford, Ohio. He was married in this state and county to Miss Mary A. McLaurin, a daughter of Peter McLaurin, formerly of South Carolina. Mrs. Shaw was born in Copiah county, Miss., and to her family of four sons and four daughters she is a most devoted and faithful mother. Mr. Shaw was a planter and merchant in this county until his death, which occurred in 1882. He was a member of the board of police, now called supervisors, for some time and held a number of other local positions of trust and honor, discharging his duties in a manner highly acceptable to his constituents. He was a member of the Masonic fraternity, and was of that moral and personal integrity, and clear, well-balanced, active intelligence, that adorns the private and public station. His third son, E. E. Shaw, is a merchant and planter at the old homestead; S. L. is also a merchant; William, the eldest, is a planter of Texas; one daughter is deceased; and the others are: Maggie A., Kate C. and Lelia. Thompson A. Shaw was given the advantages of the school of Zion Hill, and after he had obtained a good practical English education, he gave his attention to farming for several years. In 1885 he began merchandising at McNair, in a very small way, his stock of goods being quite small but well chosen, and his store building his own. He has since added to both his store and stock, and his present stock of general merchandise is of goodly proportions and exceptionally well chosen. He is a model business man, for he is methodical, punctual and energetic, and he at all times shows the utmost courtesy to his patrons, and endeavors to meet their wants and wishes. He is the soul of honor, and is now one of the substantial merchants of the town. He was married in Franklin county, Miss., on the 17th of November, 1872, to Miss E. J. Newman, daughter of J. P. Newman, and to them the following children were born: Sidney T., Vernon W., Leta L., Alma C., S. Pervis and Annie E. Mrs. Shaw is a member of the Methodist Episcopal church, and socially Mr. Shaw is a member of the Knights and Ladies of Honor.

George B. Shelby is an energetic tiller of the soil of Bolivar county, Miss., and although he was born in Madison, Miss., on the 6th of October, 1844, he has resided here the greater part of his life. He was the eleventh of thirteen children born to Marcus L. and Sarah (Barnes) Shelby, the former of whom was born in Kentucky, and the latter in South Carolina. Marcus D. Shelby came to this state about 1810, and died in 1852, at the age of forty-nine years. He was the second of four children born to Moses and Martha Shelby. George B. Shelby is a lineal descendant of ex-Gov. Isaac Shelby, who was the first governor of the state of Kentucky. In 1865 he began to make his own way in the world, and that, too, under adverse circumstances, but by closely applying himself to business, he bent the force of circumstances to his will and has accumulated a fortune. He is a very extensive planter, and is the owner of one thousand acres of land valued at $25 per acre. He is one of the oldest settlers of the county, and by all who know him is regarded as a very worthy citizen, and a safe business man. His handsome and imposing residence is situated on Holmes Lake bayou, two and one-half miles west of Shelby, which is a wideawake and enterprising town named in honor of the Shelby family, and here he and his intelligent and amiable wife, who was Janie Poilevent, of Grenada, Miss., dispense the unbounded yet unostentatious hospitality for which the Southern people have so justly become famous. Mr. Shelby is a cultured and intelligent gentleman, and the education which he received in Madison college, at Sharon, Madison county, Miss., has been broadened and strengthened by a business life, and by contact with the world. At the opening of the late war he joined Gen. Wirt Adams' regiment, but at the end of six months was detached as a scout, in which capacity he served throughout the remainder of the war, rendering valuable aid to the Confederate cause. No braver or more faithful soldier ever served in the same capacity, and he was trusted and respected by his superior officers as well as being admired and liked by his brother soldiers. He is essentially a selfmade man, has always lived an active life, and has always believed that everybody should have something to do and should endeavor to do it well. He has a brother, Marcus D. Shelby, who is now sheriff of Conway county, Ark., where he has figured prominently in politics and has held the office of sheriff for several years.

Hon. Oscar L. Shelby, merchant and planter, Huntington, Miss., was born in Henderson county, Tenn., in 1843, and inherits Welsh blood from his paternal and Scotch-Irish blood from his maternal ancestors. The grandfather, Evan Shelby, was an early settler of North Carolina and the short-lived state of Franklin. He was a planter by occupation. The maternal grandfather, Isaac McCallum, was also a native of the Old North state and a planter by pursuit. He left the state of his nativity and moved to Tennessee as early as 1818, there passing the closing scenes of his life. Wade Hampton and Judith (McCallum) Shelby, the parents of Oscar L. Shelby, were natives of North Carolina, but the father moved to Tennessee at an early period. He was a planter by occupation, but also a physician of considerable prominence. He was an earnest advocate of the whig party, a leading local politician, and served as sheriff of Henderson county for some time. His death occurred in 1854, and his wife followed him to the grave two years later. Both were devotees in the Christian church. Oscar L. Shelby grew to manhood in his native state, received his education in the common schools, and then entered upon the railroad of life as a schoolteacher. In 1858 he came to Mississippi, clerked at Bolivar Landing until 1861, and then returned to Tennessee, where he continued his former occupation. The same year he entered the company of Henderson sharpshooters, afterward attached to the Twenty-seventh Tennessee infantry, and was a participant of the desperate battles of Shiloh and Corinth. After the last-named struggle he was promoted to the rank of second lieutenant, and served in that capacity for some time. He was in the battles of Murfreesboro, Atlanta, Lovejoy Station, Franklin, and Nashville, where he was captured. At that time he was first lieutenant and was acting captain. He was retained until June 25, 1865, at Fort Delaware and then came to Mississippi, locating in Bolivar county, where he was soon appointed county assessor under Davidson. He then clerked for one year, and in 1870 was married to Mrs. Wilkerson, nee Cornelius, a native of Alabama. Later still he embarked in merchandising at Wilkerson (now Huntington), under the firm name of Shelby & Co., but carries a small stock of goods, mainly to furnish his hands. He is also interested in planting and has control of one thousand acres, with six hundred acres under cultivation. The town of Huntington has been built on the estate. He was justice in the seventies, then supervisor, and in 1889 he was elected a member of the lower house of the state legislature. He is active for general improvement but an opponent of rings and cliques. Although not perhaps a brilliant man in any respect, Mr. Shelby is exemplary in his conduct and example, and is most highly esteemed by the people of his county. He is a member of the Masonic fraternity, the Knights of Pythias and the Knights of Honor. The Shelby family is a very old and prominent one, and has produced many men of note and distinction, after whom towns and counties in both Tennessee and Kentucky are named.

Pettus W. Shell is a representative merchant of Houston, Miss., who, by his untiring industry and exceptionally fine business qualifications, has built up a large and paying patronage. He was born in Newberry district, S. C., April 13, 1841, a son of Francis A. and Mary J. (Dugan) Shell, also natives of that state and county, the birth of the former occurring January 6, 1796, and that of the latter September 19, 1803. The paternal grandfather was Stephen Shell, a Virginian, of Scotch-Irish descent, who was married to a Miss Jane Ellis, also of that state, and with her removed to South Carolina, probably about the year 1760. He was a minister of the Methodist church, devoting a considerable portion of his time to his ministerial duties, but also followed the calling of a planter, at which he became moderately well to do. He reared a large family of children, to each of whom he gave the advantages of a practical education. His son, Francis A., spent his boyhood and early manhood in the state of his birth and his marriage with Miss Dugan took place about 1822, she being a daughter of John and Nancy (Shell) Dugan. At the time of his leaving Newberry district, in 1845, he had accumulated a moderate competency at planting, and this occupation continued to receive his attention after locating in Chickasaw county, or what is now a portion of Clay county, Miss. In 1846, soon after coming to Mississippi, his wife died, having borne him ten children: John and Henry (twins), Robert L., Elizabeth, Edward C., Morgan C., William W., Margaret C., Pettus W., and Mary W. The mother of these children was an earnest Christian, and had been a worthy member of the Methodist church the greater part of her life. In 1852 Mr. Shell was united in marriage to Miss Elizabeth Harrell, by whom he became the father of one child that died in infancy, the mother's death occurring a few days after the birth of her child, about one year after her marriage. After the death of his second wife Mr. Shell remained a widower until his death in October, 1868, at the age of sixty-nine years. He was a member of the Methodist Episcopal Church South, in which he was class leader and steward. Pettus W. Shell was attending the common schools when the war broke out in 1861, but he immediately dropped his books and enlisted in the Confederate service, becoming a member of company A (Buena Vista rifles), Seventeenth Mississippi infantry, May 3, 1861, with which he served in the army of northern Virginia until the close of the war, most of the time a non-commissioned officer. He was in the battles of first Manassas, Ball's bluff, Fredericksburg, Gettysburg, Chickamauga, charge of Fort Sanders, Knoxville, Tenn.; Wilderness (where he was wounded in the left leg), Spottsylvania courthouse, Cold Harbor, the engagements around Petersburg, the battle of Perryville, in valley of Virginia and others. In the last named conflict he was severely wounded in the right leg, which terminated his active service. He was paroled at Columbus, Miss., at the close of the war, and soon after began planting on rented land, but made such a success of this business that at the end of three years he was enabled to purchase two hundred and eighty acres of land, which he tilled until the close of 1871. January, 1872, he and his brother, M. C. Shell, and brother-in-law, J. H. Smith, engaged in merchandising under the firm name of Shell, Smith & Shell, at Houston, Miss., but in 1874 Mr. Smith sold his interest to Col. J. L. S. Hill, and the firm name was changed to Hill, Shell & Brother. At the close of the year 1879 Colonel Hill withdrew, selling his interest to his partners, M. C. and P. W. Shell, and the firm has since been Shell Brothers. Mr. Shell was married January 31, 1866, to Miss Elmina Westbrook, a native of Monroe county, Miss., where she was born in 1845, a daughter of James and Elmina (Glasgow) Westbrook. Mrs. Shell died August 11, 1875, leaving one child, Maggie L., now the wife of J. M. Walker, of Oxford, Ala. Mr. Shell's second wife was formerly Miss Susie E. Matthews, who was born in Williamson county, Tenn., April 12, 1850, their marriage being celebrated on the 28th day of November, 1878. It resulted in the birth of three children: Frank A. S., Mary Matthews and Thomas Elkin. Mrs. Shell's parents, Thomas and Mary Matthews, were Tennesseeans by birth, but about 1857 became residents of Monroe county, Miss. Mr. Matthews was instantly killed by the lever of a cottonpress, October 13, 1875, in Monroe county, Miss. Mr. Shell is a democrat in politics, has been a member of the board of selectmen of Houston two terms, is a charter member of the Knights of the Golden Rule, and he and his wife are members of the Methodist Episcopal Church South, in which he is a steward. Of the children born to Francis A. Shell, only three are now living: M. C., Margaret C. (wife of Dr. James R. Ford, of McCondey, Miss.) and Pettus W. Six sons were in the Confederate army, of whom only one returned unhurt: William

W. died of fever at Richmond, Robert L. sickened and died at Lynchburg, Henry was killed at Petersburg, while retiring from picket duty, and John was the only one unhurt. After the war he engaged in milling at Aberdeen, Miss., near which place he died in 1888, leaving a wife and three children, who are still living and reside in Clay county, Miss. Morgan C., was a clerk in and near West Point for a few years after becoming grown. He was married to Miss Sallie R. Huff, a native of Mississippi and a daughter of Daniel and Elizabeth (McCullon) Huff, who were born near Pulaski, Tenn. He was called upon to mourn the death of his wife in 1870, she having borne him two daughters and a son: Daniel H.; Mary E., wife of Rev. J. C. Park, of Strong station, Miss.; and Clemmie, wife of Dr. J. A. Evans, of Houston. Morgan C. Shell entered the Confederate army in 1862, and belonged to the Thirty-first Mississippi infantry, army of the Tennessee, with which he took part in the various campaigns and battles until the engagement at Franklin, when he was wounded in the ankle by a ball, which resulted in the loss of his leg. After the war he followed the calling of a clerk until he was elected to the office of county and probate clerk, in 1866, serving until the spring of 1869, when he re-engaged in clerking. This calling occupied his time and attention until 1872, when he and his brother and Mr. Smith, P. W. Shell's brother-in-law, opened a mercantile establishment in Houston, Miss. He was married in 1872, to Mrs. Sally M. Wilcox, widow of M. Wilcox, a lawyer of Okolona. The various members of the Shell family have been strict adherents of the principles of democracy and he is a member of the Masonic fraternity and served for a number of years as master of the lodge of Houston. He is a charter member of the Knights of the Golden Rule, and he, as well as the other members of his family, is a member of the Methodist Church South.

David Shelton, one of the oldest residents of Jackson, and a prominent member of the bar, was born February 22, 1813, in Smith county, Tenn. His parents were James and Nancy (Marshall) Shelton, the latter being a distant relative of John Marshall. Both were born in Virginia, where they were married about the year 1809. The father of James, William Shelton, was a Virginian, and was a colonel in the Revolutionary war. Both families were of English ancestry. There were two children besides David, who is the eldest, who grew to maturity: William, who is a minister of the Baptist church, at present residing near Nashville, Tenn., and Henry, who resides in California. James Shelton was a planter by occupation, and passed from life in Tennessee in 1844, his widow surviving him about twenty years. The early life of David Shelton was spent on the plantation, attending the academy near home, until 1831, when he entered the University of Nashville, from which he was graduated in 1833. He then returned home, and for a year devoted himself to reading history. He then went to Nashville and became a law student in the office of Bux & Meigs. He was admitted to the bar at Nashville in the fall of 1835, and after taking part in a few law cases in Tennessee he removed to Mississippi, locating at Jackson in the fall of 1836, where he opened an office and began practicing his profession. He soon built up a large practice and was very successful at the bar. In politics he was a whig, and like the majority of that party was opposed to secession. In the fall of 1868 he was a candidate for the state senate, running under the new reconstruction measures against James R. Lynch. He was elected by the popular vote of the state, but the state rejected the constitution under which the legislature was to be held. This was the only occasion of his being a candidate for any official position, preferring always to give his attention to his profession. He was married at Jackson in April, 1845, to Lavinia, daughter of Prior Lee. The issue of this union was eight children: James, Prior L., Maria, David, Lavinia, William, Lucy and Henry, all living but James and Henry. Of the members of the bar that were in Jackson when Mr. Shelton came, none are now living. He had accumulated a good property when the war broke out, but during that long struggle he lost the greater part of it. His residence, which was in the suburbs of Jackson, was between the two lines, and the emergencies of war caused it to be laid in ashes. It was burned by order of the Confederate authorities, as it was affording a convenient protection to the Federal sharpshooters. For this loss he received no compensation from the Confederate government.

S. M. Shelton is a lawyer of the firm of Birchett & Shelton, and was born in Hanover county, Va., on August 3, 1837, being the eldest of eight children born to W. C. and Ella (Masey) Shelton, the former of whom was a successful planter and a prominent citizen of his native state, Virginia. He is still living, but his wife died in 1870, she as well as Mr. Shelton, having belonged to old and prominent Virginia families. The paternal ancestors were of English origin and the maternal ancestors of Welsh descent. S. M. Shelton was educated in Hampton and Sidney college, Virginia, and in September, 1859, came to Mississippi to seek his fortune. He soon after began the study of law with an uncle at Raymond, Miss., but upon the bursting of the war cloud which so long hovered over the country, he laid aside his books, and on April 29, 1861, enlisted in company A, Twelfth Mississippi regiment of infantry, with which he served until 1863, when he was transferred to company B, Forty-fourth Virginia regiment, and served until the battle of Spottsylvania courthouse on May, 1864, at which time he was captured and held as a prisoner of war until March, 1865, being near Appomattox courthouse at the time of Lee's surrender. In 1866 Mr. Shelton returned to Mississippi and in January of the same year was admitted to the bar at Raymond. Since 1877 he has been a legal practitioner of Vicksburg, and was first associated in his practice with a Mr. Lee, the firm being Shelton & Lee, for two years, and from that time until 1889 was associated with Mr. Crutche, the present firm being organized in 1890. This firm are the attorneys for the Alabama & Virginia railroad, the Merchants' National bank, Sengers Manufacturing company, and the Stower's Furniture company. Mr. Shelton has been married twice, first to Miss Z. Imogene Gray, daughter of Joseph Gray, Esq., of Raymond, Miss. Mrs. Shelton died in April, 1885, leaving a son and daughter: Annie E. and Samuel Percy. His second union was to the sister of his first wife, Miss Annie Gray, in 1887. Mr. Shelton and his wife are members of the Presbyterian church, in which he is an elder, and has been superintendent of the Sunday-school since January, 1878. He is the owner of a fine residence in South Vicksburg and is in good circumstances financially. Mr. Shelton is thoroughly posted in his profession, is a fluent and eloquent orator, and that his ability is known and recognized, is shown by his large clientage.

Richard Butler Hooke Shepherd (deceased) was born in Virginia while his parents were visiting there and is the son of Charles Moses Shepherd, of Shepherdstown, Va., which place was named in honor of the Shepherd of this family who first settled there. Moses Shepherd came to Louisiana at the age of seventeen years and engaged in sugar planting. He was born in 1801 and was married March 11, 1829, to Margaret Ann Hooke, of Wilkinson county, who was the daughter of Captain Moses and Harriet (Butler) Hooke, the first settlers of this county and natives of Augusta, Me., and Carlisle, Penn., respectively. Harriet was the sister of Col. Richard Butler (of whom further notice is made in this sketch), one of this county's early settlers and prominent citizens. He entered the tract comprising the Woodstock plantation from the Spanish government, and married but died in middle life and left no children. He was colonel in Gen. James Wilkinson's army, stationed at Fort Adams. His father, William Butler, was the third son of the Duke of Ormond, of Ireland. He came to Pennsylvania when a young man, where he married and reared a large family.

Capt. Moses Hooke settled the place now known as the Salisbury plantation, adjoining the Woodstock plantation, both of which belonged to R. B. H. Shepherd. Moses Hooke was a captain in Wilkinson's army, and was a man of prominence and was intimately connected with the early history of this county. He died August 9, 1821, aged forty-four years. His wife was first married to a very old gentleman, who died within a month, and she was then married to Captain Hooke, by which union were born sons and daughters as follows: Moses J. (who died January 2, 1834, aged thirty-three years), Richard B. (who died November 2, 1812, aged seven years); Sarah J. (who died September 5, 1819, aged nine years); William B. (who died September 26, 1837, aged twenty-three years); Richard B. (who died September 1, 1837, aged nineteen years); Margaret Ann Hooke, who married C. M. Shepherd, father of R. B. H.; Harriet, who first married a man named Tutle, and after his death a Mr. Bennett. She died leaving no children. Moses Hooke died at Salisbury plantation and was buried with his sons and daughters. His widow was afterward married to a Mr. Browder, of Natchez, by whom was born one daughter, Jane, who married Pierre Buller McCutcheon, of Pass Christian, Miss. Mr. Browder was supposed to have been killed by the John H. Murrell pirates. Mrs. Browder died July 16, 1830, aged forty-three years. To Mr. and Mrs. C. M. Shepherd were born four sons and one daughter, who lived to be grown and one who died young: Charles Moses, Abram, Harriet H., Henry and Richard B. H. Francis died November 28, 1837, aged seven years. Charles Moses was a captain in the Confederate army from Louisiana, Abram was an invalid, Harriet first married Dr. Follen, of Mobile, and second Mr. McClelland, of New Orleans, and lived at Pass Christian, Miss.; Richard Butler Hooke Shepherd, the subject of this memoir, entered his first school at Pass Christian, Miss., and from there to the grammar school near Philadelphia, Penn., thence to the University of Virginia and from there to Dresden, the capital of Saxony, Germany, where he attended school for several years and completed his education.

He returned to the United States during the late war, coming through the North, making his way to New Orleans, and joining the Confederate army at that place. He entered the cavalry service, and at one time was a member of General Briggs' staff. He was also commissioned second lieutenant. His brother Henry served in the same regiment, and with these two young men were the servants who went with them to serve their wants. These servants are now in the service of Mrs. K. B. Shepherd; they have always lived with the family. Mr. Shepherd served until the close of the war, and during this bloody period his uncle died, leaving him this fine plantation, where he resided until his death. He was married June 21, 1871, to Miss Kate B. Morson, a beautiful and highly accomplished lady, a native of Virginia, and daughter of Alexander and Maria (Berry) Morson, natives of Virginia, and prominent citizens on the Rappahannock, near Fredricksburg. Both of the parents are deceased; they had five children: Alexander, deceased; John Andrew, who is living in Mississippi, and is a retired planter; Arthur A, who lives near Jackson, Miss.; Susan S., who died, aged fifteen years, then Mrs. Shepherd. Her parents having died when she was an infant, she was reared by her uncle James Morson, and educated by private tutors, and at the Southern Female college. She is a lady of fine attainments, and very high accomplishments, loved by all, and one of this county's most charming women. She is the mother of four lovely children, one of whom is deceased. Arthur M., the eldest, is a student at the Episcopal school, Sewanee, Tenn., and is very bright and promising; Kate B. and Margaret H., beautiful girls, are at Pass Christian, Miss., and Richard B. died at the age of eighteen months. Mr. and Mrs. Shepherd, with their family, were members of the Episcopal church. Mr. Shepherd, at his death, owned a fine estate. He was one of the county's most active and successful men. The family are very highly respected, and own one of the most beautiful places in the county. Major Butler was a member of Gen. James Wilkinson's army at Fort Adams, and was ordered by his commanding officer to have his queue cut off, but refused to obey, and was put under arrest. He soon after sickened and died. He gave orders about his burial; "Bore a hole," said he, "through the bottom of my coffin, right under my head, and let my queue hang through it, that the infernal old rascal may see that, even when dead, I refuse to obey his orders." These directions were literally carried out.

Robert C. Shepherd, one of the most successful business men of Yazoo county, is a native of the Buckeye state. He was born in Butler county January 7, 1835, and is the second of a family of seven children of Daniel and Catherine (Clayton) Shepherd, natives of Pennsylvania and New Jersey, respectively. The father was reared in Ohio, and there received his education in the common schools. He was a contractor and builder by trade. In 1849 he removed with his family to Mississippi, and located in Tallahatchie county, where he was engaged in railroad contracting. In 1853 he went to Marshall county, and there contracted for bridges and trestles on the Mississippi Central railroad. He remained in Marshall county until 1860, removing in that year to Arkansas, where he contracted for the construction of bridges and trestles on the Memphis & Little Rock railroad. In 1862 he enlisted in the Confederate army, and served bravely until he was killed in 1864, at Arkansas Post, where he was buried. He was a son of Stephen Shepherd, a native of Pennsylvania, of Welsh extraction. Robert C. was reared and educated in Ohio. At the age of seventeen years he accepted a situation as clerk of a steamboat plying the Yazoo river, between Yazoo City and Vicksburg. He held this position until 1862, when navigation was stopped by the fall of Memphis. During the war he was engaged in the civil service of the Confederate states, as he was physically unable for active duty. After the end of the war he was offered a situation in a large mercantile establishment in Yazoo City, which he filled until the autumn of the same year, 1865, when he went into business for himself. He formed a partnership with W. H. Mangum, and in 1867 he purchased the entire stock, became sole proprietor, and the firm name was changed to R. C. Shepherd, general plantation supply business. His efforts have met with marked success, and he has accumulated a comfortable fortune, consisting of real estate, mortgages, and bank stock. Upon the organization of the Yazoo City bank, in 1876, he invested largely in the stock, and was at once made president. Under his wise supervision the institution has been highly prosperous. The present capital stock is $100,000, with $50,000 surplus. He has large real estate interests in Chattanooga, Tenn. He was married in 1865 to Mary J. Fuque, a native of Mississippi and a daughter of John W. Fuque, a native of Virginia. Mrs. Shepherd died in 1873, mourned by all who knew her. Mr. Shepherd is a Mason, and although he is not a member of any church he is a liberal contributor to all religious movements. He has no aspirations to political honors, but lives a retired life, enjoying to the fullest extent the respect of the entire community.

Dr. J. N. D. Shinkel is the third of seven children born to Isaac and Mary (Faustnight) Shinkel, his birth occurring in Brookville, Ill., March 18, 1857. The parents were both natives of Pennsylvania and were of German and French origin respectively. The father followed the occupation of a merchant and settled in Illinois at an early day. His death occurred in 1885, at the age of fifty-nine years. The mother is now residing at Aurora, Ill. Dr. Shinkel attended the Rochelle high school, and in 1878 entered the Cornell university, New York, from which he graduated in the class of 1881 in the course of science and letters. When about eighteen years of age he began the study of medicine, and when at Cornell took the medical preparation course. After graduating at the last-named institution he spent fifteen months in Europe, studying medicine at Vienna and London, after which he returned and took a regular course at Rush Medical college, Chicago, taking his degree from that college in 1884. He was surgeon for the Longford Lumber company, of Canada, for one year, and in January, 1886, he came South, locating at Friar's Point in the following month. Dr. Shinkel is a member of the Tri-State Medical society, and has been county physician for Coahoma county for the past five years. He is of literary taste and habits, often contributes to medical journals, and is a constant student of subjects relating to his profession. The Doctor contemplates another trip to Europe for especial study. Though not a specialist in surgery he has made especial study of those branches, and practices in those cases with great success. He is examiner for a number of life insurance companies and does considerable in that line. Miss Georgia Clindinning, who became his wife on the 7th of November, 1888, is a native of Arkansas, and the daughter of J. A. and J. C. Clindinning. Her father was a planter and merchant at La Grange, Ark., and her mother was a member of the Alcorn family, her maiden name being Julia C. Alcorn. Dr. Shinkel was quite a noted athlete and oarsman in his college days; was stroke oar and captain of the college crew, and for a time was commodore of the Cornell navy. He won many races, being stroke oar of a crew of four that made the best time on record. He is of medium size, compactly built, dark hair and eyes, and has a striking countenance. He is permanently located in Coahoma county, has a rapidly growing practice, and sees a bright future opening before him. Although solicited to remove to Memphis he thinks it best to remain among the people who have given him such a cordial reception here. The Doctor has recently finished a very neat cottage, one of the neatest and coziest in town. He is one of the organizers of the Bank of Friar's Point and has been a director in the same since. He is a member of the Masonic lodge and also the Knights of Pythias, Coahoma lodge No. 49.

J. N. Shirley was born in Lauderdale county, Miss., in April, 1858, the fourth in a family of eight children born to J. P. and Sarah (Martin) Shirley, the former of whom was born in North Carolina, and the latter in Greene county, Miss. The father was taken by his parents to Alabama when a small boy, and there resided until he was seventeen years of age, when he came to Mississippi and located in Lauderdale county, where he still lives. Here he was married, and on the plantation on which he is now living he reared his family. He has made planting his chief occupation throughout life, never caring to enter political life, or to hold any public office. J. N. Shirley began the battle of life for himself when sixteen years of age, and when only eighteen years of age was married to Miss Nancy Dunham, of this county, and to them four sons and three daughters have been born: Arabella, Tolitha, Charles (deceased), Arthur, Julian and Justin (twins), and Ora. Although Mr. Shirley commenced to make his own way in the world without a dollar, he has, by energy and strict attention to business, succeeded in getting a fair start in the world. In 1881 he opened a mercantile establishment, and to this calling has given the most of his attention since that time, but has also farmed more or less, and has been engaged in milling a part of the time. He began business in the southeastern part of Lauderdale county, where he remained until 1889, at which time he sold out and moved to his present location, thirteen and a half miles north of Meridian, where he had purchased a plantation of one hundred and twenty acres. On this plantation he opened his store, his stock of goods being worth at least $3,000, from which he derives an annual income of $15,000. He is a young man of excellent business qualifications, and thus far has made a success of the enterprises in which he has engaged, when many others would have failed. He is progressive, public-spirited and intelligent, and makes a point of keeping well posted on the general topics of the day, and up with the times in the business affairs of life. By his honorable methods of doing business and his many amiable and worthy traits of character, he has won the respect and esteem of all who know him, and he and his wife are gladly welcomed in the highest social circles. He and Mrs. Shirley are members of the Baptist church, and he has been liberal in his support of this as well as other churches. He is a patron of education; in fact all worthy enterprises receive his hearty support.

Jordan P. Short, planter, Melrose, Miss., is the sixth of ten children born to Monroe and Lucinda (Harrison) Short, the father a native of North Carolina, and the mother of Tennessee. Monroe Short was an extensive planter of Mississippi, and an honored and highly respected citizen. He came to this state in 1848, settled in Panola county, and at the time of his death, which occurred in 1883, he had accumulated quite a fortune. He was of Scotch-Irish origin. His parents were James and Elizabeth Short. Mrs. Short's father was W. H. Harrison, and the latter's father was a cousin of ex-President William Henry Harrison. Jordan P. Short is a native of Panola county, Miss., born on the 22d of February, 1852, and remained in the private schools of the same until sixteen years of age, when he attended school at White Creek Springs, Tenn., for two years. He subsequently entered the William and Henry college of Virginia, but at the end of two years, on account of ill health, he was obliged to leave school, and since that time has been engaged in planting. He has been successful in this occupation, and is the owner of five thousand acres of land, two thousand five hundred acres under a fine state of cultivation. He has a beautiful residence, and everything about his place indicates the owner to be a man of enterprise and progress. Aside from his planting interests he is also engaged in merchandising, and carries a stock of goods valued at $3,000. Miss Mary W. Sorrels, who became his wife in 1877, was born in Mississippi, and is the daughter of Robert P. and Mary B. Sorrels. The fruits of this union have been seven children: Mary L., Lelia A., Bennie B., Robert S., Monroe and Jordan P., Jr., and Lillian L. Mr. Short and family are members of the Methodist church, and although he is a democrat in his political views, he is not an active partisan. He is liberal with his means to further all enterprises for the good of the county, and is a live, energetic young man. He stands very high in the estimation of the people, and wields a great deal of influence in his vicinity. In personal appearance he is tall, but not powerfully built, dark hair, gray eyes, and is considered a handsome man.

Mrs. Laura Shotwell, widow of the late Bourboun Shotwell, was born in Nashville, Tenn., January 26, 1833, the elder of two children born to John G. and Anna (Work) Hay, both of whom were Kentuckians by birth. Mrs. Shotwell's marriage to Mr. Shotwell took place in 1849, her husband having been born in Madison county, Ala., September 2, 1829. His parents, Robert and Mary (Tallefano) Shotwell, were born in Georgia and Alabama, respectively. Bourboun Shotwell was reared in Lowndes and Madison counties, Miss., and was educated in Princeton and Bardstown, Ky., graduating from a college of the last-named place. After leaving school he read law, and was admitted to the bar in 1849, but his large planting interests occupied his attention so completely that he found no time to devote to the practice of his profession, and in time abandoned all thought of practice. He became the owner of large tracts of valuable land in Hinds, Scott, Holmes, Tallahatchie, Quitman and Coahoma counties, and was very thorough and practical in the management of his real estate. In 1863 he enlisted in the Confederate army, becoming a member of company A, Withers' light artillery, and was a participant in the siege of Vicksburg, where he was wounded, but not seriously. He served until the close of the war, when he returned to his home, and once more assumed the duties of a planter, a calling he followed until his death, in 1883. He was modest and retiring in disposition, and although well known and greatly admired, he was never a candidate for office, much preferring the quiet, uneventful life of a planter to one of political strife and intrigue. Of six children born to himself and wife the following are living: Anna L., wife of A. Perkins; Ellen H., wife of T. K. Green, of Natchez; Walter G., who has inherited many of his worthy father's fine business qualities and principles, is the owner of twenty-five thousand acres of land, and is one of the leading business men and substantial planters of the county of Coahoma; Bourboun, a planter, and Laura H. Robert is deceased. Mrs. Shotwell is now residing on the old home plantation, six miles from Jackson, is an estimable woman, and is an earnest and devoted member of the Christian church.

B. Shotwell was born in Hinds county, Miss., on April 15, 1865, his brothers and sisters being also born in the state of Mississippi. He was the third of his parents' seven children. His father and mother, B. and Laura (Hay) Shotwell, were born in Alabama and Tennessee, respectively, and the former when a youth, graduated with honors from Bardstown (Kentucky) college, after which he studied law under Judge Sharkey, of Jackson, Miss., and although he was admitted to the bar he never practiced his profession. He came to Mississippi in 1835, settled in Madison county, and in connection with his father, purchased a large tract of land in Madison and Coahoma counties. Prior to the war he came to Hinds county, purchased a large body of land and became very wealthy, but during the hostilities between the North and South, all his accumulations were swept away with the exception of his real estate. He enlisted in Withers' artillery, and was on active duty in Mississippi until the fall of Vicksburg, when he went to Demopolis, Ala., and engaged in some government constructions. He was wounded at Vicksburg. B. Shotwell, the subject of this sketch, attended the common schools up to the age of fifteen years, then entered the city schools of Jackson, where he remained two years. At the end of this time he returned home and took charge of the home plantation, which comprises about two thousand acres, the most of which is good productive soil. Seven hundred acres are under cultivation, which annually produce one hundred and fifty bales of cotton and four thousand bushels of corn. In the ten years that he has managed this place he has only purchased about fifty bushels of corn. He raises a sufficient number of cattle and hogs to supply them with meat for family use. He was married in 1888 on January 18, to Miss Lydia George, a native of Madison county, Miss., by whom he has one child, Walter G. Socially Mr. Shotwell is a member of the K. of H., and has always been interested in worthy enterprises. He is a genial, whole-souled gentleman, and is very hospitable and has many warm friends.

As a man of business James A. C. Shrader has become well known throughout Sharkey county and the surrounding country, but during the time that he has been connected with the business affairs of life his career has been illustrated with acts of liberality. With each vital interest of his section and his people he has been closely identified, and every step taken in the development of this section has found in him a warm supporter. He was born in Benton county, Ala., August 8, 1834, his father, Henry Shrader, being a native of Kentucky, born and reared near Lexington. The latter's father came to this country from Germany and settled near the above city, where he reared his family. Henry learned the trade of a machinist, a calling he followed for some years after settling in Alabama, and in that state was married to Miss Mary Weatherly, a native of the state, by whom he became the father of ten children— seven sons and three daughters: John W. settled in Texas, where he is a planter; Mary A. is the wife of W. A. Bevil, also of Texas; Henry A. is a resident of Arkansas and was a soldier in the Confederate army during the late war; Thomas is connected with the Shelby Iron

works of Alabama; George came to Mississippi, and was a resident of Sharkey county until 1886, when he moved to Bolivar county, where he died in 1887, leaving a wife, four sons and three daughters (he was a soldier in the Confederate army); James A. C. comes next in order of birth; Jackson V. also served in the Confederate army and is now residing in Alabama, and Isaac, who is also a resident of that state. Two little daughters died in infancy. The father of these children was born in 1799 and died in Alabama in 1882, having, during the last years of his life, followed farming. His wife was called from earth in 1838, in Alabama, both being worthy members of the Methodist Episcopal church at the time of their death. When only thirteen years of age James A. C. Shrader began earning his own living, one-half of his time being spent at farm work and the other half in going to school. At the age of nineteen years he was married and began devoting himself to farming, continuing to reside in Alabama until 1856, when, with his family, he moved to Mississippi and took up his abode in the Yazoo delta, where, after a few years, he purchased some land, on which he resided until 1865. Since that time he has been a resident of Sharkey county, but has only resided on his present plantation since 1869. He is the owner of several hundred acres of fine land, a considerable portion of which is under cultivation, and on which is located a good general store. He has been engaged in merchandising since 1876, but first conducted affairs on a very small scale, and gradually increased his business as his patronage demanded it, and now has a first-class stock of goods and is doing a prosperous business. His wife, formerly Miss Mary E. Logan, was born in Alabama, a daughter of James Logan, a planter of that state, and by her he has a family of four sons and two daughters, who are living at the present time: William Henry is married and resides on the Sunflower river; Samuel is married and lives near his father; W. P. is married, lives at home and is a bookkeeper in his father's store; James resides at home; Isabella is now the wife of Charles Lewis; she was first married to J. A. Overby (deceased), a planter; Rosa is the wife of W. J. Clark, a planter of Washington county, Miss. Mary B., another daughter, became the wife of Charles Lewis, a merchant of Percy, Miss., and died at the age of twenty years; three other children died in infancy. Mr. and Mrs. Shrader are rearing a little orphan girl, Annie Hill, who is now in her twelfth year. Her parents died when she was very young, she being their only child, and she has since found a father and mother in her good friends, Mr. and Mrs. Shrader. Mr. Shrader is a typical Southerner, and, upon the opening of the Civil war, espoused the cause he considered right and just and enlisted from Yazoo county, Miss., in Withers' light artillery, being taken prisoner at the siege of Vicksburg. He was in the Chickasaw bayou fight, just before the engagement at Vicksburg, and after the siege he went to Texas, where he remained about one year. Upon returning to what is now Sharkey county, Miss., he was appointed by the governor as one of the members of the board of supervisors of the county, which office he efficiently filled for ten years. He is a democrat, politically, and he and his wife are members of the Universalist church. An organization of that faith, known as the Vickland church, was organized in 1886 by J. C. Burruss, editor of the *Universalist Herald*, which he publishes in Alabama, with Rev. Pope as the first pastor, the latter being from Illinois. There are about twenty-five members now on the roll. Mr. Shrader is a self-made man, is very highly respected and esteemed, is well to do, and is now residing in a beautiful residence, which has just been completed.

Among the many enterprises necessary to complete the commercial resources of a town or city no one is of more importance to the community than the pharmacist, and prominent in this trade is John A. Shreve, who keeps one of the finest establishments of the kind in the town of Port Gibson, his stock of goods being exceptionally large and well selected. He was born in Nelson county, Ky., August 12, 1854, being the eldest child of his father's last marriage. A short sketch of his parents and brother Charles is given in the article immediately succeeding this. His brother, James B., is a resident of Chicago, and his sister, Ruth B., resides in Port Gibson, Miss., and is a thorough student of the New England conservatory of music, Boston, Mass., being also a preceptress in the Port Gibson Female college. John A. Shreve obtained his early scholastic training in the schools of Port Gibson and at a later period became a student in Forest academy, near Louisville, Ky., in which he received a full academic course, which has thoroughly fitted him for the active business life he has led. He made his debut in the business circles of Port Gibson at the age of twenty-two years, succeeding to his father's fine drug establishment, and has proved himself a stirring, successful and popular business man. His aim is at all times to meet the wants of the public and to make his store the central emporium of trade in his line of goods. In addition to a most complete line of pure drugs and chemicals he keeps the standard school books, stationery, etc., and in fact all articles that go to make up an admirable drug store. He is a gentleman of genial, social and refined tastes and always courteously and cordially attends upon the wants of his customers, his efforts to gratify their wishes and desires being fully appreciated, as is fully attested by the large patronage which he has gathered about him. On the 28th of February, 1877, he was married in Natchez, Miss., to Miss Sue Willie Wickliffe, a native of Kentucky, who was born in the town of Bardstown, being the next to the youngest in her parents' family. The Wickliffe family is well known throughout the state of Kentucky, her great-uncle, Hon. Charles A. Wickliffe, having been governor of Kentucky and was also postmaster-general during President Tyler's administration. Her great-grandfather, Robert Wickliffe, was a very prominent resident of Lexington, Ky. To Mr. and Mrs. Shreve a family of six children were born, only three of whom are living: Margaret H., born February 24, 1879, an attendant of Port Gibson Female college; Charles, born August 16, 1881, and John, Jr., born August 18, 1886. Mr. Shreve has not been an active politician, but has always exercised his franchise for the democratic principles, and for men whom he deemed competent and honorable. He has been a member of the board of aldermen of Port Gibson, Miss., for a number of years, and his marked ability and his individual efforts in the interests of his city were so generally observed by the citizens, his constituents and associates, that upon his resignation a beautiful tribute was paid him in the form of a testimonial which was recorded in the minutes of the municipal body and a memorial copy presented him. For a number of years he was a trustee of the Port Gibson academy, a position he also filled with distinction after the incorporation of the Chamberlain Hunt academy. In his religious views he is a churchman and is a member and vestryman of St. James Episcopal church at Port Gibson, of which church his wife is also a member. Mr. Shreve is one of that type of men who present a strong example for the younger generation to follow, for his life has been strictly upright and he has endeavored to follow the teachings of the Golden Rule. As far as he can at present judge he and his wife expect to make Port Gibson their future home, where, by their many kind, disinterested and benevolent deeds, as well as by their many admirable social qualities, they have gathered about them a host of warm admirers and friends.

"In memory of Mr. Charles Shreve, who died of yellow fever August 31, 1878; Mrs. Margaret Shreve, his beloved wife, who died September 9, 1878, and their son Charles Shreve, who died September 11, 1878. The terrible scourge of yellow fever carried to their graves these excellent people, whose demise caused a pall to spread over our entire city. The position Mr. Shreve held in this community, the integrity of his character, and his benevolent disposition render his death a serious public calamity and an irreparable loss to many who confided in him as a friend and a counselor. Mr. Shreve was born in Mount Holly, Burlington county, N. J., November 25, 1813. He was the fourth son of Charles and Rebecca (Cox) Shreve. He was left early without parental privileges, and was reared by an aunt who belonged to an old Quaker family. His paternal grandparents came to this country from Holland in the early part of the eighteenth century and settled in Burlington county, N. J. His maternal grandparents came from Scotland about the same time and settled in the same place. Dr. Alexander Ross, his great-grandfather, came to this country after completing his course in Edinburgh university. He was an uncle of the Hon. John Ross, chief of the Cherokee nation, whose descendants have been the most prominent and influential men of the nation for many years. He was married to a Miss Becket, whose mother, a Miss De Normandie, belonged to a French Protestant family who fled from France after the revocation of the edict of Nantes. His mother, Rebecca (Cox) Shreve, was the daughter of Richard and Jane (Ross) Cox. Richard Cox was a major in the Revolutionary war. Mr. Shreve was twice married—first to Miss Corianna H. Brashear, of Kentucky, July 21, 1846, who died in Buffalo, N. Y., August 13, 1850. He was married, a second time, to Miss Margaret B. Hackley, of Kentucky, in August, 1853. He left one child by his first wife, Robert S. Shreve, now of Louisville, Ky., and four by his second wife, one of whom, Charles Shreve, died a few days after his father. Mr. Shreve began life in that county's speculative age, when young men sought to lay the foundation for business by learning the principles of a profession. When about fifteen years of age he was received as an apprentice into the well-known drug firm of John Hart, in the city of Philadelphia, and there by patience and industry he qualified himself for a signally successful business man. He first came South in October, 1835, and after remaining a few weeks in Natchez came to Port Gibson and entered the drug store of Samuel P. Bernard, where he remained as clerk till 1836, when he went to Grand Gulf, where he continued in business until 1852, when he finally settled in Port Gibson. As a man of honor and integrity Mr. Shreve had no superiors. The nobility of his character won for him the highest esteem of his fellow-citizens. The ideal of his life was raised above the plane on which suspicion and criticism are wont to link. There was nothing covert or ambiguous about him. He would never allow himself to stand in a false position, and his fidelity to truth was unswerving. As a business man he was the full representative type of those old-fashioned principles which have become almost obsolete. He relied on industry, economy and strict perseverance as the elements of success. His economy was gilded with benevolence. The poor could pay a noble tribute to his memory. As a man of moral rectitude and sincerity of purpose Charles Shreve had no superior in Port Gibson. He was a thorough Christian gentleman and resigned himself complacently to his Almighty. Mrs. Shreve survived her husband but a few days. For many years she had been an invalid. She was born in Bardstown, Ky., where she continued to live until 1853, when she married Mr. Shreve, and came to Mississippi. For many years she had been a member of the Presbyterian church. She was affectionate and kind in her domestic relations, to which she particularly resigned herself. She was entirely free from all ostentation or fondness for display. There is no compensation for the loss of a loving, faithful mother. In a few days Charles Shreve, Jr., died, in the twenty-third year of his age. He was a model young man, and was just budding into useful manhood. His moral character was unimpeachable, and he at all times exerted a wholesome influence over his associates. He had chosen the medical profession as his life duty, and had been reading under the directions of Dr. Russell with a view of attending the next term of lectures in the Jefferson (Philadelphia) Medical college. He was a young man of more than ordinary attainments naturally. He was advised to flee from the terrible scourge, but sacrificed his young life to remain with his adored parents. Thus were consigned to the tomb three personages in the history of Port Gibson who were central figures in its business and social arena."

Hon. Joseph K. Shrock, a prominent farmer and merchant of Attala county, Miss., was born in Kershaw district, S. C., on the 6th of May, 1821, and is next to the youngest of seven children born to Henry and Mary (Fletcher) Shrock. The father was born in Pennsylvania, and was of German descent. When a youth he went to South Carolina, married Miss Mary Fletcher, who was of Irish descent, and in 1834 came to Madison county, Miss., entering three hundred and twenty acres of land near Camden. He served with the South Carolina troops in the War of 1812. He was a hard-working, industrious man, but owing to hard times and security debts he lost the most of his property in his old age. His death occurred in Madison county in 1854. The mother had died in 1824. Our subject's paternal grandfather was a native of Germany, and immigrated to the United States at an early day, settling in Pennsylvania. Of the seven children born to the above mentioned union, six grew to maturity, but only two, besides our subject, are now living: Elizabeth Purivance, of Camden, and Nancy A. Shrock, who makes her home for the most part with Joseph K. The latter became thoroughly familiar with the duties of farm life at an early age, but owing to his father's straightened circumstances his educational advantages were limited. However, his greatest desire was for a thorough education, and he took advantage of every opportunity to perfect himself in his studies. He was also favored in one or two instances, when he received instruction from a very thorough educator of the time. In this way he fitted himself for teaching, but owing to a delicate constitution he was obliged to abandon his intention of securing a collegiate education, being several times almost prostrated by overexertion. Having taught several terms of school with gratifying success he entered a store as clerk, in Camden, and there remained in that capacity until 1847, when he and Mr. Purviance purchased the store and stock of goods. From that time until 1859 they carried on the most extensive business of any firm in Madison county, their sales in dry goods alone amounting to from $30,000 to $40,000 per annum, while in other lines it was in proportion. In 1859, on account of ill health, Mr. Shrock sold out his interest in the business, and bought twelve hundred acres of land in the edge of Attala county, having on it a steam saw and gristmill. Living on this farm during the dark and stormy days of the Civil war, and surrounded by a community of needy white people, Mr. Shrock's mill was the means of relieving a great deal of the suffering. He assisted in clothing and feeding the destitute, and having a practical knowledge of physic he ministered to the physical wants of the community in many cases where medical skill could not be obtained. So skillful did he become in this that even to this day his advice in sickness is called into use as much as any M. D. in the vicinity. In 1865 Mr. Shrock built a store and put in a stock of general merchandise, which he has largely increased from time to time. As he is well advanced in years he has taken his sons into partnership with him, and the firm is now known as Shrock Bros. & Co. They do a general merchandise and supply business, and their stock invoices about $6,000. In politics Mr. Shrock is a conservative democrat, and in 1875 and 1876 he represented Attala county in the legislature. He was married on the 15th of October, 1848, to Miss Caroline Fitler, a daughter of William and Eliza Fitler. Mr. Fitler was born in Pennsylvania, and of a wealthy family of Philadelphia. To Mr. and Mrs. Shrock have been born seven children, six of whom are living. Mrs. Shrock died in 1880. Socially Mr. Shrock is a Chapter Mason, and he is a liberal contributor to all worthy enterprises.

Among the prominent members of the planting community of Anding, Miss., is Coleman C. Sibley. He is a native of Madison county, Miss., born September 14, 1835, and is the eldest of a family of three children. His parents were John and Matilde (Thrasher) Sibley. The father was a native of Tennessee, and was engaged in planting the greater part of his life. He was among the earliest settlers of Madison county, and was a witness to its development from a wild, uncultivated country to a fertile group of plantations. He died in 1854. The paternal grandfather was Jesse Sibley, a native of South Carolina. Coleman C. was brought up amid the scenes of his birth, and acquired his education in the private schools. He chose for his vocation in life that of planting, and is the owner of six hundred and ninety acres of choice land. He has through his own efforts places of one hundred and seventy-five acres under cultivation. He has for many years been a leader of the democratic party in his county. He was elected to the office of assessor of the county in 1865, and again in 1866 and 1867, being removed by the government. He was also justice of the peace four years. He was a soldier in the Civil war, enlisting in 1861 in company I, Eighteenth Mississippi volunteer infantry, and serving until the close of the conflict. He was in the following named battles: Manassas, Leesburg, seven days' fight around Richmond, the Wilderness, Spottsylvania, Cold Harbor, Petersburg, Sharpsburg, Chickamauga. In the battle of Petersburg he was seriously wounded in his left arm, which was finally amputated; he was carried to the hospital in Richmond, where he remained six weeks; he then returned to his home and did not reënter the service. Mr. Sibley was married in 1865 to Miss Mary E. Lee, a native of Mississippi, and a daughter of John and Susana Lee, natives, respectively, of South Carolina and of Georgia. They have had born to them seven children, Susanah I. (deceased), Carrie B., John A., Adolphus M. and Jesse E. (twins), and Edwin and Ethel. The parents are worthy members of the Missionary Baptist church. Mr. Sibley is connected with the I. O. O. F. fraternity, and also with the Farmers' Alliance. Movements of public interest have ever received his sympathy and aid, and he has always been held in the highest esteem as a citizen and neighbor.

Hon. Walter Sillers, one of the younger members of the Bolivar county bar, is a native of Jefferson county, Miss., born 1852, and the youngest of three children born to Joseph and Matilda (Clark) Sillers, the father a native of Mississippi and the mother of Ohio. The father followed the occupation of a planter and in 1854 came to Bolivar county, settling on Lake Beulah, where he opened a large plantation. He became one of the influential men of the county. In 1862 he entered the Confederate army in Colonel Montgomery's company and was promoted to the rank of lieutenant. He was taken prisoner in 1864, and died in the prison at Vicksburg in April, 1865. He was also a veteran in the Mexican war; was in Captain Crump's company and Col. Jefferson Davis' regiment. The mother was a sister of Governor Clark. The paternal grandfather, James Sillers, was a native of North Carolina. He came to Mississippi at an early period in that state's history, settled in Jefferson county, and became one of the most extensive planters of his time. He reared a large family of children, and his descendants are residing principally in Mississippi. Much of the youth and early manhood of Walter Sillers was spent in the school at Oxford, Miss., and after finishing his literary education, or in 1874, he entered the office of Colonel Montgomery, where he began the study of law. In the following year he was admitted to the bar at Rosedale and immediately began practicing his profession, although in connection he also carried on planting. He is the owner of one thousand acres of land, with six hundred acres under cultivation, and has cleared about two hundred acres himself. He owns a good residence in Rosedale and other town property. He has been twice married, first in 1880, to Miss Ida Gayden, a native of Bolivar county, who died in 1883, leaving one child, Maud, and his second marriage occurred in 1887 to Miss Florence Warfield, a daughter of Colonel Warfield, of Kentucky. Two interesting children have blessed the last union—Walter and Mary. Mrs. Sillers is a member of the Presbyterian church, and Mr. Sillers is a menber of the Knights of Honor and Knights of Pythias orders. He is an active politician, and has been county attorney for the past eight years. In 1886 he was a member of the general assembly.

Like all native Mississippians who come of prominent families, Dr. J. L. Simmons, druggist, Clarksdale, Miss., is of an energetic, enterprising and intelligent disposition. He was the third of four children born to the union of Stearne and Elizabeth (Harper) Simmons, both natives of the state of Georgia. The father came to Yalobusha county, Miss., in 1830, cleared many acres of land and became one of the prominent planters of that section. He died in 1847 and the mother received her final summons about the same time. Both were consistent members of the Baptist church. Dr. J. L. Simmons was reared in Yalobusha county, received a thorough literary education there, and began the study of medicine in the office of a physician about 1858. He soon after entered the University of Louisiana and graduated from that institution in the class of 1861; then filled with a strong desire to aid the Southern cause he enlisted in company F, Twenty-first Mississippi regiment, and was in the battles around Richmond in 1862. He also participated in the battles of Harper's Ferry, Antietam, Gettysburg, and others, about eight in all. He was captured at the last-named engagement, but was released just prior to the surrender. Afterward the Doctor located near Dublin, Coahoma county, practiced his profession there for five years and then went to Friar's Point, where he started a drug store, at that time the only one in the county. In 1884 he came to Clarksdale and started his present business, erecting a good business building. He carries a full line of drugs, cigars, tobacco, toilet articles, paints, oils and every description of druggists' sundries usually kept in a first-class store. In 1872 he was wedded to Miss Anna Davis, of Marshall county, and the daughter of Maj. W. L. Davis, a planter of that county. The fruits of this union have been three children—two sons and a daughter: Fannie, Lawrence and William. The Doctor is a member of the Knights of Pythias and the Knights of Honor orders. He is president of the Clarksdale Compress and Warehouse company, vice president of the Clarksdale Bank and Trust company, and is a stockholder in the Clarksdale Brick and Manufacturing company. In politics he is a stanch democrat, and has held a number of offices of trust and honor. He held the office of treasurer of Coahoma county for eight years, is at present a member of the board of aldermen and treasurer of Clarksdale. Dr. Simmons is the owner of six hundred acres of fine land in Texas, all well improved and an excellent piece of property. He also owns two hundred and seventy acres near Clarksdale, one hundred and thirty-five acres in cultivation. He is a good business man and has accumulated considerable property. He has retired from the practice of his profession. The Doctor is above the medium hight, has brown hair and beard and is a fine-looking man.

Hon. Peter Simmons, planter, Lexington, Miss. Captain Simmons was born in Franklin county, Tenn., on November 8, 1831, and was the eldest of a family of four sons and two daughters born to Capt. John and Ann (Hudnall) Simmons, both native Virginians. The father was born in Bedford county, in 1796, went to middle Tennessee when a young man and there received his education. He was a man of superior literary taste and ability. He followed merchandising and planting in Tennessee until 1830, when he came to Mississippi, made a location, and then returned to move his family there. They settled in Madison county in 1832, opened a large plantation, and Mr. Simmons became one of the wealthy and prominent men of the county. He resided there for forty years and then moved to Yazoo county, where his death occurred in 1880. His wife received her final summons five years later. Of the six children born to this union Hon. Peter and two sisters are the only survivors. The sons were all planters, and one of them, John, was one of Walker's soldiers and assisted in Nicarauga. Another son, William, was a soldier in the Confederate army, and Benjamin, the third son, also served in the Confederate army, holding the rank of lieutenant and was acting colonel of his regiment when killed. The two daughters, Mrs. Marietta Walker and Mrs. Bettes Cowan, are widows and are residents of Yazoo City. Capt. Peter Simmons passed his boyhood days in Madison county, and was educated at La Grange college, near Louisville, Ky., graduating in the class of 1850. He then returned home and remained with his father, assisting on the plantation, for several years. He subsequently began merchandising in Canton, sold goods there a few years, and then moved to Kosciusko county, where he carried on merchandising up to 1859. He was married in Holmes county in May of that year to Miss Margaret D., daughter of Col. W. H. Johnston, of Holmes county, but formerly from Louisiana, and a brother of Gov. Isaac Johnston of Louisiana. After his marriage Captain Simmons settled in Holmes county, near Tchula, and has been a planter in that and Yazoo counties ever since. He bought residence property and located his family in Lexington in 1865, and there has made his home up to the present time. He has a beautiful suburban home in the western part of the town, and has everything comfortable and convenient about his place. During the war he served in the state militia, and first belonged to an independent company for home protection and was stationed at Grenada and Holly Springs. He was captain of his company and was in some skirmishes, but no general engagements. He has ever been active in politics; was elected chancery clerk in 1875, and held that position four consecutive years. In 1888 he was elected to represent Holmes and Yazoo counties in the legislature, served with credit and efficiency, and during that time was a member of several committees. He is a member of the Knights of Honor and the Knights of Pythias, and he and Mrs. Simmons are worthy members of the Presbyterian church, in which she takes a deep interest. They have reared two children: Mrs. Tullia Johnson, wife of J. C. Pinkerton, of Lexington, and Miss Maggie P. Simmons, attending college at Pass Christian institute, will graduate this year (1891). Mr. and Mrs. Simmons have one grandchild, Katheryn Pinkerton.

Col. John M. Simonton Shannon has been so closely identified with the history of Lee county, Miss., that a sketch of his personal career is a desirable addition to this work. He was born in Lawrence county, Tenn., in 1830, and is a son of Gilbreath F. and Evelina (Buchanan) Simonton. The father was born May 13, 1799, in North Carolina, and was a son of John Simonton, a native of North Carolina. The paternal ancestors emigrated from Scotland to America, and served as soldiers in the Revolutionary war. The grandfather of our subject was a thrifty planter, and at one time owned twelve thousand acres of land in Tennessee, which he divided among his children. He married Jane Falls, a native of North Carolina, a daughter of Major Falls, of Revolutionary fame, who was killed at the battle of R——— mill. Gilbreath F. Simonton was reared in Tennessee, and was a merchant and planter by occupation. Politically he was a stanch Whig, but was not an aspirant to public office. In 1850 he removed to Mississippi, settling first at Carmengo; later he went to Shannon, where he passed the remainder of his days. He died July 24, 1881. His wife was born in 1814, and died March 21, 1878. She was a devoted member of the Primitive Baptist church, and was a woman of unusual force of character. They reared a family of eight children to mature years; two died in infancy: Dr. William F., G. F., Ethe Jane, Haney B., Robert Ross, Mrs. E. J. Raspberry, Mrs. Sarah A. Thomison, Mrs. Evelina M. Lowe, Margaret E. and John M. Colonel Simonton was educated in the common schools, and in the fall of 1850 he engaged in business at Carmengo, Miss. For six years he carried on a thriving trade, and then removed to Shannon, where he formed a partnership with Mr. Buchanan. In 1859 he was elected to the senate. When the war broke out he resigned his place in the senate, left his store in the hands of an agent, and went to the defense of the Southern cause. After the close of the struggle he was interested for a time in a sawmill, and also gave some attention to farming. He was united in marriage to Miss N. Ruth Potter, of Giles county, Tenn., a daughter of W. W. Potter. Her father was a graduate of Yale college, and was one of the pioneer educators of the South. Mrs. Simonton was born in 1835, and died in 1881. She was a member of the Methodist Episcopal church from childhood. Six children were born to the Colonel and his wife: Sarah E., wife of James K. Whitesides, Anna Ethe, Ruth P., John M., Jr., Gilbreath P. and William W. Our subject was married, a second time, April 8, 1885, to Miss Flora Porter, of Aberdeen, Miss., a daughter of Benjamin F. Porter. Colonel Simonton enlisted in the Confederate service, and from the beginning seemed destined to meet all the horrors of war, as well as to receive the honors and distinction which courage confers. To trace his steps through all those five years of carnage would only serve to awaken the bitterness of the saddest of experiences. He was in many of the most noted engagements of the war, and was often thrown in the closest relationship with his superior officers. His great care for the men under his command won him innumerable stanch friends, who to this day are filled with gratitude to him. He had the greatest courtesy shown him on many occasions by the officers of the opposing side, and certainly gleaned all the sweet that was mixed with the bitter. He was promoted from one rank to another, until he was finally made colonel of the First Mississippi infantry. He suffered some severe bodily ailments during his service, and had one operation which nearly cost him his life. After the war was ended he represented his district in the first session of the state senate, and was elected to the reconstruction convention in 1885. In 1866 he was elected to the senate to represent the district composed of Itawamba county, and was elected president of that body, but was not permitted to serve out his term, for reasons of disfranchisement under the reconstruction acts of congress. He was relieved from disability by the general act of congress; elected to the senate from district composed of the counties of Itawamba, Monroe and Lee, in 1884, and for five years discharged the duties of this office. In 1890 he was a member of the constitutional convention. He has been chairman of some very important committees in the senate, where his excellent judgment gives his opinions much weight. He has always taken a deep interest in the welfare of the South, and has manifested that interest by an unflinching devotion to his rights of citizenship. He is a member of the Masonic fraternity, and belongs to the Cumberland Presbyterian church.

C. A. Simpson, Pass Christian, special deputy collector of customs of the Pearl River district, Miss., was born in the city of New York, January 8, 1859, and is a son of C. A. and Mary (Malay) Simpson, natives of Ireland. The parents immigrated to America, landing in New York city; there the father died in 1859. They reared six children, three of whom are living: John (superintendent of immigration, New York city), Rosanna, and C. A. (the subject of this biographical notice). After the death of the father, in 1863, the mother removed to Mound City, Ill. She was married again in 1862 to Thomas Ryan, who was a shipcarpenter and foreman of the navy yard at Mound City. He died in Texas, and the mother came to

Mississippi in 1867, and located at Pass Christian, where she now resides. She has been postmistress at that place for eight years. C. A. Simpson was a child of eight years when he came to Mississippi, and received his education at Pass Christian college. He mastered the art of telegraphy, and was made station agent at the Pass. He filled this position for five years, and for the following fifteen years was in the employ of the Louisville & Nashville railroad. He has been prominently identified with the political history of Pass Christian, having served as postmaster and as mayor. He turned the office of postmaster over to his mother in 1881, when he was appointed deputy collector of customs at Pascagoula. In 1885 he went out of office under President Cleveland, and for two years was lessee and manager of the railroad eating house at Hattiesburg, Miss. He then purchased an English ship and took her to British Honduras, where he sold her for a good sum of money. In 1889 he was appointed to the office he now fills. Mr. Simpson has always been a stanch republican, and has worked zealously in the interest of his party. He was a delegate to the national convention of the republican party held in Chicago in 1880, 1884, 1888. Although he has hosts of friends among the democrats, he remains true to his convictions, and he is one of the republicans whom the press of Mississippi has never attacked. In 1878 he was married to Miss Mary Duke, of Jasper county, Miss., and one child has been born to them, John. In 1881 he was married a second time to Miss Nettie Manders, and three children have been born to this union: Mary L., C. A., Jr., and Margarette. Mr. Simpson is a member of the Knights of Labor and of the Knights of Pythias. The family belong to the Roman Catholic church, and are highly respected throughout the community.

F. M. Simpson, farmer and merchant, residing four miles east of Courtland, Panola county, Miss., was the youngest of nine children born to Andrew and Mary (Murphy) Simpson, both natives of Tennessee, where they spent their entire lives. The mother died when F. M. was but three weeks old and the father received his final summons in 1862. All the nine children grew to mature years, and three besides our subject are now living: Susan, wife of James Patterson, of Tennessee; Caroline, wife of John Madaris, of Arkansas, and Grace, wife of John Clamor, of Madison county, Tenn. Those deceased were: Jane, Nancy, Newton, Jasper and John. F. M. Simpson was born in Carroll county, Tenn., in 1834, grew to manhood in his native state and in 1854, when about twenty years of age, he settled in Yalobusha county, where he bought and improved one hundred and sixty acres of land. From there he moved to Yazoo county four years later and was engaged in business for other people until the beginning of the war. In 1861 he espoused the cause of the Confederacy and enlisted in the First Mississippi artillery, company B, under Capt. A. J. Herod, as a private and served five years. He was at Vicksburg, Holly Springs, Jackson, Miss., and many other engagements. He was captured at Port Hudson, retained at Enterprise until exchanged, and was then assigned to heavy artillery at Mobile, Ala., where he remained until the surrender. In July, 1865, he married Miss Laura J. Rice, daughter of P. L. Rice, and afterward resided in Tallahatchie county for about three years. He then removed to Courtland, Panola county, and for the first twelve years in this county he was engaged in merchandising and farming. In 1880 he settled on his present farm, consisting of one hundred and sixty acres, and in connection is also engaged in general merchandising, his annual sales amounting to from $10,000 to $12,000. His principal productions from his farm are corn and cotton. Mr. Simpson is also the owner of a dairy farm in Shelby county, Tenn., and has about thirty good Jersey and Holstein cows. In his political views Mr. Simpson affiliates with the democratic party, and he has been a member of the board of supervisors of Panola county. He is also a member of Stonewall Jackson Blue lodge No.

332, at Courtland. To his marriage were born ten children: Mary F., wife of William Laurance, of Hill county, Tex.; W. A., of Memphis; L. B., wife of George Baugh, of Memphis; Alonzo, Caskey, Pearl, Ada, Douglass, Bertha and Adonis, the seven youngest at home. Mr. and Mrs. Simpson are members of the Methodist church at Eureka and are liberal contributors to the same, as indeed they are to all worthy enterprises.

Judge Horatio Fleming Simrall, ex-chief justice of the state of Mississippi, was born near Shelbyville, Shelby county, Ky., February 6, 1818. Prior to the Revolutionary war James Simrall, his grandfather, immigrated to America from Scotland, settling in Virginia. He served in the war for independence and rose to the rank of captain, and after the close of the war returned to Virginia, where he spent the remainder of his life. He left three sons and one daughter. The eldest of this family was a son, James, born near Winchester, Va., where he grew to maturity and married Rebecca Graham, a native of Lancaster county, Penn., who had removed when a child with her parents to Virginia. Immediately following their marriage the young couple emigrated to Kentucky. The perilous journey was made in wagons and on horseback, and consumed considerable time, and severely tried the fortitude on the part of those undertaking it, as the country was infested with murderous bands of savages who did not hesitate to attack emigrant trains. Mr. Simrall and his wife located in Shelby county, Ky., about a mile from the city of Shelbyville, then but a flourishing village. There, surrounded by the dangers, and enjoying but the primitive advantages of the early times, they took up their permanent residence. There Mr. Simrall died, about 1823, aged about fifty-eight years. He was a prominent citizen in Shelby county, and was elected from that county to the state legislature, and was at the time of his death a general of the state militia. He raised and commanded a battalion of cavalry in the War of 1812, and served in the northwestern frontier, and during his service he contracted rheumatism which ultimately caused his death. His widow survived him a number of years, her death having occurred at Louisville, Ky., in 1871. To James Simrall and wife were born five sons and one daughter, of whom our subject is the only survivor. He is the youngest son and the fifth child in order of birth. He was but a small child when his father died, and his mother soon afterward removed to Shelbyville. There he grew to maturity. His early education becoming the especial care of his mother, who was an earnest Christian woman whose moral training exerted a powerful influence for good upon his after days. When of sufficient age he attended a select school in Shelbyville, taught by an efficient schoolmaster from New England, and continued his studies there until his seventeenth year, when he became a student at Hanover college, at Hanover, Ind., and there remained one year. Returning to his home at Shelbyville, he became a tutor at the school he had attended. When pursuing his studies at Shelbyville he had, as classmates and intimate associates, Bland Ballard and Caleb Logan, a near relative of Gen. John A. Logan. These friends, after much deliberation and consultation, chose the law as a profession and furnished a striking example of the result of determination and effort. Bland Ballard became district judge of the United States for the district of Kentucky, holding this position at the time of his death; Caleb Logan acquired prominence at the bar of Kentucky, and became judge of the chancery court of Louisville, and Mr. Simrall filled, in a most exemplary manner, the highest judicial position in Mississippi. He began reading law, while continuing his services as tutor in the school at Shelbyville, in the office of Johnston & McHenry, a prominent firm of attorneys there. In 1838 he attended the law department of Transylvania university, at Lexington, Ky., and upon returning home he stopped at Frankfort, where he successfully passed an examination before the court of appeals of Kentucky, and was licensed to practice in all the courts of the state. Late in the fall of

1838 he came to Mississippi, making the journey by boat. He stopped at Natchez, and early in 1839 located at Woodville, Wilkinson county, where he opened a law office and soon became a prominent figure in legal circles. The bar of that section was particularly a strong one. There appeared men who have become noted in the South as jurists and able expounders of the law. Among them, and with whom Judge Simrall was closely associated, were James Walker, who afterward became circuit judge; John Henderson, who afterward represented this state in the United States senate; William H. Dillingham, an accomplished lawyer; the late Judge Hiram Cassedy, Hon. John I. Lamkin, and Hon. David W. Hurst, all of whom were noted for their ability, and of whom personal sketches are given elsewhere. At Natchez were Gen. John A. Quitman; Samuel Boyd, at that time one of the ablest lawyers in the state; Eli Montgomery, and John T. McMurran, and others of prominence. During the period from 1846 to 1848 he represented Wilkinson county in the state legislature. During his term there he worked with characteristic energy for the passage of a bill establishing a public-school system in the state. In this, however, he was defeated, but he succeeded in securing the establishment of a system of public education in Wilkinson county, which continued in operation until succeeded by the present system. The system he introduced was supported by the funds derived from the lands donated by congress in the various townships for primary education, supplemented by county taxation. In 1857 he was invited to the law professorship in the University of Louisville, and removing to that city he filled that position with honor until the outbreak of the Civil war. In the summer of 1861 he returned with his family to Wilkinson county, Miss., where he still owns a plantation. Shortly after his arrival there he received a telegraphic communication from Bowling Green, Ky., stating that he had been elected lieutenant-governor of state government, which had been established in the southern portion of the state, in sympathy with the Confederacy, and invited his return to that state. Upon his arrival at Bowling Green he found General Johnston's army retreating from Kentucky, which necessarily interrupted the designs of this newly established government, and rendered its continuance impossible. The excitement of the war having passed, he resumed the practice of his profession at Woodville, remaining there until 1867, when he removed to Vicksburg, and there successfully continued his practice. During this time the courts of the state were being superceded and the administration of justice seriously interfered with by the military tribunal, whose rulings were ofttimes arbitrary and unconstitutional in this state, and Judge Simrall spent much of his time in the defense of persons unjustly tried before these court martials, contending that the law of the state should be administered by her courts alone, and that the court martial could not, with any sense of justice, punish a citizen for any act not designated as a crime in the code of the state, based upon her accepted constitution, and in this opinion he was upheld by the Federal judge, Robert A. Hill, and also by the department of justice at Washington, and this view of the case was established by the United States district judge who, at Judge Simrall's solicitation, released, on a writ of habeas corpus, parties who had been confined in the state penitentiary upon the sentence of the military tribunal for an offense not so punishable by the law of the land. The Judge had many important cases before the military tribunal, of which Gen. Adelbert C. Ames, afterward governor of the state, was the presiding officer. In 1870 he was appointed to the supreme bench, at the solicitation and earnest request of the leading members of the bar of the state, and he occupied the position nine years, the last five years as chief justice. His associates were Judges Peyton and Tarbell, and, for the last five years, Judges Josiah A. P. Campbell and Ham. Chalmers.

As a member of this court, Judge Simrall's record has been a most exemplary and honorable one, reflecting credit not only upon himself, but upon his state. The Civil war had interfered to a great extent with the affairs of the court, and as chief justice, he found an overcrowded docket and much delayed work. With characteristic energy, he applied himself to the duties of discharging the large number of cases, and won a distinction for his efficiency. It is a fact worthy of mention that no decision rendered by this court while he was at its head was ever reversed by the supreme court of the United States, although many were submitted to that body. The energy displayed did not in any way interfere with the efficiency and thoroughness of the court, for it won the confidence and admiration of the bar of the state. Particularly have his efforts been of great value to the people of the state in his decisions rendered upon equity and constitutional law, and decisions systematizing the laws of the state relative to the rights of married women in the holding of separate estates. One of the most important cases which occupied his attention was the famous lottery case of the state of Mississippi vs. Moore, which was probably the first case decided in any of the states to uphold the power of the legislature to repeal lottery grants and privileges. In this case just cited, the legislature of Mississippi in consideration of a sum of money to be devoted to educational purposes, had granted a charter to a lottery company. A subsequent legislature repealed this charter, and the case came before the supreme court of the state. Judge Simrall, after a careful review of the case, rendered a decision upholding the last act of the legislature, holding that private or corporate interests, even though instituted by a special act of the legislature, were, and rightfully should be, subservient to the public good, and as the continuance of this lottery would be damaging in its effects upon the public morals, he rendered his decision accordingly. The case was taken to the supreme court of the United States on a writ of error, and in that court his decision was unanimously sustained. Another notable case of great importance to the people of the country was that of Hawkins vs. Carroll county. The question under consideration was one of the validity of bonds voted for the improvement of the county, when all her voters were not represented at the polls. The lower courts had interpreted the provision requiring a two-thirds majority as applying to the number of votes cast. Judge Simrall ruled that the proper interpretation was that a two-thirds vote of the qualified voters of the county was necessary to grant bonds, and in this decision he was also sustained by the supreme court of the United States. The principle of this interpretation was a new one, and was afterward sustained by the supreme court in a case taken before it on a similar ruling from one of the Western states. In another case brought to recover damages for cotton burned during the war by order of the Confederate military commander, the owner of the cotton sought to recover damages from the person who set fire to the cotton, but the Judge ruled that as this was an act of war, the individual could not be held responsible for the same, and in this he was sustained by the supreme court. Adelbert C. Ames had been elected governor of the state, and had taken his seat as such. The legislature introduced articles of impeachment against him, and the constitution requiring the chief justice to act as president of the senate when that body was sitting in impeachment trials, this duty fell upon the shoulders of Judge Simrall. In this matter the Judge was devoid of any personal feelings and losing all personality, was prepared to give Governor Ames an impartial trial, but the resignation of the governor made the trial unnecessary. After the Judge had retired from the supreme bench, in 1879 he returned to Vicksburg, where for the following year he attended to his practice, and then retired. In 1881 he located on his plantation in Warren county, where he now resides, choosing to spend the remainder of his life in quietness and domestic enjoyment. In 1870 he was appointed trustee of the University of Mississippi by Governor Alcorn, and his appointment was confirmed by the senate. Again, in 1876, he was reappointed by Governor Stone, and again in 1882, and in 1888 by Governor Lowry, and is now the oldest trustee of the university in number of years of service. He is also serving his second term as trustee of the University of the South at Sewanee, Tenn. In 1881 the University of Mississippi conferred upon him the title of LL. D. In 1867 at the reorganization of the University of Mississippi after the war, he was tendered the professorship of law, which he declined, on account of pressing business at home. In 1890 he was unanimously elected a member of the constitutional convention of the state, acting as chairman of the judiciary committee, and was the author of the report of that committee as to the constitutional right of the convention to adjust the right of suffrage, notwithstanding the condition in the act of readmission of the state by the congress of the United States in 1870, that the state should not alter or change the franchise article in the constitution of 1869, abridging or denying suffrage to any person by that constitution entitled to it. The argument of the report was that the state was sovereign over the question and condition of suffrage, and that congress was without right to impose conditions of suffrage upon one state not common to all. He also reported the judiciary system which was afterward adopted by that convention. Judge Simrall has always taken an active interest in all movements of public interest, particularly in the improvement of the Mississippi river, and was president of a committee to properly lay before congress the necessity of such improvements, and the constructions of levees to protect the lower lands from overflow, and was a member of a committee of seven chosen to proceed to Washington and bring the matter before congress. February 22, 1842, he married Lydia Ann Newell, of Wilkinson county, and this union resulted in the birth of five children, three still living. The family are members of the Episcopal church of Vicksburg, and for years, the Judge has been a member of the vestry. Politically, the Judge is a republican on national matters, but in state affairs votes with the people of the state, the democratic ticket. He is a venerable appearing man, his hair being snow white, but the brilliancy of his intellect is undimmed, and his memory as active as ever.

Thomas M. Sims, an old and prominent citizen of Panola county, Miss., was the fifth of eleven children born to David and Nancy (Strong) Sims, both natives of Virginia. His greatgrandfather Sims emigrated from the Emerald isle to America and settled in the Old Dominion. David Sims followed planting in Virginia, was a man of moderate means but a good, substantial, honorable citizen, and had no political aspirations. He was a soldier in the War of 1812. He died when about sixty-eight years of age and his wife survived him a number of years later. Thomas M. Sims was born in Louisa county, Va., on the 8th of February, 1819, and passed his boyhood and youth in that state. His advantages for an education were limited, but experience and observation have taught him much. He left the state of his nativity in 1836, went to Fayette county, Tenn., and after remaining there one year removed to Marshall county, Miss., where he resided for five years. From there he went to Tippah county, remained eight years engaged in the tailor's trade, and then went to Oakland, Yalobusha county, where he continued his trade in connection with gents' furnishing business. In 1855 he came to Panola county, and here he has since resided, engaged in planting. In 1879 he began merchandising in Pope, continued this for seven years and then retired from business, since which time he has lived a retired life. He is a man of pleasant, cheerful disposition, is upright and honorable in all his relations with the public, and is universally respected. He served in the war from 1864 until the close, but was never in any regular engagement. He was a member of the board of supervisors for four years, and in 1877 he was nominated for the legislature, but as the republicans were in the majority and he ran on the democratic ticket, he was defeated by a few votes. He was married in 1843 to Miss Eunice Rogers, who was born in Tennessee and who was the daughter of Thomas Rogers, a native of Tennessee. Mrs. Sims died in 1864 leaving five children: Mary M., now Mrs. Shields, widow of Joseph Shields; Lou T., now Mrs. E. P. Collins; John I. (deceased); Frank C., in Texas, and Sue N., now Mrs. George Tinen. Mr. Sims and family are members of the Methodist church. He is a pioneer of Mississippi and has served faithfully in his sphere.

William H. Sims is a Georgian by birth, having emigrated to Mississippi from the former state just before the opening of the late Civil war. He was born in the village of Lexington, Oglethorpe county, about fifty years ago, in that middle section of Georgia which has given to the state her greatest sons. Oglethrope was the home of William H. Crawford and Thomas W. Cobb, the latter a relative, on his mother's side, to the subject of our sketch. The adjoining county of Wilkes was the home of Robert Toombs. The adjoining county of Clarke, where Henry Grady was born, was the home of Thomas R. R. Cobb, Georgia's great lawyer, and Howell Cobb, his brother, secretary of the treasury under President Buchanan. Taliaferro county, hard by, was the home of Alex. H. Stephens; while Greene county, near it, furnished Georgia a United States senator in the person of Crosby Dawson. All of these now notable citizens of Georgia were in the habit of gathering twice a year at the sitting of the circuit court at Lexington Courthouse, and the aspiring youth was wont to attend upon their great speeches at the bar or upon the hustings. Young Sims was among this number. He was the son of Dr. James Saunders Sims and Amanda Booker Moore, both of Virginia extraction. His father, Dr. Sims, was a physician of great learning and eminent in his profession in that portion of the state. His practice was not confined to his own county, but he was sent for from far and near in critical cases by the sick of surrounding regions. By middle life he had acquired such a competency through his professional success, that he retired from active professional work and gave himself to his books and scientific farming.

The early schooling of W. H. Sims was obtained at Meson academy, at Lexington. When a little more than sixteen he entered the junior class of the University of Georgia; and as he frequently regretted, graduated before he was nineteen. Shortly after graduating he became a student of law at Athens, Ga., in the office of Thomas R. R. Cobb, and in less than a year was admitted to the bar at Lexington. Being young in years and anxious to acquire greater learning in his profession before entering upon his duties, he spent a year at Cambridge, Mass., in attendance upon the Harvard law school. Returning home to Georgia, he lingered at his old home, casting about where he should enter upon the field of professional labor, and desiring to go West, he decided to settle at Columbus, Miss., whither he went in the latter part of 1859. Here he found many Georgians from the region of his birth, the Baldwins, the Claytons, the Whitfields, the Harrises, the Billupes, the Moores, the last two families being nearly related to him on his mother's side. After a few preliminary months of reading in the office of William S. Barry, at Columbus, to acquaint himself with the local statutes and decisions, W. H. Sims was numbered in the year 1860, among the young attorneys of the Columbus bar, then distinguished as one of the strongest in Mississippi, and nearly all of whom have been gathered to their fathers at this writing. James T. Harrison, Charles R. Crusoe, George R. Clayton, William S. Barry, Henry Dickenson, Isham Harrison, McKinney Irion and Beverly Matthews, were among the most distinguished members of the local bar at that time, not one of whom is now living. About this time the war clouds commenced gathering. The country was agitated with political discussions brought about by the allignment of the North and the South in separate political parties. The election of Mr. Lincoln determined the leaders in Mississippi to seek redress for her anticipated ills outside of the Federal Union. In December, 1860, Jefferson Davis and L.

Q. C. Lamar made speeches at the fair grounds at Columbus, Miss., containing much of warning and gloomy forebodings of the Southern future. The country soon became aflame with excitement; volunteer companies for service in the anticipated war between the sections began to form. Among the first in this section of the state was the formation of a company, intended for cavalry service, before the close of 1860, known as the Tombigbee rangers. Samuel Butler was its first captain, and W. H. Sims its first orderly sergeant. It was mustered into state service at Columbus, Miss., February 28, 1861. Captain Butler, having become restless to get into active service, had gone to an infantry regiment, called into service in Virginia, and J. H. Sharp, the first lieutenant of the rangers, became his successor as captain, while W. H. Sims was promoted to second lieutenant, to fill the vacancy created by the company officers moving up. After a tiresome waiting for weeks for a call as a cavalry company, the rangers finally abandoned that feature of their military purpose, and early in the spring of 1861 rendezvoused at Union City, Tenn., as infantry, as a part of a Confederate command which Gen. Frank Cheatham was there forming. Then began the active Confederate service which shifted the rangers, as company A, Blythe's battalion; afterward company A, Blythe's Mississippi regiment; afterward company A, Forty-fourth Mississippi regiment, from Union City to Columbus, Ky., during the winter of 1861–2; to the battle of Shiloh in April, 1862; to Saltillo, Miss.; to Chattanooga; to Murfreesboro, Tenn., and the seven days' fight on Stone river; and thence back to Tullahoma, Tenn.; and thence, under Bragg, to Kentucky, where as a part of Chalmer's high-pressure brigade, it joined in the daring attack upon the fortress at Munfordsville, Ky. It participated in the battle at Perrysville, Ky., and with Bragg, retreated through Cumberland Gap, and on back to near the place where it started its aggressive march. It shared the victory of Chickamauga, and the defeat at Missionary ridge; fell back and wintered at Dalton in 1863–4; stubbornly fought under Joseph E. Johnston against Sherman's outnumbering ranks from Resaca to Atlanta and Jonesboro, Ga., through four months of comparatively every day fighting, during the spring and summer of 1864. Johnston's Fabian policy having lost him nineteen thousand troops, in killed, wounded and missing, between Dalton and Atlanta, without his giving battle or obtaining any coigne of vantage; but on the contrary, in the opinion of the Confederate authorities, losing it, while in the possession of a splendid army and without daring to fight for it, he was supplanted by Hood, who had become famous in Virginia as the commander of a Texas brigade and a fighting division. W. H. Sims had shared the fortunes of his company all along through these events. At Shiloh he participated in both days' battles, commanding his company on the last day. Though not wounded there, he narrowly escaped it, having a grape shot to pass through his haversack and cut it loose from his person. The commander of his regiment, Col. A. K. Blythe, having been killed at Shiloh, Lieutenant Sims was detailed to bring his body to Columbus, Miss., for interment, and upon the reorganization of his company during his few days' absence, his captain, J. H. Sharp, was elected colonel of the regiment and W. H. Sims was elected by his comrades from the position of second lieutenant to that of captain of company A.

At Chickamauga, while in command of his company, Captain Sims received, early in the action, a severe wound in the arm, which carried him to the rear and caused his absence on leave for a month or more. He was again wounded slightly in the same arm at Jonesboro, when his horse was killed under him. During a year of the time mentioned, under Gen. Patton Anderson, Gen. Tucker, and Gen. Sharp, commanding the brigade successively, Captain Sims was on detail duty as inspector-general of the brigade, but on the flank movement of Hood's army from below Atlanta around Sherman's rear to the Tennessee river at

Decatur, he was recalled to his regiment, promoted to the rank of lieutenant-colonel, and put in command of it, and with it fought in the battle of Franklin, Tenn., in December, 1864, where he received a severe wound in the knee, which resulted in the loss of the lower portion of his leg. Shot down at the locust thicket near the breastworks, on the left of the line, about ten o'clock at night, he was several hours crawling off the field to a place of safety. Carried to an improvised hospital at a farmhouse by some cavalry men who picked him up, he lay there for eighteen days, until Hood's army was beaten from in front of Nashville and were retiring pell-mell through Franklin to the Tennessee river. Colonel Sims, having partly recovered from his wound, was taken by a friend in a wagon and endeavored to escape with Hood's army. But a secondary inflammation setting up in his leg during the two days' travel in the rain, and in an open wagon without springs, over a road originally rough, and badly cut up by artillery and wagon trains, he was obliged to stop at Columbia, Tenn., where he was captured. Here he remained three months on his back in a hospital. When he got up on his crutches, after a hard battle for life, some time after Lee's surrender, he was sent on to the Federal military prison, at Nashville (which was the state penitentiary), where he remained three weeks. Thence he was carried to the United States military prison, at Louisville, Ky., where he was detained until August, 1865, being among the few unfortunates who came under the operation of President Andrew Johnson's order, that conscious rebels should not be discharged from prison, but should be held for trial for treason. The line was drawn by President Johnson, at field officers, and those who had been at the United States military schools. Colonel Sims, when he entered the military prison, at Louisville, found himself in company with nine thousand Confederate prisoners, and saw them all discharged except three, himself, a major in an Arkansas regiment, and a captain of the Confederate navy, who had enjoyed some benefits of a military training at Annapolis. These three were detained weeks after the other body of the prisoners were paroled, during which period amusing comments were made from time to time by the editor of the Louisville *Courier-Journal*, then George D. Prentiss, concerning the ridiculous detention of these officers. Finally paroled, however, in August, 1865, Colonel Sims returned South to the home of his boyhood, at Lexington, Ga., where his parents were still living. In the summer of 1866 he came back to Columbus, Miss., and resumed the practice of his profession in partnership at law with Col. S. M. Meek. During the fall of that year, he was elected probate judge of the county of Lowndes, and held the position three years, from 1866 to 1869, when he was removed by the military governor to make room for an officeseeker in sympathy with the republican reconstruction policy in the South. Colonel Sims now gave his whole time and energy to the practice of law.

In August, 1870, he was married at Lexington, Ga., to Miss Louie Upson, daughter of Judge F. L. Upson, of that place, and granddaughter of Stephen Upson, one of Georgia's great lawyers. Their union has been blessed with one child, Harry Upson Sims, now about eighteen years of age. Colonel Sims, while often invited to counsel with his fellow-citizens on public matters affecting his county and state, was never an officeseeker, nor an active politician. But in 1875 the times of reconstruction were upon the people of his state. For ten years after the war the situation of affairs in Mississippi, like that in nearly all the Southern states, was exceedingly depraved. The state and county offices were, in the main, from the highest to the lowest, occupied by radical republican politicians. They were generally tramping carpetbaggers from the North or renegade Southerners of low origin or association, ignorant and unscrupulous. Many of the minor places and some of the higher ones, including legislative and congressional representatives, were filled by negroes, chosen not for their fitness, but for their pliant subserviency to the ends of their carpetbag and scalawag associates in office. The burden of taxation upon the white people became enormous. Official corruption was common. Respectability was cowed, and from constrained silence and submission Mississippians of the better classes nearly approached the condition of Rome to which Tacitus referred when he said: "We would have lost our memory together with our freedom of speech, had it been as easy to forget as to be silent." The iniquitous rule of carpetbagism had culminated in such enormities about the year 1875, that the white people of Mississippi came to realize that their civilization required a tremendous effort, and gathering around the banners of democracy, called upon all the good men of the state to unite and overthrow this jeopardous rule. At a meeting at West Point, in Clay county, Colonel Sims, without notice or consultation, was nominated as one of the state senators from the eighteenth district, composed of the counties of Lowndes, Oktibbeha and Clay. This nomination, with Hon. F. G. Barry, of Clay, as his colleague, was immediately endorsed by the democratic party in Lowndes and Oktibbeha counties. Fully alive to the peril of the hour, and answering to duty's call, Colonel Sims accepted the nomination, and with Mr. Barry entered upon the active canvass of his district, speaking from day to day through its length and breadth wherever occasion collected the excited multitudes. The democratic appeal and rally of good citizenship prevailed at the election in November, 1875, and Messrs. Sims and Barry were triumphantly elected state senators. The new democratic legislature assembled at Jackson in January, 1876, and promptly began the cleansing of the government corrupted by years of maladministration by the radical party. Gen. Adelbert Ames, the military governor, and his mulatto Lieutenant-Governor Davis, were successfully impeached and brought to trial for high crimes and misdemeanors. Adelbert Ames resigned to escape conviction; Davis was convicted and deposed. J. M. Stone, who had been elected president pro tempore of the senate, succeeded under the constitution, to the executive chair vacated by Ames; and W. H. Sims, who was unanimously chosen president of the senate in the place of Stone, succeeded to the lieutenant-governorship. In 1877 Governor Stone and Lieutenant-Governor Sims were nominated by the democratic party, and without opposition were elected by the people to the places they respectively held for the term of four years, from January, 1878. About this time the firm of Meek & Sims took into their law partnership Judge J. A. Orr, under the firm name of Orr, Meek & Sims. Colonel Meek withdrawing in a few years to unite with his son, the law firm of Orr & Sims was formed, and continued through the years since. The duties of member of the senate and president of that body were performed by the Hon. W. H. Sims, with great satisfaction to his constituents and friends. He soon made a reputation throughout the state as a debater of ability, fairness and force. As a presiding officer, he was recognized as one of the best who had ever presided in the senate of Mississippi. In 1882, having declined to become a candidate for re-election to the place he had then filled for six years, W. H. Sims returned to his law office and a lucrative practice at the bar, ranking among the foremost lawyers of Mississippi. At the democratic state convention at Jackson in 1885 for the nomination of a governor and state officers, Hon. W. H. Sims was unanimously chosen its temporary and permanent president. The convention was a very large one, composed of about six hundred delegates, and from disputes growing out of contesting representatives, was inclined to be turbulent. President Sims, by reason of his learning and readiness as a parliamentarian, his tact, patience, and decision of character, won golden opinions from the members of the convention and the people and press of the state. At the democratic state convention of Mississippi in May, 1888, Governor Sims was elected, by the leading majority, a delegate from the state at large to the national democratic convention called to assemble at St. Louis in June following. At St. Louis the Mississippi delegation was organized by selecting Gen.

W. T. Martin as its chairman; Hon. S. S. Calhoun, member of the committee on permanent organization; Hon. A. F. Fox, on credentials, and Hon. W. H. Sims, on resolutions and platform. This committee on resolutions and platform, composed of one delegate from each of forty-seven states and territories, organized at the Southern hotel at St. Louis by the election of Hon. Henry Watterson, of Kentucky, as its president, and W. H. Sims, of Mississippi, as its secretary. A sub-committee of nine to prepare a platform was selected by the general committee. W. H. Sims was also a member of this committee, in association with Hon. Alfred E. Burr, of Connecticut; Senator Turpie, of Indiana; Hon. Henry Watterson, of Kentucky; Gov. Leon Abbet, of New Jersey; Hon. Edward Cooper, of New York, and Senator A. P. Gorman, of Maryland. The deliberations of this committee, occupying about eighteen consecutive hours, were attended by much debate and contention concerning the expression of democratic principles to be embodied in the platform to be reported to the convention. A division arose over the tariff reform plank of the platform. Hon. Henry Watterson, of Kentucky, led the adherents of one view, and Senator Gorman, of Maryland, led those of another. The committee, nearly equally divided between these views, entered upon a debate in which a ten minutes' speech was permitted to each member, with little prospect of being reconciled. Governor Sims, who had supported Mr. Watterson for chairman of the committee, spoke to the question on the side of Mr. Gorman with such effect as to be credited with being largely instrumental in effecting that reconciliation. Senator Gorman and Hon. William L. Scott, of Pennsylvania, were very openly complimentary in their remarks concerning Governor Sims' good offices, and Senator Gorman having gone before the Mississippi delegation and communicated the facts to them, in recognition of Governor Sims' services in that behalf, the delegation adopted the following resolutions:

HEADQUARTERS MISSISSIPPI DELEGATION,
ST. LOUIS, June 7, 1888.

At a meeting of the Mississippi delegates to the national democratic convention held at these headquarters this day, on motion it was unanimously resolved that the thanks of the delegation are due and are hereby tendered to the Hon. W. H. Sims for the very able and effective service rendered by him on the national committee on platform and resolutions. And they have heard, with great gratification, of the happy influence exerted by him in producing harmony in said committee and elaborating a satisfactory platform. WILL T. MARTIN, Chairman.

Attest, C. M. WILLIAMSON, Secretary.

Full accounts of the whole proceedings and copies of the resolutions were published throughout the press of the state upon the return of the delegation to Mississippi, and Governor Sims' course was commended, and his able representation of the state emphasized.

Governor Sims, although often mentioned in connection with the highest offices of the state by the most influential portion of the press and people, has never been an office-seeker; indeed has declined, in several instances, to be put forward for public place when the way seemed open to success, because he did not wish to antagonize friends who, he stated, had more claims upon the position. It is well understood among his friends that positions, both upon the circuit and supreme court benches, have been within his reach, and he would have been appointed to them had he indicated an acceptance.

At present he resides at Columbus, busy with extensive personal interests, his books, and such attention as he chooses to give to the practice of law.

In 1888, upon the solicitations of the citizens of Columbus, he was appointed by Governor Lowry as a member of the board of trustees of the Mississippi Industrial institute and college for girls, to fill a vacancy. In 1890 he was reappointed by Governor Stone for six years. Governor Sims is a member of the Methodist Episcopal church at Columbus.

During his life W. McD. Sims (deceased) was one of the leading planters of the state of

Mississippi, and was especially well known in Claiborne (his native) county, where he was known not only as an able financier but as a man whose love of justice and right was one of his prominent characteristics. He was born on the 19th day of May, 1810, to David Sims and wife, the former of whom came to Mississippi when a child with his parents from his native state of North Carolina and located in what was known as the Red Lick neighborhood, in what is now Jefferson county, where he grew to manhood. He was one of a family of four sons and several daughters, all the members of the family coming to the state, with the exception of the daughters. W. McD. Sims inherited quite a handsome fortune from his father, but being careless of the future he soon spent it all and was then compelled to look about him for something to do in order to support himself and family, and after his marriage turned his attention to planting. He was married on the 3d of December, 1856, to Mrs. Rebecca J. (Harmon) Neal, who was born on the 9th of June, 1826, and by her became the father of two children: Louisiana E. and Carrie J., the former of whom died October 24, 1865, at the age of eight years. The latter became the wife of R. W. Magruder and died December 10, 1880, at the age of twenty years, five months and three days, leaving a son, John M. Mrs. Sims' parents, Joseph and Eliza (Sims) Harmon, were born in Mississippi, the birth of the former occurring on the 6th of March, 1795, in what is now Claiborne county, his death occurring on the 17th of July, 1834. Their marriage was consummated on November 2, 1820, Mrs. Harmon at that time being seventeen years of age, a daughter of David and Abigail Sims, early settlers of this county. To Mr. and Mrs. Harmon three daughters were born: Elizabeth Ann, who was born October 8, 1823, and died July 28, 1838; Rebecca J. (Mrs. Sims), was born June 9, 1826, and Phœbe F., who was born September 6, 1828, and died June 2, 1852, the wife of John Venable. Mrs. Rebecca J. Sims was first married to Joseph Neal, a native of Pennsylvania, whose death occurred of yellow fever, September 14, 1853. By him she became the mother of three children: Frances E., Martha and Ida (twins); Martha being the wife of Isaac Magruder. Mrs. Sims traces her ancestry back to her great-grandfather, James Harmon, who is supposed to have been born in North Carolina, October 3, 1731, inheriting English blood from his ancestors. He was one of the very earliest settlers of Claiborne county, Miss., having come here when the country was under Spanish rule and entering land on the Bayou Pierre river. He died on this plantation, September 18, 1819, over eighty-eight years of age. His son, Hezekiah Harmon, was born on the 22d of June, 1763, being the only son reared by his father, two of his brothers being killed by Indians. He attained manhood in the territory of Mississippi, where he entered land with his father, and was here first married to Miss Mercy Leonard, by whom he became the father of two sons and three daughters, all of whom, with the exception of one, lived to be grown and married: Polly, Rebecca, Elizabeth, James and Joseph (twins). They all settled in Mississippi, where they became the heads of families, but James died on the 24th of February, 1825, at the age of twenty-nine years. The mother of these children departed this life April 14, 1795, aged twenty-eight years, two months and one day. Mr. Harmon then married Mrs. Catherine Murphy, the widow of John Murphy, their union taking place on the 28th of August, 1811, and resulting in the birth of two children, one of whom died in infancy. The other, Hezekiah, lived to be grown and removed to Yazoo county, where he died soon after. Mr. Sims was one of the leading stockholders in the Port Gibson & Grand Gulf railroad, and when it was sold after the war he purchased it, putting it in good running order, after which he sold it. He was also a member of the Masonic fraternity and as a business man was shrewd and far-seeing, but strictly honorable in every transaction. He possessed a charitable and kindly disposition and gave willingly of his wealth to all who needed his aid or assistance. He took a deep interest in educational matters and besides giving his own children excellent educational advantages, he educated some nieces and nephews and gave them a start in life. He lost $75,000 by the failure of a commission merchant just before the war, but afterward retrieved much of his losses, leaving at his death, February 7, 1882, an estate comprising six thousand acres of land, of which about three thousand are under cultivation, of which R. W. Magruder has the charge. Mr. Sims at one time endeavored to settle his land with white people and sent to Germany for emigrants, but the plan was not a success. In 1872 he peopled his land with whites from the eastern portion of the state and gave them the land free of rent for a number of years as an inducement. He was a citizen of whom any community might feel proud, for he was not only industrious and honest, but he was also very enterprising in his views and had the interests of the county warmly at heart and supported her institutions with both purse and influence. His widow and children reside on the home place in a commodious, substantial and pleasant residence, fronting Russum station.

W. S. Sims, physician, surgeon and oculist of Meridian, Miss., was born in Lauderdale county, Miss., in 1854, a son of John I. Sims, a native of Georgia, who came some time in the thirties when a boy to Mississippi with his parents. His father is a planter of Lauderdale county and is the owner of considerable property. The Doctor received his literary education in the Marion school under the direction and tutelage of Captain Day, who was regarded very highly as an educator. At the age of nineteen he began the study of medicine, to which he devoted himself assiduously, graduating at Mobile, Ala., in 1878. While taking a special course on the eye and throat, he practiced his profession for three summers. He took a three years' course in his specialties in New York and New Orleans, La., since which time he has devoted himself to them almost exclusively. He has built up a fine practice, and is highly regarded both as a general practitioner and as a specialist. He is a member of both state and county medical associations, and is the vice president of the latter. He read an article before the state medical association, entitled "Operation for the extraction of hard cataract," with a report of twenty-six cases, and introduced another paper before the state board at Jackson, Miss., entitled "Penetrating wounds of the cornea in which the iris is involved and treatment for the same," accompanied by a report of five cases, which won for him a wide reputation. He is a member of the order of Odd Fellows. In 1887 he married Miss Elizabeth Mahan in Marion, Miss., by whom he has two children: Ruth and W. S. Sims, Jr.

Elbert D. Sinclair, planter, Oxford, Miss. On the 30th of June, 1810, in Chatham county, S. C., there was born to the union of Hezekiah and Sarah (Morphis) Sinclair, a son, the third in order of birth of six children. This son, who was named Elbert D. Sinclair, had very limited scholastic advantages, and what he obtained was the result of his own exertions. His father was born about 1770, and was a son of Peter Sinclair, who served during the Revolutionary war, and who acquitted himself with credit and honor in every instance. He was slain by the tories in 1779. Mr. Sinclair's maternal grandfather, John Morphis, was also a native of the Old North state, and was one of the most popular men in the section where he was known. He was public-spirited, and every worthy enterprise found in him a strong advocate and supporter. His liberality amounted almost to prodigality, and he was reverenced by all who knew him. When the Revolutionary war broke out between America and the mother country he was the first to buckle on his armor in defense of his country, and among the last to sheathe his sword after the grand victory. Mr. Sinclair removed with his parents to Tennessee, and while on the road at Bedford the father breathed his last. The mother, with her family of children, came on to Henry county, where the children all grew to maturity, and where, in 1836, Mr. Sinclair married Miss Nancy Broach, an estimable lady, who bore him six children, two sons and four daughters. Five of these children are now living, one son having died while attending the state university. In 1879 Mrs. Sinclair died, having lived a Christian life, and being at the time of her death a member of the Primitive Baptist church. Mr. Sinclair has been a member of the Primitive Baptist church since 1831, and has lived an honest, upright life, and one worthy of imitation. His honesty and truthfulness are proverbial, and he has made the Golden Rule a part of his life. Before the war he owned and operated a large plantation, but during that eventful period everything was swept away, and he began, though an old man, with energy to retrieve his fallen fortune. He has been successful, and is now the owner of a good plantation only two and a half miles from town, and attends to the management of it in person.

William R. Sivley is a Hinds county Mississippian, born on July 23, 1843, the second of five children born to Rawley and Eliza H. (Burleson) Sivley, the former born in Huntsville and the latter in Decatur, Ala. The father was reared and educated in his native city, but in 1841 became a resident of Hinds county, Miss., and here resided on a plantation until his death in 1887, at the age of eighty-one years. His widow, who survives him, is seventy-one years of age and is residing on the old homestead. Rawley Sivley was successfully engaged in agriculture and at the opening of the Civil war was worth about $250,000. Not only was he one of the most prosperous and enterprising of the planters of Hinds county, but he was also one of her most enterprising and public-spirited citizens. He was a son of Andrew and Rebecca (Denton) Sivley, who were born in Virginia and Tennessee respectively, and from his paternal ancestors, who settled in Virginia at an early day, he inherited Dutch and Welsh blood. The maternal grandfather of the subject of this sketch, Jonathan Burleson, was a native of Tennessee. This was one of the first families to settle in Alabama, and perhaps there is not a family in the state that has done more to develop its resources than the Burlesons. They are a numerous people and at the present time number about four thousand members in the United States, some of whom have been the ablest statesmen of the South, eminent divines and professional men. Among the latter may be mentioned Dr. Rufus C. Burleson, president of Baylor university of Waco, Tex., in which state the Burlesons have taken an important part in every great era for the past fifty years. This family have been the Indian fighters and pioneers of civilization, and during the Revolutionary war seven brothers, sons of Aaron Burleson, who came from Wales and settled in North Carolina in 1726, assisted the colonists in their struggle for liberty, four of whom were killed during the war. William R. Sivley was brought up in Hinds county and was educated in Clinton college. The war came on when he was about eighteen years of age and with the zeal that has ever characterized those of his race, and with the enthusiasm of youth and the native Southerner, he left school to take up arms in defense of his home and country. In 1861 he enlisted as a volunteer in company E, of the Third Mississippi regiment, with which company he remained two years, participating in the siege of Vicksburg and Baker's creek. In 1863 he was transferred to company C, Balantine's cavalry regiment, Armstrong's brigade, and was a participant in the battles of Franklin, Nashville, Atlanta, Peach Tree creek and the Tennessee campaign, surrendering at Demopolis. He was twice taken captive but was never a prisoner over ten days at a time. When the war closed he returned to his Mississippi home only to find his father's plantation laid waste and in a desolate and discouraging condition. With the same courage which he had displayed on the field of battle, he at once took upon himself the burden of repairing the broken fortunes of the family, and for four years thereafter assisted his father by every means in his power. In 1869 he purchased a plantation near where he now lives, and as he has devoted his attention to this calling ever since, and is a shrewd and far-seeing man of business, he is now the owner of four thousand acres of land of which about two thousand are under cultivation. He is also the owner of fine property in Oakley, where he lives and conducts a large mercantile business. He erected him a beautiful home at Oakley in 1884, which is one of the handsomest in the county, conveniently and beautifully arranged and fitted up with all the modern conveniences and luxuries. His plantation, Oakley, was named by his wife and is one of the finest and best tilled places in this section of the country. Mr. Sivley believes in land being self-supporting, and as a means to this end, raises a diversity of crops and vegetables and sufficient stock to supply them with meat throughout the year. He owns stock in some of the most firmly established banks of the state, is very public-spirited and is liberal and generous in the use of the wealth he has so honorably earned. His contributions to churches, charitable institutions and to the cause of education are generous, and he has ever been a friend to the poor and needy. He is a fine-looking gentleman and is a very entertaining and agreeable conversationalist. He was united in marriage in 1866 to Miss L. J., daughter of Dr. Young and Mary A. (Gray) Stokes, natives of Virginia and Alabama respectively. Mrs. Sivley was born in De Soto county, Miss., and is the mother of three children: Emma S., now the wife of Dr. Rhodes, of Learned, Miss.; Clarence L., and Lena R. The mother of these children is a worthy member of the Presbyterian church, and Mr. Sivley is a member of the A. F. & A. M., the Knights of Pythias and the Knights of Honor.

Dr. J. J. Slack, physician and druggist, Friar's Point, Miss., the second of three children born to Rev. William M. and Sarah (Johnson) Slack, owes his nativity to Madison county, Tenn., where his birth occurred in 1848. His parents were natives of Ohio and Tennessee, respectively. The father was a Baptist minister and physician, studied medicine at Louisville, Ky., and later settled at Denmark, Tenn., where the subject of this article was born. His father soon gave up medicine, and devoted his time to teaching a classical school, first at Belmont, and afterward at Denmark, where he remained in charge of a high school for eight years. In 1853 he came to Pontotoc, Miss., and became the president of the Mary Washington college, filling that position successfully for four years, having also the care of the Baptist church at that place, which he retained for more than twenty-three years. He then embarked in commercial pursuits, which he continued until the second year of the war, then resuming the practice of medicine for two or three years, after which he, with the assistance of his wife, opened the Baptist Female college, of which he made a complete success, continuing it for nearly sixteen years. This school was one of the first educational institutions in the state, and from it went out many teachers, building up colleges of their own, such as Blue Mountain college, Houston Normal and Slate Springs school, all of Mississippi. On account of failure of his voice, Rev. W. L. Slack gave up his school, and removed to Friar's Point, Miss., in 1881, where he had considerable interest in cotton planting, and engaged in the mercantile business. After a few years of retirement he went to Memphis, and assumed the care of Rowan Baptist church. Dr. J. J. Slack was reared in Pontotoc, Miss., from the age of five years, and received good educational advantages prior to the war, but during the continuance of the unpleasantness had very little opportunity for study, on account of there being no schools during the chaotic condition of the country. In 1865, though only sixteen years old, he began the management of a drug business for his father, which, under his careful handling, grew to be quite an extensive mercantile establishment in a few years. Realizing now the value of an education, he at once commenced a course of private study after business hours and at night, continuing it under many difficulties, until after several years of hard study he completed a full collegiate course. In 1867, in addition to his other studies and his extensive business engagements, he commenced the study of medicine, and continued it with unremitting assiduity for about ten years, but without an opportunity to attend college, on account of his business cares. In 1870 he was admitted as a partner in the business with his father, which was successfully continued until 1878, when the partnership was dissolved. Dr. Slack then came to Friar's Point, Miss., where he immediately opened a drug business, commencing January 1, 1879. Three years later, or in 1882, he finished his medical course, graduating at the well and favorably known Kentucky School of Medicine, at Louisville, having taken a special course each in diseases of women, gynecology, surgery and microscopy, which branches he intended to practice as specialties. His practice has been entirely satisfactory. In his drug store Dr. Slack dispensed entirely with the sale of all kinds of spirituous liquors, wines and brandies, and added in place jewelry, watches, clocks and fine watch repairing, thereby freeing his business from all the objectional features of retailing liquors, and has therefore organized a new departure by adding to the full line of drugs, medicines, paints, oils, glass, etc., a complete jeweler's stock, and has the best equipped repair department in any town of its size in the entire state, employing two skilled watchmakers constantly. In the whole list of professions there are no two usually kept distinct that admit of more satisfactory blending than that of physician and druggist, hence an appreciative public recognizes the benefit of the amalgamation, and favors the establishment of Dr. Slack in its dual capacity. The Doctor was married in 1871 to Miss Annie Suddoth, a native of Friar's Point, and the daughter of John A. Suddoth, one of the pioneers of the Mississippi delta. Mrs. Slack died early in 1878, leaving two daughters: Emma and May, the first since married to Mr. F. D. Robinson, one of the most progressive merchants of Friar's Point. The Doctor's second marriage occurred in October, 1879, to Miss Emma Suddoth, a sister of his former wife, and to this union have been born two children—a son and a daughter: Aylmer and Vera. Dr. Slack is a member of the Masonic fraternity, the Knights of Pythias and the Knights of Honor. He is president of the Friar's Point Building and Loan association (a live local investment company, which recently declared a dividend on its stock of thirty per cent.), a director in the Friar's Point Box and Woodwork factory, and is a stockholder in the bank. He bought the former residence of Governor Alcorn, which he tore down, and on its site erected a nice home. He has been engaged in cotton planting to some considerable extent, but has no desire to continue it longer, though he has a small farm near town. The Doctor is pleasing in manners and address, is of medium size, with dark hair, eyes and beard.

William David Sledge was born in La Grange, Tenn., on the 30th of June, 1837, and is the eldest of six surviving children born to the union of Norfleet R. and Catherine E. (Jones) Sledge, natives of North Carolina. The father removed to La Grange, Tenn., when a young man, married there, and in 1838 went to Marshall county, Miss., where he remained until 1847. From there he went to Panola county, settled at what is now known as Old Sledgeville, where he was engaged in merchandising and planting very extensively. In 1868 he located at Como, embarked in business there, and there continued until his death, in 1881. Since that time the business has been perpetuated by his three sons, W. D., N. R. and O. D., who had for some time been associated in business with him. Mrs. Sledge received her final summons in 1884. Mr. Sledge was prudent and temperate in his habits, was a man of excellent judgment, and was one of the most successful business men in the state. At the breaking out of the war, he was worth over $500,000, all of which he had made himself. His eldest son, William David, was reared in Panola county, and received all his schooling before fourteen years of age, for, after that, he was in his father's store at Sledgeville, until twenty years of age. He was then married to Miss Mary J. Brown, a native of Mississippi, and the daughter of Joshua T. and Clara (Grady) Brown, natives of Tennessee. To Mr. and Mrs. Sledge have been born five living children: Joshua T., now engaged in merchandising and planting at Redfork, Ark; Ruffin F., engaged in the same at Duncan, Miss.; Joseph B., at Duncan with his brother; Katie Lee, now Mrs. Ernest Taylor, of Como, and Sallie W., attending school at Memphis. After marriage Mr. Sledge began planting, and continued this until 1869, when he went into business with his father at Como, but at the same time continued his planting interests. In 1862 he enlisted in the Confederate army, company F, 28th Mississippi cavalry, but remained with this only four months, when he was discharged on account of physical disability. He was in no regular engagement, but participated in several sharp skirmishes. Mr. Sledge has been president of the board of supervisors for some time, and is one of the most prudent, clear-headed men in the county. His life has been a quiet, unassuming one, but marked with success and active business enterprises. The three brothers are associated in almost all business matters. Mr. Sledge now owns about four thousand acres of land, most of which is open land. He is largely interested in business at Memphis, under the firm title of Sledge & Norfleet, cotton commissioners, and has business enterprises at Lula, Mastodon and Como. He has an elegant home in the latter place, and considerable real estate in the county. His first wife died in 1887, and he was married again in 1888 to Mrs. Bessie N. Cruse, a native of Alabama, and the daughter of Dr. Newman, of Huntsville, Ala. Mr. and Mrs. Sledge are members of the Episcopal church, and are highly respected in the neighborhood.

Norfleet R. Sledge, merchant, Como, Miss., was the second child born to N. R. Sledge, Sr. (see sketch of W. D. Sledge), his birth occurring in Marshall county, Miss., on the 25th day of January, 1839, and was reared in Panola county, having moved with his father there when about eight years of age. He attended the University of Oxford, graduated in 1857, and afterward returned home, where he remained until 1861. He was then married to Miss Catherine E. Jones, a native of Mississippi and a daughter of F——— and Pauline J. (Moore) Jones, natives of North Carolina. In 1862 Mr. Sledge enlisted in the Confederate army, company F, Twenty-eighth Mississippi cavalry, and was soon after made lieutenant of the company. He served a considerable portion of his time as adjutant and was finally promoted to the captaincy, in which capacity he was serving when he was captured while covering General Hood's retreat from Nashville, Tenn. He was taken to Fort Delaware and retained until June, 1865. He participated in the battles of Murfreesboro, Franklin and others. While he was never wounded he had two horses shot from under him and was a daring and fearless officer. After being paroled he returned home, engaged in business with his father, and was the first one of the sons thus associated with the father, the firm name being N. R. Sledge & Co., until the other two brothers entered the copartnership, when it became N. R. Sledge & Sons. This continued until 1881, when the brothers bought the father's business and it became Sledge Bros., in which it is now conducted at Como. Mr. Sledge is also interested in the same business, of Sledge & Norfleet, in Memphis and at Lula and Mastodon, Miss. At Lula, Mr. Sledge and his brother, O. D., own a large tract of land and raise about one thousand bales of cotton on it annually. Mr. Sledge is the owner of about five thousand acres of land, much of which is under cultivation; is also the owner of considerable real estate in Como, and owns a very handsome residence between Memphis and Grenada. In business circles Mr. Sledge stands forth as an honorable and conscientious merchant, and as a citizen he is thoroughly respected and esteemed. His first wife died in

1880, leaving two children: Inez, who graduated from Ward's seminary, Nashville, Tenn., with highest honors over a class of fifty-seven when but seventeen years of age, and who the following summer, in company with Miss Clara Conway, of Memphis, made a trip to Europe, visiting London, Paris, Berlin, Vienna and other noted cities of the old world. In 1888 she was united in marriage to Dr. M. Campbell, superintendent of the East Tennessee asylum for the insane, and is now the mother of two interesting children: Lucille S. and Michael. Norfleet F. is now with his father in the store. In 1882 Mr. Sledge selected his second wife in the person of Miss Lucille Merriwether, a native of Mississippi and a daughter of James and Lucy Merriwether, natives of Georgia. To this union have been born two children: Olivette and N. R. Mr. Sledge has been a director of the Mississippi & Tennessee railroad, and is now a director of the Illinois Central railroad. Though often solicited by his numerous friends to become a candidate for office he has always declined, preferring his business at home. He owns stock in the Union and Planter's bank of Memphis, Tenn., and many other good business enterprises. Of thorough business capabilities and moral sentiments, his career has been one of modesty and yet activity. A promoter of all that is good, he brings into practice the virtues taught, and thereby commends the respect of all he meets in a business or social way. He is a liberal contributor to all religious and benevolent institutions, and is a whole-souled, pleasant, agreeable gentleman to meet.

O. D. Sledge, a prominent business man of the county, owes his nativity to Marshall county, Miss., where he was born in October, 1840, and is the youngest member of the well known firm of Sledge Bros. He was reared in Panola county, but received the principal part of his education in Florence, Ala. He espoused the cause of the Confederacy, and in 1861 he enlisted in the army, participating in the battles of Shiloh, Corinth and Fort Pillow, where he was wounded and disabled for about six months. As soon as able he joined General Forrest's cavalry, with which he remained until the close of the war, surrendering at Selma, Ala. He returned home and superintended his father's planting interests until the partnership with his father was formed, and then he and his brothers became interested in that business. In 1874 Mr. Sledge was married to Miss Dora Jones, a native of Mississippi, who died in 1886, leaving one child, Oliver Lee, who is now attending school at Sewanee, Tenn. In 1888 Mr. Sledge was married to Miss Mattie L. Brahan, a native of Mississippi, and a daughter of Col. John C. Brahan. Mr. Sledge is associated in business with the other brothers, and owns about as much property as either of the others. He and wife are esteemed members of the Episcopal church, and he contributes liberally to all laudable enterprises. He is an excellent business man, and is an adept at making money, as are also the other brothers. He has a happy, contented disposition, and is universally esteemed.

W. B. Sloan is the genial and popular clerk of the circuit court of Tate county, Miss., but is a native of Mecklenburg county, N. C., where he first saw the light of day August 13, 1835, being the third child born to John and Dovey (Barry) Sloan, also of that state and county. Finishing his education in the county of his birth, he turned his attention to business, but gave it up to enter the army, enlisting in May, 1861, in company B, Twenty-third North Carolina infantry, under Capt. George W. Seigle. Entering as sergeant of his company, he was promoted the second year of his service to second lieutenant, winning an honorable discharge at the close of the year on account of a wound received at the battle of Seven Pines. He was also in the engagement at Williamsburg. Mr. Sloan took up his residence in Coldwater in 1870, where he now resides in his own comfortable home. He was appointed and filled the office of deputy chancery and circuit clerk of his county two years—1875 and 1876. In May, 1878, he was elected mayor of the town of Coldwater, which office he filled for two years, at the expiration of which term he declined a re-election, on account of other business which occupied all of his time and attention. He was elected to the office which he now holds in 1883, serving with such merit that he was re-elected in 1887 without opposition. He is a generous, warm-hearted gentleman, and is a great favorite in local society, being a member of the Presbyterian church and the A. F. & A. M., lodge No. 76, of Senatobia. His parents, John and Dovey (Barry) Sloan, were blessed with six children, all of whom are still living. They are: Dr. A. B., of Coldwater; Dr. R. F., of Cass county, Tex.; W. B., the subject of this sketch; Ruth M., wife of J. T. Patterson, of Murphy, N. C.; Mary A., widow of T. A. Gillespie, and John D., who still resides in Mecklenburg county, N. C. Mr. Sloan, Sr., was an active, progressive farmer and an ardent democrat. He died in November, 1845, at the age of forty-five years, the death of his wife occurring the previous year, at the early age of thirty-eight years. Dr. A. B. Sloan, eldest brother of W. B. Sloan, engaged in the mercantile business in his native county of Mecklenburg, N. C., when but twenty years old, and continued in this line of business for about ten years, when he abandoned it for the profession of dentistry. In 1854 he married Miss Sarah J. Cooper, also a native of North Carolina, and in 1859 they removed to Mississippi. Three children gladdened their home and have left it to form homes of their own: J. E., a merchant in Alma, Ark.; Ida C., now Mrs. W. F. Baker, of the same place, and William T., who is in business in St. Louis. Mrs. Sloan died in 1863, and June 6, 1865, Dr. Sloan married Miss L. P. McCully, of Holly Springs, Miss. Like his brother, Dr. Sloan saw service in the war, enlisting in the Confederate army in the spring of 1863 as first lieutenant in Ballentine's regiment, Journegan's company, Mississippi cavalry. He reluctantly retired from the service after little more than one year's experience on account of a severe attack of rheumatism contracted on the field. Dr. Sloan follows his profession at Coldwater, where he is a well-known and respected citizen, as well as a skillful dental practitioner. He is active in all public enterprises, is an ardent politician, and is a Master Mason of lodge No. 409, of Coldwater. Dr. and Mrs. Sloan are members of the Presbyterian church, and take an active interest in the social life of the town.

Gen. Charles E. Smedes, Mississippi City, Miss., is a Kentuckian by birth. Nine brothers, several of whom have reached high and eminent stations in life, have contributed to the dignity and honor of the family home. Two were talented Episcopal clergymen, and two attained prominence at the bar. General Smedes studied law under S. S. Prentiss, and practiced for a short time, but tiring of the confinement, he engaged successively in the wholesale grocery business at Vicksburg, and in the cotton brokerage and commission business at New Orleans. He was a soldier in the Mexican war, a member of the historical first regiment, Mississippi rifles, Jefferson Davis commanding. At the opening of the late war he promptly entered the Confederate service, attained the rank of brigadier-general, and served with distinction to the close of the conflict. Like so many others, when he returned to his former scene of business life he found utter desolation, and only those possessed of great buoyancy of nature and untiring energy were able to regain quickly the equilibrium of commercial life. A change in the management of the St. James hotel, New Orleans, made it possible for him to secure its lease, and this he did without delay. The success following his regime was phenomenal. General Smedes notably excels in the comprehension and mastery of the innumerable details of a hotel, and the comforts and wishes of guests are of the first consideration. The cuisine is unsurpassed in the houses he has had under his control. He has been connected with the Maxwell house, Nashville; Marnes hotel, Mississippi City; Blount Springs, Ala.; Beersheba Springs, Tenn., and the Planters' house, Augusta, Ga., and has gained a reputation extending over almost the entire Union. In 1878 he secured the leasehold of what was then known as Barnes hotel, Mississippi City. He has converted it into an elegant hostelry where there is at all seasons of the year a welcome to the invalid, the pleasure seeker, the sportsman, and the stranger. The house has been rechristened Gulf View, and is largely patronized by the wealthiest classes of merchants, professional people and planters. General Smedes takes a just pride in his military career. At the battle of Monterey he was promoted from the ranks to the office of captain, and was placed upon the staff of Gen. John A. Quitman. He was a gallant, faithful soldier, and fully deserving of the honors conferred upon him.

Dr. A. H. Smith is a retired physician. He was born in Charlotte county, Va., in the year 1815, a son of John and Elizabeth (Elam) Smith, who were also natives of the Old Dominion. The father of Dr. Smith, at an early age (about fourteen years), enlisted in the cause of American freedom, and fought as a soldier in the army of the Revolution. He was a farmer by vocation, and after the war resumed his previous life, and died in Tennessee. He was the father of nineteen sons and daughters, born of two mothers. Dr. Smith was reared on a farm in Wilson county, Tenn., receiving an academic education at Laguardo academy, in the immediate neighborhood. He began to study medicine when eighteen years old, and graduated in the year 1837, in the medical department of Transylvania university, Lexington, Ky. He began the practice of his profession at Sumterville, Ala., where he remained (except six years spent at Gainesville, a neighboring town), till 1868, when he came to Meridian, Miss., and has made his home in this city ever since. On account of infirm health, Dr. Smith has not engaged actively in the practice of his profession for the last thirty years, and in 1887 was paralyzed in the right arm and leg, which has incapacitated him for walking ever since. He was elected to the legislature from Lauderdale county in 1870, and by contest was turned out after six weeks by the radicals. Dr. Smith was married in 1841 to Miss Louisa Davidson, who became the mother of three children, only one of whom, a daughter, Emma, is living. She is the wife of John D. McInnes, of Meridian. The Doctor married a second time, in the year 1858, a Miss Jane Moors. Dr. Smith is a member of the Baptist church, while his wife is a Presbyterian. He is a Mason, also a member of the I. O. O. F.

The family to which Addison B. Smith belongs was among the earliest settlers of Mississippi, and the grandfather, Judge Edmond Smith, was born in the state and was one of the early residents of old Sunflower county, in which he became a prominent and leading man in county affairs. He was an active politician, and so greatly was he admired, and so popular did he become, that he was chosen to represent the county in the state legislature, where his knowledge of law and the soundness of his propositions received immediate recognition. He also admirably filled the position of probate judge and held other offices of trust and honor to the satisfaction of all concerned. James H. Smith, his son and the father of the subject of this sketch, was born in the Yazoo delta in 1826, and there attained manhood. He was married to Miss Fannie Stubblefield, a native of Georgia and a daughter of Squire Stubblefield, one of the pioneers of Yazoo county, and there followed merchandising for a number of years, being a practical pharmacist. During the Civil war he served in the medical department of the Confederate army for about two years, but when just in the prime of life in 1863 he was called from life. He was a man of liberal, generous and high minded impulses, and manifested the instincts and training of a true gentleman in his daily walk and conversation. He was a Royal Arch Mason and throughout life was a warm admirer of that order. His widow survived him until 1885, when she was called from life. Addison B. Smith is the youngest of three sons, and although his advantages were limited in early life he has by contact with the world and the active interest he has taken in the business affairs of life become an exceptionally well informed man. At the age of seventeen years he began clerking in the county in which he is now living, and for several years this occupation received his attention. Here he received a practical business education and training and laid the foundation for future success. In 1883 he embarked in business for himself in a small way, as his capital was exceedingly limited, but so thoroughly did he attend to every detail, so honorable was he in every respect, and so earnestly did he try to please his patrons that in time success crowned his efforts. He increased his stock of goods from time to time, as his purse permitted and his patronage demanded, and now, as a reward for his early labors, he has a large store filled with a select stock of general merchandise, and commands a large trade. He is a man of superior business qualifications, for besides possessing much discernment in the selection of his stock, he takes proper care of it after it has come into his possession. In 1883 he was appointed postmaster of Indianola and since that time has served continuously in this capacity, and has made a faithful and capable official for Uncle Sam. He was married on the 29th of November, 1888, to Miss Beatrice Holt, a daughter of W. J. Holt, and by her is the father of one child, a little daughter named Mary A. Mrs. Smith was born, reared and educated in this state, and is an intelligent, agreeable and social lady. They are now residing in their handsome residence in Indianola, which has lately been erected, it being situated on a beautiful building site on the north side of the bayou.

Allen N. Smith, the popular sheriff of Issaquena county, was the elder of two children born to John and Esther (Mills) Smith, natives of Louisiana. The parents were married in their native state, and at an early day emigrated to Madison county, Miss., where Mr. Smith died when Allen N. was but a small boy. The other child, Rufus, died at the age of thirty-eight years. Mrs. Smith was a passenger on the first steamboat that plowed the waters of the Mississippi river. After her husband's death she married J. L. Mitchell, of Kentucky, a school teacher by profession. They became the parents of one child, Joseph, who now resides in Holmes county, and is a planter by pursuit. Mrs. Mitchell died at the age of forty-five. Allen N. Smith, who was born in Madison county, Miss., February 22, 1834, was fairly educated in the common schools of his native county, and at the age of seventeen years started out to follow the occupation to which he had been reared, farming, and this he has continued the principal part of the time since. He has been a resident of Yazoo and LeFlore counties, but came to this in 1887, and in 1889 was elected sheriff and tax collector, the duties of which office he is filling in a manner highly creditable to himself and to the satisfaction of the community at large, and was re-elected July 6, 1891, for the term of four years. He has been inspector of the levee, and is a man of intelligence and influence. He has a fair complexion, is about six feet tall, weighs about two hundred and ten pounds, and, although very gray, is still erect and dignified. In 1866 he was married to Miss Sidney Skidmore, daughter of C. S. Skidmore, of Madison county, and the fruits of this union have been four children: Clifton B. (deputy sheriff and a merchant of Mayersville, of this county), Sidney, Allie May and Rosa Lee.

Austin W. Smith, planter of Saragossa plantation, is a native of Natchez, Miss., born on the 22d of May, 1843, and his father, Walton Pembroke Smith, was born in Madison county, Va., on the 7th of August, 1810. The elder Smith was educated in Maryland and Middleton, Conn., and when a young man came with some of his people to Adams county, Miss., where he was married to Miss Anna Elizabeth Williams. He became the owner of large landed estates in Adams county, Miss., Louisiana, Missouri and Virginia, and held various minor offices in Louisiana. He was a stanch union man and at one time during the war, while at home sick, and with no one present but his wife and one or two small children,

his house was surrounded by about twenty-seven Federal soldiers who commenced an assault upon it. This frightened all the inmates very much except Mr. Smith, who told the others to secret themselves as best they could while he took up his trusty gun and prepared to defend his home. He fired upon them and killed two, after which the others fled. The house was riddled with bullets. He was at one time president of the police jury in Concordia parish, La., and was also a tutor of John Perkins, who became a very prominent man in the Confederate congress. Mr. Smith died in August, 1866, while in Missouri. His father, William Haslett Smith, was born in Maryland on the 9th of June, 1777, and was an educated and well informed gentleman. He was a very extensive planter but was formerly a wine merchant and importer in Baltimore. His wife, Mary Bell Madison was a daughter of Francis Madison who was a brother of President James Madison. She was born in the Old Dominion in 1773 and died in 1812. Mr. Smith died on the 15th of July, 1829. Their family consisted of three children, two sons and a daughter, Walton Pembroke Smith being the second in order of birth. In 1815, Mr. Smith took for his second wife Miss Hannah Level, a native of Kentucky, who died in 1819. He had extensive planting interests in Louisiana and Virginia, and was a man of great resources. His father, David Smith, was born in Cecil county, Md., on the 27th of August, 1739, and was a graduate of Princeton college. He was married on the 6th of December, 1768, to Miss Martha Haslett, and they became the parents of three sons and one daughter. David Smith was sheriff under George III of Cecil county a number of years and spent all his life there. He was tutor of Rutledge, one of the signers of the Declaration of Independence. His father, John Smith, was born near Londonderry, Ireland, in 1701 and died September 9th, 1772. He came to America in the early part of the eighteenth century with his father, John Smith, (of Scotch-Irish decent) who settled in Pennsylvania on the Susquehanna river. John Smith, Jr., younger brother of James Smith was a prominent lawyer in York, Pa., was one of the signers of the Declaration of Independence and was one of the committee who called that body together. He was a colonel in the Revolutionary war and a member of the Continental congress. Austin Williams, the maternal grandfather of Austin W. Smith (our subject), was born in Jessamine county, Ky., on the 24th of June, 1780, and died on the 19th of October, 1846. When a young man he came to Adams county, Miss., and was there married to Miss Caroline Matilda Routh. They spent the balance of their days there, Mr. Williams becoming quite wealthy as a planter. He was a captain at the battle of New Orleans, U. S. A. His father, Charles Pierce Williams, was born near Petersburg, Va. but moved from that state to Kentucky, where his death occurred. He married Miss Elizabeth Redd, a daughter of Mordica Redd and granddaughter of Col. John Minor of Revolutionary fame. Charles P. Williams was the son of Barney Williams, who came from Wales to Virginia in 1700. Job Routh, the father of Mrs. Williams was a very early settler of Adams county and became one of the largest land holders and planters, being the owner of forty thousand acres in Louisiana. He left a large family of well known sons and daughters.

Austin W. Smith was the second in order of birth of the following children: Dr. John Davidson (deceased) was a man of fine education. He was lieutenant in a Louisiana company of cavalry under General Taylor in the Confederate army, and was a physician at Natchez. His death occurred in 1885; William Madison was killed in a steamgin in Concordia parish, La. He was a courier for Gen. Majors in the Confederate army; Haller Routh was killed in February, 1867, by the accidental discharge of a gun at Saragossa: Austin W. Smith was educated under private tutors, among them Frank Waterhouse, president now of the high school of the city of Boston, Mass., and later attended Oakland and Jefferson colleges, also Fredericksburg, Va. In 1861 when not eighteen years of age, he joined company E, Fourth Louisiana battalion, Confederate States army, and served as corporal and sergeant. At Atlanta he was promoted to ensign and afterward served in that capacity in the Pelican regiment. He fought in the campaigns in West Virginia and in the fall of 1861 he was sent to Savannah, Ga., operating in the extreme south until 1863. After this he was around Vicksburg, Chickamauga, Chattanooga, Missionary ridge and at Resaca. He was wounded at the last named place and afterward joined his command at Atlanta. He then went back with Hood to Tennessee, was on detached service, went from there to Mobile, thence to Meridian, Miss., and started to join Johnston with his company, but was soon ordered back to Meridian to surrender. He is now the only ensign living of the fifteen in his brigade. After the war he returned to planting and in May, 1867, he married Clara Ann Montgomery, a native of Jefferson county, Miss., and the daughter of Prosper K. and Mariah L. (Darden) Montgomery. Mr. Montgomery was born in Adams county, in 1808, and was married in Jefferson county, to Miss Darden, a native of the last named county. Her death occurred in that county, in 1864, and Mr. Montgomery's death followed in 1886. Mrs. Montgomery was a daughter of Buckner Darden. To Mr. and Mrs. Smith were born, three living children. Since 1868, Mr. Smith has lived on his present property, and the house, an old Spanish building, was formerly surrounded by a brick wall, probably for protection against the Indians. The plantation consists of eighteen hundred acres, and Mr. Smith owns four hundred acres in Louisiana. He is a member of the Veteran association and his wife is a member of the Presbyterian church. He is a descendant of a very old, intellligent and aristocratic family and one of which he may well be proud.

Isaac C. Smith, a prominent farmer of Lincoln county, living three miles northeast of Brookhaven, was born in December, 1848, in the house in which he now lives. He was a son of Leonard and Lenora (Maxwell) Smith. Her mother was a daughter of Maj. Jesse Maxwell and Priscilla (Kees) Maxwell. The Maxwells had a large family of children, three sons and three daughters of which are now living. Of these, Carroll resides on Pearl river, near Monticello; Thomas K., lives near him, Joel P., is married and lives in Lincoln county, near his father's old homestead; Amanda P., is the wife of Mr. A. Price, and lives on a plantation near Bogue Chitto; Lenora, the mother of our subject, is a member of his family, having made her home with her children since the death of her husband in 1854; Pernecia is the wife of John Ray, and lives on a plantation in Lincoln county; Conway died, leaving a family of three children; Louis W. died at Grenada, leaving two daughters; Martha M. bore her husband, Fleet Cooper, two daughters, and she and her husband are now deceased; Sallie married Ambrose Bull, and both died in Arkansas, leaving four children. Carroll, Thomas K. and Amanda P. all had large families. Leonard Smith, the father of our subject, was the fifth son in order of birth of his parents' children, named as follows: Isaac, who died when young; Isham, also deceased; Lott (deceased) and leaving a large family; William, who died leaving four children; Leonard, the father of our subject, who left three sons and a daughter; Everett (deceased), who left three children; Martin, who was killed by a train while riding on a hand car, and who left one son; Sallie, who married Ambrose Bull, died leaving four children; Nancy (deceased) was the wife of Richard Coke, who is also dead; Emily J. married Anslom H. Jayne, and both are deceased, leaving one daughter; Mary (deceased) was the wife of Solomon Carpenter, who is also deceased, and left a large family; Jane is the widow of John Hart, and lives in Yazoo county, having reared a large family. Leonard Smith was born in 1808 in Georgia, and located with his parents where his son, Isaac Smith, now lives. There he made his home until his death in 1854, as above mentioned, his wife surviving him. To them were born four children, three sons and one daughter: Louisa J., who was never married, lives on the old homestead with her brother; she is a member of the Baptist church. Jesse M., who was born December 28, 1850, married Miss Julia Tyler, a native of Lawrence county, Miss., being a daughter of Marvin and Frances (Hardy) Tyler. Her father was a native of New York, and her mother of Alabama. Their children were: Julius, Martha, Julia, Emma and Thomas, the latter being deceased. Jesse M. and his wife are both members of the Baptist church. They have had three children: Ernest (deceased), Alva and Herbert. Joel I., another son of Leonard Smith, was born March 1, 1853. He received his education at the common schools of Lincoln county. He has lived with his brother Isaac, and has assisted him in planting. He cast his first presidential vote for S. J. Tilden. He is a member of the Baptist church. Isaac, the first son and the second child in order of birth in his father's family, received a limited education at the common schools, in consequence of the death of his father, which left a portion of the family support on him, and was prevented from pursuing his studies further. He was married December 21, 1876, to Miss Cornelia E. Ross, who was born in Lawrence county in 1856. She is a daughter of Simeon and Margaret (Wiley) Ross, both natives of Lawrence county. Mr. and Mrs. Ross have had three children, two daughters and one son, named as follows: John W., Susana and Cornelia. To Mr. and Mrs. Smith was born one child, Estus C., who was born November 14, 1877. His mother died December 28, of the same year. Mr. Smith is a democrat, politically, and cast his first vote for Horace Greeley. He is a member of the board of supervisors of Lincoln county, and he and his brother, Jesse M., are members of the Farmers' Alliance. He is a Baptist, and a strong advocate of the temperance cause. He contributes liberally to churches, schools and all enterprises, believing thoroughly in everything that he thinks has a tendency toward the good of the people, and the upbuilding of the cause of Christ. He has landed property, comprising in area about twelve hundred acres, and he is the owner of a steam gristmill, canemill and cottonmill combined.

James C. Smith, general merchant and vice-president of the Crystal Springs bank, was born in Edgefield district, S. C., in 1830, a son of James and Nancy (Clement) Smith, natives of North Carolina, who were married in South Carolina, in Edgefield district, and lived there until about 1838. At that time they came to Copiah county, settling four miles north of Crystal Springs, amidst a wide extent of forest, this part of the state being at that time much of it in a primitive condition. Mr. Smith cleared and improved a farm, upon which he lived until his death, which occurred in 1858, at the age of sixty-one, his widow surviving him till 1870, when she died at the age of seventy-five years. Mr. Smith was of English descent, and his family were not numerous, his sister, Mrs. Wood, who lived near Aberdeen, having been his only relative in Mississippi. He was an honest, industrious man, modest and retiring in disposition, a good citizen and successful planter. The subject of this sketch was the second of six children born to his parents, three of whom are still living: John, who was a member of the Sixteenth and afterward of the Thirty-sixth Mississippi infantry, and died at the old homestead; William J. served in company C, of the Sixteenth Mississippi infantry all through the war; Isaac served during most of the period of the war in the Thirty-sixth Mississippi infantry; Sarah Ann (deceased), who became the wife of Jack Young; Elizabeth (deceased) married William Clark. Our subject passed his boyhood days on the plantation, receiving a common-school education. At the age of twenty he began planting on his own account, which he continued for two years. He then engaged in the mercantile business near his old home, which he continued until the railroad was built in 1858, when he saw a more advantageous position near Crystal Springs, and removing to that point, became the first merchant there. His career since that time has been one of most gratifying success. He not only enjoys the distinction of being the pioneer merchant of that section, but one of the leading merchants as well. His operations before the war were so extensive that some years he did as much as $75,000 in trade, and his business now aggregates about $35,000. During the last year of the war Mr. Smith served in Mississippi in Major Roberts' cavalry. He was married, in 1851, to Matilda, a daughter of Calvin and Martha Cox, natives of South Carolina, whence they came to Alabama at an early day, removing from there to Copiah county, where they passed the remainder of their lives. Her father, who was a well-known planter, died soon after the war. Mrs. Smith was a native of Alabama. She has borne her husband nine children, seven of whom are still living: William Robert, James C., Jr., Wiley T., Augustus, Andrew, Mattie and Anna. Mr. Smith was the first president of the Crystal Springs bank, which position he held for two years, and has since been its vice president. His familiarity with the mercantile business was extensive, and his acquaintance extends through all parts of the state. Mrs. Smith died in 1889, having for many years been a member of the Baptist church, and is remembered as a most estimable lady, devoted to her children, of a charitable disposition and most pleasing manners. Mr. Smith is a consistent and helpful member of the Baptist church. In person Mr. Smith is rather tall and spare built, is courteous, affable and friendly, and has the faculty of drawing to him and retaining many friends. He has led a quiet, but in a certain sense, a very active life. He has made a great financial success. He exercises the right of suffrage for the good of the community at large, but does not neglect his business for politics. He has given much attention to the education of his children, all of whom are worthy members of society, and several of his sons are connected with his business in different capacities.

Murray F. Smith is an attorney of the firm of Miller, Smith & Hirsch, and for the past seventeen years has been a resident of Vicksburg, Miss., and one of its most eminent and successful lawyers. He was born in Milton, Caswell county, N. C., in 1850, the youngest of seven children that grew to maturity born to George A. and Adaline (McGehee) Smith, who were born in Virginia and North Carolina, respectively. The father was a merchant and a prosperous tobacco manufacturer. He died in 1860 and his wife in 1858, both having been earnest and consistent members of the Presbyterian church. The paternal ancestors for many years back were residents of Virginia, the mother's people being wealthy and influential residents of the Old North state. Murray F. Smith was educated in the state of his birth, having been an attendant of Bingham school, a noted educational institution of North Carolina, and later graduated from the Washington and Lee University of Lexington, Va., in 1870. Immediately upon leaving this institution he began the study of law in Judge Pearson's law school at Richmond Hill, Yadkin county, N. C., and graduated therefrom in January, 1872, being admitted to the bar by the supreme court of that state in 1872. He at once began practicing in Greensboro, N. C., continuing there until April, 1874, when he came to Vicksburg, Miss. He was married the same year to Miss Kate Wilson, of Vicksburg, a daughter of Victor F. Wilson, a merchant for many years of this city, who died about 1865. In the fall of 1874 he became a regular practitioner of Vicksburg, and in 1878 formed a partnership with John A. Klein, which continued for one year. In 1880 he became associated with A. B. and W. B. Pitman, the firm being Pitman, Pitman & Smith until 1883, but since January, 1884, has been associated with his present partners, they being now the attorneys for the Louisville, New Orleans & Texas railroad, the Delta Trust and Banking company, the St. Louis & New Orleans Anchor Line Steamboat company, the Yazoo & Tallahatchie Transportation company, the Refuge Oil Mill company and the Vicksburg Street Railway company. This firm have a very large private court practice and handle in a masterly manner the many large and important suits entrusted to them. Mr. Smith has been quite an active politician, has attended many conventions, and every state convention since 1880. In 1887 he was elected to the lower house of the state legislature for the session of 1888, and served on several important committees. He was a member of the state constitutional convention in 1890, and in every official position in which he has served he has added luster to his name and has shown that he is possessed of mental qualities of no ordinary merit. He is active in the affairs of the city and is in all ways an exemplary citizen. He has always been a careful and painstaking student and gives the most devoted attention to his cases. He is a member of Vicksburg lodge of the A. F. & A. M., Lee lodge of the K. of P., is an Elk, and K. of H., and also belongs to the American Legion of Honor. He is a good financier and has erected a handsome residence on Prince street, besides having an interest in a plantation in this county. He and his wife are members of the Episcopal church and are the parents of four interesting children: Victor Conway, Murray Forbes, Jr., Ada McGehee and Clarence Carroll. Mr. Smith is a director of the D. W. Froweree Ice company and has manifested much interest in other worthy enterprises.

Robert M. Smith, planter, Mayersville, Miss. This branch of the Smith family is the oldest now living in the county, the father, Robert M. Smith, Sr., having settled here in 1845, and there is but one other family now in the county who settled here at an earlier period. Robert M. Smith, Sr., was born in the blue grass regions of Kentucky, but came to Mississippi in 1832, and was married in 1847 to Miss Margaret Charr, a native of Tennessee. Mrs. Smith went on a visit to Missouri and there, in the year 1848, Robert M. Smith, Jr., was born. The elder Smith was a man of more than usual influence in the community, was firm in his convictions and was sensitive of his honor. Public offices were bestowed upon him on account of his intelligence, tact and integrity, and these talents commanded for him the respect of every citizen in public affairs. He served as magistrate for many years, also held the office of treasurer of the county, was a member of the board of county police, and was also a member of the levee board. He was not in active service during the Civil war, but was provost marshal in Issaquena county a portion of that time. He was a manager for twenty-seven years, twelve years for William Cannon, and fifteen years for Stephen Duncan. He commenced planting for himself in 1858, and during the war lost nearly all his property, having to commence almost at the beginning in 1865. He was unusually successful in that occupation, and at the time of his death, in 1877, he was one of the substantial men of the county. To his marriage were born nine children, Robert M. being the eldest. The others were: W. J. (died in 1883); Martha C., wife of F. B. Hill, of Patterson, La.; Mamie E., wife of Will E. Collins, of Mayersville; Preston H., resides in Issaquena county; Lee S., of Louisiana; L. W. (died in July, 1890); Lurena, wife of James P. Heath, of this caunty; and Hampton P. (deceased). The mother of these children is still living. Mr. Smith was a member of the I. O. O. F. and the A. F. & A. M., being a charter member of the old Preston lodge, the first in the county. Robert M. Smith, Jr., was educated in Issaquena county, and at the age of twenty-two started out to make his own way in life. His first venture was in the mercantile business at Clover Hill, this county, where he remained from 1867 to 1873, when he closed out and engaged in planting. In 1878 his father's estate demanded his attention, and he took charge of this, remaining thus employed until 1890. He has been twice married, first in December, 1873, to Miss Linda Sibley, daughter of John T. Sibley, of New Orleans, La. She died in July, 1874, and on the 1st of January, 1890, Mr. Smith took for his second wife Miss Emma Woodry, daughter of John Woodry, of New Orleans, La. Both of her parents died when she was quite small. Mr. Smith's first wife was a member of the Presbyterian church, but his second wife is a Methodist, and Mr. Smith holds membership in the same church. He is a member of the American Legion of Honor of Vicksburg, Miss. Mr. and Mrs. Smith are the parents of one child, a son, Robert M., who was born on the 13th of January, 1891. The eldest son for three successive generations has been named Robert M., thus retaining the old family name. Mr. Smith is the owner of seven hundred and eighty acres of land, with five hundred acres under cultivation, on which are annually raised about three hundred and fifty bales of cotton. He has one of the finest city residences and owns considerable property besides. He is quite a popular man in the county, and makes many warm friends wherever he goes. He is extremely fond of hunting, and always keeps a number of fine dogs. His complexion is quite fair, and he is about five feet eight inches in hight, and weighing about two hundred and twenty pounds.

No work devoted to the history and the commercial and professional interests of Mississippi could be complete without some mention of the well-known gentleman, Dr. Sidney O. Smith, a native-born Mississippian, who has attained high rank in his chosen profession. His parents were John D. and Margaret P. (Mize) Smith. The former was a native of Georgia, born in 1809, the latter of Alabama, born 1829. They were the earliest pioneers where they first settled in Mississippi, and where they spent the greater part of their lives, removing in 1870 to Covington county and thence to Lincoln county. There the father died in 1884, the mother surviving him. They were the parents of six children: Ophelia R., Lerona V., Cornelia, Neulan B., Sydney O. and another who died in infancy, unnamed. Of this family the subject of this notice was the first born September 17, 1861, and was educated principally at the Byhala high school, of Lincoln county, Miss., and in 1878 began the study of medicine, under the direction of Prof. W. H. Dixon, and Dr. E. A. Rowar, of Wesson, Miss. In the winter of 1880 and 1881 he attended lectures at the medical department of the Tulane university, at New Orleans, La., formerly known as the University of Louisiana. Later he read medicine for a time at Raleigh, Miss., under the instructions of his brother, Dr. D. L. Smith, and was at the same time engaged in teaching school. In the fall of 1881–2 he took a second course of lectures at Tulane university, from which he was graduated with high honors in March, 1882. He soon after located in Lincoln county, Miss., and, for a short time, practiced his profession there, but removed to Wesson, Miss., where he was a resident practitioner until March, 1884. From that date until June, 1884, he was engaged in the practice of medicine at Natchez, Miss. At this time his father was taken with his final illness, and Dr. Smith returned home to render him such assistance as was in his power to give. After his father's death, he returned to Wesson, Miss., where he resumed his practice, and on the 27th of November, 1884, he was united in marriage to Miss Anna M , a daughter of W. W. and Anna L. (Waddell) Robeson. In January, 1885, he again took up his residence in Natchez, Miss., where he practiced with some success until October, 1885, at which time he returned to Wesson, Miss. He removed in January, 1889, to Ellisville, where he has since remained, having acquired a successful and extensive practice, and won the confidence of the public generally, and also that of his professional brethren. In April, 1891, he formed a partnership with Dr. Robert L. Turner, a sketch of whom appears elsewhere in this work. The Doctor is a member of the State Medical association, of the Masonic order, of the Knights of Pythias and of the Baptist church, while his wife is identified with the Methodist Episcopal Church South. They are the parents of three children: Sydney W., Annie J. and Nellie L.

William M. Smith, merchant and farmer, Booneville, Miss. Between the years 1830 and 1840 the state of Mississippi received many emigrants from other states, and among those who sought out homes in the wilderness were Joseph and Nancy (Mussy) Smith, natives of Georgia and the parents of our subject. They were married in their native state, but subsequently moved to a place near Birmingham, Ala., thence to Fayette county of that state, and in 1836 they came to Mississippi, locating six miles south of Ripley, in Tippah county. The country was wild and unsettled, and Indians were numerous, but during the year 1836 many settlers poured into the state. Mr. Smith was a blacksmith by trade, but in connection with this he also engaged in tilling the soil in Tippah county, until 1844, when he removed to what is now Prentiss county, near Blackland. There he resided until the breaking out of hostilities between the North and South, when, with his wife and daughters, he moved to Fayette county, Ala. There his death occurred when eighty-three years of age. He was a stanch democrat, took an active part in politics and was well posted on the issues of the day. He was a soldier in the War of 1812 with General Jackson, of whom he was a great admirer and one of his most earnest supporters. He was a leading member of the Methodist church, as was also his wife, and was a very liberal supporter of the same. He was one of a large family of sons in Georgia, but he was the only one who came West. His marriage was blessed by the birth of seven children—five sons and two daughters—all of whom lived to be grown, and four are yet living: John died in Corinth, Miss., just before the war; Mrs. Eliza Roseman (deceased); James B. was in the army of Virginia, and was killed at the battle of the Wilderness; he left a wife and several children, one of his sons serving in the army with him. R. Allen (retired) resides in Fayetteville, Ala., and was a saddler in early life; he was born in the year 1819, and was a soldier in the Civil war, holding the rank of captain of a company at Shiloh; William M. (subject); Thomas B. was a soldier in the Civil war; he is now keeping hotel at Fort Worth, Tex.; and Mrs. Mary Ann Hubbert resides in Walker county, Ala. William M. Smith emigrated to Mississippi with his parents when fifteen years of age, received his education in the schools of the county, and in 1842 began working for himself. One year later he went from Tippah to Prentiss county, settled in Blackland in the west part of the county, and there entered wild land, which he continued to cultivate until 1880, when he came to Booneville. He was married to Miss Nancy Ray, a native of Tippah county, Miss., born in 1821, and the fruits of this union were three children, all sons, two of whom are yet living. The mother of these children died about 1855. She was a worthy member of the Cumberland Presbyterian church. The children were named: A. Gaines Smith, Franklin Smith, who died when young, and Dr. William A. Smith, the latter a practicing physician at Sherman, Miss. He served in the cavalry during the latter part of the Civil war. A. Gaines Smith, now a prominent merchant of Booneville, was born in Tippah county, Miss., and reared in what is now Prentiss county. He received a good practical education in the common schools, and during the war served in Hawkins' battery of sharpshooters in General Wood's brigade, Claiborne's division, as sergeant. He was in the battles of Perryville, Murfreesboro, Chickamauga, etc., and was captured on the 22d of July, 1864. He was carried to Camp Chase, Ohio, and retained there until May, 1865. After being released he returned to his home, began farming, and in September, 1866, he came to Booneville, where he has been engaged in merchandising ever since, with the exception of one year in Mobile, when he was interested in the produce commission business. He is now engaged in a general dry goods merchandising business. Mr. Smith is a democrat, and one of the leading men in the place. He was married to Miss Lou M. Norwood, a native of Kentucky, born near Bowling Green, and the daughter of B. F. and Ann M. (Webb) Norwood, both natives of North Carolina. Her parents were married near Carthage, Tenn., and Mrs. Smith was the eldest of the children born to this union. Her people came to Mississippi about the breaking out of the war, and the father followed the occupation of a tobacco grower to some extent. He is now deceased, but the mother is living, and resides in Mississippi. To Mr. and Mrs. Smith were born nine children: Edgar G., Jessie, Willie, Annie Lee, Lota, Ray, Dora, Douglas, Bessie and Lillian, all daughters but two. Edgar married a Miss Johnson, and resides in Monroe county, Miss. The father of these children is a member of the Presbyterian church. He is quite a prominent Mason, was master of his lodge for five years, district deputy grand master for four years, and was re-elected to that position of the first district of Mississippi in 1891. To return to the father of the above-mentioned gentleman: After the death of his first wife, William M. Smith married Mrs. Martha E. Pressley, a native of the Old North state. To this union were born two daughters: Anna P. and Dora (deceased). Anna P. is the wife of P. M. Walker, who is a merchant of Booneville, and a brother of Dr. Walker, of Baldwyn, Miss. Miss Dora, who was educated at Florence, Ala., and who was a highly accomplished young lady, died in 1886. The mother of these children died on the 24th of September, 1889, when about seventy-two years of age. She was a member of the Baptist church, in which she was a very active member and a devoted worker. She was educated at Wake Forest, N. C., and was the daughter of Oscar Pressley, a sailor on the ocean. During the war Mr. Smith took no active part. In politics he affiliates with the democratic party, and socially he is a member of the Masonic fraternity, Brownville lodge No. 305. He has held the office of taxcollector and other minor offices in the county.

Dr. A. J. Smythe, physician, Bethany, Miss., was born in old Pontotoc county (now Lee), Miss., on February 29, 1856, and was the only child born to the union of Anson G. and Caroline (Humphreys) Smythe, both natives of South Carolina. The paternal grandparents removed from South Carolina to Alabama at an early day, resided there for several years, and then removed to Carroll county Miss., near Vaiden, where the grandfather located and passed the remainder of his days, his death occurring in 1868. In connection with his occupation as a farmer he also followed the blacksmith trade. The maternal grandparents came to Mississippi in 1839. Anson G. Smythe studied medicine in the office of Dr. Cross, at Lexington, Miss., in his youthful days and subsequently attended medical lectures at New Orleans. He located in Prentiss county, near Baldwyn, in 1842 he practiced his profession there, and was married the same year in the house where his son, Dr. A. J. Smythe, now lives, one mile east of Bethany, Prentiss county. In his youthful days he followed surveying a considerable portion of his time. His wife died at Bethany in November, 1876, and was a consistent member of the Bethany Presbyterian church. The father died on July 2, 1884, at the same place. He was a free thinker and was one of the leading physicians in the county. Dr. A. J. Smythe was educated at the Kentucky Military institute near Frankfort, and in the fall of 1877 and winter of 1878 he attended medical college at New Orleans at what is now known as Tulane university, although prior to that he had read medicine for several years in his father's office. He graduated at Bellevue Hospital college, New York, in 1881, and then returned to Prentiss county; began practicing his profession at Bethany, where he has remained up to the present writing. He was married in 1878 to Miss Emma Richey, daughter of Robert Richey, of Lee county, Miss., and they had born to their union six children, two sons and four daughters: Mabel, Caroline, Nancy, Gordon, Emma and Andrew J. Dr. Smythe owns one hundred and sixty acres of land, has sixty acres under cultivation, but gives this very little attention, for his whole time is taken up with his large and lucrative practice. He has resided in the community where he now lives all his life, with the exception of a few years during the war, when his father moved with his family to Aberdeen for protection, and remained there until the war closed, when they returned to their former home. The Doctor is a member of the Knights of Honor and Mrs. Smythe is a member of the Presbyterian church.

John A. Snell is the present efficient incumbent of the office of county treasurer and was born in Lowndes county in 1847, a son of Reuben H. and Elizabeth (Love) Snell, natives of South Carolina, but early emigrants to Lowndes county, Miss., where they spent the remainder of their lives, the father having followed the calling of a planter. Their union resulted in the birth of seven children. John A. Snell was reared on his father's plantation and was given the advantages of the public schools of Lowndes county, in which he improved his time to the utmost and became a proficient scholar. In January, 1864, he enlisted in company I, Sixth Mississippi cavalry, and served until badly wounded at Harrisburg. Miss., July 14. 1864, his right leg being taken off by a shell. After being confined to the hospital for about two months he returned home and was engaged in planting until he was elected assessor in 1875, and county treasurer in 1877, the duties of the last named position being filled by him continuously and with ability ever since. The people of this section have known him from his birth and the confidence which they have in him is therefore intelligently placed, for they have had every opportunity to judge of his character and qualifications. He has shown himself to be capable and trustworthy and his kindness and courtesy have won for him much popularity and the good will of all. He is an earnest member of the Presbyterian church, and socially belongs to the K. of H.

W. P. Snowden, planter, Deerbrook, Noxubee county, Miss. W. P. Snowden is the son of James A. and Sarah S. (Holder) Snowden, who were born in Utica, Oneida county, N. Y., in 1806, and Winchester. Franklin county, Tenn., respectively. The parents were married in 1835 in Winchester, Tenn., and their son, the subject of this sketch, was born in that place in 1837. In 1845 he removed with his parents to Chickasaw county, Miss., where they settled on a farm. Here his mother died in 1849. The father, with five children, removed to Monroe county, near Aberdeen, in 1851, at which place the family resided when the Civil war broke out in 1861. W. P. Snowden was one of the first men mustered into the Confederate service in Monroe county. He went out as a private in the Eleventh Mississippi, commanded by Col. W. H. Moore, and after reaching Harper's ferry was put in the brigade of General Bee. He was in all the engagements of the Virginia army prior to the battle of Gettysburg, where he received two severe wounds, and was captured by the enemy. Previous to this battle he received three wounds, one at Malvern Hill and two at Sharpsburg. After his capture at Gettysburg he was imprisoned at Johnson's island, where he remained until exchanged, March 14, 1865. After returning to his command he succeeded to the captaincy of his company. On reaching home, after the surrender of General Lee's army, he found that all his property had been destroyed or confiscated by the Federal cavalry, not having as much as a change of clothes left. He then began life anew as a tiller of the soil, went to work and by industry and economy soon regained a part of his fallen fortune. Mr. Snowden was married in 1872 to Miss Dora Blanche Henson, of Aberdeen, who died in 1874, leaving an infant, Dora Blanche. He was afterward married to Miss Mollie G. Bush, of Noxubee county, where he now resides with his family. He has two daughters by his second marriage: Eva Bush and Corrie Delle. His family are all living with him. Mr. Snowden is now in comfortable circumstances, and has considerable landed interests in Noxubee, Lowndes and Monroe counties. The career of Mr. Snowden since the war presents an example of industry, perseverance and good management, rewarded by substantial results, well worthy the imitation of all those who start out in life, as he did after the war, with no capital except a good constitution and a liberal supply of pluck and energy.

Martin U. Sojourner, a planter of Copiah county, was born in Orange district, S. C., in 1833, the son of Roderick and Lovisa Sojourner. His father, also a native of South Carolina, led the life of a planter from his youth up. He married Mrs. Lovisa Sallie Young. This lady was three times married; her first husband, Mr. Young, was the father of four children, all of whom are deceased; to her and Mr. Bolin, her second husband, were born two children, one of whom, the widow of D. F. Fanning, is now living; by her last husband, Mr. Sojourner, she has three children: Friday W., killed at the siege of Vicksburg; Bridges H., of Copiah county, and Martin U. Roderick Sojourner was a member of the Masonic order, and he and his wife were both identified with the Baptist church. He came with his family to Mississippi, locating in Copiah county in 1841, where he remained until his death. At the age of twenty-one, our subject began life for himself by taking up the career of a planter, and he has proved himself to be a very successful farmer. His plantation is in good repair and almost invariably produces good crops. His life-long interest with the planting business has naturally inclined him toward movements that will benefit agriculture, so that one expects to know that he is a well known member of the Farmers' Alliance. In 1853 he married Amanda E. Sandifer, a daughter of William T. and Catherine Sandifer, and of a very old and estimable family of Copiah county, who has made him the father of three children: Lafayette B., of Copiah county; Mary A., wife of Albert Trayler, Copiah county; John C., who is deceased. Mr. and Mrs. Sojourner and their family are all members of the Baptist church. Our subject pursued his vocation so successfully that he is now regarded as much more than a well-to-do planter. In addition to his other operations he raises thoroughbred Jersey cattle and fine hogs. He has reached that point in his career where he is enabled to take life easily, but though having a sufficiency of this world's goods for all he needs, he does not relax one whit in his brisk business methods. He is a man who stands deservedly high in the community, and one who is equally well liked for his jovial ways.

Hon. Thomas H. Somerville, lawyer, Winona, Miss., inherits sturdy Scotch blood from his paternal ancestors, his grandfather, James Somerville, having been a native of Scotland but emigrated to the States prior to the Revolution. The latter's son, Samuel Somerville, was a native of the Old Dominion, and was reared to mature years in that state. He was married there to Miss Jennie B. Farish, also a native of that state, and the daughter of Colonel Farish, of an old and prominent Virginia family. Mr. Somerville followed farming in Culpeper county, was a successful farmer, and in that state reared his family. He was an honest, industrious citizen, and a man respected by all for his noble qualities of mind and heart. His family consisted of six sons and four daughters. One of his sons, Hon. Thomas H. Somerville, subject of sketch, was born in Culpeper county, Va., on September 19, 1850, and there passed his boyhood days, and received his education at Washington and Lee university, graduating from the law department of that institution in June, 1872. After finishing his education he came West, located first at Carrollton, Miss., where he entered into a law partnership with his cousin, Col. James Somerville, and two years later he located at Vaiden, Carroll county, where he continued practicing law until 1876. He then returned to Carrollton and continued his law practice at that place for a number of years. Mr. Somerville is a stanch supporter of the principles of democracy, and was elected to represent his county in the legislature in November, 1879, serving in the lower house. He served on a number of committees and was chairman of the committee on corporations. After his term in the legislature he resumed his law practice at Carrollton and there continued until 1887, when he moved to Winona, Montgomery county, forming a law partnership at that place with Mr. McLean, his present law partner. Mr. Somerville is also associated in the practice with Hon. Monroe McClurg, of Vaiden, and is a man of good legal ability. He is noted for his pertinacity, industry and strict fidelity to the interests of his clients, and as a safe counselor he has the confidence of the people. He devotes his entire time to the practice of his profession. Mr. Somerville was married at Carrollton on June 4, 1878, to Miss Ella Vasser, a native of Carrollton and the daughter of Dr. G. W. Vasser (see sketch). Mrs. Somerville was educated at Bardstown, Ky., and at New Orleans, La. Four children are the fruits of this union: Hugh Vasser, Theresa, Mary Hartwell and Ellen Douglas. The last named died at the age of five years.

Frank Souter, the subject of this sketch, was born in Lawrence district, S. C., in 1829, where he lived until he was eighteen years old, when he came with his parents to Pontotoc, Miss. There he made his home until his marriage, which occurred in December, 1850, to Miss Mary A. Duncan. He purchased a farm of eighty acres of land, upon which he was successfully engaged in planting until 1858, when he embarked in the sawmill and lumber business, which he continued until the outbreak of the Civil war. He enlisted in the Confederate army in 1861, and after two years' service was discharged on account of disability. Returning home, he was elected to the office of supervisor, which exempted him from further participation in the war. He was a member of the board of supervisors from 1862 till 1866. He was an ardent supporter of Governor Alcorn, believing his principles to be such as were best for the general public. In 1866, finding himself physically unable to continue in the lumber business, he began merchandising at Toccopola, in the western part of the county, where he carried on a successful trade on the same floor for twenty-two years. He was burned out in November, 1887, and shortly afterward located in Pontotoc, where he became a member of the firm of Wood & Souter, and engaged somewhat extensively and exclusively in the handling of hardware. Mr. and Mrs. Souter became the parents of ten children, only three of whom are now living: Laura, the wife of W. H. Wood, of Pontotoc; Sue, who is a member of her father's family, and J. B., who is studying medicine. Mr. Souter is an active member of the Pontotoc lodge, A. F. & A. M. He is a member of the Missionary Baptist church, and has been since 1848. As a Christian gentleman, he has ever been ready to aid in the upbuilding of the cause of his acknowledged Master. His liberality is well known in that direction, wherever his acquaintance extends.

It is with pleasure that we chronicle the history of a man whose career has been so short and yet so full of the successes of public life. Hon. Lewis M. Southworth, attorney, Carrollton, was born in Carroll county, Miss., August 15, 1863, and is a son of Judge H. H. Southworth. The father was born in Kentucky and was educated in that state at Center college; he chose the profession of law, and about the year 1847 he came to Carroll county, where he at once entered into active practice. In 1852 he was elected to the legislature of Mississippi and was twice re-elected, serving three consecutive terms. He was an old line whig, canvassed the state in the interest of the whig ticket and was a presidential elector before the war. He became a resident of Le Flore county, was elected to the office of probate judge and served in this position for a number of years. During the latter years of his life he retired to private life, residing on a plantation on the Yazoo river. His death occurred in 1878. He was united in marriage at Jackson, Miss., to Miss Mary Morgan, a daughter of Dr. J. B. Morgan, who was at one time a candidate for governor of the state on the whig ticket. Mrs. Southworth was born and reared in Mississippi. She was the mother of three sons and two daughters: Susie S. is the wife of L. P. Yerger, a well-known attorney of Greenwood; Mary S. married A. McC. Kimbrough, also a prominent attorney of Greenwood; the sons are H. H., a planter in Le Flore county; Fisher M., a law student, and Lewis M., the subject of this notice. He passed his youth and early manhood in Le Flore and Carroll counties, and was given the advantage of a thorough literary education, which he acquired in the universities of Mississippi and Virginia; he took the law course at the latter institution and was admitted to the bar in 1887, when he began his professional life. In 1883, before he was yet twenty years of age, he was appointed superintendent of education; in 1884 he was elected mayor of the city of Carrollton and in 1885 he was elected to the house of representatives from Carroll county; in 1887 he was re-elected to the legislature, and has the distinction of being the youngest man ever elected to that position in the state of Mississippi. He was presidential elector in 1888 for the state-at-large, the youngest man ever elected to that position in the United States, being only twenty-four years old, being elected over Col. W. C. Falkner, of Ripley, one of the most widely known men of the state. Mr. Southworth's abilities are recognized not only at home, but in distant states; he was invited to assist in the last presidential campaign in Indiana by the campaign committee, and also addressed a large meeting in Louisville before the canvass was closed. In 1889 he was elected to the senate of Mississippi, the opposing candidate being Col. James R. Binford, of Montgomery county, who was at that time a member of that body; the election was contested, owing to some technicality, and was finally decided at Jackson by the democratic state executive committee in favor of Mr. Southworth. Aside from his public interests he has had a large law business, has conducted some very important criminal and civil cases, in the management of which he has exhibited a superior ability. It is exceptional that the first three score years or even less of a man's life should bring honor, position and influence that usually are not attained short of sixty years. Taking the beginning of this career as an index, there is nothing possible of human attainment we might not predict for the future, with a most reasonable hope that the prophecy may be fulfilled.

Aaron Spain, planter, Booneville, Miss., who has been a resident of Prentiss county for over forty years, has lived an honorable upright life, and is one of the county's most successful planters. His father, James Spain, was a native of North Carolina, born near Raleigh, in 1805, and was one of six children born to John and Jane (Hunter) Spain, the grandfather having been married three times. The grandmother died in Wayne county, Tenn., in 1840, and the grandfather in the same county in 1860. James Spain moved to Bedford county, Tenn., at an early date, and was there married about 1827 to Miss Lydia Gambrill, who bore him eleven children, six of whom they reared: Elizabeth, Mrs. Davis, resides in Booneville; John, died at the age of twenty-two years; Henry, in the livery business in Booneville; James, in Booneville, and Mechanic. Three others, Martha, Ella and Polly, died when some age, but the others died in infancy. The father of these children moved to Mississippi in 1850, bought land, and at the time of his death was the owner of two hundred acres. He was a thrifty farmer and a self-made man. He died in Prentiss county in 1859. The mother died at Booneville, this county, at the age of seventy-seven years, and was a member of the Baptist church. Their son, Aaron, was born in Wayne county, Tenn., July 27, 1837, passed most of his school days in Prentiss county, assisted his father on the farm, and at the age of twenty-two bought land on which he began farming for himself. He is now the owner of four hundred acres of what is known as black land, and is also the owner of another tract of land east of Booneville. He was married in 1860 to Miss Margaret Rone, daughter of Samuel and Susan (Anderson) Rone, and a native of Bedford county, Tenn., of which her parents were also natives. This union has resulted in the birth of eight children, two sons and three daughters living: James William, farmer, residing near Booneville, and quite well-to-do, married Miss Mattie Elder, and is the father of two children, Ora and Clarence. John S., married Miss Ava Price, daughter of William Price, and has one child, Louise. He owns a good farm. Caddie, Mrs. Perkins, formerly Mrs. Johnson. She has two children by Mr. Johnson, Baxter and Samuel; Eugenia and Eudora, twins. Mr. Spain lost three children, Joseph, Mary and Oscar. In 1862 he enlisted in company C, Thirty-second Mississippi infantry, was in the battles of Chickamauga, Perryville, Atlanta, Franklin, Bentonville, and was paroled at Greensboro, N. C. Since that time he has followed agricultural pursuits and has been successful. He is interested in educational and religious matters, and gives liberally of his means to all worthy enterprises. He is a democrat in his political principles, and he and wife hold membership in the Methodist Church South. In September, 1885, Mr. Spain moved to Booneville to educate his children, and during that time, five years, was engaged in the livery business. In 1890 he returned to the farm.

Alexander Spain, one of the prominent planters of Prentiss county, Miss., resides three miles west of Booneville and is well and favorably known all over the county. He is a native Tennesseean, born in Lawrence county in 1838, and was early trained to the arduous duties of the farm, attending school as he could until the age of eighteen years. In 1861 he enlisted on a sixty days' service, but after that expired he returned and enlisted in company C, Thirty-second Mississippi Infantry. He was in some severe battles, among the most prominent being Chickamauga and Perryville, and also participated in a number of severe skirmishes at Missionary ridge. He took a prominent part in all actions, but was never wounded or taken prisoner. He was paroled at Columbus, Miss., at the close of the war and then came home, where he afterward engaged in the active duties of the farm. He was married, in 1859, to Miss Molly Johnson, daughter of William and Jane Johnson, and to them were born six children: Theodore, Mary, Richard, Edward, Robert and Lee. Mrs. Spain died in 1877, and his second marriage was to Mrs. Vianna Green, daughter of S. Rones. Two children, Alonzo and Oscar, were the fruits of this union. Mrs. Spain received her final summons in 1880, and Mr. Spain was married to Miss Martha Prichard, daughter of John H. Prichard. Mr. Spain has attended to his adopted calling with care and perseverance and with such energy and thoroughness, that successful results have been reaped, and he is to-day classed among the prominent agriculturists of the county. He is the son of Henry and Roena (Armstrong) Spain, natives of North Carolina and Tennessee, respectively. Henry Spain was born on February 2, 1807, and was a son of John Spain, who was an old pioneer of the Old North state. The grandfather died in Tennessee about 1852 or 1853. Henry moved to Tennessee at an early day, engaged in farming, and was there married to Miss Armstrong. Later they moved to Mississippi, and in 1850 located in Tishomingo (now Prentiss) county, where they bought 200 acres of land. He was the father of eight children by this union, seven of whom lived to be grown and who are named in the order of their births as follows: James (killed in the battle of Shiloh), Caroline (now Mrs. Stewart, of Texas), Alexander, Jane (Mrs. Parter, a widow residing in the Lone Star state), John W. (see sketch), Huldah (Mrs. Johnson, a widow of this county), and Amanda (Mrs. Gambill of Tennessee). The father of these children was married three times, Miss Armstrong being his second wife. She was a member of the Baptist church and died about 1852. The Armstrongs were a prominent family of Tennessee. Mr. Spain was also a member of that church, and died February 1, 1887. He was a successful farmer and a hard-working, industrious man. His first wife was a Miss Johnson, and one daughter, Caroline, was the result. His third marriage was to a Miss Mary E. Plaxico, who bore him two children, George F. and Francis M.

Tennessee has given to Prentiss county many estimable citizens, but she has contributed none more worthy of respect and esteem than John W. Spain, planter, Booneville, Miss. This gentleman was born in Lawrence county in 1846, and although he started out in life with limited means he is now the owner of a fine farm of four hundred and forty acres four miles west of Booneville, and has everything comfortable and convenient about his place. He is the son of Henry and Roena (Armstrong) Spain, the father a native of North Carolina and the mother of Tennessee. (See sketch of Alexander Spain.) John W. Spain attended school until sixteen years of age, and at the breaking out of hostilities between the North and South he enlisted in the sixty-day troops and went to Bowling Green, Ky. After returning home he joined the cavalry, company B, and was in active service at Jackson, near Atlanta, Ga., and at Selma. He was in a great many battles and fought all over the country and county where he now lives. He was discharged at Columbia, Miss., in 1865, and then returning home resumed work on his father's farm. In 1870 he bought land and began in earnest for himself, marrying the same year Miss Mary Lowry, a native of Tennessee, born in 1846, and the daughter of C. and E. Lowry. She came with her parents to Mississippi when a little girl, and was the eldest of five children; Green, William, Ida and Alma. Ida is now the wife of Mr. Stain, of Texas, and Alma is Mrs. Miller, and resides in Prentiss county. Mr. Lowry died about 1884, but Mrs. Lowry is residing in this county with her daughter, Mrs. Miller. To Mr. and Mrs. Spain were born three children: Modenna E., John L., and Guy W. Mrs. Spain was a consistent member of the Baptist church and died on the 7th of April, 1888. She was a descendant of one of the oldest families in the state. She was a true Christian, a kind mother, and a loving, thoughtful wife. Mr. Spain's second marriage was to Miss Ora Williams, who was one of five children: Frederick, Richard, Mary and Ethel, born to Dr. Ben and —— (Flake) Williams, formerly of Prentiss county. Both parents are now deceased. Mrs. Spain is a member of the Methodist church. Mr. Spain is a thoroughgoing planter and is advanced and progressive in his ideas. He has one hundred and seventy-five acres under cultivation and during the season has about ten plows in the field. He is a democrat in politics and alive to the interest of the party. He takes a prominent part in all enterprises tending to the advancement and growth of the county.

A. P. Sparkman, M. D., of Magnolia, Pike county, Miss., was born in Pike county, November 8, 1840. R. F. Sparkman, his father, was a native of North Carolina, and was born in 1798. He was reared and educated there, but removed to Mississippi when quite a young man, locating in Pike county. He married here Miss W. N. Pierson, a native of South Carolina. Mr. Sparkman was a well-known planter and business man of Pike county, was a colonel in the state militia, and served his county as sheriff for a number of years. He was also a prominent early merchant at Holmesville, the old county seat, where he lived until 1845, when he died. His widow still survives him, a well preserved, healthy, old lady of eighty-five years. Dr. Sparkman was one of a family of three sons and five daughters, who grew to mature years. He has four sisters living, all of whom are the heads of respectable families. He received his early education at Holmesville, later studying medicine and attending lectures at the University of Louisiana, at New Orleans, where he graduated in 1861, just before the opening of the war. In 1861 he enlisted in company E (known as the Quitman guards), of the Sixteenth Mississippi infantry, and served until wounded and permanently disabled in the battle of Cross Keys, Va. He lay in the hospital for seven weeks, and was then discharged and returned home to Holmesville. As soon as the Doctor had somewhat recovered his health, he engaged in the practice of medicine. In 1875 he was elected circuit clerk of Pike county, and has been re-elected at each succeeding election, having served at this time for twenty-six consecutive years, and having the reputation of being the best circuit clerk in the state. His attention to all the duties of his position is proverbial. Of course he had had opponents at each of the above elections referred to, but he has been victorious in each by a handsome majority. He is a candidate for re-election in the fall of 1891, and there are few who entertain any doubt of his success, for, though the clerkship of the circuit court is a very desirable position, the Doctor's popularity is so well established that there are few who will offer to make the race against him. He retired from the practice of his profession about the beginning of his official career. In March, 1863, the Doctor was married to Miss M. E. Vaught, the only sister of Chancery Clerk Vaught, and a member of another of the prominent families of Pike county. Mr. and Mrs. Sparkman have a family of four sons and three daughters: William A., N. P., J. A. (who is deputy circuit clerk), Leontine, Anna, Joseph Logan and Ruth. Miss Leontine Sparkman is a very popular young lady. Ruth is a little miss of seven years, who, at the age of four years began to play upon the piano, and has since become so expert a performer that she rivals the accomplishment of many older musicians. The Doctor and his family stand high socially, and are on terms of intimacy with the best families throughout Pike county.

J. F. Spearman, a prominent planter, lives near Tremont, in Itawamba county, Miss., was born in this state in 1835, a son of Elijah and Sidney (Cotton) Spearman. His parents were born in Tennessee and there married, coming to Mississippi at an early day. Mr. Spearman's youth was spent on a plantation. He received a limited education in the common schools, and began the stern battle of life while yet quite youthful. He married Nancy E. Stone, a sister of J. H. Stone. (A sketch of this gentleman is given elsewhere in this work). Her parents were both natives of South Carolina, and she was born in Alabama in 1843. Mr. and Mrs. Spearman have had born to them six children, of whom the following five are living: Marquis de L., Robert Lee, Manly N. O., Eva T., and Hattie. In April, 1862, Mr. Spearman enlisted at Columbus, Miss., in company E, of the Second Mississippi cavalry, which was commanded by Captain McCarty, attached to Armstrong's brigade of Jackson's division. He was in battles at Iuka, Corinth, Brookhaven, Ponchatoula, La., and for meritorious service at Vicksburg during the seige he was promoted to be first sergeant. He also fought at Clinton, Baker's creek, West Point, Jackson, Rome, Atlanta, Dallas and Jonesboro, Ga., Franklin, Nashville, Murfreesboro, Spring hill and Pulaski, Tenn., and at Okalono, Macon and Tupelo, Miss. He received his discharge from the army in 1865, never having from the time of his enlistment been absent from his company for one day without leave. He is a democrat and takes a deep interest in all public questions. He served his county one term as a member of the board of supervisors. He is a Master Mason, and his family are members of the Methodist Episcopal church. He is the owner of about fifteen hundred acres of land. He is also owner of a gristmill and a cottongin. The latter has a large capacity. He is an energetic, helpful and highly respected citizen, and he has the satisfaction of knowing that he has attained success by his own efforts.

Frederick Speed, an attorney and an active real estate owner, was born in Ithaca, N. Y., in 1841, the youngest of five sons of John J. and Anne (Morrell) Speed. The Speed family being of English descent, immigrated to America at an early day, and settled in Virginia about 1700, but the grandfather of Frederick Speed removed in New York about the year 1812. His father was a constructing engineer, and built the first line of telegraph west of Buffalo, and many other important works in the Western states. He was a member of the state legislature, a speaker of the assembly and an active politician up to the time of the defeat of Henry Clay. Having been a Harrison elector, he was a leading man in the politics of his day and time, and the town of Speedsville, N. Y., was named in his honor. He moved to Detroit, Mich., in 1847, but in 1860 he went to Maine, and while living there he constructed the United States and Independent telegraph lines from Portland to Washington, after which he retired from active business life, and made his home in Brooklyn until his death in 1867. His widow survived him until 1877, until she, too, passed away. Federick Speed was educated in the public schools of Detroit, but in 1860 went to Portland, Me., with his parents and was there residing at the opening of the war. He raised the first company for the war in that state. As he was too young to hold office he enlisted as a private soldier, but was mustered into service as sergeant major of the Fifth Maine regiment of infantry, serving in the army of the Potomac, and was soon promoted to the adjutantcy of the Thirteenth Maine regiment, Col. Neal Dow, which formed a portion of the New Orleans expedition, with General Butler. In 1862 he was made assistant adjutant general, serving on the staffs of Generals Dow, Dudley, Weitzel, Emory, Thomas W. Sherman, Dana and Canby, as they respectively succeeded to the command of the brigade, division and army corps to which he was assigned, being with the last named at the close of the war, at the headquarters of the military division of west Mississippi. He participated in the engagment at Bull run, siege of Port Hudson, and in nearly all the battles of the department of the gulf, and was at Mobile, Ala., at the termination of hostilities. In the fall of 1865 he settled at Vicksburg and the three following years were spent in sawmilling, during which time he also read law, being admitted to the bar in 1868. In 1867-8 he served as circuit and chancery clerk of Warren county by appointment, and during 1869-70 he was judge of the criminal court. From 1878 to 1885 he practiced his profession extensively in all the courts, but since that time he has given his attention principally to real estate law. In 1880 he purchased sixty-nine acres adjoining the southern part of Vicksburg, now known as "Speed's addition," and which is now one of its most beautiful suburbs, the improvements on which have been principally made by Mr. Speed's own efforts. He was married in 1871 to Miss Esther Adele Hillyer, a daughter of Col. Giles M. Hillyer, who was one of the early and successful newspaper men of Natchez. Mrs. Speed was born in Aberdeen and to them five children were born: Hillyer Roylston, Frederic Gordon, Esther Adele, Liscomb and Annie M., who died in infancy. The family are members of the Episcopal church, in which Mr. Speed has been a vestryman for some eighteen years. He is also a member of the standing committee and one of the trustees of this diocese, and has for several years been a delegate to the general convention of the church. While his legal residence was still in Maine he became a member of the Masonic fraternity in 1866, and the following year, having taken up his domicile permanently at Vicksburg, Miss., he affiliated with Vicksburg lodge No. 26, of which he has been many times worshipful master. He was grand master of the grand lodge of Masons in Mississippi in 1883, and was grand high priest of the Grand Royal Arch Chapter in 1880-1. He is now past eminent commander of Magnolia commandery No. 2, and was grand commander of the grand commandery of the state in 1888-9. He is at present grand master of the grand council of royal and select masters of the state, and has been for a number of years chairman of the jurisprudence committee of all the Masonic grand bodies of the state. He has also, for some years, filled the position of deputy of the supreme council of the thirty-third degree of the Southern jurisdiction of the United States, and is the only thirty-third degree Mason in Mississippi. A man of literary tastes and inclinations, he is the owner of one of the largest and most complete Masonic libraries south of the Potomac river, and has contributed many articles of note to Masonic, secular and religious journals. He is an elegant and forcible speaker and has delivered numerous speeches and addresses. He was the first commander of Vicksburg post No. 7, G. A. R., and is the senior vice commander of the department of Louisiana and Mississippi. Leading an active and useful life, he has endeavored by the example of an honorable and upright career to impress upon the young men of his acquaintance the importance of qualifying themselves for the duties and responsibilities of life, and it was but natural to find him unanimously chosen as the president of the Young Men's Christian association, an organization which is exerting a beneficial influence in the community and in whose behalf he is an untiring worker. One of the most influential of the Mississippi state papers in speaking of him recently said: "Judge Frederic Speed is a good lawyer, has had experience on the bench, is in the prime of life, full of energy, fertile in resources, a sound thinker and forcible speaker, and positive, but courteous, in announcing his convictions."

Another state paper, in referring to him, adds: "Judge Speed came to this state as a Federal officer during the war, but not like most of the Federal soldiers, returned North, or else remained to indulge in the rich pillage that followed, but joined his efforts as one of the victors to aid the conquered in building up and restoring the waste places. And right well has he done this in practical work, but also in the work of reconciliation and the bringing about kindly relations between the sections. A man of legal learning as well as of large general information and culture, a Christian gentleman who has been eminent in good deeds by reason of the modesty with which they were performed, largely acquainted throughout the state, and where known respected, one loyal to his party, and yet in no instance offensively antagonistic to his political opponents, he has won for himself a position of honor which commands the trust and esteem of all as a lawyer, earnest member of his party and public-spirited citizen."

Hon. Samuel M. Spencer is one of the progressive and enterprising citizens of the county of Washington, Miss., and has done a great deal to build up and improve the section in which he resides. He was born in Port Gibson, Miss., on the 19th of September, 1838, being the fifth of ten children born to Horatio N. and Sarah (Marshall) Spencer, natives of Connecticut and Mississippi respectively. The father came to Claiborne county, this state, in 1829, and for about fifteen years was an able and successful lawyer of Port Gibson, having graduated from Yale college in 1821. Retiring from the practice of law, he sought a more quiet life, accordingly purchased land and began planting. In the meantime he fulfilled the duties of president of the Port Gibson bank, and also of the Port Gibson & Grand Gulf railroad. Planting proved very congenial to him, and he continued it up to the day of his death in 1876, having, prior to the war, amassed a large property, the most of which was swept away in that struggle. His parents were I. S. and Temperance Spencer, natives of Connecticut, as were also his grandparents (the great-grandparents of the subject of this sketch). The family orginally came from England, during the early history of the colonies, settling in Connecticut. The mother's father was Samuel Marshall, a native of Pennsylvania, of Scotch and Irish ancestry. Both branches of the family were in their faith Presbyterians, and the three sons now living all are ruling elders in that church. Hon Samuel M. Spencer received his education in Center college, Danville, Ky., and in that admirable institution of learning,

Yale college. After leaving school he engaged in agricultural pursuits, and when the war opened, he warmly espoused the Southern cause, and helped to organize a company in Washington county, of which he was made second lieutenant. On reaching Bowling Green his company was organized into an artillery company, but he retained his position as second lieutenant, and was taken a prisoner at the fall of Fort Donelson, and was taken to Johnson's island where he was kept in captivity for about six months, after which he was taken to Vicksburg and exchanged. He immediately rejoined his command, and at the battle of Chickamauga was promoted to first lieutenant. So many of the members of his company were killed that the handfull that remained were consolidated with Cobb's battery, and Mr. Spencer was assigned to conscript duty, and was sent to Louisiana, which ended his fighting. He surrendered at Jackson, Miss., at the close of the war and returned home to resume his farming operations, soon after which, in 1866, he was married to Miss Carrie T. Hogg, a native of Mississippi, and a daughter of Dr. Thomas H. and Rose (Russell) Hogg, the former from Tennessee and the latter a native of Mississippi. To Mr. and Mrs. Spencer five children have been born: Rose R., who died at the age of fourteen years; Carrie M., Samuel M., Jr., Thomas H. and Mary G., all of whom are at home. Mr. Spencer is the owner of forty-six hundred acres of land, of which twenty-six hundred acres are under cultivation, about one-half of which he has himself opened, and on which he has expended a large amount of money in improvements. He is a citizen of whom Washington county may well feel proud for he has done a great deal to improve this section of the country, and on his own land laid out the little village of Glen Allan and induced the Louisville, New Orleans & Texas railroad company to build to the place. They afterward extended the line from Hampton to Rolling Fork and withdrew the passenger train from running to Glen Allan, for which reason the village has not continued to build up. The place is situated on the shore of Lake Washington and is one of the most attractive sites in the state. Mr. Spencer is a zealous member of the Presbyterian church, in which he is an elder, is especially interested in the moral training of the young, and is endeavoring to rear his children to honorable manhood and womanhood. He has served in the capacity of magistrate, has been a member of the board of supervisors, and in 1884-5 was a member of the state legislature from this county, filling these positions with ability, although he had not sought them. He has a beautiful home in Glenn Allan, fronting Lake Washington. It sets well back from the street and is surrounded by a beautiful lawn thickly dotted with handsome shade trees.

William H. Spencer. Among the many enterprises which have made Jefferson county, Miss., noted for its commercial enterprise, may be mentioned the mercantile establishment belonging to Mr. Spencer, of which he has been the proprietor since about 1878. It is complete in its appointments, and by excellent business ability and foresight he has built up one of the largest and most prosperous trades in the county. He first saw the light of day in Charlotte county, Va., in the month of October, 1843; J. B. Spencer, his father, being a native of the same state and county, where he was married to Sarah Lyle, of Prince Edward county, daughter of Rev. Matthew Lyle, a well-known and eloquent minister of the Presbyterian church. Mr. Spencer was a farmer in his native county throughout life, was a man of progressive and enterprising views, and took an active part in religious matters, being an elder in the Presbyterian church. He died in the fall of 1876, his wife having passed from life when their son, William H., was a child. The boyhood days of the latter were spent in his native county, where he received a thorough practical education, but in 1861 the clash of arms caused him to cast aside all personal considerations, and with the enthusiasm of youth he enlisted in the Confederate service in the fall of that year, being first in an independent company. He was afterward transferred to the Eighteenth Virginia infantry, and in time was promoted to the rank of sergeant in company K. At the evacuation of Petersburg he was wounded in the thigh by a gunshot, was taken prisoner and for several months was held in captivity, the most of which time it took him to recover from his wound. After being paroled he returned home, having been an active participant in the seven days' fight around Richmond, the battle of Gettysburg, all the principal engagements around Petersburg, a number of minor engagements and numerous skirmishes. The year 1867 is the date of his arrival in the state of Mississippi, his first location being in Claiborne county, where he was engaged in teaching school and planting. After following this calling up to 1872, he moved to Jefferson county, and after being a clerk in a mercantile establishment here for some six years, he became a member of the firm, and three years later became the sole proprietor of the establishment. By the honest measures he has always followed, by his methodical business habits and by his industry, perseverance and desire to please, his trade is a large and lucrative one. He was appointed postmaster at Red Lick in 1876, and this position is holding at the present date. All measures of morality, education, temperance and others of like nature find in him a strong advocate; in fact he is found among the foremost in any reliable, uplifting movement. He was married in 1878 to Miss Mary F. Barker, a daughter of John W. Barker of Jefferson county, and their union has resulted in the birth of four children: Sarah M., Lillie Lyle, John Blair, and William H., Jr. Mr. Spencer is a thorough and practical business man and since 1879 has been engaged in farming in connection with his mercantile operations. By his own endeavors he has accumulated a fair share of this world's goods and is prepared to enjoy his good fortune to the utmost. He is at present a member of the Knights of Honor.

Augustus D. Spengler was born in Vicksburg, Miss., October 22, 1870, the eldest of six surviving children of S. and Elizabeth (Miller) Spengler, natives of Germany, the former of whom came to the United States in early manhood and was first engaged in the sawmilling business in California. In 1850 he came to Mississippi, locating in Vicksburg, where he continued to reside until his death, in 1889. He was a successful business man, amassing quite a fortune, and in 1885 purchased the entire estate known as the Cooper wells, which consists of one hundred and sixty acres of good land. The famous wells which are on this property are noted for their medicinal qualities. An analysis of one gallon of the water, by Dr. J. Lawrence Smith, gives its gaseous contents: Oxygen, 6.5 cubic inches; nitrogen, 4.5 cubic inches; carbonic acid, 4 cubic inches; and the solid contents: sulphate of soda, 11.705 grains; sulphate of magnesia, 23.28 grains; sulphate of lime, 32.132 grains; sulphate of potash, .608 grains; sulphate of alumina, 6.120 grains; chloride of sodium, 8.360 grains; chloride of calcium, 4.322 grains; chloride of magnesium, 3.480 grains; peroxide of iron, 3.362; chreuate of lime, .311; chreuate of silica, 1.801, the total being 105.471. Soon after making his purchase Mr. Spengler erected near the springs two elegant buildings for the accommodation of guests, and a fine building at the springs, at a cost of about $85,000. The hotel is open from May 1 to November 1, and during this time is largely patronized by those who wish to leave the turmoil and heat of the city behind them for a time, as well as those who are afflicted by disease. A few yards from the hotel and approached by a good, substantial walk is the large two-story pavilion erected over the well, with a seating capacity for over one hundred persons. A full corps of attentive attendants are kept busy at all hours drawing by windlass and pumps fresh supplies of water, which is handed around to the guests. There is in connection with the well, a sulphur well, eighty-two feet deep, over which is a large bath house, which has lately been erected, fourteen by seventy-five feet, having cold and hot baths. The main hotel building is two hundred and twenty-five feet long, sixty feet wide, and two stories high, with large commodious double galleries on the front. The addition to the main building is one hundred and seventy-five feet long, sixty feet wide, and three stories high, with large double galleries on front and ends. The rooms are large and airy, having high ceilings, and are elegantly furnished in the latest modern style, the furniture being uniformly substantial. Every room is connected with electric call bells and ventilating blinds and patent transom lifts to insure perfect ventilation, and in the spacious dining rooms all the luxuries of the season are spread before the guests, especial attention being paid, by competent cooks and assistants, to the cuisine. There is a large billiard hall and ten-pin alley, with ample accommodations for all its guests, and the ladies' drawing room contains a fine grand piano, where, in the evenings, musical entertainments are given. The latest papers and periodicals are to be had at any time, the mail being delivered daily from all parts of the country. Augustus D. Spengler was reared in Vicksburg, and received a thorough business education in a private school. In 1889 he assumed complete control of the Cooper's well property, and has been its efficient manager ever since, it becoming very prosperous and largely patronized while under his care. Mr. Spengler is a fine business man and possesses social qualities of a high order, attributes which make him very popular in the business in which he is engaged. The wells were first dug about 1842, by a man who had a dream concerning their curative properties, and upon digging them found them to be just as he had dreamed. Not much was done with them, however, until they were purchased by Mr. Spengler's father, in 1885. Since then it has been quite a health resort for people of the South, and especially Mississippians. Mr. Spengler and his brothers and sister are interested in a large sawmill at Vicksburg. Mr. Spengler is a member of the Catholic church.

Hubert Spengler is the senior partner of the firm of Spengler & Sons, Jackson, Miss., and owners and proprietors of the Spengler house. His sons, A. H., F. C. and L. Spengler, manage the grocery business, and H. Spengler, Jr., is in charge of the hotel. Its history embraces many interesting periods and incidents and its registers bear the names of many noted people, who have found a pleasant home beneath its hospitable roof. Mr. Spengler was born in Alsace, France, in 1820, being the third son born to Joseph and Francisco (Sherno) Spengler, who came to America at an early day; the father was the owner of two large sawmills, run by water power, that did a large business, and also a lumberyard and woodyard. Hubert Spengler was the eleventh of his parents' twelve children, he and his sister, who now resides in Vicksburg, being the only ones of the family that are now living. Of this family four sons and three daughters came to America and settled at Vicksburg and Jackson. Hubert Spengler left home at the age of sixteen years to seek his fortune in the new world, and in 1836 landed at New Orleans, after an ocean trip on a sailing vessel of sixty-five days. In 1852, with his wife and two sons, he took a trip to Europe, and made the run from New York to Liverpool in ten days, and back from Havre to New York in twelve days. He at once went to Vicksburg, Miss., where his elder brother Joseph was located as a builder, for whom he at once went to work. After remaining with him about two years in Vicksburg and two years in Jackson, he, some two years later, opened a billiard hall and saloon. Some time later he added a stock of groceries to his establishment, and has since continued that business. During the Civil war he served in the Confederate States militia for a short time. In 1848 he purchased a lot at the corner of State and Capitol streets, of Jackson, on which he erected buildings covering nearly one-half square, but these were all burned by the Federal soldiers during the turbulent times of the war, the

entire stock in these stores being also destroyed. Afterward he set energetically to work to rebuild his fortunes and resumed the grocery business, at which he has been remarkably successful. In 1884 he and his eldest sons became half owners with his brother, S. Spengler, of Vicksburg, in the Cooper's well property, the firm name being S. and H. Spengler, a full description of which noted summer resort is given in the sketch of S. Spengler. Mr. Spengler owns a considerable amount of valuable city property, about twelve acres in all, on which are erected some excellent buildings. He has taken an active interest in the city's welfare; in 1859 was a member of the board of aldermen; in 1870-1 he was a member of the board of supervisors, and in 1876 was again elected alderman, in which capacity he served with great credit to himself and the satisfaction of all concerned, for nine years. In 1845 he was united in marriage to Miss Mary E. Nahrgang, a native of Hesse, Germany, only four years old when brought by her mother to America. To her union with Mr. Spengler ten children were born, seven of whom are living: A. H., who is in the grocery business, is married and has a family; F. C. is also in a lucrative business, is married and has five children; Catharine, the widow of George Muh, has six children: Hubert, Jr., who assists his father in the management of the Spengler House, in Jackson, is married and has five children; Louis and Jennie are single, and Emma is the wife of Peter Miazza, proprietor of a hotel at Greenville, and is the mother of one child. George died at the age of eleven years, and Elizabeth and Charles died in infancy. Mr. Spengler is the oldest member of the Catholic church in Jackson, and the only one of the old members now living. He remained in that city during the terrible yellow-fever epidemic in 1878, during which time he was an active worker, was fearless in regard to his own danger, and rendered valuable aid in nursing the sick and burying the dead. He and his eldest son kept the only store open during the epidemic where the sick could find something to eat. Joseph Spengler, a brother of Hubert Spengler, came to America in 1831, and after a short residence in New Orleans he went to Cincinnati, Ohio, and engaged in carpentering, but was unfortunately burned out, after which he located in Vicksburg, Miss., as a builder.

In 1838 he came to Jackson, and here soon opened a grocery establishment, which he conducted successfully. In 1852 he built a cotton factory, but before he could equip it with machinery, he died of yellow fever in 1853. He was a progressive and enterprising man of business, and had he lived would have undoubtedly become wealthy. He was married and left a family of children. Amand Spengler, another brother of Hubert's, came to America in 1836, settled at Vicksburg, and began work in the new world as a carpenter, and made considerable money at this calling. In 1839 he returned to Europe, where he married and remained, succeeding to his father's business. Seraphin Spengler, his brother, arrived in this country in the year 1841, soon after which he engaged in the sawmill business in the vicinity of Jackson. About 1850 he was taken with a severe attack of the gold fever and started for California, and in that region remained for four years. Upon his return he resumed sawmilling in Vicksburg, and in this pursuit made a large amount of money from the start. He became one of the wealthiest men of Vicksburg, and for his many admirable traits of heart and head was highly esteemed and respected. He was alderman of the city and was the first president of the first loan association. He was a partner with his brother in Cooper's wells, in addition to which valuable property he owned other real estate of value. He was accidentally killed in Vicksburg in July, 1889, by his horse running away with him. Hubert Spengler, Jr., son of Hubert Spengler, Sr., was born in Jackson in 1855, and was educated in the college at Cape Girardeau, Mo., from which institution he graduated. After clerking for his father and brother for a few years, he became a partner in the business, the firm taking the name of H. Spengler & Sons. In 1881 he was married to Miss Nannie E. Miazza, to which union five children have been born: Hubert, Thomas, Mildred, George, and Angelo. In 1884, after the completion of the new hotels at Cooper's wells, he was located at that place as manager, and did much to build up and make the place the popular resort that it now is. He has, however, been the efficient and popular manager of the Spengler house in Jackson for some time, and the whole management, the perfect system and thorough adaptation of every detail to secure the approval of guests, indicate the fact that intelligent and careful direction is exercised. He has an interesting family, and resides in a pleasant home near his parents. Antone H. Spengler, a son of Hubert, Sr., was born in Jackson, February 1, 1846, and received his initiatory training in the city of his birth, finishing his education in St. Mary's college, in Marion county, Kentucky. He left school on account of the opening of the war, after which he clerked at Jackson and Selma, Ala., until 1864, when he entered the Confederate army, and was with General Wirt Adams, in General Forrest's command, participating in the last battle of Jackson. After the war he clerked in his father's store, who, after he had become proficient in the business, as was his usual custom, took him in as a partner, when the firm became Spengler & Sons. He, like his brothers and father, before him, is a successful and honorable business man, and is thouroughly posted and up with the times. He is of the stuff of which model citizens are made, and the career of the entire family, as men of business, has been one round of success.

J. C. Spight is a worthy and representative agriculturist of Tippah county, Miss., and acquired his knowledge of the calling from his father, Thomas Spight, and the knowledge thus gained has been put to a practical experience. He was born in Jones county, N. C., in 1820, in which state and county his parents were also born, the father in 1779 and the mother, whose maiden name was Rebecca Mumford, in 1783. They were married in their native state in 1805, and there Mr. Spight, in addition to following the calling of a planter, was engaged in merchandising, in both of which he was quite successful. After the death of his wife in 1833 he took for his second wife Mrs. Evans, their nuptials being celebrated in Trenton, Tenn., in 1834. His last union was without issue but his first wife bore him nine children: Thomas, John, Pollie, James M., Simon R., J. C., E. R., Sallie P. B., wife of William Robertson; and Rebecca T., all of whom are deceased except Simon R., J. C. and Sallie P. B. The father of these children died in 1858, having, for many years, been a member of the Baptist church. J. C. Spight commenced to make his own way in the world in 1844, and during the years of 1853-4-5-6 he was also engaged in merchandising. By the opening of the war he had accumulated a comfortable competency, but like the majority of Southerners, lost very heavily during that time. He did not participate in the war owing to the fact that his eyes were quite weak. In 1845 he was married to Miss Nancy K. Chapman, a daughter of Turner Chapman, a prominent and successful planter of Jones county, Ga., and their union has resulted in the birth of the following children: Thomas (deceased), Turner C. (deceased), Elizabeth F., wife of M. L. Clark, who has borne Mr. Spight his only two grandchildren, Jodie George, and Frank Early Clark; Sallie J., wife of F. S. McKnight, James M., J. C. and Nannie L. Mr. Spight has resided on his present plantation sine 1845, and of the one thousand acres of which he is the owner he has one hundred and fifty acres in a good state of cultivation. He is a member of Ripley lodge, No. 47, of the A. F. & A. M., and he and his worthy wife and all his children are members of the Baptist church, to which they contribute liberally of their means. Mr. Spight's grandfather was also a native of Jones county, N. C. He died in 1815 in the seventy-fifth year of his age.

Capt. Thomas Spight, lawyer, Ripley, Miss., is a native Mississippian, born near Ripley, Tippah county in 1841, when the country was comparatively new. His father being a planter, Captain Spight was early trained to the duties of the farm and in the meantime had the advantage of good schools. He attended college at LaGrange, Tenn., but was prevented from graduating by the breaking out of the war, at which time he hastened home to engage in the strife. He entered the Confederate army as a private and rose step by step and was commissioned captain of infantry before reaching his majority and was in the command of the remnant of his regiment at the close of the struggle. After this he followed school teaching for a number of years and was eminently successful as an educator. In December, 1865, he was united in marriage to Miss M. Virginia Barnett whose father, A. G. Barnett, a successful merchant, was one of the pioneers of Tippah county, coming here at a time when the country was still inhabited by Indians. After his marriage the captain turned his attention to planting and from the experience gained from his early life on the farm, continued this successfully together with teaching for a number of years, but in the meantime was a diligent student and commenced the active practice of law in 1874. He served three successive terms in the Mississippi legislature, from 1874 to 1880. In March, 1879, he commenced the publication of the *Southern Sentinel* at Ripley, in the interest of the democracy against the greenback party which was then making rapid progress in Mississippi. He dealt some telling blows against the opposition and saved the county to the democracy. In 1880 he was presidential elector on the Hancock ticket and made an active and successful canvass of his district. In the fall of 1883 he was elected district attorney of the district in which he resided and was re-elected in 1887 and this position he held, giving entire satisfaction, until the close of the year 1890. He then declined re-election, preferring to devote his time to the practice of law at home and to planting, which he still conducts with the ardor of his youth. Captain Spight's father, James M. Spight, came from North Carolina to West Tennessee, thence to Mississippi at an early day, and thus became one of the pioneers of Tippah county. He became the owner of extensive plantations well stocked with mules, etc., and also had a large slave interest prior to the war. He was a man of unblemished character and one whose sterling qualities made him respected far and wide and he instilled into his son the elements which formed the basis of his future success in life. At the close of the war Captain Spight found himself, in common with most young men of his section, without means, his father having died on March 11, 1861, and his property which consisted mainly in negroes having been swept away as the result of the war; but with faith in himself, and by the help, counsel and encouragement of a noble, cultured, Christian wife who was distinguished alike for her indomitable energy and womanly virtues, he entered the arena of life determined to succeed.

Dr. J. C. Spinks, a prominent and practicing physician of Shubuta, Clarke county, Miss., was born in Wilcox county, Ala., in 1831, on the 29th of August. His father was John Spinks, and his mother was Margaret (Kelly) Spinks. His father was born in North Carolina in 1785, and was a son of Presley Spinks. During his early life his father was a carpenter, but in his later days he devoted his energies to planting. He came to Mississippi in 1834, and located in Kemper county, and engaged in farming, thus becoming one of the pioneers of that part of the state. He and his wife were members of the Baptist church. They reared nine children: Mary, Peter, Presley, Jane, Margaret, Sarah, John, Raleigh, and Enoch. His father died soon after the time of the war in Kemper county, the mother having preceded him in 1853, the latter was a native of South Carolina, and was born in 1796, being a daughter of Peter Kelly. Mr. and Mrs. Spinks were married in Wilcox county, Ala.

Of nine children only five are living. Our subject spent his boyhood days in Kemper county, where he enlisted in 1861 in the Kemper Legion, in the Thirteenth Mississippi regiment. He began his military career as a private, but in 1863 was promoted to the position of assistant surgeon, which he held during the remainder of the war. He was in the fights at Leesburg, Fredericksburg, Millword, and numerous others, important and otherwise. When Knoxville was taken by the Federals in 1863, the Doctor was in charge of a Confederate hospital at that place. He was educated at the University of Louisiana, in New Orleans, and established himself in Kemper county, in 1855, in the practice of his profession. He was married in 1866 to Laura Hand, daughter of Dr. T. J. Hand of Kemper county, who has borne him seven children, five of whom are living: Gilmore; Bertha and Sherrid, who died in infancy; John, Mary, Manley and Peter. Mr. and Mrs. Spinks are members of the Baptist church. The Doctor is a prohibitionist in his principles, though he acts and votes with the local democratic party. He has been an active worker in the prohibition cause at home. As a physician, he has been successful, having acquired a large and remunerative practice, and he is a member of the County Medical association. He is an enterprising and public-spirited man, deeply interested in everything that pertains to the welfare of his fellow-men. To churches and schools he is especially devoted, and it is known that he can always be safely counted upon to contribute of his means or otherwise aid any worthy object in which his fellow-citizens are interested.

E. E. Spinks, D. D. S., of Meridian, Miss., was born in Kemper county, of this state, in the month of October, 1835, a son of John and Margaret (Kelly) Spinks, natives of North Carolina and Kentucky, respectively. They came to Mississippi in 1833, spending the remainder of their lives in Kemper county. The father was one of the honest sons of the soil and became reasonably well-to-do. Dr. E. E. Spinks was the youngest of their nine children, and was reared in Kemper county, receiving his education in the common schools. In 1861 he enlisted in the Confederate service, the following year becoming a member of company A, Thirty-fifth Mississippi regiment, with which he served until the surrender. The first twelve months of his service he held the rank of first sergeant, after which, until the war closed, he held the rank of second lieutenant. He was captured at the siege of Vicksburg, but was soon paroled. At the battle of Franklin, in November, 1864, he was seriously wounded by a gunshot in the head, which came very near ending his life. He was given the most careful attention, and, after a long sickness, was once more restored to health. When the war was over he began the study of dentistry, and for the past twenty-five years has been an active practitioner, and in the twenty years of this time that he has been a resident of Meridian he has become widely known as a skillful and experienced dental surgeon. His office is well fitted up and furnished, and he has all the latest improved instruments for the successful conduct of his work. In 1858 he was married to a Miss Ball, by whom he has one child, Maggie. His second union took place in 1873, Miss Vallie Garner becoming his wife and the mother of his seven children: Garner, Mary, Enoch, Vallie, Henry, Virginia and Ruby. Dr. and Mrs. Spinks are members of the Baptist church, and, socially, he is a member of the A. F. & A. M., belongs to Mount Barton lodge of the K. of P., the American Legion of Honor, the K. of H., and the Knights of the Golden Rule. He has passed all the chairs in the K. of P. fraternity, and has been treasurer of the K. of H. since its organization.

Louis Spotorno, one of the progressive merchants of Bay St. Louis, Hancock county, Miss., and the present city clerk of Bay St. Louis, has been identified with the interests of the place since 1888. He was born in New Orleans in 1851, and is a son of Louis Spotorno, Sr. His father was also a merchant in Bay St. Louis from 1854 to the time of his death, which occurred in 1871. Young Louis Spotorno was brought to the Bay when a child three years of age, but was taken back to New Orleans during the Civil war. He received his education at St. Stanislaus college, Bay St. Louis. At seventeen years of age he entered a wholesale establishment at New Orleans, in which he was a clerk for eight years. He then embarked in the mercantile business on his own account. In 1888 he came back to Bay St. Louis, and has since made it his home. He carries a good stock of merchandise, and has a free delivery of goods system, which is a great convenience to the patrons of his store. Mr. Spotorno was elected city clerk in 1890, and has made an efficient officer. He is a member of the American Legion of Honor and of the Knights of Pythias. He was united in marriage in New Orleans, to Miss Matilda Olivari, by whom he has seven children.

Emory J. Spratlin, planter, was born in Arkansas county, Ark., March 7, 1863, and in his native state and Mississippi he was reared, although the greater part of his education was obtained in the schools of Tennessee. His advantages were excellent, for his father was a warm patron of education, and while acquiring his knowledge of books, his time was improved to the utmost, thereby fitting himself for a practical and useful life. In 1884, at the age of twenty-one years, he began an independent career with a small capital, but instead of squandering it, as many would have done, he gradually increased his capital, and is now the owner of a large plantation, situated on the bank of the Mississippi river, five miles west of Rolinsonville, which is a thrifty little town on the Louisville, New Orleans & Texas railroad, twenty-eight miles south of Memphis. His land comprises four hundred and eighty acres, two hundred acres of which is in a good state of cultivation, and very fertile, producing as large crops as any like amount of land in the county. He possesses many sterling qualities and habits, prominent among which are honesty, morality, industry and perseverance. He is a member of the K. of P. fraternity, and he and his brother, William A., are democrats in politics, and are deputies to J. W. Johnson, who is sheriff of Tunica county. They are reliable and trustworthy young men, and although William is an aspirant for the office of sheriff, they have taken but little interest in politics, preferring to devote their time to their business, the latter being a wideawake young business man of Tunica. In personal appearance, Emory J. is tall and slender, and has dark hair and eyes. He has been a resident of Mississippi since 1875, and on his plantation has a beautiful and comfortable residence. He was the third of five children born to John W. and Martha (Montgomery) Spratlin, the former of whom was born in Alabama, and the latter in Arkansas. John W. Spratlin was a stockman, while a resident of the state of Arkansas, and in that state was called from life in 1872. He warmly espoused the Confederate cause during the Civil war, and served throughout the entire war, making a faithful, brave and efficient soldier.

H. F. Sproles, D. D., pastor of the Baptist church of Jackson, Miss., was born in Holmes county of this state in the month of January, 1844, the second child born to Wilson R. and Mary Ann (Fortune) Sproles, who were native North Carolinians. The paternal grandfather, Richard Sproles, came to Mississippi about 1836 and settled in Holmes county, where he opened and dug the Castalian springs, which afterward became one of the finest summer resorts in the state of Mississippi. Mr. Sproles first tilled the soil, but later became a merchant, in each of which occupations he made money. He served for some time in the Confederate army, making a brave and faithful soldier. He died in 1882, his wife having passed from life in 1851. Rev. H. F. Sproles was an attendant of the common schools until the opening of the Civil war, when he enlisted in company D, First Mississippi light artillery, and served until the war terminated, being wounded on several different occasions. He was in the engagements around Vicksburg, and just two days before Lee's surrender he was badly wounded at Mobile, Ala. In 1865 he studied under Rev. C. C. Lee, of Holmes county, continuing until September, 1866. He then entered the Southern Baptist Theological seminary, and, by studying during vacations also, he graduated in May, 1870, soon after becoming pastor of the Baptist church at Carrollton, Miss. After remaining at this place for nine years, he in 1880 came to Jackson, where he has since been located. In 1890 the board of trustees of Mississippi college conferred the degree of D. D. upon him. He is president of the convention board of missions of the Baptist state convention, and since locating in Jackson he has built up the membership of the church, and is held in high esteem by his congregation as well as by his ministerial brethren. He is laboring hard for the erection of their new church edifice, and in every respect is a faithful worker in his Master's vineyard. He was married in 1870 to Miss R. A. Pickel, a native of the Palmetto state, and by her is the father of four children: Mary P., Marion Olive, H. F., Jr., and James Arthur.

Capt. John T. Stanford, Carrollton, Miss., was born in Duplin county, N. C., February 17, 1834, and is a son of Samuel and Sarah (Maxwell) Stanford, who were also natives of Duplin county, N. C. The father was born in 1799, and in the year 1840 removed to the state of Mississippi, settling in Carroll county, where he passed the remainder of his days. He died in 1880, and his wife survived until December, 1888. Our subject is the third of a family of four sons and four daughters: A. D., a planter of Warren county Miss., was a soldier in the Confederate army and was wounded in the service; J. H. was also a soldier and was killed at Harrisburg, Miss.; Sam was killed in the battle of the Wilderness, and one sister is deceased. John T. spent his youth in the neighborhood of his birth, and in 1861 he enlisted in the Eleventh Mississippi volunteer infantry, and was promoted from one office to the next until he was made captain in 1863 after the battle of Gettysburg; he participated in the engagement of Seven Pines, the seven days' fight around Richmond, Malvern Hill, Boonsboro, Sharpsburg, and Gettysburg; in the last named he received a wound which disabled him for some time; he was taken prisoner and held for fifteen months at Baltimore and Fort Delaware; he was paroled, came home, was exchanged, returned to the front, and was finally paroled at Appomattox courthouse, having followed General Lee's army through the war. After the surrender he returned to Carroll county and settled on the old home plantation. He was married here in April, 1867, to Miss Mildred Taliaferro, a native of Alabama, and a daughter of John and Celina Taliaferro. The Captain and his wife have six children: Samuel, Sarah Clementine, James H., Anna Laura, John T., Jr., and Margaret P., who is now ten years old. Before the war Captain Stanford was a member of the whig party, but he is now a conservative democrat; he is a member of the Farmers' Alliance and is president of the local Alliance. He is also a member of the Masonic fraternity, and is a council Mason. He and his wife belong to the Presbyterian church, also all of the children with the exception of the youngest. Captain Stanford is a man of high integrity of character and moral worth, and is highly esteemed in the community as a neighbor, friend, and citizen. In the time of his country's need he went to the front and fought and bled in the cause which he had so heartily espoused.

Aaron Stanton, a prominent planter of Adams county, Miss., is a resident of Stanton station, where he has a fine home, Brandon Hall. He was born on Traveler's Rest plantation, twelve miles east of Natchez, in 1840, and is the son of David and Anna (Winston) Stanton. David Stanton was born in Belfast, Ireland, in 1812, and in 1820 came with his parents to Natchez, Miss. He was educated at Jefferson college, and after marrying, settled near Washington, where he followed planting until about 1843, when he removed to Natchez. There he followed merchandising until the breaking out of the war. He then joined the Tenth Mississippi infantry as lieutenant and served until the fall of 1862, when he resigned, having fought at Shiloh, Munfordsville, Shelbyville, etc. After the war he carried on his planting industry until his death in August, 1890. He was a selfmade man, of good business ability, conservative in politics and industrious in his habits. He accumulated a fortune before the war, but met with reverses afterward. Two of his brothers, Frederick and William, came from the Emerald isle to Natchez, Miss., about 1816, engaged in merchandising, and in 1820 returned to their native country and brought over their parents, Aaron and Varina Stanton, who died here. Frederick and William became prominent and wealthy citizens and both died shortly before the war. Mrs. Stanton, the wife of David Stanton, was born at Traveler's Rest plantation in Adams county, and is still living. She is an Episcopalian in her religious preferences. Her father, Gen. Samuel L. Winston, was one of three brothers who were triplets, born in Raleigh, N. C., in 1788. In 1795 he came with a brother-in-law, Mr. Williams (who afterward became lieutenant-governor of the state) to Adams county, and there passed the life of a successful planter until his death in 1831. He served in the Seminole war and was aid-de-camp to General Jackson in the War of 1812 at New Orleans. His two brothers, Judge Lewis and William, also came to Adams county at quite an early day and were prominent lawyers. The former died here in 1825 and the latter in 1834. Judge Lewis was at one time judge of the southern district of Mississippi. Their father, Major Joseph Winston, was a native of the Old Dominion but died in North Carolina. He was a major in the Revolutionary war and was presented with a sword for gallantry at the battle of King's mountain. Ann W. Hoggatt, who became the wife of Gen. Samuel L. Winston, was also born on Traveler's Rest plantation in Adams county in 1800, and died in the same neighborhood in 1882. Her father, James Hoggatt, was born in Bedford, Va., in 1753, and from there he went to Tennessee, where he married a Miss Bell, who died in Tennessee. Afterward Mr. Hoggatt married Miss Grissella Newell, and about 1800 came to Adams county, where he purchased large tracts of land east of Washington. He became an extensive planter and a breeder of race horses and had a training track on his plantation. There he passed the closing scenes of his life in affluence. Aaron Stanton, the subject of this sketch, was one of four children, only one besides himself now living, Samuel W., who is a planter at Natchez. Aaron was educated at Jefferson and Oakland colleges and at the breaking out of the war he joined a company of cavalry and served as lieutenant, most of the time under Gen. Patrick Cleburne, until the close of the war. He fought at Murfreesboro, Chickamauga and all through the Georgia and Atlanta campaign. He went back with General Hood to Tennessee, and fought at Franklin and Nashville, and then retreated into Mississippi. He afterward rejoined General Johnston in North Carolina and surrendered with him. He was wounded at Resaca, Ga. After peace was declared he returned home and on the 12th of October, 1865, he married Miss Elizabeth Elmina Brandon, daughter of Girard and Charlotte (Smith) Brandon. The father was a son of Gov. Girard C. Brandon, born in Wilkinson county in 1818, and his wife in Adams county in 1821. They were married in the last named county about 1841, and at once settled on the plantation known as Brandon Hall, at Stanton station, where Mr. Brandon erected a fine mansion in 1856, the one in which Mr. Stanton now resides. Here Mr. Brandon spent the remainder of his days as one of the most prosperous farmers in Adams county, owning at the breaking out of the war about $1,000,000 worth of slaves. He died in 1874 and his widow three years later. Both were members of the Episcopal church. Mrs. Stanton was born at Brandon Hall, and by her marriage became the mother of four children, viz.: Charlotte S., wife of Dunbar Surget Merrill; Anna W., wife of Arthur E. Shaw, who is secretary and treasurer of Bessemer rollingmills at Bessemer, Ala.; Agnes and David Brandon. The latter is now finishing his education at the University of the South at

Sewanee, Tenn. The eldest daughter was educated at Hollings institute, Virginia, and the younger, Agnes, at Columbus college, Mississippi. Mr. Stanton lived on Cedar Grove plantation near where he was born until 1875, and since then on the old Brandon Hall place, which contains about eighteen hundred acres and produces about three hundred bales of cotton annually. Mr. Stanton has never aspired to office, but is active in the interest of his party and for the general welfare of the county. He is a typical Southern gentleman and a man of many friends. His wife and all the children are active members of the Episcopal church at Natchez.

Frederick Stanton (deceased). There are few selfmade men but what have had an interesting history connected with their early struggles, and a few facts connected with the past life of the above mentioned gentleman will give some idea of his usefulness in the different walks of life. He was born in Belfast, Ireland, in 1798, and in 1817 immigrated to the United States, forming, while on the voyage, the acquaintance of A. T. Stewart, who afterward became a merchant prince of New York city. After a short time spent at this place Mr. Stanton came direct to Natchez, where he at once began to make his own way in the world as a clerk, but by 1820 had accumulated sufficient means to enable him to embark in business for himself, and he soon after established the flourishing cotton houses of Stanton & Buckner, of Natchez, and Buckner & Stanton, of New Orleans, which at one time were the strongest firms in both cities. So in love did he become with his adopted country, and in such a prosperous condition were his business affairs, that he soon sent for the other members of his family in Ireland, and the numerous people of that name in Adams county are the descendants of this family. In addition to his mercantile interests, Mr. Stanton also gave a considerable amount of his attention to planting, and in this he likewise prospered. In 1827 he was married to Miss Huldah Helm, of Kentucky, a daughter of Thomas Helm, and by her became the father of ten children, four of whom are living: Frederick, Newton H., Elizabeth, wife of Maj. John Rawle, and Verina B., widow of Mr. Gaither. In 1857 Mr. Stanton erected the magnificent residence in Natchez, which is, perhaps, the finest private residence in the state of Mississippi to-day. The residence occupies the site of the old fort of the Natchez Indians, the grounds occupying the block embraced by High, Monroe, Pearl and Commerce streets. It was erected at a cost of $130,000, was magnificently furnished at a cost of $40,000, and the beautiful marble mantels, which adorn each room, were carved in sunny Italy. The wood carving is also very artistic, beautiful and unique, and the chandeliers are works of art. The furniture was all made in Paris, and in making a tour of the wide and spacious halls, the stately parlors, receptionrooms, the diningroom (which can seat half a hundred guests) and the sleeping apartments, the effect is, indeed, almost oriental in its beauty. The grounds are no less beautiful, for stately live-oaks shade this ideal home. Mr. Stanton did not long survive to enjoy the beauty and comfort which, by his own unaided efforts, he had acquired for his loved ones, and in 1859 he was called from the scene of his earthly labors, leaving to his children the record of an untarnished name. His widow survives him, and with her son-in-law, Maj. John Rawle, and family, still occupies the home erected for her by her husband.

Maj. William Starling, chief engineer of the Mississippi Levee district of Greenville, was born in Columbus, Ohio, in January 25, 1839, and was the third in a family of nine children born to Lyne and Maria (Hensley) Starling, the parents natives of the Bluegrass state. The father was a merchant of New York for many years, and in 1858 moved to Illinois, where he followed agricultural pursuits. At the breaking out of the war he was appointed assistant adjutant-general under General Crittenden, and later held the rank of lieutenant-colonel. He was in the battles of Shiloh, Stone river, Chickamauga, and the whole Atlanta campaign. In 1866 he came south, followed planting in Mississippi, and then bought a large estate, Sunnyside, situated twelve miles below Greenville. The plantation was one of the finest in this section, and there were one thousand six hundred acres under cultivation. Mr. Starling, who was a worthy member of the Presbyterian church, died in 1876. The mother is still living, and makes her home with her sons, William and Lyne, both residents of Greenville, where the latter is engaged in merchandising. She is also a member of the Presbyterian church. Maj. William Starling was educated at the University of New York, which he entered when fourteen years of age; graduated in 1856, and immediately began reading law in the office of Alexander & Green, then, as well as now, an eminent firm of attorneys in New York; removed with his parents to Illinois in 1858. In 1861 he entered the volunteer service as lieutenant of company G, Third Kentucky cavalry, Federal army, and was afterward transferred to the Ninth Kentucky infantry with the rank of captain. He was subsequently promoted to the rank of major, and retained that rank in the veteran corps, and besides numerous minor engagements, was in the great battle of Murfreesboro. Mr. Starling has an enviable war record, and retired from the service only on account of sickness. After the war he came South, and joined his father in Arkansas in 1867. In 1882 the estate was sold to the Calhoun land syndicate, and the same year Mr. Starling, who had removed to Greenville, entered the service of the Mississippi levee board as assistant engineer. In 1884 he was promoted to the position of chief engineer, and still continues to hold that office. He became identified with the interests of the South, and is enthusiastic as to its prosperity. He has attained considerable prominence in the Masonic fraternity. He is at present grand scribe of the Grand lodge of Mississippi; is commander of Delta commandery No. 16 of the Knights Templar, and high priest of the chapter. He is an active member of the American Society of Civil Engineers.

The Starling & Smith company, general merchants at Greenville, established their business in that city in 1888, and carry a stock of goods valued at about $30,000. They do an annual business of about $300,000, are live business men and merit the success by which their efforts are rewarded. In 1890 they erected a fine two-story brick block on Poplar street. Lyne Starling was originally from Kentucky, his birth occurring at Frankfort in 1848, and is the son of Lyne and Maria (Hensley) Starling (see sketch of William Starling). He was educated at Yale college and graduated from that institution in 1871, after which he resided on his father's plantation in Arkansas until 1882. He then came to Greenville and engaged in the Bank of Greenville as corresponding clerk until he went into business for himself. He was married in 1872 to Miss Kate C. Watson, of Kentucky, the daughter of Henry Watson, who was from one of the old families of the state. To this marriage were born four children: Henry, Lyne, Jr., Inez and Maria. Mrs. Starling and her son, Henry, are members of the Presbyterian church. Mr. Starling is vice president of the Citizens' bank and a director of the Greenville cotton compress. He is the owner of considerable town property.

Mrs. Martha Steele, who is engaged in planting, and is a well-known lady of Copiah county, is the widow of Archibald Steele, and was born in Mississippi in 1836, a daughter of James D. and Lucretia (Corley) Cammack. Archibald Steele was born in Tennessee in the year 1819, a son of Peter and Anna Steele. Peter Steele died in Tennessee about 1828, and in 1830 his wife came with her family to this state, first settling in Marion county, but after living on a plantation there for about fifteen years, they removed to Copiah county, where Mrs. Steele lived till her death. Her son was a selfmade man, who, beginning with very little capital, but a willingness for hard work, gained an enviable reputation among the planters of this state. He served during the entire period of the late war under General Lee's command as captain of company G, of the Fifteenth Mississippi regiment. At the close of the war he resumed planting, in which he was successful. He was first married to Eliza Catching, who bore him two children: Whitman, a resident of Copiah county, and Julia, wife of Dr. J. T. Alford, of Rockport, Miss. Our subject, the relict of Archibald Steele, was married to him in 1857, and to them were born eight children, six of whom are living: Mary, wife of Frank Catching, of Copiah county; James B., at home; Archella, wife of Dr. J. M. Catching, of Hazlehurst, Miss.; Abner P., at home; Oscar, at home; Bennajuh, who also lives at home. Mr. Steele was a member of the Masonic order, and was for a long time prior to his death identified with the Methodist Episcopal church, of which denomination his wife was also a devout member. The leading characteristics of Mr. Steele were industry, frugality and unswerving honesty. He was a model planter, indulgent husband and father, and as a citizen was widely known and respected.

Johan Otto Steen, father of Otto Steen of Enterprise, Clarke county, Miss., was born in Copenhagen, Denmark, in 1797. He was the son of Johan Otto Steen, Sr., who died in 1842, at the great age of one hundred and three. The first mentioned was a great machinist and a polished artisan, who executed the finest styles of work in metals. The Danish government employed him in the manufacture of the finest naval instruments, compasses, lanterns, etc. He spent ten years in visiting the shops of the famous artisans of Europe, which went far toward his preparation for his life-work. He was married to Miss Jacobini Bless, in 1826. She also was a native of Copenhagen, born in 1809. Otto Steen, the eldest son of Johan Otto Steen, Jr., was born April 5, 1834, in Copenhagen, Denmark. He attended the schools of his native city, and at fourteen years of age was apprenticed to the trade of metalworking in a shop of which his father was superintendent and head workman. Here began that training which was to develop in young Steen the finest powers as a mechanic in his chosen branch. It is not out of place here to remark that the Danish government requires all males to learn a trade. After four and one-half years of continuous service, Mr. Steen passed the required examination and was admitted to the grade of journeyman workman. Among the requirements for promotion to this rank was the execution of a most artistic and difficult piece of work in hammered brass. This exquisite piece of work, which is now in the possession of Mr. Otto Steen, has been examined by the writer, and is certainly a testimonial of the masterly skill of the maker. After serving his apprenticeship and after his graduation from the Polytechnic institute, Mr. Steen visited Germany and Great Britain, and, in the autumn of 1852, came to the United States. Landing at New York, he immediately found employment on Pearl street. He spent two years in Greenwich street, later, and, in 1854, went to New Orleans, La. In March, 1854, he removed to St. Louis, Mo., and later returned to New Orleans. Becoming interested in Mobile, Ala, he removed there in December, 1854. Here he was employed until 1857 in a steamboat shop, owned by Robert S. Kirk. He then went into the same business on his own account, which he continued until 1860. In that year he removed to Enterprise, Miss., where he continued the business of metalworking. On the outbreak of hostilities in 1861, he was employed by the Confederate government, in whose service he continued during the entire war. Mr. Steen's wide reputation as a skilled machinist caused his services to be sought by the Mobile & Ohio, the Vicksburg & Memphis, and the Memphis & Charleston railway companies, and by others also. Simultaneously he was doing difficult and finished work for the Confederate government. The close of the war found Mr. Steen, like other Southerners, well nigh broken up; but with characteristic energy he set himself about the task of rebuilding his broken fortunes. His services had now become indispensable to the roads employing him, and he was continued in the employ of the Mobile & Ohio company, which connection existed till 1870. Mr. Steen has kept in connection with his shop a stock of merchandise hardware. His services are yet sought far and near when work of most intricate character is demanded. Mr. Steen was married in 1858 in Mobile, Ala., to Miss Alena Robertsen, born in 1836, a native of Marstral, Denmark, which is not far from Copenhagen. They have had eight children: Emma, Otto, Laura, Mary, Clara, Lena, Minnie and James, of whom the first, third, sixth and seventh survive. Miss Laura married Mr. Tibbetts, a gentleman from Minnesota. In religious affiliations Mr. Steen and his wife are Lutherans, while their daughters are Presbyterians. Mr. Steen is financial reporter for the Knights of Honor, which position he has filled for the past five years. He is eminently a successful man, having never been embarrassed in business. He is one of the pillars of his town, and a citizen of whom his countrymen are justly proud.

Dr. W. J. Stegal, of Evergreen, Itawamba county, Miss., was born in this state in 1847, and is a prominent physician and planter. His parents were Stanley D. and Dollie A. (Thomas) Stegal, his father having been born in North Carolina and his mother in Alabama. Of a family of four children, Dr. Stegal was the only son. He attended medical lectures at Mobile, Ala., in the winter of 1872-3, and has been successfully engaged in the practice of his profession ever since. He was married, November 9, 1882, to Miss Mary A. Armstrong, who was born in Mississippi, February 5, 1855. She is a daughter of Maj. J. M. Armstrong. To Dr. and Mrs. Stegal have been born five children: Carrie Janet, William T., deceased, James Stanley, Annie L., deceased, and Frankie R. In 1864, Dr. Stegal enlisted in the company of Capt. F. M Armstrong, known as company C, of the Second Mississippi regiment. He served in the Confederate army until the close of the war, when he was paroled at Macon, but did not participate in any engagements. Politically, he is a democrat, and as a citizen he is public-spirited and helpful. He has a large practice, which extends over a large territory, and as a physician he has been unusually successful. He owns and operates a large plantation, raising considerable quantities of cotton and other products, and is regarded as one of the leading planters of this section. He and his wife are members of the Baptist church.

William L. Stephen is well worthy of being classed among the substantial residents of Jefferson county, Miss., for since near the close of the war he has been a leading merchant of Fayette. His parents, George and Barbara (Schneider) Stephen, were born in Germany, and a few years after their marriage immigrated to the United States, landing at New Orleans in 1832 with three small children. Unfortunately it was the year of the cholera siege at that place, and though they remained in New Orleans but about three weeks, they were called upon to morn the loss of one of their little ones. From New Orleans they went to Cincinnati, but after a residence of two years in that city they bought a farm in Warren county, Ohio, and on this farm the father breathed his last in 1845, he being at that time sixty-three years of age. He left a widow and seven children, three sons and four daughters. After his death his widow continued to reside on the farm, and with the assistance of her sons cultivated the land until 1854, when she sold out and moved with her family to Clarke county, Mo., where she remained about two years. At the end of that time she came to Fayette, Miss., and here the rest of her days were spent, her home being in the family of her son, William L. She was born May 14, 1796, and departed this life October 6, 1875. Lieut. William L. Stephen was born May 21, 1836, in Warren county, Ohio, and although his early opportunities for obtaining an education were somewhat limited, he made the most of the few months of country schooling that was afforded him each year. At the age of sixteen years, being ambitious of securing a better education, he obtained permission to work for wages on an adjoining farm in order to obtain sufficient means with which to enter the Maineville academy, a school of high order located in the eastern part of Warren county, and after completing his studies he went to Missouri and began working for his brother on a farm, remaining with him one year. At the end of this time, at the solicitation of his uncle, who was a merchant of Fayette, Miss., he came here for the purpose of assisting him in his grocery store, and to this work devoted his time and attention until the war cloud, which had so long hovered over the country, burst in all its fury, at which time he left the store to take up arms in defense of the Confederate cause, enlisting May 4, 1861. During the first year of the war he was fourth corporal of company D, Nineteenth Mississippi volunteer infantry, army of north Virginia, but the second year he was promoted to orderly sergeant, and while acting in this capacity was often called upon to command the company. The third year of the war he was made lieutenant, and discharged the duties of this position faithfully and well until the close of the war, participating in all of the battles fought by the army of north Virginia. He was the last officer commissioned for his company, and at the time of the surrender was with General Lee. He was neither wounded nor taken prisoner during his service. At the close of the war he returned to Fayette and once more engaged in the mercantile business, and so well did he succeed in this calling that he has followed it up to the present time. His stock of goods consists of an assortment of general merchandise, and as he disposes of his goods at reasonable rates, and is strictly honorable in all his transactions, he commands a large trade. In 1878 he was married to Miss Elizabeth Paul, daughter of F. C. Paul, a former citizen of Natchez, but now a resident of this county. Their union has been blessed in the birth of three sons and two daughters: Barbara, Frederick William, Adolph, Lewis W. and Isabelle. Mr. Stephen is a member of the A. F. & A. M. lodge of Fayette, and for three successive years officiated as worthy master. It is remarked by those who were members at the time he took his seat, that the lodge was in a very depressed condition, but that during his administration a new interest was awakened, many accessions were made, and the lodge brought into good working condition. He is also a member of the Knights of Honor, of which order he is now treasurer, having filled all the offices within the gift of that organization. He at present holds the position of commander in the camp of Confederate Veterans lately organized at this place, called J. J. Whitney camp No. 10. He at all times manifests a deep interest in the advancement of education, and is treasurer of the board of trustees of the Fayette high school. He has at different times held the position of alderman of the city, besides other offices of trust. His family are members of the Presbyterian church, and his wife is a most devoted Christian and is highly respected and beloved by her acquaintances. She is a devoted mother, and is endeavoring to train her children in the ways of usefulness and right living. Mr. Stephen inherits many of the sterling qualities of his German ancestors, prominent among which may be mentioned faithfulness of purpose, honesty, industry and frugality.

Col. M. D. L. Stephens, the subject of this notice, was born in Williamson county, Tenn., November 9, 1829. His father, Dennis Stephens, the son of Thomas and Martha Stephens, was born at Fort Nash, now the city of Nashville, in May, 1796. Thomas Stephens was born near Lynchburg, Va., in 1760, and his grandfather took part in what is known in history as the Bacon rebellion, in 1675, in which Bacon and his adherents were either killed or banished from the country by the British government. W. H. Stephens being one of the prominent actors in this rebellion, was banished and all of his property confiscated. He took his wife and went west, and settled on the James river, near where Lynchburg now stands, being obliged to raise his family amid the most adverse circumstances, in rugged wilds, amongst the Indians, without any schools or advantages for his family. From this family Thomas Stephens sprung, and the many families bearing this name and that of Stevens who have spread over the South and West. Georgia's great statesman, A. H. Stephens, belonged to this family. Thomas Stephens and Martha Davis were united in marriage near Knoxville, Tenn., in what was then the territory of North Carolina, in June, 1790. Soon after their marriage Thomas Stephens moved to Fort Nash, and at or near this fort Dennis Stephens was born. He was reared in Montgomery and Murray counties, with but little educational advantages. In 1822 he was united in marriage to Jane Hudson, the only daughter of John and Elizabeth Hudson. John Hudson was of Irish nativity, and his wife was Elizabeth Spratt, who was the daughter of Andrew and Elizabeth (Blythe) Spratt. Andrew Spratt was born in north Ireland and was educated for a Presbyterian minister, but when he had graduated he fled to America instead of embarking in the ministry. He settled at Charlotte, N. C., where he established a school in 1760. In a short time he was united in marriage to Elizabeth Blythe, who had a brother, Dr. Blythe, who was a surgeon in the Continental army. Andrew Spratt left his family, to serve some years in the army. At the close of the war he found himself very poor, with a large family to support. Dr. Blythe was the owner of a large tract of land in what is now Tennessee, which he gave his sister, and there this family settled. Sixteen children of this family lived to be grown. John Hudson and his wife came out to Tennessee with Mr. Spratt, and settled here in 1800. A postoffice was soon established in this settlement, named Bethesda.

The eldest daughter of Dennis and Jane Stephens was Susan T. J., born in 1825; the next child was a daughter, Martha E. N., born in 1827; Marcus D. LaFayette, the subject of this notice, was born in 1829, and Melissa A. E. was born in 1832. Dennis Stephens left Tennessee with his family and moved to what was then called the Chickasaw Nation, and settled in Marshall county, Miss., near Tallaloosa, in January, 1838. Sarah married W. H. Daniel, February 14, 1844, and became the mother of three daughters, Dora, Scott and Fannie, and three sons, Duruyter, William L. and Robert Lee. Mrs. Daniel died in 1871. The children are now residents of Nevada and California. Martha married Berry O. Best in 1847, and became the mother of five daughters and three sons. All are now residing in Tallahatchie county, Miss., being all married except one. Melissa married Jerard Burch in December, 1852. They have two daughters and one son, and all are married. R. L. Burch married Cora Weathers; Nora married R. J. Thompson; Ella married Newton Matthews. Mrs. Best and Mr. Burch are both living. LaFayette, the subject of this notice, the only son, engaged with his father in working a small farm on Pigeon Roost creek, in Marshall county, until he was seventeen years old, working on the farm, and going to school through a few months of the year. His parents were in straitened circumstances and had hard work to keep the daughters in school, but LaFayette was enabled to get a fairly good English education. He began teaching school in the neighborhood and afterward taught in Tippah and Panola counties, in Mississippi, for the purpose of making money with which to complete his education. In 1851 he took up the study of medicine in connection with teaching, and in 1853-4 he attended lectures at Louisville, Ky. His preceptor was Dr. R. M. Glover, of Tallaloosa, Marshall county. Having completed his education, he located at Banner, in Calhoun county, and entered into a large and lucrative practice. He remained at Banner until 1858, when he removed to Sarepta, in the same county, some eight miles east of Banner, and continued the practice of his profession in partnership with Dr. J. M. Lyles until 1860, when he was nominated on the union co-operation ticket for a seat in the state convention which had been called by Gov. J. J. Petters to consider the question of the secession of the state of Mississippi. He voted against the ordinance of secession in all of its various forms presented to the people of the convention, but on its final passage he recorded his vote for it with these remarks: "I was elected to this convention on what is known as the co-operation ticket, and every vote I have cast since this ordinance has been before the convention has been cast in good faith to carry out the pledges made to my people. The question now having narrowed down to secession or submission, and as between the two I am for secession, I cast my vote for the ordinance, feeling at the same time that a different course should have been pursued; but I am a Mississippian to the core—the bones of my ancestors sleep upon its hills—and all I am and have, and ever expect to be, are within her borders; and whatever my destiny may be, I am with her heart and soul."

Immediately after the state had seceded he wrote home to his partner, Dr. Lyles, that war was imminent and that they must organize to resist, and directed him to enroll his name on the muster roll of a company then organizing by Dr. Lyles. Upon his return home he found the company organized, and on the 7th day of April, 1861, he mustered into the state service under General Lowrey, of Pontotoc. At the breaking out of the war Mr. Stephens was engaged in a lucrative practice and stood at the head of his profession. February 14, 1856, he was united in marriage to Mary Jane Duff, the daughter of James Madison and Jane (Hullam) Duff, who were married in South Carolina in 1837 and settled near Sarepta. The result of this union was the birth of two daughters and two sons: Mary Jane Duff, the eldest, was born March 29, 1839; William Duff, the eldest son, joined Captain Wheeler's company of mounted men, attached to Col. Robert Pinson's First Mississippi cavalry, and was killed at the battle of Island No. 10, holding the rank of first lieutenant at the time; Mittie N. married A. McDonald, and died in 1872, leaving no children; James F. Duff joined the same regiment that his brother did and served as a private until the close of the war, taking part in all the engagements in which the regiment participated. He married Miss Mary Scott Mayes, the eldest child of W. D. and Mary Jane Mayes. He is now living in Water Valley, Miss. The Magnolia guards, the company into which Mr. Stephens enlisted, was called into active service May 29, 1861, and ordered to Corinth, Miss. Here this company was attached to the Seventeenth regiment of Mississippi volunteers, with W. S. Featherston as colonel, John M. Guirk, lieutenant-colonel, and John M. Lyles, major. Captain Lyles having been promoted, W. L. Duff was elected captain of the Magnolia guards, now company K. Mr. Stephens was tendered the position of assistant surgeon, but declined, preferring to remain with the company as second lieutenant. The regiment was ordered to Manassas Junction, Va., June 9, 1861. The regiment was attached to General Jones' brigade, which was composed of the Fourth and Fifth South Carolina regiments and the Seventeenth Mississippi regiment. July 17 Lieutenant Stephens was sent with a detachment from the Seventeenth regiment to guard Conrad's ford, on Bull Run, and he reported the enemy advancing in force, and that evening he was joined by the entire brigade of General Jones, General Longstreet guarding Mitchell's ford. On the morning of the 18th the enemy advanced on Longstreet and a sharp engagement ensued, when the enemy was repulsed and withdrew. On the morning of the 21st the heavy boom of artillery announced the attack of the enemy on the left, near the stone bridge, or above. In the afternoon the regiment advanced in the direction of Centerville, and was confronted by twelve pieces of artillery. The enemy sent shot and shell upon the regiment so heavy that they fell back in a deep ravine and there sent forward skirmishers to keep posted on the movements of the enemy, when they found that the enemy had fallen back. The regiment was then ordered back to position on Bull Run, and spent the night in bivouac. This was the first battle of Manassas, or Bull Run, as it is called.

Lieutenant Stephens' regiment was then ordered to Leesburg, Va., to report to Gen. G. Evans. Joining that brigade, they went to Levettsville on the Potomac, near Harper's Ferry, captured and sacked the town and returned to Leesburg. Here they remained in camp a few days, when the company was ordered to the Potomac to do picket duty. Captain Duff camped the company at Big Springs, near the residence of Mr. Bell. From here the regiment went back twelve miles to Grouse creek, near Aldie, where they were soon ordered to the brigade, consisting of the Eighth Virginia regiment of volunteers, Colonel Hunton; the Thirteenth Mississippi, Colonel Barkdale; the Seventeenth Mississippi, Colonel Featherston; the Eighteenth Mississippi, Col. E. R. Burt, and the Richmond hunters, with four pieces of artillery. When the brigade returned to Leesburg Captain Duff and his company were ordered back to the Big Spring, and pickets placed on the Potomac river. The evening of October 20 General Evans visited this company and told them to be on the lookout, as the enemy was making some movement, and if they crossed the river to fight them. Lieutenant Stephens asked him what was to be done if they came in overwhelming numbers. General Evans replied, "Fight them if they come twenty thousand strong." In the morning the company was notified that the enemy had crossed the river at Ball's bluff. They hastily organized, there being only forty-eight men, the rest being on picket duty. They moved rapidly in the direction of the firing and met a detachment of the Fifteenth Massachusetts regiment on the crest of Ball's bluff, with five hundred men. A sharp encounter ensued, and the enemy was driven back. The company was relieved by the appearance of two companies from the Eighteenth and Thirteenth Mississippi regiments, and with their aid succeeded in driving the enemy back to Ball's bluff. This was a complete victory for the company, as they had not a man killed or taken prisoner, and they were outnumbered by the enemy. After this engagement the regiment went into winter quarters near Leesburg. In the battle of Leesburg or Ball's bluff Lieutenant Stephens also participated. Early in February, 1862, Lieutenant Stephens was granted a leave of absence and ordered to report to Col. J. A. Orr in Mississippi. He did so, and raised company D in his, the Thirty-first Mississippi regiment, and at the organization, after several weeks, was elected lieutenant-colonel. The regiment was ordered to Corinth, soon after the battle of Shiloh, and was placed in a brigade in General Breckinridge's division, going then to Vicksburg to join General Pendleton. This was in June, and they remained there during the bombardment, until the last of July, going thence to Baton Rouge, La., where they participated in the battle at that place. Thence they went to Grand Junction, pressing the enemy back, and then returned to Davis' mill. General Breckinridge then left the regiment, and with his division went to join Bragg's army in north Georgia.

Under Van Dorn, the regiment then went to Holly Springs, and remained until after the battle of Corinth, when they went to Coffeeville, where a sharp engagement ensued, which resulted somewhat disastrously, and the regiment retreated to Grenada, Miss. Here they remained inactive until the spring of 1863. Van Dorn in the meantime took the cavalry and attacked the enemy at Holly Springs, which induced Grant to retreat to Memphis. In July, 1863, the regiment was ordered to Jackson, Mississippi, where they remained for a short time, going thence to Snyder's bluff, on the Yazoo river, and from there went up Deer creek to meet a detachment of the enemy coming through Black Bayou and Deer creek to Vicksburg, where the enemy met a defeat and was driven back to Black Bayou. The regiment then went to Grenada, Miss., and from there to Edwards depot, near Big Black river. They met the enemy at Baker's creek, where they were defeated, and the army fell back to Vicksburg. Loring's division, of which Lieutenant-Colonel Stephens' regiment was a part, retreated to Jackson, where they were joined by General Johnston, and went to Canton, Miss., where a small army was formed which moved on toward Vicksburg, when the news of the surrender reached them and they fell back to Jackson, with the enemy in close pursuit. Remaining at Jackson for some days, the regiment then fell back to Brandon, Miss. During the siege of Jackson, the Thirty-first regiment lost quite a number of men, among them being Maj. Henry E. Topp, who was mortally wounded while directing the left wing of the regiment repelling an assault from the enemy. After going to Brandon, they went to Forest, and later to Newton Station, where Colonel Orr turned over his regiment to Lieutenant-Colonel Stephens, and went home to engage in the canvass for congress. The command then went to Enterprise, Miss., and thence to Demopolis, Ala., where they remained till winter, when they went to Montevallo, Ala. In the spring they, with the rest of Johnston's army, now commanded by General Polk, went to Rome, Ga., and from there by rail, went to Resaca, where they met and repelled the enemy coming through a mountain gap. The regiment took part in two or three brisk engagements at this point, and then fell back to Adairsville and Cassville, where preparations were made for a final stand, but were ordered back to Cartersville and encamped for several days in the Altoona mountains. They met the enemy at New Hope Church, and after an engagement in which the regiment was victorious, it was mustered into Featherston's brigade, Loring's division of Polk's corps. Lieutenant-Colonel Stephens had been promoted to the colonelcy after the resignation of Colonel Orr, who was elected to congress. Colonel Stephens received his commission February 12, 1864.

The regiment then went from the line at New Hope to Lost Mountain, and from there to Noonday creek in front of Kenesaw mountain, and fell back after a short skirmish on this creek to the mountain, where they were attacked by a heavy force June 27, but repulsed the enemy at every point and then fell back to Smyrna church and fortified a line, but soon abandoned it and fell back to Chattahoochee river, and on the 17th of July crossed the river and formed a line on Peachtree creek. July 18, Johnston was removed and General Hood took his place in command. July 21, the regiment attacked the enemy on this creek and took their breastworks, but were compelled to fall back. Colonel Drane was severely wounded and Maj. F. M. Gillespie was killed, and two hundred and sixty-five men were either killed, wounded or captured. On the 22d of July, the regiment supported General Hood on the right at Atlanta, and on July 28, supported him on the left. He then encircled the city of Atlanta, and put up temporary breastworks and the siege of Atlanta began, which lasted till September, when the enemy struck General Hardee's corps at Jonesboro. On the evacuation of Atlanta, the regiment joined General Hardee at Lovejoy station, where they remained for some time, then crossed the Chattahoochee, and came to the railroad at Big Shanty, where a sharp engagement ensued between Featherston's brigade and the enemy. The regiment sustained some loss and the horse of Colonel Stephens was shot and the fort captured. Then the regiment moved on Acworth, which surrendered without a fight. General Frendi's division attacked Alatoona, and was repulsed after a severe engagement. The regiment was still with General Loring, but Gen. A. P. Stewart was the corps commander, and went to Cedartown and back across the Coosa river and struck the railroad at Resaca. The regiment then moved off up the river, tearing up the road as far as Dalton, where it deflected to the left and went to Summerville, Ga. From there it went to Summerville, Ala., and thence to Decatur, where the enemy was attacked by the brigade. The command halted at Tuscumbia, Ala., where they remained a few days. They took up the line of march for Nashville, Tenn. At Franklin General Hood attacked the enemy in his stronghold behind three lines of breastworks. Hood's army suffered a fearful loss. Colonel Stephens had his

right leg broken with a minie-ball just below the hip, and fell against the breastworks of the enemy. In this charge he lost one hundred and eighty-four men, in killed and wounded, forty-five dying on the field. He was himself captured by the enemy and taken in the direction of Nashville, across the H—— river, where he was abandoned by them in an old field. The ground was frozen and the north wind was blowing and he would doubtless have died but for the kindness of a Federal soldier, who kindly wrapped him up in a pair of his blankets, and another soldier who put a fire at his feet. This no doubt saved his life, and in the morning the men of his own regiment found him and took him to Major McGorvick's residence, where he was cared for till an uncle in the neighborhood, Miles R. Hudson, removed him to his house, where he remained till the army went to Nashville. He feels under many obligations to Mr. Barr of the One Hundred and Sixty-fifth Illinois regiment for bandaging his wound on the battlefield, and for moving him from between the lines of the enemy and for watching over and protecting him, and to Colonel Stewart, of the same regiment, for his kindness and consideration to him while in his lines, and to the soldier, Mr. Hindman, who built the fire at his feet to warm him on that bitter cold night, and to a soldier belonging to an Iowa regiment for kindly giving him a pair of United States blankets to keep him from freezing. He and these soldiers are fast friends, and have exchanged photos, and he points with much pride to these pictures of his friends in blue, who came to his relief on the battlefield in the hour of danger.

He fell back with the army across the Tennessee river, and made his way home, arriving there January 1, 1865, having ridden three hundred miles with his broken leg fastened to the horn of the saddle, with his negro boy walking in the road before him and riding behind him across creeks. He was eighteen days making the trip from Franklin to Sarepta, his home in Calhoun county, Miss. This ended his military career, as he was confined to his bed for nearly two months and was obliged to use crutches for more than a year. He took no further part in the war, but attended the session of the legislature in March, 1865, at Columbus, Miss., and took a part in its deliberations. When the surrender came he was at home with his family, consisting of his wife, a son Rudolphus and his daughter, Cleora. He was without a single dollar; the Confederate money he had was utterly worthless, and everything was gone but his family and some land, and he on crutches. He at once resumed the practice of medicine, but soon found that his broken leg would make it impossible for him to ride much on horseback. He gathered a little money and engaged in merchandising with Capt. H. L. Duncan, his former companion in arms. They soon took in a partner, S. R. Kirkwood, and opened a store in Water Valley, Miss., with a capital of $10,000. Captain Duncan soon sold his interest in the store to W. D. Mayes, and took up the practice of law. Stephens & Co. now did a large, paying business. In 1871 W. D. Mayes withdrew from the firm, and Stephens & Kirkwood continued the business. He was elected to the legislature of Mississippi in the fall of 1863, at the time Colonel Orr was elected to congress, but he kept in the field all the time except when the legislature was in session. He did not resign, for the men would not permit him to leave them. In the spring of 1865, soon after the surrender of the forces east of the Mississippi river, Gov. Charles Clarke called the legislature, and Colonel Stephens, being a member, went to Jackson with C. A. Lewers, his co-representative for Calhoun county. Neither of them had a cent of money; in fact, there was no money in the country. They got transportation on the railroad and reached Jackson, and arranged to board with the family of Col. C. E. Hooker, Colonel Stephens drawing rations from the commissary, by order of Governor Clarke, to pay the board of himself and Lewers. The legislature was in session about three days, the city full of Yankee soldiers and negroes; the legislature did nothing, could do nothing. The third day Governor Clarke informed Stephens that there was an order for his arrest, and that the boys had better scatter, and soon after that warning they adjourned The proceedings of this assembly have never been published, and are perhaps unwritten. The Colonel got home without spending a dollar. He was elected to the state senate in October, 1866, from the district of Calhoun and Yalobusha, and served one session, and until, by the reconstruction act of congress, he, together with all the officers of the state, was turned out, and the state placed under military government. His business as a merchant prospered until contraction brought ruin to the country, culminating in 1878 in suspension and the surrender of everything to his creditors, and he once more took a new start in the world, and went to clerking to support his wife and seven children.

In 1879 he was elected to the legislature and served in the session of 1880, and assisted as one of the committee in making the code of 1880. Soon after his return from the legislature he was appointed deputy chancery clerk, and served in that capacity till 1883, when he was elected chancery clerk. He served four years in this position. In 1888 he was elected recorder of the city of Water Valley, and in 1890 re-elected recorder, in which position he is now serving. His wife and seven children are still here with him. His eldest daughter, Millie, married John W. Smither, December 22, 1890. His sons are unmarried. Since he came to Water Valley he has served as alderman and school trustee; in fact he is one of the founders of the magnificent grade of public schools in Water Valley, which has now enrolled more than six hundred and fifty pupils, and there is a fine building of twelve rooms for the accommodation of the pupils. Colonel Stephens was made a Master Mason in Theodosia lodge No. 182, in Sarepta, June 18, 1855. He represented this lodge in the grand lodge of Mississippi which assembled in Vicksburg, January, 1856. He joined the chapter and council at Duncansby, Miss., in 1863, and was made a Knight Templar Mason in 1873. In 1866 he represented Theodosia lodge in the grand lodge at Jackson, and was elected grand senior warden for this year. He delivered the memorial address to the lodges of Calhoun city in the spring of 1866, which address was published in pamphlet form and is now among the records of the grand lodge. He was master of Theodosia lodge for seven years and master of the Water Valley lodge; high priest of Water Valley chapter and eminent commander of St. Cyr commandery at Water Valley. He has ever been a true and loyal Mason, and devoted much of his time in his younger days to the work of the lodge, and was a bright Mason in the various lodges to which he has belonged.

Z. M. Stephens is foremost among the lawyers of the state of Mississippi. He is a resident of New Albany upon which city his name sheds luster. He was born near Fulton, Itawamba county, Miss., in the year 1852 and lived there until 1865. Then he removed with his parents to Memphis, remaining there until 1870. In 1873 he located in New Albany and began the study of law, for which profession he was pre-eminently fitted. In 1874 he was admitted to the bar and has since practiced his profession with increasing and gratifying success. He has been engaged in some of the most noted criminal cases in northern Mississippi and, owing to the masterly manner in which he has conducted them, he has been almost uniformly victorious over his opponents. Colonel Stephens is one of the most extensive land owners in the state and is one of its leading business men. He was first elected to the state legislature in 1873 and served during the session of 1874-5. He was returned in 1883 and served with distinction during the succeeding session and has since then devoted his time almost exclusively to the practice of law. He was an elector on the Cleveland ticket in 1884. His father, Dr. Stephens, was a prominent physician and surgeon of New Albany, who during a long career won the respect of all who knew him, and died deeply lamented in January, 1891.

J. H. Stevens is one of the reliable business men of Lowndes county, Miss., and although he has only followed the calling of a merchant in Columbus since November, 1889, his efforts have been prospered and his patronage is now large and lucrative. He was born in Columbus, in the month of January, 1838, to Hardy and Elizabeth (Myatt) Stevens, who were born in Raleigh, N. C., the former of whom came to Mississippi on horseback about 1830, being one of the earliest settlers of this region. Although he was brought up to learn the details of planting he began learning the carpenter's trade upon coming to Columbus, and some of the first houses in the town were erected by him. He followed this calling for many years, and in 1889 died at the age of eighty-four years; his wife's death occurring in 1882. Their marriage was blessed in the birth of eight children, six of whom are living at the present time: Mrs. Taylor, of Kentucky; J. H., of Columbus, Miss.; Mrs. Palmer, of Columbus, Miss.; John A., of West Point, Miss.; and J. A. Stevens, and Mrs. J. B. Cobb, of Texas, all of whom are married and settled in life. Hardy Stevens was a member of the board of county supervisors for many years, was a member of the city board of aldermen and also belonged to the Masonic fraternity. J. H. Stevens was reared and educated in Columbus and at the age of sixteen years started to make his own way in the world as deputy probate clerk, a position he filled to the satisfaction of all concerned for three years. He next became a clerk in a mercantile establishment, a calling he followed until the opening of the war, when he became a member of company K, Old Columbus riflemen (which is still in existence), serving as a private until the surrender of General Lee at Appomattox. When at Bowling Green, Ky., he was clerk of a court martial, but he afterwards became a member of company H, Thirty-fifth Mississippi regiment under Col. W. S. Barry, serving six months until company K returned from Camp Douglas, when he rejoined that company and served till the close of the war. After the surrender he returned home and embarked in the mercantile business, which he continued to follow until 1874, when he was appointed deputy chancery clerk, serving throughout that year and in 1875. In 1876 he was made clerk of the circuit court, in which capacity he made a faithful and zealous official until 1888. He then turned his talents toward making a plat and index of land numbers of the county, and for the admirable manner in which he carried out this work he was well paid. In November, 1889, he once more embarked in merchandising, and is now one of the leading men engaged in this business in the county. He was married in Columbus, Miss., in 1869, to Miss Ophelia Wallace, who was born in Lebanon, Tenn., by whom he has two living children: L. W. and Allie M. He and his wife and daughter are members of the Christian church, and socially he is a Knight Templar in the A. F. & A. M., and a member of lodge of Perfection, at Columbus, and secretary in the lodge of I. O. O. F., in which position he has served fourteen years.

Capt. John P. Stevens was born in Caswell county, N. C., November 30, 1835, the third of ten children born to Rev. George and Susan P. (Richardson) Stevens, the former a native of Georgia and the latter of North Carolina. The father was a minister of the Methodist Episcopal church and moved from the state of his birth to Christian county, Ky., where he devoted his life and energies to his calling until his death, in 1854. He was a strong supporter of his church and served the cause of the Master faithfully throughout a long career. His widow survived him until 1888, when she died at the age of seventy-four years. The mother was of English descent, but the father was of Scotch-Irish lineage. Capt. John P. Stevens, was reared in Christian county, Ky., and in Hopkinsville received a common English education. At the age of fifteen years, he left the shelter of the parental roof and after spending two years in Cadiz, Ky., he came to Jackson, Miss., and from 1858 until 1861 he was a salesman with the firm of Robinson, Winelly & Co. He then became a member of company

A, Sixth Mississippi regiment, participating in the battles of Shiloh, Port Gibson, Baker's creek and siege of Vicksburg. During this time he served as captain of his company. After being paroled and exchanged, he reported to General Forrest at Corinth, was promoted to the staff of General Buford and went through Hood's campaign. Upon his return from that campaign he was sent from Iuka to Aberdeen in charge of the ordnance train, and upon reaching his destination was assigned to duty at Enterprise, to relieve Captain Freeman, collector of provisions for the army. He remained at this place until the surrender, then went to Pickensville, Ala., and followed the calling of a merchant for about ten months. He then came to Jackson, Miss., and here, in connection with John W. Robinson, he successfully followed the calling of a merchant until 1881, when Mr. Robinson died and Mr. Stevens continued the business under the name of Stevens & Saunders until 1889, when the stock of goods was closed out. Mr. Stevens and Mr. Saunders then organized the Jackson Grocery Company, in which Mr. Stevens is a large stockholder. He also owns six thousand acres of land, of which some two thousand acres are under cultivation. He is a stockholder in the Jackson Fertilizing Company, and the Jackson Compress Company, and he has been one of the thrifty and prosperous men of the city and a fine business man. He is moral, religious and honorable and his standing is high in both business and social circles. He was married in 1868, to Miss Sidney E. Green, a native of Mississippi and a daughter of Thomas and Mary J. (Stuart) Green, the former of whom was born in Baltimore, Md. To Mr. and Mrs. Stevens, two children have been born: Sue Stuart and John Price, Jr., both of whom are at home. Mr. Stevens and his wife and children are members of the Methodist Episcopal church and he is a member of the A. F. & A. M., the Knights of Honor, the A. L. of H., and the Knights and Ladies of Honor.

W. G. Stevenson is a native of the Palmetto state. He settled in Alabama in 1851, and engaged in building machinery. He then moved to Noxubee county, Miss., continuing his former business. In 1862 he joined the Forty-first Mississippi regiment, and was detailed in the ordnance department. In 1863 he was ordered to the commissary department for the erection of flouring and sawmills, and remained there until the close of service, surrendering at Meridian to General Canby. In 1865 Mr. Stevenson became a citizen of Meridian, was made a member of the city council of the rising town, and was also ex-officio trustee of the public schools. Meridian becoming a separate school district, he was elected president of the board of trustees, but prior to that had been president of the city council. He still holds the former position. Mr. Stevenson is one of the strongest advocates of education. In 1885 Meridian had five small schools, three white and two colored, with an attendance of two hundred and seventy. Now, with her three magnificent new buildings, and other structures, and two thousand students in attendance, she presents a striking example of progress and enterprise. The city has received more substantial aid in population, etc., from her schools, than through any other source. In 1884 the city did not own a dollar in school property, but she now owns $70,000 worth of fine property. The negro school, numbering seven hundred pupils, is the largest in the state. Mr. Stevenson and Prof. A. A. Kincannon, who was superintendent of the schools, were sent by the city to the northwest and northeast to investigate the progress of school architecture, etc. On returning, their plans were adopted by the trustees and city council. The system put into effect is essentially the one used at Jamestown, N. Y. Mr. Stevenson is the originator of the industrial feature of the Meridian public schools, which he considers a success. He is Anglo-German by descent, and inherits a turn for machinery.

The medical profession is ably represented in Lauderdale county, Miss., by W. J. Stevenson, M. D., for his efforts as a medical practitioner have been attended with the best of success and he is well posted and up with the times in his profession. He was born in Clinton, Green county, Ala., November 24, 1856, the son of W. G. and Eliza J. (Shepherd) Stevenson, both of whom were born in Newberry district, S. C., and emigrated to Alabama with their parents, where they met and afterward married. After remaining there several years they removed to Mississippi in 1860 and located in Noxubee county, where Mr. Stevenson followed the calling of a machinist. W. J. Stevenson was educated in the common schools of Lauderdale county, and at the age of twenty-one began the study of medicine, entering, in 1879, the Alabama Medical college at Mobile, from which he graduated in March, 1881. He entered upon his practice in De Kalb, Kemper county, Miss., but at the end of six months, or in the fall of 1881, he located at Lauderdale, Miss., where he has continued to reside up to the present time. In connection with the large practice which he commands, he is also engaged in the drug business, at which he is doing well. He is a young physician of acknowledged ability, and his agreeable and pleasant disposition fits him in an eminent degree for his calling. He is the owner of about five hundred acres of land near Lauderdale, of which about two hundred acres are improved, and his stock of drugs is valued at about $800. In 1885 he was married to Miss Sorinthia L. Simmons, a daughter of J. L. Simmons, and to their union three children have been born: Martha (deceased), Willie (deceased), and Katie. Dr. Stevenson and his wife are members of the Presbyterian church and he is also a member of the A. F. & A. M. of the K. of H. They move in the highest circles of society and are liberal contributors to all enterprises that deserve their patronage.

Isaac D. Stewart is an extensive planter and dealer in general merchandise and plantation supplies, his residence being one mile west of Fayette. He is a young man of good business ability and coming, as he does, of one of the best families of the county, he is highly respected, not only on this account, but for his own merit also. He is a son of William and Martha J. (Mayberry) Stewart, the former of whom was born in New Jersey and raised in Illinois, but came to Jefferson county, Miss., while yet a young man, this being about the year 1839. He soon became a clerk in the store belonging to J. B. Carpenter, and afterward became a partner in the concern. He married Miss Mayberry in 1849, and went into business for himself, opening a store of his own. He continued to follow this occupation with excellent success until 1855, when he sold his business in Fayette and moved to his farm four miles south of that point and lived there until his death. In company with a man named Drake, he merchandised at Rodney, Miss., in 1856 and 1857. He sold out to his partner, Drake, in 1858, and attended to his farm. He died March 1, 1859. He was a man of shrewd financial views and owned a fine plantation of about eight hundred acres. He at all times manifested a Christian spirit and for many years had held official position in the Methodist Episcopal church. He left a widow, two sons and three daughters to mourn his loss, all of whom are now residing near Fayette, Isaac D. and his family residing on his place about a mile west of the town. William C. Stewart is a dentist and is doing a large and flourishing business in that line at Fayette; Mary L., is the wife of Judson J. Gordon, a merchant of Fayette; Fanny E., is the wife of Dr. George Rembert, a dentist of Natchez; and Mattie M. is the wife of C. R. Freeman, a farmer of Jefferson county. Mrs. Stewart, the mother of these children, is the daughter of Abraham Mayberry, a planter and native of Tennessee. He became a resident of Mississippi when a young man and was here married to Miss Lucretia Boles, who was born in this county near Fayette, she being a daughter of James and Mary Boles. Mrs. Stewart has one brother and three sisters living: Henry J., Mary E.,

Kate V., and Fanny. Henry J., was a soldier in the Confederate army during the late war. The Stewart family are members of the Methodist Episcopal church and are liberal in their support of enterprises deserving their patronage, and at all times manifest a very charitable and christian spirit. A paternal uncle of Isaac D. Stewart was presiding elder of the Methodist church and died about twenty-five years ago at Mount Pleasant, Iowa, having been a powerful and eloquent divine. Isaac D. Stewart was born on the 15th of December, 1852, and was educated at Fayette. On the 10th of April, 1889, having come to the conclusion that it is not good for man to live alone, he was married to Miss Josie J. Whitney, a daughter of Wesley Whitney, a planter of the county. She was born on the 4th of November, 1867, and has borne her husband one child, a girl named Virgie. Mr. Stewart ranks among the most active business men of the county, is largely engaged in stock raising and has control or supervision of several extensive plantations. No man in the county is more universally respected and to know him is to have a high admiration for him, for he is possessed of those sterling characteristics which make a true man. Genial and hospitable in his intercourse with those around him, he has a host of warm friends and very few, if any, enemies.

Col. James D. Stewart is an influential and well-known citizen of Jackson, Miss., and is of Scotch descent, his paternal great-grandfather, James Stewart, having been a fugitive from Scotland to South Carolina in 1745. After residing for some time in that state, he removed to Tennessee, of which he was one of the first settlers, and did his full share in the development of the section in which he lived. His son, James, was born on his plantation in Tennessee; was there reared and educated, and followed in the footsteps of his father, inasmuch as he made the calling of a planter his chief occupation throughout life. His efforts were rewarded by substantial success, and his latter days were spent in the enjoyment of a comfortable competency. He died while on a visit to his sons in Mississippi, about the year 1826. His son, William, the father of Col. James D. Stewart, was also born in Tennessee, but about 1805 he came to Mississippi, and, like many of his ancestors before him, began devoting his time and energies to planting, a calling to which he had been reared, and to which he was thoroughly adapted. He was of a very active and energetic temperament; and, possessing sound and practical views, he was very successful in the enterprises in which he engaged, and became very wealthy. He interested himself in, and was a liberal contributor to worthy enterprises, and became president of a branch of the Planters' bank at Woodville, Wilkinson county, which position he was filling at the time of his death in 1835. In this state he was married to Miss Frances M. Smith, whose ancestors were among the earliest settlers of Wilkinson county, Miss., her grandfather, Peter Smith, having emigrated to this state from South Carolina about 1785. He followed the life of a planter, and at his death, which occurred in 1837, at about the age of seventy years, he left a valuable estate and a large family of children to inherit it. Among his sons, Coatsworth Pinckney Smith became a noted lawyer, and became chief justice of the high court of errors and appeals. He died in 1862. Col. James D. Stewart was born in Wilkinson county, Miss., in 1824, the fourth of his parents' children. He was educated in the University of Virginia, from which institution he graduated in 1843, after which he continued the study of law at Cambridge, under Story & Greenleaf. Upon returning to his Mississippi home, he commenced the battle of life as a planter of Wilkinson county, and in 1850 was married to Miss Amanda Yerger, a daughter of George S. Yerger, a distinguished lawyer, and about 1852 moved to Hinds county. Three years later he took up his abode in the city of Jackson, and here practiced law for a short time. In 1863 he entered the Confederate army as chief of ordinance for Mississippi, receiving his appointment from the governor, and held this position until the close of the war. He is a veteran of the Mexican war also, having served in company B, Jefferson Davis' regiment. Although the Colonel has never been an office seeker, yet he has been prominent in the affairs of his section, and the people of Wilkinson early showed their appreciation of his ability by electing him to the lower house of the state legislature, in which body he was an active and useful member during 1850. In 1879 he was elected to the state senate from Hinds and Rankin counties, discharging his duties in 1880 and 1882; and during those years he introduced bills which became laws, one being an act to prevent prize-fighting, and another for the prevention of cruelty to animals, both of which were wise and humane measures. In 1878 he was elected president of the Howard association, soon after the organization of that society, and was one of its most active and useful members during the yellow-fever epidemic of 1878. He visited patients day and night during that dark period, being utterly fearless in regard to his own danger, and many owe their lives to his faithful and watchful care. In 1885 he was appointed registrar of the United States land office at Jackson, which position he efficiently filled for four years. Of nine children born to Colonel Stewart and wife, the following are living: Ida, wife of Percy Lemly, a leading grocer of Jackson; George Yerger, a druggist; William N., a physician of Louisiana; Noland, a physician in the employ of the government, and Amanda. The family are members of the Episcopal church.

William Stewart (deceased), one of the county's very early settlers and prominent citizens, was descended from the noble family in Scotland of that name. He came to North Carolina in 1730, with several children and was at that time a widower. Soon after locating near Raleigh he met Jannet Williamson, a former lady-love of his single days who had come a widow to the Carolinas with her children. This acquaintance was renewed and resulted in their marriage, and by this union a family was reared. Patrick Stuart, one of the elder sons of William was a tory during the Revolution and a captain in the British army, and Duncan Stewart refused to spell his name as his brothers, owing to differences in political views. Thus the name is spelled by the others Stewart. Patrick Stuart was progenitor of Capt. J. Madison Bachelor, now of Vicksburg, Miss., who is the only representative of that branch of the family, being the great-grandson of Patrick. Duncan, James and Charles were the other sons of William by his first marriage, and he had also two daughters. These were: Mrs. Ventress, grandmother of the Ventress Bros., of LaGrange, Wilkinson county, Miss., and Janet, wife of John Stewart, a native of Scotland, and a half-pay British captain, who on the king's birthday always appeared in full regimentals much to the disgust of the patriots of Woodville, Miss., on one occasion narrowly escaping violence at their hands. Captain Stewart and his wife left no issue. Duncan and James emigrated to Tennessee in about 1797 or 1798, and settled in the vicinity of Clarksville. Duncan Stewart came to Mississippi territory and settled in Wilkinson county in about 1808 or 1809, and located the Stewart plantation in the southeastern portion of the county, became very wealthy as a planter and one of the most prominent citizens. He had been a member of the legislature while in Tennessee, and afterward became surveyor-general and lieutenant governor of Mississippi. He was a man of more than ordinary ability, a thorough politician, a man of learning, was very generous in his habits, brave and fearless, notably honorable and well respected, with a brilliant mind, and as a debater of public affairs had few equals in the state. He died in 1815, aged sixty years. He entered the Revolutionary army as a private, and was promoted to the rank of colonel; but owing to delicate health was compelled to quit the service before his undoubted military genius had time to develop itself. He was married to Penelope Jones, of North Carolina, daughter of Tignal Jones of that state, who was also a colonel in the Revolutionary army. Mrs. Stewart died February 25, 1843, aged sixty-four years.

By this union were born William (who died in infancy), Tignal Jones, James A., Charles D., Catherine, and Eliza. Tignal J., the eldest that lived to be grown, was well educated, and a man of fine attainments. He was elected state senator from this district, also to the house, where he was founder of the bill protecting the rights of married women in holding property, real estate, etc. He was a man of prominence, and one of this county's ablest and best citizens. He was honorable, generous and popular, and very fond of field sports, hunting, etc., and through it all, was a polished gentleman. He married Miss Sarah A. Randolph, daughter of Peter Randolph, United States district judge, of Mississippi, appointed by Andrew Jackson in 1823, and by this union was born two daughters, Sarah A. and Penelope. Sarah A. married William J. Fort, and owns a portion of the old home place. She now resides in Louisiana, West Feliciana parish, and is very highly respected, and a cultured lady. She is a widow. Penelope is the widow of Charles L. Mathews, of the same parish, where she resides, comfortable and happy. Tignal J., the father of these two daughters, died March 20, 1855. He was born April 20, 1800, in Tennessee. His widow is yet living with her daughter, Mrs. Fort, in her eighty-second year, an honored and respected lady, and one of the best of women, hospitable, kind, and loved for her many noble social qualities. James A., the second son of Duncan and Penelope Stewart, was born July 14, 1811, and died August 28, 1883. He was educated at Nashville, Tenn., and Troy, N. Y., and followed planting in Wilkinson county, where he became very prominent. He possessed fine business ability, and was distinguished for his generosity. He became very wealthy and highly respected. He married Juliana Randolph, sister of Sarah, who married Tignal J. Stewart. She was a beautiful woman, of sprightly disposition, and possessed unusual social graces. She was educated by the wife of John James Audubon, the famous naturalist, and at the Convent Ursuline, at New Orleans. She is now living with her youngest daughter, Mrs. Simpson, both of whom are members of the Episcopal church. To James A. and Juliana Randolph were born nine children, seven of whom are yet living: Penelope J., widow of J. B. Sterling, at Leland, Miss., Duncan Stewart, who married Caroline, the daughter of Judge Edward and Mary Burruss McGehee, and lives at Laurel Hill, La., where Mr. Stewart is engaged in planting and raising fine stock, among which are Devonshire cattle, and a fine grade of horses. He is among the leading planters of the parish, and one of the most honored and respected citizens. He was reared in Wilkinson county, but his birth occurred October 7, 1836, at Bay St. Louis, Miss., while his parents were there spending the summer. He was educated at home by a private tutor, and at the University of Virginia, and for a time also attended Yale college. Returning home from school he managed a sugar plantation for his father in Pointe Coupee parish, La., until the breaking out of the war; he entered the secret service of the Confederacy during the latter part of the war.

Soon after the war he located at the present place, Laurel Hill stock farm. He is a member of the police jury of West Feliciana parish, which office he has held for many years. He was chairman of the democratic executive committee of the parish, which ended carpet-bag rule. He is a Master Mason of Woodville lodge, No. 63. To him and wife were born eight children, of whom two are deceased: George McGehee, Mary B. (who died aged nineteen years), Louise F., Ida Randolph, Henry Martin, and Eugenia McGehee, Kate B. (deceased), and Edward McGehee. The family are highly esteemed, and enjoy a pleasant home. The third child of James A. is Catherine, the wife of J. Burruss McGehee, one of the prominent and leading citizens of West Feliciana parish, La., and a son of Judge Edward McGehee. They have one son, J. Stewart McGehee, who lives on the Bowling Green plantation. Tignal J., the fourth child of James A. and Juliana Stewart, was a highly respected and educated gentleman, and served during the late war in the Confederate army, in the Washington artillery of New Orleans, and was commissioned lieutenant on Deering's staff during the latter part of the war. He married Mary Heyward, and now lives in New Orleans. Rosa Stewart, the fifth child of James A., was married first to St. Clair Sutherland, of Maryland, a near relative of the Knickerbocker family of New York, and secondly to her present husband, Capt. Hiram Sharp, of Alabama. They reside on a part of the old home place. She is a lady of fine social attainments, very highly cultured and a fine conversationalist. Henry M., the sixth child of James A. and Juliana, was drowned in the Mississippi river from a burning boat, while trying to save a lady passenger, at the age of twenty-one years. He was a soldier in the late war in the Thirty-eight Mississippi regiment, was twice wounded and was distinguished for his bravery and coolness. He always kept his gun loaded, and when ordered by a superior officer to shoot a prisoner, he avoided the murder by stating that his gun was not loaded to shoot unarmed prisoners. He was the only man in the company who was known to have a loaded gun. He was a brave and daring soldier, and was loved and respected. Cornelia Randolph, the seventh child born to James A. and Juliana, a very beautiful and highly cultured lady, is the wife of Dr. Albert Bachelor, of Pointe Coupee parish, La. Ida, the eighth child born to James A. and Juliana, married Lenox Simpson, of Washington, D. C., a nephew of the celebrated Jurist Lenox, of Washington. She is a highly cultured and attractive lady, now a widow. She and her mother travel a great portion of the time and own valuable property in Birmingham, Ala. Charles Duncan, the third son of Duncan and Penelope Stewart, was highly educated and settled in Pointe Coupee parish, La., where he became wealthy. He married Julia Black, daughter of Judge Black, who became United States senator.

They have a son John Black Stewart, who has distinguished himself as an author favorably known as "Archibald Clavering Gunter," and who resides in New York city. He is the author of "Mr. Barnes of New York," "Mr. Potter of Texas," "That Frenchman," "Miss Nobody of Nowhere," "Small Boys in big Boots," "The Daughters of America," "Ten Nights in Rome," and several others. "Mr. Barnes of New York," was dramatized and brought out under the management of Frank W. Sanger, of the Broadway theatre, New York, and is one of the most successful plays now on the stage. The above novels have had, and are yet having, a phenomenal sale. "Mr. Barnes of New York," had, in 1889, reached its one hundred and ninetieth thousand, "Mr. Potter of Texas," its one hundred and fiftieth thousand, "Miss Nobody of Nowhere," its seventieth thousand, and the others in large numbers. "Small Boys in big Boots," a story for children, became at once very popular and had a large sale. His writings are characterized by vigor, boldness of conception, originality, are never dull, always singularly fresh and sparkling, and are filled with unexpected and powerful dramatic effect. The press of the United States is unanimous in his praises. Even the Thunderer, the great *Times* of London, England, of November 4, 1888, says of him: "Mr. Gunter's books are more read than perhaps those of any other living writer." He married a highly accomplished lady, from New Jersey, Miss Elizabeth Luzby. Charles D., died in 1886, aged seventy-three years and in his middle life lost a great deal of his property by losing his eyesight, but the excellent management of his estimable wife regained the fortune. Catherine, the fourth child born to Duncan and Penelope, married Judge Harry Cage, by whom she had two sons, Albert and Duncan. Catherine died February 12, 1829, aged twenty-four years, four months and nine days. Her two sons served in the Mexican war, and in the late war, Duncan as colonel and Albert as captain. They were well to do planters before the war, both of whom have since died leaving large familes, now living in Louisiana. Eliza, the fifth child born to Duncan and Penelope Stewart, and the wife of Col. W. S. Hamilton, died in 1870. She had a large family, most of them deceased. Mr. Hamilton was of excellent parentage and highly respected. His son, Col. Jones S. Hamilton, held the office of sheriff in Wilkinson county, and was state senator from this district. He was the youngest official of note ever elected to office in this county. The family of Stewart is represented in all of the Southern and southwestern states, and is connected by ties of blood or marriage with many of the leading families of the United States. Through the Randolphs they are connected with ex-President Madison, Thomas Jefferson, the Claibornes, Monroes, Pages and Nelsons of Virginia. Charles, the twin brother, of Duncan, lies buried at the Ventress place one mile north of Holly Grove, the old Stewart estate, which is still owned by the family.

Prof. W. P. Stewart is one of the able, experienced and successful educators of the South, and his place among the leading men engaged in his line of work has been won by his own persistent endeavors and indomitable perseverance. He is a native of Mississippi, a thoroughly self-made man in every respect, and, although his parents were poor and unable to give him the advantages he craved, by many diligent hours of study by the fireside he managed to secure sufficient education to teach in the public schools of his native state. In this way he secured means to pursue a higher course of education, and first attended the Buena Vista college, Mississippi, afterwards the Iuka Normal institute, and last the National Normal university, of Lebanon, Ohio, where he graduated in the college of science, receiving the degree of B. S. in 1891.

B. J. Stinson, son of John and C. J. (Clark) Stinson, was born January 18, 1859, a native of Lauderdale county, Miss., and grandson of Burwell Stinson, of North Carolina, born in 1777. In his early manhood he began teaching school, which vocation he has followed almost continuously to the present time. In 1881 he was married to Miss M. E. Pickett of Lauderdale county. He has had five children, four of whom—May, Effie, Elsie and Mary, are living. Mr. Stinson is the junior member of the firm of Stinson & Son, nurserymen, who are experimenting in the propagation of a November peach and who are sanguine of success. This firm is testing all the new varieties of fruits and berries with a view to supplying this latitude with paying stock. He has already given to the world the finest September and October peaches known in this section of the South: Stinson's September Cling and Free, and Stinson's October by name. This is an institution which promises to be of great benefit to the section in which it is located, and indeed to the whole South, over which a correspondence and patronage is fast spreading. Mr. Stinson is personally very social in his nature and has many friends. He is an educated gentleman, having graduated with the class of 1889 at Cooper Normal college. He is truly a representative, public-spirited citizen, and reflects credit on the county of his nativity.

William H. Stinson, a son of John and C. J. (Clark) Stinson, the former of whom began life in Alabama in 1825, and a grandson of Burwell Stinson of North Carolina, born in 1777, was born in Lauderdale county, Miss., in 1861. He was married in 1884 to Miss S. S. Etheredge. Providence has blessed him with two little ones—Bessie and Lawrence. Mr. Stinson deserves great credit for the patience and perseverance he has displayed in reaching his present attainments. He graduated from Cooper Normal college in 1889, five years after his marriage. Few men are so persistent for an education as to undergo like hardships, which renders Mr. Stinson's achievements all the more commendable. He has established the Pleasant Hill high school, six miles southeast from Meridian, Miss., in Lauderdale county, which has already wrought for itself a character which has reached beyond county lines. Fortunate in the selection of a site, blessed with fine water, excellent drainage, good society and a wideawake patronage, it seems that nothing should interfere to prevent its complete success. The splendid furniture and latest school equipments found in the school are proof positive of the new life that has possessed the rural districts of the South in regard to educational development. Mr. Stinson is a Baptist, but not at all sectarian in his school. At present (1891) he stands as the choice of the democratic party for one of the three legislative representatives of Lauderdale county, Miss. As to his election there can be no doubt, since he has no opposition whatever.

William B. Stinson, farmer and gardener, Canton, Miss., is a native of Kershaw county, S. C., born in 1840, and is the fourth of six children born to William and Martha (George) Stinson, both natives of South Carolina. The father followed the occupation of a farmer, was very successful in this, and died in 1845. The mother died about 1886. The children grew to mature years and four are now living: Sarah, wife of J. L. Jones of the Palmetto state; Robert S., a farmer of Madison county; George, died at Pensacola in 1861; William B., and Annette, wife of R. J. Cunningham of Texas. William B. Stinson passed his boyhood days in his native state, and received his education at a South Carolina college, graduating in 1860. The following year he enlisted in company G, Eighteenth Mississippi infantry, under Colonel Burt, and was assigned to Longstreet's corps, army of Virginia. He was in the engagements at Manassas, Leesburg and Malvern Hill, where he was wounded in the right arm. At Sharpsburg he was severely wounded in the left leg and hip and was left on the field. He was cared for by the enemy and in a few months was taken to Baltimore, where he remained until able to be exchanged. He then returned to his company, but was not able to serve. He acted as staff officer to General Humphrey, and was then assigned to the invalid corps, acting as recruiting officer for Mississippi, and remained in that position until cessation of hostilities. He entered the service as a private and served through the various ranks up to captain, while in active service, and as major in the invalid corps. His promotions were unsolicited by himself, and were the reward of bravery and faithfulness. After the war Mr. Stinson settled in Madison county, and was married in 1867 to Miss Kate Anderson, daughter of Dr. E. A. and Eliza (Green) Anderson. The result of this union has been nine children: Edward, William, Kate, Sallie, Mattie, Thomas, Louis, Annette and Eliza. Mr. Stinson engaged in merchandising in 1866, followed this occupation for several years, and was then obliged to abandon it on account of ill health. He subsequently engaged in farming and gardening, being one of the first of the place, and he has since found it both pleasant and profitable. He also has a farm of five hundred acres near this place, and has two hundred acres under cultivation. For ten years he held the office of superintendent of public instruction in Madison county, and filled that position in an efficient and highly capable manner. He is a member of the Knights of Honor, Knights of Pythias and the Masonic fraternity. He and Mrs. Stinson are members of the Presbyterian church, and he is elder in the same and is superintendent of the Sunday-school.

Mrs. Penelope J. Stirling is a lady whose many admirable traits of character, whose kindly disposition and whose Christian life has endeared her to the hearts of many. She was born in Wilkinson county, Miss., in 1835, to James A. Stewart, a native of the same state and county, of which he became a prosperous planter. He was sent to Schnectady, N. Y., to be educated, and there made a good record for himself as a student, as he did for himself in after life as a public spirited citizen. He was married to Miss Juliana Randolph, a native of Virginia, who still survives him, being seventy-four years of age. Mr. Stewart passed from life in 1885. The grandfather, Duncan Stewart, was a native of Tennessee, became a government surveyor and laid off the state of Tennessee, Stewart county being named in his honor. He became a man of considerable prominence and served in the legislatures of North Carolina, Tennessee and Mississippi, and at the time of his death was holding the position of lieutenant governor of the state of Mississippi. His wife was formerly Miss Penelope Jones, a native of Orange county, N. C. His father was descended from James I of Scotland, and was banished from his native land. The grandmother's father, Col. Tignal Jones, was a North Carolinian, and during the Revolutionary war served in the Colonial army. The mother was the daughter of Judge Peter Randolph, of the supreme bench of Mississippi, who was descended from Sir Edward Randolph, who was Queen Elizabeth's friend and adviser and ambassador to the courts of Russia and France. The maternal grandmother was a Miss Cocke, of Virginia. Mrs. Penelope J. Stirling was reared in Mississippi and was educated by tutors and governesses at home. She was married in 1854 to James B. Stirling, who was born in Louisiana, and by calling was a sugar planter. He came to this state in 1857, and successfully followed the calling of a planter in Washington county, until his career was closed in 1879. His father, Henry Stirling, was a native of Louisiana, and his grandfather was born in Scotland, who, after coming to America, was married to Miss Ann Alston, of South Carolina, and was employed by the Spanish government to lay off the state of Louisiana. He was afterward incarcerated in Moro castle, Cuba, by Spanish authorities, on account of his son's conduct in an insurrection against the Spanish government, but was afterward released by order of Napoleon. To Mr. and Mrs. Stirling ten children were born: Julia Anna, Mary Isabel, Louisa Butler, James Stewart, Henry S., Mary Cornelia, James Bowman, Penelope, and two children who died in infancy. The only ones who are now living are Julia A., Louisa B. and James B. Mrs. Stirling is the owner of a fine plantation of five hundred acres, four hundred and fifty of which are devoted to the raising of cotton, and calls her place Avondale. Beside this she owns one thousand seven hundred and fifty acres in Alabama. She lives on her plantation, all alone the most of the time, and successfully controls and manages the sixty negroes who work her land. She is very intelligent and versatile, is an interesting conversationalist, and, although she is now somewhat advanced in years, she thinks it a small matter to get on her horse and ride all over her plantation to see that everything is in good working order. She is kindness itself to the negroes who are on her place, and it is a rare thing when she has any difficulty with them. She is a strict member of the Episcopal church, and over her renters she exerts a good moral influence. She is benevolent and hospitable and her home is a favorite resort of her numerous and warm friends.

Mrs. Sarah H. Stirling was born on Lake Washington, Miss., on the 13th of April, 1836, being the second of five children born to John A. and Sallie Steen (Jefferies) Miller, natives, respectively, of Kentucky and Tennessee. When still in their early youth, they came to Mississippi, and Mr. Miller at once engaged in planting in Washington county, at which occupation he became very wealthy, being at the time of his death the richest man in the county. His daughter, Sarah H., became the wife of William H. Stirling in 1856, the latter being a native of Louisiana, and at that time operating a large sugar plantation in his native state. There he remained until 1873, when he came to Mississippi and located at the head of Lake Washington, on the plantation on which his widow now resides. Here he engaged in cotton planting, and at the time of his death was one of the wealthiest planters in the Yazoo delta. He devoted about $30,000 to improving their home shortly after their marriage, and it is now a commodious, substantial, well furnished and remarkably pleasant home. Mrs. Stirling was reared in Mississippi, and received her literary education in the city of New Orleans and Frankfort, Ky., and has given her four children excellent advantages also. Their names are Mary, Georgie Miller, Sallie Steen and Eleanor Corinne; all accomplished, intelligent and refined ladies. Mrs. Stirling is a practical business woman, and since her husband's death has successfully managed her large plantation, consisting of two thousand acres, of which about nine hundred acres are under cultivation. She is of Scotch descent, and comes of an exceptionally fine family, that settled in Louisiana while it was still under control of the Spanish government, and is a great-granddaughter of Gen. Evan Shelby of Tennessee. Her husband was a son of Henry and Mary (Bowman) Stirling, natives of Louisiana and Pennsylvania, respectively, the latter inheriting German blood of her ancestors, who came to this country at a very early period and settled in Pennsylvania. Mr. Stirling was a lineal descendant of Lord Belmore of Ireland. Mrs. Stirling and her daughters are members of the Episcopal church.

C. C. Stockard, M. D., a prominent physician of Columbus, Miss., has shown himself to be a physician of decided skill and merit, and is worthy the confidence and trust reposed in him by all classes. He was born in Macon, Noxubee county, Miss., July 24, 1853, a son of J. J. and V. A. (Rupert) Stockard, natives of Tennessee and Georgia, respectively, but about 1840 became residents of Noxubee county, Miss. Mr. Stockard opened the first mercantile establishment at Brooksville and sold the land to the Mobile & Ohio railroad for their depot at that point, and he it was who named the town Brooksville. He carried on business at this point until 1851, but was interested in the same calling at Macon until 1858. He then became a commission and cotton factor under the firm name of Rupert, Stockard & Co., at Mobile, Ala., in which business he was very successful until the opening of the war. During the early part of the war of secession he served as a cotton buyer for the government, but was subsequently in the militia, after which he again embarked in the commission business in Mobile, under the firm name of Cozart, Stockard & Co. This firm consisted of eight wealthy men who conducted business on an extensive scale, carrying on their operations at Mobile, Memphis, New Orleans and New York, and continued in existence several years. Succeeding this Mr. Stockard moved to his plantation in Chickasaw county, but after a short time removed to West Point, Miss., where he was engaged in the hardware business for some time with Messrs. Bonner & Foster. He opened the First National bank at West Point, which was the second national bank to be opened in the state, and in numerous ways was an enterprising and pushing man of business. He is now a resident of Chattanooga, Tenn., and although in his seventy-fourth year is yet hale and vigorous. To himself and wife, a family of five children were born: Rupert, M. D., of Columbus; Dr. C. C.; Sidney Lea; Thomas W., died in 1878; Arthur, and Daisy, wife of C. V. LeCraw. C. C. Stockard, M. D., was reared principally on a plantation and was an attendant of the country schools until he was seventeen years of age. He then entered the University of Mississippi at Oxford, where he took a three years course in engineering, at the end of which time this branch of study was abolished in the institution, after which he decided to study medicine. In the fall of 1875 he began attending lectures at Nashville, and in 1877 graduated in his profession from Vanderbilt university. His first practicing was done in Washington county, Miss., where he remained until January, 1880, at the end of which time he went to Europe for the purpose of taking a clinical course. He spent the most of his time at Vienna, Austria, in the hospital of that place, the largest one in the world, and during this time pursued his researches with Prof. Carl Braun, a noted man of that country.

He was absent from his native land about one year, but returned to this country with the consciousness of having improved every opportunity and of being able to take upon himself the arduous duties of a physician. He then came to Columbus, which city has since been his home and where, owing to his ability, he has built up an extensive and lucrative practice. He keeps thoroughly apace with the progress made in his profession, and is a member of the state medical association and the Lowndes County association.

Hon. Thomas Ringland Stockdale is a member of congress from the sixth district of Mississippi, and as an American is all that the word implies. In his nature are embodied all those principles of sterling integrity, determination of purpose and indomitable energy so characteristic of the American people, and these have placed him among the foremost of his fellows. Just after the war of the Revolution, when the dark cloud that for seven long years had hung over the Western continent had cleared away, revealing in all its resplendent glory the new republic, that had risen from the altar of sacrifices, to take its place among the nations and powers of the world, the oppressed and down-trodden of the Eastern dynasties saw in the new government an organization destined to become the Mecca of those who sought the blessings of fraternity, liberty and equality. Among those who were attracted by the bright gleam of the star of the new republic, was one James Stockdale, who, leaving behind him the tender associations of kindred and home, came to the new world, and located in Pennsylvania, where he soon married a Miss Weir, and became the father of one son and four daughters. His son, William, was born in Greene county, Penn., where he spent his childhood. He had scarcely attained his eighteenth year when the War of 1812 plunged the country again into all the horrors of war, and threatened with disaster the flag that had floated so proudly above a peaceful and prosperous land. The spirit of bravery and patriotism of those who called the country theirs knew no limit. Immediately following the cry for aid came the steady tramp, tramp, tramp of those sturdy pioneers marching forth for the defense of their country and their homes, and among them was William Stockdale. He was married to Miss Hannah McQuaid, a Pennsylvanian, of Scotch-Irish descent, and they lived and died in Pennsylvania. Their union was blessed by four sons and three daughters, and of these James, who is deceased, was a member of the Maryland legislature, representing a Baltimore district. John M., now a resident of Washington, Penn., was twice chosen as Greene county's representative in the Pennsylvania legislature, and in 1884 was the democratic nominee for congress from his district. Robert P. Stockdale lives at Mt. Pleasant, Iowa, and Mrs. J. B. Wise of Washington county, Penn., is the only surviving daughter. Thomas Ringland Stockdale is the sixth child in his family, and was born in Greene county, Penn., February 28, 1828. During his boyhood, which was spent upon the farm, he experienced all the hardships and privations which fell to the lot of the youth of that period. The little district school near his home afforded him but meager advantages for an education, but young Stockdale attended it for a few weeks during the winter months, applying himself to his studies with energy and diligence, and thus with the aid of his mother, a lady of exceptional culture, he laid the foundation for his education. Those early struggles of the pioneers made a lasting impression upon their after lives. It constituted the fire which separated the gold from the dross and awakened the men and women to a stern realization of the difficulties and responsibilities of life, and it may be truly said that the privations endured in his youth by Thomas R. Stockdale, and in the obstacles he met and fearlessly overcame was laid the foundation for the resolute determination, the tireless energy, and the unimpeachable honesty which were the chief attributes of his whole after life. At the age of twenty-one years he entered college at Waynesburg, Penn., and in 1853 became a student in

Jefferson, now Washington and Jefferson college, becoming in 1856 the proud possessor of a diploma from that institution. Later in the same year he came to Mississippi and soon found employment as a teacher in the schools of Covington county.

In 1857 he became a resident of Pike county, where he accepted a position in the Holmesville academy, and while performing his duties he at the same time gave attention to the study of law, and in 1858 had as his preceptor the Hon. John T. Lamkin, at that time one of the leading attorneys of the South and afterward the representative of his district in the Confederate congress. In the fall of 1858 he entered the University of Mississippi, where he applied himself with characteristic energy to the prosecution of his legal studies and by close application and assiduous effort completed both his junior and senior courses in one year, graduating in 1859. Returning to Holmesville he entered upon the practice of his profession. When the first shot crashed against the walls of Fort Sumter and awakened the people of both North and South to a knowledge of the real character of the impending conflict, Mr. Stockdale was among the first to offer his services for the defense of his state, and in April, 1861, he enlisted in the Confederate service as a member of the Quitman guards and was soon elected lieutenant of his company. He soon won the appointment of adjutant of the Sixteenth Mississippi regiment of infantry and before the close of 1861 was elected major of that regiment. Returning to Mississippi in 1862 he recruited and organized a company of cavalry and took the field as its captain. He was appointed commander of Stockdale's battalion of cavalry and in 1863 was commissioned major of volunteers. As a reward for efficient service he was soon wearing the stars of a lieutenant colonel, and in 1864 was assigned to the Fourth Mississippi cavalry. He was severely wounded while commanding his regiment at the battle of Harrisburg (one of the engagements near Tupelo), July 14, 1864. Colonel Stockdale was paroled from General Forrest's army May 12, 1865, after having performed gallant and continuous service since 1861. An amusing incident is related at the Colonel's expense, and may, perhaps, be found of interest in this connection. Upon one occasion when the regiment was drawn up in order of battle, awaiting the command to participate in the engagement, and he was riding down the line with words of cheer and encouragement for his men, he noticed a soldier, whom for the occasion we will call Smith, dodging a bullet that went whistling by in close proximity to his ear. The Colonel laughingly reproved him, telling him of the impossibility of dodging a minie ball. The Colonel had proceeded but a short distance when a huge shell from the Federal battery came shrieking through the air, and when directly above the Colonel burst with a deafening roar. Nature was stronger than military discipline, and down went the Colonel's head. Smith, who had been watching him, thereupon called out: "That's all right, Colonel, you dodge the big ones, and I'll look out for the little fellows." In the roars of laughter which followed this remark those present all forgot for the moment the dangers of the situation. The war being over, Colonel Stockdale returned to Holmesville and resumed the practice of his profession. In February, 1867, he married Miss Fannie Wicker, a native of Amite county, Miss., and a daughter of Adam Wicker, an extensive planter there. During that year they settled in Summit, Pike county, Miss., and in 1869 Colonel Stockdale became associated in the practice of law with the late Judge Hiram Cassedy, a prominent lawyer and leading jurist of the South. This partnership existed for twelve years, and the firm was widely noted for its strength and ability. In 1868 Colonel Stockdale was a member of the National democratic convention, was presidential elector on the democratic ticket in 1872, and again in 1884. In 1886 he was elected to the Lth congress; in 1888 to the LIst congress, and was re-elected in 1890. In the Lth congress he was a member of the committee on public lands and war claims, and in the LIst congress was a member of the committee on levees and improvements of the Mississippi river and public lands. The first session of the Lth congress will ever be memorable for its debates, the tariff discussion being the ablest ever had on that subject. It has shown more comprehensive grasp and more certain and detailed information among the members generally than has been heretofore displayed by even a few leaders. This has been both a school and an opportunity to the new man, and Mr. Stockade availed himself of the school and was equal to the opportunity. His speeches are marked by vigor, clearness, logic and points, and at times rise into impassioned and commanding eloquence as in the peroration of his tariff speech on May 5, and in his eulogy on the soldiers of the war. He has a strong sense of humor, tells a story well and has surprises and quaint terms in his speech which keep the listener on the qui vive.

His talking has not interfered with his work, since few constituencies have had so tireless and efficient a representative. In this long session which lasted ten months, he was absent only about a week and never missed a meeting of his committees—war claims and public lands. He voted on every proposition that came before the house. Out of the seven thousand cases before the war claims committee, he reported all from Mississippi and many from other states, and never had a report reversed by his committee, which is a most emphatic compliment to his industry, intelligence and sense of justice. He framed bills to remove the quarantine stations on the Mississippi coast; to hold a term of the federal court at Mississippi City; joint resolution to withdraw the public lands from sale; bills to build a bridge at Natchez across the Mississippi river; secured appropriations for the harbors and rivers in his district and bills giving pensions to many of his constituents.

His speech on the bill forfeiting land grants to railroads favored forfeiture for reasons clearly shown, whether the grants were earned out of time prescribed or not at all. He spoke also most effectively on the timber clause of the homestead bill. His speech on the claim of Mr. Poitevent, one of his constituents, was one of the ablest ever made on a private claim bill. He clearly exposed and unmercifully ridiculed the idea, which seems to have been the polar star of the Southern claims commission and still held by many republican members of congress, that a man in the South was necessary disloyal because a relative happened to have been a Confederate soldier, or because he was never hanged or had his house burnt over his head by the Confederate authorities. He illustrated by his own case a Confederate whose father, brothers and kin were all loyal Pennsylvanians. This speech let the light into many dark places and set Northern members to thinking. He put himself on record against extensive pleasure grounds for the few rich at the expense of the many poor, whether at Washington or in Yellowstone park, contending that the best use of the public lands is for homes for the people, and fields, woods and mines for their industry and enterprise. In his remarks upon the proposition to take the duty off of salt, he attacked the protection by the reductio ad absurdum and said that the protectionists proposed to help God and alter the plan of creation. All his speeches are full of crisp, solid sentences that stick in the memory and turn up handy for quotation.

He supported with energy the bill to create a department of agriculture. Showed that it was in no sense class legislation, and that the prosperity, wealth, and even life of the nation depended upon the farmers. This tribute to the honest farmers will be appreciated in Mississippi, which is essentially an agricultural state. Mr. Stockdale gave more study and thought, perhaps, to his tariff speech than to any other, for he realized that in that long array of able debaters and eloquent orators, if he would be heard at all, what he did say must be well said. His speech met the high expectation of his friends, was immediately recognized

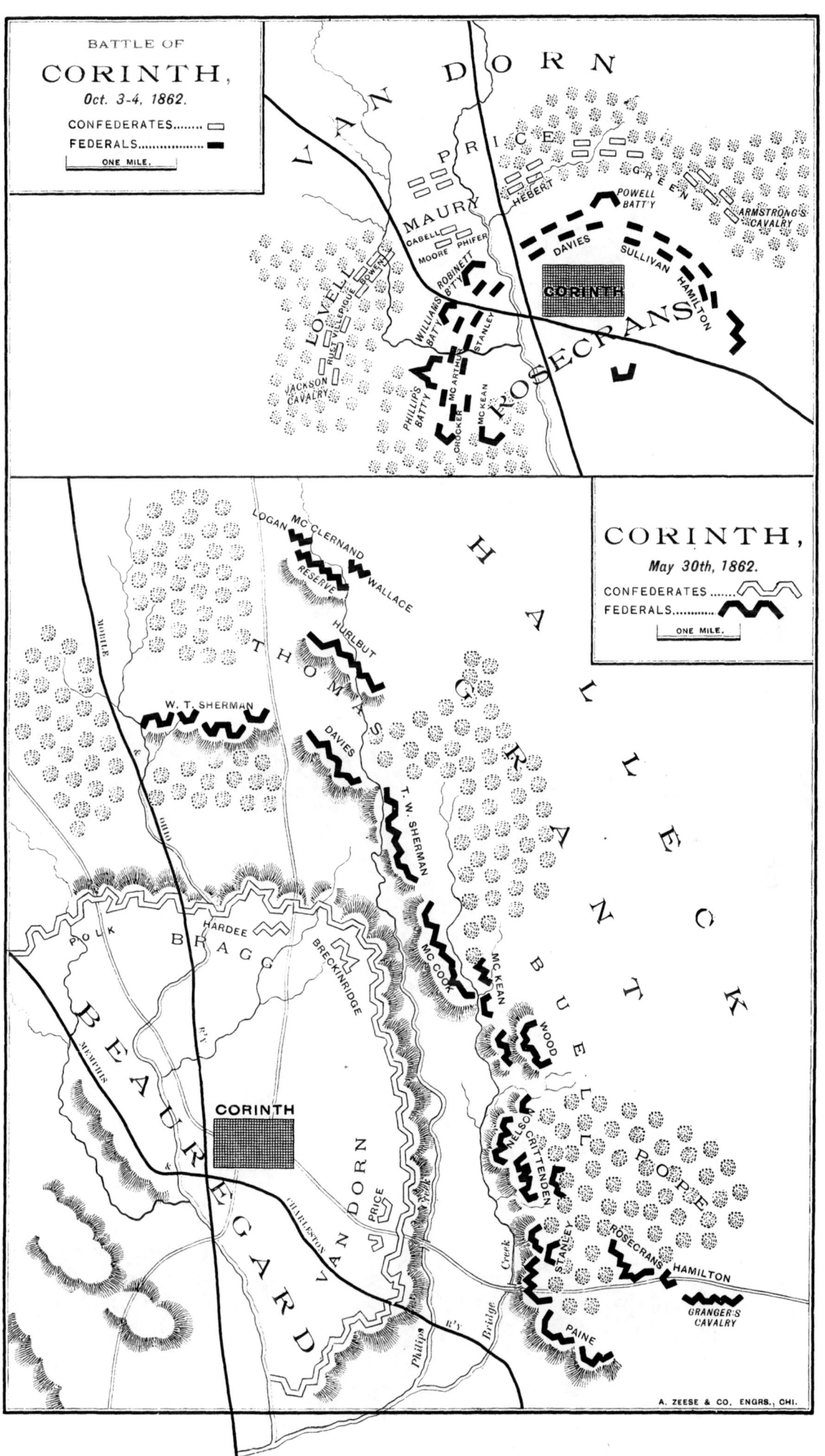

as a valuable contribution to the tariff literature, and is in great demand all over the Union by democratic clubs and speakers, and was praised in high terms by newspapers in New York, St. Louis, Detroit and elsewhere. The St. Louis *Globe-Democrat* said it was the first tariff speech by either party that clearly presented and advocated the right and interest of the negroes in tariff reform, showing that all they consumed was taxed too much and that they were still in servitude to the protected industries and needed another proclamation of emancipation before they could be free from the unjust imposition placed upon their hard earnings to enhance the wealth of the rich.

His speech on the Oklahoma bill is a masterpiece. It shows the speaker as student, lawyer and thinker, and completely answered the objections of the opposition. As a citizen he is public spirited, loves his country, state and town; as a public officer he is above suspicion, ever zealous for the right and alert to properly fill the high station to which he has been called. As a speaker he is interesting and forcible, and in society amiable and pleasing. He is a man of commanding presence, being six feet three inches in hight, and his splendid physique gives him a knightly bearing that commands both admiration and respect. Colonel Stockdale and his family reside at Summit, where they have a pleasant home, where they are considered, in many respects, the leaders of local society. Five children have blessed their union, two of whom died in infancy. One son and one daughter still survive to brighten Colonel and Mrs. Stockdale's home, and make lighter the cares and burdens of their lives. The Colonel is a loving and indulgent father, and when in his home, surrounded by his loved ones, forgets for a while the cares of a public station, and gives himself over to the enjoyment of domestic life.

Colonel Samuel Stockett, a representative citizen of Wilkinson county, settled in the county in 1801, entering from the government the plantation now known as Gretna Green, situated on the line of demarcation between the states of Louisiana and Mississippi. Upon this plantation, which is still in the possession of his descendants, he lived during his life, as a large planter, and most honored and liberal citizen. He became very prominent in the county and in military affairs, and was colonel of the militia of the county in 1812, which commission he held for some years. He was a man of fine education and conspicuous ability, a great reader and a thorough student. He was a native of Maryland, where he was born, February 12, 1775, and where he was reared and educated. He died in Wilkinson county, Aug. 17, 1822, and is buried in the family cemetery, on the Gretna Green plantation. He was descended from Sir Lewis Stockett, of St. Stephens parish, Kent county, England, who was born in 1558 and died in 1603. Capt. Thomas Stockett, a great-grandson of Sir Lewis Stockett, coming to Maryland in 1658, settling at Annapolis, and there was united in marriage to Mary Wells, and died in 1671, leaving one son, whose grandson was the father of Col. Samuel Stockett, the subject of this sketch. Col. Samuel Stockett, in company with several other members of the family, removed from Maryland to Davidson county, Tenn., about where the city of Nashville now stands. Colonel Samuel, however, remained only a short time, but before leaving, he married Elizabeth Johnson, daughter of Isaac Johnson and Mary Dunhand, and also a cousin of Postmaster general Cave Johnson. In 1801 Colonel Stockett, accompanied by his wife and her three brothers, Gov. Henry Johnson, Joseph Johnson and William Johnson, came to Mississippi, and Col. Samuel Stockett settled on what afterward became the plantation known as Gretna Green. The result of the union of Colonel Stockett and Elizabeth Johnson were the following six sons and three daughters: Mary Allen, born in Davidson county, Tenn., in 1801, come to Wilkinson county with her parents, married Joseph Smith of Maryland and died without leaving descendants, in 1885; Isaac

Johnson, born at Gretna Green in 1803, and died in 1803; Rachel Holliday, born at Gretna Green in 1805, married George Randolph, of Wilkinson county, and both died with yellow fever and without children in 1836; Joseph Johnson, born at Gretna Green in 1807, was educated in New Jersey, and was killed soon after his return from college, by the accidental discharge of his gun, in 1832; Sarah, born at Gretna Green in 1811, married Lorenzo Brown and died in 1851; William Noble, born at Gretna Green in 1813, and died in 1819. Samuel Henry, was born at Gretna Green in 1815. He was educated at Centenary college, and returned home and engaged in planting. He took great interest in the advancement of religion and was a member of the Methodist church. He was a steward in the Woodville Methodist church, and was very active in educational promotion and church work. He was a trustee in Centenary college, the Female institute at Jackson, La., and the Woodville Female seminary, and also a director in the West Feliciana railroad. He was a Royal Arch Mason. He married Lucy Elizabeth Holt, of Woodville, daughter of Dr. David Holt and Juliet White. To Samuel Henry was born eight children, four of whom lived to be grown, and who are now living with their mother. Samuel Henry died in 1871, and was laid to rest beside his ancestors. Thomas Galen, was born in Gretna Green in 1817 and died in 1879. He was educated at Centenary college and was one of the leading men of the county. He took some part in politics after the war, and was an extensive planter and a man of strong convictions. He first married Ellen Edwards, who died in 1844 with yellow fever, and by her had two sons and one daughter, all dying in infancy. He then married Mary Elizabeth Johnson, daughter of William Johnson and Elizabeth Randolph. She was a member of the Presbyterian church, in which she was very active. She was of a literary turn of mind, highly educated and had traveled a great deal. She lived for some years in Washington city, with her uncle Gov. Henry Johnson, who was then representing the state of Louisiana in the United States senate. She died in 1884, and was buried beside her husband. Isaac Johnson, was born at Gretna Green, July 19, 1819, and died March 1, 1870. Like his brothers he was educated at Centenary college, Louisiana, and followed planting for a livelihood. He took a lively interest in politics, was a strong states' rights democrat and a leading member of the Presbyterian church.

He married Mary Olivia McKenzie, daughter of Peter McKenzie and Charlotte Williams. Peter McKenzie came from Scotland originally, and had been educated at the celebrated University of Edinburgh, and became a prominent man of this county. His wife, Charlotte Williams, came from one of the old influential families of this state, she being a daughter of Daniel Williams and Miss Overton, of Tennessee, and a sister of Hon. Daniel Williams, Mississippi's first secretary of state. To Isaac Johnson and Mary Olivia were born eleven children, four of whom, Samuel Overton, Isaac Johnson, Mary Olivia and Effie Arlington, died unmarried; John, Mary Elizabeth, Joseph Smith, Kate, Henry Johnson and Charlotte Williams moved to Texas in 1872, and are now married and located at Fort Worth, in that state. Peter McKenzie, the second child born to Isaac Johnson Stockett and Mary Olivia McKenzie and their eldest living son, was born at the Gretna Green plantation, July 11, 1842, and was educated at Centenary college. While at college the Civil war broke out, so he came home and joined the Wilkinson rifles, Sixteenth Mississippi regiment, under Capt. Carnot Rosey, and was in all the battles participated in by his regiment, including all those bloody and desperate conflicts fought in northern Virginia. He was wounded in the seven days' fight around Richmond, and was disabled at the battle of Spottsylvania courthouse, May 12, 1864, after which he was made adjutant of the Eighteenth Louisiana cavalry, and commissioned by President Jefferson Davis. He was, for a third time, wounded in a skirmish at

Woodville, Miss., where he was in command of the advance of Bynum's battalion of cavalry. A great, but merited, honor was conferred on Mr. Stockett after returning from the army, by the Soldiers' Memorial association of Wilkinson county. He was chosen to write the biographies of all the soldiers who died or were killed in the late war from Wilkinson county. He has held the office of secretary since the organization of the association. This association has erected to the memory of their dead, on a beautiful lawn at Woodville, a bronze monument, that will ever stand as a fitting memorial of their memory and patriotic services. Mr. Stockett was married to Juliet Johnson, May 14, 1867. She is a daughter of William Johnson, Esq., and Elizabeth Randolph, late of Woodville, Miss. Mrs. Stockett was well educated, and is a lady of fine social graces and attainments. Mr. Stockett is a leading planter of this county, where he owns large landed interests, most of which were formerly owned by the older members of the family, all beautifully located and well improved. He is a democrat and has often been chosen to represent the county in the state, senatorial and congressional conventions. He has been for many years a member, and several times secretary, of the county democratic executive committee. Mr. and Mrs. Stockett are active members of the Presbyterian church at Woodville, Miss., of which he is an elder and clerk of the session. He has several times been a delegate to the meetings of the presbytery and synod, and was a delegate to the general assembly of the Presbyterian church, that met at Vicksburg in 1884, and was chosen alternate in 1890. Mr. and Mrs. Stockett now reside on their Rosedale plantation and have several children, as follows: William Johnson, born February 14, 1868, and was educated at Chamberlain-Hunt academy and the University of Mississippi, graduating at the latter institution in 1889; he was admitted to the bar in 1890, and is now a practicing lawyer; Samuel Overton, born January 6, 1870, also attended the University of Mississippi; he is a successful planter in his native county; Thomas Galen, born April 29, 1872, and attended Chamberlain-Hunt academy; he is at present at home with his parents; Elizabeth Randolph, born January 7, 1877, and died September 8, 1881; she was a bright and beautiful little girl.

Robert N. Stockton, of Smithville P. O., Monroe county, was born in Madison county, Ala., February, 1814. His parents are William and Sarah (Marez) Stockton. William Stockton was reared in Stockton valley, in east Tennessee, a tract of land deriving its name from that of his family, and was a farmer and merchant all his life. His wife was a native of Logan county, Ky. Both were members of the Cumberland Presbyterian church. Mr. Stockton, who saw service in the Creek Indian war, came to Mississippi in 1830, and moved on the farm where his son Robert now lives, in 1831, where he died July 27, 1833. He was a prominent Mason. His widow married Rev. Mr. Weaver, and died in 1878. Robert N. Stockton's early life was spent in farming, a practical preparation for the planter's life which he has ever led since he was sixteen years and four months of age. He has held the office of supervisor and was bailiff for fourteen years. During the late war he was a member of company B, of the Third Mississippi battalion, under command of Lieutenant Bergin. He was in the service one year and was discharged on account of sickness. He is a prominent Mason, and member of the Blue lodge No. 165, of Amory. He is one of the most successful farmers in the county, and owns about nine hundred acres of well improved land, all in one body. He was married December 31, 1844, to Mary J. Baldwin, and they have had thirteen children, named as follows: Sarah S., Affienca A., Robert C., Josephine, Amelia, Silas G., William L., Dancy M., Mary V., Nathaniel M., Fannie E., Jane V., and John C. B., who died in December, 1878, aged twenty-two years. Mr. Stockton has led an honorable, upright life and has been more than successful financially, and the same may be said of his sons who are old enough to take active part in the duties of life. He is passing his declining years in the quiet enjoyment of the fruits of his industry, held in high esteem by his large circle of friends, and loved and honored by his family.

William L. Stockton, son of Robert N. Stockton, was born in Monroe county, in 1847. His father was one of the pioneers of this section of the country, and his biographical sketch appears elsewhere in this work. In 1870 Mr. Stockton married Melissa Tubb, of Monroe county, and to them have been born nine children, named as follows: Edward, Mary E., Mattie B., Robert N., Imogene, William A., Grover Cleveland, Lockridge and Lucian L., all of whom are living. Mr. Stockton is in no sense a public man, but he is enterprising and successful, and one of the most helpful men in Monroe county.

Walter Stokes, merchant and planter, Canton, Miss., who is one of the prominent business men and successful planters of Madison county, was born in Yazoo county, Miss., on the 5th of May, 1861, and is of English descent. His father, E. A. Stokes, was a native of the Palmetto state, and his mother, Sallie (Taylor) Stokes, was a native of North Carolina. The paternal grandfather, Joseph Stokes, was born in South Carolina, and the maternal grandfather, J. A. Taylor, was a native of the Old North state. E. A. Stokes, father of subject, came to Mississippi at an early day and settled in Madison county, where he has been engaged in planting since. Of the nine children born to his marriage, Walter was the eldest in order of birth. The latter passed his boyhood days in Mississippi, and was educated in both the public and private schools of that state. When seventeen years of age he entered the Mississippi college at Clinton, remained there three years, and afterward, in 1879-80, entered the state university at Oxford. The last named year he took a course in the Eastman Business college, Poughkeepsie, N. Y. He is now the owner of eleven hundred acres of land, has eight hundred acres under cultivation, and in connection with his brother, under the firm title of Stokes Bros., is engaged in merchandising, carrying a stock of goods valued at $3,000 and doing an annual business of $20,000. Mr. Stokes was married in 1888 to Miss Eugenia Atkinson, who was born in Mississippi, and whose parents, W. H. and M. B. Atkinson, were natives of Mississippi. Mr. and Mrs. Stokes have one child, Eugenia. Mr. Stokes began the battle of life for himself with no means, and by his industry and push has made a very creditable start. He advocates the principles of the democratic party and is enterprising and public spirited.

Adolphus Stone, Eudora, Miss., occupies a position in the history of De Soto county, that entitles him to a record in this volume. His ancestors were people of great integrity of character and much force and ability, and these traits have found ready expression in this member of the present generation. He was born in Chatham county, N. C., February 7, 1846, being the youngest of a family of three children. His parents, Carney P. and Delilah (Jenkins) Stone, were also natives of North Carolina. The father was an extensive planter and a large slave-holder before the war; he is still living and holds a prominent position in the community. The paternal grandparents were John and Betsey Stone, natives of Virginia and North Carolina respectively. John Stone was one of the wealthiest planters in North Carolina. He went to the state a very poor man, but at the time of his death he was immensely wealthy. Adolphus Stone passed his boyhood and youth amidst the scenes of his birth. He attended the private schools of the neighborhood until 1864, and then entered the military school at Hillsboro. But the pressure of war finally brought an end to this advantage, and he with many others was deprived of what is the right of every one brought into this world, the highest education which he is capable of receiving. At the age of twenty-four years he bade farewell to the parental roof and went out to seek his fortune in his own way. He had a small capital and this was invested in land. To-day he owns six hundred and forty acres of land, two hundred and fifty of which he has placed under cultivation. This plantation lies one mile south of Eudora, is well improved, and is in every way a delightful home. With that hospitality characteristic of the true Southerner, visitors are always welcome to this pleasant retreat. Mr. Stone was united in marriage December 2, 1890, to Miss Maud L. Troutman, who was born in Indiana, a daughter of Henry D. and Nancy J. (Nash) Troutman. Mr. and Mrs. Troutman came from Kentucky and Indiana, respectively. The Nash family were among the first settlers of Tennessee, and the city of Nashville was named in honor of them. Our subject was in the late Civil war; he enlisted in 1864 in the Fifth North Carolina cavalry, doing service to the end of the conflict. He is a member of the Knights of Honor. Politically he affiliates with the democratic party, but takes no part in the action of that body beyond the casting of his suffrage. Mrs. Stone is a worthy member of the Methodist Episcopal church.

Edward H. Stone, merchant and planter, Canton, Miss. Prominent among the successful business men and popular citizens of Madison county stands the name of Edward H. Stone, who is a native born resident of the state, born in Madison county on October 8, 1851. He was the third of five children born to John and Eliza J. (Cohea) Stone, the father a native of Virginia and the mother of Tennessee. John Stone was a merchant in the early part of his days, but at the time of his death, in 1857, he was engaged in the hotel business. He erected the first business house in Canton, Miss. The maternal grandparents, Perry and Mary Cohea, were natives of Tennessee. The grandfather Cohea came to Mississippi when it was a territory, and assisted in removing the Indians from that state. The family is one of the oldest in the history of the state. Edward H. Stone passed his boyhood and youth in Mississippi, and secured a fair education in that state. At the tender age of twelve years he was obliged to start out for himself, and all his property has been obtained by hard work and good management. He is a man of more than ordinary ability and is shrewd and clear-headed in his business. Mr. Stone is a member of the Knights of Honor, and ever extends a willing and liberal hand to further all good movements. He was married in 1884 to Miss Mary I. Yellowlly, a native of Mississippi. To Mr. and Mrs. Stone have been born three children: Edward Y., John W. and Alma.

James Stone, attorney, Batesville, Miss. Mr. Stone's grandfather, William E. Stone, was originally from the bluegrass regions of Kentucky, but was one of the very first settlers of Panola county, Miss., where he was one of the prominent planters. He did a great deal toward the development of the county in his day, and was among the foremost to assist in all worthy enterprises. He died about 1865, at the age of eighty-five years. His son, William E. Stone, was a native also of Kentucky, and was married in that state to another native Kentuckian, Miss Elizabeth McCoy. They came to Mississippi, when this state was very sparsely settled, and there William E. became a successful agriculturist. He was a commissioned officer in the Confederate army, and was a brave and faithful soldier. He was a very strong democrat but never made himself conspicuous in politics. His death occured in 1888. His marriage resulted in the birth of one child, James Stone, who was born in Panola county, Miss., on the 29th of August, 1856. The latter attained his growth in his native county, but received his education in the military college of Frankfort, Ky., graduating in 1876. He soon after entered the law department of Oxford university, but on account of failing health left school at the end of a few months. He was subsequently admitted to the bar, and in 1880 opened an office in Batesville, where he has since practiced successfully. In 1890 he entered a partnership with P. H. Lowry, a promising young attorney at

Batesville. Mr. Stone is extensively interested in farming and now owns two thousand acres of land, of which six hundred acres are under the plow. He also has a well equipped office and a handsome residence in Batesville. He was married in 1879 to Rosamond Alston, a native of Mississippi, and a daughter P. S. Alston, of Memphis, Tenn. They have two children: William E., and James. Though a young man Mr. Stone is an able member of the bar, and is one of the foremost men of the county. He is pleasant and social and a gentleman one delights to meet, for he is not wrapped up in himself, but on the contrary is interested in his fellowman and all that is going on around him. Socially he is a member of the Knights of Honor and the American Legion of Honor. Mrs. Stone is a member of the Methodist church.

The Rev. J. B. Stone, who is well-known throughout Lee and adjoining counties, was born in South Carolina in 1831, and is a son of the Rev. Tilman and Eliza (Boyd) Stone. His father was a minister, teacher, and farmer. He was born in Spartanburg, S. C., in 1806, and was a son of William and Frances Stone. He was reared in his native state, and in 1827, was married. Eleven children were born of the union, eight of whom are living: J. B., William M., J. L., Nancy J., now Mrs. Cheek; Margaret C., now Mrs. Lloyd; Rev. Samuel C., of Memphis; Richard W., and Hilliard B. The father died in 1849, but the mother survived until 1873. Mr. Stone was a member of the I. O. O. F. The youth of our subject was not an ideal one, but his circumstances were such that the best that was in him was developed. His education was acquired entirely through his own efforts, and he did not yield until he felt that he had received the mental discipline necessary for theological study. In 1857 he entered the ministry, and has since devoted his time to preaching the gospel. He has been a Methodist minister for thirty-five years, filling circuits, stations and districts, in the Alabama, Mobile and North Mississippi conferences. Mr. Stone's first marriage took place in Monroe county, Miss., in 1857, when he was united to Miss Rebecca Mosley, a daughter of E. B. Mosley. One child was born to them, Bessie, who is now Mrs. Buder, of Columbia, Miss. Mrs. Stone died in 1864, and Mr. Stone was married to Miss Mary B. Koger in 1865. She is a daughter of Thomas J. and Bilsey Koger, and a native of Noxubee county, Miss., born in 1847. Her grandfather, Hon. Joseph Koger, was in his day one of the most prominent men in the politics of South Carolina and Mississippi; being a member of the state senate of each state for several years. Her father, Rev. T. J. Koger, a graduate of Randolph-Macon college, practiced law for a short time, then went into the ministry, was a member of the general conference that met in Nashville in 1858, and was killed in the battle at Perryville, Ky., October 8, 1862. Five children were born of the second marriage: Jefferson K., who was educated at Emory and Henry college; Lila, wife of A. D. Rogers; Clara A., Mary C., and Ruth C. Mr. Stone is a woman of more than ordinary mental endowments, and has improved all the opportunities that have come to her lot. In 1884 she was elected principal of the Verona Female college, a position she has filled with great credit to herself, and to the best interests of the institution. She was elected corresponding secretary of the Woman's Missionary society of the North Mississippi conference in 1880, which position she still continues to occupy. Mr. Stone enlisted in the Forty-third Mississippi regiment as chaplain, and served until the end of the war.

Rev. Samuel C. Stone, M. A., minister and planter, Memphis, Tenn., was born in Monroe county, Miss., on the 22d of November, 1845, and is the seventh in order of birth of ten children born to Tilman and Eliza (Boyd) Stone, natives of the Palmetto state. The father came to Mississippi in 1840, and there passed a life of usefulness as a local minister in the Methodist church. Though a slaveowner he was very kind to them and they were devoted to him. He died suddenly in 1847 in Marshall county, Miss., in a few hours after having preached an excellent sermon. He was an esteemed and honored minister in his denomination and left seven children, who are all prominent in their different callings. One son, Rev. J. B. Stone, is a minister of great usefulness in north Mississippi and has been presiding elder for twenty years, having laid himself a willing sacrifice upon the altar of the church of his choice. The maternal grandfather, Joseph Boyd, was of Irish parentage, and was a Presbyterian minister of rare attainments and unusual ability; the Boyd family being noted for their energy, integrity, piety and their activity as protestants against the state church of England. The paternal grandfather was of Welsh origin. Rev. Samuel C. Stone was reared in Mississippi and educated at Summerville, Ala., where he completed his education in 1870. Since that time he has been in the ministry of the Methodist church, and after becoming eligible to elder's orders he was at once put in charge of a district where his administrative ability became a matter of comment throughout the conference. He has been in charge of important stations of this conference from that time up to the present. In addition to his ministerial duties he has, with striking ability, carried on business enterprises and is now the owner of four different places, consisting of not less than two thousand acres of land located in the richest portion of the delta. He has seven hundred acres under cultivation and is rapidly clearing more, having himself put most of the improvements on his several places. He is also the owner of a neat residence in Memphis, Tenn., valued at about $7,000, and he is now engaged in the real estate and brokerage business in that city, in connection with chief manager of the firm, a position to which he has recently been elected. Mr. Stone was married in 1874 to Miss Bettie D. Partee, a native of Mississippi and only daughter of S. B. and Martha (Douglass) Partee, natives of Tennessee, and descendants of two of the prominent families of the state. Mr. and Mrs. Stone became the parents of three children: Joseph B., Samuel C. (deceased) and Hilliard Partee. Although Mr. Stone educated himself and was obliged to start out to fight life's battles empty handed, his work, both in the ministry and in secular pursuits has been greatly blessed and no man in the state has achieved so much under similar circumstances. He stands in the front ranks as a minister of his church in north Mississippi and his ability for usefulness extends in every direction and into adjoining states, while his name is associated with every enterprise for the advancement of the interests of his country and for the promotion of the honor and welfare of his native state. He is a man of pleasing address and is an extremely interesting speaker and a perfect type of a Southern gentleman. He is at present residing in Memphis, where he is educating his children and where he is manager of the furniture establishment that bears his name. Mr. Stone, wherever he has gone, has in a most signal manner made himself felt as a temperance worker and a leader in the cause of temperance of marked ability, having through many a hotly contested fight led his church or party to victory. Notwithstanding the fine business qualifications of which he is possessed in so high a degree, he takes no credit to himself, but points to the sacred memory of his sainted mother, recognizes her influence as the mainspring of all of his achievements; next to his affectionate sisters, who live to bless and encourage him, and with a becoming modesty and pride points to his thoroughly accomplished and highly polished wife, who has, while he was struggling against adversity and opposition, until he is now paying taxes on over $50,000 worth of real estate, situated in different towns and states, been a helpmeet to him indeed, and would give her all the glory, pointing to her as his unfailing guide, ever faithful, loyal and loving and possessed of the grandest and most praiseworthy and honorable of characteristics, standing in her presence with uncovered head. Mrs. Stone was four years a student in the State Female college, going from there to Nazareth, at Bardstown, Ky., where she received her diploma. Mr. Stone has three times been called to the presidency of important schools and of two colleges, but declined such honors.

J. H. Stone is a prominent planter, whose postoffice address is Tremont, Itawamba county, Miss. He is the owner of two thousand acres of land, and has a fine gristmill and one of the largest steam cottongins in the county, located at Tremont, about ten miles east of Fulton. His is one of several families of Stones living in this neighborhood. He is the son of D. J. and Parmelia A. (Bethany) Stone, both natives of Alabama, and he was born in that state in 1834. He removed with his parents to Mississippi, when young, and was reared to an agricultural life, and also given fair educational advantages. As his father had done before him, he chose the career of a planter, in which he has been quite successful. He was married in 1859 to Florence, a daughter of John and Eliza Cowden, and a native of Alabama, where she was born in 1842. Mr. and Mrs. Stone have had eleven children, of whom ten are living: Mary O., Josephine L., Julia M., Orville T., Walter D., Lucien Q., John H., William G., Galusha C. and Florence E. In May, 1862, Mr. Stone enlisted in Colonel Gordon's regiment and served with it during the war, receiving his discharge at Columbus, Miss. Active in local and state politics, he is a stanch democrat, and has twice been elected by his party to the office of sheriff of Itawamba county. Except during the time when he was in the war, he has been postmaster since 1859 at Tremont, where he lives, and still holds that office. He is a master and Royal Arch Mason, and he and his wife are members of the Methodist Episcopal Church South. He is everywhere recognized as a liberal contributor to churches and schools, and other laudable enterprises, having for their object the benefit of the community in which he lives. Dr. D. A. Stone, a brother of our subject, was born in Alabama in 1820, and married Jennie E. Ward, a native of Alabama, and who has one child, named Casta B. He has long been a member of the Methodist Episcopal church, and has been a practicing physician in this neighborhood. G. P. Stone, another brother, is a planter living in his near vicinity. He was born in 1836, and married Elizabeth A., a daughter of Rev. S. Mayfield, of this state. He was a soldier in the Confederate army for a short time during the late war. He is the owner of about ten hundred acres of land. It is a source of much gratification to Mr. Stone that his brothers here mentioned are good democrats and good citizens.

John Marshall Stone. Among the governors of Mississippi there has been none more popular with the people, who stood higher in their confidence and esteem, or who was more able, zealous and conscientious in the discharge of official duties than the present incumbent, John M. Stone. He is a native of Tennessee, where he was born April 30, 1830, being the second child of Asher and Judith (Royall) Stone, who were born in the state of Virginia, in which state their ancestors were prominent people. Asher Stone was born in Pittsylvania county, November 1, 1806, and Judith, his wife, in Halifax county, March 12, 1811. Asher's father was a native of the Old Dominion and of English ancestry. Judith Royall was a daughter of Nathaniel Royall, one of the old families of that state. Asher Stone died in Carroll county, Tenn., September 20, 1841, to which place he had emigrated at an early day. His widow still survives him and resides in Chester county, Tenn. There were born to them nine children: Elizabeth (the subject of this sketch), Thomas, Isaac, Rebecca, Samuel, Robert, Berry and William C. Samuel, Robert and William C. were killed in battle, fighting for the establishment of the Confederacy. The parents were not wealthy, and consequently John M. was early indoctrinated in the principles of industry and economy, which in the future were to mold his character. His struggles in early life for an education brought him into sympathy with the masses, for whose elevation and betterment he has labored during his long public career. It was not his good fortune to be sent to college, but he acquired a good education by his assiduous attention to his studies. Often the blaze of the pine knot would light up the pages of his books, over which he could be seen poring far into the night. Thus by pursuing his studies and teaching school, he managed to support himself and secure an education which enabled him in after years to discharge the high public duties entrusted to him. In August, 1855, he removed from Tennessee and located at Eastport, Miss., where he engaged with a business house until 1859. At this time the Memphis & Charleston railroad being completed, he was tendered the position of station agent at Iuka, which he accepted and filled with credit until the breaking out of the late war. Believing that his services were due to the state of his adoption, he enlisted in the Confederate service, and the early days of April, 1861, found him at the head of company K, Second Mississippi infantry. From Iuka the company moved to Corinth, the place of rendezvous. About the 1st of May his command was ordered to Lynchburg, where it remained for a short time, and then moved on to Harper's Ferry, where it became a part of the Third brigade, which was then under command of Brigadier-General Bee. His first experience in active warfare was at the battle of Manassas, where his regiment was distinguished for its gallant conduct, and where his company suffered heavily, having several killed and wounded. After this battle the command moved to Fredericksburg, where they rested, and then went on to Dumphreys, at which place they went into winter quarters. In the early spring they were ordered to Fredericksburg, and after some maneuvering about there, moved on the Yorktown. There the troops were organized, and in the reorganization, April 10, 1862, Captain Stone was elected colonel of the second regiment. This promotion was but a just recognition of his efficient services as a soldier, and of the gallant manner in which he had discharged his duties as captain of company K. Soon after the reorganization the command moved up about Richmond, from which place it was subsequently ordered to Staunton to join Jackson, who was moving around in the rear of McClellan. His next engagement was at Gaines' Mill, June 27, where, with his regiment, he had some hard fighting. After the battle of Malvern Hill, in which he participated, the command marched to near Richmond, where it went into camp. Movements of the armies brought on another battle at Manassas, in which Colonel Stone with his regiment participated, August, 1862. After this fight his command moved back to camp near Richmond, where the troops were rebrigaded and Joseph R. Davis placed in command. This brigade subsequently became known as Davis' brigade. Before returning to Richmond this brigade was in the engagements at Boonesboro and Sharpsburg (Antietam).

Early in the spring the Colonel with his command was in the field in active movement to meet the advances of the Federal troops, and was in several actions, among which was that of Bristoe Station. For a time, also, he was on detached service. When General Lee began his movement northward into Maryland, Colonel Stone's brigade, under command of Brigadier-General Heath, was ordered to join him. This offensive movement of the Confederate army brought on the memorable battle of Gettysburg, in which the Second Mississippi regiment was hotly engaged. This regiment was stationed on the left and was opposed by General Reynold's forces. Colonel Stone gallantly led his regiment in the fight, which lost heavily in killed, wounded, missing and captured. He also was wounded in the side by a piece of shell while leading his troops. This was during the first day's fight and prevented him from engaging any further in the battle. He was able, however, to witness the third day's fight, in which his regiment was in constant action, it being placed immediately to the left of Pickett's division, and was conspicuous in that famous charge for the possession of Round Top. He was near the center of action, but being unable on account of his wound to remain longer, was returning from the field to the hospital when he was again wounded. On the return of Lee's army from the fatal field of Gettysburg Colonel Stone was engaged in a sharp fight at Falling Waters. Returning, the army went into winter quarters at Mine Run, where it remained until the spring of 1864. When activities commenced, Colonel Stone was again ready and in the field, and commanding Davis' brigade participated in the battle of the Wilderness, fighting with Longstreet. He was also in the battle of Spottsylvania and all the engagements of that campaign. At the close of the above mentioned battle General Longstreet rode up to Colonel Stone and asked of him his name. Upon being told he said "Colonel Stone, you have won to-day the stars of a major-general." It is known that he could have had this appointment, but it necessitated his leaving, not only his regiment but the Mississippi troop, which he could not bear to do, and so declined the promotion. Subsequently his troops were ordered to the defense of Petersburg, where he remained in command until the evacuation of that place, except when he was called out to meet a feint of General Grant. This was at the time when the Grub mine was sprung. His command went into winter quarters at Hatchers Run. In January, 1865, he was granted a leave of absence to return to his home in Mississippi and upon his return to join his regiment, which was then near Salisbury, N. C., he was taken prisoner by General Stoneman. He had taken back with him some recruits, and at the above named place he was joined by some troops from Georgia, being shortly after confronted by forces under General Stoneman, and had (the governor says) one of the hardest little fights he was in during the entire war. The enemy numbered about four hundred, mostly belonging to a Kentucky regiment, while he only had about forty men actively engaged. He, with most of his force, was taken prisoner. They were first taken to the mountains of Kentucky, then to Camp Chase, Ohio, from which place they were afterward moved to Johnson's island, where, on July 25, 1865, they were discharged. While in the mountainous regions of Kentucky the news came of the assassination of President Lincoln. This created an intense and bitter feeling among the soldiers who guarded them and who were under the command of Colonel Kirk, of Kentucky, and the prisoners were unjustly subjected to very hard treatment.

The Confederate army having surrendered, and the cause for which he had so gallantly fought, having failed, Colonel Stone returned to his home at Iuka, Miss., and again took up the peaceful pursuits of life, beginning at his old station which he had vacated for the field four years before. Though the cause for which he fought was a lost one, he had the consolation of having done his duty, and of carrying with him to his peaceful retreat the record of a brave, gallant and able officer. Every soldier who was with him was enthusiastic in his praises, and ever found him, whether in the hottest battles or dress parade, the same courteous gentleman. In 1866, Colonel Stone was elected mayor, and subsequently treasurer of Tishomingo county. In 1869 the state held her election under the reconstruction act, and Mr. Stone, having been placed in nomination for the state senate, was elected for a term of four years, being one of the few democrats to be elected, a position to which he was re-elected in 1873. He filled this position with satisfaction to his constituents and with eminent credit to himself. In 1872 he was a candidate for congress against Lamar, but did not secure the nomination. In 1876 he was chosen president pro tem. of the senate. During this time, Governor Ames resigned and Mr. Stone, by virtue of his office as president pro tempore of the senate (Lieutenant Governor Davis having been impeached), succeeded to the governorship. He was installed as governor, March 27, 1876. In 1877 he was, by a large and popular vote, elected to the position for a term of four years. In 1881 he was a candidate for re-election, but was defeated by Robert Lowry, who was elected and re-elected, serving in all a term of eight years. Governor Stone retired from the duties of his office, carrying with him the love and confidence of the people and returned to his home at Iuka, where he began devoting himself to agricultural pursuits. In 1884 he was appointed railroad commissioner by Governor Lowry, the duties of which he discharged with his usual careful business methods. In 1889, when the campaign opened, he announced himself as a candidate for governor, and quietly and in a dignified manner presented himself before the people for their support. This was easy to secure, for his administration as governor had been popular, clean and efficient. The people responded to his call with an enthusiasm that would gratify the pride or ambition of any man, and he was nominated and elected. By the provisions of the new constitution his term of office was extended two years and will expire in January, 1896. Governor Stone was married at Iuka, Miss., in 1872, to Miss Mary G., daughter of James and Elizabeth J. (Mason) Coman. The issue of this union were two children, James Marshall and Mary E., both of whom died young. He has adopted three of his brother's children: Anna, Jennie and Maggie, whom he is carefully rearing. Governor Stone is a member of the Masonic order, a member of the Grand lodge, and has held various important positions in this society. He is also a member of the Knights and Ladies of Honor. Physically he is all that could be desired, for he stands full six feet, is as straight as an arrow, with a well-knit, muscular frame. He has a full head of hair, now turning gray, and wears a mustache only. He looks at you square out of his steel gray eyes, and in a manner that immediately secures your confidence and attention. He has a firm mouth, and an open, yet decided expression, that establishes him, every inch, a man of nerve and great decision of character. To this may be added a genial disposition and a courteous, military bearing. Governor Stone possesses great executive ability; this, with his principles of rigid economy and his financial skill, has enabled him largely to reduce the debt of the state and place her on the high road to prosperity. Though now in his third administration as governor, no breath of scandal has ever touched him; he still holds the love and confidence of the people of the state and it is thought that he has not an enemy within its borders. Hamlet says: " Give me that man that is not passion's slave, and I will wear him in my heart's core, ay, in my heart of hearts." So the people of the state feel in regard to their governor, and it may be truthfully said that he is one of the ablest and most popular governors that ever sat in the executive chair of the state of Mississippi.

Rev. Lewis Maxwell Stone, Shuqualak, Miss. The subject of this sketch was born in Noxubee county, Miss., July 6, 1844. His parents were Col. J. M. and Mrs. Sarah M. Stone, who had born to them twelve children—eight sons and four daughters—Lewis Maxwell being the youngest son. The father was a native of Georgia, the mother, of South Carolina, and the daughter of Mr. John Bradley. They lived for several years in Florida, immediately after their marriage, moving later to Mobile, Ala., where they resided for some years. In 1843 they moved to their prairie farm in Noxubee county, Miss., and the second year, following, they removed to Pickens county, Ala. The early boyhood of Lewis was spent on the Stone-ferry farm near Fairfield. In his fourteenth year he entered the Springhill academy under Prof. A. C. Boken, his family having moved into the locality of Springhill, for the benefit of the school. Eighteen months later the Civil war broke out. In the fall of 1861, young Mr. Stone entered the army, joining the company raised by Capt. Newton N. Davis, which proceeded to Mobile, Ala., and connected itself with the Twenty-fourth Alabama regiment, under command of Col. W. A. Buck. The young man was in the active service until his health gave way, when he was assigned to post duty at Columbus, Miss., where he surrendered in 1865. Immediately after the war, he decided to go to work, to make money enough to finish his education. He taught school with Professor Baker, at Artesia, two sessions, taking private lessons as part pay for his services. He taught the school as principal two sessions following, and that to the great satisfaction of his patrons. He then, in association with young Frank Critz, a graduate of the University of Mississippi (and later the honored chancellor of the fifth district), started a male school at Starkville. Mr. Stone, after a successful beginning of this enterprise, turned it over to his associate and went to Marion, Ala., where he entered the Hawood college. Here he stood high in his classes as a hard and apt student. His education receiving its finishing touch in this famous school of Alabama, he entered upon the work of the ministry as pastor of the Baptist church at Gainesville, Ala. He was ordained to the ministry by his home church at Springhill the fall he entered college. His pastorate was a successful one for the two years he served here. In 1872 he was married to Miss Mary High, of Gainesville. They have three children living: Sallie Leslie, Edna Montgomery and Edward Sholl. In 1873 he was called to take charge of the Meridian Baptist Female college located in the city of Meridian. Three years of vigorous and successful labor were given to this school, which greatly enlarged its patronage. A general depression coming upon the city, Professor Stone was induced to remove to Starkville and join Dr. T. G. Sellers in the proprietorship and teaching of the Female institute there. Two years later, 1877, he was tendered the presidency of the Gainesville (Ala.) Female college, the place of his first public service and of his marriage. Here he had an unexpected degree of success in building up and commanding a fine patronage. In 1879 the branch road of the Mobile & Ohio railroad was abandoned. This meant ruin to Gainesville as a business place. Professor Stone at once decided to change locations. He came to Shuqualak, Miss.—on the Mobile & Ohio railroad —and with some aid from the citizens founded the Shuqualak Female college, of which he has been proprietor and president for eleven years. In the true sense of the word, Professor Stone is a selfmade man. The college for young ladies he founded and presided over for eleven years is a standing monument to his indomitable will, force of character and good judgment. This school has worthily won a place alongside the oldest and best colleges of its class in the state. It commands a large patronage from abroad, including many counties of its own state and other states. The conduct of the college is noted for its splendid system in all particulars. It is doing a wonderful amount of good in developing the educational interest of the state on a high plane of religious morals, economy and practicability. Professor Stone is a modest, unobtrusive, polished gentleman, and must be well known to be fully appreciated for all he is worth. His father, now in his eighty-eighth year, and who enjoys a fine flow of spirits and is stout and healthy, lives with him in the college. His mother died in 1881, in her sixty-seventh year.

Few, if any, industrial or professional pursuits have, within the last few years, made such rapid strides as that of the profession of medicine, and among the leading physicians of Washington county, Miss., who have availed themselves of all new ideas and put them in practice is Dr. Owen W. Stone. He was born in Boone county, Mo., on the 8th of May, 1850, to Caleb S. and Ann W. (Wilson) Stone, both of whom were born on bluegrass soil. Caleb S. Stone was a true Southerner in every sense of the word, and upon the opening of the Civil war, in 1861, cast his fortunes with the Confederacy, and for valiant service was promoted to the rank of colonel. At the battle of Pea Ridge, Ark., he was captured and retained a prisoner for six months, at the end of which time he was released. For further history of this gentleman see sketch of Captain Stone of Jackson. Dr. Owen W. Stone was reared in Missouri, and received his education in the State university at Columbia. In 1872 he began reading medicine, soon after which he graduated from the Alabama Medical college of Mobile, and in 1875 began practicing on Deer creek. At the early age of twelve years he began making his own way in the world, leaving school to take upon himself the duties of a laborer, in order to support his mother while his father was in the army, their property having been swallowed up in security debts, so that they were in very poor circumstances even at the opening of the war. He had to surmount many difficulties and disappointments during his career, but has battled manfully against adversity, and is now reaping the reward of a useful and well-spent life, in the shape of a substantial income and the respect and esteem of all who know him. He owns two hundred and forty acres of land on Deer creek, two hundred of which are under cultivation, and since owning the place it has been improved to the extent of about $3,000. Dr. Stone was married, in 1881, to Miss Mary Holt, a native of Mississippi, and a daughter of Dr. A. C. and Mary W. (William) Holt, both of whom are Mississippians, the former being one of the leading physicians of New Orleans until his death, which occurred in 1881. The union of Dr. Stone has resulted in the birth of four children, the eldest two of whom died in infancy, Orville Walker and Eleanor, living. Dr. Stone is a member of the Christian church, and his wife is a Presbyterian. He belongs to the K. of H., the K. of P., and has been deeply interested in the progress of both orders. He has been a resident of Washington county since he was fifteen years of age, and is now the health officer of the county. He went through the yellow-fever epidemic of 1878, volunteering as a physician for the city and, while doing heroic service in that capacity, was stricken with the malady himself. He is a finely educated gentleman, and is a credit to the profession of which he is a member.

As an example of the usefulness and prominence to which men of character and determination will attain, we have but to chronicle the life of Capt. W. W. Stone, who is the intelligent and efficient auditor of the state of Mississippi. He is a descendant of a long line of illustrious ancestry, and worthily fills his position in this line. The Stones originally came from England to America in the seventeenth century, one brother pitching his tent in Connecticut, another in Maryland and another in Virginia. James Stone, the paternal grandfather of Captain Stone, was a Virginian and a pioneer settler of Madison county, Ky. His father also settled in this county, and, in time, there became a large settlement of the Stones near Boonesboro. Caleb S. Stone, son of James and father of Capt. W. W. Stone, was born on bluegrass soil, but in 1830 left the home of his birth to seek his fortune in the then wilds of Missouri, and after merchandising in Columbia for a few years, he turned his attention to tilling the soil and became wealthy. He interested himself in politics to some extent, became a prominent and leading democrat of Boone county (of the Calhoun and Jacksonian stripe), but never aspired to any prominent political position. At the opening of the Civil war he was appointed adjutant-general of the Missouri state guards, and while serving in this capacity he was captured at Elkhorn, and before being exchanged, in September, 1862, he was kept for some time in the prison at Alton, Ill. He served in the quartermaster's department during the remainder of the war, after which he returned to his home at Columbia, Mo., where he died in 1873, at the age of sixty-three years. He was married to Miss Ann Wilson, a native of Kentucky, who removed to Missouri when young, and she survived her husband until 1883, both being worthy members of the Christian church at the time of their deaths. She was also descended from English ancestry and one of the F. F. V.'s, her people having settled in the Old Dominion as early as 1624. Through the Woodsons, with whom she was closely related, she was connected with the noted Jefferson and Randolph families. Capt. W. W. Stone, the fifth of their twelve children, was born in Boone county, Mo., July 20, 1840, and received his initiatory training in a log schoolhouse in

Columbia. He afterward fitted himself for the active duties of life in the University of Missouri, from which he was graduated in 1859, soon after which he began the study of law. When the war broke out he, with the enthusiasm of youth, determined to become a votary of Mars, and soon became second lieutenant of a local company, which was afterward attached to the Confederate army. After serving six months he joined another company, and although he was at one time captured he succeeded in making his escape, after which he joined the Confederate army at Tupelo, Miss., and took service in the quartermaster's department. In December, 1862, he joined the army of General Hindman at Fort Smith, Ark., and while participating in the varied fortunes of that command he was, in a few months, made lieutenant, and was shortly afterward promoted to the rank of captain of company E, Ninth Missouri infantry. He was in the battles of Prairie Grove, Ark.; Mansfield, Pleasant Hill, and in all the engagements in which General Price participated on his Missouri raid. He did much staff duty under the various commanders of the brigade, and surrendered at Shreveport, La., in 1865. After some time Captain Stone returned to his old Missouri home, but after a very short stay there he came South to Mississippi (1866), and although his finances at that time were at a very low ebb, he began merchandising at Greenville in a small way, soon after turning his attention to planting, which occupation has received the greater part of his attention ever since. That he is admirably fitted for this calling is undoubted, for he is now owner of six thousand acres of some of the most valuable and fertile land in the state, the twenty-five hundred acres which are under cultivation being almost wholly cleared and improved by himself. This land is in four plantations, all of which are favorably situated for agricultural purposes, and show that a man of enterprise and energy has the management of affairs.

Since 1875 he has taken an active interest in politics, and in 1882 he was elected to the state legislature. So ably did he discharge his duties in this capacity that in 1885 he was elected state auditor, the same distinction being conferred upon him in 1889, which term will expire in 1896. The functions of this office he fills to perfection, for in every detail the most perfect arrangement is manifested, showing the workings of an intelligent and well-directed mind. He is efficient, punctual and honorable and uniformly courteous to all with whom he comes in contact. He has been many times a delegate to state conventions, and has otherwise interested himself in the political affairs of his section. His marriage to Miss Ella Holt took place in 1869, she being a daughter of Dr. Holt, of New Orleans, an eminent physician and a member of the secession convention of Mississippi. He died in 1881. To Captain and Mrs. Stone a family of nine children have been born, the following of whom are living: Alfred Holt (who is now practicing law in Greenville, Miss.), Annie, Lillian, Ella and Aimee. Captain Stone has been quite active in promoting the commercial development of Greenville, and is a stockholder in several of its most important enterprises. Socially he is a member of the A. F. & A. M., the K. of H., and has been a member of the K. of P. He is a member in good standing of the Christian church, while his wife holds to the Presbyterian faith.

The Stonewall Manufacturing company, manufacturers of 4-4 A. A. sheeting, 7-8 A. A. shirting, C. C. drills, 8-oz osnaburgs, carpet warps and yarns, has its extensive cotton mills at Stonewall Station, Clarke county, Miss., immediately on the line of the Mobile & Ohio railroad, three and a quarter miles south of Enterprise, eighteen miles south of Meridian, and eight miles north of Quitman, Miss. The locality is as healthy as the average of this section of the state. Women and children compose fully three-fourths of the working force in the mills, very few men being needed, who have to be skilled in cotton manufacturing. Boys and girls from ten to fifteen years old are employed in spinning, doffing, and other light work, which children can do quite as well as grown people, and are paid usually by the piece, and earn from $8 to $12 per month, the average being about $10 at these ages. Boys and girls from fifteen to sixteen years do similar work, and earn from $10 to $15 per month. Grown young ladies are employed at weaving, spooling, reeling, speeder and warper tending, all light and easy work, but requiring skill and close attention, at which they earn from $15 to $25 per month according to their capacity, all being paid by the piece. The above prices are for skilled help. While learning they are paid less, say $5 to $8 per month for boys and girls, and $10 per month for grown young ladies. It usually requires two to four weeks to learn the work, after which they are paid for all they do. A few industrious young ladies earn from $25 to $30 per month. The cost of living is low. Rents for houses range from $2 to $7.50 per month, according to size of house. A house of two rooms and two fire-places, with gallery, etc., rents for $3.25; three rooms and two fire-places, $4.25; four rooms and two fire-places, closets and gallery, $5.25 per month. Yards and gardens are neatly fenced in, and all repairs to houses, fencing, wells, etc., are done free, and kept in good order. Young ladies can get board in private families at $8 to $10 per month. A resident physician lives on the place, and is subject to call at all times to any member of a family, for which medical services a charge of fifty cents per month is made for those only who work in the factory. As the work is light and genteel, and inside of a comfortable building, it is specially suitable for women and children.

The morals of the village are as good as those of any place in the South, no drunkenness, profanity or other immoral or unbecoming conduct being tolerated. There are two very handsome church buildings—one Methodist and the other Baptist—both of which have services regularly, and Sunday-schools every Sabbath. There is also a public free school, maintained four months in the year, and occasional private schools in the intervals. The management of the mills is as lenient and conservative as is consistent with good discipline and well-established business principles. The mills have been in operation about twenty-two years, and have never passed a pay-day without having paid off the operatives in full. The entire management and employes are Southern people, and nearly all from the surrounding counties in Mississippi and Alabama. The company is under the management of Dr. O. F. Cawthorn, president and treasurer, and T. L. Wainwright, superintendent and secretary. Dr. O. F. Cawthorn has been president since May, 1879. He is a man of worth and the highest order of business and executive ability; being the pioneer successful manufacturer of artificial ice, and the first to establish a successful electric light plant in Mobile, Ala. Mr. T. L. Wainwright, youngest son of W. D. and Mary A. Wainwright (nee Taylor), was born in Greene county, Miss., November 30, 1851. His parents removed to Washington county, Ala., when he was two years old. He grew to manhood in Alabama, and at twenty years of age came to Clarke county, Miss., and settled at Stonewall. In youth he attended country schools and at twelve years of age went to boardingschools. After attending other schools, he entered a special school at Beaver Meadow, Ala., under W. J. White, a graduate of Chapel Hill. Here he pursued special branches, viz.: Latin, bookkeeping and civil engineering, for two years. On coming to Stonewall he became accountant for the Stonewall Manufacturing company, and continued in that capacity until March, 1875, when he became superintendent and secretary to succeed Mr. R. N. Taylor, which position he now holds. The mill formerly contained thirty-one hundred and sixty-eight spindles and one hundred looms, and the machinery was mostly old style and much worn. In 1879, under Dr. Cawthorn's management, new machinery, engine, etc., were added and the mill became a paying investment. In 1882 its capacity was increased to fifty-nine hundred and fifty-two spindles, and in 1889 it was brought up to seventy-three hundred and fifty-six spindles, consuming thirty-five hundred bales of cotton annually. About two hundred hands are employed. Steam is the motive power employed and wood is used for fuel. The products of the mills are sold chiefly in Northern markets: at St. Louis, Mo., New York, Philadelphia and in Mobile, Ala., some being exported to South America and to China. The capital stock of the company is $200,000.; its annual output amounts to $250,000, its pay-roll aggregating $4,000 per month. Mr. Wainwright married Miss Rosa Harvey, of Clarke county, Miss., a native of Holmes county, November, 1875. They have had five children: Cecil, Helen, Ralph, Orville and Zoe. He is a Missionary Baptist, a democrat, a member of the Masonic fraternity and a Knight of Honor, while Mrs. Wainwright is a Baptist.

Of the many prominent citizens of Bolivar county who are of foreign birth Edward Storm, merchant and planter, Stormville, Miss., stands among the foremost. His birth occurred in Prussia, in 1842, and he was the second child born to the marriage of Morris Storm, who with his wife resides in Prussia at the present time. Edward Storm came to the United States when seventeen years of age to join his elder brother, Samuel, who was located at Greenville, Miss. He landed at a point on the Mississippi river where he now resides and which has since been called Stormville. This was then a wilderness, but it has since been cleared by Mr. Storm, who is now the owner of twelve hundred acres of fine land, with four hundred acres under cultivation. He has a gin and sawmill, and in addition to this is interested in merchandising, having started this business in 1869. His stock of goods is valued at $10,000, and his annual sales bring him about $30,000. In 1862 he enlisted in the Confederate army, Washington cavalry, under Captain Hunt, was captured at Atlanta and paroled and exchanged at Natchez at the close of the war. He was married in 1880 to Miss Kuhn, of Greenville, Miss., who has borne him four children, all daughters: Frankie, Emelie, Lula and Ollie. Mr. Storm is a member of all secret societies. He has always been quite active in politics and was elected a member of the board of supervisors, serving as president of that body for ten years. He erected his fine residence in the seventies, has a pleasant, comfortable home and has the confidence and respect of all. He is postmaster at Stormville. His brother, Saul, was on the steamer Kentucky when it blew up at Columbus, Ark., in 1862, and was killed. He was a prosperous merchant at Bolivar.

John C. Stowers, member of Adams county board of supervisors from the fourth district and one of the county's leading planters and stockbreeders, resides on his plantation, Oakland, ten miles north of Natchez, in the house in which he was born, in 1832. His father, Caleb Stowers was probably born in the same neighborhood in 1785, and his first marriage was to Miss Elizabeth Wade, who was born in Adams county, and who died there, leaving three sons and three daughters: James, John, Abijah, Margaret, Eliza and Emily, all deceased except the last named, who is the widow of Col. Richard Parkinson, and now resides in Bowling Green, Claiborne county, Miss. In 1826 Mr. Stowers married Miss Anna M. Montgomery, mother of the subject, who was born in Concordia parish, La., in 1806. Both spent the last years of their life on the farm where John C. now lives. Mr. Stowers was one of the successful and enterprising planters of Adams county, and at the time of his death, which occurred in 1860, he left a very handsome estate. He enlisted in the War of 1812, but was not called into service. He assisted in the capture of Aaron Burr in Jefferson county. He was a member of the Presbyterian church, and his last wife, who died in 1842, was a member of the Methodist church. His father, John Stowers, who was probably born in the Palmetto state, was one of the first American settlers of Adams county, where he died a well-to-do planter.

He had four sons, all of whom became wealthy planters, viz.: Caleb, Lewis, James and Joseph, and three daughters, Louisa, Nancy and Mary, all deceased. Our subject's maternal grandfather, Joseph Montgomery, was a native of Louisiana, it is thought, and he there reared a large family and became a wealthy planter. John C. Stowers, subject of this memoir, was the third of eight children born to his parents: Amanda (deceased), Joseph, Louisiana, Indiana and three others who died when small. He received his education in the common schools, was early taught the duties of farm life, and in 1861 he joined the Jeff Davis legion as a private soldier, serving in the Virginia army in Butler's division and Hampton's corps. The last two years he was orderly sergeant and fought at Seven Pines, the seven days' fight around Richmond, Sharpsburg, Brandy's Station, Boonsborough, Md.; Fredricksburg, the battles around Petersburg, Wilderness and many others until January, 1865, when he was sent South and joined Johnston's army. He fought at Bentonville, N. C.; Raleigh and other places, and surrendered with Johnston. He had two horses shot from under him, but was never wounded or captured. After the war he came home on horseback and resumed his farm duties. On the 6th of June, 1866, he was united in marriage to Miss Mary Kurtz, a native of Louisville, Ky., whose father died when she was an infant and her mother in 1840, the latter dying from injuries received in the tornado that swept over Natchez during that year. She was then residing on Natchez island. Mrs. Stowers, being left an orphan, was adopted by a Mrs. Patterson of Natchez, where she was reared and principally educated. She was afterward a teacher of mathematics in Fayette academy. To Mr. and Mrs. Stowers have been born six children: Martha C.; John C., Jr.; Samuel P., died in 1889, the day before he would have graduated from Jefferson college; John died at the age of four years; Mary P. died at the age of nine years, and one died in infancy. Mr. Stowers has spent all his life on the farm of his birth, and is the owner of about four thousand acres, one thousand two hundred acres being in Louisiana. This is principally the result of his own energy. He does not make a specialty of raising cotton, but devotes his attention more to stockraising, breeding the Booningle and the Lewis E. Smith horses (trotting stock), Durham cattle and Berkshire hogs. He is also a stockholder in the Rosalie cottonmills. He was master of the Pine Ridge grange during the existence of that order, and since 1886 he has been a member of Adams county board of supervisors, having been elected three times. He is a member of Harmony lodge No. 1, A. F. & A. M., Bluff City lodge No. 1145, Knights of Honor, Natchez lodge No. 3, Knights of Pythias, and he is an elder in the Presbyterian church at Pine Ridge. Mrs. Stowers is also a prominent member of that church. Mr. Stowers is not an aggressive politician but an active worker in local political affairs. He is giving his children the advantages of the best local schools.

Rev. Joseph Buck Stratton, the pastor of the Presbyterian church of Natchez, Miss., comes of good old English stock, and members of his family have been known in the history of this country almost since the landing of the Pilgrim fathers. Upon braving the dangers of an ocean voyage in a sailing vessel and the unknown horrors and privations of a new and unknown country, they settled in New England. John Stratton, one of the early ancestors of the immediate subject of this biography, removed to Long Island in 1649 and founded East Hampton, after which the family moved to New Jersey, where they lived for many years. Nathan Leake Stratton, the father of Rev. Joseph Buck Stratton, was born in New Jersey, and was there married in the early part of 1815 to Miss Hannah Buck, also a native of that state, and for many years after his marriage followed the occupation of a merchant at Bridgeton. He was a man of most estimable character, did much to improve and benefit the county in which he lived, and in the year 1862 died very suddenly, mourned by a large circle of friends as well as his immediate family. His wife had passed from life about 1854, both having been worthy and active members of the Presbyterian church. The maternal ancestors were also English, and Joseph Buck, the grandfather, was an officer in the Revolutionary war, was with Washington at Yorktown and witnessed the surrender of Cornwallis. He was in many of the noted battles of that war, and tradition has it that he was a brave and intrepid soldier. He afterward became sheriff of his county. Rev. Joseph Buck Stratton was born in Bridgeton, N. J., December 24, 1815, and in his youth was given educational advantages far above the average. After enjoying the advantages of the high school at Lawrenceville, N. J., he completed his course of study at Princeton college, receiving the degree of A. M. in the year 1833. Subsequently he entered upon the study of law, the first two years of his study being under Judge L. Q. C. Elmer, of Bridgeton, the remaining two years being spent under the able guidance and instruction of Hon. John Sergent, of Philadelphia, Penn. In this city he was admitted to the bar in 1837, and there continued to practice until about 1840, at which time he joined the Presbyterian church, and in the fall of that year entered the theological seminary at Princeton, with the intention of making the ministry his life calling. While in this institution his career was characterized by a devotion to his work, and in the spring of 1843 he was graduated. He had been invited to take charge of the church at Natchez, Miss., which invitation he accepted and in the month of May, 1843, he arrived at his destination. He had had no experience in the saving of souls but his heart was in his work and he eagerly and hopefully entered upon his duties. In December, 1843, he was formally ordained and installed as pastor of the church, and here has been expounding the doctrines of his denomination and the principles of Christianity with fervor and zeal for nearly half a century. During this time he has been the pastor and the faithful friend and adviser of one of the most important Presbyterian churches in the South, and although he is now advanced in years he yet shows the fire, life, and eloquence of his younger years. His labors in the vineyard of the Lord have not gone unrewarded, and besides having the love, confidence and esteem of his large congregation he has been the means of bringing many to the feet of Christ. He has often been urged to take other positions, but has always declined and will in all probability end his ministerial career where it began. He has been a close student all his life, possesses literary tastes of a high order, and has written largely for the periodicals of the day, besides publishing several works on theological subjects. In 1856 he received the degree of D. D. from his alma mater, Princeton college. Miss Mary L. Smith, a native of Philadelphia, Penn., became his wife in 1844, but after a married life of four years she died, leaving her husband with two small children to care for, their names being Sidey V., now a prominent architect in New York city, and Mary, who died in 1863. Dr. Stratton's second marriage took place in 1852, Miss Caroline M. Williams, a native of Natchez, Miss., becoming his wife. To them one child was born, whom they named Joseph B. He died on the 16th of September, 1888, having been married to Miss Ruth A. Britton, by whom he had three children.

H. M. Street, of Meridian, Miss., was born in Moore county, N. C. His parents, Donald Street and Lydia McBryde, were natives of the same county. His grandfather, Richard Street, was a native of Virginia, and moved with his parents, Richard Street and Elizabeth Clapton, to North Carolina, where he married Ann McQueen, who came over from Scotland when quite young with her father, Murdoch McQueen. Donald Street was a farmer. While in North Carolina he represented his county in the legislature and filled other places of trust. His wife, Lydia, was the daughter of Hon. Archibald McBryde, a native of Scotland. He came to America in early manhood and married Lydia Ramsey, of Chatham county, N. C. He was a large planter and a lawyer of ability, and represented his district in congress. H. M. Street was educated at Carthage academy, a high school in his native county, and in his early days devoted himself to agriculture. He came with his father to Mississippi in 1853, and settled in Tishomingo county. He enlisted in the Confederate army in 1861, and remained in the service until the final surrender. He was elected in 1869 to represent Tishomingo county in the legislature. In response to the wishes of his constituents he secured the passage of a bill dividing his county, putting himself in the new county of Prentiss, which he represented for five successive terms. During this time he was twice elected speaker of the house of representatives. In 1882 he removed to Meridian, and in 1889 was elected to the legislature from Lauderdale county. He prepared the bill calling the constitutional convention which met at Jackson, August 12, 1890. He was elected one of the three delegates from Lauderdale county, and assisted in framing the present constitution of the state. He has been nominated by the democrats for re-election to the legislature. The election takes place in November, 1891, and the nomination is considered equivalent to an election. He has been engaged for the past seventeen years in the fire insurance business, and for several years has had general charge of the interests in Louisiana and Mississippi of the Phenix Insurance company, of Brooklyn, N. Y. He is a director in the Citizens' bank, and identified with other interests. He is a Presbyterian, a member of the Masonic fraternity and of the Knights of Honor. In 1858 he married Miss Charlotte Prindle, by whom he has five children living: Charles Richard, Albert Jackson, Bessie Lee, Ethel McQueen and Lottie Prentiss. His sons both reside in Chicago. In 1887 he married for his second wife Miss Charlotte Ryder, a first cousin of his first wife. Richard Street, a brother of our subject, was killed in battle in front of Atlanta, July 22, 1864. He was a member of the Thirty-second Mississippi regiment, Lowry's brigade of Cleburne's division. H. M. Street was named in honor of his great-uncle, Hugh McQueen, once attorney-general of North Carolina, and afterward a resident of Texas.

Maj. William M. Strickland, of Holly Springs, Marshall county, Miss., is a native of North Carolina. He came to the state with his father, Matthew Strickland, who settled in Panola county, in January, 1837. Major Strickland is recognized as one of the prominent citizens and leading lawyers of north Mississippi. He is well informed upon all subjects connected with agriculture, the principal industry of the state, and has engaged actively, as a democrat, in every political campaign since the war. He has never been an aspirant for office, but has acted upon the maxim, that the post of honor is the private station.

Thomas H. C. Strong, planter, Batesville, Miss. In Monroe county, Miss., on June 1, 1844, there was born to the union of Gen. Elisha and Ann S. (Hill) Strong, a son, whom they named Thomas H. C. The latter was the fifth of six children and passed his boyhood days in his native state. He was a student in the University of Alabama, at Tuscaloosa, when the struggle between the North and South began, but he laid aside his books and in 1861 enlisted in company K, Second Mississippi battalion, with which he remained two years. He was then changed to Armstead's regiment, company I, and remained with the same until peace was declared. He enlisted as an orderly sergeant, but in 1863, at the battle of Lafayette, Ga., he was made lieutenant for gallantry on the field. He afterward served as captain for two years and was in the following engagements: Manassas, Cedar Creek, Leesburg, Harper's Ferry, Sharpsburg, Frederick City, South Mountain, Marietta, Resaca, Atlanta, Lafayette, Rome, Spanish Fort, Blakely, Oxford, Gadsden, Whistler and Mobile. He was slightly wounded in the foot by a shell at Sharpsburg, but was not disabled from service. He was paroled at Gainesville, Ala., about one month after General Lee surrendered.

Mr. Strong then returned to his home, engaged in merchandising for two years, and then started out as a planter, which pursuit he has since continued. He is the owner of four thousand acres of land, one thousand three hundred and seventy-five acres under cultivation, and he is now one of the largest planters of the county. Besides his landed interests he with a company erected a large warehouse at Aberdeen, Miss., covering one and one-quarter acres of land, and at a cost of $14,000. He was married in 1867 to Miss Susan A. Strong, a native of Georgia, as were also her parents, Charles and Adaline (Kennon) Strong, and to this union have been born five children, two living: Charles and Leila. Mr. Strong and family hold membership in the Methodist church, and are highly esteemed in the county. Mr. Strong is a member of the Masonic fraternity and a member of the Knights of Honor. In politics he affiliates with the democratic party. He is one of the county's substantial citizens, and is ever ready to give his weight to any enterprise that will assist the same. His parents were both natives of Georgia, and the father was a very extensive and wealthy planter. He was the owner of a great many slaves prior to the war. He came to Mississippi in 1835 and died in 1878. His wife, who was also a native of Georgia, died in 1878. The father was quite a noted military character, having served as colonel in the War of 1812, and was also general of the state troops. The paternal grandparents, Charles and Sarah (Thompson) Strong, were natives of the Old Dominion. The grandfather was in the Revolutionary war with General Washington and was present at the surrender of Lord Cornwallis. The maternal grandparents, Thomas and Sallie (McGehee) Hill, were born in Georgia.

Edward Stuart is one of the pioneers of Coahoma county, Miss., but was born in Russellville, Ala., April 13, 1823, the eldest of seven children born to Samuel D. and Elizabeth (Louis) Stuart, the former of whom was born in North Carolina and the latter in Tennessee. The father was a wheelwright and spent the most of his life in Alabama and Tennessee, dying in the latter state in 1849. His father was a Scotchman, who came to America from his native land and made his home in the Old North state. Edward Stuart was reared in middle Tennessee and was educated in a private school. At the age of twenty-three, or in 1845, he was married to Miss Winnie A. Baugh, whose birth occurred in the Old Dominion, of which state her parents, William and Sarah (Cheatham) Baugh, were also natives. To Mr. and Mrs. Stuart a family of seven children have been born, six of whom are now living: Mary E., Martha A., Emma G., Lou Lee D., William E. and John H. At the age of nineteen years Mr. Stuart began to make his own way in the world, and for twelve years worked in a wagon and carriage shop in Fayette county, Tenn., at the end of which time he engaged in the lumber business, continuing for eight years. He then came to Coahoma county, Miss., and here commenced his mercantile career, which he has continued with success up to the present time. In connection with this he has planted to some extent, and is now the owner of a good residence and his place of business in Lyons, his stock of general merchandise being valued at about $4,000. He is also the owner of some real estate in Shufordsville, Miss., and has always been found to be a safe and reliable man of business. He is an active and devoted member of the Methodist Episcopal church, in which he has held the position of steward for some time. Although he has lived a quiet and peaceful life, his career has been one of honor and usefulness, and when called upon to serve in any public capacity he has shown sound judgment and an earnest desire to discharge every duty faithfully and well. He has been a member of the board of supervisors, and in this capacity won the respect and esteem of all, for he evinced a thorough knowledge of county affairs, and his desire to make Coahoma one of the leading counties of the state was undoubted. He is well informed on general topics, and in his modest and unassuming way endeavors at all times to do his duty.

During his long residence in the county naught has ever been said derogatory to his honor, and for his many estimable qualities he has many warm personal friends. He has done his part in converting the wilderness into productive fields of cotton, and no more worthy pioneer can be found in the county.

Col. William R. Stuart, an old resident of Ocean Springs, Miss., is entitled to distinction as the chief promoter of pecan culture in the South. He is a plain, unpretentious man, with strong convictions of right and wrong. Politically he affiliates with the democratic party. He has been prominent in public affairs, and was a member of the Louisiana constitutional convention of 1852. He was born near Centreville, Kent county, Md., November 18, 1820, a son of William R. and Ariana (Frazier) Stuart. His paternal and maternal grandfathers were both natives of Scotland, and early settlers in Maryland. In that state Mr. Stuart was reared, and there he remained until he was twenty years of age. In 1840 he came down the river from Wheeling, Va., during which journey he made the acquaintance of Col. Nolan Stewart, who resided in Baton Rouge, La. At the invitation of Colonel Stewart, who had taken a fancy to the young man, Mr. Stuart visited him, and remained with him between two and three years. During that period he received some excellent commercial training, and when he left the Colonel was well equipped for the struggle of life. He went to New Orleans, and embarked in the sugar business, and also did some trading in cotton. He conducted this business until 1871, and then came to Ocean Springs, Miss. While a resident of Louisiana he owned a fine plantation. Since coming to Mississippi he has done much to improve the breeds of livestock in this state, and has given a great impetus to the culture of the pecan tree. He sells plants and seeds from Maryland to California, and in Jamaica and Australia. He has fifty acres of trees, and in an excellent paper read before the executive committee of the Mississippi horticultural society, he gives an interesting bit of his experience. He says: "Pecan culture is my hobby. When I was fifty-six I bought the largest and best paper-shell pecans I could find, paying $1 per pound for them, and planted the nuts. When sixty-eight I sold $305 worth of pecans; when sixty-nine, I sold $700 worth. This year I will get $1,500 to $2,000 from the sale of my young trees and nuts. Pecans have off years. A planter putting out five hundred trees in a grove, ought to plant one hundred trees every year, then he will have plenty of pecans every year." The Atlanta *Constitution* said of him recently: "Mr. W. R. Stuart, of Ocean Springs, Miss., is the father of pecan culture in the South. 'I began,' said he, 'at fifty-six years of age. I am now seventy-one, and make more money out of pecans than I do out of cotton. The young men of the South ought to think of this. There is unlimited money in pecan culture in the South, and I am anxious to see our people plant pecan trees just as they do apple or peach trees. They will make the South rich.'"

The report of the secretary of agriculture for 1890 contains a full-page illustration of Colonel Stuart and his pecan orchard and makes complimentary mention of his enterprise:

The Hickoria pecan is one of the best of all nuts, and is found wild only in North America. It abounds in the rich river and creek bottom lands of the Mississippi valley, especially in Texas, Louisiana and Mississippi, Indian territory, Arkansas and Missouri. Even as far north as southeastern Iowa it grows wild; but the region of profitable culture does not probably extend so far north as the other species of the hickory family. In the Gulf states is found the best climate for this nut, and already there are considerable orchards of it planted there. It is needless to expect success in poor soil, for like all nut trees the pecan grows to the greatest perfection in rich, moist alluvium. Many of the lands subject to periodical floods along the Mississippi river and tributary streams might be planted to the pecan with great profit. Once well established, these orchards in rich bottoms would yield large quantities of the very best nuts, and would not be injured by the floods, which usually occur long before the time of gathering the crop. There is great variation in the nuts as to size, shape, thickness of shell, and quality of the kernel. The illustration plate 1, fig. 1, shows the character of the ordinary wild nut; and fig. 2, the large, choice, wild nuts sent to market. Fig. 3 is a very choice variety named Stuart, in honor of the originator, Col. W. R. Stuart, Ocean Springs, Miss. This is one of the largest and best in quality and thinnest shelled of any that I have yet examined. Fig. 4 represents another variety by the same originator, named Van Deman by him, as a compliment to myself. It is also very large, and thin shelled. Either of these varieties can be crushed in the hand. Fig. 5 is a cut of a choice variety received from Louis Biediger, of Idlewild, Tex., and named Idlewild by me, as I thought it well worthy of propagation under a distinct name. A very choice variety is also shown in fig. 6, which was obtained from E. E. Risien, of San Saba, Tex. Distinct differences will be noticed in the shape of the varieties, and these are only a few of a large number of choice kinds which have been sent to this office. It is only just to mention that in addition to the above the following persons have large and delicious pecans, which it will pay any one who contemplates growing this nut to procure: T. V. Munson, Denison, Tex.; O. D. Faust, Bamburg, S. C.; B. M. Young, Morgan City, La.; Arthur Brown, Bagdad, Fla. The illustration on plate 2 is of a tree thirteen years old, on the farm of Col. W. R. Stuart, of Ocean Springs, Miss., and shows the typical size and shape of a pecan tree grown in the open field. It has been bearing for three years past.

Dr. W. W. Stuart, physician, Clarksdale, Miss., for many years a leading physician at Clarksdale, Coahoma county, Miss., was the second of seven children born to Enoch and Ann (McNeill) Stuart, his birth occurring in North Carolina in 1835. The parents were also natives of North Carolina and the father followed the occupation of a farmer the principal part of his life. The elder Stuart moved to west Tennessee in 1839, and from there to Coahoma county, Miss., in 1856, receiving his final summons there in 1864. Upon coming to Coahoma county he settled in the eastern part, opened a farm, and was among the early pioneers, the country being at that time wild and unsettled. The mother died in Tennessee in 1849. Both were consistent members of the Methodist Episcopal church. Dr. Stuart passed his boyhood and youth in west Tennessee and was well educated at La Grange, of that state. In 1856 he began the study of medicine, and attended lectures at Cincinnati, Ohio, graduating in 1858. In 1859 he began practicing in the vicinity of what is now Clarksdale, and has been in constant practice here since. He ranks among the oldest physicians (in practice) of Coahoma county, and has been identified with the section of country in the vicinity of Clarksdale since his early manhood. He is of studious habits, is highly esteemed in the community and has always had a large and lucrative practice. Several years ago he opened a drug store at Lyons, this county, and though not giving it his personal supervision, still conducts the business here. He has a good store and a fair share of the trade. He is a member of the Masonic fraternity, Shufordsville lodge, and is a member of the Knights of Honor. He is also a member of the National Association of Railway Surgeons, and health officer of his county. Dr. Stuart is of medium stature, with fair complexion, and has dark hair, eyes and beard.

Marlen Stubblefield, one of the leading agriculturists of the farming community of Benton, Yazoo county, was born in Dallas county, Ala., in 1818, and is a son of William H. and Agnes (Etherage) Stubblefield, natives of the state of Georgia. The father came to Yazoo county, Miss., in 1832, and settled seven miles east of Benton on a quarter section of land, where he spent the remainder of his days. He was very successful in his farming, and at one time owned ten thousand acres of land in this county. He died in 1858, and his wife died in 1826. He married a second time, and this wife lived until 1883. He was the father of six children, five of whom are living: Marlen, the subject of this notice; W. Henry, ex-sheriff of Yazoo county; Stephen, who lives in Texas; David, a farmer of this county; and Simon, a son of the second marriage, who lives on the old homestead. Mr. Stubblefield came to Yazoo county with his parents at the age of thirteen years, and grew up amid the scenes of pioneer life. At the age of twenty-four years he bade farewell to his father's home, and started out in the world for himself. He was first employed as overseer and manager of plantations, and by economy and good management he succeeded in saving money to invest for himself. He purchased eight hundred acres of land and four negroes. At the breaking out of the Civil war he owned twenty-five slaves and stock enough to work the whole farm. He raised all the meat and provisions, and all the supplies that could be home-made. During the war he was in the home militia, being first lieutenant of cavalry. At the close of the war he resumed his agricultural pursuits. For the past eight years he has lived on his present farm; it consists of three hundred and twenty acres, but he has owned as high as fifteen hundred acres of land, which he has divided among his children. He has always taken an active part in the political affairs, and has ever been an ardent supporter of home industries. He was married August 3, 1847, to Miss Elmira McCormick, a daughter of John C. and Sarah (Dukes) McCormick, natives of Georgia. Three children have been born of this marriage who have lived to mature years, and three died in infancy. William Henry is a farmer in this county, Fountain B., resides at home, and Wyech F. lives at Benton. Mr. Stubblefield is a member of the Masonic order, and of the Farmers' Alliance. He and his wife belong to the Baptist church, and the sons are members of the Methodist Episcopal church. He is a man of more than ordinary experience, and is well informed on all the topics of the day. He has been identified with the growth and development of the county, and has contributed liberally of his means to all charitable purposes.

Thomas B. Stubbs was born in the state of Georgia, February 20, 1820, and is a son of Thomas B. and Catherine P. Stubbs, also natives of Georgia. His father was a merchant and planter, and before the war was possessed of great wealth. He died in 1863, at the age of seventy-four years, and his wife passed away in 1867. Both were buried in the family graveyard in Tippah county, Miss. Thomas B., Jr., is the third child and the first son of a family of fourteen. He came to Mississippi in 1841, and embarked in the mercantile trade at Holly Springs; he remained there about a year, taking his stock at the end of that time to Pontotoc, where he was but a short time; thence he moved to Carrollville, where he carried on both a mercantile and agricultural business until 1871. In that year he located in Baldwyn, Lee county, and has devoted his time and attention to commercial interests. For fourteen years he has been postmaster, and has made a faithful and efficient officer. In August, 1852, he was married to Miss Virginia L. Marks, a native of Virginia, born August 3, 1827, and a daughter of Lewis L. and Mary Marks. Eight children have been born to Mr. and Mrs. Stubbs: Sarah E.; Thomas F., who married Miss Mollie Elliott; Catherine P., deceased; Mary L., wife of Robert E. McKinney; Edward P.; M. E., deceased; Rozelia D., deceased, and Charles H. Mr. Stubbs is a democrat, but has never aspired to public office. His first vote for president was cast for General Harrison. He is a Mason of high degree, and belongs to the Methodist Episcopal church. Mrs. Stubbs, Sarah E. and Mary L. are members of the Christian church, while Thomas F. is a Baptist. The war played as serious havoc with Mr. Stubbs' fortunes as it did with so many others, but by energetic effort he has succeeded in regaining a portion of his property. He is an advocate of all enterprises that tend to the elevation of the masses, and the progress and growth of the country.

Capt. Zacheus P. Stutts, Yazoo City, Yazoo county, Miss., is the youngest of a family of five children, born November 23, 1835, to Henry and Elizabeth (Burroughs) Stutts, natives of North Carolina. The father was a wealthy planter; he died in 1852, and his wife passed away in 1848. The paternal grandparents were Jacob and Frances Stutts, of Pennsylvania. The maternal grandfather, Zacheus Burroughs, a very wealthy planter, was a native of North

Carolina. Our subject was reared and educated in the place where he was born, Moore county, N. C., and was trained to the business of planting; he has always followed this vocation, and is the owner of five hundred acres, two hundred being under cultivation. He also owns an interest in three thousand two hundred and eighty acres known as Tyrone plantation. He has been twice married: October 26, 1856, he was united to Mrs. R. L. Pruitt, of Alabama; July 13, 1886, he married Miss Josie V. Carter, of Mississippi, a daughter of R. N. and Elizabeth Carter, natives of Alabama. In 1862 he raised a company of cavalry, of which he was chosen captain; he held this position until 1864, when he was compelled to resign on account of ill health. In 1861 he had volunteered his services to his country but was refused admittance to the army, on account of disability. In his political opinions he adheres to the principles of the democratic party, with whose action he has been prominently connected in this county. He was twice elected a member of the board of supervisors, in 1887 and 1889, and made president of the board both times. He is now a candidate for the state legislature, and bids fair to win in the race, having received the nomination by a large majority over all his opponents. He and his wife are members of the Missionary Baptist church, and he belongs to the Masonic fraternity. He has been a stanch supporter of home enterprises, and has been a telling factor in the development of the county. He is honored and respected as a citizen, is kind, hospitable, and obliging as a neighbor, and an ornament to his community.

John A. Suddoth, mayor of Clarksdale and secretary and treasurer of the Clarksdale Compress and Warehouse company, is a native-born resident of Mississippi, his birth occurring in Chickasaw county in 1849. He was the eldest in a family of seven children born to John O. and Mildred (Taliaferro) Suddoth, the former a native of the Old Dominion and the latter of South Carolina. The father emigrated to the state of Mississippi at an early day and engaged in merchandising at Houston, Chickasaw county. In 1859 he came to Friar's Point, opened a store and became a most extensive merchant, continuing in trade until his death in 1865. He was an active citizen, and in his personal appearance was rather tall, with auburn hair and brown eyes. His people were among the prominent families of Virginia and other members of this family are now residing in Coahoma county. The mother died in 1888. Both were members of the Baptist church. John A. Suddoth was ten years of age when he came to Coahoma county, and as his educational advantages during youth were rather limited he is mainly self educated. He began clerking at an early age and followed this for a long time, continuing the same occupation after coming to Clarksdale in 1873. In 1878 he began business for himself and carried this on until early in 1890. In 1880 he was appointed the first mayor of Clarksdale, and so ably and well has he filled that position that he has been re-elected each successive year. By his marriage, which occurred in 1880, to Miss Ruby Miles, a native of Mississippi and a niece of Governor Alcorn, Mr. Suddoth became the father of four children: Ittaline, Gertrude, Marie and Norwood. He has been quite active in politics and was a member of the board of supervisors of Coahoma county from 1878 to 1881, being for two years president of that body. He is one of the leading and public-spirited citizens of Clarksdale. In all enterprises that promise to contribute to the good of Clarksdale or Coahoma county Mr. Suddoth may be counted on to take a leading part. In 1889 he was one of the organizers of the Compress and Warehouse company, and he was then elected secretary and treasurer of that corporation. He is the president of the Clarksdale Building and Loan association, and is a stockholder in the Clarksdale Bank and Trust company. He is the owner of considerable city property.

John L. Sullivan, Greenwood, Miss. The subject of this notice is a native of Mississippi, and was born November 14, 1864, in Calhoun county. His father, Jesse S. Sullivan, was also a native of Mississippi, born about the year 1817; he married M. C. Baily, a daughter of Samuel Baily, and also a native of Mississippi. The father died about 1867, when John was yet a small boy; the mother is still living. John L. Sullivan is one of a family of five sons and one daughter. He spent his youth in Tallahatchie county, where he received a fair business education. In January, 1881, he came to Le Flore county. In 1883, although he had been a resident of the county but two years, he was appointed to the responsible position of deputy sheriff, serving under Mr. Terry and Captain Bashet. He did a large portion of the office work, and became familiar with all the details of the business. At the general election in 1889 he was elected sheriff of the county, and has filled the office with great credit to himself, and to the entire satisfaction of his constituency. He is a candidate for re-election, and will in all probability succeed himself. When he came to the county he was a poor boy, his only capital being that with which nature had invested him. He has, however, used that to the best advantage, and has made his way to a position of influence in the county. Mr. Sullivan was united in marriage in Le Flore county, November 27, 1888, to Miss Ella O. Lucas, a native of Grenada, Miss., and a daughter of John O. Lucas, now deceased. Mr. Sullivan is said to be the youngest sheriff in the state of Mississippi, and is a member of the Association of Sheriffs of Mississippi, of which he is secretary, and of which A. E. Anderson, sheriff of Sunflower county, is president. He is a member of the Knights of Pythias, and of the Knights of Honor. He is a young man of unusual qualifications, and extraordinary business talent. He is possessed of sterling traits of character, and there is little that may not be anticipated for a man who has made so striking a record so early in life.

Jacob Sumrall, a prominent farmer and miller of Clarke county, was born in that county November 28, 1835, the eldest of six children of Elisha Woods and Margaret (Watts) Sumrall. His father was born while his parents were en route from North Carolina to Tennessee, in 1809, a son of Levi and Agnes (Gibson) Sumrall. He was reared to farm life, and in 1832 settled with his parents in Clarke county, the father dying in that county in 1849. Mr. and Mrs. Sumrall were married in 1830, the mother having been a daughter of James and Nancy Watts. Her father was a native of South Carolina who moved to Georgia; her mother, born in South Carolina, came with her parents to Mississippi at an early day, locating in Wayne county. There Mrs. Margaret Sumrall was born in 1815, and there married at the age of fifteen years. Mr. Watts was a planter all his life, and lived in Clarke county from 1836 to 1862, when he died, his wife having died the previous year. The father of our subject died in 1849. He was a life-long member, and from 1841 to the time of his death was a minister of the Baptist church. His mother is still living at the age of seventy-six, making her home with Jacob Sumrall. The six children born to this union were: Jacob, Nancy, Elisha, Elijah, John and James. Of these John, Jacob and James are living. Their maternal grandfather, James Watts, served in the Indian war. Mr. Sumrall was reared and educated in Clarke county. He entered the employ of the Mobile & Ohio Railroad company at the age of eighteen, remaining with that corporation twenty-one years, becoming one of their most trusted and popular conductors. In 1875 he resigned this position and was then engaged in farming and in the manufacture of turpentine until 1888. In 1890 he established a saw, gin and gristmill. He began to buy land in 1856 and gradually added to his possessions, until he is now the owner of about one thousand acres in Clarke county, about one-tenth of which is under cultivation. He is also largely interested in stockraising. In 1856 he married Mary, a daughter of Thomas and Lucinda (Raspberry) Sumrall, who were old residents in Clarke county, their grandparents having been pioneers in this state. Mrs.

Sumrall was born in this county in 1837. She has presented her husband with seven children: Melissa E., now Mrs. Rogers, of this county; Gehu, a resident of Texas; Rufus W., of Clarke county; Grace E., now Mrs. Meeks, also a resident of Clarke county; Milton B., Jerusha and Laura, who are living at home. Mrs. Sumrall is a member and her family are attendants upon the services of the Baptist church. Mr. Sumrall is a successful, selfmade man, who, while acquiring a competency for himself, has been liberal in his aid to all general interests. His public spirit is proverbial. Politically he is a democrat, a member of the Masonic order, also of the county fair committee, upon which he is active and influential.

James Surget, planter and fine stockbreeder, in Adams county, Miss., is the son of James and Catherine (Lintot) Surget. The father was born in Baton Rouge, La., in 1785, and the same year he was brought by his parents to Adams county, where he spent the balance of his days as a very successful planter, accumulating all his property by push, economy and industry. He became quite wealthy. His death occurred in 1855. His wife, who was born in Adams county, died in 1838. She was the daughter of William Lintot, a native of Connecticut, in which state he married Miss Grace Mansfield, also a native of Connecticut. They came to Adams county at a very early day, passed through all the hardships of pioneer life and passed the closing scenes of their life here. He was a well-to-do planter. Peter Surget, the grandfather of our subject, was a native of Rochelle, France, and while a young man came to New York, where he married Mrs. Catherine Hubbard. While there Mr. Surget was engaged in merchandising, trading with the West India islands. He afterward removed to Baton Rouge and from there, in 1785, he came to Adams county, where his death occurred in 1796. He was a man possessed of indefatigable will power, energy and industry. He was thoroughgoing and a very successful business man, as well as a shrewd trader. He was the father of six sons and five daughters: Peter, Jacob, Frank, William, Charles, James (father of our subject), Mrs. Jane White, Mrs. Stocker, Frances, Mrs. Catherine Charlotte Bingaman and Catharine Pilmon. Several of these sons became successful planters. James Surget, Jr., was born in Adams county, in 1837, and was the second of three children—a son and two daughters. One of the daughters died in infancy and the other, Mrs. Kate S. Minor, is the widow of the late John Minor, who was born at the old Concord, or Governor Gayoso place, near Natchez, in 1831. The latter was educated at Natchez and later graduated from Princeton college. He was married in 1855 and spent the remainder of his days in Adams county as a prominent planter and stockbreeder. He resided at Oakland, near Natchez, but at the time of his death, which occurred in 1869, he was in New York, whither he had gone for his health. He was a son of William J. Minor, who was a son of Don Steven Minor, who was prominent in the Spanish times of Mississippi (see sketch). James Surget was educated in Adams county, and at an early age was left a handsome property by his father. This he has since managed with success, owning two fine plantations in Louisiana, viz.: Ashley and Waterloo, and four in Adams county, viz.: Featherland, in part; Cherry Grove, the home place, eight miles southeast of Natchez; Linnwood and Rokeby. For twenty years or more Mr. Surget has been extensively and successfully engaged in the breeding of fine stock, thoroughbred running horses, perhaps the best in the state, also Ayershire and Devon cattle, Southdown sheep and Essex hogs. One of his plantations he devotes almost wholly to the breeding and raising of stock. He was married in 1873 to Miss Catharine Boyd, a native of Adams county, and a lady possessed of all the qualities that make a cultured and noble woman. She was the daughter of the late Judge S. S. Boyd, a native of Portland, Me., where he remained until a young man. He then came to Natchez and was there married to Miss Catherine C. Wilkins, a native of Adams county and still a resident of

Natchez. She is an accomplished and refined lady. Judge Boyd was a lawyer of great ability and of widespread reputation. In his death the state lost one of its brightest legal lights.

Capt. Micajah Surratt (deceased) was a prominent lawyer, a prosperous merchant and a very successful farmer, of Prentiss county, Miss. He was born in Alabama, graduated from the North Bend, Indiana, school, and became the husband of Miss Amanda Surrell, a native of Georgia. They became the parents of one child, Thomas, who was killed in war. Mr. Surratt was elected to the legislature from Tishomingo county a number of terms, before the war. He was a secessionist, and when the war came he volunteered in the spring of 1861 as a private in the Second Mississippi regiment infantry, under Colonel Faulkner, and B. B. Boone as lieutenant-colonel. He was promoted in the latter part of 1861 to regimental quartermaster, and continued to serve in that capacity until the surrender. He was in the campaign of Virginia, and was a true man to the cause he fought so bravely to defend, holding the love and esteem of all by his many noble qualities of mind and heart. After the war he was appointed express agent at Booneville for the Mobile & Ohio railroad, and at the same time carried on a large merchandising business in that place. He was also quite deeply interested in agricultural pursuits in Prentiss county. He practiced law before the war, but after that eventful period abandoned it, preferring to pass the remainder of his days as a planter and merchant. His death occurred on his farm in Prentiss county and he was interred at Booneville. Mrs. Surratt is still living, and resides with her sister, Mrs. Fannie Cobb, near Athens, Clarke county, Ga. She is a member of the Methodist church, and he also held membership in the same. Mr. Surratt was a distant relative of Mrs. Surratt, who was hanged for conspiracy in the assassination of President Lincoln. Mr. Surratt reared a number of homeless children, and was one of the kindest and most hospitable of men. His doors were ever open to the distressed and needy, and a warm welcome was accorded to one and all.

Samuel R. Swain is a South Carolinian, born in 1838, but since his boyhood he has been a resident of the state of Mississippi. His father, William B. Swain, was born in the Palmetto state in 1811, was a planter by occupation and followed this calling in Mississippi and Texas, moving to the last named state in 1871, passing from life in Hunt county in 1887. His wife was formerly Miss Susan Williams, of South Carolina, and two years prior to the death of her husband was called to her long home. The paternal grandmother was a Miss Ray, a native of Ireland, and the maternal grandfather was John B. Williams, of Scotland, who became a planter after becoming a subject of Uncle Sam. The wife of the latter was Drucilla Johnson, also of Scotland. In the common schools of the state of Mississippi Samuel R. Swain was educated, and in the year 1863 began an independent career. Being a warm supporter of the Confederate cause, he, with youth's enthusiasm, enlisted in company D, First Mississippi light artillery, afterward participating in the battle and siege of Vicksburg, the engagements at Mobile and Pensacola, and a number of skirmishes. He was married in 1860 to Miss Harriet A. Sales, a native of South Carolina, and a daughter of William M. Sales, also of that state, whose wife was Janes A. Guffin. To Mr. and Mrs. Swain a family of six children were born: William B., Mary Ray, Jennie Olivia, Nettie Arthur, Alonzo Paul and Sally. Mr. Swain has devoted his life to the occupation of planting, and now owns a half interest in six thousand three hundred acres of land, two thousand acres of which are under cultivation, and one thousand five hundred acres in woodland. On Walnut bayou he has one thousand four hundred acres of land, and of this one thousand and fifty acres are cultivated, three hundred and fifty acres being woodland. Mr. Swain is an excellent financier, is very practical in his views, and keeps fully apace with the progress of his adopted calling in every particular, and, as a reward, is in affluent circumstances. He is much esteemed by all his acquaintances, and is especially liked by his farm hands. In the occupation of planting he is connected with Capt. W. W. Stone, the present auditor of the state of Mississippi, and on their largest plantation they principally employ convict labor. Mr. Swain is an affable and pleasant gentleman, and as a conversationalist is intelligent and entertaining.

Henry Clay Swayze, planter and stockraiser residing on Fairview plantation, is a descendant of old and honored families on both sides of the house. He was born near Kingston, Miss., in 1830, and his father, Solomon Swayze, was born in the same neighborhood on July 4, 1777. Solomon was married, in 1825, to May Custard (née Boyd), a native of North Carolina, born on May 3, 1792, and they passed the closing scenes of their lives in Kingston neighborhood, Mr. Swayze dying on September 7, 1833, and his wife in 1854. Mr. Swayze was the first American child born in the settlement. He was educated at home, and although he started out for himself with limited means he became quite a wealthy planter. He was the son of Richard Swayze, who came from New Jersey with a brother, Samuel, in 1772 and a colony of about thirty families settled on the Mandamus grant, which consisted of about twenty-five thousand acres, made by the English government to Capt. John Ogden. Samuel Swayze was a local Congregational minister and an active and prominent man. They left many descendants, and at one time there were twenty of the Swayzes in Kingston precinct. Grandfather Boyd came with his family from Tennessee down the river on a flatboat and settled on what is known as Boyd's lake, near Hutchins' landing, where Mr. Boyd became quite an extensive planter and where he probably spent his last days. Solomon Swayze was married twice, first to Elizabeth Carter, who was of the colony, and two children were born of this marriage: Richard and William Swayze; and his second marriage was to the mother of our subject, who had also been previously married to Morris Custard, who was one of the Swayze colony too. Henry Clay Swayze is the youngest of three sons living: Benjamin F., a planter of Wilkinson county, and Alexander Montgomery, a planter of Adams county. Henry Clay secured a fair education in Brighton, Adams county and was married in 1861, to Miss Catherine I., daughter of Hardy and Missouri (Thomas) Lajourner, the father born in the Palmetto state and the mother in Tennessee. Mr. Lajourner was a brickmason by trade, and also followed the occupation of a planter. He left four sons and four daughters, his daughter Catherine having been born in Adams county. To Mr. and Mrs. Swayze and wife were born twelve children, six sons and three daughters now living. For fifty years Mr. Swayze has lived on the old Mandamus plantation, and now has five hundred and thirty-three acres, with about four hundred and fifty acres cleared. He has been a member of the A. F. & A. M. fraternity, Harmony Lodge No. 1, for many years, and is a respected and law-abiding citizen.

H. S. Swayze, planter and dealer in livestock, Evans, was born in Yazoo county, in 1842, and has passed all his life within the borders of this county. He received his education in the common schools, and was trained to agricultural pursuits. In 1862 he entered the Confederate service, enlisting in company B, Withers' artillery. He was in the siege at Vicksburg, and at Port Hudson he was taken prisoner; was paroled and exchanged, and at Mobile was again captured and held until the surrender; he was taken to Ship island, where he passed many weary days until the release came. In 1866 he was wedded to Miss Jennie Handley, a daughter of Sebourn and Elizabeth (Stubblefield) Handley. When he began farming on his own account he had three hundred and twenty acres of land. By wise management and habits of industry he succeeded admirably, and to-day is the owner of twelve hundred and twenty acres, all of which is well improved, and one-half under excellent cultivation. He gives special attention to the breeding and raising of fine horses, and has made a record in this branch of husbandry. He takes an active part in local politics, and is a member of the democratic county committee. He is an honored member of the Knights of Honor. Mr. and Mrs. Swayze are the parents of seven children: Josephine, wife of James D. McKie, of Yazoo county; Hayes, a student of medicine under Dr. Blundle; Lizzie, Nathan, Hardy, Clayton and Katie. The father and mother are consistent members of the Midway Methodist Episcopal church. Mr. Swayze has been steward of this society for sixteen years, and has always contributed generously to the support of religious and educational movements in the community. His parents, Richard and Mary E. (Sojourner) Swayze, belonged to the earliest and most prominent of Yazoo county families.

Among the legal practitioners of Montgomery county, Miss., stands the name of Capt. David L. Sweatman, whose long residence here and his intimate association with the various affairs of importance have gained for him an extensive acquaintance. He was born in Hancock county, Miss., on the 25th of December, 1832, and is the son of D. L. and Penelope (Jolly) Sweatman, both natives of Georgia and she a daughter of Peter Jolly. Mr. Sweatman located in the southern part of the state, on the coast, in 1825, and there he resided until his death, when Capt. David L. was but a child. After the death of her husband Mrs. Sweatman returned to Alabama. Capt. David L. Sweatman grew to mature years in Alabama, received a good education in the private schools, and when a young man returned to Mississippi. There he taught school in Noxubee and Winston counties for some time, and subsequently read law with Gen. W. F. Brantley, at Greensboro. In 1860 he was admitted to the bar and afterward formed a partnership with General Brantley, which continued until the death of the latter in 1871. During the late unpleasantness between the North and South, Captain Sweatman entered the Confederate army in 1861, Fifteenth Mississippi regiment infantry, and after serving with the same about two years and a half, on the reorganization of his regiment he was made first lieutenant of company D. After a year and a half with this regiment he was transferred to the quartermaster department, and the following years he was quartermaster of his regiment with the rank of captain. After this he joined General Brantley and served on his staff until the close of the war, following that general in the varied fortunes of the soldier until the surrender. He participated in a number of important engagements: Shiloh, where he received two wounds and was disabled for some time; Vicksburg; and at Baker's Creek, where he was with Long's division, and with him made his escape. He also participated in the battles of Franklin, Nashville and Resaca. After termination of hostilities Captain Sweatman formed a law partnership with Judge Williamson, now circuit judge of this judicial district, and this partnership continued until the appointment of Mr. Williamson as chancery judge. The Captain then formed a partnership with Walter Trotter, and this has since continued. They have a good law practice, and have had a number of important criminal and civil cases. Captain Sweatman has been the attorney for the Illinois Central railroad for a number of years, and stands at the head of his profession in that part of the state. He has been quite active in politics, and has ever given his support to the principles of the democratic party, but he has never been an aspirant for office. He was first married in Choctaw county, Miss., in 1867, to Miss Mary Peebles, a native of Choctaw county, Miss., and the daughter of Alpha Peebles. She was educated in Alabama, was a devoted wife and mother, and was a consistent member of the Methodist church. She died in 1881. There were born two children to this union, both daughters: Mary A. and Davis, both attending the Female institute at Jackson, Tenn. Captain Sweatman's second marriage occurred in 1882, to Mrs. Mary E.

Kittrell, a native of Georgia, but who was reared in Mississippi, receiving her education principally at Jackson. Mrs. Sweatman has four children by a former marriage and they are nearly all grown. This family are members of the Methodist church. Captain Sweatman is a member of the Masonic fraternity, Blue lodge, chapter and council, and has represented his lodge in the grand lodge at different times. He is a member of the Bench and Bar association.

James M. Switzer has been a resident of Bolivar county, Miss., almost from the time of its formation, and is one of its substantial and progressive planters. He was born in Montgomery county, Ind., September 8, 1831, the fourth in a family of eight children, born to John and Mary (Randolph) Switzer, the former a native of Kentucky, and the latter of Virginia. John Switzer was a mechanic by trade, which occupation he followed all his life. His father was a native of Germany, and came to America at a very early day, identifying himself with the interests of his adopted country, and proving a useful, progressive and highly honorable citizen of the state of Kentucky, where he finally located. The maternal grandparents were Virginians, in which state their ancestors settled in colonial times. In the year 1845 James M. Switzer became a resident of the state of Mississippi, but prior to this was educated in the public schools of the state of Indiana. Upon his arrival in the state of Mississippi, he had little or no means, but by close application to business, he soon began to accumulate some means, and now his property, which is value at about $8,000, all the result of earnest, persistent and determined effort. He has two hundred acres of fine land, of which one hundred and fifty acres are under cultivation, besides a valuable amount of personal property, and is one of the substantial citizens of this section. In 1854 he was married to Miss Sarah Betty, by whom he became the father of nine children, three of whom are living at the present time: Alice F., Charles H. and Hattie D. Mr. Switzer has always thoroughly identified himself with the South, and when the late war opened, espoused the Confederate cause, and in 1862 became a member of the Forrest Scouts, under General Forrest, and was in active service until General Lee's surrender, proving himself a courageous, faithful and competent soldier. Upon his return home he commenced to upbuild the fortunes of his family, and his labors have placed them beyond the reach of want. He is beloved and popular throughout the section in which he resides for his many worthy traits, and his kindness and simplicity of manner. He is an excellent neighbor, a faithful friend, and has proved himself a thorough gentleman and Christian in his walk through life.

Col. E. T. Sykes, of Columbus, is one of the foremost attorneys of Lowndes county, Miss. For nearly twenty years he has been associated in the practice of law with Capt. W. W. Humphries, under the firm name of Humphries & Sykes, and is in command of a large clientage. He was born in Decatur, Ala., March 15, 1838, and is a son of Richard and Martha A. Sykes, who were natives of Greenville county, Va., and cousins, the maiden name of Martha being likewise Sykes. The family connection was a large one. About the year 1834, the first of the name moved to Decatur, Morgan county, Ala., where in a few years all of the immediate family connection had moved and become extensive planters, as they had been in Virginia. In a few years thereafter, the Sykeses had also become large owners of the rich prairie lands in Lowndes and Monroe counties, Miss., and by 1842 most of the name had removed to the latter state, taking up their residence in Columbus and Aberdeen, Richard settling in Columbus. The Sykeses were among the first settlers of this section, and all of them became extensive and prosperous cotton planters, and though they lost quite heavily by the results of the war, they were nevertheless in good circumstances at its close. Richard, the father of Col. E. T., died December 19, 1870. His wife, who died September 4, 1866, bore him ten children, only three of whom are now living, viz.: Col. E. T. and Dr. R. L., of Columbus, and Dr. W. S., of West Point, Miss. The eldest of the ten children, Maj. A. J. Sykes, died in Aberdeen, Miss., on September 14, 1882, leaving, as his widow, Mrs. Georgia A. Sykes, one of the most accomplished ladies of the state, and four promising children; the eldest of whom, and who bore his name, has since died, while attending the law department at the Vanderbilt university, Nashville, Tenn. He also left a large estate, which has been successfully managed by his widow and eldest son, Clifton R. Sykes. Richard Sykes, a great-uncle of Capt. E. T. Sykes, was an officer in the Revolutionary war, and was killed in one of its battles. Colonel James, a maternal uncle of the subject of this sketch, was a colonel in the War of 1812. E. T. Sykes was reared and obtained his early education in Columbus, Miss., but in 1858 he graduated from the literary department of the University of North Carolina, after which he became a law student in the University of Mississippi, at Oxford, from which he graduated in June, 1860. On March 27, 1861, he enlisted in Capt. George Lipscomb's company, which responded to the first call for troops by the president of the Confederacy, and as color bearer of the company left on same day for service at and near Tuscola, Fla., under Gen. Braxton Bragg, Confederate States army. He was soon after promoted to the position of adjutant of his regiment, in which capacity he served until after the battle of Shiloh, when he was made captain of company K, Tenth Mississippi infantry, and so continued until after the campaign in Kentucky in November, 1862, at which time E. C. Walthall was made brigadier-general, and Captain Sykes was commissioned and assigned to duty upon his staff as adjutant-general. He remained on General Walthall's staff as adjutant-general until June, 1864, when, and during the Georgia campaign, he was transferred to W. H. Jackson's division of cavalry, with which he served as division adjutant-general until the close of the war. Upon the cessation of hostilities he returned to Columbus, Miss., and once more entered upon his legal practice, where, in 1883, his knowledge of his profession, and his popularity with all classes, led him to be elected to the state senate, in which body he served with distinction and honor for a term of four years. He is one of the leading attorneys of the state, is an able, forcible and eloquent speaker, is wise in counsel, cool in judgment, and is well qualified in every way to become eminent at the bar. He is a Knight Templar, is past grand chancellor in the K. of P., which order he has represented in the supreme lodge, and is also a member of the K. of H. He has been an ardent friend and promoter of all public enterprises, and his zeal and influence in everything affecting the general weal, either of his city, county or state, has given him a wide and popular reputation. On November 16, 1863, he was united in marriage to Miss Callie, daughter of Col. Isham Harrison, who was killed July 14, 1864, at the battle of Harrisburg, Miss., and Julia R., daughter of ex-Gov. James Whitfield, of Columbus. Of five Harrison brothers, two, viz.: James and Thomas, of Waco, Tex., were brigadier-generals of cavalry; Richard, a twin brother of Isham, was colonel of infantry, and Moses K., a brigade surgeon. Colonel and Mrs. Sykes have four children, viz.: Isham H., who is married to Miss Lida Williams, of Greenville, Miss.; Julia T., wife of William B. Hamilton; Augusta J., and E. T., Jr. Although Colonel Sykes has all the while been interested in planting, he never gives his farming interest his personal attention, but devotes his time exclusively to his profession. He is and has been for several years a member of the city council, is adjutant-general of the Grand Camp of Confederate veterans of Mississippi, and he and his accomplished wife are worthy church members—he of the Methodist and she of the Baptist.

Capt. Thomas B. Sykes, attorney at law, Aberdeen, Miss., was born in Decatur, Ala., in May, 1834. He was the son of Dr. William A. and Rebecca J. (Barrett) Sykes, who were natives of Virginia. Both the great-grandfather and the grandfather were patriotic soldiers of the Revolutionary war. The parents of Captain Sykes emigrated to Virginia in 1830 and to Monroe county in 1844, where they purchased a plantation. The father was a physician, being a graduate of a medical college in Philadelphia, but after coming to Mississippi, he gave up his practice and devoted himself exclusively to planting. He died in 1873 and his wife died in 1850. Only five of his ten children are living, viz.: Thomas B., Mrs. R. J. Morgan (of Memphis), Capt. E. O., Mrs. Paulina Cunningham and Dr. W. G. Captain Sykes was but nine years of age on coming to Mississippi, where he lived the life of a farmer's boy, going regularly to school; afterward he attended the University of Mississippi, where he graduated in 1854. He immediately entered the law department at Lebanon, Tenn., graduating in 1856. In the fall of that year he went to Leavenworth, Kas., in time to see the bloody scenes enacted in the border warfare which tore that state almost asunder. He practiced his profession in Kansas till 1861, also acting as agent for the Delaware tribe of Indians for the last two years of his stay there. In May, 1861, he returned to Mississippi and enlisted in company B, of the Twentieth Mississippi regiment. He went out as lieutenant and was promoted as captain of the company, but was soon transferred to the adjutant-general's department, serving as inspector of infantry; he was again transferred to Jackson's division of cavalry, where he remained till the surrender. He took an active part in all the engagements of the Tennessee army. He was captured at Fort Donelson, and kept a prisoner for six months, principally at Johnson's island. He was selected from this prison as a delegate to meet delegates from other prisons to arrange about making an exchange of prisoners. Fifty in all were chosen, but this number being considered too large, it was cut down to nine by General Wood. Captain Sykes was one of the nine, and going to Richmond, brought about the only general exchange of prisoners that took place during the war. After the close of the war he returned to Aberdeen, Miss., where he farmed for two years and then resumed the practice of his profession. He has been the recipient of many honors at the hands of his townsmen, being twice elected to the office of the mayoralty of Aberdeen. He has been a member of the Methodist Episcopal church with his entire family for years, and the superintendent of its Sunday-school for eighteen years; president of the board of stewards, and president of the board of trustees for ten years. He is a member of the Masonic fraternity, Knights of Honor, and Knights and Ladies of Honor. In February, 1865, he was married to Miss Maria H. Jones, of Hinds county, Miss. They have two daughters: Corinne and Mary D. He and his charming family live a quiet life on the plantation his father bought so many years ago, and where he died. It is one of the oldest and also one of the most beautiful places in Aberdeen. One of the most attractive and endearing features of the place are the magnificent groves of magnolia trees which were planted by the mother's hands so long ago, and which serve to keep her ever in fragrant remembrance.

Dr. William G. Sykes, of the firm of Clopton & Sykes, fire insurance agents of Aberdeen, was born in Monroe county in 1845, the son of Dr. William A. and Rebecca J. Sykes. Dr. W. A. Sykes, the elder, was born in Northampton county, Va., where he was married and moved to Decatur, Ala., and about 1842 came to Monroe county and settled on the prairie, seven miles southwest of Aberdeen, where he died in 1873, his wife having died in 1850. Both were devout members of the Methodist church. After the death of his first wife Dr. Sykes was married, a second time, to Miss S. A. Hobson, of Columbus, Miss. Dr. Sykes was a farmer's lad and received his common-school education in his native state, afterward graduating from the University of Pennsylvania at Philadelphia, and practiced medicine with great success till he moved to Aberdeen, when he retired from active life and devoted himself to his plantation, thereby accumulating a handsome property. He was a man of sound judgment, good financial ability and active in all public duties; was a prominent democrat, but not an officeseeker; was the mayor of Aberdeen and a power in all church affairs. Our subject is the youngest of nine children, of whom six are still living. The Doctor was educated principally at La Grange, Ala., where he was when the war broke out. He immediately left school, and joined company F, of the Forty-third Mississippi infantry, and served in the capacity of sergeant for a short time, when he was made an aid-de-camp to Gen. W. S. Featherstone, which position he held till just before the close of the war, when he was made adjutant of the Third Mississippi regiment. After the war he attended the University of Toronto, Canada, one year, and then graduated from the University of New York city in 1870. After practicing about one year, he gave up his profession, and devoted himself to his planting interests. He owns two fine farms, one of which is the farm on which he was born. He owns in all about eighteen hundred acres of land, a portion of which he inherited, but to which he has added largely by his own effort. He has been in the insurance business for several years. He is president of the Mississippi Exposition and Fair convention at Aberdeen, and stands high in social circles. He is a prominent member of the Knights of Honor, Eureka lodge No. 719, at Aberdeen, and was first dictator of the lodge. He is now the representative to the grand lodge, and for six years was a representative to the supreme lodge of the United States. He is also worshipful master of the Aberdeen lodge No. 32, F. & A. M., in which he stands high. He was married in 1872 to Eliza Brandon Clopton, a daughter of William H. and Cornelia W. Clopton, who came from Alabama to Aberdeen about 1840. Mr. Clopton was a prominent planter, and died in 1879. Mrs. Sykes was born in Aberdeen, where she received her early education, later graduating with high honors from the Columbus Female college. She was a lady of high attainments and amiable disposition. She died in 1886, leaving three sons and one daughter to mourn her loss. Dr. Sykes is a man of fine presence and very elegant manners. He is deservedly one of Aberdeen's most popular and representative citizens. His fellowmen have entire confidence in him as a business man; his political record is unblemished, and he is among the foremost in social circles, and is a worthy member of his noted family.

CHAPTER XX.

CONSPICUOUS RESIDENTS OF THE STATE, T.

YALOBUSHA county has a prominent citizen and a successful planter in the person of James B. Talbert, who was born on the plantation on which he now resides, February 1, 1836. He was a son of Michael D. and Mary (Truitt) Talbert, the former of whom was born in Edgefield district, S. C., in 1799, the latter in 1807. They were married in 1822, and ten years later they moved to Tennessee, and in the same year, Mr. Talbert came to Yalobusha county, where the following year he bought his home, which was then surrounded by a forest. There he passed the remainder of his life, dying in 1853. His wife died in 1877. He was a well-to-do planter and trader, and one of the prominent men of the county. He was the only one of his family except his sister, Mrs. Hartwell, who came to this state. Mr. and Mrs. Hartwell were both members of the Primitive Baptist church. Mr. Smith, the maternal grandfather of the subject of our sketch, lived and died in South Carolina. James B. Talbert was the eighth of twelve children of his parents, who lived to maturity. Of these five were sons and seven were daughters, and of this large family only Mr. Talbert and three of his sisters are living. Mr. Talbert and all of his brothers served during the war in the Confederate army. Edmund died at home, after one year's service, in the Twenty-ninth Mississippi infantry. Pinckney rose to the rank of captain, and died while a prisoner of war. John R. was discharged after a few months' service for disability. He was in the Twenty-ninth Mississippi infantry. His death occurred in 1869. Joseph T., who had served from 1863 as a scout, was killed February 23, 1867, in Tallahatchie bottoms. Our subject was educated at home, and began life for himself as a farmer and planter at the age of seventeen. October 29, 1861, he married Maggie E., daughter of Allen and Angelina Gattis, who came to Yalobusha county at a very early date. They passed their lives in this county, both dying near Oakland, the first in 1858, the other in 1867. Mr. Gattis, who was a well-known planter, was the son of Samuel Gattis of this county, who was a soldier during the Revolutionary war. Mrs. Talbert's mother's father, Olsimus Kendrick, was also an early settler of this section, who had also served the colonies during the Revolution, and who died in Tallahatchie county. Mrs. Talbert was born in this county, one of eight children of her parents, who grew to manhood and womanhood. She has five children, four sons and one daughter, all of whom are well educated: Minnie L. became the wife of J. E. Aldridge, of Washington county. She was educated at the public school at home, and at the State Female college, of Memphis, Tenn. Robert B. began life for himself at the age of thirteen, and has made his own way with success ever since. He has been a resident of Texas for several years, and during the last few years has served in different capacities in banks, having been at one time cashier of the First National bank of St. Angelo, Tex., and having been then known as the youngest national bank cashier in the United States. Joseph T. was educated at Oxford, and is now assistant cashier in a bank at Fort Worth, Tex. James B. received his education at Buena Vista, and in a common school, and is now a telegraph operator for the Louisiana, New Orleans & Texas railroad. Barksdale was educated at Hardy, and at the Capital Commercial college of Jackson, Miss. In 1862 Mr. Talbert joined company E, of the Twenty-ninth Mississippi infantry, and fought at Corinth and at Munfordville, Ky., where he was wounded in September of that year so severely as to disable him from further service. Since his return home, he has devoted his energies entirely to planting. He is the owner of about fifteen hundred acres of well-improved land, producing about one hundred bales of cotton yearly, and sufficient hay, corn and other products to meet his demands for home consumption. This fine property he has accumulated since the war, being a man of great business ability, everywhere recognized as one of the best planters of this section. His standing as a citizen is high, and he is a liberal supporter of every movement for the general good. Strictly temperate in his habits, he gives his entire attention to his business affairs, and his success has been the success of a selfmade man. If there is one thing in which he takes more pride than in all others, it has been in properly rearing and amply educating his children, and his concern for the advancement of all the interests of his county has been deep and abiding. He has given considerable attention to blooded horses, of which he is a lover, and those he drives are among the best in the town. Mrs. Talbert is a lady of culture and intelligence, and amiable disposition, a model wife and mother, hospitable to the last degree.

David S. Tankersley, College Hill, Miss., whose name heads this short biography, was born in Birmingham, Ala., in April, 1829, and is the sixth of a family of ten children. His parents, Reuben and Aisley H. (Scott) Tankersley, were natives of Virginia and Alabama, respectively; they were married in Alabama where they lived for many years. Reuben Tankersley was magistrate there for a number of years, and was also interested in agricultural pursuits. He removed with his family to Lafayette county, Miss., in the fall of 1842, and bought wild land there; he and his three sons cleared and improved his place, converting it into one of the most desirable plantations in the county; he lived only two years after coming to the county, his death occurring in 1844; he was an elder in the Presbyterian church, of which he was a worthy and consistent member; he left a wife and nine children— three sons and six daughters: Jane C., wife of Newton Buford; James M.; John F., Margaret, wife of Benjamin Smith; Mary M., wife of Yancey Wiley; David S., the subject of this sketch; Nancy E., wife of Oliver Smith; Martha A., wife of Robert Gray, of Pontotoc county, Miss., and Sarah S., wife of Jones Brooks, who resides near Waterford, Miss. The mother lived to see all of her children grown; she died in July, 1866; she was also a member of the Presbyterian church. At the age of twenty years David S. began life on his own responsibility, taking up agriculture. In the spring of 1862 he enlisted in the Confederate army and served with his command until he surrendered at Charlotte, N. C., in April, 1865. He was under Bragg from Corinth until his removal; then with Johnston, through his campaign through Georgia, until his removal; then with Hood, through Tennessee, and until his surrender at Charlotte, N. C., during the whole period in the quartermaster's department. He then returned to his home in Lafayette county, Miss., and resumed his occupation of farming. He was married March 4, 1869, to Mary S. Henlon, and of this union seven children were born—one son and six daughters—four of whom are now living: Sallie S., Ella W., Maggie L. and David N. Mr. Tankersley owns two thousand acres of land, one thousand of which are under cultivation. He has been a plain, practical farmer all his life, and has left public life to other aspirants. He has lived on his present plantation since coming to the state in 1842, and has a host of friends who esteem him for his sterling traits of character. He has always contributed liberally to all laudable public enterprises, and is a generous supporter of the Presbyterian church, of which he and his wife are members.

Charles W. Tatum, of Missionary, Jasper county, Miss., was born in Greene county, Miss., in 1836. When but two years of age he located in Jasper county, where he grew to maturity and was educated at the public schools. He was married in 1858 to Miss Martha McCormick, a daughter of that honored pioneer, J. J. McCormick. In 1861 he enlisted in company C, of the Eighth Mississippi regiment, under Colonel Flint. At the close of the war he returned home and engaged in planting, and which he has continued with such success that he is now the owner of nearly a section of land. Mr. and Mrs. Tatum have had born to them a family of three children: James J., M. D., a practicing physician of this county; Lillian C., who married W. H. Munger, and lives in Newton county; and William C. Mr. Tatum is a member of the local lodge of A. F. & A. M., and has long been connected with the Methodist Episcopal Church South. He does a general planting business, raising cotton, corn and other farm products, besides a large amount of stock.

Col. Caleb W. Taylor, who is now deceased, was born near Lexington, Ky., in 1811. He moved to Alabama when he was a young man, locating in Greene county, where he remained for a few years. Here he married Miss Lizzie Morton. Their union was blessed with two children—sons—one whom died during the war, near Lynchburg, Va., the other son will be spoken of later in this sketch. Col. Caleb W. Taylor came to where Morton now stands about the year 1850, and busied himself in planting until the outbreak of the war. He was intensely loyal to the cause of the Confederacy, doing all in his power to aid it. His home, which stood only about one-fourth of a mile from Morton, was the only place where travelers through the then sparsely settled country could find refreshment for man and beast. As he was a typical Southern gentleman, it is needless to say that all comers were welcomed, particularly in those troublous times. He was not an extensive farmer, but lived that happiest of all existences, an independent plantation life. Politically he was a whig; was a man very prominent in politics, and was a member of the seceding convention which was held at Jackson, Miss., March, 1861, and at which he earnestly advocated the right of secession. He was also a member of the Methodist Episcopal Church South, in whose service he was earnest and active, and it is not too much to say that he was a man whom everybody respected and honored in the highest degree, and one who, though dead, is not forgotten. J. A. Taylor, the second son of Col. Caleb W. Taylor, was born in Monroe county, Miss., in 1844, and came with his parents to Scott county in 1850. He has made this country his home ever since. He has been a most successful business man, owning at the present time an interest in a good paying mercantile business in the town of Morton, and he also has an interest in a store at Pelahatchee, Rankin county, Miss., while he is also an extensive land owner in Scott county. In the fall of 1861 Mr. Taylor enlisted in company G, of the Twenty-eighth Mississippi regiment, serving the first year under the command of Peter B. Stark. Later he joined the Tennessee and Georgia division of the army, and remained with it until the close of the war. The service left him, as it did thousands of others, in a debilitated condition, and he has never recovered from its effects.

Capt. Hillary L. Taylor, Bentonia, was born in Greenville, Ala., October 15, 1843, and is the third of a family of ten children. His parents, Dr. Marion D. K. and Elizabeth (McDaniel) Taylor, were natives of Georgia and Alabama, respectively. The father was a well-known physician and a successful planter. He removed to Cass county, Tex., in 1846, and was for seventeen years speaker of the legislature of that state. When his county was divided Marion county was named in his honor. He was also a member of the state senate, and has for many years presided over the democratic state conventions. He is now living at the age of seventy-three years, holding a high place in public estimation. In all the duties of life he has acquitted himself with great honor and credit. Captain Taylor was reared in Texas, receiving only a common-school education. He remained under the paternal roof until 1861, when he enlisted as a volunteer in company G, Third Texas regiment. He was promoted to the office of lieutenant, and finally to the command of his company. He participated in the battle of Oak Hill, Mo., and other engagements in the West. He was transferred to the army of the Tennessee, served under Generals Bragg, Johnston and Hood through Tennessee and Georgia, until the close of the war. He was wounded at Iuka, Miss., and was paroled at Liverpool, Yazoo county, Miss. He then settled in Yazoo county, where he has since resided. He has been engaged in planting and in mercantile pursuits. In 1875 he was elected sheriff of Yazoo county, and re-elected in 1877. In 1879 he was made president of the board of county supervisors, and in 1886 he represented the people of Yazoo county in the legislature. Captain Taylor has been twice married. First to Miss Mary G. Calvit, in November, 1865. She was a native of Mississippi, and a daughter of Charles Calvit. She died in 1879, having borne four children: Nettie H., Marion D. K., Lizzie K. and Mary G. The Captain was married a second time, in 1881, to Mrs. A. E. Harris, a daughter of Col. J. R. Mosley. Two children were born of this union, only one of whom survives, Annie Ross. Mrs. Taylor passed away in 1883. Captain Taylor owns about five thousand acres of land, and large mercantile interests, doing about $60,000 business annually. He is a member of the I. O. O. F. and of the Knights of Honor. He is a man of public spirit, benevolent and hospitable, and a citizen whose influence for good would be felt in any community.

John Taylor (deceased), one of the early settlers of old Tishomingo county, Miss., was born in Leesburg, Loudoun county, Va., in February, 1776. He was married to Miss Mary Knott in Granville county, N. C., on the 20th of May, 1801, her birth having occurred in the county in which she was married December 23, 1784, and her death on the 4th of August, 1827. In 1818 or 1819 they moved to Caswell county of the same state, but afterward became residents of Clarke county, Ga., locating near Salem, but at a still later period they settled in Jackson county, where they purchased land and resided until the fall of 1838. They then removed to Tishomingo county, Miss., and settled near the town of Old Danville, where the father continued to make his home until his children had grown to maturity and started out in life for themselves. At the time of his death in 1864, he was living with his youngest son. He lived a life of usefulness, and by attending strictly to his farming interests he raised large crops, for which he received good prices. Although an old line whig and a great Henry Clay man, he was not an active politician, and after the whig party went down he remained neutral. He was a strong Union man, and opposed secession with all the strength of his will, but at the time of his death, was the owner of quite a number of negroes. Although not a member of any church he believed in the Christian religion, and was upright and moral in every respect. He was strictly temperate, a rare thing in his day, and was never heard to take an oath. One of his elder brothers was killed while serving in the Revolutionary war, and one of his sisters married a Mr. Dorr and settled in the East. Mrs. Taylor was reared in the county of her birth, being a daughter of James Knott, who became the father of four sons: John, James, David and Robert, all of whom reared families, and lived to be old men, and settled in Georgia, with the exception of Robert, who emigrated to Tennessee, in which state many of his descendants yet live. Mrs. Taylor was an earnest member of the

Methodist Episcopal church, and was a kind and faithful wife and mother, as well as an exemplary Christian. She bore her husband thirteen children, whose names are as follows: Frances was born August 8, 1803, in Caswell county, N. C., and on the 24th of December, 1823, was married to George Swain, a brother of David Swain, of North Carolina, who afterward became governor of that state, and at her death, which occurred the same year as her mother's, left her husband with one child to care for. This child afterward was reared by her grandfather Taylor, and, upon reaching womanhood, married Dr. Long, of Athens, Ga., who became a prominent physician, and was said to have been the discoverer of anesthesia. He died a few years ago, in Athens, members of his family having moved to San Antonio, Tex. His wife was killed in a railroad wreck near San Antonio, Tex., after having borne him two sons and four daughters, all of whom are living. The second child born to Mr. and Mrs. Taylor, was Robert Knott, who was born May 3, 1804, and died in July, 1820, soon after his parents had moved to Georgia; Franklin was born May 3, 1805, and was married in Georgia, July 7, 1831, to Miss E. A. Baring, and by her became the father of four sons and seven daughters. He moved to Chambers county, Ala., during the early settlement of that region, afterward to Claiborne parish, La., where he followed planting. In 1853, with a brother, he began merchandising, a calling he very successfully followed until the opening of the war. He afterward moved to Texas, where he died in 1871, leaving a large family of children; Elizabeth Taylor was born November 22, 1806, and died in October, 1807; John Taylor, Jr., was born May 8, 1808, removed to Mississippi with his parents, and after a short residence at Columbus moved to Jacinto, the old county seat of Tishomingo, where he followed merchandising with a brother; he died at the home of his brother in 1875, a single man; Mary Ann, the next child, was born December 1, 1809; was married October 6, 1835, to Coday Fowler, who died in Tishomingo county, Miss., shortly before the war, leaving her with three sons and three daughters to care for, some of whom still reside in this vicinity; Martha was born May 26, 1812, and died in February, 1813; Calvin A. was born in Caswell county, N. C., January 6, 1813, emigrating to Georgia with his parents when six years of age, and to Mississippi with them in 1838. He was educated in the common schools and at Randolph-Macon college, Virginia, but soon after returned to Mississippi, his health having become very much impaired while in school. In 1839 he began teaching in Old Farmington, and in 1840 opened a private school in Marshall county. The following year he was elected circuit clerk of Tishomingo county, and in 1842, while holding this office, he opened a mercantile establishment which he conducted for several years, being associated during this time with his next eldest brother. He also followed the same calling with his brother in Claiborne parish, La. In 1861 he was elected to the state legislature for the second time, which office he held throughout the war. Since that time he has held the office of county treasurer of Tishomingo county, besides various other offices of importance. After the forming of Prentiss county, in 1869, he removed to Rienzi, and until 1875 conducted a mercantile establishment at that place, being now a member of the firm of John R. Moore & Co., of Booneville. He has also been successfully engaged in planting near Rienzi. He was married in Tishomingo county to Miss Elizabeth Haigh, a native of Tuscumbia, Ala., she being the daughter of Jacob Haigh, a leading merchant of that place, and a German by descent. He removed from Alabama to Mississippi about 1836, and in 1857, became a resident of Arkansas county, Ark., where he died in 1870, leaving a large family. The wife of Calvin Taylor was his eldest child. She was reared in Mississippi, and has borne her husband five children who lived to maturity, their names being as follows: John J., who is married, and is engaged in merchandising in Booneville; George C., who is living in Nashville, Ark.; James F., who is in the store of John R. Moore & Co.; Katie married R. F. Arnold, a well-known attorney of Graham, Tex., and judge of the circuit court; and Mollie, who became the wife of G. M. Street, and died in 1885, leaving three children, one of whom has since died. Katie E. and Mary E. have resided with their grandfather, Calvin Taylor, since their mother's death, their father being in business at Little Rock, Ark. Calvin Taylor and his wife are members of the Methodist Episcopal church; he is a democrat in politics, and since 1884 has been mayor of Rienzi. The ninth child born to John and Mary (Knott) Taylor was Elsa, born November 24, 1814, and on November 26, 1839, married James Rosamond, by whom she became the mother of five children. The next was Luther R., born November 24, 1816, married Miss Louisa Brewster, December 23, 1843, by whom he had four children. Sarah C., the eleventh of the family, was born September 28, 1818, and on July 7, 1840, was married to A. B. Dilworth. William A. was born January 26, 1821, in Jackson county, Ga.; was married on June 6, 1849, to Miss H. P. McCrory, by whom he had two sons, one of whom is now deceased, and James M., who was born January 12, 1827, in Jackson county, Ga., being married on October 8, 1851, to Miss Mary E. Cox.

Dr. William A. Taylor is a son of John Taylor (deceased), a sketch of whom immediately precedes this, and although born in Georgia he was principally reared in Mississippi, whither he came with his parents. After receiving a good practical education in the common schools of Tishomingo county he began the study of medicine, and after attending lectures in the University of Louisville, Ky., he was graduated as an M. D., after which he returned to his home in Mississippi, for fourteen years thereafter practicing his profession at Danville, and Jacinto. Since that time he has been an active medical practitioner of Booneville, and in his professional capacity has entered the homes of many of her citizens. His long experience (since 1860), his thorough knowledge of his profession and his sound good sense, have placed him among the foremost medical practitioners of the state, and he has been exceptionally successful in the treatment of diseases to which the human body is heir. While at Jacinto he was engaged in the mercantile and manufacturing business, but since leaving that place he had devoted his attention to his profession, with the best results. On the 6th of June, 1849, he was married to Miss Hannah P. McCrory, a native of Tennessee and a daughter of Robert McCrory, who settled in this section in 1846, following the calling of a planter near Rienzi. Mrs. Taylor was one of a large family and was reared in Mississippi. She has borne the Doctor two children, one of whom is deceased. Marcus E., their living son is a surgeon in the United States army, and is located at Vancouver barracks, opposite Portland, Ore., where he is post surgeon. He prepared himself for his profession at home under his father, took lectures at Louisville, Ky., for a time, after which he taught school in Jackson, Tenn., for a time, in order to obtain means with which to continue his medical studies, and later entered the Bellevue Hospital Medical college of New York, from which institution he graduated in 1875. While in this college he made application for a position in the United States army, was commissioned and sent to Jackson barracks, New Orleans, where he remained for three years. At the end of this time he was ordered to the Missouri department, thence to Fort Bliss, El Paso, Tex., remaining there four years, thence to Jefferson barracks, Mo., and afterward returned to his home in Mississippi on leave of absence. He was next sent to David's island, thence to Fort Stanton, N. M., remaining at this place four years, next to Boise City, Ida., and in 1890 to Vancouver barracks, where he now is. His literary education was acquired in the University of Mississippi at Oxford, from which he graduated with honors in 1871. Clay Taylor, the other son, died at the age of ten years. Mrs. Taylor is a member of the Cumberland Presbyterian church. Dr. Taylor is a member of lodge No. 305, of the A. F. & A. M., of Booneville, is a member of the State Medical association and the American Medical association. Prior to the war he was a whig, but has since been a democrat. He keeps himself posted on all the issues of the day, and is alive to all matters of importance, both of a political and social nature, but is not an office seeker, preferring to devote his time to his profession. He has a pleasant home and has given considerable attention to planting and stockraising, his cattle being of the Devonshire breed. He was appointed a commissioner of the state lunatic asylum, while B. G. Humphries was governor, and is a particular friend of Governor Stone. He is a man of unblemished reputation and well liked.

Dr. J. M. Taylor is an eminent physician of the state, but is especially well known in Alcorn, and surrounding counties, where he has resided the most of his life. He is the youngest of the thirteen children born to John Taylor, whose sketch appears above. He came to Mississippi with his father in 1839, and settled in the vicinity of Old Danville, now in Alcorn, then in Tishomingo county, where he attained his majority on the home farm and his education at home. Owing to the newness of the country at that time and the scarcity of schools, his advantages were very limited, but being possessed of a strong will and a determination to become a well-informed man, he applied himself diligently to his studies, whenever he could find the time, and, with the assistance of his father, made quite a thorough study of astronomy, philosophy, etc. Although his father was somewhat opposed to more than an ordinary education, he was persuaded by an old friend to allow his son, J. M., to enter a good school, although it was understood that after one year's attendance he was to return home and assist his father for one year. This J. M. Taylor readily agreed to do, after which he took a thorough course in Greek and Latin. He remained with his father until he commenced the study of medicine, reading under an elder brother, Dr. W. A. Taylor, at Old Danville, attending his first course of lectures in 1848-9 at Louisville, Ky. He began practicing his profession at Jacinto, the county seat of Tishomingo county at that time. Upon his return from college and in the eighteen months that he remained at this place, his skill and success in his practice made him very popular. He obtained enough money during this time to enable him to enter the Jefferson Medical college of Philadelphia, Penn., from which institution he was graduated as an M. D. Soon after this he located at West Point, Ga., where he was engaged in the drug business for some time with a cousin, but he soon after gave up this work and went to Griffin, Ga., where he was married on the 8th of October, 1851, to Miss Mary E. Cox. A short time after the celebration of their marriage they came to Jacinto, Miss., where he resumed his former practice, but had only resided there a short time when they returned to Georgia, settling at McDonough. A short time after this he was urged so strongly by his many friends at Jacinto to return there that he did so, but with the intention of locating permanently at Rienzi, then a prosperous village on the line of the Mobile & Ohio railroad, then under construction, where he successfully practiced his profession until the war opened. He then sold his property and came to Corinth in 1870, which place has since been his home and where he has built up an extended practice. Fate has always been the Doctor's friend. Indeed, his superior talents seemed to mark him as her favorite for his efficiency, skill and signal success are too well known to elaborate, suffice it to say that he does a large practice both in Corinth and adjoining towns, as well as in the country and on the railroads leading into the city. Although he has always done a general practice, circumstances early forced him to devote special attention to surgery and the diseases and accidents peculiar to women, branches very much neglected in the country, especially until the last few years. He has several times performed the operations of lithotomy, tracheotomy, hemitomy, resection of bones, cataract, excision of tumors, etc., also a great many operations in plastic surgery. His office has been the starting point for several young men scattered over different states, who have become ornaments to the profession. His first pupil, Dr. Elvis McCrory, became a distinguished surgeon in the Confederate army. Having volunteered as a private in the Second Mississippi regiment soon after returning from college, he went immediately to the front in Virginia, where he was soon made a full surgeon. He died early in the war, with the rank of brigade surgeon. His funeral was one of the most imposing ever held in the army. Dr. T. L. Patterson, a prominent physician in Charleston, Mo., studied medicine in Dr. Taylor's office before the war. Dr. W. H. McDougal and Dr. D. T. Price were students when the war began and went out with their preceptor, through whose influence they were retained in the medical service until the battle of Fort Donelson, at which place Price was captured with Dr. Taylor and retained as a prisoner of war until the general exchange. After the close of the war they returned to the Doctor's office and completed their studies, after which Dr. McDougal located at Rienzi, where he recently died, and Dr. Price at Boonville, Miss., where they soon became leading physicians and citizens. Dr. Feemster, another pupil located in Lee county, Miss., stands fair in the profession in his locality. Dr. W. C. Steele, after passing through his pupilage, did a general practice for a few years and then made a specialty of the eye, ear and throat, and located in Chattanooga, Tenn., where he does a good practice and occupies a professorship in the medical department of the U. S. Grant university. Dr. M. A. Taylor, a nephew and namesake is located in Honey Grove, Tex., and ranks with the best physicians in that country. Dr. Brewer, another pupil is doing a good practice in the Indian territory. Dr. G. C. Chandler, of Nacogdoches, La., has made considerable local reputation, both as a physician and surgeon. Dr. B. M. Bishop, after going through the ordinary course of study, commenced practice with his preceptor, and at once entered into a large and varied practice. Within the first year of his practice, when only twenty-three years of age, he performed the operation of ovariotomy and also Tait's operation with complete success, and entire relief in both cases. The Doctor's son, Charles M. and I. T. Bynum, have recently commenced the practice, the former at Kossuth, Miss., and the latter in middle Texas, with satisfactory prospects. These young men were all famous sons, and obtained their preliminary education in the schools in their respective neighborhoods. Dr. Taylor always has taken a deep and personal interest in all his pupils, and succeeded admirably in infusing into them his own enthusiasm and devotion to his profession. He received most of them into his house, treating them as part of his family, and they have ever retained for him the profoundest respect, gratitude and confidence. He omitted no opportunity to impart instruction as far as he could, both by precept and example, and did not hesitate to employ restraint and correction whenever he deemed it necessary. He is one of the founders of the State Medical association, has done a great deal for the society, and is well and favorably known throughout the state, having been, from its organization, an active member of the state board of health, its organization being brought about in great part by his earnest efforts. He was for some time chairman of the executive committee of the State Medical association, which committee is the nucleus of the board of health; was president of the State Medical society in 1874; has taken a deep and abiding interest in both organizations, and has been a member of the American Medical association since 1873. He was vice president of the State Medical association for some time, and has always believed in medical legislation, having written many articles of note for medical journals while advocating this movement. His wife died after the war, having borne him four children: Robert M., a druggist; Charles

M., a practicing physician of Kossuth; Mary M., who is the wife of a Mr. Rogers and resides at Grand Junction, Tenn.; and Andrew B., who died at the age of nineteen years, besides four others who died in early infancy. Dr. Taylor was married, the second time, to Miss Sallie Murray, a cousin of his first wife, she being reared and educated in Griffin, Ga. She has borne the Doctor three children, only one of whom is living at the present time: Beatrice M., the wife of Dr. Bishop, who is associated in the practice of his profession with his father-in-law, Dr. Taylor; Glenmore, a little daughter, died when less than a year old, while her mother was on a visit to friends in Georgia; and Rush died at the age of nine years, a handsome and promising lad. The Doctor and his wife are members of the Methodist Episcopal church, in which he is president of the board of trustees. He was a member of the A. F. & A. M. When the war opened he volunteered as a surgeon in the Twenty-sixth Mississippi Volunteer infantry and served as such until the fall of Fort Donelson, when he was captured and taken to Mound City hospital, where he was kept for a short time. He was then removed to St. Louis, where he was paroled to go to Camp Chase. While there, General Halleck kindly changed the order and sent him, at his request, to Indianapolis, where he remained but one month. From that time until the prison on Johnson's island was ready for occupancy, he was at Camp Chase, after which he remained at the former place until surgeons were released, when he signed the cartel for the exchange of prisoners and was ferried across to Sandusky. Here he was left without friends or money, but he managed to make his way to Indianapolis, thence to Kentucky and home, but as the Federal troops occupied Corinth and vicinity including his home, he was compelled to procure another parole from the Federal commanders. After they had evacuated Corinth he reported for duty, but was not again called on for duty, as his health was greatly impaired by the hardships he had undergone. The Doctor says his treatment by the Federal officers was very good, the commanding officers being very lenient with him, and recites many interesting and pleasant incidents of prison life. Before the war he was a whig in politics, but since that time he has been a democrat, although he takes no active interest in political matters. The Doctor has a very large and valuable medical and literary library. He is a profound and earnest student on general as well as medical topics, and although a highly educated gentleman, he is modest and unassuming in manners.

Leroy T. Taylor, Verona, a substantial citizen of Lee county, Miss., was born in Itawamba county, Miss., December 10, 1845, and is a son of Col. Clark W. and Louisa J. (Keys) Taylor. His father was born in Oglethorpe county, Ga., in 1820, and was one of two children of Col. Swepson and Sarah T. (Mitchell) Taylor. The grandfather of our subject was a native of Virginia, born in 1796, and was a son of Clark Taylor. Sarah T. (Mitchell) Taylor was a daughter of Randolph Mitchell. The Mitchell family were of Scotch-Irish descent, and the Taylors were of English ancestry. Clark W. Taylor was educated in Georgia, and in 1842 embarked in the mercantile trade in connection with his agricultural interests. He was elected to the state senate before the war, and in 1839 he removed to Mississippi. He was a Mason, and in his political views he sympathized with the democratic party, although before the war he was a whig. He died at Verona, Miss., in 1886, at the age of sixty-six years. He served in the Civil war for one year. He was a member of the Baptist church, and was a zealous supporter of any cause which he espoused. He and his wife had these children: Leroy T., William C., Samuel M., Lilla B., wife of W. C. Raymond, and Charles H. living. James S. was killed at Fort Donelson, and was eighteen at the time of his death; Samuel T. died at the age of eleven years; Zachariah W. died in 1877; Joseph died in 1888. The mother of our subject, Louisa J. Keys, was a daughter of Judge James and Susan M. (Thomas) Keys. Her father was judge of the probate court, and was a prominent planter. She came to Mississippi at the age of seventeen years, and has resided here since that time. She lives in Verona. Leroy T. Taylor was reared to the life of a farmer, and received his education in the schools of his native state. At the age of sixteen years he enlisted in company B, First Mississippi volunteer infantry, and was in some of the most severe service of the war. He was captured at Fort Donelson, and was afterward released. He was in the battle of Shiloh; was honorably discharged at Tupelo, and assisted in forming a company, of which he was elected second lieutenant. He was in many of the most noted engagements, following that period, until April 2, 1865, when he received a gunshot wound in the head. He was paroled in the May following. In 1865 he embarked in the mercantile trade at Mooreville, and in the next year he removed to Shannon. In 1867 he sold out the entire concern, and went on the road as a traveling salesman. He still retains a small territory, in which he travels in the interest of B. Sonenshein & Bro., of Memphis, Tenn., but devotes the greater portion of the time to agriculture. In December, 1868, he was united in marriage to Miss Sallie C. Calhoun, a daughter of Dr. William H. and Jane S. (Orr) Calhoun. Dr. Calhoun was born and reared in South Carolina, and was a son of James and Sarah (Caldwell) Calhoun, and a nephew of John C. Calhoun. The Calhouns were of Scotch-Irish descent. The doctor was a planter and practicing physician. He represented Pontotoc county in the legislature of the state, and was a citizen whom all honored and respected. His wife was a sister of James S. Orr, speaker of the house before the war, governor of South Carolina after the war, and subsequently minister to Russia, in which country he died, at St. Petersburg, in 1871. Mrs. Taylor was born April 19, 1847, and was one of a family of six children, four of whom are living: Cornelia, now Mrs. Tankersley; John C., William H. and Mrs. Taylor. To our subject and wife have been born two daughters and one son: E. L., the wife of V. C. Kincannon; Nellie, a student at college; and Swepson D., a student at Iuka, Miss. The parents are members of the Baptist church. Mr. Taylor devotes his time to planting and to some business interests which he has in Plantersville, Lee county. Politically he affiliates with the democratic party and strongly supports all its measures. He is a man of sterling traits of character, and has a host of friends and admirers in the community.

Hon. Robert Hudson Taylor, attorney, Sardis, Miss., is second in order of birth of five children born to Lawson G. and Augusta (Rawlings) Taylor, the father a native of Halifax county, Va., and the mother of North Carolina. Lawson G. Taylor came to Mississippi, when Robert Hudson was less than a year old, and located in Panola county, where he continued his occupation as a planter. His life was one of quiet, honest industry, and he died in 1871, at the age of sixty-five years. He was a modest, unpretentious man, and one of the county's best citizens. His father was a native of the Old Dominion, and his grandfather, Taylor, was a native of Wales, coming to this country at an early date and settling in Virginia. On the Rawlings side, Robert H. Taylor is of English extraction. The latter received a fair education in Panola county, where he was reared, and at the age of twenty-three years, while in the office of deputy circuit clerk of the county, he began the study of law. At the breaking out of war he enlisted in company H, Seventeenth Mississippi regiment of Panola vindicators, and was first lieutenant of the same, his company participating in the first battle of Manassas, Leesburg, and other sharp skirmishes. His company drifted down on the peninsula, between the York and James rivers. In 1862 he joined the cavalry, and was given command of company K, Valentine's regiment, and was in constant service until peace was declared. He was in the Georgia and Tennessee campaigns, was at Holly Springs when General Van Dorn attacked General Grant's depot of supplies, etc., and was in front of Vicksburg, under

General Johnston. In fact he was in almost constant engagements, from the time he enlisted until the South laid down its arms. He was in the last fight of Forrest's command at Selma, Ala., and was in command of his regiment, which was surrendered by Gen. Dick Taylor in Alabama. Returning from the war, Mr. Taylor practiced law and farmed at Old Panola, then the county seat of Panola county. He selected as his life companion Miss Belle Alston, who was born in Mississippi, and who was the daughter of William and Mary (McLeod) Alston, natives of Georgia. The fruits of this union have been nine children: Mary Belle, Eugene B., Blanche Irene, Robert Hudson, Jr., James A., Clair and Edith. In 1873, the courthouse being removed to Sardis, Mr. Taylor followed and has since been a resident of that place. The same year he was elected to the state senate, held that honorable position for four years, and in 1890 was a member of the constitutional convention. As a lawyer, Mr. Taylor is straightforward, clear-headed, well-balanced and persevering. He has a large practice, and is noted for pertinacity and strict fidelity to the interests of his clients. He is the owner of about five thousand acres of land in Panola county, and of this has about two thousand five hundred acres under cultivation. He is president of the Bank of Sardis, which has a capital of $75,000, with $10,000 surplus; it is doing a large business and is one of the most prosperous institutions in the county. Mr. Taylor is an excellent business man, and in all circumstances he has been an earnest disciple of progress and enterprise, hence his life has been one of thrift and prosperity. As the guardian of the people's interests he has zealously prosecuted his undertakings, and has ever held the love and high esteem of his constituency. He is interested in whatever pertains to the welfare of his people. Mr. Taylor is an able attorney, an enterprising business man and a citizen of whom any country might well feel proud. He is pleasant and congenial and a fine conversationalist. Socially he is a member of the Masonic fraternity.

Judge L. Temple, Nettleton, Miss., was born in North Carolina, in 1814, and is a son of Burrel and Harriet Temple, also natives of North Carolina. The father was a democrat in his political belief, and a member of the Primitive Baptist church for fifty years. He was the able editor of two papers, known as the *Primitive Baptist* and the *Freedom's Blade*. He was connected with the former twenty-seven years, and with the latter fifteen years. He died in 1879, in North Carolina, on the place where he was born. His wife, Harriet, was the daughter of Henry Ivy, a native of North Carolina, born about 1705, and died in 1854. The subject of this notice received his education in the common schools, and was trained to the occupation of a farmer. In 1833, October 24th, he was married to Lydia Powell, who was born in North Carolina, March 20, 1811, a daughter of Matthew and Elizabeth Powell, natives of the same state. Five children were born of this union. The mother died October 12, 1879. The children were named as follows: Harriet, wife of Wesley Strickland, had seven children; Lucy A., deceased, married S. A. Shackford, and they had nine children; M. M. married Louisa Roberts, and they had born to them nine children, six of whom are living; Martha H. is the wife of J. G. Marlo, and the mother of three children; M. D., married Miss P. A. Riley, and they have five children, all of whom are living; he is a successful farmer, controlling one thousand acres of land, over three hundred of which are in a high state of cultivation. He is one of the leading agriculturists, a liberal supporter of all public enterprises, and a citizen whom all honor and respect. All of the Judge's children are well settled in life, and are rearing children who will be an honor to their ancestry. Judge Temple has been prominently identified with the political history of his county. He is a stanch democrat, and has figured conspicuously in all the deliberations of that party. He has been justice of the peace three terms, and supervisor of the court seven terms. As he was president of court, at the time Lee county was organized, it became his duty, according to the existing laws, to order an election to vote upon organizing Lee county. He belongs to the Farmers' Alliance, and is a prohibitionist. He is a member of the Primitive Baptist church, and has always been a zealous worker in the cause of his Master. The Judge makes his home with his son, M. D. Temple, on the old plantation where he settled in 1848. He has witnessed a wonderful change in the face of nature since that time; then he could stand in his doorway and shoot deer, turkey, and other wild game, while the redman roamed at will, comprising the greater portion of the inhabitants. The Judge is still able to assist in overseeing the plantation, and is comparatively strong and hearty. His friends and admirers insist upon his allowing his name to be used as a candidate for the state legislature, but he has no ambition or inclination in that direction. Too much cannot be said in praise of those hardy souls who took upon themselves the burden of going to the frontier in pioneer days and laying the foundation of the present advanced civilization, and the generation of this day should not forget the debt of gratitude they owe to their ancestry for the comforts and luxuries they now enjoy.

Moses R. Temple is one of the progressive planters of Lauderdale county, Miss., where he is the owner of one thousand two hundred and sixty acres of land, of which three hundred acres are under cultivation. This land is among the best in the county, and Mr. Temple being enterprising and energetic, it yields him large crops yearly. He was born in the county in which he now resides, in October, 1852, the fourth in a family of twelve children born to John W. F. and Sarah (Jones) Temple, the former of whom was born in North Carolina and the latter in Alabama. The mother was taken from the home of her birth to Kemper county, Miss., by her parents, when quite small, but Mr. Temple came to this section when a young man, and in Kemper county they met and married, remaining there about one year after their union. They then purchased land in Lauderdale county, and Mr. Temple made that the chief business of his life, accumulating a fair share of this world's goods. He was a member of the board of county supervisors for a number of years, and for about fourteen years filled the office of justice of the peace. He was well known throughout the county, and had the respect of all who knew him, for he possessed numerous worthy qualities. After a useful and well-spent life, he died at his home in this county, in 1880, his widow surviving him only three years. Of the children born to them, six sons and one daughter survive them. Moses R. Temple remained under the shelter of the parental roof until he was eighteen years of age, at which early age he was married to Miss Ella Shepherd, a daughter of William and Ann (Cochran) Shepherd, natives of Mississippi and Alabama, respectively, the former of whom was killed while serving in the Confederate army at the battle of Atlanta. His widow afterward married Reuben Smith, and at the present time is residing in Lauderdale county. After his marriage Mr. Temple set energetically to work to make a competency for himself and family, and as above stated, is now the owner of one of the finest plantations in the county. He held the office of justice of the peace for two years, and at one time was bailiff for a short time. Like his father before him he has many warm friends, and ranks high in the estimation of all who know him. He is deservedly considered a high-minded and honorable gentleman, and he and his wife are active and worthy members of the Methodist Episcopal church. He is also a member of the A. F. & A. M. and the Farmers' Alliance, and contributes liberally of his means to worthy causes. To himself and wife two daughters have been born: Hattie and Mabel.

Judge Samuel H. Terral, of Clarke county, Miss., was born in Jasper county of that state in 1835. His parents were James S. and Alletha (Heielburg) Terral. His father was born in Wayne county, in 1809, a son of Edward Terral, of Welsh descent, who was born in South Carolina, but moved to Mississippi, going there at an early day and settling in Wayne county. He fought in the Revolutionary war, in which he enlisted from the state of South Carolina, where he then lived. His wife was a member of the Stevens family. The father was one of five children reared by his parents, the most of whom were born in this state. He was one of the early settlers in this section of the state, and became a prominent planter. He was married in Perry county of this state, in 1831, and reared a family of five sons and three daughters. Of these, John H. died in 1861; James S. Terral, who in 1858 was elected district attorney of the eighth district, over a very popular incumbent. In 1861, when the call for volunteers was made, he left his circuit and raised a company for the war, of which he was elected captain. It was designed for an infantry company, but the need in that arm of service being supplied, he turned over the company to Capt. Melancthon Smith, a graduate of West Point, for the artillery service. In the fall of 1861, a new call for troops being made, with the aid of Major Welborne, he raised the Seventh Mississippi battalion, composed of seven companies from southeastern Mississippi, of which he was elected commanding officer, lieutenant colonel. After a short training, the battalion was attached to Little's division of General Price's army. It was in the affair at Iuka, September 19, and in the battle at Corinth, October 3, 1862. On the latter day, while leading his battalion, with spirit and gallantry, he was wounded in the left breast, and was still leading and encouraging his men in the thickest of the fight, when he was stricken to the ground by a minie-ball, which broke the bone of the thigh, just above the knee. His left leg was amputated and his wound had nearly healed when erysipelas set in, of which he died November 2, 1862. He was generous and brave to a fault and had the full confidence of his men. When death approached he sent a loving remembrance and farewell to his family, in which he expressed his content to die, in that he died for his country. The next in order of birth is the subject of this sketch, Edward S. Terral, who lives in Texas and was lieutenant of the Sixteenth Mississippi regiment; Milton was lieutenant of the Thirty-seventh Mississippi regiment, company C, and was killed at Corinth, October 4, 1862; Ardelissa was married to Mr. Munger and died in Jasper county; Nannie became the wife of Mr. Smith, and is living in Jasper county; Lucretia, who also married a Mr. Smith, is residing in Heidelburg. The father of these children died in Jasper county, February, 1879. He was a Mason of high standing and a member as well as a minister of the Baptist church. The mother, who was a daughter of Thomas C. Heielburg, was born in the state of Georgia, of which her parents were both natives, they coming here at an early date and locating for a time in Perry county, whence they removed to Jasper county, where they died, the mother at Quitman, in 1885. The early life of Judge Terral was passed in Jasper county. He was educated in the common-schools and later attended Oxford university. Still later he studied law and hung out his shingle as a legal practitioner at Quitman, in 1858. He was district attorney of this county for eight years, and in 1861 was a member of the secession convention of this state. At another time he represented his county in the legislature. In 1882 he was appointed judge of the circuit court, a position which he has held with credit up to the present time. In February he enlisted in company C, of the Thirty-seventh Mississippi regiment, of which company he was elected captain and served with that rank till 1863, when he was promoted to the rank of major. He was present at the engagements of Iuka, Corinth, Vicksburg, Atlanta, the Atlanta courthouse affair, Franklin, and Nashville, Tenn. Immediately after the war he settled permanently at Quitman, and engaged in the practice of law. He was married in 1859 to Mary E. McLeod, a daughter of Alexander McLeod, of Winchester, whose wife was Lydia Avera.

Mr. McLeod was a native of South Carolina, who came with his parents to Mississippi when he was a small boy, the family locating in Greene county. He was a son of John and Mary (Bethune) McLeod. Mrs. Judge Terral's mother was born in Greene county, Miss., in 1819, a daughter of Powell Avera and wife, who was formerly a Miss Susana Middleton, who early settled in Wayne county. They were married in Greene county, Miss., in 1836, and Mrs. Terral was her only child. Mrs. McLeod died in February, 1837, in Greene county, and her father married a second time, and by that union had four children: Kenneth, John, Laughlin and Margaret, who was named for her mother. Mrs. McLeod's parents, as were also her grandparents, were among the early pioneers of this state. Her father was a physician and died in 1855. Mrs. Terral was born in Greene county, in 1836, and has borne her husband six children, of whom four are living: James A., a railroad man residing at Meridian, Miss.; he married Maud Massingale, of this county, who died leaving him one son, James A.; Joseph E., a successful attorney at law; Mary A. and Samuel H., who are living at home with their parents; John S. and Milton K. are dead. Judge Terral has been interested in politics all his life, and has always done his full share toward the general development and improvement of the county. Many years ago he united with the Masonic fraternity, and he and his wife are both members of the Methodist Episcopal church.

Dr. George A. Teunisson, now president of the Farmers' Alliance of Mississippi, is a practicing physician and life-long resident and planter of Lawrence county. He was born within six miles of Monticello, August 21, 1841. He is a son of John Henry and Mary Ann (Kennicott) Teunisson. His father was born in Amsterdam, Holland, July 4, 1800, and his mother was a native of Connecticut, born December 31, 1811, and was reared in Cattaraugus county, N. Y. John H. Teunisson was a son of John Teunisson, a Danish sailor, who married Susan Van Bergen, a native of Holland, and who followed a seafaring life between Holland and Denmark, dying in the latter place in 1802. At one time during his life, he had been very wealthy, but his fortune became so reduced that, at his death, his family was left in very moderate circumstances. His wife died in Holland at a very advanced age, in 1855, after fifty-three years of widowhood. She had several children, of whom the father of our subject was the youngest. He was apprenticed to learn the trade of chair-making. Later he took up the shoemaker's trade. When quite a youth he left home with a theatrical troupe, but, after a short time, returned to his mother, only to leave again in a short time for the sea. Embarking on board of ship, the vessel was wrecked on the coast of Cuba, and he and one other were the only ones saved. They were rescued by a ship bound for Brazil. In that country, the father of our subject remained for about one year, when he shipped for New Orleans, going soon to north Louisiana, where he engaged in planting and trading. He was at that time about eighteen years of age. He removed thence to Pike county, Miss., where he followed the same occupation. In 1828 he engaged in merchandising, on Canal street, New Orleans, but later he sold out his store and invested his money in goods, intending to bring them to Monticello, Miss., and there engage in merchandising, but the schooner on which his goods were loaded was wrecked on Lake Ponchatrain, and all on board, except Mr. Teunisson and the captain lost their lives. They were obliged to remain three days in the rigging, before being rescued. Mr. Teunisson, having lost all of his possessions, was obliged to begin life anew. He began planting for a time, in 1830, carrying out his original intention of engaging in the mercantile business, which he continued until about 1840, when he again engaged in farming, which he followed for some years. After a time he relinquished this occupation, and again turned his attention to the mercantile pursuits, in Monticello, where he continued with success until 1867, when he retired from business and removed to New Orleans, possessed of considerable property. He lived there quietly until 1873, when in Keokuk, Iowa, he was attacked with cholera, and died. He was a man of great energy and force of character, honest in every sense, in all of his dealings. He was a member and an elder in the Presbyterian church, and was a member of the Eastern Star lodge, A. F. & A. M., of Monticello, Miss. In politics he was a whig, and a Union man in sentiment and influence. His favorite recreation was chess playing, at which he was skillful.

The mother of our subject still survives, and is a resident of New Orleans, though she is now quite feeble. She has been for many years a member of the Presbyterian church. Mr. and Mrs. Teunisson had ten children, four of whom are still living: Isabella E. married John S. Lamkin, of Magnolia, Miss.; Charles E. is a merchant at Summit, Miss.; Alice E. is the wife of Wallace Wood, of Madison, Wis.; James and Eugene died in childhood; Willie H. was a member of General Gordon's staff, acting as a courier, was captured by the Federals at Nashville, Tenn., and died at Camp Chase, Ohio, at the age of eighteen years; he was the youngest of the family and a general favorite with all who knew him; Helen L. married Col. M. A. Oatis, and lived in Monticello, where she died in 1866, leaving her husband two children. Two other children died in infancy, being unnamed. Dr. George A. Teunisson was reared in Monticello, Miss., and was educated at the common schools near his home and at the Monticello academy, he studied medicine, which study was interrupted for four years by the war. While a student at what is now Tulane Medical college, he enlisted in company A, of the Twenty-second Mississippi regiment, with which he served until the close of the war. He took part in the campaigns around Vicksburg, at Baton Rouge, and in the campaigns in Kentucky under General Johnston, being present at the battles of Corinth, Vicksburg, Rolling fork, Baton Rouge, Baker's creek, Jackson, Resaca, Atlanta, New Hope church, Peachtree creek, Decatur, Columbia, Franklin, and Nashville. He was in the rear guard, to which is given the credit of having saved Hood's army when retreating from Nashville. After the return of Hood from Tennessee, Dr. Teunisson received a furlough of sixty days and returned to his home, but rejoined the army at Demopolis, Ala., and was paroled at Meridian, May, 1865. He was regularly promoted from fourth sergeant of his company to that of adjutant of the Twenty-second regiment, but upon the reorganization of the regiment he was appointed first lieutenant of company A, Twenty-second Mississippi regiment.

Returning home at the close of the war, he re-entered Tulane Medical college, but his studies were interrupted, this time by illness in his family, and he was prevented from immediately returning to the institution, from which he finally graduated in 1884. Soon after he began the practice of his profession in Monticello, and he has come to be regarded as one of the leading physicians of his county. He was married April 5, 1866, to Miss Anna C. Daughtry, a daughter of Enos Daughtry, a native of Anson county, N. C. Mr. Daughtry was born December 6, 1806, and came to Mississippi when a child, with his parents, Enos and Catherine (Bryant) Daughtry. He was a member of a Quaker family, of Irish and French ancestry, who went to Ireland as refugees from France, and thence to America, at the time of the Huguenot massacre. The family landed at Natchez, and were residents near there for a time, later removing to Pike county, Miss., where Enos, the father of Mrs. Teunisson, was reared. He was married in Pike county, and then removed to Hinds county in 1839, and thence to Lawrence county in 1846. He was a planter, a hotel-keeper and a merchant, during different periods of his life. His wife was Mary Ann, daughter of Richard and Anna (Stovall) Ratliff, who was born in South Carolina, August 30, 1816, and came, when a child, with her parents to Pike county, where she grew to womanhood. To this

union have been born five children, three of whom are living: Dr. J. B. Daughtry of Brookhaven; J. H. Daughtry of Houston, Tex., and wife of Dr. George A. Teunisson; Roy T. served as a soldier in the late war and was a prisoner of war for seven months at Point Lookout, and died at the age of thirty-two years; Clara died at the age of two years. To Mr. and Mrs. Teunisson have been born six children, five of whom are living: Mary A., who graduated from Whitworth college in 1891; and Alice, Rose, George E. and John H. are members of their parents' home. Dr. Teunisson is a democrat in politics and has twice represented his county in the state legislature, having been reëlected in 1880 and again in 1886. He was elected vice president of the Farmers' Alliance of the state of Mississippi, and succeeded to the presidency on the death of R. C. Patty, the former president. The Doctor is also much interested in Masonry. He was elected master of the Eastern Star lodge in 1868, and has held that position for twenty years. He is now a district deputy grand master of this order, a position which he has filled for the past ten years. He and his wife are members of the Presbyterian church, in which he has held the office of elder for twenty years, being also superintendent of the Sunday-school. He has been acting superintendent of education for two years, as a substitute for the appointed superintendent, who is a lady. Outside of his professional duties, the Doctor is engaged in planting, having a fine home near Monticello. His practice is large and lucrative. He is a member of the State Medical association.

Dr. Andrew H. Thomas (deceased) was a very prominent physician, living near Cumberland, Webster county, Miss., whither he had removed in 1857, but was a native of Nashville, Tenn., born in 1818. His father, Andrew Thomas, removed to the Lone Star state many years ago, followed farming and trading, and there received his final summons. Dr. Thomas left his home in Nashville when about fourteen years of age, went to Pickens county, Ala., and worked there for a short time. He started life a poor boy and earned his first twenty-five cents by carrying brick all day. He afterward learned the blacksmith's trade, and worked at the forge until he earned money enough to buy a negro, who was taken sick on the day he paid for him and died in a few days. He continued to work at his trade until he made money enough to buy another negro, for whom he paid $1,800. This negro he taught the blacksmith trade, and this way the Doctor continued to carry on blacksmithing, and in connection, also, engaged in farming, for a number of years investing the proceeds in negroes, etc. About 1840 he married Miss Martha E. Walker, who was also born near Nashville, Tenn., in 1824. She went with her parents to Lowndes county, Miss., where she was married to Dr. Thomas. From boyhood, Dr. Thomas had had a taste for the medical profession, and prior to his marriage had taken a course of lectures, not with an intention, however, of making that his profession, but merely for his own satisfaction. An occasional professional call to a sick neighbor soon gave evidence as to his skill and ability as a physician, and after the Civil war, his slaves having been freed, he placed his farming interest in the hands of other men, he, himself, devoting his entire attention to his profession. This he followed with marked success until his death in January, 1891. He was a man of strong and vigorous mind and those who knew him best, loved and appreciated him most. The willing heart and ready hand that so often ministered to others in the alleviation of suffering and the prolonging of life was helpless before the Great Reaper. He left a devoted wife and a family of interesting children to mourn their loss.

Noble, generous and hospitable, he had a kind word for everybody, and the child of want never went empty-handed from his door. He was influential and active in all that went toward the advancement of the town and county, and was ever ready to give his weight to any worthy enterprise for the public weal. He was a devout Methodist, and was formerly a member of the Masonic fraternity. He was a good financier and left a handsome property. Soon after his marriage he settled in Nashville, Miss., where he resided until about 1857, when he removed to what is now Webster county, where he made his future home. He was one of a large family of children. His widow, who still resides on the old farm near Cumberland, is an excellent lady and a devout Methodist, also. Her father, Mr. Walker, removed many years ago from Tennessee to Lowndes county, Miss., where he died when Mrs. Thomas was a girl. Dr. Thomas was the father of ten children, viz.: John, died at nine years of age; Mary, now deceased, was the wife of Dr. F. N. Arnold, of Walthall; Sallie, wife of D. T. Hartley, a planter near Cumberland; Andrew H. was born in Lowndes county, in 1851, and passed his boyhood in assisting on the farm and in attending the common-schools. In 1868 his father placed him in his dry goods store at Bellefontaine, as a clerk, and after serving two years in that capacity he returned to his father's farm. In 1873 he engaged in merchandising at Cumberland, where he has been in business ever since, and is perhaps the leading merchant of the county, carrying a very heavy stock of general merchandise; he also has large planting interests. He is one of the most successful business men of northern Mississippi, is an excellent financier and is a gentleman in every sense of the term. The next child, in order of birth, born to Dr. Thomas, was John A., also a prominent merchant at Cumberland. The latter was born in Lowndes county, Miss., in 1853, received a common-school education, and since 1870 has been merchandising. He also has large planting interests, and is a man not only respected and honored for his upright and honest dealing, but is one of the county's best citizens. The doctor's sixth child was Catharine C. (deceased), who was the wife of A. W. Dominick, of Houston. James L. died in infancy. James Walker was burned to death in a building in Winona, October 6, 1889. He was a merchant also, and had been to Memphis to purchase goods, and on his return stopped over night at that place to wait for the train. He was a young man of excellent habits, fine business ability, and had a bright future opening before him. He was educated at Cumberland and at the state university. Laura E., wife of J. E. Clark, an attorney, of Walthall, and Dr. Sylvester S., who is a practicing physician now on the old homestead. Sylvester S. received his education principally at Cumberland and graduated in his profession from Louisville (Ky.) Medical college.

C. L. Thomas is a Hinds county Mississippian, born in the month of July, 1829, and throughout life he has followed the calling of a planter, at which he has been reasonably successful. He is the fourth of eight children born to Andrew Thomas, a native of Tennessee, who came to the state of Mississippi when about eighteen years of age, and eventually became the owner of a large amount of real estate in Hinds county, and was one of its most substantial citizens prior to the opening of the Civil war. C. L. Thomas, like the majority of youths, was an attendant of the common schools during his youth, but at the age of fifteen years he entered Mississippi college at Clinton, where he spent four years, but did not complete the course. At the age of nineteen years he engaged in general merchandising at Clinton, continuing until 1861, when he closed out his business, which had been a very profitable and prosperous one. After the war he became assistant superintendent of the Alabama & Vicksburg railroad, continuing until 1866. Mr. Thomas' first purchase of land was on the Big Black river in 1868, a tract of ten hundred and eighty acres, on which he engaged in farming, and has been so occupied ever since. In 1870 he purchased another valuable tract of land, containing eleven hundred acres, the most of which is in pasture, and which he uses as a stockfarm. He is quite extensively engaged in the raising of horses, mules and cattle, about thirty colts being foaled each spring. He has two fine thoroughbred horses, also two pedigreed jacks, and his herd of Jersey and Holstein cattle is an exceptionally large and fine one. His home place, which contains six hundred acres, was purchased in 1885, and on this place is a handsome and comfortable residence, pleasantly located. He has about fifteen hundred acres under cultivation, on which he annually raises about two hundred and fifty bales of cotton, and has three hundred acres devoted to grass, from which he secures two hundred and fifty tons of hay, which he is now selling at $16 per ton. Five hundred acres of his land are heavily covered with timber, the most valuable woods being oak, hickory and walnut. He is enterprising and progressive in every respect; is intelligent, well posted and up with the times, and has always been strictly honorable in all his business transactions. He has always manifested much interest in the cause of education, and for at least twenty years has been trustee of Central Female institute and Mississippi college. He was married in 1864 to Miss Cabbell, of Hinds county, which union has not resulted in the birth of any children. He is a worthy and earnest member of the Baptist church, in which he is a deacon, and socially is a member of the A. F. & A. M.

B. F. Thomas, merchant, and manager of Chamberlain hotel, Grenada, Miss., was born March 23, 1846, in Sumter county, Ala., and was the youngest of a family of nine children born to Morrison and Patience (Horn) Thomas, natives of the Old North state. Morrison Thomas was born April 17, 1802, and was the second son of a family of eight children, seven sons and one daughter, born to the marriage of Theopolis Thomas, who was a native of the famous old Edgefield district, N. C. The latter's eldest son, Archibald, was the first husband of Mrs. Dr. Trimble (see sketch); Wade R., the third son, died in Meridian, Miss., leaving a wife and two children; John R. died in Alabama during the latter part of the war, and left a wife and child, both of whom were soon laid to rest; Edwin resides in Gainesville, Ala., where he is engaged in merchandising; Bennett B., makes his home in Sumter county, Ala., and there follows the occupation of a planter; James R. died in 1867, leaving a wife and two children, and Margaret R., the daughter, married W. B. Barnes, who came to Mississippi in 1850, and who died eighteen years later, leaving a large family, two of whom are now living, Willie and Margaret. Morrison Thomas resided in Alabama for a number of years, and then, in 1849, immigrated to Mississippi, coming overland to this state. He settled on a place eight miles west of Grenada, and became one of the leading planters of the county. He was a stanch whig and kept himself well posted, being a constant reader of the news. He was a member of the Presbyterian church and a liberal contributor to the same. He was also a member of the I. O. O. F. lodge of Grenada, and a Mason of the same place. His death occurred on April 17, 1872, in Mississippi, after a long and useful life. His wife, whom he married in North Carolina, was born in 1805 and died on December 31, 1869, in full communion with the Presbyterian church. Both were kind, generous and hospitable, and won the respect and esteem of all with whom they came in contact. Of the large family of children born to this union, four lived to be grown and three survive at the present time: A. V. B., the eldest (see sketch of J. T. Thomas), and Rebecca F., who is the wife of C. C. Peete, formerly of Parson's station, and who is now keeping a hotel, the Brinkley house, at Greenwood, Miss. She was educated at the Female institute. Her husband is one of the very early settlers of this county, having located and settled a place near what is now Parson's station, and this was named Peete postoffice, for him. B. F. Thomas came to Mississippi, with his parents, when but three years of age, and supplemented a common-school education by attending the Masonic academy, where he received a thorough education. After the war he commenced for himself as a farmer, followed this occupation for about six years on the old home place, and on coming to Grenada clerked for Lake Bros., until 1876, when he was made deputy sheriff under Capt. R. N. Hall, continuing in that capacity until 1879, when he was in the brokerage business for a short time. He formed a partnership with his brother, A. V. B. Thomas, in the grocery business in 1882, and this they still continue. In 1889 they took charge of the Chamberlain hotel, and are now keeping one of the best and most popular houses in the state, our subject having full charge of the same and his brother, A. V. B., of the store. B. F. Thomas was married first to Miss Flora Lewis, daughter of John Lewis, a native of Tennessee and the niece of J. M. Dunkin (see sketch). She was born in 1847 and died in 1869, leaving one child, Effie. She was a member of the Methodist Episcopal church. Effie Lewis became the wife of R. W. Mullin, but is now deceased, leaving one child, Mary Mullen (see sketch of R. W. Mullin). Mr. Thomas was married the second time to his present wife, whose maiden name was Annie Poston, of Shelby county, Tenn., and who was the daughter of William King and Mary (Park) Poston, both decendants of wealthy and distinguished families. Mrs. Thompson was educated at the Female college, Memphis, and is a lady of culture and high social standing. Her father was a very eminent lawyer, but had never held public office, except that of member of the legislature in 1866-7. To the union of Mr. and Mrs. Thomas was born two children: Frank and Morrison. Mrs. Thomas is a member of the Methodist church. Mr. Thomas entered the Confederate army, during the last eighteen months of the war, in Ballentine's regiment, Armstrong's brigade, Jackson's division, and participated in all the battles fought by that regiment from that time until the retreat from Resaca to Atlanta. He is a member of the I. O. O. F., Grenada lodge No. 6, Knights of Pythias No. 8, and the Masonic lodge No. 31, in which he is a Knight Templar. Mr. Thomas has been treasurer of the grand lodge of Knights of Pythias for eleven years, and in 1889 he was elected past grand chancellor of the state of Mississippi. He takes a great deal of interest in society work. In politics Mr. Thomas is a democrat and is well posted on all the political issues of the day. He attends closely to business and is popular and highly respected by all. He is a descondant of one of the most prominent families in the state.

J. Talbert Thomas, cashier of Grenada bank, chancery clerk of the county and secretary of the Central Fair and Livestock association, the meeting of which was held at Grenada, Miss., and which embraces the counties of Grenada, Montgomery, Carroll, Le Flore, Tallahatchie, Yalobusha, Calhoun, Choctaw and Webster, is a native of Mississippi, born in what is now Grenada county and reared in the city of Grenada. He is a son of Adrian V. B. and Mary E. (Nason) Thomas, grandson of Morrison and Patience (Horn) Thomas, and great-grandson of Theopolis Thomas, who was of Edgefield county, N. C. Morrison Thomas was born in the Old North state in 1802, and moved to Mississippi in 1849. He was a stanch whig in politics, and after moving to the last named state settled on what was afterward known as Whig island, on the Yalobusha river, where he reared his family and opened a large farm. He soon became the owner of large tracts of land, many negroes, and was one of the representative citizens of the county. Although a man of prominence and very active in political affairs, he was no officeholder. He was a leading member of the Presbyterian church, and died on the 17th of April, 1872, at the age of seventy years. His wife was born in North Carolina in 1805, died on the 31st of December, 1869, at the age of sixty-four years. She was also a member of the Presbyterian church. Of their eight children Adrian V. B. Thomas was the eldest, and is one of the three now surviving. His birth occurred on the 31st of March, 1835, and he was educated in Grenada. He served during the last three years of the war in Ballentine's regiment, Armstrong's brigade, Jackson's division, Mississippi cavalry, and was wounded and captured at the battle of Selma, Ala., on the 1st of April, 1865. He was shot in the leg, below the knee, and from this injury he has never fully recovered. Soon after the war he settled at Grenada as a merchant, and was elected chancery clerk in 1876, holding that position in a satisfactory and creditable manner for eight years, or two terms. He is one of the best and most popular men in the county, as well as one of its oldest citizens; has a host of warm friends, and his uprightness and integrity are proverbial. He is social, kind, and very charitable. He is one of the leading merchants of Grenada, owns a one-half interest in Chamberlain hotel, is a director of the Merchants' bank of Grenada, and is also engaged in planting. He married Miss Mary E. Nason, of Grenada county, who was left an orphan when a child. Her grandfather was of Irish ancestry. This union was blessed by the birth of six children, five of whom are now living. The parents are leading members of the Presbyterian church, in which Mr. Thomas has been an elder for many years. He has been a member of the I. O. O. F. lodge No. 6, for nearly thirty years, and in politics is a democrat, having been very active in political affairs in early life. J. Talbert Thomas, the second in order of birth of the above mentioned children, is a selfmade man. At the age of sixteen years he commenced clerking in a store, and one year later was made deputy chancery clerk under his father, and at the early age of twenty-one years he was made circuit clerk. In 1887 he was elected chancery clerk and this office he is holding at the present time. The Grenada bank was organized in July, 1890, with J. W. Griffis, B. C. Adams, Edgar Wert, Walter Trotter and Judge A. J. Roane as directors, and Mr. Thomas was made cashier in September, of the same year. This bank has a paid-up capital of $60,-000. Mr. Thomas is not only one of the county's most energetic, thorough-going business men, but, having the public interest in view, is foremost in the support of charitable, progressive and praiseworthy enterprises. In politics he is strictly democratic. He is a member of the I. O. O. F. lodge No. 6, and is at present deputy grand master of the state of Mississippi, having attended all the meetings of the grand lodge since his election to the office. He is also a member of the Knights of Pythias. Like his father and grandfather before him, he is a worthy member of the Presbyterian church. He was married to Miss Ruth A., youngest daughter of Dr. and Mrs. R. L. Jones, on May 19, 1891.

J. V. Thomas, of Cardsville, ex-sheriff of Itawamba county, was born in Hickman county, Tenn., August 30, 1819. He is a son of Samuel and Nancy (Sparks) Thomas, who were natives of Georgia. His parents were members of the Missionary Baptist church, and they had six sons and two daughters, seven of their eight children living to be grown. Of this family, J. V. Thomas was the first born. He was educated in Hardeman county, Tenn., and began life for himself, as a mechanic, at an early age. December 28, 1843, he married Miss Martha A. Bourland, who was born in Mississippi, a daughter of James S. and Mary (Hudspeth) Bourland, and who has borne Mr. Thomas six children, five of whom lived to maturity: Samuel J., Mary E., Rebecca, Eulalia, Eliza and Fleming H., who is deceased. Mr. Thomas has lived on his present homestead since 1844, and was one of the early settlers of this part of the county. He accumulated considerable property, and his influence in local matters is recognized by all his fellow-citizens. Politically he is a democrat, and on the democratic ticket was elected to the office of sheriff of Itawamba county, a position which he held with great credit during a period of seven years. His wife is a member of the Presbyterian church, and he is a Master Mason of long standing. Liberal and progressive in his views, and generous and helpful by nature, he has done much to aid all worthy local causes, and has contributed his full share to the establishment and maintenance of churches, schools and other means of public advancement and enlightenment.

Rev. R. S. Thomas, D. D., the present pastor of the Cumberland Presbyterian church of

Coffeeville, Miss., is one of the most highly respected citizens of Yalobusha county. He was born in Wilson county, Tenn., in October, 1820, and is the son of Jacob and Mary (Donnell) Thomas. The parents were born in the state of North Carolina, and removed with their parents in childhood to Tennessee, settling in Wilson county; there they grew to mature years and were married. They had born to them fifteen children, thirteen of whom lived to be grown; there were nine daughters and six sons, all of whom are now deceased, excepting our subject and Mrs. McLean. Thomas D. and G. B., two of the brothers, also entered the ministry. R. S. Thomas was the fifth child born, and was educated in the University of Lebanon, Tenn. He did his first ministerial work at Dryesburg, Tenn., and thence came to Coffeeville, Miss., where he has since been engaged in the work of the Master. He has preached upward of sixteen hundred sermons and has been actively interested in educational affairs. He was the founder of the Coffeeville academy in 1852; this institution flourished until the breaking out of the war, Dr. Thomas being president and Misses Patton and Ingals assistant teachers. The school was re-opened, and continued until the present school was founded in 1870. Dr. Thomas had the degree of A. M. conferred upon him in 1859, and that of D. D. in 1877. He was married in Coffeeville to Miss Elizabeth L. Carr, a native of New Hampshire, who came to Mississippi in her childhood with her parents; she was reared and educated in Yalobusha county, and was a most efficient worker in the Cumberland Presbyterian church. She died in 1871. Dr. Thomas was married a second time to Miss Annie Rayburn, a daughter of D. M. Rayburn, one of the very earliest settlers and founders of Coffeeville. He donated the land for the site of the place in 1834. He was the first clerk of Yalobusha county, and held the office for a number of years. He was the first merchant to do business in Coffeeville. He was a member of the Cumberland Presbyterian church, and was one of its most liberal supporters; he was an elder at the time of his death. Mr. Rayburn was a native of Obion county, Tenn. He married Miss Harriet L. Buntin, a Virginian by birth, who came with her parents to Mississippi. She died in 1866, having had born to her five children, three of whom lived to maturity, and only one of whom now survives, the wife of Dr. Thomas. One of the sons, Rutilius, died in the war in Tennessee. Mrs. Thomas is the eldest child, she was reared and educated in Coffeeville. The Doctor and his wife are among the most highly respected people of the county, and rank with the leading citizens of Coffeeville. Dr. Thomas at one time was a member of the Masonic fraternity, belonging to the Blue lodge and chapter.

William B. Thomas is a native of Dinwiddie county, Va., where he was born on the 5th of December, 1858, the fifth in a family of six, born to Edward and Agnes E. (Thompson) Thomas, natives of Virginia. Edward Thomas was a planter, a calling he followed until the opening of the Civil war, when he enlisted in the Confederate service, serving until his death, which occurred in 1863, at the age of forty-seven years. The paternal grandparents, David and Annie Thomas, were also Virginians, their parents having been early settlers of that state, and among its most prominent citizens. William B. Thomas was educated in the private schools of his native state, and in 1880 became a resident of Mississippi, where he has since made his home. When only fifteen years of age he began to fight the battle of life for himself, and owing to his pluck, perseverance and energy he is now worth about $50,000. He is the owner of some eleven hundred acres of land, of which he has five hundred acres under cultivation, and is worthy the reputation he has won as a progressive, industrious and enterprising agriculturist. He is very practical in his views, keeps fully apace with the progress made in his calling, and is ever ready to adopt new and improved methods upon his plantation. In 1887 his marriage to Miss Pattie Connell was celebrated, and their union has been blessed in the birth of two little daughters: Eveline P., who died August 3, 1888, and Agnes E., who is an interesting and promising child. Mrs. Thomas is a daughter of W. C. Connell, who was born in Wilkinson county, Miss., November 26, 1821, in which state he is still making his home, having thoroughly identified himself with its interests. Mr. Thomas is a member of the Methodist Episcopal church. As a citizen his reputation is untarnished, and in all the affairs of life he has borne himself in an upright manner, and is now recognized as a man of true worth. He is extremely well informed and naturally intelligent, and as a conversationalist is very interesting and entertaining. His manners are easy, courteous and pleasant, and he has the grace and tact of putting all at their ease who enter his presence. He is a member of the Knights of Honor, of which he is a warm supporter, and he thoroughly approves of worthy secret organizations. He is of medium stature, and is of rather fair complexion.

Bishop Hugh Miller Thompson, now at the head of the Episcopal church of Mississippi, was born in the city of Londonderry, Ireland, June 5, 1830. While he was yet a child his parents immigrated to the United States, locating first at Caldwell, N. J., where they remained eight years, when they removed to Cleveland, Ohio. John Thompson, the father of Hugh, was a contractor by occupation, and came to the United States with the view of having a better and a larger field for carrying on his business. The Thompson family were purely English, and belonged to the church of England. The mother, whose maiden name was Ann Miller, was of Scotch origin, and the family were strong Presbyterians. While on their way to the United States they were shipwrecked in the bay of St. Lawrence, losing everything they had. The father died in Columbus, Ohio; the mother is still living. The subject of this sketch received an academical education in the schools of Cleveland, and took his theological course at Nashotah house, Wisconsin. He was ordained deacon at that place June 6, 1852, by Bishop Kemper, and priest in St. John's church, Portage, Wis., August 31, 1856. During his deaconate he had charge of Grace church, Madison, Wis. In 1853 he removed to Maysville, Ky., where he remained one year, and then returned to Wisconsin, where he was assigned to mission work at Portage and Baraboo. Immediately on his ordination to the priesthood, he became rector of St. John's church, at Portage. In 1858 he was elected rector of St. Matthew's church, at Kenosha, Wis., and after remaining there one year removed to Galena, Ill., and became rector of Grace church at that place. In 1860 he was made professor of ecclesiastical history of Nashotah and founded Kemper hall. In the same year he became editor-in-chief of the *American Churchman*, published at Chicago, Ill., and continued in this office until the *Churchman* was merged into the *Churchman*, at Hartford, Conn. In 1871 he became rector of St. James' church, at Chicago, which was burned in the great fire of that year. In January, 1872, he removed to New York and took charge of Christ church, and with these duties were added the editorship of the *Church Journal* and *Gospel Messenger*. In 1875 he became rector of Trinty church, at New Orleans, La., where he remained until he was consecrated assistant bishop of Mississippi, February 24, 1883. Four years later, upon the demise of Bishop Green, he succeeded to the position of bishop, and the following year attended the pan-anglican conference, in London, and in August, of that year, delivered the funeral oration of Bishop Harris, of Michigan, which was received by the clergy and laymen with great favor. Bishop Thompson was united in marriage in February, 1853, at Madison, Wis., to Caroline Berry, and two children were in time born to them: Annie, now the wife of James Pearce, of New York; and Frank who is a minister of the Episcopal church, and is at present chaplain in the United States navy, assigned to the flagship Charleston. Mrs. Thompson died in 1857, and the Bishop's second marriage was consummated at Kenosha, in the year 1859, the maiden name of his wife being Anna Hinsdale, daughter of Henry B. Hinsdale, late secretary of the Northwestern Telegraph company. The issue of this union was the following children: Mary, wife of William T. Howell, of Wisconsin, attorney for the Northwestern railroad; and Hugh G., a planter in Mississippi. Bishop Thompson is a man of medium stature, with a solid frame, a large intellectual head, covered with a liberal growth of hair turning gray. He is a man of deep thought and extensive research, and as a pulpit orator ranks high, his equals in the state being few. His command of language is excellent; his diction pure and engaging, and his conclusions forcible as well as logical. His imagery, when indulged in, is brilliant and captivating. He is a ready conversationalist, his thoughts which come quick, either sparkling with wit or laden with wisdom. He is genial in character, courteous in manner, and a good entertainer. In the suburbs of Jackson he has an elegant home, where he is surrounded with those attractions that are essential to the happiness of a gentleman of culture. The church which he represents is indeed fortunate to have so able and so popular a man at its head. Notwithstanding the onerous duties, incumbent upon him as rector and bishop of his church, he has found time to enter the literary field and is the author of several valuable books. In 1860 he published "Unity and its Restoration," and in 1862, "Sin and its Penalty," following this, in 1868, was published "First Principles," and in 1872, "Absolution." In 1873 he brought out his work, "Is Romanism the Best Religion for a Republic?" also "The Kingdom of God," and a volume of lectures published in 1885. "The World and the Kingdom" was issued in 1888, and in 1890 "The World and the Man" was published, which is now in its third edition.

Jacob Thompson, Lafayette county, Miss., was born in Caswell county, N. C., May 15, 1810. His father, Nicholas Thompson, was descended from a family which emigrated from England to the state of Pennsylvania, more than two centuries ago. In his youth Mr. Thompson was prepared for college at Hillsboro, N. C., and entered the university at Chapel Hill in his seventeenth year, graduating in 1831, with the first honors of his class. He was at once appointed tutor of the university, and discharged his duties faithfully for eighteen months, when he resigned and began the study of law in the office of Judge John M. Dick, of Greensboro. He was admitted to practice in 1835, when he removed to Mississippi and established himself at Pontotoc, where the United States land office had just been opened. His first political speech in the state was made at Pontotoc at a public meeting which was called for the purpose of favoring the policy of the state's endorsing the Union bank bonds for $5,000,000, and also for instructing the representatives in the legislature to vote for the endorsement. He was bitterly opposed to the proposition, and at the meeting in Pontotoc made a speech against it which attracted wide attention and brought him prominently to the notice of the people of the state. Banks at this time were springing up everywhere over the state; banking had already become a craze. He predicted ruin and disaster to flow from it, and placed the Union bank in the same category with the rest. The current, however, could not be stemmed, and the resolution favoring endorsement was passed. This came to be one of the most vital questions that has ever affected the life of Mississippi, and much was heard of it in the years that followed. The general collapse of the banks came in 1837, and gloom brooded over the state. In 1839 Mr. Thompson was first elected to congress on the democratic ticket with Hon. Albert G. Brown. The public lands of Mississippi having but lately been settled there was much confusion in the perfecting of titles, and numberless conflicts of various kinds. It being a new country there were a great number of contracts for surveying and for carrying the mails, new postoffices having been opened and new routes located. All these matters, in which Mr. Thompson's constituency was interested, needed adjustment and settlement, and he being in Washington, as their representative, was situated so he could give his personal attention to the many necessary demands upon him, a task which he undertook with diligence and determination and accomplished to the satisfaction of each and all who called upon him for his friendly aid. By this means he won many friends among the masses of the people at home, and "after this period," says one, "his popularity was greater than his party strength."

In 1840 he took an active part in the presidential canvass between Van Buren and Harrison. He was an ardent supporter of the former. He desired to retire from public life on the expiration of his congressional term, but in 1841 he was unanimously renominated by his party convention, together with Hon. William M. Gwin. The great question of the states making good the Union bank bonds, which the state had rashly endorsed, forced itself into the canvass of this year. The bank had become bankrupt and its bonds dishonored. The catastrophe had come which Mr. Thompson had predicted and warned against. Payment of the bonds was refused by the governor on the ground that the state was not legally or morally bound. Says Mr. Claiborne, in his history of Mississippi: "Mr. Thompson, being a candidate for congress, was called upon for his views, and in a letter to Mr. Webster, of Vicksburg, he maintained that the governor was right in his refusal to admit the binding obligation of the state's endorsement. This letter," continues the same author, "stated the whole case with so much clearness, force and eloquence that it satisfied the public mind, and from that day to this no one has been or could be elected to any position of honor by the people of the state who did not endorse the sentiments of that letter. The succeeding legislature, in proclaiming the position it took in regard to the Union bank bonds, embodied in substance the whole letter." In November of this year, Mr. Thompson and his colleague, Mr. Gwin, on the democratic ticket, were elected to congress; and at each succeeding election thereafter Mr. Thompson was a candidate for congress, on the democratic ticket, and triumphantly elected until 1851, during which year, on the 4th of March, his sixth term closed, making for him twelve years of continued service in the house of representatives. For one term he was chairman of the committee on public lands, and for two terms was chairman of the committee on Indian affairs. He reluctantly consented to become a candidate again in 1851, having previously published a letter announcing his intention not to run again. This time he and the entire democratic ticket were defeated. In 1852 he was a delegate to the Baltimore convention which nominated Franklin Pierce for president, and was one of the committee who officially notified Mr. Pierce of his nomination. The latter, during his presidential administration, tendered to Mr. Thompson the consulship to Cuba, but it was declined. Governor Brown, of Mississippi, offered him the commission of United States senator on the resignation of Hon. Robert J. Walker, who, while Mr. Thompson was still serving as representative in congress, resigned his seat in the senate to accept a place in President Polk's cabinet. This commission was also declined. In 1855 he was prevailed upon to become a candidate for the United States senate, but in the party caucus it was decided to nominate Hon. Jefferson Davis. He was an active supporter of Mr. Buchanan for the presidency in 1856. After his election, President Buchanan tendered him a place in his cabinet, inviting him to take charge of the interior department, which position he accepted. As secretary of the interior he systematized the work of the department and infused new life into it. The treacherous conduct of a trusted clerk in the interior department served at one time as sufficient foundation for false and malicious charges against Mr. Thompson. The secretary of the interior was the custodian of the Indian trust fund, which consisted principally of the bonds of different states and amounted to more than $3,000,000. The actual custody of these bonds, as were customary, was left in the hands of a clerk of the Indian bureau. Mr. Goddard Bailey, a young man whose character was above suspicion and reproach, was made appeal and disbursing clerk of this bureau and was given charge of this trust fund. For nearly four years, until near the end of Mr. Thompson's term, he discharged all his duties faithfully and acceptably. In the meantime a certain business firm, known as a transportation company, Russell, Majors & Waddell, had entered into large contracts with the war department, amounting to millions of dollars. The funds of the company, for a long time thought by every one to be almost inexhaustible, in course of time began to run short, and in order to raise money the company secured permission of the secretary of war to anticipate its earnings, and to draw drafts for the amounts on the secretary. These drafts the secretary accepted and they were known in money circles as acceptances of the war department.

In 1860 the earnings of the company proving less than what was anticipated, the leading members of the company applied to Mr. Bailey, the custodian of the Indian trust fund, to let him have these bonds; first, $150,000; at another time, $387,000; and various sums at other times, and to take in lieu thereof the company's notes, in order to save from protest the acceptances of the secretary of war. To this proposal, strange to say, the custodian of the bonds acceded, all without the knowledge of Mr. Thompson, and on each request delivered, to the party applying, the bonds asked for. Whenever it became necessary to do so the clerk would submit his accounts all neatly and accurately made out as if everything was in proper order, in a manner easy to be done so as to excite no suspicion. Finally, Mr. Bailey, the clerk and custodian of the bonds, learning that Mr. Thompson was soon to resign, presumed that the time had come when the safe itself would be examined, and believing that he would soon be detected, hastened to make a confession of his guilt to the secretary of the interior and to explain why he had committed the crime. This was the first intimation Mr. Thompson had of the abstraction. With the secretary of state and attorney general, Mr. Thompson made an examination of the safe and found it all as represented. He on the next day informed the house of representatives officially of the matter, and asked an investigation. A special request he made of the speaker was that he select a committee to be composed only of those who were known to hold political opinions adverse to his own (the secretary's), which request was complied with, a committee of five being appointed. After a thorough examination, unanimous report was made, from which the following extract is taken:

"They (the committee) deem it but justice to add that they have discovered nothing to involve the late secretary, Hon. Jacob Thompson, in the slightest degree in the fraud, and nothing to indicate that he had any complicity in the abstraction, or that he had any knowledge of it until the time of the disclosure of Goddard Bailey."

This, however, was not to be the last of it. It afforded material sufficient for his political enemies to work slander out of from time to time when needed. The circumstance was brought fresh to the public mind again in 1876, when Secretary of War Belknap was impeached, and when he resigned his office in order to escape conviction. The argument of General Belknap and his supporters was that having resigned, and being no longer an official, he could not be impeached. Mr. Chandler, then secretary of the interior, insisted that if congress should claim the right to prosecute General Belknap after he had resigned his office, that it had a right also to prosecute Mr. Thompson, even at that late date, after he had resigned, charging at the same time that Mr. Thompson had, while secretary of the interior, abstracted a large amount of bonds belonging to the Indian trust fund. Not only this, but Mr. Chandler stated that he would insist on Mr. Thompson's prosecution, if congress should continue the Belknap prosecution. On seeing a report of this, Mr. Thompson immediately went to Washington. After conferring through friends with Mr. Chandler, the latter promised to withdraw the charge as publicly as he had made it, but after Mr. Thompson had left the city, instead of withdrawing the charge as promised, he instituted a civil suit against Mr. Thompson for recovery of $2,000,000 instead of a criminal action. To this civil action Mr. Thompson filed his plea of non assumpsit. A presidential campaign was on hand during that year, and this case was continued upon the docket through the campaign. It was used both for campaign purposes and for Belknap's protection. As soon as the presidential canvass was over the bubble burst, the case was ordered by Mr. Chandler to be dismissed at the cost of the government, which was accordingly done. Mr. Thompson's vindication on this occasion was complete, and these old charges thus suddenly brought forward failed to serve the purpose for which they were renewed.

When Mississippi seceded from the Union, January 9, 1861, Mr. Thompson resigned and returned to his home in Oxford, Miss. During the war he served for short periods in various capacities, and after the fall of Vicksburg he returned to his home, and represented Lafayette county in the legislature for two terms. In 1864 he was sent to Canada on a secret mission by the Confederate authorities; this mission failed, and in 1865 he started back to the Confederacy; on his way from Montreal to Halifax he heard of the assassination of President Lincoln. To divert suspicion from Mr. Johnson, charges were made that implicated Mr. Thompson, and a proclamation was made offering a large reward for him and others. He and his family sailed for Europe at once and passed several years there. When he did return he removed from Oxford, Miss., to Memphis, where he lived a retired life as far as politics were concerned; he was engaged in mercantile pursuits until his death, which occurred in 1885. He was a member of the Episcopal church, was a zealous supporter of all movements of an educational character, and served as a member of the board of trustees of the University of Mississippi from 1844 to 1864, with one interval of four years; he was the second president of that body, and filled that office until the law went into effect which made the governor of the state president ex-officio.

William Thompson, Oxford, Lafayette county, Miss. The gentleman whose name is found at the head of this sketch was born in the state of North Carolina, in the year 1818. He received his education in the university of his native state, and was graduated in the class of 1840. Having determined upon the profession of law as his calling in life, he began its study under Judge Pearson at Mucksville, N. C., and was admitted to the bar in 1842; he practiced there until 1845, and in that year he came to Mississippi, and settled in Pontotoc county. His residence there was of short duration, however. In 1846 he volunteered as a private in the Mexican war, and participated in the battle of Buena Vista. In 1847 he returned to Mississippi and settled in Oxford, where he resumed his professional work. The following year he was united in marriage to Miss Martha A. Jones, a native of Georgia, and a daughter of William S. Jones, a pioneer of this county. Mrs. Thompson died in 1877, leaving a family of seven children: Maria L., wife of Dr. Chandler, a sketch of whom appears elsewhere in this volume; William J., a resident of Mexico; Annie T., wife of Ed Dial, of Meridian, Miss.; Nicholas O.; Jacob, Lewis W. and Kate. The family are worthy and consistent members of the Episcopal church. Mr. Thompson belongs to the Masonic order. In 1863 he raised a company in this county for the Confederate service, being elected captain. In connection with his professional work he has given a great deal of time and attention to agriculture. He owns thirty-eight hundred acres of creek and river bottom lands; this is in three different tracts, and five hundred acres are in an advanced state of cultivation. Mr.

Thompson is a man of a genial disposition, and has a host of friends in Oxford and vicinity, where he has resided since his coming to Mississippi. The brothers and sisters of Mr. Thompson will be mentioned in the following order: A full sketch of Jacob Thompson will be found on another page of this history; James Y. was born in North Carolina in 1808, and was graduated in the university of his native state. He was married in Alabama to a Miss Shanklin, and afterward settled in Monroe county, Miss., where he practiced the profession of medicine; became a prominent citizen, and was elected to the state legislature from that county. Dr. John Thompson was born in North Carolina, about the year 1816, and was graduated in medicine from the University of Pennsylvania. In 1842 he began to practice in Lafayette county, Miss. He married Miss Laura E. Hunt, of Panolo county; he farmed quite extensively in Calhoun county, and during the war served as a surgeon in the army. After the surrender he returned to Oxford, where he lived until his death, which occurred about 1875. He was also a surgeon in the Mexican war, and was in attendance upon Jefferson Davis at Buena Vista. The eldest brother, Joseph Sidney, spent his entire life in North Carolina, where he accumulated a large fortune; he was born in 1805. The youngest brother, George Nicholas, was born in 1833, and was graduated from the University of North Carolina; he studied law and is now practicing at Leasburg, N. C., residing on the old homestead; Ann Eliza Thompson married Yancy Wiley; Sarah Thompson married Abner Lewis; the sisters were both natives of North Carolina.

John S. Thompson, a merchant and planter of Quitman, Clarke county, Miss., was born February 4, 1838, in Sumter county, Ala. He was the second child in a family of five children born to William H. and Alice (Rosser) Thompson. His father was born in Washington county, Ala., in 1808. He spent his early life in that state, and was married there. In 1845 he removed to Clarke county, Ala., and settled on a farm, where he lived through life. He was a successful planter, and an extensive landowner, a public-spirited citizen, who died in 1871, in Newton county, Miss., having been for many years a member of the Methodist Episcopal church. The mother of our subject was born in 1817, in Sumter county, Ala., and died in Newton county, Miss., in 1879. She was a daughter of Eleazer Rosser, and her father and mother both died in Alabama. Mr. Thompson's father removed to Newton county in 1867. His children are named as follows: Eliza J., John S., William D., Sadie E. and Martin J. The early life of John S. Thompson was passed in Clarke county, Miss., where he came with his parents at the age of seven years. He was educated at Quitman, and began life for himself as a soldier in 1861, enlisting in company D, of the Fourteenth Mississippi regiment, in which he was a sergeant. He was in the battles of Fort Donelson, Jackson, Miss., and in the engagements of the Georgia campaign and in those of the Tennessee campaign. At Fort Donelson he was captured and taken to Camp Douglas, at Chicago, where he was held a prisoner for seven months, until he was exchanged. After the war he settled at Quitman, and engaged in farming for the next two years. He then engaged in mercantile business, at which he prospered very well. He is the owner of a large tract of land in Clarke county. Mr. Thompson was first married in 1866, to Miss Mary McDonald, a daughter of William McDonald, of this county. Our subject has one child by this marriage, William A., who is living in Quitman, and is a clerk in his father's store. Mrs. Thompson died in 1869. Mr. Thompson married again in 1870, to Miss Millie Bowen, the daughter of Rev. P. Bowen, of the Baptist church, who is now dead. By this marriage there were seven children born; there names are Nora E., Charles B., Henry C., Stella, John S., Sallie and Nellie. Mr. and Mrs. Thompson are members of the Methodist Episcopal church, of which Mr. Thompson is recording steward. In politics he is a democrat, and, although he has never sought office and is in no sense an active politician, he was at one time elected mayor of the town of Quitman. He is an enterprising, public-spirited citizen, deeply interested and always ready to aid any cause, which in his opinion has a tendency to advance the interests of his fellow-citizens, and he is especially interested in schools, churches and charitable institutions. He can properly be termed one of the pioneers of Clarke county, and here he has lived during the greater part of his life, and built up a reputation for honesty and integrity which causes him to be highly regarded by all who know him.

J. R. Thompson was born in October, 1841, in Monroe county, and is the son of William J. and Elizabeth (Rommoly) Thompson, natives of South Carolina. His father moved to Monroe county in 1839, and died in 1871. Mr. Thompson was reared on a plantation, and planting has been his only occupation through life. He received a fair education in the public schools, and was a student in 1861, when the war began. When the first call was made for volunteers he enlisted as private in the Fourteenth Mississippi infantry. The first fight in which he was engaged was the Fort Donelson fight, where he was captured and taken to Camp Douglas, Chicago, and there held prisoner of war for eight months, at the end of which time he was taken to Vicksburg, and there exchanged. Rejoining his regiment he participated in the battles of Clinton and Jackson, Miss., after which he was detailed to go to Choctaw county, Miss., on conscription service, in which he was employed for eight months, afterward joining General Johnston's command, at Marietta. Later he was in the battles of Altoona, Atlanta, Franklin and Nashville. At the close of the war he returned to Monroe county, and was employed on his father's plantation until 1869. May 5, 1870, he married Ella, daughter of Joseph and Mildreth Johnson. They are the parents of eight children, and have lost one by death; those living are named: Willie J., Ruth A., Horace L., Sybil C., Guy, Russel R., Tolbe and Isma. Mr. Thompson, after his marriage, engaged in planting on his own account until 1863, when he removed to Carlville, Tenn. He remained there only a short time, however, when he returned to Monroe county, and purchased the plantation on which he now lives. Politically he is a democrat, but takes no active part in public affairs, his home interests demanding and receiving his undivided attention. As a planter he is successful, and as a business man has won the regard of the entire community in which he lives.

J. T. Thompson, one of the oldest citizens of Chickasaw county and a planter, was born in Franklin county, Ala., in 1837, a son of John I. and Ann (Williams) Thompson, the former a native of Virginia and the latter of Kentucky. They located in Franklin county, Ala., with their parents, the former at the age of fifteen, the latter in childhood. To their union eleven children were born, only seven of whom lived to maturity: Sarah L., wife of R. Longest; Evelina E., wife of J. W. Hamilton; James T., Mary Adaline, wife of John Curry; Hannah H., wife of R. T. Humston; John L., who died in the army at Chattanooga, and Susan D., wife of A. Delishment. John I. Thompson removed to Chickasaw county, Miss., with his family in the fall of 1838, at which time there were comparatively few settlers in this region. He chose a fine body of land two miles north of Houlka, which he cleared and on which he resided until his death in 1876, owning at this time a section of land. His widow still survives him, a worthy member of the Methodist church. The boyhood days of J. T. Thompson were spent in Chickasaw county, mostly on his father's plantation, but he received only such education as the schools of that time and place afforded, and acquired a common-school education. In 1860 he began farming for himself, on land which is now a part of his present plantation, his first purchase of land amounting to a quarter of a section. At the opening of the Civil war he entered the service with the first company sent out from

Chickasaw county under Captain Tucker, and in January, 1861, found himself in Pensacola navy yard. The company was afterward placed in the Eleventh Mississippi volunteer infantry and served in the army of Virginia. Owing to failing health Mr. Thompson was discharged in July of the same year, and returned to his home in Mississippi, where he soon regained his accustomed vigor and once more entered the service, becoming a member of Company L, Forty-first Mississippi infantry. In the battle of Murfreesboro he was slightly wounded and he also took part in the engagements at Atlanta, Chickamauga, Resaca, Franklin, as well as numerous minor engagements and skirmishes. He surrendered at Greensboro, N. C., and upon returning to his home at once began to till and improve his land, which had been laid waste during the war. He has devoted his attention to planting throughout life, at all times aiming to be a practical farmer, and that he has succeeded is shown by his well-kept and productive plantation. For a short time he was interested in a store for grangers, but the entire stock of goods afterward passed into his possession and for some time he conducted the business, but with little success. In his planting operations he has made cotton his principal crop, but has made his place self-sustaining. He is the owner of about eleven hundred acres, eight hundred of which are in Chickasaw county and the remainder in Cross county, Ark. He was a charter member of the Houlka Grange, and has been a member of the Masonic fraternity, since he attained his majority, and at one time was senior warden for a number of years, and although elected worshipful master declined to fill the position. He is a member of John S. Kane lodge No. 259, of Redland, formerly, but now located at Houlka. Mr. Thompson, his wife, and family are members of the Baptist church, of which he became a member and was baptized while in the army during the war, being immersed by Dr. T. C. Teasdale, in Duck river, Tenn. He was married in 1867 to Miss Carrie Delishment, a native of Chickasaw county, and a daughter of Seley and Mary A. (Rawes) Delishment, both of whom were born, reared and married in South Carolina. They came to Chickasaw county, Miss., about 1835, and here became well to-do planters. Mr. Thompson and his wife have seven children. Annie L., John Seley, James F., Robert L., W. Henry, Mary, Sue and Benjamin A.

Julius Thompson, the subject of this sketch, well and favorably known to a host of acquaintances in this section, was born in 1845, and, like many of the other residents of Washington county, is a native of North Carolina, Bertie county being the place of his birth. His father, Louis W. Thompson, was born in that state also, in the year 1812, being the third of four children, all of whom came to Mississippi in 1846, remaining here until their death, with the exception of Noah Thompson, who went to Alabama in 1863. All were planters with the exception of a half-brother, Dr. William Sutton, who became a physician of Madison county, Miss. The brothers are now deceased. A sister, Margaret L., married John T. Johnson, of North Carolina. The father of these children became a prosperous planter of Madison county, Miss., which place was his home from the time of his arrival in the state until his death in October, 1888, at the age of seventy-six years. He was a successful financier, and at the time of his death left a fine property to be divided among his heirs. He was a Baptist. His wife was Martha Ellen Britton, of North Carolina, and their union resulted in the birth of eleven children, whose names are as follows: Margaret E. (who married Augustin Chew, a native of Maryland; he spent the most of his life as a planter of Mississippi, and died in February, 1889; his widow, now residing in Washington county, near Holandale), Louis W. (died in infancy), Ellen (also dying when a babe), Henrietta E. (became the wife of Edward Tarry, of Virginia; both being now deceased), Lucius A. (lives in Washington county), Mary E. (is the wife of John D. Britton, a Virginian; now a cotton merchant of New Orleans), Parmelia (wife of Henry Moorman, a native of Kentucky), Louis W. (died in infancy), Hattie (deceased, was the wife of G. A. Baldwin), and Herbert (who is now dead). The Thompsons are of Scotch descent, and the Brittons are English. Julius Thompson was reared to man's estate in Madison county, Miss., and received his education in its public schools. In 1868 he began for himself as a planter of Washington county, Miss., and by his own endeavors he has become the owner of two hundred and forty acres of land, besides three hundred and fifty acres inherited from his father's estate, two hundred and fifty acres of which he has put under cultivation himself, building thereon a residence begun in 1868, at a cost of $2,000. His marriage, which took place in 1870, was to Miss Hettie Moorman, a native of Owensboro, Ky., and a daughter of Mercer Moorman, also of that state, and a merchant by occupation, his wife being a Miss Talbott, of Tennessee. To Mr. and Mrs. Thompson six children have been born: Louis W., Sarah M., Mercer M., Edward, Julius, and Herbert, all of whom are at home. This family are all members of the Baptist church, and are favorites in the social circles in which they move. In 1863 Mr. Thompson enlisted in the late war, becoming a member of company B, Third Mississippi cavalry, as a private, serving until the close of the war, and taking part in the following battles: New Hope church, Kenesaw mountain, and the engagements around Atlanta. At the surrender he was near Natchez, where he had been sent as a scout in Bradford's battalion, never having been seriously wounded during his entire service. Mr. Thompson is a very agreeable and entertaining gentleman to meet, and is a very strict member of the Baptist church, taking great interest in religious matters and in training his children to be Christian men and women. No man in the county stands higher in public esteem than does he, and this good opinion he fully deserves. Although he gives proper attention to his plantation, he does not devote all his time to the accumulation of gain, for he has a higher idea of life than simply the acquirement of wealth, and believes that home is the place for a parent, and is usually found within the family circle.

Dr. M. J. Thompson, of the firm of Thompson, Hyer & Partin, physicians and surgeons of Meridian, Miss., was born in Choctaw county, Ala., a son of William H. and Alice (Rosser) Thompson, natives of Georgia and Alabama, respectively. His father was a planter and removed to Mississippi in 1847, locating in Clarke county, though he ended his days in Newton county. He had five sons, of whom Dr. M. J. Thompson was the fourth born. The Doctor was reared in Clarke county, and educated in private schools. At the age of twenty-one years he began the study of medicine, and graduated at Mobile, Ala., in the year 1872. He took post-graduate courses at the New York polyclinic, 1886-8. He practiced for a time in Lauderdale county, and removed to Meridian, Miss., in 1880. Seven years later he formed a partnership with Dr. I. P. Partin, and in November, 1888, Dr. W. F. Hyer was admitted to the firm, which then became known as Thompson, Hyer & Partin. Dr. Thompson takes high rank in his profession. He has served as vice president of the State Medical association, and as president of the Lauderdale County Medical association, and is, at this time, vice president of the Alumni Medical association of Alabama. He has also served as a member of the board of health of the city of Meridian, Miss. He has been too much devoted to his profession to take much part in other affairs, and he has attained to a high place in the esteem of his fellow practitioners. He has been especially prominent in the department of surgery, and has established at Meridian a private infirmary for surgical cases and the diseases of women. This was opened about two years ago and has accommodations for about fifteen patients. Dr. Thompson is a member of the Masonic fraternity and of the Knights of Pythias. He was married in 1875 to Miss Augusta Stennis, of Lauderdale county, Miss., who has borne him seven children, six of whom are living: Sidney, Stennis, Gussie, Ida, Mamie and Ethel. The family are members of the Methodist Episcopal church.

Pharaoh Carter Thompson. In the very early settlement of the state of Mississippi, among the families who were closely identified with its affairs and associated with its progress and development, were the Thompsons, and a respected representative of this family is found in the subject of this sketch. He is a prominent planter and breeder of Holstein cattle and fine saddle horses and mules, and at the present time is the owner, in connection with his uncle, C. F. Thompson, and general manager of the *Southern Progress*, a weekly newspaper, published at Garden City, the official organ of Franklin county. He was born in the neighborhood in which he is now residing, in 1852, to Bartlett C. and Adeliza A. (Carter) Thompson, the former of whom was also born in this county in December, 1819, and is still residing on the farm on which he was born, having led the industrious life of a planter. He was educated in the common country schools, and in time became noted throughout this region as a man of sound judgment, and much executive ability. He served some years as a member of the board of supervisors, and was also magistrate for some time. He was called upon to mourn the death of his worthy wife in 1862, she having been a true helpmate throughout their married life. His father was Col. John L. Thompson, who was born in South Carolina, but came with his parents to Franklin county, Miss., at a very early day, spending the rest of his life here. He was made a colonel while serving in the War of 1812, and after settling down to the life of a civilian, became a successful pioneer planter. His wife was Elizabeth Callahan, who was born in Franklin county. Maj. David Thompson, the father of John L., was born in the Old North state, in 1758, but was married, in South Carolina, to Miss Frances Longmire, of that state. In the early history of this region they came hither, and here Mrs. Thompson was called from life soon after. Mr. Thompson then married again, Miss Nancy Sojourner becoming his wife. He afterward moved to Amite county, where he passed from life July 4, 1840. He had been a soldier in the Revolutionary war, and was major of militia in the War of 1812. He reared two large families. Mrs. Adaliza Adelia Carter was born in Adams county in February, 1823, and was a daughter of Pharaoh Carter, who was, in all probability, a North Carolinian, and when a young man came to Adams county, Miss., where he married Miss Susanna Griffing, and resided until just prior to the war, when he removed to Pike county, and was there called from life in 1888, at the extreme old age of ninety-one years. He was a planter and mechanic, and was exceptionally skillful in the use of tools. Pharaoh Carter Thompson was the fifth of seven children, three sons and four daughters, five of whom are now living: Elizabeth, wife of Henry K. Aldridge; Laura, wife of William J. Laughman; John B., of Shelby county, Texas; Susan E., wife of Samuel R. Farrell, and Pharaoh C. The latter was given the advantages of the common schools, and at about the age of eighteen years he began trading for himself whenever opportunity afforded, though he lived with and acknowledged the right of his father to dictate until he was twenty-one years old, doing for himself as a trader, being also engaged in trapping for many years, sold books and dealt in stock, in fact, he engaged in anything honorable that came in his way, and promised reasonable compensation. In the spring of 1883, after a winter's hunt or trapping campaign, he embarked in the mercantile business near Knoxville. The following year he moved his business to Knoxville, where he ran a store and carried on a farm. This he continued with success until January 26, 1886, when he was severely injured by the closing of an opening in a freight train, at Knoxville depot, on the New Orleans & Tennessee railroad, the result of carelessness and gross negligence on the part of the employes of the road, which was proven by the decision of the circuit court, the following fall, which gave a verdict of $15,000

damages. This decision was sustained in the supreme court the following spring, 1887, which augmented the cost, making the total damages allowed $16,200. After this injury, which resulted in breaking his thigh bone in two places and his pelvis bone in two places, and causing a considerable wasting of the muscles, necessitated his abandonment of the mercantile business, though he kept up his farm. He finally settled down to planting and stockbreeding, and is now one of the most extensive and successful followers of these callings in this part of the state. He is the owner of two thousand eight hundred acres of land, his residence being very pleasantly situated on the Leland plantation, at Garden City, making one of the most attractive homes in Franklin county. On the 1st of January, 1889, he purchased the Hamburg *Herald*, removed the press to Knoxville, and began the publication of the *Southern Progress*, where he continued until June 26, 1890, when he removed his plant to Garden City, and here has since continued the publication of his journal. In 1887 he was married to Miss Mary S., daughter of Samuel G. and Sina Marshall, who were born in Madison county, Ala., in 1834, and Hinds county, Miss., respectively. Mr. Marshall came to Mississippi when a young man, and he and his wife have since lived in different parts of the state, his principal business being that of a druggist. He was for some years deputy chancery clerk of Hinds county, was a faithful, painstaking and zealous official, and discharged the duties incumbent upon the office in a manner highly satisfactory to all. Mrs. Thompson was born at Raymond, in Hinds county, and by Mr. Thompson is the mother of two children. She is a Methodist, but her husband is a member of the Baptist church—a deacon. Mr. Thompson is one of the most progressive men of Franklin county, and, although he commenced life a poor boy, by his untiring efforts has become one of the foremost planters of the county. He has always been active in the general up-building of the county, is deeply interested in the progress and development of the same, and is a genial and agreeable gentleman to meet. He is kind, generous and hospitable in disposition, in the domestic circle is a model husband and father, and for this reason, has won numerous friends and lost few.

Robert H. Thompson, a prominent lawyer residing at Brookhaven, Lincoln county, was born in Copiah county, Miss., August 25, 1847. He is the son of J. Harvey Thompson and Margaret Ann (Watson) Thompson, both natives of Mississippi, and both are still living. His grandfather, Jesse Thompson, who married a Miss Margaret Harvey of that state, was a prominent planter of Georgia, and came from there to Mississippi when it was a territory. The father of the subject of our sketch was a man of prominence in the ante-bellum days of the state. He was the youngest of quite a large family, while the mother (Margarat A.) was the eldest of such a family. To these parents were born seven children; one son and six daughters. Julia is the widow of Capt. T. J. Chrisman, who was killed at the siege of Vicksburg, a Confederate soldier, leaving two children: Anna C. and Agnes. Anna C. lost her life in the Johnstown, Penn., flood, while on her way to Brazil as a missionary. Agnes and her mother are schoolteachers at Wesson, Miss. Mrs. Maggie T. Butler, the second sister, is the wife of Dr. John T. Butler, of Oregon, Mo. Laura, Emma, Margaret and Mary, sisters, are all dead. Robert H. Thompson received his primary education in Copiah county; he attended schools at Gallatin, Hazlehurst and other points until February, 1864, when he enlisted in the Confederate army, in Capt. T. J. Hargrave's company of the Twenty-fourth Mississippi regiment, under the command of Col. George Moorman. This regiment was in Wirt Adams' brigade of Forrest's command. Mr. Thompson served with it until the surrender, at Gainesville, Ala., in April, 1865. He was paroled April 12th, of the year last mentioned, and returning home engaged in planting. During the same year he entered the old Summerville institute, of Noxubee county, Miss., as a student, and

EEE

remained there two years. Entering the junior class of the University of Mississippi, at Oxford, in September, 1867, he graduated in June, 1869, with the degree of A. B. After his graduation from the literary department he remained as a student of law, which department was then in charge of Professor Lamar, now justice of the supreme court of the United States. In 1889, twenty years after his graduation, Mr. Thompson returned to the university and delivered an able address to the alumni association. He is now a trustee of this university, his alma mater, and takes much interest in the institution. He began to practice law in January, 1871, at Brookhaven, only a few days after receiving his license at Gallatin, then the county site of Copiah county, Miss. Since that time he has been engaged unremittingly in the practice of his profession. He is now regarded as one of the leading lawyers of the Mississippi bar, and one of the best judges of law in the South. He has prepared several papers of more than common interest for the Mississippi Bar association, of which he has been the president and is one of its leading spirits. He was married December 21, 1871, to Miss Mary Lou Coleman, of Madison county, Miss., a daughter of E. H. and Mary (Gilchrist) Coleman, who died shortly afterward. Mr. Thompson was married the second time, in 1876, to Mrs. Fannie P. Myers, widow of the late Hamilton Myers. This lady was reared in Natchez, Miss., and was a daughter of L. M. Patterson, a merchant of that city, but who was a native of Maryland. Her mother, Miss Lucy Gridley, was from New York. Of their eight children Mrs. Thompson was the youngest. Mrs. Thompson can trace her family genealogy on the maternal side back to the Mayflower. Three brothers, named Richard, Samuel and Thomas Gridley, came with the Pilgrims, and were among the fathers who settled the city of Hartford, Conn. Mrs. Thompson is descended in direct line from the last mentioned of these brothers. To Mr. and Mrs. Thompson have been born four children: Harvey, Robert, Gertrude and Mildred, all of whom, the eldest being only fourteen, are living with their parents.

Mr. and Mrs. Thompson are members of the Presbyterian church, and, with their family, are attendants upon its services. Mr. Thompson has had a somewhat interesting political career. He is a stanch democrat, and, on account of his age, was one of those who were compelled to cast his first presidential vote for Horace Greeley. In 1875 he was elected to the state senate by a large majority, to represent Pike, Lincoln and Lawrence counties. The campaign of that year in Mississippi is known as the political revolution, and the senate of which he was a member has passed into history as the historical senate. Of this body Mr. Thompson was the youngest member. He served with credit until the end of his term, comprising four years. In 1890 he was elected to represent Lincoln and Jefferson counties in the state constitutional convention, and acted as chairman of the legislative committee of that body. The report of this committee, brought in by Mr. Thompson as such chairman, was widely commented upon, and everywhere regarded as the ablest report of the convention. At the close of the session he was made chairman of the committee on revision, which was charged with the duty of arranging the various ordinances that had been passed, and with making the constitution harmonious and consistent in all its parts. This committee received the unanimous thanks of the convention for the able manner in which it performed its duties. The constitution then formulated required the governor to appoint a committee of three learned lawyers to revise the statute laws of the state, and prepare such other laws for adoption by the legislature as should be found necessary to put the new constitution in full operation and force. Of this committee Mr. Thompson was made chairman, and he is now engaged upon the work of preparing a new code of laws for Mississippi. In view of the facts that we have stated, it would be superfluous to say that Mr. Thompson is an influential and widely known citizen of Mississippi. At home, and where he is most intimately known, he is perhaps held in highest esteem; and there are few local interests that have not received his helpful support. He was unanimously elected the president of the Mississippi state democratic convention, which met at Jackson, in July, 1891, and presided over its deliberations with ability and grace. He was elected by the convention itself, an unusual but great honor, the chairman of the democratic state executive committee, which office he now holds.

E. W. Thornton, planter, Sardis, is a native born resident of the county, his birth occurring on November 28, 1863, and although young in years he is foremost among the planters of his locality. He is of English descent and the eldest of four children born to Benjamin W. and Jane (McKinney) Thornton, the father a native of North Carolina and the mother of Mississippi. Benjamin W. Thornton immigrated to Panola county, Miss., before the Indians had left the state, engaged in planting, and continued that occupation until his death on September 28, 1885. He was very successful, and accumulated quite a fortune. His father, Wright Thornton, was also of the Old North state. Mrs. Thornton's parents, Michael and Susan McKinney, were natives of Tennessee, and the family is of English origin. E. W. Thornton was left motherless when quite small, and what he has won in the way of this world's goods is wholly due to his own good fighting qualities, for he started out for himself at the age of eighteen with no capital. He selected the occupation of a planter, and by his industry and good management has become the owner of three hundred and sixty-eight acres of rich land, one-half of which is on the Tallahatchie bank and is extremely productive. He has one hundred and forty acres under cultivation. He is wideawake, energetic and thoroughgoing, and believes that what is worth doing at all is worth doing well. He is considered one of the best farmers of his age in the county, and contributes liberally of his means to all worthy enterprises. In personal appearance he is tall, strongly built, black hair, dark eyes, fair complexion, and is a prepossessing young man. He is a democrat in political views.

James B. Thornton, one of the most practical and progressive planters of Tallahatchie county, was born in the valley eight miles north of Charleston, in the neighborhood near where he now lives, in 1854. He is the son of Philip H. and Eliza A. (Bailey) Thornton, both of whom were natives of Tennessee. Mr. Thornton came as a young man to Tallahatchie county, Miss., and was twice married; first to a Miss Baker, by whom he had one daughter, and who is now deceased; for his second wife he married Eliza A. Bailey, a sister of Col. James S. Bailey. (See sketch of Col. James S. Bailey, which will be found in this work.) Mr. Thornton first lived some miles south of Charleston, and then a few miles above the same city, where he died while in the service of his country. His death took place in 1863. He was a good man and a progressive planter. He was the only son of his parents, and the only one of his family that came to Mississippi. The subject of this sketch was the fourth of five children: Sallie, who died young; Belle, now of Sardis, the widow of Judge J. G. Hall, who died in 1890 (he was a promising attorney, and had served as chancellor of his district); Eliza A., wife of C. S. Merriweather, a lawyer of Scranton, Miss.; the subject of this sketch comes next in order, followed by Philip H., a merchant at Charleston. James B. Thornton received a common English education, and resided with his aunt, Mrs. Caruthers, after the death of his father. When he was fourteen years of age he left the shelter of his aunt's home and went to Texas, where he lived about six years with his eldest sister, who had married and settled there. He then returned home and lived with Colonel Bailey for about one year, till he reached his majority, when he engaged in farming on his own account. He was married in 1882 to Maggie, a daughter of J. R. and Mary A. Davis, of Vaiden, Carroll county, Miss. His wife's parents were natives of Mississippi, and for many years they lived in Carroll county, where Mr. Davis has been circuit clerk for many years and still holds that office. Both of them are Presbyterians. The daughter, Mrs. Thornton, was born in Carroll county, one of three children. Since his marriage Mr. Thornton has lived on his present plantation, which can in truth be said to be one of the finest if not the finest plantation in this county. The energetic habits and progressive mind of the owner are easily seen by the prosperous condition of things in general about the farm, such as good substantial buildings, good fences, and all that goes to make up a first-class plantation. There are eleven hundred acres in this plantation, which produce about one hundred and fifty bales of cotton annually. He inherited a part of this fine old place from his father, but the most of it has come through Mr. Thornton's own unaided efforts, a fact of which he may well be proud. On this plantation are eighteen tenement houses, a steam sawmill, a gristmill and a cottongin. Mr. Thornton is a member of the Knights of Honor, of A. Macon Leigh lodge No. 3233, of Charleston, while his wife is a strong Presbyterian.

Dr. J. J. Thornton, Gulf Port, Miss., was born in Troop county, Ga., in 1833, and is a son of Jordan and Jemima (Mabry) Thornton, natives of Georgia. The father was a soldier in the War of 1812, and was promoted to the rank of major. He was a farmer by occupation. He emigrated to Montgomery, Ala., and died there in 1880. His wife died in 1854. They reared a family of six sons and two daughters: Mrs. Mary McCane, P. M., Mrs. Georgia Horrelson, Andrew J. and J. J., the subject of this notice, are the only surviving members. The Doctor was reared in Wetumpka, Ala., and received his elementary education there. He began the study of medicine at an early age, and was graduated at Mobile, Ala., in his twenty-first year, from the Alabama Medical college. He engaged in practice at Buyckville, Ala., where he remained several years. There he was married to Miss Sarah Buyck, and eight children were born to them: Buyck, Alice, Finlayson, Thomas M., Mary G., Clower, Laura and Jennie. In 1857 the Doctor removed to Scott county, Miss., and settled at Hillsboro, but at the end of the year he went to Conehatta, Miss., and practiced there until 1870. His next place of residence was at Hattiesburg, Miss., where he practiced medicine and managed a hotel until 1888. In that year he came to Gulf Port, and built the Thornton house, which is a well equipped and managed hotel. The Doctor has abandoned professional work, and attends to the hotel; it is kept up in first-class style, and is a credit both to the proprietor and to the town. Dr. Thornton was married, in 1875, to Margaret Buyck, and one child was born of the marriage—Minnis. Mrs. Thornton died in April, 1889. The Doctor is a member of the Knights of Honor and of the Masonic fraternity. While a resident of Hattiesburg he was mayor for one term.

Hon. Stephen Thrasher. This eminent attorney is one of the leaders of his profession in this section of the state, for his long experience in the practice of law, his brilliant intellect and his powers as an orator, have tended to place him on the topmost round of the ladder. He possesses all the fire, vim and eloquence of the native Kentuckian, for in that state he was born February 24, 1833, being the eldest of seven children born to William and Henrietta (Hook) Thrasher, who were born in Kentucky and Maryland, respectively. The former was the fourth child born to his parents, and grew to manhood in Kentucky, where he was educated, and where he settled, his attention being devoted to trading. He was born in April, 1804, and is now a resident of Indiana, and makes his home with his grandchildren. His wife died in 1869, in that state, whither they moved about 1850, being an earnest and worthy member of the Christian church at the time of her death. Their children are as follows: Stephen; Sarah (deceased); Mary, wife of Oscar Turner, is a resident of Eau Claire,

Wis.; Henrietta, wife of a Mr. Golding, is a resident of Minnesota; John is a resident of Shelbyville, Ind., and David is a resident of Texas. Stephen Thrasher, the father of William, was born in Maryland, and after the Revolutionary war removed to Kentucky, where he became colonel of a Kentucky troop and participated in the War of 1812. He was a member of the Kentucky legislature, and was a very prominent man in his day, taking an active interest in politics. He was a participant in the early Indian struggles in Ohio, and was at the battle of Miami when Anthony Wayne was in command. He died about 1830, in his sixtieth year, his ancestors having been natives of England. His wife was a Miss Boyd, a grandniece of General Montgomery, of Revolutionary war fame. They reared a small family of children. Stephen Thrasher, whose name heads this sketch, began the battle of life for himself in the year 1852, at which time he came South. After remaining here a short time, he returned to Bloomington, Ind., where he entered an excellent institution of learning, and graduated in 1857. He then once more returned South, and settled at Port Gibson, where he followed the practice of law until the breaking out of the late war, at which time he cast aside personal considerations to enlist in the Claiborne guards, of Port Gibson, which was afterward incorporated in the Twelfth Mississippi regiment, with which he served until the close of the war, participating in the battle of Seven Pines, the seven days' fight around Richmond, and Chancellorsville, where he was wounded in the left arm and side, and for some time was confined in the hospital at Richmond and Petersburg. After obtaining a furlough he came home, and later rejoined his regiment at Rapidan, and took part in the battles of Wilderness and Spottsylvania. He was captured in front of Petersburg, and was taken to Point Lookout, where he remained until hostilities had ceased. Upon his return home he formed a copartnership with his uncle, J. B. Thrasher, in the practice of law at Port Gibson, and since 1875 had been at his present stand. His plantation, on which he now resides, the property of his wife, is one of the finest and most valuable in the county, and was first settled by Capt. Thaddeus Lyman, it being a portion of the land granted by George III, of England, in 1775, and was among the first land grants made in the county, consisting of twenty thousand acres. In addition to the property of Mr. Thrasher, Mrs. Thrasher owns a fine plantation of about one thousand acres, under a high state of cultivation. Mr. Thrasher is a lawyer of experience, and possesses broad and liberal views. His mind is acute, and his reasonings void of sophistry, and his reasons for his convictions are always clear and well defined, he has at all times the courage to express his views. He was first elected a member of the state senate in 1886, and was returned in 1889, serving two terms in succession, being a very strong supporter of the soldiers' monument appropriation. He is very conservative in his views, and does not seek political favors, being elected to the legislature much against his will. His reputation as a pure and intelligent legislator was of the very best, and while a member of that body he discharged the duties of his position with eminent ability, and to the satisfaction of all concerned. In 1875 he was married to Mrs. Lizzie (Belknap) Hamilton, a native of Tennessee, the Belknap family being noted throughout the South, and becoming early citizens of Mississippi. Mrs. Thrasher came with her mother to Grand Gulf in 1849, at which place she was married to C. D. Hamilton in 1853, his death occurring in 1869, having been an extensive planter. To them seven children were born, five of whom are living: Richard; Mary J., wife of Amos Burnett; Nannie, wife of S. C. Humphreys; Bettie, wife of B. E. Humphreys; Charles (deceased), and R. E. Lee, living near Grand Gulf. Mr. and Mrs. Thrasher have a beautiful home overlooking the Mississippi river, and are enjoying their prosperity as only people of education and refinement can do. They are members of the Episcopal church, and to every worthy project or institution they contribute liberally of their means. Mr. Thrasher is a man who has made his way to the front by sheer force of will and native talent, and it is acknowledged by competent judges that he ranks among the highest civilians. He is a stockholder in and president of the oilworks, and a stockholder in the brickyard and the bank at Port Gibson, and socially is a Knight Templar in the A. F. & A. M., in which order he has held various chairs. His uncle, J. B. Thrasher, with whom he was associated in the practice of his profession for some time, came to Mississippi in 1826, and became very prominent in the legal circles of this section as well as in all matters of a public nature. He died of yellow fever in 1878, at the age of seventy-eight years.

Cassius L. Tillman, the popular treasurer of Adams county and the surviving member of the well known and reliable firm of I. Lowenburg & Co., the only exclusive wholesale dealers in groceries, tobacco, etc., in Natchez, is a man of good practical judgment and business acumen which are the cardinal points of success. This business was established in 1864, and has an extensive and rapidly growing trade, competing with many of the wholesale houses of the larger cities. Mr. Tillman was born in Natchez in 1852, and is the son of J. L. and Ricka (Deutsch) Tillman, both of whom were natives of Bavaria, Germany, where they were reared. The parents came to Natchez, Miss., in the years 1832 and 1848, respectively, were married in that city and there made their future home. Mrs. Tillman is still living, but Mr. Tillman died in New York city in 1869, while there temporarily. The father followed merchandising in Natchez for many years and was very successful in this pursuit. Of the five children born to this union, Cassius L. was the third in order of birth, and is the only one now living. He received his early education at Natchez, and in 1865 graduated from Gurkeim college, Bavaria, after which he attended Gerke institute in New York city. After completing his education he connected himself with the firm of I. Lowenburg & Co., with which he has continued ever since. Since the death of Mr. Lowenburg Mr. Tillman has been the sole proprietor of this immense business. Although yet a young man he has long been recognized as identified with the business interests of the city, and the position he now occupies in social as well as business circles is a very high one. He has taken an active part in every measure or enterprise for the good of Adams county, and being public spirited, enterprising and intelligent by nature, his career has been both successful and honorable. He is a director in the First National bank, was city alderman one term, and since 1880 he has filled the office of treasurer of Adams county in a very efficient and satisfactory manner. He stands high in social orders, having held all the offices in Andrew Jackson lodge No. 2, A. F. & A. M., and is a member of Royal Arch Chapter No. 1; Bluff city lodge of Knights of Honor No. 1145; the Knights and Ladies of Honor; the Knights of Pythias No. 3, and he is a member of the following Jewish orders: B'Nai B'rith and Kaisher. Mr. Tillman's wife, to whom he was married in 1880, was formerly Miss Mamie Hyms, a native of Charleston, S. C. They have four interesting children.

Henry Tindall, planter, merchant and lumberman, of Grenada county, Miss., and one of the most progressive, thoroughgoing business men of the same, is the eldest of nine children born to James and Sarah (Gant) Tindall, both natives of the Old Dominion. The parents were married in North Carolina, and moved from there to Bedford county, Tenn., at an early day. There they resided, with the exception of a few months in Illinois, until 1849, when they removed to what is now Grenada county. There the father died in 1885. He had been married twice, his first wife being our subject's mother. She died in 1850. Both were Cumberland Presbyterians for many years. Mr. Tindall followed the life of a successful planter, although in North Carolina he engaged in milling for some time, and never aspired to publicity. His father, James Tindall, died when comparatively a young man. The children born to Mr. and Mrs. Tindall were named in the order of their births as follows: Henry; Anderson, died before the war; William, resides near Carrollton, Miss., and is a mechanic and planter. He served all through the Confederate army, Fifteenth Mississippi infantry, company E, as a private, and was in the Georgia and Atlanta campaign; James, a planter of Grenada county, was in the Fifteenth Mississippi also during the war; Thomas, was in the same company in the Confederate army, and is now a planter of Grenada county; John, a planter of this county, was not in the war; George, was a private in the Thirty-first Mississippi infantry and was killed at Murfreesboro; Mary E., wife of Maxey Caffee, of Duck Hill; and Victoria, wife of William Bradford, of Walthall. Henry Tindall secured a fair education in the common schools of Mississippi and Tennessee, and when twenty-one years of age started out to fight life's battle's for himself. He first began as an overseer, continued this until the breaking out of the war, when he took about one hundred and sixty-three negroes and worked a few months on the fortification at Fort Pillow. He then returned home, and soon after joined company E, Fifteenth Mississippi infantry, Tennessee army, and engaged at Corinth and the siege of Vicksburg as commissarian. He was captured and paroled, and was in parole camp at Demopolis, Ala., for about two months. He was then ordered to join his command near New Hope church, and was in the Georgia and Atlanta campaign. He then went back with Hood to Tennessee; down to Tuscumbia, Ala., and then got a furlough and went home to look up clothing, etc. He was in Mississippi at the time of the surrender, and afterward returned to Carroll county, where he engaged in farming. In 1867 he embarked in the sawmill business at Duck Hill, and in 1869 built a mill at his present stand, then in the woods, and has followed this business ever since, now being the owner of four different mills: one steammill near Duck Hill, a watermill seven miles east of that town, a steammill at home, and a watermill in Webster county. He also owns a good gin at each place. For eight years he has operated a good store on his place, and does an annual business of about $12,000. He is the owner of three thousand one hundred and forty acres of land in Grenada county, three hundred and twenty acres in Montgomery county, one hundred and twenty acres in Webster county, and has a two-acre block and a business block in Duck Hill, all the fruits of his own labor since the war. He is now one of the most prosperous planters and business men of the county. He is thoroughgoing, public-spirited, and has a host of warm friends. He was married in 1870 to Miss Josephine Neal, a native of Carroll (now Montgomery) county, Miss., and the daughter of Robert Neal, who came from Tennessee to Carroll county, Miss., and followed the life of a planter. There his death occurred. To Mr. and Mrs. Tindall have been born twelve children, seven sons and five daughters, all of whom he has spared no pains to educate. He is postmaster at Misterton, which was established at his store about seven years ago. Mr. Tindall has often been urged to run for office, but as often refused.

Col. William Henry Haywood Tison, of Baldwyn, Miss., the subject of this sketch, was born in Jackson county, Ala., November 6, 1822. He was the son of Richard and Nancy Tison, natives of North Carolina, who first emigrated to Georgia, thence to Tennessee, thence to Alabama and finally to Mississippi. They both possessed iron constitutions, indomitable wills and untiring energy, which they transmitted to their son in whose home they spent their old age. The father was a soldier in the War of 1812; he died October 15, 1876. His mother, a most lovable character, died March 15, 1872. Col. Tison was a self-made man. He was reared without early educational advantages, and in his youth met and overcame impediments which an ordinary man could not have surmounted. The school facilities of the county in which he lived were poor, and his father was unable to give him opportunities above those known as old fieldschools. He served as an apprentice to learn the saddler's trade, in which he proved himself a master workman. While following this vocation in the now extinct village of Carrollville, he was married to Miss Sarah S. Walker, an estimable young lady, who showed her faith in the ambitious, rising young man, who even then was a hard student of books as well as men. How fortunate that he didn't spend his energy on material things! He entered the printing business in 1855 as editor of the *Eastport Republican*, with D. C. White as publisher. In the winter of 1855 the paper was moved to Jacinto, and the name changed to the *Republican*. He continued the paper through the year 1856 and sold it. In the year 1855 the democratic party was confronted by a secret organization known as the know-nothing party, and the warfare was bitter and uncompromising. Colonel Tison wielded a trenchant pen, and was never so happy as when throwing shot and shell into the know-nothing camp. He fought know-nothingism to the bitter end, and contributed as much as any other man to its defeat and destruction in the state of Mississippi. Being a democrat of the Jacksonian school, he soon became the leader of his party. His first canvass was for representative from Tishomingo county, and resulted in his election. He prosecuted his canvass with the same zeal that he ever displayed in all his undertakings throughout life. Upon his entrance to the legislature he took a leading part in all of the deliberations of that body, which numbered among its members some of the foremost intellects of the state at that time. He was repeatedly returned to the legislature before the war, and the journal of the house contains no record of service more faithful and more beneficial than his. In 1857 he was appointed, by President Buchanan, United States marshal for the northern district of Mississippi. In his application for the place he had the earnest and active support of Hon. Jacob Thompson, secretary of the interior, who was then, and ever remained his constant and devoted friend. When the war broke out he organized a company early in 1861, for the Nineteenth regiment of Mississippi volunteers, the Jake Thompson guards, which served under the gallant Mott in many of the battles of Virginia. After serving a year in Virginia, he was made colonel of the Thirty-second Mississippi regiment, and was transferred to Bragg's army in Tennessee. He participated in most of the prominent battles in that state and in Georgia, and was twice wounded, once at Resaca, and again at Franklin. As a soldier, he was as true and brave a man as ever drew a sword. His courage was Spartan, and his skill as an officer commanded admiration. His bearing on the field was superb. He was always at the front and dared to lead where any dared to follow. His spare slight figure, erect in his saddle, could always be seen where the battle raged fiercest. He became known throughout the army for conspicuous gallantry, and received from his commanding generals complimentary notices in their reports. At the close of the war he returned to his home and engaged in active business pursuits. Being disfranchised, he could not enter politics as an aspirant for office, but he took an active part in all that pertained to the welfare of his state, and exerted a controlling influence in the affairs of his county. He organized the democratic party and again became its leader. He was prominent in his opposition to the regime of that day (at the close of the war), but such was his honesty and courage that he commanded and maintained to a conspicuous degree the respect of his adversaries. This was notable in the first legislature of which he was a member during that eventful period.

On the removal of his disabilities he was again elected to the legislature, and continued to represent his county till his death. At its last session he was elected speaker of the house, the duties of which he discharged with eminent ability. No man in the state has attained greater distinction as a legislator. The statute books show the imprint of his superior wisdom in many of the measures of substantial benefit to the people, especially in those measures looking to retrenchment in expenditure of the public funds. He was gifted with a peculiar wisdom and acumen in this branch of legislation. In his death, the community in which he lived lost its most distinguished and useful citizen. As a husband he was gentle, faithful and true; as a father he was loving and kind; as a brother he was devoted and constant; as a Mason he lived up to the highest standard of the order. He was a proud man and erected a lofty standard to which he strove to elevate his family, and may his two sons and two daughters fill the full measure of his hopes. As a neighbor he was generous and considerate; as a friend he was warm hearted and true. When he once placed his friendship, it become lasting and steadfast, and under it his confidence was given without reserve. He was conspicuous in deeds of charity. It is said of him that there was scarcely a poor man within reach of him, whom he had not materially befriended. His character was marked by strong traits. To a casual observer he seemed austere and imperious. To those who knew him well he was yielding and placable. Nature made him an honest man, free from all dissembling and pretention. He abhorred all shams and alluring devices. He had no guide save principle; he was deep and strong in his convictions of right and duty, and obeyed them with earnest energy and unfailing courage. His will was inflexible and his nerve was iron. It was these noble traits that made him invincible before the people. He was truly a man of the people; he was ambitious, but subordinated his desire for preferment to a genuine respect for the people and their interests. In their behalf there was no task too laborious, no sacrifice too great for him to make. In their service he comprehended and felt the sternest and loftiest sense of duty and held in supreme contempt any allurements from its pathway. His large heart was always with them and its honest yearning was to serve them faithfully. In educational matters his views were broad and comprehensive. He was a leading advocate of measures designed to enlarge and build up that great cause, and bring its blessings within the reach of the whole people. The death of such a man is, under any circumstances, a sad event, but when so illustrious a citizen falls by the hand of violence, his death is a most deplorable calamity. The state has lost one whose deeds in her councils and on the tented field have shed luster on her fair name and added to her glory and renown. He was killed in Baldwyn, December 4, 1882. Like J. G. Holland he lived to accomplish his early wish: "To occupy a pure place in the popular heart; to be welcomed in God's name, into the affectionate confidence of those for whom life has high meanings and high issues; of being recognized as among the beneficent forces of society." We drop a tear to the memory of a wise statesman, a pure patriot and a noble Christian man.

Among the residents of Washington county, Miss., the name of Dr. R. Saunders Toombs has become almost a household word, for so often has he entered their homes in his professional capacity, and so successfully has he practiced the healing art, that their confidence in him has become unbounded. He was born in Copiah county, Miss., August 12, 1844, to George H. and Winnie (Green) Toombs, who were born in Georgia and North Carolina, respectively, the former being a planter by occupation. When a young man he came to this state, and was married here soon after to Miss Green, dying in Copiah county in 1851. The paternal grandfather and grandmother were from England and Ireland, respectively, and were pioneer settlers of Georgia, North Carolina and Virginia. The Toombs family became very well known throughout Georgia; Robert Toombs being in the United States senate from that state for about twenty years, and for some time was secretary of state for the Confederacy, during the early part of the war, but afterward resigned to take the rank of brigadier-general in the Confederate army, distinguishing himself in the second battle of Manassas. The maternal grandparents of the subject of this sketch were William and Mary (Taylor) Green, natives of the Carolinas. Nearly all the male members of the Green family were ministers of the Baptist church, becoming distinguished for their ability as divines, and for their sturdy habits and morals. They prided themselves upon maintaining a high standard of morals and Christian integrity, and possessed many of the characteristics of their Huguenot ancestors, who left their native land on account of their religious belief. Dr. R. Saunders Toombs was reared in Mississippi, and received his education in Pleasant Hill academy, afterward pursuing his medical studies in Vicksburg, and graduating in medicine in the Washington university, of Baltimore, Md., in 1868, after which he began practicing, and has since been one of the leading physicians of the state. When he was six years of age his mother was left a widow, and as his father had become security for many friends, the most of his fortune was swept away, and his family was left with comparatively nothing to maintain them. For this reason the Doctor had not only to support and educate himself, but to assist in supporting his mother besides. There was no such word as fail in his vocabulary, and the success that has attended his efforts and his many accomplishments are due to his ambition and his indomitable energy. During a time that he should have been in school the war came on, and in 1862, at the age of eighteen years, he enlisted in the Confederate army, becoming a member of company K, Thirty-sixth Mississippi regiment, and soon showed himself to be a young man of undoubted courage and trustworthiness. Having manifested considerable ability as a scout, he was sent with important dispatches on various occasions, and at one time rode sixty-eight miles through snow and sleet, swimming his horse across three streams, nearly losing his life by his horse becoming entangled in driftwood. On this occasion he was bearing important news from Gen. Wirt Adams to Colonel Scott. He was at the battle of Jackson, but soon after entering the army ill health caused him to give up heavy service, and he was assigned to light duty, and was made hospital steward in field service, under Chief Surgeon John M. Allen, of the division of cavalry. He was the first to reach General Goblson after he was wounded in the fierce fight near Jackson, but just prior to this was engaged as superintendent in the cartridge manufacturing department in the arsenal at Jackson.

While in Jackson he had a most miraculous escape from death in the terrible explosion which occurred in that city, killing every inmate in the building, in which about forty children lost their lives, he being the only one left to tell the cause, which he thinks resulted from recharging some old shell. He had only thirty minutes before been transferred to the state treasury, and he considers his escape as a special act of providence, for his transfer was effected by telegram by one of his friends in authority, who had a premonition of his danger. Dr. Toombs was married in April, 1876, to Miss Fannie Ray, a native of Carrollton, Miss., and a daughter of Capt. William and Mary (Latham) Ray, both of whom were born in Mississippi. To their marriage four children have been born: William Ray, Percy Walthall, Robert Henry, and Frederick S. The Doctor is the owner of a large landed estate in Washington county, and besides this he owns several residences and one business house on Walnut street, besides several vacant lots on the same street, and the most of Toombs addition to the city of Greenville. He has property in Memphis and Chattanooga, Tenn., and in Sheffield, Ala. He is a stockholder in the Merchants and Planters' bank and Citizens' bank at Greenville. The Doctor came to this point just at the outbreak of the terrible yellow-fever epidemic of 1878, and was at once made secretary of the city board of health, and is now a member of the state board of health, and was appointed by Governor Lowry to represent that board in the inter-state quarantine convention, held in Montgomery, Ala., in 1889. His practice has been equal to that of any physician in the county, for he has acquired great proficiency in his profession, and has contributed many valuable articles to the medical literature of the day. In 1886 he was elected president of the State Medical association of Mississippi by acclamation, and is now vice president of the National Association of the Railway Surgeons of America. He and his wife are prominent members of the Baptist church, and were instrumental in the founding of the flourishing church of that denomination in Greenville. He has always taken great interest in church work, and was a liberal contributor to the endowment of Mississippi college (Baptist) at Clinton, which is one of the best and most prosperous institutions of the state. He is a member of the A. F. & A. M., the K. of H. and the A. L. of H. Dr. Toombs possesses perfect manners, and at all times manifests the instincts and training of a true gentleman. When engaged in conversation he at once impresses one as a gentleman of intelligence, for his ideas on all subjects are shrewd and sound.

John Torrey. Among the first pioneers to settle in the east part of Jefferson county, was the Torrey family, the date of their arrival being 1806. Dugald Torrey, father of John, was born in Robinson county, N. C., in 1780, and in that state and county grew to manhood, marrying, in the month of September, 1804, Miss Flora Gilchrist, who was also of that state, and of Scotch parentage. Sometime after their marriage they removed to Tennessee, where they resided about one year, then came to Claiborne county, Miss., settling near Port Gibson, but at the above mentioned date settled in Jefferson county. Here he opened a very large plantation on which he reared his family, and on this farm, which he, himself, put in an admirable state of cultivation, he breathed his last in 1853, his wife having passed from life ten years earlier. He was a son of George Torrey, a native of Scotland, who emigrated to the states, and was one of the pioneers of North Carolina, rearing his family in Robinson county. John Torrey is one of a family of three sons and six daughters, but is the only surviving member of the family at the present date. One brother, George Torrey, who died in Fayette, was well known, having been a former sheriff of Jefferson county. Wm. Torrey died on the Island of Cuba in 1843. After attaining manhood in this county, John Torrey was married in the month of October, 1846, to Miss Margaret C. Cameron, a native of the county and a daughter of Archibald Cameron, one of the settlers of 1810. Mr. John Torrey has been engaged in planting his entire life, and in following this calling has met with a more than average degree of success. He has been a resident of the plantation on which he is now living since January, 1850, on which place was some open land that had been under cultivation for about forty years. Mr. Torrey commenced at once to clear more land and on this property erected a good residence, steam cottongin, and in other ways greatly improved it, making it one of the most desirable plantations in his part of the county. His land amounts to about one thousand acres at the present time, although he at one time owned over five thousand acres. He owned a large number of slaves during ante-bellum days, and over eighty-three were set free by the emancipation proclamation. Mr. Torrey is a man possessing much energy and decision of character and his judgment in matters of business, as well as upon all other topics, is shrewd, far-seeing and intelligent. A family of five children in time gathered about his board: Florah Ann, wife of John S. Gillis, a farmer of the county; Alice, wife of J. M. Riggs, a schoolteacher of the Lone Star state; Arlone Maddux, a widow; Dugald A. and Mary C. Like the majority of Scotch people, the Torreys are members of the Presbyterian church, and are frugal, industrious and acquisitive, although not in the least penuriously so. They are among the most substantial of the county's residents and are hospitable, charitable and kindly people.

Hon. William D. Torrey has been long and worthily identified with Jefferson county, Miss., and no satisfactory history of his immediate vicinity would be complete which failed to make proper mention of his career. He was born on the 5th of August, 1850, and in his early days was given better advantages than the average boy, and for some time was an attendant of the University of Mississippi. After deciding to make the practice of law his profession, he began studying in the office of Shackleford & Cassidy, and on the day that he arrived at his majority, August 5, 1871, he was admitted to the bar. His views on legal questions soon won for him golden opinions, and while serving in the capacity of justice of the peace, which he did for several years, he became noted for the excellent decisions he made in all cases that appeared before him. He was not long allowed to remain as a mere practitioner, for his brilliant mind and thorough knowledge of all legal technicalities were needed in the legislative halls of Mississippi, and in 1880 he was elected by his numerous friends to that body and for some time was a member of the committee on education and corporations. He was a conscientious and scrupulously honorable legislator, and on all occasions endeavored to use his influence for the benefit of his state. He is now residing on the old homestead, a beautiful place situated about one and one-half miles north of Fayette, which he purchased after the death of his father. Here he is extensively engaged in planting and stockraising, and the seven hundred acres of which he is the owner, have been made very productive by his system of farming. In 1881, Miss Mary F. Hunt, a daughter of Abijah Hunt, one of the early settlers of the county, became his wife and their union has resulted in the birth of two sons. He and his wife are members of the K. and L. of H., of which lodge Mr. Torrey is the chief officer. His father, George Torrey, was also born in this county, his birth taking place in the year 1808, and the wife of the latter, Mary Ann (Barker) Torrey, was born on the 7th of March, 1821, their union taking place in 1840. Six of their children grew to maturity and two sons and one daughter are living at the present time: William D., George, who is a planter residing near Fayette, and Effie, the wife of George D. Forman. George Torrey was an extensive and successful planter and was a man well known for his intelligent views on all matters. For this reason, and from the fact that he possessed undoubted courage and determination, he was elected to the office of sheriff, and for eight years filled this position with credit. He served in both houses of the state legislature, was for many years a member of the senate, and throughout his entire manhood he was prominently before the public as a supporter of all matters pertaining to the welfare of the state and his county. He was chosen commissioner of immigration, and during his term of office made three trips to England, for the purpose of inducing white laborers to immigrate to the state of Mississippi. In this he was quite successful and many good families of this section came here owing to his influence. He lived an active and useful life, and for many years before his death, September 12, 1886, he had been a member of the Presbyterian church. His wife was left an orphan at a very early age, and from her native state of Kentucky she came to this state with an uncle, Dr. E. W. Harding, who settled in Greenville, formerly the county seat of this county, where he built up an extensive practice and died in 1887 at the age of ninety-one years. Mrs. Torrey was finely educated, was an exemplary Christian, and died on the 16th of September, 1889.

James Clinton Totten, Holly Springs, a native born citizen of Marshall county, Miss., has become one of its most promising attorneys, and although young in years, he has practiced throughout the entire judicial circuit for some time. His parents, Benjamin and Olivia

(Brooks) Totten, were born in Tennessee, but came with their parents to Mississippi when small children. They grew up, were married in Marshall county, and the fruits of their union were two children: James C., and Maggie, who is the wife of Dr. S. D. Hamilton of Waterford. The paternal grandfather was a native of Tennessee and of English descent. He had two brothers, A. O. W. Totten of Tennessee, for many years one of the judges of the supreme court of that state, and Clinton Totten of Arkansas, who had served as circuit judge for many years in Tennessee, and was a prominent politician and lawyer in Arkansas at the time of his death. James S. Totten, our subject's grandfather, came to Mississippi at an early day and he was repeatedly elected a member of the legislature from Marshall county, being speaker of the house for a number of years, before the war. He removed from Mississippi to Arkansas and was a very prominent attorney of that state for a number of years. There his death occured in 1866. Benjamin Totten followed planting in Marshall county until the opening of the conflict between the North and South, and then, in 1861, enlisted as a private. He was in the battles of Corinth, Shiloh and many others, and in the last-named engagement received a wound in the foot, which incapacitated him from further service in the infantry, consequently he entered the cavalry. He was killed near Holly Springs, Miss., in 1863, by his horse falling on him. His wife had died several years previous and this left our subject and sister to be taken care of by their grandfather, Alfred Brooks, who was very kind to them, and to whose aid our subject acknowledges much credit for his success in life. James C. Totten was born on April 29, 1857, and at the age of nineteen went to Oxford, obtained his literary training in the State university, and in 1879 he took a commercial course at Bryant and Stratton Commercial college at Louisville, Ky., graduating in 1880. After this he returned to Holly Springs, studied law with the firm of Watson & Smith, and was admitted to the bar in 1882. He then formed a copartnership with J. W. C. and E. M. Watson, of Holly Springs, but E. M. Watson was appointed assistant attorney-general, under Attorney-General Garland, in 1884. Mr. Totten has continued to practice his profession up to the present time and has also been engaged in agricultural pursuits, being the owner of one-half interest in one thousand acres of land in Marshall county, with five hundred acres under cultivation. His principal crop is cotton, and in 1890 he raised seventy-five bales and two or three thousand bushels of corn. He has never been elected to any office in the county, but is at present chairman of the democratic county executive committee. He has given almost his entire attention to the practice of his profession, and his efforts have been crowned with a reasonable degree of success. He is a member of both the Masonic and Odd Fellows fraternities. His grandfather Brooks was born in North Carolina in 1802, and died in Marshall county, Miss., in 1887. He was a very extensive farmer.

Capt. John V. Toulme, Bay St. Louis, Miss., proprietor of the Crescent hotel, and mayor of Bay St. Louis, Miss., was born in this place in August, 1827, and is a son of John B. and Uranie (Sancier) Toulme, natives of France and of the Dominion of Canada, respectively. The father immigrated to America in 1812, and the mother had come to the states two years before. They were married in Bay St. Louis, and Mr. Toulme carried on a large mercantile and stockraising business for many years. He was identified with all public movements, and was a member of the state legislature for one or two sessions. He was also mayor of the city for some time. He and his wife both died here. They reared a family of seven children, six of whom are living. John V. is the fourth child and the only son. He was educated at St. Mary's school, near Lebanon, Ky., and after completing his studies he engaged in mercantile trade and the raising of livestock. These he conducted successfully until the breaking out of the Civil war. At that time he paid taxes on five thousand head of cattle, and was the largest stockraiser of the state. However, when the call came, he abandoned his private interests, raised company F, Third Mississippi volunteer infantry, and went out as captain of the company. He served in this capacity until 1863, when he resigned and returned to his home. The desolation and destruction wrought by war would have completely discouraged many a man, but, realizing the uselessness of despair, he set to work at once to retrieve his fortunes. He opened a hotel, and has kept the best house in the Bay. He has just completed a large hotel of fifty-six rooms with all modern improvements. The management is excellent in every department, and the comfort of guests is of the first consideration. The house is known as the Crescent hotel, a name it has had since 1866. Captain Toulme has been mayor of Bay St. Louis, and has proven himself an efficient officer during the several terms he has filled the chair. In 1850 he was married to Martha E. Carr, and three children were born to them, all of whom are living. He was married a second time, in 1879, to Mrs. C. W. List. Five children have been born of this union. The Captain is a member of the Masonic fraternity. He is now captain of company C, First artillery battalion, Mississippi national guards, which he raised and organized in March, 1889. During the time of his service in the Confederate army he was captured in his home while on a furlough, but he managed to make his escape. He was a brave soldier, and is a loyal progressive citizen, zealously supporting all home interests.

W. L. Treadwell was born in Rutherford county, N. C., on the 19th day of June, 1828, the second in a family of nine children who came to the home of T. L. Treadwell and Eliza (Allison) Treadwell, who were natives of North and South Carolina, respectively. The paternal grandfather was a soldier in the Revolutionary war, serving under the famous General Marion. The parents of W. L. Treadwell were married in North Carolina, where they lived till the year 1836, when they moved to Marshall county, Miss., thus earning for himself the title of being one of the pioneers of this part of the state. He bought land here and engaged in farming, also opened up a store, trading principally with the Indians, as there were but few white people in and around old Lamar, the town he chose for his residence. He was quite successful both as a planter and a merchant, accumulating considerable property, and prior to the war owning one hundred slaves. As he was so well and favorably known, he was naturally elected to fill the offices at the command of his fellow townsmen. He was a man noted far and wide for his extreme generosity, especially to aught which pertains to the betterment of his community. After the war he engaged in merchandising in the new town of Lamar, and was thus employed at the time of his death in 1870. His wife died at old Lamar, in 1848, and he married Elizabeth E., widow of Samuel Haney. This wife died in 1889, in her eighty-seventh year; by his last wife there was no issue. Of his offspring there are only six living: Our subject; Allison C., Memphis; Robert A., of Jackson, Tenn.; A. B., engaged in the wholesale grocery business at Memphis; A. E., wife of H. P. Maxwell; and Francis M., farmer in Marshall county; B. D. having died at Memphis, Tenn., leaving a family, and Mary A. (wife of W. B. Smith), and Amelia F., (wife of F. P. Long), having both died near Lamar. The subject was educated at Chapel Hill, N. C., and was a graduate in the class of 1851, after which he took a course of law under a private tutor, Judge Pearson, of Rockford, N. C., and began the practice of his profession in Memphis in 1854, remaining there until 1860. In this year he abandoned the practice of law and moved to Marshall county, Miss., where he had bought land, and turned his attention to its cultivation. In 1862 he enlisted in company A, of the Seventh Tennessee cavalry, under Col. W. F. Taylor, this regiment being known as Jackson's escort. He served until the close of the war, and was paroled at Gainesville, Ala., when he returned home and resumed his interrupted occupation of planting to which he added the charge of the mercantile business, left at loose ends by his father's death at Lamar, and which he continued to oversee up to the year 1884, when he closed up this branch of his business, and retired to his farm. Later he gave up the management of this also, and had it worked by renters. He owns twelve hundred acres of land, six hundred of which are under cultivation. It is situated two miles southeast of Lamar, in what is now Benton county. He was married in 1858, to Miss Lou A. Farabee, a daughter of F. B. Farabee, of Shelby county, Tenn. They have three children: Lucy, Robert D., and Eliza A., wife of J. M. Aldrich, of Michigan City, Miss. Miss Lucy was educated at Bethlehem academy at Holly Springs, graduating in 1877. Miss Eliza received her education at the Huntsville Female college at Huntsville, Ala. Robert went to school at Memphis and is now engaged with the wholesale dry goods house of Lemmon & Gale as traveling salesman. The faithful wife died in 1887, a consistent member of the Episcopal church, to which denomination the family all belong. The family occupy an enviable position in the county, and their home is the resort of the elite of that part of the state. Mr. Treadwell is a Mason and is a man who delights in using his means and influence to better the condition of his county, to such an extent that he is deserving of the name of the generous man, which is applied to him. He is a man to whom honor is due and to whom honor comes, but he prefers to use his influence in a private way, always declining his services for any office of profit.

Hon. James M. Trice is a general merchant of Okolona, and also gives considerable attention to the calling of a planter, his land amounting to over one thousand five hundred acres. Mr. Trice was born in Lawrence county, Ala., in 1825, to James A. and Rhoda (Smith) Trice, natives, respectively, of Hanover and Louisa counties, Va., in which state they were reared, educated and married. In 1816 they removed to Madison county, Ala., and in 1818 settled in Lawrence county, where Mr. Trice passed from life in 1853, and his wife in 1864, both having been earnest members of the Methodist church. The father received only an ordinary education in his youth, but possessing much natural ability he became an exceptionally well-informed and intelligent man. He possessed a strong will and a decisive character, and being industrious and honorable he became well-to-do. He was a soldier in the War of 1812. His father, William Trice, was a Virginian, but died in Madison county, Ala., whither he had moved in 1816, a well-to-do planter. He was married twice and reared a large family of children, his first wife being the grandmother of Hon. James M. Trice. The maternal grandfather, Noah Smith, was also a Virginian, but in an early day removed to Roane county, Tenn., where he died, a worthy tiller of the soil. Hon. James M. Trice was the eighth of nine sons and three daughters, only two members of this family being now alive. One of the sons, Robert L., now a resident of Verona, Miss., served faithfully in the Confederate army, being in the army of the Tennessee, and participating in the engagements of the Georgia and Atlanta campaign. James M. was reared on a farm, receiving a fair English education, and at the age of nineteen, or in 1844, he came to Monroe county, Miss., and for several years was engaged in trading. He was first married in 1846 in Lawrence county, Ala., to Elizabeth, daughter of John M. and Martha McGaughey, who were born and married in Tennessee, from which state they removed to Lawrence county, Ala., where they died, the father having been a prosperous planter. Mrs. Trice was born in this county and died in 1862, having borne a family of six children: Zachariah T., a merchant of Okolona, was in the state militia during the latter part of the war; Laura, wife of B. T. Clark, of Nettleton; Anna, widow of Charles Smith; John, of the John Trice Banking company, of Okolona, one of the most thoroughgoing and successful financiers of the county; Mollie, wife of Thomas M. Walton, a planter of Monroe county, and James A., a planter of Nettleton. James M. Trice resided in Monroe county, on the old plantation, until 1883, since which time he has been a resident of Okolona, where he has been connected with the mercantile business since 1876, the firm for some years being J. M. Trice & Co., but for some time he has conducted affairs on his own responsibility. He is one of the most energetic, progressive and practical of business men, and the handsome fortune which he now enjoys is the result of his own efforts. In 1862 he served for some time in Col. William Inge's regiment of Mississippi cavalry, but owing to the failing health of his wife he was compelled to return home, and afterward hired a substitute. His second marriage was celebrated, in 1872, to Mrs. Margaret T., a daughter of Joseph Pickens, a native of South Carolina, who removed to Huntsville, Ala., where he passed from life prior to the war, his widow still surviving him. Mrs. Trice was born near Huntsville and is a member of the Cumberland Presbyterian church. Although Mr. Trice has never sought office his many friends deemed him a fitting man to represent them in the state legislature, and in 1875 they elected him to this position, being again elected from Monroe county in 1881, during which session he was chairman of the committee on agriculture. After removing to Chickasaw county he interested himself in every worthy enterprise and soon became well known for his sound and practical views on all subjects, and in 1889 was chosen as a representative to the legislature from this county, and while a member of that body displayed such sound and practical views that he became a conspicuous figure in the legislative halls. He made an enviable record for himself and was an able and incorruptible legislator. He was a member of the committee on conventions, and worked for the interest of the bill providing for the new constitutional convention. He was formerly a member of Carnargo lodge No. 118, of the A. F. & A. M., of which he was worshipful master; but he is now a member of Prairie lodge No. 87, of Okolona, in which he is a Knight Templar.

Dr. G. W. Trimble, a prominent physician and surgeon of Grenada, county health officer, surgeon for the Illinois Central railroad and president of the State Medical association, was born in Limestone county, Ala., in 1822, and is a son of Archibald and Margaret (Reese) Trimble, the father a native of the Old Dominion, and the mother of Tennessee. Archibald Trimble, who was of Scotch-Irish parentage, had three brothers in the War of 1812. He moved from Tennessee to northern Alabama, was one of the first settlers of that state, and died there in 1827. He was a selfmade man. His wife died in Alabama in 1836. She had been married twice, Mr. Trimble being her last husband. The paternal grandfather, John Trimble, of Augusta county, Va., moved to Tennessee at an early day, and thence to Claiborne county, Miss., where his life terminated. The maternal grandfather, Rev. Solomon Reese, was a Cumberland Presbyterian minister, and at an early day emigrated to northern Alabama, his death occurring in Franklin county of that state During the principal part of his life he ministered to the spiritual wants of his fellowman, and also wielded the ferule in the schoolroom. He was of Scotch-Welsh descent. Dr. G. W. Trimble, the only child born to the above mentioned union, was educated in a printing office in Nashville, Tenn., and Tuscumbia, Ala., beginning when but a small boy, and continuing the printing business until he was twenty-three years of age. He then closed his editorial career at Aberdeen, where he published the Aberdeen *Independent* and the Aberdeen *Bee* for a few years. He began the study of medicine with Dr. J. A. Trimble, a half-brother, of Russelville, Ala., and graduated from the medical college of Louisville, Ky., in 1852, since which time he has practiced in Grenada and vicinity, being the oldest resident

practitioner there. He was assistant surgeon in the Second Mississippi infantry, but was soon after disabled by getting his leg broken at Bowling Green, after which he did no further service, except at home. He has been a prominent member of the State Medical association since its formation. He was married, in 1842, to Miss Ella Barksdale, a native of Pickens county, Ala., and the daughter of John and Anna Barksdale, natives of the Old Dominion, where they were reared and married. Later the parents moved to Pickens county, Ala., and there both received their final call. The father was a planter by occupation. Mrs. Trimble was a member of the Baptist church, and died in 1846, leaving one son, Joseph H. The latter was educated in Alabama, and served as a private in the Confederate army. He was a trader, and died in 1875. Dr. Trimble's second marriage occurred in 1856 to Mrs. Rebecca Thomas, daughter of Frank Bullock, a native of South Carolina, who was a successful planter and merchant of Sumter county, Ala., where his death occurred. Mrs. Trimble was born in Old Fort, S. C., and by her marriage to Dr. Trimble became the mother of two children: Mary T., wife of Curtis H. Guy (see sketch), and Charlie. The Doctor has been a member of the Grenada lodge No. 6, I. O. O. F., since 1853, is a very prominent member, and is past grand master of the state, also past grand representative. Mrs. Trimble is a member of the Presbyterian church. The Doctor has planting interests and is one of the foremost men of the county. He is learned in his profession, and his career, as a practitioner and thorough student of medicine, has won for him no less a reputation than has his personal characteristics, as a citizen and neighbor. His advantages for schooling were very limited while growing up, for he was left an orphan when very young, and was compelled to be his own custodian; thus it may truly be said that he is a selfmade man.

Like many of the prominent citizens of Winston county, Nimrod D. Triplett, planter, Perkinsville, Miss., owes his nativity to the Palmetto state, his birth occurring in Chester county, in 1839. His parents, Nimrod, Sr., and Dorothy (Moore) Triplett, it is supposed, were natives also of that county, and there they were reared and married. In the winter of 1848 and 1849, they removed to Winston county, Miss., whither the father had gone to purchase land in 1845, and settled on what was known as the Gentry place. They remained there only a short time, however, and then moved to the place where their son, Nimrod D., now resides. There the father's death occurred in September, 1861, at the age of seventy-one years. His wife is still living at the advanced age of ninety-nine years, and is doubtless the oldest person in the county. The father was a man of ordinary education, and in early life had followed the shoemaker's trade. This he had to abandon on account of ill health, but he afterward ran a still in South Carolina for some time, although his principal occupation during life was farming. He was a very temperate and industrious man. His father, Nimrod Triplett, was of Welsh descent, and was probably born in the Old Dominion, where he was married. From there he removed to North Carolina, thence to South Carolina, and settled in Chester county, where he followed agricultural pursuits. He was the father of two sons. The maternal grandfather, Thomas Moore, was born in Chester district, S. C., and there passed his entire life engaged in farming. He was but a boy during the Revolutionary war, and he and his father were captured by the tories. The father was killed, but the boy escaped, and afterward wreaked vengeance upon his father's murderer. Nimrod D. Triplett, subject of this sketch, was the tenth of thirteen children, four of whom are now living: George W., of Leake county, was in the Confederate army with General Ferguson; Solomon R., of Kemper county, was in the cavalry during the Civil war. Nimrod D. Triplett was reared on a farm, and received an ordinary education in the common schools. He began for himself at the age of twenty-one as an overseer, and early in 1861 he joined company F, Fourteenth Mississippi infantry in the western army, and fought at Fort Donelson. He was captured and spent about seven and a half months in Camp Douglas. He was exchanged at Vicksburg, and afterward fought at Coffeeville, Baker's creek, Jackson, Dalton, and was in the Atlanta campaign. He then went back with General Hood to Franklin and Nashville, and afterward joined General Johnston in North Carolina, with whom he surrendered after four years' hard service. Returning home after the war he engaged in farming, and in 1868 he was united in marriage to Miss America Richards, a native of Choctaw county, Miss., and the daughter of George W. and Lucinda Richards, the father a native of Alabama, and the mother of Georgia. The parents removed to Choctaw county, Miss., and afterward to Noxubee county, where Mr. Richards died in 1887. Mrs. Richards died about 1877. Both were Baptists, and he had followed planting all his life. They saw twelve of their children grow up and marry. To Mr. and Mrs. Triplett were born seven children, all of whom are living: Beulah A., wife of James M. Smith; George Edwin, Nimrod D, Samuel Orr, Laura Belle, Thomas Moore and John Henry. Since his marriage Mr. Triplett has lived on his present farm consisting of one thousand one hundred acres, and in connection with farming is quite extensively engaged in raising stock. He owns two hundred acres in another tract. He is a member of the Masonic order, formerly of Winstonville lodge No. 277, was a charter member of Parkersville lodge No. 336, and has been secretary twelve years. He and Mrs. Triplett have been members of the Baptist church for many years, and are highly esteemed citizens.

William E. Trotter is a successful planter and merchant of Clay county, Miss., and is well and favorably known to the majority of the residents of this section, for he has been a resident of the county since 1854. He was born in Lincoln county, Tenn., in 1816, and when about five years of age was taken to Alabama by his parents and was there brought up on a plantation. Notwithstanding this, upon starting out in life for himself, it was as a clerk, and in 1852 he was sufficiently familiar with the business to embark in merchandising for himself at Moscow, Ala. Since becoming a resident of Mississippi he has carried on planting in connection with merchandising, and his plantation is a valuable one and beautifully located on the bank of the Tombigbee river. In 1842 he was married to Miss Sarah A. Moore, of Tennessee, a daughter of Maj. James Moore, of that state, and their union has resulted in the birth of these children: Mary F. (Kirk); John, who died at the age of two years; Charles M., also died when two years of age; James M., of Aberdeen; Sarah A. (Hodo), of West Point; Mattie A., wife of Dr. White, of West Point, Miss.; Ida (Dukeminer), who is deceased; Richard M., of West Point; Benjamin, a resident of Vinton, Clay county, Miss.; Henry C., who died when two years old; Susie (Watts), of Starkville. Mr. Trotter is a member of the Masonic order, which he joined in Alabama in 1836, and while a resident of Moscow, Ala., in 1838, was appointed postmaster of that place by Martin Van Buren, who was then president of the United States. He has been postmaster at different places in Alabama and Mississippi ever since, a period of over fifty-three years. He and his wife are members of the Methodist Episcopal church and are respected and honored by all who know them. Mr. Trotter is now in his seventy-fifth year, but carries his age remarkably well and looks much younger. He is a son of Dr. Thomas L. and Mary S. (Quarles) Trotter, who were born in 1777 and 1784, respectively. The former practiced medicine in Virginia, North Carolina, Tennessee and Alabama, and being well posted in his profession, as well as on all the general topics of the day, he was successful and accumulated a comfortable competency. He was a member of the Masonic fraternity, died in 1831 and his wife in 1861.

Hon. Jeff. Truly has early become a distinguished member of the bar, and during his career as an attorney he has shown himself to be endowed with superior ability, and his words are accompanied with weight and vigor. By hard study and conscientious practice his position is so well established that it is conceded by all competent judges that he ranks among the highest civilians. Mr. Truly has been deeply interested in everything pertaining to the welfare of Jefferson county, for in the town of Fayette he was born on the 21st of July, 1861. His father, R. H. Truly, was also born here, and was here united in marriage to Miss Mary Key, a native of Alabama, but reared in Mississippi. R. H. Truly is a man of strong character, and intellectually is far the superior of the average man. He is personally acquainted with and has met socially nearly all the great statesmen of Mississippi and the nation, and as he is very fond of traveling, and believes this to be a liberal education in itself, he has visited nearly all the great cities of the United States. He is of a very social and agreeable disposition, and his pleasant, winning manners, his kindly disposition and his intelligent conversation make him a most agreeable companion, and have won for him innumerable friends. Hon. Jeff. Truly had only limited school advantages in his boyhood, and is principally self-educated. Having always possessed a strong inclination for the study of law, he began the study of that profession in his native town, but later continued to pursue his studies at St. Joseph, La., under Steele & Garrett, eminent attorneys of that place, and still later took a complete course in the law department of the University of New Orleans, completing the course before he attained his twenty-first birthday. After the completion of his course he returned to his home in Mississippi, and formed a partnership with W. D. Torrey, his present partner, their union being blessed with abundant success from the first. He has had some very important cases which he has brought to a successful issue, and the echo of his name and fame have extended over a wide territory. He has evinced quite an active interest in local politics, and in 1885 was chosen by his numerous friends to the state legislature, being one of the youngest members of that body, and distinctly in opposition to the administration at that time. He served as a member of the state campaign committee, also the state democratic committee, in both of which he distinguished himself. He is able and earnest in advocacy of what he thinks best calculated to promote the best interests of the country, and as he is studious and attentive to his business, abstemious in his habits and laborious in research, he has never permitted the interests of his clients to suffer. He is at all times thoroughly prepared in his cases, and is rarely taken by surprise. His clients rely implicitly upon his word and his counsel. He was married in Fayette, October 23, 1889, to Miss Mattie Whitney, a daughter of Dr. P. K. Whitney, who is a native of Jefferson county and a member of one of the oldest and best known families in the county. Mr. and Mrs. Truly have one child, Everette. Mr. Truly is a member of the Masonic fraternity and the Knights of Honor, and as he is a man of much native ability there is a bright future before him.

John Thomas Trusty, Pine Valley, Miss., a successful merchant and planter of Yalobusha county, was born in the state of Tennessee in the year 1840, and is a son of James G. and Eliza F. (Speary) Trusty, also natives of Tennessee. The maternal grandparents were natives of Pennsylvania and Canada. John Speary, the grandfather, was a millwright who emigrated to Mississippi soon after 1830, and purchased a large tract of land in Pontotoc county, where he became an extensive real estate dealer. He afterward settled in Yalobusha county and put up a mill on Hurricane creek. There he lived until death, which came to him in 1858, at the age of sixty years. He was a Universalist in his religious faith. He accumulated a considerable property, and was highly respected by all who knew him. He had two children: the mother of our subject and Mrs. Francis Tatum. Martha Speary, his wife, was born in Pennsylvania; she lived to be past seventy years of age. She was one of the charter members of the Methodist Episcopal church of Pine Valley, which was organized in 1840. The parents of Mr. Trusty were married in Williamson county, Tenn., and came to Mississippi after the Speary family had removed to that state. The father is yet living, and is engaged in farming, being the owner of a considerable estate. He is a member of the Baptist church, of which he has been a deacon since its organization. During the war he belonged to the militia, and in his political opinions he is democratic. His wife died in 1875. To them had been born thirteen children, five of whom are yet living: John Thomas is the eldest of these. He remained under the parental roof until the breaking out of the late war, when he enlisted in the Fifteenth Mississippi volunteer infantry, company F. He served until he was discharged at Chicago after the surrender. He was taken prisoner at Nashville, Tenn., while under Hood. He was wounded in the battle of Shiloh, by a spent shell, and again, in the battle of Corinth, he was knocked down by a spent shell, but was not disabled more than a few days. He was also at Franklin and Nashville, and in several skirmishes. In 1867 he was married to Mrs. Anna H. Bell, nee Palmore, a native of Virginia. She is one of a family of three sons and three daughters. Her mother died when she was but three years of age. She was first married to William A. Bell, a native of Winslow county, S. C. Of this marriage one child was born, Helen, the wife of Charles W. Wright, a resident of Arkansas. Of the second marriage five children have been born: Virginia, John L., William T., Joseph H. (who died at the age of five years) and James R. Mr. Trusty is a member of the Tabernacle lodge No. 340, A. F. & A. M. Politically he affiliates with the democratic party, and in religious faith he is a Baptist. Since 1880 he has been engaged in the general mercantile trade, and is the proprietor of the Pine Valley store. He was commissioned postmaster December 31, 1885, and has conducted the office in connection with his other business. He is the owner of several hundred acres of land, a large portion of which is under cultivation. Stockraising is also carried on extensively on this place. In these various industries our subject has call to exercise all of his business faculties, and that he has made a success of it is to be seen in the thrift and air of prosperity which pervades all his possessions.

Joel A. Tucker owes his nativity to Marshall county, Miss., his birth occurring on the 7th of October, 1852, and although young in years, he is one of the substantial men of the county. He was the eldest in order of birth of four children born to Asa E. and Amanda E. (Ingram) Tucker, both natives of the Old Dominion. The father is a planter, has been very successful in life, and is one of the representative men of the county. He was president of the Bank of Sardis, where he resides, until on account of age and ill health he refused to serve any longer. He came to Mississippi at an early day, and became quite a noted character in Panola county. Joel A. Tucker grew to manhood in Panola county, received his education in both public and private schools, and at the usual age of twenty-one years he began for himself as a planter. He started with some capital, and is now the owner of one thousand nine hundred and fifty-five acres of land, with four hundred acres under cultivation. This farm is in a fine state of cultivation, and is considered one of the best in the county. Mr. Tucker is also the owner of a saw, gin and gristmill, a cotton and seedhuller. He was married in 1879 to Miss Irene F. Caldwell, who was born in Mississippi, and who is the daughter of Hon. W. W. and M. C. (Fowler) Caldwell, the father a native of Tennessee, and the mother of Alabama. Mr. Caldwell represented Panola county, Miss., in the state legislature in 1884. Mr. and Mrs. Tucker's union has been blessed by the birth of four children: Willie B., deceased; Mary E., Asa C. and Casey L. In his political views Mr. Tucker adhers closely to the democratic party. He is a member of the Masonic fraternity, and he and his family hold membership in the Methodist church. He gives his hearty support to all enterprises tending toward the growth and prosperity of the county. Mr. Tucker is the owner of a stone building in Courtland, a busy little town on the Illinois Central railroad, sixty-five miles south of Memphis, and Mrs. Tucker is the owner of forty acres of land, two brick buildings in Batesville, and an interest in three hundred acres of land on Tallahatchie river. Mr. Tucker comes of one of the oldest and most respected families in the county, and by his sociable ways has won a host of friends.

J. W. Tucker, merchant, Chulahoma, Miss. Prominent among the successful business enterprises of Chulahoma stands that conducted by Tucker Bros., the firm consisting of J. W. and his brother, Robert L., both live, industrious merchants. They engaged in this enterprise in Chulahoma about 1880, and carry a stock of goods valued at $3,500, their annual business amounting to $20,000. Aside from this J. W. Tucker is the owner of one thousand three hundred and twenty acres of land, five hundred acres under cultivation and his principal crop is cotton. His farm is operated by renters principally. Mr. Tucker was born near Chulahoma, Marshall county, Miss., on the 24th of December, 1847, and is a son of Jesse C. and Mary E. (Fort) Tucker, the father a native of Alabama, and the mother of North Carolina. They came to Mississippi with their parents when small, grew up and were married in Marshall county. They reared a family of thirteen children, eight sons and five daughters. The Tucker family was one of the earliest pioneers of the country, having removed from Tennessee to Mississippi in the thirties, when the country was full of Indians. Grandfather Tucker was a Baptist minister, and organized the church at Chulahoma and others in the surrounding country. He died in 1841, near Chulahoma. Jesse C. Tucker became a successful planter and died in 1868. The mother died in July, 1874. Ten of their children are now living, J. W. being third in order of birth. In 1864, when but sixteen years of age, the latter enlisted in the Confederate army, Colonel Withers' regiment, and served until the close of the war. He afterward followed farming near Chulahoma. Previous to entering the army he had received a good practical education in the common schools, and his brother, Robert L., who had taught in the public schools for two years, took a commercial course at Memphis. The latter, who is the youngest of the boys, is six feet six inches in hight and weighs two hundred and thirty-four pounds. He was married in 1889 to Miss Matilda M. Odell, daughter of Denton and Fanny E. (Bloodworth) Odell, and they have one daughter, Robina E. He is the owner of farm land and a fine residence at Chulahoma. The Tucker family is well and favorably known all over Marshall county, and are excellent citizens and successful business men. J. W. Tucker is a member of the Methodist church, but his brothers, R. L. and B. C., are members of the Baptist church. J. W. is also a member of the Masonic fraternity.

Kate Tucker institute. The Kate Tucker institute, located at Byhalia, Miss., was founded in 1882 by Mrs. Kate E. Tucker, and is a shining monument that deserving merit has won its principal. By her indefatigable energy and industry, in the face of strong opposition and without capital, this institution has steadily grown in numbers, character, and especially in the esteem of its patrons, till it stands now among the first schools of the state. The great success of its noble work is realized in the many young teachers it has sent out, who are engaged in remunerative positions in this and other states. Their pride in their work reflects great credit upon their alma mater, whose training has fitted them for such success. The institution was chartered in 1889, and by special request of its patrons its present name was selected. The principal, Mrs. Kate E. Tucker, was raised and educated in the school-famed city of Shelbyville, Ky. Her father, Mr. John Ross Doolan, died in 1854, when she was but six years old, leaving her mother with five small children to rear and educate. But the mother must have been animated by the enterprise that so eminently characterizes the daughter, for she not only reared, but she secured them the best educational advantages the town afforded. The father being a Baptist the children were educated at the Baptist college of Shelbyville, then the most progressive, under that model teacher, the Rev. B. F. Hungerford. That the children responded to the ambition of the mother to leave them the priceless fortune of an education, is manifested in the fact that two of them, Prof. T. J. Doolan, of Finchville, Ky., and Kate Eugenia, became teachers before they were seventeen. The latter filled with distinction a position as teacher in Bardstown, Ky., from 1867 to 1870, when she came to Holly Springs, where she taught four years. Failing health obliged her for a period to abandon her loved profession. Like many others who visit the South, she became so charmed with the genial climate and the hospitality of its people that she determined to make it her future home. Again, in 1875, she accepted a position in the Winona Female college for one year, after which she returned to Marshall county, where she has since taught. From the first she has been a diligent reader of educational literature. She has taken several normal courses, besides lessons in art, mathematics and penmanship from celebrated specialists. In 1881 she was married to Hon. J. H. Tucker, of Marshall county, and the fall of the next year commenced the nucleus of Kate Tucker institute.

Hon. J. H. Tucker, who is co-principal of Kate Tucker institute, was born near Petersburg, Va., in 1840. His father, Joseph Tucker, moved to Marshall county in 1844. His mother, who became a widow when he was ten, managed admirably the estate left her, and spared no expense in the opportunities procured for her children. The greater portion of his education was acquired in Marshall county, till he entered the sophomore class in the University of Mississippi. He enlisted in the Eleventh Mississippi regiment soon after the first gun from Fort Sumter resounded, and served in General Bee's brigade in the first battle of Bull Run, where he lost his brother, Thomas Emmet. He was discharged, but soon re-enlisted in the Tenth Mississippi regiment, and served in Gen. James H. Chamlers' brigade, until he again resigned, and, on returning health, re-enlisted in General Forrest's cavalry. He was paroled at Gainesville, Ala., and returned to his home to find it in ashes, and a comfortable fortune wasted by the ravages of war. He has been twice elected to the legislature of his state, which were the only interruptions in his vocation of planting, till 1882, when he became connected with the Kate Tucker institute.

Hon. Edward Turner (deceased) was a man whose memory has been kept green in the hearts of the many who knew and loved him in life. His reputation remained unblemished throughout a long and useful public career, and his acts of charity, his liberality, his kindness of heart and his brilliant mental endowments, made him a favorite of all with whom he came in contact. He was born in Fairfax county, Va., on the 25th of November, 1778, but in 1786 was taken by his parents to the state of Kentucky, and in the healthful bluegrass regions of that state he was brought up. He was given the advantages of excellent schools, and in his early manhood graduated from the Transylvania college, soon after which he began the study of law with Col. George Nichols, and at the end of three years, when in his twenty-eighth year, he began practicing his profession. In 1802 he came to Natchez, Miss., and as his ability soon became known, he was elected a clerk of the house of representatives, and was also the private secretary of Governor Claiborne. In September, 1802, he married a daughter of Col. Cato West, of Jefferson county, and to that county Mr. Turner removed and made his home. After a wedded life of nine years his wife was called from him, and in December, 1812, his union with Miss Eliza B. Baker, a native of New Jersey, was consummated. In 1815 he was elected to represent Adams county in the state legislature, and so admirably did he fill the obligations that were imposed upon him that for many years he was honored by re-elections. In 1816 the legislature confided to him the preparation of a digest of the statute laws, and at the time of the admission of Mississippi into the Union as a state, he was a member of the convention. He was twice elected speaker of the house of representatives, and in 1822 was appointed judge of the criminal court of Adams county, which led to his being elevated to the bench of the supreme and superior courts of the state by Governor Leake, and in 1830 received the appointment of attorney general. In 1834 he was elected chancellor of the state, but at the end of five years was elected judge of the high court of errors and appeals, during which time he displayed very superior mental endowments. Having a thorough knowledge of all the intricacies of the law, the most abstruse and complicated subjects were handled with ease and grace, and through his clear, forcible and convincing manner of expressing himself, were made plain and perceptible to the most ordinary understanding. When he retired from the bench he lacked three weeks of being sixty-five years of age, but, notwithstanding his advanced years, he was not long allowed to remain in retirement, but in 1844 was called to the state senate and for four years thereafter sat in the legislative halls of the state and assisted in making the laws by which he was to be governed. At the age of seventy years he withdrew from public life and spent the remainder of his days at Woodlands, his pleasant home, situated one mile from Natchez, where he passed from life on the 23d of May, 1860, being then in his eighty-second year. He was a man of exceptionally noble character, generous to a fault, kind and considerate to his family, and a faithful and generous friend. He was fond of society and in social circles was esteemed for his rare conversational powers, his gracious and deferential manners. He possessed decided literary tastes, and had been an extensive reader on most subjects. He was a thirty-second degree Mason and for many years had been a devout member of the Episcopal church. In person he was of commanding presence, being six feet two inches in hight, and his complexion was fair. His widow survived him until September 16, 1878, when she, too, was called from life, having borne her husband four children: Mary Louisa, now the widow of John T. McMurran; Edward, who died in the month of August, 1823; Elizabeth Frances, who was born in July, 1827, and died the following year, and Elizabeth Frances (second), born December 7, 1829, and now the wife of Lemuel Parker Conner, a talented and successful lawyer. These two sisters live on the old homestead, which has been the abiding place of some member of the family since 1856, but the estate now comprises seventy-five acres. It was in former times a large cotton plantation and was very valuable.

Henry C. Turner, merchant and planter, Canton, Miss., is one of the prominent men of Madison county, Miss., who, singlehanded, have had to carve out his own career in life, and that he has been successful thus far is not to be doubted for a moment, when a glance is cast over his well-kept farm. He owns fourteen hundred acres of land, with eight hundred acres under cultivation, and he is also engaged in merchandising, carrying a stock of goods valued at $500. He is wideawake and industrious, and being honest in his dealings and representations merits the esteem with which he is regarded. He is one of the substantial citizens, and is ever ready with his means and influence to further any good cause. He was born in Wilcox county, Ala., on the 16th of August, 1844, and is the fifth of six children born to Reuben

P. and Phœbe A. (Bishop) Turner, natives of Georgia. The father, who followed planting all his life, came to Mississippi in 1858, and died in 1875. His wife died in 1870. His father was A. J. Turner, also of Georgia, and her mother was Patience (Alford) Bishop, of that state also. Henry C. Turner was reared in Georgia and Mississippi, and received his education in the private schools of the same. He has been married twice, first, in 1868, to Miss Emma P. Pace, a native of Mississippi, and the daughter of James M. and Amanda J. Pace, natives of Tennessee. They had one child, Emma M., now deceased. In 1872 Mr. Turner married Miss Mattie E. Holliday, who was born in Mississippi, and who is the daughter of Isaac N. and Elizabeth A. Holliday, both also natives of the Bayou state. To Mr. and Mrs. Turner were born four children: Trocher S., Ruloff P., Hooker and Grady S. Mr. Turner served during the late unpleasantness between the North and South, enlisting in 1863, in company C, Withers' light artillery, and was with the same a short time before the war ended. He was discharged in 1864 on account of ill health. Mr. Turner takes a prominent part in politics and is a nominee for the state legislature for his county on the democratic ticket. He and his family are members of the Methodist church.

L. R. Turner is a native of Grenada county, Miss., where he was born on the 2d of April, 1856, the eldest of five children born to the marriage of R. H. Turner and Martha Miller, the former of whom was born in South Carolina, and is by occupation a farmer. L. R. Turner was an attendant of the common schools of his native county up to the age of twelve years, at which time he entered college at Columbia, S. C., in which institution he completed his junior year. He then read law for some time, but was not admitted to the bar, as he did not like the profession. In 1884 Mr. Turner was elected chancery clerk of Grenada county, Miss., for one term, at the expiration of which he opened up a general mercantile establishment at Grenada, and for about one year his business was quite prosperous. He then removed to his farm near the town of Grenada, where he remained for eighteen months, actively engaged in fitting it up for occupation. Of the nine hundred acres of land, of which he is now the owner, he has six hundred acres under cultivation. Mr. Turner came to Hinds county in September, 1890, but until the month of January, 1891, remained in Raymond, when he purchased and moved to the Mrs. Estes' property, which contains two thousand two hundred and seventeen acres, of which nine hundred acres are at the present time given to pasture, the rest being under cultivation. His is one of the best improved plantations in Hinds county, the house alone costing $10,000 just after the war. Mr. Turner also has a five thousand acre tract in Tallahatchie county, but it is unimproved. Mr. Turner is a Master Mason and he and his estimable wife are members of the Episcopal church. He was married February 22, 1887, to Miss Evelyn Summers, a native of Hinds county, by whom he has one child: Lewis S. Mrs. Turner received her education chiefly at Bardstown, Ky., but did not get to complete her course of study on account of sickness. Mr. Turner is of a practical turn of mind, very wideawake and progressive, and although he is still a young man he has a beautiful and comfortable home, and bids fair to become very wealthy.

Robert H. Turner, planter, and the present treasurer of Grenada county, was the youngest of five children born to his parents, Robert and Lovinda (Childs) Turner, his birth occurring in Abbeville district, S. C., on the 8th of October, 1825. The father was born on the Atlantic ocean in December, 1786, while his parents, Alexander and ——— (Hood) Turner, were on their way to Charleston, S. C., from Dublin, Ireland. Soon after landing at Charleston, Alexander's wife died, and he went on to Georgia, settling near Atlanta. The little son, Robert, who was left motherless, was taken and reared by his aunt, Mrs. Anderson, in Abbeville district, where he grew to manhood. He was married there to Miss Childs, a native also of that district, who died in 1826, leaving five children: Robert H. Turner being six months old at that time. The other children were Matilda, now the widow of Samuel Major, resides at Greenwood, Abbeville district, S. C.; John C., served as a soldier in the war and died at Tuscahoma, Miss., in 1870; Judith, was the wife of Wesley Major, and died at Abbeville, S. C., and Alexander died in South Carolina when young. The father was married the second time to Miss Dorotha Klugh, a native of Abbeville district, who bore him ten children, only one of whom is now living, Alexander K., who is a planter, and resides near Grenada. Those deceased are Paschal D., who died of consumption at the age of fifty years; he served during the Civil war, and received a medal for being the best and bravest soldier in a cavalry company during a march from the siege of Vicksburg; William A., was also a soldier in the Civil war, and was wounded and taken prisoner at Fisher's creek, but who was soon after paroled; he then remained with a family by the name of Jones until able to return to the company; he died in December, 1889; Rebecca, was the wife of Willis Davis, and was the mother of four children, all born in Mississippi; Carrie, was the wife of Stephen Dunlap, who resided near Grenada, and there she died, leaving two children; Mollie, was the wife of D. L. Holcombe, who resided at Tuscahoma, this county, and there she died leaving two children; Wesley was killed at the battle of Shiloh; he was a young man; James died at Tuscahoma, at the age of twelve years, and an infant, named Wesley, died in South Carolina. Mr. Turner came to Mississippi, with the younger members of the family, in 1846, settled at Tuscahoma, and opened up a large tract of land. There he reared his family. His death occurred in 1868, but his wife had passed away five years previously. Both were worthy members of the Methodist church. In politics he was democratic. Robert H. Turner attained his majority in South Carolina, and came to Mississippi on horseback when a single man. He located at Tuscahoma, and there continued to reside until 1880, when he moved to Grenada, Miss. He selected as his life companion Miss Martha S. Miller, who was born in Tennessee in 1831, and who was the daughter of Lewis and Sybil Miller, both natives of the Palmetto state. Mrs. Turner was a well educated lady, having attended James A. Girault's school, and the school at Spring Hill, Miss. She was a member of the Methodist church, and was a noble and exemplary Christian. Her death occurred in December, 1876. To this union were born six children: Lewis R., who is cashier at the bank at Bolton, Miss.; Matilda, wife of B. R. Turnipseed, resides in South Carolina; Venie, is single, resides at Grenada, and is a highly accomplished young lady; Ellen, is the wife of Dr. J. H. Bitzer, of Temple, Tex.; Donna, married Harry O. Rollins, and resides at Greenwood, Miss., and Johnnie W. died in 1878. During the late unpleasantness between the South and North, or in 1862, Mr. Turner entered Gwaltney's company, Brumley's regiment, and soon after, when the Third Mississippi cavalry was formed, he became a member of it, and was in Colonel Barksdale's company. He was made captain by election of the company and participated in the following battles: Collierville, Jackson, Harrisburg, Atlanta and Jonesboro, besides numerous skirmishes. Mr. Turner received a contusion wound in his right arm at Collierville, Tenn. From Pollard, Ala., to Pensacola, his regiment had a running fight with the Union soldiers and put them to flight. Captain Turner was paroled at Ramsey, Ala., on the 12th of May, 1865, and then returned to the homeplace, where he has since been engaged in planting. In 1889 he was elected county treasurer, which position he has held successfully up to the present time. He is a public-spirited citizen and is deeply interested in educational matters. While a resident of Tuscahoma he was a trustee of the schools, and held other positions of like character.

He owns a large tract of land, but is now manager for Captain Mister on the latter's plantation, although he resides in Grenada. He is quite active in politics and votes with the democratic party.

Dr. R. J. Turner, physician and surgeon, Bay St. Louis, Hancock county, Miss., was born in Murfreesboro, Tenn., July 30, 1841, and is a son of Thomas J. B. and Sarah (Jetton) Turner. The parents were natives of middle Tennessee, where they lived and died. The father was a planter by occupation. He reared a family of five sons, three of whom served in the late war. The Doctor was the eldest of the family. He was reared in Murfreesboro, and received his literary education there. He began the study of medicine at an early age, and was graduated from the medical department of the University of Tennessee at the age of nineteen years. When the war began he enlisted as a private in company I, First Tennessee regiment. He was afterward appointed assistant surgeon, Confederate States Army, and served until the close of the conflict. He had charge of a hospital at Kingston, Ga. While on field duty at Chickamauga he was wounded by a cannon shot and was picked up for dead. He finally survived, and was in the hospital as a patient only two weeks. He was twice captured and left in the lines with his wounded. After the surrender he returned to Murfreesboro and began practice at Salem, a little town near Murfreesboro. Desiring to perfect himself further in his profession he entered Vanderbilt university and took a course of medical lectures. In 1878 he removed to Nashville, Tenn., and practiced there until 1881. He then came to Hancock county, Miss., and settled at Nicholson, where he was physician to the Northeastern railroad until 1883. In that year he removed to Bay St. Louis and has established himself in a large and paying practice. He is president of the board of health and is physician for several insurance companies. He is a member of the Masonic fraternity, and he and his wife are worthy members of the Methodist Episcopal church. The Doctor was married in 1865, to Miss Laura Butler, of Rutherford county, Tenn., a daughter of Capt. William S. Butler. They have one son living, F. B. Turner. Dr. Turner is a man who is interested in all the enterprises tending to the development of the county, and is a liberal contributor to benevolent movements.

Robert L. Turner, M. D., of the firm of Smith & Turner, physicians and surgeons, Ellisville, Miss., was born in Jasper county, Miss., July 8, 1865. His parents were the Rev. Martin and Susan M. (Thompson) Turner, natives of Alabama and Georgia, respectively. The father was born in Wilcox county of the state just mentioned, November 1, 1838, and was the son of Martin D. and Harriet (Haddol) Turner, who were natives of Georgia and South Carolina, respectively, and removed to Mississippi in 1841, and thence to Texas in 1865, where the mother died in 1868, and the father in 1869. They were the parents of thirteen children, twelve of whom grew to be men and women. Rev. Martin C. Turner came with his parents to Mississippi in 1841, and has resided in the state ever since that date. In May, 1861, he enlisted in company F, of the Sixteenth Mississippi regiment, known as the Jasper grays, and served in that organization until the close of the war. April 2, 1865, he was taken prisoner at the battle of Port Gregg, near Petersburg, and was taken to Point Lookout, Md., where he was kept until June, 1865, when he was released and returned home. During the service he returned home on a furlough in 1864, and was married, September 16, 1864, to Susan M., a daughter of Zachariah and Charity (Duckworth) Thompson, who was born in Georgia, November 16, 1836. In 1866 Rev. Mr. Turner was elected assessor of Jasper county, and served in that capacity four years. He was afterward elected again and served three years. He has been a member of the Baptist church since 1853, and was licensed to preach in 1867, and was regularly ordained in 1874. In 1879 he was elected to the office of chancery clerk of Jasper county, Miss., and served two successive terms, during which time he attended to his ministerial duties also. In March, 1891, he removed to Ellisville, Miss. He has had born to him the following named children: Martin F., William A., Eugene L., Susan M., Ida L. (deceased), and Dr. Robert L., above mentioned, the eldest member of the family. Dr. Turner was educated at the Agricultural and Mechanical college at Starkville, Miss., from which he was graduated in 1887. In 1888 he began reading medicine under Dr. C. W. Bufkin, of Vossburg, Miss., and in the winter of 1888-9 he attended lectures at the University of Pennsylvania, at Philadelphia, after which he returned to Mississippi, and resumed his studies, which he continued there until the winter of 1889-90, when he attended lectures at the Tulane university, at New Orleans, La. In the winter of 1890-91 he took his concluding course of lectures at the institution last mentioned, and the degree of M. D. was conferred upon him April 1, 1891. He returned immediately to Ellisville, Miss., and entered into a partnership with Dr. Sidney O. Smith. Drs. Smith and Turner rank among the best educated, most skillful and most successful physicians and surgeons in the county, and have a large and increasing practice.

The social, political and business history of this section is filled with the deeds and doings of selfmade men, and no man in Jefferson county is more deserving the appellation than Robert Tweed, for he marked out his own career in youth, and has steadily followed it up to the present, his prosperity being attributable to his earnest and persistent endeavor, and to the fact that he has always consistently tried to follow the teachings of the golden rule. He was born in Ayrshire, Scotland, June 2, 1821, his parents, William and Mary (Orr) Tweed, being also born in that country, the father following the occupation of merchandising at Irvine, Ayrshire, until his death, which occurred when the subject of this sketch was an infant. After Mrs. Tweed became a widow she bravely took up the duties of life and continued her husband's business until she was called to her long home, which was in the year 1831. Robert remained in his native town until he was ten years of age, and after the death of his mother he spent four years in an adjoining village, Stevenson, attending school. He then went to the city of Glasgow, where he engaged in clerking, continuing for about four years, when he decided that in the New World there were better things in store for him, and time has proved the wisdom of his views. In 1839 he immigrated to the United States, and in the month of January, 1840, arrived in Rodney, Miss., and his first efforts in the way of making a living here was as a school teacher, a calling he followed for some four months, then accepted a position as clerk in a mercantile establishment, and during the four years that were given to this calling he managed to save some of his earnings, and in 1844 engaged in business for himself. After following that calling in Rodney up to 1850, he moved to the city of New Orleans, and there for a number of years followed the same occupation. From 1857 to 1860 he was in business in New York, but in 1861 again returned to New Orleans, and in that city and Mexico he resided up to 1869, when he once more returned to Rodney, at which place he again opened a mercantile establishment. Here he has been in business ever since; and although he commenced life a poor boy, and obtained only a small salary by clerking, he acquired excellent and methodical business habits, and these, in connection with a naturally fine mind, perseverance and industry, have acquired for him a comfortable income. In former years he did a business at this point of from $50,000 to $60,000 annually, but of late years business has been reduced, by the railroads cutting off the more distant trade, and his sales have not been nearly so large, amounting to about $30,000 each year. He was married in Philadelphia, in 1851, to Miss Virginia Van Uxem, a native of Pennsylvania, reared and educated in the city of Philadelphia, a daughter of Louis Van

Uxem, a merchant of that city. For a number of years prior to her marriage, Mrs. Tweed was a teacher in Mississippi. She and her husband have two children: Mary, wife of Rev. J. J. Chisholm, of Winchester, Ky., and Robert Tweed, Jr., a merchant of Wilkesbarre, Penn. Mr. and Mrs. Tweed are members of the Presbyterian church, and in this church Mr. Tweed is an elder, and is superintendent of the Sunday-school, in which capacity he has served for some forty years. They are earnest Christians; and although Mr. Tweed is nearly seventy years of age, he is remarkably well preserved, and gives promise of spending many more years of usefulness in this vicinity. The sons of Scotland are fairly represented in Jefferson county, and although with characteristic modesty they do not assume the brilliancy in the forum, yet they hold conspicuous places in many pursuits, which makes the county of Jefferson a substantial star in the galaxy of Mississippi's many interesting counties; and prominent among these is Mr. Tweed. He and his wife lost two children: Louisa, who died in Brooklyn, N. Y., at the age of four years, and Clara, who died in Rodney.

Col. F. A. Tyler, a well-known citizen of Holly Springs and a man universally esteemed and respected, is the eldest child born to Nathan and Eliza (Brooks) Tyler. His paternal ancestors were of English descent, and settled in Massachusetts soon after the Pilgrims. On the maternal side the Brooks came over in the Mayflower. Col. F. A. Tyler was born in Massachusetts in March, 1812, and was educated in Brown's university, Providence, R. I. He began the study of law at Bangor, Me., and also attended the law school at Cincinnati, being admitted to the bar by the supreme court of Ohio, in 1835. He then went to Vicksburg, Miss., and entered the office of Prentiss & Guion. In 1836 or 1837 he purchased the Vicksburg *Register*, the first paper published in that place, and conducted this until 1839, when he sold to William H. McCargle. In May, 1839, he located in Grenada, Miss., formed a partnership with E. H. Fisher, and after practicing there one year bought a paper which he conducted for several years. He subsequently removed to Panola, started the first paper in that place, did well, and remained there for two years. He then bought a plantation twelve miles north of Grenada, and after two years began the study of theology, at the Lane seminary at Cincinnati. During this time he boarded with Dr. Lyman Beecher. He was licensed and ordained in Mississippi in 1848, and began preaching at Grenada, spending twelve years in the ministry. He then removed to Memphis, having been elected by the Memphis synod to establish a church paper, called the *Presbyterian Sentinel*, at that place. This he conducted up to the war. He later became connected with the Memphis *Appeal*, of which he was for a time editor in chief, and he was also president of the Appeal Publishing company. He was elected superintendent of the schools of Shelby county, Tenn., during 1871 and 1872, and then went to Washington city, where he edited the *Sunday Gazette*. In 1878 he came to Holly Springs, and took charge of the Holly Springs *South*, with which he continued until about 1886. During that time he did much to advance the interests of the place. He was married, in 1840, to Miss Virginia Ann Townes, daughter of Armstead Townes, of Virginia, a prominent man in the early days of the state. Mrs. Tyler died in 1879 leaving a son, who now resides at Gainesville, Tex., and who is a prosperous merchant. They had five children, all of whom died previous to the death of the mother. Mr. Tyler was married at Holly Springs in June, 1880, to Mrs. Rosa Goodlow, daughter of Roger Barton (see sketch), and one child is the result of this union, Roger Barton. Socially Colonel Tyler is a member of the Masonic and Odd Fellows orders. It is said that he gave more to the Confederate cause, according to his means, than any man in Memphis. He is now living a semi-retired life, though ably filling the office of magistrate of Holly Springs, and is engaged in literary work. He is a well-preserved and courteous gentleman.

James M. Tyler, the proprietor of a sawmill, farmer and postmaster of Bogue Chitto, Lincoln county, Miss., is a son of Derrell M. and Elizabeth (Jones) Tyler. He was born in 1847, in what was then known as Lawrence county, within ten miles of his present residence. He is now one of the most prominent and popular men of this town and county. His father was born in 1822, and was a son of Daniel Tyler, a native of South Carolina, who came to Mississippi among the pioneers of this section, bringing with him his wife, who was Miss Elizabeth Sistrunk, also a native of South Carolina. They lived to a good old age, and reared a large and respectable family. He was a whig in politics, and was a member of the Baptist church. Derrell M. Tyler was the youngest child but one, and was reared within a short distance of where he now lives, and is engaged in farming. He served in the militia during part of the late war. From principle he was a strong Union man, and for many years he has been connected with the Baptist church. His wife, Miss Elizabeth Jones, was a daughter of Vincent Jones, of South Carolina, and who was a soldier in some of the early wars. He came to Mississippi soon after his marriage, where he accumulated some property, consisting of land and negroes, becoming what was considered well-to-do. He died just before the war, and professed religion on his deathbed. His wife died about two years afterward. She was a member of the Baptist church. Politically her husband was a lifelong whig. They had children named as follows, four of whom are yet living, including the mother of our subject: Martha, became the wife of Rev. Bailey, a very aged mininster, who lives in this county; Mrs. Emily Busby, a widow, residing in this county, and who has raised a large family; Margaret, who became the wife of John A. Grear, of this county. Those deceased were Andrew V., Zacharias Berry; Mrs. Dolly Grear, Mrs. Phebe McLendon and Mrs. Cynthia Brister, who was the eldest child, and who died in 1871 (see sketch of B. E. Brister). To the parents of Derrell Taylor were born eight children, four of whom were sons: William M. died in 1888, leaving a wife and three children; Mrs. D. Summers; Mrs Dolly McCullough, and Mrs. Emily Bailey, three of the daughters are residents of this county; Vincent Lafayette, who was accidentally shot in 1889, was postmaster of Brookhaven, his wife being appointed to succeed him, and is holding that office at the present time; another daughter, Mrs. Martha Norman, is a resident of Pike county; Ira W. Tyler is a merchant at Bogue Chitto, Miss. Our subject is the second child in order of birth, and he attained his majority in this county, living on the home place until he was twenty-two years of age. He received his education principally at the common schools of his home. He was married February 21, 1871, and began farming in Lincoln county, near the old plantation. In the fall of that year, he was elected a member of the board of supervisors. In 1873 he was elected assessor, after which he was again elected a member of the board of supervisors. He was re-elected assessor in 1879. Mr. Tyler is the owner of a fine plantation near Bogue Chitto, and of a sawmill four miles distant from his plantation, which is connected with Bogue Chitto by a tramway. He is also largely engaged in ginning. He was married to Miss Mary L. Brent, a native of Pike county, who was reared in what is now Lincoln county. She was a daughter of Jesse M. Brent, also a native of Pike county, and whose wife was Miss Mary Williams, and who was born in Lawrence county. Her mother died in 1860; her father is yet living. To her were born two children: James M., a miller and a farmer of this county, and Mrs. Tyler. Mr. Brent is now living with his third wife, by whom he has had five children, and he also had two by his second wife. To Mr. and Mrs. Tyler have been born nine children: James C., Amanda Belle, Frankie E., Louis I., Jesse M., Derrell M., a baby called Pet, Willie W., aged five, and Mary E., who died at the age of ten years. Mr. and Mrs. Tyler are members of the Baptist church, of which he has been clerk almost continuously ever since his identification with that organization, in 1871. He is a member of the Masonic order and a Knight of Honor. Politically he is a republican.

Rev. John Tyler Christian, D. D. The subject of this sketch was born in Fayette county, Ky., near old Fort Boonesboro, December 14th, 1854. His mother was a Miss Martinie, a granddaughter of Charles Tyler. He thus comes of two of the oldest families of the state—the Christians and Tylers having emigrated to Kentucky either with Daniel Boone, or soon after that historical pioneer went to the state. Dr. Christian was born on a farm, and remained upon the farm until his seventeenth year. He then entered Bethel college and graduated with distinction from that institution in 1876. Soon after his graduation he moved to Mississippi and took the pastoral care of the Baptist church at Tupelo. It had been his intention to practice law, and he was already preparing himself for the bar, when he was called to preach. He consulted not with flesh or blood, but enthusiastically entered upon his work as a preacher. While pastor at Tupelo he was married to Miss Evylyn Quin, of West Point, Miss., and to her wise counsel and help he owes much of his distinction. After having preached six years in Mississippi with much success, he became pastor of the First Baptist church, Chattanooga, Tenn. The church grew rapidly, and nearly five hundred members were added to its fellowship during his pastorate. For over four years he has been the efficient missionary secretary of the Baptist denomination for Mississippi. In 1890 he received from Bethel college the honorary degree of doctor of divinity. As a man Dr. Christian is sunshiny and genial, and consequently numbers his friends by hundreds. He is one of the best known men in the state, and while he is progressive and pronounced in his opinions, he is popular with all. He is a strong preacher and eminently evangelical. He has marked ability as a writer, and has been a frequent contributor for newspapers and magazines. During the present year he has published a volume upon Immersion, the Act of Christian Baptism. The book is having a remarkable sale. Three editions have already been called for, and the press is very pronounced in its praise. He is scarcely yet in the prime of life, and if he lives out the allotted time allowed man upon the earth, many years of service are doubtless yet before him.

H. L. Tynes, M. D., Tynes, Tishomingo county, Miss., was born in Tuscaloosa county, Ala., February 20, 1850, a son of Robert F. and Eliza Ann (Berry) Tynes. His father was a native of Virginia, and his mother of Georgia. They were married in Alabama and lived there for twenty years thereafter, where Mr. Tynes was engaged in planting and a portion of the time held a position as a bookkeeper for Robert Jamison, of Tuscaloosa county, a mail contractor who operated several stage lines and mail routes. Mr. Tynes and wife had twelve children, seven sons and five daughters, of whom six sons and two daughters lived to maturity. The family removed from Alabama to Mississippi in 1855, and bought land and located in Itawamba county, where Mr. Tynes engaged in planting, and accumulated considerable property in the period before the war, owning a good quantity of land, about fifty slaves, and having a snug sum of money at interest. He was a practical, progressive man of affairs, who had no political aspirations whatever. He took a deep interest in educational and religious matters and was a consistent and helpful member of the Presbyterian church. He died in 1888 in Itawamba county, his wife having died in the same county in 1874. H. L. Tynes, M. D., began life for himself at the age of eighteen as a clerk in Brownville, Miss., a connection which he continued for four years. At the end of that period he became a drug clerk in the same town in the employ of Smith & Brown. There he remained for the next two years, reading medicine in the meanwhile, and in 1874 he went to Mobile, Ala., where he took a course in the Alabama Medical university. Returning home he soon afterward located in Union county, where he practiced his profession with considerable success until 1877, when he returned to Mobile and finished his course, graduating in the spring of 1877, with the degree of doctor of medicine. After this he again took up the practice of medicine in Union county, where he remained until the spring of 1880, when he came to Tishomingo county and located near Bay Springs. He built up an extensive practice and had a reputation among the people of being one of the most successful physicians in the county; while in the profession he was regarded as being a man of much ability and undoubted skill. He was married, in 1872, to Miss Mattie A. Rogers, a daughter of Hugh Rogers, who has borne him nine children, five sons and four daughters: Carrie L., Myrtle V., Roxie N., Humbert A., Robert R., Lucien Q. C. L., Clara Ann, Henry L. and James S. The Doctor is the owner of two hundred and forty acres of land, eighty acres of which are under cultivation. He pays very little personal attention to planting, however, his practice consuming his entire time. Though he is in no sense a practical politician, he takes a keen interest in all movements inaugurated for the benefit of his fellow-citizens. He has never been an aspirant for any official position, but, as a matter of convenience to his neighbors, he has for the past six years acted as postmaster of Tynes postoffice, which was named in his honor. The farmers' movements attracted his attention to a great extent, and he was the organizer and first president of the first wheel organized in Mississippi, of which he was at the head for two terms. He has always been a liberal contributor to schools, churches and all laudable enterprises, and is regarded as a useful and helpful citizen, whose presence in the community is a benefit to its general interests and an aid and encouragement to its citizens.

CHAPTER XXI.

A FEW SPECIAL NOTICES, U.

SPECIAL sketches in this work would be incomplete without mention of Alfred Augustus Ulman of Waveland, Miss., who has given a greater impetus to the manufacturing interests of the state than any other one man. He was born in New Orleans, La., December 19, 1846, and is the son of James A. and Ellen (McDonald) Ulman. His father was born in Boston, Mass., and came to New Orleans in 1836, where he was a contractor and builder for some years. In 1848 he removed to Bay St. Louis, Miss., where he carried on the same business. He has been prominently identified with the history of the place since his residence there began. For a number of years he was mayor of the place, and has also served on the board of supervisors. Having more than attained his three score years and ten, he has retired from active business pursuits, and leads a quiet life at the Bay. His wife was a native of Ireland. They reared a family of two sons and three daughters, of whom Alfred A. is the eldest. He was but five years of age when his parents removed to the place. He was educated at St. Stanislaus college, and early in life started out to seek his fortune. His first enterprise was a blacksmith shop and a blackingbrush factory; he carried on this business for some years. He served in the latter part of the Civil war under General Forrest. He was but sixteen years of age. When the war was over, instead of yielding to despondency, he promptly began prospecting for the future. He went North, and after a thorough examination of the great industries of that section, returned to his home, fully convinced that the natural advantages of the South were superior to those of the North, and that the employment of the same means would insure similar results. Buoyed by this inspiration, he threw into the enterprise all his energies, and the end of the beginning was the woolen mills at Ulmanville, which are located within the corporation of Waveland. The spacious warehouses, the business offices, the extensive stores, and the operatives' cottages are models of convenience and taste. The factories are furnished with modern machinery, and the product of the looms finds a ready market throughout the South. When the woolen mills were established, a general store and sawmill were also put into operation, and the whole is conducted with an exactitude and harmony of which no common man is master. Mr. Ulman was elected mayor of Waveland in August, 1890. He adheres to the principles of the democratic party, and was a delegate to the convention of the state for 1891. In 1890 he was a delegate to the constitutional convention. He is vice president of the Homestead Building and Loan association, and was one of the originators of the Gaslight and Ice factory. In fact there is no home enterprise of importance that has not felt a strong impetus from his touch. He is the largest individual taxpayer in Hancock county, owning a vast amount of land and real estate. Mr. Ulman is a man of many fine traits of character; he is generous and charitable, and his friends are the masses. He is deeply appreciative of the loyalty of his operatives, which he has rewarded by liberal gifts and the kindest consideration. He was married in 1873 to Miss Emma Nicholson. He is a devout member of the Catholic church.

James A. Ulman, Bay St. Louis, Miss., was at one time one of the most active business men of Hancock county, but he has retired, and is now enjoying the fruits of his labors. He was born in Boston, Mass., in 1819, and is a son of Melchi and Martha (Smith) Ulman, natives of England. The parents were early settlers of Massachusetts, where they passed their last days. The father was a mechanic by trade. They reared a family of nine children, three of whom are living: Mary A., resides in Cambridgeport, Mass., and is now eighty-two years of age; Maria J., lives in the same place, and James A., the subject of this sketch. He was reared and educated in Boston, and was trained to the occupation of a builder. At the age of twenty years he went to New Orleans, La., and soon made a place for himself among the best known builders and contractors of the South. He had large contracts in Louisiana and Texas, and was very successful in all his dealings. In 1848 he removed to Bay St. Louis, Miss., and two years later he brought his family, and has since made it his home. He has put up a vast number of buildings in the surrounding territory, which will be a monument to his industry and ability for years to come. During his residence in the South, Mr. Ulman has passed through many trying periods. In the epidemics that have at different times swept the South, he has nursed the sick and buried the dead; the latter office he has performed unaided when there were none to help. During four years of the war he was at Selma, Ala., when he was in the state service. Since his residence in Bay St. Louis he has been prominently identified with the public affairs of that place. He was mayor for several terms, and was appointed mayor by Governor Ames for a short time. In 1852, 1853 and 1854 he was a member of the board of supervisors, and did most efficient service to his

county. In 1845 Mr. Ulman was married in New Orleans to Ellen McDonald. They have five children living: A. A., Clara A., Rosabella, Mary E., and James A. The father is a member of the Masonic fraternity, and was master of his lodge for a number of years. Mrs. Ulman died in 1889.

S. R. Upshaw, Craigs, Miss., was born in Holmes county, Miss., in 1856, and is a son of Samuel W. and Margaret A. (Terrall) Upshaw, natives of Virginia. The father removed with his family to Holmes county about the year 1845, and engaged in farming, and to some extent in the mercantile trade. He then disposed of his commercial interests, and devoted himself exclusively to agriculture. He died in 1865, but the mother still survives. They reared a family of ten children, seven of whom are still living. Young Upshaw grew to manhood in the midst of husbandry, receiving but a limited education. The common school had not then reached its present advanced development, and many a lad of pioneer days was but poorly equipped for the battle of life, so far as literary attainment was concerned. At the age of nineteen years he began life for himself, hiring out on a plantation; he has always been industrious and economical, and was enabled to save a considerable amount from his wages. In 1885 he was married to Mrs. Betty Upshaw, widow of W. E. Upshaw, a brother of our subject. Mrs. Upshaw is a daughter of Thomas and Adaline (Hill) Singleton, and upon her mother's side is connected with one of the earliest families of Yazoo county and one of much prominence in South Carolina. Mr. Upshaw now owns, on Silver creek, a fine farm of four hundred acres in cultivation, and as much more in timber. It is one of the best improved plantations in the county; he has a pleasant dwelling house; his tenant houses and barns are neat and in good repair, and all his surroundings are indicative of the thrift and wise management of the owner. In the cultivation of his lands he employs all the modern improvements in machinery, and reaps abundant harvests.

Mrs. Elenora C. Urquhart was born on Lake Washington, in Mississippi, in 1838, to John A. and Sarah Steen (Jefferies) Miller, the former of whom was born in Georgetown, Ky., and the latter in Mississippi. Mr. Miller came to this state at the age of seventeen years, and after a time engaged in banking in Natchez, later removed to New Orleans, La., where he was in the coffee business for a number of years, at the same time following the occupation of a planter in that state, a calling he continued until his death, which occurred at his home, Lelna plantation, in 1875, at which time he was the owner of a large estate. His father was John Miller, a native of Kentucky, a planter by calling, who lived and died near Georgetown, in his native state. The Millers are of German descent and possess the thrift, perseverance and energy characteristic of the German people. The maternal grandparents were James and Priscilla (Shelby) Jefferies, the town of Shelbyville, Ky., being named for the latter's family. She died near Port Gibson, being the owner of a large plantation at the time of her death. Mrs. Urquhart was reared principally in this state, for some time attending school at Port Gibson, being afterward a student at Patapsco institute, near Baltimore, Md., from which institution she was graduated at the age of seventeen years. She was married in 1859 to William Urquhart, a cotton merchant of New Orleans, and from the time of her marriage until the death of her husband, was a resident of that city, with the exception of two years during the war, which they spent in Europe. His father, David Urquhart, was born in New Orleans, he and his wife becoming the parents of ten children: David, who died in New Orleans when a lad; Anna, who married Baron De Boigne, and is now residing in Paris, France; Emma, Rosalie and Eloise, who died in Paris, France, and were buried in Pere la Chaise cemetery, of Paris; Georgine was married to Robert McLane, minister to France under Cleveland, having formerly been minister to China and Japan under Buchanan. He was also minister to Mexico when the war began, being afterward a member of congress from Maryland, and still later filled the position of governor of that state; Robert was a sugar planter in Louisiana, and is now deceased; James also followed the same occupation in that state, and is now deceased; Angelica, also deceased, married Henry Livingston, a native of New York; William, the husband of the subject of this sketch, comes next in order of birth; and David, the latter being now a retired cotton merchant of New Orleans. Mrs. Urquhart inherited her father's home, and has lived on it since 1875. She is the third of four daughters, the eldest of whom, Martha Priscilla, married F. A. Metcalfe, a native of Mississippi, of which state he was also a planter; Sarah Hannah married William Stirling, a planter of Louisiana, and Mary Georgiana married C. H. Smith, a native of Missouri. Mrs. Urquhart bore her husband six children: Sadie Steen, wife of J. B. Ferguson, a native of Kentucky, now living in Kansas City, Mo.; William, who is located near Bristol, Tenn.; Eloise, wife of McDuffin Hampton, a son of Gen. Wade Hampton, of South Carolina, who now resides in Bristol, Tenn., a civil engineer; Corinne, wife of William Griffin, a lawyer in Greenville; John, who died in Kansas City, Mo., in 1890; and George, who is in Bristol, Tenn. Mrs. Urquhart and her children are members of the Episcopal church, and are highly esteemed wherever they have made their home. She is the owner of two thousand acres of land, one thousand two hundred acres of which are under cultivation, three hundred of which have been opened under her direction, and on this place she has put about $10,000 worth of improvements, her home being now a beautiful and comfortable one. She makes a charming and entertaining hostess, for all who enter within the portals of her home are made to feel welcome. She has always endeavored to make her home a happy one for her children, and that she has succeeded is abundantly testified in the warm affection and honor they bear her.

S. T. Ussery is a planter who, in his operations, displays those sterling, characteristic and honorable principles so necessary to a successful career in any calling. He was born on the 2d of November, 1848, to Samuel and Mary D. (Shotwell) Ussery, both natives of South Carolina. The father removed to Tennessee about 1820, and after remaining there two years came to Mississippi, and entered and purchased about two thousand acres of land. Although he began life a poor man, before the war he paid tax on nearly $75,000 worth of property. He was a practical business man throughout his life, never following any occupation but farming, and died in 1878. He had four sons who served in the Confederate army during the war. One died at Danville, Ky., and another, who held the rank of lieutenant, was killed at Jonesboro, Ga. S. T. Ussery attended the common schools near his home until he was about twenty years of age, attending mostly during the winter months, at the end of which time he began planting for himself. His father gave him one hundred and sixty acres of land, loaned him a mule for one year, and boarded him for the same time. With heart and soul he entered upon his work and at the age of twenty-three began dealing in mules, buying and selling in Tennessee and St. Louis, and continued to carry on this business until he attained his twenty-eighth year, when he gave up this calling. He sold one year for J. P. Brownloe, on commission, in Missouri. During the one winter that he followed this calling he made considerable money, his operations as a stockdealer and planter being also prosperous. Of the nine hundred and forty acres of which he is now the owner, he has five hundred acres under cultivation, and on this land is a fine artesian well one hundred and forty-five feet deep, which throws a stream of water one and one-half inch in diameter. There are also good springs on the place. Mr. Ussery has just completed a dwelling house at a cost of $2,500 and a barn that will shelter forty head of mules, both of which buildings are among the best and finest in this part of the state. Formerly Mr. Ussery operated a sawmill for twelve years, during which time he marketed all his valuable timber, a fact which he now regrets very much, although the money which he thus obtained was very much needed, for, a short time prior to this, he had lost by fire in Columbia about thirty-six bales of cotton. He now has on his plantation a steam cottongin, which has a capacity of about three hundred bales of cotton a year, about sixty of which he controls as the product of his own land. Mr. Ussery is also quite an extensive raiser of mules, but does not give as much attention to raising horses as formerly, for he finds they are not as remunerative as the mules. He has fourteen mule colts, which were foaled in the spring of 1890-91, and sired by a wellbred jack of which he and his brother are the owners. About 1881 he opened a mercantile establishment on his plantation. He carries a well-selected stock of general merchandise, which brings him in an annual sum of about $5,000. On account of his youth his service during the war was very slight, but he lent considerable aid in the way of collecting and driving stock for the use of the Confederate army. While our subject was visiting in west Tennessee Hood invaded middle Tennessee. Mr. Ussery followed in his wake with a beef supply. He received for his services $3,000 per day in Confederate money. In October, 1879, he was united in marriage to Miss Jennie Nichols, a daughter of N. H. Nichols, a native of South Carolina, who was a well-to-do planter. This union resulted in the birth of two children: Mary Lena and Oscar Burdette. Mr. Ussery is a member of the Methodist Episcopal church, but his wife is a member of the Cumberland Presbyterian church. He is the postmaster of Cherokee, the office being in his store, but is not interested in politics and has never been an aspirant for office.

CHAPTER XXII.

A GLANCE AT INDIVIDUAL RECORDS, V.

IN the commercial circles of Jackson county, Miss., is R. A. Vancleave, of Ocean Springs, who was born in Hinds county, Miss., June 9, 1840, and is a son of Jonathan and Elizabeth (Rowland) Vancleave. The father was a native of Maury county, Tenn., born April 1, 1800. The mother, a sister of Dr. David Rowland, of Louisville, Ky., was born in Kentucky in 1805. They were married in Hinds county, Miss., in 1837, having settled there in 1825. Their families are of English, French and Scotch-Irish descent. Jonathan Vancleave was a grand-nephew of Daniel Boone. He was a very prosperous planter, and was well known among the merchants and farmers of the county. He died in 1886. By his first marriage he had a large family, all of whom are deceased. Four children were born of the second marriage, two of whom are living: Mellison R., and R. A., the subject of this sketch. He spent his early youth in Hinds county, where he attended the common schools. He finished his education in Yazoo City, whither his father had removed. He remained under the parental roof until he had reached his majority, and then, in 1861, he enlisted in the Confederate service under General Price. He afterward joined the First Mississippi light artillery, and was taken prisoner at the fall of Vicksburg. He was soon paroled and spent three years in active service. In 1867 he removed to Ocean Springs, and engaged in the mercantile trade. In 1872 he was appointed postmaster and held the office nearly ten years. This position was petitioned for by the citizens without his own personal solicitation. In 1885 he was appointed by President Cleveland special agent of the general land office of the United States, and assigned to duty in Mississippi, with headquarters at Ocean Springs. The duties of this office were to protect the public timber lands. He held this office until 1889, when he was removed by President Harrison, and the office was filled by a republican. Mr. Vancleave is one of the oldest merchants at Ocean Springs, having carried on the business there for twenty-four years. He now has two sons, George A. and Robert A., Jr., associated in business with him. He established a postoffice at Vancleave in 1868; this place was named in his honor, and is located twelve miles northeast of Ocean Springs. He was married in 1865 to Miss Eliza R., a daughter of William Sheppard, a pioneer merchant of Yazoo City, Miss. Mr. and Mrs. Vancleave are the parents of seven living children: Fannie, the wife of Walter H. Covington; George A., Robert A., Jr., William S., Richard S., Sarah and June P. They have a beautiful residence, and are surrounded with all the comforts of life. Mr. Vancleave has a cousin in Chicago, James R. B. Vancleave, who is a prominent man throughout the state of Illinois; he is the present city clerk.

Rev. J. H. Van Court was an early settler of the town of Natchez, Miss., coming from New Jersey about the year 1823, and for many years was a minister of the Presbyterian church and school teacher by profession. In disposition he was modest and retiring, but was earnest and indefatigable in his labors in the cause of the Master. His sincerity of purpose was manifested during the many years that he filled the position of clerk of the Presbyterian synod, and showed that he was a man of ability and popularity. He was married in this state to Mrs. Catherine (Smith) Swayzie, her father, Philander Smith, being a son of Rev. Jedediah Smith, who came to New Orleans from Massachusetts, with a family of ten sons. In the city of New Orleans, he was robbed of his library and much of his possessions by the Spaniards who were hostile to his religious views, and without them he started in an open boat up the Mississippi river to Natchez, this being in 1776, but owing to his advanced age, the exposures and hardships he was compelled to endure were too much for his strength and he sickened and died before he reached this place. Through his sons he has numerous descendants in this section, who are thrifty people, and who have been largely instrumental in developing and improving this section. Rev. J. H. Van Court turned his attention to planting, near Baton Rouge, La., after his marriage, but his latter years were devoted to teaching school. He died in this county, in 1867, his wife having been called to her long home in 1859; and their son, E. J. Van Court, was educated in Oakland college, from which he was graduated. He later turned his attention to the study of medicine and in 1853 graduated from the Medical university of Pennsylvania. He was married on May 25, 1870, to Miss Adeline B. Mitchell; a native of Adams county, and a daughter of Philo Mitchell and Varina (Stanton) Mitchell, both of whom are members of well-known families of this region. To Mr. Van Court and his wife four children have been born: Catherine S., E. J. Jr., Adeline Baker and David Benjamin Swayzie. The family are members of the Presbyterian church, and move in the highest social circles of Natchez. The paternal ancestors of Mr. Van Court were of Holland descent, and originally came from the Island of Guernsey to New Jersey, in 1710. E. J. Van Court has in his possession a testament, printed in the French, which was given to an ancestor of his, nearly two hundred years ago, and has descended to him.

The town of Shuqualak is to be congratulated on her good hotels, among which, Central hotel, conducted by A. M. Van Devender, ranks prominent. To the traveler the name of Central hotel has about it the ring of a true and tried friend. The genial proprietor, Mr. Van Devender, was born in Kemper county, Miss., in 1844, and when but seventeen years of age he enlisted in the Confederate army, with Major Nunn of Shuqualak, Miss. (see sketch). He was in nearly all the engagements of the army of Tennessee and surrendered with General Johnston in North Carolina. In 1867 he was married to Miss Magarah E. Kellis and became the father of nine children: Walter, Horatio, Willie, Addie, Carrie, Eugene, Lillie J., Ruth and John J., all living except the eldest. In 1883 Mr. Van Devender rented and opened to the public the Shuqualak East Side hotel at Shuqualak, Miss., and by rare management became proprietor of this property, now known as the Central hotel. As a manager of this enterprise he is a genuine success. Eight years ago he began the business without a dollar, under most unpropitious circumstances. To-day he is, by his energy, perseverance and enterprise, an illustration of what may be done under adverse surroundings, with will power and industry for capital. Mr. Van Devender is in the highest degree a representative man of his vocation and therefore entitled to recognition in these pages. He has a son in the employ of the Western Union at Atlanta, Ga., who stands among the best of his profession. A daughter graduated at Shuqualak in the class of 1891. Mr. Van Devender was the son of Jacob and Elizabeth J. (Pace) Van Devender, the father born in Virginia in 1809, and the mother of Tennessee. Jacob Van Devender removed to Alabama in 1829, or 1830, and later to Noxubee county, Miss. There he was married in 1841.

It is truly said that a man can never be too wise or too learned to be a lawyer, for sooner or later, in the practice of his profession, his first and last resources will be called into action. Owing to this fact the profession of law has attracted the best talent of the country, and has brought into play the most brilliant talents, the most extensive knowledge and the strongest sentiments, moral, spiritual and material, of which humanity can boast. An instance of this is seen in Hon. H. S. Van Eaton who stands high with the bar in the state of Mississippi. He was born in the Buckeye state in 1826, being the eldest in a family of six children, but at the age of six years was taken by his parents to Morgan county, Ill., and was brought up on a farm near Jacksonville. He attended the common and subscription schools until he attained the age of sixteen years, at which time he entered the preparatory department of Illinois college at Jacksonville, and six years later graduated with honors in a class of seven. At this time the South possessed great attractions for him and here he determined to cast his lot. He soon came to Mississippi and near the town of Woodville became an instructor in a common school, which position he retained to the general satisfaction of the patrons of the institution, for five years. During this time he formed a taste for the study of law, and began laying a solid foundation for his present enviable legal reputation. After reading law with Judge Stanhope Posey, the then circuit judge of the district, he was admitted to the Mississippi bar, this being in the year 1854. He at once opened an office in Woodville where, four years later, he formed a partnership with John P. Dillingham, a native of Maine and a man of no little legal ability. Their connection was very amicable and mutually satisfactory and lasted until the opening of the Civil war, at which time, as he had fully indentified himself with the South, and admired and loved her people and institutions, he cast his lot with the Confederacy, becoming a private soldier in company K, Sixteenth Mississippi regiment. He served with credit and distinction in the engagements at Winchester, Cross Keys, Malvern Hill, the seven days' fight before Richmond, and Fredericksburg, the second battle of Manassas, where he received a flesh wound from a piece of broken shell, and one contusion wound by grape shot. In February, after the battle of Fredericksburg, he was promoted to the rank of captain and was transferred to the commissary department. He was as such in the campaigns at Chancellorsville and Gettysburg, and later was transferred from the army of northern Virginia to the western division under the command of Gen. Joseph Johnston, and was assigned to duty as post commissary at Mt. Carmel, Miss., where he remained until the surrender. Prior to the war, in 1854, he was elected mayor of Woodville, was chosen state's attorney three years later, and in 1859 was elected to the state legislature. In the last named year he was united in marriage to Miss Anna Blount, who was born in Louisiana, May 21, 1838, her native parish being West Feliciana. She received her education in St. Mary's hall, Burlington, N. J., and upon graduating was considered one of the most brilliant and accomplished young ladies that ever left that institution. She was especially gifted in art and music and has all her life been a lover of good literature, and is considered an acquisition to any society. She moves in the highest social circles, and her manner is at all times characterized by grace, ease and dignity. Her father, Levi Blount, was born in North Carolina, but after leaving his native county of Beaufort, he took up his residence in Louisiana, where he became a wealthy planter. He traced his ancestry back to the time of Charles I, of England, through the following men: Nathaniel Blount, an Episcopal minister of prominence who was ordained in St. Paul's church, London, England, in 1772-3; Reading Blount, Thomas Blount of Chocminity, N. C., Thomas Blount of England, and Sir Walter Blount, who was created baronet by Charles I on October 5, 1642. About 1669 three of Sir Walter Blount's sons emigrated to America, one settling in Virginia, where he became the head of a long line of descendants, but the other two, James and Thomas crossed over into North Carolina, and settled in the country bordering upon Albemarle sound, Thomas becoming the father of a large family that he reared at Chocminity. One of his sons, Col. Jacob Blount, became the father of William Blount, who was an able officer in the Continental army during the Revolution, and was a member of the Continental congress and a member of the convention that framed the constitution for the United States. He afterward became governor of the territory south of the Ohio river, and was a senator in congress from 1783 to 1797, from the state of Tennessee. Willie Blount, his younger brother, who was his private and official secretary while senator, and who succeeded him in the administration of the duties of governor of Tennessee, (which position he filled for many years), were cousins of Levi Blount, the father of Mrs. Van Eaton. The latter's mother was a native of Boston, Mass., and lived to be eighty-three years of age. Mr. and Mrs. Blount were active members of the Episcopal church, and will long be remembered for their many generous, charitable and kindly deeds. Rev. Nathaniel Blount became distinguished as a divine and was the founder and builder of the church in Washington, N. C., which still stands as a memento of his labor, and is still known as Parson Blount's church. In 1880 Mr. Van Eaton was appointed to the office of chancellor of the district by Governor Stone, and in 1883, while on the bench, was nominated and elected to the XLVIIIth congress of the United States, and was afterward returned to the XLIXth congress, which position he filled with credit to himself and his constituents.

He has advanced the interests of the section where he has so long made his home by every means in his power, and has been an earnest champion of all measures for the improving of his state. He was a strong advocate of the Morrison tariff bill, and all measures tending to political reform, and his reasons for his convictions are alway clear and well defined. During the campaign of 1889, when the question was asked, "Whom shall we have for governor of Mississippi?" Major Van Eaton's name was frequently heard mentioned as an admirable man for that responsible position of trust, but he steadily refused to allow his name to go before the convention as a candidate. While he was grateful to his many friends and for the flattering remarks made of him in the journals of the state, and particularly the delta and southwestern portions, he thought it better to live in retirement from public life for a time. While chancellor of the tenth district he was considered a conscientious and impartial judge, and soon won encomiums from all for the correctness of his decisions. He was one of the directors of the West Feliciana railroad, as well as their attorney for upward of twenty years, before it fell into the hands of the present owners. In connection with his practice much of his attention is devoted to planting. He is a member of Woodville lodge No. 63, of the A. F. & A. M.; the K. of H. and the I. O. O. F., and has held various chairs in each order. He has been high priest of the chapter, worshipful master of his Masonic lodge and grand master of the state in the I. O. O. F. He has a very valuable souvenir, which was presented to him by the two lodges of Woodville, as a token of their esteem, which he values very highly. He has always been a warm patron of education, and was elected one of the trustees and treasurer of the board of the McGehee Female college. From 1853 until 1856 he edited the Woodville *Republican*, and being an able writer, as well as an eloquent and forcible speaker, his editorials on the current topics of the times were read with much interest and profit. He was appointed by President Cleveland as one of the board of visitors to the naval academy at Annapolis, in 1887, and was appointed by him, in 1888, as one of the commissioners to view the completed portion of the Northern Pacific railroad. Mrs. Van Eaton accompanied her husband on this trip, joining the party at the Palmer house, Chicago, and went by special car to and from the Pacific coast. Mr. and Mrs. Van Eaton are worthy members of St. Paul's Episcopal church, in which Mr. Van Eaton is a vestryman. He and his amiable wife are highly esteemed in social circles, and in their beautiful and attractive home, where good taste and refinement prevails, they dispense the generous and true-hearted hospitality for which the South is famous.

Mrs. Thirmutheus H. Van Eaton is an accomplished and refined lady, and is a member of one of the leading families of Coahoma county. She was born in Colbert county, Ala., March 1, 1858, being the youngest of seven children born to Asa and Adaline (Ligor) Cobb, natives of Tennessee and Alabama, respectively. Asa Cobb came to Coahoma county, Miss., in 1858; was one of the first settlers of the county, and became one of its most influential citizens. He was for a number of years a member of the board of supervisors, and was a large slave and landowner before the war. He did not take an active part in the struggle between the North and South, but his eldest son Thomas was an active participant, was a member of a scouting company, and once distinguished himself by routing an entire company of Union soldiers who were intent on his capture, and were about to overtake him. He turned suddenly and began firing into them, shouting, come on boys, and they, thinking doubtless, that he had led them into the ranks of his own company, beat a precipitate retreat, and he then made his way to his company. The maternal grandparents were James and Mary (Ganneway) Ligon, of Alabama, the former of whom was one of the most prominent citizens of Colbert county, Ala., and held the office of sheriff of that county for twenty years, in the discharge of which duties he distinguished himself as a brave, tried and true custodian of the public's interest. Mrs. Van Eaton was reared in Coahoma county, Miss., and was educated at Pontotoc. In 1874 she was married to Frank R. Van Eaton, a native of Alabama, and the youngest of three children born to Dr. Isaac and Sarah E. (Martin) Van Eaton, the former a native of North Carolina, and the latter of Cincinnati, Ohio.

Isaac Van Eaton came to Mississippi in 1872, and located in Coahoma county, where he practiced medicine, having graduated from the Ohio Medical college of Cincinnati. He arose to eminence in his profession, but died three years after locating in this section. Frank R. Van Eaton came to this state in 1870, having received his education in the schools of Lebanon, Ohio, and graduating from the same medical institution as his father. They practiced together in Mississippi, until the father's death, after which Frank R. practiced alone, and also followed the occupation of planting, until he was called from life in 1891, at the age of forty-two years, his birth having occurred on the 31st of July, 1848. He was a cousin of Judge Henry Van Eaton, of Greenville. His maternal grandfather's real name was Emanuel Suezza, but when a lad of nine years he was stolen from his home by a crew of Englishmen, who brought him to America, landing at New York, where he managed to escape from them and found refuge with a man by the name of John Martin, whose name he afterward adopted. At the age of twenty-eight years he went to Cincinnati, Ohio, where he married and lived for some time. Mrs. Van Eaton's union resulted in the birth of three children: Lula Lake, Isaac Hampton, and Addie Cobb, all of whom reside with their mother. Mrs. Van Eaton is the owner of eighteen hundred acres of land, seven hundred of which are under cultivation, and in the management of her property has shown herself to be shrewd and practical. She is an earnest member of the Baptist church, and is a talented and handsome woman.

Thomas H. B. Van Hoozer, Torrance, Miss., is one of the oldest settlers of Yalobusha county, and is fully entitled to a space in this record of the pioneers of Mississippi. He was born in Limestone county, Ala., in 1842, and is a son of John and Elizabeth (Powell) Van Hoozer, natives of Tennessee and Alabama, respectively. Mrs. Van Hoozer was a relative of the Burneys, of Oxford, Miss. She and her husband emigrated from Alabama to Mississippi in 1845, making the journey by wagons; they settled in the neighborhood of Torrance, and two years later purchased land near the same place. The father died in January, 1869, aged fifty-nine years; the mother died December 11, 1868, at the age of fifty-seven years. Ten children were born of this marriage, all of whom lived to maturity: Robert S., a farmer, lives in Water Valley, Miss.; Ira L., lives west of Coldwater, Miss.; he is a farmer; Mattie is the wife of John Gillon, and resides near Torrance; Thomas H. B. is next in order; Tabitha E., is the wife of Daniel G. Anthony, and resides with the subject of this sketch; Elizabeth is the wife of Frank M. Spears, and lives in Grenada county; Rosa married O. P. Farrell, and lives in Yalobusha county; John B. is a farmer near Torrance; Agnes, married Charles Farrell, and lives in Grenada county; Mary, the eldest child, married G. W. Williams; both are deceased, leaving eight children. Our subject was reared in Yalobusha county, Miss., within six miles of the place on which he is now living. His educational advantages were somewhat limited, but he acquired sufficient information to meet the demands of ordinary business life. He remained under the paternal roof until the beginning of the war when he enlisted in the Fifteenth Mississippi volunteer infantry. He was wounded in the battle of Franklin, Tenn., and at New Hope, Ga.; at the former place he was captured, and was held prisoner until June, 1865. He was with Hood on his campaign from Georgia to Tennessee; he was taken to Nashville, Tenn., in December, 1864, and, as before stated, was not released until June, 1865. He resumed farming as soon as he was recovered from his wounds, which he continued until March, 1873, when he located in Torrance, and embarked in the general mercantile trade; at one time he was postmaster, and he has not wholly relinquished his agricultural pursuits. Mr. Van Hoozer was married in 1868, to Miss Olivia Horton, a native of Mississippi, and a daughter of Robert Horton, one of the very earliest settlers of this county; he assisted in the building of the first courthouse in the county. He married Louisa Ridley, and to them were born thirteen children, nine of whom lived to maturity. He died at the age of seventy-six years, and Mrs. Horton lived to be seventy-two years old. Mr. and Mrs. Van Hoozer have had born to them eight children, four of whom have died; those living are: Willie, Mamie, Alama and Ethel; Louisa, Thomas, Vincent and Benton are dead; the last named was burned to death at the age of two years. Mrs. Van Hoozer was educated at Grenada, Miss., and she is a member of the Baptist church. Mr. Van Hoozer is a member of the Masonic lodge at Coffeeville No. 83. He is a man of deep integrity of character, and holds a place in the esteem of his fellow-citizens of which any one might well be proud.

John O. Vann, who has for many years been identified with the commercial and agricultural interests of Yalobusha county, will next claim the attention of the reader. He was born in Gates county, N. C., April 28, 1828, and is a son of Harrison and Julia Ann (Field) Vann, also natives of North Carolina. The father was born in 1790, and was the son of John Vann who immigrated to this country, from England, with his father, and settled in North Carolina, where he engaged in farming. He lived to be an old man, and reared a family of three sons and one daughter. Harrison, the father of John O., passed his youth on a farm, and in later years was occupied with house carpentering. He came to Mississippi in 1870, and died in January, 1871. His wife was born in 1800, and died in the state of Mississippi in the spring of 1870, before the arrival of her husband there. She was the daughter of Mills R. Field, a well-known citizen of Gates county, N. C. He was a man of fine education, and much more than ordinary ability. He lived to be more than seventy-five years of age and reared a family of four sons and one daughter. John O. Vann has now in his possession the first dollar ever owned by Mills R. Field, and it is about one hundred and twenty-five years old. Harrison Vann and wife had born to them eleven children; one died in infancy, and the others lived to maturity. John O. is the youngest of the family, and grew to manhood in Gates county, N. C. He had but few opportunities for acquiring an education, as his parents were in moderate circumstances. At the age of twenty years he bade farewell to his home and friends and came overland to the state of Mississippi. He traveled with a man and family who were looking for a new home. At first he worked at anything that offered until 1850, when he went to Oxford and worked at his trade. The following year he spent in school at Mount Vernon, and June 3, 1852, he was united in marriage to Miss Ellen Spearman, a daughter of Robert Spearman, a native of South Carolina. Mrs. Vann was born in 1817, February 19, and came with her parents to Mississippi, in 1842. She died September 20, 1885, leaving two children: John E. of the enterprising firm of Vann & Beadles, dealers in general merchandise, and Julia Ann, wife of W. D. York, a resident of Yalobusha county. The mother of these children was an earnest Christian, and a consistent member of the Baptist church. Mr. Vann was married a second time to Mrs. S. A. York. She was born in the state of Alabama in 1828, and is a daughter of Robert Perkins, who emigrated from Virginia to Alabama when a young man; there he married Elizabeth Hooper, a native of Georgia, and they came to Mississippi in 1848, and settled near Coffeeville. They had ten children, all of whom lived to be grown. Mrs. Vann was the second child, and she was first married to Daniel York, a native of Tennessee. He was born in 1810 and died in 1870 leaving a family of eight children: William, Lucy, John, Sally, Elisha are still living; those deceased are Lizzie, Harriet and James. Mr. and Mrs. Vann are both members of the Baptist church. Mr. Vann enlisted in the regiment of Colonel Gordon, participated in many engagements, was taken prisoner at Selma, Ala.; sent to a place near Atlanta, and finally paroled, after which he returned to his home. He is now one of the largest planters of the county. In 1880 he embarked in the general mercantile trade at Coffeeville, and has since turned that business over to his son, J. E. Vann. He owns twenty-three hundred acres of land, one thousand of which are under good cultivation. He is a man of excellent business qualifications, and has made a success of life from every standpoint. Politically he affiliates with the democratic party. Mrs. Vann has a farm of eight hundred acres in her own name. This is also in a high state of cultivation.

Samuel T. Van Norman. The family of Van Norman is originally from Holland, and the first member of the family of whom much is known is Aaron Van Norman, who was born in the state of New York. At an early day he became a resident of Indiana, and from that state came to Mississippi in the year 1831, and became a resident of Amite county. He served his country in the War of 1812, and made a faithful and efficient soldier. Hiram Van Norman, his son and father of the immediate subject of this sketch, was also born in New York, and during his father's different changes of residence he removed from place to place with him, but attained his manhood in the state of Indiana, where he was married to Miss Elizabeth Waldon, daughter of Moses Waldon. Mrs. Van Norman was reared in Kentucky, but soon after her marriage she and her husband came to Mississippi and engaged in planting and milling a few miles west of Liberty. Mr. Van Norman afterward moved to the town and established a tan yard and soon built up an extensive trade and a lucrative business. He continued this calling up to the breaking out of the late war. He was an honorable and useful member of society, was a man whose views of life were worthy and to his credit, and every enterprise in which he took an interest, was practically benefited by his notice. His brother, William Van Norman, was quite a prominent politician of Amite county, which he represented in both houses of the state legislature. He afterward took up his residence in the Lone Star state and there was called from life. S. T. Van Norman, whose name stands at the head of this biography, is the youngest son of a family of four sons and four daughters, and in Liberty, Miss., he first saw the light of day, September 5, 1837. He received but limited educational advantages in this county, but in 1858, with a determination to change this state of affairs, he went to Missouri and for one year attended school in Chillicothe, where he improved rapidly in his studies. In his early youth he had learned the harness-maker's trade but abandoned that business for a few years to engage in planting, after which he returned to his native town and for a short time previous to the war was engaged in merchandising. The coming clash of arms caused him to cast every personal consideration aside, and with the enthusiasm of youth he, in September, 1861, enlisted in the Seventh Mississippi infantry, company C, and until the close of the war served the cause he espoused with that intrepidity, courage and fidelity for which the Southern soldier was famous. He was in the bloody and disastrous battle of Shiloh; at Murfreesboro, in the engagements around Atlanta, at Jonesboro; the two day's fight at Nashville, also taking an active part in many engagements of less importance. He served on detached duty for over one year, and surrendered with his regiment at Greenville, N. C., after which he returned to Amite county and settled down to the peaceful pursuit of planting on the plantation where he now resides. He has devoted his time and energies to this calling and as a reward for the indomitable industry, push and enterprise he has always displayed, he is the owner of seven hundred acres of valuable land adjoining the town of Gloster, which was laid out on his land, and here he sold quite a number of acres to advantage for town purposes. He has used his influence to build up the town and advance the interests of the place, and as the town of Gloster is a thriving and prosperous place, he may be said to have succeeded. Mr. Van Norman is a man of good business habits and at all times manifests an enterprising spirit and a deep interest in the welfare of the county. He has always upheld the principles of democracy but has never been an aspirant for office. He has shown his approval of secret organizations by becoming a member of the Masonic fraternity, and has been much interested in the workings of this order. In the month of January, 1861, he was married to Miss Naomi, daughter of G. B. McLain, one of the early and prominent farmers of Mississippi, and in time a family of eleven children gathered about their board, their names being as follows: Leila, Amanda, Albert, Florence, wife of J. B. Cason; Bessie, Robert, Jennie, Samuel, Curtis, Anna and Myrtle. Leila, the eldest daughter, married W. T. Caston. In the Baptist church of Gloster, of which Mr. Van Norman has long been a member, he holds the positions of deacon, church-clerk and treasurer. In the various affairs of the county Mr. Van Norman exerts an influence which all feel, and as his friends are numerous, this speaks in an admirable manner of his many worthy qualities of mind and heart.

John H. Vanslyke, an enterprising and wideawake merchant of Ellisville, Miss., was born at Raleigh, Smith county, Miss., February 19, 1855. His parents were Jesse and Mary E. (Connerly) Vanslyke, natives of New York and South Carolina, respectively. They came to Mississippi at an early day, and were married in Smith county, and there passed the remainder of their lives. They became the parents of three children: Margaret E.; Morgan, and John H. Of these, John H., our subject, was the eldest. He attended the home district schools in his county, and by diligent study and close application to his books, he acquired a thorough, practical education, which he supplemented by a course at Johnson's Commercial academy. In 1877 he secured employment as a salesman in the store of John F. Champenois, of Shubuta, Miss., with whom he remained in this capacity until the 1st of March, 1883, at which time he became a partner with his employer and removed to Ellisville, opening a store at that place. In February, 1885, he purchased the interest of Mr. Champenois, and has since conducted the business and is sole proprietor. He has gained an extensive trade, and in connection with the mercantile business is largely engaged in planting and stock-raising. He owns two thousand five hundred acres of land, which is very valuable. He was married at Shubuta, March 4, 1882, to Lulu E., the daughter of John and Fannie R. (Copeland) Champenois, who was born in Shubuta, May 12, 1864. Mr. Vanslyke is a member of the Masonic order, and he and his wife are members of the Methodist Episcopal Church South. Our subject is an enterprising citizen, of good principles, and has been successful in every enterprise which he has taken in hand. He enjoys, to a marked degree, the respect of his fellow citizens, and as a merchant and man of affairs, he has the confidence of all classes with whom he comes in contact.

In the front ranks of Carroll county's professional men is Dr. George W. Vasser, physician and surgeon, Carrollton, Miss., whose career will be briefly outlined in the following page. He was born in Halifax county, Va., April 4, 1826, and is a son of Elijah H. Vasser, also a native of Virginia. The father of Elijah H. Vasser was a Virginian by birth, and of English descent. The Vassers are among the F. F. V.'s of Virginia. Elijah H. Vasser married in Halifax county, Va., Mary H. Womack, a native of that state and county, and a daughter of Capt. William Womack. He removed to Alabama about the year 1838, and located at Athens, where he resided five years, and then went to Monroe county, Miss., settling near the present site of Egypt station; his death occurred there in 1847. George W. Vasser passed his youth in Mississippi and Alabama, receiving his education at a private seminary in Athens, Ala. After completing his literary studies he began to study medicine in Monroe county, Miss. He took his first course of lectures at the University of Pennsylvania, and was graduated from this renowned institution of learning in 1848. He then returned to Monroe county, Miss., and entered upon his professional career. In 1854 he removed to Carroll county, continuing his practice. Since 1861 he has been a resident of Carrollton. He is a skillful, conscientious physician, and has won a large patronage. He is a student to this day, never having abandoned the attitude of seeking information and advanced opinions, which he occupied in the beginning of his professional studies. He is a member of the State Medical society, where his skill and experience render his attendance of great benefit to younger members. He fills the office of health officer of Carroll county. Dr. Vasser was united in the holy bonds of matrimony, in Monroe county, Miss., in 1851, to Miss Eliza Roseborough, a native of South Carolina, but a Mississippian by adoption. One child, a daughter, Ella, has been born to the Doctor and his wife; she is the wife of the Hon. T. H. Somerville, of Winona, Miss. In his fraternal relations, our subject is identified with the Masonic order, being a Royal Arch Mason. He is past master, and has represented his lodge at the grand lodge of Mississippi on several different occasions.

Dr. B. A. Vaughan's name has become almost a household word in Columbus, Miss., for he has been an active medical practitioner of that city since 1854, his many estimable qualities of heart and head drawing around him many warm friends and an extended medical practice. He was born at Scotland Neck, N. C., September 18, 1829, to George W. and Felicia (Norfleet) Vaughan, who belonged to prominent families of Virginia and North Carolina. They were of Scotch-English descent. His father was a soldier in the War of 1812 as a surgeon, and lost a thumb and finger in the service, the same ball penetrating his hip and causing a severe wound, from which he suffered all his life. In early manhood he emigrated to North Carolina where he practiced his profession until his death. He was a graduate of the University of Pennsylvania. To this union three children were born, of whom Dr. B. A. Vaughan is the only survivor. Dr. Vaughan's general education was received in Columbus, Miss., at the Franklin academy. He attended medical lectures at the University of Virginia and the Jefferson Medical college of Philadelphia, Penn., from which he graduated in 1854. Although practicing in every branch of his profession he makes a specialty of gynecology. He is a member of the American Medical association, the State Medical society of Mississippi and the Lowndes County Medical association, of which he was president in 1874–5, and is at present secretary and treasurer of a similar society. He was president of the State Medical society in 1877–8, and in 1876–7 was secretary of the section of practice of medicine and materia medica, of the American Medical association. He has written articles on the following subjects: Air as a physician; Water as a disease producing agent; Chemical thermometry; Quinine, its therapeutic characteristics (on which he has written a second paper); Uterine colic and improvement in the treatment of uterine diseases; Antagonism of remedies; Amblyopia caused by quinine, and other articles that have been widely read by physicians throughout this country. He was the principal of Franklin academy at Columbus, before he was grown, and has been alderman of the city. He held the position of chairman of the district executive committee (in 1873), and was a member of the same committee for Lowndes county in 1875–6, and was president of the board of school trustees of the city of Columbus. During the war he was surgeon of the Fourteenth Mississippi regiment, post surgeon at Macon and Lauderdale, Miss., surgeon in chief of the hospitals of Macon and Lauderdale Springs, and surgeon in charge of the camp of paroled and exchanged prisoners at Jackson, Miss. He was also chief surgeon of the Blind Asylum hospital at Jackson, Miss. Was surgeon for the state of Mississippi at Atlanta, Ga., and was medical director of the state of Mississippi at close of the Civil war. A volunteer company was organized at Columbus, August 11, 1837. This company served during the late war and is still in existence, being a company of the Second regiment, First brigade of national guards. The Doctor has been a member of this company for some forty-four years. He is chief health officer of Lowndes county, and is assistant surgeon general of the First brigade of national guards. He is a member of the Masonic fraternity and is a past master, past high priest, past commander and past grand commander of Knights Templar, Mississippi; and is a thirty-second degree of the Scottish Rite. He also belongs to the U. S. B. fraternity. the K. of H., and is the president of the Tombigbee Railroad company. He was married, in 1853, to Miss M. Wade, a daughter of P. B. Wade, of Columbus, Miss., by whom he has one child, Jeannie. Doctor Vaughan is pursuing the practice of medicine among a people who have known his childhood, his boyhood and his professional life. He has lived in Columbus, Miss., since 1837.

Henry B. Vaughan, planter and stockraiser of Commencement plantation, near Kingston, was born here in 1849, and is the younger of two children born to his parents, Charles N. and Ann Eliza (Farrar) Vaughan, the former born in Southampton county, Va., in 1818, and the latter born in Kingston vicinity in 1827. The grandfather, John Vaughan, was a native Virginian, and a planter by occupation. Charles N. Vaughan was educated at Charlottesville and the University of Virginia, being there at the time of the Turner insurrection, in which several members of the family were killed. The parents had died previous to this. Mr. Vaughan left college and joined the troops for the Mexican war, but at Vicksburg they were disbanded, and he, after stopping at various places in the state, finally came to Adams county, Miss., where he married about 1844. He settled in the Kingston vicinity, and there he carried on planting very successfully, until his death, in November, 1862. He was a member of the Masonic fraternity, and a man of wonderful energy, very industrious habits, and one who stood well in the community in which he resided. Mrs. Vaughan died in September, 1889. After the death of Mr. Vaughan she had married Capt. George C. Comstock, deceased. To her first marriage were born two children, a son and a daughter, the latter, Ann Eliza, dying at the age of fifteen years. The son, our subject, was educated in the home schools at Kingston, and also attended school at Natchez for some time. At the age of fifteen years he joined company C, Fourth Mississippi cavalry, and operated with General Forrest in many severe engagements, being frequently sent on light duty, on account of his youth. He surrendered at Gainesville, Ala., at the close of war, and in 1866 went to Europe, where he spent a year or two in France and England. After returning to the United States he passed a year in Bryant & Stratton's Commercial college in New Orleans, and subsequently spent three years, or until 1871, engaged in merchandising. He then went to Clinton, La., where his mother was living, and resided there for twelve years. Ten years of the time he and his stepfather operated the Clinton & Port Hudson railroad, in which they had a controlling interest. Since that time he has resided on his estate, near Kingston, one of the finest upland plantations in Adams county. This magnificent plantation is well improved, and everything about the place indicates the presence of a thrifty and practical owner. He has one thousand three hundred acres in Commencement plantation, and one thousand acres in another tract, all the result of his own exertions, having started with nothing. In looking after the interests of his large plantation he does not lose sight of the stock industry, improving his cattle with the Holstein breed. He married Miss Bettie A. Slaughter, a native of East Baton Rouge parish, Louisiana, and the daughter of William and Elizabeth Slaughter, natives of Bowling Green, Ky., and East Baton Rouge parish, La., respectively. When a boy Mr. Slaughter went with his parents to Louisiana, and there he married, and spent the remainder of his days near Port Hudson, as a wealthy planter and merchant. He was a practical business man and was conservative and liberal in all his views. To Mr. and Mrs. Vaughan have been born three interesting children. In 1886-7 Mr. Vaughan served as a member of the board of supervisors of Adams county. He has shown his appreciation of secret organizations by joining the Knights of Pythias, American Legion of Honor, the I. O. O. F. and the A. F. & A. M., all at Clinton, La. He has been through the chair in the I. O. O. F., and has held various offices in the Knights of Pythias organization. Mrs. Vaughan has been a member of the Presbyterian church from youth.

James Vaughan has been a resident of Yazoo county, Miss., since his birth in 1842, and is the seventh of a family of twelve children. His parents Henry and Emma (Reese) Vaughan, were natives of South Carolina, but emigrated to Mississippi in 1832, and settled on the plantation now occupied by the subject of this notice; there they spent the balance of their days; the father died in 1870, at the age of seventy years, and the mother passed away ten years later, at the age of three-score and ten years. Nine of their twelve children grew to maturity, and three of them are still living: Mrs. Mary S. Guion, Mrs. Margaret Moore, deceased; Betsey, who died in infancy; Dr. Henry Vaughan, deceased; John A., who died in childhood; Charles B., who was killed in the siege of Vicksburg; H. R. captain of company B, Eighteenth Mississippi volunteer infantry, who fell at Gettysburg; James; Mrs. Alice Burroughs of Yazoo county; Emma, deceased at the age of fourteen years; Frank, who died at the age of twenty-six years, and William R., who died at twenty-one years of age. James Vaughan grew to manhood in this county, and received a good education. He was a member of the sophomore class of Oxford university at the time the Civil war broke out, and left the schoolroom for the field of battle. He enlisted in company B, Eighteenth Mississippi volunteer infantry, and for one year served as sergeant; he then joined Wirt Adams' cavalry, and served until the end of the conflict. He participated in the first battle of Manassas, in the siege of Vicksburg, and many skirmishes both in Mississippi and Alabama. After the declaration of peace he returned to his home, and resumed his farming. The plantation consists of fourteen hundred and forty acres, one thousand of which are under excellent cultivation; cotton and corn are the principal crops, but Mr. Vaughan is planning to devote more of his time to the raising of livestock with a view to improving the breeds of the county. He was married in 1867 to Miss Mary E. Anderson, a daughter of John W. and Adaline (Newell) Anderson, who were early settlers of Yazoo county. By this union nine children have been born, seven of whom are living: Emma, wife of H. F. Russell of Washington county, Miss.; John A., Samuel, H. Y., Mary, James and Charles. Mr. Vaughan is a member of the P. B. Tutt lodge No. —— A. F. & A. M., and is also a Knight of Honor. He takes an active part in local politics, but is not an officeseeker. He and his wife are members of Bowman's chapel of the Methodist Episcopal church, to which they are liberal contributors. They have been foremost in all movements calculated to benefit the community in which they live, and are numbered among the leading familes of the county.

James Alexander Ventress was born in Robertson county, about twenty-five miles from Clarksville, Tenn., in 1805, and was the youngest son and second of the children of Lovick Ventress, who settled in that state in 1796. His paternal grandfather came from England about 1760, and settled first near Norfolk, Va., where several of his children were born, and removed thence to North Carolina. His mother, Elizabeth Stewart, was of the Stewarts of Scotland, of noble lineage. While James A. Ventress was yet a small boy (in 1809), his parents accompanied his uncle, Duncan Stewart, afterward lieutenant-governor, and other members of the family, to the territory of Mississippi, settling in what was known as the Mount Pleasant neighborhood, near what is now Centerville, Wilkinson county. After his removal to Mississippi, Lovick Ventress bought a plantation and engaged in planting, but, his health soon failing, he returned to Tennessee, where he died in the prime of life. His worthy widow survived him many years, and died in Wilkinson county, having been a faithful and affectionate mother and a worthy friend, guide and counselor to her fatherless children. Their eldest son, William C. S. Ventress, moved to Louisiana, and served his parish in the legislature of that state. He became a wealthy planter, his sugar plantations being very extensive and profitable. He lived to a ripe old age, and, dying, left two daughters, both of whom still survive him. He had two sons in the Confederate army, and one, James A. Ventress, attained the rank of major in that service. Eliza A. Ventress, the only daughter of Lovick and Elizabeth Ventress, became the wife of Major A. M. Feltus, who was a prominent planter, merchant and banker of Wilkinson county and was at one time quite wealthy. He was a native of New York, and he and his wife became the parents of a large family of children, four sons having been soldiers in the Confederate army. One, Abram M. Feltus, Jr., held the rank of lieutenant-colonel in the Sixteenth regiment of Mississippi volunteers, and on May 12, 1864, was killed at Spottsylvania Courthouse, Va. Another, P. Gassner Feltus, being the senior officer present, commanded and surrendered two regiments at Appomattox. Major and Mrs. Feltus were residents of Woodville. The former died at a good old age in 1861, and the latter in 1889, aged eighty-two years.

After attending the schools which then existed in the county, and an academy in New Orleans, the subject of this sketch took passage for Europe, where he spent nine years in the prosecution of his studies, and with marked success. At the University of Edinburgh he was a pupil of the celebrated John Wilson—Christopher North—author of Lights and Shadows of Scottish Life; Noctes Ambrosianæ, etc., who wrote of him that he was "an assiduous and successful student," and became so much impressed with his aptitude for philosophical studies that he urged him to remain and devote himself to that branch of learning, with a view of succeeding him in the chair of moral philosophy in that university. While a student in Scotland, he formed the acquaintance of Sir Walter Scott, and had the honor of being a guest at the banquet when Lord Meadowbank forced from that distinguished writer a confession of the authorship of the Waverley novels. After leaving Scotland, he spent several years in Paris, a student at the *Academie* and a pupil of Jean Baptiste Say, the political economist, through whose kindness and influence he made the acquaintance of and was enabled to receive instructions in his studies from Jeremy Bentham, for whose philosophy he ever afterward entertained a high regard. While in Paris he was a frequent visitor at La Grange, the home of La Fayette, whose friendship he gained, and to whom he was indebted for many courtesies. It was during his stay in Paris that the revolution of 1830 occurred, and, being an exceptionally fine rifle shot himself, he readily noted the inferiority of the French troops as marksmen. He often remarked, when speaking of that occasion, that the people who had ascended to the housetops for safety, were in more imminent danger that were those in the streets, at whom the muskets were aimed, and that a single company of Mississippi riflemen would have done more execution. During his stay in Paris Mr. Ventress had the distinguished honor of being elected by the Conseil d'Admistration, on account of his *lumieres et zele*, a collaborateur correspondent of the *Revue des Deux Mondes*. He was also a contributor to several of the English and French scientific and literary magazines and had papers read before the Institute of France, receiving the commendation of the scientific lights of Europe. He also translated several works and wrote several plays, which were highly praised. After leaving Paris, he spent some time in Rome, and was a student for two years at the University of Berlin. Having already mastered the German language, he went there to continue the study of jurisprudence, carrying with him letters of introduction to Baron Humboldt. After his return from Europe, where he had devoted a large portion of his time to the study of jurisprudence, he prepared himself for admission to the bar, and received his license to practice law, in 1841, from that eminent jurist, Wm. L. Sharkey, then chief justice of the supreme court of Mississippi. Being in affluent circumstances, however, he practiced but little, devoting himself instead to his planting interests, and his leisure to the study of general literature and the development of his taste for mechanics. His study and experiments resulted in numerous inventions, some of which he had patented, but it being a labor of love rather than of profit, he never attempted to make money out of them, though he permitted the use of some of them by manufacturers who were friends of his. While a student in Berlin, he presented to and received the thanks of the patriot government of Poland, then at war, for an improvement on the cannon then in use, and for a substitute for the cuirass worn by the soldiers of that unfortunate country. During the Civil war he invented a patent bullet, which he presented to the Confederate government. While he was an omnivorous reader, he devoted himself principally to works on science, politics and history, and the library he collected and bequeathed to his children is probably the finest, if not the largest collection of rare works in the state. Endowed with a fine memory and unusal powers of ratiocination, he digested thoroughly and remembered accurately what he read. Mr. Ventress was a man of profound erudition, and throughout his useful and well-spent life he was a close and painstaking student. He was deeply interested in the political questions of his day, and his brilliant intellect, which was strengthened and enriched by the highest culture, was admirably displayed while in the arena of politics. He was prominent in the counsels of his party, and no one's opinion and advice in political matters was considered more weighty, or was more sought after than his. He was a fluent, eloquent and convincing speaker and writer, and during his public career he had an opportunity of displaying the originality and versatility of his genius.

He became a presidential elector and state senator, was elected a member and had the additional honor of being chosen speaker of the house of representatives, at a time when it numbered among its members the brightest minds that have adorned the history of the state and nation. He was, at one time, also offered the nomination for governor. Stimulated by a laudable ambition to be useful in his day and generation, he was sometimes impatient of opposition, but invariably acted on principles which he believed to be founded on justice and truth, and from the defense of which he could never be swerved. This trait and a habit of expressing his opinions with the utmost freedom on all questions, regardless of consequences, doubtless, in a great measure, contributed to prevent the political preferment to which his eminent abilities entitled him. To the wiles of the politician he was a stranger. In public as well as in private life, he was a constant friend to education and to his exertions while in the legislature was probably due, more than to those of any other one man, the establishment of the University of Mississippi, at Oxford, of which institution he was a trustee from the time of its organization in 1844 until his death. In politics he was a states' rights democrat and Union man. While he believed and maintained that the constitution of the United States guaranteed the right of secession, he was very much opposed to the exercise of the right, believing it to be best that there should remain one country; best for the South and best for the North. As a member of the convention called by the legislature, in 1851, to take

measures for the redress of grievances, he labored earnestly for the preservation of the Union. While North, in 1860, he wrote an open letter to the mayor of Philadelphia, which was copied by the press throughout the country and pronounced by competent judges one of the most statesmanlike papers of the day. After the die had been cast, however, and his state had severed its connection with the Federal Union, true to his states' rights principles, he gave his allegiance to her and the Confederate states of which she had become a member. In private life Mr. Ventress was known as a man of integrity, high sense of honor and great kindness of heart, one whose charities were as generous as they were unostentatious, and whose friendship was as unselfish as it was lasting; socially he was a delightful companion, being a most interesting and instructive conversationalist and raconteur. In 1848 he married Miss Charlotte Davis Pynchon, daughter of Hon. Stephen Pynchon, of Massachusetts. On the paternal side, she was a lineal descendant of Col. William Pynchon, who came to America in 1630, was a charter member, first treasurer and assistant governor of Massachusetts Bay colony; was author of several theological works and the founder of Springfield, which was named in honor of his home in England; and of his son, John Pynchon, known as the worshipful major, commander of the troops of western Massachusetts in King Phillip's war, associate justice of the supreme court of the colony; one of the commissioners appointed by the British government in 1664 to receive the surrender of New Amsterdam, N. Y., from the Dutch, and a member of the council of King James II. The ancestor of the Pynchon family came to England in 1066, with William the Conqueror, and received, among other returns for his services, a grant of manors at Thorpet, in Kirby, Lincolnshire. In 1167, Hugh Pincheun held seven knight's fees in that county. The family drifted after several generations to Northamptonshire and afterward to Essex. A grandson of one of them was Henry Chicheley, first privy councilor under King Henry VI.; archbishop of Canterbury from 1414 to 1443; the founder of All Souls' college, Oxford, and who built the western tower of Canterbury cathedral at his own expense. The branch of the family that emigrated to America was descended from Nicholas Pynchon, high sheriff of London in 1533, whose son, John, married Jane, daughter of Sir Richard Empson. From them were descended the earls of Portland, Sir Edward Pynchon and William Pynchon, the emigrant. On the paternal side, Mrs. Ventress was also a lineal descendant of Rev. William Hubbard, the early historian of New England, and of Gov. George Wyllys, colonial governor of Connecticut and owner of the celebrated Charter oak.

The mother of Mrs. Ventress was Miss Sarah Trask, daughter of Dr. Israel Trask, of Brimfield, Mass., a Revolutionary veteran and member of the Massachusetts constitutional convention. His wife was Miss Sarah Lawrence, daughter of Dr. James Lawrence, a descendant of Sir Robert Lawrence, of Ashton hall, Lancashire, England, who accompanied Richard Cœur de Lion to the Holy Land, and at the siege of Acre was the first to plant the banner of the cross on the battlements, for which he was knighted. Stephen Pynchon, the father of Mrs. Ventress, was a graduate of Yale college, receiving his diploma in 1789. He afterward studied law and was admitted to the bar in 1791, settling in Brimfield, of which place he was a citizen the balance of his life. In 1805 he was chosen a representative to the general court, and in 1819 was appointed by Gov. John Brooks chief justice of the court of sessions of Hampden county, Mass. He served his county for sixteen years in the state legislature, of which body he was a member at the time of his death in Boston, February 5, 1823. He was a prominent Free Mason. The order was then a social and political power, and under its rites he was buried. He was a noble, worthy and generous man, and for his day was exceptionally well educated and intelligent.

HHH

After completing her education in Springfield, Mrs. Ventress, at that time a beautiful and accomplished young lady, came to Mississippi with a cousin to make her home with her uncle, Maj. James L. Trask, who was a bachelor, and remained with him until his death. Major Trask settled in Mississippi in 1805. He was a veteran of the War of 1812, and served under General Jackson at the battle of New Orleans. A man of remarkable energy and business tact, he amassed a large fortune, most of which he bequeathed to his niece. His brothers, Augustus and Dr. William P. Trask, also lived in Wilkinson county, and are buried in the family burying ground, as is also his eldest brother, Col. Israel E. Trask. Col. Trask was a man of considerable ability. Harvard university conferred on him the honorary degree of A. M. He represented his county in the legislature and constitutional convention of Massachusetts, and was one of the incorporators of Amherst college. As was the case with the planters throughout the South, the emancipation proclamation, and the amendments to the constitution passed in confirmation thereof, swept out of existence the slave property of Mr. Ventress, which constituted the major part of his wealth. Losing his property at an age when men usually retire from business, and worried beyond expression by the changed and unsettled condition of the country, his health, which had not been good for some time, gradually declined, and he at last succumbed to general bodily prostration, passing away quietly at La Grange, his home, on the 26th of June, 1867. His widow survived him until the 10th of May, 1877, when she, too, was called from a life of Christian excellence, having been for many years a worthy and honored member of the Presbyterian church. Their family consisted of five children, three of whom lived to manhood; a son and a daughter dying in childhood. Those living are Lawrence T., born Aug. 5, 1850, educated at home and in the State university at Oxford; James A., born February 14, 1853, and William P. S., born May 28, 1854, both of whom were educated at home in the Norwood high school and the University of Virginia. After leaving college the latter graduated in law from the University of Mississippi, at Oxford. He is at present a practicing attorney of Woodville. These sons reside at the La Grange plantation, and give their friends a royal welcome to the luxuries and comforts of their magnificent home.

They are among the largest and most successful planters in Wilkinson county. Lawrence T. is the only one of the brothers who is married. His wife was Miss Mary Ellen Holmes, a finely educated and talented lady, eminently fitted, by virtue of her intelligence, grace, ease and dignity, to do the honors of her beautiful home. She is a charming and gracious hostess, and is highly esteemed in social circles for her conversational powers and her winning manner, which inspires ease and confidence in her presence. She is the daughter of Capt. Richard Holmes, of Natchez. Mr. and Mrs. Ventress have a beautiful little daughter, Charlotte E., now five years of age, and a son, Lawrence T., Jr., born May 6, 1891, in whom their hopes and affections are centered. Lawrence T. Ventress was elected a member of the board of supervisors in 1887, and re-elected in 1889 and 1891. During this time he has served as president of that body. William P. S. was elected to the state legislature in 1891. At an early day Major Trask built the first story of the now palatial residence occupied by the Ventress family. This building was raised one story, and an observatory added just before the war. This is one of the most beautiful, attractive and costly of Southern homes, and is provided with a fine billiardroom, spacious halls, library, parlors, drawing and sleeping rooms, and lighted with gas, and in this abode of refinement and good taste hospitality of the most generous and truehearted, yet unostentatious description, is extended to all.

Newet J. Vick. The Vick family has been prominent in the history of Mississippi since the year 1806, at which time, or a little before, Newet Vick, the grandfather of the subject of this sketch, became a resident of Jefferson county. This gentleman, like his father before him (Thomas Vick), was a Virginian, and when just in the vigor of early manhood removed to Raleigh, N. C., where, for a short time, he was engaged in merchandising. The state of Mississippi next became his home, but after residing near Washington for some time he came to near what is now the city of Vicksburg, where he purchased a large tract of land, his plantation taking the name of Open Woods. He also purchased a body of land fronting the Mississippi river, including, for the most part, what is now Vicksburg, seven miles distant from Open Woods. He came to this state as a local minister of the Methodist Episcopal church, and being a man of excellent parts and of original and intelligent views, there was strong talk among his neighbors of his making the race for the governorship of Mississippi, and he was urged to stand for the nomination, but he would not allow his name to go before the convention, for he was very much averse to coupling the gospel with politics. He was warmly welcomed in high social circles, as a business man was quite successful, and was an esteemed minister of the gospel. Mississippi at this time was not specially lawless, being mostly settled by citizens from Virginia, and their families, trained to the usages of old society, though subsequently Vicksburg and other river towns earned an unenviable reputation from the misdeeds of floating or transient characters. The first Methodist Episcopal conference ever held in the state was at his residence on the Open Woods plantation. He died of what was believed to be yellow fever in 1818, at the age of forty-seven years, having lived a most useful and truly Christian life. To Open Woods he was accompanied by his relative, Foster Cook, a civil engineer and afterward planter, whose son, Colonel Cook, a venerable octogenarian, is still living. Thomas and Burwell Vick, brothers of Newet J. Vick, came to Mississippi about the same time as himself, or perhaps before, the former (Uncle Tommy, as he was familiarly called) living to be a very old man. He was noted throughout this section for his generosity, kindness and nobility of heart, and the affection, good will and respect which were bestowed upon him by all were fully merited.

He became a well-to-do planter, but his wealth was not selfishly hoarded for his own benefit, but was lavished freely in behalf of those less fortunate than himself. Burwell Vick has descendants now living who are large landowners: Captain John Willis, at Panther burn, and Mrs. Dr. Phelps, at Nitta Yuma, neighboring stations to Anguilla, on the Louisville, New Orleans & Texas railroad, owning all property outside the depot belongings, although Nitta Yuma has been recently laid off into town lots, a few of which have been sold. Newet Vick was married in Virginia to Miss Elizabeth Clark, a very handsome, accomplished and amiable lady, and when they attempted the journey to Mississippi they traveled overland to the Muscle shoals of the Tennessee river, in northern Alabama, where Mr. Vick built a flatboat, on which they embarked and floated down to a point below Natchez, making their first settlement in Jefferson county. Mrs. Vick died within a few hours of her husband, also of that dreaded scourge, yellow fever. They left a family of twelve children, the eldest of whom, a daughter, was not more than eighteen years of age. All lived to maturity, and two members are still living: Mrs. Dr. C. K. Marshall, wife of an eminent divine of the Southern Methodist Episcopal church, lately deceased, and Mrs. E. F. Anderson, both of Vicksburg, each of whom has now a daughter living with her, Anne and Willie. The eldest son of this family was John Wesley Vick, the father of the immediate subject of this sketch, who was born in Jefferson county, Miss., March 1, 1806. He died on the 2d of March, 1888, in extreme old age, being at the time of his death eighty-two years and one day old. The formation of an internal tumor, due to a fall, was the immediate cause of his death, while for a year or more he had been in an enfeebled condition after an attack of dengue, or "break-bone" fever, from which he never recovered his wonted vigor. He was reared in Warren county, where he spent the greater portion of his life, except while away from home at school. He received his initiatory training in the schools of Warren county, but finished his education in Transylvania college, of Lexington, Ky., and in the University of Virginia. He would have graduated in a short time at the university, well up in his classes, and while in that institution was one of the captains of the cadets. He was called home by the necessities of business. After some time he purchased land at Mount Albon, near Vicksburg, on which he resided a number of years, engaged in planting. He purchased the land comprising the Anguilla plantation about 1840, at which time but little of the land had been cleared, but he was very successful in his business operations and rapidly developed this property, so that at the opening of the Civil war he was the owner of two thousand four hundred acres of land in one body, nearly one-half of which he had succeeded in reducing to a fine state of cultivation, eight hundred acres more being cleared and put under cultivation since 1880. This land was kept under one management until 1886, with the exception of the land now owned by Junius Parham, which was sold some few years before. Besides this land, at different times he owned several other tracts, including his home place, known as Mount Albon plantation, near Vicksburg, already referred to, on which is erected a fine brick residence, the residence which he built in Vicksburg being still one of the finest in the city, and is now the home of his daughter, Mrs. Dr. S. D. Robins, whose husband has charge of the United States and Mississippi State hospital service, besides railroad and other corporation practice. He was the owner of about two hundred slaves and was considered a very wealthy man, but, like other members of his family, he was generous and charitable, giving freely of his wealth to churches, schools and charitable and public enterprises. The lot on which the present Methodist Episcopal church of Vicksburg now stands, one-fourth of a square, was contributed by him, and many other enterprises which tended to the building up and improvement of the city found in him a most liberal patron. While the original company was organized for the building of the Memphis & Vicksburg railroad, now a part of the great Huntington system, he was its last president, and, owning a majority of the paid-up stock, he sold the franchises, which were finally bought by Northern capitalists, and by them the road was constructed in 1880 and 1881, stipulating in the sale that the road should pass through Anguilla and a depot be there maintained. In the will of Newet Vick it was stipulated that the present site of Vicksburg should be laid out in town lots and divided among his children. Thus Newet Vick was the founder of the place, and it was left to his children to develop the city, they being the sole owners of the land on which Vicksburg now stands. Newet Vick's will became the subject of a rather notable litigation respecting the title to certain valuable tracts in the young city of Vicksburg, which involved an interesting construction of law, and was decided by a bare majority of the supreme court of the United States, being argued by that celebrated orator, S. S. Prentiss, and other legal luminaries. Of this decision The Life and Times of Sergeant Smith Prentiss speaks as follows:

The 17th day of June, 1845, was, so far as Mr. Prentiss' pecuniary condition was concerned, the day of doom. To comprehend this we must now take up the dropped stitch in the thread of our narrative and return to 1837, when, the reader will remember, Prentiss had by the decision of the supreme court of Mississippi recovered the commons in front of Vicksburg, valued then at from $100,000 to $350,000. On these he had put up large and extensive buildings, estimated to be worth $100,000. It will be remembered that in that case the title of Vick's daughters came into the question collaterally, and the opinion of the court was that they had no interest in the two-hundred-acre tract reserved for the city in Vick's will. It will be remembered further that the city of Vicksburg claimed the commons partly in virtue of the dedication by the administrator, Mr. Lane. No sooner had the court decided that the city of Vicksburg was not entitled than a new question sprang up in the minds of the daughters of Mr. Vick. Rev. John Lane, who had married one of them, had moved into the state of Louisiana. The other sisters were residents of the state of Tennessee. Being thus residents of different states they could bring suit against the parties claiming the commons in the United States court. Accordingly, as early as 1838, Rev. John Lane and wife and some of the other daughters of Newet Vick filed their bill on the equity side of the circuit court of the United States for the Southern district of Mississippi, setting out the will, the administration of Lane, the payment of all the debts, the sale of the town lots, and that the commons were still left; that the complainant's were entitled to a partition of them, or a sale and division of the proceeds, etc., and praying for a construction of the will. To this suit Prentiss and others were made parties. Some of the defendants answered the bill and concurred in the prayer for division; others concurred generally, and prayed that their parts might be allotted to them. But the parties made defendant as cendes, to wit, Prentiss, etc., demurred to the bill. The cause being set down for hearing on this state of preparation, the court, in June, 1842, sustained the demurrer and dismissed the bill. From this decree the complainants appealed to the supreme court of the United States. In law phrase, they, Prentiss, etc., demurred to the bill, or, in other words, they said, admitting all the bill alleges, it is evident from the face of the will that the four sons alone of Newet Vick are entitled to this two-hundred-acre tract, the daughters are not at all entitled to it or interested in it, and that the will had been so construed by the supreme court of Mississippi. The reader will perceive, therefore, that the question now presented before the court was very different from the one presented in the case heretofore described, although the same elements entered into the discussion. There the question was: Did Newet Vick dedicate the commons in his lifetime, or did Lane do it under proper authority? Both these questions were decided against the city. But in this case the naked, bold question was: Did Newet Vick in his will devise this two hundred acres to his sons exclusively, or to his sons and daughters? If the latter, then the daughters were entitled to nine shares of it. The third clause, as will be seen by reference to it, gives to each of his daughters one equal proportion with his sons and wife, of all of his personal estate as they come of age or marry, and to his sons an equal portion of said personal estate as they come of age, together with all his lands, all of which lands were to be appraised, valued, and divided when Westley arrived at twenty-one years of age; the said Westley having one part, and the son William having the other part, of the tracts unclaimed by the wife Elizabeth, and the son Newitt to have, at her death, the one she had chosen to occupy. Hartwell was to keep the part he already had in possession. Had this clause stood alone the question would have been beyond doubt, but the fourth clause, after appointing the executors, etc., wishes—that is, directs—his executors to remember the town lots hereafter to be laid off on the aforementioned two hundred acres of land, should be sold to pay his debts or other engagements, in preference to any other of his property, "for the use and benefit of all his heirs" (interlined in the will). The fate of the cause hung upon the construction of these two clauses. The demurrer was sustained in the court below, and Lane appealed to the supreme court. Hon. Benjamin Hardin, of Kentucky, represented the complainants' appellants and John J. Crittenden the defendants'. The reporter says: "This is one of the cases which was argued during his unavoidable absence, and, although he is enabled to give Mr. Hardin's argument, he regrets that he could not furnish Mr. Crittenden's. Of the eight judges, Story was absent and Nelson had not taken his seat. Of the six who presided, four, that is, McLean, Wayne, Catron and Daniel, held that the fourth clause entitled the daughters to share equally with the sons in the two-hundred-acre land tract, while two of the judges, to wit, McKinley and Chief Justice Taney, held to the contrary. Judge McLean delivered the opinion of the court, and the critical reader will observe that the reasoning of the court is sustained in one part by the hypothetical interlineation of the little word "and" before the interlined words in the will, "for the use and benefit of all my heirs." And Justice McKinley, in his dissenting opinion, comments with cautious words of judicial severity against this hypothetical interlineation, "I deny the power of the court, in such a case as this, to add the word 'and.'" He held that all the lands passed to the sons under the third clause of the will, unmodified by the interlined words of the fourth clause, and that the will, having been adjudicated by the supreme court of Mississippi, was *res adjudicata*. The above synopsis shows upon what slight circumstances sometimes hang not only the fate of great cases in law, but also the destiny of men. Had Story and Nelson been upon the bench, the court might have stood four to four, and thus the complainant's cause might have been lost, as it requires a majority to overrule a decision of the court below. As it was, the decision of the court below was reversed and the case sent back.

John Wesley Vick was married in the year 1827 to Miss Maria Brabston, a native of Mississippi, and a member of a well-to-do family, descendants of which are still living around Vicksburg. She died in 1832, having borne three children—two sons and one daughter: Thomas Vick, the eldest, was a graduate of the Military Academy of Kentucky, and of Center college of Danville. He became a physician of considerable prominence, and for some time was employed as surgeon on board a United States steamer. He traveled quite extensively in Europe, and during the great Civil war of this country he first served in the capacity of captain of a volunteer company, later as colonel of a regiment, and afterward as brigadier-general of the Louisiana militia. Before and after the war he turned his attention to sugar planting in Louisiana, also practicing his profession, and in 1867, after escaping the perils of battle, while making a business trip on board the steamer Carter, it blew up, and he is supposed to have been killed, as he has never since been heard from. He was last seen at about one o'clock at night, reading a paper. Prior to the war he had so improved his inheritance as to have a large property, which, for the most part, was lost by the business calamities incident to that great conflict. He never married. He was very popular and well liked, for his many noble qualities could not fail to win him many warm friends. Hartwell O. Vick, another son, was a planter on the Sunflower river, where he resided until 1880, during which year, being overtaken by sickness on a business trip, he stopped at Vicksburg, where he died, a single man. Harriet, the daughter, a bright and beautiful child, died at the age of nine years. Mr. Vick's second marriage was to Miss Letitia Booker, a daughter of Judge Booker, a prominent politician of Kentucky, and to this union one daughter was born, Letitia, who first married James R. Downs, of Mississippi, by whom she became the mother of two sons: Alfred and James R., both of whom are residents of Chattanooga, Tenn., and were educated in Kentucky, and in the law department of the University of Michigan. Alfred is a member of the law firm of Marchbanks, Taylor & Downs, and is a very promising young attorney. Both he and his brother are married, and each have two children. James R., Jr., is a broker, and he and his brother own large tracts of land in Washington county, Miss. After the death of their father, their mother was married to Col. John Cowan of Danville, Ky., an ex-lieutenant-colonel of a Kentucky regiment of the Union army, that participated in the siege of Vicksburg, where he was wounded in the foot. His wife died in April, 1880. She was a most devoted wife and mother, a highly cultured and refined lady, and possessed grand and noble traits of character. After the death of his second wife, Mr. Vick was married to the mother of the immediate subject of this sketch, her maiden name being Catherine Barber. She was born and reared in Danville, Ky., and was a sister of Lewis G. Barber, who is a professor in Central university of Kentucky, and James Barber, a prominent attorney and banker of Maysville, that state. She bore Mr. Vick six children. Kate, the eldest, is a highly accomplished woman, and is now traveling in Europe. She owns a part of the Anguilla plantation, on which she has nearly one hundred acres devoted to fruit, which is being added to from time to time, fifty acres being a pecan orchard. She was the first to attempt fruit raising on Deer creek, in Sharkey county, but as her venture proved successful, others have attempted it, and now the owners of Anguilla have all large orchards, except one. Martha D. is the wife of R. Perry, a merchant of Russellville, Ky., by whom she has two children, Wesley and Kate. Mary Ellen is the wife of O. S. Robins, a prominent attorney and real estate agent of Vicksburg, by whom she has two daughters, Mamie and Fannie. Amanda is the wife of Dr. S. D. Robins, and lives on the old home place in Vicksburg. She has three children: Vick, Kate and Amanda. Wesley Vick died at the age of three years, and Newet J. is the youngest of the family, and is the only male member of the Vick family that is now living. The mother of these children died in 1867, at the age of forty-nine years, a firm believer in the Presbyterian faith, although a member of the Methodist Episcopal church, by mutual consent of the Presbyterian and Methodist Episcopal churches. Mr. Vick was a leading member of the last named church, and for a great many years before the war was Sunday-school superintendent.

He was a whig in politics, was a strong Union man in sentiment, and was much opposed to secession, although after the war was precipitated his sympathies, as was generally the case at the South, were naturally on the side of his neighbors and friends, although, personally, he took no part in the struggle. His former slaves, having been kindly treated, came back home, as they called the plantation, and remained with him, so that being able to keep his place under cultivation his losses by the war, though great, were less than with many. He was a man with fine perceptions, was just and liberal in his views, was devoted to his home and family, and in the domestic circle was a model husband and father. He was a model host, for besides being hospitable and cordial, he was naturally kind, and had sufficient tact to at once put at their ease those who entered his presence, and to enable them to show themselves at their best. Newet J. Vick, whose name heads this sketch, was born at Vicksburg in the year 1858, and was reared in his native town, and at Anguilla plantation during the war, but was educated at Russellville and Danville, Ky., and in the Southern university of Greensboro, Ala., graduating from the last named institution, with the degree of A. M., in 1877. The same year, and also the year succeeding, he was offered the position of principal of the preparatory department in his alma mater, but preferred other occupation. He graduated from the law department of the University of Michigan at Ann Arbor with the degree of LL. B. in the class of 1880, which numbered about one hundred and seventy-five, and was licensed to practice in that state. He settled on his present plantation in 1881, which, together with other parts of the Anguilla plantation, he has been managing, until of late he has begun to devote his attention largely to the raising of fruit, about ninety acres being now given to this enterprise; and is, moreover, engaged still in planting, and is considered one of the thrifty, progressive and successful planters of this section. He has an excellent store-building under rent in Anguilla village. The village of Anguilla was laid out adjoining his plantation by his father and was named after the plantation. The word Anguilla is understood to be derived from an island of that name which was early identified with the growth of cotton, and signifies, when translated into English, an eel. Mr. Vick is a finely educated gentleman; possesses, in an eminent degree, that courtesy for which the Southern people have become famous, and better than all, is a gentleman of excellent habits and reputation. He is unmarried, and the greater portion of the time makes his home in Vicksburg, where he has hosts of acquaintances and friends. Among the other children of the founder of Vicksburg may be mentioned his eldest child, Sallie, who married Judge Lane, appointed administrator to carry out the provisions of the will, whose descendants are now living at Vicksburg and vicinity; Lucy, who married Mr. Erwin, some years speaker of the Mississippi house of representatives; Eliza, the wife of Mr. Morse, one of the first merchants of Vicksburg; Matilda, who married Dr. McCray, a leading physician in early times; and among the sons, General William Vick, a popular planter and man of affairs, and Newet Holmes Vick, somewhat noted for his fine appearance and aptitude for business, who died on his plantation in Yazoo county, Miss., at the early age of thirty-six years.

CHAPTER XXIII.

BRIEF NOTICES OF PROMINENT PERSONS, W.

NEAR Macon, Jones county, Ga., July 6, 1810, John C. Wade was born. He is a son of Micajah and Sarah (McCormack) Wade, both natives of North Carolina, the former being born in 1777, and the latter in 1785. Micajah Wade's parents were Benjamin and Amy (Jourdon) Wade, his father having been a son of Andrew Wade and they came from southern Virginia. Micajah was reared near Oxford, N. C., passing his early years on a farm, and, owing to his father's early death, received only a limited education. His father left a family of nine children—three sons and six daughters—all of whom grew to maturity. The sons' names were, Memucan, Charles and Micajah. The latter followed farming all his life. He removed to Georgia in January, 1802, stopping in Hancock county, where he was married in 1803. About 1808 he removed to Jones county, Ga., and thence to Butler county, Ala., in January, 1819. Eleven children were born to him, named: James W., Benjamin J., Martha Ellen, John C., Benjamin D., William M., Rebecca E., Charles A., Augusta, Susan and Milton. In 1839 he removed to Holmes county, Miss., where he purchased a section of land and engaged extensively in planting. He was for a number of years a magistrate, serving in that capacity both in Georgia and Alabama. His wife was a finely educated woman, and he was thoughtful and studious, and made up for his lack of educational training by the acquisition of a wide range of general information. He was an energetic, pushing, thoroughgoing man, and at the time of his death, in 1848, left a considerable property. His wife died in 1844, both being members of the Methodist church, and he was a member of the Masonic fraternity. John C. Wade was reared and educated in Butler county, Ala., the schools there affording him a fair English education. Later he studied Latin for two years and gave considerable attention to the higher mathematics. At about the age of twenty, he began to read law in the office of James La Fayette Cottrell, with whom he remained about one year. In 1834 he was married to Miss Annie E. Tomlinson, who was a native of Mississippi, being born August 31, 1814. She was a daughter of Jacob and Eleanor (Graves) Tomlinson. Of this marriage were born the following named children: Byron L. F. (deceased), John A. (deceased), Micajah T. (deceased), Eleanor (deceased), Annie T. (deceased), Zorada (the wife of A. L. West, of Copiah county), Benjamin (deceased), William A. (deceased), Leonora J. (deceased) and Edward T. (a dentist living at Wesson). Mrs. Wade died July 24, 1851, having been for many years a consistent member of the Methodist church. After his first marriage, Mr. Wade engaged in merchandising at Pine Bluff, Copiah county, Miss., in which he continued three years. Later he taught school in Copiah county, until his election to the office of sheriff in 1845, when he located in Gallatin. At the expiration of the term for which he was elected he was again chosen to the same office, but he declined a re-election and purchased a place upon which he resided, in 1849, and engaged in farming. His original plantation contained between two and three hundred acres. He has added to it until he is now the owner of eight or nine hundred acres. Cotton and corn are the principal products. In 1849 he was elected a member of the board of supervisors, of which he was president for four years. He was married, the second time, to Miss Sarah Wright, the daughter of Elijah Wright and a native of Franklin county, Miss., and born May 10, 1818. Mr. Wade and his wife are both members of the Methodist church, of which he has been recording secretary. Mr. Wade is still vigorous, though the snows of four-score years have whitened his hair and beard. His step is light and elastic and his form is erect. He attributes being spared many of the ills of old age to his having led a temperate, careful life. He retains his mental vigor perfectly, his memory being phenomenal. He is of medium hight and build, and his eyes are as clear and bright as those of a boy. He has a bright, well-trained mind, and is strong in his convictions, and is a good reasoner. In his long career he has always enjoyed the esteem and respect of his fellowmen, and he has a wide acquaintance throughout the state.

W. A. Wade was born near Fayetteville, Moore county, N. C., in 1816. His father, Mark Wade, was a native of this county, and was born May 17, 1776, and was there married to Miss Celia Wright, also a native of Moore county. When Mr. Wade was about four months old, his father moved to Clarke county, Ala., where he remained about four years and engaged in farming. From this county he removed to Copiah county, Miss., in 1821, settling about five miles north of where our subject now lives, in what was then known as the Choctaw purchase. The country was then in its natural state, the nearest settlement was ten miles distant and the nearest mill was ten miles away. The Choctaw Indians were roaming about the forests and were seen almost daily. Mr. Wade took up about one hundred and sixty acres of land, which he improved and added to its area, until at the time of his death he owned five or six hundred acres. He had five children: Penelope, Nancy, Mary, Elizabeth, and W. A., our subject. Of these, only the youngest two are living. Mrs. Mark Wade died some time in the fifties, her husband dying in 1866. They were members of the Methodist Episcopal church for many years. W. A. Wade was reared and educated in Copiah county, attending school whenever a teacher could be secured, at an old-fashioned, pioneer log schoolhouse. At the age of sixteen he became a clerk in a store at Gallatin, where he remained seven or eight years, when he was elected justice of peace, and served in that capacity about nine years, when he began farming. In 1843 he married Miss Elizabeth Carns, who was born in Copiah county in 1826. He began his career as a planter where he now resides, which was the homestead of his wife. He has added to his possessions here and is now the owner of a large tract of land, the principal productions being cotton, corn and potatoes; and stockraising, including horses, mules and cattle, also claims his attention. His plantation, four and one-half miles west of Hoylehurst and about one-half mile west of Gallatin, consists of three thousand four hundred and forty acres, about seventy-five per cent. of which is under cultivation. Mr. and Mrs. Wade have had ten children, of whom the following five are living: Mark; Nannie, the wife of J. W. Richardson, of Texas; Mary, the widow of Capt. A. B. Lowe; William and Walter. Mr. Wade is a sensible, matter-of-fact man, strong in intellect and of retentive memory, and noted for his stern and unflinching integrity. In person, he is tall, slender, smooth shaven and is erect and as vigorous as a young man.

Daniel R. Wagner, president of the Bank of Water Valley, secretary and treasurer of the Yocono mills, and member of the firm of Wagner & Leland, occupies a conspicuous position in the business circles of Yalobusha county, and is more than justly entitled to a biographical sketch in this record of the leading men of the state of Mississippi. He was born in Union county, Penn., in 1840, and is a son of Andrew and Catherine Wagner, natives of Wittenberg, Germany. They were married in their native land, and soon after sailed for America, settling near Philadelphia; thence they went to Union county, Penn., and some years later returned to Philadelphia, where they died in the year 1849. Andrew Wagner, the grandfather of Daniel R., was a native of Germany; he immigrated to the United States about the same time his son came, and located in Philadelphia, where he lived the rest of his life; his death was in 1868. He reared a family of ten children, of whom Andrew, Jr., was the seventh. Daniel R. Wagner is one of a family of eight children, all of whom lived to be grown, and six of whom are yet living. He passed the greater portion of his youth in Philadelphia, and at the age of nineteen years he came to Mississippi. He first worked in the express office of the railway company, and at the breaking out of the Civil war he enlisted in company F, Fifteenth Mississippi volunteer infantry, and went to the defense of the stars and bars. Later he was with General Chalmers' escort. When General Price was retreating through Water Valley with his army, Mr. Wagner was taken prisoner and was carried to Alton, Ill., where he made his escape, going thence to Port Hudson, La.; there he rejoined the army. He was twice wounded, once at the battle of Shiloh, while his regiment was charging a battery, and on the retreat from Nashville, Tenn. After the first wound—a gunshot wound in the ankle—he was transferred to the cavalry. After the surrender he settled in Water Valley, where he embarked in the mercantile trade on a very small scale, laying the foundation, however, of his future success and prosperity. The first firm was composed of W. H. Brister, W. B. Wagner and D. R. Wagner. Mr. Brister soon withdrew from the business, and the Wagner brothers built a fine two-story brick, which the firm now occupies. After several years of business success W. B. Wagner died, and D. R. Wagner became sole proprietor of the business, which had grown to immense proportions. He has, however, proven fully equal to the demand upon his judgment, tact and capacity. In 1887 Mr. Wagner was elected president of the Bank of Water Valley, a state institution, chartered under the laws of the state of Mississippi, with a cash capital of $35,000. Since he was chosen to fill this responsible position the business has increased from $18,000 to $100,000 per year. To him is also due the resuscitation of the cotton factory, which stood idle for several years. The value of this property to the city may easily be estimated, when it is known that seven hundred and fifty thousand pounds are used annually, and that the gross earnings amount to nearly $40,000 yearly. Mr. Wagner was united in marriage to Miss Maria G. Young, a daughter of Dr. John Young, a native of North Carolina and one of the oldest physicians of Water Valley. Mrs. Wagner was born and reared in Yalobusha county. She has had born to her six children: John H., assistant cashier of the Bank of Water Valley, is a graduate of the well-known Bingham school, of North Carolina; Jessie E., Corinne, Calista, George and Eugene. The parents are members of the Presbyterian church, and are among the most zealous and liberal supporters. Mr. Wagner takes no special interest in politics further than to exercise his right of franchise; he votes the democratic ticket. The family are highly esteemed throughout the community.

George I. Wainwright, a well-known planter and the present treasurer of Clarke county, Miss., was born June 28, 1843, at Quitman, where he now resides. He is the third in a family of eight children of John V. and Martha (Risher) Wainwright. His father, a native of Mobile, was a son of Hastings Wainwright; his mother was a Singleton. The former passed his early life in the place of his nativity and came to this county about 1834, locating at Quitman, where he married. His mother was a daughter of James Risher, one of the earliest settlers in Clarke county, who became a prominent planter during the early period of the county's history, dying in 1858, his wife having preceded him in 1832. His father was a life-long planter, dying in 1879, his widow surviving him and living at Quitman. The father was a member of the Baptist church; his mother was connected with the Methodist Episcopal denomination. They had five children: Mary J. (who died young), Louise E., George I., James J., Sarah A., Green M. George I. Wainwright passed his early life as a farmer's boy of all work—acquiring such an education as was afforded by the public schools of the county. Before the war began he enlisted in the state's service. When war was formally declared in 1861, he re-enlisted in company B, of the fourteenth Mississippi regiment as a private, but was soon promoted to the rank of a sergeant. He participated in the battles at Iuka, Corinth, Vicksburg and Franklin, Tenn., where he was wounded in the right arm by a shell. He was confined in the hospital only sixteen days, and when the army left Nashville he walked from Franklin, Tenn., to Columbus, Miss. Returning to Clarke county he found employment at farming work. It was not long before he began planting for himself, and he is now the owner of quite a tract of land, located near Quitman. He is prominent as a planter; is a useful member of the Farmers' Alliance; has long been identified with the democratic party; is a Knight of Honor and a member and trustee of the Methodist Episcopal church, of which his wife is also a member. He was elected to the office of county treasurer in 1882, and has been re-elected at each election since. In March, 1866, Mr. Wainwright took unto himself a wife in the person of Mrs. Mary E. Walker, a daughter of Robert and Margins (Ezell) Walker, who is a native of Mississippi, born in the month of October, 1844, and who has had the following children: Elyett P., Leona, John A., William H., Arthur, Charles E., Edwin and Katie (who were twins).

P. M. B. Wait has served in the capacity of sheriff of Tate county, Miss., since 1881, which fact speaks volumes as to his ability, efficiency and popularity. He has made a beau ideal public official, for, besides being faithful in the discharge of every duty, he possesses undoubted courage and pluck, attributes very necessary for his calling. He was born in Greenville, S. C., the third child born to John C. and Jane A. (McCollough) Wait, who were born, reared and married in the Palmetto state, from which they moved to Mississippi in 1850, locating first in Panola county and in 1860 in Tate county. The father was called from earth in February, 1867, but is still survived by his widow, who bore him seven children, five of whom are living. P. M. B. Wait spent his youthful days in Tate county, and from here he enlisted in the Confederate service in 1862, being then but fifteen years of age. He was a member of company G, Adams' regiment of cavalry, in which he served throughout the entire war, participating in the siege of Vicksburg, the battles of Jackson, Champion Hill, Port Hudson, Selma, Shiloh, Guntown, Bear Creek, Port Gibson, Coleman's Cross Roads, and Oxford, Miss., where he was wounded in the right shoulder by a minieball. He was mustered out of the service at Selma, Ala., May 5, 1866, after which he returned to Senatobia and engaged in planting, which he followed for some time. He was elected to his present position by the democrat party, of which he has long been a member, and, as above stated, has discharged the duties of this position in a highly satisfactory manner. He was married, in 1870, to Miss Alice Day Fuqua, a daughter of W. Y. and Martha (Brown) Fuqua. He lost his wife in 1878, after she had borne him four daughters. His second union took place in December, 1880, Mrs. Mary Stowers, widow of James Stowers, becoming his wife, her maiden name having been Matthews. This union has resulted in the birth of two sons. Mr. Wait is a member of the K. of H., the K. & L. of H., and the I. O. O. F. He and his wife belong to the Baptist church of Senatobia, and are highly esteemed in the social circles in which they move. Mr. Wait is a genial, whole-souled gentleman and has many warm friends.

Dr. James S. Walker is a gentleman who has become well known throughout the state as a practitioner of medicine and surgery, a safe and reliable banker and as a business man of sterling principles. He was born in Richmond, Ky., on the 12th of April, 1845, being the third son born to William Jason and Sarah (Stone) Walker, natives of Kentucky. The father was a merchant, planter and banker of note, and spent his entire life in Madison county, where he died in 1879, in the sixty-ninth year of his age. He lived a life of usefulness to his country and state, and his death was felt to be a great loss to the community in which he resided. His parents were William and Ann (Bates) Walker, who were of English descent, their ancestors coming from England and settling in Virginia during the colonial history of this country. The maternal grandparents, James and Katie (Harris) Stone, were also among the very early residents of Kentucky. Dr. James S. Walker was educated at Center college, Danville, Ky., and the University of Missouri, and subsequently graduated in medicine from the Jefferson Medical college of Philadelphia, Penn. He began practicing in Richmond, Ky., in 1865, but at the end of two years came to Greenville, Miss., and here was a very extensive and successful practitioner, until 1890, when he retired from practice and became president of the Merchants and Planters' Bank of Greenville. He was elected to this position in 1888, but did not take active charge until 1890. He was chief health officer of the county for about six years, but at last resigned the position, having in the meantime interested himself in planting. In addition to being a large landowner, he is a stockholder in the Delta Insurance company, of which he is also director and treasurer, and is the largest stockholder in the bank of which he is president, which has a capital of $150,-000. Although his father was a wealthy man, he was compelled to look out for himself to a considerable extent in his youth, and it is in a great measure owing to this that while he was still young he was independent in thought and action and learned to rely upon his own resources. Although he has not united himself with any church, he is a liberal contributor of his means to worthy enterprises, and is a man of strictly moral habits. Having come to Greenville in the days of its infancy, he passed through the yellow-fever scourge of this region in 1878. His first marriage was consummated in 1870, Miss Frances E. Dye, a native of Arkansas, and a daughter of William H. Dye, of Virginia, becoming his wife. To them one child was born: Frances, who is now residing at home. He was called upon to mourn the death of his wife in 1871, and in 1878 he was married a second time, to Miss Belle O. Blanton, who also died, in 1884, a native of Washington county, and a daughter of Dr. O. M. and Martha R. (Smith) Blanton, for a sketch of whom see Dr. Blanton's sketch. His second union also resulted in the birth of one child, Sarah Stone, who resides with her parents. In personal appearance Dr. Walker is prepossessing, has a fine physique, and handsome and intelligent grayish eyes. His conversational powers are excellent, and although dignified, he is very easy in his manners and inspires others with ease and confidence. He is highly cultured, and his naturally brilliant mind has been broadened and strengthened by mingling with the world and by contact with the business affairs of life. While a practitioner of the healing art his reputation was most enviable, and his services were in demand over a very large scope of territory. As a business man, his honor has been unassailable, for any transaction not straightforward is looked upon by him with contempt. Being of a modest and quiet disposition, he does not seek or desire public notoriety, but nevertheless is deeply interested in the welfare of his county and in the wellbeing of his fellow mortals. The bank of which he is the efficient president is a prosperous one, and is situated in one of the most desirable locations in the city in a handsome building on Poplar street, between Washington avenue and Main street.

Hon. Joel P. Walker, a prominent lawyer of Meridian, Miss., was born in Lauderdale county, of this state, October 3, 1840, a son of John R. and Martha A. (Felton) Walker, natives of North Carolina. His father was a member of the North Carolina legislature and some of his ancestry figured quite prominently in the Revolutionary war. John R. and his brother Joel P. came to Mississippi in the year 1836 and located in Lauderdale county, where they purchased land near Lauderdale Springs. They were extensive slaveowners and everywhere noted for being mild masters. They both died in this county. John R. Walker had twelve children—six sons and six daughters—of whom nine are still living. The eldest of them was the subject of this sketch, who was reared on a farm, and received his primary education in the public schools. In 1858 he entered Chapel Hill college, in North Carolina, and was a student there at the time of the capture of Fort Sumter by the Confederates. Being fired with a martial spirit, he immediately started for home and a few days thereafter joined the Lauderdale zouaves. He was in the fight at Leesburg, where his lieutenant was killed and succeeded him in that office, and later, through the influence of Colonel Barksdale and others, he was commissioned as captain, with a view to recruiting a new company, but the conscription act having come into effect, this design was thwarted. He next joined the Second Mississippi cavalry and was elected second lieutenant of his company. He was captured at Oxford, Miss., with the majority of his company, and taken to Alton, Ill., and thence to Camp Chase, and thence to Baltimore, Md., being kept a prisoner for four months, when he was exchanged at Petersburg. He rejoined his regiment at Spring Hill, Tenn., and was under the command of Generals Armstrong and Forrest most of the time until the close of the war, and was himself in command of a body of men detailed to him from different brigades. After the surrender he came back to Lauderdale county, and was elected a member of the first legislature that convened after the war. He served three successive sessions and was the second youngest man in that body. While a student in college at North Carolina he had read law, and after the expiration of his legislative term he resumed his study, which he pursued diligently in connection with planting, and being duly admitted to the bar began his practice. He was district attorney under appointment by Governor Alcorn, and filled this office until the expiration of his term in connection with his legal practice, seeking no other official position until, in 1883, he was elected to represent his district in the state senate for a term of four years, at the expiration of which he was re-elected for another term of the same duration, and this office he accepted only at the earnest solicitation of friends. During all of his active career he figured quite prominently and had a strong influence in local and state politics, though he has followed his profession as closely as possible and devoted his attention as little as possible to public affairs, except during his terms in office, when he filled the various high positions to which he had been chosen with credit to himself and to the entire satisfaction of his constituents. His name was strongly discussed in his district at one time as an available one for a congressional canvass. He has many warm friends throughout the state. He is prominent in Masonic circles and is a member of the Knights of Honor. He was married in 1867 to Miss Mary Johnson, who lived but eleven months after their union. April 4, 1871, he married Miss Sallie, a daughter of Dr. Joseph M. Reynolds of Hinds county, Miss. By his first marriage he had one daughter, who is the wife of E. C. Williams. He has three sons and two daughters living by his second marriage: Joseph P., Hallie C., Wallace R., Paton E. and Sallie R. The family are communicants of the Episcopal church. The law firm of Walker and Hall, of which our subject is the senior member, stand deservedly high at the Mississippi bar, and are the attorneys for the Meridian National bank of Meridian, Miss.

Hon. John A. Walker, of Walker's Bridge, Pike county, Miss., is among the substantial merchants and planters of this part of the state. He was born in Pike county, near where he now resides, May 6, 1843. His father, Hon. Elijah Walker, was a native of Georgia and was born in Lincoln county, and there he was educated and passed his early years. While yet a young man he came to Mississippi, and was married at Columbia, to Miss Hester Adams, a daughter of John Adams, one of the pioneer families. After his marriage he located in Pike county, near the present home of our subject, where he improved a plantation and reared a family, and passed a prosperous and commendatory life, which terminated in 1858, his widow surviving him until January, 1871, when she died at an advanced age. Mr. Walker was a prominent member of the Baptist church, with which his wife was also long identified. They were consistent Christian people, whose lives were in accordance with their professions. Mr. Walker was for a number of years a justice of the peace, and filled other local positions creditably to himself and to the satisfaction of his fellow-citizens. John A. Walker is the youngest son of a family of two sons and three daughters, the fourth child in the order of nativity, born to his parents. His brother, Andrew Walker, was a soldier in the Sixteenth Mississippi infantry, and died near Carterville in 1861, early in the Civil war. Our subject spent his youth in his native county, and received his primary education in the public schools near his home. In 1861 he enlisted in the Quitman guards of the Sixteenth Mississippi regiment, with which he served in the army of Virginia under Generals Lee and Jackson, participating in a number of engagements, among which were those at Cross Keys and Winchester, Va., the seven days' fight around Richmond, and the second battle of Bull Run. In the last named engagement he received a gunshot wound through the leg, which disabled him from further service for six months, during which time he was in the hospital. After his recovery he returned to his regiment, and participated in the battles of Fredericksburg, Antietam, Gettysburg, the battle of the Wilderness, Spottsylvania Courthouse, Cold Harbor, and the siege of Petersburg. He was captured by the Federals at Weldon railroad, and held a prisoner at Point Lookout, Md., until the close of the war, when he was paroled. While a prisoner, Mr. Walker attended a private school taught in the prison by Professor Morgan, of South Carolina, who was also a prisoner of war. Mr. Walker had the advantage of this fine educational opportunity for about five months before the surrender. After the close of hostilities he returned to his home in Pike county, and engaged in planting. In 1872 Mr. Walker built a store, and engaged in merchandising at his present location. He embarked in this trade in a small way, and his progress has been such that he has since not only had to frequently increase his stock, but also to build additions to his place of business. His sales now reach $75,000 annually. As a matter of historical interest it may be stated that he was the first one engaged in merchandising at this point. A business man of superior ability and a skillful manager of affairs, Mr. Walker has acquired a fine property, and now ranks among the wealthy men of Pike county. He has ever taken an active interest in politics, and has always supported the principles and candidates of the democratic party. He has held several local offices, having served as a magistrate and as a member of the board of supervisors for eight consecutive years and as a delegate to the county and state conventions, and to him is given the honor of having cast for Pike county the vote for Governor Stone. At this time, August 8, 1891, Mr. Walker is a candidate for representative of Pike county in the lower house of the legislature. He is a man of ability and unquestioned honor, and if elected to represent the county, will do so with dignity and credit. Mr. Walker was married in Pike county, in 1866, to Miss Mollie McGehee, daughter of S. C. McGehee, a prominent and influential man and a member of one of the leading families of Mississippi. He is an active member of the Masonic order and of the K. of P., in both of which he has been connected officially.

Benjamin J. Walker was born in Edgefield district, S. C., in 1790, and was married in Wayne county, Miss., in 1818, to Catherine Huston, who was born in the state of Kentucky in 1800. They had born to them eleven children, of whom Henry Walker, the subject of this biographical notice, is the eldest. They removed to Simpson county, Miss., in 1826, and thence, in 1834, to Newton county, Miss., where they were among the earliest settlers. The father engaged in farming, in which he was more than ordinarily successful. He and his wife were members of the Baptist church, to which they contributed liberally. Henry Walker received a common-school education; he was born in 1820, and in the year 1841 he engaged in agricultural pursuits. In 1847 he was united in marriage to Miss D. Evans, a daughter of Henry Evans, a prominent farmer of the community. Eleven children were born of this marriage, eight of whom are living: Elizabeth (wife of William Pierce), Frances C. (wife of Thomas Peoples), Watson F., Mary J. (wife of J. Chapman), H. B., Archie E., William E. and Jo E. In 1862 Mr. Walker responded to the call for men, and enlisted in Captain Carleton's company for six months; at the end of that time he enlisted in Captain Grimes' cavalry company, Ninth Mississippi. He was captured at Savannah, Ga., December 21, 1864, and after his release he returned home and turned his attention to farming. He owns about twelve hundred acres of land, the cultivation of which he superintends, and runs a cottongin and a gristmill. He is a man of unusual business qualifications, and has been prosperous in all his undertakings. He is a member of the Masonic fraternity, and the family belong to the Baptist church. Mr. Walker is a liberal supporter of all worthy enterprises, and is a highly respected member of the community in which he lives.

Capt. Nelson Simmons Walker is a name that is well and favorably known through Claiborne and adjoining counties, and it may with truth be said that he inherits many of the characteristics for which the natives of the Empire state have become famous throughout the length and breadth of America—enlighted and progressive views, energy, honesty and courage. He was born in Herkimer county, N. Y., August 21, 1835, the fourth of six children whose names are as follows: Mary (deceased), became the wife of a Mr. Murray, a planter; Dwight B. was a successful business man of West Winfield, N. Y., and died at the age of forty-five years; George F. is a prosperous merchant of Melbourne, Australia (he first emigrated to that distant land in 1850; was there married and retured to America, after which he again returned to Australia, and is there now living); Edward Everett resides at Grand Rapids, Mich., where he is engaged in merchandising; Julia is the wife of Horace Kinney, of Saginaw, Mich., and Nelson Simmons. The father of these children, Ira Walker, was born in York state in 1798, and as a merchant amassed quite a fortune. His wife, Julia (Foster) Walker, was also born in that state, and both were educated in the public schools, and throughout their lives were patrons of education. Their deaths occurred March 7, 1873, and 1881, respectively. Nelson Simmons Walker received his early educational training in the common schools of New York, after which he entered the West Winfield academy of Herkimer county, and took a full English and business course of instruction, which admirably fitted him for the practical life he has led. He finished his schooling in

1854, and then commenced the voyage of life for himself at the age of nineteen years as a salesman in a general store without any capital whatever, so far as money was concerned. He, however, possessed a stout heart, willing hands and a determination to succeed, and has kept steadily to this determination until he is now one of the prosperous men of the county in which he resides. He remained in business until the opening of the Civil war, when he enlisted as a private in a Mississippi regiment, and was promoted through the various stages of third lieutenant, second lieutenant and was made captain of company E, after the second battle of Manassas, his commission coming direct from the hand of the Southerner's ideal of a chieftain, Gen. Robert E. Lee, a man whose fame, honor, bravery, integrity and true worth will ever be perpetuated in song and story. Mr. Walker took an active part in the following battles: All the engagements around Yorktown, Williamsburg, second Manassas, Seven Pines, seven days' engagement around Richmond, Chancellorsville, Fredericksburg, Mine Run and the three days' engagement at Gettysburg. Mr. Walker was in thirty-two engagements during the war. He was wounded in the left leg at the battle of second Manassas, which confined him about one month in the hospital. The retreat from Pennsylvania was one continuous fight, and during this time he was in the siege of Petersburg, Burgess Mill and the sieges of Forts Baldwin and Gregg. He surrendered with Lee at Appomattox Courthouse, and afterward went to Washington, D. C., via City Point, thence to New York, and from there to New Orleans. While they were in Washington, on account of the intense excitement over the death of President Lincoln, the Southern troops that had surrendered and been paroled were arrested and placed in prison at Alexandria, where they were confined for thirty days. They were then released, owing to a letter that was sent privately to General Grant, and in charge of an officer came to New Orleans.

Mr. Walker once more commenced at the bottom of the ladder as a salesman, but was soon after elected to the position of treasurer of Claiborne county, and held the position from 1867 until Governor Ames compelled him to evacuate the position to make room for a republican. In 1875 he was chosen clerk of the circuit court, but after he had ably filled this position for two years, J. P. Briscoe, then chancery clerk, was killed, and he was appointed to fill the unexpired term, making him the incumbent of two important county offices at one time. In 1878, the sheriff, Dr. Charles E. Buck, was killed and he was succeeded by Mr. Heslip, who died one month later, upon which Mr. Walker was appointed to fill the vacancy by Governor Stone, a position he has filled by re-election up to the present time, which fact speaks in an eloquent manner as to his efficiency, courage and popularity. November 26, 1867, he was married at Port Gibson, Miss., to Miss Frances Kennard, the ceremony being solemnized by Rev. J. A. B. Jones. Mrs. Walker was born October 3, 1844, and received her education in the Port Gibson Female academy, from which she graduated in June, 1861. She possessed great natural ability, stood remarkably high in her classes and would have been selected as valedictorian of her classes, but, on account of her youth, her parents objected. Her parents, Joseph L. Kennard and Araminta B. (Palmer) Kennard, were born January 22, 1815, and April 11, 1818, in Queen Anne and Kent counties, Md., respectively. The latter was a very finely educated lady, and received her scholastic training in Baltimore, Md. Her marriage with Mr. Kennard took place at Cincinnati, Ohio, November 28, 1837, their license being obtained from William Henry Harrison (the grandfather of President Benjamin Harrison), who at that time was a justice of the peace. Their marriage resulted in the birth of seven sons and seven daughters. Mr. and Mrs. Walker have been blessed in the birth of four children: Nettie K. is the wife of W. B. Hopkins, of Columbus, Miss., is an exceptionally fine musician and is well educated;

E. F. Lowe M.D.

Fannie Belle died at the age of twenty-two months, Florence died at the age of six weeks, and Nelson, who is a bright little lad of seven years. Mrs. Walker is an ardent member of the St. James' Episcopal church at Port Gibson, and she and her husband are very charitable, contributing liberally to all worthy enterprises.

Mr. Walker is a member of the A. F. & A. M., being worshipful master of Washington lodge No. 3, having ably filled all the subordinate offices of his lodge. He is a member of Clinton chapter No. 2, of which he has been high priest twice, has held all the official positions of Port Gibson council No. 36, and was one of the charter members of the Cœur de Lion commandery No. 13, having been several times eminent commander of the same. He was elected grand treasurer of the grand commandery of the state of Mississippi, a position he held for several years, and in 1888 was elected grand commander of the grand commandery of the state of Mississippi for one year, and at present is a member of all the above named lodges. He is also a member of Franklin lodge No. 5, of the I. O. O. F. of Port Gibson, having filled all the chairs of his lodge, and at the present time is its treasurer. He belongs to the K. of H., the K. of P. and the A. L. of H. He is an earnest worker in the Episcopal church, and since the organization of the Sunday-school in 1868, he has been its superintendent. It opened with an attendance of three, but now has on an average sixty members. He is a director of the Port Gibson bank, the Port Gibson Brick company, and in every respect is a public-spirited man, and an honored, useful and influential citizen. He is in easy circumstances, financially, and has an income sufficiently ample for all necessary expenses. During the negro insurrection in 1875, Mr. Walker displayed much coolness and courage in quelling the turbulent spirits of the negroes and whites, and his deliberation and knowledge of human nature were instrumental in saving the lives of many.

Dr. W. E. Walker, a successful dentist of Bay St. Louis, was born in New Orleans, La., in 1868, and is a son of Dr. J. R. Walker, deceased. The father was born in Tompkins county, N. Y., August 7, 1830, a descendant of ancestors distinguished for intelligence, learning and integrity. In 1834 the family removed to Michigan, where the son acquired the rudiments of a good education. His seventeenth year he spent in teaching and study in Illinois. There he also began the study of dentistry, which he continued the following year at Albion, Mich., while he was attending the academy at that place. The next year he was under Dr. Foster, of Jackson, Mich., who was one of the best dentists of that day. In order to perfect himself further in his profession, he went to the Eastern cities, where he made the acquaintance of the finest operators, and familiarized himself with their latest improvements and discoveries. He then resumed his literary studies at Antioch college, Ohio, and in the year 1854 went to Texas, where for four years he enjoyed a lucrative practice. At the outbreak of the Civil war he enlisted in the Confederate cause. He served until the end of the conflict, gaining the reputation of a cool, daring and reliable scout. After the surrender of General Lee he returned to New Orleans, where he had taken up his residence in 1858. In May, 1861, he was married to Miss Camille Viavant, whose death occurred a few months later. August 7, 1865, he was united in marriage to Miss Jeanie Mort, a woman of refinement and education, who was born of English parents. She is a native of the state of New York, but, before the war, came South as a governess. She has made some contributions to literature that show much study and natural ability. She is the author of Captain Fry, the Cuban Martyr, and Letters from a Mother to a Mother, on the formation, growth and care of children's teeth. She has contributed to and edited departments in various newspapers and scientific and dental journals, being well and favorably known to the dental profession as Mrs. M. W. J. She is an honorary member of the Southern Dental association and of the State Dental societies of Georgia, Alabama and Mississippi. Five children were born to the Doctor and his wife: Lizzie A., Dr. W. E., Flora C. (deceased), Katie R. and J. Mort. In 1866 Dr. J. R. Walker was elected a fellow of the New Orleans academy of science; in 1870 he became a member of the American Association for the Advancement of Science, and in 1875 a fellow of the same body. In 1857 he was made a member of the Mississippi Valley Dental association, and in 1870-71 he was vice president of the American Dental association. In 1875 he was president of the Southern Dental association. He was one of the regents of the Maryland Dental college from the foundation of that institution. In 1876 he was elected professor of operative and dental surgery in the New Orleans Dental college. It will thus be seen that the position he held, both in scientific and professional circles, was no inconsiderable one, and that his ability and attainments were highly esteemed. In 1866 he became a member of Merchants' lodge, I. O. O. F., and soon after joined Hobah encampment, passing rapidly through the official chairs of the order to that of grand patriarch of the state of Louisiana, in 1871. Closely devoted to his profession, science and literature, he took but little interest in politics, although he was a bitter enemy to fraud and corruption. He was liberal in his religious views, courteous and genial in his manner, and a general favorite with all whom he met. Dr. Walker died June 22, 1887. Dr. W. E. Walker was educated in the various schools of New Orleans, and, while a youth, began the study of dentistry. He entered the Baltimore college of dental surgery, and was graduated from this institution in 1889, receiving the degree of D. D. S., receiving also a handsome gold medal. He began his practice at Bay St. Louis, Miss., and in a short time has built up a patronage almost phenomenal. He also has an office at Pass Christian, and is always closely engaged. At the annual meeting in 1891 he joined the Mississippi State Dental association, and was elected secretary of that body. He is a young man of unusual intelligence, and thoroughly understands his business. While a student in the dental college he gave some time to the study of the science of medicine, but did not complete the course. Dr. Walker is unmarried.

William Henry Wall, merchant, Sardis, Miss., was born near Lynchburg, Va., on the 29th of June, 1838, and was the eldest of five children born to Charles B. and Henrie A. (Davies) Wall, natives also of the Old Dominion. The father was a merchant by occupation, removed to Iowa in 1840, and there his death occurred in 1854. He was a successful business man, never failed, and never ran in debt. William Henry Wall remained in Iowa until eighteen years of age and then received an appointment to the Naval academy at Annapolis, Md., and remained there two years. During this service he made one cruise at sea, going to the Azore islands on the United States sloop of war, Preble. At the end of two years and while on leave he resigned his position, came South, and located in Sardis, Miss., in 1859. When the war broke out Mr. Wall enlisted in the Sardis Blues and was made first lieutenant of his company. On reaching Corinth the company was formed into the Twelfth Mississippi regiment of volunteers under Colonel Griffith and started to the first battle of Manassas, but arrived too late to participate in it. Mr. Wall was then made adjutant and after serving in that capacity for twelve months was sent as adjutant of Hughes' cavalry regiment to Port Hudson, La., to fortify that point. One month later he was appointed lieutenant in the Confederate States navy and ordered to report at Savannah, Ga., for duty on board the gunboat, Atlanta. One month later he was detached from the boat and ordered to report for duty at Charleston, S. C., on board the Confederate States ironclad Chicora, where he remained for two years, participating in all the bombardments of that place. He was then ordered to Richmond, Va., to take command of the Confederate States gunboat Drewry, and participated in all the engagements there until his vessel was destroyed by the enemy's battery. Then he and Capt. Charles W. Read were ordered to go to Shreveport, La., to take charge of the Confederate States gunboat Webb, and run her down Red river, past New Orleans to sea, to be used as a privateer. In this daring move they went twenty-seven miles below New Orleans before they were captured. They set the vessel on fire and then surrendered. In that exceedingly dangerous trip, when the enemy had complete control of the Mississippi river and their gunboats were stationed all along its banks, every ten or fifteen miles, not once were they fired upon by the enemy until they reached New Orleans. This expedition was regarded as one of the most daring of blockade running of the war. After being captured he was taken as a prisoner of war to Fort Warren in Boston harbor, and when General Kirby Smith surrendered he took the oath of allegiance and came home. In 1869 he was united in marriage to Miss Adelle Coleman, a native of Panola county, Miss., and a daughter of Edwin and Amanda (Pope) Coleman, natives of Kentucky. The six children born to this union are named in the order of their births as follows: Adelle B., Nettie C., William D., Charles E., Kate G. and Pope C. Miss Nettie is quite an artist and is now teaching art and shorthand in Lexington, Miss. Miss Adelle makes music a specialty and has taught music for some time. Mr. Wall has given all his children good educational advantages. Since the war Mr. Wall has been engaged in merchandising and was for twelve years cashier of the Bank of Sardis. He is now its vice president. At the present time he is in the hardware and furniture business in Sardis. He has a handsome residence in Sardis, is a stockholder in the Sardis bank and in the American Building and Loan Association of Memphis, in which he is also a director. Mr. Wall and family are members of the Methodist church and he is steward in the same. He is also a school director. He has repeatedly represented the state of Mississippi in the supreme lodge of the Knights of Honor. He is also a Mason, an Odd Fellow, a member of the American Legion of Honor and the Knights and Ladies of Honor. He is one of the most energetic, enterprising men in the county.

Of the many prominent citizens of Leake county, Miss., who owe their nativity to the Palmetto state, stands the name of R. L. Wallace, circuit clerk, Carthage, Miss., who was born in Chester district on the 14th of June, 1831. His father, W. L. Wallace, was a native of the same state and district, born in 1783, and was of Scotch descent. The latter grew to manhood and was educated in Chesterville and was a soldier in the War of 1812. He was married in South Carolina to Miss Elizabeth Love, who was a native of that state, born in York district. After his marriage Mr. Wallace moved to Alabama, settled in Perry county in 1833 and there he resided a number of years. In 1846 he moved to Mississippi, settled in Leake county, engaged in farming and there his death occurred in 1857. His wife received her final summons in 1868. The paternal grandfather was a native of the Keystone state, but at an early day emigrated to South Carolina. Of the six sons and one daughter born to Mr. and Mrs. Wallace only two now survive, viz.: R. L. and Thomas A. R. L. was the eldest of this family, grew to manhood and received his education in Leake county, where he has carried on farming ever since. In 1871 he was elected clerk of the circuit court of Leake county for four years, was re-elected at the expiration of his term, and has now served for twenty consecutive years in that capacity. He has the enviable and merited reputation of being the best circuit clerk in Mississippi, and is very popular with the people of the county. He attends strictly to the duties of his office, is courteous, social and pleasant to all, is the most accommodating of men, and has a host of warm friends. He was married in this county in November, 1853, to Miss Mary Hall, a native of South Carolina, where she was reared and educated, and the fruits of this union were six children, viz.: Irene, wife of J. A. Boyd of Leake county;

Sarah F., wife of E. C. Angling; R. H., married; N. F., also married; Minnie F., wife of L. L. Wallace, and Mary A., a young lady. Mrs. Wallace, who was a devoted and consistent member of the Methodist church, died in May, 1886. Mr. Wallace is a Royal Arch Mason, and has filled different positions in that organization. He owns a good farm on Pearl river, near Carthage, and has followed agricultural pursuits for some time.

Eric William Wallin is one of the oldest settlers of Vicksburg, Miss., and is now retired from active business. He was born in Stockholm, Sweden, in 1822, and was educated in that country. He came to America in 1839, and having learned the trade of a machinist in his native land, he began working in the shops in New York city, but was afterward with the noted inventor, Captain Ericsson, and worked on some of his patents. In 1840 he enlisted in the United States navy on the ship North Carolina, but three years later came to Vicksburg. The following year he returned to Stockholm on a visit, and remained there a year and then returned to Vicksburg, and since that time has made a permanent settlement here, and has followed various occupations, in which he has been fairly successful. He has held various positions of trust and responsibility, and was elected to the honorable position of mayor of Vicksburg in the year of 1866. This was the first election held after the reconstruction of the state, and the majority he received over his competitors gave abundant proof of his great popularity. In 1866, while holding the position of mayor, he introduced the first steam fire engine in the city, which the citizens called the E. W. Wallin, out of compliment to his untiring energy for the success of Vicksburg. He has been most active in advancing the interests of the city, and is one of her most substantial, progressive and respected citizens. During the war he was a city officer, and was not in the army. During the siege of Vicksburg many balls passed through his residence, evidences of which are still apparent. He was married in 1848, and his wife, Mrs. Barbara Wallin, noted for her Christian charity, died on the 15th of January, 1891, at the advanced age of sixty-six years. He has a beautiful Southern home in the northeastern part of the city called Springfield, where he resides with his daughter, Mrs. Wilhelmina M. Halpin. His other children have long since gone to the silent city of the dead. His son Robert Henry died in 1857, Maria Regina died in 1863, and his son Gustave William died in 1873.

Harvey W. Walter. In all human existence there is no blending of virtues so rare and admired as those which characterize the true philanthrophist, which eliminate all idea of self from human actions, and devote an individual to the service and welfare of his fellow-creatures. Such was the character of the Savior of mankind, and one may only look for such along the path in which He trod, among those who, like the subject of this sketch, have imbibed His spirit, and followed His teachings which enjoin "that greater love than this has no man, to lay down his life for his friends." Harvey W. Walter was born in Fairfield county, Ohio, on the 21st of May, 1819, while his parents, who were natives of Virginia, were temporarily residing in that state, and at an early age removed with them to Kalamazoo, Mich., where they settled and lived to a venerable age. Both father and mother were noted and highly respected for their noble and generous qualities, and it was from this source that Mr. Walter imbibed in his earliest youth that noble spirit which adorned his character and stamped his life upon the pages of virtue and of fame. During his early years his father enjoyed the possession of wealth and afforded his son every advantage, but having suddenly lost the greater portion of his property by an unfortunate investment he could no longer render him assistance. At the tender age of fourteen years young Walter found his fate depending upon his own resources, but buoyed up by his genius and ambition, and supported by the staff of a virtuous resolution, he stepped out upon the journey of life, and while no glittering prospects charmed his view, his destiny was hallowed with the devout benisons of a father's blessing, and the guerdon of a mother's prayers. These were his only patrimony. With them he went forth, and with his energy and determination soon cleared away the untoward circumstances that clustered along his youthful pathway. He alternately taught and attended school, and by this means obtained a collegiate education. Having completed his course in college, and seeking for a propitious field for his future labors, he turned his attention toward the South, as if impelled by those warm and generous feelings which sought the accord and mutuality always vouchsafed by that people with whom his lot was destined to be cast. About 1838 he joined the throng of emigrants who were pressing into the beautiful country which had recently been acquired from the Indians in north Mississippi, and having determined upon the profession of law, he taught school two years at Salem, in Tippah county, as a means of support while preparing for the bar. In 1840 he obtained his license and located in Holly Springs, where every prospect which energy, integrity and latent will could engender in a fruitful field smiled immediately upon his career. He soon took his position in the front rank of his profession, and achieved pre-eminence at a bar which was scarcely excelled by any in the South. His remarkable talents and indomitable energy were kindled and fueled by the able competition amid which he began his forensic career, and the blaze of his eminence continued in the ascendant. His ability extended in every direction of usefulness, and his name became associated with every enterprise for the advancement of the interests of his country, and for the promotion of the honor and welfare of Mississippi. It was mainly through his exertions that the Mississippi Central (now Illinois Central) railroad was projected and pushed to completion, an enterprise which he foresaw to be necessary to the development of his section of the state, and to the accomplishment of which he devoted his energy and means liberally and unweariedly.

Mr. Walter was an ardent friend to the interest of education. He took great pride in the prospects of the University of Mississippi, and was, at the time of his death, one of its trustees. Refined and elevated in his sentiments, temperate in his habits, lofty in his aspirations, he was a devoted Christian, and the patron of every moral and religious promotion. He was long a conspicuous member of the Masonic fraternity, and after having presided over its various subordinate bodies, was, in 1844, made grand master of the state lodge. He was a Mason, not only in the mere superficialities of the order, but in heart, in practice and in all the walks of life. Mr. Walter was intensely Southern in his principles, yet, as a whig, he opposed the doctrines of secession until he considered that measure an inexorable alternative to the dishonor and political degradation of his people, and then he was ready, as he was in every thing that engaged his sympathies, to sacrifice whatever its promotion might demand. No sooner had the tocsin of war sounded than he girded himself for the struggle, and as lieutenant of a company of infantry he responded to the first call of his state for troops in 1861. He was ordered to Pensacola, and soon after reaching there was transferred to the staff of General Bragg as judge advocate, serving in that position with distinguished efficiency until the close of the war. Colonel Walter accepted the conclusion of the conflict with the same conscientious and abiding faith with which he had drawn his sword, and returning to Holly Springs he resumed the practice of his profession, counseled a conservative and dignified policy, and devoted himself to the amelioration of the rigorous circumstances of his people. As a lawyer he was well read and profound. His comprehension was ready and acute; the succession of his thoughts was logical, and his argumentative powers clear, vigorous and incisive. The versatility of his legal genius was remarkable, and he seemed to be equally qualified for eminence in either branch of the profession. His high sense of duty and devotion to the interests of his clients engaged at all occasions his utmost powers. The distinguished jurist, Hon. A. M. Clayton, speaking of Colonel Walter, said: "He possessed to an eminent degree the two most requisite characteristics of a lawyer, patience and perseverance. He saw his end clearly, and never grew tired in pursuing it. He never saw but one side of a case, and that was his own. He overlooked all obstacles that stood in his way, and drove on to the conclusions regardless of their presence, and if not always successful, he always presented the strongest and most favorable view of the case." His logical learning and powers of analysis are amply exhibited in his briefs in the reports of the supreme court. These are too well known to the profession to require more than a passing reference. His knowledge was ever at his command, and he was never at a loss for replication or retort. His stores of preceding were comprehensive, and which the quickness and alertness of his memory and mental operations enabled him to call to his support in every emergency. He was a clear reasoner, an eloquent speaker, and possessed a mesmeric influence over the minds of juries. As a citizen, Colonel Walter had no superior in his sphere of neighborly usefulness. While he was conspicuous in every public assembly, he was the center of the social circle and the welcomed and honored guest of every private entertainment. Generous and magnanimous in principle, he was courteous and affable to all classes, and his opinion was deemed the criterion of propriety and expediency. But the crowning gem in his chaplet of exalted virtues was the jewel of charity, which sparkled more brilliantly than that which blazed in Diomede's crest or flamed in the imagination of the alchemist. He was at all times noted as a man of good deeds, but it was when that besom of death with its ministers of grief and pain swept over his devoted town in 1878 that this divine quality of his nature was exemplified with more than mortal radiance. When the neighboring town of Grenada had fallen into the arms of the inexorable fiend, and its shrieks reached the gates of Holly Springs, they were flung wide open to its flying, homeless people, and Colonel Walter was mainly the author of the deed. He opposed all quarantine regulations, and opened his heart, his hands and his house to the terror-stricken refugees, and when the fatal malady, lurking in the garments of the strangers, reached forth and seized upon his own people, he counseled them all to flee for their lives, but said: "As for me and my sons, we can not go; we must fight this foe; we must succor our people and administer to the sick, the dying and the dead."

Col. Walter's family was a remarkably interesting one. He was married in 1849 to Miss Fredonia M. Brown, daughter of Col. James Brown, of Oxford, a lady of rare accomplishments and of an exceedingly amiable character. From this marriage were born ten children, nine of whom lived until the visitation of the scourge. He had promptly, at the outbreak of the fever, sent his family away except his three sons, who partook of the heroic spirit of their father and shared his glorious death. While in the midst of his charitable labors Colonel Walter was himself stricken down, on the 19th day of September, 1878, and his three sons followed him within the same week. The noble young men had but recently graduated with distinction at the state university, and Frank was a law partner with his father. He and Jimmie, who was acting as postmaster, died on the same day, the latter praying that his life might be spared for the sake of his mother and little sisters. Avent, who passed away a few days before, died rejoicing at the thought of meeting his mother, his father, his brothers and sisters in heaven. The pious death of this young man would furnish a theme for a sermon that would echo against the walls of eternity. Thus perished this noble family while endeavoring to ward from others the shafts more fatal than the arrows of Apollo sent into the Grecian camps on the plains of Troy. Amid all these scenes of terror, when the eyes of heaven seemed averted from the doomed people, Colonel Walter still bowed to the will of his Maker. On one occasion a young wife who had just lost her husband, and who now saw other members of her family dying, half crazed with grief, wandered through the streets in desperation at her calamities. Colonel Walter met her and endeavored to soothe and comfort her agonizing distress, but in the bitterness of her grief she cried out against the justice of God. His eloquent and only reply was, "Though he slay me, yet will I trust him." No nobler martyrdom was ever recorded upon the pages of history, or hallowed the memory of mortal than that which crowned the death of this good man and his three noble and promising sons, but they have their reward. Frank C. Walter was born October 23, 1854, and died of the fever on the 26th of September, 1878. He was among the most prominent of those kind, true, noble-hearted ones who sacrificed their lives during the epidemic of Holly Springs in endeavoring to alleviate the sufferings of those who had been stricken down with the plague. In the fall of 1871 he entered the sophomore class at the University of Mississippi, and owing to his firmness and great decision of character, his purity of thought and his high sense of honor, his integrity and liberality of heart, he soon became the favorite of all, both professors and students, and being possessed of an extraordinary ability, as well as an ambitious energy, a discriminating mind and the power of concentrating thought, he graduated in the summer of 1874 in two distinct courses, the A. B. and B. S., in the former with the third honor and in the latter with the second. Shortly after his return home he commenced the study of law, under his father, and soon after was admitted to the bar in Holly Springs, his native place. As a young attorney he managed his cases with wonderful ability, and his argument of them was not only forcible but also analytical and logical. His manners toward all, whatever may have been their station in life, were kind, polite and refined. His social nature was of a remarkable development, and he delighted in making himself pleasant to all around him. Had he lived, he was destined to be a leader among men. When refugees from the yellow fever came to Holly Springs and were taken sick by that direst of diseases, he was one of the first to offer his services to nurse them. After the fever broke out in his own city, and the people were fleeing from its poisoned atmosphere in which death had planted its destroying germ, he was asked if he was not going to leave also. His reply was: "No, let my epitaph be duty." How grand, how sublime, how noble is the sentiment! With the unswerving energy of a Titan he adhered to his motto, ministering to the unfortunate sick and afflicted, burying the dead and cheering those who were mourning for loved ones, until at last, he too, after having buried his father and brother, was seized by death and ushered into eternity.

Edward Cary Walthall, United States senator from Mississippi, was born at Richmond, Va., April 4, 1831. He received his education at Holly Springs, Miss., studied law in that city, and at the age of twenty-one years was admitted to the bar of the state. Establishing himself at Coffeeville, his talents soon won recognition, and in 1856 he was elected attorney for the tenth judicial district of the state. Three years after he was reëlected, but in less than two years resigned the office to take part in defending the property of the Southern people against the fanaticism of a powerful minority in the North. In 1861 he entered the Fifteenth Mississippi infantry as lieutenant, and made such a brilliant record that promotion followed promotion in quick succession. He was a lieutenant-colonel in 1862, and commanded the Fifteenth Mississippi infantry at Fishing Creek, Ky., January 19, that year. Immediately after he was commissioned colonel of the Twenty-ninth Mississippi infantry, and on December 13, 1862, was raised to the rank of brigadier-general. His services in the field won general recognition throughout the Confederacy, and his name was not unknown among the legions of the North. Prompt in war as genial in peace, he won the hearts of the Southern people, and drove those of the North to admire his courage and his methods. On June 6, 1864, he was promoted major-general in the western army, and at Missionary Ridge undertook the forlorn hope of holding the divide against the Federal mass of eighty thousand men, until the defeated army was beyond pursuit. From this dangerous position he led his brigade in perfect order, that night of October 25, 1863, and next day was hailed as the savior of the western army. Late in the afternoon of that terrible day three divisions of General Thomas' army, led by Phil. Sheridan, attacked the Confederate center and right on this ridge, broke through the Confederate lines, and would have captured or killed the defeated army of Hood had not Walthall's brigade interposed and checked the pursuit until night brought relief. This strategic movement rescued a great army for future work in 1864, when Hood re-occupied Tennessee and fought the terrific fight at Franklin. After the defeat of Hood there, General Walthall played almost a similar part to that at Missionary Ridge, for, forming the rear guard of that army, he protected it against the attacks of the victors until a secure position was reached. These are only a few instances of the brilliant and valuable services rendered by him in the field.

In 1868 he was delegate at large to the national democratic convention. In January, 1871, he established himself at Grenada as a member of the bar, and won high honors in the profession for the ensuing sixteen years. In 1876 he was chosen delegate at large to the democratic national convention; again in 1880 and again in 1884. On the resignation of United States Senator Lamar to accept the position of secretary of the interior, in 1885, General Walthall was appointed to fill the vacancy in the United States senate by Governor Lowry, on petition of the people, and in January, 1886, the Mississippi legislature elected him United States senator, and in January, 1888, he was elected senator for the term ending in 1895, without a dissenting vote. The share taken by the senator in defeating the sectional bill, commonly termed the force bill, is recorded by the Washington (D. C.) *Post* in the following language:

The speech of Mr. Walthall, of Mississippi, against the Federal elections bill, delivered in the senate on December 19, 1890, was a clear, logical and dispassionate presentation of the case from a Southern standpoint. As a citizen of a state where, perhaps, to use his own language, "the heaviest calamities would fall" in case the proposed legislation is enacted into law, his remarks commanded close attention, and the keenest partisan scrutiny will fail to detect in them, or even between their lines, a single thought or sentiment that does not bear the impress of sincere and patriotic conviction, even though it fail to agree in all respects with his conclusions. His appeal to the senate and argument to the country were characterized by no less candor than force, and an earnest conservatism, in the presence of which sectional prejudice must confess itself practically disarmed. Mr. Walthall makes no concealment of the fact that in times past illegal acts have been committed in connection with elections, nor does he claim that even now the elections in Mississippi are wholly free from "reprehensible practices and lawless methods," but he does insist, with a strenuousness borne out by the record, that the tendency is "away from violence, and toward tolerance and justice." As evidence in support of this position, he produces the statement of Governor Lowry to the effect that during the past five years not a single instance is found in any of the seventy-four counties of the state, where anybody has been killed or injured on account of elections or politics. The senator's main point is that under circumstances like these, with the reasons for Federal interference fast disappearing, if they ever existed, it would be the hight of unwisdom to resort to measures altogether at war with the situation and calculated to retard instead of advancing it. Nothing, he holds, can justify an arbitrary and dangerous interruption of the relations which now exist between the whites and blacks in the Southern section of the Union, nor can the difficulties of the race problem be worked out by iron rules.

The Machiavellian proposition to enact laws which would crush out the Caucasian race in the Southern states owes its defeat largely to the reasoning powers of Senator Walthall and his fellow-senator from Mississippi. The friends they made, in and out of congress, aided them in the battle, and won for General Walthall, among his own people, the title, the Corinthian Column, and for Senator George, the Gothic Pillar. The same sincerity, earnestness, promptness and ability which in 1863 and 1864 distinguished General Walthall, were not wanting in this emergency; for as he saved an army then, he saved half a nation now from the horror of legalized terrorism.

In October, 1891, when it was rumored that General Walthall would retire from the senate, a distinguished Mississippian, high in the official circle of the United States, paid the following tribute to him:

Mississippi ought not to tolerate for a moment the idea of acquiescing in the retirement of Senator Walthall. Of all the splendid men that she has ever presented to the nation, General Walthall is the one beyond all competition in moral purity, strength of mind, heroism of soul, and commanding influence among men. I know that the expression of my admiration for General Walthall has been ascribed to the enthusiasm of friendship. But no. My friendship is only the effect, not the cause, of my estimate of his qualities of mind and heart. I can tell you in this private letter my sober opinion, that all that General Walthall lacks of being the first man in America is the highest official station in America. You know this is not said for political effect. I heard Gen. Joseph E. Johnston once say, "If the Confederate war had lasted two years longer General Walthall would have risen to the command of all the Confederate armies." This remark was elicited by one of my own in his presence, when I was asked who, among all the distinguished men, I had known, excelled in strength of mind and moral force of character, I replied that, "in vigor of intellect, simplicity of character, and unwavering moral rectitude, I regarded General Walthall as the greatest man I ever knew." General Johnston then said, "I am not surprised to hear you say that," adding what I have quoted above.

This is simply the echo of Mississippi. The same sentiment prevails wherever his record is known and it is acknowledged by his political opponents in congress.

For twenty years Edwin Smith Walton, Sardis, has been engaged in the insurance business in Panola county, Miss., and his principal business at the present time is adjusting fire losses for some of the best companies of the world. His fine business acumen has peculiarly fitted him for his present occupation, and he has the reputation of being one of the best adjusters of fire losses in the South. Always cool and deliberate, he weighs all business propositions with care and discretion. He is another of the representative citizens of the county who owe their nativity to North Carolina, his birth occurring in Gates county on the 31st of March, 1833, and is the eldest of four children born to Benbury and Ann K. (Montgomery) Walton, natives also of the Old North state. The father removed to La Grange, Tenn., in 1835, and from there, in 1850, to Oxford, Miss., for the purpose of educating his children. In 1854 he located in Panola county, Miss., and there died in 1879, at the age of seventy-eight years. His wife had died in 1850. He was quite an extensive planter. The paternal grandparents, John B. and Esther (Roberts) Walton, were natives also of North Carolina, and the grandfather was of English descent. Edwin Smith Walton was reared in La Grange, Tenn., and Oxford, Miss., entering the university at the latter place in 1850, and graduating with the class of 1853. He remained with his father as manager of the plantation until the beginning of the war, when he entered the Confederate army, mustered in May, 1861, into Pettus' flying artillery, commanded by Capt. Alfred Hudson, with which he remained until the close of the war. However, after the battle of Belmont, the company was attached to Bowen's brigade and called Hudson's battery. After the battle of Shiloh, where Hudson was killed, this battery was commanded by Sweeney and Mr. Walton, alternately, until the siege of Vicksburg, where Sweeney was killed and Mr. Walton badly wounded. In the winter after this engagement Mr. Walton was paroled and ordered to report to General Forrest at Como, Miss. He then took command of the company, and it bore his name until the close of the war. He entered the ranks as a private, was promoted to a lieutenancy, which position he held until after the siege of Vicksburg, when his great ability as a commander was recognized and he was singled out to fill important positions, in all of which he manifested great bravery and skill. He participated in all the battles of his army in Mississippi and Tennessee, including Fort Pillow, the burning of Johnsonville and the capture of the boats there, which was mainly conducted by Mr. Walton. He was in almost constant engagements from the time of his enlistment until the surrender at Gainesville, Ala. He then returned home, resumed his work on the plantation which had been badly wrecked during the war, and in 1866 was married to Miss Fannie Shaw, a native of Tennessee and a daughter of Wiley and Eliza (Malone) Shaw, natives of Tennessee and North Carolina respectively. The result of this union has been one child, Lona, aged twelve years. In 1871 Mr. Walton came to Sardis, engaged in the fire insurance business, but at the same time has continued to carry on his planting interests. He is the owner of about one thousand acres of land with six hundred acres under cultivation, and he has a neat residence in Sardis, erected in 1888. He and Mrs. Walton are members of the Methodist church, and he has been steward in the same for about twenty-five years. Socially he is a member of the Masonic fraternity and the American Legion of Honor. He is cultured and refined, a zealous Christian, and is devoted to his family, sparing no pains to surround them with all the comforts in his power, but with no ostentation or show. He is generous almost to a fault, is liberal in his views and is charitably inclined toward his fellowman. While he is ambitious to fill his mission in life and to do something and be somebody, he scorns the idea of being built on another's downfall.

J. T. Walton, planter, Acona, Miss., was born in Georgia, as were also his parents, J. B. and Mary (Moss) Walton. His birth occurred in 1831, and in 1836 his parents moved to Mississippi, settling near Lexington, where young Walton received the rudiments of an education. He subsequently entered the state university and remained there two years. On the 10th of September, 1853, he was wedded to Miss Thurman, who bore him six children: J. B. (died on the 1st of January, 1864), James D., Mattie T., H. W., L. A. and Johnnie M. Mr. Walton's occupation has always been that of a planter, and his fine farm, consisting of five hundred acres with two hundred acres under cultivation, is kept in excellent condition. He takes an active part in politics, but has never aspired for office, preferring the quiet, steady life he is now following instead. In April, 1862, he enlisted in the Confederate service as a private and was taken prisoner at Lookout mountain. He was held in Rock Island prison for eighteen months and was then shipped to New Orleans, where he was released. He also took part in the battle of Murfreesboro. Returning home after the war he resumed his former occupation, which he has continued successfully up to the present time. His father was also a planter, took an active part in political affairs, but, like his son, never cared for office. The paternal grandfather, Benton Walton, was born in North Carolina but moved to Georgia and there passed the closing scenes of his life. His wife died in Mississippi. The maternal grandfather, John Moss, was a native Virginian and was a splendid specimen of manhood, standing six feet two inches and being well proportioned. His wife was a native of Georgia and in that state both passed the remainder of their days.

Douglas Walworth needs no special introduction to the inhabitants of Adams county, Miss., for he was born here on the 14th of June, 1833, and is now the popular and well-known editor of the *Democrat*, which is an admirably conducted and ably edited journal. He was the second child born to John P. and Sarah (Wren) Walworth, the former a native of New York and the latter of Illinois. The paternal grandfather, Judge John Walworth, of Cleveland, Ohio, was born in Connecticut and was one of the first judges of the

Western reserve. He was a very prominent man of his day, and passed from life in Cleveland. He was of English descent, his ancestors having come to America during colonial times. John P., Jr., father of the subject of this sketch, was educated in the state of New York, and in 1819 came to Mississippi, settling at Natchez, where he at once became a clerk in the postoffice, and after a time engaged in business for himself as a merchant. About 1833 he began planting extensively on land owned by him in Louisiana and Arkansas, but at the same time acted as president of the Planters' bank of Natchez. He was one of the active spirits of his times and was popular, public-spirited and very prominent. At the time of his death, in 1883, he was a venerated and respected resident of Natchez. He was married to Miss Wren in 1827, she being a daughter of Woodster Wren, a native of Virginia, who came to Natchez about ———. Mr. Walworth was active in city improvement, was a man of wide experience and extended knowledge, and through the long term of years that he resided in this region he was esteemed as one of its most valuable citizens. His widow, who still survives him, is an earnest member of the Presbyterian church, and is in the enjoyment of good health. Douglas Walworth attended school in Natchez until 1851, when he entered Harvard college, where he remained two years, after which he was in Princeton college for one year. He was admitted to the bar of Jackson, Miss., in 1855, having pursued this study in the office of General Martin, of Natchez, and here he remained in the active practice of his profession until the opening of the war. In 1859-60 he was elected by his numerous friends to the state legislature, and while a member of this body displayed mental qualities of a high order. At the opening of the war he assisted in raising the Light Guard battalion and was elected captain of company I, of the Sixteenth Mississippi regiment, and was sent to northern Virginia, where he served one year in the infantry. He was then transferred to General Martin's staff as adjutant-general, and was in the battles of Thompson's Station, Knoxville, Farmington, Chickamauga, and many smaller engagements. After his return from the war he resumed the practice of his profession, but also followed planting. He was first married in the month of January, 1856, to Miss Rebecca Conner, a daughter of William Conner, a member of a prominent old family of this county, but he was called upon to mourn her death in 1868, she leaving him with one son and four daughters, all of whom are living. His second marriage took place in 1873, Miss Jeannette Haddermann, a daughter of Prof. Julius Haddermann, becoming his wife. She was reared principally in the city of Natchez, and here also received her education. She began a literary life when quite young, and her first book, Forgiven at Last, was issued in 1869, and was soon followed by Dead Men's Shoes. She has produced many other books, all of which have become popular, and her magazine articles also show power and are very meritorious. After about eight years spent in Natchez Mr. Walworth moved to New York city, and during the four years that he resided there he was engaged in legal and editorial work. Since 1888 he has been a constant resident of Natchez, and has been the able editor of the *Democrat*. He also edited the Natchez *Courier* in 1868-9. The family are members of the Presbyterian church, and Mr. Walworth is a worthy member of Harmony lodge No. 1, of the A. F. & A. M.

Augustus M. Wansley, Decatur, Miss., was born in Elbert county, Ga., in 1823, and is a son of Thomas and Jemimah (Means) Wansley, natives of Albemarle county, Va., and Elbert county, Ga., respectively. He grew to maturity in the county of his birth, and received his education in the common schools. In the days of the whig party he adhered to their principles, and cast his first vote for Henry Clay, when he was a candidate for president of the United States. Since the war, however, he has been an active democrat, energetically supporting all its measures. In 1853 he was married to Miss Theresa A. Harris, a native of

South Carolina, and a daughter of James S. Harris. In 1857 he located in Newton county, Miss., near Decatur, and in 1867 he removed five miles north of Decatur. There he owns two hundred and eighty acres of land, one hundred of which he has placed in a high state of cultivation. In 1862 he enlisted in Captain Carleton's company, and served in the fight at Vicksburg, where he was captured; he was afterward paroled and came back home, but did not re-enlist. When the war closed he began planting again, and has been very prosperous. He has been prominently identified with the Masonic fraternity for thirty-five years, being a member of the lodge at Decatur. He and his wife are both members of the Methodist Episcopal Church South. Mr. Wansley's farm is considered one of the most desirable in the county; it is the product of a long period of thought and labor, and is a satisfactory reward for all the effort that has been expended upon it. All his interests being agricultural he is naturally a strong Farmer's Alliance man, and is giving that body a hearty support.

William F. Ward, the father of Dr. Benjamin F. Ward, physician, Winona, Miss., was a native of South Carolina, and was of Irish parentage. He grew to manhood in his native state and was there married to Miss Martha Mecklin, also of Irish ancestry, and the daughter of Hugh Mecklin. Mr. Ward was one of the honest and successful yeomanry of his district and state, where he passed his uneventful life, dying when the Doctor was an infant. The Wards were nearly all members of the Presbyterian church, one of Mr. Ward's brothers being a minister of that denomination, but he also had a brother a minister in the Methodist church. Dr. Benjamin F. Ward, the youngest of five sons and two daughters, was brought by his mother to Mississippi in 1846, after the death of the father, and she settled in Cherokee county. There the Doctor spent his youthful days and received a primary education in the private schools. The Doctor, however, is principally self-educated since reaching years of maturity. He went to Carroll county when a young man, taught school, and began the study of medicine. He took his first course of lectures in the University of Louisiana and his second course at Atlanta Medical college, from which he graduated in 1859. After completing this course, the Doctor located in Carroll county, where he began the practice of his profession and this continued until the breaking out of the war. In 1861 he entered the Confederate service as a private, and soon after was promoted to the rank of surgeon and later brigade surgeon of Gen. Joseph R. Davis' brigade. He was made a member of the army medical board of health, serving his battalion all through the campaigns of Virginia, Maryland and Pennsylvania. He was taken prisoner at Gettysburg and held five months at Fort McHenry at Baltimore. After being exchanged he rejoined his battalion. He surrendered with General Lee at Appomattox. After the war he located at Winona, and has been actively and successfully engaged in his practice since. He keeps thoroughly posted in his profession, is a correspondent for a number of popular medical journals, and he often lectures, not only in medical, but other colleges in Mississippi. His reputation as a speaker, writer and lecturer is quite extended and he is often solicited to lecture in other states. An article, written by the Doctor, and published in 1886, was quite extensively copied and commented on both North and South. It was entitled the Old South, and was conceded to be a very able production. The Doctor is not only a physician and litterateur of prominence and ability, but is a man of excellent principles, and one who is held in the highest estimation by all whom he chances to meet. He is a member of the State Medical association and the state board of health. Although never an aspirant for office, he takes quite an active and prominent part in politics and is a strong advocate of his party. He was married on the 3d of June, 1886, to Miss Mary H. Hardeman, daughter of William Hardeman, of Tennessee, in which state Mrs. Ward first saw the light of day. She was left an orphan when but an infant, and was reared in Mississippi by an uncle. She and the Doctor are both members of the Presbyterian church. Their union has been blessed by the birth of four interesting children.

Among the professional men of prominence in Leake county, Miss., stands the name of Dr. B. N. Ward, physician and surgeon, Carthage, Miss., who was born in Edgecomb district, N. C., on the 2d of February, 1829. His father, Needham Ward, who was also a native of that state, grew to manhood and was married there to Miss Sallie Beaman, a daughter of Noah Beaman, who was also a native of the Old North state. Mr. Ward removed to Mississippi about 1833, settled in Noxubee county, and there followed farming for several years. In 1856 he moved to Leake county and continued his former occupation there until his death in 1858. His wife survived him until 1872. Their family consisted of three children, one of whom is deceased and only one besides our subject now surviving—Mrs. Martha Susan Smythe, a widow. Dr. Ward passed the first years of his life in Noxubee county, received a good education in the University of Alabama, and then studied medicine in Noxubee county. Later he attended lectures at the Medical College of the State of South Carolina, located in Charleston, graduating in the class of 1851. After this he located at Macon, where he engaged in the practice of his profession for about a year, and then removed to Winston county, Miss., where he remained till 1854, and in 1856 settled in Carthage, Miss. His sympathies were with the South, and he enlisted in the Confederate army in 1862, fortieth Mississippi infantry, as a private. He was soon promoted to regimental surgeon and served in that capacity until the close of the war. He served as brigade surgeon on the staff of General Featherston during the Georgia campaign. After cessation of hostilities the Doctor returned to Leake county, where he had located in 1856, and resumed the practice of his profession, and in 1858 he took a supplemental course at Tulane Medical college, New Orleans. Since that time the Doctor has practiced in Leake county, and has met with flattering success. In connection with his practice he has been engaged in merchandising, and is one of the largest merchants of the county. He is also the owner of a fine drug store. The Doctor is the chief health officer of Leake county. He is democratic in his political views and takes quite an active part in local politics. He has served as a delegate to numerous conventions, but is not an aspirant to office. He was married on the 18th of May, 1866, to Mrs. Caroline Sharkey, a native of Tennessee, and the daughter of Dr. James Dismukes. Mrs. Ward was reared and educated in Mississippi, and died here on the 19th of June, 1884, leaving three children: Benjamin N., a graduate of the University of Alabama, who after taking one course of lectures in the medical department of the University of Virginia will complete his medical education in the College of Physicians and Surgeons, New York; Sallie Agnes, wife of Dr. Frank D. Smythe, of Kosciusko, Miss., who is a young surgeon of fine promise; and Mattie C., a young lady now attending college. Dr. Ward is well read and posted on all subjects relating to the medical profession, and is a superior business man.

Enoch J. Ward, druggist, of Ellisville, Miss. This gentleman was born in Marion county, S. C., August 14, 1860. His parents were Enoch B. and Elizabeth J. (Gaddy) Ward, natives of Robertson county, N. C. They were married in South Carolina and subsequently returned to Robertson county, N. C., where they now live. They were the parents of eight children: Elizabeth E., Susan J., Enoch J., John W., Florence L., Katie P., Homer B. and Annie B. Enoch J. was educated in the public schools of Moore county, N. C., and afterward engaged in the drug and general merchandising business with his father and brother, at Rowland, N. C., for a number of years. In 1885 he began business for himself near that place, which he continued with considerable success until February, 1886, when he came to Ellisville and became a member of the drug firm of Peacock & Ward, Dr. W. M. Peacock being his partner until 1887, when Mr. Ward acquired his partner's interest and admitted J. J. Malady to a partnership in the enterprise. In November, 1888, he bought Mr. Malady's interest, and has since been sole proprietor. His drug store is the largest in the town, and he has the reputation of being the ablest and most reliable druggist in the county. Polite and accommodating, he has won the esteem of all, and his devotion to his business is such that it absorbs all of his time and energy. He was married at Meridian, Miss., January 25, 1887, to Miss Mollie V. McClain, a daughter of Col. Robert McClain (deceased), a biographical sketch of whom appears elsewhere in this work. Mrs. Ward was born in Enterprise, Miss., June 13, 1861, and is a highly accomplished and most popular lady. She has borne her husband two children: Edmund J., March 29, 1889, and Laura, September 11, 1890. Mr. Ward's interest in Ellisville is great, and since his residence here he has done his full share toward its development and improvement. In 1890 he was elected a member of the board of aldermen of the town, and as such served to the entire satisfaction of his fellow-citizens until the expiration of his term of office. Mr. and Mrs. Ward are members of the Presbyterian church, and contribute liberally toward the support of its several interests, doing so with great heartiness and an earnest desire to do their share in helping to make the world better.

George V. Ward is justly conceded to hold an enviable position among the successful planters of Washington county, and the admirable state of cultivation of his land has been brought about by his own earnest efforts, for although at the close of the war he was the owner of some real estate he had no means of working it, for all his slaves were freed and other help was next to an impossibility to obtain. With undaunted energy he commenced to build a home out of the wreck of his fortunes and now has a landed estate amounting to eight hundred acres, four hundred of which are under cultivation. His present residence, worth $12,000, was only saved from being swept away by the river (the land at that point caving in in an alarming manner) by razing it to the ground and moving it to another site. Mr. Ward was born in Scott county, Ky., April 25, 1832, the third of nine children born to Junius R. and Matilda (Vila) Ward, who were also born in that state. The father came to the state of Mississippi when quite a young man and located at Natchez, where he engaged in merchandising. In 1823 he purchased some land on Lake Washington, and until his demise, in 1886, followed the calling of a planter. He was for some time a member of what is now called the board of supervisors, and in other ways identified himself with every worthy interest of the county. His father, William Ward, was born in Maryland and for a number of years was Indian agent to Mississippi for the Choctaw nation. George V. Ward was reared in Kentucky and received his education in the Western Military institute at Georgetown, one of his instructors being Hon. James G. Blaine. After giving his attention to his father's business for a number of years he began doing for himself at the age of twenty-five years, and has since been one of the leading planters of Washington county. In 1857 he was married to Miss Maria L. Williams, a native of Kentucky and a daughter of Minor and Mary C. (Viley) Williams, who were also Kentuckians. To Mr. Ward and his wife two children have been born: James W. and Junius R., Jr. Mr. Ward is a member of an old Kentucky family, but came to Mississippi when a boy, and has ever since made his home in this state, where he is highly esteemed and respected. (For further particulars of the Vileys see sketch of Merritt Williams.) Mr. Ward is of a social temperament and is a very agreeable and pleasant gentleman to meet.

Junius R. Ward, planter, Erwin, owes his nativity to Washington county, Miss., his birth having occurred on the lake in 1844, and is the sixth child born to Junius R. and Matilda (Vila) Ward, the parents originally from the bluegrass regions of Kentucky. The father was perhaps the earliest settler on the lake, having located there about 1825, and began farming on a very extensive scale, becoming the owner of a magnificent plantation. He passed his summers in Kentucky, but returned to Washington county, Miss., to pass the winter months. He opened up several other places and became prominently identified with the agricultural interests of the county. He and wife both died in the year 1881. They were of representative families of Kentucky and were upright, honorable citizens. Junius R. Ward was reared in Kentucky, educated in the schools of that state and at the breaking out of the war enlisted in company B, Second Kentucky regiment, under Captain Breckinridge. He was in the bloody battle of Shiloh, in Morgan's command, with whom he remained for a year and a half. He then returned to his home in Mississippi and there remained until 1865, when he went to Kentucky. Shortly afterward he again returned to Mississippi and began planting for himself. In 1879 Mr. Ward bought his present plantation, consisting of six hundred acres, with two hundred acres under cultivation, and is one of the progressive men of the county. He is single and resides quietly at home.

Zack Wardlaw is one of the progressive and leading citizens of Hinds county, Miss., but was born in Warren county, of this state, December 22, 1844, the eldest of five children born to Zack Wardlaw, Sr., and his second wife, Falba L., who was the widow of a Mr. Wilkins, and the daughter of Thomas S. Moore, a native of Alabama. Mr. Wardlaw, Sr., was a native of Alabama, born in 1804, and devoted his life to agriculture. Although he commenced life with no means, he was industrious, thrifty and painstaking, and prior to his death, which occurred in 1854, he had accumulated a comfortable competency. He was a great admirer of fine horses and always had some blooded stock about him. He was of a modest and unassuming demeanor, and at the time of his death he was an earnest member of the Baptist church, in which he had been deacon for a number of years. He was descended from an old and well-known Scotch family, his ancestor in America having come here with two brothers and settled in South Carolina, in which state some of his descendants became eminent. Among these may be mentioned Judge L. Wardlaw, who was supreme judge of South Carolina for some time. Zack Wardlaw, the subject of this sketch, was educated in Hinds county, whither his father moved from Warren county, and here he began attending the common schools, but his education was cut short by the opening of the war. With the enthusiasm of youth he espoused the cause of the Confederacy, enlisting as a private in company B, Twenty-second Mississippi regiment, and served faithfully and well until the last gun was fired. At the battle of Shiloh he received quite a severe wound, which confined him to the hospital for some thirty days. He rejoined his command at Vicksburg, participating in the marine siege of that place, after which he was at Baton Rouge, La., Deer Creek, Baker's Creek, Jackson, Corinth, the Tennessee campaign and the Georgia campaign, during which time he was in almost constant service. He surrendered at Greensboro, N. C., and, walking about eight hundred miles, reached home on the 8th of May, 1865. He soon after began teaching school, but at the end of three months he gave it up to enter a commercial college at New Orleans, La., graduating in 1866. For a short time thereafter he followed the calling of a bookkeeper, then went to Memphis, Tenn., and engaged in the tobacco and cigar business, and also kept a restaurant for a short time. He then returned to Hinds county, Miss., and here was married, in 1871, to Miss Laura A. Cook, a native of Mississippi, and a daughter of M. L. and Jenett (Scott) Cook, both natives of North Carolina. To

Mr. and Mrs. Wardlaw three children have been born: Falba J., Mary J. and Zack, Jr. After his marriage Mr. Wardlaw farmed exclusively for ten years, but in 1882 also engaged in general merchandising in Utica, which calling he has continued with excellent success. He does an annual business of about $25,000, and has real estate to the amount of eight hundred acres, of which five hundred acres are under cultivation. In 1886 Mr. Wardlaw erected a handsome residence, and in this lovely and ideal Southern home he and his wife dispense a generous and free-hearted hospitality. He is a very congenial and agreeable companion, and he, as well as his wife, is highly esteemed in social circles. He has always believed that what is worth doing at all is worth doing well, and in the different enterprises in which he is engaged no department of his work has been neglected. He also owns some valuable real estate in Chattanooga, Tenn. He and his wife are members of the Baptist church, in which he is deacon, and socially he belongs to the A. F. & A. M., the Good Templars, the A. L. of H., and the K. of P.

D. Cameron Warren, M. D. The profession of the physician is one which operates effectively in time of need in arresting and alleviating the most acute pains and ailments to which the human body is heir, and therefore deserves the most appreciative consideration on the part of the public. In this profession the gratitude of hundreds is due to the skill and talent of Dr. Warren, who is deservedly ranked among the leading practitioners of the healing art in Jefferson county. The Doctor is a native Mississippian, and was born in the county in which he is now residing on the 6th of February, 1851, his parents being J. J. and Sarah J. (Cameron) Warren, the former being born and reared in Windham county., Vt., and the latter a native of Jefferson county, Miss. After reaching his majority, J. J. Warren determined to seek his fortune elsewhere than in his native state, and finally found himself in the state of Mississippi, and, being pleased with this section, settled in Jefferson county, where he met and married Miss Cameron, a daughter of Archibald Cameron, a pioneer planter of this county. He soon after opened up a farm in this county, and for a period of forty years was one of the honest sons of the soil of this region. He and his worthy wife, though quite aged, are still living, and make their home in Franklin county, where they are surrounded by everything to make their declining years comfortable and easy. To them a family of five sons and eight daughters were born, of whom two sons and seven daughters are living: Eugene, a farmer of Franklin county; Dr. D. Cameron; Mrs. F. M. McNair, of Fayette; Mrs. B. D. Knapp, of Harriston; Mrs. A. L. Torrey, of Hermanville; Mrs. W. A. Newman, of McNair; Mrs. E. M. Williams, of Meadeville; E. J.; M. L., a teacher at Harriston; and Marquis D., who grew to mature years, married, and moved to Texas, where he died. The other children died in early childhood. Dr. D. Cameron Warren grew to manhood in Jefferson county, and spent his youth in attending the common and high schools and in learning the intricacies of farm work. After attaining a suitable age, and always having had a desire for the medical profession, he began studying with Dr. McNair, of Fayette, a sketch of whom appears in this volume. In the winter of 1873-4 he took his first course of lectures at Tulane university, of Louisiana, to which institution he returned the two following winters, taking three courses of lectures, and graduating from the institution in March, 1876. He soon after took up his location where he now resides, and has since devoted his time and attention to attending to the bodily wants of his fellowman. In this calling his efforts have been blessed with success, and he now has all the practice that he can give proper attention to. He was married in the month of March, 1871, to Miss Mary I. Torrey, a daughter of R. D. Torrey, of one of the oldest and best known families of Jefferson county (see sketch of John Torrey). Dr. and

BLIND ASYLUM, JACKSON.

Mrs. Warren have four children: Mary, Lucy, Lottie and George. The Doctor, his wife, and their eldest daughter are worthy members of the Presbyterian church, and socially he belongs to the K. & L. of H., and is examining physician for the lodge at Union Church. Dr. Warren has a pleasant country home, a place he settled and improved, it being situated about two miles from Union Church.

Dr. N. B. Warren, Marietta, Miss., is one of Prentiss county's most trustworthy physicians, and as he has ever had a liberal share of public favor, it is one of the best proofs of his skill and care. He was born in Alabama on the 10th of April, 1834, and is next to the youngest of twelve children born to John S. and Sarah (Robinson) Warren, the father a native of Kentucky and the mother of South Carolina. John S. Warren was married twice; first in Kentucky to Miss Gentry, who bore him seven children—three sons and four daughters. He resided in the Blue Grass state for several years, and there his first wife died. His next marriage was to Miss Robinson, their nuptials being celebrated in Tennessee. Twelve children were the fruits of this union, Mr. Warren being the father of nineteen children in all. He was a farmer by occupation, and after removing from Tennessee to Alabama engaged in the stock business for several years. From there he removed to Itawamba county, Miss., located near Fulton, the county seat, and there bought a large tract of land. He engaged extensively in farming and stockraising, selling a great many horses and cattle, and also ran a distillery on his farm. He was one of the pioneer settlers, and was held high in the estimation of all who knew him as an honorable, high-minded citizen. He never aspired to any official positions, and was a consistent member of the Primitive Baptist church. His death occurred in Itawamba county in 1863. His wife is still living, and is in her eighty-seventh year. There are now only six of the nineteen children living. Dr. Warren began working for himself when fifteen years of age, and engaged with the firm of Rhynic Brothers, of Fulton, Miss., to peddle dry goods and notions. He followed that part of a year, and afterward began teaching school and going to school at intervals until he had acquired a fair English education. He was educated mainly at the Euclid academy, in Tishomingo county, Miss. In the fall of 1854 he began reading medicine, and in 1855 entered the office of Dr. Choate in Tishomingo county, with whom he remained one year. In 1856 he entered the Louisville Medical university, took only one course, and then returned home, beginning to practice near Fulton. The following year he went back, took another course, and again returned to his practice, locating at Ryanswell, in the same county, where he continued to practice for four years. In 1860 he returned to Louisville, took another course, and graduated in the spring of 1861. He again resumed his practice at Ryanswell, and remained there until April, 1891, when he removed to Marietta, Prentiss county, where he is now located. He has an extensive practice and is doing well. He was exempt from service in the army on account of being a cripple, and during that stirring period remained at home and kept up his practice, being the only physician for many miles around. He had frequently to make visits thirty and forty miles away. The Doctor has never married, but has two adopted sons, Robert J. and George B. Warren, whom he reared from infancy. The former is twenty-four years of age, and is a farmer by occupation. He was educated at Fulton, Miss. The latter is sixteen years of age, and was educated at Oakland Normal institute. Dr. Warren is one of the directors of Oakland Normal institute. He has never aspired to official positions of any kind, but devotes his entire time to his practice and his farming interests. He is a large landowner, having nearly twenty thousand acres, embracing several farms in Itawamba, Tishomingo and Prentiss counties. The Doctor was engaged in the drug business at Iuka for one year, also engaged in the same business at Fulton for two years, and was in partnership with George B. Walker in general merchandising at Walker's Bridge for seven years. He sold that out in 1872 and bought an interest in the dry goods business at Pleasanton, continuing there for two years. He was appointed administrator of his father's estate in 1863, and in 1870 he was appointed administrator of the estate of his brother. The Doctor is acknowledged by the medical profession as a physician of ability and prominence, and as a citizen he is esteemed and honored by all. He has been a member of the Masonic fraternity since June, 1857, and an able supporter of schools, churches, etc.

J. W. Waterer, Free Run, has been a lifelong resident of Yazoo county, Miss., where he first saw the light of day November 8, 1848. He is the eldest of the three children born to Needham and Louise (McCormack) Waterer. The father was a native of Twiggs county, Ga., and there grew to manhood. At the age of twenty-one years he left kith and kin, and rode seven hundred miles through a comparatively wild country, inhabited by Indians, until he came to Yazoo county, Miss. He decided to tarry here a while and finally settled near Free Run, where he was employed as an overseer. At the breaking out of the Civil war he owned fifteen slaves and fifteen hundred acres of land. He was married in 1846 to Miss Louise McCormack, and by this union three children were born, only one of whom grew to maturity. Mrs. Waterer died in 1852, and after some time he was again married, his second wife being Miss Amanda McCormack, a sister to the first wife. Six children were born to them, five of whom lived to be grown: Needham C., of Texas; Heibunia, wife of Henry Gorden; S. F., a planter of this county; Virginia L.; and H. Y., a farmer of Holmes county. The father died in August, 1873, at the age of fifty-six years. He was a man of many sterling qualities, and by his industry and economy made a success of life. The subject of this notice, J. W. Waterer, grew up surrounded by the industry of husbandry, and early received a bent in this direction. At the tender age of fifteen years he entered the Confederate service in Capt. Ed. Berry's company of cavalry, and gallantly lent his aid in the defense of the Southern cause. After the surrender, in 1865, he went into agriculture, which he followed until 1888. During four years of this time he was assessor of the county. His next business venture was in the mercantile trade, in partnership with the Hon. D. Bunch, of Benton. He now has the entire business in his own name, carrying a stock of $2,500, and doing an annual business of $10,000. He owns a well-improved plantation of six hundred acres in addition to his mercantile interests. Mr. Waterer was wedded, in 1869, to Miss Ella Reed, daughter of J. H. and A. L. (Hurst) Reed, prominent early settlers of Mississippi. Four children have been born to Mr. and Mrs. Waterer who lived to maturity, and four died in infancy. Those living are, Nellie L., Lizzie, Fannie and J. B. Mrs. Waterer passed from this life September 14, 1890, lamented by her family and a large circle of friends. She was an estimable Christian woman, and a devoted member of the Baptist church. Mr. Waterer is a member of the Free Run lodge No. 2994, Knights of Honor. He is one of Yazoo's enterprising, progressive citizens, and has always contributed to the support of all public movements that have been of general benefit.

Dr. Benjamin D. Watkins, physician and surgeon for the state and the city Charity hospital at Natchez, and a general practitioner, was born in Natchez in 1862, and is the son of Rev. William H. Watkins, D. D. The elder Watkins was born in Jefferson county, Miss., in 1815, was educated for the ministry (Methodist), and for a number of years was president of Centenary college at Jackson, La., a Methodist institution, and was afterward in the New Orleans conference. While in that city he met and married Mrs. Elizabeth Johnson, nee Jones, who was a native of Liverpool, England, born in 1818, where she had married her first husband, who was a ship captain. Mrs. Watkins is still living and makes her home among her children. She is an excellent lady and a devout Methodist. After leaving New Orleans Mr. Watkins was placed on the Mississippi conference, and was stationed at Natchez, Woodville, Jackson and Vicksburg, continuing in the ministry with unabated success until his death in 1881. His father, Asa Watkins, was born in Jefferson county, Ga., in 1777, and at a very early day came to Mississippi, locating in Jefferson county, where his death occurred in 1840. He was a planter by occupation and a pronounced Baptist in his religious belief. Dr. Benjamin D. Watkins is the youngest of six sons and five daughters, six of whom are living, born to his parents. They are named as follows: Dr. William H., a successful physician and surgeon of New Orleans; Thomas H., a planter of Louisiana; Dr. John M., a physician of New Orleans; Rev. Alex. F., a prominent divine of Jackson and agent for a college, and Olive B. Dr. Benjamin D. Watkins was educated at Centenary college, La., and then, afer a three years' course, graduated from the medical department of Tulane university at Baton Rouge, La., in the meantime spending a portion of two years in the Charity hospital, New Orleans. After finishing his course he at once located in the city of Natchez, where he already ranks among the foremost of his profession. He has an extensive and lucrative practice. He is a prominent member of Harmony lodge No. 1, A. F. & A. M., and also of Natchez lodge No. 3, of Knights of Pythias. He selected Miss Eloise Reimer, a native of Natchez, as his life companion and their nuptials were celebrated in June, 1889. She is the daughter of Daniel and Minnie Reimer, early settlers of Natchez, where Mr. Reimer died a number of years ago. He was a planter. Mrs. Watkins is an earnest and active member of the Methodist church. Dr. Watkins is a public-spirited citizen and stands high in his profession and in social circles. He was pension examiner for about two years under the Cleveland administration.

Erskine Watkins, merchant, of Jackson, Miss. In giving a history of Hinds county, Miss., the name of Mr. Watkins deserves honorable mention, for he has always been industrious and public spirited, and has ever aided enterprises which tend to the interests of his city and section. He was born in Huntsville, Ala., on the 8th of November, 1838, the fourth of six children born to Dr. Miles S. and Sallie D. (Shelby) Watkins, the former a native of Virginian and the latter of Tennessee. Dr. Watkins was brought up in the state of his birth, but about 1820 removed to Alabama, and, having graduated from the Jefferson Medical college, of Philadelphia, Penn., he practiced his profession in Huntsville until 1850, when he removed to Mississippi, taking up his abode near the city of Jackson, where he engaged in planting until the opening of the war. During the great conflict between the North and South all his property was swept away, after which he lived a retired life, until his death, in 1866, at the age of seventy-five years. He lived the life of a true Christian, having for many years been a member of the Presbyterian church and an elder in the same, and although not an aspirant for political favors, he was very public-spirited and a very prominent man of the county. He was very successful in business until the war swept his accumulations away, possessed decided literary tastes, being an omnivorous reader, and was a graduate of Hampton Sidney college, of Virginia. He was a model husband and father, was devoted to his children and gave them all good advantages. He was a true and tried soldier of the War of 1812, and in every respect ranked among the highest civilians. He was of Scotch descent, and a nephew of his, Benjamin Watkins Leigh, was one of the ablest men of his times. Erskine Watkins has been a resident of Mississippi since his twelfth year, but the most of his education was obtained in Huntsville, Ala. He left school at the age of sixteen years to enter a general mercantile store in Jackson, and from 1855 to 1861 he was with the firm of Fearn & Putnam. Upon the opening of the Civil war he enlisted in company K, Eighteenth Mississippi regiment (which was the second or third regiment organized in the state), as lieutenant of his company and served until the last gun was fired, and made an enviable record as a brave and faithful soldier. He took part in the first battle of Bull Run, the first battle of Manassas, and was afterward transferred to company I, Thirty-ninth Mississippi, with which he remained until captured at Port Hudson. He was a participant in the bloody battles of Vicksburg, Corinth and Baton Rouge. He was severely wounded in the engagement at Corinth, and was disabled for over three months. He was captured at Port Hudson and kept as a prisoner of war until the surrender of General Lee, after which he was released and returned to his home. He soon after opened a mercantile establishment, and to this calling has industriously devoted his attention ever since. He is the sole proprietor of the house of E. Watkins, which is the largest hardware establishment of Jackson, and does an annual business of $50,000. In every respect he has shown that he is a man of discrimination and judgment, and his upright and honorable business career is a worthy example to the rising generation. He has always endeavored to follow the teachings of the golden rule and his many admirable qualities of heart and head, and his kindly, courteous and pleasing manners, make him an agreeable and desired companion, and one who holds an enviable position in the religious and social circles of Jackson. He is extremely public-spirited, and to aid in the improvement of his section and to assist and encourage worthy enterprises, he gives generously of his means. He has been a member of the board of aldermen for some years, in which position he has used his influence for justice and right, and for the good of the city. In addition to managing his hardware establishment, he also successfully conducts a fine plantation of one thousand acres, and thus finds that his time is fully and profitably occupied. Besides his fine store building he owns a beautiful residence in Jackson, which he erected in 1881, and here he and his intelligent and amiable wife dispense a generous and free-hearted hospitality. In 1875 he was united in marriage to Miss Alice Petrie, a native of Jackson, Miss., and a daughter of Lemuel W. and Rosa (Farrar) Petrie, the former a native of Maine and the latter of Virginia. To Mr. Watkins and his wife three children have been born: Rosa F., Marian S. and Alice P., all of whom are at home. Mr. Watkins and his wife are worthy members of the Presbyterian church.

Jesse Watkins (deceased) was originally from North Carolina, his birth occurring in Richmond county in 1813, and he there grew to maturity, receiving a common-school education. He was early trained to the duties of farm life, and it was but natural perhaps that that should be his chosen vocation when starting out for himself. He was married in 1835 to Miss Sarah A. Morgan, daughter of Richard and Annie (Ewell) Morgan, natives of Virginia and Maryland respectively. To Mr. and Mrs. Watkins were born four children, three of whom are still living: James, Mary A., (wife of M. A. Cooper, of Neshoba county, Miss.) and Edmond (who is a prominent business man of Chattanooga, Tenn.) Mr. Watkins came with his family to Neshoba county, Miss., in 1849, located in the woods and on the exact spot where the old home now stands. He began opening up land, and in the short space of two years he had a good farm opened and was making considerable money. At the breaking out of the war he owned about two thousand acres of land and about twenty-five slaves. He thought slavery wrong, and when he had to give up those belonging to him he never lamented the loss. He opposed the ordinance of secession, but when the die was cast went with his people. He was an old-line whig in politics, but although active he never sought office and never allowed his name to come before the people. He died in 1885, after having lived a useful and Christian life. His son, James Watkins, was born in Richmond county, N. C., in 1836, and removed with his parents to Neshoba county, Miss., at the age of thirteen years. Here he labored on his father's farm, and was educated in what was then known as Carolina academy, near his father's home. In 1857 he was married to Miss Martha, daughter of Jones Brantley, a native of Georgia, but who came to Mississippi in 1855. The fruits of this union were five children, four of whom are still living. In 1861, when the war between the two sections broke out, Mr. Watkins enlisted in company K, Fifth Mississippi regiment, and served until the close. He was in the battle of Pensacola, Fla., Farmington, Miss., and Chickamauga, where he was wounded in the arm and prevented from further service. Returning home after the war Mr. Watkins followed farming and in 1867 moved to Meridian, where he opened a general merchandising store. He was burned out in 1868, after which he returned to the farm, where he has since remained. He owns immense tracts of land, between ten and fifteen thousand acres, and is the largest landowner in the county. He is a devout, religious man, and one who gives his liberal support to every worthy enterprise. He believes in educating the young, and puts this into practice by giving all his children liberal educational advantages. He has the good will and esteem of all who know him. He is a member of the Masonic fraternity. Mr. Watkins' paternal grandfather, Israel Watkins, was probably a native of the Old Dominion, but located in North Carolina when young. He was an active Revolutionary soldier and served his country well. The maternal grandfather, Richard Morgan, was also a soldier in the Revolution.

Among the prominent farmers of Copiah county is William A. Watkins, who resides near the eastern border of the county, on the Pearl river, on the plantation upon which he was born in 1838. He is the son of Henry and Anna Watkins. His father was born in South Carolina, May 4, 1802, a son of William and Sarah Watkins, both natives of that state. In 1822, after the death of his father, Henry Watkins came to Mississippi with his mother. After a few years devoted to planting interests, he was appointed warden of the state penitentiary, at Jackson, Miss., which position he held for eleven years. Upon his retirement he purchased a farm in Copiah county, upon which he located and lived till his death, which occurred February, 1878. He was married in 1836 to Mrs. Anna (Carter) Young, a daughter of Burrel and ———Carter, of Pike county, Miss. To this couple was born one child, a son, William A., the subject of this sketch. Mr. Watkins was prominent in the Masonic order. William A. Watkins began life for himself at the age of twenty-one as a farmer, which vocation he now follows, owning the farm upon which he first started out for himself, and upon which he has lived during that whole period, except two years, when he was merchandising in Brookhaven. He was married in 1859 to Margaret Conn, a daughter of Matthew and Ada Conn, of Copiah county. They had two children, Benjamin A. and Nannie, wife of Francis Barlow. In 1861 Mr. Watkins enlisted in Gray's battalion for the Confederate service, but soon after joined company K, of the Twentieth Mississippi infantry, with which he served until the close of the war. He is a member of Charles Scott lodge No. 136, A. F. & A. M. Mr. Watkins, although well advanced in life, is well preserved, and though somewhat stout is quite active. He is rather tall, quite erect, with clear blue eyes and gray hair, and a long gray beard, presenting an appearance no less striking than pleasing. His business reputation is of the highest character, and the esteem in which he is held by his fellow-citizens would be flattering if it were not deserved.

Dr. W. W. Watkins, physician and planter, is well known in Monroe county, where he was born in 1849, the son of Bryant and Susan (Whitfield) Watkins, the former of whom was born in Dublin county, and the latter in Wayne county, N. C. They came to Monroe county in 1837, where they were married and passed the remainder of their lives. Mr. Watkins died in 1852, his wife in 1878. They were members of the Methodist Episcopal Church South for many years, and Mr. Watkins was an Odd Fellow. The grandfather of our subject was John Watkins, supposed to have been born in North Carolina, where he lived till he came to Monroe county, in 1837, becoming a well-to-do planter, and dying in what is now Clay county, in 1866. He was of Welsh descent, his family consisting of seven sons and six daughters, two sons and one daughter of whom are living. Several of his sons, and quite a number of his grandsons, did service for the Confederacy in the Civil war. His maternal grandfather, Hatch Whitfield, was born in North Carolina, and in 1835 also came to Monroe county, settling near Aberdeen. He engaged in planting with considerable success, and died in 1883. He will long be remembered as being a veteran of the War of 1812, during which he served under General Jackson, at New Orleans. He was of English descent, but thoroughly American in his ideas, and active in all matters of public importance. He was twice married, and had ten children, nine of them by his first wife. Mr. Watkins' mother was married, a second time, to D. Wiley Howe, now deceased. Our subject was the third of three sons and one daughter, named as follows: Amelia, who became the wife of Mason Cummings, now deceased, dying in 1858; John H., a planter who served during the war in Lander's battalion of Ferguson's brigade, and died in Lauderdale county in 1882; William W.; Bryant Y., a planter of Monroe county, who died in 1890. Mr. Watkins obtained a common-school education, but became a practical planter on his own account at the age of nineteen, continuing that business till 1870, when he began studying medicine with Dr. Thomas B. Elkin, graduating in March, 1872, from the Tulane university at New Orleans. He practiced afterward in the vicinity of his birth, for seventeen years, when he relinquished the active duties of his profession and again turned his attention to planting, with which he combined the merchandise business, being a member of the firm of Mitchell & Watkins, of Aberdeen. He owns two thousand two hundred and forty acres of land in Monroe county, as well as several other valuable tracts of prairie land in Clay and Monroe counties, aggregating about six thousand acres. He was married in 1873 to Miss Anna, a daughter of Benjamin and Anna Knowles, who were born, reared and married in Rhode Island, and came from there to Monroe county about 1830, where Mr. Knowles died, in 1866, and his wife in 1869. He was a merchant, and both he and his wife were members of the Christian church. They had two daughters and one son. One of the daughters was Mrs. Watkins, who was born in Monroe county, but received her education at Wilbraham, Mass. She has five children. During the last four years the family have resided in Aberdeen. Dr. Watkins is of an old and highly respected family. He is known as a successful business man, and is perhaps the largest single planter in Monroe county, one thousand eight hundred acres of his land being cleared. It is crossed by both the main line and the Aberdeen branch of the Mobile & Ohio railroad. He gives this place his personal supervision, and under his superb management it is one of the most productive plantations in the whole of Monroe county.

Maj. Augustus C. Watson. In the preparation of this brief outline of the life history of one of the most cultured and honorable men who has ever made his home in Jefferson county, facts appear which are greatly to his credit. His intelligence, enterprise and integrity, and many estimable qualities, have acquired for him a popularity not derived from any fictitious circumstances, but are a permanent and spontaneous tribute to his merit. In the space allotted in this sketch it is impossible to mention in detail all the services he has rendered to his much-loved South, but they are of much interest and show that he has always been ready to identify himself with what he considered justice and right. He was born in the county in which he is now residing, on the 14th of July, 1825, but his father, James H. Watson, was born in the Old North state, and, after making his home in that state until he was a young man, he determined to devote his energies to the accumulation of a competency in a different state, and the year 1779 found him in what is now Jefferson county, Miss. He was a man who possessed intelligence of a high order, and upon the large and valuable plantation which he opened near Rodney, he brought all his native intelligence and knowledge of agriculture to bear, and, as a natural result, became wealthy. He was called from life in 1841, and his wife, whose maiden name was Anna M. Cable, died a few years earlier. She was born in Jefferson county, her father, Fred Cable, being one of the pioneers of the state. Maj. A. C. Watson is the youngest of a family of five sons and four daughters that grew to mature years, he, his brother, William, a planter of Louisiana, and their sister, Mrs. Anna Hunt, widow of George Hunt, a sketch of whom appears in this work, being the only ones of the family who are now living. Major Watson attained man's estate in Jefferson county, and, owing to his father's excellent financial circumstances, he was privileged to devote his time to his books, and received a thorough and practical education in Oakland college. After completing his studies he was married to Miss Polivia McGill, in 1850, daughter of Jeremiah McGill, but after a married life of two years he was left a widower. Soon after the celebration of his nuptials he located on a plantation in Louisiana, and for a number of years was successfully engaged in planting in Tensas parish. Being a firm believer in state's rights, and enthusiastic in his love for the South, he immediately responded to the call of the Confederacy for troops at the opening of the Civil war. In 1861 he raised what was known as Watson's battery, and, as he was wealthy, he uniformed and equipped his men and furnished two hundred head of horses, the entire amount he spent being about $60,000. He went at once to the front, and, with his battery, took part in the battles of Belmont, Shiloh, Corinth, Baker's Creek and Port Hudson, his battery being captured in the last named engagement in 1863. Major Watson then served with different commands until the close of the war, a short time prior to which event he was commissioned by Jefferson Davis to raise and organize a new command in Louisiana, and was following out these commands when he heard of the surrender of General Lee. Although the war was at an end, and the North victorious, Major Watson returned to his home with the consciousness of having performed every duty faithfully and well, and, although he was considerably impoverished, he did not fold his hands and uselessly repine, but set energetically to work to retrieve his fortunes by locating on a plantation in Louisiana, his attention being devoted to this calling until 1882, when he sold out and bought his present place, known as Woodlawn. This is one of the most beautiful and best places in Jefferson county, and is situated about half way between Fayette and Rodney. Besides being beautiful and well appointed in every particular, it is a home of true and unbounded hospitality, where love, kindness and unselfishness reign supreme. Major Watson was happy in his choice of a wife, and in Louisiana was married, in 1865, to Miss Louisa Mason, a native of the Pelican state, but who was reared and educated in Boston, Mass., her father being a well-known physician, Dr. Josiah Mason. Major Watson became the father of two children by his first wife: A. C., a planter of Louisiana, and Frank, a business man of New Orleans. To his last union three children have been born: A. J., a merchant of Louisiana; Lulie A., and Albert Sidney Johnston, a prosperous young business man of Louisiana. One son, James M., died at the age of fourteen years. Major Watson has all his life appreciated the liberal education he received in his youth, and has given all his children excellent advantages, which they did not fail to improve, being a credit to themselves and their parents. Mrs. Watson is a member of the Episcopal church, and, socially, the Major is a Master

Mason. His reputation for honesty has been tried and not found wanting. His financial ability has been more than once put to the test, but never without credit to himself. His social qualities are well known and appreciated, and he has hosts of friends, whose confidence and esteem are his highest eulogium.

Dr. James R. Watson, physician, Lexington, a prominent citizen of Holmes county, Miss., was born in that county on the 10th of May, 1848. His father, Joseph H. Watson, was a native of North Carolina born in Jones county, in 1818, and was there reared and educated. He came to Mississippi in 1837, when a young man, settled on a farm in Holmes county and was there married to Miss Ann Eliza James, who died when her son, Dr. James R., was but three years old. Mr. Watson served as a member of the board of police for a number of years and also as magistrate. He took quite a prominent part in politics. During the war he served in the militia for home protection, Confederate service. He was a successful and prosperous farmer and accumulated a nice estate. His death occurred on the 22d of February, 1870. He had been twice married, his last wife living at the present time. Dr. James R. Watson was one of two children, his brother, Dr. J. H. Watson, being also a physician of Holmes county. He has one half-brother and three half-sisters. Dr. Watson received his education mostly by private tutors, studied medicine in this county and took his first course of lectures at the University of Louisiana in 1868 and 1869, graduating from that institution in the spring of 1870. He subsequently located in Holmes county, twelve miles south of Lexington, practiced his profession there for thirteen years and in connection carried on farming. He moved to Lexington in 1881, bought residence property, and in connection with farming has given his attention to the raising of thoroughbred Jersey cattle, his herd now numbering about thirty head. The Doctor has been unusually successful in all his enterprises, is the owner of several plantations and has a small farm of about one hundred and seventy acres near town. He has about seven acres in strawberries and about the same number of acres devoted to orchard peach, pear and plum trees. His political principles are purely democratic and he served as a member of the board of supervisors for several years, being president of the same most of the time. He was also a member of the city court. On the 5th of May, 1870, he married Miss Alice C. Stewart, a native of Holmes county, Miss., where she was reared and educated, and the daughter of John M. and Elizabeth Stewart. There were six children by this union. Mrs. Watson died on the 31st of December, 1882. The Doctor took for his second wife Miss Fannie L. Dyer, who was born, reared and educated in Holmes county, and who is a daughter of Judge J. M. Dyer. Three children are the fruits of this union. Dr. Watson is a Master Mason, a member of the Knights of Honor and the Knights of Pythias. He is a member of the Methodist church, and has been steward in the same for some time. Mrs. Watson is a member of the Presbyterian church. The children by his first wife are named as follows: Anna A., John Stewart, Bettie Ford, Mattie May, Alice Lee and James Raford, and those by the second union: Julia Dyer, Eloise and Joseph D.

James W. Watson has been a resident of Claiborne county, Miss., since his birth, which occurred in Port Gibson in 1824. His father, James Watson, was a Tennesseean, but became a resident of Mississippi while it was still a territory. The latter's father, James Watson, was born in the Old North state, but at a very early day removed to Tennessee, and afterward to Mississippi, being among its very earliest settlers. To this gentleman a large family of children was born, all of whom grew to maturity and reared families of their own, with the exception of two. One of the sons, Isaiah Watson, served in the state legislature about 1839 or 1840. The eldest son was James Watson, the father of the immediate subject of this sketch, and was one of the first and leading merchants of Port Gibson, being associated with a Mr. Pope. Three months before his son James W. was born, while in New York city purchasing goods for his mercantile establishment, he was taken ill, and died soon after returning home, in the fall of 1823. After the birth of their son, their only child, Mrs. Watson lived only two weeks. Her maiden name was Malinda Crane, the daughter of Waterman Crane, one of the county's earliest settlers and most prominent men. Mr. Crane was a member of the first county court, and took an active part in the affairs of the county. He became the father of a large family, all of whom were more or less connected with the early history of the county, and are now deceased. After the death of his parents, James W. Watson, who was at that time two weeks old, was taken to raise by his mother's sister, Mrs. Clarissa (Crane) Young, wife of William Young, and with his uncle and aunt, who took the place of his father and mother, he remained until grown. William Young was a native of Scotland, and when he was about twenty-one years of age he came to America and settled at Port Gibson, where he followed the occupation of a merchant for a few years. There he was married to Mrs. Christie, a native of the county, after which he turned his attention to planting, at which he has been very successful, becoming wealthy. He was very highly educated, and while in his native land became a member of the Presbyterian church. He was very benevolent and open-hearted with his means, contributing freely to what he deemed deserving his support, and so sound was his judgment and so true his convictions that he did untold good with his means. He was called from life during the war, his widow surviving him many years, being an active member of the Presbyterian church throughout her life. By a former marriage to a Mr. Christie she became the mother of one child, a daughter named Caroline, who became the wife of Rev. S. R. Bertron, by whom she became the mother of two daughters, who lived to be grown and married, Mary, the youngest, marrying William Hughes, who now resides near Bethel, Miss., and Clara, who became the wife of Charles T. Purnell, her union resulting in the birth of one son. Mrs. Purnell is a widow, and is a resident of Virginia. James W. Watson received his early training in a country school, after which he entered Oakland college, and still later that noted institution of learning, Princeton college, New Jersey, from which he graduated in 1844, several members of his class afterward becoming eminent, among whom may be mentioned Representative Hooker and Senator Colquit. After his graduation Mr. Watson returned to Claiborne county, Miss., and commenced planting in the neighborhood of Bethel. Several years later he purchased his present home place, which at that time was unimproved, but by industry and good management he has succeeded in putting under cultivation ten hundred of his eighteen-hundred-acre plantation. On this place is a good steam cottongin, but the first gin put up by him was run by horsepower. He was a strong Union man until his state seceded, and although he was a member of the convention that passed the ordinance, he opposed secession with all the strength of his energetic nature, but bowed to fate when the ordinance was passed, and went with his people. He has never taken any particular interest in political matters, but votes the democratic ticket, and has made speeches for his party during the campaigns. He was at one time a trustee of the Chamberlain-Hunt academy, and a director in the Grand Gulf & Port Gibson railroad. He was married in 1848 to Miss Miriam Buck, a daughter of William R. Buck, who served in one of the early wars (1812), and for the bravery he displayed in the capture of an English vessel in the Mediterranean sea he was awarded a sword. He was an early settler of Claiborne county, and was a very honest, conscientious, kind and modest gentleman. His children are: William H., was a captain of artillery in the Civil war, and C. E., was first lieutenant of a company of cavalry. The latter was a graduate of Princeton college, N. J., and of a medical college of New Orleans, and William H. was also a graduate of Princeton. C. E. is now deceased. William is residing in Louisiana and is a well-to-do planter. Caroline resides on the old home place (where the battle of Port Gibson was fought) and is unmarried. Mrs. Watson, his eldest daughter, was born and reared in this county and was educated in the Nazareth college of Bardstown, Ky. She has borne Mr. Watson the following children: James W. was educated in the West Point Military academy, graduating in 1880 and is now at San Carlos, Arizona territory, held the rank of first lieutenant (he was recommended to the war department as captain for bravery, and for gallant and distinguished service while in a fight with the Apache Indians near Salt river, Arizona; March 7, 1890, he was promoted to the rank of captain of the Tenth cavalry); Samuel D. was educated in Nashville, Tenn., and is now a successful planter of Louisiana; William Y. was educated at Port Gibson and Oxford, Miss., and is now at home; Maria F. is the wife of Capt. E. P. Briscoe, and was educated in New Orleans; Linda, who was educated at Port Gibson and the Female college of Fairmont, Tenn., is an accomplished young woman. William Y. has a plantation adjoining his father's, which he is engaged in tilling in connection with looking after the home place. Mr. Watson has an extensive library and is one of the best read men in the county, keeping thoroughly apace with the times. His residence, which was erected in 1848, is still in good repair and is beautifully situated on an elevated tract on the north fork of the Bayou Pierre river. Mrs. Watson is a member of the Presbyterian church.

Hon. John W. C. Watson (deceased). Death brings its sorrowful pangs unfailingly to the hearts of those bound to the departed by ties of relationship and bonds of affection, but when the icy hand is laid upon a citizen of distinction and widespread influence, the result of a long and well-spent life which has clustered around it valuable and distinguished public services and cherished private virtues, this sorrow is not confined alone to those who mourn because of the tender ties of relationship, but brings sadness alike to the citizens of the entire community. Hon. John W. C. Watson was born in Albemarle county, Va., on the 27th of February, 1808, and died at his residence at Holly Springs, Miss., on the 24th of September, 1890. His early educational advantages were only such as could be obtained in the country schools of the time, but he improved them well, and afterward graduated in the law department of the University of Virginia, then in charge of Prof. J. A. G. Davis. In 1831, soon after his admission to the bar, Mr. Watson married Miss Catherine Davis, sister of Professor Davis, a lady of lovely character who was richly endowed with personal attractions. Her companionship was the chief joy of his life for nearly sixty years and her death occurred scarcely twelve months prior to his. A short time after their marriage the young couple removed to Abingdon, Va., where Mr. Watson continued in the successful practice of his profession until 1845, at which time he removed to Holly Springs, Miss., where a law partnership had been tendered him by J. W. Clapp, formerly a student in his law office. He here assumed, upon the very day of his arrival, the active duties of his profession, which he continued to perform with almost phenomenal assiduity and ability until well nigh the time of his death. In the resplendent galaxy of legal talent of which Mississippi can boast, his name shines with conspicuous luster. The official reports of the supreme judicial tribunals, both state and national, indicate the frequency with which he appeared as counsel in the most important cases and bear ample evidence of that untiring industry, zeal and learning as a lawyer which frequently elicited high and well-merited encomiums from the bench.

In May, 1876, Mr. Watson was appointed a judge of the circuit court of the state by the governor, an office he held for a term of six years. As a judicial officer he was inflexible in his adherence to what he believed to be right, and yet, as far as he felt he might do so, he tempered judgment and justice with mercy, and always exhibited a conscientious and considerate recognition of the rights and feelings of all. His integrity and uprightness as a judge were proverbial, and no stain ever sullied his judicial ermine, nor breath of obloquy dimmed the brightness of his official escutcheon. Among his professional brethren he was distinguished for his urbanity and sympathetic aid to the younger members of the profession, as well as for an honorable bearing and appreciation of the dignity and responsibilities of the legal profession which his surviving brethren may well aspire to equal.

In politics Judge Watson was a whig as long as that party had a recognized existence, and was active and earnest in his opposition to the secession of the Southern states, preceding the late Civil war. But when the die was cast he adhered to the fortunes of his state, and was equally active and earnest in his efforts to promote the interests of the South. In 1863 he was elected by the legislature of Mississippi to the Confederate senate, and served in that capacity until the close of the war. He also, both before and after the war, filled various responsible positions, such as delegate to the national convention of his party, member of the state legislature and state constitutional conventions, and commissioner in behalf of the state to Washington, D. C., with a view to obtaining relief from the arbitrary and oppressive measures adopted by the Federal government toward the seceding states after the war. This lively and watchful concern in public affairs he continued to manifest to the close of his life, as was evinced by the interest he expressed and the suggestions he made during his last illness as to the proceedings of the constitutional convention of Mississippi, then in session. The moral and religious aspect of Judge Watson's life is a feature deserving especial comment. In his early manhood he professed his faith in Christ as his Redeemer, and became a member of the Presbyterian church, and throughout his long and useful life he was conspicuous for the fidelity with which he maintained his allegiance to his Divine Master, and for the interest and zeal which he manifested in the cause of religion and good morals. While he cherished a profound reverence and affection for the church of his choice and was an ardent supporter of its doctrines, he was tolerant toward other denominations, and ready at all times to extend the hand of fellowship to all whom he believed to be sincere Christians. Whatever cause or pursuit he espoused, whether in matters of state or church, of law or morals, he never entered into it by halves, but took hold of it with characteristic energy and ardor. Among other matters of public concern and vitally affecting the welfare of society to which he directed his attention, was that of the sale and use of intoxicating liquors. He was known as a zealous temperance worker for many years, and it was through his invitation that Miss Willard first visited Mississippi. He wrote her in 1882 and secured a hearing before the legislature, where she won over men who have ever since been stanch allies to the temperance cause. As an advocate he was persuasive and logical, not unfrequently rising to the hights of true eloquence and lofty oratory. His arguments upon legal propositions before the various courts were analytical expositions and enforcements of legal principles which rarely failed to carry convictions. One of the most brilliant achievements of his career as a lawyer was his success before the superior courts of the United States, in what is known as the railroad commission cases, argued October, 1885. Judge Watson represented the state of Mississippi by appointment of Governor Lowry. The railroad corporations were represented, respectively, by the ablest legal talent of the country. Chief Justice Waite pronounced the opinion of the court, reversed the decision of the United States circuit court judge, and dismissed the bills of the several railroad corporations, holding, as contended by Judge Watson, that the act of the Mississippi legislature creating the railroad commission was constitutional. So brilliant was this last great argument of Judge Watson before the august tribunal, that the chief justice, in a private conversation, attested his profound legal learning and forensic power. His unswerving fidelity to truth, his conscientious discharge of duty, from which no temptation could seduce him, was a characteristic which specially endeared him to all those who knew him. Socially, Judge Watson was the courteous, affable gentleman, the faithful friend, the conservative, trustworthy public-spirited citizen, and the open-handed sympathizer with those in distress. In domestic life, his home was the haven of repose and happiness, where his loving nature found full gratification in the devoted affections of wife and children. Of the latter, eight were born as the fruit of his marriage, only two of whom now survive: James H. Watson, a prominent member of the Memphis bar, and Miss E. D. Watson, principal of Maury institute, at Holly Springs. Few men have left behind them a record more stainless and enviable in all the walks of life than has Judge Watson. A friend makes this statement: "That those who knew him best loved him most."

Capt. Robert H. Watson, proprietor of the Iuka Springs house. Iuka has over a thousand inhabitants and is situated on the Memphis & Charleston railroad, one hundred and fifteen miles east of Memphis, six miles from the Alabama line, seven miles from the Tennessee river; upon one of the most elevated sections of Mississippi, readily accessible by the Memphis & Charleston and its connections. The country around is hilly and has been termed the Switzerland of Mississippi. The corporation is one mile square. Every house is surrounded by ample grounds of orchard, park and garden. There are five churches, all with active, earnest membership, and a flourishing normal school. Cordial, hospitable, wide-awake and energetic, the inhabitants of Iuka are pleasant people with whom to cast your lot. The Springs house is a magnificent, four-story brick structure, to which has been added, to meet the increased patronage, a large frame addition, together with a square of neat, cool, three-roomed cottages. The open court around which they are built is a beautiful grass-covered plot, shaded from the summer's sun, the place for croquet and other out door games. Balconies above and below furnish a cool, delightful place throughout the summer days for quiet thought, jolly conversation or social promenade. One steps from the train into the entrance of the hotel. In the front central part is the office. On this floor are a number of choice rooms. On the second floor is an elegant ballroom, well fitted to the fancy of those who worship at the shrine of Terpsichore. Conveniently near is the parlor. The diningroom is large and airy, the tables are supplied from the city markets supplemented by the rich, fresh store of good things from the country. The management is now in the efficient hands of Capt. R. H. Watson, which of itself is assurance to every one of perfect satisfaction. Captain Watson has thoroughly refitted and repaired the hotel property from top to bottom. Those who have been there before will hardly recognize the place, it has been so much improved from roof to foundation, new clothed with what of beauty the painter's hand can give. Captain Watson is a courteous, enterprising, successful business gentleman, and his name guarantees that no pains or expense will be spared to make Iuka Springs the most delightful summer resort of the South. This gentleman was born in York district, S. C., August 5, 1832, a son of Matthew and Eleanor (Love) Watson. His father was a native of Ireland and was born in 1778. He came to this country when about twenty-five years old and located in Tennessee, whence he removed to Mississippi, where in the early days he became prominent as an educator. He was married in South Carolina about 1820, and raised five children: Margaret, John L., Catherine, Mary J. and Robert H. His wife was born in South

Carolina, in 1797, a daughter of John and Drucilla Love. They were married in South Carolina, previous to the removal of Mr. Watson to Tennessee, and came together to this county in 1838. They were both members of the Methodist Episcopal church. Mr. Watson died in 1842, and his wife died in 1852. The former was politically an old-line whig. The early life of Captain Watson was spent in Tishomingo county, and at the age of twenty he went to East Port and became a clerk of R. B. Brown, where he remained for three years. He then went to Pleasant Site, Ala., where he became a merchant, planter and miller, being successful in each of the three occupations. There he remained until 1884, when he came to Iuka, where he established a mercantile business, which is now managed by his son C. L. Watson. In October, 1890, he purchased the Iuka Springs house and the property connected with it.

In 1859 he was married to Miss Martha J. Harrison, one of the five children of John and Polly (Harrison) Harrison, who was born in Lauderdale county, Ala., in 1836. Of this marriage five children were born, the two following of whom are living: John H., and Charles L. John H. has, since his father's retirement from the active management of the mercantile business, been in charge of that important interest. John H. married Miss Mary William, and lives at Pleasant Site, Ala. Charles L. is bookkeeper in his father's store. Mrs. Watson died January 16, 1878, and in 1879 Captain Watson married again, this time to Morilla Cross, daughter of Dr. S. E. Cross and his wife, Margaret (Shelby) Cross, and she was born in Lauderdale county, Ala., in 1855. By this marriage he had four children: Mattie B., William C., Mary W. and Morella C. Mr. and Mrs. Watson are members of the Methodist Episcopal church. Politically Captain Watson is a stanch democrat. He acquired his title as captain by gallant service for the Confederate cause during the Civil war. He was in command of company B, of the Twenty-seventh Alabama infantry, for a year. For two years thereafter he was captain of a cavalry company. He was one of the first to answer the call for troops in 1861, and he participated in battles at Fort Henry, Fort Donelson, Jackson, Miss., Port Hudson and numerous other engagements and skirmishes. He was taken prisoner at Fort Donelson, but an opportunity soon presented, and he made his escape. After taking command of his company's cavalry, he served under General Forrest, and took part in the fighting at Tupelo, Cross Roads and Selma. He was paroled at Iuka, in 1865. Captain Watson has an enviable record as an honorable and successful business man, and is a public-spirited and useful citizen. He is largely interested in the improvement and development of the county, and has been especially helpful to schools and churches. His political influence is recognized, and though not an officeseeker, he has taken an active part in the public history of his county, and was a delegate to the state convention when Stone was nominated as governor.

Wheeler Watson is a native of Monroe county, Miss. He was born about three miles from his present residence, February 16, 1847. His father, Asa Watson, was born in Rhode Island in 1812, and was descended from colonial ancestry of sterling and sturdy characteristics. They settled, in the latter part of the seventeenth century, on a tract of land in Rhode Island, which is still owned by a member of the family. They were an energetic, industrious, highly educated, honorable family, and stood in the foremost rank of Rhode Island's best people, many of them filling the most responsible positions in the gift of the people. Wheeler Watson's grandmother, on his father's side, was Mary Peckham, a descendant of the noted family of Peckhams of New York, so many of whom have adorned the bench and the bar of the state. Judge Malborne Watson and Judge Rufus Peckham, both judges of the supreme court of New York, are cousins of Wheeler Watson. His father, formerly a merchant in Albany, N. Y., came South and married a cultivated, refined Southern lady, a sister of Hon. John M. Taylor, of Tennessee, and niece of Hon. Christopher Williams, of Tennessee. His father became a planter, and identified himself thoroughly with the people of the South. His qualifications as a man of business were of the highest order, and he possessed a comprehensive intellect, boundless self-reliance, unflagging industry and energy, and withal was strongly armed with honesty and integrity—a conjunction of qualities which, employed in his orderly and exact methods, could not fail to bring him into the foremost ranks of honorable and successful planters. Wheeler Watson's boyhood was spent partly in Monroe county, Miss., and in traveling over the North. He was educated in Columbus, Miss., at La Grange college, in Alabama. He is a worthy descendant of a long line of honorable ancestors, and in him is a happy mingling of the best traits of the North and the South, for he has all the genial, courteous kindness and chivalry of a Southern gentleman, combining the untiring energy, industry and sterling characteristics of his Northern ancestors. He is progressive, hospitable and a good liver. In his home life he is indulgent. He enjoys the esteem of his friends, and is an altogether honest, useful citizen of whom his neighbors may well feel proud. He has been for years extensively engaged in cotton planting. He is now very much interested in planting large pecan groves and in seeding a large tract of land in grasses. He is an enterprising and progressive planter. In 1871 he married Miss Alice Clay, of Monroe county, a daughter of Thomas and Caledonia (Oliver) Clay. In the early part of 1863, when he was only sixteen years of age, he entered the army, enlisting in the Seventeenth Tennessee battalion, which consolidated with Stied's battalion, forming the Thirteenth Mississippi regular cavalry. His service began below Tupelo, Miss., whence he went into the north Alabama campaign. Later he served near Vicksburg, participating in the fights about there, and went thence to Jackson and Canton, whence he went to Rome, Ga. Still later he served under Johnston and Hood in Georgia. He went from there to Savannah, and later served under General Johnston, in North Carolina. After the surrender of Lee and Johnston, he returned with his regiment to Greensboro, N. C., waiting for President Davis, with whom the regiment went as a bodyguard to Washington, Ga., where the members were paid $25 each in specie, and the regiment was disbanded. He was a gallant soldier and did his duty faithfully and well. Mr. Watson is of an inventive turn of mind, and has originated several useful machines. His first patent was granted September 25, 1888, on a fruit gatherer; the next, granted January 20, 1891, was for a plow; another, granted February 3, 1891, was upon a peanut picker. These are practical working machines invented as aids in carrying on the work on his home plantation. He has never made any effort to bring them into general use, being so deeply engrossed in the affairs of his plantation that he has no time to attend to outside business. He is thoroughly posted upon current events, and enjoys a wide acquaintance with prominent men.

Robert H. Watt belongs to that sturdy, honest and independent class, the planters of Mississippi, and is now engaged in cultivating an estate comprising about three thousand six hundred acres, of which some one thousand acres are under cultivation, on which are annually raised four hundred bales of cotton and three thousand bushels of corn. He was born in Warren county, being the second of four children born to Hugh and Nancy S. (Clark) Watt, the former of whom was a native of Ireland, and came to America about 1829, settling in Pennsylvania, where he met and married his wife. He was a carpenter, and worked at his trade in Pennsylvania, and also after coming to Mississippi, but in 1835 opened a carriage, wagon, plow and general repair shop, near where Dr. Naylor is now living, nine miles southeast of Vicksburg, where he conducted his business affairs with success for eight years, the three following years being spent at the same calling near the home of Ninion Klein. He then purchased the plantation of Dr. Crawford, which consisted of four hundred and eighty acres, and on this plantation resided until his death, which occurred, very suddenly, in Vicksburg. His wife was a Canadian by birth, and moved to Pennsylvania when young. She died July 3, 1870. He was a whig in politics, and was a strong Union man prior to the war. He died February 14, 1862. Robert H. Watt attended a private school until seventeen years of age, the two subsequent years being spent in college in Springville. N. Y. At the end of this time, on account of his father's enfeebled condition, he returned home to look after the interests of the plantation. In 1862 he dropped his farming implements to don the weapons of warfare in defense of his home, and became a member of company H., Capt. L. C. Moore's Forty-seventh Mississippi infantry, army of Virginia, and was in the battle of Seven Pines and other engagements around Richmond, in one of which he was wounded in the thigh by a shell, which produced permanent injury. After remaining in the hospital two weeks he was furloughed home, and although he made an effort to rejoin the Confederate army in April, 1864, at Petersburg, he was rejected, and was compelled to return home. He was at once captured by a Wisconsin regiment, and was incarcerated at Vicksburg for two months, but was paroled and discharged by General Dana, and returned at once to his home, where he set himself to work to improve his mother's war-worn plantation, preparatory to an energetic era of planting. In 1868 he purchased part of the Randall Gibson place, and continued to make purchases from time to time, until he now owns the entire tract, with the exception of ten acres. In 1874 he bought the Gibson place of over three hundred and seventy acres, and has at different times purchased land from the Hilderbrands, the Whittingtons, Stocktons, Hulloms and Stevenses, aggregating fully three thousand six hundred acres. On this admirably conducted plantation he raises a sufficient amount of stock for his own use. He takes no active part in politics, much preferring to devote his attention to his plantation. He is very highly esteemed in the section in which he resides, and is unmarried.

David S. Watts, M. D., of Madison county, Miss., was born in Wilkes county, Ga., on the 29th of December, 1833, and is the only child born to the union of David S. and Martha C. (Billingslea) Watts, both natives of Georgia also. The father died one month before David S., Jr., was born, and the latter remained in Georgia until twelve years of age with his grandfather Billingslea. The grandfather then removed with him to the Lone Star state in 1845, and two years later came to Mississippi. David remained with his grandfather until eighteen years of age, received his education in Canton, and subsequently spent one session in a medical institution in Louisville, Ky. He then finished his course at Georgia Medical college, Augusta, and in 1856 began the practice of medicine in Madison county, where he has since, a period of about thirty-five years, carried on a successful country practice. He was married in November, 1859, to Miss Ana N. Sutherland, daughter of P. R. and Louise (Olive) Sutherland, and this union resulted in the birth of eleven living children, one having died in infancy, viz.: Mattie L., wife of C. J. Dancey, of Greenville, Miss.; Aurelia S., wife of J. W. Brown, of Sunflower county; Anna Bell, wife of O. H. Billingslea, Sunflower county; Walter W., at home; Ollie E., wife H. T. Cassell, of Canton; David S., of Bolivar county; Charles D., at Mississippi college; Hallie M.; Clifford P. (deceased); Bertha M.; Johnson Olive and James Reid. In December, 1861, Dr. Watts volunteered as a private in the state service under Capt. R. B. Campbell, and was detailed to the hospital service, but on account of ill health was discharged at the end of one year. He is now the owner of about twelve hundred acres of fine land, has about six hundred acres under cultivation and three hundred acres in pasture. He raises improved stock of all kinds. He takes an active interest in politics, but has never aspired to office, and just lately declined the nomination to represent Madison county in the legislature. Dr. Watts was master of Camden Royal Arch lodge No. 74 during the time of its greatest activity, is a member of the Knights of Honor, and has held numerous offices in the Farmers' Alliance. He and Mrs. Watts are members of the Baptist church of Canton. The Doctor has seen the full development of the country, has contributed liberally to all laudable public enterprises, and is one of the county's best citizens.

Capt. James Watts was born in Wayne county, Miss., May 1, 1829, a son of John and Elizabeth (Chapman) Watts, the former of whom was a North Carolinian by birth and came to Mississippi when a boy, where he grew to manhood and married. He became a prominent and well-known citizen of Wayne county, filled the position of district attorney for a number of years and was circuit judge for twenty-five years. He was also a member of the state senate for some time and throughout his life was a warm personal friend of Judge Sharkey. He was a local preacher of the Methodist Episcopal church, of which he had long been a member, and died in full communion with that church at Newton, in Newton county, Miss., in 1875. He was a son of Josiah and Margaret (Evans) Watts. His wife was a South Carolinian by birth and a daughter of Thrashley and Catherine (Edwards) Chapman, with whom she came to Mississippi when a child of six years. Her marriage was celebrated in Wayne county in 1826, and resulted in the birth of ten children: Josiah, James (the immediate subject of this sketch), John B., Thomas, Julia, Cornelia, Olcott S., William S., Mary and Elizabeth A. The early life of Capt. James Watts was spent in Jasper county, his education being obtained at Paulding academy, but left school in 1846 and began the study of law, being admitted to the bar of Mississippi in 1850. He commenced practicing at De Kalb, Kemper county, but during 1866-8 he was one of the ablest lawyers of the city of Meridian. He is now a resident of Scooba, Kemper county. He was married in 1851, to Miss Eleanor Bell, a daughter of Dr. Samuel Bell, of Kemper county, of which he became a resident in 1844. Her mother, Jane Parke, was a native of England. Mrs. Watts was born in North Carolina in 1832 and has borne her husband four sons and six daughters: Elizabeth, wife of B. F. Ormond of Meridian; Ella W., wife of W. H. Ormond, of Meridian; John B., at Lauderdale; Clifford H.; Mamie L. wife of J. W. Brooke, of Meridian; Julia B.; James E.; Hallie A., wife of J. P. Lipscomb; Florence C. and Samuel T. Mr. Watts and his wife are members of the Methodist Episcopal church, and although he was formerly an old line whig, he is now a member of the democrat party. Socially he belongs to the I. O. O. F., of which he has been a member since he was twenty-one years of age, and he has attained the thirty-second degree in the A. F. & A. M. fraternity. In 1862 he organized what was known as company A, of the Thirty-fifth Mississippi infantry, commanded by William S. Berry, of Moore's brigade, Maury's division, Price's command, army of the West, and one of the principal engagements in which he took part was the battle of Corinth, Miss. He afterward resigned and returned to his home on account of ill health.

John B. Watts, the third child born to Captain James and Eleanor (Bell) Watts, whose sketch appears above, was born in Kemper county, Miss., in the month of April, 1856. He began life for himself at the age of sixteen years (after he had obtained a fair education), as a clerk in the store of B. F. Ormond & Bro., at Lauderdale, Miss., with whom he remained four years. At the end of this time he entered the University of Mississippi, at Oxford, and after remaining in that institution for one year he returned home and engaged in farming, which calling he followed with fair success for three years. He then went to the Lone Star state and worked for the Texas Pacific railroad company for nearly two years, returning to Lauderdale county, Miss., in 1882, and for some time thereafter kept books for J. L. Simmons, whose daughter he married in 1882. They have two sons and two daughters: Kitty B., Eleanor, John and James. Mr. Watts began the mercantile business for himself in Lauderdale in 1887, and by honest toil, persistent endeavor, upright methods of conducting his affairs and desire to please his patrons, he has established for himself a lucrative business. In 1891 he was elected mayor of Lauderdale, but respectfully declined the position, as his business occupied his time and attention. The stock of goods that he carries amounts to about $6,000, and he does an annual business of $20,000, besides which he owns four hundred acres of good land near the town of Lauderdale, of which one hundred and fifty acres are improved and under cultivation, and some good and valuable residence property within the corporation. He is superintendent in the Methodist Episcopal Sunday-school, of which church he is an active member, and he is also one of the working members of the A. F. & A. M. and the K. of H. His wife is a member of the Presbyterian church, and they are highly esteemed in the social circles in which they move. They are hospitable, generous and liberal and are among the worthy, useful and substantial citizens of the county.

Capt. S. B. Watts, a prominent lawyer of Lauderdale county, Miss., residing at Meridian, was born in Jasper county, Miss., April 13, 1843, a son of Samuel B. and Mary A. (Mayers) Watts, natives of Mississippi. His paternal grandfather was one of the pioneers of Wayne county, Miss., where he became a well-known and successful planter and merchant. He died in 1843, leaving two sons, Maj. A. B. Watts and Capt. S. B. Watts, both of whom are now residents of Meridian. Captain Watts, who was but an infant at the time of his father's death, received his primary education in the private schools in Jasper county, and later attended a school at Brandon, Miss. In 1861, when but eighteen years of age, he enlisted in the Rankin rifles, with which organization he served until the reorganization of the army, when he entered the Confederate service and served until the close of the war. He entered the struggle as a private and rose to the rank of captain. At Franklin, Tenn., he was taken prisoner and surrendered his sword to Captain Knapp, of Martin, Ohio. He was confined at Johnson's island, Ohio, until June, 1865, about six months altogether. Twenty-two years after the war, while he was visiting in Ohio, his sword was returned to him by Captain Knapp's daughter. He participated in the battles of Shiloh, Murfreesboro, Mumfordsville, Resaca, Jonesboro, Chickamauga, Missionary Ridge and Franklin. He was three times wounded by gunshot at Mumfordsville, Chickamauga and near Marietta. After his return home he began reading law and was admitted to the bar at Brandon, Miss. He located at Meridian, Miss., in 1867, and there he has been engaged principally in the practice of his profession. He was United States commissioner for about fifteen years, and is now candidate for the office of state senator. He has been a member of the city council of Meridian, and has otherwise taken an active interest in the growth and development of the city. He has been for many years president of the board of trustees of the East Mississippi Female college, which he was largely instrumental in founding. He is also president of the board of trustees of the state insane asylum, which is located at Meridian. Politically he is a democrat. He is a communicant of the Methodist Episcopal church, a member of the I. O. O. F., of the Knights of Honor and of the Knights and Ladies of Honor. He was married in 1868 to Kate McLaurin, of Rankin county, Miss., by whom he has five children: A. M., Sadie Z., Kate McL., Mary I. and Louise L.

Hiram E. Weatherbee is a leading merchant of the town of Greenville, and has, by his keen business foresight, built a business second to none within the limits of Washington county, Miss. He was born in Boone county, Ky., December 31, 1842, to Tarable W. and Sally A. (Woodberry) Weatherbee, both of whom were born in the state of New York, the former being a mechanic by trade. He moved to Kentucky in 1844, and of this state he has since been an honored, industrious and esteemed resident. The paternal grandfather, Oliver Weatherbee, and the grandmother, formerly Miss Willard, were born in some of the New England states, the paternal great-grandparents having come from England in the pioneer days of America, taking up their abode in New England. Hiram E. Weatherbee was reared principally in Indiana and Illinois, but his schooldays were very much broken up on account of the war, which was in full progress at just the time when he should have been devoting his attention to his studies. Since that time, by close application, he has become one of the most intelligent and best informed men in the county. He began the battle of life for himself at the age of eighteen years, but his capital consisted solely of a good constitution, pluck and a knowledge of the tinner's trade, which he followed closely for six years. He then opened an establishment of his own in Greenville, Miss., and since that time has been one of the leading hardware merchants of the place and is doing a thriving business on Walnut street. He is the owner of about three thousand acres of land in Washington, Sunflower and Bolivar counties, six hundred acres of which land are under cultivation, and besides this he is the owner of a considerable amount of real estate in the city of Greenville, including three of the best business houses in the place. He carries a stock of goods valued at about $1,200, his annual sales being large and netting him a handsome profit. He erected a handsome residence in Greenville in 1882, on Washington avenue, and in this pleasant and comfortable home he and his estimable wife dispense hospitality with true Southern liberality. In 1862 he enlisted in the Union army, becoming a member of company E, One hundred and Twentieth Illinois regiment, for he believed that the Southern states had no right to secede, and remained true to the stars and stripes until the war closed. The most important engagement in which he took part was the siege of Vicksburg. He was in Memphis, Tenn., when the news reached him of the surrender of Lee. Miss Dora McCoy, a native of Illinois, became his wife in 1874, she being a daughter of Job W. and Eliza (Richey) McCoy, the former a Virginian and the latter a native of Tennessee. Mr. McCoy was a merchant. To Mr. Weatherbee's union two children have been born: Harry L. and Edna, both of whom are at home with their parents. The town of Greenville has been Mr. Weatherbee's home since 1867. He is interested in the banks of the place, the Street Railway Compress company, and, in fact, all worthy enterprises have received encouragement from him. Notwithstanding the fact that he commenced life a poor boy, he has made a comfortable fortune and is considered by all a leading and substantial citizen of Greenville. He is a man of whom it might well be said he has not lived in vain, but with a purpose ever before him, and with a full knowledge of the fact that one has a mission in life, he has not passed his days in idleness, or, like Micawber, waited for something to turn up, but has manfully put his shoulder to the wheel, and as a reward has become possessed of an ample income and has a kindly and charitable feeling toward all men; while he has been diligent in business, and is, as are also his wife and son, a zealous member and worker of the Presbyterian church, socially he also belongs to the A. F. & A. M., the K. of P. and the K. of H. In personal appearance he is above medium hight, is of graceful and easy address, and is an intelligent and entertaining conversationalist. He was the fourth of nine children born to his parents, all of whom attained maturity, five of whom are now living in different parts of the Union. He lost two brothers during the yellow-fever epidemic of 1878.

Albert G. Webb, Columbia, Marion county, Miss. John H. Webb, deceased, was born in the state of Georgia about the year 1801, but in his youth removed to Mississippi, where he grew to manhood. He settled in Marion county, and there married Miss Elizabeth Hammond. They reared a family of ten children, seven of whom lived to maturity: Mary S. married Thomas Edmonson, a prominent man, and at one time sheriff of Marion county (he died and she married Thomas Allen); Walter B., the eldest son, died a few years since; William T., M. D., who became captain of company D, Seventh Mississippi infantry; Courtney A. married W. J. Sones, of Lawrence county; Henry W., who was killed in the battle of Murfreesboro; Albert G., the subject of this notice; and Louie E., who married W. J. Bass; the other three children died in infancy, and all of this family are dead except Mrs. Mary S. Allen, who is now a widow, and Albert G. Webb, the subject of this notice. The maternal grandparents, Benjamin and Mary (Cooper) Hammond, were both natives of Tennessee, and were among the early settlers of Marion county; they reared a family of twelve sons and one daughter; Gordon and Jackson Hammond are still residents of this county. Albert G. Webb, son of John H. Webb, was born in Marion county, Miss., October 23, 1843. When the Civil war broke out, he enlisted in the first company that went from Marion county, and served until the surrender. He was in the battle of Shiloh, and went through the Kentucky campaign with General Bragg. When the war was ended he returned to his home and embarked in the mercantile trade as bookkeeper and salesman. This he continued six years, in the employ of W. B. Webb and A. E. Foxworth, taking a course of instruction in the business college at New Orleans, from which he was graduated. In 1874 he was married to Miss Nannie H. Regan, and taught school that year in the original Pearl county. For three years, from 1875 to 1878, he served as clerk of this county, but at this time its existence as a county ceased. Captain Webb then removed to Marion county, and took charge of the clerk's office at Columbia, as deputy. He discharged the duties of this position until 1879, when he was appointed clerk of the county to fill the unexpired term of Paul L. Gusman. In the autumn of the same year he was elected to the office, and has held it continuously since that time. In the summer of 1890 he was elected a delegate to the constitutional convention. He is a man of excellent business ability, and has always worked for the success of his party. As a citizen he is loyal and public-spirited, and has contributed both his means and influence to those enterprises which have tended to the growth of the county and its general development. Captain and Mrs. Webb have a family of six children—five daughters and one son. He is a member of the Masonic order, and of the Knights of Honor. The family belong to the Methodist Episcopal church.

W. S. Webb, president of Mississippi college, was born in Le Roy, N. Y., on the 14th of November, 1825, the youngest of fourteen children born to Benoni and Betsey (Phillips) Webb, natives of Massachusetts, the father's ancestors being Welsh and the mother's German. The father, who was a blacksmith and farmer, died in 1867. After attending the common country schools until he was eighteen years of age, W. S. Webb left home to take a course of study in Kingsville academy, preparatory to a college course, after which he entered Colgate university in central New York, where he spent four years, graduating in 1849. He then went to Tennessee to engage in teaching in Stewart's Creek academy, near Murfreesboro, and after remaining there two years was elected president of a female college in Grenada, Miss., taking upon himself the duties of this position in the fall of 1851, where he remained six years. While at that place the present large and commodious brick building was built under his direction and the attendance was built up from seventy-five to one hundred and eighty pupils. He left this institution in a flourishing condition, to take a position in the Starkville high school, but after two years spent in this place he removed to West

Point, where he became pastor of the Baptist church. Six years later he removed to Crawfordsville, remaining pastor of the church at that place for fourteen years, during which time he took a prominent part in organizing the Confederate Orphans' Home, located at Lauderdale Springs, Miss., about 1864, and was corresponding secretary of the board of trustees. On the 1st of January, 1872, he came to Clinton to act as pastor of the Baptist church and to deliver lectures to the theological students. About one year after coming hither, Dr. Hillman, then president of the college, resigned and Mr. Webb was elected to fill his place and continued in the successful discharge of his arduous duties till July of the present year (1891), when he resigned the presidency of the college and was appointed emeritus professor of psychology and ethics. This is considered an honor and most worthily bestowed. There are, it is thought, but four such professorships held in the world and this is the only instance on record where such an honor has been bestowed by a Baptist institution of learning. In 1882, the title of D. D. was conferred upon him by the Mississippi State university at Oxford, and also by the Howard college, Marion, Ala. Dr. Webb's struggles to build up the college while it had no endowment, in the midst of pestilences, political revolutions and financial crises, have been nothing less than heroic, and his success has been wonderful. He has proved to be the right man in the right place, and under his able and efficient management the college has come to have a national reputation. During his administration about $60,000 has been secured toward an endowment fund for the college. President Webb possesses the entire confidence of the people, for, besides being an admirable disciplinarian, he is a talented, thorough and well-posted educator. The course of instruction is thoroughness itself, and the college seems now to have entered upon an era of unusual success. The grade of scholarship is being constantly raised, requiring a higher degree of proficiency to enter the institution. The present number of students attending the institution is about two hundred and fifty, which greatly increases their need of better facilities, and this fact is coming to be recognized and work in that direction is being pushed forward. President Webb was married in Tennessee, in 1850, to Miss Adelphia Wheeler, of New York, and their union resulted in the birth of two children: C. W., and Fannie A., wife of Rev. R. A. Venable, pastor of the First Baptist church of Memphis, Tenn. Mrs. Webb died in 1855, and in 1857 Mr. Webb married Miss Mary McMath, by whom he became the father of two children: Mrs. H. R. Granberry, whose husband is chancery clerk of Copiah county, and Mrs. S. M. Dodds, wife of Senator Dodds. The mother of these children was called from earth in West Point in 1863, and two years later President Webb's third marriage was celebrated at Marion, Ala., Miss M. J. Sherman, a sister of Professor Sherman, of Howard college, becoming his wife and the mother of his six children: Maggie, W. S., Thomas L., Myrtle, Henry D. and Nelson G. The eldest daughter is teaching in Kelhie college, Louisana. Sherman attended medical college in Louisville, Ky., and upon graduating took the highest honors in his class, being now a successful practitioner in the hospital. Thomas L. is in Coleman, Tex., and Henry is captain of the Mississippi College rifles.

F. M. Weed, agent for the Louisville & Nashville railroad at Ocean Springs, Miss., is a native of New England, born in the state of Vermont in 1850. He is a son of Judge F. A. Weed, of Burlington, Vt. Believing the West afforded greater opportunities for the rising generation, our subject went to Texas in his early manhood and engaged in cattle and sheepraising. Finding the frontier life extremely severe, he determined to return to his home and re-enter school. This he did, and was graduated from the high school of Hinesburg, Vt. He then secured a situation with a railway company, and has since been devoted to this business. For fourteen years he has been in the employ of the Louisville &

Nashville railroad company, stationed during this period at Ocean Springs, Jackson county, Miss. No higher tribute could be paid to him than the fact of his being kept in charge of the business at this point for so great a length of time. He has been faithful to the interests of his company and has never shirked a duty. He is a master of all the details of the business, and is well worthy of the confidence which his employers repose in him. Politically he is an uncompromising democrat. He was chairman of the last county convention, and is chairman of the present senatorial convention, comprising Hancock, Jackson and Harrison counties. In all the deliberations of that body his counsel is sought and his opinions carry conviction. He is one of the most promising men in political circles in Jackson county, and a bright future is predicted for him. He is a prominent member of the Knights of Pythias, in which he holds a high official position. Mr. Weed was united in marriage to Miss Alice A. Lyon, of St. Albans, Vt.

Robert S. Weir, Vaiden, Miss. Among the pioneers to settle in Carroll county, Miss., was the family of Dr. H. H. Weir. The Doctor was a native of Virginia, and was educated in his native state, graduating from the Washington college, now Washington and Lee university, and from the medical department of the University of Pennsylvania. He was married to Jane T. Steele, also a Virginian. He settled in Carroll county about the year 1834, when Indians were numerous, and wild animals roamed at will. The tavern at which he boarded was not graced with a door, and at night a barricade was made of tables and other furniture to keep out the beasts of the field. When, finally, the Doctor built a residence with the luxuries of planed floors and doors, some of the settlers said he was stuck up and was putting on airs. The territory in which he practiced covered many miles. He was very successful in his practice, and won many warm friends. He was an active member of the Presbyterian church, and served as an elder in the same. He was very liberal in his support of the church, and gave generously to all charitable purposes. He died in Carroll county, Miss., in 1858. His wife survived him many years; her death occurred in 1881.

Robert S. Weir, son of the above, is one of a family of five sons and one daughter. One brother died just as he reached maturity; one died at the age of fifteen years. Of the living members, one brother, William Weir, is a merchant in Texas; Rush C. is a successful druggist at Vaiden; the sister, Ophelia, is the widow of Samuel T. Lockhart. The two brothers are unmarried, and they, with the widowed sister and her daughter, constitute a happy family. They have a beautiful home in Vaiden. Robert S. was educated at the University of Oxford, and was graduated from that institution in the year 1858. He entered the Confederate army in 1861, enlisting in the First Mississippi cavalry as a private. After a year and a half he was transferred to the commissary department, in which he served until the close of the war. He then returned to Carroll county, and in 1865 he engaged in the drug business in Vaiden. In a few years he disposed of his interest, selling to his brother, who still continues the business. He then embarked in the general mercantile trade, and carries a large and well-selected stock of goods. He is one of the solid, substantial men of Carroll county. He is generous and accommodating to his patrons, is of the highest moral character, and is justly esteemed one of the leading citizens of the county.

William S. Weissinger, M. D., Hernando, Miss. In reviewing the lives of those men in the three great professions, ministry, medicine and law, none command greater respect than the members of the medical fraternity. It may well be doubted if any one enters so fully into the soul life of another as he whose care is for its vehicle, the body. William S. Weissinger, one of the most honored physicians of the state of Mississippi, was born in Carroll county, Miss., June 17, 1847, and is the third of a family of ten children. His parents,

Alexander and Cordelia (Strong) Weissinger, were born and reared in Perry county, Ala. The father came to Mississippi about the year 1846, and located at old Middleton. In the latter days of his life he engaged in planting. Before the war he was a large owner of slaves, and hired his negroes out. He enlisted in the Confederate army in 1861, being a member of the Fourth Mississippi regiment. He served until the close of the conflict, and passed from this life in 18—. His father was a very wealthy planter, and for thirty-three years was a member of the legislature of Alabama. He and his two brothers emigrated from Germany to this country, landing at Charleston, S. C., near which point they settled. The maternal grandparents were George J. and Caroline (Nall) Strong, natives of Georgia and North Carolina, respectively. Theirs was a family of agriculturists, and commanded vast wealth; they were of English extraction. Dr. Weissinger was reared in Carroll county, Miss., and there received his education. In 1863 he enlisted in the service of his country, and served until the declaration of peace. He was a member of Captain Dun's company of state troops under Gen. J. Z. George, and was afterward in the Vaiden artillery, First Mississippi regiment. He was at Meridian at the time of the surrender. When the opportunity came to settle to more peaceful occupations the Doctor began teaching school, reading medicine during his leisure hours. After pursuing this plan for two years he attended a course of lectures at Louisville, Ky., and in 1869 he began the practice of his profession in De Soto county. After two years he received the degree of M. D. from the Tulane Medical college, of Louisiana. He has devoted his efforts to a thorough understanding of the science, and has been a close student of all advanced methods of treatment. He has built up a large and profitable practice, and takes a front rank among his brothers. He is the first vice president of the Tri-State Medical association of Mississippi, Arkansas and Tennessee, and is now serving his second term in this office. During three terms he was president of the De Soto County Medical association. The Doctor was united in marriage in 1872, to Mrs. L. A. Holmes, a native of Tennessee, and a daughter of Raiford and Harriet (Boone) Whitley. Her father was from Kentucky, and the mother, a descendant of Daniel Boone, was born in North Carolina. Dr. and Mrs. Weissinger are members of the Methodist Episcopal church. He belongs to the Knights of Honor, and is the medical examiner of the fraternity at Hernando. In addition to his professional duties he conducts a considerable amount of planting; he owns eleven hundred and eighty acres of land, eight hundred of which are in a high state of cultivation. He also owns his residence and office. The Weissinger family is well known for the strict integrity and uprightness of its members. Many have been men of talent and ability, notably George J. Weissinger, an uncle to the Doctor, who was junior editor of the Louisville *Journal* with George D. Prentice, and who wrote some of the ablest articles that ever appeared in that publication. Two of the Doctor's brothers were faithful soldiers in the late war. Although Dr. Weissinger has made a great deal of money in his practice, he has been a liberal supporter of all worthy enterprises, and is exceedingly benevolent. The poor and needy and less fortunate always find in him the most generous aid and sympathy, and he is beloved both by his patrons and the citizens of his county.

John R. Weissinger, one of the selfmade men and a prosperous planter of Coahoma county, Miss., was born in Carroll county, Miss., December 4, 1857, being the eighth of ten children born to Alexander and Cordelia S. (Strong) Weissinger, both native Alabamians. Alexander L. Weissinger became a resident of the state of Mississippi about the year 1849, and in Carroll county was engaged in planting until his death, in 1865. He was of German descent and a worthy and respected citizen. John R. Weissinger was reared in Mississippi, and was educated in the public schools of this state and at Oxford, and upon leaving school he began for himself as a planter in Montgomery county, later in Le Flore county, and then in Coahoma county. In 1889 he opened a hardware house in Clarksdale, and has since done an annual business of about $35,000, his stock of goods being valued at about $15,000. He owns his business house, which is one of the best in the city, and in addition to his mercantile establishment operates three hundred and seventy-five acres of land. Upon starting out to make his own way in the world he had no means, but through his own perseverance and industry he has been very successful, and is now wealthy. He is eminently a selfmade man, for in addition to earning his own living and caring for his mother, he has educated himself, and is a remarkably well-informed and intelligent gentleman. His property has not been the result of speculation, but has been the result of hard and persistent endeavor, and the accumulations of many years. Notwithstanding his success as a man of business, he is modest and unassuming, but possesses sufficient confidence to at all times rely upon his own judgment and to think for himself. Socially he belongs to the K of H. and the K. of P., in both of which organizations he holds official position. He was married in 1886 to Mrs. Julia Stone, a native of Mississippi and a daughter of John J. and Matilda W. (Allen) Fort, both of whom were born in Tennessee. To Mr. and Mrs. Weissinger three children have been born: John Fort (deceased), John Robert and Julia Cordelia. Mr. Weissinger has cared for his mother for a great many years, and is a devoted son as well as a faithful and considerate husband and father. His father, with three brothers, served in the Confederate army until the close of the war; were gallant defenders of the Confederacy, the former being an officer of rank.

Dr. Jacob P. Welch. The earliest member of the Welch family of whom authentic history is known, lived near the Welsh border in England over two hundred years ago. Jacob Welch, the great-great-grandfather of Dr. J. P. Welch, was born in England in 1662 in sight of the Welsh mountains. He was the first of the family to attempt a settlement in the new world, but his religious belief was very dear to him and on account of the persecution he was compelled to undergo he sought a home for himself and family in the, then, wilds of America, locating near Richmond, Va., about 1690. He reared five sons, of whom Dempsey, the youngest, was the great-grandfather of Dr. Welch of this sketch. Dempsey Welch was born on the old homestead in Virginia and his posterity, and that of his four brothers, are residents of the Western and Southern states. He was married to Miss Priscilla Perry, a near relative of Oliver Hazzard Perry and James Lawrence of naval fame. After his marriage he moved to South Carolina and later to Georgia, where he passed the remainder of his life, his death occurring in 1792. Together with his sons he fought throughout the Revolutionary war, willingly offering his life for the country he loved. He left a family of five sons and two daughters, Jacob Welch, who was probably his eldest son, being born about 1740 and died about 1807. He was of very handsome and commanding presence, possessed elegant and courtly manners, being, in fact, a gentleman of the old school. He has three sons and five daughters. His son Warren was born in 1780 in Johnson county, N. C., and was exceptionally gifted in the use of the violin, handling the king of instruments with a skill that was the admiration of all. He was married to Miss Mary McCullers on Christmas day, 1805, after which he settled in Burke county, Ga. When the War of 1812 came up he enlisted in the service, and after it was over he removed to Warren county, Ga., later to Lawrence county of the same state and finally to Wilkinson county, Ga. In 1815 he removed his family on packhorses to Montgomery, Ala. (then called New Philadelphia), and afterward floated on a barge to Monroe, Ala., where he remained a few months, afterward removing to Amite county, Miss., and years later to the state of Louisiana. In January, 1821, he returned to Alabama in order to make arrangements to remove to that state. His wife was a noble woman of rare attainments, was a model wife, mother and friend, and was a devoted Christian. She died in St. Francisville, La., in 1821, only a few days after the departure of her husband for Alabama. Her children soon found homes with different families throughout the neighborhood and after the death of their father, which occurred in Monroe county, Ala., in 1832, they were compelled to fight the battle of life for themselves single handed. Dr. Jacob Perry Welch, the eldest child, was born in Burke county, Ga., in 1807, and with the seven other members of his parents' family, was given the advantages of the common schools in his youth, and was reared on a farm. Dr. Welch has inherited his father's taste for music, and in early life was quite famous as a violinist. In 1836 he entered the medical department of the University of Pennsylvania, after first studying with Dr. Wimberly of Twiggs county, Ga. After finishing his medical studies he began practicing in Jefferson county, Ga., and was soon after invited by Dr. Stokes, of Cool Springs, Ga., to engage in a copartnership, which lasted one year. Dr. Welch then located in Washington county, Ga., and during the year and a half that he remained there he built up a good practice. He next went to Saundersville, of the same county, where he also obtained a good practice and remained until 1851, since which time he has been a resident of Lauderdale county, Miss., a period of forty years, having during that entire time been a resident of his present homestead. He successfully followed his profession until age and its attendant infirmities demanded his retirement in 1870. He has been an agriculturist the most of this time also and has, at different times, owned over four thousand acres of good land. He arose to eminence in his profession, for he believed in the old saying that what was worth doing at all was worth doing well, and this seemed to have been his motto through life, for he showed sound judgment in everything in which he engaged. He was married July 14, 1840, to Miss Martha S. Whitaker of Georgia, by whom he has had twelve children: Mary C., Warren P., William Thomas, George W., Sarah C., Jacob W., Martha S., Samuel W., Eugenia A. and James M. Two children died in infancy. Four children are married and five are living. The Doctor is a Mason of over fifty years' standing, in which he has attained to the chapter. He has been a member of the Missionary Baptist church for thirty-seven years, being baptized with his daughter, Mary C. Dr. Welch was at one time a candidate for legislative honors, and was defeated by only one vote, although he was prevented by sickness from making the canvass. He is benevolent, charitable, and has always been a patron of education. He is in every sense of the term a selfmade man, and throughout life has been the soul of honor, never owing a cent that he did not pay.

James N. Welch was born in Covington county, Miss., and there grew to maturity. He is the only child born of the union of Caleb and Susan (Robertson) Welch. Caleb Welch was born in Covington county, Miss., near the plantation he occupied for so many years, in 1829. He received a limited education, and was trained to the vocation of farming. When the Civil war broke out he enlisted, but was soon discharged on account of disability; he re-enlisted twice afterward, but with the same result. He was then commissioned to look after the families of soldiers. This office he performed faithfully, and with the greatest consideration and kindness. In 1870 he was appointed treasurer of the county, as a democrat, and held the position until the impeachment of Governor Ames. After that he was elected for one term. He died in 1885. His parents, James and Martha (Hill) Welch, were natives of South Carolina and Georgia, respectively. They reared a family of twelve children, and lived to a ripe old age. Their last days were spent in Covington county, Miss. Susan (Robertson) Welch was a daughter of Norval Robertson, a native of Georgia, born in 1797. He removed to Mississippi at an early day, and was one of the pioneer ministers of the gospel. He was a preacher for forty-five years, and for forty-four years was pastor of one church. He died in Lawrence county, Miss., in the eighty-second year of his age. He was a man of unusual ability, and of marked force of character. He wrote a little work on parliamentary law, and was the author of a little work, entitled The Church Member's Hand-Book of Theology. The latter had a wide circulation, and reached a second edition. James N. Welch, at the age of twenty-two years, was married to Miss Anise Rogers, a daughter of Timothy Rogers, of Covington county. Since his marriage he has devoted his time to farming and milling. He owns eleven hundred acres of land. He has been a member of the Missionary Baptist church from his twenty-fourth year, and a deacon since 1880. He has four living children, and is highly in favor of progress in education, and all other progressive moves.

B. R. Wells has been a resident of Hinds county, Miss., all his life, for here he was born on the 8th of September, 1838. He is the fourth child born to William and Mary (Wade) Wells, the former of whom was born in the Old North state in 1806, and came to Mississippi about 1832, purchasing and entering land in Hinds county. He accumulated a considerable amount of real estate, which he has since divided among his children. He is residing on a good and valuable plantation, and is in the enjoyment of a comfortable competency and a hale and hearty old age. The Wells family is of English descent. B. R. Wells obtained his first knowledge of the world of books in the common schools, but at the age of sixteen years he entered Mississippi college at Clinton, in which institution he remained two years. He then engaged in planting and managing his father's affairs, continuing until he attained the age of twenty years, when he was married and began the battle of life for himself. His father kindly gave him five hundred and eighty-seven acres of land and all the slaves on it, and his prosperity has been such that since the war, although at that time he lost a great deal of valuable property, he has added at different times about six hundred acres, and now cultivates four hundred acres, averaging about one hundred and thirty bales of cotton and twelve hundred bushels of corn yearly. He raises cattle for the market, and also sells quite a number of horses each year, in fact, he is a wideawake, progressive and enterprising man of business, and has a valuable plantation which he is constantly seeking to improve. In 1885 he took an interest in a stock of general merchandise at Bolton, which he continued to hold for three years, but the most of his attention has since been given to his plantation. In 1862 he enlisted in company I, sixty days' troop, but when this time expired he re-enlisted, and went to Virginia with company I, Eighteenth Mississippi infantry. After remaining with this command for about five months he returned to his home, and joined the Twenty-eighth cavalry, in which he served during the remainder of the war. He was a participant in the engagements at Malvern hill, Savage station, the Atlanta campaign, and was with Hood at Franklin. He was then furloughed home for thirty days, after which he became a member of Chalmers' division at Columbus, Miss. He was paroled at Gainesville, Ala., after which he returned to his home to resume the management of his plantation and to build his fortunes anew. He was married in 1859 to Miss Robertson, of South Carolina, and by her has had a family of twelve children, nine of whom are living: B. H. (a lawyer, of Raymond), Ida C., Sudie, W. S., Eva, Maggie, Cecil, Clifford and Sidney. Mr. Wells is a member of the A. F. & A. M. and the K. of H., socially, and is quite active in local politics.

William M. Wentworth (deceased). This gentleman was well and favorably known to the majority of the residents of this section, for he at all times identified himself with the interests of this county, and it is but just to say that his good name was above reproach and that he won the confidence and esteem of all who knew him. He was born in Franklin county, Miss., on the 24th of April, 1816, and on a plantation on Dry bayou, in the western part of this county, he was reared to manhood. His entire schooling amounted to only about three months, but, notwithstanding this fact, he became a well-informed man and took an active part in the affairs for the progress and development of the county. He was married here to Miss Lucretia Atkins, and here followed the occupation of a planter until 1849, when he removed to Meadville, where he spent the rest of his life, seventeen years of his life being spent as sheriff of the county, with but one intermission. At the commencement of the reconstruction period he resigned this position and for a few years held the office of justice of the peace, being elected in 1876 chancery clerk and ex-officio recorder, the duties of which office he was ably discharging at the time of his death, December 20, 1889. He filled this position in a most able manner. As a public servant he was efficient, honest, punctual and industrious, and to all with whom he came in contact he was uniformly courteous. He was a stanch Union man during the war, and at first worked earnestly for its preservation, strongly opposing secession, but during the latter part of the war served a short time in the Confederate army, although exempt from service. He was in every respect a selfmade man, and by his honesty and the moral courage which he displayed in at all times expressing his views, he became very popular throughout this region and wielded considerable influence. Although he was not identified with any religious creed, he was a liberal supporter of the church, and all measures of morality, education, etc., received from him a hearty support. His parents were early settlers of the county, and here his mother passed from life, the father dying in the state of his birth while there on business, this being when William M. was a boy. Mrs. Wentworth was born in Franklin county, Miss., and was called from life on the 18th of May, 1888, being at the time of her death a devout member of the Methodist Episcopal church. Her father, John Atkins, came from South Carolina, and died in Franklin county many years ago a well-to-do planter. William M. Wentworth was the eldest of two sons and one daughter, the other members of the family being Rowan, who died in Lauderdale county, Miss., and Nancy (deceased). After the death of their father their mother married again, becoming the wife of Benjamin Dorsey, by whom she reared a family, all of whom are now deceased. To William M. Wentworth and his wife ten children were born, five of whom survive: Nancy (wife of E. L. Middleton, of Natchez), William J. (a planter, of Concordia parish, La.), Wiley M., Ernest H. and Anthony D. Ernest H. was born in Meadville in 1857, was given a good education in his youth, and after becoming competent became his father's deputy, remaining so until the latter's death. In January, 1890, he was elected to fill the unexpired term, and is making a very creditable official. He was married on the 25th of December, 1886, to Miss Lula A., daughter of Rutillias K. and Margaret Scott, from Alabama, who became residents of Franklin county since the war, Mrs. Scott dying here in April, 1890. Mr. Scott is still living. Mrs. Wentworth was born here and has borne her husband one child. They are the owners of eight hundred acres of land in different tracts, and are well calculated, by temperament and inclination, to enjoy their prosperity. Mr. Wentworth is a member of Ben Franklin lodge No. 11, of the A. F. & A. M., which he joined in 1886, and is now secretary in and a member of the Methodist Episcopal church, his wife being a Presbyterian in faith. Mr. Wentworth's long experience as his father's deputy made him very familiar with the duties of that office, and to say that he has followed in his father's footsteps is bestowing upon him the highest praise. He is courteous and genial in disposition, and by the many people whose acquaintance he has made in his public capacity he is universally esteemed and admired.

Gen. Absolom Madden West was born in Alabama in 1818. His parents were natives of the Palmetto state, and his grandparents were from North Carolina. His grandsires were both Revolutionary soldiers, one of whom fell bleeding at King's mountain and was carried from the field by a young woman, who took him home to her parents, where she nursed him back to health. After the war they were married, and from this union General West is descended. The family, however, were Americanized about 1613, when John West, brother of the then governor of Virginia settled in the colonies, and from whom most of the name descend. It is not a little singular that of all the colonial governors Thomas West (Lord Delaware) alone impressed his name upon an American state. West Point still preserves the family name, and Delaware the title. He died at the mouth of the bay which bears his name. General West received a limited education in such schools as were provided by private enterprise in a new and undeveloped state. His irregular educational advantages ended in his fourteenth year, but, impelled by a love of knowledge, he read much, and being an ardent patriot, most of his time was devoted to works bearing upon the origin and structure of our government and the wants and necessities of the people. In the year 1837 he settled on a farm in Mississippi, and has continued his identification with an interest in agriculture to the present day, and by his success has shown himself to be one of the most practical and efficient farmers of his adopted state. In 1845 he married Miss Carrie O. Glover, of Alabama, a young lady of superior mind and rare literary attainments, who proved a helpmeet indeed in all the relations of life, and to her the General is greatl indebted for his gradual advancement in public usefulness and confidence. In politics he was a Union whig. In 1847 he was elected to the legislature by an unprecedented majority, where he soon took rank as a thinker and debater with the leading members of the house. He was twice elected to the senate in a democratic district over a worthy and honorable opponent. After secession, and under order of the state, he was appointed a brigadier-general and ordered to organize a brigade, which he did with great alacrity. His practical usefulness rendered necessary the employment of his services by the state, and indirectly by the Confederate States, in various departments. He was appointed quartermaster-general, paymaster-general and commissary-general, holding all three offices at the same time. He was also charged with the duty of providing salt for families of Confederate soldiers and the indigent families of the state, and putting the works under a skillful manager, manufactured salt with great rapidity.

No man in the state shared so largely the confidence of the governor for practical usefulness as did General West, notwithstanding they had always been on opposite sides in politics. At the instance of General West the legislature provided for the appointment of a commission, consisting of one lawyer and two practical business men, to examine and audit the books and papers of his several officers. General West made a final settlement with the state in accordance with the report of the commissioners, squaring up his accounts with the state. His was the only final settlement made during the war by any state officer. In 1864 General West was called to the presidency of the Mississippi Central railroad company. This road was used and destroyed alternately by the belligerent armies during the war, and at its close the road bed was a wreck. General West, with that will-power which has always characterized him, brought all his energies to bear to rebuild the road bed and to re-equip the same with sufficient rolling stock, etc. His success was regarded as the crowning glory of his life. Without his solicitation the people elected him to congress over two able lawyers, but congress refused to seat him and his colleagues, as it did all others at that time. In 1876 he was appointed by Governor Stone to deliver an address upon the growth and history of the state of Mississippi at the International exhibition at Philadelphia. The address, which was one of the ablest productions of that memorable occasion, was delivered July 10. In the same year he was an elector for the state at large on the Tilden and Hendricks ticket, and his speeches, founded in the great idea of reform, were able, convincing and eloquent. After the purchase of the Mississippi Central railroad by the Illinois Central railroad company, General West retired from active life, but was soon after elected to the state senate by an unanimous vote of the people of his district. The national party in convention assembled at Indianapolis, Ind., on May 29, 1880, unanimously nominated him for vice president of the United States and the anti-monopoly party nominated him for the same high office in 1884. It is a noteworthy fact that during his eventful life his integrity has never been questioned nor has he ever been sued. In 1876 he identified himself with the National Labor union, and has ever since held to its principles and objects with unfaltering fidelity. He has always been the friend of the poor, and a bold, fearless defender of the rights of the people. His views are broad and natural, with no sectional animosity or race hatred. In 1837 General West settled in Holmes county, and at the close of the war removed to Oxford for school privileges. In 1870 he located in Holly Springs, Marshall county, and there he has since resided. Since being a resident of this county he has represented it in both branches of the state legislature and served as chairman of the committee of state and Federal relations in the house of 1890. He declined to be a candidate for the constitutional convention, continued farming from choice, and declined all professions to devote himself to planting, of which he is very fond. He has ever been the farmer's friend. The family homestead is one of the handsomest in the state; seventeen acres surround it, on which he raises fruit and flowers, a large space being devoted to the latter, of which he has many choice varieties. His chief occupation since moving to town has been of a literary character, writing on politics, and studying history and biography. He has a large plantation of twenty-five hundred acres in Holmes county, seven hundred acres cleared and occupied by his sons, Benjamin G. and Charles. Mrs. West died July, 1889; she was a member of the Methodist church. To General and Mrs. West were born four sons and two daughters living, and two died in infancy: Olivia is the wife of W. T. McCarty, lawyer of Kansas; A. M., Jr., professor of chemistry in the Medical college at Memphis; Edgar, a prominent citizen of Grenada, having represented that county in the legislature; Benjamin G., now stationed in Memphis as the business agent of the State Alliance of Mississippi; Mrs. Carrie W. Smith; Charles, on the place near Durant, and Sidney Y., deceased. A. M., Jr., and Edgar are both graduates of the State university and the former of the University of Virginia. He also graduated at the Philadelphia Medical college, closing his collegiate career with high honors. He is now a practicing physician of prominence in Memphis, Tenn. General West's father, Anderson West, removed to Tennessee early in the century and from there to Alabama in 1817, where he was engaged in planting near Marion. On the organization of Perry county he was elected its first sheriff and later held various other county offices. In connection with his planting interests he was also engaged in merchandising, and was a man of great energy and business qualifications. He was quite an active politician, was a state's rights man in 1836 and later a whig. He died a well-known man. General West is a natural orator, generous to a fault, impulsive and sanguine in temperament, a selfmade man and also self educated. He has always been prominent in all things for the good of Holly Springs or the state or nation. He has a distinguished and commanding appearance, possessing strong mental as well as physical powers. His complexion is rather dark, his eyes bright and piercing, and he has a broad, intellectual looking head.

M. M. West, a native of Copiah county, Miss., was born in 1844, a son of James M. and Mary A. (Simms) West. The father was born in Georgia December 25, 1801. He was left an orphan at an early age, and was reared partly in Georgia and partly in Mississippi. He was twice married; first to a Miss Taylor, by whom he had five children, two of whom are now living: Eleanor, wife of Clinton Atkinson, and Nancy E., wife of Bellfield Simmons. Mrs. West died in 1836, and in 1839 Mr. West again married a Miss Mary A. Simms, a native of Louisiana. This lady was born in 1826, a daughter of Jose and Sarah Simms, both of them being natives of the same state in which their daughter was born. Five children were born to Mr. and Mrs. West by this second marriage: Maud, Phillip, Matthew M., Albert, Sarah, wife of A. B. C. Patrick, and Jose. The father was a farmer and a practicing physician of the botanical school. He was not a graduate of any college, but he was a diligent student and a firm believer in the efficacy of nature's remedies. He was a successful practitioner of more than fifty years, principally in Copiah county. He and wife were both members of the Methodist Episcopal church, of which he was for a number of years a steward and trustee. He died February 12, 1889, his wife following him August 22, of the same year. Matthew M. West was educated in the common schools, and at the age of seventeen years enlisted in company D, of the Twelfth Mississippi volunteer infantry, in which he served until the close of the war, participating in the battles of Seven Pines, Fredericksburg, Chancellorsville, Gettysburg, Spottsylvania Courthouse and in the fighting before Petersburg and just preceding the surrender at Appomattox, taking part also in many minor engagements. At the battle of Seven Pines he received a gunshot wound in the neck which disabled him for seven months. At the battle of Gettysburg he received a wound in the leg. Returning home after the war he engaged in agricultural pursuits and in milling. Locating on his present place he began with eighty acres for a farm; he has now increased his landed possessions until he has a plantation of four hundred and eighty acres. He plants corn and cotton and raises stock sufficient for all domestic use. At the time of locating here he became the owner of a steam saw and gristmill, which he still operates. In 1871 he married Mary E. Simms, a native of Louisiana, who was born in 1856. They have eight children living, and have lost two by death: Olivia, Walter, Margaret, Verner, Allsie, Pierce and Payne (twins), Mary, Martin and Dudley C. Mr. and Mrs. West are members of the Methodist Episcopal church, Mr. West being recording steward and superintendent of the Sunday-school. Mr. West is a member of the Smyrna Sub-Alliance, of the Farmers' Alliance, of which he is lecturer. He is of medium hight, strongly built and of a fine personal appearance. Politically he is a democrat, and has always taken an active part in all political questions, and his social standing is high.

Richard D. West, horticulturist, Durant, Miss., was one of nine children born to his parents, Nathaniel and M. A. (Sanders) West, his birth occurring in Pickens county, Ala., near Bridgeville in 1837. The father was born in the Palmetto state in 1803, was reared and educated there, and was there married to Miss Sanders, also a native of that state. By occupation Mr. West was a farmer, although in connection he carried on the carpenter's trade, and at an early date he moved to Alabama, then in 1857 to Mississippi, settling in Carroll county. He there engaged in farming and died in 1889. Mrs. West had died in 1879. Their family consisted of seven sons and two daughters, all of whom grew to mature years, and all of the sons were in the Confederate army: W. J. was first lieutenant of the Forty-second Mississippi and was killed at the battle of the Wilderness; N. C. was in the Thirtieth Mississippi, and is now a planter of Carroll county; B. F. served in the Forty-second Mississippi with his brother, was wounded at the battle of the Wilderness and died from his wounds two months later; G. W. was brigade surgeon in the trans-Mississippi department; J. D. was a private in the Fifth Alabama, and was killed at the battle of Chancellorsville; and F. B. was in the Thirtieth Mississippi and was killed in the battle of Murfreesboro in January, 1862. The two daughters are: Miss J. F. West, residing with our subject, and Mrs. W. Boon (deceased wife of John W. Boon). Richard D. West passed his youthful days in Carroll county, where he received his education, and first enlisted in the Fourth Mississippi infantry in 1861, serving in that for two years. He was in the fights at Vicksburg, Forts Henry and Donelson, and was taken prisoner at the last named place. He was held for seven months at Camp Morton, Indianapolis, and after being discharged rejoined his regiment, participating in the battles of Baker's Creek and Vicksburg. At the last mentioned place he received a flesh wound in the shoulder, which disabled him for six weeks, after which he joined the Twenty-eighth Mississippi cavalry and was with that until the close of the war. He was in the fight with General Forrest at Kenesaw mountain, was also at Atlanta and received a scalp wound in that engagement, but was not disabled. He was discharged at Lexington, Ala., and retired to Carroll county, Miss., where he followed planting for several years. He moved to Durant in 1877 and settled on his present property. He engaged in cotton planting up to 1884, opened up his place, and in that year began strawberry culture in a small way. He now has twenty acres devoted to berries and has a fine pear orchard of five hundred and fifty four-year old trees. He also has out some choice plum, apple and peach trees. He cultivates other small fruit and vegetables and is making a success of this business. He has eighty-seven acres, nearly all in a fine state of cultivation, and has a good residence. He was married in Holmes county, in 1876, December 20, to Miss Mary E. Lockhart, a native of Holmes county, and the daughter of Thomas Lockhart. She died on June, 1, 1890, leaving two children: Cora Belle and Vernon R. Mr. West is a Master Mason, a member of the Knights of Honor and the Alliance. He and sister are members of the Baptist church.

Judge R. R. West, Hernando, Miss., who has been closely connected with the political history of De Soto county for many years, was born in Perry county, Ala., January 16, 1818, and is the son of William and Mary (Howard) West. There were eleven children in the family, of whom he is the sixth. His father moved from Alabama to Mississippi in 1837, and located in Marshall county, where he engaged in planting, and spent the greater portion of his remaining days. He died in White county, Ark., at the residence of his son, W. C. West, in 1856. The paternal grandfather was William West, who was of English lineage. John Howard, the maternal grandfather, was of Irish extraction. The Judge passed his youth in Alabama, and there received his education; his advantages in this direction were meager enough, but a life of varied experience has developed his many qualifications. He remained with his father, assisting in the support of the family, until he was twenty-one years of age. He then started out in life for himself. He has been engaged in many different occupations, and his career has been dotted with many changes. He was first a clerk in a dry goods store for Dr. J. D. McCray for one year. He then went to eastern Texas, and worked for a company of civil engineers for two years. At the end of that period he returned to Mississippi, and was united in marriage to Miss N. J. Roberts, a native of North

Carolina, and a daughter of John and N. J. (Jeffress) Roberts; her father came from North Carolina, and the mother was born in Virginia. Of this union nine children have been born, only two of whom are living: John B. is editing the *Tate County Record* at Senatobia, Miss.; Mary E., is the wife of A. M. Lauderdale, of Hernando, a teacher by profession. After his marriage Judge West dealt for a time in livestock, and then had the charge of a blacksmith shop. He had some experience in bookkeeping, and when in 1855 he was elected to the office of clerk of the probate court he discharged his duties with great efficiency for five years. He was then elected judge of the same court, and acted in this capacity for three years, and for two years he was engaged in general practice of law. He next invested in a mercantile business, but disposed of this and gave one year to agriculture. At this time he returned to Hernando, and was elected clerk of the chancery court in 1875, and is the present incumbent of that office. The Judge belongs to the Masonic order. In all the public offices which he has held he has preserved the strictest integrity of character, and no man stands higher than he in the estimation of the people of De Soto county. His first wife, Mrs. N. J. (Roberts) West, died in 1878, and in 1879 he married Miss America (Mecca) C. Clark, who is still living, and is a consistent member of the Christian church, and a superior woman. She was the daughter of Thomas C. and Sarah Clark. Her father was of English and Irish extraction, and his forefathers were Virginians in Revolutionary times, and removed thence to Tennessee, Alabama and Mississippi, in the order named.

Thomas J. West, Water Valley, Miss. The gentleman whose history is here outlined is the senior member of the firm of T. J. West & Co., and has a business career older than that of any other business man in the city. He has survived the shock of Civil war, and the still greater strain of the confusion of the financial crisis that swept over the country by the famous policy of the government in resumption. He has steadily maintained a reputation for strict business habits, and deep integrity of character. Mr. West was born in Madison county, Tenn., in 1827, and is a son of George West, a native of Maryland, whose parents came from Scotland to America before the Revolutionary war. The father was a soldier in that conflict, and died in the service, leaving a wife and one child, George West. The mother was married, a second time, to a Mr. Hubbard, by whom she had two children. George West passed his youth in North Carolina, and received his education in the common schools. He was apprenticed to learn the tailor's trade, which he followed until his marriage. He then engaged in farming and in 1827 he removed to Tennessee, locating in Madison county. In 1841 he came to Mississippi, making his home in Lafayette county until his death, which occurred in 1860. Politically he affiliated with the whig party. He did service in the War of 1812. He was a member of the Baptist church, and a man of considerable means. He was married to Lucretia Childress, who was born in Georgia in 1789, and died in 1847. She was a daughter of Thomas Childress, who served in the Revolutionary war, and was one of a family of ten children. She became the mother of ten children, four of whom are still living: John M., Holman F., James H. and Thomas J. (the subject of this notice.) In the beginning of his business life he was a clerk in a country store, where he remained until 1858; he then removed to Water Valley and engaged in the mercantile trade. At the present day few young men would have the courage to make the beginning which he did. His first year's salary was only $100, but he managed to save the most of that, and with this capital he embarked in business. By energy and close attention he soon gained a foothold, and is now doing a business of $40,000 a year, handling upward of twelve hundred bales of cotton. Mr. West was married in 1855 to Miss Telitha Boydston, a native of Yalobusha county, Miss., and a daughter of the Rev. John P. Boydston. The father was a native of Tennessee, and removed to Mississippi at an early day, where he followed the ministry; he died in 1871, at the age of seventy years. His wife's maiden name was Wilson, and to her were born four daughters and two sons. Mrs. West is the fourth child, and was reared in Yalobusha county, and educated at the Oakland academy. Mr. and Mrs. West are the parents of six children: Eva S., Nellie T., Fred M., Alice M., William Thad. and Hugh J. When there was a call for men to go to the defense of their country Mr. West was found willing and ready to leave his family and home interests. He enlisted in January, 1863, in the Eighteenth cavalry, under General Forrest. He had charge of the provisions and wagons; was in the battles of Fort Pillow, Harrisburg, Selma, Ala., and other smaller engagements. He and his wife are members of the Methodist Episcopal Church South, of which he has been steward since its organization at this place. He is a member of the Masonic order, and has been high priest of his chapter for a number of years. In addition to his commercial interests he finds time to give to agriculture, and he is one of the directors of the Water Valley bank.

Judge Thomas Jesse Wharton. It is a fact clearly established that a man's language is a part of his character, that his speech is an index to his mind and heart. It opens his character to the light and discloses his disposition, his temper and modes of thought. The Greeks were correct in their teaching, that as a man lived so would he speak. Ben Jonson has said that no glass renders a man's form and likeness so true as his speech. His discourse is an open window through which his soul can be seen. So it can be said of Judge Thomas J. Wharton, that distinguished citizen and eminent jurist of Mississippi, whose name stands at the head of this sketch. No person can pass an hour in conversation with him without feeling that he is in the presence of a gentleman of deep culture, pure thoughts and noble aspirations; one who is broad in his humanity, charitable and merciful. Judge Wharton was born at Nashville, Tenn., May 18, 1817, and is the son of Jesse and Elizabeth (Rice) Wharton, who were natives of Virginia, from Albemarle county. The elder Wharton was a lawyer by profession, and a highly educated man. He took a prominent part in the political affairs of Tennessee, to which state he removed in 1795, locating in Nashville. In fact, he was one of her leading and most honored citizens. He was a member of both houses of the state legislature, also both houses of congress, and retired from public life at the age of forty. This was when he was in congress, and during James Madison's administration. During his active professional life he had the largest practice of any lawyer in Tennessee, and accumulated a large fortune. He died in 1834, his widow surviving him but a few months. The Whartons were of Welsh descent. Judge Wharton attended the primary schools of Nashville and then entered the University of Nashville, where he was graduated with high honors in the fall of 1834. He began the study of law and was admitted to the bar of Mississippi, before the supreme court, in January, 1837, soon after opening a law office at Clinton, where he remained for six years, meeting with marked success in his profession. From Clinton he removed to Raymond, where he continued his practice for six years, after which he located at Jackson, his present home. His younger brother, Francis A. R. Wharton, who studied law with him, was a partner from the time he was admitted to the bar (1842) until 1882, when Judge Wharton was appointed to the bench. He is now in practice at Raymond, Miss. In 1857 Judge Wharton received the nomination from the democratic party to the position of attorney-general and was elected. In 1861 he was re-elected without opposition, and served until he was removed by Federal authority in the spring of 1865, under the reconstruction measures. He then resumed his practice, which he continued with distinguished success until 1882, at which time he was appointed judge of the circuit court, of the ninth judicial district, by Governor Lowry. Before the expiration of his term the legislature passed an act retiring three circuit judges and five chancellors. The ninth district was merged into the eighth, which retired Judge Wharton, and he returned to his private practice. He was a believer in the right of the states to secede, and supported the Confederate cause with all the earnestness of his character, but when the cause went down and the Federal authority was again established he was active in the reconstruction of his state, and recommended strongly the adoption of the reconstruction measures. He was appointed by Governor Clarke one of the commissioners to Washington in behalf of the state to accept the reconstruction measures of the government. The reconstruction government adopted by the state was rejected by the Federal government and she was put under a provisional government. Judge Wharton regards the assassination of President Lincoln as the greatest calamity that could possibly have happened to the South next to the defeat of its cause. He was a great admirer of President Lincoln, and believes that in his death the South lost her best friend.

The Judge was married at Nashville, Tenn., June 15, 1837, to Mary T., daughter of Rev. John T. Edgar, D. D., who for thirty years was pastor of the Presbyterian church of that city. Her mother was Mary Todd, of Kentucky. The children born to the Judge's marriage, who are living at the present time, are: Thomas J., Jr., assistant postmaster at Jackson; Iva, wife of J. J. Hampton; Margaret E., wife of George S. Green; Louisa E. and Sallie G. In hight Judge Wharton is about five feet eleven inches, thin and straight in form, exceptionally dignified in carriage. His well-shaped head is ornamented with a liberal growth of gray hair, and a mustache is the only adornment of his intellectual countenance. His eyes are blue and expressive, and although he is well along in years his mind is still vigorous and his step elastic. He is courteous and warm in his manner, especially to his acquaintances, and his generous heart is filled with the milk of human kindness for all. To a man possessed with these qualities it is hardly necessary to add that his hospitalities have made many persons happier and better, that his domestic relations have been and are of the best order, and that he is a devoted and affectionate husband and father. He has given much time and study to subjects outside of his profession, and often lectures to delighted audiences. His historical and biographical paper of Mississippi, from 1801 to 1890, has won for him the applause of thousands. He is a gifted orator; his language is choice, rich and full of thought, his sentences well rounded, and delivered in a clear, cultivated voice. There are few men of to-day so well versed in the history of Mississippi, or so well qualified to discuss it as he. He has witnessed the erection of her capitol at Jackson, attended every convention held there, and has heard every speech of importance that has been delivered within its walls. He has also been a member of almost every democratic convention held there, and could have had, unquestionably, any political position within the gift of the people of his state, had he sought it. The dying advice of his distinguished father was never to aspire to or hold any political office, and this advice he has faithfully kept. It is in the legal forum that Judge Wharton is at his best, for his learning is profound and complete, and is greatly enhanced by a natural gift or an intuitive perception of law. He rarely, if ever, becomes entangled in any case, however intricate, but takes up the most difficult problems of law, and with his clear analysis goes to the bottom of them. The vast resources of his mind are always at his command, and in the discussion of a cause he is never at a loss for ideas or words to give force to his arguments or authorities to sustain them. He is possessed of a rich and varied elocution, and in his arguments is ever respectful to the court and courteous to his opponents. While he dignified the ermine of justice it was thought that no just cause could fail. His integrity, ability, learning and calm equipoise of head and heart were assurances that the cause before him would be tried and adjusted upon its own merits. As a judge he combines some of the best elements that have been united in that office. Among these may be mentioned his deep learning, his knowledge of the fundamental principles of law, his calm, dispassionate mind, his ceaseless endeavor to get at the truth, and his fervent zeal for justice, as the end and intended fruit of all law.

William B. Wheatley is a substantial resident of Washington county, Miss., but is especially well and favorably known in the vicinity of Arcola, in which place he keeps a well patronized hotel. He was born in Wheeling, Va., in 1837, being the second of four children born to Warren Wheatley, a native of Westmoreland county, Penn., which was once a part of the Old Dominion. He later resided in Illinois and Missouri, and died of cholera in St. Louis in 1849. The maiden name of his wife was Johanna Cool, a daughter of George Cool, a Pennsylvanian, and a millwright by trade; he was in the War of 1812, under Gen. Anthony Wayne. The paternal grandfather, George Wheatley, also a soldier in 1812, was born in Virginia, was also a millwright, and was called from life in the city of St. Louis, Mo., in 1845. His wife was a Miss Leggett, of Va., of which state, his father, William Wheatley, was also a native shipcarpenter, a millwright by trade, and was one of four brothers who settled at Red Stone, now McKeesport, Penn., who built the first model keelboats there, and started the first shipyard. They were Revolutionary soldiers. They came west of the Alleghany mountains after the war and bought land with their land warrants issued by the state of Virginia to her soldiers. They built and ran flatboats and keelboats to New Orleans, when Louisiana belonged to Spain, our subject's great grandfather dying on a trip to New Orleans on one of his boats, and being buried at or near Ellis cliffs, near Natchez, Miss. Their names are as follows: Isaac, Thomas, John and George. George Wheatley, the grandfather of William B., was one of a large family of children: George, Samuel, John, William, Elijah, Nancy, Sarah, Mary and Margaret, being the only ones remembered. The sisters of William B. Wheatley are as follows: Sophia, the wife of Thomas Griffith, resides in Monroe county, Ohio; Sarah, is the wife of McKinley Blayney, of Washington, Penn., and Elsie R. Amos, who died in 1880, leaving four children. William B. was reared in Pennsylvania and St. Louis, Mo., and was educated at West Alexandria, Penn. In the winter of 1853 he began life for himself as a cabin boy on board a vessel called the Allegheny Clipper. He remained on the river for about twelve years steamboating, and in 1861 opened a hotel at Cape Girardeau, Mo. At a later period he engaged in the produce business in Memphis, from which place he moved to Vicksburg, and in 1866 he took up his residence at Greenville, where he conducted a hotel until 1881, since which time he has been a resident of Arcola, the most of his time being given to merchandising. He was married in 1863 to Miss Emma Holt, a native of Missouri, and a daughter of Thomas Holt, of Virginia, a successful architect. To Mr. Wheatley and his wife three children have been born: Colin, who died in 1864; Belle Lee, who died in 1868, and William W., who now resides at home, and is the agent at the Grand Pacific depot. Mr. Wheatley has always been a democrat in politics, and socially belongs to the Masonic order. He and his wife are worthy members of the Baptist church, and in the different localities in which they have resided have won many friends. Mr. Wheatley has been quite a traveler, especially in the central and western states, and as he was of a rather restless disposition he did not settle down permanently until 1865. He has journeyed up the Mississippi river above Minneapolis, Minn., the Missouri river from its mouth to the head of navigation, the Ohio from Cairo to Pittsburgh, the Red river from its mouth to the northern part of the Indian territory, the Ouachita river as far as Camden, Ark., the Arkansas river to Fort Smith, and the White river to Batesville. He was also on the Gulf of Mexico for six months, on the Morgan line of steamers, from New Orleans to Galveston, Tex. His anecdotes of his travels and adventures are very interesting, and are made doubly so, for Mr. Wheatly is a fine conversationalist, and relates a story well. He has seen many sides of human life, but his experience has not hardened his heart or made him forgetful of the wants of his fellowmen. In personal appearance he is decidedly prepossessing. He weighs one hundred and seventy-five pounds, is five feet seven inches in hight, has brown hair, and dark gray eyes full of intelligence and kindly humor. As a host he is careful of the wants and wishes of his guests, and at all times endeavors to make their stay with him comfortable and pleasant, and that he does so is testified by the many who patronize his house. He owns his home and several business houses in the town, and in all is worth about $5,500.

George W. Wheeless. The history of every community is made up, so far as its more interesting features are concerned, of the events and transactions of the lives of its leading representative citizens. In any worthy history of Claiborne county, Miss., an outline of the career of Mr. Wheeless should not fail to be given. He was born in this county on September 18, 1846, his youthful days being employed in obtaining an education which is a decidedly practical and useful one. His parents, G. B. and Elizabeth (Davis) Wheeless, were born in Georgia February 10, 1804, and Claiborne county, Miss., in 1826, respectively, their union taking place in the mother's native county in 1843. Mr. Wheeless followed the noble and independent calling of an agriculturist, and by his upright, manly and consistent life, did much for the elevation of that calling. Although not an active or bitter politician he favored democratic principles, and always supported the representatives of that party with his vote and influence, which was considerable. He invariably tried to do as he would be done by, and although he expressed his mind freely when occasion so demanded, he was not in the least disputatious, but was careful of the feelings of others. His life was daily illustrated with deeds of kindness, and it may be truly said of him that he never violated a friendship or willfully wronged one of his fellowmen. He lived to an advanced age, dying July 3, 1889, and his remains now rest in the cemetery in Port Gibson. The homestead is still the abiding place of his widow, a kindly, Christian lady. The family that in time blessed their union are as follows: Henry S., a promising young business man of Port Gibson, died during the yellow-fever scourge of 1878; George W., the immediate subject of this biography, comes next in order of birth; Martha, is the wife of S. P. Patterson, a successful planter of the county; Mary died of yellow fever in 1878; Sallie is the wife of Sanford Bloomquist, who is head engineer and superintendent of the oilmills at Port Gibson; G. B. is a planter of the county and is unmarried; Joseph D. is also a resident of this county; Samuel died in 1876, at the age of fourteen years; Charles F. is unmarried and is the proprietor of the Wheeless hotel, a popular hostelry in southwest Mississippi; Lizzie is the wife of P. L. Shaifer, a planter of Claiborne county, and John A., the youngest of the family, makes his home in this county also, but is at present attending Mississippi college in Hinds county; Frank is deceased. In the family cemetery is erected a beautiful monument sacred to the memory of the dearly loved father, brothers and sister. George W. Wheeless, being the eldest living member of his father's family, remained with and cared for his parents until he attained his twenty-fifth year, then began making his own way in the world, and to his own well-balanced, active intelligence and unswerving perseverance he owes his present prosperity. His first work was as an agriculturist, but after some years given to this work he determined to engage in more congenial employment, and accordingly opened a mercantile establishment, a calling to which he devoted his attention with undeviating attention for a period of two years. He has been one of the pushing business men of the place up to the present date, and his sterling honesty and superior capability have long been well and justly noted. In his daily walk and conversation his kindness of heart and liberality are manifested, in both of which he is eminently deserving of mention as above the average of mankind. He was married on May 23, 1888, to Miss Irene Watkins, their union being solemnized at the home of Mrs. Wheeless' parents in Jefferson county, the ceremony being performed by Rev. J. P. Hemby of the Baptist church of Fayette, Miss. Mrs. Wheeless was born in Jefferson county, being the eldest of three daughters born to her parents; Leota, wife of Fred L. Schoeber, a bookkeeper of Adjer, Ala., and Laura, aged eighteen. Their parents, B. F. and Anna (Le Gette) Watkins, were born in Mississippi in 1842, and South Carolina, respectively. Mr. Watkins is a planter, owning four hundred acres of land, and is a finely educated gentleman, being a thorough scholar in Latin and Greek, having obtained his education in Oakland college. His father was a Georgian and his mother came of old Virginia stock. J. N. Le Gette, Mrs. Wheeless' grandfather, was a native of France and she inherits much of her beauty, intelligence and vivacious manners from her Huguenot ancestors. She was educated at home by private tutors and was also for some time a student at Port Gibson Female college, where she acquired an education which has admirably fitted her for the enviable social position she is filling. She is noted for her grace and beauty, and the nobility of her character and the kindly and generous impulses of her heart and mind are reflected in her face, which is of almost perfect contour and expression. Mr. and Mrs. Wheeless occupy a high social position, and in their beautiful home make an agreeable and gracious host and hostess. Mr. Wheeless is a warm democrat, and socially is a member of Franklin lodge No. 5, of the I. O. O. F.

John Whitaker (deceased) was a native of North Carolina, born in the town of Enfield, December 13, 1798, and was one of a large family of sons and daughters born to Eli B. Whitaker. The latter was the son of John Whitaker, who was born in Warwick county, Va., and who was the son of Richard Whitaker, who came from England to America about the time Cromwell was beheading a number of the leading citizens of England. Richard Whitaker, on coming to this country, settled in Warwick county, Va., bringing his wife and two of his cousins with him. In Warwick county they reared large families, many descendants of whom afterward settled in Tennessee. Richard had a small family, lived to be quite old, and died before the Revolutionary war. His son, John, when a young man, left the paternal roof, going to North Carolina, where he entered land in the vicinity of Enfield. He was the first settler in that district. He entered very large tracts of land in that vicinity, where he reared his family. One of his sons, Eli B., father of the subject, was brigadier-general of the militia of North Carolina, and served in the Revolutionary war in that capacity. His wife was a sister of Gov. John Branch, of North Carolina, who was one of its most prominent politicians and citizens. To Eli B. and wife were born nine sons and six daughters, all of whom but one lived to be grown. Several moved to Alabama, others to Florida, and still others to Louisiana, and the father to Mississippi in 1818. Only two of this family are now living: Lizzie and Martha, who live in Oswichee, Ala. Eli, the youngest son, was in the Confederate army during the war, and was captured in the battle of Gettysburg and died in some Northern prison. The others followed planting and were leading and representative citizens in the counties where they settled. The father of these children died at an advanced age in Tallahassee, Fla., and was a very earnest worker in the Methodist church. John, the subject of this sketch, attended the college of Chapel

Hill, N. C., and in 1818 came overland to Mississippi, bringing about forty slaves with him. One of the negroes, Phil Branch, is still living on the home place. He claims to have been born in 1796, and is a smart old fellow, and used to be the carriage driver of the family. Mr. Whitaker, when he first arrived, camped where Mrs. Lewis now lives in Woodville, but from there he soon went to Louisiana, settling near Laurel Hill, where he purchased a plantation and remained until 1838. He then came to the present place, where he remained the rest of his life, devoted to his family and home. He was a stanch Whig, and a man of broad views and noble principles and was well posted in the public affairs of his day. He was a liberal contributor to all charitable institutions, and was an active worker and supporter of the Methodist Episcopal Church South. He was a class-leader and steward in the church, and died in 1857, a just and good man and a good neighbor, loved by all. He was an ardent follower of the chase, and while out so carried the respect of his associates that even the most profane would not swear in his presence. He was married to Mrs. Rodgers (nee Verbenia Stewart), a descendant of one of the oldest resident families in the state. By this union was born one child, Nolans. Mr. Whitaker's next wife was a Miss Caroline Saunders (the daughter of Augustus Saunders, who was auditor of public accounts at Jackson, Miss., at his death), who was educated at Sharon, Miss., and at Nashville, Tenn., a graduate of both institutions. She had a superior intellect and a finished education, was highly cultivated and refined, and died in 1881, having been a member of the Methodist Episcopal church and a devoted Christian. By this union were born seven children: one, Elizabeth, died in infancy; Anna Augusta, another, is now the wife of Dr. W. D. Wall, of Jackson, La.; James W., was reared on the home place and was educated in Edinburgh, Scotland, where he remained for three years. Returning home he was married to Sallie Robert, sister of Dr. Robert, of Centerville, Miss. By this union were born nine children: James, Robert, Joseph, Anna, Rebecca, Sally, Esther, William S. and Eloise (who is deceased). James entered the Confederate army at the age of fifteen years, and served until the close of the war; he now resides on his farm, and is engaged in planting; Martha R. (now deceased) was the wife of Dr. J. C. Robert, of Centerville; Eli B. is traveling and prospecting in the mining districts of the West; James owns the old homestead and married Miss Lizzie Fanver, and is engaged in planting; Richard is a merchant and planter at Whitaker Station, on the New Orleans & Texas railroad, in Wilkinson county. He was born in 1854 and educated at Trenton, Ark. In 1872 he began for himself at planting on the home place, and was married in 1877 and located on this place, where he remained one year, then moved to Louisiana, where he engaged in planting and merchandising in East Feliciana parish. He located at the present place in 1881 and engaged in planting and merchandising, and in 1888 at Whitaker Station, of which place he is the founder. He is also engaged in sawmilling, ginning, etc., and has about two thousand five hundred acres of land well under cultivation. He was married to Antoinette Mitchell, of Amite county, where she was born and reared, the daughter of Antoine and Henrietta J. (Dunn) Mitchell, natives of Louisiana and Mississippi, respectively. They were early settlers of Amite county. Her grandfather, Henry Dunn, was one of the very early settlers of that region, and entered the land upon which Clinton is now built, and was very prominent in social and public matters. Mrs. Whitaker was educated in Clinton, her home and birthplace. To Mr. and Mrs. Richard Whitaker were born three sons and four daughters: Antoinette, Antoine M., Anna H., Martha R. and Mary (twins), John, and a baby boy, born January 20, 1891. Mr. Whitaker is a member of the K. of H. and K. of P., and is a Democrat in politics. He devotes his time and attention to his plantation, and is one of the largest planters of this portion of the county.

John J. White was unanimously elected president for the third time of the Yellow Pine Lumber association, which held its meeting at Montgomery, Ala., March 6, 1891, was born in Anderson county, S. C., April 1, 1830, a son of William Moore White. The organization which insists that he stand at its head, has for its range on membership sawmill men in the states of Georgia, Florida, Alabama and Mississippi, and represents an aggregate capital of immense proportions—that which is operating an industry now conceded to be one of the most important of what is popularly termed "the great South." Mr. White is also vice president, for the state of Mississippi, of the Southern Lumber Manufacturers' association, which embraces the principal manufacturers of lumber in the states of Missouri, Arkansas, Louisiana, Texas, Mississippi, Alabama and Georgia. His father, William Moore White, was born in Ireland in September, 1803, and came to America at the age of eighteen years. Locating in Charleston, S. C., he engaged in carpentering for a time, having first served an apprenticeship at that trade in that city. He afterward went to the northern portion of the state and indentified himself with the milling business, later associating himself with his brother in the manufacture of cotton fabrics and a general line of cotton goods. There he met and married, about 1828, Miss Elizabeth J. McMurtray, of Scotch descent and a native of South Carolina. In 1838, having lost his factory by fire, Mr. White moved with his family to Mississippi, locating in Madison county and engaged in the manufacture of lumber. His mill, which was operated by water power, was a primitive affair, but his business for those days was an extensive industry. There he sawed the most of the lumber used in the construction of the first houses erected at Canton, Miss. He afterward turned his attention to farming, in which he was engaged until his retirement from business. He now lives near Camden, within a few miles of his original settlement in the state, and although at the advanced age of eighty-eight years, is quite active for one of his years. Mrs. White died in Madison county at the age of forty-three, in 1847. Mr. White afterward married, and his second wife is now living. To Mr. White and Elizabeth J. McMurtray White, were born four sons and three daughters, of whom the first born is the subject of this sketch, John J. White, who was about eight years of age when his father moved from South Carolina to Mississippi. His educational advantages were good, however, and he received a thorough training in the public schools of his neighborhood. He passed his boyhood days upon the plantation, growing to maturity in Madison county, and remained with his parents until after he attained his majority. A particular incident of his boyhood is the following: The school which he attended was quite large and of a high grade for the time and locality. Young White took great interest in his studies and with characteristic energy directed all his efforts toward a mastery of the highest branches, and was soon so far advanced as to be chosen his teacher's assistant, and afterward there being a vacancy, caused by the death of the former teacher, he was placed in charge of the school which he had previously attended and continued for several years as its teacher. His push and determination to make a place for himself in the world were such that he could not think of remaining for an indefinite time in such employment; and in partnership with his brother, Robert E. White, he soon branched out in the sawmill business near Summit, Pike county, Miss., where he had removed in 1859. The war came on two years later and cut him off, temporarily, from the hope of the fruition of the ambitious desires which were, no doubt, cherished in the heart of the young man. During the dark days of "61" when the question of secession was paramount in the minds of the people of the South, Mr. White was an earnest and consistent Union man and opposed secession in all its forms, but when his state decided to withdraw from the mother government, he felt his first allegiance due to her and he at once became her earnest supporter.

Robert E. White, his brother, enlisted in 1861 in the McNair rifles, which were mustered into the Confederate service and attached to the Thirty-eighth Mississippi regiment. He was stricken with brain fever at Murfreesboro and died in a tent on the field before he could be removed to the hospital. The withdrawal of his brother from the business caused its entire responsibility to fall upon the shoulders of John J. White, who conducted it successfully for some time, and supplied a considerable amount of timber used in the construction of Confederate gunboats, but in 1862 he laid aside his peaceful pursuits and enlisted in the Wilson guards, and was mustered into service as a member of company H, of the Thirty-ninth Mississippi regiment. He was soon commissioned lieutenant of his company, and participated in the fights at Corinth and elsewhere. With his regiment he was at the siege of Port Hudson after the taking of Vicksburg, and fell a captive into the hands of the enemy and was carried to Johnson's island, near Sandusky, Ohio, where he was confined as a prisoner of war until the close of hostilities. Undaunted and unflinching, he shouldered his musket and fought gallantly for the Confederate flag, taking part bravely in some of the hottest battles. Mid whistling bullets and flying missiles of death, blinding smoke and horrifying scenes, he endured to the end, having risen from the ranks to the proud position of a commissioned officer. Returning to his home in Pike county, he began with redoubled energy to re-establish his ruined business and re-engaged vigorously in the manufacture of lumber. He began making money, and has been remarkably successful up to the present time, though he has had several very destructive fires, by which he has sustained losses amounting to nearly $100,000. In 1881 he was completely burned out, but rallied again, and at that time supplied himself with a new outfit throughout, consisting of improved modern machinery, dry kilns, etc. His sawmill is of the steam-feed kind, and has a capacity of fifty thousand feet per day, and his planingmill has a capacity of thirty thousand feet, and he uses four Sturtevant dry kilns. He has fourteen miles of railroad equipped with iron and steel rails, and two locomotive engines. His present plant is located on the main line of the Illinois Central railroad, one mile south of Macomb City, Miss. He owns about fifty thousand acres of timber land in Pike and Marion counties, and has a kind of little city under his feet, as it were, everything being under his control, which is called Whitestown, in contradistinction to Macomb City. He employs nearly two hundred operators, the inhabitants of his place numbering between five and six hundred persons. Mr. White has taken an active interest in educational matters, and at his little place near McComb City he has two public schools, one for white and one for colored children, which are maintained by him principally. He has also erected a large Union church building, in which Christians of all denominations are privileged to hold meetings. Mr. White's residence sets well back in the distance, perhaps half a mile, but not so far off but that he can hear the whistles of his own locomotives of his own road, and at the same time listen to the hum and buzz of the sawmill, or to the continuous sound emanating from the planingmill (all of these, no doubt, being music in the ears of the average sawmill man), and watch the even flow of his business, as each employe goes forth attending strictly to his own duties. Thus the mind grasps the entire scene: bustling business, without which the wheels of progress can not be made to turn, and by which a livelihood is earned; schools and education—that which is so necessary to the upbuilding and refinement as well as success of any community of people; churches and religion—that which is indispensable in cultivating that high moral sentiment necessary to insure future safety and happiness. In 1870 Mr. White married Miss Helen E. Tyre, who has borne him seven children. Mr. White is one of those quiet, unassuming men who accomplish magnificent results without ostentation or effort. Public-spirited and generous to the last degree, he is conceded to be one of Pike county's most universally respected citizens, and in his business relations he is known widely and favorably throughout the entire lumber sections of the United States. Mr. White stands pre-eminent amongst his fellowmen. Every movement tending to elevate those about him, every movement for the public good, finds in him not only an earnest advocate but a liberal supporter. Mr. White is strong and active, and though time has tinged his hair with gray, it is but the silver crown of a life well spent.

Col. Thomas W. White was born in Elbert county, Ga., January 8, 1824. He was a son of William and Concord H. (Brown) White, natives of Virginia and Georgia respectively. William White removed to Mississippi about the year 1845, and settled in De Soto county, where he resided until his death, which occurred in 1864. He was highly esteemed, and was one of the most substantial merchants of Hernando. Colonel White received his early education in Georgia, and was afterward graduated from the law school of Harvard university. He then taught for a short time, and in 1847 he opened an office in Hernando, where he practiced his profession up to the time when the hand of death fell upon him, July 26, 1889. He was a democrat, and took deep interest in political affairs. He was a member of the legislature before the war, the only time he was induced to accept public office. His last public service was as president of the board of levee commissioners of the Yazoo (Miss.) delta. He came to Mississippi a young, modest, studious lawyer, and grew with the passing years until he was long since recognized as the foremost of the community. He was a wise, prudent man, noted for the justice of his dealings and the integrity of his conduct. He was highly cultivated in his tastes, well read, and widely traveled. He was possessed of a quick and ready sympathy, which won him the allegiance of all who came within the charmed circle of his acquaintance. He loved home and family, and few men had more friends. In 1861 Colonel White built an elegant residence in Hernando, where his wife, formerly Miss Mina Meriwether, of Georgia, and family still reside, surrounded by all the comforts which his loving forethought could suggest.

W. H. White, M. D., Brandon, Miss., was born at Steen's creek, Rankin county, October 17, 1848. His father, Thomas S. White, was descended from Scotch-Irish ancestry and emigrated to Alabama when it was a territory, and later to Rankin county, Miss. He was a man of local prominence, and an old line whig, who represented Rankin county in the legislature one term, having been elected in the memorable campaign in which H. S. Foote defeated Jefferson Davis. Although a slaveholder he doubted the righteousness of slaveholding and was opposed to the war and secesssion. Dr. W. H. White received the best education the schools of his section afforded, and by dint of assiduous application, aided by a strong native talent, he acquired a wide range of practical information. In 1869 he matriculated in the University of Louisiana (now Tulane university), from which institution he received the degree of M. D. in 1873, after having attended four consecutive courses of lectures. Dr. White located in Brandon in 1883, where he has built up a large and devoted patronage. He is thoroughly imbued with a love for his profession, is a hard student and keeps well up with the advance of medical science. He is an honored member of the Mississippi State Medical association, of which he has been vice president; has been a delegate to the American Medical association; has been a frequent contributor of essays which have been read to the state association, and has occasionally contributed articles for the medical press. Dr. White is at present health officer for Rankin county, having received his appointment in 1884 from the state board of health. Socially, as well as professionally, he is deservedly popular with all classes. He loves his friends and holds that, like the king, "they can do no wrong." Toward his opponents he is tolerant, and toward his enemies indifferent. His highest ambition is to merit the confidence and esteem of his patrons, to prove himself worthy of the high regard entertained for him by his friends, and to do his whole duty in the sphere of life in which his lot is cast. In religious views he is, as were his ancestors, a Methodist and a zealous worker in his church. In politics he is a modern democrat. He is a close student of political economy, and an interested observer of the current history of his country. He has been an ardent Free Mason for many years and occupied the chair of worshipful master of Evening Star lodge for several terms. Dr. White was married, in 1874, to Miss Mary E. Allen, a daughter of Col. Daniel Allen, a man of sterling character and influence, and a veteran of the War of 1812. The Doctor's home is a model of domestic happiness, and it is there that he receives inspiration and courage for the arduous duties of life.

Among the most reliable and substantial merchants of Lee county, Miss., is W. R. Whitesides, Nettleton. He is a native of Mississippi, born March 8, 1852, and is a son of Thomas and Martha A. Whitesides. His father was a native of South Carolina, born March 20, 1824, and was a son of James and Sarah Whitesides. During his infancy his parents removed to Alabama, and there he received his education. When he was sixteen years of age they went to Itawamba county, Miss., and he engaged in planting. In 1849 he was married to Martha A. Keys, a daughter of James and Susan E. Keys, born in Lawrence county, Ala., March 30, 1830. They had born to them six children, one of whom died in infancy: Susan E., deceased; James K., who married Sallie E. Simonton; Lou Ollie, wife of I. E. Sykes; and Annie M., wife of W. G. Francis. The father continued farming until the Civil war broke out, and in March, 1861, he enlisted under Capt. James Bullard in the Tenth Mississippi regiment. When his time expired he organized a company of state troops, went out as captain, but was soon elected colonel. He served until the surrender. He was paroled May 1, 1865, after which he settled with his family in Itawamba county. In 1869 he removed to Lee county, and located at Shannon, where he embarked in the mercantile trade in connection with his agricultural interests. In 1883 he was elected treasurer of Lee county, and held the office two terms. He was a democrat in his political opinions. In 1871 he received injuries from falling out of a wagon, and never fully recovered. He died April 7, 1891, at Shannon. He was a Mason of high degree, and a deacon in the Missionary Baptist church.

W. R. Whitesides assisted his father on the farm, and attended the common schools during his youth. He was united in marriage to Miss Alice Borum, a native of Mississippi, born August 20, 1853, and a daughter of Richard M. and Emeline Borum. Three children were born of this union: Joseph B., was born October 13, 1875, and died November 3, 1875; Arthur W., was born December 12, 1887; Daisie Emma, was born May 29, 1881, died October 2, 1885. Mr. Whitesides continued farming until 1882, when he engaged as a clerk for W. B. Redus of Shannon; he was employed in this capacity until October, 1887, when he took charge of a stock of goods at Nettleton, the firm being W. B. Redus & Co. August 1, 1889, Mr. Whitesides and E. R. Wiygul bought out the business, which they have since conducted. They carry a well-selected stock of goods, and have built up a prosperous business. Mr. Whitesides is a democrat in his political opinions, and cast his first presidential vote for Samuel J. Tilden. He is a member of the town council and is also town treasurer; he is treasurer and trustee of Providence college of Lee county, and belongs to the Knights of Honor. For many years he has been a member of the Missionary Baptist church, and like his father, has been a generous contributor to all religious and educational movements. He is a man keenly alive to the public needs, and a citizen who would not disregard his duty to his fellowman.

North Carolina has contributed many of her sons to distant states who have shed luster and honor on their adopted home. But the Old North state never contributed one more universally liked and respected than the subject of this sketch. At White Hall, Wayne county, N. C., on the 6th of June, 1822, was born Dr. N. H. Whitfield. His father, Maj. Edmond Whitfield, was no stranger to the legislative halls of North Carolina, but his sturdy, independent spirit would never permit him to be an office holder, though more than once his native state endeavored to honor him with an office of high trust, the state treasurership being among the honors tendered him. Major Whitfield married Miss Penelope C. Holmes, of Clinton, Sampson county, N. C. Through the veins of Miss Holmes coursed the blue blood of aristocracy; she was a granddaughter of the distinguished General Clinton. From this union was born Dr. N. H. Whitfield. The early ancestors of Dr. Whitfield were conspicuous cavaliers, who refused to bend their necks to Cromwellian tyranny. They took refuge in the untrodden wilds of America, and the colonial history of New York, Virginia and North Carolina attests the valor, the energy and the intelligence they displayed in carving out the fortunes of America. Under the United States government they have always been bravely aggressive, ready to defend her liberty and advance her prosperity. As an evidence of the aid they have extended their country, William Whitfield, a great-uncle of Dr. Whitfield, contributed one hundred and twenty sons and grandsons to the American cause during the last war with England; they were conspicuous in expelling the foreign foe from the soil. The Whitfields have always been successful in the financial world, and honorable and upright in their business relations. Many of them have accumulated fortunes. William Whitfield, from whom the Doctor is a lineal descendant, came from England about the eighteenth century. He married a Miss Goodman, and settled in Nansemond county, Va. When North Carolina was still in its virgin state, and the Indian roamed unmolested through its unbroken wilds, a descendant of William Whitfield moved hither from Virginia, and settled on the Neuse river. He named his home White Hall. This spot is now designated as a flourishing town, and around this town have lived and flourished for two hundred years the descendants of this brave and progressive pioneer, who, like Boone, knew no fear and acknowledged no master. It is noteworthy to state that though five generations have come and passed over the river of death, the Whitfields still own the place settled by their honored forefather. On December 9, 1793, was born at this place Edmund Whitfield, the father of Dr. Whitfield. Edmund Whitfield, inheriting the pioneer spirit of his early ancestor, moved West in 1840, with his family, and settled at Aberdeen, Miss. At that period railroads were an unknown factor, and transportation was effected by wagons. But Major Whitfield safely made the trip through dense forests and an unbroken wilderness until he reached the home of his adoption. Major Whitfield was a large and successful planter, and an honor and a credit to the society of Aberdeen. He lived quietly and happily in the midst of his ample possessions until September 14, 1867, when death ended his existence. He died as he had always lived, an honorable Christian gentleman. His career had never cast one blot on the escutcheon of his distinguished family. The mother followed her departed husband January 6, 1875. Six children were the result of this union, two of whom are now living, the subject of this sketch, and Mrs. Mary A. Holmes, a true wife, a loving mother and an earnest cultivated Christian. One of the sons, O. H. Whitfield, achieved distinction in the legal world, not only carving his way to the top of his profession, but was appointed chancellor judge of his district, which office he filled with distinguished ability and with honor and credit to himself and family. Dr. N. H. Whitfield was educated in North Carolina. He is a fluent and interesting conversationalist, and his striking and well-rounded periods clearly show the careful and classical training he received. At the age of twenty-one he developed a taste for materia medica, and began the study under a private tutor, Dr. B. L. Hatch, an able practitioner of Aberdeen. Untiringly and with energy did he pursue his profession as a science for two years. He here laid a foundation on which he built his eminent success in future years as a surgeon. Being carefully prepared he entered the University of Pennsylvania, where he graduated with the first honors of his class in 1846-7. He began the practice of medicine near Aberdeen, and his ability being quickly recognized he rapidly built up a lucrative practice. His devotion to his profession soon caused his health to fail, and he reluctantly turned his attention to agriculture, being compelled to give up medicine. In this new field his natural ability and common sense soon asserted itself, and he rapidly made money for seven years; but longing for the social amenities of town life, he sold out his farming interest, moved to Aberdeen and embarked in the mercantile business. His genius of success did not desert him here, for until the war broke out he was known as a successful merchant. When the South, in 1860, was convulsed with excitement over the war soon to burst forth, Dr. Whitfield, with heroic courage and with prescient knowledge, fought the dismemberment of the Union. "It will bring," said he, "nothing but ruin and destruction in its wake, and inevitable calamity will be the portion of the South." How truthful and prophetic were his words! He said slavery was doomed, that our so-called free government was the laughingstock of all Europe; why not abolish slavery, and why shall we plunge this beautiful Southland of ours in a destructive war? But like his native state he fought manfully the war issue until the ordinance of secession was declared, when he offered his services and his talents for the protection of his people. He first entered the Confederate service as a quartermaster, with the rank of major. This position being distasteful to him he resigned and was immediately appointed surgeon, and was ordered to take charge of a large number of hospitals at Grenada, Miss. This duty was ably and efficiently discharged by him.

When General Grant made his first attack on Vicksburg, the Confederate service recognizing the eminent fitness of Dr. N. H. Whitfield as a surgeon, ordered him to report thither immediately, when he was appointed chief surgeon on Gen. M. L. Smith's staff. This position was filled with perfect satisfaction to the Confederate service, and with distinguished credit to himself. As an evidence of the importance and magnitude of the post held by Dr. Whitfield it is only necessary to state that it was connected with the second largest division in Lieutenant-General Pemberton's army, which embraced eight thousand privates, besides the various commanding officers, twenty-seven surgeons and a large number of hospitals filled with the sick and wounded. In the thickest of the fray, when death and destruction stared every one in the face, and when the tenure of life was slight to both friend and foe, we find this heroic surgeon ever at his post of duty. No danger was too great for him, no duty too severe. After a destructive siege of forty-six days, Vicksburg was forced to surrender to an overpowering force, and the enemy were in possession of the city. Dr. Whitfield was invited by a friend to call on General Grant, at his headquarters. "As soon as we arrived we sent in our cards by the servant, who immediately invited us into General Grant's sittingroom, who met us and gave us a cordial welcome. We soon engaged in a pleasant conversation. During this time we conferred freely about the war. He regarded it as a great calamity, and manifested a strong desire to see it terminated and peace and harmony restored to the country. I could not fully realize that I was conversing with General Grant. He was so very plain in conversation and in his manners. He did not seem to be aware of his own power, or the influence he would have or exert in controlling and shaping the future destinies of this country, either for good or evil, if he lived. The more I saw of him and became acquainted with him, the more I became thoroughly impressed with the very extraordinary combination of rare elements of character which he exhibited. He manifested a strong sympathy for the South, and thought the South had made a very great mistake in withdrawing from the Union." After conversing for some time the Doctor thought he had trespassed too long upon General Grant's time; he arose and bade the General good-bye, at which time the General handed him the following order, written and signed by himself:

HEADQUARTERS DEPARTMENT, VICKSBURG, MISS.
TO THE COMMANDING OFFICERS OF THE UNITED STATES GOVERNMENT AND ARMY:

Please allow Dr. N. H. Whitfield to pass in and out and through our lines at the various posts; to travel on all government railroads and steamers; to visit my headquarters at discretion, free of charge.

Very respectfully,
U. S. GRANT, General Commanding.

Dr. Whitfield carefully and deliberately read the order. He calmly looked at the General and said: "General Grant do you mean to attack my loyalty, or do you give me this simply as a matter of courtesy and kind feeling, and to protect me against the casualties of this war? If the latter I accept it with pleasure." Such acts of kindness endeared General Grant to all who met and knew him. "A more noble, generous foe I never met. It was certainly very fortunate the South had such an adversary. I regarded him as a true, sincere patriot, and I believe that whatever he did was for the good of his country." After the surrender of Vicksburg he reported to General Pemberton, at Demopolis, Ala., for hospital work, but was soon transferred to Enterprise, Miss., where he was assigned to conscript duty, which office he held until the death of the Confederacy. Having been paroled at Gainesville, Ala., with General Forrest and others, he returned to Aberdeen, Miss. At the close of the war the Doctor found himself a financial wreck, without a home to retire to, but still in possession of his untiring and dauntless energy. By close economy and judicious management he rapidly recovered from his financial embarrassments, and is to-day in possession of a handsome income and a beautiful home. The rapid recovery of his wealth the Doctor attributes to the faithful and loving assistance of his cultured and amiable wife, to whom he was married in 1849. She was at all times faithful and true, and she followed his pathway through life knowing no higher duty than to administer to the wants of him who was her guide and helpmeet. Her death, which was a sad blow to the Doctor, took place in 1867. She was a Miss Anna Hill, and was descended from a family prominent in politics, social position and wealth. Dr. Whitfield is a brilliant, aggressive writer, and the journalistic world, both North and South, has felt the effect of his cold, persuasive logic. During the political struggle of Mississippi, when negroism and carpetbagism were grinding the existence out of his beloved state, he came boldly to the front a second time, and defended her rights and liberties with his pen. He is a prominent member of the Presbyterian church, and a Mason. Dr. Whitfield has a very social disposition, and nothing delights him more than to entertain his numerous friends. He dispenses his hospitality in a brave and liberal manner. From the quiet haven of rest in his beautiful home at Aberdeen, he looks back over his eventful life and quietly awaits the time when his Creator shall call him to partake of the joys of an eternal happiness.

Hon. J. J. Whitney, attorney, of Fayette, Miss. From his early manhood Mr. Whitney has given to Jefferson county the very best energies of his life and in his career at the bar he has achieved an excellent reputation. He is a native of Jefferson county, Miss., where he has resided all his life. His father, John M. Whitney, was born in South Carolina, and when a stripling of sixteen years old came to Mississippi, in the year 1808, and located at Greenville, or what is now called Old Greenville. After his marriage, in 1815, he engaged in farming and became one of the most successful and prosperous planters of the county. His strong intellect and excellent judgment soon became known and he was elected to the position of probate judge, in which capacity he served ten years, and through his whole life enjoyed the highest confidence and esteem of the people. He was married in Jefferson county to Miss Clarissa Montgomery, a native of this county and a daughter of Alexander Montgomery, a pioneer of the county, and on his fine plantation near Fayette he resided until his death in 1867, his widow surviving him until 1871, when she, too, passed away. Six sons and three daughters were born to them, three sons and one daughter being now deceased. The eldest son, Rev. Alexander Whitney, was a minister in the Methodist Episcopal church and died in Louisiana. John was a lawyer and died in Decatur, Ill. F. S. was a planter and died in Claiborne county, Miss. Of the living sons Dr. P. K. Whitney is a successful practitioner of Fayette; C. W. is a merchant and planter of Louisiana, and Capt. J. J. is an attorney and planter of Fayette. The latter attained manhood in his native state and county, and as his father was in good circumstances he had plenty of time to devote to the acquirement of an education and graduated from Oakland college, Miss., in the class of 1853. He then began following in his father's footsteps, that is, he engaged in planting, and this calling received his attention till 1862, when his love for the South and his sympathy with the cause of secession caused him to enlist in the Confederate army. He became a member of the Fourth Mississippi cavalry and was elected lieutenant of company H, after which he was promoted to the rank of captain, in which capacity he served until the close of the war. He participated in numerous battles and skirmishes and surrendered at Gainesville, Ala., after which he returned home, changed his sword into a plowshare and once more engaged in agricultural pursuits. In 1874 he was elected treasurer of Jefferson county, and with the efficiency, faithfulness and honor which have ever marked his career he discharged the duties incumbent upon this office. In 1882 he was honored by an election to the state legislature, and at the end of two years was chosen state senator and held the office four years. Later he was once more elected to the legislature, serving in all eight consecutive years, and having always the confidence of the people. In 1873 he was admitted to the bar and has been one of the leading attorneys of the Jefferson county bar. In the month of February, 1858, he was married to Miss Josephine Darden, daughter of John P. Darden. She was born and reared in this county, liberally educated and in all respects is eminently worthy of the old and honored family of which she is a descendant. Her eldest brother, Capt. Put Darden, was a brave and distinguished Confederate soldier, being commander during the whole war of the Jefferson artillery battery from this county. After the war he engaged in farming, and at an early day enlisted in the order of Patrons of Husbandry. With untiring energy and great ability he devoted his life to the cause, soon rose to eminent distinction, and at his untimely death, July, 1888, was master both of the state and of the national grange. Her surviving brother, Hon. T. L. Darden, is treasurer of the Mississippi State Alliance and represents his county in the state legislature. Mr. and Mrs. Whitney have five children: Annie; C. C., a railroad agent at Leland, Miss.; Lena, Della and Eula. The family move in the best social circles and are attendants and members of the Christian church.

William H. Whittle, a prominent physician and surgeon of Clarke county, Miss., was born in Kemper county, February 12, 1860, a son of William J. and Mahala (Flora) Whittle. His father was a native of Mississippi and son of Richard Whittle, who was an early settler of Kemper county. He had a family of three children: Winnie J., James and William J. The paternal grandfather died in Smith county, Miss., and the mother in Kemper county, near De Kalb. His father removed from Kemper county to Smith county, where he died in March, 1865. He served as a soldier in the Confederate army during the war. He was a prominent Mason and was a member of the grand lodge of Mississippi. He was an active, selfeducated and selfmade business man and prominent farmer, who was also interested in other important enterprises. His wife, mother of our subject, was born in South Carolina, about 1830, a daughter of E. Flora, who moved to Kemper county probably about 1836. She was one of seven children, of whom Lawson N., is a planter of Kemper county; Richard A., also is a planter in the same county; Minnie T. is now Mrs. Coolidge, of Noxubee county; William H. is next in order of birth; James J. is a dentist in Gholson, Noxubee county; Winnie J. is living in the old home in Kemper county; John N. is a teacher of this county. Mrs. Whittle, mother of the above, is living in Scooba, Kemper county. She is a devout member of the Primitive Baptist church. Our subject passed his youth in Kemper county. He was educated at Cooper institute at Daleville, Lauderdale county, and graduated in medicine at Baltimore, Md., in 1882, and entered upon the practice of his profession at Coffadeliah, Neosha county, where he remained two years, removing to Peden, Kemper county, where he practiced successfully until 1890, when he came to De Soto, where he continued his medical practice in connection with the mercantile business, starting a general store in the year just mentioned. He is also half owner in a mill and turpentine distillery, the output of the last-mentioned establishment being about five hundred barrels per year. He was married November 16, 1886, to Miss Anna B. Wright, of Lake Burnside, Neshoba county, a daughter of Col. A. R. Wright and Mary L. (White) Wright, natives of Georgia, in which state Mrs. Whittle was born in 1864. They have two children, Clara H. and Mary L. The Doctor is a member of the State Medical association and is very prominent in the County Medical association. Politically, he sides with the democratic party. He is a member of Chickasaw lodge, A. F. & A. M. Besides his other interests above mentioned, he has a fine farm in Clarke county and other interests in the town of De Soto. His partner in the milling business is Joseph McGee, and Lee Ethridge is his partner in the turpentine enterprise. The Doctor is a young man of much public spirit and he has made his own way in the world with marked success, not only professionally but socially and commercially. He and his wife are both members of the Episcopal church and contribute largely to its various interests.

Whittington Brothers. Among the pioneer families to come to Amite county, Miss., and engage in planting were the Whittingtons, who were led by Moses Whittington, a Georgian, who took up his abode here in the early part of the present century. His son, William J. Whittington, was born in this state and county March 16, 1818, and was here united in the bonds of matrimony to Miss Permelia Evelyn Bolin, a native of this county, and a daughter of William Bolin, who was a Jefferson county Mississippian, born in 1793. He was a soldier in the War of 1812, and was in the engagement at New Orleans with General Jackson. He removed from Jefferson to Amite county in an early day, became well known here, and here spent his declining years. After his marriage, William J. Whittington was engaged in planting near Liberty for a number of years, and there lost his wife, in Franklin county, May 4, 1887, after which he moved to Gloster, where he now resides. Notwithstanding the fact that he is now seventy-three years of age, he is in the enjoyment of fairly good health, his mental vigor being also unimpaired. To himself and wife a family of six sons and two daughters were born, all of whom are living at the present time. N. C. Whittington, his son, is a member of the firm of Whittington Brothers, and was born near Liberty September 8, 1841. He was given the advantages of the schools of this county, but finished his education in the New Orleans Commercial college. In the early history of the Civil war he responded to the call for troops, and was a member of the Seventh Mississippi infantry, Confederate States army, and took part in a number of important engagements, among which may be mentioned Shiloh, where his clothing was riddled with bullets; Murfreesboro, where he was wounded in the leg by a gunshot; Chickamauga, where he was seriously wounded in the shoulder and hand and permanently disabled, and one or two other engagements of less importance. Soon after this he returned to his home, and was here married in 1869 to Miss Anna M. Robertson, a daughter of Joseph Robertson. Mrs. Whittington was born and reared in Jackson, Miss., and upon her marriage to Mr. Whittington removed with him to Natchez. The latter was engaged in merchandising at this point for about one year, then moved his goods and established a country store in Jefferson county, four years being spent here. At the end of this time his establishment was destroyed by fire, and he then turned his attention to farming, near Mount Zion, in Franklin county. Since 1885 he has been a resident of Gloster, and has been associated in the mercantile business with his brother, their house being one of the first to be established in the place. Mr. and Mrs. Whittington are members of the Methodist Episcopal church. J. Monroe Whittington, the other member of the firm, was born in Amite county, August 29, 1846. His youth was spent in obtaining an education and assisting on his father's plantation, where he learned lessons of industry, patience and economy, which have since stood him in good stead. He was first married in Jefferson county, in 1874, to Miss Ollie A. Fowler, a daughter of Col. Gabriel Fowler. His wife was born, reared and educated in Jefferson county, and was an intelligent, accomplished and amiable lady. She died August 23, 1878, leaving three children: Lucien N., Gortie M. and Anna C. Mr. Whittington married his present wife in Rodney in 1881, she being Mrs. Sallie Haley, a daughter of Dr. E. R. Manuels. Mrs. Whittington was brought up and educated in Fayette, Miss., and has borne her husband two children: Melenium Eloise and James Monroe. Mr. Whittington has followed merchandising since quite a young man, and from Fayette removed to Franklin county, locating near Meadville, where he sold goods and also carried on a farm, continuing for about nine years. In 1885 he moved to Gloster, and here has since been associated with his brother in the mercantile business. Their stock of goods is well chosen, is extensive, and as they dispose of the same at reasonable rates, are honest, and endeavor at all times to please their patrons, they now command a very large trade. They are public-spirited, enterprising gentlemen, and are very social, cordial and agreeable, qualities that are very essential for success in any calling. The latter named member of the firm erected one of the finest residences in the town, but sold out recently and purchased other property. He and his wife are members of the Baptist church. They have a brother, Rev. J. R. Whittington, who is a minister of the Methodist Episcopal church. He is a man of superior intelligence and education, and in addition to attending to the spiritual wants of his fellowmen, he has, in times past, looked after their physical welfare also, being a graduate and a practitioner of medicine. Another brother, Walter W., is a farmer of Franklin county; Alexander is a merchant of Roxie, Miss.; Thomas L. is a farmer of Jefferson county; Indiana is the wife of Alexander Thomas, of Franklin county, and M. E. is the wife of L. J. Imes, an agriculturist, of Jefferson county.

John Lawrence Wiggins, attorney, of Rosedale, Miss., was born in Ashley county, Ark., in 1859, and was the third son born to the union of Samuel B. and Mary G. (Wade) Wiggins, the father a native of South Carolina, and the mother of Tennessee. The father moved to Mississippi in 1836, followed farming and speculating, and later became a prominent planter and slaveowner in Louisiana. He subsequently moved to Arkansas and there followed the same occupation successfully. The town of Hamburg, Ark., was built up on his place, and his old residence, the Wiggins home, is historic in Hamburg at the present time. His death occurred in 1871. His wife had died in 1862. Both were church members, he of the Baptist and she of the Methodist persuasion. The paternal grandfather was a native of North Carolina, and the grandmother, whose maiden name was Ricks, was a native of the Palmetto state. The maternal grandfather was a native of Tennessee and of an old and prominent family. John Lawrence Wiggins is practically self educated, having clerked and worked at other occupations to obtain the means to educate himself. He came to Mississippi in 1872 and first clerked for Nance Bros., of Bolivar, for a few months. He followed this business at other places for a number of years, and in 1879-80 attended the University of Oxford. After this he engaged as clerk and bookkeeper, and also carried on planting until 1886, when he entered the Louisville Law school. Finishing the study of law in 1887, he at once entered upon the practice of his profession at Rosedale. On the 1st day of January, 1891, he formed a partnership with W. B. Roberts. In the spring and summer of that year the state witnessed a very warm political fight in the democratic party, the alliance of Bolivar county indorsing Mr. Roberts for the state senate on the sub-treasury platform in opposition to the views of his partner, Mr. Wiggins, who favored the renomination of George and Walthall for the United States senate, in opposition to the sub-treasury and the alliance candidates, and in consequence thereof, Mr. Wiggins ran for the state legislature and was successfully nominated by the county democracy, the result of which was a defeat for Mr. Roberts and a final dissolution of their partnership in July. Mr. Wiggins enjoys a good practice and is keenly alive to the interests of his clients. He is a member of the Methodist Episcopal church, and is also a member in good standing in the Knights of Pythias organization. He is alive to progress and improvement.

George M. Wilburn, Pickens, was born in Yazoo county, Miss., May 14, 1856, and is the third of a family of six children. His parents, William W. and Elizabeth (Crutcher) Wilburn were natives of Virginia. The father emigrated from his birthplace to Yazoo county, Miss., in 1832, and was engaged in planting there until the time of his death in 1885. He was a son of James and Sallie (Wyche) Wilburn, also natives of Virginia. The maternal grandfather of George M. was Reuben Crutcher. Young Wilburn was reared in the state of his birth, and attended both the public and private schools. After leaving school he gave his energies to planting, and now owns six hundred and forty acres, three hundred being under cultivation. Later on he embarked in the mercantile trade, and carried a stock of $1,200. He has been very successful in his business, and has given generously of the means he has accumulated for the aid of public works and the needs of the less fortunate. Politically he affiliates with the democratic party. He is a member of the board of supervisors of Yazoo county, having been elected in 1889. He has proved a very efficient and able member, and has given entire satisfaction to his constituency. Mr. Wilburn was married in 1878 to Miss Alice Pepper, a native of Mississippi and a daughter of A. G. and Amanda (Stuhlefield) Pepper. They have had three children born to them: William W., Carrie and Gwin Pepper. They are worthy and consistent members of the Missionary Baptist church, in which they are zealous workers. The Wilburn family is of Irish and English origin, and is among the older settlers of Mississippi.

R. H. Wildberger, banker, Clarksdale, Miss., the efficient cashier of the Clarksdale Bank and Trust company and an energetic and reliable gentleman, was originally from Tennessee, his birth occurring in Memphis in 1852. His parents, John and Caroline (Cheek) Wildberger, were natives of Switzerland and Virginia respectively. The father came to the United States in 1830 and three years later made a permanent settlement at Memphis, where he was engaged in the clothing business, which he carried on until the outbreak of the war. He then enlisted in the Confederate army and served as lieutenant of an artillery regiment for two years, after which he was discharged on account of poor eyesight. He died in 1866. The mother is still living and makes her home in the Blue Grass state. R. H. Wildberger was reared to mature years in Memphis, educated at the Kentucky Military institute near Frankfort, and was for two years steamboat clerk on the Mississippi river. After this for eight years he was professor of natural sciences and commandant of cadets at the Kentucky Military institute. In 1882 he was engaged in planting near Memphis, continued this for two years and in 1884 moved to Clarksdale, where he became secretary of Sunflower Oil company for four years. In 1888 he was one of the organizers of the Clarksdale Bank and Trust company and was elected to his present responsible position as cashier. He is president of the Yazoo Delta Investment company, director of the Clarksdale Brick and Manufacturing company, and is also a director in the Clarksdale Compress company. He is a member of both the Masonic and Odd Fellow fraternities. He is notary public and insurance agent for fifteen companies, being the only agent in this part of the country. Insurance has of late years assumed such a degree of importance as to now constitute an important factor in commercial pursuits, and Mr. Wildberger adds efficiency in this line to his many other business accomplishments. He is a leading spirit in every enterprise looking to Clarksdale's future greatness. He is an unusually busy man and one of the shrewdest business men in Mississippi. He has been the life and spirit of every enterprise of Clarksdale and is an officer or a stockholder in every corporation of the town. He is tall and dark and is gentlemanly and courteous in his manner.

One of the most efficient members of the board of supervisors of Adams county and its present president is Capt. Oliver N. Wilds, who comes of one of the oldest families of the state. He was born in Natchez on the 18th of August, 1839, the youngest of a family of four children born to Richard and Mary (Myers) Wilds, the former of whom was born near Manchester, England, and the latter in West Virginia. About 1834 the father came to the United States, and after a short time spent in New Jersey he came to Natchez, and here in 1836 he started a foundry, the first in the city. The works stood near the site of the old, or first, cottonpress under the hill, where he did a good business. He died in 1866. His wife died in 1839, soon after the birth of the subject of his sketch, after which Mr. Wilds married a Mrs. Gipser. Oliver N. Wilds was reared in Natchez, at which place he attended the public schools and the institute, the latter being under the management of Messrs. Gaines and Cornish, under whom he graduated. He learned the trade of a machinist and engineer, serving an apprenticeship of four years, after which he worked at the same for the same length of time. He finished his trade in Cincinnati, after which he studied draughting for some time, and was there at the opening of the war. He returned to Natchez early in 1861; for sixty days was a member of a company, after which he joined the Natchez Southrons under Capt. Richard Inge, and was at the battle of Shiloh, where he was badly wounded, and was afterward discharged from the service, being unable to enter the service again. In 1862 he was married to Miss Barbara Koerber, a native of Natchez, and a daughter of Lewis Koerber, an early pioneer of that city. After his return from the army Captain Wilds began planting in Adams county on a small scale, and although he only raised six bales of cotton the first year he rapidly extended his business until he became one of the most extensive planters in the county, his crop of cotton amounting to three thousand five hundred bales one year. He is now the owner of four plantations in Louisiana and one in Adams county, of which one thousand nine hundred acres are under cultivation. In 1876 he bought his fine residence in the suburbs of Natchez, a beautiful place of some twenty-five acres in extent. The residence is beautifully situated and surrounded by majestic oaks, making it one of the loveliest places of the city. In 1876, in partnership with A. G. Ober, he purchased a number of fine plantations, and was very extensively engaged in farming until 1887, when he sold out to Mr. Ober. In 1876 he was elected a member of the board of supervisors, and upon the death of Mr. Pollock was made its president, and has been the presiding officer of that body ever since. He has been instrumental in making many improvements in the way of roads and bridges in the county, as well as reducing the tax rate and advancing the county's credit. To Captain Wild's union ten children have been born: Lena Marcella, who died in infancy; Mary Virginia, the wife of Dan Reagan, now residing in Terre Haute, Ind.; Richard S. is now the manager of his father's plantation; Stella is an accomplished and popular young lady, and was educated in the convent near Mobile, Ala. (the Mississippi river steamer, Stella Wilds, was named in her honor); Oliver K. is attending a college of Bay St. Louis; Aurella; Louisa, who died in infancy; Albert J.; Edna, who died in infancy, and Eva Hillary. Mrs. Wilds and all of her eldest children are members of the Catholic church. Mr. Wilds is one of the wideawake business men of Natchez and has always been an active citizen and an enthusiastic supporter of all things for the good of Adams county. He is popular and well liked wherever known, and in the bosom of his family is a model husband and father.

L. and N. Wilczinski, wholesale dealers in dry goods, groceries, etc., and cotton commission merchants at Greenville, carry a stock of goods valued at $100,000 and do an annual business of $500,000. This business was started in Greenville in 1868, under the firm title of L. Wilczinski & Co., general merchants, and their annual business was very large from the very start. Since then this has steadily increased, and the firm is now the largest in the Yazoo delta. They began exclusively in the wholesale business in 1887. Leopold Wilczinski, senior member of the above mentioned firm, was born in Germany and came to America when a boy. He resided for some time in Tennessee and Louisiana, where he mainly followed planting and merchandising, but in 1868 he came to Greenville and at once formed the present business. In 1885 the firm erected their storehouse, a large two-story brick, and in 1889 they erected the finest block in Greenville, at a cost of $50,000. This firm is the only one on the delta that own their cotton yard and fireproof cotton warehouse, the latter having a capacity of ten thousand bales, and they also own several plantations, consisting of ten thousand acres with four hundred acres under cultivation. Leopold was married in 1876 to Miss Levenson, a native of the Blue Grass state, of a very prominent family, and three children have been born to this union: Joseph, Junius and Louis. Mr. Wilczinski is a member of the Masonic fraternity. In 1872 and 1876 he was mayor of Greenville, and started the first improvements ever instituted. During the time he was in office the first railroad (the Georgia Pacific) was commenced and Mr. Wilczinski did all in his power to promote that and to attract foreign capital to Greenville, besides taking a leading part in all other enterprises of a laudable nature. His partner and brother, Nathan Wilczinski, was married in 1880 or 1881 to Miss Levenson, of Kentucky, a sister of Leopold's wife, and the fruits of this union were two children: Fred and Hortense. There were five brothers of the Wilczinski family who came to Washington county, Miss., about the same time. One resides on a plantation in the country and the others are living in Greenville. When they first located in this town it was a hamlet of perhaps five hundred people, and no one has done more in various ways to advance and develop her resources than the members of this family. Their new building, Wilczinski block, is a most tasty edifice, and their large two-story office building, consisting of offices and storerooms, with its highly ornamental and artistic tower, adds much to the looks of the town. A few years ago they laid out part of Greenway plantation, which was one of the finest in the state, and which adjoins the town of Greenville, into five hundred city lots, and this they called Wilczinski's addition to the city of Greenville. A number of tasty residences have already been erected, and from present indications many more will undoubtedly soon be built. A line of street cars passes through this addition and terminates in a beautiful park on which there is a large, handsome grove, the only one in the county. Streets are being laid out and graded and it has been only a year or so since it was a productive cotton field; its prospects for building up and improving from now on are very great indeed.

Col. Drury D. Wilkins, planter and merchant, Duck Hill, Miss. The Wilkins family is of English descent, and among the earlier settlers of North Carolina was the Colonel's grandfather, who was an officer in the Revolutionary war. The Colonel's father, A. S. Wilkins, was born in the Old North state on the 18th of March, 1812, and was the youngest of a family of nine sons. He attained his growth in his native state, and was married in Lincoln county of the same to Miss Levina Warlick, who was born in the Palmetto state in 1814, and who was of German parentage. In 1838 Mr. Wilkins moved to Tennessee, settled in Hamilton county, near Chattanooga, where in connection with planting he followed the blacksmith trade, conducting a general wagon and repair shop. He left there during the war, but returned after peace was declared and continued his former business there until his death in May, 1889. His wife survived him only a few months and died in 1890. They were the parents of seven children—four sons and three daughters—all of whom lived to be men and women; one son, W. W., was a soldier in the Confederate army and held a commission, dying in the service of his country in 1863. Another son, L. B. Wilkins, was also a soldier and held a commission; he was killed at Fort Donelson. The other two sons, Dave A. and Drury D., are in partnership in the mercantile business at Duck Hill. The latter, the youngest in order of birth of the above mentioned family, was born in Cleveland county, N. C., on the 18th of March, 1834. He secured a fair common-school education and remained with his father until nearly grown, when he engaged in railroading with Gray, Dent & Co., contractors. Mr. Wilkins was their manager of construction until 1860, working on the Illinois Central road, and the following year he enlisted in the Confederate army, Brand's battalion. He was under Colonel Dent the first year and in 1862 he was detailed to the quartermaster department, where he was engaged in the manufacture of salt for the army in the Tennessee Salt works until the close of the war. After returning from the war, Colonel Wilkins took his family to Tennessee in a wagon while his wife went the entire distance, two hundred miles, on horseback. In the fall of 1865 Mr. Wilkins returned to the West and located in Montgomery county, Miss., where he has since been extensively engaged in planting. He is the owner of several plantations and is one of the largest landowners in the county, having about twelve thousand acres of land in Montgomery, Carroll and Grenada counties. In 1867 Mr. Wilkins embarked in merchandising in connection with his planting interests, and he carried on a large mercantile establishment at Winona for a few years. He now has a large brick store at Duck Hill, and is doing a general mercantile business. He resides on one of his plantations, about four miles from Duck Hill, and devotes his time to the management of the same. He is an excellent business manager, has accumulated a large estate and is one of the wealthiest men in Montgomery county. He is well known and respected for his many excellent qualities as a business man, citizen and member of society. The Colonel was married in Montgomery county on the 9th of April, 1861, to Miss Mary R. Eskridge, a native of Montgomery county, Miss., and daughter of Tolive and Sophia (Butler) Eskridge, who were formerly from South Carolina, and who were of an old and prominent family. Mr. Wilkins' marriage resulted in the birth of seven children: Lula, wife of D. R. Branch; Waddie, wife of Thomas A. Williams; William, Emma, attending school; Belle, also attending school at Winchester, Tenn.; Drew and Erne E. The Colonel, his wife and most of the children are members of the Baptist church. Colonel Wilkins is a Knight Templar in the Masonic fraternity and is also a member of the Knights of Honor.

Charles Williams, proprietor of the Pearl river foundry in Jackson, Miss., was born in England in 1827, the youngest of three sons born to Paul and Elizabeth (Norham) Williams, the former of whom was a machinist by trade. He came with his family to America in 1829, and settled at Philadelphia, where he built the first worsted machinery in the United States. He continued in business in the city of Brotherly Love until his death, in 1834, his widow surviving him until 1862. Charles Williams was educated at Manayunk, near Philadelphia, and learned the machinist's trade at Reading, Penn. At the age of twenty-one years he had completed his trade, and became an engineer on the Philadelphia & Reading railroad, and the next year (1849) was engaged as master mechanic of the Illinois Central railroad, the construction of which was then begun, and six months later he was made superintendent. After serving in this capacity for one year he returned to Reading on account of sickness, and again became engineer on the Reading railroad, running a locomotive for a few months. At the end of this time he was engaged by the Pennsylvania railroad to take charge of the railroad shops at Miflin, Penn., remaining in their employ until 1853, when he was engaged by the Mississippi Southern railroad to come to Jackson and become superintendent of the road. Three years later he became general superintendent of the combined line from Vicksburg to Meridian, and was the youngest general superintendent of a railway in the United States. In that capacity he served until he resigned of his own accord, in 1859, to enter other business. During the war he ran a gristmill for the Confederate government, five miles east of Jackson, and at the close of hostilities he at once started the Pearl river foundry on the west bank of the beautiful Pearl, which he christened with the name which its pellucid waters suggested. He and his enterprise were among the pioneers in an undeveloped forest, and although obstacles which invariably beset the pioneer and explorer strewed his pathway, they were courageously met and successfully overcome. This enterprise, in every respect, breathes the spirit of energy and intelligence that animated the veteran proprietor, Mr. Williams, which attributes have characterized his course throughout an honorable and successful business career of over a quarter of a century. The following article was published in the Jackson *Clarion* on December 12, 1867, and was written by the now Hon. Ethel Barksdale:

This establishment deserves a more than passing notice. Its founder and proprietor, Mr. Charles Williams, belongs to that class of men who are destined to become famous as the architects of the future material prosperity of the South, if it be recorded in the book of fate that she is ever to arise from the dust and ashes of her defeat in her struggle for independence.

This class embraces the stanch, solid, laboring men of the country who have apprehended the requirements of the times, and consequently addressed themselves to the task of supplying what is needed.

No man deserves more credit than the agriculturist who, nothing daunted by the destruction of the labor system of the country, gathered courage from adversity, and entered upon the hard task of wresting from the bosom of mother earth her fruits with the poor materials that were left him. For it is from her undeveloped resources, at least, that the elements of a restored prosperity must be secured.

But not less deserving of reward is the manufacturer, who, amid the wrecks which surround him, essays to build up such enterprises as the one over which Mr. Williams presides.

The farmer will toil in vain to restore the prosperity of the country if he is wholly at the mercy of foreign interests and dependent upon them for the implements with which he works. The great object of our people should be to make what they need at home, and the money which is expended to supply their wants will circulate among themselves. Last season tens of thousands of dollars were sent outside of the state for agricultural tools. It went to enrich the people of Louisville, Pittsburgh and other communities, and hundreds of thousands were expended in the Western markets for provisions. In meeting these expenditures the cotton crop of the state has been almost wholly absorbed.

The Pearl River foundry is a complete establishment. By reference to his advertisement it will be seen that the proprietor has determined to leave no pretext for purchasers to seek other markets in order to supply themselves with the various descriptions of articles which are manufactured there. They are very numerous and are afforded at lower rates than usual. A thoroughly practical man, he has accumulated all the latest labor-saving improvements by which work can be done expeditiously and at the lowest cost, and has gathered around him a corps of experienced and skillful craftsmen. The best evidence of his success is found in the fact that at the recent exhibition at Kosciusko his plow (which he offers at from $5 to $7) took the prize from six other manufacturers, and his ornamental work has been purchased by some of the most imposing buildings that have been erected in Vicksburg, as well as this city, since the close of the war. When the superior facilities of Vicksburg for cheap river transportation from the largest establishments of Pittsburgh, Cincinnati and other Northern cities are considered, it will be imagined what a triumph Mr. Williams has achieved by his success over other competitors in that city.

We need not doubt the success of this enterprising and thoroughgoing citizen. It is an assured result, if our beautiful and glorious land is not forever lost in gloom and darkness, and this sad fate will not overtake her if other classes of our countrymen will display but one-half of his energy, skill and courage in useful undertakings.

In 1873 he erected his present building, occupying some four acres on South State street, and from this establishment turns out annually a large number of plows. His plow, called the Pearl River, has taken the premium wherever exhibited. He makes all kinds of agricultural machinery, at which he is an adept, and in his establishment, which is the largest of the kind in the state, he does all kinds of repairing, and also makes machinery to order. He has been very successful financially, and is the owner of a fine tract of land in Jackson, on which are erected seven houses, and he also owns a farm of eighty acres near the city. He is very courteous and kind to his employes, and is very thoughtful of their comfort, his factory being supplied with everything for their convenience. When running full force he employs about forty men, the majority of whom are skillful and practical mechanics. Mr. Williams is very tasteful and methodical in all his ways, and is a very desirable gentleman with whom to have business dealings, for he believes in and practices the teachings of the golden rule. He is a stanch democrat of the Jacksonian type, but has never been an aspirant for public office, although he was a member of the city council for a number of years. He was at one time appointed mayor of Jackson by Governor Ames, but respectfully declined the office. In 1857 he was married to Miss Rosa Spangler, a daughter of Joseph Spangler and a native of Vicksburg. She died in 1886, without issue, an earnest and worthy member of the Catholic church.

C. C. Williams, president of the Meridian Sash, Door and Blind factory, one of the leading manufacturing concerns of the city and the largest of its kind in the South, was born in Hawkins county, Tenn., February 12, 1826, a son of George Williams, who was a native of the same county, having been born at Red Bridge, Tenn. He was reared, educated and died in his native county, and was regarded as one of the best planters in that part of the state. His wife was Sarah Moore, who bore him eight sons and three daughters, who grew to maturity, four sons and two daughters surviving until the present time. Of this large family of children the subject of this sketch was the fifth in the order of nativity. He was reared and educated in Hawkins county, Tenn., completing his studies at the Emory and Henry college. He came to Mississippi in 1849, and located at Okolona, Chickasaw county, and there engaged in planting. In 1862 he enlisted in company C, of the Twelfth Mississippi cavalry, and served until the close of the war. He came to Meridian, Miss., in 1871, and bought an interest in a small sash, door and blind factory. This concern, largely through Mr. Williams' management, has developed into the present great Meridian sash, door and blind plant. It has always been recognized as the leading manufactory of this class of goods in the South. This being a distributing point, the products of this concern reach all of the surrounding states, and they have been sent as far as Cairo, Ill., on the north, and to Texas, on the southwest. The gentlemen composing the company which owns this large plant are thoroughly conversant with their business, and keep constantly in stock the very best material in the country, their ample capital enabling them to carry a large supply of lumber which is not manufactured until it is thoroughly seasoned, and for this reason gives the very best of satisfaction. Their main factory building is 112x210 feet, being two and three stories high, while their brick warehouse is over two hundred feet long, with over forty thousand feet of floor space. Their planing department has a capacity of about fifty thousand feet of dressed lumber daily, and the concern carries over two million feet of lumber in stock, and is prepared to execute unlimited orders. Its work can not be surpassed for beauty, style and finish, and is made from designs which are models of taste and elegance. The company manufactures and keeps in stock sash, doors, blinds, moldings, newels, balustrades, brackets, stairs, and all kinds of inside finish, as well as office and bank furniture of the most tasteful character; in fact everything that the building trade demands which can be manufactured out of wood. One hundred and twenty-five men are employed, and about seventy-five machines are in operation. Mr. Williams, besides being the president of this concern, owns stock in nearly every enterprise in the town. He was married in 1861 to Miss Ardenia Pullen, of Giles county, Tenn., and they have four children living: F. W., E. C., Mrs. Lillie Smith and Mrs. Daisy Weems. Mr. Williams is a deacon in the Meridian Baptist church.

Charles D. Williams, one of the most substantial and progressive citizens of Hinds county, Miss., was born near Auburn, Ala., May 18, 1848. His father, the late Samuel Moore Williams (born 1805, died 1889), was a native of South Carolina, an architect; he planned and erected many of the courthouses of his own state and in Georgia. In the latter state he married Emeline, daughter of Dr. Pleasant Philips, whose ancestors were English. The subject of this sketch is the eldest of their seven children, and until he was thirteen years old he attended school, but on the outbreak of the Civil war the school was closed and his education was practically finished. Shortly before his eighteenth birthday, he enlisted in the Georgia cavalry as a member of Cheatham's staff. Three days later a severe scalp wound disabled him, and before he was again able to be in the saddle, General Lee had surrendered. His parents, who had been wealthy at the beginning of the struggle, now found themselves poor, and with their family they came to Mississippi where they engaged in farming. This they pursued until 1868, when they removed to Texas. Charles, having obtained a situation as clerk in Raymond, remained behind. For his first year's services he was paid his board and $6.25 per month. But he had made himself the trusted friend of his employer, who raised his salary a few dollars the ensuing year. This he divided with his mother. Four years thereafter, he was engaged by Messrs. Harrison & Lewis, of Edwards, where he was joined by his younger brother, Philips, who was employed by the same firm. Together they saved sufficient money to buy a farm in Texas, which they presented to their parents, who were thereby rendered independent. They remained in Edwards until 1878, when with a capital of $450 each they formed a copartnership with C. L. Robinson, of Bolton, to conduct a general furnishing business. Here they prospered, and at the expiration of two years they dissolved the partnership with Mr. Robinson and carried on the business in their own name and according to their own ideas. In 1885 J. M. Black was admitted as a partner. The following summer, the interest of P. P. Williams (who removed to Vicksburg) was purchased by his brother. In December, 1889, he also bought the stock owned by Mr. Black, and now conducts the business under the firm name of C. D. Williams & Co. (the company is nominal). He carries a stock of general merchandise, the inventory of which is $6,000; with this he does annually a business of $125,000. During thirteen years his business has grown from $450 the first year to $150,000 at the present writing (1891), and from handling fifty bales of cotton in 1878 to three thousand five hundred in 1890. He owns stock in two of the best banks in Jackson and one in Vicksburg, besides a liberal share of life insurance. Each year he retires from $1,000 to $5,000 for outside investments, and expends a great deal in charity. His landed estates to the amount of fifty-five hundred acres are under his personal supervision and are growing in beauty and value. His plantations are furnished with the latest and best farming implements and are excellently stocked. He expects soon to retire from mercantile life and devote his attention to the management of his plantations. He belongs to several fraternities, the Masons and the Knights of Honor among them. He is also a member of the Methodist church. In 1890 he married Miss Lula Bates, whose father, F. A. Bates, was one of the first physicians of Alabama.

Hon. C. W. Williams, a prominent citizen of Alcorn county, and one of the oldest settlers of northeast Mississippi, was born in Marshall county, Tenn, in 1813. His father, William Williams, was a native of the Old North state, and came to Tennessee in 1798, settling on Mill creek, near Nashville. From there he moved out on an old Indian trail, about fifty miles south, near the Nashville & Huntsville road. He had been previously married in Granville county, N. C., to Miss Elizabeth Allison, a native of that state and the daughter of Robert and —— (Oglesby) Allison, also of North Carolina, the father of Scotch descent. Mr. and Mrs. Allison lived to be old people, he dying at the age of ninety-six years, and she at the age of ninety. They were the parents of nine children, the youngest one living to be sixty years of age before a death occurred in the family. The father of our subject followed farming after coming to Tennessee, although in his early life he had followed merchandising. He started with a small stock of goods early in the present century, and gradually increased his business until he became a very successful merchant. He also engaged in the same business at what is now known as Belfast, in about 1831; was succeeded by his son, Robert Williams, who in turn was succeeded by his son-in-law, Joseph Orr, who was succeeded by his widow, Mrs. Orr, the latter now carrying on the business. Thus the business has been conducted by some member of the family since its foundation. Mr. Williams died where he settled in Tennessee in 1842 or 1843, at the age of sixty-eight years, and was a consistent member of the Methodist church. His father was of Welsh descent, and probably a native of Wales. His wife died in Marshall county, Tenn., at an advanced age and was also a member of that church. Their family consisted of ten children, seven of whom lived to be grown, but only C. W. Williams now living. They were named in the order of their births as follows: Mrs. Nancy McCrory, the mother of Mrs. Dr. Price and Mrs. Dr. Taylor, of Booneville; Benjamin, died in Mississippi; Robert, died at Belfast, Tenn.; William, died in Mississippi; C. W., subject; John, died at Louisburg, Tenn.; Mrs. Sarah Nowlin, died in Mississippi; and Alfred O., died in Tennessee. The others died young. C. W. Williams was reared in his native state, educated in the common schools, mostly in log cabins, and received a civil engineering education from a Scotchman by the name of James R.

Brown, a man of education. Mr. Williams was an inveterate reader, and was devoted to his books. In 1834 he commenced for himself, and came to Pontotoc, Miss., where he sold goods for some time. He then sold out, and having a knowledge of surveying, was engaged in looking after land for some time. In June, 1837, he married Miss Mary L. Boone, the only daughter of Col. R. H. Boone, and sister of Judge Boone, of Booneville, Miss., and afterward settled on his present property, where he has resided since. He purchased his land from a Mr. J. N. Niles, and this was all unimproved, there being only a small cabin on it. Mr. Williams constructed a log house and continued to live in that after additions were added. Until the war Mr. Williams was engaged in farming and selling goods, and founded a manufacturing establishment that was burned before it was well under way. He was a heavy contractor in the building of the Mobile & Ohio railroad, by which he lost a large amount of money, and followed merchandising until 1889. He was elected to the legislature in 1861, but is not an officeseeker, and takes only a fair amount of interest in political matters. He was elected county surveyor of Tishomingo county at the first general election after 1837, and was the second surveyor of that county. He held that office many times, but since the division of Tishomingo county he has not held any office. However, he has been engaged as surveyor in the several counties, and has surveyed many of the towns in northeast Mississippi, including Corinth, Iuka and Booneville. Mr. Williams' wife died in December, 1859, leaving four children, three of whom are living: William L., county surveyor of Alcorn county; Charles W., Jr., and Walter, who resides in Rienzi, Miss. Reuben B. was in the Twenty-sixth Mississippi regiment, afterward attached to another Mississippi regiment, and was killed at Petersburg, near Richmond, Va., on the 22d of April, 1865, while on a retreat, not being able to hold the fortifications. Mr. Williams' second marriage was with Mrs. Fannie R. Martin, nee Moores, the widow of Dr. Martin, who was a native of Williamson county, Tenn., and who died with cholera in Lincoln county, Tenn. One child was born to Dr. and Mrs. Martin, C. B. Martin, who is now residing near Rienzi, Miss. To Mr. and Mrs. Williams were born five children, three now living: James H., married and resides at Memphis; Julia A., and Hetty, now attending school at Staunton, Va. Those deceased were: M. F., who died at the age of seventeen years, and Robert, who died at the age of one year. Mr. and Mrs. Williams are members of the Methodist church, and in politics he is a stanch democrat. He was the first postmaster at Rienzi, while Hon. Amos Kendle was postmaster-general.

John R. Williams, planter and stockraiser, Williamsville, Miss. Mr. Williams belongs to one of the earliest and best known families of Grenada county and is now one of the largest planters of the same. He was born in Yalobusha county, Miss., in 1835, and is the son of Major John and Lurana (Lowry) Williams, the father born in the Palmetto state in 1800 and the mother in Georgia in 1809. The parents were married in the last named state and about 1833 moved to what is now Grenada county, where the father farmed as a tenant for a number of years. They then moved to Yalobusha county and about 1838 or 1839 removed to the farm on which their son John R. now resides. There the father died in 1842. He was, in his younger days, a successful merchant in South Carolina and Mississippi, but he finally engaged in planting and became quite rich. He was major of the militia in the Palmetto state and was a member of the Masonic fraternity. When he first settled in Grenada county the country was a vast canebrake teeming with bears, panthers, deer and wolves, and he and family experienced all the hardships incident to pioneer life. Mrs. Williams was left a widow in 1842 and all the care and responsibility of this family fell on her shoulders. She was equal to the task, and, although difficulties and privations beset her way, she reared her little family in the wilderness and was honored and highly esteemed by all. She was a member of the Baptist church for many years and died in 1873. The paternal grandfather, Robert Williams, was of Scotch-Irish parentage and was born in North Carolina. He was a planter and died in South Carolina. The maternal grandfather, Rev. James Lowry, was a native of Georgia, where he spent his entire life and was a minister in the Methodist church. He reared a large family. The six children born to the above mentioned union are named in the order of their birth as follows: James died in youth, Ann Eliza also died when a child, Tobitha F. is the wife of J. J. Andrews, John R., Mary (deceased), and Elizabeth (deceased) was the wife of O. H. Perry. John R. Williams received his primary education in the common schools and at Grenada and finished at the University of Mississippi. In 1861 he assisted in organizing a company of which he was made lieutenant, but he was not called into service. The company was disbanded and Mr. Williams went to Knoxville, Tenn., where he served as an independent in the Fifteenth Mississippi infantry. He was wounded at Fishing Creek in January, 1862, and then returned home, where he raised company G, Twenty-ninth Mississippi, and served as lieutenant in General Bragg's raid until December of the same year, when he was compelled to resign on account of the effects of his old wound. From that time he acted as scout for General Forrest in Mississippi, Tennessee and northern Alabama. He had many thrilling adventures and hair-breadth escapes and was wounded once while serving as a scout. He was paroled near Vicksburg, and at once returned to the old farm, consisting of about four thousand acres, all, with the exception of about two hundred and forty acres, the result of his own exertions. From the eight hundred acres cleared he raises from one hundred to one hundred and twenty bales of cotton annually and corn and hay to supply the place. He is also quite extensively engaged in stockraising. He is a member of the Masonic fraternity, a charter member of Graysport lodge No. 289 (now defunct). Mr. Williams is well known all over the county and has many associates and friends. He frequently engages in the chase, of which he is very fond.

John Williams, merchant, Philadelphia, Miss., son of Samuel and Jane (Slaughter) Williams, was born in Kemper county, Miss., in 1836. The same year his parents removed to Neshoba county, Miss., located near Philadelphia, and there John passed his youthful days. He received a common-school education and then read medicine with Dr. J. S Smythe, of Gholson, after which, in the winter of 1859–60, he attended medical college at New Orleans. He selected as his companion in life Miss Lavinia Lewis, daughter of James and Katie Lewis, and their nuptials were celebrated in January, 1861. The same year Mr. Williams enlisted in company K, Fifth Mississippi, under General Bragg, but immediately after the battle of Shiloh he was discharged on account of disability. When he first entered the army he was made lieutenant, in which capacity he served until the close of his service. He subsequently went to High Hill, Leake county, engaged in merchandising, and there remained until 1879, when he sold out and went to Meridian. There he embarked in business and continued for eight years, when he came to Philadelphia, where he has since been engaged in merchandising. He carries a good stock of general merchandise, and low prices and superior goods have assured him one of the largest trades in the city. He has a family of three living children: Louie V., who has recently graduated at the University of Tennessee; Katie and Gertrude. Mr. Williams is an affiliating member of the Masonic fraternity and American Legion of Honor. He is a member of the Methodist Church South, as are all his family. His father, Samuel Williams, was a native of Pendleton district, S. C., born in 1810. The latter removed with his parents to Tuscaloosa county, Ala., and at the age of sixteen years located in Pickens county, where he remained until after his marriage in 1832 to Miss Jane Slaughter. In 1836 he located in Neshoba county, Miss., and there reared his family. When he first settled in the county the nearest mill was in Winston county, twenty-five miles from his home, and he had to pay $2.50 per bushel for corn. Game of almost every kind abounded, and the people had little trouble in providing a plentiful table. Mr. Williams was but a child when his parents died, and he was reared by strangers, never seeing a blood relative from the time he was six until twenty-six years of age. He was an energetic man, and before the war had accumulated considerable property. Both himself and wife are still living and are in comfortable circumstances.

Merritt Williams was born in Scott county, Ky., on the 24th of August, 1841, being the seventh of eight children born to Miner B. R. and Mary C. (Viley) Williams, who were also born on bluegrass soil. They continued to make their home in Kentucky until 1853, when they removed to Missouri, where they continued to reside until Mr. Williams' death, which occurred in St. Louis in 1870, his life having been devoted to the occupation of planting. His parents, Charles P. and Elizabeth (Reed) Williams, came from England in the early history of the colonies and settled in Maryland. George Viley, the mother's father, was of Scotch-Irish ancestry and was a native of Maryland. Merritt Williams was reared in Kentucky and Missouri, and while attending William Jewell college, of Clay county, Mo., the war opened and he dropped his books to take up arms in defense of the Confederacy, enlisting, in 1861, in company F, Third Missouri regiment, participating in the battles of Lexington, Springfield, Pea Ridge and both battles of Corinth, in fact was in all the engagements that occurred in Mississippi. At the time of Lee's surrender he was at home on furlough, so he immediately began tilling the soil on the plantation on which he is now residing on Lake Washington. Like numerous others at the close of the war, he began life anew with some land but no means whatever of working it, for all his slaves were emancipated and help was hard to obtain. By honest industry he has acquired his present large property, and he now has land to the amount of seven thousand four hundred acres, one thousand two hundred acres being in Louisiana and the rest in Washington county, Miss. Besides this valuable property he owns real estate in Superior, Wis., valued at $40,000. By his own efforts he has opened up about one thousand two hundred and fifty acres of land, and on his place has put about $40,000 worth of improvements, erecting his present elegant home in 1885. On account of the flooding of the Mississippi river one thousand eight hundred acres of his land were washed away. On account of the continual caving in of the land on the river, near where his residence stood, he was forced either to move it or eventually lose it, so he took the initiative and moved it to its present site, which is a most beautiful one. His residence is beautifully fitted up with furniture that was hauled in wagons years ago from Pennsylvania to Kentucky, and in this typical Southern mansion is extended a hospitality for which those of Kentucky birth alone are noted. He was married in 1876 to Mrs. Irene Bullitt, a native of Mississippi and a daughter of Austin and Caroline (Ruth) Williams, of Natchez. His bridal tour was a trip to Mississippi in a two-wheeled rockaway or gig. Mr. Williams has one stepdaughter, Fannie Bullitt, and one son, Charles P. Williams, the latter of whom is now attending school in England, the daughter being the wife of Dunbar Marshall and a resident of Boston, Mass. Mr. Williams has always taken great interest in his children and has spared no pains to give them all the educational advantages possible. His wife is an earnest member of the Christian church and is a cultured and refined lady. Mr. Williams has been a member of the levee board for several years.

Nehemiah Williams, of Summit, was born in Pike county, Miss., August 25, 1814. He is the eldest of four children born to Reuben and Elinder (Waldin) Williams, natives of South Carolina. His father came to Mississippi in the pioneer days and was one of the earliest settlers here. He died in 1817. Mr. Williams was born within a mile of his present home, to which he removed with his parents when he was but six months old, and where he has lived continuously ever since, being now seventy-seven years of age. He is one of the oldest men of the county who were born here. He is a well-to-do planter, owning six hundred acres of land, one hundred of which are cultivated. He served a short time in the Confederate army during the Civil war. He was married in 1837 to Miss Mary A. Hart, who is still living, being now seventy-four years of age. She is a daughter of James Hart, a native of South Carolina, who has borne her husband seven children: Jackson, Martha, James, Isaacher, Robert, Haseltina and William. Mr. Williams and his family are members of the Missionary Baptist church. Mr. Williams has been for forty years connected with the Masonic fraternity. He has always been an active, industrious man, and even at his present advanced age he does a great deal of work on his plantation, frequently boasting that he can accomplish about as much work now as he could in his younger days. He enjoys in an eminent degree the respect of his fellow-citizens of all classes.

R. P. Williams is noted as one of the most capable members of the bar in Lauderdale county, Miss., for he has been eminently successful in practice and is known as a conservative and prudent counselor, whose advice can safely be relied upon. He is a member of the firm of McIntosh, Williams & Russell, which has an excellent reputation in legal circles. He was born in Chickasaw county, of this state, April 14, 1857, a son of Dr. U. S. Williams, who was a Kentuckian, and at an early date became a resident of Mississippi, becoming one of the earliest settlers and finest medical practitioners of Chickasaw county. He was a graduate of the medical college of Philadelphia, Penn., but gave up the practice of his profession before the war. Of six sons born to him the subject of this sketch is third to the youngest. He was brought up in his native county and received his initiatory training at the Gathright school, afterward graduating from Emory and Henry college of Virginia, in 1878. He afterward entered the law department of the University of St. Louis, graduating in 1881, after which he entered upon his practice in Nebraska. Eighteen months later, or in 1882, he returned to Mississippi and located in Okolona, where he formed a partnership with Col. J. R. McIntosh, which was continued harmoniously and profitably until the latter's removal to Meridian in 1884, to which city Mr. Williams also came the ensuing year. The firm of Woods, McIntosh & Williams was then organized and continued until 1887, when Woods & Williams continued alone the following year. Mr. Woods was then called to the supreme bench and the present partnership was formed. In 1889 Mr. Williams was elected city attorney and was re-elected in 1891. He is an able lawyer and he has every reason to be proud of the practice he has gained. He is a member of the A. F. & A. M., the I. O. O. F., the K. of P., and has passed all the chairs in the last named fraternity. December 13, 1883, he was married to Miss Alice, daughter of Col. J. R. McIntosh, and by her is the father of two children: Robert S., and Thomas W. He and his wife are members of the Presbyterian church. He is a stockholder and director of the First National bank, a stockholder and director in the Meridian Land and Industrial company, a stockholder and director in the Meridian Fair and Exposition association, besides owning stock in numerous other enterprises.

S. B. Williams, senior member of the mercantile firm of Williams & Elliott, of Magnolia, is a Mississippian in everything except nativity. He was born in Connorsville, Ind., October 4, 1841. He is a son of John Williams, who was a native of Kentucky, but who removed to

Indiana when a young man, and there met and married Ada N. Reid, a native of South Carolina, who had come to Indiana with her parents. In 1842 John Williams moved to Mississippi, locating in Amite county, where he lived until 1860, when they removed to Pike county, and settled on a plantation near Summit, where Mrs. Williams died in 1867, at the age of sixty-five years. Soon after his wife's death, Mr. Williams retired from the life of a planter, and took up his residence in Summit, where he died in 1887. S. B. Williams is the seventh child in order of birth, in a family of five sons and three daughters, born to John and Ada (Reid) Williams. He was a diligent attendant at the public schools until in his seventeenth year, when he entered upon a course of study at Franklin college, at Franklin, Ind. His studies were interrupted by the outbreaking of the Civil war, which necessitated his leaving college and returning home. In 1862 he enlisted in the Confederate service, as a member of company D, of the Tenth regiment of Mississippi volunteers. He participated in engagements at Murfreesboro, Chickamauga, Missionary Ridge, Franklin, Mumfordsville, Nashville, Jonesboro and in several minor battles and skirmishes. At the battle of Murfreesboro he was severely wounded, a fragment of shell striking him in the face. He served until the close of the war, at which time he had attained to the position of second lieutenant of the company. Returning to Mississippi, he became a teacher in the public school, and later he began the study of medicine. He attended lectures at the New Orleans School of Medicine, and when about to graduate, turned his attention to the mercantile pursuits, accepting a position as salesman and bookkeeper. In 1883 he established himself in the mercantile business at Magnolia. In 1887 J. W. Elliott, his brother-in-law, became associated with him in the business, and the firm has since been known as Williams & Elliott. Mr. Williams was obliged to begin business on a small scale, with a very limited capital, but by good management and close attention to all of the details of his enterprise he has placed it among the leading mercantile concerns in this part of the state. In 1886 Mr. Williams was married to Miss Eliza J. Elliott, a daughter of Wiley and Caroline E. Elliott. Only one child has been born to them, a daughter, who died in infancy. For many years Mr. Williams served as a member of the board of aldermen of Magnolia. At present he occupies the office of secretary and treasurer of the city. Mr. and Mrs. Williams are recognized as among the leaders of society in their present place or residence. Their home is one of the most hospitable, and they are universally respected. Mrs. Williams is a constant member of the Baptist church. Mr. Williams is interested in everything pertaining to the public welfare and he has probably done as much for the upbuilding of his city as any one man thereabout.

Dr. Sidney H. Williams, physician, Carthage, Miss. Rev. John P. Williams, a minister in the Cumberland Presbyterian church, was born in Tennessee in 1818, and in 1839 removed to Mississippi, locating in Leake county. He was a man of education, and was one of the pioneer preachers of Leake and adjoining counties. He was also engaged in farming. He came to Mississippi when a young man, and was married in Leake county to Miss Elizabeth Boyd, daughter of Hon. John P. Boyd, one of the pioneers of Leake county. Rev. Williams made his home in Leake county, reared his family there, and there his death occurred about 1881. His wife died several years previous (1872). Dr. Sidney H. Williams was one of a family of four sons and three daughters born to the above mentioned union, all of whom grew to mature years. The eldest brother, D. F., was a soldier in the Confederate army, and died in 1863, while in service. Finis E., the second son, is the proprietor of the Arlington hotel, at Carthage. He married Miss M. A. Jordan, daughter of Isaac Jordan, and a sister of John L. Jordan, Sr., of an old and prominent family. To this union were born seven children. Dr. Sidney H. was the third in order of birth. J. D., the fourth son, is a merchant at Carthage. There is only one sister living, Mrs. E. H. Jones, wife of E. H. Jones, deputy sheriff of Leake county. Dr. Sidney H. Williams reached years of discretion in his native county (Leake), and received a good English education in that and Attala county. He then studied medicine at Carthage with Drs. Plunket and Ward, and took his first course of lectures in the medical college at Mobile, Ala., in the class of 1874-5. Dr. Williams then began practicing in Leake county, continued there a short time, and in 1878 he returned to Mobile, where he took his second course, graduating in the class of 1879. He then returned to Leake county, and resumed the practice of his profession. In 1883 he moved to Carthage, and has practiced his profession there since. His patronage has been constantly growing, and he is counted among the successful professional men of the county. Although he started a poor man, he has met with success, and is in very comfortable circumstances. He is a man of superior character, pleasant and agreeable, and has many warm personal friends. In 1889 the Doctor formed a partnership with Dr. B. B. Ward (see sketch), and has continued the practice with him. Both these gentlemen are prominent and successful physicians. They have recently also engaged in the drug business. Dr. Williams was married in Carthage December 23, 1876, to Miss Hattie Allen, daughter of J. E. Allen, one of the pioneers of Leake county, and one of the esteemed citizens of Carthage. Mrs. Williams died in April, 1890, leaving five children: Alice E. (a young lady), John E., Albert F., Sidney H. and Allen B. Dr. Williams is a member of the Knights and Ladies of Honor, is examining physician for the lodge, and also for the New York Life Insurance company. He is secretary of Leake County Medical association.

Dr. Uriah S. Williams is a well-known physician of this county, but in addition to successfully looking after his extended practice he is also engaged in merchandising and planting, being quite successful in all three occupations. He was born in Pulaski county, Ky., in 1812, a son of Smith and Sarah Williams, who were born, reared and married in the Old North state, the maiden name of the latter being Ashbrook. To their union eight children were born, of whom is living Sarah (De Hoof), of Somerset, Ky. His father died while a resident of the Blue Grass state in 1846, the mother's death occurring some two years later, both having been worthy members of the Baptist church, in which he was a deacon for some time. Dr. Uriah S. Williams was educated in the schools of Pulaski county, Ky., but his medical education was obtained in Transylvania university, of Lexington, Ky., from which institution he graduated in 1837. His career while there was marked by earnest application and rapid advancement, so that upon leaving that college he was well calculated to enter at once upon a successful career as a medical practitioner. After practicing two years in Kentucky he came to Houston, Chickasaw county, Miss., at which place he followed his calling successfully for about five years. At the end of this time he came to Buena Vista, and in 1846 built the first house where the town now stands. He was the first postmaster of the place, chosen the same year, and discharged the duties of this position for some fourteen years. He has a good general mercantile establishment in Buena Vista, but gives much of his attention to planting also. Although he has almost reached the eightieth milestone of his life and is somewhat feeble physically, his mind is as clear and active as in days of yore, and being well posted on all the topics of the day, and possessing original and practical views, his counsel and advice is often asked by those who know him. He was married in 1844 to Miss Martha B. Pulliam, of Houston, by whom he has eight children, the names of those living being as follows: John C., Homer L., Robert P., U. S., Jr., Charles B. and Dixie. Dr. Williams is a member of the Presbyterian church.

W. B. Williams, a planter of Strong's station, Miss., was born in Alabama on October

5, 1844, a son of Moses and Mary (Smith) Williams, both of whom are natives of Alabama, the former born in February, 1822, in Jefferson county, the son of Lightfoot Barton Williams, a Georgia planter, who, though not a politician, was prominent in his state. Moses Williams received his common English education in Pickens county, and as soon as he attained to manhood engaged in farming. He was married in 1841 to Mary Smith, a native of Pickens county, Ala., by whom he had two children, of whom W. B. Williams was the eldest, the other, Mary Vernon, becoming the wife of John Appling, of Le Flore county, Miss. The mother died in 1847, having lived a consistent Christian life, and having been for years a member of the Baptist church. Mr. Williams married a second time, in 1848, Mary Hollimar, of Pickens county, Ala., becoming his wife, and bearing him one child, Thomas A. Williams, now a planter of Monroe county, Miss. She died in 1850. In 1858 Mr. Williams again married, this time to Mrs. Sarah R. Coker. The union resulted in the birth of five children: Fannie H., Myrtle L. (who married Cary Tucker, and has died), Henry N. (now residing in east Tennessee), Matthew and Moses. Eugene lives in Birmingham, Ala. Moses Williams, Sr., died in February, 1888. He had long been a member and was for some time a deacon in the Baptist church. He was a member of the Vinton lodge, A. F. & A. M., and of Palo Alto chapter, R. A. M. He was a democrat in politics, but never sought nor accepted office. W. B. Williams entered the army at the age of sixteen, thereby losing all the opportunities he might otherwise have possessed of acquiring an education. He joined company C, of the Second Mississippi battalion, in 1861, and served until 1864, when he was severely wounded, after which, though he remained in the service, he took no active part in it. He took part in the battles of Yorktown, Seven Pines, Cold Harbor, Gaines' farm, Malvern Hill, Manassas Junction, Harper's Ferry, Sharpsburg, Fredericksburg, Chancellorsville, Gettysburg, the Wilderness, Locust Grove and Spottsylvania Courthouse. The wound mentioned above he received at Sharpsburg, and he received two severe wounds at Spottsylvania Courthouse. He was paroled at Columbus, Miss., in May, 1865, and returning home was married in the following year to Miss Eliza Burrett, a daughter of James and Mary (Davis) Burrett, of Monroe county, Miss. He has five children living and has lost two by death. Those living are named Thomas B., Mary V. (wife of P. W. Strong, of Strong's station), John M., Moses and Eliza. The names of those who died are Julia and Edwin. Mr. Williams is a member of Vinton lodge, A. F. & A. M., of which he has been senior warden for a number of years. He is a member of the Baptist church and is superintendent of the Sunday-school at Pain's chapel, while his wife is connected with the Methodist Episcopal church. He is a modest, unassuming man of sound judgment, progressive, public-spirited, eminently sensible, and very highly esteemed by all who know him. He is a true citizen in all that the words imply, a zealous worker in the church and generous and indulgent husband and father.

Dr. William G. Williams, one of the leading and prominent citizens of Claiborne county, was born in Philadelphia, Penn., July 17, 1814, a son of William Williams, a native of New York, who married Miss Mary Dorsey, who was born near Richmond, Va. Of this union two sons were born: George W. and the subject of this biography. The former graduated in medicine from Transylvania university, Lexington, Ky., in 1844, after which he went West and practiced his profession until his death, which occurred in Sacramento, Cal., in 1855. Dr. William G. Williams also graduated in medicine from Transylvania university, in 1835, and in June, 1836, came to Rodney, Miss., where he was in the active practice of his profession until 1861. He continued to make his home in Rodney until November, 1868, when he was united in marriage to Mrs. Catharine S. Daniell, nee Freeland.

After his marriage the Doctor removed to the Bethel neighborhood, where he has since made his home, his time and attention being given to planting. In 1860 he made the race for the legislature as a Union man (this being in Jefferson county), but was defeated by nine votes. He is conservative in all his views, and although not a member, is a strong supporter and a prime mover of the Farmers' Alliance. His leading characteristics are extreme frankness, integrity, honesty of purpose and indomitable will, and as he is free from selfishness he is ever ready to sacrifice his own convenience to give comfort and pleasure to others. He is highly esteemed in social life. He is an able newspaper correspondent, and as his style is smooth, eloquent and convincing, weight and power accompany the articles he has contributed to the press. His wife, who was formerly Miss Catharine Freeland, was born in Claiborne county in 1830, and was educated in the Bishop Elliott school of Georgia. She was married in 1839 to Smith C. Daniell, of Mississippi, a native of Claiborne county, who received his education in that admirable institution of learning, Oakland college, from which he graduated, later graduating from the law department of the University of Virginia. Being a very extensive landholder, his planting interests occupied his time to the exclusion of the law. He died in 1861, leaving a large estate. The palatial residence which he erected on what is now the Windsor plantation was planned by the architect, David Shroeder, and was erected at a cost of $140,000. This magnificent home, together with the library and all else it contained, was consumed by fire in February, 1891. During the war this place was used as a hospital for General Grant's army, and over thirty deaths occurred in the house, out of some four hundred men that were quartered there. A part of General Grant's army stayed all night in the house and on the grounds, the dead being buried on the place, but were afterward moved to Vicksburg.

Hon. C. M. Williamson, attorney at law of Jackson, Miss., was born in Marshall county, this state, in the year 1856, being the eldest of three children born to A. S. and Mary (Meek) Williamson, both of whom were born in the Palmetto state. A. S. Williamson settled in Panola county upon first coming to Mississippi, but afterward located in Marshall county, where he remained for some time, then returned to Panola county, where he resided until the year of his death, 1869. His wife died in 1862, both being earnest members of the Presbyterian church at the time of their deaths. The father was an extensive planter, was an active man of his day, and wherever known was highly esteemed. He was twice married, the first time in South Carolina, and by this wife became the father of three sons and a daughter, all his sons serving in the Confederate army during the Civil war, two of whom held the rank of captain and were in many hard-fought and bloody battles. C. M. Williamson was educated in the state university of Mississippi, graduating in the literary department in 1875, after which he taught school for two years, during which time he also read law during his leisure moments, and in December, 1877, was licensed as a lawyer by the supreme court, after which he at once entered upon his practice at Raymond. Here he remained successfully and profitably employed until 1887, when he moved to Jackson, which city has since been his home, and where he has built up an excellent reputation as a legal practitioner. He is an attorney for the British and American Mortgage company, and is successful and promising in his calling. He has been quite active in politics, and was for two years the efficient and popular mayor of Raymond. He was a member of the house of representatives in 1886, and of the state senate in 1888, during which time he was one of the authors of the local option bill, and made a faithful, intelligent and incorruptible legislator. He has been re-elected to the state senate. He is in good financial circumstances and is one of the stockholders of the Jackson Grocery company. In 1887 he married Miss Mamie Robinson, of Jackson, Miss., daughter of John

W. Robinson (deceased), at one time a prominent merchant of that place. To Mr. and Mrs. Williamson the following children have been born: Elise and Chalmers, both of whom are bright, interesting and handsome. Mrs. Williamson belongs to the Episcopal church, and Mr. Williamson is a Presbyterian in faith. Socially, he is a member of the A. F. & A. M. and the K. of P.

Dr. Lea Williamson, physician, Como, is one of the most successful physicians of Panola county, Miss., and, although his birth occurred in York district, S. C., on April 6, 1837, he has identified himself with the interests of Panola county since early childhood. His parents, James S. and Jane M. (Hicklin) Williamson, were natives also of the Palmetto state (see sketch of S. Z. Williamson). Dr. Williamson came to Panola county with his parents in 1846 and received the principal part of his education in the University of Virginia, where he also took a course of medical lectures. He subsequently attended Bellevue hospital, New York, and graduated from Jefferson Medical college, Philadelphia, in 1859. The following year he began practicing at his home in Panola county, and at the breaking out of the war he enlisted as private in Bartlett's regiment and was soon afterward made assistant surgeon of his regiment in General Alcorn's brigade, remaining with his regiment one year. Upon the reorganization, he attached himself to the Fourteenth Mississippi artillery battalion, with which he continued as surgeon until the close of the war, first under Major-General Van Dorn till the siege of Vicksburg, next under Major Preston, of South Carolina, who was killed in the battle of Peach Tree creek, and finally under Major Truehart, who was captured at Nashville, Tenn., December 16, 1864. After this the battalion, being without horses or guns, was ordered to rendezvous near General Hood's army at Columbus, Miss. In February, 1865, his battalion went to Mobile, Ala., to defend that place, and there they remained till April 9, when all of them that could escaped at the fall of Spanish Fort and retired to Mobile and thence to Demopolis. Ten days later they were removed to Meridian and were there paroled on May 11, 1865. Dr. Williamson returned home and resumed the regular practice, which he has continued ever since with more than usual success. He is no dishonor to the medical profession, and stands high both as a citizen and a physician. In connection with his practice he has planted to a considerable extent and is now the owner of about four thousand acres of land in Mississippi and Arkansas, with nearly twelve hundred acres under cultivation. Miss Helen Howard, who became his wife in 1868, was born in Grenada, Miss., and is the daughter of Col. Nat. Howard, who was at Winthrop, Me., in 1805, and descended from the John Howard who came to the new world in that well-known historical ship, the Mayflower, as one of this country's first settlers. Being well educated, he went to Nottoway county, Va., in 1824, and teaching there two years, removed to West Tennessee, and in 1828 from there to Vicksburg, where he made friends of such young men as S. S. Prentiss, Henry S. Foote, Robert J. Walker and William Sharkey, who afterward became men eminent in law and national politics. In 1832 Colonel Howard bought in Cincinnati a boatload of goods which were keeled from Mississippi river, near Helena, down the Yazoo pass to Coldwater river, thence down Tallahatchie to Yalobusha and up that stream to the canebrake where Grenada now stands. Colonel Howard pitched the first tent and opened the first store in what afterward became a somewhat noted town. Colonel Howard was a man of very extensive reading and information, of superior colloquial power, fond of his friends and dispensed a generous hospitality, and was one of the projectors, and, until his death, a director of the Mississippi & Tennessee railroad. Dr. Williamson's marriage resulted in the birth of three children: Howard, now in the University of Mississippi; Louise and Lea. Dr. and Mrs. Williamson are worthy members of the Presbyterian church. The Doctor is railroad surgeon for the Illinois Central railroad, and is a member of the A. M. Railroad association. He is a Mason and the trustee from the second congressional district of the Industrial institute and college for girls at Columbus, Miss. He comes of a representative family and has done credit to it.

One of the most promising young men of De Soto county is Hon. Lucanus W. Williamson of Pleasant Hill, Miss., who was born in this county April 24, 1856. He is the second of a family of seven children of Charles W. and Ann (McMillan) Williamson, natives of South Carolina and Alabama respectively. The father came to Mississippi in 1843, and is still living in De Soto county. Lucanus W. received his education in the private schools of his native county and enjoyed more than ordinary advantages. At the age of eighteen years he secured a position as clerk in a store at Pleasant Hill, and with the savings of two years' work he went to school for some time longer. He is a planter, stockraiser and merchant, and owns considerable landed estate. He and his brother, J. C. Williamson, are engaged in the mercantile business and they carry a large stock of goods and are doing a large and profitable trade. In 1883 he was united in marriage to Miss Ora L. Webber, a native of Tennessee, and a daughter of John and Linnie (McAlexander) Webber. The father was a merchant in Memphis, Tenn. Mrs. Williamson died in 1844. Our subject is a member of the Methodist Episcopal church, belongs to the Masonic order, and also to the Knights of Labor and the Knights and Ladies of Honor. He has been a liberal supporter of all movements tending to the growth and advancement of the county. Although a young man, he has twice represented his county in the state legislature—in 1888 and in 1890—and has just been elected to serve a third term. He has represented his constituency with honor and credit, and has discharged his duties with great zeal. He is considered one of the political leaders of the county. In consideration of the disadvantages under which Mr. Williamson has labored from his youth, too much can not be said in praise of his efforts and the strides he has made toward success. He was needed by his father to assist on the farm until he had arrived at mature years, and when he came to enter the struggle for a place in the world, he was illy prepared, and had no capital to fall back upon. But with courage worthy a Spartan he went to work, and the reward has been a generous one. He occupies a position in the community which has been won through a life of the strictest integrity, and his name is honored where it is known.

Judge R. W. Williamson. In no profession do men attain greater prominence than that of law. The amount of good accomplished is a subject we will leave to the discussion of others. R. W. Williamson was born in Rutherford county, Tenn., January 11, 1832. His father, George W. Williamson, was a native of Virginia, born in 1804, and he was the son of Ludi Williamson, also a native of Virginia; the latter removed with his family to Tennessee about the year 1811, and was one of the pioneers of Rutherford county. There George W. grew to manhood, and married Edna De Jarnatt, a native of Tennessee, and a daughter of James De Jarnatt, another of the pioneers from Virginia. George W. Williamson removed to Mississippi in 1834, and settled in Carroll county, where he was engaged in planting. He was located in that portion of Carroll that is now embraced in Grenada county. There he reared his family, and resided until his death, which occurred in 1884, his age being eighty years. His widow still survives, and is aged eighty-two years (1891). Judge Williamson is one of a family of two sons and four daughters who grew to mature years. He received a liberal education at Union university, a Baptist college at Murfreesboro, Tenn., being graduated in the class of 1852. The following year he was engaged in teaching at Grenada, and the next year was devoted to the study of law at Carrollton. He was admitted to the bar in 1854, and until 1870 he was closely identified with the legal profession in Carroll county. At that time he removed to Winona, where he practiced for six years. In 1876 he was appointed chancellor by Governor Stone, was reappointed by Governor Stone, and was once so honored by Governor Lowry. He filled this responsible position for twelve years, exhibiting that decision of character that has marked his administration of public office. In 1888 the Judge removed to Greenwood, where he has resided since that time. He was appointed judge of the fourth judicial district by Governor Stone in 1890, and is now serving his first term in this capacity. He is an able and efficient lawyer, and a just judge, and in the discharge of his duties has given the greatest satisfaction throughout the entire district. He was united in the holy bonds of marriage in De Soto county, Miss., in 1866, to Mrs. Mary E. Howze, daughter of Robert and Ann White, and a native of Rutherford county, Tenn. The Judge and his wife have had born to them five children: George W., a clerk in the town of Greenwood; Annie, the wife of F. Barksdale; Edna, the wife of James A. Howze, of Denver, Colo.; Mary W. and Robert W. Mrs. Williamson has one son by her former marriage, Arthur R. Howze, a merchant of Winona. Judge Williamson and family are active members of the Baptist church. April 19, 1861, our esteemed subject enlisted in the Eleventh Mississippi volunteer infantry, and went to the service of the Confederate cause. He was promoted from the office of sergeant to that of captain at Corinth, Miss., and remained with the Eleventh Mississippi one year. He then returned home and joined the Thirtieth Mississippi volunteer infantry, was transferred to the Twenty-ninth, and was again elected captain, and was afterward made colonel of the Twenty-fourth, a consolidated regiment, serving in this position until the close of the war. He participated in a number of important battles, the most noted being Perryville, Resaca, Nashville and Murfreesboro, where he received a slight wound. At Resaca he was shot through the body, and was in a dangerous condition for some time. He did gallant service in the cause of the South, and has every reason to be proud of his war record. He is a member of the Masonic fraternity, being a Royal Arch Mason.

Robert Patton Willing, of the firm of Willing, Ramsey & Willing, lawyers of Hazlehurst, Miss., was born in Copiah county in 1836. He is a son of William J. and Malinda A. (Patton) Willing. His father was born on the eastern shore of Maryland, in 1810, his mother in 1817, in Claiborne county, Miss. Mr. Willing received a liberal education, and came when a young man, about 1830, to Mississippi, and engaged in merchandising at Gallatin, the old county seat of Copiah county. Afterward he became a planter, and continued to be one until his death in 1870. He was a successful business man, active and helpful in all public matters. He was one of a large family of children born to Phillip M. Willing, who died in Maryland. The Willings are of English descent, and as a family became quite widely known and influential, some of them having been prominent in Philadelphia. His wife was a daughter of Francis Patton, who came from Georgia at an early date to Claiborne county, where he became a planter and reared a large family. One of his daughters married Justice Ephraim G. Peyton, one of the most distinguished judges of Mississippi in his day. Mr. Willing was for many years a member of the Methodist church, and was a prominent Mason. He married his wife in 1835. Robert P. Willing is the eldest of ten children who were born to his parents, two sons and four daughters of whom are living. From an early age he rendered his father such assistance as was in his power in the management of his plantation affairs. He received a creditable rudimentary education in the common schools near his home, and graduated from the state university in 1856. Immediately after he began the study of law, but had been only a short time engaged in the practice of his profession when the war commenced. He joined the Pettus relief, which was attached to the Twelfth Mississippi regiment, and which formed a part of the regiment. He reached the seat of war soon after the first battle of Bull Run, and took part in the battle of Seven Pines and in many others, including those at Chancellorsville and Gettysburg. Just prior to Lee's surrender he was captured near Petersburg, and taken to Washington, and thence to Johnson's island, where he was kept a prisoner until July, 1865, when he was released after four years of hard service as a soldier. He held the rank of lieutenant, but was in command of his company in several engagements. In 1862 he returned home on a furlough, and in October of that year he married Mary A., the daughter of Michael M. and Carrie Durr. Her father was a native of South Carolina, but removed to Mississippi when a young man, and was married in Simpson county. He became a well-to-do planter, and reared a large family, each of whom received a good education in the colleges. He died in Simpson county. Mrs. Willing was born in that county, and educated partly at Clinton and at Holly Springs, graduating at Memphis with high honors. She has borne her husband nine children, seven of whom are living: Robert Patton, Jr., graduated with distinction from the state university in 1883, and is now a member of the firm of Willing, Ramsey & Willing (he taught school for a while at Jackson, Miss., and was later for three years principal of the public school at Fort Worth, Tex. He married Miss Willie F. Flowers, who was born in Copiah county, and who was educated at Stanton, Va., and at the Ward seminary of Nashville, Tenn.); Carrie is the wife of J. S. Ramsey, who, with her father and brother, comprise the firm of Willing, Ramsey & Willing; (he was born in Copiah county, and educated at the Mississippi college at Clinton); Mary was educated at the Newton seminary at Crystal Springs; Lizzie is the wife of John C. Ryan, a capitalist at Fort Worth, Tex.; Myra and Nellie are unmarried. After the war Mr. Willing located at Gallatin, and engaged in the practice of law. Not long after he was elected district attorney, in which office he served with credit for eighteen months, when he was reconstructed out of office. In 1869 he removed to Crystal Springs, and thence, in 1885, to Fort Worth, Tex., where he was attorney for the Fort Worth & Denver railroad company, having besides a considerable private practice. In 1891 he returned to Copiah county, and with his son and son-in-law organized the present firm of Willing, Ramsey & Willing. He is the oldest legal practitioner in Copiah county, and one of its oldest and most prominent citizens. His standing at the bar is high, and his son, Robert Patton, Jr., is one of the most promising young lawyers in this part of the state. Mr. Willing is a member of the order of Knights of Pythias.

C. O. Willis is a member of the firm of Willis, Moore & Co., cotton factors of Vicksburg, and he has also been president of the Merchants' National bank since its inception, he being one of its organizers. He was born in Maryland, May 1, 1848, being the youngest of five children that lived to maturity, born to Thomas and Mary (Mace) Willis, who were also born in Maryland, the father being quite an extensive farmer. He died in 1880, and his wife in 1850. C. O. Willis was educated in Mechanicsville, Penn., and in 1870 came to Mississippi and located in Warren county, where he engaged in planting until 1880, at that date removing to Vicksburg, where he began dealing in cotton. In 1882 he established himself in business with the father of his present partner, and the same year assisted in organizing the Vicksburg Compress company, and was for some time its president. In 1890, when the two compresses were combined, Mr. Willis was elected president of the new corporation, now known as the Vicksburg Cotton Compress association, and he is also one of the directors of the Vicksburg Hotel company. He is one of the active younger business men of the city, is a reputable and valuable citizen, and is a thoroughly selfmade man. He has proved himself a successful financier, and is now the owner of about two thousand acres of land, one thousand of which are under cultivation. He was married in 1877, his wife being Miss Mary B. Hogan, of New Orleans. She died in 1890, leaving five children: Florence Keene; Ethel Miles; Lucille Moore; Rosalie, and Hazel Cameron. Mr. Willis is prepossessing in personal appearance, is rather portly, and is of fair complexion.

La Fayette Willis, of Aberdeen, Monroe county, Miss., was born in February, 1823, less than one mile from where he now lives, and is the only son now living of Austin Willis. His father was born in Virginia, and lived there until his marriage with Miss Wood, by whom he had six children. After her death he married Evalina Wood, her sister. This family of Woods were of German and English descent, and traced their ancestry back to George III, of England. Mr. Willis came to Mississippi in 1816, and located in Monroe county in 1823. He was a veteran of the War of 1812, and had one son, Austin W., Jr., who served in the Mexican war. He was a strong democrat, of the old Andrew Jackson style; a man of strong physique, enjoying unusually good health almost to the day of his death. La Fayette Willis now owns and lives on the plantation formerly owned by his father. It consists of some of the best land in the Tombigbee river bottoms, there being four thousand acres in the plantation. His father died when he was about fifteen years old, and, while his education is somewhat limited, it is yet sufficient to enable him to transact the business of life with a success that has been more than flattering. In 1847 he married Fannie Quarles, of Alabama, who is connected with the Butler family, of South Carolina—one of the best of the many distinguished families of that state. At the outbreak of the Civil war he was fired with the patriotism which moved the Southern heart at that period, and equipped a company, which he turned over to Captain Baker, but before the close of 1861 he was found in active service. He participated in the Georgia campaign, and, among other engagements, took part in the fighting around Atlanta. His health became impaired, and he was sent home a few months before the close of the war. Though he was long in active duty, and a participant in many closely contested engagements, he was never wounded nor taken prisoner. Before the war he was a whig, but since that time he has been a democrat. His plantation is in a high state of cultivation, and there are living and engaged upon it in work about three hundred negroes, many of whom he owned before the war. Mr. Willis is a natural-born sportsman, and from boyhood has taken part in the sports so much enjoyed by Southern gentlemen. He owns one of the finest packs of hounds in the state, and, although now somewhat advanced in life, has frequent foxhunts upon his plantation, in which he takes great interest, and which are an attraction to many of the best citizens round about. Mr. Willis is of a cheerful, contented disposition, and, although he has always lived childless, he has by no means been friendless, for, it is safe to say, there are few more popular men in his part of the state. He is, in the highest degree, hospitable, and his home is open to all comers. Mrs. Willis, of whose high personal character and many admirable social qualities her husband is justly proud, is a lady of education and refinement, and very popular among a large circle of acquaintance.

Dr. William T. Willis, father of R. B. Willis, planter and stocktrader, Graysport, Miss., was born in Orange county, Va., and was a worthy son of that state, having inherited the enlarged views of government, liberty and law from those ancestors who sought out homes in obedience to impulse prompted by lofty ambition and sincere desire to benefit their race. When a young man he went with a brother to Alabama, and was there married to Miss Frances E. Starke, a native of South Carolina. About 1832 he and family immigrated to Mississippi and settled in the eastern part of what is now Grenada county, on the farm where R. B. Willis now resides, when the country was a perfect wilderness. He was truly one of the pioneers of the county and was a man of noble character, kind disposition, generous and progressive, but did not live long to enjoy the home he had established in the wilderness. He died about 1841, leaving a large tract of land—about two thousand acres. He was a man of considerable literary ability and was a graduate of both the Jefferson and Philadelphia medical colleges. He practiced with success for some time in Alabama, but abandoned his practice after coming to Mississippi. His father, William Willis, was born in Fredericksburg, Va., and there passed his entire life as a wealthy planter. This was one of the prominent families of the Old Dominion. The maternal grandfather, Turner Starke, was a native of South Carolina, but an early settler of Alabama, where he received his final summons. Mrs. Frances E. (Starke) Willis, wife of Dr. William T. Willis, and the mother of our subject, died in 1879. She had been a member of the Methodist church for many years. Their family consisted of four children, the eldest of whom died when quite young. The second in order of birth, Amanda B., became the wife of Robert H. Golladay, a prominent attorney of Coffeeville; R. B., our subject, was third in order of birth, and the fourth was John W., who was a planter and died in Sevier county, Ark., about 1888. He served as a private in an Arkansas regiment, Confederate army. R. B. Willis was born where he now resides, in Grenada county, in 1836, received the rudiments of an education in Grenada county and then entered Union college, at Murfreesboro, Tenn. After this he attended the state university, at Oxford, but left that institution when about sixteen years of age to take care of his mother's estate. This he did until the breaking out of war, when he joined the Mobile cadets, Third Alabama, as a private, serving in that command until the spring of 1862, in the army of northern Virginia, and fought at Seven Pines and many other places. In the spring of 1862 he joined the Forty-second Mississippi, company H, and remained in the Virginia army until the battle of Gettysburg, when he was severely wounded. This disabled him from further service and he was in the hospital at Baltimore for probably two months as a prisoner. He was then exchanged and spent some time with his relatives in Virginia, after which he returned home. In 1870 he married a cousin, Miss Rosalie Willis, daughter of Richard Henry and Lucy A. Willis, her father being a brother of Dr. William T. Willis. Mr. and Mrs. R. H. Willis were natives of Orange county, Va., where they spent all their lives. He was a very progressive planter and an excellent citizen. Mrs. Willis, subject's wife, was also a native of Orange county, Va. To this union were born three children. Since his marriage Mr. Willis has lived on the farm of his birth, six miles east of Graysport, and now owns over two thousand acres. He raises annually two hundred bales of cotton and plenty of corn and hay to supply the plantation, and is one of the leading planters of the county. For about six or eight years he was engaged in merchandising on his plantation, and then for about two years he followed the same business in Graysport, but the fall of 1890 he sold out. He has never aspired to office, but has led a quiet, industrious life. He was a charter member of Graysport lodge, A. F. & A. M., No. 289, and was once junior warden. He and his estimable wife are Episcopalians, holding membership in All Saints' church, Grenada. He is a whole-souled gentleman, noble, generous, and one of the most practical and successful planters in the county. He spares no pains to make his home pleasant and cheerful. Mrs. Willis is a lady of culture and taste and has many warm friends.

Born on May 5, 1858, near Union Church, Rankin county, Miss., Edgar Stewart Wilson spent his early boyhood on his father's farm. Descended on both sides from Scotch-Irish ancestry, his father, Joseph Wilson, being a native of Ireland, and his mother, Elizabeth Ellen Evins, a native of Tennessee, his home surroundings were in keeping with that sturdy stock. When he had reached the age of eleven the family moved to Brandon, the county seat, to secure for the younger members such educational advantages as the troubled condition of the state could then afford. The death of his father, in 1876, not only took him from school, but also threw him on his own resources, and he began in earnest the battle of life. Determined to learn the printer's trade, he commenced as "devil" in the office of the *Eastern Argus* at Brandon, where he remained until he found employment with Col. Fleet Cooper, on the Meridian *Gazette* (soon to become the *Comet*), and continued to work on that paper at Brookhaven and at Jackson. Upon its removal to the latter place, young Wilson took a position on the editorial staff, which he retained until 1880. In that year, after a temporary engagement with the Grenada *Sentinel*, he bought the Walthall *Pioneer*, and went into business for himself. In 1881 he was elected secretary of the Press association, at its meeting in Aberdeen, and in January, 1882, he was elected, after a close and spirited contest, clerk of the Mississippi house of representatives, over some of the most popular gentlemen in the state, being the youngest man ever chosen to that important and lucrative place. On March 1, 1882, Mr. Wilson was married, at Jackson, Miss., by Rev. Dr. Galloway (now Bishop Galloway), to Miss Elizabeth Buckley, daughter of Hon. James M. Buckley, and the wedding was so numerously attended by members that the legislature was left without a quorum. Toward the close of the legislative session Mr. Wilson attempted to buy the *Comet*, the paper with which he had been so long, and which he had helped to build up. Failing in this, he established the *New Mississippian*, its first issue appearing March 1, 1882, and marking an era in the journalism of his state. The new venture met with phenomenal success, and attracted wide and favorable comment from the progressive press of the South. The New Orleans *Picayune* pronounced it the most serviceable engine of independent journalism in the state. Its conservatism and candor commanded the respect of the public, and it speedily attained the honor of being the home organ of that progressive, unsectional and constitutional democracy of which Hon. L. Q. C. Lamar, then in the senate, now on the supreme bench of the United States, was recognized as the foremost leader in the South, and which in Mississippi had come to bear his name. True to the policy he announced, Mr. Wilson fearlessly assailed the abuses which he saw in his own party, and severely criticised and steadily opposed the state administration of that day as extravagant and violative of its pledges. This course led, subsequently, to his defeat by the unsparing use of administration influence, when he became a candidate for reëlection as clerk of the lower house of the state legislature; yet the result was barely accomplished, the vote standing, just before the decisive ballot, fifty-one for Wilson, fifty-two for his successful competitor and two for a gentleman not in the race. In the fall of 1884 Mr. Wilson was called to Washington, to become private secretary to Senator Lamar, and remained with that distinguished statesman until he accepted a position in Mr. Cleveland's cabinet. Mr. Lamar tendered Mr. Wilson the choice of Federal positions in Mississippi, but Mr. Wilson desired to see something of the Northwest, and asked for an appointment in Wyoming. He was appointed receiver of public moneys at Evanston in June, 1885, but after visiting Wyoming in September of that year, declined the position, and asked for the registership of the United States land office at Cheyenne. He was immediately appointed, and entered upon his duties October 21, 1885, being the youngest register in the service. As prior to taking up his official residence in Wyoming, Mr. Wilson had been appointed annual orator of the Mississippi Press association, he returned to fulfill his engagement, and at the annual session of that body at West Point, in May, 1886, delivered an oration more widely quoted and highly eulogized by the newspapers of the state, Memphis and New Orleans, than any similar effort before or since. It was also freely copied with favorable comment by the Wyoming press. In the administration of his office, Register Wilson discharged its important and difficult duties in such a manner as to receive merited commendation from President Cleveland, Secretary Lamar, Commissioners Sparks and Stockslager and the Wyoming public, irrespective of party, and to provoke the criticism only of those whose hostility attested his personal integrity and absolute fidelity to official trust. Upon this subject the Laramie *Sentinel*, the oldest republican paper in Wyoming, said:

"Register Wilson possesses to an eminent degree the courage of his convictions. In the fearless discharge of duty it is natural that he should offend the landgrabbers and their organs; but the people will the more admire him for the enemies he has made, and if he is the man we take him to be, he is proud of his enemies. He is just the man for the place. Honest, intelligent and courteous, upon his induction to office he saw his way clearly laid down before him, and has pursued it, through criticism and slander, with a step that has never faltered and a courage that has never failed. And he is right—all honest men indorse an honest administration of the land laws."

Commenting on the changes incident to the election of a republican president, the Platte Valley (Wyo.) *Lyre* used the following language:

"In the case of Mr. Wilson, the man was found for the position, not the position for the man. Eminently capable, perfectly fearless, and always vigilant, the register of the Cheyenne land office has been a shield and buckler to the threatened rights and interests of the bona fide and honest Wyoming settler. Unhesitatingly accepting the gage of battle so impudently and aggressively thrown down by the powerful land robbers who had entrenched themselves on Wyoming soil, he has met and completely worsted them. To-day the name of Edgar S. Wilson is a terror to the Wyoming land sharks, however high their estate or masked their designs. For public duties well performed and public interests well defended, Mr. Wilson reaps throughout the territory the grand reward of grateful appreciation and hearty thanks. In accordance with the powerful decree of political preferment, Mr. Wilson may step down and out of the Cheyenne land office, but the memory of his name and works will forever abide in the heart and home of the Wyoming settler."

Upon the induction of President Harrison, Mr. Wilson, under date of March 4, 1889, notified the President by letter of his desire "to relinquish the official trust confided to me as a democrat by a democrat." His resignation was accepted subject to the appointment and qualification of his successor, which did not occur until the following September. Mr. Wilson immediately returned to Mississippi, where he re-embarked in journalism at the state capital. This new paper, the *Commonwealth*, at once became one of the leading journals of the state, exhibiting all of his early pluck, enthusiasm and devotion to the true principles of democratic government, coupled with a riper judgment and, perhaps, a more forceful and pungent style. He made of it all that could be expected or desired as an earnest, elevated and able champion of the public good. Its record was never stained by even the suspicion of a job, nor its columns prostituted to the purposes of selfish favoritism. Although respectful to opponents, it was always bold, and the divinity that doth hedge a king was no protection against the scorpion lash it laid upon official misdoing. On November 4, 1890, the *Commonwealth* was consolidated with the *New Mississippian*, Mr. Wilson's old paper, the title of the new paper being the *Mississippian*. Its management purchased the subscription list and good-will of the *New Farmer* of Winona, then the official journal of the state Farmers' Alliance. Of the papers thus merged, Mr. Wilson became, and is now, the editor-in-chief, and he has made the *Mississippian's* name so widely known, and its public usefulness so fully recognized, that it hardly needs further mention. It was made the official organ of the Farmers' Alliance of the state, with the understanding, however, that it would suffer no dictation from that body touching its political course as a democratic paper, and when it became evident that the alliance leaders were going to insist upon an active support of the sub-treasury scheme and other heresies set out in the Ocala platform, the managers of the paper promptly severed all official connection with the alliance. In the stirring canvass of the present summer (1891) for the seats in the United States senate to become vacant on the expiration of the terms of Hons. J. Z. George and E. C. Walthall, it has been a tower of strength to the opponents of the wild and visionary schemes of financial reform by which the people are sought to be allured from the plain teachings of common sense and experience, and for the victory won it is entitled to credit in no small degree. On this subject the Raymond *Gazette*, the oldest and most conservative journal of the commonwealth, while the senatorial campaign was at its hight, said: "The *Mississippian* was the first paper in the state to assault the sub-treasury, and it never quailed under circumstances that would have blanched the cheek and struck dumb the heart of many a journalist. It declined to be coerced into a support of the sub-treasury by a powerful secret organization, assuming a political phase, stating it would speak its conscience, 'though hell itself should gape, and bid it hold its peace.' No braver words were ever spoken, especially when it is considered that it staked its very existence in defense of its principle. In the fight now raging, its white plume ever nods in the forefront. It is the idol of the state democracy. Edgar S. Wilson is a brilliant Mississippian. His devotion to democracy is a passion. His hostility to the sub-treasury is as sincere as his opposition is powerful." As a paragrapher, Mr. Wilson is particularly strong and incisive, and his political adversaries know the danger of this sharpshooting no less than that of the general and more sweeping onslaught of his leaders. The response by Mr. Wilson on behalf of the press to the address of welcome at the press convention in Yazoo city, in May, 1891, has been widely commended for strength of thought and elegance of diction. As a speaker his manner is forcible and impressive, but by no means lacking in grace. Mr. Wilson is a man of wide general reading, as well as practical information, and is a constant student. His acquaintance with the best authors, particularly Shakespeare and the other great English classics that have enriched and molded that noblest of tongues of men, is particularly full and accurate. His personal acquaintance with the public men of the day in his own state and the country generally is large, and the estimation in which he is held commensurate with his force of character, influence and knowledge of governmental affairs. In person he is large and sturdy of frame, with a massive head and a large, bright, steel-gray eye, expressive of every passing emotion. He is a devoted family man and domestic in his tastes, devoting much of his leisure to the culture of his young olive branches, of whom there are four—two boys and two girls—named respectively: Elizabeth, Edgar S., Jr., Joseph Buckley and Bethany Craft.

Samuel J. Wilson, Anding, Yazoo county, Miss. Joseph Wilson was a native of east Tennessee, and was there married to Lucinda Cook. He removed to Lawrence county, Ala., and thence to Mississippi in 1836, and settled in Kemper county. At the end of one year he went to Neshoba county, Miss., where he was engaged in agriculture until his death in 1864. His son, Samuel J. Wilson, is the eldest of nine children. He was born, June 26, 1831, in Lawrence county, Ala.; went to Mississippi with his parents in 1836. When he had arrived at the age of twenty-one years he bade adieu to the roof that had shielded him through childhood, and went out into the world for himself. He had a small amount of capital, and by judicious investments he has accumulated a considerable estate. He owns six hundred and twenty acres of land and has placed under cultivation two hundred and fifty acres. He was united in marriage, January 5, 1854, to Miss Caroline Kelly, a native of Alabama, and a daughter of Albert and Permelia Kelly, of Tennessee. Three children are the result of their union: Francis P., Joseph B. and Albert K. When the late Civil war broke out Mr. Wilson, with the loyalty of true citizenship, went into the service. He enlisted in company A, Thirty-seventh Mississippi volunteer infantry, and was with this regiment until 1864, when he was captured; he was carried to Camp Douglas, Chicago, Ill., where he was held until the declaration of peace. He participated in the battles of Iuka and Vicksburg, and was in several engagements in Georgia. After the close of the war, a large part of his property having been invested in slaves, by their freedom his financial condition was wrecked, like that of many others. He then removed to Yazoo county, where he has since lived. He and his family are members of the Missionary Baptist church. Politically he affiliates with the Democratic party, and he is a member of the Farmers' Alliance. He is one of the men who have helped to make Yazoo county what it is to-day, and his record as a citizen is above reproach. His maternal grandparents are of Irish birth. Their names are James and Margaret J. Cook.

Rev. William Winans, D. D. (deceased), was one of the most illustrious divines in the entire South. He was born near Braddock's grave, Penn., November 3, 1788, and at two years of age he was left to the sole care of his mother, having three sisters and a brother, all older than himself. The sisters were Elizabeth, Martha and Asenath, and the brother Obediah, all of whom married and reared families. From his autobiography and from a diary kept by himself from 1808 are gleaned the following facts: "My mother was poor and dependent upon the labor of her own hands, with the slight assistance of her older children. She was, I believe, the most industrious human being I ever knew. I scarcely ever saw her unoccupied, day or night. She usually lulled me to sleep at night with the sound of her Scotch wheel, and aroused me in the morning with the bustle of housekeeping occupations. We never wanted bread to eat nor raiment to wear; and, besides this, our careful mother taught, or had us taught, to read. By some means, I do not know how, my brother, four years older than myself, learned to write, and from him I learned enough, by dint of persevering application, to write in a plain, artificial manner. This is the amount of the education I received, except that, when I was about eighteen years old, I received instruction in arithmetic during fifteen and a half days. This enabled me to return the obligation conferred upon me by my brother in teaching me caligraphy, as I initiated him in the science of figures and calculations. When I was two years old my mother removed to Ten-mile creek in Greene county, Penn., where she remained some seven years, and then removed to George's creek, Fayette county, Penn., near Union Town. Here we continued until I was sixteen years old and then removed to Clermont county, Ohio, where I remained until I entered the itinerant ministry in the Methodist Episcopal church. While in this county I united with the church. My excellent mother was sincerely pious, long before I was born, and she diligently imparted pious and moral instruction to her children as soon as their minds could receive it. There were, however, quickenings and accessions to the strength of the impression so made upon my mind by the preaching of the gospel at sundry times and by various ministers. When eight or nine years old I heard Valentine Cook and James Smith and was deeply impressed, so that I earnestly desired to be a Christian. But during the following six or seven years my associations were as bad as any out of the infernal regions, and led me into many vicious habits. Dancing, Sabbath breaking, card playing, and even drunkenness, were vices in which I frequently indulged with keen and increasing relish. I lived in the vicinity of large iron works and was employed in them; and in those days, the characters of those employed were perhaps unparalleled for wickedness. In 1803 or 1804 a young man, named Davidson, came to my mother and proposed to make her house a preaching place on the circuit. He prayed with us with great fervor and unction and left an appointment to preach; but severe affliction prevented him from doing it and I never saw him again. His manner, his conversation and his prayer made a deep and lasting impression upon my mind and heart. Soon after Simon Gilespie, James Hunter, William Knox, Thornton Fleming and Anderson Hemphill successively preached at my mother's house, and formed a small society, of which I was a member. In 1805 we removed to Ohio, and I took with me the proper voucher of my membership in the church. But the dissipating influence of immigration and a protracted separation from the ordinances of religion had brought me into so careless a state, that when I had an opportunity to claim my membership in the church I declined doing so, under a conscientious presumption that I was unfit for the relation. My love to the church and my desire to become a Christian continued, however, and I was, perhaps, as punctual as any member in attending the means of grace, including love feasts and class meetings. This continued till Christmas day, 1806, when I was shut out of love feast by John Collins, a preacher whom I revered more than all others. Determined that I would not again be excluded from love feast, my certificate of membership being a nullity, I joined the church that same day on trial. I was sincerely desirous to be a Christian, but not very earnest in my efforts to that effect till March, 1807. Then I became truly penitent and sought diligently in the bitterness of soul for pardon. On Easter Sunday, March 29, at a prayer meeting at night, and when I was leading in prayer, God spoke peace to my soul and wrought a wonderful change in my whole moral nature, shedding His love abroad in my heart. I was soon after appointed class leader, and on the 29th of August received license to exhort. I first made an attempt to preach in a private house, my mother and all the rest of her family in the congregation, on, I think, the 6th of June, 1808. The presence of my family, my mother especially, embarrassed me more than would that of the president and congress have done. I have not dared to preach on the same text again, though I have written a sermon on it. It was Ephesians v: 8. On the 27th of August, 1808, I received license to preach, and immediately entered upon the work of the itinerant minister, though not formally admitted into it till the following October. My first regular appointment was the Limestone circuit, including Augusta, Washington and Marysville, and, before the year expired, by a uniting of the Limestone and Fleming circuits, Flemingsburg in Kentucky." He preached his first funeral sermon at Washington, that of Mrs. Mary Magruder, daughter of Eliza and John Dunbar, son of Joseph Dunbar, Esq. His first marriage ceremony was performed while on this circuit, May 16, 1810. "My second appointment was to the Vincennes circuit, Indiana. This circuit included all the settlements on the Wabash and White rivers, from the Indiana line to the Ohio river. I went to this circuit October 17, 1809, and left it October 23, 1810. I was the second preacher appointed to this circuit, and during the whole year never saw an itinerant preacher, and had but little assistance from local preachers, of whom there were three on the circuit. Here my acquaintance with President Harrison commenced, and I was enjoying his hospitality at the time of his council with Tecumseh, which met on the lawn before Harrison's door. This council was held between two men, than whom few have lived who were more patriotic, wise or brave. They viewed the matter in debate (a late land sale to the United States by the Miami tribe) from different standpoints, and both honestly believed they were defending the right. Tecumseh had spoken very ably from 10 A. M. till 2 P. M. (his speeches being twice interpreted), and Harrison had spoken by way of introduction ten minutes, and had entered upon the merits of the dispute in a second speech, when, upon the interpreter translating it into the Indian language, Tecumseh, who was sitting on the ground, sprang to his feet and said fiercely, 'That's a lie.' Immediately the Indians who were of his party also sprang up and as fiercely assented to his negative. I happened to be standing at the back of General Gibson's chair and heard him whisper to the officer in command of a guard of fifteen men, 'Have your men ready. Those fellows intend mischief.' (He had lived twenty years among the Shawnees.) The men were brought immediately in front of Tecumseh and his confederates, with arms presented and ready for instant action. Had the Indians attempted violence all their chiefs would probably have fallen, as the guards were not more than five paces from them and covered them with their muskets. But for the presence of the guards I have no doubt there would have been a horrible massacre of the whites, as few of them had any arms, and as the Indians were well armed for close conflict, though without firearms. The 'Life of Harrison' does my gallantry more credit than it is entitled to. It represents me as going to the door to defend the women and children, whereas, in fact, I do not know that I thought of them. I had seen a musket, with a fixed bayonet, standing at the door, and thither I went that I might arm myself if a conflict ensued. The door was within a few feet of where the council was held. I came to Mississippi on horseback from Vincennes via Shelbyville, Ky., the seat of the conference that year, and arrived at Port Gibson December 5, 1810. My fields of labor have been as follows, viz.: Claiborne, Wilkinson, Natchez and Claiborne, two years; New Orleans, 1813 and 1814; Natchez, Claiborne and Wilkinson; local, five years, on account of ill health; Natchez circuit, 1821; Mississippi district, four years; Washington station, Washington district, three years; missionary agent, three years; superannuated, 1833; New Orleans district, one year; Wilkinson, supernumerary, one year; Woodville station, one year; agent from New Orleans church, 1837; New Orleans district, one year; Natchez district, four years; New Orleans district, three years; agent for Centenary college, 1846; Natchez district, two years; Woodville district, agent for Centenary college; superannuated, four years. I have been a delegate to the general conferences nine times, and a delegate to the convention which organized the Methodist Episcopal Church South." While in attendance at the general conference at New York city he was the guest of Harper Brothers, and soon after 1846 was presented with a fine large family Bible, with their kind wishes. This work was profusely illustrated and a masterpiece of topography. A. B. Hyde, D. D., professor of Greek in the University of Denver, speaks of Rev. William Winans, D. D., in the story of Methodism as "the greatest of the Methodists of the Southwest. His gifted mother taught him to read well the two books, the Bible and Pilgrim's Progress. In the Southwest he was the right man for the region, and here for forty-five years he employed his wonderful energies of mind and body. His personal appearance was striking. In his later years he became feeble, yet when he could hardly sit upon a saddle, he would preach with wonderful power. A delegate to the general conference, on the separation of the Southern Methodists, he took a lively interest, being himself a slaveholder. He was very negligent of his dress, his collar without stock or cravat slouching about his neck. In this shellbark interior was a mind of strange energy, grasping and molding the most difficult of subjects and uttering itself in a rhetoric equal to that of our best writers." As a writer he issued a wide and choice circle of Biblical literature, including a volume of Discourses on Fundamental Subjects, an enduring monument (large octavo, about seven hundred and fifty pages), besides many fugitive publications. He would go miles to get a book he wanted to read, though his own library was large and comprised many rare and valuable works. They were of a choice selection and said to be one of the best in the South. He received the degree of D. D. first from Baton Rouge college, La., and afterward from Randolph, Macon, Ga., Dr. Winans was the second Methodist preacher in New Orleans, going there during the struggle for liberty and renting a small room in which he taught school and held religious service evenings and Sundays. The firing of a gun for the cock fight was the hour his services on Sunday were to commence. He was afterward very intimately associated with Judge Edward McGehee in the building of the Carondelet Street church. He was also engaged in schoolteaching in Wilkinson county near the place of this settlement, where he taught for several years with a large attendance. In his diary kept by himself, dated 1808, is the system of shorthand used by him in taking notes and writing his sermons. He was the first elder commissioned in Mississippi, by Bishop R. R. Robert, bearing the private seal, at Pine Ridge, Miss., October 13, 1816. In the same diary are found the number of volumes he read and re-read, some of them as high as ten times, numbering one thousand three hundred and ten, with the number of pages one million three hundred and forty-four thousand five hundred and five, the Bible ninety-seven times, and the New Testament one hundred and ninety-four times up to within a short time before his death, well preserved on the fly-leaf of his Bible, with date of each reading, now in the hands of his son's family at Columbia, Mo. The number of miles traveled by him, mostly on horse-back, up to within five years before his death was one hundred and thirty-nine thousand eight hundred and fifty two, and the number of marriages performed one hundred and thirty-three, for which he received $1,853.25; the number of chapters read by him before he commenced the ministry of the gospel, from October 22, 1808, to 1811, was eleven thousand one hundred and seventy-two. He performed the marriages of many of the leading families of this county: Noland Stewart (of Louisiana), Judge Henry Cage (of this county), Judge H. F. Simrall, Judge McGehee (second marriage), J. W. Burruss, Hon. B. H. Drake, Judge James Walker and many others. He came to Wilkinson county in 1814 and settled the present home place, where he reared his family. Here he was married September 14, 1815, to Martha Du Bose, a native of South Carolina, born at Darlington April 20, 1797, and died March 22, 1802. She was a daughter of Daniel and Mary (Nettles) Du Bose, natives of the same place. Daniel was the son of Isaac of Dieppe, Normandy, and came to South Carolina in 1689, with his six sons and one daughter, the youngest of whom was Daniel, by whose union with Mary Nettles was born Martha, who became the wife of Dr. Winans. Elias, the living brother of Daniel, married Lydia Capers, by whose union was born Elizabeth, who married Stephen Miller, afterward governor and United States senator from South Carolina. Martha, the wife of the subject, was of a family of five children—four daughters and one son—all of whom grew to maturity and married. Elizabeth married Robert A. Shackleford, Margaret married John C. Richardson, Mary N. married Dr. William Langley, and Martha married the subject of this memoir. Samuel Du Bose, the eldest child, married Jane Dick and settled in Alabama. Martha, wife of Dr. Winans, came to this territory with her mother in 1809 (she being a widow) and settled in the Midway neighborhood, where she reared and educated her daughter. She was a woman of sterling integrity and very devoted to her family, a good Christian mother and noble woman. She was beloved by all and very highly esteemed. By this union were born six children, four of whom lived to be grown, two of whom are yet living. The eldest, Mary S., married Mr. Isaac Wall, and is now living in Clinton, La., the mother of nine children, five of whom are yet living. The eldest daughter of Mrs. Wall, Sarah C., married W. F. Kernan, a prominent lawyer of Louisiana, and now an ex-circuit judge of one of the judicial districts of that state. Mrs. Kernan was the eldest grandchild of Dr. Winans, and on one occasion, when he introduced little Sallie Wall to Henry Clay at Baton Rouge, he said: "This is my eldest grandchild." Henry Clay smiled and said: "He is very particular to say eldest; he doesn't want to be thought old." Margaret L. C. married W. P. Dickson, of Tennessee, but reared in Mississippi; by this union were born six children, three of whom are deceased. W. P. Winans was a lawyer of prominence in Louisiana, and married Jane Harper, by whom he had four daughters, all in Columbia, Mo. His widow became the wife of Dr. G. W. Riggins. W. P. Winans was killed at Missionary Ridge, Tenn., November 23, 1863, and at the time of his death held the commission of colonel in the Nineteenth Louisiana regiment; he was a man of fine ability and education. The fourth child born to Dr. Winans is Annie E., born in 1828. She was reared in this county, and finished her education in Shelbyville, Ky., and is a woman of fine attainments, hospitable and kind. She and her sister, Mrs. Wall, are the only survivors of Dr. Winans' family. She was married, January 4, 1849, to Nolan S. Dickson, a native of Tennessee, by whom were born three children: Mary L., who died at fourteen years of age; Lucy W., at home, and William A., the present representative of this county, born and reared on the home place, and educated at Centenary college and at Vanderbilt university, Nashville, Tenn. He was married to Lucy B. Hampton, of Tennessee, where she was born and reared and educated at Hopkinsville. By this union they have one son, Stewart H. Mr. Dickson is one of the county's most enterprising young men. He was elected to the legislature in 1888, which office he still holds, having succeeded himself for the second time. Mr. and Mrs. Dickson resided on the home place, where they kindly cared for Dr. Winans during his last feeble years, and until his death, August 31, 1857. Nolan S. Dickson died June 9, 1870, and was one of the county's representative planters. Mrs. Dickson is one of the county's most noble women, a Christian mother and a faithful worker of the Methodist Episcopal church. She has a son of her niece-in-law Anna Dickson, Wall Henry, whom she has reared from an infant since the death of his mother, a bright lad of twelve summers. The New Orleans *Christian Advocate*, speaking of the death of William Winans, D. D., said: "Dr. Winans is dead! We are slow to realize the fact with its announcement. The church mourns, not as for a servant, but a father, and the county for one of its greatest citizens.

> "Servant of God, well done!
> Rest from thy loved employ,
> The battle fought, the victory won,
> Enter thy Master's joy."

J. W. Winborn, sheriff of Benton county, was born in what was at the time Marshall county, in 1840. His parents were Richard W. and Rebecca (Floyd) Winborn, natives of North Carolina. His father was born in 1806, and grew to maturity in the state of his birth, moving to Marshall county, Miss., in 1836, and locating twelve miles east of Holly Springs, where he lived for many years, and reared a family of eight sons and two daughters, only five of whom are living at the present time, all within the boundaries of Carroll, Holmes and Benton counties. He died in 1888 Sheriff Winborn was reared in this county, and received as good an education as the public schools afforded. In the beginning of the war he enlisted in company K, of the Thirty-fourth Mississippi volunteers, under Capt. D. B. Wright, and served until the close of hostilities, taking part in the engagements at Farmington, Prairieville, Chickamauga, Resaca and Atlanta, receiving a wound in the latter engagement which necessitated his being placed in the hospital, but he had no sooner recovered than he again reported for active duty. He was married in 1860 to Cornelia M. Hoover, an estimable lady, who has borne him nine children, eight of whom are living. On the 1st of January, 1892, he will have held the office of sheriff for fourteen years, having been re-elected at election after election, which indicates more clearly than anything else could do the fidelity with which he has discharged the trust reposed in him by his fellow-citizens, and he has been nominated for another term of four years. He has been a Mason since 1875, and all of his friends who are Masons testify that he is a Mason in principle as well as in name. The career of Mr. Winborn shows what may be achieved by an intelligent, honest, industrious and ambitious young man, not only in Mississippi, but in any other of the states of our glorious Union.

W. D. Windham is a native of Jasper county, Miss., and was born September 15, 1839. His father was James Windham and his mother was Christiana McLeod, the former being a native of Georgia and the latter of North Carolina. They moved with their respective families to Mississippi at an early day. They were married in Perry county, Miss., coming thence to Jasper county about the year 1833. Mr. Windham was a man of considerable prominence in his day, especially in connection with the old state militia. He died at Columbus, Miss. His wife still lives, residing in Jasper county. They were the parents of ten children: Murdock, William D., Jared C., James S., George, Susan, Effa, Elizabeth, Caroline and one daughter who died very young. W. D. Windham was educated at the public schools of Jasper county. He began life for himself at the age of eighteen years, but was able to get only a fair start before the war, being obliged after the war to start anew. In May, 1862, he enlisted in company A, of the Fortieth Mississippi infantry, in which he served until near the close of the struggle. Returning to Jasper county he interested himself in agriculture. In August, 1869, he was married to Miss Colen V., daughter of William and Elizabeth (Moss) Hossey. Shortly after they located upon the plantation which they now occupy, and which Mr. Windham has operated successfully ever since that time. He owns in all about six hundred and forty acres of land, of which nearly one-half is in the highest state of cultivation. Mr. and Mrs. Windham are members of the Baptist church, and Mr. Windham is a useful and in every way a highly respected citizen, who commands the esteem of the entire community.

Col. William Winston, a hardware merchant of Columbus, Miss., was born in Boone county, Ky. (near Cincinnati, Ohio), June 20, 1839, a son of Robert P. and Rebecca (Pollard) Winston, both of whom were born in Hanover county, Va., and relatives of Patrick Henry. The paternal grandfather, William Winston, was in the War of 1812 and by occupation was a planter, following this calling the latter part of his life in Kentucky. Robert P. Winston was likewise a planter, and at the time of his death, which occurred of cholera in Louisville, Ky., in 1849, he was an extensive coal merchant and owned what is now known as the Mulford mines, which he purchased from ex-President Tyler. His wife also died in Louisville and was buried at Cave Hill. Of four children born to them, the subject of this sketch is the only survivor. He was reared principally in the Old Dominion, being an attendant of Hampton-Sidney college, in which institution he completed his studies. His health was very poor at this time, but with the determination that has ever characterized his career he entered upon the study of law, but his body failed to uphold the burden which the brain imposed upon it, and he was compelled to abandon his legal studies. He then embarked in the hardware business as a clerk in Richmond, Va., but came West before he had attained his majority and entered into business with his brother, Thomas P., continuing with him for some time. In 1861 he enlisted in company D, Third Kentucky regiment, and after serving a short time was made aid-de-camp on General Tillman's staff, but afterward took charge of an independent company between the Cumberland and Ohio rivers, stationed at Princeton, Ky. He was but twenty years of age at this time, and after he had lost all his men at the battle of Fort Donelson he went to Virginia, where he was made lieutenant-colonel under General Floyd, who commanded the state line when the state troops were turned over to the Confederate service. As Colonel Winston was in very poor health at this time he came West and acted on General Wheeler's staff, notwithstanding the fact that he was exempt from service on account of his health. Upon recovering his health to some extent, however, he enlisted as a private in the Eighth Kentucky regiment, serving about thirty days, when he was put upon the staff of General Lyon, with whom he served until the surrender in 1865 at Columbus, Miss. In the latter part of the same year he opened business in Columbus and has continued the same up to the present time, being now the oldest resident merchant of the town. He is well to do, and besides the valuable property which he owns in Columbus he is extensively engaged in the stock business and is interested in an orange grove in Florida and in several other places. In 1865 he was married to Miss Lucy A. Harris, by whom he has two children: William, attending military academy at Huntsville, Ala., and Corinne. In 1887 he was married to his present wife, formerly Miss Virginia S., daughter of Col. Joseph Taylor, of Alabama. Colonel Winston is a member of the A. F. & A. M., and he and his wife are members of the Episcopal church.

Within the limits of Jefferson county, Miss., there is not a man of greater personal popularity than Hiram L. Winters, a man of recognized worth and substantial and progressive spirit. He was born in Ohio county, Ind., May 4, 1823, but his father, Levi Winters, was born in the Keystone state, where he also grew to manhood. After reaching manhood he went to Vermont and in that state was married to Miss Phœbe Clark, and afterward removed with his bride to what was then the wilds of Indiana, and became one of the pioneers of Ohio county. There he was called from life in 1827, his widow surviving him several years. Hiram L. Winters, their son, spent his youth at Rising Sun, Ind., and at that place began learning the tinner's trade, and as his employer and instructor was engaged in running a flatboat on the Ohio river and down the Mississippi river to New Orleans, selling his wares, Mr. Winters may be said to have learned his trade on these rivers, several years of his life being spent at this work and in this manner. In 1853 he located at Grand Gulf, Claiborne county, Miss., with the purpose of following his trade, but the first year was taken with yellow fever, and although very ill, his time had not yet come and he gradually recovered and once more took up the burden of life. He was one of a very few that survived that dreaded scourge, for in the little village of Grand Gulf there were sixty-four deaths. In 1857 Mr. Winters removed to Rodney, then a thrifty little town of five hundred souls, and there commenced business with a very small capital, but pushed his venture to a successful issue and accumulated property very rapidly. Unfortunately he lost the most of it during the turbulent times of the war, and in 1864 removed with his family to Indiana, two years being spent in his native state. In 1866 he returned to Rodney to once more engage in the tin business, and although he has met with severe loss by fire on three different occasions and has been, each time, left in reduced circumstances, he has, with undaunted determination, resumed business each time and has succeeded in bending circumstances to his will. By shrewd management and devotion to his business he has recovered his losses, and with renewed strength and courage looks forward to a prosperous future. In 1875 he put in a small stock of general merchandise in his hardware establishment, and this has increased from time to time, he now being a prosperous general merchant with a bright outlook for the future. He was first married in Indiana, July 21, 1850, to Miss Elizabeth Schofield, a native of England, who came to the United States with her parents when a child of ten years, meeting and afterward marrying Mr. Winters. She died in 1880, having borne a family of eleven children; six are still living:

Arabella P., wife of John Mackey; Henry L., married, and a merchant of Rodney; Rosa W., wife of Samuel J. Schofield, of Madison, Ind.; William S., married, and a prosperous merchant of Alabama; Joe S., a successful physician of Rodney; and Hannah L., who is at this writing (spring, 1891) attending school in Madison, Ind. Mr. Winters married his present wife, Miss Victoria Harper, in May, 1888. She was born in Mississippi to Rev. Miles Harper and wife, the former being a minister of the Methodist Episcopal church. Mr. Winters is a member of the Masonic fraternity, in which order he has held a number of important offices, and he also belongs to the I. O. O. F. and has represented his lodge in the grand lodge of the state. He and Mrs. Winters are members of the Presbyterian church, and although he has reached his sixty-eighth year he is yet in the enjoyment of good health. He has made his way through life by his native talents and deserves much credit and honor for the position he has attained, for it is truly an enviable one.

John Wise, from 1840 to 1856, sixteen years, justice of the peace at Quincy, Monroe county, Miss., and one of the prominent planters of this section, was born in Bedford county, Tenn., June, 1811, the son of William and Katherine Wise, and came to Monroe county with his father's family in 1818, when only five years of age, his father being one of the first white men to locate permanently on the present site of Quincy, and, in fact, one of the earliest settlers thereabouts. His location was then covered with dense forests, and very little was in a fit state for cultivation, and in the end of the year following his arrival there provisions became so scarce that he was compelled to make the journey back to Tennessee after corn and other necessaries. Before he completed the journey, he was killed and robbed, his assailants supposed to have been Indians. The burden of the family's support fell upon his widow and children. Our subject remained with his mother until he was twenty-five years of age, helping to rear and educate his younger brothers and sisters. In 1836 he married Margaret, daughter of John and Margaret Tucker, and has since been engaged for the most of the time in planting on his own account. In 1861 he was commissioned by the government officers to take care of the women and children residing within the boundaries of the county during the war, a position he filled during all that eventful period from that date to 1865, discharging his duties in a manner that commanded the admiration of all classes of citizens. Mrs. Wise died in 1870, having borne him three children, as follows: Laura (deceased), Catherine, and Martha E. (deceased). In 1872 Mr. Wise was again married, to Elizabeth Dillingham. She is a daughter of James and Mary Dillingham. Politically Mr. Wise is a democrat. He is a member of the Methodist Episcopal church, and contributes liberally to its support. He is a kind husband and father, and ranks high as a business man and citizen.

Capt. Albert Q. Withers, farmer, Victoria, Miss., is a member of a well-known and highly esteemed pioneer family of Marshall county, Miss., was born in Sussex county, Va., April 6, 1819, and his parents, Sterling and Elizabeth (Moyler) Withers, were also natives of the Old Dominion. The paternal grandfather came over from England with Governor Dinwiddie, colonial governor of Virginia, and was his private secretary. The maternal grandparents were of French descent. The parents of our subject were married in their native state and remained there until all their children, four in number, were born. They were named in the order of their births as follows: Albert Q.; Emily (deceased), was the wife of Jesse M. Tate; Mary E., wife of C. C. White, and Sterling A., deceased. The parents removed from Virginia to Alabama in 1835, remained there one year engaged in farming, and then, in 1837, removed to Marshall county, Miss. The father bought land, erected houses and he and his two sons opened up a large estate. He was an honest, upright citizen, and was noted for his hospitality, that being a predominant characteristic of the Withers family. He and Mrs. Withers were members of the Methodist church. She died in 1846 and he in 1862. There are now only two of the family living, one besides our subject, Mrs. White. Capt. Albert Q. Withers received his literary training in the state of Virginia, and when nineteen years of age engaged in merchandising at Raleigh, Tenn., continuing in business there for five years. He returned to Mississippi in 1843, located on the farm where he now lives, and was married the same year to Miss Matilda Caroline Jones, daughter of William and Phalba C. (Howard) Jones. The Howard family were from the same county in Virginia that the Withers family hailed from, and they were old acquaintances. To Captain and Mrs. Withers were born seven children: Emile Q., William L., Elizabeth P., Mary H. (deceased), Lulu T., (wife of William H. Cannon), Sallie M. and Cora M. Captain Withers owns nine hundred and sixty acres of land and has six hundred acres under cultivation. He was elected a member of the legislature from Marshall county in 1859, and re-elected again in 1861, making four years' service in that capacity. He was a member of that honorable body when the ordinance of secession was passed and strongly opposed that measure. However, he acquiesced and bent his energies in support of the cause of the South, enlisting in the service in 1863. He raised a company of cavalry, was elected captain of the company, and was on detached duty mostly in the state of Mississippi, under General Wright. He remained in the service until the close and was paroled at Grenada, Miss. Returning to Marshall county he removed his family to Holly Springs, for his houses, fencing, etc., were destroyed by the armies, and his loss was at least $150,000 worth of property. At the breaking out of the war he had one hundred slaves, and was reputed to be worth at that time $300,000, having an annual income of $12,000 besides the ordinary increase in property. While a resident of Holly Springs he engaged in merchandising, remained there until 1878 (the time of the yellow fever scourge), and then returned to his farm, where he has since resided. His estimable wife and family are members of the Presbyterian church, and move in the best circles of society. The Captain is well known throughout the county as one of its very best citizens, and is noted for his hospitality and marked individuality. He educated his children in the best schools of the country. He has been a member of the Masonic fraternity for many years, and has taken all the degrees in that order. He was largely instrumental in inducing the building of railroads in the state. The Mississippi river bottom and other abandoned lands were allowed to be redeemed, and the same held free of taxation for fourteen years; and he drew up the bill that passed both houses of the legislature, and became a law, allowing this bonus and at the same time replenishing the treasury.

John P. Withers, Blythe, Miss. In the early settlement of the state of Mississippi members of the Withers family settled within its borders, and with that bravery and courage characteristic of the pioneer, made homes in Marshall county, in the midst of the wilderness. From these good people is descended the subject of this biography, John P. Withers. He was born in Marshall county, Miss., July 25, 1850, and is one of a family of four children. His parents, Sterling A. and Emily C. (Caruthers) Withers, were natives of Virginia. The father, the son of Sterling Withers, was a planter, and one of the early settlers of De Soto county. He died in Marshall county in 1852, when John P. was two years old. The maternal grandparents of John P. were John P. and Ann C. Caruthers, natives of Virginia; they were also early settlers of Mississippi. John P. Withers was brought up in De Soto county and received a good education in the private schools of the neighborhood. When he had reached man's estate he left his mother's home, and started out in life for himself. He had a small amount of capital to sow for the future, and an unusual amount of native energy and pluck. He is now farming on his mother's place. He was married in 1874 to Miss Adda B. Thompson, of Mississippi, a daughter of Benjamin F. and Camilla J. Thompson, natives of Tennessee. Six children have been born of this union: Camilla G., Sterling A., Frank T., Emily C., deceased, Ada B. and John P. Mr. Withers is a member of the K. H. S. In 1888 he was appointed a member of the Yazoo Mississippi levee board, and still holds that position. He has been president of the board of supervisors of De Soto county for one year and a member of said board for four years. He has always been actively interested in politics as a democrat, and has given much attention to the issues which have most affected the welfare of the people. His broad, public spirit and his generous support of all philanthropic measures have won for him the respect and honor of the entire community.

R. S. Withers, a prominent Mississippian, was born in Jackson, May 27, 1857, a son of William T. Withers, and the fourth of his family of ten children. His father, a native of Kentucky, came to Mississippi about 1848, and being a talented attorney, he became a partner of Judge Wiley P. Harrison, with whom he remained associated for about seven years, after which he returned to Lexington, Ky. He then abandoned the profession of law to engage in the raising of blooded horses, and his fine stock farm near the city of Lexington he named Fairlawn. Although he began on a small scale, he had an aptitude for the work and did it well, being at one time the owner of Almont and Happy Medium, paying for the former $15,000, and for the latter $20,000. Some of his finest animals were sold to King Humbert, of Italy, to the king of the Sandwich islands and to the khedive of Egypt. When Mr. Withers came with his wife to Mississippi they were among the first settlers of the old town of Grand Gulf. R. S. Withers first attended the common schools, but finished his education in the academic department of the University of Kentucky, but left this institution in 1874, and spent two years in California. He then returned to Kentucky, but being of an adventurous disposition, he was not yet disposed to settle down, so made a trip to the Sandwich islands, taking with him some of his father's finest horses, which he disposed of to the king, whose guest he was for one year. The latter gave him a sinecure on board an emigrant ship, whereby he secured a good fee, although he had nothing to do, and visited many of the most important islands in the Pacific ocean. When King Kalakaua was on a visit to this country he visited the Kentucky home of William T. Withers. R. S. Withers has also traveled throughout Mexico and the Central American states. When his desire for travel had become somewhat satisfied he returned to his home in Kentucky, where he remained until 1886, when he launched his canoe and drifted down the rivers to Vicksburg, Miss. In this state he has since made his home, and is now the owner of five thousand acres of land, about two thousand of which are under cultivation, which he devotes to the raising of cotton and corn, exclusively. He has four hundred and ninety acres in a stock farm, which he stocked with horses he brought from his Kentucky home, they being of the Hambletonian and Mambrino breed. In 1890 he opened a large general mercantile store on his plantation, in order to simply supply his own tenants, and from his $8,000 stock of goods, which he keeps constantly on hand, his annual sales amount to $75,000. In June, 1890, he was married to Miss Minnie Robb, a daughter of R. B. Robb, a native of Ireland. Mr. Withers is a wideawake, pushing and enterprising man, and expects soon to drop planting altogether and devote his time and attention to the raising of stock, and should he do so he will no doubt be remarkably successful, for he has been brought up to the business. He has some valuable papers in his possession which were written by General Johnston to his father during war times, asking for a statement of facts concerning the battle of Baker's Creek.

William T. Withers enlisted in the Confederate army at the opening of the war, enlisting in the First regiment of Mississippi light artillery, with which he remained until the surrender of Vicksburg. He was then paroled and stationed at Blakely, Ala., on Mobile bay, until the war closed. He was on Pemberton's staff, and participated in all the battles in and about Vicksburg. After the war he opened a law office in Jackson, as above stated.

E. H. Wiygul is a well known planter, whose postoffice address is Boland, Itawamba county, Miss. He was born December 9, 1827, a son of Alfred and Nancy (Mayfield) Wiygul. His parents were natives of Tennessee, and both were members of the Methodist church. Of their eleven children the subject of this notice was the eldest. He got his education over pine, as he was denied the privilege of school facilities, and by perseverance obtained a good business education, and was married July 3, 1857, to Miss Elizabeth C. Conwill, who was born in South Carolina October 22, 1832, a daughter of J. G. and Mary (Shumpert) Conwill. She was one of twelve children who lived to maturity. Joseph A. was educated in Mississippi and has taught school since 1879. He was married October, 1883, to Miss Tabitha Monts, who was born March 25, 1866, and has had five children, three of whom are deceased. Mr. Wiygul is located on a farm near his father's plantation. He is a Mason and a member of the Farmers' Alliance. Politically he is of the democratic faith, and his first vote for president was cast for Samuel J. Tilden. He and his wife are members of the Methodist Episcopal Church South. William E. was elected county treasurer of Itawamba county in 1883 and held the office two terms. He took the place of his recently deceased brother, E. R. Wiygul, in the mercantile firm of Wiygul Brothers, general merchants, and lives in Nettleton, Miss. J. A. Wiygul now lives in Nettleton, Miss., and is interested with his brother, W. E., in business. Elbert Riley, a merchant of Nettleton and a member of the firm of Wiygul Brothers, died recently at his residence in Nettleton. His death was a gloriously victorious one, and he said he was going home to glory, and besought his family and friends to meet him in the sweet bye and bye. Starting a poor boy, he had accumulated a good property for a young man, for he was yet in his twenties and single. Dora A. married J. D. Springer, of Itawamba county, and has three children. John P. married Miss Lillie M. Tally, daughter of M. Tally, of this county. Nancy M. graduated at the industrial institution of Columbus, Miss., and with James M. and Isaac G., is a member of her parents' household. Mary E., Amanda M., and J. M. and Henderson B. are deceased. Mr. Wiygul is a democrat, politically, but has never aspired to any official positions, though he has been offered offices of honor, which he has declined, preferring to be with his family on the farm, teaching them the importance of an agricultural life, though his children have been so well educated as to prepare them for any walk of life. He cast his first presidential vote for Martin Van Buren. He is a Royal Arch Mason and a member of the Farmers' Alliance. He and his wife are communicants at the Methodist Church South, upon the services of which his children are regular attendants. He has lived on his present homestead since 1834. He located in this county at a time when the playmates of his boyhood were Indians and the country was full of wild game. He lived through the period of settlement and development to see civilization firmly planted where, at his coming, the wilderness covered a large extent of territory. He is honored as the oldest settler of this part of the county. To the work of development he has been a liberal contributor, both of his influence and of his means. No man in the county is more deserving of the high respect which is paid him than is Mr. Wiygul.

Hon. Thaddeus A. Wood, an attorney of Clarke county and a well-known resident of Quitman, was born in Lauderdale county, March 13, 1852. He was the fourth child in a family of six children born to James H. and Mary (Smith) Wood. His father was a native of South Carolina, and was born about 1812, being a son of Reese Wood, and he removed to this state about 1852, locating at Lauderdale county, having previously married in South Carolina, and to him were born the following named children: James D., Martha J., John R., Francis and Lee. Before coming to Mississippi Mr. Wood located for a time in Alabama. He died in Smith county in 1867, where he had been for some years a resident. He was a planter, a Free Mason, a democrat and a member of the Methodist Episcopal church. The mother of our subject was born in South Carolina, in 1807. She was a daughter of Dempsey Smith, a well-known planter and slaveowner of that state. Before her marriage to Mr. Wood she had been married to Mr. Hill, by whom she had six children, the eldest two of whom died in infancy; the others were: Thomas T., Elam, William H. H. and Mary. She died in Pulaski county, Ark., in 1887, having been long a consistent member of the Baptist church. William H. H. Hill was a prominent physician of Sylvania, Smith county, and a graduate of the New Orleans medical college, who had a successful career and amassed a considerable fortune. Lee Wood, brother of T. A. Wood, is also a successful and well-known physician of the same place, and is a graduate of the Nashville Medical college. James is a wealthy planter residing in Arkansas. The boyhood, youth and young manhood of our subject were spent in Smith county. In 1867 he removed to Arkansas, where he lived till 1877. He was educated at Jacksonville college in Arkansas, and was a student there in 1873. In 1874 and 1875 he attended the Sylvania institute, and in 1876 he was again a student at Jacksonville college. Later he entered the Southwestern university at Georgetown, Tex., where he remained during the years 1877, 1878 and 1879. Returning to Mississippi in the last mentioned year, he taught school at Sylvania in 1880, and at Quitman in 1881. He studied law under Maj. Samuel Terral, of Quitman, in 1881–2, and was duly admitted to the bar. Mr. Terral having been appointed judge, Mr. Wood remained in his office and took charge of his large practice. September 29, 1886, Mr. Wood was married to Miss Anna L. Hassell, a daughter of John and Mary (Hunter) Hassell, who was born in Choctaw county in 1867. Her father and mother were natives of Tennessee, the latter being a graduate of Columbia college, Tennessee. Her family moved to Mississippi in 1883, and located at Heidelberg, in Jasper county. Mrs. Wood was educated at Martin college. She has borne her husband two children: Mary, who died in infancy, and Florence, who is living. Mr. Wood's career as a legal practitioner, which has extended through the past nine years, has been a markedly successful one. In 1887 he was elected to the state senate of Mississippi. In addition to his legal and miscellaneous practice he has upon his hands the legal business of the Enterprise Manufacturing and Development company, having been appointed attorney for that corporation. He is a man of great public spirit, and has done his full share toward the advancement of the general welfare of the community. He is a member of the Baptist church, and his wife is a member of the Presbyterian church.

Hon. Thomas H. Woods, associate justice of the supreme court of Mississippi, is a native of Kentucky. Born in the quiet town of Glasgow, Ky., in 1838, the first ten years of his life were passed there. In 1848 his father, Rev. Hervey Woods, removed from Glasgow, Ky., to Kemper county, Miss., where Justice Woods received a common-school education, and where he resided until the winter of 1871–2, when he removed to Meridian, Lauderdale county. The promise of his youth warranted his father in sending him to Williams college, Massachusetts, and during his term of two years in that college he demonstrated clearly his strength of mind and endurance of physical powers. On returning to Mississippi, he turned his studies directly to law and in the winter of 1859–60 was admitted a member of the bar. With all the hope and pride of a young lawyer he determined to begin professional life among a people who knew his father and himself, and accordingly established his office at De Kalb, the seat of justice of Kemper county. Little time was given to assert his claim to prominence among his seniors of the bar. Within a year he was chosen a representative of Kemper in the historic convention of 1861. Within a year the Confederacy of the Southern states called all men to arms, and among the very first to respond to this loud, deliberate, daring call, was the young advocate of De Kalb. No commission urged him to enter the army, for his military career commenced as private in the first military company raised in Kemper county for the Confederate service. He did not subsequently seek promotion, but as virtue brings its own reward, slowly but certainly his personality rose above influence, and by gradual promotion he attained the rank of captain in his old company before Appomattox decided the fortunes of war. Singularly fortunate in being permitted to carve his own way upward in the military scale, he was equally fortunate in escaping the prison and the soldier's grave. A serious wound, received at Malvern Hill during the terrible combat at that point, is the reminder of the perils through which he passed and of the manner in which he answered the bugle calls to battle for rights and customs which he believed inalienable. He was earnest in the constitutional convention of 1861—he was the youngest member of that body—earnest in following the lessons which the convention inculcated, and earnest as a soldier of that western army which it brought into existence; he was always and everywhere faithful. It is not a matter for surprise to learn of the esteem and honor which waited on him in the years since the war. Immediately after his discharge from the army he was chosen attorney for the Third Mississippi district to fill a vacancy, and in 1866 was elected for a full term. His administration was forcible to such a degree that no guilty man escaped, criminals feared the law for that reason and good men learned to admire its rigorous administration. The rule of the carpetbaggers now commenced, the zealous attorney was ousted under their forms of law, and a reign of legalized terror instituted. The victors claimed the spoils in word and deed. In 1869, when he was nominated for the state senate by the unanimous democratic voice of his district, the new forms of law militated against his election and he went down with the other democratic candidates. Everywhere the Federal bayonet and the negro enforced the law after the system of the Moors and Saracens. They were evil days in Mississippi, but the shadows were passing and intolerance was marching toward its end. He was elected district attorney in 1871, for the full term, and eclipsed his record as such in 1865 and 1866. The district was cleared of ruffians and desperadoes and the law, as administered by him, taught men to control their tempers and observe the rules of civilized life. In 1875 he was re-elected district attorney and the record of exact justice was not only maintained, but also extended until 1876, when he resigned the office to devote himself to his practice. Success followed success, and a few years brought him to that high position which his day dreams as a young lawyer in 1860 pictured for his future. In 1882 he was chosen representative in the legislature almost by acclamation. From the point of view of himself and friends, it was an honor dangerous to accept, and during the session he every day denounced his own folly in accepting the honor. In 1885 he declined the office of United States district attorney, offered by President Cleveland, and in other affairs showed a decided disinclination to seek public office. In 1889 Governor Lowry appointed him judge of the supreme court, to fill an unexpired term, and he became chief justice on going on the bench by operation of law. In 1891 Governor Stone reappointed Judge Woods for the full term of nine years. Since 1889, in common with his associates on the bench, he has bent his energies to reflect the glories of the great old bar of Mississippi and present to the Union opinions and decisions equaling in words and logic any ever delivered in the English tongue. He it was who delivered the opinion in the Hemingway case in 1890, a production as literary as it is legal, abounding in beautiful ideas of justice and in language strong and irrefutable. A volume could be written on the life of this Mississippi jurist, each page of which would portray a man of intense convictions, well ordered ideas, logical, learned, soldierly, and withal genial and beneficent.

Dr. A. V. Woolverton, a practicing and prominent physician of Enterprise, Miss., was born in Broadalvin, Fulton county, N. Y., in 1828. He is a son of Dr. Asher and Jane (Kennedy) Woolverton. His father was born on the Hudson river in New York in 1779 and served in the War of 1812. He became a practicing physician, finally locating at Rochester, N. Y., where he died in 1851. He reared a family of eight children, of which our subject was the last in the order of birth. The mother was born in the same town as her husband, and died in Rochester about 1854. The children were named Dennis, Thomas, Stephen, Asher, Servius, Orpha, Samantha and Almira J. Dr. A. V. Woolverton's early life was passed in Rochester, N. Y. He received his early education in the state of his birth, and in 1851 came to Mississippi and located at Enterprise, Clarke county. In 1853 he entered the Medical college of the state of Louisiana at New Orleans, at which he graduated in 1854, establishing himself in the practice of his profession in Enterprise during the same year. He was married in 1858 to Miss Cornelia E. Hand, of Clarke county, and a daughter of John F. Hand, who was one of the pioneers of the county, on one of the original purchases of land. Mrs. Woolverton was born in this county in 1841, and is one of a family of ten children. The maiden name of her mother was Sarah Everett, and one of her aunts was the first wife of Commodore Vanderbilt. Her parents were early settlers in this part of the county, where they became extensive planters and where they ended their days. Dr. and Mrs. Woolverton have had three children, whose names are: Walter, who died in 1880 at the age of twenty-one; Stella, now Mrs. J. W. Dyes, of Enterprise, and who has had children, whose names are: Christopher R., Almira and Walter; and Almira, who is living at home with her parents. In 1861 the Doctor became connected with the surgical department of the armies of the Confederate States, and served as assistant surgeon in the hospitals during the war. He was at the siege of Vicksburg, and his duty called him often to the field of battle. He located in Enterprise after peace was declared and engaged in the practice of his profession, with which he combined, however, the duty of bookkeeper. He is everywhere recognized as a successful medical practitioner, who has the confidence of his patients and the respect of the general public. He is generous in his support of public enterprises, and takes a special interest in schools, churches and all kindred institutions. He and his family are members of the Presbyterian church, of which he is an official. He is a Royal Arch Mason. He has a pleasant home, about two miles south of Enterprise, which is one of the most hospitable in the country.

Thomas Worthington, planter, Leota Landing, was born in Leota, Miss., in 1855, and of the twelve children that blessed the union of Isaac and Ann (Taylor) Worthington he was the youngest in order of birth. The father and mother were originally from Kentucky and the paternal grandfather was also a native of that state and of a distinguished family. The maternal grandfather, Ben. Taylor, was lieutenant-governor of Kentucky and of a prominent family of that state. Isaac Worthington was educated in his native state, where his birth occurred in 1792, and was a soldier in the War of 1812. He came to Mississippi in 1825 and with his negroes made a permanent settlement at Leota, which he named himself, in 1829.

He had about fifteen hundred acres, but afterward bought more and cleared one thousand acres. He then bought an adjoining place with five hundred acres cleared. He was quite a prominent man and was elected to the office of judge of the county court. He died in 1855, an active member of the Methodist Episcopal church and the organizer of the same near Leota. His wife received her final summons in 1882. Their children were named as follows: Macie (married Cyrus R. Johnson), Theodocia (married Judge L. B. Valliant of St. Louis, Mo., now circuit judge in that city); William H. (married Miss Baldwin and lived and died at Enterprise, Miss.), Ben. T. (married Miss Mary Elly and both are now deceased), Isaac M. (married May Johnson and now resides in Chicot county, Ark.). The remainder of the children died in infancy. Thomas Worthington was reared in Washington county and graduated from the University of the South at Sewanee, Tenn., in 1877. He subsequently went to St. Louis, Mo., studied law for one year, but in 1878 began planting on his present place. He was married in 1883 to Miss Rosine Adams, of New Orleans, daughter of R. W. Adams, a merchant of that city. In 1886 Mr. Worthington erected his fine residence on his place and has now twelve hundred acres with nine hundred acres cultivated. He has a steam gin and all the modern improvements. He has a small orchard, but raises a good variety of fruit. He has a fine Percheron stallion, one of the best horses in the country, and is aiming to raise a good breed of stock. On his place the town of Leota has been built and the first merchants, Mott & Scarey, began business there in 1867. There are now twelve stores, postoffice, etc., and it is quite a thriving place. In 1858 Mr. Worthington's mother built a splendid brick mansion, which later, with six hundred acres of cleared land, caved in the river. To Mr. and Mrs. Worthington have been born three beautiful and interesting children: Annie, Henriette and Thomas, Jr. Mr. Worthington has been a member of the board of supervisors and has been active in the welfare and improvement of the county, and is a member-elect to the legislature. His father and uncles were pioneers of the Lake Washington country and did much to develop Washington county in its early day. Their children, Mr. Worthington and his cousins, are among the prosperous planters and prominent citizens of the county at the present time. Mr. Worthington is a fine looking and intelligent gentleman.

E. H. Wray, who is engaged in the sawmill industry at Huntington, Bolivar county, Miss., is the son of Levi Wray, who was a native of Halifax county, Va., and who came to Madison county, Miss., when a young man. There he was soon married to Miss Julia Eleanor, a native of North Carolina, and the fruits of this union were seven children, E. H. being the second in order of birth. The father planted extensively, became very prosperous and his plantation on Bogue Chitto is still known as the Wray place. He moved to Lawrence county in 1858, and there his death occurred on the 9th of February, 1865. After this the family moved back to their former place of residence, and the mother died in Hinds county in 1879. She was a worthy and exemplary church member. The father was a Mason of high standing. The maternal grandparents of E. H. came to Madison county, Miss., in 1841, followed planting, and there both passed the remainder of their days. E. H. Wray began life for himself in 1879 by coming to Washington county, Miss., and engaging in the timber business for Edward Richardson. In 1882 he contracted to furnish pilings for the Mississippi river commissioners, and was thus engaged for three years, making considerable money in that time. In February, 1886, he came to Huntington, erected a first-class sawmill, thoroughly equipped in every way, and has followed this business ever since. This mill has a capacity of twelve thousand feet daily, and saws principally for local trade and for most of the buildings erected in Huntington. In 1888 Mr. Wray bought his present residence, one of the many neat cottages of Huntington; also owns a business house and lot, and a house and lot in Moores. In April, 1888, he was married to Miss Lela Atkinson, daughter of William Atkinson, of Madison county. She is a member of the Methodist Episcopal church. Mr. Wray has served as mayor of Huntington, and filled that position in a creditable and satisfactory manner. He is pleasant and accommodating, and a very agreeable person to meet.

G. L. Wrenn, planter, Gunnison, Miss., the youngest of six children born to Theodore and Elizabeth (Kirk) Wrenn, was originally from the Palmetto state, his birth occurring at Waxhaw settlement in 1838, and is of Danish extraction. The parents were natives of Virginia and South Carolina, respectively, and the father came to South Carolina with his parents when but a child. He followed the occupation of a planter, and received his final summons in that state in 1838. He and wife were members of the Methodist Episcopal church. The paternal grandfather, with others, established one of the first Methodist Episcopal churches in South Carolina at Waxhaw, and it was called Wrenn's Wesleyan chapel. It is now called Waxhaw church. G. L. Wrenn came to Mississippi in 1855, made his home with his uncle, J. C. Kirk and Mrs. N. R. Simmons until 1858, when he entered La Grange college, Tennessee, and there remained until 1860. He enlisted as a private in McGehee's rifles, in June, 1861, was in the battles of northwestern Virginia with Generals Floyd and Lee, and then in the western army, under Gen. A. S. Johnston. He was captured at Fort Donelson, taken to Chicago, Ill., and there kept in confinement for seven months. He was exchanged at Vicksburg, and afterward joined his command at Grenada, Miss. He was in all the battles around Atlanta, and was in the Tennessee campaign. He was taken sick at Tupelo, Miss., and was home on a furlough at the time of the surrender. The ensign of the regiment was killed at Fort Donelson. Mr. Wrenn served as color-bearer the remainder of the war. He was captured the second time at Port Gibson, sent to Alton, Ill., and after being exchanged, joined the army at Resaca, Ga., to participate in the concluding engagements, as above stated. At the death of his aunt, Mrs. Simmons, in 1863, Mr. Wrenn inherited an interest in the Waxhaw plantation, and after returning from the war he bought other property. He purchased Hudson plantation in 1876, and this fine property, consisting of one thousand acres, with eight hundred acres under cultivation, he has cleared and otherwise improved until it is now called one of the finest in the delta. In April, 1886, Mr. Wrenn was united in marriage to Miss Nora W. Cousar, a native also of the Palmetto state, and whose people now reside at Chester, S. C. To this union was born one child, who died unnamed. Mr. and Mrs. Wrenn are members of the Methodist Church South. He is a member in good standing in the Masonic fraternity, has been a member of the levee board and the board of supervisors. He is rather large and fair, and is pleasant, genial and courteous. Mrs. Wrenn is handsome and refined, and one whose graces and virtues are well known. Mr. Wrenn is a thorough and most successful planter and his clean and well-improved fields, with the many neat tenant houses, remind one of the suburb of some large city, while his beautiful residence, erected near Gunnison in 1890, at a cost of $14,000, is built in artistic villa style, and with its graceful minarets and towers, attracts and pleases the eyes of all. The twenty commodious rooms are furnished in the best of style and with exquisite taste, and are finished in the natural wood and oil. They are well lighted from many large windows, the grates are ornamented with tile, and the highly polished halls reflect every object. This home is all that the heart of man could desire or that a refined and educated taste could wish. Aside from his large farming interests, Mr. Wrenn is the owner of a good steam gin and sawmill.

J. H. Wright, vice president and manager of the Meridian National bank, Meridian, Miss., since its opening, is a native of New York state. His ancestors were among the early settlers of New England. His parents, John Sheldon and Amoret (Moses) Wright, are residents of Palmyra, N. Y. His mother was a daughter of Zebina Moses, of Marcellus, N. Y. (See "John Moses, of Plymouth," pages 70-71. Ed.) This Moses family are descended from John Moses, who came from Wales in 1640. Possessed of a liberal education, Mr. Wright began his business career in the employ of the United Pipe lines, in Olean, N. Y., and Bradford, Penn., where for years his characteristic signature was seen on the face of orders for oil certifying the same as authentic and good in the market. In 1881 he married Mattie Waller Hersee, of Buffalo, N. Y. He removed to Meridian, Miss., in 1884, and opened the Meridian National bank for Eastern and local capitalists. This is a strong concern, capitalized at $100,000, with a surplus and undivided profits aggregating $75,000. Its officers are: T. Wistar Brown, of Philadelphia, president; J. H. Wright, of Meridian, Miss., vice president; E. B. McRaven, cashier; and J. M. Jameson, assistant cashier. The directors are: T. Wistar Brown, J. H. Wright, B. F. Ormond, I. Marks, George S. Covert, A. B. Wagner, G. Q. Hall, W. W. Lowry and J. A. Wetherbee. Under Mr. Wright's management this institution has grown in favor from day to day. The history of the bank since its organization has been the history of Meridian, which it has certainly done more to develop than other similar agency. A critical investigation of the financial standing of the list of stockholders will show it to be the most responsible bank in the Southern states, without exception. Backed by ample capital and unlimited resources, both eastern and local, with an officiate and directtorate comprising the best business elements of Meridian, and others with national reputation, the city is certainly to be congratulated upon the possession of such an able and enterprising institution. The bank occupies its own building, at 2313 Fourth street, one of the most imposing in the city. The interior of the bank itself is magnificent, the furniture being of the most modern style, well fitted for a metropolitan concern. In its enterprise and its influence on Meridian and its indomitable spirit we find a revelation of the genius and the impress of the personality of Mr. Wright.

O. P. Wright (deceased) was born near Lawrence, S. C., in 1810, the eldest of twelve children born to Gen. Thomas Wright, a native of the Palmetto state. The latter was married to Miss Simpson, of South Carolina, an aunt of Chief Justice William Simpson. O. P. Wright came to Mississippi at the age of twenty-one years and settled in Hinds county, where he was engaged with his aunt as manager of her planting interests for about ten years. In 1852 he married and moved to a plantation two miles west of Jackson, and to himself and wife, who was formerly Miss Kate Barrett, a native of Hinds county, and the adopted daughter of Richard Cordell, seven children were born, the following of whom are living: T. C., Mary W. (Mrs. Winslow), Katie B. (Mrs. Holland), Sallie C. (Mrs. Ballew, of South Carolina), Daisy L. (Mrs. Dorsey). Mr. Wright, by honest toil, became quite wealthy before the war, but during that time he lost everything but his land, but afterward managed to retrieve his losses to some extent. He was not a participant in the Civil war. He died in August, 1876. His widow is the owner of four hundred acres of land, has one hundred and fifty acres under cultivation and two hundred acres in meadow land, on the former of which she raises both cotton and corn. She is interested to some extent in the raising of Jersey and Ayrshire cattle for dairy purposes, her meadow land thus proving quite profitable. Mrs. Wright is a devoted mother and endeavored to give her children the advantages of a good education. All of her daughters have attended Central Female college of Clinton, are accomplished and intelligent young ladies, and are now engaged in teaching school. T. C., the son, is in the government service in the United States marshal's office in Salt Lake City, Utah.

Dr. William Wright, physician, Sardis, Miss., the fifth in order of birth of seven children born to Dr. John and Sarah (Dunn) Wright, was originally from Greensboro, Ala., his birth occurring on the 25th of March, 1833. The parents were both natives of the Old North state, the father born on the 21st of December, 1801, and both were reared in their native state. The father received his education there but graduated in medicine at New York city in 1822. He then practiced in North Carolina until about twenty-five years of age, when he married and removed to Greensboro, Ala., where he practiced several years. In 1835, having previously bought land at the Choctaw land sales, he removed with his family and effects to Grenada, Miss., and in connection with a large and successful practice, was engaged in farming, accumulating considerable property before his death, in 1848, when in the prime of life. He was a charter member of the Masonic lodge, No. 31, at Grenada, Miss., one of the oldest in the state, having been organized in 1836. The paternal grandparents, David and Sarah (Hill) Wright, were natives of Maryland and removed to North Carolina in 1786. He was a merchant and planter. His father came from England about 1750 and located in Maryland. The maternal grandfather, James Dunn, was a native of Maryland and of Scotch descent. Dr. William Wright attained his growth in Yalobusha county, Miss., and received his education in the high schools of the same. He subsequently graduated in medicine from Louisville, Ky., (in 1857) and in 1858, after having made a trip to Texas and North Carolina prospecting, he located in Grenada, Miss., where he remained one year. He afterward came to Panola county and there he has since made his home. In 1861 he entered the Confederate army as surgeon of the Fifteenth Mississippi regiment, in which capacity he remained until cessation of hostilities. After cessation of hostilities he returned to his farm and resumed a large and lucrative practice. In 1870, having built a handsome residence in Sardis, he removed to that town and there has since made his home. He first engaged in the drug business, which he conducted until 1880 under the firm name of Kinchloe & Wright, and was very successful in this venture. After the death of his partner in 1879, he closed out part of his business and has devoted his time wholly to his profession. He was married in 1858 to Miss Mary B. Walton, a native of Tennessee and a daughter of Benbury Walton, who was born in North Carolina. She was a graduate of the Wesleyan Female college, Macon, Ga., one of the oldest female institutions in the United States. Two children were born to this marriage: Ellen (deceased), and Dr. Edwin Wright. The latter received his literary training in Virginia Medical institute of Lexington, Va., graduating in 1884, and his medical education in Tulane university, New Orleans, La., from which he received his diploma. He is now practicing in partnership with his father. Dr. Wright is the owner of four hundred acres of land, has two hundred acres under cultivation, also owns his office and ten acres of valuable lots within the corporation limits of Sardis. Dr. and Mrs. Wright are members of the Methodist church, and he is a Knight Templar in the Masonic lodge, is a member of the I. O. O. F., the Knights of Honor and Knights and Ladies of Honor. He is a member of the state board of health. The Doctor is an excellent physician and is well posted on all points of his profession.

William M. Wroten, a physician and surgeon of Magnolia, Pike county, Miss., was born near Magnolia, May 15, 1847, a son of Hon. V. J. Wroten, M. D., who was born in Copiah county, Miss. He chose the medical profession for his life work, and, after receiving his education, began the practice of his profession, in which he continued with great success for more than half a century. He is still an active man, but has retired from the practice of medicine. He represented Pike county in the legislature in 1872. He is a member of the Masonic order and of the Methodist Episcopal church. He was married in this county to Elizabeth Quinn, who was born here, a daughter of Colonel H. Quinn, formerly of South Carolina. William M. Wroten, M. D., was reared and educated in this county. He read medicine with his father, and after two courses of lectures graduated from the medical college at Louisville, in 1872. For several years, until the retirement of his father, he was his professional partner. He has a large and lucrative practice, and enjoys the reputation of being one of the most successful physicians and surgeons in this part of the state. For a number of years he was a proprietor of a drug store which did a very large trade, but his professional duties were so numerous that he had to relinquish that business. He is a member of the board of health, and has acted as surgeon for a railroad company. He is also a member of the board of aldermen of Magnolia. In August, 1862, he enlisted in company I, of the Fourth Mississippi regiment, as a private, and served until the close of the war, participating in the engagements at Springfield Landing, La., at Harrisburg and in Forrest's campaign. He was married in Liberty, Amite county, Miss., November 21, 1872, to Miss Eleanor Lea, a daughter of Robert Lea, of St. Helena parish, La. Mr. and Mrs. Wroten have three children: V. J., Lillian and Hugh. They are members of the Methodist Episcopal church and the Doctor is an Odd Fellow, Knight of Pythias and Knight of Honor. He is the medical examiner for his lodge of the Knights of Honor, and is noble grand of his Odd Fellows' lodge, having served the last named order as district deputy. The business and professional standing of the Doctor is deservedly high, and his family move in the best social circles.

F. A. Wyatt, farmer, Tchula, Miss., is in every way worthy of being classed among the prosperous planters of Holmes county, Miss. He is the owner of five hundred acres of excellent land near Tchula lake, and he also owns residence property in Lexington, where he makes his home. He is a native Mississippian, born in Yalobusha county on the 14th of April, 1841, and is a son of J. R. Wyatt (see sketch of Capt. T. J. Wyatt). F. A. Wyatt came to Holmes with his parents, passed his youthful days in assisting his father on the farm, and received a good practical education in this county. During the late unpleasantness between the North and South, his sympathies were with the Confederate States, and in 1861 he joined company A, Twenty-eighth Mississippi cavalry, and served until the final surrender. He participated in a number of engagements and skirmishes—those around Vicksburg, fighting the gunboats on the Mississippi river during the entire summer of 1862, the raid at Grenada that drove General Grant back from that place, and the charge at Franklin, Tenn., in 1863. Mr. Wyatt was then ordered back to Mississippi to reinforce Johnston, who was back of Vicksburg. Mr. Wyatt received a gunshot wound in the knee at Barr creek, July 3, 1863, was disabled from further duty, and was obliged to use crutches for several years after the war. Returning home to Holmes county, he engaged in planting in connection with his brother, Capt. T. J. Wyatt, and he has followed that pursuit in the county ever since. He is a thriving, industrious citizen, and is considered one of the substantial men of the county. He was married, in Holmes county, on the 12th of December, 1867, to Miss Lydia Ann Walton, who was born, reared and educated in Holmes county, and who was the daughter of Jesse Walton. Her death occurred on the 17th of February, 1882, and was a great blow to her afflicted family. She was a noble woman, and her virtues were many. She left three daughters and a son. On the 1st of February, 1889, Mr. Wyatt was married to Miss Georgia Cole, a sister of his former wife. Mr. Wyatt is a member of the Masonic fraternity, Tchula lodge. He was elected a member of the board of supervisors of Holmes county in 1889, and is a member of that body at the present time. Mrs. Wyatt is a member of the Presbyterian church.

Capt. Thomas J. Wyatt, farmer, Tchula, Miss. Among the early families to settle in Holmes county, Miss., was that of James Wyatt, who moved to this state about 1820, settled in what is now Holmes county and opened up a plantation near Tchula lake. There his death occurred, near old Fort Rankin. He was a soldier in the Revolutionary war and lost a leg in the service of his country. His son, J. R. Wyatt (father of subject), was born in Tennessee in 1816, and when but a child came to Mississippi with his parents. The state was at that time almost a wilderness, wild animals abounded and the Indian children were his playmates. He was married in Yalobusha county, Miss., to Miss Phebe Nations, a native of that county and the daughter of Capt. James Nations, one of the pioneers of Yalobusha county. After his marriage Mr. Wyatt removed to the Lone Star state, accumulated much wealth and was one of the prominent men of that state. He died in 1856, in the prime of life, and two years later Mrs. Wyatt followed him to the grave. This union was blessed by the birth of five children, all sons, who grew to mature years: The eldest brother, W. W., joined the Confederate army, became lieutenant of company A, Twenty-eighth Mississippi regiment, and was killed in the battle at Pulaski, Tenn., on the 25th of December, 1864. The second son, F. A., was also a soldier (see sketch). Robert N. served in the same company and regiment and was badly wounded in the same engagement in which his brother was killed (his death occurred in 1872); the next in order of birth was Capt. Thomas J. (subject), and the youngest, W. R., grew to manhood and died in 1873. Capt. Thomas J. Wyatt attained his growth in Holmes county and received a good education at the Kentucky Military institute, completing his studies there in 1870. He then returned to Holmes county, engaged in planting in partnership with his brother until 1881, when the partnership was dissolved and he bought the plantation where he now resides. He has a fine place and everything about it indicates the enterprise and thrift which have ever characterized his efforts. He cultivates about eight hundred acres of land and for the last two years has worked state and county convicts, from thirty-five to forty annually. He has good houses, which are kept in a clean and healthy condition for the convicts, the food is good and wholesome and every precaution is taken in regard to their sanitary condition. Captain Wyatt is a democrat in politics, and was elected sheriff and collector of Holmes county in 1885. So efficiently did he fill that position and so prompt was he in the discharge of the duties of that office, that he was re-elected and made a model officer. He was faithful, honest and fearless in the discharge of his duties, and his many friends speak very highly of his official record. After serving four years in that capacity Mr. Wyatt retired from public life and returned to his plantation. He is a Royal Arch Mason and a prominent member of Tchula lodge No. 122.

Prof. Lewis A. Wyatt, the efficient founder of the Capital Commercial college, of Jackson, Miss., was born in Grayson county, N. C., March 5, 1850, the fourth of eight children born to Solomon and Caroline (Maxwell) Wyatt, both of whom were also born in the Old North state. Solomon Wyatt was reared in the state of his birth, and about 1851 removed to Jackson county, Mo., where he is now residing at the advanced age of eighty-two years. He has had a prosperous career as a farmer and is now in the enjoyment of a hale and hearty old age. He is a son of William Wyatt, a North Carolinian of Irish descent. Caroline Maxwell was descended from Scottish ancestors, her grandfather, Alexander McMillan, having been born in the land of thistles and oatmeal. He represented North Carolina in the United States senate before the late war, being elected by whigs. In the state of Missouri Prof. Lewis A. Wyatt was reared, but his education has been acquired by his own efforts and since he was grown. He obtained his commercial training at Spalding's English and Commercial college of Kansas City, completing his course in 1870, from which time until

1880 he was engaged in teaching in literary and business schools in Missouri. In 1880 he removed to the Lone Star state, where he was employed in expert accounting in Dallas and Fort Worth for three years, after which he came to Jackson and established the college of which he is now senior principal, Prof. J. M. Sharp, formerly of Mississippi college, being associated with him at present. This is one of the best colleges of the kind in the South, and under Professor Wyatt's able management has prospered from the beginning. Professor Wyatt is purely selfmade and certainly deserves great credit for what he has accomplished, and the pluck and energy he has manifested in building up an institution that is not only prosperous and a great credit to the city, but has afforded opportunity for Mississippians to educate their sons and daughters in the business branches without having to go out of the state. The institution was opened to the public and to the reception of students November 3, 1884, and from a small beginning it, in time, passed the experimental stage, and becoming established in the confidence of the people, it was incorporated in 1886 under the laws of the state of Mississippi to award diplomas and confer degrees. Since then it has increased in efficiency, and consequently in patronage, and is now in a very prosperous condition. The aim of the management is to furnish a course of study directly adapted to the exigencies of the times and the necessities of its patrons, complete in all its appointments, and having advantages and facilities unexcelled for practical and substantial training for business and in carrying out this purpose, Professors Wyatt and Sharp recently revised and improved the course of study and increased their facilities for educating the young and middle-aged of both sexes for a successful start in business life. Besides the regular business course shorthand, typewriting and telegraphy are also taught by efficient and competent instructors. Professor Wyatt is attentive to his business and is always found at his post of duty, hence his success. He was married in 1888 to Miss Lelia Burch, a daughter of S. D. and Frances (Jones) Burch. The Professor and his wife have one child, John C. Professor Wyatt and his wife are worthy Christians, but the former is a member of the Methodist Episcopal church and the latter of the Christian church.

Capt. Benjamin L. Wynn, a planter of Tallahatchie county, was born near Coffeeville, Yalobusha county, in 1839. He is the son of Hon. Robert Edward and Mary (Williams) Wynn, born in Virginia and South Carolina, respectively. Mr. Wynn was the youngest of his family, and was left an orphan at an early age. His youth was passed on a farm, and his education was only such as was afforded him by the common schools. While yet little more than a boy he came with an elder brother, Col. William T. Wynn, to Mississippi, and when but eighteen years old was married in Yalobusha county, and located five miles south of Coffeeville on a small improvement. He lived in Grenada during the war, and afterward returned to Yalobusha county, where he died in 1866, aged about forty-five, having been successful and become a well-to-do planter. He was a man of no little ability and influence, and in 1854 was a member of the legislature, to which he was again elected in 1862. His father, Lyttleton Wynn, was a native and life-long resident of Virginia, where he died when Robert E. was a small boy. Mr. Wynn's paternal grandfather, Benjamin Williams, was a native of South Carolina, who, some time early in the thirties, came to Yalobusha county, where he became a planter, and died while our subject was yet in his teens. His wife died in Yalobusha county also. Captain Wynn's mother died in 1863, being for many years a member of the Methodist church. She had ten children, of whom our subject was the eldest. Robert E., a planter of Tallahatchie county, was educated at La Grange, Tenn., and fought during the Civil war in the Fifteenth Mississippi infantry under Gen. E. C. Walthall. William T. was a planter and superintendent of education in Yalobusha county. He was educated at the University of Virginia, where he was a student at the breaking out of the war. He joined the Vicksburg Southrons and served until the end of the struggle, being assigned, after the battle of Seven Pines, to the signal service, in which he was useful until the close of the war. He was with Gen. Stonewall Jackson at the time of his death, and was one of the two who carried his body from the field. John Wynn died when a young man. Kershaw, a merchant of Cass county, Tex., was educated principally at Charlotteville, Va. Watkins was also educated in Virginia, and was a resident of Yalobusha county. Mollie died young, but had, in her life, attended a female college at Columbia, Tenn. Susan, who was a sister of St. Mary's order in Memphis, Tenn., was educated by a private tutor. Katie, now Mrs. Gordon, of Phillips county, Ark., received her education at Jackson, Tenn. Maud, who resides at Coffeeville, was also educated at Jackson. Our subject attended the public schools at Coffeeville, and later was a student at the Kentucky Military school near Frankfort, but did not graduate on account of the opening of the war. As several of his brothers had done, he also offered his services to the Confederate government, and enlisted in the Vicksburg Southrons, fighting in the army till 1862. After the battle of Seven Pines he was transferred to the signal department, in which he served till the close of the war under General Jackson and Gen. Jubal A. Early in the Second army corps. The only really hard engagement in which he participated was the battle of Seven Pines. He was captured in October, 1862, by General McClellan's body guard, and taken to the General's headquarters. He was sent to Washington, D. C., and was there kept a prisoner about two months, when he was paroled and sent to Petersburg, and then to Richmond, where he was soon after exchanged and joined his command at Fredericksburg. At the close of the war he surrendered at Petersburg and returned to Mississippi.

In 1866 and 1867 he was in the commission business for about fifteen months and was in the firm of Edmondson & Wynn, of Memphis, Tenn., and during that time, 1867, married Fannie E., daughter of Armstead and Fanny E. Leigh, both natives of Amelia county, Va. Mrs. Wynn's parents were reared in Virginia and were there married. In 1843 they came to Yalobusha county and Mr. Leigh was engaged in the practice of law in Coffeeville until his death in 1854. He was a graduate of the University of Virginia and was a very eminent attorney. His wife died in 1858, having been for a long time a member of the Episcopalian church. She was a daughter of John Lane, a native of Buckingham county, Va., who passed all of his life in that state. Mrs. Wynn's grandfather, John Leigh, also a native of Amelia county, Va., moved to Mississippi about 1833 and died in Yalobusha county, now Grenada county, about twenty years later. He had been a prominent man in Virginia and had served for many years as a clerk in Amelia county. Mrs. Wynn was the eldest of three children—two sons and a daughter. She was born in Yalobusha county and educated at Staunton and Richmond, Va. She has four children—two sons and two daughters. In 1868 and 1869 Captain Wynn lived on his farm, but afterward returned to Yalobusha county and resided there for some years. Then he again removed to his farm. He has about two hundred acres of land, about two-fifths of which are under cultivation. In 1875 and 1876 he represented Yalobusha county in the legislature and was a member of the committee on printing, etc. He was one of a committee of two members of the house appointed to go to Washington, D. C., and bring back the remains of Judge Sharkey. He is a member of the lodge of A. F. & A. M. at Coffeeville, of which he has been warden and secretary. Captain Wynn was for some years justice of the peace in Yalobusha county. He received his title of captain through his appointment as captain of the militia company by Governor Humphreys during the troublesome times that are fresh in the memories of the citizens of this section. Mr. Wynn is of good family, and his standing as a citizen is deservedly high. His natural ability is above the average. He is exceptionally well informed. He has taken a deep interest, not only in the education of his children, but in education generally. Mrs. Wynn, who is a member of the Episcopal church, is also of a prominent family and is widely known as a lady of much culture and high literary attainments.

Capt. W. T. Wynn, Coffeeville, Miss. The subject of this sketch is the present superintendent of the public schools of Yalobusha county, having been once elected to the office, and twice appointed to it. He was born in this county, December 20, 1843, and is a son of Robert E. Wynn, a native of Sussex county, Va., born February 2, 1820. The latter immigrated to Mississippi in the year 1836, having been left an orphan, and for a time lived with his brother-in-law near Coffeeville; when he became of age he started out in life upon his own responsibility, settling on the place where B. R. Winters now lives; there he remained until 1856, and then went to Grenada, where he reared and educated his family. He was elected to the legislature, from Yalobusha county, in 1854, and re-elected, in 1862. He was an ardent whig, and a man of great breadth and strength of character. During the late war he was a member of the home militia, and was exempted from active duty. He was a man strictly temperate and moral in his habits, and universally honored and respected. He died in 1866. He was united in marriage, in February, 1838, to Miss Mary Williams, a native of South Carolina, and a daughter of Benjamin Williams, one of the early settlers of this county. A full sketch of Mr. Williams will be found on another page of this volume. Mrs. Mary Wynn was born in 1822, and was but sixteen years of age when she was married. She had born to her eleven children—six sons and five daughters. All but one lived to be grown, and eight are still living: Benjamin L., William T., Robert E., John (deceased), Kersha, Watkins, Mary E. (deceased), Susan A., Kate G., Maud, and Martha (deceased). William T. was educated in the common schools of Grenada and in the University of Virginia. He was graduated from the latter institution in 1861, and went immediately to Richmond, Va., where he enlisted in the Vicksburg Southrons, company A, Twenty-first Mississippi regulars. He served as a private until after the siege of Richmond, when he was put on Stonewall Jackson's signal staff. His experience during that fearful conflict was not unlike that of thousands of other brave sons. He participated in many engagements, and distinguished himself by gallant service. He was recommended to a captaincy by Jackson, but the General died before the order was issued. His brothers, Robert E. and Benjamin L. Wynn, were also in the service, and the former was wounded and they were both taken prisoners. After the surrender Captain Wynn returned to his home, and remained with his parents a year. He was then married to Miss Judith M. Jones, a Mississippian, and a daughter of William S. Jones. She was born in 1845, and died in 1872, leaving one child, William T., who was educated at Oxford and is a very bright young man. Mr. Wynn was married, a second time, to Miss Sally M. Cock, a native of Virginia, and a member of one of the most distinguished families of that state. Her father was a man highly educated and of very polished manners. He was descended from the French Huguenots, and was regarded as the Chesterfield of his age. The Captain and Mrs. Wynn have had born to them three children: Juria, Roland Edward, and Helen Archer (deceased). The mother died in 1887; she was a member of the Baptist church, and was a most earnest Christian, honored and loved by all. Captain Wynn affiliates with the democratic party. As before stated, he is the present superintendent of the public schools of the county, and he has made a most efficient officer. To him must be attributed the successful reforms inaugurated, which place the schools among the best of the state. Yalobusha county is to be congratulated upon the possession of so able a superintendent. He was appointed by President Cleveland to compile the commercial and agricultural statistics of the state of Mississippi. He has held the office of chief magistrate of district No. 4 for a period of twelve years, his election being unanimous. The black people in this district outnumber the whites ten to one, and Captain Wynn has always been their choice. In his official capacity he has always discharged his duties with a rare fidelity, and with an ability quite out of the ordinary. He has won for himself a host of friends and admirers, and made a reputation second to none in the state.

Judge James Harper Wynn. This gentleman is one of the most brilliant and talented lawyers in the state of Mississippi. He is a man of advanced ideas, liberal and progressive, and while pursuing the practice of his profession takes an active interest in every move for the development of his state. He was born in Tallahatchie county, Miss., to William T. Wynn and wife, the former having come from his native state of Virginia to Mississippi when a young man, locating in Jackson, where he became connected with some of the leading banks. He was very successful as a business man, became possessed of considerable wealth, and at his death, which occurred in his native state in 1855, he was in good circumstances. He was married to Coralie, daughter of Maj. J. N. Harper, who is still a resident of Tallahatchie county, although born in the state of Georgia. The latter's wife was a Miss Jones, of Georgia, and her father, Col. William Jones, won his title in the Revolutionary war, and was a native Georgian. Judge James Harper Wynn attained manhood in Tallahatchie county, but was educated in the University of Mississippi at Oxford. In 1873 he began teaching school, and after following this occupation for two years, and in the meantime studying law, he began practicing the latter calling in Charleston, Miss. Two years later he moved to Friar's Point, Miss., at which he continued his practice until 1886, when he was appointed judge of the circuit court of the delta district, a position he filled until 1889, proving himself a most eminent jurist. Being full of charity and generosity, he rarely suspected others of sordid motives, and his criticisms, when provoked, were tempered with mildness and forbearance. Since 1889 he has been a practitioner of Greenville, and as he gives every attention to his business, he never permits the interests of his clients to suffer. He was elected mayor of Greenville in 1889, and has discharged the duties of this position very creditably up to the present time. He was married in June, 1880, to Miss Mattie Kinman, a native of Memphis, Tenn., but a resident of Newport, Ark., being a daughter of Captain Riley and Mattie (Hooker) Kinman, the former a planter and the latter a native of Nashville, Tenn. To Judge and Mrs. Wynn three children have been born: Robert Harper, Mattie Kinman and William Thomas. Judge Wynn is the owner of one thousand acres of land. In 1888 he erected him a residence in Greenville at a cost of $5,000, which is a handsome, commodious, substantial and very pleasant residence. He has the satisfaction of knowing that he is not beholden to any man for the property of which he is now the owner, for he began life with limited means and has earned it all by his own efforts. He inherits English and French blood of his parents, and in his religious views is a Presbyterian, his wife being an earnest member of the Catholic church. Socially he belongs to the K. of P., the K. of H. and the American Legion of Honor. He is one of the ablest lawyers in the Yazoo delta, if not in the state, is intelligent, highly educated, and bears an enviable reputation as a citizen and jurist. Since becoming mayor of Greenville he has been diligent in his efforts to rid the city of the moral vampires that have infested it, and has done much to raise the standard of morality in this section. He has at all times manifested a spirit in keeping with Christian principles, and as he possesses very superior natural endowments, strengthened and enriched by the highest culture, he is eminently capable of filling any position within the gift of the people. In social life he is highly esteemed for his conversational powers, and for the ease, grace and dignity of his manners, and in the domestic circle he is a model husband and father, making the happiness and comfort of his family his chief aim and object in life. His many admirable qualities of head and heart have won him many warm friends, and when once won they are rarely lost. He has achieved an excellent reputation, both professionally, socially and as a citizen, and it may with truth be said that no one has gained more fully the confidence of the people, and certainly no one has been truer or more loyal to public trusts.

CHAPTER XXIV.

CONCLUDING INDIVIDUAL AND FAMILY NOTICES, Y.

CONNECTED with his practice, which he has made a complete success, Dr. A. S. Yarbrough, Como, Miss., is also engaged in farming, and is possessed of those advanced ideas and principles which can not fail to place him in the front ranks as an agriculturist. He was born in Marshall county, Miss., on the 12th of October, 1840, and is the son of Charles and Sallie B. (Anderson) Yarbrough, the father a native of Franklin county, N. C., and the mother of Lunenburg district, Va. The Yarbrough family is of English extraction, and the first immigrants to this country made their appearance here prior to the Revolution. Many descendants now reside in North Carolina. Charles Yarbrough was reared in North Carolina, was married in Tennessee to Miss Anderson, and in 1839 he moved to Marshall county, Miss., where he followed the occupation of a farmer. He became quite wealthy, and died in Marshall county in 1873. The mother is still living, and is seventy-eight years of age. Seven of the eleven children born to this union grew to mature years, and are named as follows: Martha G., wife of James Sims of Holly Springs; Beatrice (deceased), was the wife of the late Dr. W. M. Compton; Charles G., a farmer of Marshall county; Dr. A. S.; G. W. and J. Henry, both farmers of Marshall county, and John W. (deceased). Dr. A. S. Yarbrough spent his boyhood days on his father's farm in Marshall county, and when eighteen years of age, owing to ill health, he went to Texas, where he spent a year with the cow boys. He then returned to Mississippi, studied medicine under the late Dr. William M. Compton, and took a course of lectures in the medical college at Nashville, Tenn. At the commencement of the late war he entered the Confederate army as a private in company I, First Mississippi infantry, commanded by Captain Milams. Soon after, on making an application to be examined in medicine and surgery, he was appointed surgeon in 1862. He was in the engagement at Fort Donelson, was captured and taken to Mound City, Ill., where he was left with the wounded of his command. Subsequently, fearing that he should be taken farther north, Dr. Yarbrough made his escape, crossing the Ohio river when it was eight miles in width, (this was before it was agreed upon that physicians should not be considered prisoners of war), and then reported to his colonel, who was at Shannon, Miss. He was granted a furlough. He joined his regiment as soon it was enchanged, was a participant of the siege of Port Hudson, and was again captured. Upon being released he reported to Gen. Joseph E. Johnston, who was near Jackson, Miss. His regiment was soon exchanged, and his command joined the army of Tennessee, taking part in all the fights around Atlanta, Ga., and being with Hood in the Tennessee campaign. He was in the battles of Franklin and Nashville, and after retreating from the latter place to Vernon, Miss., he was given a furlough. He was on the way to join his command when he met Jefferson Davis on his retreat from Richmond, near Washington, Ga. Dr. Yarbrough was then paroled, and returned to the peaceful pursuits of farm life. In 1865 he wedded Miss Texana J. Wilbourn, daughter of Elijah and Eliza Wilbourn, and to them were born three children, all daughters: Mattie B., wife of J. B. Davis, of Nashville, Tenn.; May B., wife of J. B. Wardlaw, of Como, Miss.; Minnie L., at home, single. Dr. Yarbrough lost his estimable wife in 1873. His second marriage was to Miss Emma McGee, daughter of Edward and Sarah (McGee) McGee, a very prominent pioneer family of Panola county. By his last union the Doctor became the father of one son, Archie. Dr. Yarbrough has been a resident of Panola county since 1865, and of his farm for about ten years. He was elected to the state legislature by the democratic party in 1889. He has one of the largest and best improved plantations in the county—two thousand three hundred acres, with one thousand five hundred acres under cultivation, and has all the latest improved machinery for conducting the same. He stands high in the estimation of all who know him.

Daniel T. Yates was born in Hinds county, Miss., January 14, 1838, the youngest of nine children born to Daniel and Mary (Dyson) Yates, natives of the Old North state. The father was born in 1795, and was reared in the state of his birth, there receiving only such advantages as the common schools afforded. He was a man of great will power, and engaging in agricultural pursuits, by industry and good management he accumulated, prior to the war, a fortune of $150,000 in slaves, land, stock, etc., most of which was swept away during the terrible struggle between the North and the South. He was not a political aspirant, and lived a quiet and uneventful life upon his plantation. Upon his removal to Mississippi, in 1816, he located in Covington county, but afterward removed to Hinds county, where he spent the rest of his days, dying in 1875. He was a son of Luke and Helen (Flowers) Yates, of North Carolina, the Yates family being of English ancestry. He gave all his sons a collegiate education. He and his wife belonged to the Christian church. Daniel T. Yates was reared in Hinds county, and was educated in Bethany college, of Bethany, Va., graduating from this institution in 1858, following which he clerked in a general mercantile store for about one year. In 1861, at the beginning of the war, he enlisted in the Confederate army, attaching himself to company A, of the Twelfth Mississippi regiment—Raymond fencibles—and served until the close of the war, participating in the battles of Spottsylvania, the seven days' fight before Richmond, Chancellorsville, Seven Pines, Fredericksburg, Gettysburg, Sharpsburg, the second Manassas and Petersburg. He was wounded in the head at Gettysburg, and in the side at Seven Pines, but not dangerously either time, and in the seven days' fight near Richmond he lost a finger. He surrendered at Meridian, Miss., and returned home in April, 1865, where he almost immediately began planting and merchandising, notwithstanding the fact that the country was desolated by the war. He began anew with the same courage that had upheld him in many battles and throughout the long period of the war, and by undeviating effort he soon began to accumulate means, and in time his broken fortunes were mended. Through his own business ability he has become the owner of thirteen hundred acres of land, of which about six hundred acres are under cultivation, devoted to the raising of the usual Southern products. This plantation is admirably conducted, and everything about it indicates that a man of thrift, intelligence and enterprise is at the helm. Added to all the advantages of a college education, Mr. Yates' experience as a soldier, and his subsequent contact with the world, were excellent teachers, and had their uses, for they taught him to think and act for himself. He is a refined and intelligent gentleman, a pleasant and instructive companion, and a fluent and interesting conversationalist. He is a member of the Knights of Honor, and is insured in the New York Life Insurance company, also in the New York Mutual Life Insurance company, and he and his wife and children worship in the Christian church. In December, 1866, Mr. Yates was married to Miss Maggie Murchison, a native of Mississippi and a daughter of John and Catherine (Evans) Murchison, the former a Virginian, and the latter a native of Mississippi and a graduate of Brashear academy, Mississippi. To Mr. and Mrs. Yates the following children have been born: Alexander, a teacher; Katie, a graduate of Wood's seminary, Nashville, Tenn.; Daniel T., Jr., a commercial traveler; John R., a teacher; Mary H., at the Convent of Mercy, Vicksburg, Miss.; Simon M.; Dan Voorhees, and Alonzo Lewis. Simon M., Dan Voorhees and Alonzo Lewis are at home attending school. The Yates family stand socially among the best people of the county.

Rucks Yerger, attorney, Friar's Point, Miss., was born in Bolivar county, Miss., November 22, 1859, and was the youngest child that reached maturity born to Alexander and Elizabeth B. (Rucks) Yerger, the father a native of Tennessee, and the mother of Mississippi. Alexander Yerger was a man of thorough education, and was very prominent in the politics of Mississippi. Many members of the Yerger family, an old and prominent one, have been eminent attorneys, and have held high legal offices in the states of Mississippi and Tennessee. Mrs. Yerger was a native of Washington county, Miss., her father being the owner of the plantation on which the town of Leland now stands. Rucks Yerger, who was named after his grandfather, Judge James Rucks, was mainly educated at home, and for a time was clerk in the law office of Charles Scott, of Rosedale, Miss. In June, 1882, he graduated in law from the University of Mississippi, graduating second in his class. He soon formed a partnership with W. S. Farish, locating at Mayersville, Miss. Two years later he took a summer course at the University of Virginia, and in July, 1884, located at Friar's Point, where he has since resided. Mr. Yerger is one of the most prominent legal lights of Coahoma county, and for soundness of views and clearness of intellect he stands second to none. In 1886 he formed a partnership with George Winston. This continued under the firm name of Winston & Yerger until 1889, when Mr. Winston was appointed circuit judge. Mr. Yerger is a stockholder in the bank of Friar's Point, and in the Friar's Point Box and Woodwork factory. He is attorney for the Friar's Point Building and Loan association, treasurer of the Friar's Point Land, Loan and Improvement company and president of the Friar's Point Packing company. He was married November 13, 1889, to Miss Hyacinth W. McGuire, a native of Mississippi, and daughter of Charles L. and Hyacinth McGuire. Mrs. Yerger was principally reared in New York. From there she moved to New Orleans, where she resided at the time of her marriage. One child, Charles Alexander, has been born to this union. Mr. Yerger owns a large quantity of wild lands in Coahoma county, and is a firm believer in the future of the Mississippi delta. He is a member of the K. of P., Coahoma lodge No. 49. The family are members of the Episcopal church.

Hon. William Gwin Yerger, senior member of the well-known firm of Yerger & Percy, lawyers of Greenville, Miss., was born in Vicksburg on the 22d of July, 1840, and was the fourth in a family of nine children born to Judge Jacob Shall and Mary H. (Bowen) Yerger, the father a native of Pennsylvania and the mother of Tennessee. Judge Yerger was one of the most prominent men of Mississippi, and so great was his popularity that he could have been elected to any office to which he aspired. The following is taken from the *Bench and Bar* of Mississippi: "Judge Jacob Yerger was born in the town of Greensburg, Penn., on the 11th of January, 1816, and removed with his parents to Lebanon, Tenn., where he was reared and educated. He was one of eleven children, and in consequence of the poverty of his father his educational advantages were sparse and limited. Full, however, of the workings of an innate genius and the ambition of conscious talents, on attaining his majority he selected the profession of law, and began its study in the office of his brother, George S. Yerger. Having, after a thorough preparation, obtained his license to practice, he located in the city of Nashville and entered at once upon his prosperous and brilliant career. In spite of the most flattering prospects he removed to Vicksburg in the winter of 1837, and there, among some of the brightest legal lights of the state, he was soon recognized as fully equal to the task before him, and the expectations which his reputation engendered. He was one of the most profound lawyers at the bar of Mississippi, and practiced in the Federal courts, in the high court of errors and appeals, and in the superior court of chancery, being perhaps the largest and most lucrative in the state and which he retained until his election to the circuit bench in 1855. As a judge, he was a wise and faithful expositor of the law, a stern and unswerving vindicator of justice, and upright arbiter before whom the weak and oppressed found an ample and sure redress of their wrongs. He possessed the unbounded confidence of the bar and the people, and his decisions were received as emanations from the fountain of wisdom and justice. His addresses to the grand jury were models of legal expositions and moral commentary and the dignity and decorum which he maintained in his courts were elevating to the bar, admonishing to the people, and an honor to judicature. At the expiration of his first term as circuit judge of the then third judicial district of Mississippi, he was re-elected and continued in that office until his death, on the 14th of July, 1867. In every sphere of life, Judge Yerger maintained the same high character which embellished his career on the bench. He was a true patriot, and though widely differing from a majority of his fellow-citizens on many vital issues of his day, so lofty was his integrity, so firm were his convictions and so sincere were his motives that they commanded respect from the fiercest opposition. In politics he was a whig, and his services to that party both in Tennessee and Mississippi were great and lasting. He was twice elected to represent the city of Vicksburg in the legislature of the state, and while a member of that body, in 1841, he moved to reject the measure of Governor McNutt, which suggested the policy of repudiation. He was convinced that the payment of the bonds of the Union and Planters' bank was legally binding on the state, and advocated the payment. At this same session he introduced a bill for funding the indebtedness of the state, the wisdom of which was exemplified in the gradual recall of a large amount of outstanding warrants from a depucelate circulation and consequently to a speedy restoral of the credit of the state.

"In 1845 Judge Yerger removed to Washington county, Miss., and was soon restored to the legislature. In 1852 he was sent as a delegate to the whig convention at Baltimore, Md., and on his return was made one of the electors-at-large from the state. In the canvass which followed, his vigor and eloquence added greatly to the strength of his party and increased his reputation for consummate ability. On taking his seat on the bench Judge Yerger discarded all his party enthusiasm and carefully avoided all participation in politics, but when the question of secession began, in 1860, to assume a serious aspect, he used all his ability and influence in opposition to that measure. He considered it unnecessary, impolitic and ruinous, and in the March convention of 1861 he stemmed almost alone the revolutionary tide that swept over that body. While he deeply felt the wrongs of his people, he loved the Union and was willing to rest satisfied with the obtaining of further constitutional guarantees of equality within its folds. But when the die was cast and the fatal consequence thrust upon the country, he sent three of his sons to answer the call for troops of his state, in 1861, and afterward, as soon as he became of proper age, he buckled on the armor of a fourth son who was killed in battle in 1864. In 1865 Judge Yerger was unanimously elected as a delegate from his county to the convention for reorganizing the state government, and was chosen president of that body, over which he presided in a manner dignified and satisfactory. In private life his conversation was enlivening and entertaining, his manner attractive, and he possessed a rich vein of humor. He was popular among all classes of people, and to such an extent that at his re-election to the bench, in 1861, he is said to have lacked but one vote of being the unanimous choice of the district, and that one vote was not cast against him. He was the friend of the widow and orphan, and his charity was large and open handed. The Judge was married in 1833 to Miss Mary H. Bowen of Smith county, Tenn., and to them were born nine children. He died of congestion of the brain while holding court in Vicksburg." Hon. William G. Yerger was reared in Washington county, Miss., and received his literary education at Lebanon, Tenn., and Princeton, N. J. He began the study of law before the war, and in April, 1861, he entered the Confederate army as aid-de-camp to General Alcorn. He subsequently resigned and went to Virginia, where he enlisted in company K, Eighteenth Mississippi infantry, as a private, and served in that capacity until after the battle of Manassas, when he was elected second lieutenant, mainly commanding the company for a year. He then came to Mississippi and enlisted in Washington cavalry, company D, as a private, but was elected lieutenant. He surrendered with General Forrest on the 12th of May, 1865. While in Virginia he was in the battles of Bull Run, Manassas, Leesburg and Williamsburg, and in the West he was in the battles around Atlanta. He then returned home, was admitted to the bar at Greenville in 1865 and at once began practicing in this county. In 1865 he located at Greenville, and here he has since resided. He was in partnership with W. L. Nugent for six years, and then with Colonel Percy for sixteen years. At the latter's death he continued the firm with his son as Yerger & Percy. Mr. Yerger was mayor of Greenville at an early day; was elected state senator of Washington county in 1886, being the first separate senator that said county had; was a delegate to the state constitutional convention in 1890. The firm of Yerger & Percy are counsel for the board of levee commissioners, general counsel for the Louisville, New Orleans & Texas Railroad company, and counsel in the western part of Mississippi for the Georgia Pacific Railroad company. Mr. Yerger was married on the 6th of December, 1866, to Miss Jennie Hunter, a native of this state, and daughter of Ambrose and Jane Hunter, of Aberdeen, Miss. The fruits of this union were five children, two sons and two daughters living: Mary Louise, William Nugent, James Allen and Jennie. Annie died in infancy. The family are members of the Episcopal church. Mr. Yerger is a member of the Masonic, Odd Fellows, Knights of Pythias and Knights of Honor fraternities. He is a selfmade man, having started with nothing after the war; he has risen to the front ranks in his profession, and is held in high estimation by all.

A. F. Young, planter, Sessumsville, Miss., was born in Columbus, Miss., on the 4th of July, 1846, receiving the principal part of his education in that city, and then spent one year in the University of Alabama. When in his eighteenth year he was adjutant of a post at Meridian, Ala., and served in that capacity for eleven months, or until the close of the war. Afterward Mr. Young followed farming for a year, and then he attended Washington college, at Lexington, Va. (now Washington and Lee university), where he took one course. Returning then to Lowndes county he again began farming, and this has continued to be his chosen occupation since. He was married on the 15th of November, 1877, to Miss Emily M. Fox, a native of Monroe county, Miss., born in 1846, and the daughter of Henry A. and Emily M. (Gay) Fox, early settlers of Mississippi. Both are now deceased. In August, 1878, Mr. Young removed to Oktibbeha county, Miss., to his wife's homestead and is engaged in general farming. He also raises a good grade of livestock. His marriage resulted in the birth of one child, Hampton Gay, who is now attending school at Artesia, and is eleven years of age. Mr. Young is a member of the Farmers' Alliance, is president of the sub-alliance and also of the county alliance. He is chairman of the democratic executive committee and is captain of Oktibbeha rangers. He has never united with any church, although a strong believer of the Presbyterian doctrine. In all his ideas and tendencies Mr. Young is progressive and enterprising, a useful member of society, personally and in business circles. His parents, A. F. and E. L. (Davis) Young, were natives, respectively, of Tennessee and South Carolina, the former born on the 27th of March, 1809, and the latter on the 5th of May, 1817. A. F. Young, Sr., was reared in his native state, and when grown came to Mississippi. He received merely a common education, for he was left an orphan when quite young, and although he was a lawyer by profession he followed the occupation of a planter. He met and married Miss E. L. Davis, a daughter of John Davis, who was one of the earliest settlers of Columbus, and who built the first brick house in that city on the 7th of March, 1835. A. F. Young, Sr., purchased a large tract of land (two thousand acres), in the southwest portion of Lowndes county, and after engaging in farming he abandoned his law practice. This he continued until his death, on the 31st of August, 1862. His wife only survived him six months, dying February 7, 1863. To his marriage were born three daughters and two sons, who are named in the order of their births as follows: Ella Wright, wife of E. J. McGavock, of Nashville; Lelia A., wife of J. H. Sykes; Laura V., wife of Henry B. Whitfield, of Columbus; Alexander Frank (subject), and John Davis (deceased). The father of these children was a prosperous farmer and amassed a considerable fortune in land and negroes. He was a member of the Masonic fraternity and still takes a deep interest in the workings of the order. He and wife are members of the Presbyterian church.

A native Mississippian, Dr. J. W. Young, physician and surgeon, Grenada, Miss., was born in Carroll, now Montgomery county, Miss., in October, 1846, and was the son of Samuel H. and Kate (Small) Young, the father born in Albemarle county, Va., in 1821, and the mother in Tipton county, Tenn., about 1826. The parents were married in Carroll county, Miss., in 1845, and there Mr. Young passed the remainder of his days, his death occurring in 1861. He was a planter and bookkeeper and was once mayor of Old Middleton. He was an elder in the Presbyterian church. Mr. Young had two brothers, John O. and David Lucian, both of whom came to Carroll county, and there the former spent the balance of his days. John O. was a successful merchant at Middleton and held the office of sheriff for seven years. His death occurred in 1866. David Lucian is now living and is engaged in merchandising at Winona. He was postmaster there under Cleveland. Grandfather Harry Small was probably born in Montgomery county, Tenn., and died in Tipton county of that state when Mrs. Young was but six years of age. The latter came at once to Carroll county, Miss., with her uncle, Maj. John T. Brown, and there she grew to womanhood. She now makes her home with her son, Dr. J. W. Young. She was one of the pioneers of Carroll county and has seen its development from a wilderness to its present prosperous condition. She is a devout member of the Presbyterian church and a lady highly esteemed. To her marriage were born six children—three sons and three daughters—who are named in the order of their births as follows: Dr. J. W.; Samuel H., of the firm of Gauss & Shelton, of St. Louis; Harry S., now a prominent attorney of Covington, Tenn., was educated at Davidson college, N. C.; Mary J., wife of James W. Green, a planter of Tipton county, Tenn.; Elizabeth A., wife of John McCain, the present sheriff of Carroll county, and Nannie W. Dr. J. W. Young was educated at Old Middleton, and in 1864 he joined Armstrong's brigade, First Mississippi cavalry, and joined Johnston's army at Rome, Ga., fighting all the way to Atlanta, and was sent back with Hood. He was left on detached service in northern Alabama and was afterward captured at Selma, of that state, but was soon after paroled at Columbus, Ga. He then returned home and assisted his mother, who was left a widow with several small children to provide for and no visible means of support, as the property was all destroyed. The Doctor being the eldest, the means of support devolved upon him, and but for his indefatigable will and good management he would have given up in despair, for it was a hard struggle for many years. He succeeded in educating the children and keeping them together, and in the meantime studied medicine with an uncle, Dr. W. W. Lidell, of Carroll county, graduating from the medical department of the University of Louisiana, at New Orleans (now Tulane university), in 1869. He practiced at Smithville, in Carroll county, for a year, and then at Teoc until February, 1890, after which he removed to Grenada for better educational privileges. There he formed a partnership with Dr. G. W. Trimble, which at once brought him into prominence and a good practice. He is a leading member of the State Medical association and is a man of energy and enterprise. He is a man of good habits, is moral and upright, has made a success of life and is very popular in the community. He is the owner of a fine plantation of about one thousand five hundred acres in Carroll county and is devoted to stockraising, principally Jersey cattle. He was married in 1873 to Miss Mollie L. McCain, daughter of N. H. and Jane (Topp) McCain, born in Mecklenburg county, N. C., and Tennessee, respectively. Her parents came to Mississippi and were married in this state. The father followed planting in Carroll county and there died in 1881. Soon after he came to this state he was for a number of years teacher in the Female school, at Columbus. He was a fine scholar. His wife lives at Teoc, in Carroll county. Mrs. Young was born in Columbus, Miss. To the Doctor and wife have been born eight children, one son and six daughters living. He and wife are members of the Presbyterian church, in which he is an elder. He is a member of Ivanhoe lodge No. 8, Knights of Pythias, and is also a member of the Farmers' Alliance. He has always been active in politics and has frequently been solicited to run for office, but as often refused. He is the present chairman of the state senatorial democratic committee, was chairman of Carroll county democratic central committee, also of prohibition executive county committees, and is a member of the congressional committee. He has been a delegate to state conventions several times and represented his congressional district in the democratic national convention at St. Louis in 1888.

Robert Semple Young, planter, Natchez, Miss. Mr. Young's father, Dr. Benjamin Farar Young, was born in Philadelphia, Penn., in 1798, although the home of his parents was in Pointe Coupee parish, La., and he received an academic education at the University of Pennsylvania. He also graduated in physic from that institution, but did not practice his profession, preferring rather to devote his time and attention to his large planting interests in Louisiana and Adams county, Miss. He was married in Wilkinson county, Miss., in 1824, to Miss Catherine Semple, who was originally from West Feliciana parish, La., born in 1806.

The fruits of this union were two children: Jane Semple, who became the wife of James W. Metcalfe (deceased), and Robert Semple, the subject of this sketch. Mrs. Young, who was a consistent member of the Episcopal church, died in 1833, and soon after Mr. Young married Miss Martha J. Wade. In 1835 they came to Adams county, Miss., and settled on the Beaux Pres plantation, where he made a lovely and attractive home. He died in 1860 and was also a member of the Episcopal church. He was a man of positive character, clear, intellect and excellent business ability, and was fitted in every way to make life a success. He was quiet and unassuming and never aspired to office. He left a handsome property. His father, Hon. Samuel Charles Young, was born in Philadelphia, Penn., in 1771, was educated and married there, and in 1795 removed to Pointe Coupee parish, La., thence to New Orleans, where he died in 1832. He was educated as a lawyer, but inherited a large estate and for about fifteen years was engaged in planting in Pointe Coupee parish, but afterward devoted his attention to his profession, becoming a very successful lawyer in New Orleans. He was at one time an alderman of that city and while in that office was sent as a special commissioner to Washington city in behalf of his adopted city, to obtain from congress the grant to the city of New Orleans of all the public property within the city limits, including the public grounds, wharfs, etc. He was afterward sent to Europe in behalf of the city to whose interests he was devoted, greatly to the neglect of his own. He was a leading attorney and was well known and esteemed. He was the son of Samuel Young, a native of Philadelphia, who there spent his entire life as a successful merchant, and who in turn was the son of John Young, a native of England. The last named when a child came to America and very successfully pursued the business of ship chandler at Philadelphia, where he spent the remaining years of his life. Mr. Young's grandfather, Robert Semple, was a native of Carlisle, Penn., and began life as an ensign under Gen. Anthony Wayne in his northwestern Indian campaign. He afterward came to the Southwest as adjutant of the First United States infantry and was located at Fort Adams, where he died. He was a wealthy planter and was prominent in public affairs, having held various local offices. He was county magistrate and captain in the mounted cavalry, etc. His wife died at Fort Adams also. She was formerly Isabella Turnbull, a native of Mobile, Ala., and was a daughter of John Turnbull, who was a Scotch adventurer connected with the English army in west Florida for a number of years. The latter passed the closing scenes of his life in Baton Rouge as an extensive land speculator and Indian trader and became very rich. The father of our subject had four children by his second marriage: Margaret A. died in 1875. Samuel Charles, now district judge at St. Joseph, La., an able lawyer and well-to-do planter, was educated at Oakland college and at the University of Pennsylvania. He was a soldier in General Forrest's cavalry. Wade Ross was educated in the University of Virginia and is now a lawyer and planter of Vicksburg. He was a soldier in the Virginia and Tennessee armies. William Conner is the present sheriff of Tensas parish, La., which position he has held for ten or twelve years. He was a lieutenant in the Second Louisiana cavalry in the Tennessee army and was afterward on Red river. Robert Semple Young was born in Wilkinson county, Miss., in 1832, graduated from Yale college in 1853, and began life as a planter on his father's plantation in Louisiana, making that his principal occupation through life. At the breaking out of war he joined the Jeff Davis legion and served one year in the Virginia army, being in many of the principal engagements. He then served one year with Adams' cavalry in the Tennessee army and was captured during the siege of Vicksburg as a spy. He soon escaped, however, and although he was captured several times after this, he escaped soon after. After his service of one year in the Tennessee army he served about a year on Red river in the Second Louisiana cavalry. During Cleveland's administration Mr. Young served as inspecting officer in the surveyor's department of the customhouse at New Orleans. He is still a resident of the old Beaux Pres plantation, eight miles southeast of Natchez, which consists of five hundred acres. Mr. Young is an intelligent gentleman whom it is a pleasure to meet. He is single.

The following sketch was received too late for alphabetical insertion:

Dr. Robert J. Lyles, Byhalia, Miss. The subject of this sketch is the fifth son of Archibald M. Lyles, of Baltimore, Md., and Harriet Feaster Lyles, of Virginia, who moved to Kentucky in 1831. Locating in Logan county, the father engaged in the practice of law, where continuous success elevated him to the position of district judge. Every worthy enterprise won his earnest, liberal support, and his generosity and hospitality amounted almost to prodigality. He was a devout Christian, a member of the Presbyterian church, and much of the success that attended his long, happy life, reflected the Christian influence of his amiable wife. Dr. Robert J. Lyles was born near Russellville, Ky., in 1842. Here his education was begun, and even at an early age gave evidence of the genius that marked his career in later years. When the vicissitudes of the Civil war came on he joined Colonel Hunt's Fifth Kentucky regiment, General Hanson's brigade, Breckinridge's division, and followed the changing fortunes of the South till the close of the struggle, bearing home the proud consciousness that he had done his duty, and a wound in the side to attest his valor for the lost cause. After graduating at the School of Physicians and Surgeons in New York, with the class of 1868, he located at Triune, Tenn., where he remained until 1870. In 1871 he married the accomplished Mrs. S. C. Parr, a daughter of Joseph Abernathy, a prominent lawyer and member of the legislature of Missouri, who moved to Tennessee prior to his daughter's marriage. The Doctor then located at Byhalia, Miss., where, by his social magnetism and superior qualifications, he has built up an extensive practice. Thoroughly devoted to his profession, and happily blending the practical and theoretical, we find in him all that pre-eminently characterizes the true physician. Indeed, in all that pertains to the progressive steps of his profession, he is a leading spirit and an active worker in its associations. To courteous manners, a candid, fearless spirit, and high intellectual attainments, he joins the lavish generosity of his worthy father, and his home, blessed by an entertaining, hospitable wife, a fascinating daughter and two sons, offers a hearty welcome to hosts of friends.

Errata, Omissions, Additions, Etc.

Page 22. In line three read "Liberia" instead of "Siberia."

Page 24. "Amos B. Johnston" should be "Amos R. Johnston."

Page 29. "E. N. Yerger" should be "E. M. Yerger."

Page 235. The word "Okolona" is misspelled.

Page 243. "Marsckalk" should be "Marschalk," and "I. F. H. Claiborne" should be "J. F. H. Claiborne."

Page 245. "John I. McRae" should be "John J. McRae."

Pages 246 and 249. "Samuel D. Harper" should be "Sam D. Harper."

Page 247. The date in the top line should be 1866 instead of 1870.

Page 248. "J. M. Partridge" should be "I. M. Partridge," "E. W. Yerger" should be "E. M. Yerger" and "J. L. Powers" should be "J. L. Power."

Page 249. "I. M. Howry" should be "J. M. Howry" and "L. W. Garrett" should be "L. M. Garrett."

Page 250. In line nine from the bottom there should be no comma after "Miss."

Page 251. "A. B. Hurst" should be "A. B. Hurt."
Page 273. Vol. I. Although the name came from the War Department as "Capt. James Kemps" the publishers think the name should be "Kemper."
Page 310. The date in line twelve should be "1833" instead of "1883."
Page 315. Third line from the bottom read "union school" instead of "university school."
Page 316. Third line from the bottom read "four" instead of "forty."
Page 323. In lines four and five read "Early in 1848" instead of "In January, 1848."
Page 325. In ninth line from the bottom read "Confederate States army" instead of "Confederate States of America."
Page 329. In line fourteen "LL. B." should be "B. L. U."
Page 332. In line three from the bottom read "Lipsey" instead of "Tipsey."
Page 334. In line ten from the bottom read "Featherstun" instead of "Featherston."
Page 344. In line twelve read "William W. Rivers" instead of "Rev. William Rivers."
Page 346. In line twenty-two read "Lexington Normal college" instead of "Lexington Normal school."
Page 347. At the close of the chapter it speaks of "two" chapters on education and of a "corresponding" chapter in Volume I. The two chapters were united in one in Volume II.
Page 395. In line nine from the bottom the word "Manor" should follow the word "Saunders."
Pages 399–400. The given name of the mother of the Marshall brothers was given differently by them; the publishers could not reconcile the discrepancy.
Page 423. In the sixth line read "Mayers" instead of "Myers."
Page 427. Read "Mrs. Dona Meeks" instead of "Miss Dona Meeks."
Page 430. Read "Merrill" instead of "Merill."
Page 682. The date of the birth of Reuben J. Right should be 1834 instead of 1884.
Page 762. In line twelve read "fifth" instead of "third" and in line thirty-one read "Lida" instead of "Lydia."
Page 769. "John M. Simonton" should be followed by a comma.
The map in Vol. I. entitled "Map of the Mississippi country in 1764" should be entitled "Copy of a map of the Mississippi country made in 1764."

SUPPLEMENTARY INDEX FOR VOLUME I.

The matter indicated below for Volume I, was, much of it, received or returned revised too late to be indexed in its due order; hence this supplementary index.

	PAGE.		PAGE.
Addenda, Errors and Omission	1247	Harvey, W. H.	888
Alcorn, William A., Jr.	291	Hill, Robert Andrews	922
Allen, David J.	300	Hudspeth, George W.	970
Anderson, William W.	306	Ivy, J. W.	1007
Berry, Rev. W. E. and the Berry family	1159	Johnson, J. E.	1036
Buck, Edward Jefferies, Nathaniel Jefferies and William Henry	453	Johnson, Mrs. Mary	1041
		Johnson, Matthew F.	1029
Buckley, James M.	1163	Johnson, Samuel M.	1037
Campbell, William R.	498	Lemly family, Percy, Samuel, Col. Samuel and William Steele Lemly	1118, 1119
Campbell, William R., Sr., and William R., Jr.	499		
Carmack, Dr. Frank T.	512	Ligon, B. T.	1131
Carr, John W.	514	Lowry, Dr. M. J.	1160
Cato, Edwin	533	Lynch, James D.	1164
Cauthen, John B.	534	McCarty, Michael	1175
Chalmers, Gen. James R.	535	McFarland, Baxter	1088
Cochran, M. D., Thomas J.	560	McGehee, Hon. J. Burruss	1203
Collins, Elisha P.	574	McGehee, M. D., Thomas W.	1203
Cowan, Capt. J. J.	596	McLeod, John W.	1227
Forman, George D.	758	McNeill, Dr. G. H.	1235
Foxworth, John and Eugene E.	765	McNutt, Gov. Alex. G.	1236
Grafton, J. M.	808	McRee, Samuel P.	1240
Harrison, LL. D., M. D., William H.	882	Taylor, Mrs. Dr. Littleton L.	1180

POPULATION OF MISSISSIPPI BY MINOR CIVIL DIVISIONS.*

DEPARTMENT OF THE INTERIOR,
CENSUS OFFICE,
WASHINGTON, D. C., October 13, 1891.

This bulletin gives the population of the state of Mississippi in detail by counties, beats, cities, wards of cities, towns and villages according to the official count of the returns made under the eleventh census, taken as of June 1, 1890; also the population of the same divisions according to the census of 1880, in order to show the increase or decrease during the decade. The population of the state under the census of 1880 was 1,131,597; under the present census the population returned is 1,289,600, an increase of 158,003, or 13.96 per cent. Since 1880 Pearl River county has been organized from parts of Hancock and Marion counties. The name of Sumner county has been changed to Webster. Of the seventy-five counties in the state eleven show decreases. The summary which follows gives the population of each county according to the censuses of 1890 and 1880, and the increase or decrease in number and per cent.:

COUNTIES.	POPULATION.		INCREASE.	
	1890.	1880.	Number.	Per cent.
The state	1,289,600	1,131,597	158,003	13.96
Adams	26,031	22,649	3,382	14.93
Alcorn	13,115	14,272	a1,157	a8.11
Amite	18,198	14,004	4,194	29.95
Attala	22,213	19,988	2,225	11.13
Benton	10,585	11,023	a438	a3.97
Bolivar	29,980	18,652	11,328	60.73
Calhoun	14,688	13,492	1,196	8.86
Carroll	18,773	17,795	978	5.50
Chickasaw	19,891	17,905	1,986	11.09
Choctaw	10,847	9,036	1,811	20.04
Claiborne	14,516	16,768	a2,252	a13.43
Clarke	15,826	15,021	805	5.36
Clay	18,607	17,367	1,240	7.14
Coahoma	18,342	13,568	4,774	35.19
Copiah	30,233	27,552	2,681	9.73
Covington	8,299	5,993	2,306	38.48
De Soto	24,183	22,924	1,259	5.49
Franklin	10,424	9,729	695	7.14
Greene	3,906	3,194	712	22.29
Grenada	14,974	12,071	2,903	24.05
Hancock	8,318	6,439	1,879	29.18

* Special report to the Goodspeed Publishing Company.   a Decrease.

SUMMARY BY COUNTIES—Continued.

COUNTIES.	POPULATION.		INCREASE.	
	1890.	**1880.**	Number.	Per cent.
Harrison	12,481	7,895	4,586	58.09
Hinds	39,279	43,958	a4,679	a10.64
Holmes	30,970	27,164	3,806	14.01
Issaquena	12,318	10,004	2,314	23.13
Itawamba	11,708	10,663	1,045	9.80
Jackson	11,251	7,607	3,644	47.90
Jasper	14,785	12,126	2,659	21.93
Jefferson	18,947	17,314	1,633	9.43
Jones	8,333	3,828	4,505	117.69
Kemper	17,961	15,719	2,242	14.26
Lafayette	20,553	21,671	a1,118	a5.16
Lauderdale	29,661	21,501	8,160	37.95
Lawrence	12,318	9,420	2,898	30.76
Leake	14,803	13,146	1,657	12.60
Lee	20,040	20,470	a430	a2.10
Le Flore	16,869	10,246	6,623	64.64
Lincoln	17,912	13,547	4,365	32.22
Lowndes	27,047	28,244	a1,197	a4.24
Madison	27,321	25,866	1,455	5.63
Marion	9,532	6,901	2,631	38.12
Marshall	26,043	29,330	a3,287	a11.21
Monroe	30,730	28,553	2,177	7.62
Montgomery	14,459	13,348	1,111	8.32
Neshoba	11,146	8,741	2,405	27.51
Newton	16,625	13,436	3,189	23.73
Noxubee	27,338	29,874	a2,536	a8.49
Oktibbeha	17,694	15,978	1,716	10.74
Panola	26,977	28,352	a1,375	a4.85
Pearl River	2,957	......	2,957	......
Perry	6,494	3,427	3,067	89.50
Pike	21,203	16,688	4,515	27.06
Pontotoc	14,940	13,858	1,082	7.81
Prentiss	13,679	12,158	1,521	12.51
Quitman	3,286	1,407	1,879	133.55
Rankin	17,922	16,752	1,170	6.98
Scott	11,740	10,845	895	8.25
Sharkey	8,382	6,306	2,076	32.92
Simpson	10,138	8,008	2,130	26.60
Smith	10,635	8,088	2,547	31.49
Sunflower	9,384	4,661	4,723	101.33
Tallahatchie	14,361	10,926	3,435	31.44
Tate	19,253	18,721	532	2.84
Tippah	12,951	12,867	84	0.65
Tishomingo	9,302	8,774	528	6.02
Tunica	12,158	8,461	3,697	43.69
Union	15,606	13,030	2,576	19.77
Warren	33,164	31,238	1,926	6.17

a Decrease.

SUMMARY BY COUNTIES—Continued.

COUNTIES.	POPULATION.		INCREASE.	
	1890.	1880.	Number.	Per cent.
Washington	40,414	25,367	15,047	59.32
Wayne	9,817	8,741	1,076	12.31
Webster	12,060	9,534	2,526	26.49
Wilkinson	17,592	17,815	a223	a1.25
Winston	12,089	10,087	2,002	19.85
Yalobusha	16,629	15,649	980	6.26
Yazoo	36,394	33,845	2,549	7.53

The population of the nineteen cities and towns having 2,000 or more inhabitants, in the order of their rank, is as follows:

CITIES AND TOWNS.	COUNTIES.	POPULATION.		INCREASE.	
		1890.	1880.	Number.	Per cent.
Vicksburg city	Warren	13,373	11,814	1,559	13.20
Meridian city	Lauderdale	10,624	4,008	6,616	165.07
Natchez city	Adams	10,101	7,058	3,043	43.11
Greenville town	Washington	6,658	2,191	4,467	203.88
Jackson city	Hinds	5,920	5,204	716	13.76
Columbus city	Lowndes	4,559	3,955	604	15.27
Aberdeen city	Monroe	3,449	2,339	1,110	47.46
Yazoo City	Yazoo	3,286	2,542	744	29.27
Biloxi city	Harrison	3,234	1,540	1,694	110.00
Wesson town	Copiah	3,168	1,707	1,461	85.59
Water Valley town	Yalobusha	2,832	2,220	612	27.57
West Point town	Clay	2,762	1,786	976	54.65
Grenada town	Grenada	2,416	1,914	502	26.23
McComb City town	Pike	2,383	1,982	401	20.23
Holly Springs city	Marshall	2,246	2,370	a124	a5.23
Brookhaven town	Lincoln	2,142	1,615	527	32.63
Canton city	Madison	2,131	2,083	48	2.30
Corinth city	Alcorn	2,111	2,275	a164	a7.21
Okolona town	Chickasaw	2,099	1,858	241	12.97

a Decrease.

The following table gives the population of each county in detail by minor civil divisions; also the population of all incorporated places, and of all unincorporated places having two hundred inhabitants or more, as far as it has been possible to make the separation from the returns of the enumerators:

MINOR CIVIL DIVISIONS.		1890.	1880.
ADAMS COUNTY		26,031	22,649
Beat 1, including Natchez city		15,393	12,058
Natchez city		10,101	7,058
Ward 1	2,351		
Ward 2	4,329		
Ward 3	1,736		
Ward 4	1,685		
Beat 2		2,574	2,600
Beat 3		1,930	1,834
Beat 4		2,850	2,679
Beat 5		3,284	3,478
ALCORN COUNTY		13,115	14,272
Beat 1, including Corinth city and Wenasoga town (a)		3,811	4,174
Corinth city		2,111	2,275
Ward 1	270		
Ward 2	952		
Ward 3	193		
Ward 4	554		
Ward 5	142		
Beat 2		2,634	2,567
Beat 3, including Rienzi town (a)		2,136	2,713
Beat 4, including Kossuth town		2,384	2,938
Kossuth town		165	132
Beat 5		2,150	1,880
AMITE COUNTY		18,198	14,004
Beat 1, including Liberty town (a)		4,161	3,823
Beat 2		3,483	2,648
Beat 3, including Gloster town		4,779	2,798
Gloster town		1,142	....
Beat 4		3,183	2,586
Beat 5, including Gillsburg town		2,592	2,149
Gillsburg town		95	....
ATTALA COUNTY		22,213	19,988
Beat 1. Kosciusko, including Kosciusko town		4,968	4,230
Kosciusko town		1,394	1,126
Beat 2. Northeast, including McCool town		3,752	3,122
McCool town		246	....
Beat 3. Mitchell Mills		3,766	3,166
Beat 4. Newport, including Newport and Sallis towns		5,172	5,724
Newport town		52	107
Sallis town		156	132
Beat 5. Center		4,555	3,746

a Not separately returned.

MINOR CIVIL DIVISIONS.	1890.	1880.
BENTON COUNTY	10,585	11,023
Beat 1	2,121	2,082
Beat 2, including Lamar town (a) and Michigan City	3,095	3,803
Michigan City	129	91
Beat 3, including Ashland town	2,227	2,557
Ashland town	138	174
Beat 4	1,175	1,242
Beat 5, including Hickory Flat town	1,967	1,339
Hickory Flat town	293	
BOLIVAR COUNTY	29,980	18,652
Beat 1	4,729	2,276
Beat 2, including Concordia town (a)	6,817	3,956
Beat 3, including Cleveland (a) and Rosedale towns	7,359	3,980
Rosedale town	376	
Beat 4, including Bolivar town	4,159	4,036
Bolivar town	102	
Beat 5, including Huntington and Shaw towns	6,916	4,404
Huntington town	155	
Shaw town	201	
CALHOUN COUNTY	14,688	13,492
Beat 1, including Pittsboro town (a)	3,070	2,915
Beat 2	2,517	2,217
Beat 3, including Banner town (a)	2,939	2,803
Beat 4	3,409	3,103
Beat 5	2,753	2,454
CARROLL COUNTY	18,773	17,795
Beat 1	2,132	1,948
Beat 2	2,411	2,002
Beat 3	4,026	3,690
Beat 4, including Carrollton town	5,365	5,122
Carrollton town	488	394
Beat 5, including Vaiden town	4,839	5,033
Vaiden town	533	526
CHICKASAW COUNTY	19,891	17,905
Beat 1, including Houston town	3,108	2,425
Houston town	893	480
Beat 2, including Houlka town	3,382	5,413
Houlka town	99	
Beat 3, including Okolona town	4,694	3,523
Okolona town	2,099	1,858
Beat 4, including Buena Vista and Egypt towns (a)	4,325	3,860
Beat 5, including Atlanta town (a)	4,382	2,684
CHOCTAW COUNTY	10,847	9,036
Beat 1, including Chester town (a)	2,290	2,327
Beat 2	2,490	1,854
Beat 3, including French Camp village	2,214	1,862
French Camp village	267	420
Beat 4, including Weir town (a)	1,338	1,341
Beat 5, including Ackerman town (a)	2,515	1,652

a Not separately returned.

MINOR CIVIL DIVISIONS.	1890.	1880.
CLAIBORNE COUNTY	14,516	16,768
Beat 1, including Port Gibson town	4,954	4,790
Port Gibson town	1,524	....
Beat 2	2,366	2,180
Beat 3	2,360	2,466
Beat 4	2,616	4,198
Beat 5, including Martin town	2,220	3,134
Martin town	76	....
CLARKE COUNTY	15,826	15,021
Beat 1. Quitman, including Quitman town	2,492	2,521
Quitman town	395	410
Beat 2. Shubuta, including Shubuta town	4,115	4,324
Shubuta town	589	754
Beat 3. Enterprise, including Enterprise town (a)	4,690	4,226
Beat 4. Energy	1,750	1,050
Beat 5. Maxville	2,779	2,900
CLAY COUNTY	18,607	17,367
Beat 1	3,006	2,921
Beat 2, including West Point town	5,913	5,251
West Point town	2,762	1,786
Beat 3	3,786	3,668
Beat 4	2,979	3,237
Beat 5	2,923	2,290
COAHOMA COUNTY	18,342	13,568
Beat 1	2,480	1,744
Beat 2, including Friar Point town	4,456	3,333
Friar Point town	674	676
Beat 3, including Jonestown town	3,908	2,919
Jonestown town	286	147
Beat 4, including Clarksdale town	4,743	4,060
Clarksdale town	781	....
Beat 5	2,755	1,512
COPIAH COUNTY	30,233	27,552
Beat 1, including Gallman and Hazlehurst towns (a)	6,237	7,518
Beat 2, including Beauregard (a), Hewitt Springs (a), and Wesson towns	6,530	5,523
Wesson town	3,168	1,707
Beat 3	4,659	3,882
Beat 4	5,426	4,171
Beat 5, including Crystal Springs village	7,381	6,458
Crystal Springs village	997	915
COVINGTON COUNTY	8,299	5,993
Beat 1. Williamsburg	1,830	1,164
Beat 2. Watts	1,155	898
Beat 3. Holloday Creek	1,508	974
Beat 4. Mount Carmel	2,239	1,913
Beat 5. Ocoha	1,567	1,044

a Not separately returned.

MINOR CIVIL DIVISIONS.	1890.	1880.
DE SOTO COUNTY	24,183	22,924
Beat 1 (b), including Olive Branch village	5,960	6,556
Olive branch village	199	73
Beat 2, including Pleasant Hill town (c)	4,247	3,430
Beat 3	4,819	3,475
Beat 4, including Eudora town	3,483	3,013
Eudora town	106	
Beat 5, including Hernando city, Love (a), and Nesbitt towns	5,674	6,450
Hernando city	602	583
Nesbitt town	152	117
FRANKLIN COUNTY	10,424	9,729
Beat 1, including Knoxville and Roxie (a) towns	3,314	2,965
Knoxville town	91	
Beat 2, including Hamburg town (a)	1,626	2,040
Beat 3, including Meadville town (a)	1,790	1,791
Beat 4	1,847	1,592
Beat 5	1,847	1,341
GREENE COUNTY	3,906	3,194
Beat 1. Leakesville	584	455
Beat 2. State Line	940	942
Beat 3. Washington	957	672
Beat 4. Vernal	845	649
Beat 5. Salim	580	476
GRENADA COUNTY	14,974	12,071
Beat 1, including Grenada town	5,653	4,867
Grenada town	2,416	1,914
Beat 2	3,405	2,476
Beat 3	1,916	1,654
Beat 4, including Hardy Station town (a)	2,058	1,634
Beat 5	1,942	1,440
HANCOCK COUNTY (d)	8,318	6,439
Beat 1. Pearlington, including Logtown village	1,598	1,301
Logtown village	353	
Beat 2. Gainesville	1,413	1,295
Beat 3. Yamacraw	1,069	599
Beat 4. Jordan River	1,143	809
Beat 5. Bay St. Louis, including Bay St. Louis and Waveland cities	3,095	2,435
Bay St. Louis city	1,974	1,978
Ward 1 452		
Ward 2 884		
Ward 3 442		
Ward 4 196		
Waveland city	328	
HARRISON COUNTY	12,481	7,895
Beat 1. Biloxi, including Biloxi city	3,839	2,061
Biloxi city	3,234	1,540
Ward 1 708		

a Not separately returned.
b Pleasant Hill town returned as in beat 1 in 1880.
c Not separately returned; returned as in beat 1 in 1880.
d Part taken to form Pearl River county in 1890.

MINOR CIVIL DIVISIONS.	1890.	1880.
Ward 2... 1,074		
Ward 3.. 489		
Ward 4.. 963		
Beat 2. Mississippi City, including Handsboro and Mississippi City towns	2,695	1,989
Handsboro town...	1,021	519
Mississippi City town..	534	265
Beat 3. Pass Christian, including Pass Christian and Wolf towns.......	3,654	2,702
Pass Christian town..	1,705	1,410
Wolf town...	471	....
Beat 4..	1,317	606
Beat 5..	927	537
Cat, Deer, and Ship islands (e).......................................	49	....
HINDS COUNTY...	39,279	43,958
Beat 1, including Clinton town (a)....................................	6,711	7,173
Beat 2, including Bolton and Edwards towns (a).......................	8,624	8,334
Beat 3, including Utica town..	6,327	8,237
Utica town...	370	230
Beat 4, including Learned and Raymond (a) towns.....................	5,453	9,121
Learned town..	119	....
Beat 5, including Byram town (a), Jackson city, and Terry town (a)....	12,164	11,093
Jackson city...	5,920	5,204
Ward 1... 1,298		
Ward 2... 2,223		
Ward 3... 1,126		
Ward 4... 1,273		
HOLMES COUNTY..	30,970	27,164
Beat 1, including Franklin (a), Gray Mill (a), and Lexington towns.....	6,127	5,497
Lexington town..	1,075	798
Beat 2, including Durant, Emory (a), and West Station (a) towns.......	5,813	5,044
Durant town...	1,259	724
Beat 3, including Ebenezer, Goodman, and Pickens (a) towns...........	3,679	5,583
Ebenezer town...	127	....
Goodman town...	354	378
Beat 4, including Mileston and Thornton towns (a)....................	6,881	4,294
Beat 5, including Howard Station and Tchula towns (a)................	8,470	6,746
ISSAQUENA COUNTY...	12,318	10,004
Beat 1..	2,253	1,400
Beat 2..	1,402	1,110
Beat 3..	1,958	2,156
Beat 4, including Mayersville town (a)................................	2,534	2,139
Beat 5, including Duncansby town (a).................................	4,171	3,199
ITAWAMBA COUNTY..	11,708	10,663
Beat 1..	2,843	2,153
Beat 2..	2,578	2,559
Beat 3..	2,113	2,160
Beat 4..	1,916	1,769
Beat 5..	2,258	2,022

a Not separately returned.
e Not located in beats.

MINOR CIVIL DIVISIONS.	1890.	1880.
JACKSON COUNTY	11,251	7,607
Beat 1. Northeast	1,156	572
Beat 2. Central	755	813
Beat 3. Southeast, including Scranton town	5,228	3,654
Scranton town	1,353	1,052
Beat 4. Southwest, including Ocean Springs town	3,466	2,208
Ocean Springs town	1,148	849
Beat 5. Northwest	638	360
Horn Island (a)	8	....
JASPER COUNTY	14,785	12,126
Beat 1. Center	3,048	2,790
Beat 2. Northeast	2,660	2,452
Beat 3. Northwest	1,633	1,412
Beat 4. Southwest	2,940	1,939
Beat 5. Southeast, including Heidelberg town	4,504	3,533
Heidelberg town	216	....
JEFFERSON COUNTY	18,947	17,314
Beat 1	2,976	3,409
Beat 2	4,129	3,844
Beat 3, including Fayette and Harriston towns (b)	5,064	4,036
Beat 4	2,825	2,411
Beat 5, including Rodney town	3,953	3,614
Rodney town	702	733
JONES COUNTY	8,333	3,828
Beat 1. Ellisville, including Ellisville town	1,773	381
Ellisville town	961	37
Beat 2. Laurel, including Laurel town (b)	2,563	1,297
Beat 3. Erata	1,460	795
Beat 4. Southeast	597	465
Beat 5. Southwest	1,940	890
KEMPER COUNTY	17,961	15,719
Beat 1. Scooba, including Scooba town (b)	4,663	4,362
Beat 2. Gainesville	3,516	2,766
Beat 3. Moscow	3,412	2,860
Beat 4. Kellis Store	2,972	2,585
Beat 5. De Kalb, including De Kalb town	3,398	3,146
De Kalb town	240	....
LAFAYETTE COUNTY	20,553	21,671
Beat 1, including Oxford city	4,953	6,121
Oxford city	1,546	1,534
Beat 2	2,321	2,796
Beat 3, including Abbeville town (b)	4,996	5,618
Beat 4, including Taylor town (b)	4,018	3,662
Beat 5, including Paris town (b)	4,265	3,474

a Not located in beat.
b Not separately returned.

MINOR CIVIL DIVISIONS.		1890.	1880.
LAUDERDALE COUNTY		29,661	21,501
Beat 1, Meridian, including Meridian city		16,925	9,110
Meridian city		10,624	4,008
Ward 1	2,847		
Ward 2	2,141		
Ward 3	3,078		
Ward 4	1,315		
Ward 5	1,243		
Beat 2. Lauderdale, including Lauderdale town		3,571	3,580
Lauderdale town		322	266
Beat 3. Daleville		3,341	3,080
Beat 4. Tunnel Hill		2,610	2,650
Beat 5. Hurricane Creek		3,214	3,081
LAWRENCE COUNTY		12,318	9,420
Beat 1		2,193	2,083
Beat 2		1,076	852
Beat 3		2,020	1,468
Beat 4		4,480	3,003
Beat 5		2,549	2,014
LEAKE COUNTY		14,803	13,146
Beat 1. Edinburg, including Edinburg town		3,465	2,392
Edinburg town		123	....
Beat 2. Carthage, including Carthage town		3,390	3,857
Carthage town		322	285
Beat 3. Thomastown		2,276	2,066
Beat 4. Good Hope		1,980	1,800
Beat 5. Walnut Grove, including Walnut Grove town		3,692	3,031
Walnut Grove town		166	....
LEE COUNTY		20,040	20,470
Beat 1, including part of Baldwyn town (c) and Guntown (b)		3,641	3,717
Beat 2, including Birmingham and Saltillo towns (b)		3,015	3,564
Beat 3, including Tupelo town		5,095	4,692
Tupelo town		1,477	1,008
Beat 4, including Verona town		4,053	4,677
Verona town		465	596
Beat 5, including Shannon town		4,236	3,820
Shannon town		329	232
LE FLORE COUNTY		16,869	10,246
Beat 1		3,241	1,864
Beat 2		3,537	2,273
Beat 3, including Greenwood town		3,954	2,117
Greenwood town		1,055	308
Beat 4		2,875	1,965
Beat 5, including Sidon town		3,262	2,027
Sidon town		119	....

b Not separately returned.

c Not separately returned; in beat 1 Lee county, and beat 3 Prentiss county.

MINOR CIVIL DIVISIONS.		1890.	1880.
LINCOLN COUNTY		17,912	13,547
Beat 1, including Bogue Chitto and Brookhaven towns		7,175	5,733
Bogue Chitto town		300	143
Brookhaven town		2,142	1,615
Beat 2		2,064	1,321
Beat 3		2,423	1,455
Beat 4		2,131	1,643
Beat 5		4,119	3,395
LOWNDES COUNTY		27,047	28,244
Beat 1			4,762
Beat 2, including Columbus city			5,519
Columbus city (d)	4,559		
Ward 1	716		
Ward 2	605	b14,703	
Ward 3	804		
Ward 4	1,579		
Ward 5	303		
Ward 6	552		
Beat 3			3,649
Beat 4, including Crawford town		5,580	6,056
Crawford town		225	304
Beat 5, including Artesia and Mayhew towns		6,764	8,258
Artesia town		313	150
Mayhew town		106	197
MADISON COUNTY		27,321	25,866
Beat 1, including Canton city		8,647	8,597
Canton city		2,131	2,083
Beat 2. Vernon, including Flora town		3,615	2,978
Flora town		228	
Beat 3. Livingston		5,779	6,002
Beat 4. Sharon		4,018	3,360
Beat 5. Camden		5,262	4,929
MARION COUNTY (a)		9,532	6,901
Beat 1, including Columbia town (b)		2,058	1,659
Beat 2		2,061	1,267
Beat 3		1,471	1,167
Beat 4		1,825	1,447
Beat 5, including Purvis town		2,117	1,361
Purvis town		287	
MARSHALL COUNTY		26,043	29,330
Beat 1, including Holly Springs city		7,859	8,823
Holly Springs city		2,246	2,370
Ward 1	486		
Ward 2	377		
Ward 3	366		
Ward 4	452		
Ward 5	565		

b Not separately returned.
d Population in 1880, 3,955.
a Part taken to form Pearl River county in 1890.

MINOR CIVIL DIVISIONS.	1890.	1880.
Beat 2, including Mount Pleasant town	4,135	6,393
Mount Pleasant town	110	135
Beat 3, including Byhalia town	5,526	6,028
Byhalia town	474	346
Beat 4, including Chulahoma and Wall Hill towns (b)	4,797	4,546
Beat 5, including Bethlehem, Potts Camp and Waterford towns (b)	3,726	3,540
MONROE COUNTY	30,730	28,553
Beat 1, including Amory and Cotton Gin Port (b) towns	4,253	3,593
Amory town	739	....
Beat 2	3,285	3,052
Beat 3	4,374	3,517
Beat 4, including Aberdeen city	12,576	12,456
Aberdeen city	3,449	2,339
Ward 1 410		
Ward 2 320		
Ward 3 738		
Ward 4 582		
Ward 5 622		
Ward 6 777		
Beat 5	6,242	5,935
MONTGOMERY COUNTY	14,459	13,348
Beat 1. Winona, including Winona town	5,482	4,496
Winona town	1,648	1,204
Beat 2. Duck Hill, including Duck Hill town	2,661	2,787
Duck Hill town	332	151
Beat 3. Lodi, including Lodi town (b)	2,128	2,046
Beat 4. Mayfield	2,098	1,666
Beat 5. Poplar Creek	2,090	2,353
NESHOBA COUNTY	11,146	8,741
Beat 1. Philadelphia	2,390	1,602
Beat 2. Lees	1,427	992
Beat 3. Moguehesha	2,345	2,051
Beat 4. Hay	3,408	2,698
Beat 5. Riley	1,576	1,398
NEWTON COUNTY	16,625	13,436
Beat 1	3,157	2,596
Beat 2	2,758	2,151
Beat 3	3,362	2,744
Beat 4	4,107	2,995
Beat 5	3,241	2,950
NOXUBEE COUNTY	27,338	29,874
Beat 1	7,684	8,609
Beat 2	4,533	4,537
Beat 3, including Macon town	5,509	6,351
Macon town	1,565	2,074
Beat 4, including Shuqualak town	4,809	4,938

b Not separately returned.

MINOR CIVIL DIVISIONS.	1890.	1880.
Shuqualak town	601	352
Beat 5, including Brookville town	4,803	5,439
Brookville town	424	284
OKTIBBEHA COUNTY	17,694	15,978
Beat 1, including Starkville town	5,429	4,105
Starkville town	1,725	1,500
Beat 2	3,174	3,506
Beat 3	2,685	1,871
Beat 4, including Sturges town	2,385	2,161
Sturges town	203	....
Beat 5	4,021	4,335
PANOLA COUNTY	26,977	28,352
Beat 1, including Como town	6,508	7,367
Como town	178	149
Beat 2, including Longtown town (b)	4,484	3,627
Beat 3, including Courtland and Pope towns (b)	4,328	4,177
Beat 4	4,752	5,171
Beat 5, including Batesville and Sardis towns	6,905	8,010
Batesville town	705	442
Sardis town	1,044	986
PEARL RIVER COUNTY (c)	2,957	....
Beat 1, including Poplarville town	568	....
Poplarville town	232	....
Beat 2	853	....
Beat 3	705	....
Beat 4	263	....
Beat 5	568	....
PERRY COUNTY	6,494	3,427
Beat 1. Augusta	1,204	885
Beat 2. Monroe, including Hattiesburg town	2,375	90
Hattiesburg town	1,172	....
Beat 3. Tallahala	690	1,005
Beat 4. Thompson Creek	1,124	670
Beat 5. Black Creek	1,101	777
PIKE COUNTY	21,203	16,688
Beat 1	3,807	2,961
Beat 2	3,605	2,608
Beat 3	2,458	2,084
Beat 4, including McComb City and Summit towns	7,210	5,863
McComb City town	2,383	1,982
Summit town	1,587	1,604
Beat 5, including Magnolia and Osyka towns	4,123	3,172
Magnolia town	676	567
Osyka town	742	542

b Not separately returned.

c Organized in 1890 from parts of Hancock and Marion counties.

MINOR CIVIL DIVISIONS.	1890.	1880.
PONTOTOC COUNTY	14,940	13,858
Beat 1, including Sherman town	1,933	2,379
Sherman town	79	
Beat 2	2,416	1,932
Beat 3, including Toccopola town	3,086	2,477
Toccopola town	190	
Beat 4, including Chesterville (b) and Pontotoc towns	3,812	3,801
Pontotoc town	535	447
Beat 5, including Troy town	3,693	3,269
Troy town	175	
PRENTISS COUNTY	13,679	12,158
Beat 1, including Booneville town	2,710	2,827
Booneville town	748	603
Beat 2	2,823	2,725
Beat 3, including part of Baldwyn town (a)	3,303	2,939
Beat 4, including Marietta town (b)	2,401	1,911
Beat 5	2,442	1,756
QUITMAN COUNTY	3,286	1,407
Beat 1	445	194
Beat 2, including Belen town	1,225	334
Belen town	184	
Beat 3	700	437
Beat 4	443	242
Beat 5	473	200
RANKIN COUNTY	17,922	16,752
Beat 1, Steen Creek	4,335	3,549
Beat 2, Brandon, including Brandon town	4,025	4,195
Brandon town	835	864
Beat 3, Fannin	2,831	2,926
Beat 4, Pelahatchie, including Pelahatchie town	2,873	2,574
Pelahatchie town	139	117
Beat 5, Cato, including Cato town (b)	3,858	3,508
SCOTT COUNTY	11,740	10,845
Beat 1, including Forest, Harperville and Hillsboro villages	3,230	2,787
Forest village	547	
Harperville village	138	
Hillsboro village	112	
Beat 2	1,998	1,614
Beat 3, including Morton village (b)	2,338	2,829
Beat 4	2,354	1,932
Beat 5, including Lake village (b)	1,820	1,683
SHARKEY COUNTY	8,382	6,306
Beat 1	851	543
Beat 2	1,241	749
Beat 3 } (b)	3,200	{ 1,135
Beat 4 }		{ 2,305
Beat 5	3,090	1,574

a Not separately returned; in beat 3 Prentiss county, and beat 1 Lee county.   b Not separately returned.

MINOR CIVIL DIVISIONS.	1890.	1880.
SIMPSON COUNTY	10,138	8,008
Beat 1	2,042	1,488
Beat 2	1,602	1,067
Beat 3	3,246	2,454
Beat 4	1,255	1,209
Beat 5	1,993	1,790
SMITH COUNTY	10,635	8,088
Beat 1	3,576	2,603
Beat 2	1,441	1,054
Beat 3	1,970	1,439
Beat 4	1,863	1,734
Beat 5	1,785	1,258
SUNFLOWER COUNTY (c)	9,384	4,661
Indianola town (in beat 3)	249	
TALLAHATCHIE COUNTY	14,361	10,926
Beat 1, including Harrison town (b)	2,497	2,282
Beat 2, including Charleston town	3,070	2,407
Charleston town	412	368
Beat 3	3,729	2,957
Beat 4	3,113	2,167
Beat 5	1,952	1,113
TATE COUNTY	19,253	18,721
Beat 1	3,719	3,163
Beat 2, including Arkabutla town	3,073	2,648
Arkabutla town	148	
Beat 3, including Coldwater town	4,081	4,106
Coldwater town	518	397
Beat 4, including Senatobia town	4,161	4,457
Senatobia town	1,077	935
Beat 5	4,219	4,347
TIPPAH COUNTY	12,951	12,867
Beat 1	2,835	3,047
Beat 2, including Ripley town	3,923	3,687
Ripley town	574	637
Beat 3, including Blue Mountain town (b)	2,762	2,642
Beat 4	1,653	1,741
Beat 5	1,778	1,750
TISHOMINGO COUNTY	9,302	8,774
Beat 1, including Iuka town	2,946	2,932
Iuka town	1,019	845
Beat 2, including Burnsville town	1,848	1,995
Burnsville town	318	240
Beat 3	1,189	1,150
Beat 4	1,732	1,338
Beat 5	1,587	1,359

b Not separately returned.   c Not returned by beats.

MINOR CIVIL DIVISIONS.	1890.	1880.
TUNICA COUNTY	12,158	8,461
Beat 1	2,867	2,060
Beat 2, including Tunica town	2,702	849
Tunica town	198	
Beat 3, including Austin town (b)	2,576	2,531
Beat 4	2,577	2,321
Beat 5	1,436	700
UNION COUNTY	15,606	13,030
Beat 1	2,482	1,985
Beat 2	2,972	1,668
Beat 3, including New Albany town	4,431	4,208
New Albany town	548	250
Beat 4, including Blue Springs and Poplar Springs towns (b)	4,064	3,548
Beat 5	1,657	1,621
WARREN COUNTY	33,164	31,238
Beat 1 (coextensive with Vicksburg city)	13,373	11,814
Beat 2	8,286	5,197
Beat 3	4,311	5,640
Beat 4	3,508	4,861
Beat 5	3,686	3,726
WASHINGTON COUNTY	40,414	25,367
Beat 1	4,403	5,968
Beat 2	8,121	4,566
Beat 3, including Greenville town	8,902	7,451
Greenville town	6,658	2,191
Beat 4, including Leland town	14,520	4,381
Leland town	485	
Beat 5	4,468	3,001
WAYNE COUNTY	9,817	8,741
Beat 1	1,644	1,760
Beat 2, including Waynesboro village	1,981	1,597
Waynesboro village	458	156
Beat 3	2,690	2,682
Beat 4	2,512	1,948
Beat 5	990	754
WEBSTER COUNTY (a)	12,060	9,534
Beat 1, Walthall, including Eupora and Walthall towns	2,955	2,098
Eupora town	432	
Walthall town	122	101
Beat 2, Cadaretta	2,554	1,820
Beat 3, Greensboro	2,430	2,070
Beat 4, Spring Valley	1,956	1,488
Beat 5, Cumberland, including Cumberland town (b)	2,165	2,058

a Formerly Sumner.   b Not separately returned.

MINOR CIVIL DIVISIONS.	1890.	1880.
WILKINSON COUNTY	17,592	17,815
Beat 1, including Woodville town	6,013	5,578
Woodville town	950	965
Beat 2	3,789	5,311
Beat 3, including Centerville town (b)	4,649	4,301
Beat 4	1,483	949
Beat 5	1,658	1,676
WINSTON COUNTY	12,089	10,087
Beat 1, Louisville, including Louisville town	3,433	2,467
Louisville town	484	418
Beat 2, Southeast	2,643	2,043
Beat 3, Webster	2,540	2,123
Beat 4, Northeast	974	912
Beat 5, Plattsburg	2,499	2,542
YALOBUSHA COUNTY	16,629	15,649
Beat 1, including Coffeeville town	3,340	3,062
Coffeeville town	465	749
Beat 2, including Water Valley town	5,733	5,555
Water Valley town	2,832	2,220
Beat 3, including Oakland town	3,065	2,506
Oakland town	327	288
Beat 4, including Garner Station town	3,112	2,565
Garner Station town	124	166
Beat 5, including Air Mount town (b)	1,379	1,961
YAZOO COUNTY	36,394	33,845
Beat 1, including Anding, Bentonia and Satartia towns (b)	7,333	6,264
Beat 2, including Benton town (b)	5,603	5,315
Beat 3, including Yazoo City	11,297	10,604
Yazoo City	3,286	2,542
Ward 1	1,438	
Ward 2	1,848	
Beat 4	6,213	5,746
Beat 5	5,948	5,916

b Not separately returned.

ROBERT P. PORTER,
Superintendent of Census.

INDEX.

A

	PAGE.
Abbott	204
Aberdeen	190
Abernethy, H. B.	235
Act for the encouragement of agriculture	27
Act for the government of insurrectionary states	27
Academies of the various counties	302–347
Administration of Governor Sargent	18, 127
Administration of Governor Claiborne	18, 127
Administration of Governor Williams	18, 127
Administration of Governor Holmes	19, 127
Administration of Governor Poindexter	19, 129
Administration of Governor Leake	19, 129
Administration of Governor Brandon	19, 129
Administration of Governor Scott	19
Administration of Governor Fountain	19
Administration of Governor Runnels	19
Administration of Governor Lynch	19
Administration of Governor McNutt	19, 130
Administration of Governor Tucker	19
Administration of Governor Brown	19, 132
Administration of Governor Matthews	19
Administration of Governor Quitman	19, 133
Administration of Governor Foote	20, 133
Administration of Governor McRae	20
Administration of Governor McWillie	20
Administration of Governor Pettus	20, 134
Administration of Governor Clarke	20, 135
Administration of Governor Sharkey	20, 136
Administration of Governor Humphreys	20, 136
Administration of Governor Ames	20, 138
Administration of Governor Alcorn	20, 138
Administration of Governor Powers	20
Administration of Governor Stone	20
Administration of Governor Lowry	20
Africans, what to do with them	22
Agricultural and Mechanical college	20, 341
Agricultural statistics	104–115
Alabama Great Southern railway	89
Alabama & Vicksburg railroad	87
Alcorn Agricultural and Mechanical college	339
Alcorn's remarks to the legislature of 1871	99
American Legion of Honor	59
Ames, Impeachment proceedings against	140
Ancient Order of United Workmen	60
Armistead, W. H.	263
Ashland	240
Associations at Meridian	154
Asylum for the insane at Jackson	39
Asylum for the insane at Meridian	40
Attorneys-general of the state	32
Augusta	239
Australian system adopted	16, 36

B

	PAGE.
Baldwyn	208
Banking facilities and statistics	46
Banks of Jackson	177
Banner	238
Baptist church	369
Bar of Natchez, The old	161
Batesville	232
Bay St. Louis	200
Beck, R. F.	486
Belen	232
Benela	237
Bethany	209
Bethel church	526
Big Creek	237
Black and tan convention	14, 29, 137
Black code, the	25
Blind asylum	40
Blue Mountain Female college	337
Boatmen and boats	71
Bogue Chitto	218
Bolton	185
Booneville	231
Booth, D. W.	263
Bowie family	503
Branches of the Illinois Central railway	82
Brandon	232
Brandon college	329
Brookhaven	217
Buena Vista Normal college	236–345
Buildings at Jackson, Public	175
Buildings at Vicksburg	151
Burr, Experiences with	18, 127
Business at Columbus	186
Business of Greenville	169, 170
Business of Meridian	155
Business of Port Gibson	214

C

	PAGE.
Cage, A. H.	267
Calhoon's address in 1890	15, 35
Campbell's codification of the laws	35

Campaign of 1875, The	139
Canton	198
Capitol, The present	18
Carrollton	234
Carthage	239, 241
Catholic church, Roman	374
Cemeteries of the war	45
Centenary college	319
Chalmers, H. H	32
Chamberlain-Hunt academy	525
Chancery and circuit courts	30
Chancery judges of the state	33
Charleston	233
Chester	236
Christian church	368
Christian, Rev. J. T	936
Churches of Natchez	161
Churches of Vicksburg	151
Church statistics	378–9
Circuit judges since the war	33
Cities, towns and villages	147
Clarke, Governor	453
Clarkes, The	593
Clarksdale	224
Cotton crop, A big	523
Cotton at Natchez	166
Courthouse at Greenville	169
Columbus	186
Coffeeville	193
Corinth	194
Confederate veterans of Mississippi	59
Council of Masons	56
Colored soldiers	93
Colored population	95
Commercial statistics	105
Cotton production	102–12
Corn, The culture of	112
Constitutional provisions and changes	130
Columbia	240
Compton, W. McC	265
Cooper Normal college	335
Common schools, The	338
Corinth Female college	341
Colleges	300, 347
Convention of 1865	12, 24
Constitution, A new	13
Convention of 1890	14, 143
Constitutional provisions	16, 142
Commissioners to locate the capital	17
Codification and revision of state laws	19
Constitution of 1832 adopted	19
County officers appointed during the military era	23
Courts created by commissions	24
Constitution of 1869, Provisions of	30
Commissioners appointed to revise laws, 1870	31
Constitution of 1890, Provisions of	35
Code of 1892, Preparation of	36
Convict-lease system, The	39
Congressmen of Mississippi, List of	41
Confederate congressmen	43
Craft, M. S	279
Creek Indian wars	19
Creekmore, Dr	626
Cumberland Presbyterian church	358
Cyclone at Wesson	203

D

Dairy products	121
Dancy, F. W	285
Davis, J. S	272
Deaf and Dumb asylum	40
Decatur	239
DeKalb	231
Delegates to the Montgomery convention	135
Democratic convention of 1876	141
De Nouaille's trip up the Mississippi	61
Distribution of apartments of the Capitol	17
Digest of Mississippi reports	34
Disbursements of the state	45
Dinner service, A costly	523
Duck Hill	205
Durant	241
Dulaney, W. J	271
Diseases prevalent	287, 298
Dueling	586

E

Earthquake of 1811	70
East Mississippi Insane asylum	20
East Mississippi Female college	340
Election of governor and others in 1869	13, 30
Effects of the military government	13
Effects of the election of 1875	14
Election of 1867 for a constitutional convention	29
Ellet, Judge	32
East Tennessee, Virginia & Georgia railway	89
Exhibition of Mississippi at the centennial	93
Enterprises at Meridian	154
Emmaville	224
Enterprise	225
Ellisville	241
Ellis, J. W	280
Elkin, T. B	283
Educational history	300
Errata, etc	1091

F

Fant, J. C	284
Federal aid to education, The first	303
Franklin Female college	329
Fourteenth amendment, refusal to ratify it	27, 137
Fourteenth amendment, Ratification of	31, 138

	PAGE.
Financial condition	50
Farmers' organizations, societies, etc.	53
Fruitgrowing	117
Fertilizers	125
Fishery interests	125
"Flush times," The	130
Fayette	210
Friar's Point	224
Forest	233
French Camp schools	236
Fulton	241
Fitzgerald, P. F.	267
Finley, W. P.	273

G

Galloway, C. B.	368
Galloway, W. A.	283
Georgia Pacific railway	86
Giles, S. H.	504
Glass sand	125
Governmental epochs	21
Governmental form, Consideration of	142
Grand chapter of Masons	55
Grange societies of the state	114
Grant of land for Jackson	17
Graves, Defalcation of	19
Grasses of the state	119
Green's emancipated slaves	98
Greenville	168
Greenwood	223
Grenada	195
Growth and development of the state	90
Gulf & Chicago railway	89
Gunter, Archibald Clavering	835
Guntown	210

H

Hall, W. W.	266
Halls of learning	300-347
Hampton Roads conference	537
Harbors of Mississippi	76
Hart, W. W.	281
Harriston	212
Hartford	237
Hattiesburg	239
Haynes, F. B.	527
Hazlehurst	202
Hernando	240
Herron, J. N.	554
Hicks, J. R.	264
High court judges appointed in 1867	29
High schools	300-347
Hill, S. V. D.	284
Historical Society of Mississippi	52
Holly Springs	197
Holman, J. W.	273

	PAGE.
Holmes, John	598
Homœopathy	286
Horticultural Society, The	53
Hospitals, first in the state	39
Hotels of Jackson	179
Houston	235
Hughes, E. W.	264
Humphreys elected governor	12
Hunt-Poindexter duel	398
Hueston-Le Branch duel	515

I

Immigration, Statistics of	94
Impeachment of Governor Ames	13
Impeachment proceedings	140
Incorporation of Columbus	188
Incorporation of Natchez	160
Indebtedness of the state	51
Indigo, The culture of	111
Indian population	92
Indianola	231
Industrial institute and college	344
Industrial institute at Columbus	187
Industrial institute for girls	20
Institutes of learning	300-347
Iuka	227

J

Jacinto	195
Jackson, City of	172
Jackson enthusiastically received	19
Jefferson college	300
Journalism of the state	248
Johnston, Judge A. R.	31
Judiciary reorganized	31
Judges of the high court bench	26
Jurisdiction of courts after 1865	25
Justices, Jurisdiction of	26

K

Kansas City, Memphis & Birmingham railway	88
Kate Tucker institute	927
Kavanaugh college	343
Keelboats and barges	63
Kells, Robert	280
Ker family	521
Kilgore, Benjamin	698
Kinchloe, D. A.	265
Knights and Ladies of Honor	59
Knights of Honor	59
Knights of Pythias	59
Knights Templar	57
Knutt family	518
Kosciusko	225
Kosciusko Masonic Female college	333

L

	PAGE.
Labor organizations	53
Labor, Problems of	116
Lamar in the secession convention	134
Land, Sales of	103
Laws declared in force by Governor Sharkey	23
Lawyers, other great ones	36
Lea Female college	341
Lea, W. M	264
Leakesville	240
Leatherman, Zach	503
Library of the state	41
Lee Female college	543
Lee, T. J	283
Legal holidays	43
Legislature of 1861	11
Leland	171
Levee commissioners, Powers of	73
Levees, how built	75
Levee system, The	72
Lexington	241
Liberty	240
Liberty Male and Female college	345
Literature of Mississippi	250
Lopez' expedition to Cuba	20
Louisville	233
Louisville, New Orleans & Texas railway	86
Lowry's address to doctors	276
Lumber statistics	123
Lyles, Dr. Robert J	1091

M

	PAGE.
Mackay, John	384
Mackay, Charles	384
Macon	200
Maddox, James H	384
Maddox, James	384
Madison, James S	385
Madison college	332
Madison, John E	386
Magee, E. C	386
Magee, L. R	386
Magee, Robert	386
Magee, J. W	386
Magee, Chester	387
Maggard, M. G	387
Maggard, David	388
Magnolia	230
Magruder, J. H	388
Magruder, A. F	388
Magruder, T. B	388
Magruder and the Indians	389
Magruder, R. W	390
Magruder, W. T	390
Magruder, R. H	391
Magruder, B. H	391
Magruder, Thomas	391

	PAGE.
Mahorner, Mathias	391
Mahorner's stock and crops	392
Majet, L. C	392
Majet as a sportsman	392
Malone, T. J	393
Mangum, S. H	394
Manley, T. J	394
Manor, S. J	395
Manor, Levi	395
Manufacturers of Vicksburg	149
Manufacturers	124
Manufacturers of Jackson	178
Manumission of slaves	97
Marshall, C. H	395
Marshall, W. L	395
Marshall, J. P	396
Marshall, L. R	397
Marshall, S. D	397
Marshall, G. M	398
Marshall, T. A. M	399
Marshall, Martin	400
Marshall, George	400
Marshall, T. D	401
Martin, E. J	401
Martin's library	406
Martin, E. L	402
Martin, J. H	402
Martin, John	403
Martin, J. McC	404
Martin, J. E	404
Martin, W. M	404
Martin, C. H	404
Martin, W. H	405
Martin, Norman	407
Martin, T. N	407
Martin, W. B	409
Martin, A	409
Martin, J. A	409
Martin, W. F	409
Marye, T. S	411
Mason, Presley	411
Masons of Mississippi	53
Massingale, G. M	412
Mastodon	221
Mathis, Edwin	413
Mathison, Neill	414
Matthews, Joseph	414
Matthews, R. F	414
Matthews, S. A	415
Mattingly, J. B	416
Mattingly, Walter	417
Maxwell, H. P	417
Maxwell, P. J	418
Maxwell, W. L	419
May, A. Q	419
Maybin, J. W	420

	PAGE.
Maybin, W. H	420
Maybin's speech	421
Mayers, A. G	422
Mayersville	241
Mayes, Edward	423
Maynard, G. F	423
Maynard, Decatur B	424
McCallum, G. C	264
McCardle, W. H., The case of	28
McKie, N. W	266
McLaurin, H. C	271
McWillie, James	283
Mead, J. A	285
Meadville	230
Medical schools	287
Medicinal plants	299
Meek, S. M	424
Meeks, T. M	426
Meeks, J. T	426
Melton, A. J	428
Melvin, E. W	429
Members of the convention of 1865	24
Mendenhall, T. L	430
Mendrop, E. W	430
Mendrop, R. V	430
Meridian	153
Meridian, Growth of	157
Merrill, D. S	430
Merrill, A. P	431
Merritt, J. F	432
Metcalfe, O	432
Methodist church	362
Miazza, P. S	433
Mickle, D. A	434
Middleton, E. E	434
Middleton, R. M	435
Middleton, E. S	435
Miles, J. D	436
Military control assumed	11, 23
Military governor appointed	13
Militia, Ante-bellum	38
Militia, Post-bellum	38
Mineral products	125
Miller, E. D	437
Miller, H. R	437
Miller, Irvin	438
Miller, J. C	439
Miller, J. H	439
Miller, E. L	440
Miller J. C	440
Miller, J. T	440
Miller, W. D	441
Millsaps, R. W	442
Millsaps, Uriah	443
Millsaps' college	346
Mims, W. D	445

	PAGE.
Minor, D. S	446
Minor, H. A	446
Mississippi Normal college	343
Mississippi Female college	315, 331
Mississippi college	307
Mississippi State Medical association	255
Mississippi City	201
Mississippi admitted to the Union	128
Mississippi mills, Wesson	674
Mississippi citations	34
Mississippi owned by one man	45
Mississippi compared with other states	90
Mississippi Manufacturing company	533
Mister, M. K	447
Mitchell, E. S	448
Mitchell, J. C	449
Mitchell, T. J	449
Mobile & Ohio railway	86
Montgomery, A. A	450
Montgomery & Co	529
Montgomery, D. C	451
Montgomery, W. E	451
Montgomery, F. A	452
Montgomery, L	454
Montgomery, W. A	455
Monument at Jackson	18
Monument at Jackson, Confederate	181
Monticello	231
Monette, W. E	265
Moore, B. S	456
Moore, C. C	456
Moore, E. H	458
Moore, James	458
Moore, Henry	459
Moore, G. D	459
Morgan, J. B	460
Moore, J. M	460
Moore, J. F	461
Moore, J. S	462
Moore, J. W	462
Moore, J. R	463, 464
Moore, J. F	465
Moore, Lod	466
Moore, L. R	466
Moore, O. J	467
Moore, R. J	468
Moore, Nelson	468
Moore, T. J	469
Moore, W. W	469, 470, 472
Morehead, B. H	473
Morgan, J. D	474
Morgan, J. H	475
Morris, J. H	475
Morris, J. W	476
Morris' reports	34
Moseley, J. T	477

	PAGE.		PAGE.
Mosley, R. J	477	Noel, E. B	510
Moss, B. F	478	Noel, E. F	511
Moss, L. A	478	Noland, H. P	512
Moss, R. P	479	Noland, Pierce	512
Mott, C. H	480	Noland, T. V	512
Muldrow, W. C	480	Nolen, J. R	513
Muldrow, H. L	481	Norrell, T. N	514
Mulligan, J. J	483	North Mississippi college	321
Mullin, Robert	483	Northrop, A. K	514
Mullin, R. W	484	Nugent, W. L	515
Mulvihill, P. W	484	Nugent, John	515
Myer, J. P	485	Nugent, R. J	517
Myers, C. H	486	Nunn, E. F	518
		Nutt family arms	518
N		Nutt, William	519
Naron, G. W	488	Nutt, Rush	519
Nash, W. N	489	Nutt, The writings of	519
Nash, S. E	489	Nutt's cotton	519
Nash, W. N	490	Nutt, Rittenhouse	520
Natchez	159	Nutt, Haller	520
Natchez, Jackson & Columbus railway	89, 165	Nutt, J. K	520
Nations, Calvin	496		
Nations, J. L	496	**O**	
Neel, G. W	491	Oakland college	310, 524
Negro marriages legalized	30	Oatis, C. E	526
Negus, J. E	497	Oatis, J. H	526
Neilson, C. A	498	Obryant, T. T	527
Neilson, J. C	499	Odd Fellows of Mississippi	58
Nelson, B. F	500	Odd Fellows' Female college	334
Nelson, F. C	501	O'Dell, Denton	528
Nelson, J. C	502	Oden, J. B	529
Nelson, L. L	503	Odeneal, J. H	529
Nelson, Samuel	503	O'Ferrall, J. J	530
Neshoba	231	O'Ferrall, J. W	531
Nettleton	207	Officers of the state militia	38
Neville, S. S	504	Officers of the Illinois Central railway	85
Newspapers at Greenville	170	Officers of the state, qualifications	128
Neville, William	505	Officers of Jackson	173
Neville, J. H	505	Office, Tenure of	130
Newberger, Joseph	506	Okolona	235
Newberger, Edwin	506	O'Leary, Richard	531
Newberger, Charles	507	Oliver, William	532
Newbery, John	507	Ormond, B. F	535
Newman, D. B	508	Ord, Military Commander	28
Newman, Maxwell	508	Ordinance of secession	134
New Orleans & Northeastern railway	87	Orendorff, T. T	535
New Orleans, Mobile & Chattanooga railway	88	Orr, J. A	536
New Albany	238	Orr, Christopher	537
Newton college	333	Orr, James L	537
Nicholson, J. M	508	Orr's resolutions	538
Nicholson, T	508	Orrick, E. C	540
Noble, J. E	509	Orrick, N. C	540
Noble, W. S	510	Orrick, Nicholas	540
Noel, Leland	510	Orrick, William	540
Noel, James	510	Otken, C. H	542
Noel, E. F	510	Owen, R. A	544

	PAGE.
Owen, R. T.	544
Owen, T. G.	544
Owen, S. D.	545
Owen, W. E.	545
Owens, G. W.	546
Oxford	221

P

	PAGE.
Pace, J. R.	547
Pace, R. B.	547
Paden, H. G.	548
Paden, Alexander	548
Page, G. R.	549
Page, L.	549
Paine, Robert	367
Parham, J. G.	550
Parker, J. T.	551, 552
Parker, R. A.	553
Parrish, E. A.	553
Parsons, W. E.	555
Parsons, D. C. M.	555
Parsons, Frank	555
Partee, C. W.	556
Partin, I. P.	557
Partin, C. P.	557
Pass, W. N.	557
Passmore, B. F.	558
Patterson, P. W.	559
Patton, J. V.	559
Patton, W. E.	560
Patton, J. W.	560
Patton, W. H.	560
Patton, J. J.	560
Patty, R. C.	563
Paulding	232
Paxton, A. G.	564
Paxton, A. J.	565
Paxton, W. G.	566
Paxton, C. B.	566
Payne, G. H.	567
Payne, J. A.	567
Payne, L. C.	568
Peace commission, The	539
Peace, J. H.	569
Pearce, R. N.	569
Pearcefield, J. B.	570
Pearcifield, A. V.	571
Pearlington	200
Pearman, W. L.	571
Pearson, C. A.	572
Pearson, C. W.	573
Pearson, W. J.	573
Pearson, I. C.	573
Pearson, L.	573
Pearson, W. E.	574
Pease, J. B.	574

	PAGE.
Peatross, A. C.	575
Peek, G. F.	576
Peel, R. H.	576
Peel, T.	578
Peel, V.	578
Peel, A.	578
Peets, G. H.	578
Pegram, W. C.	580
Penitentiary, The	39
Pepper, R. B.	580
Percy, W. A.	581
Percy L. R.	582
Percy, W. A.	582
Perkins, W. P.	586
Perkins, C. H.	583
Perkins, R. S. G.	583
Perkins, E. M.	584
Perkins, E. O.	584
Perkins, Jesse	585
Perkins, W. W.	587
Perkins, J. W.	587
Perry, J. C.	588
Perry, O. H.	588
Pettit, T. H.	589
Pettit, A.	589
Pettus, T. F.	589
Pettus, W. P.	589
Petty, G. M.	590
Peyton, E. G.	32
Phelps, A. J.	591
Phelps, O. J.	591
Phelps, W. G.	593
Phillips, Eli	593
Phillips, G. C.	594
Phillips, F. W.	594
Phillips, H. W.	595
Phillips, S. F.	595
Physicians and their associations	252
Piazzo, V.	596
Pickett, M	597
Pipes, James	598
Pitard, The case of	26
Pitchford, J. C.	599
Pittsboro	237
Planchet, G.	599
Planters' bank bonds	19, 20, 47, 129
Plantations, The size of	114
Poindexter's code	129
Poitevent, W. J.	601
Political and social status	21
Political history	127
Pollock, G. W.	601
Pollock, W. A.	601
Pontotoc	227
Pool, S. P.	602
Pope, Jacob	602

	PAGE.
Pope, John	602
Poplarville	238
Population of 1880-1890, in detail	1094
Population of Jackson	173
Population of Natchez	160
Population, statistics of	91
Porter, C. A	603
Port Gibson	212
Porter, J. C	604
Port Gibson Female college	325, 603
Pou, J. G	605
Powell, A. C	605
Powell, I. C	606
Powell, J. F	609
Powell, J. M	608
Powell, John	606
Powell, W. H	609
Powell, William	283
Powell, William	606
Power, J. L	610
Powers, H. C	612
Prather, J. T	613
Prather, L. C	613
Pratt, F. B	614
Presbyterian church	354
Presidential majorities	43
Press, History of	242
Preston, J. R	614
Price, A. M	617
Price, Armead	615
Price, Bem	616
Price, D. T	618
Price, G. W	619
Price, J. J	621
Price, John	619
Price, J. R	620
Price, J. W	620
Price, Richard	618
Price, W	616
Price, W. D	620
Priddy, M. C	622
Priestly, J. T	623
Prince, F. M	623
Prince, Robert	625
Prince, W. B	624
Productions, total of the state	126
Program of concert at Jackson	183
Protestant Episcopal church	348
Provine, L. F	627
Provine, R. N	625
Provine, Samuel	625
Prowell, J. W	628
Pryor, James	630
Pryor, J. T	628
Public buildings at Jackson, first	17
Public school system	19

	PAGE.
Purnell, J. C	630

Q

Quin, D. C	633
Quin, D. H	632
Quin, H. M	632
Quin, L. J	632
Quin, P. C	633
Quin, Richard	632
Quitman	225

R

Radgesky, J. C	634
Ragland, S. E	634
Ragsdale, W. A	635
Ragsdale, G. W	635
Railway commission established	20, 89
Railway transportation	77
Railways on paper	78
Railway mileage	79
Railway, The Illinois Central	79
Railway appropriations	80
Railroads of Jackson	176
Rainey, W. F	636
Rainey, I. S	636
Raleigh	234
Ramsey, T. J	636
Randall, L	637
Randolph, W. F	638
Raney, W. T	639
Rankin, W. M	639
Ratcliffe, S. S	640
Ratliff, J. S	640
Ratliff, W	641
Ratliff, W. P	642
Raum, W. C	642
Rawle, John	643
Rawle family	644
Raymond	185
Rea, R. W	645
Reaves, J. J	647
Reconstruction acts	12, 136
Receipts of the state	45
Recent political events	146
Redhead, Joseph	648
Redhead, J. A	649
Redmond, D. M	649
Redus, W. B	650
Reed, Thomas	651
Reed, W. S	654
Rees, W. H	654
Reeves, J. J	655
Refusal to ratify the fourteenth amendment	12
Regan, W. S	656
Registration of voters	30
Reid, H. P	656

	PAGE.
Reid, Joseph	657
Reid, T. B.	657
Reinach, D.	658
Religious history	348
Religio-fraternal societies	53
Rembert, I. P.	658
Rembert, I. B.	659
Reports of the courts of the state	34
Representatives of Mississippi, List of	42
Resignation of the high court judges	28
Resolutions for political harmony	139
Revolution, The great	14
Rew, E. J.	660
Reynolds, R. O.	661
Reynolds, Colonel	34
Reynolds' reports	33
Republican convention of 1876	141
Rhodes, J. H.	662
Rice, A. H.	663
Rice, J. W.	663
Richards, E. P.	664
Richards, W. C.	664
Richardson, Edmund	665
Richardson, James	666
Richardson, J. S.	667, 669
Richardson, J. P.	672
Richardson, W. B.	678
Ricketts, S. R.	679
Ricketts, R. B.	679
Ricks, B. S.	680
Rienzi	195
Rife, W. W.	681
Rigby, Thomas	681
Right, R. J.	682
Riley, Sr., F. L.	683
Riley, Jr., F. L.	684
Ripley	225
Roach, Benjamin	684
Robert, J. C.	685
Robert, W. H.	685
Robert family tree	686
Roberts, Charles	687
Roberts, H. C.	688
Roberts, P. B.	688
Roberts, S. E.	689
Robertson, C. H.	689
Robertson, J. C. N.	689
Robertson, G. M.	690
Robertson, S. D.	690
Robertson, W. T.	691
Robinet, J. R.	691
Robins, J.	692
Robinson, F. D.	693
Robinson, J. D.	693
Robinson, J. L.	694
Robinson, J. W.	694

	PAGE.
Robinson, J. F.	695
Robinson, L. B.	696
Robinson, V. W.	696
Robinson, W. W.	697, 698
Roby, M. T.	698
Rochester, J. U.	699
Rogan, L. W.	700
Rogers, Timothy	701
Rogers, W. A.	702
Rohmer, W. B.	702
Rolling Fork	239
Roosevelt's voyage and experiences	64
Rosedale	238, 240
Rose, Emanuel	703
Rosenbaum, Marx	703
Rosenbaum, Charles	704
Ross–Gibbs duel	389
Ross, G. W.	704
Routh family	522
Routh, Job	522
Row, Benjamin	705
Rowan, E. A.	707
Rowan, J. H.	708
Rubel, E.	710
Rush, A. F.	711
Rushing, C. E.	711, 712
Russell, L. V.	713
Russell, E.	713
Rust university	339

S

	PAGE.
Sabougla	237
Sadler, W. R.	717
Sadler, J. M.	717
Salaries of governors	43
Sallis, J. G.	718
Sallis, John	718
Saltillo	207
Sample, A. D.	718
Sanders, J. W.	720
Sanders, G. F.	719
Sanger, Charles	719
Sardis	232
Saunders, R. L.	720
Savery, P. M.	721
Scales, W. H.	722
Scanlan, T. M.	723
Scanlan, Edward	723
Scarborough, I. W.	723
Scarborough, J. W.	724
Schaefer, Emile	725
Schools of Meridian	154
Schools of Port Gibson	215
Scott, Charles	725
Scott, E. M.	726
Scott, G. Y.	727

Scott, Charles	728
Scott, D. A.	728
Scott, F. M.	729
Scott, N. B	730
Scranton	221
Scruggs, S. A.	730
Scurr, W. B.	731
Seal, Roderick	732
Seal, D. B	732
Seale, E. B.	733
Seaman, S	734
Secession convention	134
Siege of Vicksburg	150
Selby, T. H	735
Selman, B. A. P.	735
Seminaries of learning	300, 347
Semmes, J. H	736
Senatobia	234
Senator elected in 1871	13
Senators of Mississippi, List of	41
Sessions, C. E	737
Sessions, J. F.	737
Settlement of Vicksburg	148
Settlement of Natchez	159
Settlement of Greenville	168
Settlement of Port Gibson	213
Seutter, E. von	738
Seward, E. R.	740
Sexton, J. F	742
Sexton, F. M	743
Sexton, J. S.	743
Sexton, L. M.	744
Shackelford, R. J.	746
Shackelford, T. H	746
Shackelford, C. C.	32
Shackleford, Lee	267
Shaifer, A. K	747
Shands, G. D.	749
Shannon	209
Shannon's address	267
Sharkey appointed governor	12
Sharman, J. R.	750
Sharon college	316
Sharp, J. M	750
Sharp, J. T.	751
Sharp, J. W.	752
Shaw, T. A	752
Shelby, G. B.	753
Shelby, O. L.	754
Shell, P. W	754
Shell mound	224
Shelton, David	756
Shelton, S. M.	757
Shepherd, R. B. H	757
Shepherd, R. C.	759
Sheppardtown	224
Shinkel, J. N. D.	759
Shirley, J. N	760
Short, J. P.	761
Shotwell, B.	761
Shotwell, Mrs. L.	761
Shrader, J. A. C.	762
Shreve, J. A.	763
Shreve, Charles	764
Shrock, J. K	766
Sibley, C. C.	767
Sidon	224
Sillers, Walter	767
Simmons, J. L.	768
Simmons, Peter	768
Simonton, J. M	769
Simpson, C. A.	770
Simpson, F. M	771
Simrall, H. F.	772
Sims, T. M	775
Sims, W. H	776
Sims, W. McD.	780
Sims, W. S	782
Sinclair, E. D	782
Sivley, W. R	783
Slack, J. J	784
Slave population	92
Slaves prohibited from meeting	96
Sledge, W. D	785
Sledge, N. R.	786
Sledge, O. D.	787
Sloan, W. B.	787
Smedes, C. E	788
Smith, A. H.	789
Smith, A. B.	789
Smith, J. H	789
Smith, A. N.	790
Smith, A. W	790
Smith, S. B.	283
Smith, W. P	790
Smith, I. C.	792
Smith, J. C.	793
Smith, M. F.	794
Smith, R. M.	795
Smith, S. O.	796
Smith, W. M	797
Smythe, A. J	798
Snell, J. A.	799
Snowden, W. P.	799
Societies of Port Gibson	215
Societies of Fayette	211
Societies of Grenada	197
Societies of Aberdeen	191
Societies of Jackson	180
Societies of Greenville	171
Societies of Columbus	189
Societies of Natchez	164

	PAGE.		PAGE.
Sojourner, M. U.	800	Stewart, John B.	835
Solution of the colored problem	22	Stewart, W. P.	836
Somerville, T. H.	800	Stinson, B. J.	836
Souter, Frank	801	Stinson, W. H.	836
Southworth, L. M.	801	Stinson, W. B.	837
Spain, Aaron	802	Stirling, P. J.	837
Spain, Alexander	803	Stirling, S. H.	838
Spain, J. W.	804	Stockard, C. C.	839
Sparkman, A. P.	804	Stockdale, T. R.	840
Spearman, J. F.	805	Stockett, Samuel	843
Special courts of the constitution of 1865	26	Stock statistics	109, 119, 120, 122
Speed, Frederick	805	Stockton, R. N.	845
Spencer, S. M.	807	Stockton, W. L.	846
Spencer, W. H.	808	Stokes, Walter	846
Spengler, A. D.	809	Stone, Adolphus	846
Spengler, H.	810	Stone, E. H.	847
Spight, J. C.	812	Stone, James	847
Spight, Thomas	813	Stone, J. B.	848
Spinks, J. C.	813	Stone, S. C.	848
Spinks, E. E.	814	Stone, J. H.	850
Spotorno, Louis	814	Stone, John M.	850
Spratlin, E. J.	815	Stone, Lewis M.	853
Sproles, H. F.	815	Stone products	125
Stanford, J. T.	816	Stone, O. W.	854
Stanton, Aaron	816	Stone, W. W.	855
Stanton, Frederick	818	Stonewall Manufacturing Company	856
Staples, J. D.	285	Stonewall	857
Starkville	201	Storm, Edward	858
Starling, William	818	Stowers, John C.	858
State Normal school	339	Stratton, J. B.	859
Statistics of growth	102–108	Street, H. M.	860
State board of health	287	Streets of Jackson named	17
State Springs Male and Female college	340	Strickland, W. M.	861
Steam used to navigate the rivers	64	Strong, T. H. C.	861
Steamboats, The first	66	Stuart, Edward	862
Steele, Martha	819	Stuart, W. R.	863
Steele, Archibald	819	Stuart, W. W.	864
Steen, J. O.	820	Stubblefield, M.	864
Stegal, W. J.	821	Stubbs, T. B.	865
Stephen, W. L.	821	Stutts, Z. P.	865
Stephens, M. D. L.	822	Suddoth, J. A.	866
Stephens, Z. M.	828	Sullivan, John L.	866
Stevens, J. H.	829	Sumrall, Jacob	867
Stevens, John P.	829	Summit	158
St. Aloysius college	346	Suspension of the laws	23
St. Stanislaus college	333	Supplementary index for Volume I	1093
Stevenson, W. G.	830	Supreme court formed	30
Stevenson, W. J.	831	Surget, James	868
Stewart, I. D.	831	Surratt, Micajah	869
Stewart, J. D.	832	Swain, S. R.	869
Stewart, William	833	Swayze, H. C.	870
Stewart, T. J.	834	Swayze, H. S.	870
Stewart, J. A.	834	Sweatman, D. L.	871
Stewart, Duncan	834	Switzer, James M.	872
Stewart, H. M.	835	Sykes, E. T.	872
Stewart, Charles D.	835	Sykes, T. B.	873

	PAGE.
Sykes, W. G	874
Sykes, L. M	270

T

	PAGE.
Talbert, James B	876
Tankersley, D. S	877
Tatum, C. W	878
Tax to build levees	73
Taxation, note of	51
Taxpayers' conventions	139
Taylor, C. W	878
Taylor, H. L	878
Taylor, John	879
Taylor, Franklin	880
Taylor, C. A	880
Taylor, L. R	881
Taylor, W. A	881
Taylor, J. M	882
Taylor, L. T	884
Taylor, R. H	885
Teachers' associations	336
Temple, Judge L	886
Temple, M. R	887
Tenant farming	100
Terral, S. H	887
Territorial government first established	127
Teunisson, G. A	889
Thomas, A. H	891
Thomas, John A	892
Thomas, J. W	892
Thomas, C. L	892
Thomas, B. F	893
Thomas, J. T	894
Thomas, J. V	895
Thomas, R. S	895
Thomas, W. B	896
Thompson, H. M	897
Thompson, Jacob	898
Thompson, William	901
Thompson, J. S	902
Thompson, J. R	903
Thompson, J. T	903
Thompson, Julius	904
Thompson, M. J	905
Thompson, P. C	906
Thompson, R. H	907
Thornton, E. W	909
Thornton, J. B	909
Thornton, J. J	910
Thrasher, Stephen	910
Tillman, C. L	912
Timber statistics	122
Tindall, Henry	912
Tison, W. H. H	913
Tobacco, the production of	110
Toombs, R. S	915

	PAGE.
Torrey, John	917
Torrey, W. D	918
Totten, J. C	918
Tongaloo university	337
Toulme, J. V	919
Traffic on the rivers	72
Treadwell, W. L	920
Treasury notes declared void	29
Trice, J. M	921
Trimble, G. W	922
Triplett, N. D	923
Trotter, W. E	924
Truly, Jeff	925
Trusty, J. T	925
Tucker, J. A	926
Tucker, J. W	927
Tucker, R. L	927
Tucker, J. H	928
Tucker Institute, Kate	927
Tunica	236
Tupelo	206
Turner D. B	269
Turner, Edward	928
Turner, H. C	929
Turner, L. R	930
Turner, R. H	930
Turner, R. J	932
Turner, R. L	932
Tweed, Robert	933
Tyler, F. A	934
Tyler, J. M	935
Tynes, H. L	936

U

	PAGE.
Ulman, Alfred A	937
Ulman, James A	938
United States district courts	33
Union bank bonds	19, 20, 47, 131
Universities of the state	300–347
University of Mississippi	322
University of Columbus	336
Upshaw, S. R	939
Urquhart, E. C	939
Ussery, S. T	940

V

	PAGE.
Vaiden	234
Vancleave, R. A	941
Van Court, J. H	942
Van Devender, A. M	943
Van Eaton, H. S	943
Van Eaton, T. H	945
Van Hoozer, T. H. B	946
Vann, John O	947
Van Norman, S. T	948
Vanslyke, John H	949

	PAGE.		PAGE.
Vasser, G. W	949	Watkins, E	989
Vaughan, B. A	950	Watkins, Jesse	990
Vaughan, H. B	951	Watkins, James	990
Vaughan, James	952	Watkins, W. A	991
Vegetable products	117	Watkins, W. W	991
Ventress, James A	952	Watson, A. C	992
Ventress, W. P. S	956	Watson, J. R	994
Ventress, L. T	956	Watson, J. W	994
Vick, Newet J	956, 961	Watson, J. W. C	996
Vick, Thomas	957, 960	Watson, J. H	998
Vick, Burwell	957	Watson, R. H	998
Vick, John W	957, 959	Watson, C. L	999
Vick's will and property	958	Watson, Wheeler	999
Vick, H. O	960	Watt, R. H	1000
Vicksburg	147	Watts, D. S	1001
Votes of parties compared	44	Watts, James	1002
Voyageurs, The first	61	Watts, J. B	1002
		Watts, S. B	1003
W		Waynesboro	230
Wade, John C	962	Weatherbee, H. E	1003
Wade, W. A	963	Webb, Albert G	1004
Wagner, Daniel R	963	Webb, W. S	1005
Wainwright, George I	964	Weed, F. M	1006
Wainwright, T. L	857	Weir, R. S	1007
Wait, P. M. B	965	Weissinger, W. S	1007
Walker, James S	966	Weissinger, John R	1008
Walker, Joel P	967	Welch, J. P	1009
Walker, John A	968	Welch, James N	1010
Walker, B. J	969	Wells, B. R	1011
Walker, N. S	969	Wentworth, W. M	1012
Walker, W. E	971	Wesleyan Female college	326
Wall, W. H	972	Wesson	202
Wallace, R. L	973	West, A. M	1013
Wallin, E. W	974	West, M. M	1015
Walter, H. W	974	West Feliciana railroad	77
Walthall, E. C	977	West Point	204
Walthall	229	Westville	234
Walton, E. S	979	West, R. D	1015
Walton, J. T	980	West, R. R	1016
Walworth, Douglas	980	West, T. J	1017
Wansley, A. M	981	Wharton, T. J	1018
War with Mexico	132	Wheat, the cultivation of	112
Ward, W. F	982	Wheatley, W. B	1020
Ward, B. F	982	Wheeless, G. W	1021
Ward, B. N	983	Whitaker, John	1022
Ward, E. J	983	Whitaker, J. W	1023
Ward, G. V	984	Whitaker, James	1023
Ward, J. R	985	Whitaker, Richard	1023
Wardlaw, Zack	985	White, John J	1024
Warren, D. C	986	White, Robert E	1025
Warren, N. B	987	White, T. W	1026
Washington	167	White, W. H	1026
Water transportation	60	Whitehead, P. F	263
Water Valley	191	Whitesides, W. R	1027
Waterer, J. W	988	Whitfield, N. H	1028
Watkins, B. D	988	Whitney, J. J	1030

	PAGE.		PAGE.
Whittle, W. H.	1031	Winborn, J. W.	1063
Whittington, N. C.	1032	Windham, W. D.	1064
Whittington, J. M.	1033	Winona	205
Whitworth Female college	335	Winston, William	1064
Wiggins, J. L.	1033	Winters, H. L.	1065
Wilburn, G. M.	1034	Wise, John	1066
Wildberger, R. H.	1034	Withers, A. Q.	1066
Wilds, O. N.	1035	Withers, John P.	1067
Wilczinski, L.	1036	Withers, R. S.	1068
Wilczinski, N.	1036	Wiygul, E. H.	1069
Wilkins, D. D.	1037	Woman's Christian Temperance Union	83, 379
Williams family	521	Wood, T. A.	1069
Williams, Barnet	521	Woodruff, Z. T.	264
Williams, Charles	1038	Woods, T. H.	1070
Williams, C. C.	1039	Woodville	218
Williams, C. D.	1040	Woolverton, A. V.	1072
Williams, C. W.	1041	Worthington, Thomas	1072
Williams, J. R.	1042	Wray, E. H.	1073
Williams, John	1043	Wrenn, G. L.	1074
Williams, M.	1044	Wright, J. H.	1074
Williams, N.	1045	Wright, O. P.	1075
Williams, R. E.	678	Wright, William	1076
Williams, R. P.	1045	Wroten, W. M.	1076
Williams, S. B.	1045	Wyatt, F. A.	1077
Williams, S. H.	1046	Wyatt, T. J.	1078
Williams, U. S.	1047	Wyatt, L. A.	1078
Williams, W. B.	1047	Wynn, B. L.	1079
Williams, W. G.	1048	Wynn, W. T.	1081
Williamsburg	240	Wynn, J. H.	1082
Williamson, C. M.	1049		
Williamson, Lea	1050	**Y**	
Williamson, L. W.	1051		
Williamson, R. W.	1051	Yarborough, A. S.	1083
Williamson, W. B.	265	Yates, D. T.	1084
Willing, R. P.	1052	Yazoo City	227
Willis, C. O.	1053	Yellow fever	295
Willis, Lafayette	1054	Yerger, Rucks	1085
Willis, W. T.	1054	Yerger, W. G.	1085
Willis, R. B.	1054	Yerger, E. M., The case of	29
Wilson, E. S.	1055	Young, A. F.	1087
Wilson, S. J.	1058	Young, J. W.	1088
Winans, W.	1059	Young, R. S.	1089

CPSIA information can be obtained at www.ICGtesting.com
Printed in the USA
LVOW09s1328070515

437616LV00007B/192/P